THE ALMANAC OF AMERICAN PHILANTHROPY

Karl Zinsmeister
The Philanthropy Roundtable

AlmanacOfPhilanthropy.org

Published by The Philanthropy Roundtable, 1730 M Street NW, Suite 601, Washington, DC, 20036.

Free copies of this book are available to qualified donors. To learn more, or to order more copies, call (202) 822-8333, e-mail main@PhilanthropyRoundtable.org, or visit PhilanthropyRoundtable.org.

Books are available for purchase at amazon.com. Online versions of all book sections are available at PhilanthropyRoundtable.org/almanac.

Cover: © Megin/shutterstock, jgroup/istockphoto, Kativ/istockphoto, James Hayes/istockphoto, jorgeantonio/istockphoto

ISBN 978-0-9861474-5-6
LCCN 2015956045

First printing, January 2016

TABLE

of

CONTENTS

PREFACE

The Almanac of American Philanthropy is the product of a major, multiyear commitment from The Philanthropy Roundtable and some long-sighted donors. We wanted the great American undertakings of private giving and voluntarism to have a worthy standard reference, one that captured the power of these institutions and the fascinating citizens who have creatively practiced philanthropy to improve our country in thousands of ways.

This is an entirely new work, of a sort that has never previously existed. No doubt there are elements of this compilation that can be improved, expanded, or amended. In any gathering of great achievers, major accomplishments, and crucial ideas, a certain amount of subjective judgment must obviously be employed. We've cast a broad net and included all philanthropy that has had social consequences, whether or not it seemed wise to us. But we are very open to improvements, corrections, and new information. If you have suggestions, please contact us at the address below. We intend for this *Almanac* to be a living document, continually updated and extended, serving as an important and trusted window into one of the most distinctive aspects of American civilization.

The Philanthropy Roundtable exists to serve donors of all sorts, to equip them with information that will make them as discerning and efficacious as possible in all of their charitable actions. If you know of donors who could benefit from the information contained in this book, let us know and we will share a copy with them.

We would like to thank the following generous supporters of The Philanthropy Roundtable for underwriting the production of the *Almanac* during its three-year gestation of research and writing: Anonymous, Carnegie Corporation of New York, Duke Endowment, Earhart Foundation, Hertog Foundation, Kinder Foundation, F. M. Kirby Foundation, Kresge Foundation, Leon Lowenstein Foundation, John Templeton Foundation.

Please enjoy this lively and important new book!

Adam Meyerson
President, The Philanthropy Roundtable

Feedback welcome:
AlmanacEditor@PhilanthropyRoundtable.org

INTRODUCTION

HOW PHILANTHROPY
Fuels
AMERICAN SUCCESS

By Karl Zinsmeister

This rollicking essay introducing *The Almanac of American Philanthropy* races through America's fascinating tradition of private giving and describes why it is so effective and important to our nation. You can read this argument in six distinct sections, one flowing into another:

HOW PHILANTHROPY FUELS AMERICAN SUCCESS

By Karl Zinsmeister

Philanthropy is a huge part of what makes America America.
Start with the brute numbers: Our nonprofit sector now employs 11 percent of the U.S. workforce. It will contribute around 6 percent of GDP in 2015 (up from 3 percent in 1960). And this doesn't take into account volunteering—the equivalent of an additional 5 to 10 million full-time employees (depending on how you count), offering labor worth hundreds of billions of dollars per year.

America's fabled "military-industrial complex" is often used as a classic example of a formidable industry. Well guess what? The nonprofit sector passed the national defense sector in size way back in 1993.

And philanthropy's importance stretches far beyond economics. Each year, seven out of ten Americans donate to at least one charitable cause. Contributions are from two to twenty times higher in the U.S. than in other countries of comparable wealth and modernity. Private giving is a deeply ingrained part of our culture—a font of social creativity and crucial source of new solutions to national problems. Voluntary efforts to repair social weaknesses, enrich our culture, and strengthen American community life are and always have been a hallmark of our country.

Yet, somehow, there exists no definitive resource that chronicles American philanthropy broadly and explains it in a context where it can be fully understood and appreciated. Until now.

This entirely new *Almanac of American Philanthropy* offers everyday citizens, givers, charity workers, journalists, local and national leaders, and others the information needed to put in perspective the vital role that philanthropy plays in all of our daily lives. The facts, stories, and history contained in these pages can fill gaping practical and intellectual holes in our self-awareness.

You will find here an authoritative collection of the major achievements of U.S. philanthropy, lively profiles of the greatest givers (large and small), and rich compilations of the most important ideas, statistics, polls, literature, quotations, and thinking on this quintessentially American topic.

There are also *Iliad*s and *Odyssey*s of human interest in this volume. Some tremendously intriguing Americans of all stripes have poured time and treasure into helping their fellow man. You'll meet lots of them here.

Absent the passion and resources that our fellow countrymen devote to philanthropy, it's not only our nation that would be less thriving. Our individual days would be flatter, darker, uglier, more dangerous, and less happy. You'll find vivid evidence of that in machine-gun presentations throughout this volume. Let's get a taste by meeting a few of the hundreds of philanthropists who live in the middle of this book.

LARGER-THAN-LIFE CHARACTERS

Ned McIlhenny, born and raised on a Louisiana bayou, was an expert on camellias, on alligators, on the hundreds of varieties of bamboo that grow around the world, and on wild turkeys. He was an Arctic explorer. His skills as a hunter once helped save the lives of 200 ice-bound sailors. He was an ornithologist who personally banded more than a quarter of a million birds. He also had a day job selling the hot-pepper condiment invented by his family: McIlhenny Tabasco sauce.

It turns out there is real money in burning mouths, and McIlhenny used his for an amazing array of good works. For one thing, he got very attached to a fellow native of Louisiana's bayous: the snowy egret. When McIlhenny was young, hats bearing egret plumes were for ladies what Coach handbags are today. This fashion mania had the effect of nearly driving the snowy egret to extinction, and no one was doing anything about it. So the philanthropist swung into action.

McIlhenny beat the bushes in wild parts of the island his family owned, and managed to find eight baby egrets in two nests. He raised these hatchlings in a protected area, paid for their care over a period of years, and by 1911 had built up a population of 100,000 egrets on his private refuge. He simultaneously recruited John Rockefeller, Olivia Sage, and other philanthropists to buy up and preserve swampy land in Louisiana that is important as winter habitat of migratory waterfowl, including egrets. And in this way he rescued a magnificent creature that was on the verge of disappearing from the Earth.

Later in his life, McIlhenny took action to stave off a very different kind of extinction. He had been raised with Negro spirituals in his ears, and loved them dearly. Around his 60th birthday, McIlhenny realized that these songs were dying out and at risk of being forgotten forever. So he again sprang into action with both his checkbook and his personal involvement.

He used his contacts to find two elderly singers who still remembered many of the songs—which until then had existed only in an oral tradition—and he hired a musicologist to sit with him as these ladies performed so the lyrics and melodies could be written out. The two men took care to preserve the music in scrupulous detail, exactly as it had been handed down among generations of slaves.

McIlhenny then published these songs as a book, which became a classic of the genre. All but a handful of the 125 spirituals he captured were unrecorded in any other place—he single-handedly saved these soulful artifacts of American history for future generations. McIlhenny's songs included one that provided Martin Luther King Jr. with his most famous line:

> When we allow freedom to ring…from every village and hamlet… we will…speed up that day when all of God's children, black men and white men, Jews and Gentiles, Protestants and Catholics, will be able to join hands and sing in the words of the old Negro spiritual:
> *Free at last! Free at last!*
> *Thank God Almighty, we are free at last!*

Another red-blooded American philanthropist who helped freedom last was Alfred Loomis. His philanthropic field was national defense. Many of us think of defense as the ultimate government responsibility, and a place without room or need for philanthropy, so it may come as a surprise to learn that throughout our history private donors have played important roles in securing our nation. Private donors financed our Revolution. They created the modern field of code-making and -breaking. Donors single-handedly developed the field of rocketry, and fanned private space launch into fiery success. (See "Donors Who Come to the Aid of their Country" in the

Summer 2015 issue of *Philanthropy* magazine for details on how philanthropy has repeatedly bolstered our national defense.)

No donor was more crucial in building America's military strength than Alfred Loomis. After financing much of the electrification of rural America as a Wall Street dealmaker, he became convinced that the stock market was overvalued and converted everything he owned to cash and T-bills in 1929. When the October 1929 Crash came he was not only protected but in a perfect position to go shopping at bargain prices. By the early 1930s Loomis was one of the richest men in America, and at age 45 he retired from finance to put all of his time and energy, and much of his money, into his true love: science. He set up one of the world's great science labs in a mansion near his home, invited top researchers from around the world to experiment there, and conducted his own state-of-the-art investigations.

While visiting Berlin in 1938, Loomis was disturbed to find how popular Hitler was, and how good German scientists were. He returned home convinced that war was brewing, and that science would have a lot to do with who won. He poured himself and his money into one new field in particular: using radio waves to detect moving objects. His lab quickly became the national leader in what we now call radar. Thanks to Loomis's funding and leadership, practical radar sets were

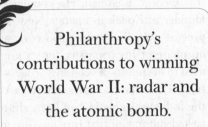

Philanthropy's contributions to winning World War II: radar and the atomic bomb.

created under his supervision and delivered to the Army and Navy by the thousands, turning the tide of World War II.

If radar won the war, the atomic bomb ended it. And as it happens Alfred Loomis had a lot to do with that as well. The method he used for his radar triumphs was to relentlessly gather the best scientific minds, without regard to their prior specialties, give them rich resources, and protect them from bureaucratic interference. When it became apparent how powerful Loomis's modus operandi was, it was directly copied for the Manhattan Project; indeed most of his scientists were transferred over to work on the bomb. Franklin Roosevelt later said that aside from Winston Churchill, no civilian did more to win World War II than Alfred Loomis.

By the way, it isn't only Alfred Loomis's brilliant model for conducting crash research that lives on today. He also left behind a flesh-and-blood embodiment of his whirlwind entrepreneurial philanthropy. His great-grandson is Reed Hastings—who as CEO of Netflix, and one of the nation's most influential progenitors of charter schools as a donor, has been a huge game-changer in both business and philanthropy.

DONORS + PASSION = POTENT ACCOMPLISHMENT

Another entrepreneurial philanthropist who put deep imprints on America was George Eastman. He popularized photography in the early 1900s as founder of Kodak in upstate New York. When he began, the photographic process was all art and guesswork, and no science. During the frantic start-up phase of his company, for example, a calamitous failure of the gelatins used in his photo-developing process threatened to kill his firm. It eventually turned out that the cows whose carcasses were being boiled down to create the industrial gelatin had been shifted to new pastures where their forage lacked sulfur, and that tiny missing ingredient was enough to wreck the delicate chemical process.

Determined to figure out the basic chemistry of photography so he wouldn't be prisoner to these inconsistencies, Eastman started hiring chemists from an obscure little school in New England known as Boston Tech. Grateful for the well-trained minds he came to rely on, Eastman later funded much of the transformation of Boston Tech into today's MIT, including building the entirely new campus where that university now resides. Eastman likewise nurtured the University of Rochester into a great research and educational facility, including creating its medical school from scratch.

Eastman adored music, and had a huge pipe organ installed in his home and played every morning to wake him as his alarm clock. One friend who accompanied him on a New York City trip where they took in 12 operas in six days described Eastman as "absolutely alcoholic about music." This passion led to one of the great cultural gifts in American history, as Eastman methodically created and built to world prominence the Eastman School of

Music at Rochester, which currently enrolls 500 undergraduates, 400 graduate students, and 1,000 local child and adult students. The Eastman School was important in Americanizing and popularizing classical music, which had previously existed as a European transplant, and remains one of our country's top cultural institutions.

Another great American donor was Milton Hershey. Many readers will insist that his crowning gifts to humanity came in brown bars and silver kisses. By transforming chocolate from expensive rarity to treat affordable by all, he did create an explosion in new ways of making Americans feel happy.

Hershey's deepest passion, though, was his remarkable school for orphans, which he and his wife created and ultimately gave their entire company to. Hershey's father was a neglectful drinker, and the separation of his parents turned his boyhood into a shoeless and hungry trial. To relieve other children of similar ordeals he built up his orphanage in a gradually surging ring of family-like houses encircling his own home, where each small group of youngsters was overseen by a married couple who lived with them. The school also provided a thorough basic education and excellent training in industrial crafts.

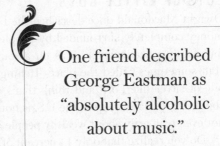

One friend described George Eastman as "absolutely alcoholic about music."

Hershey was a constant physical presence among his youngsters until his death in 1945. At one point he announced, "I have decided to make the orphan boys of the United States my heirs." And he did—endowing the Milton Hershey School with a nest egg currently worth $11 billion. That allows the school to serve 2,000 endangered children from around the U.S. every year, putting many of them on a dramatically elevated life path.

Philanthropists come in all stripes. That's one of the field's strengths: Different givers pursue different visions, so you get many solutions to problems rather than just one. If Milton Hershey's cure for child neglect was large-scale fostering, Katharine McCormick's attempt was to make orphans rarer by manipulating biology. It's pretty widely known that medical breakthroughs like the polio vaccine and hookworm eradication were products of philanthropy. But how many people know that the birth-control pill was the creation of a sole private funder?

A reaper of the International Harvester fortune, McCormick was an early women's rights activist. She initiated a connection with Gregory Pincus, a brilliant biologist who had been fired by Harvard for ethical lapses, to discuss whether it might be possible to prevent pregnancy by means as easy as taking an aspirin. Before leaving the room after their first meeting, McCormick wrote Pincus a check for $40,000.

She funded his private laboratory steadily thereafter, eventually investing the current equivalent of about $20 million in their quest to develop a daily birth-control pill. McCormick was the sole and entire funder of this work, and hovered constantly over the lab, influencing many of its research choices. By 1957 this duo had an FDA-approved pill, and the Earth wobbled a little on its axis. McCormick reveled in her accomplishment, even taking her own prescription to be filled at a local pharmacy—despite being a matron in her 80s at that point—just for the sheer frisson.

LOTS OF LITTLE GUYS

Dwight Macdonald once described the Ford Foundation as "a large body of money completely surrounded by people who want some." (Back when the foundation's headquarters was on a southern California desert estate, the staff sometimes called the place "Itching Palms.") It's easy to look at a big pile of silver like Ford and think that's what American philanthropy is all about. But philanthropy in the U.S. is not just a story of moguls. In fact, it is not even primarily about wealthy people or (even less) big foundations.

Do you realize that only 14 percent of charitable giving in the U.S. comes from foundations? And only 5 percent from corporations? The rest comes from individuals—and the bulk of that from everyday givers, at an annual rate of about $2,500 per household. Even among foundations there is a strong tilt toward the small. Less than 2,000 foundations (2 percent of all) have assets of $50 million or more today. Most foundations are modest in size. And most giving is even smaller—but it is practiced very widely.

It is inexorable giving by humble Americans that constitutes the main branch of U.S. philanthropy. Take Gus and Marie Salenske, a plumber and nurse who lived quietly into the first decade of the new millennium in a small house in Syracuse, New York. Their one indulgence was weekly square dancing; other than that they were savers. After they died, this simple couple left more than $3 million to good causes, mostly their beloved Catholic Church.

Anne Scheiber was a shy auditor who retired in 1944 with just $5,000 in the bank. Through frugal living and inspired stock picking she turned this into $22 million by the time she passed away in 1995 at the age of 101. She left it all to Yeshiva University so that bright but needy girls could attend college and medical school.

Minnesota farmer Harvey Ordung consumed modestly and invested prudently. When he passed on, he left $4.5 million to 12 charities in his home region. The largest portion went to a program that gives college scholarships to local kids.

Elinor Sauerwein painted her own home, kept a vegetable garden, and mowed the lawn herself until she was in her 90s. She eschewed restaurants, cable TV, and other expenses as unnecessary luxuries. But when she died in 2011, she left $1.7 million to the local Modesto, California, branch of the Salvation Army. "Her goal for years and years was to amass as much as she could so it would go to the Salvation Army," reported her financial adviser.

Millicent Atkins earned a teaching degree in 1940, but eventually left that profession to help manage the family farm in South Dakota. She developed a keen eye for productive land and an appetite for buying, eventually owning 4,127 acres. When she died in 2012 she left $38 million to two nearby universities and her church.

Albert Lexie has shined shoes in Pittsburgh for more than 50 years, and made a decision decades ago to donate every penny of his tips to the Free Care Fund of the Children's Hospital of Pittsburgh, which benefits families who can't afford treatment. Since 1981, Lexie has handed over more than $200,000 to Children's Hospital—a third of his total earnings.

> Can anything consequential really be accomplished by little givers? The clear answer from American history is yes.

One of these humble givers you may have heard of is Oseola McCarty. I tell her story in detail in our Philanthropy Hall of Fame section. Her life could not have started much harder—she was conceived when her mother was raped on a wooded path in rural Mississippi. And it didn't get easier with age. She started to work ironing clothes in elementary school, and dropped out at sixth grade to support her ailing aunt by taking in washing.

Hers wasn't a standard-issue home laundry. McCarty scrubbed her clients' clothes by hand on a rubboard. She did try an automatic washer and dryer in the 1960s, but concluded that "the washing machine didn't rinse enough, and the dryer turned the whites yellow." After years of boiling shirts and linens and then doing four fresh-water rinses, that wasn't good enough to meet her high standards. So she went back to her bubbling pots, Maid Rite scrubboard, and 100 feet of open-air clothesline.

Early in her life, McCarty reported, "I commenced to save money. I never would take any of it out. I just put it in…. It's not the ones that make the big money, but the ones who know how to save who get ahead. You got to leave it alone long enough for it to increase." This was a life secret she mastered, and when she retired in 1995, her hands painfully swollen with arthritis, this washerwoman who had been paid in little piles of coins and dollar bills her entire life revealed another secret: She had $280,000 in the bank. Even more startling: She decided to give most of it away—not as a bequest, but immediately.

Setting aside just enough to live on, McCarty donated $150,000 to the University of Southern Mississippi to fund scholarships for worthy but needy students seeking the education she never had. When the community found out what she had done, more than 600 men and women in Hattiesburg and beyond made donations that more than tripled her original endowment. Today, the university presents several full-tuition McCarty scholarships every year.

THE POWER OF LITTLE GUYS
AND BIG GUYS JOINED TOGETHER

Can anything large and consequential really be accomplished by these little and middling givers, or by the very limited population of big givers? The clear answer from American history is yes. Many remarkable things have been achieved by dispersed giving, which often aggregates in formidable ways.

Once upon a time, our country even built its naval ships via dispersed giving. When newborn America was having terrible troubles with pirates in the Mediterranean and revolutionary French raiders off our coasts, many communities took up subscriptions and gathered voluntary funds to build warships and hire captains. The good people of Salem, Massachusetts, for instance, contributed $74,700, in amounts ranging from $10 given by Edmund Gale to a pair of $10,000 donations from Elias Derby and William Gray, and built the frigate *USS Essex*, which became one of the most storied vessels in our new navy.

When the War of 1812 arrived it was dispersed giving that saved us from calamity. As the conflict broke out, the U.S. Navy possessed a total of seven frigates and less than a dozen other seagoing ships. The British Navy at that same moment numbered a thousand warships, including 175 double-gundeck "ships of the line," of which the United States had none. The comparison by firepower was even starker: a total of 450 cannons carried by the U.S. Navy versus 27,800 afloat in the Royal Navy.

So how did America avoid obliteration by the English juggernaut? Individually funded, decentralized warfighting—in the form of privateers. Not long after hostilities were declared there were 517 privately equipped and manned corsairs defending the U.S. "Let every individual contribute his mite, in the best way he can to distress and harass the enemy, and compel him to peace," urged Thomas Jefferson in 1812. During the course of the War of 1812, the U.S. Navy captured or sunk about 300 enemy ships, while U.S. privateers captured or sunk around 2,000, blasting British trade.

The American merchants and ordinary sailors who voluntarily organized themselves into fighting units got everything they hoped for. No more impressment of U.S. seamen. A restoration of free trading. And deep respect for the ability of America's small colonies—weak of government but strong of civil society—to defend their interests.

That same pattern has been followed in many other sectors of American society. In chronicling the astonishing bloom of colleges in the U.S., author Daniel Boorstin noted that the state of Ohio, with just 3 million inhabitants, had 37 colleges in 1880. At that same time, England, a nation of 23 million people, had four. Why the difference? Education philanthropy.

Education philanthropy in the U.S. stretches back to our earliest days, a century and a half before we even had a country. The New College was established in the Massachusetts Bay Colony in 1636. Three years later it was renamed, after young minister John Harvard donated his library and half of his estate to the institution.

America's first recorded fund drive was launched in 1643 to raise money for the college; after 500 British pounds were collected it was deemed a "great success." The next year, colonial families were asked to donate a shilling in cash or a peck of wheat to support the citadel of higher learning in their midst. These voluntary donations, known as the "college corne," sustained Harvard for more than a decade.

> Ohio, with just 3 million inhabitants, had 37 colleges in 1880. At that same time, England, a land of 23 million people, had four. Why the difference? Education philanthropy.

Fast forward to 2015. Nearly 50 American colleges were in the midst of fundraising campaigns aimed at raising at least a billion dollars in donations. Private gifts power even our public universities—institutions like the University of Virginia and the University of California, Berkeley now receive more revenue from voluntary giving (gifts and interest off previous gifts) than they do from state appropriations.

Relying on private individuals to train up the next generation of leaders, rather than leaving that responsibility to the crown or church, was an entirely new development in higher education. It burst forth across our new land, producing the College of William & Mary in 1693, the precursor to St. John's College in 1696, Yale in 1701, and many others. Sub-innovations followed, like the spread of the endowed professorship from a first example in 1721. The pervasiveness of the endowed chair in the U.S. today tempts one to assume that this practice must be common everywhere, but actually it remains rare outside America, where it has helped drive our universities to international pre-eminence.

Our nation's great bloom of universities illustrates perfectly the fruitful mixing of little and big givers. Institutions like the Rensselaer Polytechnic Institute in upstate New York—a pioneer of science-based education that granted the first civil engineering and advanced agriculture degrees in the English-speaking world—relied on big gifts from major patrons like Stephen Van Rensselaer. Other places such as Western Reserve University in Ohio, founded just two years after Rensselaer and likewise destined to become a science powerhouse, relied on an entirely different philanthropic model—the sacrificial giving of thousands of local neighbors on the frontier. One supporter spent a whole winter hauling building supplies to the school from a quarry ten miles away. Another typical family pledged a portion of their annual milk and egg sales.

Starting in the 1840s, hundreds of eastern churches began to pool small donations to support collegiate education across the western frontier. Within 30 years they had raised more than a million dollars to sustain 18 colleges. Hillsdale College was built up at this same time after professor and preacher Ransom Dunn circled through more than 6,000 miles of wild lands collecting nickels and dimes and dollars from settlers.

THE POWER OF PERSONALISM

Pledging your family egg sales to a local institution. Hauling stone all winter for a good cause. Donating your shoeshine tips. In our country, giving is often very *personal*.

Michael Brown was a Broadway lyricist with a hit musical under his belt, so his family was enjoying a burst of unanticipated prosperity. For their 1956 Christmas celebration he and his wife and two sons hosted a close friend, a young writer who was far from her home in the South. At the end of their gift exchange, the Browns handed their guest an envelope. Inside was a note that read: "You have one year off from your job to write whatever you please. Merry Christmas."

The writer's name was Harper Lee. When she had decided to try to make it as a novelist, she relocated (like many before her and since) to New York

City. After getting there she found (like many before her and since) that she was so preoccupied with paying her rent—by working at an airline office and bookstore—that she had little time left over to focus on her literary craft. The Browns noticed this, and through some very personal philanthropy changed the course of U.S. literature.

With their donation in hand, Harper Lee quit her retail jobs. And during that gift year she wrote *To Kill a Mockingbird*. It won the Pulitzer Prize in 1961 and became one of the most influential American books of all time.

While this was an especially intimate contribution, this kind of personalism is not at all unusual in American philanthropy. In fact, gifts where the givers and recipients are involved with each other, familiar with one another's characters, committed to each others' flourishing, are some of the most successful forms of philanthropy. You can see this yourself any day. Volunteer at a Habitat for Humanity building project and you will often work next to the person who is going to occupy the house as soon as you get the roof on and the oven in. Sponsor a child in an inner-city Catholic school (or an overseas village) and you will have opportunities to follow the life progress of the beneficiary, share in his or her dreams, and perhaps attend a graduation.

Knowing the character of the person you are trying to help—strengths and weaknesses, needs and temptations—allows the giver to focus his help much more effectively and to avoid wasteful or mistaken or perverse forms of "help." As William Blake put it, "If you would help another man, you must do so in minute particulars." One man's medicine can be another man's poison; donors must prescribe for particular people, not treat "mankind" as some cold, interchangeable abstraction. Much of the best anti-poverty work carried out during America's immigrant waves and transitions to industrialism during the 1800s and early 1900s took highly personal forms, where givers rolled up their sleeves and offered not only money but mentoring and guidance and support to specific men and women in need.

Stephen Girard was one of the five richest men in American history, when his wealth is measured as a percentage of GDP. But when the yellow-fever epidemics swept his home town of Philadelphia—as they did many summers in the years before anyone realized that the deadly malady was carried up from the tropics on sailing ships, and spread by mosquitoes—Girard was a tireless personal leader in the efforts to tamp down the disease. This required courage, as the terrifying affliction would kill hundreds of people per day in a horror of delirium and bloody vomiting.

Residents who could afford it generally fled the city when epidemics roared through. Not Girard. He stayed in Philadelphia in 1793, 1797-1798, 1802, and 1820 to guide relief efforts, fund hospital operations, and provide direct care for individuals—often bathing and feeding the dying himself. He routinely put his personal and business affairs on hold during outbreaks. "As soon as things have quieted down a little you may be sure I shall take up my work with all the activity in my power," he wrote to a friend in 1793. "But, for the moment, I have devoted all my time and my person, as well as my little fortune, to the relief of my fellow citizens."

Nicholas Longworth grew up poor, apprenticed to a shoemaker for a period, before eventually earning great wealth. He gave much of it away to what he called "the devil's poor," whom he identified and helped in extremely personal ways. "Decent paupers will always find a plenty to help them, but no one cares for these poor wretches. Everybody damns them, and as no one else will help them, I must," he concluded.

Longworth distributed food directly to these most abject cases, built apartments to salve their homelessness, and held personal sessions where he would listen patiently to sad stories and offer solace and assistance. When he died in 1863 in Cincinnati, Longworth's funeral procession numbered in the thousands, a great many of them outcasts. Drunkards, prostitutes, beggars, and criminals sobbed at the loss of their one true friend.

The Tappan brothers, Arthur and Lewis, were successful New York merchants and among this country's most accomplished philanthropists at changing society and politics. They worked on a much more national scale than Longworth or Girard. Yet their machinations were often just as personal.

Fired by their evangelical Christian convictions, the Tappans were leading donors to the cause of abolishing slavery. After their funding turned the American Anti-Slavery Society into a mass movement with 250,000 members, mobs attacked their homes and businesses. Arthur escaped with his life only by barricading himself in one of the family stores well supplied with guns. Lewis's home was sacked that same evening, with all of his family possessions pulled into the street and burned by slavery apologists.

The brothers did not buckle. Lewis left his house unrepaired—to serve, he said, as a "silent anti-slavery preacher to the crowds who will flock to see it." More substantively, the two men decided to flood the U.S. with antislavery mailings over the following year. This brought them more death threats and harassment, none of which slowed them down.

When a group of Africans who had been captured by Spanish slavers rose against the crew of the ship transporting them and eventually came ashore on Long Island, Lewis immediately organized their defense against murder charges for having killed a crewmember. He decamped to Connecticut, where he clothed and fed the defendants, located and hired an interpreter of their African dialect, and brought in Yale students to tutor them in English, American manners, and Christianity. Then he retained top lawyers to represent their interests. He attended the court proceedings himself every day, organized a public-relations campaign, and eventually got the Africans freed after pushing their case all the way to the U.S. Supreme Court. His personal devotion and single-handed financing turned abolitionism into a cause célèbre.

If the campaigning of the Tappans on behalf of slaves was impressively personal, the devotion of Joseph de Veuster to miserable lepers was out-and-out heroic. Better known as Father Damien after he became a Catholic priest, de Veuster thought it inhumane that when leprosy reached the Hawaiian Islands victims were forced to live in isolation on a wild peninsula without any buildings or goods or services. The newly diagnosed would be dropped off with nothing but a few tools and some seeds, and proceed to live miserably in shelters made of sticks.

Father Damien moved into the leper colony himself in 1873, brought anti-social residents into line, rescued orphans, provided medical care, and organized building and gardening efforts. He organized large fundraising campaigns by mail that brought in donations sufficient to pay for his many improvements, and to decently bury the 1,600 people whose funerals he presided over in a period of six years. He died himself at age 49 from complications of leprosy. The sacrifices made by Father Damien are especially piercing, but there are many examples of philanthropists who risked happiness, health, and even life itself to carry out their good works.

Philanthropy regularly grows out of pain. The death of John Rockefeller's grandson from scarlet fever in 1901 cemented his desire to build a medical research facility that could banish such afflictions. The result was the great Rockefeller University, whose researchers over the years have been awarded dozens of Nobel prizes. The organizer and funder of today's wildly successful National Kidney Registry, which matches donors to patients with organ failure, acted after his ten-year-old daughter was nearly lost to kidney disease.

America's most fecund artist colony, known as Yaddo, was created by Thomas Edison's financial partner Spencer Trask and his wife, Katrina, as a cathartic effort after the couple endured the profound pain of losing all four of their young children, in separate incidents, to disease and early death. The Trasks envisioned a place where "generations of talented men and women yet unborn" would be "creating, creating, creating." Since its opening in 1926, Yaddo has nurtured 71 Pulitzer Prize winners, 68 National Book Award winners, a Nobel literature laureate, and countless other productive musicians, playwrights, and novelists. The Trasks sweetened and softened a world that may have felt hard and bitter when they started giving.

Though it sometimes grows out of pain, philanthropy is more frequently sparked by opposite emotions like gratitude and joy. The first charity hospital in America was created in, of all places, 1735 New Orleans—at that point a ragingly ragged and largely ungoverned city first populated just 18 years earlier by people drawn from jails, poorhouses, and urban gutters. The hospital benefactor was a dying sailor named Jean Louis, who had made some money for the first time in his life by going into the boatbuilding business in the brand-new French colony. He wanted to pass on his good fortune. And his Charity Hospital offering free care to the indigent became one of the most useful of its type, finding a vast market in a town known even then for creativity in vice.

Sticking to that same unlikely place and time, we can easily pluck up another example of great philanthropy growing out of gratitude. Judah Touro arrived in New Orleans in 1801, where he set up as a merchant and rode to great fortune the city's rise and incorporation into the United States of America. Touro became a noted patriot and philanthropist, gratefully donating all across the country to a society that offered freedom and fair play to Jews like him. In his appreciation for the value of sincere faith, Touro financed synagogues and churches alike. He built hospitals, orphanages, almshouses, asylums, schools, and libraries. He bequeathed even more when he died in 1854, a human advertisement for what a determined donor can accomplish.

GOOD CHARITY,
BAD CHARITY?

Some activists today are eager to define what is good or bad, acceptable or unacceptable, in other people's giving. Princeton professor Peter Singer has lately made it almost a career to pronounce that only certain kinds of philanthropic contributions ought to be considered truly in the public interest. Only money given directly to "the poor" should be counted as charitable, he and some others argue.

Former NPR executive Ken Stern constructed a recent book on this same idea that charity must be "dedicated to serving the poor and needy." Noting that many philanthropists go far beyond that limited population, he complains that it is "astonishingly easy to start a charity; the IRS approves over 99.5 percent of all charitable applications." He disapprovingly lists nonprofits that have "little connection to common notions of doing good: the Sugar Bowl, the U.S. Golf Association, the Renegade Roller Derby team in Bend, Oregon, and the All Colorado Beer Festival, just to name a few."

Is that a humane argument? Without question, the philanthropy for the downtrodden launched by people like Stephen Girard, Nicholas Longworth, Jean Louis, the Tappans, Milton Hershey, Albert Lexie, and Father Damien is deeply impressive. But the idea that only generosity aimed directly at the poor (or those who agitate in their name) should count as philanthropic is astoundingly narrow and shortsighted. Meddling premised on this view would horribly constrict the natural outpouring of human creativity.

Who is to say that Ned McIlhenny's leaps to preserve the Negro spiritual, or rescue the snowy egret, were less worthy than income-boosting? Was the check that catalyzed Harper Lee's classic novel bad philanthropy? Were there better uses for Alfred Loomis's funds and volunteer management genius than beating the Nazis and Imperial Japanese military?

> Who is to say that Ned McIlhenny's leaps to preserve the Negro spiritual, or rescue the snowy egret, were less worthy than income-boosting?

Even if you insist on the crude utilitarian view that only direct aid to the poor should count as charity, the reality is that many of the most important interventions that reduce poverty over time have nothing to do with alms. By building up MIT, George Eastman struck a mighty blow to increase prosperity and improve the health and safety of everyday life—benefiting individuals at all points on the economic spectrum. Givers who establish good charter schools today are doing more to break cycles of human failure than any welfare transfer has ever achieved. Donors who fund science, abstract knowledge, and new learning pour the deep concrete footings of economic success that have made us history's most aberrant nation—where the poor improve their lot as much as other citizens, and often far more.

And what of the private donors who stoke the fires of imagination, moral understanding, personal character, and inspiration? Is artistic and religious philanthropy just the dabbling of bored and vain wealthholders? Aren't people of all income levels lifted up when the human spirit is cultivated and celebrated in a wondrous story, or haunting piece of music, or awe-engendering cathedral?

When a donation is offered to unlock some secret of science, or feed an inspiring art, or attack some cruel disease, one can never count on any precise result. But it's clear that any definition which denies humanitarian value to such giving, because it doesn't go directly to income support, is crabbed and foolish. Much of the power and beauty of American philanthropy derives from its vast range, and the riot of causes we underwrite in our millions of donations.

To illustrate this rather than just claim it, let's take a somewhat random whirl through some of the evidence packed into the back of this book. We'll scroll through a few dozen of the thousands of philanthropic accomplishments accumulated in this volume. We will begin with very tangible products like historic buildings and parks, consider services like medicine and education, and touch on more ethereal accomplishments in fields like the arts.

> The Brown family changed the course of U.S. literature with some very personal philanthropy.

THE WILD RICHNESS OF AMERICAN PHILANTHROPY

How many readers know that some of America's top cultural treasures—the homes of our founders—are preserved and kept open to the public not by the National Park Service or other agency of government but rather by privately funded nonprofits? George Washington's Mount Vernon was saved from ruin by thousands of small donors and today thrives under the ownership of the Mount Vernon Ladies' Association, a wonderful story told later in this book. The separate home where Washington was born was also retrieved from oblivion by a mix of small donors plus John Rockefeller Jr. Likewise, Monticello—Thomas Jefferson's residence sometimes described as his "greatest creation"—has been protected and interpreted to visitors for about a century by a private foundation that receives no government funding. Ditto for Montpelier, the nearby home of the father of our Constitution, James Madison.

The summer cottage where Abraham Lincoln spent a quarter of his Presidency and made some of his most momentous decisions, including formulating the Emancipation Proclamation, was a neglected part of American history until private donors came along to restore it and open it to the public in 2008. Williamsburg, Virginia; Touro Synagogue; Greenfield Village; Mystic Seaport; Sturbridge Village; Plimoth Plantation; Old Salem—these beloved historic sites and scads of others have been saved for future generations by philanthropy, not taxpayers.

Our great cathedrals are products of private giving. St. John the Divine, one of the most monumental Christian edifices in the world, was begun in New York City with gifts from J. P. Morgan, and then raised up over decades via thousands of small donations. Riverside Church, a grand gothic pile just another ten blocks up Broadway, was a gift of John Rockefeller Jr. On the other hand, the National Cathedral in Washington, the second-largest such church in the country after St. John (and probably the last pure Gothic cathedral that will ever be built), was a flowering of mass philanthropy, and built over a period of 97 years as small funds donated by the public pooled up.

Our cathedrals of human learning—libraries—are also an invention of philanthropy. Ben Franklin promulgated the idea that in a democratic nation like America, everyday people should have easy access to books, and that making them available is a worthy calling for the generous. Even the rough-and-ready city of New Orleans in 1824 got a Free Library courtesy of Judah Touro, who also helped endow the Redwood Library in Newport. John Jacob Astor, James Lenox, and Samuel Tilden gave millions between 1849 and 1886 to create what became the New York Public Library. Financier Joshua Bates launched the Boston Public Library, and Enoch Pratt provided brilliant planning as well as money for a magnificent multibranch library in Baltimore that inspired Andrew Carnegie to create more than 2,500 other libraries in the decades following. Today there are 16,000 public libraries in the U.S. and they are visited a billion and a half times every year.

Many magnificent parks are also fruits of philanthropy. In the mid-1850s, donors started giving lovely botanical gardens to the public in various cities. The list of national parks sparked by donors is long and stretches from Maine's Acadia to the Virgin Islands, from Great Smoky to Grand Teton.

A recent research report declared that thanks to philanthropy we are currently living in the golden age of urban parks. Inspired by the success of the Central Park Conservancy, which donors created to bring New York's green haven back from the brink of disastrous decay and disorder, conservancies have spread all across the country, creating parks that delight citizens by the millions. Manhattan's High Line, Discovery Green in Houston, Chicago's

606 trail, the new $350 million oasis springing up in Tulsa, Dallas's Klyde Warren Park carved out of thin air over a busy freeway—these are all new gifts. And tired or underdeveloped older recreation areas like Shelby Farms in Memphis, Piedmont Park in Atlanta, Buffalo Bayou in Houston, the Olmsted parks in Louisville, and our National Mall are also being renovated and expanded in much-loved ways thanks to generous givers.

Clever private ideas as well as private money have been at the center of miraculous recoveries of several endangered species. The peregrine falcon is the fastest creature on earth when flying, but as a reproducer it had become such a snail that it was flirting with extinction. Government biologists tried to speed its breeding but failed. Then a grant from the IBM Corporation mixed with small donations from falconry hobbyists allowed birders to experiment with some unconventional ideas (including that city skyscrapers might be among the best places for the height-loving, pigeon-dining creatures to make their comeback). Today, the peregrine is out of danger. Fresh ideas and donor funds were similarly crucial in the comebacks of the wolf, the bluebird, whooping cranes, wild turkeys, the swift fox, and many threatened waterfowl.

> Many of the most important interventions to reduce poverty have nothing to do with alms. They are gifts that increase the prosperity of everyday life—benefiting individuals at all points of the economic spectrum.

Philanthropy isn't going to bring dinosaurs back to life. It has, however, fueled much of the paleontology that has dramatically transformed the field in recent decades. Jack Horner has levered $12 million of donations into radical new understandings that some dinosaurs exhibited mothering behaviors, that millions-of-years-old bones can contain soft tissue residues that explain biological secrets, that the T. Rex may have been as much scavenger as predator. And voluntary donations have been vital in making dinosaurs real for their fans, via imaginative new museum exhibits in places like Montana, the Smithsonian, and New York City's Museum of Natural History.

THE PHILANTHROPY OF SCIENCE

Science in general is deeply entwined with philanthropy in America. Take the high-end telescopes with which astronomers and astrophysicists have made many of the most important discoveries about our universe. They have all been filled with light by philanthropy. Donors created the Lick and Yerkes Observatories before the twentieth century. It was Carnegie money that placed 60-inch and later 100-inch reflecting telescopes on Mount Wilson, and Rockefeller funding that built the 200-inch Hale telescope on Mount Palomar. The Keck Foundation made possible the pair of 33-foot reflectors that opened in Hawaii in 1993. And the two massive instruments under construction today—the Giant Magellan and the 30-Meter Telescope—are both being built with donations. *Big* donations, like the $250 million that Intel founder Gordon Moore slapped down to design and kick off the 30-Meter instrument (which will produce images *12 times* sharper than NASA's Hubble telescope).

Certain large areas of science have been spurred especially hard by donors. Aeronautics, for instance. The Guggenheim family took a very early interest in the field, and in the first half of the 1900s created most of America's infrastructure for supporting flight, including nearly all of our original university aeronautical engineering departments. The Guggenheims were also virtually the sole funders, starting with a 1930 grant of $100,000, of Robert Goddard—the world's greatest genius in rocketry, and the man most responsible for putting the U.S. on the path to world leadership in space flight.

Oceanography is another field mostly created by donors. Ellen Scripps made possible the Scripps Institution of Oceanography in San Diego, and the Rockefellers spawned a similar research operation on the Atlantic at Woods Hole in Massachusetts. There are likewise great research aquariums on both the West Coast (thanks to David Packard) and the East Coast (paid for by Bernie Marcus).

It would be hard to exaggerate the importance of some of these science gifts. In 2013, *Philanthropy* magazine undertook some deep historical investigation on John Rockefeller's pioneering funding for medical research, which commenced in 1901. We found that an astonishing 47 Nobel science-prize winners had received significant financial support from Rockefeller before they earned their awards. Another 14 Nobel laureates were supported by Rockefeller money sometime after their award, allowing them to expand their research or to mentor a new generation of scientists. The discoveries made by these men and women included blood typing, penicillin, the yellow-fever vaccine, electrical signaling in the nervous system, the operation of optical nerves, fundamental understandings of DNA and genetics, and much more.

These kinds of breakthroughs fueled by intensive philanthropy are by no means just something from history. A number of philanthropists have of late made brain research a high priority of their giving. Four donors alone have put a billion and a half dollars into this area in recent years, and their efforts are beginning to cumulate in important findings. When President Obama announced a human-brain initiative as a $100 million federal project in 2013, his roadmap was drawn by researchers involved in the much larger philanthropic brain-science blitz already underway.

SAVING LIVES

Medical philanthropy has had many splendid triumphs. After World War II, the entire budget of the National Institutes of Health was less than $10 million, and the major forces in biomedical research were smart donors. The John Hartford Foundation was smart indeed, catalyzing many advances in health care during the 1950s, '60s, and '70s with its grants in areas like immunology, organ rejection, development of the artificial heart, microneurosurgery, and cancer research.

Hartford was a special savior for the many people suffering from kidney failure. They funded some of the world's first successful kidney transplants at Boston's Brigham Hospital, and underwrote creation of the important professional societies where kidney specialists exchange information. Hartford made kidney dialysis practical, funding the machines created for the world's first out-of-hospital dialysis center. For the one out of every 100,000 Americans who experience kidney failure, these gifts lifted a death sentence.

In similar fashion, Uncas Whitaker more or less willed the new field of biomedical engineering into legitimacy by leaving $700 million for that sole purpose when he died in 1975. The trustees of his bequest pushed the money out the door quickly and wisely, at a time when most universities and the government medical-funding agencies opposed a blending of engineering and medical disciplines. The Whitaker efforts created curricula for the new field and funded inaugural research projects. They paid for classrooms, labs, and 13 entire buildings. They gave dozens of colleges the money to hire dual-purpose faculty, fellows, and interns, and otherwise encouraged talented people to take up work at the intersection of technology and medicine. They spawned professional societies and launched the careers of 1,500 biomedical engineers who founded more than 100 companies and accumulated over 400 patents or property licenses.

The results are dramatic. Biomedical engineering has become the fastest growing specialty in all of engineering. And revolutionary products like lab-grown skin and organs, laser surgery, advanced prosthetics, large-scale joint replacement, cochlear implants, and hundreds of other miracles are now commonplace.

Like overlooked medical disciplines, philanthropy has been helpful in bringing new attention to overlooked diseases. Autism was barely understood when philanthropists offered the funds for deeper research and wider public education. Schizophrenia, certain kinds of blindness, and prostate and breast cancer have all receded in the face of donor pressure.

Huntington's disease afflicts one out of every 10,000 Americans, and there is no cure for the slow, suffocating killer. It gets modest attention from the NIH. Throughout the past decade and a half, though, philanthropist Andrew Shechtel has stimulated expansive new research on the affliction via $732 million in donations.

Philanthropists have also done marvelous things on the social side of medical care. They have, for instance, funded giant advances in palliative care and patient comfort—creating the Fisher Houses, which now unite wounded servicemembers with their families during treatment, and the Ronald McDonald houses, which do the same for sick children. Humane hospice care was brought to America by philanthropists starting in 1974.

It isn't just in the field of medicine that donors have been able to save and improve lives. Literally hundreds of millions of people have avoided starvation thanks to the crucial foundation investments that created the Green Revolution.

> Uncas Whitaker willed the new field of biomedical engineering into legitimacy with $700 million and a determination to buck the university, government, engineering, and medical establishments.

Today, the Gates Foundation is putting money into extending the agricultural progress of the Green Revolution across Africa.

It is estimated that tobacco could kill a billion people globally during the present century. Philanthropists are investing hundreds of millions of dollars in educational efforts to head off many of those deaths. Dangerous roads that kill thousands of people in developing countries every year are another area where donors have recently started working creatively to save lives.

Disaster zones are one of the most visible realms where the philanthropic impulse does battle against danger and chaos. From the Red Cross and Samaritan's Purse to World Vision and Doctors Without Borders, there are many vehicles and vessels through which the generous now act to rescue the perishing. Entries later in this book chronicle multiple philanthropic out-pourings in response to earthquakes, for instance: San Francisco in 1906, Italy in 1909, Armenia in 1989, Haiti in 2010, and so on. The largest recent charitable gushes in response to cruel twists of fate were the $2.8 billion donated by Americans after the 9/11 attacks and the $5.3 billion offered up after Hurricane Katrina.

ELEVATING MINDS

Philanthropy doesn't just fill bellies and fill pockets. It also fills heads with productive knowledge, and souls with inspiration and ideas. Education, religion, giving to culture and the arts are primeval philanthropic imperatives.

Philanthropy is, for instance, the central factor behind the greatness of American universities. Donors like Mary Garrett didn't just give the money to create learning citadels (in her case, the Johns Hopkins medical school), they also demanded business-like procedures and reforms that separated U.S. colleges from their European predecessors. Garrett insisted, in return for her support, that Hopkins raise academic standards, and accept women into its medical school on equal footing with men, making it the first place those two things were accomplished.

As I am writing, more than a half-billion dollars of private giving is creating a remarkable new campus on New York City's Roosevelt Island where cutting-edge engineering and entrepreneurship training will be combined under the aegis of Cornell University. Donors also brought in as a partner Technion, the Israeli university that has proven one of the most effective in the world at spinning off lab discoveries as useful products. Cornell Tech, as the new institution will be called, has great promise of becoming a hub that not only provides superb student training but also generates a flood of economic productivity in the surrounding region, à la MIT or Stanford (two other products of entrepreneurial philanthropy).

In addition to dominant universities, philanthropy has yielded many remarkable academies for younger students. From the Catholic schools that serve as lifelines for families stranded in neglected urban neighborhoods, to superb vocational instruction at institutions like the Williamson School, to alternative programs like Waldorf schools, to many privately supported schools that provide top-flight academics, generous scholarship and endowment gifts have done wonders for generations of American children. Donors have created and sustained distinctive American institutions like the Hershey School and the Kamehameha Schools in Hawaii. The Hawaiian institution was bequeathed 365,000 acres of land by Bernice Bishop, allowing it to educate more than 7,000 youngsters every year at almost no charge to their parents.

Within just the last 20 years, donors have powered what I suspect historians will someday categorize as the most important social invention of our time—the charter school. As this book is published, 3 million children are attending 7,000 charter schools, and both of those numbers are rising rapidly (from zero just a couple decades earlier). Even more remarkably, the top charters have invented starkly original techniques and procedures that allow them to take children with harsh life disadvantages and dreadful conventional schools in their neighborhoods and lift them into well-above-average academic results.

The 9,000 students at the Uncommon Schools charter network are 98 percent minority and 78 percent low-income, yet all seniors take the SAT and their average score is 20 points above the college-readiness benchmark. At KIPP schools, 95 percent of their 70,000 students are minority and 86 percent are low-income, yet 83 percent go to college. In New York City, the average charter-school student now absorbs five months of extra learning per year in math and one extra month in reading compared with counterparts in conventional public schools.

CREATIVE JUICES

In the U.S., philanthropy is the rain that keeps the tree of artistic life in bud. Consider symphony orchestras. Fully *half* of their income today comes from donations (33 percent from annual gifts, 16 percent from revenue off of endowments given previously). Only 6 percent of symphony funds come from local, state, or federal government support. (The rest comes from concert income.)

> Philanthropy is the rain that keeps the tree of artistic life in bud.

The story is about the same for other arts. Nonprofit arts institutions as a whole currently get 45 percent of their budgets from donors. Subtract the philanthropy and our lives immediately become duller, flatter, darker, more silent.

Voluntary support for artistic activity in our country sprawls across a delightful range of fields. The little gems are often just as sparkly as the big diamonds. Take the Van Cliburn piano competition. Established in Fort Worth, Texas, in 1962 by local donors anxious to encourage gifted players like their native son Mr. Cliburn, it is a kind of Olympiad for amateur piano players. Every four years, the greatest non-professionals in the world descend on Bass Hall and play until their fingers can flutter no more. Spectacular performances are available not only to the live listeners but also to broadcast, Internet, and film audiences.

George Eastman's pet project, his School of Music and the 3,100-seat hall he built for it, remains one of the treasures of American culture. He created the venue to be much more open and welcoming to audiences than European concert halls, and programmed it from the very beginning not only with classical music but also with other arts like film (which was then considered a vulgar and unserious trifle). Eastman made Martha Graham's career by bringing her in to choreograph avant-garde dances that could be presented between film reels to mass audiences who would never darken the door of a ballet performance.

Now that it is recognized as both a potential art form and a potent shaper of popular culture and opinion, film has become a field of interest to other savvy philanthropists. The individual most committed at present is the former co-founder of eBay, Jeff Skoll, who has poured hundreds of millions of his dollars into an operation that makes popular movies with a message. He also funds a "social-action campaign" for each release, which encourages people to alter their thinking and behavior based on what they have seen. Skoll has convinced big names like Matt Damon, Julia Roberts, and George Clooney to take roles in his filmanthropy, which has hit some popular and creative nerves. A charmed Hollywood establishment has given more than 30 Oscar nominations to his pictures—which include works like *The Help, Syriana, Lincoln, Charlie Wilson's War, Waiting for Superman,* and *An Inconvenient Truth* (which brought Al Gore his Nobel Peace Prize).

> **Fully 47 Nobel science-prize winners received significant financial support from Rockefeller before they earned their awards.**

Creative work undertaken under the banner of art and culture can also yield practical progress in unexpected ways. In the days before mass media, two donors—library and art patron Ada Moore, and the Carnegie Corporation—gave money to the American Foundation for the Blind to fund a crash program to bring books to the sightless in some practical audio form. The foundation decided to see if a brand-new patent for what was being called the "long-playing record," or LP, might work.

LPs were much larger and slower-spinning than the 78-rpm records that were then popular, and thus allowed four times as much material on each side, making them practical for extended readings from books. The AFB experimented with making discs out of various materials, seeking one durable enough to stand up to shipping from house to house among blind subscribers. They eventually settled on vinyl. The foundation also had to build the first players for the records.

This philanthropic product-development effort succeeded, and "talking books" began to be shipped around the country, leaving blind Americans wide-eyed with wonder at the joys of literature. For the first 14 years of its existence, the LP record funded by Moore and Carnegie was enjoyed exclusively by the blind. Only later did CBS turn it into a medium for the general public to play music. A charitable creation thus became a big part of American pop culture.

FIXING PROBLEMS VIA PHILANTHROPY VS. GOVERNMENT

Philanthropy is not interchangeable with government spending. It typically takes quite different approaches to solving problems.

John Updike once wrote an essay about how government administrators view change—noting that their every incentive is for continuation of the status quo. Change disrupts bureaucracies and creates work for those who man them. People working in government thus tend to shun departures from prevailing procedure, and to seek more of the same, *not* innovation. Updike writes poetically that "the state, like a young child, wishes that each day be just like the last." Whereas an inventive private actor "like a youth, hopes that each day will bring something new."

This pierces to the heart of why government problem-solving is generally so sluggish and uninspired. Of course, philanthropy can also become bureaucratic and timid—as can any human activity under certain conditions. But there are fundamental structures and incentives to private giving that, in the main, make it much more imaginative, flexible, and interested in transformation, as well as more individualized, more pluralistic, more efficient. One at a time, let's look at some of the distinctive qualities of private giving that set it apart from public spending.

PHILANTHROPY IS INVENTIVE

Both in its approach to problems and in the forms through which it operates, American philanthropy has shown itself to be highly experimental and creative.

For instance, the institution of the charitable foundation itself—which allowed donors to codify their giving and extend it to future generations—is an invention of American philanthropy. The first foundations emerged in the U.S. around the turn of the twentieth century. By 1915 there were 27 in operation; in 1930 the total was over 200. The British began to copy the foundation structure in 1936; it was 1969 before the French and Japanese got some of their first examples. Today the foundation (and U.S.-style philanthropy in general) is just beginning to be understood and copied in places like China, the Middle East, Russia, and India.

Heaps of examples illustrate the inventiveness of private philanthropy in substance as well as form. Take just the past decade of grantmaking in a single field—education. Five donors recently set up a fascinating effort to trim the soaring costs of college by producing top-quality, low-cost textbooks for the country's 25 most-attended college courses. They will use the open-source method commonly applied to producing great software, along with an expert-review process. And the resulting books will be free to students. Given that college students spent an average of $1,200 on texts in the 2013 school year, this effort is expected to save collegians $750 million in its first years. The donors are now expanding it to the high-school level.

In the same year that this clever venture was launched, other donors paid to bring a new testing yardstick to schools so they can measure their performance against peers in other countries. Yet others provided the means to set up MOOCs—massive open online courses from top colleges that can be taken for free by anyone—thanks to philanthropic sponsorship. Simultaneously, philanthropists concerned about the low quality of many of the colleges that train schoolteachers created a new guide, in collaboration with rating expert *U.S. News and World Report*, that scores every one of the nation's 1,668 teacher colleges for effectiveness.

There were creative educational thrusts by other givers at about the same time. One donor paid for a major experiment in Chicago that is testing whether at-risk preschoolers get a bigger academic boost from long-term training for parents, or from special financial incentives for teachers who produce results in a year, or from small weekly payments that reward specific achievements by parents, teachers, or children. Other givers paid for Khan Academy to offer "a free, world-class education for anyone, anywhere" via thousands of free online seminars. A contemporaneous donor-driven innovation was a practical new system that allows school districts to measure how far students progress from their starting point during a school year, and then to reward the teacher accordingly.

Meanwhile, several radically different and effective new ways of drawing fresh talent into teaching were created with charitable funds. Philanthropy invented a superb math and science initiative that spread rapidly to 560 schools in its first seven years. (It causes the number of students earning passing scores on math and science Advanced Placement exams to jump 85 percent in the first year, on average, and to nearly triple within three years.) And it was thanks to generous givers that less than a decade after Hurricane Katrina wiped out every one of its miserable public schools, New Orleans had an entirely new 100-percent-charters school system in place that allowed the city's students to mostly catch up with the performance of students in the rest of the state, for the first time in state history.

And so on. We could walk through similar bursts of philanthropic invention in medicine, economic development, overseas aid, and other areas. You'll find examples of all of these in the Major Philanthropic Achievement lists at the heart of this book.

> The LP record was a charitable creation to aid the blind before growing into a big part of American pop culture.

PHILANTHROPY IS NIMBLE

Private giving is light years quicker than government action, and it tends to adapt effectively to changing conditions on the ground. A simple example is donor John Montgomery's provision of lifesaving radio gear in central Africa. Residents of that region had been terrorized for years by warlord Joseph Kony and his mercenary army that routinely popped out of the jungle to kill, steal, and kidnap children from remote villages. Montgomery suggested that if a radio network were created so information on Kony's movements could be quickly shared, imperiled villagers could be warned in time to flee. In very short order he had tribal chiefs equipped with the necessary transmitters and receivers, and many families were spared.

Another illustration of the responsiveness of philanthropy came during the 2014 Ebola scare. As the disease swept into new nations, neither the international nor American health bureaucracies showed much capacity to adjust or speed up their distribution of resources. Enter philanthropist Paul Allen with an almost instant $100 million pledge, rapidly matched by $50 million from the Gates Foundation, $25 million from Mark Zuckerberg, and other gifts. By, for instance, immediately establishing protocols for aid workers who get infected, providing financial support for their evacuations and insurance-coverage gaps, and paying for the dispatch of 500 emergency respondents and their equipment to west Africa, Allen's quick gift was credited by experts with stanching the bleeding (literally). The comparative speed of charities is often visible in disaster relief—where organizations like Samaritan's Purse and Team Rubicon are routinely able to put supplies and help-teams on the ground days faster than public authorities.

Interestingly, the nimbleness and speed of philanthropy coexist with a proven ability to be patient and take an extraordinarily long-term approach when appropriate. "Unlike business and the state, foundations can 'go long,'" writes Stanford professor Rob Reich. He cites the multigeneration creation of public libraries, the decades-long Green Revolution, the painstaking creation of our national 911 emergency call system by philanthropists, and other examples.

PHILANTHROPY IS INDIVIDUALIZED

Howard Husock once wrote in *Forbes* that "the more individualized attention a problem calls for, the less well-suited government is to dealing with it—and the more likely that independent, charitably supported groups can help." This is indubitably true.

Many of the most successful mechanisms in the charitable world—like microlending circles, Alcoholics Anonymous, the successful mentoring programs for prisoners, college-dropout preventers like the Posse Foundation, and good job-training programs for welfare moms and the homeless—rely heavily on one-to-one human linkages and accountability. They take advantage of all the useful information that becomes available when you actually know someone, instead of dealing with a stranger. And they use the power of relationships to help people change behavior.

I once did a study of the informal lending circles that many immigrants use to build economic success after they come to the U.S. Typically, a group of six to ten individuals who are related or know each other will band together, and each month every participant will put a few hundred dollars into the circle. When your turn comes up you get to collect that month's kitty—which recipients typically use for things like starting a business, or making a downpayment on a car or house, or buying some equipment or education that can be used to make a living. These circles almost never have contracts or receipts or any legally binding structure. So what prevents someone from walking off with the pot then refusing to kick in their share of contributions in the future? Relationships!

There is the pressure of not letting down your relatives or friends or neighbors whom you will see in the future. There is also the confidence that comes from entering the circle with valuable knowledge of the character of the other people in it, making it less likely you will be taken advantage of yourself. These are not anonymous strangers in a transfer program, they are people whose strengths and weaknesses are known to each other. These are personal, not impersonal, transactions.

"I never think about crowds. I think about individuals," Mother Teresa used to say. The administrator of a government helping program, on the other hand, has to focus wholly on the crowd. Government programs can't have different approaches and different rules for different kinds of people; they are all about equal opportunity, about being strictly the same for all participants in all places at all times. Cramped minds sometimes romanticize this "consistency" of government programs, and contrast it favorably to the "patchwork" variations of charitable aid. But consistency is not really how humans work.

> Gifts where the giver and recipient are involved with each other, familiar with one another's character, and committed to each other's flourishing are some of the most successful forms of philanthropy.

If you have one child who needs a very structured environment, and another who blooms when left to navigate on her own, and a third who doesn't do any kind of book learning well but has vibrant creative skills, you don't want "consistent" schools; you don't want one size fits all. You want individualized services that recognize and work with intimate differences of personality. You'll have a hard time finding that in government-run programs, but it's a hallmark of philanthropic efforts.

Great philanthropists know all of this. That's why many donors prefer to work in their own backyards, where they know the characters of many recipients. When allying themselves with social entrepreneurs, donors tend to seek out neighborhood operators who have intimate acquaintance with the problem at hand, and the persons suffering through it. Donors sift through competing petitions for help and choose those where they have some direct knowledge, and confidence the transactions will be personal enough to keep people accountable and tuned in to real needs.

Successful benevolence uses the power of intimate knowledge. That greatly improves the chances of social success. An individually tailored approach is often the central difference between philanthropy done right and ineffective government check writing.

The great giver Julius Rosenwald once described the aim of philanthropy as "healing the sore spots of civilization." This is easier to achieve by working in personal rather than impersonal ways. Consider the story of a young woman named Liz Murray who grew up as the neglected daughter of two drug addicts.

In her teenage years Murray began reaching out to potential allies for help in saving herself. On one particular day she had two back-to-back human interactions that were climactic in her life. The first was in a New York City welfare office where she attempted to qualify for aid for the first time so she could have an apartment instead of living on the street as she had been for two years. The transaction was all about forms and rules. It was impersonal. And it ended in yelling, her being mocked by the government caseworker, and a refusal of aid—which was disastrous given her precarious circumstance at that moment.

> "I never think about crowds. I think about individuals," Mother Teresa used to say.

Murray's next interview that day was at the *New York Times* headquarters, where she sat down with the committee in charge of awarding the charitable college scholarships handed out every year by the New York Times Company Foundation. This transaction was highly personal. She told them how her mother sold their donated Thanksgiving turkey for drugs; how she had slept in stairwells since her mother died of AIDS; about not eating and living off a food pantry; and about what kept her spirits intact throughout these trials. She was soon awarded one of the foundation's six scholarships (with which she eventually graduated from Harvard). And when a very personal story about her life was published by the *Times*, donations poured in which not only allowed Murray to occupy an apartment and start eating regularly, but also provided the means for the foundation to award 15 more college scholarships than expected.

Murray herself makes clear how important personal factors are in any helping interaction. "During my more vulnerable moments, I was always seeing myself through the eyes of others." If they looked at her as a failure, "then I was one." And if they looked at her as "someone capable, then I was capable. When teachers like Ms. Nedgrin saw me as a victim—despite her good intentions—that's what I believed about myself too. Now I had teachers who held me to a higher standard, and that helped me rise to the occasion. The deeply personal relationships in this intimate school setting made me believe." With the help of just a few well-placed helping hands—philanthropists as it happens, though that is too cool and greek a word to capture the intimacy of what they did for her—Murray eventually wrenched herself out of a death-spiral. It could not have been done without human closeness.

PHILANTHROPY FREQUENTLY SEEKS TO TRANSFORM, NOT JUST TREAT

Philanthropists are often driven by a deeper, wider, more comprehensive ambition than just giving aid. Instead of merely compensating for ills, philanthropy often tries to correct them. It works preemptively to stop the flow of hot lava, rather than simply putting out the fires it creates.

An early advocate for this aspect of American philanthropy was Ben Franklin. His own extensive giving aimed not so much to relieve men in their misfortune as to reform them into a healthier state. "The best way of doing good to the poor is not making them easy in poverty, but leading or driving them out of it," he wrote. Improving the world that strugglers live in was Franklin's notion of the best way to do good for fellow men. Libraries, schools, occupational training, and all forms of education, self-improvement, and character-building were his favorite causes.

This connects to the previous point about philanthropy being individualized and intimate. If improving private behavior and building self-governance is what you are trying to do, a personal approach is essential. And in our country, the goal of charity has always been individual competence and independence, not just social quiet.

As a Polish journalist who traveled across the U.S. in 1876 observed to newspaper readers back in Europe, the charitable impulses of Americans are very specific. "A man who is old and infirm, a woman, or a child receive more assistance in the United States than anywhere else," he noted. But "a healthy young man will almost invariably hear one piece of advice: 'Help yourself!' And if he does not know how to follow this advice, he may even die of starvation."

Strong citizens and strong communities make most palliative aid unnecessary. In law enforcement it is a truism that heading off bad behavior is much preferable to cleaning up after a crime. American philanthropists often take a similar approach to social reform—better to help people build sturdy habits than to rescue them after they fall.

In a free society, one doesn't really want government, with its coercive powers, to get into the business of personal transformation. There's too much risk of Big Brother authoritarianism in that. But donors can do this work well on a voluntary basis. They offer carrots that encourage individual reform, while at the same time assisting recovery from prior mistakes. This has great value to society.

In 2015 The Philanthropy Roundtable published a book called *Clearing Obstacles to Work* which catalogues the secrets of hundreds of successful charities that help homeless people, released prisoners, welfare moms, and other at-risk populations succeed economically and stand on their own two feet. These effective charities don't just give out jobs and apartments and checks. Without exception, they require their clients to rise to the occasion—they expect them to learn and cooperate and expend effort. In short they treat them as equal partners and ask them to contribute, rather than patronizing them with undemanding alms.

> Better to help people build sturdy habits than to rescue them after they fall.

PHILANTHROPY IS PLURALISTIC

Polyarchy. That's a great $50 word for any American to know. It refers to a society in which there are many independent sources of power. Contrast it to monarchy. The United States has a notably polyarchic culture, and independent grassroots philanthropic giving is one big aspect of this.

The polyarchy fed by philanthropy increases variety in our lives and protects non-mainstream points of view. There is only one federal government, and it necessarily applies a uniform approach to all who approach the throne. At the state level we have 50 power centers but only one applies to our own life. If you count every single school board and village administration and water district in the U.S. there are about 100,000 government entities all told, but again only one holds sway where we live, and we usually have no alternative to what it presents us.

Meanwhile, there are about *two million* independent organizations in our civil society, and *hundreds of millions* of separate adult donors. These overlap and compete; none have an exclusive franchise; we can pick and choose, mix and match. And as alternate sources of resources and organizing power these voluntary elements are antidotes to any uniform authority that could become oppressive, or just ineffective. ("The legislator is obliged to give a character of uniformity…which does not always suit the diversity of customs and district," observed Tocqueville.)

Yale law professor Stephen Carter points out that "the individual who gives to charity might measure the needs of the community by different calipers than centralized policy makers, and will therefore contribute to a different set of causes. These millions of individual decisions lead to a diversity in spending that would be impossible if we adopted the theory that the only money spent for the public good is the money spent by the state." Philanthropy "also helps resolve an information problem: Government officials, no matter how well-intentioned, cannot know all the places where donations are needed, or the form that will be most useful." Philanthropy is thus "democracy in action."

Give away houses built by bleeding-heart church volunteers! Ask small business owners to have coffee with a prisoner every month, and college kids to spend a day with his children! Adapt Mormon welfare programs to other hungry and homeless people! Recruit school teachers from the Ivy League! It is much easier for private givers to invent and experiment in these sorts of ways. They can try liberationist models, authority-based models, religious approaches, mentoring influences, and other strategies that would be off-limits to public agencies.

The sprawling, multidimensioned society that America has grown into is often too complex for government-provided single-solution answers. In areas like family life, schooling options, health, and so forth, many citizens would prefer to choose from independent and voluntary social solutions rather than have a government-provided version forced on them. Do we really want public authorities deciding what's in our art galleries, who trains our children in moral virtues, and the size of soda we should drink? It will often be more realistic and desirable to address these sorts of issues through multifarious private voluntary efforts. Let a thousand flowers bloom.

Philanthropic solutions, right-leaning professor Les Lenkowsky has pointed out, are "especially important for people with ideas that may be unpopular, innovative, or directed at a minority of the population…. Philanthropy, in short, is an expression of pluralism." Left-leaning professor Rob Reich makes the very same point. Because they "decentralize production of public goods and curtail government orthodoxy," he writes, philanthropists provide "pluralism of public goods."

In addition to reinforcing freedom and innovation, this aspect of private giving has many practical advantages. What works to reverse homelessness or alcoholism or loneliness in old age may be quite different in Nebraska than in Newark (or Namibia). Yet in public programs it's hard to allow different rules and pursue varying strategies. In philanthropy that's easy. Indeed that's one of the field's inherent strengths.

One of the distinctive (and for many of us encouraging) aspects of contemporary life is the rapid "nicheification" of choices. Not long ago we had three national news networks, and three national car makers, and three national entertainment channels. Many neighborhoods had one hospital choice, one public school, one department store, and one dominant employer. Today we have many more options, allowing us to select from quite different priorities, and values, and tastes. Philanthropy has always enjoyed this rich variety.

Another subtle way that philanthropy protects diversity and options is by giving the social visions of different time periods their chance to chip away at problems, allowing points of view that are out of fashion, or just forgotten, to retain a foothold. "The great thing about the legal protection of charitable trusts over time is that we don't all have a bunch of institutions in 2013 that are wholly determined by what trustees happen to think in 2013. That would lead to an appalling homogenization of our cultural, social, and educational landscape. Instead, people set up different projects in 1880, or 1938, or 1972, and those visions, sometimes gloriously out of step with how we currently think...continue to thrive."

So wrote a trustee of a college in the rural West whose founder stipulated a hundred years ago that it had to be one of the most academically selective in the country, yet require its students to put half of their time into ranch work, that it had to be all male, and never bigger than a few dozen students per class. We wouldn't want every American college to have that signature, but how wonderful that there is one that does. Thanks to its donor's rules, Deep Springs College offers a rare and perfect education for a special type of student, while producing results and insights that the rest of the educational establishment can learn from.

PHILANTHROPY IS FLEXIBLE

If you talk to problem-solvers who rely on both private donors and government grants to support their operations, they will tell you that one of the most invaluable things about philanthropy is its flexibility, its trust in social entrepreneurs, its comparative lack of red tape, its willingness to adapt.

This can be seen with crystalline clarity in science philanthropy. It was donors like John Rockefeller, John Hartford, and Lucille Markey who created modern biomedical research and set the template for the way government funders like the National Science Foundation and the National Institutes of Health operate today. Even after the federal science agencies began gushing billions of dollars in all directions, philanthropy remains crucial to the field because it is more flexible.

MIT professor Fiona Murray recently studied the 50 universities that top the list for science-research spending in the U.S. She found that private donors now provide about 30 percent of the total research funding at these places. So the sheer volume of dollars is consequential.

But what's even more important about science philanthropy is the way it is structured. Private funders often take up work that is neglected by federal funders because it is too experimental, too obscure, pursued by scientists too young to have a record, and so forth. "Government research is powerfully conservative. I've been an NIH researcher for decades, and to get an NIH grant today you essentially have to already have solved the problem in question," says Charles Marmar, a top medical scientist at New York University. Private funding is not only more willing to take risks, it is also much faster and less bureaucratic, according to Marmar. "On the philanthropic side donors tend to have business acumen and know how to get things done," he notes.

Philanthropic money often functions as venture capital, supporting high-risk, high-payoff science that is at an early stage or taking an unconventional approach. "What I've always loved about philanthropy is it's money that has a potential to be flexible. It's money that can catalyze new ideas. It's money that lets you push the frontiers, follow the leading edge," states Leroy Hood, one of today's leading biologists. "At the National Institutes of Health, if you haven't completed two thirds of your research, you're probably not going to get a grant, because everything is so competitive and so conservative. So a philanthropist who is willing to say 'Yes, I'll step in and help you find something new' is a jewel."

Hood has relied on donors over and over in his illustrious career. When he was creating a machine to automate the labor-intensive process of sequencing DNA, he applied for NIH grants and "got some of the worst scores the NIH had ever given. People said it was impossible, or they said, 'Why do this? Grad students can do it more easily.'" So Hood turned to Sol Price, the entrepreneurial whiz who originated the warehouse superstore concept that produced Costco and Sam's Club, and then later Bill Gates. With support from these two donors, Hood produced the technology that made much of today's genomic revolution possible.

There are many simple things that make science philanthropy so valuable. For example, the federal bureaucracies are hugely biased toward scientists who have already made their mark—the average age at which researchers receive their first federal grant is 43, and only 1 percent of NIH grants go to researchers 35 or younger. Yet most science breakthroughs originate from precisely those young inquirers who haven't yet fallen into conventional ways of approaching topics. Private funders are vastly more likely to support young investigators.

Private donors are also vastly more willing to buy machines, and erect buildings, and hire technology aides—creating the infrastructure within which discoveries can take place. Government grants are notoriously unwilling to pay for this sort of foundation-laying. Federal grants must be tailored for one discrete experiment and its immediate costs only. That makes it hard for directors to keep their labs operating and continuously improving.

Philanthropy has special importance in bringing resources to new fields, new places, new approaches. Ignoring conventional advice that they give only to established health centers, donors have built top-flight new medical facilities from scratch in places like Kansas City, San Diego, and Houston. Eminent neuroscientist Steven Hyman, who is investigating the genetic bases of mental illness, wanted to do work in Africa because of its unusually diverse genetic pool, "but it would take a huge administrative or bureaucratic effort to run federal grants there. We couldn't think of doing that without private money."

> Science lab directors describe private giving as "gold" and "magic"—for one thing, because it usually arrives without onerous strings attached.

As easily as it fills geographical gaps, philanthropy fill gaps in popularity, conventional wisdom, and intellectual fashion. The list of "orphan" maladies that neither government nor corporate funders were much interested in before donors became involved is long. Trachoma, schistosomiasis, Guinea worm, onchocerciasis, and many other tropical diseases. Geriatric medicine. Retinitis pigmentosa blindness. Huntington's disease. Malaria. "Diseases like schizophrenia, bipolar disorder, and autism have moved out of this black box," reports Hyman. "Without private philanthropy, we wouldn't be able to take risks or get our research up to scale."

The medical establishment was dismissive of his idea when George Papanicolau used a "highly speculative" grant from the Commonwealth Foundation to invent the Pap smear. The AIDS epidemic was still a blurry terror when the Aaron Diamond Foundation ripped into it with a nimbleness, speed, and tolerance for risk that allowed it to pioneer many of the key research and treatment findings needed to battle the disease.

Lab directors prize the fact that private giving usually comes without onerous strings attached. "Unrestricted funds are gold; they're magic," says Eric Lander, director of the Broad Institute and another of the nation's top scientists. "We're able to say when we have a good idea, 'Let's start investing in it now rather than write a grant and start working on it two years from now after it wends its way through the NIH system.'"

In combination, these practical advantages can have remarkable effects. The trust set up by Lucille Markey to support biomedical careers is an excellent illustration. It operated only from the mid-1980s to 1997, when it shut its doors for good after distributing more than $500 million in 200 grants.

The Markey funding was everything that government granting isn't. It was tremendously flexible. Preliminary investigations and risky science of the sort that give NIH or NSF funders lockjaw? No problem. Spend money recruiting great new scientists or graduate students whose exact roles will be determined in the future? Can do. Build or equip a lab before the exact experiments that will unfold there have been plotted? Sure. Shift money from one year to another, or one project to another, to fuel the most promising avenues as they open up? Yup. Dramatically change research directions in response to unexpected experimental results? You'd be stupid not to! Yet almost none of those things can be done with government funding.

The rules which allowed the Markey grants to fuel so much innovation by recipients were explicit: favor young investigators with promise and nurture them through the "valley of death" that extends from the end of their training until their reputations are established. Trust outstanding researchers with wide discretionary powers in using their funds. Support fields with the biggest upside. Fund areas that are important but not popular. Allow not just basic science but also "translational" research that turns new discoveries into useable treatments and technologies. Pay for the infrastructure necessary for great research, not just the research itself. Be patient.

The Markey Scholar Awards offered funding for five to seven years to each recipient, plus money to establish his or her own lab. The 113 Markey awardees turned out to be extraordinarily successful and productive. Eric Lander is an example—during his fellowship he refined new concepts of gene mapping in the lab Markey supported, and today he heads the largest genome center in the world.

A current example of how different philanthropy-funded science can be from state-funded science is the Howard Hughes Medical Institute. The eccentric billionaire who founded it created the institute primarily to conduct its own research instead of handing money to facilities with their own agendas. A 1985 sale of gifted stock made it the wealthiest medical philanthropy in the country.

About 350 Hughes Investigators operate at more than 70 universities, hospitals, or labs across the country in an unusual organizational structure. Their dispersal allows them to benefit from cross-fertilization of ideas, yet they are employed by the institute rather than their host, and benefit from its independence and patience. As a companion to these investigators working far afield, Hughes recently created a major research campus of its own outside Washington, D.C., where it has concentrated more than 400 biologists to do high-risk, long-term research in large interdisciplinary teams. Their more corporate style of investigation is quite different from the traditional individual-researcher model favored by government funders (and by Hughes in its other support), and brings special advantages to certain kinds of discovery work.

A 2009 study by the National Bureau of Economic Research found that these philanthropic models are unusually effective. "Investigators of the Howard Hughes Medical Institute, which tolerates early failure, rewards long-term success and gives its appointees great freedom to experiment...produce high-impact papers at a much higher rate than a control group of similarly accomplished NIH-funded scientists," the study concluded. This meshes with many other observations. "Philanthropy fuels new opportunities in exciting ways," concludes Leroy Hood. "At really excellent places like MIT or Caltech or Harvard, new innovation almost always comes from philanthropy."

> The goal of charity in our country has always been individual competence and independence, not just social quiet.

PHILANTHROPY IS EFFICIENT

A few years ago, academics collected 71 different studies comparing the efficiency of offerings when the same basic service was available from both public agencies and private organizations. They found that in 56 out of the 71 cases, the philanthropic provider was more cost-effective. In ten cases there was no clear difference, and in only five cases was the public provider more efficient.

The public senses and understands this reality, which is one root of its deep affection for charitable operations. Americans know most philanthropic efforts get a lot of bang for the buck. That's why they voluntarily handed $360 billion to charities in 2014.

Asked in 2011 "Which do you think is more cost-effective in promoting social good—private charities or the government?," 73 percent of adults nationwide said charities were the most cost-effective, while 17 percent selected government agencies. (Perhaps you've heard the old definition of social science: "Elaborate demonstrations of the obvious, by methods that are obscure.") Asked in 2010 whether they most trust government, business, or nonprofits to solve "the most pressing issues of our time," 71 percent of Americans picked nonprofits.

To gather more evidence on public attitudes toward philanthropy, The Philanthropy Roundtable commissioned its own national poll in 2015. The results revealed deep public confidence in both the effectiveness and the efficiency of private giving. The results are laid out in a separate section later in this book.

COMMON CRITICISMS OF PHILANTHROPY

It's very easy to underestimate philanthropy. After all, it is carried out in radically decentralized ways, and most of us rarely see anything other than small fragments in operation. Most philanthropy takes place on a local level. It is often private, anonymous, or simply happening out of the public eye.

Even most donors and nonprofits grossly underestimate the problem-solving power of charitable action and how crucial it is to our national flourishing. So not surprisingly there are plenty of out-and-out critics who discount or even mock the idea that major concerns can be addressed via private responses. Philanthropy can be cute, but if you're *serious*, they suggest, get big and governmental or go home.

You've all heard the complaints: Philanthropy is a drop in the bucket! Philanthropy is amateurish! Philanthropy is chaotic and uncoordinated! Its programs are a crazy patchwork! Some donors are mean, or vain, or in it for all the wrong reasons!

Let's look at a few of those claims.

IT'S A DROP IN THE BUCKET!

The next time you hear the gibe above, recall the numbers at the very beginning of this Introduction: The U.S. nonprofit sector now totals to 11 percent of our workforce and 6 percent of GDP, making it much bigger than the "military-industrial complex" and many other important sectors of our society. Let me add one more number: Nonprofits currently control total assets of about $3.5 trillion. That's trillion with a "t."

And here's a little perspective: The Gates Foundation alone (which is just a tiny sliver of our entire philanthropic apparatus) distributes more overseas assistance than the entire Italian government. It is estimated that in just its first two decades, the Gates Foundation's overseas vaccine and medical program (only one element of its total giving) will directly and immediately save the lives of 8 million preschool children. Is that a drop in the bucket?

Then absorb this: Members of U.S. churches and synagogues (who are, in turn, just one part of America's philanthropic army) send *four and a half times* as much money overseas to needy people every year as the Gates Foundation does! Indeed, private U.S. philanthropic aid of all sorts sent overseas now substantially exceeds the official foreign aid of the U.S. government. As of 2011, the annual totals were $39 billion of philanthropy versus $31 billion from government. (And on top of that, individual Americans, mostly immigrants, sent an additional $100 billion abroad to support relatives and friends in foreign lands.)

When Tocqueville made his classic visits across America he wrote, "In the United States I am even more struck by the innumerable multitude of little undertakings than by the extraordinary size of some of their enterprises.... One is therefore in daily astonishment at the immense works carried through without difficulty by a nation which, one may say, has no rich men." The power of innumerable little undertakings is even clearer today—when wealth and power are spread all across our sprawling continental nation.

Getting seduced by giantism is easy, but it's an egregious mistake. Just because something is big and shiny and official doesn't mean it is effective. And just because certain actions are small doesn't mean they can't accumulate into mighty rivers of joined effort. When private citizens in every community take care of little things, nearby things, civic needs in their own towns, the net result will often be mightier than any bureaucratic mobilization.

The best metaphors for the achievements of philanthropy are not marching armies or triumphant grand-slam home runs. Think instead of the gradual changes wrought by nature. "For many years a tree might wage a slow and silent warfare against an encumbering wall, without making any visible progress," writes Lloyd Douglas in his novel *The Robe*.

Then one day the wall topples over. "The patient work of self-defense… had reached fulfillment."

In one of his poems, Arthur Clough offers a similar image of the power of subtle, gradual action:

> …while the tired waves, vainly breaking,
> seem here no painful inch to gain,
> far back, through creeks and inlets making,
> comes silent, flooding in, the main.

These descriptions capture well the way that philanthropy works. Drop by drop, yes. But inexorable, omnipresent, and adding up forcefully.

IT'S AMATEURISH!

It's easy to caricature grassroots solutions. You've probably seen the wise-guy bumper stickers saying things like "It'll be a great day when social issues get strong public funding and the Pentagon has to hold bake sales to buy bombers." Well, I'm here to tell you that bake sales, and other small-scale acts like them, can do great things.

Lizzie Kander was working as a truant officer in Milwaukee in the 1890s when she discovered that the home conditions of Russian immigrant families were "deplorable…threatening the moral and physical health of the people." Believing that women were the keys to household success and acculturation, she devoted herself to charitable initiatives teaching cleanliness, child education, good nutrition, household skills, and economically useful trades to Russian women. By 1900 she was deeply involved in running a settlement house that assimilated Jewish immigrants using funds donated by Milwaukee businessmen.

> The Gates Foundation alone (which is just a tiny sliver of our entire philanthropic apparatus) distributes more overseas assistance than the entire Italian government.

When additional money was needed, Kander compiled a 174-page cookbook-cum-housekeeping-guide to sell as a fundraiser. The board of directors would not pay the $18 needed to print the book, so she paid for production by selling ads. It became known as the *Settlement Cook Book*, with the very politically incorrect subtitle, "The Way to a Man's Heart." Goofy little bake-sale project, right? Well, the book eventually sold two million copies. And the revenue stream from this idiosyncratic effort paid for the mainstreaming of Jewish immigrants in the upper Midwest for 75 years, along with many other charitable projects.

Let me extend the point with another example from the same era and a similar cause. Amid the turmoil of World War I and pogroms breaking out in Eastern Europe and the Near East, many American Jews became concerned for the safety of co-religionists abroad. So, in classic American fashion, a charitable fundraising committee was formed to help resettle refugees, and a goal of $5 million was announced. To kick things off, four anonymous donors pledged $100,000 each if another $600,000 could be raised in New York at a single event. A gala was scheduled at Carnegie Hall for December of 1915. Very soon, requests for tickets were triple the hall's capacity. On the day of the fundraiser more than 3,000 people congregated outside the building in the hope of being admitted at the last minute.

The event featured a string of speakers describing the dangers Jews faced abroad. Then people began walking to the stage one by one to drop off donations. In addition to cash, slips of paper pledging monthly gifts piled up. The *New York Times* reported that some in attendance left rings, necklaces, and earrings. When the event ended, the gifts exceeded $1 million. This inspired major donors like Julius Rosenwald, Jacob Schiff, Nathan Straus, and Felix Warburg to make big pledges. Throughout the next few years an estimated 3 million Americans donated, raising many millions for this urgent cause.

Even when they don't make a big wave like the Carnegie Hall fundraiser, or Lizzie Kander's cookbook-fed-charity, quirky human-scale projects can do lovely things. There is a little $5 million foundation in Baltimore called the Anna Emory Warfield Fund that has one simple mission: help elderly women who want to stay in their homes do so "in the style to which they are accustomed." Grants can be as little as a few hundred dollars to pay for a handyman to repair overflowing gutters, or a few thousand dollars to catch up on mortgage payments or weather a temporary health crisis. No one has any illusions that these grants are changing the world. But for a widow at risk of outliving her savings, or a retired teacher who doesn't have the means or inclination to enter a nursing home, this quiet support can be a godsend that prevents life from spiraling out of control.

Programs that grow naturally from the bottom up rather than the top down not only collect together into larger actions, but have overlapping qualities that can magnify their effect. Piece together a handyman grant here, a meal-delivery service there, and a volunteer program for driving people to doctor's appointments, and independent life remains possible. Add a video-medicine program that lets you consult with out-of-town specialists, and a hospice when the end draws near. A family-building effort down the street, an alternative school across town, and a county-wide college scholarship program might make all the difference to a young person. Take an inspiring donor-funded museum nearby, and a devoted effort to get local kids out of foster care, and your community feels different. Cumulate these kinds of philanthropic projects and soon you have a gorgeous, continually regenerating, transcontinental quilt that covers millions of local needs and longings.

Amateur webs of giving and volunteering make every one of our home towns more livable, richer, safer, more charming, more interesting. The varied and sometimes underappreciated gifts that donors offer their fellow citizens fill human hungers that would otherwise be ignored or foisted on impersonal and less effective state agencies. This work is a great strength of our country.

IT'S UNCOORDINATED!

Even loyal donors will sometimes complain that the factor limiting philanthropy is that it's not coordinated. Rules vary all over the place. It lacks uniformity. There are holes. Everybody gets to make their own decisions. People go off in many different directions. No one's in control. Chaos! The Wild West! Some observers are really bothered by a lack of standardizing forces that get everyone marching in the same direction (as government programs do).

There's one problem with that rather authoritarian critique: Non-coordination can just as easily be considered an advantage as a problem. Recent decades have taught us that in economics, technology, social practice, and community life, decentralized multiplicity can be a saving grace. That is even truer in philanthropy than in many other areas.

I worked for three years in the West Wing, overseeing domestic policy for the President, and one of the deepest impressions that work made on me was how heavy the tread of the federal government is. We'd take up a problem and I'd realize, "whatever we do, however well-considered our reforms, we are going to discombobulate millions of people." Since the entire federal apparatus swings in one direction with any rule change, it is very hard to test competing policies, to turn faucets on slowly, or to allow differing solutions in different places. Almost every new federal policy turns over the apple carts of many completely innocent parties and disrupts the settled expectations of large numbers of families and communities. I left the White House hungry for less monolithic, less uniform, more decentralized ways of attacking problems.

Humans are not predictable robots, so the healthiest forms of society-building often proceed in an empirical way: test, experiment, undertake lots of trials, recognizing that many—perhaps most—will fail. But so long as our whole society isn't swerving in unison in one direction, the errors will generally cancel each other out, the failures will be exposed, and the successful ventures will become visible and then be copied.

This is an argument for dispersal of resources. For divided attacks. For independent assessment. Exactly the things that private philanthropy provides.

> Humans are not predictable robots, so the healthiest forms of society-building often grow out of small tests, divided attacks, independent assessments—exactly the things that private philanthropy excels at.

Yes, you will be told that breaking the responsibility for social problem-solving into hundreds of pieces and then handing these off to thousands of charities and foundations and private doers of good is medieval, and will never be effective in our modern world. Critics will portray it as mere dabbling in the face of giant pressures. Such criticism, however, seriously misunderstands the power of the human anthill, at least under American organization.

A wonderful new word was coined in 2005 to describe a reliance on dispersed authority to fix things: crowdsourcing. The effectiveness of chewing through big issues via lots of small bites by dispersed participants is a fundamental reality understood by wise humans for millennia. But it has been brought into high relief by aspects of the computer revolution.

In the early years of computing (not very long ago), the largest supercomputers were extraordinarily complex centralized devices, where all the wires led to one extremely expensive custom-made processing chip. Today, there is no king processor in a supercomputer. The latest versions are made with around 40,000 plebeian, everyday chips just like the one in your Dell, all working in democratic parallel. And this so-called "distributed intelligence" has turned out to be vastly more potent than the elegant genius of the old centralized Cray supercomputers that worked from the top down.

Forms of distributed computing are being applied to many of today's most difficult problems. For instance, the vast amounts of astronomical data that need to be sifted through in order to discover a possible planet transiting a distant sun, or a possible radio signal from another civilization, are being processed by hundreds of thousands of volunteers on their home computers.

Or take the Linux computer operating system—the computer code which has become the backbone of the digital business world. There is no master control over what goes into Linux. Software drafts are passed around over the Internet, where thousands of informal contributors just add and subtract and tinker with the code and then put the result out there in the marketplace. If that sounds like chaos, you haven't been paying attention. This so-called open-source method of creating software solutions has turned out to be remarkably orderly and powerful, and the result is that Linux quickly turned into the most flexible and effective computer operating system available.

The pattern of complex problems being solved by small actors working locally and independently without heavy central direction is not just the story of the Internet, it is a phenomenon common to much of technology, and biology, and human history.

Some years ago, I read a book called *Ants at Work*, written by a Stanford entomologist who spent 17 years studying a large colony of harvester ants. The author's goal was to learn how these tens of thousands of tiny creatures coordinate the specialized tasks essential to colony health—food harvest and storage, care of offspring, tunnel digging, garbage toting, war fighting, etc. Who's directing the show to make sure the right work gets done at the right time?

The answer, she discovered, is that *nobody* is in charge. No insect issues commands to another. The colony operates without any central or hierarchical control. These complex societies are instead built, she reports, on thousands of simple decisions made by individual creatures based on what they see around them, with those many microdecisions melding together to yield an efficient macro-result. I suggest the right term for this is *self-organization*, and it's something of an iron rule throughout the natural world, not only among bugs, but also at the very top of nature's pyramid—in human society.

As a simple example of the general superiority of decentralized problem-solving, consider what happens every fall weekend in football stadiums. Even a boozy crowd can drain itself from a packed oval in a matter of minutes. Yet emptying that stadium by commanding each person from some master perch, as readers with some background in mathematics or statistics will know, is an almost insoluble problem. You could cover the field from goal post to goal post with computers and programmers, and you'd end up frustrated. There are just too many variables—80,000 people, 25 exits, scores of stairways, thousands of stairs, pillars that block certain routes, backups in specific aisles; it's just too much to orchestrate.

Yet leave each Joe to himself and he'll be opening the door to his Chevy before the scoreboard lights are cool. He may not realize that he's exhibiting what scientists call "large-scale adaptive intelligence in the absence of central direction." But he is. Less trivial examples abound: vast and absolutely crucial human tasks like food distribution, for instance, are managed in the U.S. without any central organization. This is not just acceptable, it is an *advantage*, increasing variety and innovation and customization to meet specific circumstances.

Thanks to technology making the mechanics easier, crowd-based problem-solving is on a sharp upswing today, including in philanthropy. Did you know that way back in 2012, Kickstarter roared past the National Endowment for the Arts in providing money for arts and culture projects? Charities like DonorsChoose.org offer remarkable opportunities for Americans to fund grassroots educational help. The fascinating philanthropy SpiritofAmerica.net collects ideas from U.S. Special Forces operators in poor, dangerous countries on ways to enhance stability and reduce

> The decentralized multiplicity of philanthropy increases variety in our lives, and protects non-mainstream points of view.

the temptation to violence and radicalism by making small improvements in community life. Donors view choices online and sign up to send sewing machines to Iraqi women, or educational supplies to a school destroyed by terrorists in the Philippines, or handheld spotlights for police working the Pakistan-Afghanistan border. Even the Smithsonian launched a crowdfunding campaign in 2015, seeking $500,000 to restore the space suit worn by Neil Armstrong on the moon. The effort quickly exceeded $720,000, given by 9,500 people.

Dispersed authority and funding may be new to military work, or to the Smithsonian. But it is the longstanding backbone of philanthropy. I'll plant my little seeds over here, and you till your garden over there, and soon the world turns green and lovely.

This is not a matter of ideology, or of sweet-breathed philanthropists trumping wicked government officials. It is a simple matter of practicality and surrender to the facts about how humans accomplish things most effectively. Local citizens tend to have better information than remote authorities on the optimal ways to solve their problems. Trying to separate good schools or good doctors from poor ones is a very hard task from Washington, but people in the neighborhood can usually steer you right away to either. Nearby helpers are also likelier to tailor solutions to specific circumstances and to create varied answers instead of just one template for everybody. Decentralized solutions tend also to be more respectful of individual sovereignty and personal preferences.

So lack of coordination and uniformity needn't be considered a problem. Indeed, it is often helpful. To take just one example, philanthropists can take much bigger risks than a government program creator would dare because the philanthropist knows he's not betting the entire national farm. He can try something new, retune as it unfolds, and expand or walk away depending on how it succeeds.

What do you suppose ran through the minds of the foundation officials who were first pitched on the idea of a bank built on $27 loans to rag pickers and fruit-cart pushers in Bangladesh? Probably that it sounded wildly improbable. Thank goodness they gave it a shot anyway. And thus was microfinance born, which grew quickly into a strapping poverty-squashing grownup.

IT'S A PATCHWORK!

Our society has rapidly moved beyond the old industrial-revolution paradigm of the one big factory. We now rely much more on networks and ecosystems of smaller providers working in loose synchronization. A perfect example of this is one of the great philanthropic creations of the last generation—charter schooling.

The very largest charter-school chain in the nation, KIPP, operates a total of 183 schools. Meanwhile, there are now more than 7,000 charter schools in total. So this is a radically decentralized sector. Most schools are solo operations or part of a very small group running just a handful of campuses.

And this allows a riot of choices. There are math and science schools. Schools built around the Great Books. Hippie schools without walls, doors, or other controlling features! Work oriented schools! Quasi-military schools where the all-male student body wears uniforms and has ranks! Academies that only assign books by gentle left-handed poets! The charter movement is built on the idea that there is no single definition of what constitutes a good school, that education is an exercise in matching each child's temperament and gifts with an institution that can bring out his or her best self.

Part of this bubbling variety is churn. Every year now, about 650 new charter schools open their doors and offer their new neighborhood some fresh approach. And in that same year, more than 200 schools will close down, because their offerings were not well embraced.

Here's a Rorschach test: Are those wildly different schools, and that annual churn, signs of inconsistency, patchwork, and trouble? Or are they healthy signs of adaptation to what people want? If you prize stability and predictability, the conventional public school (which is basically impossible to close down even when it's abysmal!) may be your preference (at least for other people's children). But if it seems humane to offer citizens more of what they prize, and less of what they are choosing to walk away from, then the constant gurgling and gap-filling may be a reflection of the very kindest and gentlest sort of philanthropy.

Within the charitable sector itself there are even further levels of customization and "inconsistency." The KIPP schools are an example. While they have a few bedrock principles and uniform high standards, schools in various regions are given a wide degree of independence and autonomy for coping with their own particular needs.

Goodwill Industries, another extraordinarily successful charity, is likewise more interested in results than in uniform rules and operations. Goodwill's operation is vast: workforce training provided to 26 million persons annually in a great variety of fields; over $5 billion in revenues; more than 3,000 stores in the U.S., Canada, and 13 other countries. Yet each of the 165 Goodwill regional branches is autonomous in policy and funding, and has its own board of directors. Local branches can assist each other, and can request advice or aid from the world headquarters. But the central office's budget is dwarfed by those of affiliates in cities like Milwaukee and Houston.

This same lack of monolithic uniformity can be seen across the philanthropic sector—in everything from the 1,500 independent local chapters of Habitat for Humanity, to the very different regional branches of the Appalachian Mountain Club that maintain thousands of mile of hiking trails in their own distinctive ways. This locally varying "nicheification" of service provision is also a strong trend in private business today. The Netflix company actually has a catchphrase for the way it puts this principle to work inside the firm. It wants its various corporate teams to be "highly aligned, yet loosely coupled." The vision, in other words, needs to be shared, but the execution should be decentralized.

This longstanding hallmark of charitable work is nothing that philanthropists should feel embarrassed or apologetic about. A riotous patchwork can be a thing of great beauty.

SOME DONORS AREN'T NICE!

Another reality which sometimes gets critics fulminating and makes philanthropists defensive is the fact that certain donors are mean, or selfish, or seem more interested in getting their name on a building, or a tax break, than in altruism. In my experience, human kindness and empathy are commoner among loyal donors than among an average cross-section of the population, but it is definitely true that there are some philanthropists who do their good for not so good reasons. Indeed, certain of these men and women are laughably far from angelic in their motivations.

J. Paul Getty was a cheapskate who made visitors to his estate use a pay phone at a time when he was one of the richest men in the world. He was a serial womanizer whose own father didn't trust him. When his grandson was kidnapped for $17 million ransom he kept dickering for a lower payment until the criminals cut off the boy's ear and mailed it to grandpa. Even then, Getty only put up as much of the ransom as was tax-deductible ($2.2 million), and gave his son the rest

> Trying to separate good schools or good doctors from poor ones is a very hard task from Washington, but people in the neighborhood can usually steer you right away to either.

as a loan—at 4 percent interest. Yet Getty gave the world one of its most sublime collections of Greek and Roman art, a gift that will elevate souls for centuries to come.

Russell Sage was a notorious miser and convicted usurer. He cheated his wife's father in business. When a mad extortionist dynamited his office, he used a clerk as a human shield, then refused to pay compensation for the man's injuries. Yet Sage's fortune created one of the most influential early charitable foundations in the country.

There is no denying that corruption made Leland Stanford rich. To build his railroad fortune he employed kickbacks, bribes, stock watering, collusion, monopolization, and political manipulation. Yet genuine grief over the death of his son motivated Stanford to use his ill-gotten lucre to benefit the children of California (and ultimately all of humanity) by creating Stanford University.

George Eastman could be as cold-blooded as he was brilliant and generous. He asked his doctor to outline the exact location of his heart on his chest. Later he reclined on his bed, centered a pistol where the doctor had drawn, and committed suicide rather than face old age.

So philanthropists are not always pretty. And even when they do bring the best of motives to the task, their efforts can disappoint. As Andrew Carnegie established the Carnegie Endowment for International Peace with a $10 million grant, he optimistically included a stipulation on what the group should do after it ended all armed conflict: "When the establishment of universal peace is attained, the donor provides that the revenue shall be devoted to the banishment of the *next* most degrading evil."

He wrote that in 1910. Oops.

> The genius of the philanthropic mechanism is that it takes people just as they are and helps them do wondrous things, even when they're not saints.

Are there stupid or cruel givers? Are there dumb projects launched by donors? Of course. But charitable programs that don't produce results soon die or transform into something more useful. When was the last time you saw a dumb government program die?

And here's the fascinating secret of philanthropy: Charity doesn't have to come from people who are charitable. You don't need to be an angel to participate. In fact, motivations of any sort aren't that important. The genius of the philanthropic mechanism is that it takes people just as they are—kind impulses, selfish impulses, confusions and wishes and vanities of all sorts swirling together in the usual human jumble—and it helps them do wondrous things, even when they're not saints.

Philanthropy is a machine that is able to convert the instincts and actions of even the meanest of men into truth, uplift, and beauty. Adam Smith taught us that freely conducted commerce can take normal human behaviors, including ugly and mercenary ones, and turn them to broadly productive uses. This is as true in the world of philanthropy as in business. Base impulses like greed, insecurity, image-laundering, and egotism can become gold, or at least good useful brass.

Happily, most philanthropy is the work of decent and earnest men and women. Even the worst misanthropes, however, are regularly redirected into doing useful, and even great, things for all of society. That is part of the power of America's charitable structure.

BIG-PICTURE BENEFITS OF PHILANTHROPY

Let's close this introduction by looking at some of the broadest and deepest ways that philanthropy makes our lives and our nation better. I don't mean the good done to recipients of aid, or the pragmatic value of donated money and time, or other obvious advantages. In this final section we'll look at some of the philosophical, moral, and political gains to America that grow out of our giving tradition.

PRIVATE GIVING SATISFIES DEEP HUMAN NEEDS

It's easy to overlook the fact that philanthropy doesn't just help the recipients—it offers profound life satisfaction to givers as well. It opens avenues to meaning and happiness and ways of thriving that aren't easily found otherwise. When I was in college I had a philosophy professor named Louis Dupre who told me a story I've never forgotten. He had a wonderfully generous friend from whom he eventually fell away for the most paradoxical reason: this friend was unable to let Dupre be generous and giving in return. Receiving gifts and favors can be lovely, but there is also a potent and irreplaceable joy of giving that most people need to express.

The joy of giving is captured frequently in literature:

> It is one of the most beautiful compensations of life that no man can sincerely try to help another without helping himself.
>
> ↝ *Ralph Waldo Emerson*

> As the purse is emptied the heart is filled.
>
> ↝ *Victor Hugo*

If you want happiness for a year, inherit a fortune. If you want happiness for a lifetime, help someone else.

↝ *Confucius*

The best recreation is to do good.

↝ *William Penn*

If you want to lift yourself up, lift up someone else.

↝ *Booker T. Washington*

A man there was, though some did count him mad, the more he cast away, the more he had.

↝ *John Bunyan*

Giving is an ancient impulse. Way back in 347 B.C., Plato donated his farm to support students at the school he founded. It is also a widespread impulse. Even people who have very little money are eager to give, and feel good when they do, as documented in several places later in this *Almanac*.

The book *Breaking Night* tells the true story of a neglected girl and the kind people who intervened to help her succeed in spite of her horrendous upbringing. "What was most moving about all of this unexpected generosity," writes the now-grown child, "was the spirit in which people helped. It was something in their moods and in their general being…how they were smiling, looking me right in the eyes."

She describes a woman named Teressa who came up to her and said, "Since I didn't have any money to help you out, I thought I couldn't do anything for you at all. And then last night, I was doing my daughter's laundry, and I thought, how silly of me, maybe you had laundry I could do for you." Every week for the remainder of the author's time in school, Teressa picked up dirty clothes and returned them clean and folded, taking great pleasure in this little thing she could do to help.

Lots of research shows that this is a common phenomenon. A 2014 book by two Notre Dame social scientists called *The Paradox of Generosity* combined national surveys with in-depth interviews and group observations. It concluded that "the more generous Americans are, the more happiness, health, and purpose in life they enjoy. This association…is strong and highly consistent.… Generous practices actually create enhanced personal well-being. The association…is not accidental, spurious, or an artifact of reverse causal influence." They conclude with the observation that "People often say that we increase the love we have by giving it away.... Generosity is like love in this way."

In a 2008 paper published in *Science*, three researchers gave study participants money, asking half of the group to spend it on themselves, and the other half to give it to some person or charity. Those who donated the money showed a significant uptick in happiness; those who spent it on themselves did not. In his book *Who Really Cares*, economist Arthur Brooks cites a host of similar studies showing that Americans who make gifts of money and time are much more likely to be satisfied with life than non-givers who are demographically identical.

PRIVATE GIVING IMPROVES CAPITALISM

Capitalism and philanthropy have always been closely tied. In the 1600s when the Netherlands was gestating free trade and many modern business patterns, there were alms boxes in most taverns (where business negotiations generally took place), and a successful deal was expected to conclude with a charitable gift.

Philanthropy and business are entwined especially tightly in America. One of the most distinctive aspects of American capitalism is the deep-seated

> Philanthropy doesn't just help the recipients— it offers profound life satisfaction to givers as well.

tradition of philanthropy that has evolved among American business barons. Our capitalism also differs from the capitalism practiced in other countries in two other important ways—in its linkage to religiosity, and its preference for entrepreneurial forms. Both of these are also connected to philanthropy.

Let's unpack this a bit, starting with religion. In 2014, the Pew Research Center released data comparing the per capita wealth of nations with the religious beliefs of their people. The U.S. stands out like a sore thumb:

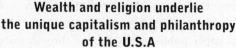

Wealth and religion underlie the unique capitalism and philanthropy of the U.S.A

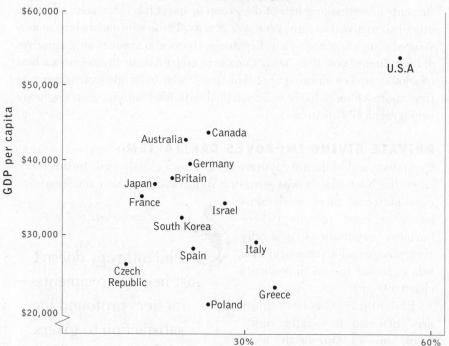

Percent of population saying religion
plays a very important role in their lives

Source: *Pew Research Center, 2013 data*

The Calvinism that came to the U.S. with the Pilgrims (and continued to dominate our religious views for generations right up to the present) treats wealth as something that passes through the hands of a successful person—with the steward expected to apply it to uplift his fellow man. Thus John Rockefeller gave away 95 percent of his fortune by the time he died. Bill Gates is in the process of giving away tens of billions of dollars, leaving his three children only $10 million each.

That is different from the pattern in Europe, where many of the same dynasties have dominated the rolls of the wealthy for generations. The Howard family, for instance, has been one of Britain's richest for more than 500 years. In the U.S., wealth tends to be extremely transient. Only 15 to 20 percent of the individuals on today's *Forbes* list of richest Americans inherited wealth. About half the the *Forbes* 400 had parents who didn't go to college at all. Even the foundations left behind by the previously wealthy rapidly get eclipsed in America: the Rockefeller Foundation, once our richest, now ranks a mere number 15, while the Carnegie Corporation has fallen to number 24.

A second distinctive aspect of American capitalism is its entrepreneurial bent. As economists Zoltan Acs and Ronnie Phillips write, "American capitalism differs from all other forms of industrial capitalism" in two ways. One is its emphasis on the creation of new wealth via entrepreneurship. New firms, new ideas, and nouveau riche wealthmakers are at the core of our economic success.

This can be demonstrated in many ways. If you look at the 500 largest companies in the world today, you find that 29 percent of the U.S. firms were founded after 1950, compared to just 8 percent of the European firms. On a per capita basis, the U.S. has four times as many self-made billionaire entrepreneurs as Europe.

Entrepreneurialism and philanthropy are often tightly connected, and linked directly with economic success. In their book *Super-Entrepreneurs*, Swedish researchers Tino and Nima Sanandaji investigated about 1,000 self-made billionaires from around the world. They found "a very strong correlation" between entrepreneurship, wealth, and philanthropy.

> Dispersed authority is the backbone of philanthropy. I'll plant my little seeds over here, and you till your garden over there, and soon the whole world turns green and lovely.

Acs and Phillips argue that in addition to its distinctive means of creating wealth through new enterprises, the U.S. has a distinctive means of "reconstituting" wealth via philanthropy. "Philanthropy is part of the implicit social contract that continuously nurtures and revitalizes economic prosperity," they write. Philanthropy is a very important mechanism for recycling wealth in America, agree the Sanandajis. "The notion exists that wealth beyond a certain point should be invested back in society to expand opportunity for future generations," they write. "'The legitimacy of American capitalism has in part been upheld through voluntary donations from the rich'.... Much of the new wealth created historically has thus been given back to society. This has had several feedback effects on capitalism. For one, the practice has limited the rise of new dynasties. Another positive feedback mechanism is that the donations to research and higher education have allowed new generations to become wealthy."

PRIVATE GIVING STRENGTHENS DEMOCRACY

Civil society and charitable action sprang up in the U.S. even before government did. In most of our new communities, mutual aid among neighbors was solving problems long before there were duly constituted agencies of the state.

> Americans of all ages, all conditions, and all dispositions constantly form associations...religious, moral, serious, futile, general or restricted, enormous or diminutive. The Americans make associations to give entertainments, to found seminaries, to build inns, to construct churches, to diffuse books, to send missionaries to the antipodes; in this manner they found hospitals, prisons, and schools. If it is proposed to inculcate some truth or to foster some feeling by the encouragement of a great example, they form a society. Wherever at the head of some new undertaking you see the government in France, or an aristocrat in England, in the United States you will be sure to find an association.

That was Tocqueville's observation in *Democracy in America* close to 200 years ago.

As the title of the French visitor's book suggests, what impressed him about voluntary action in the U.S. was not just its practical ability to solve problems, but the way it exercised and built up the social muscles needed if people were to govern themselves in a healthy democracy. Tocqueville considered American voluntary associations not just signs, but the *source*, of effective self-rule. He wished aloud that this American tradition could be transferred to Europeans, who had lost "the habit of acting in common" on their own, due to generations of smothering by the state.

Some people, Tocqueville wrote,

> claim that as the citizens become weaker and more helpless, the government must become proportionately more skilled and active, so that society should do what is no longer possible for individuals.... I think they are mistaken.... The more government takes the place of associations, the more will individuals lose the idea of forming associations and need the government to come to their help. That is a vicious circle of cause and effect.... The morals and intelligence

of a democratic people would be in [danger]. Feelings and ideas are renewed, the heart enlarged, and the understanding developed only by the reciprocal action of men upon another.

Edmund Burke also viewed local association as the nursery for broader loyalty to one's fellow man. "The little platoon we belong to in society is the first principle (the germ as it were) of public affections. It is the first link in the series by which we proceed towards a love to our country, and to mankind," he wrote.

The great advantages that accrue to America from possessing a bubbling voluntary sector that acts independently have been under threat since the Great Depression, cautions author Richard Cornuelle. The economic crash gave American confidence a knock and planted the idea that "only government seems big enough" to solve serious social issues. "Our habit of sending difficult problems to Washington quickly became almost a reflex" and parts of the public and some of our leaders have turned their back on our deep tradition of indigenous alternatives to government action.

Cornuelle complains that we often now

> speak of American life in terms of only two "sectors": the public sector (government), and the private sector (commerce). We leave out the third sector in our national life, the one which is neither governmental nor commercial. We ignore the institutions which once played such a decisive part in the society's vibrant growth... [which] made it possible for us to build a humane society and a free society together.

This third sector, operating in the space between the individual and the state, between the coercion of law and the profit-seeking of commerce, goes by various names: civil society, the voluntary sector, charitable action. Back in 1970, the Peterson Commission pointed out the crucial need for "institutions standing outside the frame of government but in support of the public interest." Cornuelle called these philanthropic institutions the "independent sector," and warned that they have

> a natural competitor: government. Both sectors operate in the same industry: public service and welfare.... The quality of life in the U.S. now depends largely on the revival of a lively competition between these two natural contenders for public responsibility. The struggle would enhance the effectiveness of both.

In some quarters, Cornuelle observes,

> the very idea of competition with government is, by a weird public myth, thought to be illegitimate, disruptive, divisive, unproductive, and perhaps immoral…. Far from being illegitimate, lively competition with government is essential if our democratic institutions are to work sensibly….
>
> The government doesn't ignore public opinion because the people who run it are naturally perverse. It isn't wasteful because it is manned by wasteful people…. Without competition, the bureaucracy can't make government efficient…. Innovation painfully disrupts its way of life. Reform comes only through competitive outsiders who force steady, efficient adjustment to changing situations.
>
> The independent sector will grow strong again when its leaders realize that its unique indispensable natural role in America is to compete with government. It must be as eager as government to take on new public problems.

There are times and places where governmental rulers feel threatened by the philanthropic process. Philanthropy practiced on a mass level, as in America, becomes a kind of matrix of tens of thousands of private legislatures that set goals and priorities, define social ills, and methodically marshal money and labor to attack them—without asking the state's permission. Some rulers prefer dependent citizens who are *consumers* rather than *producers* of governance.

Certainly tyrants hate philanthropy. They want the state to be the only forum for human influence and control. "Everything within the state, nothing outside the state, nothing against the state," was Mussolini's encapsulation. Independent associations and private wielders of resources must be co-opted or suppressed. The charitable sector is not only denied a seat at the table, it is put on the menu to be eaten. One of the first things every totalitarian government has done upon assuming power—from Nazis, to communists, to radical imams—is to destroy charities, private giving, and voluntary groups.

We're seeing the same phenomenon today in authoritarian countries like Russia, China, and Iran, where charities are being shut down out of fear that they will provide alternate sources of ideas, cultural solutions, and social legitimacy. Only the freest societies have had flourishing philanthropic sectors. In America, our freedom to expend charitable resources without supervision or control is ultimately sheltered by the First Amendment of our Bill of Rights, which protects our right to assemble and act outside of government, to dissent, to take heterogeneous, unpopular, or minority-supported action to redress grievances.

Enlightened, practical, democratic leaders shouldn't just tolerate the independent actions of donors and volunteers, they should embrace and encourage them. Social entrepreneur Neerav Kingsland, who gained prominence by helping build the nation's most extensive web of independent charter schools in New Orleans after the Katrina disaster, has argued that the most effective and humane thing that many public servants can do today to help needy populations is to let go of their monopolies on power. He uses the term "Relinquishers" to describe progress-minded officials who are willing to transfer authority away from centralized bureaucracies in order to allow experimentation and improvement driven by philanthropy, commerce, grassroots activism, and other independent forces.

To illustrate how quickly societal conditions can improve when intelligent Relinquishers cede power to civil actors, Kingsland cites examples from the U.S. and abroad. He charts the explosion of per capita income in India since 1991, where economist and then Prime Minister Manmohan Singh promulgated new policies that made him "one of the greatest Relinquishers of the modern world. Over the past 20 years, his work in transferring power to India's citizens...improved the well-being of hundreds of millions."

> Tyrants hate philanthropy. They want the state to be the only forum for human influence and control. "Everything within the state" was Mussolini's encapsulation.

Another Relinquisher triumph unfolded in New Orleans after philanthropists were allowed to pour resources and expertise into restructuring that city's schools. Government continued to provide funds, fair rules, and accountability, but it allowed independent operators to take over the running of classrooms and academies. The result was that the number of classroom seats rated "high-quality" quadrupled in four years. The fraction of students testing at the proficient level leapt from 35 percent to 56 percent. The ACT scores of graduating seniors hit an historic high.

Sharing responsibility for societal improvement with funders and volunteers in civil society will often be a government policymaker's speediest path to excellence and success—as well as a more democratic course.

IT'S NOT WISE TO RELY SOLELY ON GOVERNMENT

"Every single great idea that has marked the twenty-first century, the twentieth century, and the nineteenth century has required government vision and government incentive." That's Vice President Joe Biden. "The ballot box is the place where all change begins in America." That was Senator Ted Kennedy.

These speakers overlook the vast improving powers of free enterprise. (Government didn't produce the air conditioning that transformed the South, or the mobile phone that is now revolutionizing everything from news to conversation to human attention spans.) They also ignore the profound role of independent philanthropy in altering American history.

Let's take the civil rights movement—a favorite example of advocates who would have you believe that nothing good happens unless government does it. Back in 1704—when 1,500 African Americans in New York City were held as slaves with full government sanction, and educating them was forbidden, private donors set up schools to instruct hundreds of slaves on the quiet. In the early 1830s, when state and federal governments still made it a crime to teach a slave to read, private donors like Arthur Tappan were paying for African Americans to go to college. Less than two years after the bullets of the Civil War stopped flying, philanthropist George Peabody was distributing millions of his own dollars across the South to train teachers and set up schools without racial considerations so that freed slaves and other illiterates could get learning—despite the ferocious antipathy of state and local governments for that cause. In 1891, philanthropist Katharine Drexel gave her entire fortune (half a billion dollars in contemporary terms) to create a new religious order devoted to assisting blacks and Indians. She established 50 schools for African Americans, 145 missions and 12 schools for Native Americans, and the black college Xavier University in New Orleans. In these same years, governments at all levels were doing little more than breaking promises to Native Americans and neglecting African Americans.

As the twentieth century opened, hundreds of governments were fiercely enforcing Jim Crow laws that stunted the education of blacks. But John Rockefeller was pouring money into his new creation for providing

> Philanthropy is crucial to keeping America operating as that exceedingly rare society where most individuals can steer their own lives.

primary education to African Americans. Then he boosted up 1,600 new high schools for poor whites and blacks. He eventually put almost $325 million of his personal fortune into the venture. Simultaneously he was spending millions to improve the health of poor blacks and whites by nearly eliminating hookworm.

Numerous private givers followed the leads of George Peabody and John Rockefeller and donated millions of dollars to improve the education and social status of African Americans at a time when they had no friends in government. The philanthropic help came from Anna Jeanes' Negro Rural Schools Fund, the Phelps Stokes Fund, the Virginia Randolph Fund, the John Slater Fund, and others. These all continued their work until government finally caught up and started desegregating schools in the 1960s.

African American children whose education and social conditions were being wholly neglected by the state got their biggest lift of all from philanthropist Julius Rosenwald. Starting in 1912, he donated the current equivalent of billions of dollars to build schoolhouses in hundreds of counties where black education was ignored. In less than 20 years, the Rosenwald program erected 4,977 rural schools and 380 companion community buildings in most of America's locales with a substantial black population. At the time of Rosenwald's death in 1932, the schools he built were educating fully 27 percent of all the African American children in our country.

Many economic producers and sensible leaders were produced by these philanthropic projects. Absent these private efforts by donors, racial improvement and reconciliation in our country would have been delayed by generations. Government not only had little to do with this philanthropic uplift—many arms of government did their very best to resist or obstruct it.

A curmudgeon might say, "Well that's nice, but it's ancient history. Today, the government leads all necessary change." That is gravely mistaken.

Guess where America's most segregated and often most inadequate government-run schools are located at present? All in northern cities with activist governments: Detroit, Milwaukee, New York, Newark, Chicago, and Philadelphia, research shows. According to the UCLA Civil Right Project, New York is the state with the country's most segregated schools—thanks to New York City, where the proportion of schools in which at least 90 percent of the students are black or Hispanic rose sharply from 1989 to 2010.

The government-operated schools in New York City drip with rhetoric about "social justice." But it is private philanthropy that is shaking up the city's complacently bad educational establishment today—by launching charter schools. As of 2014, there were 83,200 New York City children in charters, nearly all of them minorities and low-income, and 50,000 more remain on waiting lists. Stanford investigators and others find that these children are receiving significantly better educations than counterparts in conventional government-run schools, in some cases outscoring comfortable suburban schools in annual testing. Yet donors and charter-school operators continue to have to fight through the resistance of reactionary progressives in city hall and the New York City Council.

Or let's look at another area where conventional wisdom says nothing important will happen except under governmental banners: Who saved the refugees disrupted by the two World Wars and the ethnic genocides of those decades? When the U.S. Ambassador to Turkey discovered that Ottomans were starving and killing Jews in Palestine, he sent an urgent telegram to philanthropist Jacob Schiff in New York. A fundraising committee was set up, and over the years to come it distributed hundreds of millions of dollars, donated by more than 3 million private givers, saving many thousands of Jews.

> Philanthropy has a long history of taking up crucial burdens in the face of government failure.

It wasn't only Jews who needed saving. At that same time, Muslims were carrying out a jihad against Armenian Christians that ultimately took 1.5 million lives. The U.S. government did little, but everyday Americans, missionaries, church members, and philanthropists sprang into action to both save lives immediately and then sustain the Armenians dislocated by the genocide. Nearly 1,000 Americans volunteered to go to the region to build orphanages and help refugees. They assumed responsibility for 130,000 mother- and fatherless children, and rescued more than a million adults.

It was a similar story when fascism swept Europe. The U.S. government dragged its feet and failed to organize any speedy effective effort to save the Jews, gypsies, Christians, and others targeted by the Nazis. Private donors jumped into the breach. The Rockefeller Foundation, for instance, established two special funds that worked, under the most difficult wartime conditions, to relocate mortally endangered individuals to Allied countries.

As with our civil-rights example, philanthropy taking up crucial burdens in the face of government failure is not just a story in the past tense. In 1993, all Western governments were pathetically slow and inadequate in their response to the ethnic cleansing in Bosnia that killed tens of thousands. The most effective actor by far was philanthropist George Soros—who used $50 million of his own money to insert a highly effective relief team into the city of Sarajevo while it was under siege, re-establishing gas and electric service during the bitter winter, setting up an alternate water supply, and bringing in desperately needed supplies. It has been estimated that Soros's gift saved more lives than the efforts of all national governments plus the United Nations *combined.*

The list of great ideas and dramatic improvements instigated by philanthropy while government was AWOL could be expanded endlessly, from the Green Revolution and invention of microlending abroad, to domestic achievements like the recovery of desolated urban parks, control of drunk driving, and creation of the country's best job-training programs for economic strugglers. And philanthropic change tends to come with much less friction. As one social entrepreneur has put it, philanthropy generally practices "the politics of addition and multiplication," while government action often comes via "the politics of subtraction and division."

WHY PHILANTHROPY IS INDISPENSABLE TO AMERICAN FREEDOM

Let's open this final section with a bit of extended historical analysis by Richard Cornuelle, from his book *Reclaiming the American Dream*:

> We wanted, from the beginning, a free society, free in the sense that every man was his own supervisor and the architect of his own ambitions. So our founders took pains to design a government with limited power, and then carefully scattered the forces that could control it.
>
> We wanted as well, with equal fervor, a good society—a humane, responsible society in which helping hands reached out to people in honest distress, in which common needs were met freely and fully. In pursuit of this ambition, Americans used remarkable imagination. We created a much wider variety of new institutions for this purpose than we built to insure political freedom. As a frontier people, accustomed to interdependence, we developed a genius for solving common problems. People joined together in bewildering combinations to found schools, churches, opera houses, co-ops, hospitals, to build bridges and canals, to help the poor. To see a need was, more often than not, to promote a scheme to meet it better than had ever been done before.
>
> The American dream was coming true. Each part of it supported another part. We were free because we limited the power of government. We prospered because we were free. We built a good society because our prosperity yielded surplus energy that we put directly to work to meet human needs. Thus, we didn't need much government,

and because we didn't, we stayed uniquely free. A sort of supportive circle, or spiral, was working for us.

The part of the system least understood, then as now, was the network of non-governmental institutions that served public needs. They did not leave an easy trace for historians to follow. They did not depend on noisy political debate for approval, nor did civil servants have to keep very detailed records of what they did. [Yet] they played a significant role.... They took on almost any public job and so became the principal way Americans got things done.

For years the leading colleges and universities were created by the churches. Hospitals began in a variety of ways, and in the era before the Civil War, under Clara Barton's leadership, they blossomed into today's major system of independent institutions. Many of our giant commercial firms, notably in insurance and mutual savings, grew out of early self-help organizations.

Urgent problems filled the agenda of public business in early America. Citizens, acting on their own, took the heavy load. Localities and states took most of what was done by government. We rarely needed the federal government, a distant thing to the frontiersman. We limited government, not only because people knew its limitations and wanted it limited, but because we left little for it to do.

This description of America's social order, and its dual devotion to freedom and goodness, is helpful in understanding why philanthropy is indispensable to American society. I view it as indispensable in two senses: 1) Philanthropy is not able to be replaced by something else. And 2) bad things will happen to the nation if it is not adequately continued.

The aspect of America that many of us cherish most is the latitude allowed individuals to chart their own course, to be responsible for themselves, sometimes to reinvent themselves if they choose and are able. Historically, this degree of individual independence and freedom is highly unusual. Every preceding society was in one fashion or another paternal. On the wide spectrum stretching from starchy monarchy to socialist beehive, all pre-American governments basically took responsibility for every individual, and in return reserved the right to tell him or her how to live. More specifically, a small caste of strongmen at the top of the heap (king, tribal chief, warlord, bishop, emperor) told everyone else how to live.

One can't really claim that's unfair—it's how all but a thin sliver of humanity has always existed. The individual liberty and self-reliance carved out in America was the anomaly. And one of great preciousness, because it has allowed a quality of life and existential autonomy never approached by people in other times and places.

Our non-paternalized freedom is also a somewhat frail arrangement, however. For the reality is that all of us will occasionally misuse our independence in various ways, and a substantial minority of us will make a complete hash of our lives under a system of profound freedom. And when elderly profligates start dying in the street, or neglected children peer up at us with starving eyes, all the old solutions to governance will immediately be proposed.

Monarchy or socialism or blanketing welfare-state all boil down in one way or another to setting up a paternal fief under which individual freedoms will be traded away in exchange for more secure and predictable lives. Then the shirkers and the drunks and the abandoned are no longer at risk of perishing on the street. But personal liberties also evaporate, and the ceiling under which we must all fly falls down to match the lowest common denominator. Life becomes less risky, but all citizens are debased—not only the failures who are henceforth ordered how and where to live, but also everyone who had succeeded independently, and even members of the master class who must cage and feed the failures. All experience a decline in dignity, self-determination, and life satisfaction.

> The miserable must be lifted up from the sidewalks where they sprawl. Empathy will not tolerate the alternative. Yet when the lifting is done in conventional collective ways, it leads to enslavement on both sides of the transaction.

Lovers of freedom object: "That's too high a price, we must therefore let the failures fail, else our whole system will tumble into busybodying oppressiveness." But stepping over wasted children or dead bodies will soften many citizens to the idea of trading independence for security. Which is why nearly all human societies have ended up in one of the many paternal structures.

It's just a fact of human empathy: one way or another, the miserable *must* be lifted up from the sidewalks where they sprawl. Common decency will not tolerate the alternative. Yet when the lifting is done in conventional collective ways, it leads to enslavement on both sides of the transaction.

It was voluntary action and private giving that allowed America to escape this terrible dilemma. We made the magical discovery that voluntary action can be a non-enslaving kind of paternalism, enabling us to meet Judeo-Christian and humanitarian responsibilities to fellow men without setting in motion the statist spiral which kills individual sovereignty. In solving basic security hungers and primal fears of a "jungle" freedom, philanthropy thus enabled enormous liberty. Philanthropy turned out to be indispensable to personal independence and national success. It kept America functioning as that exceedingly rare society where average people can steer their own lives.

This is why philanthropists are different from doctors, or teachers, or businessmen, who also do social good, and different from soldiers or ministers or others who sometimes sacrifice their own interests to aid fellow citizens. Doctors, businessmen, and soldiers are valuable contributors, but they are not essential to maintaining America's basic social contract. They are not indispensable.

Effective philanthropists are indispensable. They allow us to have a good society without a paternalist state. They are the prophylactic against public lurches for freedom-killing security blankets.

Philanthropy is the guardian of our self-rule. It is one of just a few sine qua nons essential to our national health. Without it there is no America as we know it.

As you amble through the multifarious and sometimes quirky human actions described on the pages of *The Almanac of American Philanthropy*, and absorb the colorful stories of charity as it has been practiced in our land over four centuries, I hope you will also keep sight of this profound reality that underlies voluntary giving in America.

GREAT MEN & WOMEN
of
AMERICAN PHILANTHROPY
1732-present

On the pages following you will find, first, a list of America's most active living donors. Most of these 149 individuals or couples have donated several hundred million dollars, or more, in recent years. After that comes a series of 56 profiles, bringing to life the greatest donors from American history. These include individuals like Franklin, Rockefeller, Carnegie, Rosenwald, Packard, and many others you have never heard of. They all made large imprints on the course of our country and the texture of our lives.

PROMINENT
U.S. LIVING DONORS

There is no way to say with certainty who America's top living donors are today. Many philanthropic gifts are made quietly, even anonymously, and are never widely known.

Givers who make lots of moderate-size contributions also tend to be less visible—even though they may give away larger total sums than persons who get noticed for one or two huge donations.

So the 149 names that follow should not be considered the final, definitive universe of America's top donors. However, the lion's share of our nation's most generous and influential living practitioners of philanthropy are listed here.

These individuals were compiled from several sources. We started with the Philanthropy 50 list of biggest annual donors, cumulated all of the gifts reported there from 2000-2014, and then identified those persons who gave at least $175 million over that period. To these, we added top givers over that same period from the "Million Dollar List" published by Indiana University. Then we included all of the American signers of the Giving Pledge who were not already showing up on those top-giver lists. Recall that Giving Pledge signers are billionaires who have promised to donate at least half of their fortune to charity; while some are already well on their way to meeting their promise, others will do most of their giving in the future—but they will all be heard from. Finally, we added two smaller groups of donors who have earned plaudits for the perspicacity of their charitable work: Recipients, who are still living, of the William E. Simon Prize for Philanthropic Leadership, and selected contemporary donors identified by the Bridgespan Group as "Remarkable Givers."

Bill & Karen Ackman

Sheldon & Miriam Adelson

Paul Allen

Philip & Nancy Anschutz

John & Laura Arnold

John Arrillaga

Stephen Bechtel

Marc & Lynne Benioff

Steve Bing

Sara Blakely

Arthur Blank

Michael Bloomberg

Geoff Boisi

David & Suzanne Booth

Donald Bren

Sergey Brin

Eli & Edythe Broad

Charles Bronfman

Warren Buffett

Ben Carson

Steve & Jean Case

Raymond Chambers

Steve & Alexandra Cohen

Claudia & William Coleman

Lee & Toby Cooperman

Joe Craft

Joyce & Bill Cummings

Ray & Barbara Dalio

Robert Day

John DeJoria

Michael & Susan Dell

Desh Deshpande

Richard & Helen DeVos

Barry Diller & Diane von Furstenberg

John & Ann Doerr

David & Dana Dornsife

Stanley Druckenmiller

Glenn & Eva Dubin

David & Cheryl Duffield

Larry Ellison

Charles Feeney

Doris Fisher

Phillip & Patricia Frost

Ira & Mary Lou Fulton

Bill & Melinda Gates

David Geffen

Dan & Jennifer Gilbert

Jeff & Mei Greene

Ken Griffin

Llura & Gordon Gund

Harold Hamm

Frank Hanna

Reed Hastings & Patty Quillin	Duncan & Nancy MacMillan
Roger Hertog	Alfred Mann
Lyda Hill	Joe & Rika Mansueto
Barron Hilton	Bernie Marcus
Amos & Barbara Hostetter	Richard & Nancy Marriott
Karen & Jon Huntsman	Craig & Susan McCaw
Pitt & Barbara Hyde	Red & Charline McCombs
Irwin & Joan Jacobs	Robert Meyerhoff
Charles Johnson	Michael & Lori Milken
Paul Tudor Jones	Tom Monaghan
George Kaiser	Gordon & Betty Moore
Vinod & Neeru Khosla	John & Tashia Morgridge
Sidney Kimmel	Dustin Moskovitz & Cari Tuna
Rich & Nancy Kinder	Charles Munger
Beth & Seth Klarman	Elon Musk
Phil & Penelope Knight	Jonathan Nelson
David Koch	Pierre & Pam Omidyar
Charles Koch	Natalie & Paul Orfalea
Jan Koum	Bernard & Barbro Osher
Elaine & Ken Langone	Larry Page
Liz & Eric Lefkofsky	Sean Parker
Gerry & Marguerite Lenfest	Bob & Renee Parsons
Lorry Lokey	John Paulson
George Lucas & Mellody Hobson	Pete Peterson
Ann Lurie	Ron Perelman
Peter & Carolyn Lynch	Raymond Perelman

Jorge & Darlene Perez

T. Boone Pickens

Emily Pulitzer

Ernest & Evelyn Rady

Jan & Trevor Rees-Jones

Julian Robertson

David Robinson

David Rockefeller

Edward & Deedie Rose

Robert Rosenkranz

Stephen Ross

David Rubenstein

John & Ginger Sall

Henry & Susan Samueli

Sheryl Sandberg

Herbert Sandler

Denny Sanford

Vicki & Roger Sant

Lynn Schusterman

Stephen Schwarzman

Walter Scott

Tom & Cindy Secunda

Tom & Stacey Siebel

Craig Silverstein & Mary Obelnicki

Jim & Marilyn Simons

Paul Singer

Jeff Skoll

John & Susan Sobrato

Michelle & Patrick Soon-Shiong

George Soros

Ted Stanley

Mark & Mary Stevens

Tom Steyer & Kat Taylor

Jon Stryker

Tad Taube

Ted Turner

Walton family

David Weekley

Sandy & Joan Weill

Shelby White

Oprah Winfrey

Nicholas & Jill Woodman

Charles & Merryl Zegar

Mark Zuckerberg & Priscilla Chan

Mortimer Zuckerman

THE PHILANTHROPY HALL OF FAME

56 GREAT DONORS WHO CHANGED OUR NATION AND WORLD

The great deceased donors described in this section transformed society through their charitable giving. In the entries that follow we offer brisk biographical profiles that capture the essence of each man and woman, the sources of their fortunes, and the motivations, tactics, and results of their philanthropy.

BERNICE BISHOP

Bernice Pauahi Bishop was a Hawaiian princess, the last direct descendant of the Royal House of Kamehameha. With her husband, Charles, she is remembered as one of the most remarkable philanthropists in the history of the Islands. Her bequest endowed the Kamehameha Schools, which to this day specialize in educating the children of native Hawaiians. After her death, Charles Bishop spent many years bringing her vision to fruition.

She was born in December 1831, the great-granddaughter of King Kamehameha the Great, conqueror and unifier of the Hawaiian Islands. In her earliest years, she was raised as an *ali'i* (noble), steeped in native traditions. At the age of seven, however, she was sent to the Royal School. Run by a pair of married Protestant missionaries, the school was committed to providing the children with the finest possible course of Western education. "Miss Bernice" quickly became a star pupil, excelling in both academics and etiquette, and a devout Christian. She was often compared favorably to her spoiled, misbehaving *ali'i* classmates—including Prince Lot Kapuaiwa, the future King Kamehameha V.

In 1846, Charles Bishop arrived in Hawaii. The 24-year-old clerk had sailed from New York aiming for Oregon, but after a rough passage through Cape Horn the ship put in at Honolulu for provisions. Bishop decided to wait out the winter in the Islands. He found work with local Yankee merchants, then became a clerk at the U.S. consulate. He met Pauahi and soon began regularly calling on her at the Royal School. Though her family firmly reminded her of her obligation to marry Hawaiian royalty, Pauahi resisted. In June 1850, in a small ceremony which her parents refused to attend, Pauahi became Bernice Bishop.

Bishop reconciled with her family within a year, and by 1857 had inherited from them an estate totaling 16,011 acres. With it came a wide range of responsibilities. Throughout her mid-20s, Bishop served as a traditional Hawaiian philanthropist, offering guidance, support, and assistance to those who approached her. She spent many working hours in her garden, seated under a tamarind tree, taking visits from fellow islanders and working through their problems in her native Hawaiian tongue.

At the same time, Bernice grew ever more involved in American forms of civic engagement. She was a leader in several charitable organizations, including the Stranger's Friend Society, which aided sick travelers, and the Women's Sewing Society, which provided clothing for the poor. An accomplished contralto singer and pianist, she conducted performances of the works of Haydn and Verdi with the Amateur Musical Society, and gave music lessons at the Royal School. A devout Protestant, Bishop regularly taught Sunday school at Kawaiaha'o Church.

Charles Bishop, meanwhile, found mounting success as a businessman, opening a bank that profited from the booming sugar trade. (It would eventually become First Hawaiian Bank, which remains the oldest and largest bank in the state, with assets totaling $16 billion and branches in Guam and Saipan.) Before the islands were annexed, he held a series of public offices, even serving as minister of foreign affairs from 1873 to 1874. With her royal lineage and his growing fortune, the Bishops were the social leaders of Honolulu.

In 1872, Bernice was summoned to the deathbed of King Kamehameha V, where he named her successor to the throne. Bishop refused, simply saying, "Do not think of me." Rather than assume the crown, she spent the next decade traveling the world. In 1883, the royal governess of the Islands passed away, leaving nearly 353,000 acres to her cousin Bernice. Bernice was instantly the largest landowner in Hawaii, possessing about 9 percent of its landmass.

> Bernice Bishop bequeathed a huge swath of land—totaling nearly one tenth of the Hawaiian landmass—to endow schools that now educate nearly 7,000 students annually.

With this newfound wealth, the Bishops decided to write their wills. Bernice made individual provisions for a number of charities, friends, and servants. The great bulk of her estate—some 378,569 acres of land—was to be held in trust, for the purpose of opening "two schools, each for boarding and day scholars, one for boys and one for girls, to be known as, and called the Kamehameha Schools." Her will further stipulated that the schools give preference to "Hawaiians of pure or part aboriginal blood," providing them with an English-language education and inculcating strict Protestant morality. It was an ambitious project, unprecedented in Hawaiian history.

The future of the schools was left to five trustees, including her husband. An accomplished philanthropist in his own right, Charles Bishop had already helped found the Hawaiian Historical Society, the Honolulu Public Library, and dozens of kindergartens throughout the Islands. In 1889, he founded the Bishop Museum, home to the world's largest collection of Polynesian cultural artifacts. To launch the Kamehameha schools, Bishop drew on his previous service on the board of the Punahou School, where he funded the construction of several buildings and labs.

In November 1887, 39 students formed the first class at the boys' school; in 1894, 35 students filled out the first class at the girls' school. Today the schools have campuses on Oahu, Hawaii, and Maui, educating nearly 7,000 children annually. Thus do Charles and Bernice Pauahi Bishop, childless themselves, rank among the greatest patrons of Hawaii's children.

⌐ Mithun Selvaratnam

Further reading

○ George Kanahele, *Pauahi: The Kamehameha Legacy* (Kamehameha Schools Press, 1986)
○ Harold Kent, *Charles Reed Bishop: Man of Hawaii* (Pacific Books, 1965)

ANDREW CARNEGIE

Andrew Carnegie may be the most influential philanthropist in American history. The scale of his giving is almost without peer: adjusted for inflation, his donations exceed those of nearly anyone else in the nation's history. The magnitude of his accomplishments is likewise historic: he built some 2,800 lending libraries around the globe, founded what became one of the world's great research universities, endowed one of the nation's most significant grantmakers, and established charitable organizations that are still active nearly a century after his death. And, perhaps uniquely among businessmen, the seriousness of his writing has ensured that his thoughts on philanthropy have been continuously in print for more than a century, and remain widely read and studied to this day.

Carnegie was born in 1835 in Scotland, one of two sons of a linen weaver and his wife. Advances in looming technology rendered his father's occupation obsolete, threatening the family with dire poverty. Seeking a better future, in 1848 the Carnegies borrowed money to go to the United States. They settled near Pittsburgh, where young Andrew began an extraordinary rags-to-riches business career.

Starting as a "bobbin boy" in a cotton mill for a weekly salary of $1.20, he advanced rapidly, eventually becoming a manager with the Pennsylvania Railroad Company. There Carnegie came to appreciate the importance of iron and steel for the future of the American economy and shifted his efforts toward producing them.

Carnegie had consummate—some might say ruthless—financial and organizational skills, as well as an unremitting appetite for cost-efficiencies and a keen eye for innovations (most notably the Bessemer process, the first industrial method for converting pig iron to steel). He consolidated several smaller manufacturers and mines to create the largest maker of steel and iron products in the world. In 1901, Carnegie sold his business to financier J. Pierpont Morgan for nearly $500 million. His stake was almost half the total. Thus did the poor son of a laboring immigrant become one of the wealthiest individuals in American history.

As his fortune increased, Carnegie came to associate with the most eminent political, financial, and intellectual figures of the time, both in the United States and abroad. Especially after moving to New York City in 1870, he became a patron of numerous schools, museums, libraries, and churches on both sides of the Atlantic. (Though not particularly religious himself, Carnegie adored the hymnody of his youth, and provided some 7,500 organs to congregations around the world.)

Carnegie is best known for the nearly 3,000 public libraries he helped build. As a young man in Allegheny City, Carnegie spent most of his evenings in the book collection of Colonel James Anderson, a prosperous local businessman who gave working boys free access to his 1,500 volumes. It was clearly a formative experience, and one which Carnegie later attempted to re-create for similar benefit to others. Starting in 1885, Carnegie began funding the construction of thousands of libraries. At the time of his death in 1919, the tally stood at 2,811 libraries, roughly two thirds of which were in the United States. To ensure that communities were invested in the success of these institutions, he would only pay for buildings—and only after local authorities showed him credible plans for acquiring books and hiring staff.

During his lifetime, Carnegie created a number of charitable institutions that bore his name. In 1900, he founded the Carnegie Technical Schools, later the Carnegie Institute, and known today as Carnegie-Mellon University, one of the world's great research universities. In 1904, he created what he called his "pet child," the Carnegie Hero Fund Commission, which recognizes and rewards individuals who spontaneously risk life and limb to aid others. A year later, he launched the Carnegie Foundation for the Advancement of Teaching, whose many accomplishments include the Flexner Report, which revolutionized American medical education, and the provision of pensions to college faculty members (which increased the attractiveness of an academic career).

Other organizations would bear his name, including the Carnegie Relief Fund (for the benefit of injured steelworkers), the Carnegie Dunfermline Trust (to support his hometown), and the Carnegie Trust for the Universities of Scotland (to bolster higher education in his native land). The Manhattan concert venue was not supposed to bear its patron's name, but when European notables declined to perform in a simple "music hall," its benefactor relented. In 1893 the facility was renamed Carnegie Hall.

Not all of Carnegie's efforts were successful. For much of the final third of his life, he devoted his fortune and personal influence to encouraging the peaceful resolution of international conflicts. He created and closely attended to the Carnegie Endowment for International Peace and the Carnegie Council for Ethics in International Affairs. The outbreak of World War I dashed his hopes of world amity and precipitated his retreat from the public stage.

A somewhat ambiguous achievement was the creation of the Carnegie Corporation. This foundation was among the first (and remains among the largest) grantmaking foundations in the United States, with consequential achievements including early support for the National Bureau of Economic Research, the research of Gunnar Myrdal, and the development of "Sesame Street." And yet, creation of a perpetual foundation represented a failure of sorts for Carnegie, whose stated goal was to give away his entire fortune while living, and die penniless.

The fact that Carnegie's philanthropic goals are well known is a testament to the third source of his enduring influence: his extensive public writings. In several widely read books, articles in serious British and American magazines, and frequent newspaper interviews and speeches, the colorful Scot's opinions on a range of economic, political, and philosophical issues attracted public attention.

None of his writings had more influence than those about philanthropy, which were published as two articles in the *North American Review* in 1889 and collected in a 1901 book called *The Gospel of Wealth and Other Timely Essays.* His views grew out of an economic and political philosophy that owed a lot to English classical liberalism and social theorists such as Herbert Spencer.

Carnegie attributed his business success not only to his own talents, but also to an economic system that valued enterprise, protected property, and encouraged competition. This system brought dramatic improvements in living standards to the public at large, while enabling successful competitors like himself to become extremely wealthy. Yet Carnegie acknowledged that there were costs as well as triumphs, which included a wide gap between rich and poor and social frictions between employers and workers.

Carnegie saw philanthropy as essential for addressing these shortcomings. He called on those enjoying the largest fruits of the economic system to use their wealth "to produce the most beneficial results for the community." This would ensure that all of society benefited, reducing resentments that could ultimately lead to replacement of a bountiful system of free enterprise with a less productive one built on envy and redistribution.

Carnegie believed, however, that just giving away money was not enough—in fact, it could make things worse. "Of every thousand dollars spent in so-called charity today," he opined, "it is probable that nine hundred and fifty dollars is unwisely spent—so spent, indeed, as to produce the very evils which it hopes to mitigate or cure." The problem, as he saw it, was "indiscriminate charity"—providing help to people who were unwilling to help themselves. That sort of philanthropy only rewarded bad habits rather than encouraging good ones. He argued that philanthropy should instead support universities, libraries, hospitals, meeting halls, recreational facilities, and similar projects that strengthened and refreshed individuals so they could become more independent and productive themselves.

Carnegie urged his wealthy peers to provide for themselves and their dependents and then make it their "duty" to use the rest of their funds for their communities. They should apply their "wisdom, experience, and ability to administer" to lift up "poorer brethren" who "would or could not do for themselves." He warned successful men who failed to help others that "the man who dies thus rich dies disgraced."

> Successful men should help lift the unsuccessful into more productive lives, thought Andrew Carnegie, and a man who neglects this duty and dies rich "dies disgraced."

Carnegie's "gospel" has attracted generations of successful businessmen, including the one whose current wealth rivals that of the steel magnate— Bill Gates. By linking giving not just to religious and moral imperatives to care for the needy, but also to preservation of the American economic and political system, Carnegie extended the rationale for philanthropy. In the process, he imbued charitable giving with an extra appeal for the generations of entrepreneurs and self-made men and women who came after him.

— Leslie Lenkowsky

Further reading

○ *Philanthropy* magazine article, philanthropyroundtable.org/topic/donor_intent/the_carnegie_corporation_turns_100

◦ Andrew Carnegie, *The Autobiography of Andrew Carnegie* (Northeastern University Press, 1986)

◦ David Nasaw, *Andrew Carnegie* (Penguin Books, 2006)

PETER COOPER

Peter Cooper was a first-rate inventor who also—uncharacteristically of inventors—was a first-rate businessman. He became an industrialist, a civic leader, and a philanthropist. Cooper knew what he wanted to make of his life. In his old age, he said he spent the first 30 years of his life getting a start, the next 30 making a fortune, and the last 30 doing good with that fortune.

Cooper was born in 1791, the fifth of nine siblings. His father worked at various occupations—as a hatter, storekeeper, brickmaker, and brewer. He was not particularly good at any of them, however, and the family eventually left New York City for Peekskill upstate. As a result, young Peter became widely acquainted with business practices as he tried to help the family breadwinner in creative ways. While still a child, he constructed a device for pounding laundry, perhaps the world's first washing machine. He also designed a machine for mowing lawns, in an age when lawnmowers were called "sheep."

Because his family was always short of money, Cooper received only one year of formal education, a lack he felt keenly. But he studied on his own and, when he could afford it, hired tutors to teach him subjects. Apprenticed to a carriage maker, Cooper proved so valuable an employee that the carriagemaker voluntarily doubled—and then *tripled*—his salary. Shortly after completing his apprenticeship, Cooper married Sarah Bedell. It would be a long and happy marriage, producing six children, although only two lived to maturity.

When he was 30 years old, Cooper acquired a glue factory, just north of the settled part of Manhattan. He paid $2,000 in cash, a considerable sum at that time. Adept at chemistry, Cooper greatly improved the product line. That proved immensely rewarding, yielding him $10,000 in profit the first year. Among the new products he developed was instant gelatin. (His wife developed recipes for mixing it with fruit, so in a sense it can be said they invented Jell-O.) Soon he was earning $100,000 annually, a vast income for the 1820s.

Cooper lived simply and poured his profits into his business and investments. With two partners, he bought extensive waterfront property in Baltimore, hoping to benefit from the increased commerce between the harbor and then-under-construction Baltimore & Ohio Railroad. When the steam locomotives arrived from Britain, however, it was discovered that they could not climb the steep grade and make the narrow turns west of the city. Cooper was undeterred. He built from scratch a steam engine—later nicknamed the "Tom Thumb"—that was capable of handling American conditions. It was the first steam engine built in the United States.

By the 1850s, he was among the richest men in the country. He remained open as ever to new ideas and new technology, including the trans-Atlantic telegraph cable project of his neighbor Cyrus Field. Cooper invested in the cable—which was successful only after four failures and 11 years.

Contemporaries of Cooper sometimes observed that he had no sense of humor whatsoever. He never joined any of the men's clubs that were springing up in mid-nineteenth-century New York. His idea of leisure was to spend an afternoon discussing the finer points of Protestant theology with clergymen. The great joy of his life, it appears, was philanthropy.

As Cooper approached middle age, charitable work became increasingly important to him. He sat on numerous boards of eleemosynary institutions and was a generous contributor to his church and to worthy causes throughout the city and state. In 1853, he laid the cornerstone of his signature project, Cooper Union.

Cooper intended for his school to provide a practical education, free of charge, to working people who wanted to improve themselves. Modeled after the École Polytechnique in Paris, the Cooper Union offered many of its classes at night so that those who had to earn a living could fully avail themselves of the school. And thanks to Cooper's extraordinary generosity, the college was completely tuition-free.

When Cooper Union first opened its doors in 1859, more than 2,000 people applied to take classes. The Union's reading room was also open to the public and, unlike New York City's other libraries at that time, was open until 10:00 p.m., again so that working people could use it. As many as 3,000 people took advantage of the reading room every week.

Cooper required that there be no discrimination on the basis of race, religion, or sex—almost unprecedented in the mid-1800s—and that the institution provide an education "equal to the best" available. Among its early alumni was Thomas Edison. The impoverished Edison could never have afforded tuition at a regular engineering school.

The building, located at Astor Place in Manhattan's East Village, is itself interesting. It was the first fireproof building in New York, constructed with iron I-beams invented and manufactured by Cooper himself. It contained an elevator shaft, though commercial elevators were not yet in existence, because Cooper was confident that a safe elevator mechanism would soon be developed. Soon enough, the circular shaft was fitted with a mechanism created by Elisha Otis, which is still in use.

Cooper Union's Great Hall occupied the basement level and immediately became one of the most important venues in New York for major political addresses. Abraham Lincoln gave his "House Divided" speech there early in 1860, propelling him into serious contention for the Republican nomination that year. Many Presidents have spoken there since.

Cooper devoted over half of his fortune to the Union's endowment, including much Manhattan real estate, which has allowed the endowment to grow along with the city. (Cooper Union, for instance, owns the land under the Chrysler Building, from which it derives a considerable rent.) Prominent among the school's later benefactors was Andrew Carnegie, who praised Cooper in *The Gospel of Wealth* and donated $600,000 to the institution in 1902. Cooper Union became one of the premier engineering, architecture, and art schools in the country.

> Peter Cooper's great goal in setting up a free college in New York City was to boost up poor people ambitious to improve themselves. Thomas Edison was an early alum.

"I have always recognized that the object of business is to make money in an honorable manner," wrote Cooper not long before his death in 1883. "I have endeavored to remember that the object of life is to do good." He remembered that well, and tens of thousands of young men and women over the last 150 years have benefited as a result.

— John Steele Gordon

Further reading

- Edward Clarence Mack, *Peter Cooper: Citizen of New York* (Duell, Sloan, and Pearce, 1949)
- Rossiter Raymond, *Peter Cooper* (Houghton Mifflin, 1901)
- J. C. Zachos, *A Sketch of the Life and Opinions of Mr. Peter Cooper* (Murray Hill, 1876)

BILL DANIELS

Bill Daniels was a pioneer of the cable TV industry and a major philanthropist in Denver and the Rocky Mountain region. Throughout his life, his charitable giving ranged widely. He reached out to those down on their luck, those who abused alcohol and drugs, and those who suffered from mental and physical disabilities. He provided scholarships, with a focus less on academic achievement and more on demonstrated character and leadership potential. He funded efforts to integrate ethics into business schools and created a bank meant to teach young people the principles of finance and personal responsibility. Through it all, his giving was largely personal; Daniels routinely enclosed a note with each check, explaining to the recipient what he hoped his money would do.

Born in 1920, Daniels grew up in Hobbs, New Mexico. He became a rowdy, rough-and-tumble teen who needed discipline, and he found it at the New Mexico Military Institute. Daniels entered the Navy after graduating and became a highly decorated aviator, serving in combat at Guadalcanal, Midway, and the Coral Sea.

In 1952, after serving in the Korean War, Daniels moved to Casper, Wyoming, where he made the discovery that would yield his fortune. The two-time Golden Gloves state champion stopped at Murphy's Bar in Denver one night. To his surprise, a fight at Madison Square Garden was visible on a television behind the bar. It was the first time he had seen a television. He was instantly transfixed.

But, as was the case with many small rural communities, there was no television available in Casper—a mountain range prevented the signal from reaching his town. Daniels did some research and found that several towns in the eastern United States had resolved the same issue by transmitting TV signals through coaxial cable. A single large antenna might be set up on a mountaintop or hill to pick up the nearest signal, which would then be run through cables strung on telephone poles to the homes of subscribers.

In 1953, Daniels started a cable system in Casper, at great initial expense. But his bet paid off. For a single black-and-white channel that broadcast for only eight hours daily, he won 4,000 subscribing households—about a third of the total homes in the area. Before long, he found himself traveling all across the West, securing investors, finding customers, and recruiting talent. In 1958, as small cable systems began to proliferate, Daniels sensed the need for a coordinating firm for the nascent industry. In Denver, he founded Daniels and Associates, which became a center of the burgeoning industry.

"Bill may have been the prime architect of cable's capital structure—the whole way in which the cable industry decided to make money," explained

Daniels Fund

cable entrepreneur John Malone. "In the very early days, the theory was that you charged people a lot to hook them up and then you'd charge them hardly anything after that. Bill took it the other way, arguing we'll have much more success if we treat it as an ongoing revenue stream."

With the cable boom in the 1980s and '90s, Daniels's fortune exploded. He had always been generous to his employees and to people in need. He would anonymously make cash gifts to families whose homes burned down, or who were suffering medical emergencies. He also gave generously to homeless shelters, food pantries, and organizations that served the disabled. But his wealth made philanthropy on a large scale possible.

Daniels had a soft spot for kids—like him—who needed a hand up to succeed, and he often gave scholarships to put these young people through school. They need not have been straight-A students. Daniels was looking for hard-working kids with strong values and leadership potential. He did expect satisfactory grades to keep the scholarship funds coming, and he also expected the student to live by high moral standards and hold down a part-time job.

> Daniels had a soft spot for kids who needed a second or third chance to succeed (as he had), and often gave scholarships to put these "diamonds in the rough" through college.

In 1986, the work-hard, party-hard playboy faced a reality check when his closest friends and business associates confronted him about his drinking. He committed himself to the Betty Ford Center, where he kicked alcohol for good. He never forgot hitting rock bottom, and for the rest of his life he attended Alcoholics Anonymous meetings, sponsored drug and alcohol addicts, referred friends to the Ford Center, and even paid for their treatment. In 1988, he became the first Ford Center alumnus to join its board. At the time of his death in 2000, he was one of the center's largest funders.

Daniels sensed after his recovery that he had much more philanthropic work ahead of him. In the 1980s, he became concerned that the nation's leading business schools did not teach business ethics. In the 1980s and 1990s, he gave over $22 million to what became the Daniels College of Business at the University of Denver, where he insisted that ethics and etiquette become a mandatory part of the MBA curriculum—one of the first business schools in the nation to do so.

Daniels created Young Americans Bank with the hope of preparing young people to participate in the free-enterprise system. Daniels personally backed the bank, which he insisted would be fully functioning, state-chartered, and FDIC-insured. After two years of wooing skeptical regulators, Daniels opened YAB in 1987. The bank serves people under 21, who can open checking and savings accounts, apply for credit cards designed to teach them how to spend wisely, and obtain small-business loans. By 2011, YAB had served nearly 70,000 young customers.

As the bank grew, so did its mission—YAB spun off its financial literacy teaching into an elementary-school classroom curriculum and created Young AmeriTowne, where students run model businesses and learn how to be financially responsible citizens. When asked in 1996 what his proudest accomplishment was, Daniels didn't miss a beat. "Young Americans Bank," he said.

"I think God told me as a young man to share my good fortune with others," Daniels said near the end of his life. "I have tried to do it. And my foundation will see to it when I die. Believe me, it is a real joy to me to be able to help people."

☞ *Evan Sparks*

Further reading

○ *Philanthropy* magazine article, philanthropyroundtable.org/topic/donor_intent/back_to_bill

○ Daniels Fund, *The Life and Legacy of Bill Daniels*, danielsfund.org/Legacy.asp

○ Stephen Singular, *Relentless: Bill Daniels and the Triumph of Cable TV* (Daniels Estate, 2003)

KATHARINE DREXEL

Katharine Drexel of Philadelphia is known for many things: She was heiress to a banking fortune, a fierce advocate for the poor, a foundress of the American religious order Sisters of the Blessed Sacrament, and a canonized saint in the Catholic Church. Her greatest accomplishment may have been her role in helping blacks and Native Americans improve their lot.

Drexel's birth in 1858 was traumatic; her mother died a month later and doctors expected to lose the baby as well. But the weak newborn battled back and eventually was sent, with an older sister, to live with relatives. After her father's remarriage she and her sister came home, and it would be years before the girls realized that their father's new wife, Emma Bouvier, was not their biological mother. They were soon joined by a third sister.

Drexel's family was one of the wealthiest in America, and Katharine was related to many prominent figures in American financial and political history. Her great-grandfather founded the firm that eventually became Drexel Burnham Lambert. Her grandfather partnered with J. P. Morgan to found the banking giant Drexel, Morgan & Co., later renamed J. P. Morgan. Her uncle founded Drexel University. Drexel is also related to Nicholas Biddle—the great Philadelphia banker, president of the Second Bank of the United States, and scourge of Andrew Jackson.

The Drexels were a French-Catholic family, deeply religious and intensely philanthropic. Her father had an active prayer life; her mother opened up the family house three times every week to feed and care for the poor. They gave roughly the equivalent of $11 million to charitable causes annually. The family lived on a 90-acre estate not far from Philadelphia, in a house dominated by a large stained-glass window depicting the archangel Michael.

> After growing up in one of the wealthiest families in America, Katharine Drexel became a nun and devoted her inheritance and talents to charitable work among Native Americans and African Americans.

At the death of Katharine's parents, the three Drexel sisters inherited the bulk of their massive estate. Picking up the thread of an earlier trip to the West, Katharine began to devote a significant amount of her personal fortune to missionary and charity work among American Indians, starting with the establishment of the St. Catherine Indian School in Santa Fe in 1887. Later, she visited Pope Leo XIII to ask him to send missionaries to staff the Indian missions she had financed. He turned the request back on her: the missionary she needed, the Pope suggested, was herself. To the disbelief of Philadelphia society, she decided to become a Catholic nun and devote her inheritance and talents to missionary and charitable work among Native Americans and African Americans.

Drexel entered religious life in 1889 with the Sisters of Mercy in Pittsburgh. The death of her sister in 1890 momentarily shook her resolve, but in 1891 she and 15 companions took their vows and founded a new order: the Sisters of the Blessed Sacrament for Negroes and Indians. Added to the normal vows of poverty, chastity, and obedience was a special vow, not to "undertake any work which would lead to the neglect or abandonment of the Indian or Colored races."

Drexel postponed sending sisters to missions in the American West until she felt they were well prepared. The first step for the order was to open a home for parentless African-American children at her family's estate. The home provided both a refuge for these orphans and a place to train her young novices before they were sent off into the still-wild West. Ahead of her time when it came to the education of women, Drexel arranged for the sisters to take classes at Drexel University so they could be prepared to teach their young charges when the time came.

To Katharine, education was the key to opportunity. The bulk of her order's efforts went into developing a network of 145 missions, 12 schools for Native Americans, and 50 schools for African Americans throughout the South and West. These Catholic schools were staffed by laypersons, often attached to a local church, and offered religious instruction and vocational training. Unlike many religious mission schools, students did not have to be or become Catholic to enroll.

In 1915, with a $750,000 grant from Katharine, the sisters founded Xavier University in New Orleans. The only historically black Catholic college in the United States, Xavier was designed to train teachers who could staff the order's burgeoning network of schools. Much of the cost of opening these schools, as well as Xavier, was covered by Drexel's personal fortune, and it is estimated (there is no official figure) that she gave nearly $20 million during her lifetime to support the work of her order, or more than $500 million today.

Drexel was also an outspoken advocate for the rights of poor blacks and Native Americans. She supported petitions to Congress to increase aid to reservation schools, wrote letters to newspaper editors whose reporting on Indian affairs she found to be biased, and started a letter-writing campaign in support of a federal anti-lynching law.

The wealthy heiress displayed a hard-headed pragmatism when dealing with local authorities in the segregated South. Adopting the maxim "render to Caesar what is Caesar's," Drexel decreed that the order's churches in the South, instead of the customary roped-off section in the rear for blacks, would have two long pews running front to back for the races. This tactic kept the sisters within the letter of local segregation laws—and protected the schools from closure—while flouting their racist spirit. She also used dummy corporations and other legal shell games to hide her land purchases until the schools were too entrenched for local authorities to close. Nonetheless, there were regular conflicts with local bigotries: the order's mother house in Bensalem, Pennsylvania, received a bomb threat when it was under construction; an order school in Rock Castle, Virginia, was destroyed by arson in 1899; and the Ku Klux Klan threatened the same for another in Texas in 1922.

Katharine's travels and work continued until 1938, when a stroke left her almost completely immobile and forced her to give up leadership of the sisters. Because she died without issue, the corpus of her father's estate passed not to the order she founded, but to various charitable and religious institutions designated in his will.

In 2000, Pope John Paul II canonized Drexel, the second native-born American to be named a saint. The ceremony in St. Peter's Square likely would have pained Katharine Drexel, servant of the poor, whose only request when Xavier University was founded was that the school make no mention of her bequest, and who, at the college's dedication, sat in the back of the room, quiet and unnoticed.

         Justin Torres

Further reading

○ Katherine Burton, *The Golden Door: The Life of Katharine Drexel* (P. J. Kennedy, 1958)
○ Daniel McSheffery, *Saint Katharine Drexel* (Catholic Book Publishing, 2002)
○ Ellen Tarry, *Saint Katharine Drexel: Friend of the Oppressed* (Farrar Strauss, 1958)

JAMES DUKE

James Buchanan Duke built two massive fortunes, the first in tobacco and the second in hydroelectric power generation. He became one of the greatest philanthropists in the history of the Carolinas, perhaps best known today as the patron of Duke University.

Born in December 1856 near Durham, North Carolina, Duke grew up on a small farm with a widowed father. After the Civil War devastated the Carolina countryside, the Duke family began growing, curing, and selling tobacco. In 1874, the Dukes opened a tobacco factory in Durham, where they were among the first cigarette manufacturers in the South. The family was—at young J. B.'s recommendation—among the very first to adopt machine production on a large scale. The Dukes were able to produce much faster than manufacturers using older methods, and to build consumer demand for the Duke brands they pioneered national cigarette advertising, including tradable "cigarette pictures" and billboards. J. B.'s devout Methodist father was concerned about the suggestive pictures, and his competitors sniffed at "this damned picture business" that "degraded" the cigarette industry, but smokers across the country increasingly asked their local tobacconists for Duke brands by name.

Like many of his era's industry titans, Duke sought to limit competition. His firm joined four others in 1890 to form the American Tobacco Company, which accounted for upwards of 90 percent of the domestic cigarette business. Duke, who had orchestrated the merger, was at the helm of the new monopoly. In 1901, he bought a major British tobacco company. He again joined forces with competitors and formed the British-American Tobacco Company. "Duke's keenest satisfaction from this international triumph," said business partner William Whitney, "came to him in the knowledge that he had gotten an almost unlimited and more lasting market for the tobacco made by his own people on their small farms." But in 1911 the federal government dissolved his conglomerate under the Sherman Antitrust Act.

Duke was already planning his next enterprise: hydroelectric development of the western Carolinas. Lasting growth and prosperity in the South would require cheap, abundant electricity, he believed, especially in the textile-producing regions. Duke's foresight put him a generation ahead of government efforts to electrify the Tennessee River Valley during the Great Depression. He bought land and built dams, then persuaded mill owners to use the new source of energy. By the 1920s, Duke's Southern Power Company was the leading electric utility in the western Carolinas. Today the firm is known as Duke Energy.

Duke's brother, Ben, handled most of the family's giving. ("I am going to give a good part of what I make to the Lord," J. B. Duke was fond of saying, "but I can make better interest for Him by keeping it while I live.") But in 1924, Duke gave $40 million to create the Duke Endowment. Unlike many of his peers who created foundations with vague mandates, Duke's indenture gave his trustees very specific instructions: they were to support hospitals, orphan care, rural Methodist churches, and four Carolina colleges. The men and women who have run the Duke Endowment since have hewed loyally to Duke's designs.

These philanthropic interests grew out of Duke's life. He always attributed his family's success to its Methodist faith. ("If I amount to anything in this world," he would say, "I owe it to my daddy and the Methodist church.") His interest in orphans came from his own experience without a mother. And the Duke family had for many decades generously supported Trinity College, which Duke had

> James Duke channeled his large donations tightly into the Carolinas—where he had made his fortune, and where the limited scale gave him chances to exert a clear positive influence.

designated to receive the gifts that would transform it into Duke University as a memorial to his father and brother. "I have selected Duke University as one of the principal objects of this trust because I recognize that education, when conducted along sane and practical, as opposed to dogmatic and theoretical, lines, is, next to religion, the greatest civilizing influence," he wrote. He intended that Duke University attain "a place of real leadership in the educational world."

Duke even allocated specific percentages of his endowment's payout to each charitable category: 46 percent devoted to higher education, 32 percent for hospitals, 10 percent for orphan care, and 12 percent to Methodist causes. He also limited his endowment's giving to the Carolinas—to give elsewhere, he thought, "would be productive of less good by reason of attempting too much." Duke also produced a statement of principles to guide his trustees, with many details—urging, for instance, that "adequate and convenient hospitals are assured in their respective communities, with especial reference to those who are unable to defray such expenses of their own." As for orphans, he wrote, while "nothing can take the place of a home and its influences, every effort should be made to safeguard and develop these wards of society."

Per Duke's instructions, the Duke Endowment's trustees are paid for their service. Every year, they read aloud the full text of Duke's indenture. "After the reading, there is always a time of reflection and comment about Mr. Duke, his ideas, and our mission," said the late Mary D. B. T. Semans, a longtime board member and grand-niece of Duke. "This closeness to the founder renews us and gives us a sense of new energy." Duke's successors have continued the program he laid out, with some adjustments for changes in how health care and orphan care are delivered.

In its early years, the endowment helped North Carolina's hospitals to grow at twice the rate of other southern states. It also helped make Duke University one of the world's highest-ranked institutions. "Trinity was a small Methodist college," notes endowment president Eugene Cochrane. "Mr. Duke said, 'I want it to become a great university'—and it has."

James Duke is memorialized in a statue in front of Duke University's monumental chapel. In the years before his death in 1925, he took a special pleasure in the design of Duke's Gothic campus. "Don't disturb me now; I am laying out the university grounds," he said to his nurse days before he died. "I am looking to the future, how they will stand and appear a hundred years from now."

↞ *Evan Sparks*

Further reading

○ *Philanthropy* magazine article, philanthropyroundtable.org/topic/donor_intent/duke_of_carolina

○ Robert Durden, *Bold Entrepreneur: A Life of James B. Duke* (Carolina Academic, 2003)

○ *Lasting Legacy to the Carolinas: The Duke Endowment, 1924–1994* (Duke University Press, 1998)

○ John Wilber Jenkins, *James B. Duke: Master Builder* (George Doran Co., 1927)

HARRY EARHART

Harry Earhart made his fortune as a manufacturer of lubricating oils, and used that fortune to support some of the most influential thinkers of the twentieth century through his philanthropy. He established two foundations, Earhart and Relm, to support free-market and American ideals. He also exercised bold leadership in structuring his board, thereby ensuring that his work would continue after his death, and providing a model for organizing philanthropic entities to safeguard donor intent.

Earhart was born in 1870, one of 11 children, the son of a respected local businessman (and the first cousin once removed of pilot Amelia Earhart). Earhart started several businesses, including stints brokering cargo and designing logging machinery. But his greatest success came from the lubricant industry. He took a job with the White Star Refining Company, a struggling oil company based in Buffalo, New York. In 1909, he was sent to Detroit as the company's sales agent.

Earhart saw the opportunity. With the automobile industry about to take off, he bought White Star and moved the company to Detroit. Thirsty for lubricants, auto manufacturers soon made White Star a thriving business. Under Earhart's leadership, the company operated its own refineries and sold petroleum products throughout the Midwest and into Canada, becoming one of the largest oil refining companies in the region. In 1930, Earhart sold White Star to the Vacuum Oil Company (a company later acquired by Mobil); he retired shortly thereafter. The White Star logo earned a good reputation, and would remain on Mobil gas station signs and maps until well after World War II.

Earhart and his wife, Carrie, settled into retirement in Ann Arbor and began to devote their full attention to philanthropy. They founded the Earhart Foundation in 1929 and gave it a broad charitable and religious mandate. It was a conventional family foundation, with their children included on the board.

As time passed, however, Earhart became concerned about the structure and future of his foundation. He saw increasing threats to free enterprise and traditional American values. Though he tried to get his children to see the urgency of promoting free-market ideals, he met with little success.

In 1949, Earhart moved boldly to refocus the work of his foundation—and ensure that it would continue long after him. He asked all of his children to step down and appointed a new and independent board to oversee the Earhart Foundation. He then established a second board made up of family members who shared his vision. The purpose of the second board was to elect trustees to the operating board, and to see to it that the trustees of the operating board remained true to the founder's vision. It is one of the first known instances in which a donor reconfigured his board to ensure future compliance with his intent.

At the same time, the Earhart Foundation instituted a new strategy of influencing ideas and scholarship. It would restrict its activities to funding fellowships for individual scholars whose work advanced the principles of a free society. The foundation's "talent scouts" were to identify promising students, writers, or researchers engaged in uncovering the role of economic freedom in creating a free society. Since Earhart established the fellowship program, it has funded the work of more than 2,500 graduate students.

> Nine winners of the Nobel Prize in economics were supported by Earhart fellowships in early phases of their careers.

A year later, Earhart also established the Relm Foundation, which funded institutions devoted to furthering economic freedom, like the London-based Institute for Economic Affairs and the Mont Pelerin Society. It also supported individual scholars like Leo Strauss, Eric Voegelin, and Peter Bauer. Relm was given a limited life of 20 years, and in 1977 the foundation was closed and all of its remaining assets went to the Earhart Foundation.

The Earhart Foundation has a peerless record for identifying talented, influential scholars. Nine winners of the Nobel Prize in economics were supported by Earhart fellowships early in their careers: Friedrick Hayek, Milton Friedman, Gary Becker, James Buchanan, Ronald Coase, Robert Lucas, Daniel McFadden, Vernon Smith, and George Stigler.

Though Harry Earhart died in 1954, his foundation remained true to his vision by supporting hundreds of individuals and playing a key role advancing freedom. The foundation's board decided to spend down its assets and close at the end of 2015. That decision would likely have pleased Harry Earhart, who insisted that "giving should serve to strengthen recipients rather than to make them increasingly and perhaps permanently dependent upon help from others."

↳ *Kari Barbic*

Further reading

○ *Philanthropy* magazine article, philanthropyroundtable.org/topic/excellence_in_ philanthropy/measuring_success_in_generations

○ Lee Edwards on the Earhart Foundation, *FirstPrinciplesJournal.com/* articles. aspx?article=561, December 22, 2011

○ Elizabeth Earhart Kennedy, *Once Upon a Family* (Fithian, 1990)

GEORGE EASTMAN

His talented but erratic father died when he was seven years old, leaving debts. His devoted mother coped as widows had for millennia: she took in boarders. The young boy had two older sisters, one of them afflicted with polio. Thus, when George Eastman dropped out of school in 1868 and took a job at age 14 as an office boy, he did so as the man of the family, with weight on his shoulders.

George was serious, extremely orderly, and thrifty, and he made himself useful at a pair of insurance companies and then a bank, where he rose from clerk to bookkeeper. His private passion was the brand new hobby of photography. He experimented with the variety of crude techniques available in the 1870s, haunted photo shops, and swapped tips with professional portraitists.

Eastman was a methodical self-educator, and began to experiment with the tricky chemistry and mechanics of creating photographic emulsions, which were then coated by hand on glass plates. He tinkered, invented, and even took a trip to England (then the technology center for photography) in an attempt to procure partners and patents for his innovations. He was racing scores of other nascent entrepreneurs situated around the world, trying to figure out the science and business model of a brand-new and rapidly emerging field.

Fortunately Eastman was a worker with enormous stamina. He would toil at the bank all day, six days a week, then spend his evenings in a rented room where he was experimenting tirelessly with various photo emulsions— devilishly sensitive concoctions subject to mysterious failure given the slightest variation in the chemical recipe or production process. He would work into the night, grabbing catnaps in a hammock he strung in one corner of the room and waking himself to stir the emulsions at exact intervals.

Soon he was building his own business producing photographic supplies and cameras, in an industry where the engineering was in constant flux, and the commercial competition was cutthroat. He moved aggressively and became the leading force in the sector during the 1890s. From the beginning, he worked to establish a presence not just in the U.S. but in countries around the world. By early in the twentieth century, when hobby photography was exploding in popularity, and filmed movies were emerging as mass entertainment, the Eastman Kodak Company had become one of the first firms to dominate a market across the globe.

Throughout it all, Eastman remained humble, shy, and unassuming. His reticence and boyish face gave him a low profile for many years, even in his hometown of Rochester, New York. When he identified himself, at the peak of his success, to a newly hired gate guard outside his own factory, the watchman scoffed, "Glad to meet you; I'm John D. Rockefeller." One of his friends observed that he "could keep silent in several languages." It took 25 years of close collaboration before Eastman and University of Rochester president Rush Rhees began to address each other by their first names. Eastman could be brisk and unemotional, and he never married, though he enjoyed his extended family and a number of close friendships.

He was a stern and no-nonsense businessman, but generous in sharing successes with employees and shareholders. He was a pioneer in creating sick pay, disability compensation, pensions, and hospital benefits. After one highly successful stock offering he set aside a large sum from his personal proceeds and had it distributed to 3,000 startled Eastman Kodak employees with a note reading: "This is a personal matter with Mr. Eastman and he requests that you will not consider it as a gift but as extra pay for good work." It was one of the first corporate bonuses.

Eastman was a high mix of homebody and adventurer. He would work ceaselessly in Rochester, relaxing only in mundane house and garden duties, then explode into some exotic and extended foreign jaunt. He bicycled across Europe several times (and also enthusiastically bicycled to work much of his life, even in Rochester winters). He would go on music and theater jags where he'd attend several performances or plays each day. On African safari once he stood filming a rhino on an early hand-cranked movie camera, and calmly continued as the snorting animal charged directly at him, simply sidestepping and actually brushing the animal as it passed. As the very large rhino began its second charge, with Eastman still methodically filming, the terrified hunter-guide accompanying him shot the creature dead just a few paces from his intrepid client.

By the time Eastman Kodak became a secure juggernaut in the early 1900s, its founder had lost interest in accumulating wealth. He was one of the richest men in the world, but much of his fortune sat in low-interest bank accounts. Instead of wanting more money he was now gripped by a powerful desire to put his funds to work in the rest of society. Over the next couple decades he would give away more than anyone except John Rockefeller and Andrew Carnegie. In current dollars, his gifts totaled in the range of $2 billion.

Eastman built brand-new campuses for two universities that became among the best of their kind. He established a medical school, and did pioneering work in improving the dental health of children in the U.S. and Europe. He built one of the greatest music schools in the world. And he was the largest contributor to the education of African Americans during the 1920s.

He also strayed into a few of the dead ends and dangers of those who become hypnotized by "science" and "progress" and "reason." He insisted that Kodak abandon tradition and lead the rest of mankind into use of a new rational calendar of 13 equal months of 28 days each. Kodak found it a lonely parade, but continued through the 1980s to use the so-called Cotsworthian calendar for accounting, sales, planning, and other purposes. More seriously, like others in the progressive era, he became a major funder of eugenics. And when his health began to fail, his utilitarian approach to life led Eastman to commit suicide, at age 77, via a pistol shot to the heart.

In general, though, Eastman was an exceptionally thoughtful and effective philanthropist. As much as or more than any other large American donor he worked hard at being a wise giver. "A rich man should be given credit for the judgment he uses in distributing his wealth, rather than in the amount he gives away," he stated in a rare public speech. To discipline his giving he followed several crucial principles.

> Donors should give while they are living and able to intelligently guide the use of their money, Eastman insisted. And he worked hard at being a wise patron, researching groups personally and making his own decisions with great care.

Along with Julius Rosenwald, his contemporary and confrère on this topic, Eastman believed strongly that donors should give while they are living and able to intelligently guide the application of their money. "Men who leave their money to be distributed by others are pie-faced mutts," he once said famously (just before signing away $39 million in one sitting). Eastman would never have locked up his money in a foundation, like Rockefeller and Carnegie, with money to be dribbled out after his death, in perpetuity, by succeeding waves of professional staff and trustees favoring who knows what causes. Eastman distributed the vast bulk of his fortune before he died in 1932, and bequeathed the remaining $25 million or so by last will and testament.

Rather than hiring a professional manager or teams of functionaries to distribute his largesse, Eastman did it himself, with very personal attention. He researched carefully, often acted without being asked, and made all of his own decisions. In addition to giving them money, he actively advised, guided, and assisted groups and causes. One of the reasons he concentrated his giving in the Rochester area was so he could personally supervise the execution, completion, and operation of his good works. He also took pains to avoid "scattering" his resources, and tried instead to "bunch" them for greatest effect.

Eastman ultimately had as much effect as any giver in America. He was a catalytic funder of universities. His $51 million in gifts made the University of Rochester into a top-tier school, and the $20 million he gave to MIT built its campus and reoriented it from local commuter facility to international leader. His adoption of MIT (and much of the rest of his philanthropy) was carried out anonymously, so many Americans then and now lacked awareness of his huge philanthropic footprints.

In addition, Eastman gave hefty sums, without solicitation, and loyally over decades, to black colleges like Tuskegee, Hampton, Howard, and Meharry. He also acted close to home, for instance, creating a model school for the black children living around his hunting camp in North Carolina. Between his college and lower-school gifts, George Eastman became the largest donor to African-American schooling of his era.

He was also a pioneer in medical philanthropy, with an ahead-of-his-time emphasis on prevention. He established many dental clinics serving children around the globe. He single-handedly created the University of Rochester School of Medicine and Dentistry. He built extensive hospital complexes throughout Rochester (which he identified as "the town I am interested in above all others," and where two thirds of his public gifts were centered).

George Eastman's most personal gift blessed Rochester and the world alike. "GE is absolutely alcoholic about music," wrote one friend, after accompanying him on a 1925 culture trip to New York City. They attended 12 operas and plays in six days, as well as visiting the Morgan Library, the Metropolitan Museum, the Frick Museum, and taking in two movies. ("The rest of the time we loafed," Eastman summarized in his own account.)

Eastman described listening to music as "a necessary part of life," and actually installed a large organ in his house and paid an organist to play it every morning as a kind of alarm clock and then breakfast accompaniment.

"There are no drawbacks to music: you can't have too much of it," he opined. "There is no residual bad effect like overindulgence in other things."

The charmed donor loved to share beautiful music with others, and made many innovative efforts to expose everyday citizens to great performances. He created elaborate music-instruction programs for the community at large, purchased hundreds of instruments for children, and subsidized the best ensembles to play in Rochester. He insisted tickets at all performances he had anything to do with should be sold first-come/first-served to avoid any "class distinctions." He required that operas be sung in English so people could understand them. He sent the conductor of the local orchestra to Europe for a year of full-time study and practice, then brought him back to lead a large professional orchestra in popular concerts.

With intense attention to detail, Eastman painstakingly created the Eastman Theater, still one of the largest and most wondrous concert halls in the country, into which he introduced imaginative programming. He popularized a new art form—and scandalized many in an era when movies were considered disreputable and trivial—by marrying his two loves of music and film. Every week in his 3,500-seat auditorium a fine orchestra was assembled to accompany the screening of silent films.

In philanthropy and in business, George Eastman was unusually open to novel creative combinations, while always insisting on excellence and the highest of standards. With the Eastman School of Music he was as demanding as he was generous; 12 years after his death this entity, which he had created from scratch by sheer willpower and financial devotion, was named the best graduate conservatory in the nation (and one of the best in the world). Eastman likewise aimed to make MIT a world paragon in technology education. He also got that wish.

Observers sometimes characterized George Eastman as having a "success complex." Hard achievement was everything for him. Failure was not to be tolerated. Remarkably, he often met his own lofty standard.

→ *Karl Zinsmeister*

Further reading
- Elizabeth Brayer, *George Eastman: A Biography* (Johns Hopkins University Press, 1996)
- Kodak corporate biography for founder, kodak.com/ek/US/en/George_Eastman.htm
- PBS profile, "The Wizard of Photography," pbs.org/wgbh/amex/eastman/index.html
- George Eastman Papers, University of Rochester, lib.rochester.edu/index.cfm?page=864

THOMAS EDDY

Thomas Eddy, one of New York City's top financiers, led some of the most innovative philanthropic efforts of the early nineteenth century. He founded the first mutual insurance company in New York, and was among the first commissioners of the Erie Canal. But Eddy was best known for his charitable work. He guided the efforts to reform penal laws. He helped construct the New York Hospital. And he founded the New York Savings Bank, a spectacularly successful charitable bank designed specifically to serve the working poor.

Born in 1758 to Quaker immigrants from Ireland, Eddy grew up in Philadelphia. During the Revolutionary War he sided with the Loyalists, and remained engaged in commerce as hostilities flared around him. When he turned 21, he moved to New York City, where he and his brothers set up a merchant house. The business prospered for a while, and Thomas opened a satellite office in Philadelphia. He won a lucrative contract for transporting remittance money from the British headquarters in New York to the troops who were taken prisoner after the fall of Yorktown.

In 1791 Thomas returned to New York, where he set himself up as the city's first insurance underwriter. He made a fortune speculating in the first issue of federal debt, and was asked to become a director of the Mutual Insurance Company. As his reputation grew, he was invited to join other boards, including that of the Western Inland Navigation Company, which had been established in 1792 for the purpose of developing a navigable route along the Mohawk River to Lake Ontario. When it proved impractical, he proposed building a canal rather than relying on river navigation. His idea became the basis for the Erie Canal. When the project was presented to the legislature in 1810, Eddy was appointed one of the project's first commissioners.

"There is no benevolent or charitable institution founded of which he was not the serious promoter," proclaimed New York grandee Cadwallader Colden in 1833. Eddy was chosen to meet with the Indians of the Six Nations, negotiating treaties and working to alleviate distress. He was a charter member of the New York Manumission Society. He was a founding trustee of the New York Bible Society. He established and served as the primary benefactor of the House of Refuge, one of the first charities dedicated to turning around the lives of juvenile delinquents.

One of Eddy's most notable philanthropic achievements was the reform of New York's penal laws. In the early 1790s he began a campaign to end branding, whipping, and solitary confinement in state prisons. In 1796, he shepherded a bill through the state legislature that established new standards for the penitentiary system. He was appointed to oversee the construction of the first state prison and served from 1797 to 1801 as its first director. On the basis of those experiences, in 1801 he published *An Account of the State Prison or Penitentiary House in the City of New York*, a landmark book in the history of prison reform.

Equally significant were his efforts to open the New York Hospital. Efforts to build a free hospital for the poor of New York City were begun in 1771. A fire destroyed the first building; the Revolutionary War interrupted the construction of its replacement. Progress stalled. Eddy took it upon himself to drive a new charitable subscription, to which he contributed liberally, to get the project finished. For his efforts, he was made governor of the hospital in 1793. In 1815, he launched another such project, establishing a humane mental asylum in Bloomingdale, New York.

But Eddy's greatest philanthropic accomplishment was almost certainly the Savings Bank of New York. Largely forgotten today, the mutual savings banks of the nineteenth century were invaluable to the working poor. "The utility of these institutions to industrious persons of small means," wrote Samuel Knapp, "fired his soul" and opened Mr. Eddy's checkbook.

> Eddy was one of New York City's earliest philanthropists, and a leader in nearly all of the good causes of his day.

Unlike commercial banks of the era, mutual savings banks sought out small depositors of modest means, investing their funds at minimal risk while providing at least a 5 percent return. The banks did not pay dividends, and most were run by trustees who volunteered their time. At a time when banks were unsecure, deposits were not guaranteed, and the only other method of saving was to hoard cash, the mutual savings bank offered a safe way for persons of modest income to accumulate capital.

Eddy did not invent the idea of a mutual savings bank. By the time he floated his first proposal in 1803, Boston and Philadelphia had already pioneered the model. Eddy's great accomplishment was making the Savings Bank of New York an unparalleled success. Optimistic predictions suggested that the bank would accumulate $50,000 worth of deposits in its first year. Instead, writes historian Kathleen McCarthy, "it drew $155,000 in the first six months. And its resources grew exponentially thereafter. In 1825, 9,000 investors had $1.4 million on deposit; ten years later, the number of investors had risen to 23,000, with $3 million in funds; by 1860 over 50,000 passbook holders had nearly $10 million on deposit."

Thomas Eddy died at age 69 in 1827. "His death was as sudden as his life was serene," wrote his biographer Samuel Knapp. "He who had done so much to alleviate the sufferings of others was not doomed to suffer much himself."

↪ *Christopher Levenick*

Further reading

○ Freeman Hunt, *Lives of the American Merchants* (Derby & Jackson, 1856)
○ Samuel Knapp, *The Life of Thomas Eddy* (Conner and Cooke, 1834)
○ Alan Olmstead, *New York City Mutual Savings Banks: 1819-1861* (University of North Carolina, 1976)

DON FISHER

Don Fisher founded the Gap, one of the most successful retail chains of the twentieth century, and became the savviest education-reform philanthropist of his era. Born in 1928 to a middle-class family in San Francisco, Fisher always credited his parents with encouraging him to take risks while making practical, smart decisions. "Change or fail" was the lesson he often said he learned from his father, a cabinetmaker and businessman.

Fisher had the opportunity to go into the family business when he graduated from the University of California, Berkeley, but instead chose to branch off on his own. He tried real-estate development for a while, then noticed an unfilled niche in retail fashion. While leasing space to a Levi's store in one of the properties he owned, Fisher found that he could not find a pair of jeans that fit him right. He had a 31-inch inseam, but the pants in the store only came in even numbers. He went to other stores and found a similar lack of selection.

"What if," he wondered, "someone put together in one store all the styles, colors, and sizes Levi Strauss had to offer?" In 1969, he secured space on Ocean Avenue in San Francisco and opened up a clothing store that was comprehensive and geared specifically toward young people. His wife Doris suggested that they capitalize on the perceived generation gap, and perhaps the gap in retail choices. "The Gap" was emblazoned on their tags and signs.

The Fishers learned the retail business as they went along. Within a few years, they had launched their own line of clothing. By the time Don Fisher passed away at age 81, he had expanded that single store into a worldwide chain with more than 3,100 outlets, nearly $15 billion of annual sales, and more than 134,000 employees.

In 1995, when he stepped down as CEO, Fisher began to think strategically about ways to improve K-12 education in America. A graduate of San Francisco public schools, Fisher considered excellent education a moral imperative. But public-school results were crying out for application of his father's "change or fail" mandate.

Fisher approached Scott Hamilton, who was then working in Massachusetts as associate commissioner of education for charter schools, asking about schools that had real quality and the potential for replication. "I want to do something where we can touch a lot of kids," Fisher told Hamilton. "I don't want to support just one school; I want to support something that has a broad opportunity around the country."

Hamilton found the "Knowledge Is Power Program," or KIPP, which at that point consisted of two fledgling charter schools. It was clear they were getting powerful results. According to Hamilton, KIPP's track record of success, its central belief that skin color or family income should not limit a child's ability to learn, its focus on college as a goal for all students, and its ferocious commitment to excellence made it different from anything else offered in urban public education.

> The pioneer in finding, founding, and funding effective school reforms over the last generation, Don Fisher was a lead supporter of nearly all of the major educational innovations of the last 20 years.

Over the next decade, the Fishers donated more than $70 million to KIPP—which allowed the chain to grow to 183 top-flight schools by 2015. While 87 percent of its students are eligible for subsidized school meals, and 95 percent are African-American or Latino, more than 90 percent of KIPP middle-school students graduate from high school and more than 80 percent of KIPP alumni go on to college—vastly higher numbers than in other urban schools.

Recognizing that new networks like KIPP could succeed only if they were able to recruit talented educators, Fisher turned his attention to Teach For America, eventually donating more than $100 million to that organization, which recruits top students to take up the teaching of disadvantaged students as a calling. Thanks in no small part to Don Fisher's generosity, the TFA corps has grown to around 10,000 active instructors in classrooms as of 2015, most of whom hail from the nation's most selective colleges and universities.

Just as in his business, Fisher was always concerned with both quality and scale in his philanthropy. To make sure that excellent charter schools grew beyond the occasional curiosity, he co-founded the Charter School Growth Fund with the late John Walton. This venture has made early-stage investments of over $100 million to high-promise charter school networks that have shown the ability to grow. Today, CSGF is invested in 32 networks serving over 100,000 students. These networks operate the highest-performing schools in their cities, and many have completely closed the achievement gap between low-income and affluent students.

Fisher also helped found the California Charter School Association, whose membership is open only to those schools that meet exacting educational standards. The movement "mustn't accept mediocre or poor charter schools," Fisher explained, "because they'll bring down the rest of the schools."

Don and Doris Fisher were active donors outside of education too. They assembled a large collection of contemporary art—some 1,100 works by the likes of Alexander Calder, Roy Lichtenstein, Gerhard Richter, and Andy Warhol—which they donated to the San Francisco Museum of Modern Art. Fisher was a major booster of the Boys & Girls Clubs of America, where he served as governor. He endowed the Fisher Center of Real Estate and Urban Economics, as well as the Fisher Center for the Strategic Use of Information Technology, both at Berkeley's Haas School of Business.

Don Fisher was one of the most consequential education reformers of the last century. He was first to find and fund almost *all* of the pioneering ideas and top programs of the last 20 years. His uncanny knack for discovering effective people was coupled to a fierce independent streak that encouraged him to back brave mavericks long before anyone else would.

↳ *Naomi Schaefer Riley*

Further reading

- *Philanthropy* magazine article, philanthropyroundtable.org/topic/excellence_in_philanthropy/closing_the_gap
- Jay Mathews, *Work Hard. Be Nice: How Two Inspired Teachers Created the Most Promising Schools in America* (Workman, 2009)
- Gap website founder bio, "Don Fisher, 1928–2010," gapinc.com/content/dam/gapincsite/documents/DonFisher_Bio.pdf

ZACHARY FISHER

Zachary Fisher, with his brothers Martin and Larry, built a fortune as a real-estate developer in New York City. That fortune has since been devoted to a wide variety of philanthropic initiatives, from supporting the New York Police Department to funding charitable projects in Israel. But the Fisher family, and Zachary himself, are best known for their extensive work on behalf of America's military servicemembers and veterans.

Zachary Fisher was born in 1910, the son of Jewish immigrants from Lithuania. His father was a general contractor, and at 16 years of age Zachary dropped out of high school and went to work as a bricklayer. Soon he joined his brothers in forming Fisher Brothers, a company that initially focused on building residential properties around the boroughs of New York. The firm flourished. By the early 1950s, it had expanded to commercial real estate, and within two decades was involved in financing, erecting, and leasing properties throughout the city. Fisher Brothers came to construct, own, or manage upwards of 10 million square feet of New York real estate. The Fishers, proclaimed the *New York Times* in its obituary for Zachary, rank among "the royal families that over two or three generations have molded the Manhattan real-estate market."

Throughout their lives, Zachary and his wife, Elizabeth, had an unusually deep respect for the men and women of the United States military. "It's a privilege to live in this great country of ours," Fisher said in an interview late in life. "I owe them."

Zachary Fisher never served in the military. After the bombing of Pearl Harbor he attempted to enlist in the Marine Corps. He was denied, however, because of a knee injury he sustained while working as a teenager on a construction site. Undeterred, Fisher volunteered his building expertise for civil defense, helping build coastal fortifications along the Atlantic seaboard.

In the late 1970s, Fisher learned that the *USS Intrepid*—a storied aircraft carrier which had survived several kamikaze attacks, played a critical role in the Pacific during World War II, served in Korea and Vietnam, and even recovered two NASA space capsules—was scheduled to be retired and sold for scrap metal. Fisher hated the idea that the nation would "cut up our own history for razor blades."

He decided to acquire and rebuild the *Intrepid*, converting it into a floating museum moored off the banks of Manhattan. It was a monumental undertaking. He put up the first $25 million. Then he shepherded along an act of Congress. (Since this would be the first time an aircraft carrier had ever been sold to a private party, it required a federal statute to complete the transaction.) Next he battled the New York City building commission. (Lacking any precedent for an aircraft-carrier museum, the city inspectors originally treated the *Intrepid* as a multi-story skyscraper lying on its side.) Five years later, the Intrepid Sea-Air-Space Museum opened—the world's largest naval museum. "I watched kids in sneakers wandering all over this piece of history," remarked Fisher on the *Intrepid*'s opening day. "I wondered if any of them would be inspired to do something for their country."

Soon after the 1983 bombing of a U.S. Marine barracks in Beirut, the Fishers offered an additional $10,000 beyond the standard government death benefit to each of the families of fallen service members. Having come to the conclusion that these death benefits given to families of fallen military personnel were too low in all cases, the Fishers created the Intrepid Fallen Heroes Fund. Its mission was to supplement the government's benefits, in all future cases, with as much as $25,000 cash. The Fishers continued these efforts for more than two decades, closing the direct-payment program only after the federal government significantly increased the monetary benefits offered to the families of service members killed on active duty.

> Zachary Fisher launched some of the most inventive efforts ever seen to honor and aid men and women of the United States military.

Zachary and Elizabeth Fisher are perhaps best known for launching the Fisher House Foundation. In 1990, Fisher learned about a servicewoman who had recently received medical treatment at a military hospital. Her husband, unable to afford a hotel, spent the duration of her hospitalization sleeping in his car. Fisher was shocked to learn that the military made no provision for the families of hospitalized veterans and servicemembers—and he decided to do something about it.

With an initial donation of $20 million, Zachary and Elizabeth began building "comfort homes" within walking distance of V.A. and military medical centers. These multi-unit complexes were designed to provide free housing for families of military personnel and veterans who were hospitalized at nearby medical facilities. Fisher limited his mission to building the houses, a task for which he had proven expertise. By the time of Zachary's death in 2000, the Fisher House Foundation had built 26 houses. The program continues to expand; as of 2012 there were 57 houses in operation and five more in the process of being built.

Fisher was deeply involved in creating new philanthropic ventures of all sorts throughout his life. After his wife developed Alzheimer's, he joined forces with David Rockefeller, donating $5 million to establish the Fisher Center for Alzheimer's Research. Based at Rockefeller University, it focuses on supporting research that addresses the cause, care, and cure of Alzheimer's, as well as providing public education programs on the disease.

After Zachary's death, the Fisher family continued and expanded his philanthropic mission of supporting the military and veterans. Between 2000 and 2012, the Intrepid Fallen Heroes Fund provided $120 million in support to wounded servicemembers and their families, first through direct payments to the families of soldiers lost in war, and later through the construction of new medical research and rehabilitation facilities for wounded military personnel. The Center for the Intrepid in San Antonio is focused on treatment of soldiers with amputations, burns, or loss of limb use. The National Intrepid Center of Excellence in Bethesda, Maryland, is focused on the care of brain injuries and psychological health. In 2012, it was announced that several satellite centers will be constructed to bring advanced brain-injury care to other parts of the country.

Also in 2012, the Fisher House program was expanded to Great Britain, where local partners helped build a facility to serve the families of British military patients. There was already a facility at a U.S. Army post in Germany. There is also a house for grieving families receiving the remains of loved ones at Dover Air Force Base.

As of 2015, the Fisher House Foundation has provided the families of hospitalized servicemembers and veterans with 9 million days of free lodging. In addition to saving those families a great expense, the opportunity to commune with other families in similar situations has proven invaluable for many beneficiaries. The foundation also administers complementary programs sponsored by others—such as Hero Miles, which uses donated frequent-flyer credits to pay for loved ones to travel to wounded servicemembers, the Newman's Own Award, which provides grants for projects to support troops at local military bases, and Scholarships for Military Children.

Zachary Fisher never sought any special recognition for his work on behalf of American servicemen and women. The work was its own reward. Six months after his death, though, Fisher was honored with a new law that conferred upon him the honorary status of veteran of the Armed Forces of the United States.

➻ *Thomas Meyer*

Further reading

○ John Culhane, "The Man Who Bought an Aircraft Carrier" (*Reader's Digest*, 1990)
○ *New York Times* obituary, nytimes.com/1999/06/05/nyregion/zachary-fisher-88-dies-helped-alter-new-york-skyline.html

HENRY FORD

Henry Ford ranks among the most important figures of the industrial era. He founded the Ford Motor Company, which pioneered assembly-line production, driving down costs and making automobile ownership a staple of middle-class American life. Through it all, he maintained a highly idiosyncratic style of charitable giving. He saw work as the purpose of human existence, and he deeply disliked anything—especially something well-intentioned, like philanthropy—that seemed to undermine its discipline. He distrusted organized charities, although he created a few himself. Despite his misgivings, Ford seems to have dedicated about one third of his income to philanthropy.

Henry Ford was born on a Michigan farm in July 1863. He absorbed the farmer's tireless work ethic but hated agriculture. His inclination was mechanical, and as a boy he would strip down and reassemble any machine he could find. ("Every clock in the Ford house shudders when it sees Henry coming," a friend once quipped.) At the age of 16, he left the farm and headed to Detroit, where he found work first as a machinist, and later as an engineer.

Ford settled into a comfortable middle-class life in Detroit, marrying Clara Bryant in 1888 and getting a job at the Edison Illuminating Company in 1891. Every night, he tinkered in the garage behind his house. The neighbors called him "Crazy Henry" for his obsession, but in 1896 he rolled out his first self-propelled vehicle: the Ford Quadricycle. With encouragement from Thomas Edison, Ford kept experimenting—and began to believe he could create his own automobile company.

By the time Ford turned 39 he had founded two car companies. Both had failed—one with a bang, the other with a whimper—yet he was undeterred. In 1903, he borrowed $28,000 to establish the Ford Motor Company. The early cars produced by this firm generated enough profit to make Ford wealthy, and to give him time to take on a more long-range project: the Model T.

When it rolled off the assembly line in October 1908, the Model T revolutionized the automobile industry. In relentless pursuit of efficiency gains, Ford had developed unprecedented production methods. He used machine-made, standardized parts, which were put together along a continuously moving assembly line. The results were staggering. At a time when cars regularly sold for $1,000, he was soon selling the Model T for $345. Orders poured in. By 1915, about half of all cars on earth were Fords. Eventually, some 15 million Model Ts were sold.

Henry Ford owned the Ford Motor Company until his death. By the mid-1920s, his net worth was estimated around $1.2 billion, and though Ford's market share gradually diminished, the company's stunning success made its namesake one of the wealthiest men in American history.

Yet Ford seemed almost indifferent to money and all it could buy. A dry cleaner once returned a $125,000 check Ford had accidentally left in his suit pocket. Ford once declined a dinner invitation at the White House to honor the King and Queen of England. His wife, he explained, had a previously scheduled meeting of her garden club.

Being unimpressed by money may help explain Ford's extensive charitable giving during his lifetime. In average years, Ford gave away about 33 percent of his income. By way of comparison, most people in his tax bracket gave away 5 percent. What Ford himself considered to be the most genuine philanthropy were small gifts to individuals, of which he gave many. Biographer William Greenleaf records "impulsive and warm-hearted acts of individual generosity that saw him give away money, food, automobiles, or other articles." While driving through the Massachusetts countryside, for example, Ford came across an elderly couple whose farmhouse had just been destroyed in a storm. He asked a few questions, then reached into his pocket and gave the farmers all the cash he had on him, some $200.

To Ford's mind, writes Greenleaf, charitable giving should be "a private and individual act," one

> In average years, Henry Ford gave away about a third of his income, and he preferred to give money to individual people, face to face and with a firm handshake.

that is "spontaneous on the part of the giver, unanticipated and unsought by the beneficiary, and a gratuitous gesture without any element of calculation." By contrast, Ford despised virtually all institutional charity. To his mind, it "degrades recipients and drugs their self-respect," while creating a "feeling of resentment which nearly always overtakes the objects of charity." He preferred to give money to individual people, face to face and with a firm handshake.

Ford did launch a few projects of his own. In 1911, he and his wife created Valley Farm, an 80-acre home for orphan boys. During the First World War, he housed Belgian war refugees at Oughtrington Hall, and in 1915, he headed a "peace ship" that sailed for Europe with 120 American representatives, hoping to persuade the European powers to quit the conflict. He built a trade school in Detroit and a school for African Americans in Georgia. During the Great Depression, he paid for two work camps for boys.

Two of his philanthropic projects, however, were particularly conspicuous, because of both their size and their strategy. The first was the Henry Ford Hospital in Detroit. In 1914, the residents of Detroit started a subscription campaign to build a modern medical facility. Construction began, but was halted when the half-completed facility foundered in debt. Ford took over, completed the project with his own funds, served as its first president, and over the course of his lifetime gave it about $14 million. To this day, it remains one of Detroit's largest hospitals.

Ford wanted the Henry Ford Hospital to reflect his philosophy of work and self-reliance. The hospital's patients were workingmen and their families—solid citizens who wanted excellent health care but did not want to beg for charity to settle the bills. He thus subsidized some of the cost of the medical care, but took pains to ensure that patients would still have to bear some of the costs they incurred. "There are plenty of hospitals for the rich," Ford explained. "There are plenty of hospitals for the poor. There are no hospitals for those who can afford to pay only a moderate amount and yet desire to pay without a feeling that they are recipients of charity."

Ford's other major philanthropic passion was historical preservation. Many biographers have noted the irony of the industrialist who brought about the future spending money to preserve the past. His interest was whetted in 1919 when he restored his family's homestead in Dearborn. His first major preservation endeavor was the Wayside Inn, near South Sudbury, Massachusetts, a tavern celebrated in verse by Henry Wadsworth Longfellow. To enhance the property, Ford bought up surrounding buildings and restored them, too, at a total cost of $15 million.

Ford was a lifelong collector of Americana, and in 1926 he decided to house his collection in Dearborn. For over 20 years, Ford had collected everything from locomotives to fabric samples to historic buildings—including the courthouse where Abraham Lincoln practiced law and the Wright Brothers' bicycle shop. His collection opened to the public in 1929, with President Hoover officiating. It remains one of the country's great living-history museums, known as Greenfield Village.

Ford was born in 1863, a few weeks after the Battle of Gettysburg; he died in 1947, a few months before Chuck Yeager broke the sound barrier. His life spanned from the steam engine to the jet engine—and Ford himself was responsible for much of that technological revolution. Yet his vision for philanthropy tended toward the nineteenth century. "I have no patience with professional charity or with any sort of commercialized humanitarianism," Ford wrote in 1923. "The moment human helpfulness is systematized, organized, commercialized, and professionalized, the heart of it is extinguished, and it becomes a cold and clammy thing."

↦ *Martin Morse Wooster*

Further reading

○ Peter Collier and David Horowitz, *The Fords: An American Epic* (Simon and Schuster, 1987)

○ Garet Garrett, *The Wild Wheel: The World of Henry Ford* (Cresset Press, 1952)

○ William Greenleaf, *From These Beginnings: The Early Philanthropy of Henry and Edsel Ford, 1911-1936* (Wayne State University Press, 1964)

BENJAMIN FRANKLIN

Benjamin Franklin is perhaps the greatest polymath of American history. He was known by turns as a scientist and satirist, an inventor and entrepreneur, a printer and politician. Within his lifetime, Franklin won international admiration for his discoveries relating to electricity, optics, thermodynamics, and other elements of science. He was a skilled diplomat and distinguished public servant, an intimate of many of the eighteenth century's most significant political and intellectual leaders. He was a profligate inventor, who devised the Franklin stove, the lightning rod, bifocals, and the glass armonica—an instrument for which Mozart, Handel, and Beethoven all composed works. And not least among his many accomplishments, Franklin is often considered the father of American civil society.

Franklin was born in Boston in 1706, the youngest of ten children. His father, a soap- and candlemaker, wanted Franklin to attend college but was only able to afford two years of formal education. At the age of 15, Benjamin was apprenticed to his brother James, a newspaperman. The brothers often clashed, and after two years Benjamin broke his apprenticeship and left New England, moving first to Philadelphia and then to London. In 1726, he returned to the City of Brotherly Love and soon began publishing the city's leading newspaper and the popular annual *Poor Richard's Almanac*.

Franklin also started methodically acquiring property. His investments in real estate in Philadelphia, plus holdings as far afield as Boston, Ohio, Georgia, and Nova Scotia, made him one of the colonies' wealthiest men. By some estimates, indeed, Franklin became one of the wealthiest men in American history.

Franklin retired from active business at the age of 42, and devoted himself to public service. He rose rapidly through a series of appointments: councilman, justice of the peace, assemblyman, and deputy postmaster general for North America. During this same period, Franklin was studying and writing about the properties of electricity, for which he was awarded honorary doctorates from St. Andrews and Oxford. He eventually returned to London, where he worked at the highest levels of government, eager to advance the interests of the British Empire.

As relations with the North American colonies deteriorated, Franklin tried to ameliorate tensions, becoming an ardent patriot only after being attacked before the king's Privy Council in 1774. He returned to Philadelphia, where he helped draft and then signed the Declaration of Independence. The Continental Congress appointed him Ambassador to the Royal Court at Versailles, where he achieved what may be the most remarkable success in the history of American diplomacy: winning French support for the independence of the United States. At the conclusion of hostilities, he helped negotiate the peace treaty with Britain, returned to the United States, and represented Pennsylvania at the Constitutional Convention. He died in 1790, one of the most accomplished men of our Founding era.

> "It is prodigious the quantity of good that may be done by one man, if he will make a business of it," Franklin observed.

Throughout his life, but most notably while living in Philadelphia, Franklin led a number of private, voluntary initiatives to enhance civil society. "It is prodigious the quantity of good that may be done by one man, if he will make a business of it," he once observed. Historian Edmund Morgan suggested he "was behind virtually every scheme that made Philadelphia an attractive place to live."

The city was in many respects an ideal laboratory for Franklin's experiments in civil society. For most of his life, Pennsylvania lacked capable governing institutions. The province was essentially a feudal possession of the long-absent Penn family. Philadelphia nevertheless flourished—by 1750, it was a major center of trans-Atlantic commerce and ranked among the largest cities in the British Empire—and its surplus wealth made large philanthropic initiatives possible. Civic life was further bolstered by the Quakers' strong communitarian ethic.

Back in 1727 when he was a young man, Franklin organized a group of 12 artisans—including a glazier, a shoemaker, a printer, a cabinetmaker, two surveyors, and several clerks—who began to meet for the purpose of mutual betterment. Calling themselves the Junto Club, the men met on Friday evenings to share dinner and engage in edifying conversation. "The rules that I drew up," Franklin noted in his *Autobiography*, "required that every member, in his turn, should produce one or more queries on any point of

Morals, Politics, or Natural Philosophy, to be discuss'd by the company; and once in three months produce and read an essay of his own writing, on any subject he pleased." A recurring topic of conversation involved opportunities for civic improvement.

One of the Junto's first such projects was the creation of a public subscription library. Members of the group shared books among themselves and soon decided to coordinate their efforts and share it with the public. In 1731, they incorporated the Library Company of Philadelphia, the first such library in British North America. Franklin initially found it difficult to arouse public interest in the project. The problem, he realized, was "the impropriety of presenting one's self as the proposer of any useful project." He resolved to "put myself as much as I could out of sight" and thereafter adopted the lifelong habit of presenting his ideas as a "scheme of a number of friends."

In December 1736, Franklin conceived and founded the Union Fire Company, the first volunteer fire brigade in Pennsylvania. All of the company's 30 charter members pledged to protect one another's homes against fire. Each member agreed to keep at the ready two leather buckets (to carry water) and four heavy cloth bags (to rescue endangered property). Failure to maintain the required equipment resulted in a fine—five shillings per infraction—and the fire company met eight times annually to review its procedures. In 1751, Franklin convened representatives from the other volunteer fire companies that had sprung up across the city and organized the Philadelphia Contributorship Fire Insurance Company.

Franklin also played a crucial role in the movement to bring higher education to Philadelphia. Around 1743, he began circulating his proposal for the Academy of Philadelphia. Unlike other colonial colleges, which preferred the sons of leading families, Franklin's college would be open to all deserving young men. It also differed from other schools in that it lacked a denominational affiliation. Franklin was elected president of the nascent institution, and saw it through to its opening day. The Academy of Philadelphia, later the University of Pennsylvania, opened its doors in 1750 and had 300 students within two years.

Once the academy was underway, Franklin turned his attention to founding a charitable hospital. "In 1751," he recalled in the *Autobiography*, "Dr. Thomas Bond, a particular friend of mine, conceived the idea of establishing a hospital in Philadelphia, for the reception and care of poor, sick persons, whether the inhabitants of the province or strangers—a very beneficent design, which has been ascribed to me but was originally his." When it began admitting patients in 1756, this organization became the nation's first hospital, a philanthropic enterprise that served all comers, regardless of their ability to pay.

In addition to the many institutions he founded, Franklin supported scores of others. Franklin's name, notes one of the editors of his collected writings, appears "at the head of many a subscription list, whether for the College of Philadelphia, to support the botanizing of John Bartram, or to construct a synagogue for Mikveh Israel Congregation. (He was often the most generous contributor as well.)" Although not himself a churchgoer, he funded any denomination that sought his aid. And even late in life, he was an inveterate joiner. Only a few years before his death, Franklin became the president of the Society for Promoting the Abolition of Slavery and the Relief of Negroes Unlawfully Held in Bondage.

"Liberality is not giving much," Poor Richard wrote in 1748, "but in giving wisely." Franklin was a tireless improver, and his inventiveness made lasting contributions to American philanthropy. For example, Franklin led the first effort in British North America to offer tax relief to charitable activity. Encouraged by the success of the Union Fire Company, and eager to see the model replicated throughout Philadelphia, Franklin persuaded municipal authorities to offer a property tax abatement in exchange for participation in a volunteer fire company.

Franklin likewise pioneered the concept of the matching grant. While raising funds for the Pennsylvania Hospital, he approached the colonial legislature to propose that once the hospital had raised £2,000 in private contributions, the colonial government should contribute another £2,000 to the effort. "Every man's donation would be doubled," Franklin later wrote. "The subscriptions accordingly soon exceeded the requisite sum."

Perhaps Franklin's best-remembered charitable donation was his final bequest. Franklin left £1,000 to his native Boston and another £1,000 to his adopted Philadelphia. Both bequests were held in trust, to gather interest for 200 years. At the end of the first century, each city had the right to withdraw capital from the trust; by the close of the second, each was directed to spend it down. In 1990, the trusts were required to sunset. Philadelphia elected to spend its remaining $2 million on scholarships for local high school students. The $5 million in Franklin's Boston trust was used to establish a trade school: the Franklin Institute of Boston.

In the first pages of *The Protestant Ethic and the Spirit of Capitalism*, Max Weber describes Franklin's essay "Advice to a Young Tradesman" as an expression of the capitalist ethos in "almost classical purity." Weber, however, recognized that Franklin did not always adhere to the unrelenting profit-maximizing ethic he seemed to champion. The example of Benjamin Franklin offers a deeply American symbiosis between energetic profit-seeking and creative not-for-profit activity, and between enlightened self-interest and charitable concern for others.

Christopher Levenick

Further reading

○ Whitfield Bell, "B. Franklin on Philanthropy" (American Philosophical Society, 2006)

○ Edmund Morgan, *Benjamin Franklin* (Yale University Press, 2002)

○ Gordon Wood, *The Americanization of Benjamin Franklin* (Penguin Books, 2005)

○ The Papers of Benjamin Franklin, franklinpapers.org/franklin

MARY GARRETT

Mary Elizabeth Garrett ranks among the nation's most significant benefactors of higher education for women. Born in 1853 to wealth and privilege, Garrett was the third child of railroad tycoon John Work Garrett, the president of the Baltimore & Ohio Railroad. Mary Garrett's inheritance would make her one of the wealthiest women in the United States, but it was her business savvy and shrewd philanthropy that helped her to achieve some of the greatest social improvements of her generation.

As John Garrett's daughter, Mary could not enter the family business or exert influence on their financial empire. She nevertheless gained invaluable business training as her father's personal secretary. She would accompany him on many of his business trips, recording his correspondence and meeting some of the most influential businessmen of the time, including titans like Andrew Carnegie, J. Pierpont Morgan, and Cornelius Vanderbilt.

John Garrett also taught his daughter by example in his philanthropy. Garrett's giving was influenced by his friend George Peabody, and he maintained close ties with Johns Hopkins, serving as a trustee of both Hopkins' university and hospital. Mary Garrett would employ the lessons she gleaned from the example of her father and his friends when she inherited nearly $2 million upon her father's death and became a philanthropist in her own right.

She relied heavily on her intimate circle of friends, known as the "Friday Evening." The intellectually curious group included Carey Thomas, Mamie Gwinn, Elizabeth "Bessie" King, and Julia Rogers—all but one of them daughters of trustees of Johns Hopkins University, the hospital, or both. It was with this group that Garrett collaborated on her two key philanthropic achievements: the Bryn Mawr School and Johns Hopkins Medical School.

The Bryn Mawr School was Garrett's first philanthropic undertaking. The Friday Evening group was appalled by the lack of a serious college preparatory school for girls in Baltimore. Garrett's inheritance provided the means to remedy the situation. They decided to act.

They named the new preparatory school for Bryn Mawr College in Philadelphia, and acquired the school's permission to do so. (They also maintained close ties to the college, and Bryn Mawr school students were required to pass the college entrance examination in order to graduate.) Garrett not only provided the necessary funds to establish and build the school, she also closely oversaw the project. Her hands-on involvement extended to the selection of gym equipment and artwork for the school, which was located but a few blocks from Garrett's home in Baltimore. The Friday Evening served as the governing body of the school. Garrett was its president.

Garrett and the Friday Evening then set their sights higher—the education of women at Johns Hopkins University. Garrett first attempted to open the doors of Johns Hopkins to women in 1887 by offering the university $35,000 to establish a coeducational school of science. The university president and trustees rejected her offer. Just a few years later, however, Johns Hopkins found itself on unsure financial footing. The opening of its medical school had been delayed due to insufficient funds. The Friday Evening saw an opportunity.

> Garrett cleverly mastered the art of "coercive philanthropy" to promote high standards and fairness at the same time.

Garrett enlisted her friends and sought support from other influential women around the country (including Frances Morgan, Jane Stanford, and Caroline Harrison) to raise funds to approach the university with a new offer. Garrett offered the trustees $100,000 (half of which she contributed personally) to pay for the opening of the medical school on one condition: that men and women would be admitted on equal standing. The board accepted the offer, but told the group that the school could not open with less than $500,000.

When the university and the newly formed Women's Medical Fund Committee struggled to approach this number, Garrett stepped in and covered the difference with a donation of $307,000. But her additional funding came with additional conditions. These new conditions required that the medical school be a full graduate program leading to a medical degree and that all applicants be required to have a bachelor's degree in the field of science. (Neither of these stipulations were normal for medical schools at the time.)

Garrett's funding and her clearly outlined conditions not only opened medical education to America's women, they also turned Johns Hopkins into the first modern medical school in the United States. In his history of the school, Alan Chesney concludes: "To this lady, more than any other single person, save only Johns Hopkins himself, does the School of Medicine owe its being."

Throughout the rest of her life, Garrett would continue to use her wealth and influence to promote women's education and opportunity. She gave generously to Bryn Mawr College and later became a major funder of the cause of women's suffrage. Her final years were spent at Bryn Mawr with her close friend Carey Thomas, who was president of the college, to whom Garrett left her fortune upon her death in 1915.

For her bargain with the Johns Hopkins medical school, Garrett is sometimes criticized as America's greatest "coercive philanthropist." William Osler, one of the school's four founding physicians, famously replied: "It was a pleasure to be bought."

⊱ Kari Barbic

Further reading

○ Alan Chesney, *The Johns Hopkins Hospital and the Johns Hopkins School of Medicine, A Chronicle* (Johns Hopkins Press, 1943)

○ Helen Horowitz, *The Power and Passion of M. Carey Thomas* (Alfred Knopf, 1991)

○ Kathleen Sander, *Mary Elizabeth Garrett: Society and Philanthropy in the Gilded Age* (Johns Hopkins Press, 2008)

J. PAUL GETTY

J. Paul Getty was one of America's most successful oilmen who was, if anything, an even more successful art collector. Getty acquired a number of oil companies before discovering and mining major oil deposits in Saudi Arabia, a feat which made him for some years the richest living American. Getty then used his fortune to assemble one of the world's greatest collections of art and antiquities, a collection that today forms the core of the Getty Villa and the Getty Museum in Los Angeles.

Jean Paul Getty was born in Minneapolis in 1892. His father, George Getty, was an insurance-agent-turned-wildcatter, and J. Paul grew up wealthy. Sent to Oxford by his father, J. Paul became a committed Anglophile—indeed, he spent the last 25 years of his life in a sixteenth-century Tudor estate near Guildford. After college, the younger Getty returned to the States, where he worked in his father's oil fields before striking out on his own. He made his first $1 million at age 24.

Despite his son's manifest talents, George never quite trusted him. J. Paul was a serial womanizer—"A lasting relationship with a woman is only possible if you are a business failure," he proclaimed—and George worried his son's string of hasty marriages and casual divorces (three by the time George died in 1930) would destroy the family business. J. Paul received just $500,000 of his father's $10 million estate.

Luckily for J. Paul, the Great Depression was a buyer's market, and even a diminished inheritance could go a long way toward acquiring cash-poor businesses. Getty began systematically acquiring assets. He started with oil companies: Pacific Western, Tidewater, Skelly. Then he bought Manhattan's Hotel Pierre; later he set up a realty company. During the Second World War, the Navy asked him to take over and turn around Spartan Aircraft, an aircraft-parts supplier; he did, and after the war made it a mobile-home manufacturer.

> Getty was haughty, cheap, and cruel. But his great philanthropic achievements in presenting classical art to the public were something nobler.

The majority of Getty's fortune came from an investment he made in 1949. Getty obtained a lease from King Ibn Saud to drill on a sandswept tract of barren land adjoining Kuwait. In exchange for $9 million up front and $1 million annually, Getty purchased exclusive mineral rights for 60 years. Four years and $18 million of sunk costs later, Getty struck oil. The wells produced such quantities that by 1957, *Fortune* placed Getty's net worth somewhere between $700 million and $1 billion. "A billion dollars isn't what it used to be," Getty quipped, but it did not change the fact that he was now the wealthiest citizen in the land.

After his success in Saudi Arabia, thousands of unsolicited requests for money poured in every week. They grated on him, not least because he had little use for what he considered soft-headed humanitarianism. "If I were convinced that by giving away my fortune I could make a real contribution toward solving the problems of world poverty, I'd give away 99.5 percent of all I have immediately," he wrote in one of his many articles on wealth and business. "But a hard-eyed appraisal of the situation convinces me this is not the case…. However admirable the work of the best charitable foundation, it would accustom people to the passive acceptance of money."

He was similarly suspicious of higher education. He was once approached by several members of the Rockefeller family, who urged him to make a large contribution and suggested that he consider giving to an institute of higher education. Getty sat silently for a moment. Then he burst into a tirade, demanding to know why the Rockefellers had not expelled the socialists from the University of Chicago.

If charitable giving could do little to remedy poverty and was a dubious way to promote learning, to Getty's mind it still had one distinct advantage: it could help preserve the artistic achievements of Western civilization. Philanthropy provided the means by which his private collection could become a public resource, which was precisely what Getty hoped to do with it. "As I learned in my youth," he wrote, "a gift—whether to the public or an individual—is something given of one's own volition and without strings attached. Otherwise, it is no longer a gift but a business transaction. And if I had wanted to do business with my collection, I would have gone all-out and sold it off."

A serious art collector since the 1930s, Getty had a good command of art history and criticism. He wrote a history of nineteenth-century Europe and was fluent in German, French, and Italian. He could speak passable Arabic, Greek, Russian, and Spanish, and he was able to spot-read Latin and ancient Greek. He was disciplined in his collecting, restricting himself largely to a few categories: Greek and Roman marbles and bronzes, Renaissance paintings, sixteenth-century Persian carpets, and eighteenth-century French furniture and tapestries. He owned three of the Elgin Marbles and acquired the Lansdowne Herakles, a first-century A.D. Roman sculpture that was a personal favorite of the Emperor Hadrian.

Getty had exhibited some of his art in his California mansion, but in 1968 he decided to house it in a permanent museum. He told his trustees: "I refuse to pay for one of those concrete-bunker type structures that are the fad among museum architects—nor for some tinted-glass-and-stainless-steel monstrosity." Getty also insisted that his museum have free admission and free parking. (The museum continues to offer free admission but has reversed Getty's latter commitment.) He followed its construction closely, even once berating his architect for the unauthorized purchase of a $17 electric pencil sharpener.

The original Getty Museum, now the Getty Villa in Malibu, was completed in 1974. A reproduction of a Roman villa, it is considered a masterful reproduction of classical architecture. Getty, aged 82 and in poor health when the building opened, never saw it complete. On his death in 1976, he left most of his estate to the museum, and after a nine-year probate fight (which included the 1984 sale of Getty Oil to

Texaco for $10 billion), it became the best-endowed museum in the world. In 1997, the J. Paul Getty Trust opened a second facility, the Getty Center, at a cost of $1.3 billion. With stunning views of Los Angeles, this Brentwood museum houses the collection's non-antiquarian holdings, as well as a research library, conservation laboratories, sculpture gardens, and educational facilities.

J. Paul Getty was haughty ("One is very nearly always let down by underlings," he often said), cheap (visitors to his estate had to use a pay phone), and cruel (when a grandson was kidnapped, he paid only as much ransom as was tax-deductible: $2.2 of the $17 million). But his great philanthropic achievement aspired to something nobler. "In learning about ancient Greek and Roman art," Getty wrote, "one cannot help but also learn about the civilizations and the people who produced the art. This will unquestionably serve to broaden the individual's horizons and, by increasing his knowledge of past civilizations, greatly aid him in knowing and understanding his own."

↳ *Martin Morse Wooster*

Further reading

○ J. Paul Getty, *As I See It: The Autobiography of J. Paul Getty* (Prentice-Hall, 1976)
○ J. Paul Getty, *The Joys of Collecting* (Hawthorn Books, 1965)
○ Robert Lenzner, *The Great Getty: The Life and Loves of J. Paul Getty* (Crown, 1986)
○ Russell Miller, *The House of Getty* (J. Curley, 1987)

STEPHEN GIRARD

Stephen Girard amassed enormous wealth as a merchant and banker; if his wealth is viewed as a percentage of GDP, he was one of the five richest men in American history. That fortune was dedicated to an extensive program of philanthropy. Girard was the patron of a variety of charitable causes in his adopted home of Philadelphia, most notably offering comfort to the sick, at real personal risk, during the city's yellow fever outbreaks. During the War of 1812, Girard staked virtually everything he owned on bond purchases for the federal government; in doing so, he saved the nation's credit, less in pursuit of profit than as an act of patriotism. And his final bequest funded the creation of a college for orphaned boys, which was at the time the best endowed charity in the country.

Born in Bordeaux in 1750, Girard was the son of a sea captain and merchant. At 14 years of age, he followed in his father's footsteps, serving as an apprentice pilot on a voyage to the West Indies. For over a decade,

J. R. Lambdin

he plied the seas, traveling between France, the West Indies, and North America. In 1776, Girard moved to Philadelphia, where he started his own shipping business. He instituted a number of revolutionary business practices, including warehousing goods until he was satisfied with prices and offering ship captains a straight wage rather than a percentage, thereby encouraging speed rather than market timing. His business expanded worldwide, and his ships traded in China and South America as well as Europe and the Caribbean.

When the charter of the First Bank of the United States expired in 1811, Girard purchased a majority of its shares (as well as its headquarters on Philadelphia's South Third Street). The timing was fortuitous. Over the next few years, the newly established financier effectively saved the U.S. Treasury.

As the War of 1812 ground on, confidence in American credit collapsed. In late 1813, Albert Gallatin, Secretary of the Treasury, was only able to sell $6 million worth of a $16 million bond issue. Gallatin approached Girard in Philadelphia and John Jacob Astor in New York, pleading with them to purchase the remainder. Girard and Astor consented, on the condition that the Madison administration agree to re-charter the Bank of the United States. It was not philanthropy in the strict sense—Girard ultimately turned a tidy profit—but it was nevertheless a saving grace to the American people, undertaken largely from patriotic motives, with a high likelihood of costing Girard his fortune.

During his lifetime, Girard supported a wide variety of civic associations in his adopted hometown of Philadelphia. He contributed to (among many other groups) the Pennsylvania Hospital, the Society for Relief of Distressed Masters of Ships and Their Widows, the Société de Bienfaisançe Francaise, the Public School Fund of Philadelphia, the Pennsylvania Institution for the Deaf and Dumb, the Fuel Saving Society, and the Orphan Society. He joined the Masons, and donated his time and money to its various charitable activities.

Such close, personal involvement was evident in the charitable efforts for which Girard was best known during his lifetime. Girard was a tireless leader in the efforts to contain and combat the yellow fever epidemics that hit Philadelphia in 1793, 1797-98, 1802, and 1820. Nineteenth-century medicine was all but helpless against the disease. Those who could afford to simply fled the city.

Not Girard. When epidemics broke out, he stayed in Philadelphia, leading relief efforts, funding hospital operations, and providing care for individuals—even bathing and feeding the dying. He routinely put his personal and business affairs to the side during epidemics. "As soon as things have quieted down a little you may be sure I shall take up my work with all the activity in my power," he wrote to a friend in 1793. "But, for the moment, I have devoted all my time and my person, as well as my little fortune, to the relief of my fellow citizens."

But Girard is perhaps best remembered today for his final bequest. Composed five years before his death at age 81, it left $140,000 to family members, lifelong income to several household servants, and $800,000 for various civic improvements in Philadelphia. An additional $1 million was divided among many of the charities he had supported throughout his life. The largest share by far—some $7 million—was earmarked for the creation of "a college for poor white male orphans."

> One of the five richest men in American history, Stephen Girard was known for his personal involvement in charitable efforts— like throwing himself into care for victims during periodic yellow-fever outbreaks at great personal risk.

It was a project that had long been close to Girard's heart. There is evidence in his papers that Girard was planning the school as early as 1807—fully 24 years before his death. His painstaking instructions for the school suggest that considerable time and attention went into the plans. He spelled out a preference, for instance, that students be taught French or Spanish rather than Greek or Latin.

Girard's heirs challenged the validity of the will, arguing that it unlawfully excluded ministers from the college. The case went to the Supreme Court, where Justice Joseph Story ruled against the heirs. His opinion was a landmark ruling in the history of American philanthropy, which reaffirmed the principle of donor intent.

When Girard College opened its doors in 1848, its endowment was larger than that of any other educational institution. The school has since graduated 30,000 of the most vulnerable students imaginable. "For seven years," reflected one graduate in a 1997 *Wall Street Journal* op-ed, Stephen Girard "fed, clothed, sheltered, and educated me. He bought the milk and cereal, baked the casseroles and the cookies, provided the soap and toothbrushes, furnished the sneakers and baseball gloves, darned the socks and sweaters, sent me to the barber and the doctor, provided the books and lab supplies, and much more."

To this day, the school continues to offer a superb education to low-income students in Philadelphia—and impart to them its founder's sense of civic duty. "I desire," he wrote, "that by every proper means a pure attachment to our republican institutions, and to the sacred rights of conscience, as guaranteed by our happy constitutions, shall be formed and fostered in the minds of the scholars."

⌐ Monica Klem

Further reading

o "The Father of Philanthropy," *Wall Street Journal* essay, girardcollege.edu/page.cfm?p=863
o Cheesman Herrick, *Stephen Girard: Founder* (Girard College, 1923)
o John McMaster, *The Life and Times of Stephen Girard, Mariner and Merchant* (J. B. Lippincott Co., 1918)
o George Wilson, *Stephen Girard: The Life And Times of America's First Tycoon* (Da Capo Press, 1996)

EDWARD HARKNESS

Edward Harkness is one of the least well-known of the major American philanthropists of the first half of the twentieth century. His relative obscurity is all the more surprising given the scale of his charitable giving; he was among the very largest donors of his era. The John Rockefellers, father and son, each gave away over $500 million, while Andrew Carnegie's gifts amounted to $325 million. They were followed by a handful of contemporaries whose lifetime giving exceeded $100 million: James Duke, George Eastman, Nettie McCormick—and Edward Harkness.

Harkness inherited his wealth; he was the last surviving heir of a massive fortune created by his father's early investment in Standard Oil. His privileges as a child did not prevent him from becoming a serious, orderly man. "A dollar misspent is a dollar lost," he often said. Harkness appeared to take his greatest pleasure in philanthropy, which was the principal occupation of his lifetime.

Biographer James Wooster estimates that Harkness gave away roughly $129 million before his death in 1940. (Wooster only counted gifts of more than $5,000, so Harkness's total was almost certainly higher.) Harkness dedicated his giving to three principal causes: fine arts, health care, and top educational institutions. Wooster concludes that Harkness is unknown today because his philanthropy was largely guided by a "passion for anonymity."

Born in 1874, Edward was the youngest of five children born to Stephen Harkness, a prominent Cleveland merchant who had success in distilled spirits. In 1867, he agreed to invest $100,000 in a fledgling company headed by an ambitious young man named John Rockefeller. When Standard Oil offered its first 10,000 shares of stock, Rockefeller ended up with 2,667 shares to Harkness' 1,334. (After several recapitalizations, Harkness' ownership evened out at around 10 percent.) As Standard Oil boomed, Harkness remained a silent partner.

In 1888, Stephen Harkness died without a will, leaving a $150 million fortune. His wife, Anna, inherited a "widow's third," which was administered by two of her sons, Charles and Edward. Anna had for many years quietly supported local churches and charitable organizations, but eventually became a leading philanthropist in her own right. Edward's initial work in philanthropy came from serving as the manager of his mother's large-scale charitable giving.

When Charles died in 1916, Anna and Edward gave $3 million to Yale University for the construction of Memorial Quadrangle in his honor; four years later, they gave the college another $3 million to increase faculty salaries. Support for higher education and cultural institutions remained a central element of the family's philanthropy, with notable contributions to the Tuskegee Institute, Metropolitan Museum of Art, Museum of Natural History, New York Public Library, and New York Zoological Society. In 1922, Edward and Anna Harkness acquired a 22-acre site in Washington Heights and donated the land to Columbia-Presbyterian Hospital (later merged into New York-Presbyterian). As late as 1992, undeveloped land from this donation was being turned into auxiliary facilities for the hospital.

> Support for higher education and cultural institutions were central elements of the philanthropy of the Harkness family, heirs to Standard Oil money.

Perhaps the most visible achievement of Edward and Anna Harkness was the creation of the Commonwealth Fund in 1918. Endowed with $10 million, the fund was chartered with the almost comically broad mandate of doing "something for the welfare of mankind." Among its first commitments was support for medical research, and the Commonwealth Fund supported the work of scientists pursuing (among other things) the causes of hypertension, the treatment and prevention of pneumonia, and the causes of tooth decay.

The Harkness family traced its roots to Dumfriesshire, and Edward retained a lifelong love of Great Britain. In 1925, Harkness set up a series of fellowships, administered by the Commonwealth Fund, to enable graduate students from Britain and its dominions to study in the United States. One of the first scholarships went to Alistair Cooke, who subsequently spent decades at the BBC explaining America to the British listening public. Harkness supported a range of other charities in the United Kingdom. In 1930, during the depths of the Great Depression, he donated £2 million to create the Pilgrim Trust, which to this day preserves historic sites, offers university scholarships, and funds treatment for those experiencing drug and alcohol addiction.

With encouragement from his wife, Mary Harkness, Edward became a leading patron of the Metropolitan Museum of Art. They were lifelong collectors of Egyptian art and antiquaries, and their contributions to the Met, begun in 1913, were rivaled only by those of J. P. Morgan. In 1917, they donated a ceramic turquoise hippopotamus from the Middle Kingdom; it has since been the museum's unofficial mascot, affectionately nicknamed "William."

Perhaps Harkness's most significant accomplishments were in the field of elite education. He was a benefactor of America's most prestigious secondary schools, including his alma mater St. Paul's, Lawrenceville, Taft, Hill, and especially Phillips Exeter. He grabbed headlines in 1930 with a $5.8 million donation to Phillips Exeter, a gift that capped class size at 12 students, all of whom were to share a common table with their instructor. The "Harkness Table"—with, as he put it, "no corners to hide behind"—remains a core element of the school's pedagogy.

The same concern for collegiality informed Harkness's extensive giving to higher education. (Beneficiaries included Harvard, Yale, Columbia, Brown, Oberlin, Connecticut College, and scores of others.) He saw American universities adopting the model of the large German research institutions, and feared that students were losing the sociability of collegiate life. Harkness's preferred solution was to promote the British model, in which a university was divided into smaller residential houses where students would live, dine, study, and gather.

In 1926, having already endowed the drama school, he approached Yale, offering to donate $12 million to build a series of residential colleges on the Oxbridge model. After a year of negotiations, Yale declined. Harkness immediately met with Harvard president Lawrence Lowell, offering to fund a similar scheme of residential houses. "It took Lowell about 10 seconds to accept," Samuel Eliot Morison noted in a 1942 history of Harvard. "Thus a Yale man became the greatest benefactor to Harvard in our entire history." Harvard built seven residential houses with the Harkness gift—and Yale soon after accepted $15.8 million for the construction of eight residential houses, which remain an integral part of campus life.

"One of the most difficult tasks in the world is giving away money wisely," wrote Lowell, in a tribute shortly after Harkness' death, "and philanthropic multimillionaires usually, and quite correctly, avoid it by forming a board or committee to do the work for them. Not so Mr. Harkness."

↪ Martin Morse Wooster

Further reading

○ Lewis Perry, "Edward and Mary Harkness" (*Bulletin of the Metropolitan Museum of Art*, October 1951)

○ George Pierson, *Yale: The University College, 1921-1937* (Yale Press, 1955)

○ James Wooster, *Edward S. Harkness* (Commonwealth Fund, 1949)

MILTON HERSHEY

Milton Hershey made milk chocolate a treat all Americans could afford, and in the process cooked up a great fortune. Hershey used his wealth to beautify his company's hometown and to build a remarkable orphanage that would take poor boys, give them a good home and sturdy lessons in character, and teach them to make their way in the world.

Hershey was born in Hockensville, Pennsylvania, in 1857. His parents had been raised as Reformed Mennonites, and young Hershey grew up among the devout, thrifty, and hardworking Pennsylvania Dutch. But his father was a dreamer and a drinker, and his family suffered from neglect. Young Milton grew up shoeless and hungry. Eventually his parents separated. Later in life, when asked about his gifts to orphans, Hershey would remind people, "I was a poor boy myself once."

Hershey took his first job at age 14, apprenticing with a small, German-language newspaper in Lancaster. He hated the work and promptly got himself fired. Then he took a job at Joseph Royer's Ice Cream Parlor, where he learned the basics of candy-making. By the time he was 25, he had launched two businesses, a cough drop company and a candy company. (Both failed.) His third attempt, Lancaster Caramel, was vastly more successful. By the early 1890s, he had 700 employees and three processing plants.

Everything changed in 1893. Hershey visited the World's Columbian Exposition in Chicago, where he first laid eyes on the industrial equipment of J. M. Lehmann of Dresden, Germany. Lehmann had built a full-scale chocolate-manufacturing plant, from roasting-oven for the cocoa beans to forming-presses for the molten chocolate. "The caramel business is a fad," Hershey declared, and he paid $20,000 to buy every single piece of equipment

Bettmann / Corbis

that Lehmann had on display. When he left Chicago, the machinery went with him.

Hershey began making chocolate alongside caramel, all the while systematically experimenting with new recipes. By 1900, he was confident he had a winning product, and he sold the caramel business for $1 million. With his new liquidity, he wanted to build a factory that could mass-produce milk chocolate. Three years later, he broke ground near Derry Church, right in the middle of Pennsylvania dairy farming country.

Hershey did not discover milk chocolate. What he discovered was how to make it affordable. He achieved the feat through gains from efficiency, populating his plant with the latest technology and designing the facility on the basis of Frederick Taylor's principles of industrial efficiency. The result was a steep cut in the per-unit cost of producing milk chocolate. Before Hershey opened his production lines, it was a delicacy. After Hershey, a milk chocolate bar could be enjoyed by anyone with a spare nickel.

Success came instantly. In its first year of operations, the company netted $1 million; five years later, with the introduction of the Hershey's Kiss, profits topped $2 million. As money poured in, Hershey worked to build a model city around his rural factory. He sponsored a nationwide contest to come up with a name for the town.

> "I have no heirs, so I have decided to make the orphan boys of the United States my heirs," said Milton Hershey.

(Entries included Ulikit, Etabit, Chocolate City, and St. Milton.) The winner was Hersheykoko, which the Post Office rejected as too commercial. So the town became Hershey, Pennsylvania.

Hershey oversaw most every aspect of the town's construction: tree-lined streets, handsome homes, extensive public transportation, and first-rate public schools. In 1907, he opened a park (today known as Hershey Park); in 1915, he built the nation's largest free private zoo. During the Great Depression, he launched a massive building campaign, something like a privately funded New Deal program. More than 600 men worked to build the Hershey Hotel, as well as a community building, sports arena, community theater, and high school.

As the Depression ground on, Hershey gave $20,000 to each of the town's five churches in 1935 to help them relieve the suffering of their congregants. That same year, he established the M. S. Hershey Foundation to support local educational and cultural charities. One of the foundation's first projects was creating the Hershey Gardens, a major botanical garden completed in 1942. The foundation also built (and still manages) the Hershey Theatre, the Hershey Community Archives, and a historical museum dedicated to the life and achievements of Milton Hershey.

Hershey's best-known philanthropic accomplishment, however, was his orphanage. Originally located on his homestead, it surrounded Milton and Catherine Hershey with the children they were never able to have. In 1909, the Hersheys executed a tightly constructed deed of trust for the Hershey Industrial School. In November 1918, they secretly placed all of his shares of the Hershey Chocolate Company into a trust whose sole purpose was to benefit the school. The stock was worth roughly $60 million; by way of comparison, notes biographer Michael D'Antonio, in 1918 Coca-Cola sold for $25 million.

Although Hershey made his gift in 1918, he did not reveal it until a 1923 interview with the *New York Times.* "I am 66 years old and do not need much money," Hershey said. "I have no heirs, so I have decided to make the orphan boys of the United States my heirs." Hershey explained that the Industrial School would provide "a thorough common school education, supplemented by instruction in the useful crafts"— blacksmithing, farming, the "rudiments of electrical work."

His interviewer then asked about college preparation for the students. "We do not intend to turn out a race of professors," Hershey replied, although he allowed that boys "of special promise" would be prepared for higher education. "The thing that a poor boy needs is knowledge of a trade, a way to make a living. We will provide him with the groundwork. Of what use is Latin when a fellow has to hoe a patch or run a lathe?"

Hershey was a constant presence at the school before his death in 1945. Since then, with an endowment worth $11 billion in 2015, the Milton Hershey School has become one of the wealthiest educational facilities in the United States. It offers a superb boarding school education to 2,000 elementary and secondary students, all from troubled backgrounds.

Hershey died with very little personal wealth, mostly his home and its furnishings. He had given away everything else during his lifetime. "I never could see," he once observed, "what happiness a rich man gets from contemplating a life of acquisition only, with a cold and legal distribution of his wealth after he passes away."

↳ *Martin Morse Wooster*

Further reading
∘ Joel Brenner, *The Emperors of Chocolate: Inside the Secret World of Hershey and Mars* (Random House, 1999)

○ Michael D'Antonio, *Hershey: Milton S. Hershey's Extraordinary Life of Wealth, Empire, and Utopian Dreams* (Simon and Schuster, 2006)

○ Joseph Snavely, *The Hershey Story* (Privately published, 1950)

CONRAD HILTON

Conrad Hilton was born on Christmas Day, 1887, on the banks of the Rio Grande in the tiny frontier town of San Antonio, New Mexico Territory. Connie, as he was called, was the second child of eight, the oldest boy of A. H. ("Gus") Hilton and Mary Laufersweiler Hilton.

From his father, Hilton learned the imperative of hard work. Gus Hilton was a trader and merchant, which in those days and in that place meant engaging any and all legitimate business that came his way. He sold goods behind the counter of his general store, at mining outposts, trappers' encampments, or the haciendas of old Spanish ranchers. As Hilton would later write of his father, work was "precisely as necessary to him as food and air, an ever present refuge in trouble…. He never connected it with the sweat of the brow nor the punishment of the sons of Adam. He was all for the joy of the thing." So it would be with the younger Hilton.

From his mother, a devout Catholic, Hilton came to view prayer as no less a necessity and no less a sanctuary than work. "Some men jump out windows, some quit," his mother told him during the Great Depression. "Some go to church. Pray Connie. It's the best investment you'll ever make." Even in the darkest, most difficult moments of his life, Hilton always found strength and consolation in his faith.

In 1912, New Mexico became the 47th state in the Union, and at age 23 Hilton was elected to the state's first legislature. But politics did not much appeal to the budding entrepreneur, who decided two years later to try his hand at banking. That endeavor was interrupted by the start of World War I, throughout which he served as an Army officer. Then, with $5,011 to his name, he moved to the booming oil fields of Texas, where he hoped to buy a bank and resume his pre-war career. What he bought instead was the dilapidated Mobley Hotel in Cisco, Texas. It was Conrad Hilton's "first love."

In just 20 years, Hilton's hospitality business grew from small reclamation projects to newly constructed million-dollar high-rises. Like many entrepreneurs, his business acumen sprang less from acquisitiveness than from a spirit of ingenuity, creativity, and awe in the face of human possibilities. By 1929, he owned hotels all over Texas, with plans to expand beyond the Lone Star State.

The crash of 1929 nearly erased all of it. By 1933, Hilton retained only one hotel, and that barely. Yet he survived.

Recovery was slow at first: paying down debts and reacquiring lost properties. But as the Depression lifted, and the post-war boom started in earnest, the Hilton Hotel Company reached new heights. In 1946, a corporation was formed, and a year later, it became the first hotel traded on the New York Stock Exchange. In 1949, Hilton purchased the "Greatest of Them All": the Waldorf-Astoria. In 1954, Hilton Hotels Corporation acquired the Hotels Statler Company for $111 million, the largest real-estate transaction in history at that time. Hilton eventually owned 188 hotels, including the Palmer House in Chicago, the Mayflower in D.C., and both the Plaza and the Waldorf-Astoria in New York City. Hilton hotels could be found in 38 American cities and 54 locations overseas.

The Depression had taught Hilton humility, and reinforced in him the importance of faith. "When everything material failed," he wrote, "faith remained the only gilt-edged security." Moreover, the Depression impressed upon Hilton the trust and good will of those who had seen him through his most trying times. A man whose success had been made possible by so many others could not help but return the kindness.

In 1944, Hilton started the Conrad N. Hilton Foundation. The day after the fund was established, Hilton received a request from one of the Catholic Sisters of Loretto, who had taught him his catechism as a child in New Mexico. She was raising money to build a new gymnasium and hoped he might help. "Dear Sister," Hilton replied, "I received your letter of recent date. I am sure you have been praying extra hard, for your campaign has begun and ended." There would be more such letters to follow.

Over the next 35 years, the Conrad N. Hilton Foundation would award many small grants, with special solicitude for the work of Catholics sisters and those who help children. Even more than through his foundation, Hilton gave generously from his personal wealth and talents. In his last will and testament, Hilton wrote:

> Be ever watchful for the opportunity to shelter little children with the umbrella of your charity; be generous to their schools, their hospitals, and their places of worship. For, as they must bear the burdens of our mistakes, so are they in their innocence the repositories of our hopes for the upward progress of humanity. Give aid to their protectors and defenders, the Sisters, who devote their love and life's work for the good of mankind, for they appeal especially to me as being deserving of help from the Foundation.

In addition to his support for Catholic education, Hilton was generous to charitable health-care providers, both Catholic and non-Catholic. He led the capital campaign for St. John's Health Center in Santa Monica, California. In 1972, Hilton committed $10 million to build a research center at the Mayo Clinic.

Hilton was a staunch opponent of communism. As he bluntly told the National Conference of Christians and Jews in 1950: "The essence of communism is the death of the individual and the burial of his remains in a collective mass." Hilton firmly believed that his hospitality business could be an example of cooperation and goodwill in a perilously divided world. "Each of our hotels," Hilton said, "is a 'Little America,' not as a symbol of bristling power, but as a friendly center where men of many nations and of good will may speak the language of peace." Hilton also made sure his international hotels sourced local materials, and trained and hired local workers. Display the decency and goodness of American values in the communists' own backyard, Hilton thought, and the world would note the contrast.

> "Charity," wrote Conrad Hilton, is "the great channel through which the mercy of God is passed on to mankind."

Hilton believed that prayer was a vital force in what he called the "Battle for Freedom." On July 4, 1952, at the height of the Korean War, he published in magazines across the country a humble prayer for peace and forgiveness in a darkening world, titled "America on Its Knees." It received an overwhelming response, and a year later, Hilton hosted the first National Prayer Breakfast, alongside President Eisenhower. That event has become a Washington, and national, institution.

When Hilton died in 1979, he left virtually his entire fortune to the foundation. "Charity is a supreme virtue," he wrote, "and the great channel through which the mercy of God is passed on to mankind. It is the virtue that unites men and inspires their noblest efforts."

— Stephen White

Further reading

o Conrad Hilton, *Be My Guest* (Prentice Hall, 1958)

o The Hilton Legacy, *hiltonfoundation.org/images/stories/About/Publications/LegacyBooks/Hilton_History_Book_Final.pdf*

IMA HOGG

Ima Hogg ranks among the best-known and most admired philanthropists in the history of Texas. For much of her life, she was affectionately known as the "First Lady of Texas," owing to her family's long tradition of public service. Her grandfather helped write the Texas state constitution and her father, James ("Big Jim") Hogg, went on to become the Lone Star State's first native-born governor. Her service to Texas was principally philanthropic—made possible by the discovery of large oil deposits beneath her family's plantation.

Born in 1882 in Mineola, Texas, Ima Hogg would spend most of her life contending with wisecracks that she had sisters named "Ura" and "Hoosa." (She didn't.) She had one older brother, William, and two younger ones, Michael and Thomas. At the age of 13, she cared for her mother as she died of tuberculosis, and 10 years later nursed her father as he struggled unsuccessfully to overcome injuries sustained in a train accident. After her mother's death, she took over her father's household and cared for her younger brothers. The Hoggs were a tight-knit family, and, for nearly 70 years, she was its head.

The inheritance Ima received upon her father's death in 1906 made her financially independent; he had made a small fortune through his work as an attorney, as well as investments in land and oil. But the Hoggs' philanthropic activity was greatly accelerated by the discovery of oil on the West Columbia property left to them by their father. In 1919, a supply of oil that would yield his children $225,000 per month was discovered.

Ima's first philanthropic efforts centered on fostering an appreciation for the arts in Texas. Early in her life she had hoped to become a concert pianist, and spent two years at the National Conservatory of Music in New York and two more in Vienna and Berlin studying piano. But she returned to Houston in 1909, where she began teaching piano instead. Increasingly her interests centered on being actively involved in civic life. In 1913, she helped to found the Houston Symphony Orchestra, and in 1917 became president of its board. She continued to support the symphony for the rest of her life and worked to increase public exposure to music and the arts. When elected to the Houston Board of Education in 1943 she arranged symphony concerts for public school audiences, and increased the offerings of music and art classes.

The Hogg family's philanthropic efforts centered on their home state. An avid collector of early American antique furniture and decorative art, Ima declined to lend the pieces she acquired to East Coast exhibitions, saying, "They've got plenty of these things up there." She placed much of her collection at

Bayou Bend, a house she built in 1927 as a home for herself and her brothers Will and Mike in the River Oaks neighborhood of Houston. Nearly 30 years later, after the deaths of both brothers, she decided to give the house to the Houston Museum of the Fine Arts, along with a $750,000 endowment. It opened as the MFA Bayou Bend Collection and Gardens in 1966.

But of all the causes Ima supported, the one closest to her heart was probably the promotion of mental health. She had a lifelong concern for those who were then called "mentally disturbed," and, at a time and in a place where it was not especially popular, she promoted the study and treatment of mental illness. Her first major effort took place in 1929, when she founded the Houston Child Guidance Clinic. Open to people of all races and income levels, it represented a real advance in the field of child psychology. She would later say that, of all her endeavors, it was the one that satisfied her most.

When her brother Will died unexpectedly in 1930, he left $2.5 million to the University of Texas, but he was unclear about how the money ought to be used. In response, Ima and Mike put forward a plan for the Hogg Foundation for Mental Hygiene, which came into being in 1940. Administered by the University of Texas, its initial purpose was to provide mental health education campaigns in small towns. In 1964, she founded

> She devoted her life to enriching the cultural life of her native state of Texas, and her home city of Houston.

the Ima Hogg Foundation, also administered by the University of Texas, to fund projects benefiting children's mental health in Harris County; it would eventually be the primary beneficiary of her will.

Ima also contributed to the preservation of Texas history. In 1953, she helped to found and was appointed a member of what became the Texas Historical Commission. She lovingly restored and donated to the state of Texas several properties owned by her family.

Ima Hogg died in 1975 at the age of 93. A woman of unfailing poise, she once caught a burglar in her bedroom—and gave him the name and telephone number of a man who would give the thief a job. ("He didn't look like a bad man," she would later say.) A woman of great generosity, she devoted her life to preserving and enriching the cultural life of her native state, and to improving the education and mental health of Texan children and their families.

☞ *Monica Klem*

Further reading
○ Mary Kelley, *The Foundations of Texan Philanthropy* (Texas A&M University Press, 2004)
○ Gwendolyn Neeley, *Miss Ima and the Hogg Family* (Hendrick-Long Publishing Company, 1992)

HERBERT HOOVER

Herbert Hoover was an entrepreneur, philanthropist, and the 31st President of the United States. The humanitarian services for which he is perhaps best remembered were public-private efforts to relieve misery and suffering in the wake of war and disaster. He was also a significant philanthropist in his own right. His personal charitable giving centered on two areas: character-building for children, and creating one of the nation's oldest and most distinguished think tanks, the Hoover Institution on War, Revolution, and Peace.

Hoover was born in 1874 in the small village of West Branch, Iowa. Orphaned at a young age, he went to live with an uncle in Oregon. His character was shaped by the Quaker faith, from which he gained a strong sense of moral virtue, an appreciation for voluntary service, and a relentless work ethic. He enrolled in the inaugural class at Stanford University and was quickly fascinated by the study of geology. Years later, he authored the first English translation of *De Re Metallica*, Georgius Agricola's once-authoritative work on mining.

Soon after his graduation in 1895, Hoover found himself in Western Australia, where he applied new technologies to gold mining. His career soon took him to China, Russia, and South Africa. (Hoover and his wife mastered Mandarin Chinese during their years abroad, and would speak the language in the White House to keep aides from understanding their conversations.) One business success followed another and, according to George Nash, Hoover's leading biographer, Hoover's net worth in 1913 was approximately $4 million.

On the eve of World War I, Hoover was working in England. When the conflagration began, he found himself on what he later called the "slippery slope of public life." Hoover was distraught over the suffering of civilians and organized the Commission for the Relief of Belgium. The effort fed millions of Europeans during and after the Great War; on two continents, Hoover was called the "Great Humanitarian." On the basis of his experience, write historians Richard Norton Smith and Timothy Walch, Hoover "developed a unique philosophy—one balancing responsibility for the welfare of others with an unshakable faith in free enterprise and dynamic individualism."

Throughout his life, Hoover would be called upon to assume the role of public humanitarian. In 1927, for example, the Mississippi River flooded, leaving 1.5 million Americans homeless. Although it did not fall under the jurisdiction of the Commerce Department, which Hoover then headed, six governors asked President Calvin Coolidge to put Hoover in charge of the relief effort. He marshaled a massive private-sector response. ("I suppose I could have called in the Army to help," he said years later, "but why should I, when I only had to call upon Main Street?") Two decades later, in the wreckage of postwar Germany, he led a similar effort to bring food and medicine to that devastated nation. He oversaw the distribution of 40,000 tons of emergency meals in what was a crucial precursor to the Marshall Plan.

But Hoover's involvement in public humanitarian projects (to say nothing of his political career) should not overshadow his generosity as a private citizen. With his wife, Lou Henry, he had a strong moral sense of responsibility for his fellow citizens. As many biographers have noted, however, Hoover had an equally strong moral sense that his private good deeds should be kept out of the public eye.

Even during the Great Depression, when Hoover was blamed for the worst economic crisis in American history, he never allowed his many charitable activities to be made public or politicized in any way.

> Herbert Hoover, whose high character was shaped by his Quaker upbringing, is best remembered as a philanthropist for his work to relieve misery in the wake of war and disaster.

The nation, notes Smith, "saw nothing of his private anguish, or the dozens of personal bequests he made to individuals in need." According to historian and biographer Glen Jeansonne, "Hoover did not simply save Belgium, much of Central Europe, and the Soviet Union from famine during the era of the Great War; he performed small acts of kindness virtually every day."

A central focus of Hoover's philanthropy was organizations that fostered character among young men. After leaving the Presidency, he became an active supporter of the Boys Club of America, including service as chairman. "The boy is our most precious possession," he wrote in 1937. But the life of the contemporary city boy meant "stairs, light switches, alleys, fire escapes" and "a chance to get run over by a truck." Through the Boys Club, he hoped to introduce young men to the wholesome pleasures of the great outdoors. Hoover, notes Smith, "devoted thousands of hours to the organization, building it up from 140 clubs to more than 600 at the time of his death."

Hoover was likewise committed to understanding the principles and policies that led to war or peace, deprivation or prosperity. In the aftermath of World War I, he donated $50,000 to Stanford University to begin collecting documents related to the issues and ideas that had caused the Great War. The Hoover Institution gathered materials on a variety of topics, but came to be a leading repository for scholarship on the dangers of communism. It soon became one of America's leading think tanks, defending the constitutional order and offering public-policy solutions rooted in the principles of liberty and limited government, wielding real influence on foreign and domestic policy throughout the twentieth century.

"Hoover," writes George Nash, "practiced the philanthropic virtues that he professed. As President, he declined to spend any of his salary on himself. Instead, he gave it away to charities or as income supplements to his associates. During their long marriage, he and his wife extended charitable assistance to countless needy recipients, usually anonymously and through surrogates. In the 1930s, Hoover's brother concluded that he had given away more than half of his business profits for benevolent purposes. Characteristically, however, Hoover concealed most of his benefactions, with the result that their full extent may never be known."

While in the White House, Hoover received a letter from a ten-year-old boy who was seeking advice on how to become President. His reply was revealing. "The first rule is just to be a boy getting all the constructive joy out of life," Hoover wrote. "The second rule is that no one should win the Presidency without honesty and sportsmanship and consideration for others in his character—together with religious faith. The third rule is that he should be a man of education. If you follow these rules, you will be a man of standing in your community even if you do not make the White House. And who can tell? Maybe that also."

        ↝ *John Hendrickson*

Further reading

○ Gary Best, *The Life of Herbert Hoover: Keeper of the Torch, 1933-1964* (Palgrave Macmillan, 2013)

○ Glen Jeansonne, *The Life of Herbert Hoover: Fighting Quaker, 1928-1933* (Palgrave, 2012)

○ George Nash, *The Life of Herbert Hoover* (W. W. Norton, six volumes, 1983-1996)

EWING KAUFFMAN

Ewing Marion Kauffman was a pharmaceutical entrepreneur and major Kansas City philanthropist and civic leader. Known for many philanthropic contributions related to K-12 education and human services in Kansas City, near the end of his life Kauffman discovered a new field for philanthropy: the promotion of entrepreneurship. Today, the Ewing Marion Kauffman Foundation is the largest foundation focused principally on fostering economic growth by supporting entrepreneurs.

Ewing Kauffman was born in 1916 into a farm family in western Missouri. As a boy, his salesmanship helped his strapped family to make ends meet. Kauffman sold eggs and magazines door-to-door and went "noodling"—diving into the Grand River's muddy underwater burrows to wrassle big catfish to the shore and sell them. When he was 11, a year of forced bed rest during a health crisis turned Kauffman into a lifelong speed-reader. Kauffman worked his way through junior college at a laundry service and continued there after graduating. He served in the Navy in World War II, and in the long stretches aboard ship, the shrewd poker player put away $90,000 in gambling winnings. His wife saved the money and invested in real estate, and when the war ended, Kauffman had the leisure to find the right job.

That job was in sales at the pharmaceutical firm Lincoln Laboratories. It didn't look like much—no salary, no benefits, only 20 percent commission—but Kauffman warmed to it immediately. He was a natural salesman, and by the end of his second year, he was earning more in commissions alone than Lincoln's president. The president cut Kauffman's commission and reduced the size of his territory, which naturally chafed at the star performer. He began planning his escape.

In June of 1950, Kauffman quit Lincoln and started Marion Laboratories in his basement. It was a pharmaceutical firm, a perhaps unusual choice for a man who, in his own words, "had no pharmacy background and not very much scientific education." But Kauffman loved the unique challenge of selling to doctors.

Os-Cal was Kauffman's first big hit. A calcium supplement that included ground-up oyster shells, its success came through Kauffman's innovative marketing. "He was in a business that was rooted in science and fueled by research, and he had only a smattering of the former and could not afford the latter," writes one biographer. "He knew how to sell drugs, and he was confident he could learn the rest." In the 1950s, Marion Labs grew on Os-Cal variants and by licensing and bringing others' products to market. It reached sales of $1 million by 1959, and added new blockbusters in the 1960s, during which decade it went public.

"Mr. K," as Kauffman was known to his employees, was a popular boss. He offered a profit-sharing plan, stock options, and education benefits. By 1968, 20 of Marion's employees had become millionaires (including a widow in the accounting department). In 1989, when Marion merged with Merrell Dow, it had annual sales of over $1 billion—and hundreds of employees had become millionaires.

Through it all, Kauffman was a leading benefactor of Kansas City. In 1969, he bought a Major League Baseball expansion club: the Kansas City Royals. He had little interest in baseball; he acquired the team for the benefit of the city. Kauffman took to the sport quickly—and he applied his vaunted marketing techniques to making the Royals a K.C. favorite. Kauffman propelled the Royals to a powerful decade starting with an American League division championship in 1976 and culminating in a World Series victory over the St. Louis Cardinals in 1985. The Royals were not "a part of his financial portfolio," explains biographer Anne Morgan. "It was a part of his civic philanthropy."

> Ewing Kauffman set up the largest U.S. foundation focused on fostering economic growth by encouraging entrepreneurs.

After Marion went public, Ewing and Muriel Kauffman began to engage in serious giving in Kansas City. After the Royals' embarrassing drug abuse scandals in 1983, Kauffman launched STAR, an evidence-based drug abuse prevention program in Kansas City schools. STAR reduced marijuana use by 43 percent compared to a control group. He also launched Project Choice, which used a carrot of college or vocational training funds to incentivize high school completion.

An entrepreneur to his fingertips, Kauffman learned from his mistakes. One of his first major philanthropic initiatives involved co-funding a campaign with Hallmark to underwrite home heating bills for the poor. The campaign succeeded; nobody in town went without heat. But he decided not to participate again. After all, he observed, winter comes every year—and the program "didn't solve the problem. They just threw money at it." Kauffman preferred solutions-based giving.

"Even as he began to fund substance-abuse awareness and to offer postsecondary education to those who completed high school, he was always conscious of the need to create more and better paying jobs for those young people as they prepared to enter the workforce," observed Morgan. As a Kauffman Foundation report at that same time put it, "We've got to do something to help encourage the creation of jobs." That effort became the next act of the Kauffman Foundation.

In 1990, Kauffman directed his foundation to research what could be done to help entrepreneurs. He eventually created a Center for Entrepreneurial Leadership to train entrepreneurs, form networks, develop curricula, and foster research on entrepreneurship. The center's 1992 launch event would mark one of Kauffman's last public appearances. "We cannot finance everybody who wants to get into business," he explained. "But we have the capability of guiding them to the point where they can get seed money."

With this commitment, Kauffman set his foundation on a path of pioneering philanthropic specialization. With assets of more than $2 billion, Kauffman became the largest foundation in the country to focus on fostering entrepreneurship—and helping dreamers become the next generation of Ewing Kauffmans.

↳ *Evan Sparks*

Further reading

○ Anne Morgan, *Prescription for Success: The Life and Values of Ewing Marion Kauffman* (Andrews McMeel, 1995)

W. K. KELLOGG

Will Keith Kellogg invented corn flakes and stoked America's appetite for the convenience of dry breakfast cereal. His business became wildly successful. And from its profits, Kellogg poured a fortune into improving health care and education for children.

Born in 1860, Kellogg was one of 14 children of a strict Seventh-day Adventist family. They observed the Sabbath on Saturday and abstained entirely from alcohol, tobacco, coffee, tea, and meat. Schooling for W. K. (as he liked to be called) ended at age 13, when he was apprenticed to his father's broom-making business. It was a childhood filled with work and responsibility. "As a boy," he later recalled, "I never learned to play."

W. K. worked for his father until he was 16 years old, at which time he was hired by his older brother John. In 1876, the newly minted physician Dr. John Kellogg was named superintendent of the Battle Creek Sanitarium in Battle Creek, Michigan. He hired W. K., eight years his junior, as a bookkeeper. Combining elements of the Seventh-day Adventist diet with insights from late-nineteenth-century medicine, the sanitarium was a sort of live-in spa where visitors could eat healthily, exercise vigorously, and rest soundly. For the next 30 years, it was where the brothers worked side by side.

It was not an easy relationship. John required W. K. to run beside him while he bicycled around the sanitarium, for example, and to take dictation while he used the toilet. John was a relentless self-promoter, who cajoled the great and the good to come to the sanitarium (a word he coined). Fascinated by holistic medicine, electrotherapy, and hydrotherapy, John became obsessed with digestion, administering frequent enemas of water (to flush the system) and yogurt (to supply healthy bacteria). He was also a rigid opponent of onanism, and prescribed a bland diet to ward off the temptations he associated with spicy and savory foods.

Food was a central concern at the sanitarium. Like many Seventh-day Adventists, the Kelloggs relied on a low-fat and low-protein diet that centered on fiber, whole grains, and nuts. In the mid-1890s, John told W. K. to develop a grain product more easily digestible than bread. W. K. started tinkering— boiling wheat, spreading the mixture on grinding rollers, and toasting it. Later he started using corn, and added salt and sugar. The flaked corn was served with cold milk and fruit, a far cry from the hot porridge or bacon and eggs that then greeted most Americans at the breakfast table.

> Kellogg's giving was a response to the poverty, strictures, and labor of his own boyhood.

The cereal was popular with patients, and the brothers started a small production and mail-order operation. John was too busy running the sanitarium, fighting onanism, and promoting eugenics (his other passion) to notice the commercial potential of corn flakes, but the upside was not lost on W. K. In 1904, a former sanitarium patient named C. W. Post launched a commercial line of cornflakes. W. K. could no longer stand by. In 1906, he founded the Battle Creek Toasted Corn Flake Company, which is known today as the Kellogg Company.

By the mid-1920s, W. K. Kellogg was the cereal king of America, and a very wealthy man. The final third of his life was dedicated to philanthropy. In 1923, he created the Fellowship Corporation, which quietly funded charities throughout Battle Creek and southern Michigan. In the late 1920s, as Kellogg was approaching 70, he wanted to create a more organized enterprise. This was the start of the W. K. Kellogg Foundation, which began operations in 1930.

Kellogg confined the foundation's giving to "the health, education, and welfare of mankind, but principally of children or youth...without regard to sex, race, creed, or nationality." In large part, this was a response to the poverty, strictures, and labor of his own boyhood. But there was another reason. In 1913, his grandson, a toddler named Kenneth Williamson, fell out of a second-story window. The boy nearly died, and was physically disabled for the rest of his life.

Kellogg was astounded that, despite his wealth, he could not find adequate medical care anywhere in southern Michigan. In a letter to a Battle Creek physician, Kellogg wrote that Kenneth's accident "caused me to wonder what difficulties were in the paths of needy parents who seek help for their children when catastrophe strikes, and I resolved to lend what aid I could to such children." A central focus of Kellogg's philanthropy would be children's health care.

A year after opening its doors, the Kellogg Foundation launched the Michigan Community Health Project. Focused on the seven counties of southern Michigan, the 17-year initiative built new hospitals in rural areas, helped organize public health departments, and provided nurses and doctors for remote towns. In 1942, the State Department asked Kellogg to expand the program to Latin America as a wartime gesture of goodwill. Kellogg willingly complied. "In doing so," notes historian Joel Orosz, "the foundation curiously became international in scope before it became national."

Over the last 21 years of his life, Kellogg donated a total of some $66 million to the foundation. He initially funded its activities from his checkbook, refusing to endow the foundation until it had proven its effectiveness. (When he did endow the foundation, he gave it nearly all of his equity in the Kellogg Company—some 54 percent of the common stock.) Though glaucoma left him legally blind at age 80, he attended every board meeting, worked closely with his staff, and frequently visited with grantees, always accompanied by one of his faithful German shepherds, all of whom were descendants of Rin-Tin-Tin.

Through his foundation, Kellogg also created the Ann Kellogg School, named for his mother, one of the first elementary schools to teach children with disabilities alongside children without disabilities. He likewise used his foundation to donate his Arabian horse farm to the University of California. In 1949, it became the home of California State Polytechnic, Pomona, which remains devoted to the teaching of technical arts and applied sciences. Although Kellogg conducted most of his philanthropy through his foundation, he funded a few projects from his checkbook, including his support for summer camps for low-income families, the creation of the Kellogg Bird Sanctuary, and the establishment of an experimental demonstration farm at Michigan State University.

"Dollars do not create character," W. K. Kellogg often said. But he knew that dollars could help in many other ways, and he charged his foundation, today one of the largest in the nation, with helping "children face the future with confidence, with health, and with a strong-rooted security in the trust of this country and its institutions."

~ *Martin Morse Wooster*

Further reading

○ Gerald Carson, *Cornflake Crusade* (Rinehart, 1957)

○ Mary Cohen, *W. K. Kellogg Foundation, 75 Years of Philanthropy* (W. K. Kellogg Foundation, 2005)

○ Horace Powell, *The Original Has This Signature—W. K. Kellogg* (Prentice-Hall, 1956)

SEBASTIAN KRESGE

Sebastian Kresge was among the most successful retailers in American history. The founder of what would become the K-Mart chain of discount stores, he was also an accomplished philanthropist who focused on capital grants and building projects.

Kresge's background was the definition of "hardscrabble." Born in 1867 to ethnically German farmers, he was raised in rural Pennsylvania to be upright and God-fearing. His parents instilled lifelong habits of piety, thrift, and industriousness in their son, but hard work was no proof against crop failures and depression. When Sebastian was eight years old, his parents lost the family farm to foreclosure, victims of the Panic of 1873.

In his teens, Kresge set his sights on becoming a teacher. To finance his education, he struck a bargain with his parents: if they would pay his tuition, he would sign over his wages until age 21. In the meantime, he would live on the proceeds of his beekeeping business, which Sebastian had started as a boy.

He kept the bargain, finished college, and spent one term teaching before he decided that his real interest was business. After a brief stint as a deliveryman and clerk in a Scranton hardware store, Kresge became an itinerant tin and hardware salesman, which brought him into contact with a group of men who would later become his mentors in the retail sales business: F. W. Woolworth, S. H. Knox, and John McCrory.

For an initial investment of $8,000, paid out of savings the young man had assiduously accumulated over the years, Kresge acquired two struggling five-and-dime stores. A dozen years later, he had spun his foothold in Detroit into 85 stores. Kresge was on his way to building the retailing empire that eventually became K-Mart.

Kresge's genius, most business historians agree, was in finding and occupying an unfilled retailing niche, the middlebrow space between low-cost five-and-dimes and more expensive brand-name retailers. He was personally involved in almost every aspect of his expanding empire, showing himself especially adept at finding cheap real estate, usually just months before the middle-class customers that were his bread and butter moved out to the newly built suburbs surrounding his shopping centers. Kresge was one of the first retailers to offer paid vacations, pensions, and profit-sharing. Eighty years after its founding, at its 1979 high-water mark, K-Mart Corporation posted sales of $11.7 billion in 1,891 stores across the United States, Canada, and Australia.

Kresge was notoriously frugal—his two early marriages foundered because of his personal stinginess, and he gave up golf because he couldn't stand the lost balls. He was nevertheless profoundly generous to civic and charitable causes all his life. A lifelong Methodist, he was weekly to be found in the pews of a particularly austere country church in Monroe County, Pennsylvania, near his birthplace. Early on, he confided to fellow churchgoers that he hoped to give away his entire personal fortune. His philanthropic credo was simple. I want, he would say, "to leave the world a better place than I found it."

> One distinction of Sebastian Kresge and his foundation was giving large grants to support building projects at well-established charities.

While simply derived, his approach was anything but simplistic. Befitting a man who created a whole new retailing niche, Kresge also developed a distinctive philanthropic identity. As a relatively young man, he became known for his opposition to alcohol. Kresge was a lifelong teetotaler who abhorred the damage that liquor caused in the lives of the working poor. He supported anti-liquor groups long after the temperance movement ceased to be popular, and even after it became evident that Kresge's anti-liquor politics were hurting his bottom line.

When he funded the Kresge Foundation with an initial $1.3 million in 1924, he decided to focus on supporting mature charitable organizations like the YMCA and Girl Scouts, leaving to other foundations the task of identifying new approaches and groups. Not surprisingly for the man who founded a beekeeping operation before he turned ten, Kresge's foundation also focused on self-help charitable efforts that enabled the poor to lift themselves out of poverty. And driven by his devotion, Kresge favored religious organizations that without his support would be forced to rely on government funding—and the secularization that accompanied it.

Under Sebastian's close personal guidance—he remained an active member of the board until his death—the Kresge Foundation has especially distinguished itself in giving large grants to support major brick-and-mortar projects. The Kresge name is inscribed on the walls of many large universities, medical centers, and arts institutions. It has supported hospital expansions from Columbus to Fresno; built wings on museums and concert halls in Albuquerque and Indiana; and supported a medical school in Ann Arbor, a law library at Notre Dame, and a chapel at the Claremont Theological School in California. One of the Kresge Foundation's largest brick-and-mortar grants brought it back to the birthplace of the Kresge retailing empire, Detroit, where in 2002 the foundation donated a $50 million challenge grant to an ambitious downtown riverfront renovation.

Nearly 100 years old when he died in 1966, Kresge gave his foundation a total of $60,577,183 during his lifetime. That alone made him one of the largest donors in the country. And he almost achieved his wish to divest himself of the wealth he worked so long and intently to accumulate: when he died, his personal estate was worth less than a tenth of what he had given to the foundation that bears his name.

☞ *Justin Torres*

Further reading
○ Stanley Sebastian Kresge and Steve Spilos, *The S. S. Kresge Story* (Western Publishing, 1979)
○ "The Pinch-Penny Philanthropist" (*Time*, October 28, 1966)

ELI LILLY

Eli Lilly transformed a sleepy family business into a pharmaceutical powerhouse, proving along the way that economic pragmatism and generosity are often complementary. Eli's namesake grandfather—called "Colonel Lilly" for his Civil War service—founded the family drugmaking business in Indianapolis in 1876. Lilly's father followed, starting as a bottle washer. After graduation from the Indianapolis public schools, grandson Eli was sent to school in Philadelphia to learn the pharmacy trade. All his life, Lilly would regret that he never received a fuller liberal education.

But Lilly grew the company in ways his father and grandfather never imagined. A practitioner of the scientific management techniques of

Frederick Taylor, Lilly was named head of the company's newly created economics division. Lilly brought in industrial specialists to cut costs and increase production. Even more crucially, he moved the company away from its roots as a patent-medicines manufacturer and toward advanced pharmaceutical research.

In the 1920s, this new focus paid off when Lilly & Company played a crucial role in the development of insulin for the treatment of diabetes. Lilly went on to equally instrumental roles in creating the polio vaccine and mass-producing penicillin, liver extract, and thimerosal, a preservative in medicines and vaccines. He retired as head of the company in 1948, but remained closely involved in its affairs until his death in 1977.

Lilly believed that it was the duty of the wealthy to support charitable causes. He brought to his many philanthropic efforts the same drive and attention to detail that made him successful in the drug business. But he also brought some pronounced personal passions.

Despite having assured financial success, thanks to the development of the insulin patents, Lilly was an unhappy man as he entered middle age. He was burdened with personal troubles: two sons died in infancy, his first marriage ended in divorce, and his daughter Evie suffered from mental instability and alcoholism throughout her life. Never a warm person—one of his closest friends, the president of Wabash College in Indiana, noted that Lilly used his dry sense of humor and business acumen to keep people at arm's length—Eli could be harsh and short-tempered.

> The Lilly Endowment is notable for its support of community-service organizations in Indiana, and its unusual portfolio of religious giving.

In 1927, though, Lilly remarried, and he and his wife, Ruth, were a much happier couple. They stayed together until her death in 1973. A buoyant Lilly then set out, as he wrote in a 1934 essay, "to broaden and brighten my life and surroundings." The mid-life turn started with a deliberate course of self-education in areas that were never broached in pharmacy school. Lilly became a learned autodidact in fields ranging from archaeology and historic preservation to Chinese art and comparative religion.

He began to publish books and monographs on topics of interest, making small but real contributions to various fields. Typical topics included "Prehistoric Antiquities of Indiana" and an interpretation of Lenape Indian pictographs. One of his personal heroes was Heinrich Schliemann, the amateur archaeologist who bested the "smug professionals," as Lilly put it in his article "Schliemann in Indianapolis," by discovering the site of ancient Troy in western Turkey.

These pronounced intellectual interests and personal enthusiasms would guide Lilly's personal giving. Like his grandfather and father before him, he supported historical and educational institutions in Indiana—like the liberal-arts institutions Earlham College and Wabash College, and the Indiana Historical Society. He was also a generous benefactor of Christ Church in Indianapolis, where he had been a choir boy as a child and where he attended services his entire life. He donated his extensive Chinese art collection to a local museum. Children's causes were especially dear to his wife Ruth, and Lilly supported a local children's museum and private religious groups that ministered to poor and needy children.

Unlike his father and grandfather, though, Lilly turned his philanthropy into a systematic activity. He had a keen eye for what we would today call "venture philanthropy"—a phrase that likely would have appealed to the man who once wrote a detailed manual for Lilly employees on the best way to fill gelatin capsules. Philanthropy, he told his daughter, "sounds easy, but the catch is that it takes lots of time and study" to learn what projects "are worthwhile and what are not."

Usually working anonymously, Lilly would seek out small organizations that seemed to be doing good work and could benefit from his giving. He was especially interested in character education, finding and supporting the work of Ernest Ligon, author of the popular mid-century character-education curriculum for religious schools called "A Greater Generation." With Lilly's support, Ligon founded the Character Research Project at Union College in upstate New York. Over more than a quarter century, Lilly supported Ligon's work conducting research, writing articles, and convening youth congresses to study and advocate for character education.

In 1937, along with his father and brother, Eli founded the Lilly Endowment, comprised of Lilly stock and closely controlled by the Lilly family. It is still one of the largest philanthropies in the country. The Lilly Endowment is notable for its support of community-service organizations in Indiana and its unusual portfolio of religious giving, including support for scholars working on religious topics and financial aid to divinity and theology students. (For more information on Lilly's continuing work in support of religious communities, see "Placing the Call," *Philanthropy*, Spring 2010.)

Because he frequently made anonymous donations, it will never be possible to know the full extent of Eli Lilly's philanthropy. When he died in 1977, he left his estate of $165 million to be distributed to his and Ruth's favorite causes, including Wabash College, historical and religious institutions throughout Indiana, and community service groups in the city of Indianapolis. Modest to the end, Lilly particularly requested that there be no eulogy at his funeral. So his bequests spoke for his life.

           ☛ *Justin Torres*

Further reading

○ E. J. Kahn, *All in a Century: The First Hundred Years of Eli Lilly & Co.* (Eli Lilly, 1976)

○ James Madison, *Eli Lilly: A Life, 1885-1977* (Indiana Historical Society, 1989)

NICHOLAS LONGWORTH

Nicholas Longworth is best remembered, insofar as he is remembered at all, as the father of American winemaking. Longworth popularized the Catawba grape and created a widespread, if short-lived, enthusiasm for the sparkling wines of the Ohio River Valley. He was also a well-regarded attorney, a massively successful real estate investor, and a tireless philanthropist who dedicated his enormous fortune to those whom he affectionately called "the devil's poor."

Longworth was born in Newark, New Jersey, in 1783, the son of a once-prominent merchant. Unfortunately for the family, his father had been a stalwart Loyalist during the American Revolution. After the war, virtually all of the family's property was confiscated. Nicholas spent his boyhood in poverty, bearing the stigma of his father's loyalty to the Crown. He learned hard work from an early age. For a while, he was apprenticed to a shoemaker; later, he was sent to clerk for a relative in South Carolina.

When he was 19 years old, he moved west, eager to distance himself from the shame and poverty of his youth. In 1804, he arrived in Cincinnati, Ohio, where he began to study law. His mentor was Jacob Burnet, a leading figure in Ohio politics—often called the "Father of Ohio's Constitution"—and one of Cincinnati's wealthiest men. In short order, Longworth passed the bar and began an energetic law practice. What money he made he used to buy real estate.

The investments proved immensely profitable. As Cincinnati boomed, the value of Longworth's property exploded. By 1819, he retired from his legal practice; his properties demanded his full attention. In 1850, Longworth paid more than $17,000 in taxes, the second-highest tax bill in the nation.

Retired from active business, Longworth was able to devote decades to his favorite pastime: experimental horticulture. His greatest success was the Catawba grape. In 1828, his friend John Adlum sent him specimens from Washington, D.C. They flourished along the banks of the Ohio River. Longworth pulled down his other vines, replacing them with the late-ripening, purplish-red grapes.

With bumper crops of Catawba, Longworth began to make wine, employing armies of German immigrants and introducing the first large-scale winemaking operation in the New World. When a sparkling variant was created by accident, wine enthusiasts from San Francisco to Paris toasted the pink bubblies from Ohio. (In 1858, Henry Wadsworth Longfellow wrote an ode to "Catawba Wine" and dedicated the poem to Longworth.) By the time of his death, Longworth's vineyards were producing 150,000 bottles annually.

The great bulk of Longworth's wealth went to his idiosyncratic program of philanthropy. Longworth, explained an 1863 obituary in *Harper's Weekly*, "had a whimsical theory that those whom everybody will help were not entitled to any aid from him, and that he would confine his donations to the worthless and wretched vagabonds that everyone else turns away from." These, he would explain, were "the devil's poor." They were the beneficiaries of virtually all of his charitable giving.

> He dedicated his enormous fortune to those whom he affectionately called "the devil's poor," the "wretched vagabonds that everyone else turns away."

Much about Longworth's giving is anecdotal, but the stories that remain are revealing. "A committee of Mormons, on a begging expedition, was once sent to him by a friend," noted the *Harper's Weekly* obituary, "with a note intimating that, as these people were not Christians, and seemed to be abandoned by everybody that professed to be, they probably came within his rule, and he could consistently assist them. He did so without hesitation."

Every Monday morning Longworth was known to give away 10-cent loaves of bread to anyone who would ask for one; most weeks he reportedly gave away between 300 and 800 loaves. He built a four-story brick boarding house over his wine cellars, with 56 neatly appointed apartments that he rented below cost to poor laborers and their families. If a man could not afford the rent, Longworth would often allow him to stay, free of charge, for months and sometimes even years.

Unsurprisingly, "the devil's poor" often failed to reciprocate Longworth's good will. At one of his Monday morning distributions of bread, riots nearly broke out when the crowds realized that the loaves had been topped off with rye. (Told that the wheat "was running high"—meaning that the loaves were baking with large air pockets—Longworth had ordered the bakers to plump the bread with grain.) As for the boarding house, one of Longworth's biographers noted that the tenants were "most ungrateful and troublesome" and that they "used to annoy him incessantly, and frequently broke into the wine-vaults below and stole his choicest wine."

Despite the frustration, despite the ingratitude, Longworth persisted in his course of charitable giving. "Vagabonds, drunkards, fallen women, those who had gone far into the depths of misery and wretchedness, and from whom respectable people shrank in disgust, never appealed to him in vain," wrote James McCabe. "He would listen to them patiently, moved to the depths of his soul by their sad stories, and would send them away rejoicing that they were not utterly friendless. 'Decent paupers will always find a plenty to help them,' he would say, 'but no one cares for these poor wretches. Everybody damns them, and as no one else will help them, I must.'"

Longworth also made some more conventional philanthropic efforts. In 1842, he donated the land on which the Cincinnati Observatory was built. In his last public appearance, a 77-year-old John Quincy Adams traveled to Cincinnati to lay the cornerstone. When the institution opened in 1845, it was one of the finest facilities in the world. This project was unusual for Longworth, though; he preferred to help the poor—especially those who could not, or would not, help themselves.

Longworth died in February 1863 at 81 years old. Tributes poured forth, praising and honoring the son of a disgraced Loyalist. None, it seems likely, would have moved Longworth so much as the sight of his funeral procession, with thousands of outcasts—drunkards and prostitutes, beggars and criminals—sobbing at the loss of this, their one true friend.

☞ *Christopher Levenick*

Further reading

○ Clara Longworth Chambrun, *The Making of Nicholas Longworth: Annals of an American Family* (R. Long & R.R. Smith, 1933)

○ *American Studies* biographical essay, journals.ku.edu/index.php/amerstud/article/view/4203/3962

○ "The Late Nicholas Longworth" (*Harper's Weekly* March 7, 1863)

ALFRED LOOMIS

Alfred Loomis came from a philanthropic family. They created sanitariums for tuberculosis patients, funded medical research, and built up NYU, among other causes. The son and grandson of experimental physicians, young Loomis had a powerful scientific bent. He distinguished himself in mathematics at Yale, but after his father died while he was still an undergrad Loomis decided he needed a career that could support his family. So after graduation he enrolled at Harvard Law School.

Blood will tell, however, and soon the young Alfred Loomis found himself profoundly bored with the practice of law. He returned to his earlier fascination with science, befriending internationally prominent researchers and conducting his own quite-advanced investigations in garages and basements. Eventually concluding that he needed a fortune if he was going to experiment on a large scale, the restless genius made a plan. He would launch a Wall Street firm with his brother-in-law, pile up cash, and use it to pursue pure science.

Applying a mathematical approach, Loomis quickly built one of the largest investment banks in the country by financing rapid development of the brand-new electric-utility industry during the 1920s. From almost nothing, his firm grew to underwrite almost a sixth of all the securities issued in the U.S. Then Loomis became convinced that the stock market was overvalued and likely to collapse. In early 1929 he and his partner began transferring all their money into cash or Treasury bills. When Black Thursday hit in October of that year Loomis was not only safe, but well-positioned to bargain shop. It is estimated that he made the modern equivalent of more than $700 million in the first years of the Depression, ending up one of the wealthiest and most powerful men on Wall Street, in a league similar to the Rockefellers and Morgans.

Now well able to subsidize high-level scientific research, Loomis cashed out in 1933 and threw himself into the work of the private lab he set up during the mid-1920s in a rehabbed mansion near his home north of New York City. The Loomis Laboratory became one of the world's great research institutes, better equipped than top academic or corporate labs, and visited by many of the world's leading scientists.

Loomis had a special ability to crash-study a new subject and quickly become expert. Throughout the 1920s and 1930s he used his fortune to conduct pathbreaking experiments, alone and with other scientists, on ultrasound, radiometry, the precise measurement of time, and many other subjects. He created the techniques for monitoring brain waves, discovered

MIT Museum

new sleep states, and co-invented the microscope centrifuge. He also funded scores of other researchers and built up the science departments at universities like MIT. When Yale gave him an honorary degree, the citation compared him to the American who had best combined science and philanthropy: "In his varied interests, his powers of invention, and his services to his fellow man, Mr. Loomis is the twentieth-century Benjamin Franklin."

Travels to Germany in the late '30s left Loomis disturbed over both the popularity of Hitler and the gathering technical might of the Germans. Biographer Jennet Conant summarizes his next dramatic move: "Long before the government moved to enlist scientists to develop advanced weapons, Loomis had assessed the situation and concluded it was critical that the country be as informed as possible about which technologies would matter in the future war. He scrapped all his experiments and turned [his lab] into his personal civilian research project, then began recruiting the brightest minds he could find to help him take measure of the enemy's capabilities and start working on new gadgets and devices for defense purposes."

Loomis put his main focus on using radio waves to detect and fix the location of objects—what eventually became known as radar. He immersed himself in the field, recruited academics, studied England's successes, then launched a series of intensive practical experiments. This work drew on several areas of science where Loomis personally was a scientific leader—wave behavior, electromagnetic-spectrum research, and precise measurement of time. Within a year the Loomis Radiation Laboratory had completed basic research, achieved breakthroughs in making radio-detection practical, and created a working prototype radar mounted in a converted diaper-delivery truck.

At just this point, bombs rained down on Pearl Harbor, kicking Loomis into overdrive. Back in World War I he had volunteered for service and been sent to test new weapons at the Army's Aberdeen Proving Ground. The experience left him amazed at the sluggishness and resistance to change within the military establishment, and within government generally. As this next, more terrible, war broke out, Loomis understood as few others did how important technical breakthroughs would be in determining the winner, and how much America's deep bench of scientists could contribute to victory. He made it his personal philanthropic mission to ensure that America's magnificently inventive industrial machinery would produce vital military innovations without getting gummed up by government bureaucracy.

In this, Loomis's leadership skills were even more essential to his success than his checkbook and his scientific perspicacity. When a small group of British scientists arrived in the U.S. on a covert mission to share their radar secrets in the hope that the Americans could make the technology more useable, precise, and widely available to Allied fighting forces, Loomis was the catalyst in instantly understanding their crucial breakthroughs, pressing U.S. military and civilian authorities to build on them, and then orchestrating important refinements and advances beyond the British technology.

He moved all of his valuable personal equipment and prototype findings to MIT, which had its own radar project (funded by him). When Congress was slow to approve the support needed to ramp up the MIT lab, Loomis began paying expenses out of his own pocket. Then he convinced MIT, on whose board he served, to advance the project $500,000, and he appealed to his friend John Rockefeller Jr. to advance another half million. (When government funding finally came through, MIT and Rockefeller were repaid.) Most importantly, Loomis and his close friend Ernest Lawrence, the Nobel-laureate physicist, used their credibility with many of America's top scientific minds to recruit them to drop everything and go to work in Loomis's new radar lab. Nearly all agreed.

> President Roosevelt described Alfred Loomis as second only to Winston Churchill in civilian contributions to victory in World War II.

"They had no official appointment from the federal government to do this. But Loomis got them all talked into doing it," one observer wrote later, "and it's a good thing they did." Loomis, who recognized the power and efficiency of "American individualism and laissez-faire" and believed that most progress came from "free agency and freedom from politics," fiercely protected the scientists from interference in their work and encouraged them to follow their own individual and team judgments to make the fastest possible progress. One scientist described Loomis's laboratory as "the greatest cooperative research establishment in the history of the world." Lawrence later stated, "If Alfred Loomis had not existed, radar development would have been retarded greatly, at an enormous cost in American lives.... He used his wealth very effectively."

Very soon, the Loomis lab had not only mastered the science and technique of radar, but had designed nearly 100 different lifesaving and war-ending products. By June 1943, the Army and Navy had ordered 22,000 radar sets from the lab. These had many vital effects. Radar shot down Luftwaffe planes and kept the Germans from defeating England. Radar ended the U-boat menace, saving tens of thousands of lives and allowing the crucial output of American industry to be transported to our European allies. Radar negated Germany's leading technical breakthrough, the V-rocket. Radar gave our pilots and ship captains the ability to detect threats, to direct fire, and to survive bad weather and night conditions that would otherwise have thwarted or killed them.

Loomis also personally dreamed up the pioneering long-range navigation system called LORAN. Perfected in his lab over the original indifference of military agencies, its debut in combat changed everything for American and Allied wartime navigators. Until the recent arrival of satellite GPS, LORAN continued to serve for decades as the exclusive global positioning system. Fourteen years after World War II ended, Alfred Loomis was awarded patent #2,884,628 for inventing the original system of long-range navigation.

Contemporary observers concluded that "radar won World War II; the atom bomb ended it." As it happened, Alfred Loomis also had a lot to do with that latter triumph. He was a friend and important supporter of Enrico Fermi as Fermi led investigations into nuclear fission. And Loomis was the key champion and lead private funder of Ernest Lawrence's development of cyclotrons at the University of California, Berkeley. In addition to putting his own money behind Lawrence, Loomis made it his mission to convince other donors to back this highly speculative project—eventually sweet-talking a climactic $1.15 million contribution out of the Rockefeller Foundation.

As soon as Lawrence's cyclotron was funded, Loomis plucked off his philanthropist cap and donned his entrepreneur/financier hat in order to beg and bully America's leading industrial corporations into finding the large quantities of iron, copper, electronics, and other war-constrained commodities needed to build the giant machine. Lawrence was astonished by the Wall Street titan's ability to marshal commercial cooperation. The cyclotron Lawrence and Loomis built together was subsequently used to laboriously purify the uranium for the first atomic explosions.

Loomis's broader contribution to the Manhattan Project was the modus operandi he pioneered in his private lab and then expanded on a large scale in the MIT radiation lab he oversaw during the war. The race to create the atomic bomb followed the Loomis formula to a tee: collect the best minds without regard to their immediate expertise, give them superb equipment and material support, guard their freedom to experiment, and encourage collegial exchanges of information and shared problem-solving. Nobel physicist Luis Alvarez, who worked in the radar lab and then created the A-bomb detonator for the Manhattan Project, credited Loomis's interventions for "the remarkable lack of administrative roadblocks experienced by…the builders of the atomic bombs."

Nearly all of Loomis's top hand-picked physicists were quietly pulled out of his radar lab when the Manhattan Project was launched, and sent to Los Alamos or one of the other project sites. Loomis acquiesced because he had long been pushing for exactly this crash program, alarmed as he was by military complacency that viewed atomic weapons as something to think about for "the next war," the dawdling pace of government research to that point, and the real possibility of German scientists being first to the bomb.

President Roosevelt later described Loomis as second only to Winston Churchill in contributions to Allied victory in World War II. After the war, Loomis helped institutionalize his entrepreneurial style of defense research by becoming an influential founding trustee of the RAND Corporation, a nonprofit established to apply the best scientific ideas to national defense. With funding from the Ford Foundation and other donors, RAND promoted multi-stage rockets, intercontinental missiles, magnetic-core computer memory, the building blocks of the future Internet, and many other innovations. The Loomis imprint can also be seen on DARPA, the Defense Advanced Research Projects Agency that picked up the mantle of the Loomis lab and carried it throughout the post-war era.

Alfred Loomis also left behind a flesh-and-blood embodiment of his whirlwind entrepreneurial giving. His great-grandson is Reed Hastings— who as CEO of the Internet pioneer Netflix, and one of the most influential progenitors of the rise of charter schools, has been a huge game-changer in both business and philanthropy. (See 2000, 2005, and 2006 entries on our list of Major Achievements in Education Philanthropy.)

☞ *Karl Zinsmeister*

Further reading

- *Philanthropy* magazine reporting, philanthropyroundtable.org/topic/excellence_in_
  philanthropy/donors_who_come_to_the_aid_of_their_country
- Jennet Conant, *Tuxedo Park* (Simon and Schuster, 2002)

OSEOLA MCCARTY

Oseola McCarty was born into the world in 1908, and it was a raw start. She was conceived when her mother was raped on a wooded path in rural Mississippi as she returned from tending a sick relative. Oseola was raised in Hattiesburg by her grandmother and aunt, who cleaned houses, cooked, and took in laundry.

As a child, Oseola would come home from elementary school and iron clothes, stashing the money she earned in her doll buggy. The three women relied completely on each other, and when the aunt returned from a hospitalization unable to walk, Oseola dropped out of sixth grade to care for her, and take up her work as a washerwoman. She never returned to school.

"Work became the great good of her life," explained one person who knew her. "She found beauty in its movement and pride in its provisions. She was happy to have it and gave herself over to it with abandon."

McCarty herself put it this way: "I knew there were people who didn't have to work as hard as I did, but it didn't make me feel sad. I *loved* to work, and when you love to do anything, those things don't bother you…. Sometimes I worked straight through two or three days. I had goals I was working toward. That motivated me and I was able to push hard… Work is a blessing. As long as I am living I want to be working at something. Just because I am old doesn't mean I can't work."

And hers was not a standard-issue job. McCarty scrubbed her laundry by hand on a rub board. She did try an automatic washer and dryer in the 1960s, but found that "the washing machine didn't rinse enough, and the dryer turned the whites yellow." After years of boiling clothes and then doing four fresh-water rinses, that wasn't good enough to meet her high standards. The machine was almost immediately retired, and she went back to her Maid Rite scrub board, water drawn from a nearby fire hydrant, and 100 feet of open-air clothesline.

Asked to describe her typical day, McCarty answered: "I would go outside and start a fire under my wash pot. Then I would soak, wash, and boil a bundle of clothes. Then I would rub 'em, wrench 'em, rub 'em again, starch 'em, and hang 'em on the line. After I had all of the clean clothes on the line, I would start on the next batch. I'd wash all day, and in the evenin' I'd iron until 11:00. I loved the work. The bright fire. Wrenching the wet, clean cloth. White shirts shinin' on the line."

This extraordinary work ethic, pursued straight through to her retirement at age 86, apparently produced results her customers appreciated.

In 1996, Hattiesburg businessman Paul Laughlin wrote that "I know one person who still has several shirts that were last cleaned almost two years ago by Miss McCarty. He says that he does not intend to wear them; he just takes them out periodically to look at them and to enjoy the crisp fabric and its scent." McCarty, concludes Laughlin, was a walking object lesson "that all work can be performed with dignity and infused with quality."

"Hard work gives your life meaning," stated McCarty. "Everyone needs to work hard at somethin' to feel good about themselves. Every job can be done well and every day has its satisfactions…. If you want to feel proud of yourself, you've got to do things you can be proud of."

Shortly after she retired, McCarty did something that made many Americans very proud of her. She had begun to save almost as soon as she started working at age eight. As the money pooled up in her doll buggy, the very young girl took action. "I went to the bank and deposited. Didn't know how to do it. Went there myself. Didn't tell mama and them I was goin'."

"I commenced to save money. I never would take any of it out. I just put it in…. It's not the ones that make the big money, but the ones who know how to save who get ahead. You got to leave it alone long enough for it to increase."

Of course that requires self-control and modest appetites. "My secret was contentment. I was happy with what I had," said McCarty.

These sturdy habits ran together to produce McCarty's final secret. When she retired in 1995, her hands painfully swollen with arthritis, this washerwoman who had been paid in little piles of coins and dollar bills her entire life had $280,000 in the bank.

Even more startling: she decided to give most of it away—not as a bequest, but immediately.

Setting aside just enough to live on, McCarty donated $150,000 to the University of Southern Mississippi to fund scholarships for worthy but needy students seeking the education she never had. When they found out what she had done, over 600 men and women in Hattiesburg and beyond made donations that more than tripled her original endowment. Today, the university presents several full-tuition McCarty scholarships every year.

Like a lot of philanthropists, McCarty wanted the satisfactions of giving while living. And she succeeded. The first beneficiary of her gift, a Hattiesburg girl named Stephanie Bullock, was president of her senior class and had supportive parents, but also a twin brother, and not enough family income to send them both to college. With her McCarty Scholarship, Bullock enrolled at Southern Miss, and promptly adopted McCarty as a surrogate grandmother.

Like a lot of philanthropists, McCarty felt a powerful impulse to act in her home region. When asked why she picked Southern Miss, she replied "because it's *here*." The campus (though she had never visited) was located just a couple blocks from her home.

Prior to making her gift, Oseola's one long trip had been to Niagara Falls. Here is her recollection: "Law, the sound of the water was like the sound of the world comin' to an end. In the evening we spread blankets on the ground and ate picnic dinners. I met people from all over the world. On the return trip, we stopped in Chicago. I liked it, but was ready to get back home. I missed the place where I belonged—where I was needed and makin' a contribution. No place compares to the piece of earth where you have put down your roots."

Like a lot of faithful philanthropists, Oseola McCarty was forgiving. Reminded that the university she was giving her money to had been white-only until the 1960s, she answered with equanimity: "They used to not let colored people go out there. But now they *do*. And I think they should have it."

Like a lot of philanthropists, Oseola McCarty had a strong and virtuous character and good habits. She lived frugally, walking almost everywhere, including more than a mile to get her groceries. When she stayed in a hotel for the first time after coming to public attention, she made the bed before checking out.

> "I can't do everything. But I can do something to help somebody. And what I can do I will do."

In addition to the dignity of work, McCarty's satisfactions were the timeless ones: faith in God, family closeness, and love of locale. One friend described McCarty's faith as "as simple as the Sermon on the Mount, and as difficult to practice." She was baptized at age 13, dunked in a local pond while dressed all in white (a mixed blessing for someone who washed her clothes by hand).

"I start each day on my knees, saying the Lord's Prayer. Then I get busy about my work," McCarty told one interviewer. "You have to accept God the best way you know how and then He'll show Himself to you. And the more you serve Him, the more *able* you are to serve Him."

"Some people make a lot of noise about what's wrong with the world, and they are usually blamin' somebody else. I think people who don't like the way things are need to look at themselves first. They need to get right with God and change their own ways…. If everybody did that, we'd be all right."

Like a lot of philanthropists, Oseola McCarty knew that giving is its own pleasure. When a journalist from *People* magazine asked her why she didn't spend the money she'd saved on herself, she smiled and answered that, thanks to the pleasure that comes from making a gift, "I am spending it on myself."

"I am proud that I worked hard and that my money will help young people who worked hard to deserve it. I'm proud that I am leaving something positive in this world. My only regret is that I didn't have more to give."

Like a lot of philanthropists, McCarty hoped to inspire others to similar acts. And she did. In addition to the local outpouring that more than tripled her endowment, cable TV mogul Ted Turner decided to donate a billion dollars to charity after hearing her story. He was quoted in the *New York Times* saying, "If that little woman can give away everything she has, then I can give a billion."

And like a lot of philanthropists, Oseola McCarty knew she didn't have to save the whole world. She cast her buckets down and fixed what was at hand. "I can't do everything. But I can do something to help somebody. And what I *can* do I *will* do."

......

Oseola McCarty deserves to be recognized not only for her own accomplishments, but as a representative of millions of other everyday Americans who give humbly of themselves, year after year. There are Oseolas all across the U.S.

Gus and Marie Salenske were a plumber and nurse who lived quietly in a small house in Syracuse, New York. Their one indulgence was weekly square dancing; other than that, they were savers. When they died, it was reported in 2012, this simple couple left more than $3 million to good causes, mostly their beloved Catholic church.

Anne Scheiber was a shy auditor who retired in 1944 with just $5,000 in the bank. Through frugal living and inspired stock-picking she turned this into $22 million by the time she died in 1995 at the age of 101. She left it all to Yeshiva University so that bright but needy girls could attend college and medical school.

Minnesota farmer Harvey Ordung consumed modestly, and invested prudently. When he passed on, he left $4.5 million to 12 charities in his home region of Rock County. The largest portion went to a program that gives college scholarships to local kids.

Elinor Sauerwein painted her own home, kept a vegetable garden, and mowed the lawn herself until she was in her 90s. She eschewed restaurants, cable TV, and other expenses as unnecessary luxuries. But when she died in 2011, she left $1.7 million to the local Modesto, California, branch of the Salvation Army. "Her goal for years and years was to amass as much as she could so it would go to the Salvation Army," reported her financial adviser.

Millicent Atkins earned a teaching degree in 1940 but eventually left that profession to help manage the family farm in South Dakota. She developed a keen eye for productive land, and an appetite for buying. She eventually owned 4,127 acres. When she died in 2012 she left $38 million to two nearby universities and her church.

Albert Lexie has shined shoes in Pittsburgh for more than 50 years, and made a decision decades ago to donate every penny of his tips to the Free Care Fund of the Children's Hospital of Pittsburgh, which benefits families who can't afford treatment. Since 1981, Lexie has handed over more than $200,000 to Children's Hospital—a third of his total earnings.

Gifts like these cumulate with millions of others from ordinary Americans in a powerful way. Between 70 and 90 percent of U.S. households make charitable contributions every year, with the average household contribution being $2,500. That is *two to 20 times* as much generosity as in equivalent Western European nations. In addition, a quarter to a half of all U.S. adults volunteer their time to charitable activities at some point in a year, giving billions of hours in total.

The result: A massive charitable flow of more than $360 billion per year, with 81 percent coming from generous individuals. Only 14 percent of all annual charity in the U.S. comes in the form of foundation grants. Just 5 percent is contributed by corporations.

One may quite accurately say that it is Oseola McCarty and similarly modest partners who make America the most generous nation on earth.

☞ *Karl Zinsmeister*

Further reading

○ "Oral history with Miss Oseola McCarty," University of Southern Mississippi Center for Oral History and Cultural Heritage (1997), lib.usm.edu/legacy/spcol/coh/cohmccartyo.html

○ *New York Times* reporting, nytimes.com/1995/08/13/us/all-she-has-150000-is-going-to-a-university.html

○ *Oseola McCarty's Simple Wisdom for Rich Living*, edited by Shannon Maggio (Longstreet Press, 1996)

NETTIE MCCORMICK

Nancy ("Nettie") Fowler McCormick never expected to lead a life of ease. Orphaned at age 7, she learned early on to make the most of her days. Her firm moral purpose continued to steer her through life, even after her marriage to one of the wealthiest men in American history, Cyrus McCormick, inventor of the mechanical reaper.

Nettie was born in 1835, the youngest of three children. Her father was a dry-goods merchant in northwestern New York. After he died, her mother ran the business until her own death a few years later. At that point, the little girl was sent to live with her uncle and grandmother—both devout Methodists and generous givers in their community.

These early tragedies, combined with her subsequent upbringing, did much to shape her future philanthropy. Raised to be a faithful Methodist, she felt responsibility to God to be a good steward of her resources and time on earth. The young Nettie once wrote in her diary, "Usefulness is the great thing in life—to do something for others leaves a sweeter odor than a life of pleasure."

Her uncle Eldridge Merick's prosperity afforded new opportunities for young Nettie. His involvement in the church and community and his keen business sense had a prevailing influence on his niece, and his wealth provided her the opportunity for further education and training. Nettie attended Falley Seminary in Fulton, Emma Willard's Troy Female Seminary, and the Genesee Wesleyan Seminary in Lima, New York. As a student at Genesee Wesleyan, Nettie took on a leading role in the school's missionary society and was honored by the school as a lifetime member.

> McCormick held that any gift should have a moral purpose, provide a spiritual or educational benefit, and enable the recipients to better themselves.

At the age of 21, while on a trip to visit friends in Chicago, Nettie met Cyrus McCormick, an inventor, businessman, and faithful Presbyterian. McCormick was over twice her age when the two began courting, and the couple married a year later, in 1858. Both were strong-willed individuals, and their marriage was by many accounts a challenging one. Nevertheless, it proved to be a formidable business partnership. Nettie was her husband's closest business associate.

She was also active in their joint philanthropic activities. They directed most of their charitable giving to religious organizations, usually churches and schools. McCormick gave away $550,000 in his lifetime to the Presbyterian Church, McCormick Theological Seminary, and other church colleges.

In October 1871, the Great Chicago Fire destroyed the McCormick Harvesting Machine plant. Then aged 62, Cyrus was ready to retire. Nettie, however, devoted her considerable energy to rebuilding the business. She oversaw the construction of the new plant, and formed the reorganized International Harvester Company. She was the untitled director and president of the company until her husband's death in 1884.

Nettie McCormick faithfully followed the directions of her husband's will, which stated that she and Cyrus Jr. were to keep the estate intact for five years and make donations to charitable purposes that they believed Cyrus Sr. would have made if he was still living. Then she turned her attention to her own philanthropic causes.

She felt strongly that any gift she made should have a moral purpose, provide a spiritual or educational benefit, and enable the recipients to better themselves. Over time, her focus broadened to a greater variety of institutions but her pattern of giving to education, youth, and religious institutions remained. Orphanages, schools, colleges, hospitals, and relief agencies were all beneficiaries of her generosity, and she supported causes at home and abroad. She gave gifts to institutions such as Moody Bible Institute and Princeton University. She helped establish hospitals in Persia and Siam, and gave large gifts to religious colleges overseas, including Alborz College in Tehran and a theological seminary in Korea.

Nettie carefully managed her giving and investments. At Tusculum College in Tennessee, she helped select faculty, devise curricular offerings, and appoint a new college president. Among her many charitable projects at the school, Nettie spearheaded the construction of a new women's dormitory, named for her daughter Virginia McCormick. Nettie gave specific stipulations as to how her money was to be spent on this project, and she oversaw the building process, even choosing the architect, to ensure that Tusculum had a fully modern facility for women. As a result, the school's enrollment of female students jumped from nine to 102. To this day, Tusculum holds a Nettie Fowler McCormick Service Day, focused on charitable works and improvement of the school grounds.

Upon her death in 1923, the obituary in the *Chicago Daily Tribune*, giving evidence of her private nature, grossly underestimated the scope of her philanthropy. It credited her with supporting six schools, whereas she is known to have been a major funder of at least 46 schools, and possibly more. Over the course of her life, Nettie McCormick gave away millions of dollars without expecting or wanting any recognition—in this life, at least.

☞ *Kari Barbic*

Further reading

○ Charles Burgess, *Nettie Fowler McCormick: Profile of an American Philanthropist* (State Historical Society of Wisconsin, 1962)

○ Stella Roderick, *Nettie Fowler McCormick* (Richard R. Smith Co., 1956)

ANDREW MELLON

Andrew Mellon was one of the most prominent financiers in American history. Mellon investments helped launch the aluminum, coke, and carborundum industries; by the 1920s, he paid the third-highest income tax in the United States. Mellon dedicated his fortune to several favored charitable causes, including the University of Pittsburgh and what became Carnegie Mellon University. But Mellon also loved art, and was, in effect, an artist in the field of philanthropy. Nowhere is this clearer than in his crafting of one of the world's great museums: the National Gallery of Art.

Mellon's key insight was that charity differs only somewhat from for-profit business. He therefore applied his own business principles to the shaping of his charitable gifts. Mellon principles were, in no particular order: Compete with the private sector, and honor it. Forget your ego. Ruthlessly exploit the mechanism of compounding. Always go up-market. To these fundamentals, Mellon added a final principle: When in doubt, make it marble.

After great success as a Pittsburgh banker and industrialist, Andrew Mellon came to Washington, D.C., in 1921, to serve as Secretary of the Treasury for President Warren Harding. Harding died in office, but Mellon stayed, serving first Calvin Coolidge and then Herbert Hoover as the Treasury Secretary. During this time, he settled on the contribution he wanted to make to the nation's capital: a grand art gallery.

The need was clear. Anyone strolling past the random ramshackle structures on Pennsylvania Avenue would see that Washington fell short of other national capitals in welcoming visitors with dignified edifices and inspiring attractions. Officials had ambitious plans for what we now know as the Federal Triangle, where the National Mall was to be fringed with architecture that would boast "the glory of Washington."

Mellon's aim was more than aesthetic. Many of the structures rising across Washington were monuments to government. Mellon thought private effort should help create a prominent landscape on the National Mall itself.

The art gallery Mellon envisioned would reinforce points he had made in his efforts at the Department of the Treasury. He warned that vigorous taxation snatched productive capital from the hands of private citizens who would have employed it to create compound gains. Leaving more cash in private coffers, he argued, would in the end benefit the public better than immediate federal outlays. The gallery would be a monument to the power of private investment, creation, and societal benefit.

In the 1930s, while President Franklin Roosevelt was assigning the private sector more blame than praise, Mellon offered the nation a gift from the fruits of private enterprise: a stunning assemblage of 152 works, with an offer to build a museum on the Mall worthy to house them. Construction began in 1937, and Mellon spent an extra $5 million on pink Tennessee marble—an order so large it constituted, in Depression time, an economic stimulus all by itself. Few other expenses were spared at the gallery, whose architectural details gave much thought to citizen comfort. Understanding that some tourists would have difficulty handling stairs, for instance, Mellon kept his structure as horizontal as possible.

It was in amassing the content of the gallery that Mellon's intelligence and cunning most exerted itself. Crossing the globe with the opportunistic eye of an eagle, Mellon grabbed up value where he found it, including in Lenin's Bolshevik Russia. Some have said his large purchases from Petersburg's Hermitage Museum made Mellon more buzzard than eagle, but the Pennsylvania banker classed his acquisitions differently. Lenin and the communists stole art from owners and denigrated the processes that produced it, Mellon believed, so preserving and displaying the works respectfully in the United States for all people to enjoy was both wise and fair.

As with the construction materials, so with the content: Mellon chose only top paintings for his gallery, like the Alba Madonna of Raphael, and Pietro Perugino's triptych. With fewer than 200 such objects meeting this standard, Mellon thus "had an art museum six blocks long on his hands, and enough paintings to decorate a good-sized duplex apartment," as critic S. N. Behrman quoted a Mellon friend saying. Mellon was wagering that if he gave samples of the highest quality work from many periods, he would provide the seeds for an eventual full collection. His gift would draw other gifts.

> Mellon offered the nation a stunning assemblage of artworks, then built a museum on the National Mall worthy to house them.

And he was right. By the time President Roosevelt dedicated the gallery in 1941, several other great business leaders—Samuel Kress, Joseph Widener, and Lessing Rosenwald—had already made major contributions. Mellon's inspiration eventually drew one donor who all philanthropists hope will follow them: his own son. Paul Mellon's 1999 bequest of 100 pictures and $75 million was the largest gift ever offered to the National Gallery.

The National Gallery was an immediate success. Ready by wartime, it provided a welcome refuge to soldiers on leave, and a haven to many seeking beauty and peace in a world lacking both. Even President Roosevelt, author of so many tax increases, could not hide his enthusiasm at Mellon's gift. "The giver of this building has matched the richness of his gift with the modesty of his spirit, stipulating that the gallery shall be known not by his name but by the nation's," said Roosevelt at the opening. "And those other collectors of paintings and of sculpture who have already joined, or who propose to join, their works of art to Mr. Mellon's…have felt the same desire to establish, not a memorial to themselves, but a monument to the art that they love and the country to which they belong."

— *Amity Shlaes*

Further reading

- David Cannadine, *Mellon: An American Life* (Alfred Knopf, 2006)
- David Finley, *A Standard of Excellence: Andrew W. Mellon Founds the National Gallery of Art at Washington* (Smithsonian, 1973)
- Amity Shlaes, *The Forgotten Man: A New History of the Great Depression* (Harper, 2007)

J. P. MORGAN

John Pierpont Morgan ranks among the preeminent financiers in American history. He was born in 1837 and raised in Hartford, Connecticut, heir to two of New England's most distinguished families. Educated in Boston, Switzerland, and Germany, he was groomed by his father for a career in international finance. In 1857 Morgan went to work in London at his father's bank. He moved to New York a year later, where he was based until his death in 1913.

Morgan was a central figure in many of the most important transactions of the Industrial Revolution. He was an active investor in railroads, reorganizing the Albany & Susquehanna (1869), the New York Central (1885), the Philadelphia & Reading (1886), and the Chesapeake & Ohio (1888). In 1892, Morgan arranged the merger of Edison General Electric and Thomson-Houston Electric, leading to the creation of General Electric. In 1901, he led the consolidation of Carnegie Steel Company with several other similar concerns, creating history's first billion-dollar corporation in U.S. Steel. When a financial panic gripped Wall Street in October 1907, Morgan took charge, convincing New York bankers and businessmen to pledge their own assets to provide liquidity to the faltering financial system. Thanks to his intervention, the crisis was averted, and by November financial markets returned to relative stability.

Morgan was among the most maligned of the so-called "robber barons." He is remembered as a beefy, red-faced bully, fierce and lonely, possessed of small ideas and consumed by enormous greed. All of this is deeply unfair to Morgan. Recent biographers—most notably Jean Strouse—have looked at Morgan with fresh eyes, finding a much more subtle and interesting character than his caricature would allow. He was a genuine polymath, fluent in French and German, steeped in literature and the arts, whose aptitude for mathematics prompted one of his professors at the University of Göttingen to encourage him to consider an academic appointment. He was remarkably generous, and devoted his considerable wealth and energy to a few favored causes.

At the turn of the century, Morgan was America's greatest patron of the fine arts. He began collecting art while touring Rome, not long after finishing at Göttingen at the age of 19. It was the start of a lifelong love affair. He was the driving force behind the rise of the Metropolitan Museum of Art, serving as president and donating extensively from his personal acquisitions. His reputation, however, was established by a bitter enemy, the artist and critic Roger Fry. Fry belonged to the Bloomsbury Set, and had once been a curator of paintings at the Met. He suspected—not without reason—that Morgan was behind his firing. "A crude historical imagination," Fry icily pronounced, "was the only flaw in his otherwise perfect insensibility."

> J. P. Morgan was America's greatest patron of the fine arts in the early twentieth century.

As Strouse notes, the letters Fry wrote to his wife during a purchasing tour of Europe in 1907 tell a rather different story. They praise at surprising length the artistic sensibilities of the "Big Man." Contemporary critics increasingly agree with this pre-embittered assessment. "Almost single-handed, Morgan turned the Metropolitan from a merely notable collection into one of the three or four finest anywhere," writes historian Paul Johnson. "Morgan obviously employed experts…but it is astonishing how few mistakes he allowed them to make on his behalf."

Morgan was a man of truly catholic charitable interests. In addition to his lifelong engagement with the arts, he was deeply interested in the natural sciences. A trustee of the American Museum of Natural History for 44 years, Morgan served on the board from the museum's opening in 1869 until his death in 1913. He was often the museum's lead donor—frequently giving under condition of anonymity—and he served at various times as vice president, treasurer, and finance committee chairman. Among his many contributions to the museum, notes Strouse, were "collections of minerals, gems, meteorites, amber, books, prehistoric South American relics, American Indian costumes, fossil vertebrates, skeletons, and the mummy of a pre-Columbian miner preserved in copper salts."

Third among Morgan's great philanthropic interests was the Episcopal Church. Throughout his working life, he set aside three weeks every third year to meet with Episcopalian bishops and discuss theology. He served as treasurer and senior warden at St. George's Episcopal Church. In 1886, he was appointed to a committee responsible for revising the Book of Common Prayer, which, writes Strouse, "he knew practically by heart." He quietly underwrote the salaries of scores of Manhattan clergymen and contributed heavily—$500,000 in 1892 alone—to the construction of Manhattan's (as-yet unfinished) Cathedral of St. John the Divine.

Morgan was born in 1837, a year after the Second Bank of the United States lost its charter; he died in 1913, a few months before the creation of the Federal Reserve Bank. In his lifetime, there was no central bank. That role was filled, with considerable moral seriousness, by Morgan himself. Perhaps the least noted but most enduring testament to his public-spiritedness was how little he abused that trust. When Morgan died, the newspapers estimated the value of his estate at about $80 million (or about $1.7 billion in 2011), a fraction of the wealth of the businessmen he financed. ("And to think," marveled John Rockefeller upon learning the news, "he wasn't even a rich man!") For Morgan, finance and philanthropy were different, but never opposite, forms of service.

☞ *Christopher Levenick*

Further reading

○ Jean Strouse, *Morgan: American Financier* (Random House, 1999)
○ Ron Chernow, *The House of Morgan: American Banking Dynasty and the Rise of Modern Finance* (Atlantic Monthly Press, 1990)
○ Frederick Lewis Allen, *The Great Pierpont Morgan* (Harper Brothers, 1949)

JOHN OLIN

John Olin was an entrepreneur and industrialist who went on to become one of the twentieth century's most influential philanthropists in public policy.

Olin was born in 1892, in Alton, Illinois, the son of a businessman who owned a gunpowder mill. He attended Cornell University, majoring in chemistry. Upon his graduation in 1913, Olin joined the family business, which had grown into the Western Cartridge Company, a maker of ammunition.

Dan Weiner / gettyimages

Early on, Olin showed a flair for developing new products. Twenty-four patents bear his name, all for arms and ammunition manufacture and design. His best-known innovation was the Super-X shotgun shell, which extended firing range and became popular among hunters.

Olin's real genius, however, was in finance and executive leadership. During the Depression, his company acquired Winchester Repeating Arms. In 1938, Olin helped build the large St. Louis Ordnance Ammunition Plant. When the Second World War erupted, his family firm, rechristened Olin Industries, became a major provider of ammunition to U.S. and allied forces.

After the war, the company expanded into chemical production and other areas. Olin was fiercely competitive: "Show me a good loser and I'll show you a loser," he liked to say. In 1957, *Fortune* ranked Olin and his brother Spencer at #31 on its list of the wealthiest Americans, estimating their net worth at $75 million.

In his spare time, Olin was an avid sportsman. He was featured as a hunter on the cover of the November 17, 1958 edition of *Sports Illustrated*. In 1974, his horse, Cannonade, won the Kentucky Derby.

The John M. Olin Foundation was started in 1953. For several years, it was a conventional rich man's philanthropy, supporting

> Olin decided to use his fortune to defend America's tradition of free enterprise and individual liberty.

the Cornell University Alumni Fund and several other causes. By 1973, however, Olin decided on a special mission: "I would like to use this fortune to help to preserve the system which made its accumulation possible in only two lifetimes, my father's and mine," he told Frank O'Connell, a company employee who coordinated foundation activities in the 1970s. Olin decided to deploy his money to defend America's tradition of free enterprise and individual liberty, and bring its benefits to as many Americans as possible.

Over the next three decades, the Olin Foundation dispensed hundreds of millions of dollars to scholars, think tanks, publications, and other entities. Its savvy underwriting shaped the direction and aided the growth of the modern conservative movement that first sprang into visibility in the 1980s. Perhaps more than any other philanthropist of the modern era, Olin succeeded by clearly defining a mission (he was as clear about what he did *not* want to do as what he hoped to achieve), establishing a timeline, and carefully selecting dedicated partners who shared his vision.

In 1977, Olin stepped down as his foundation's president. William E. Simon, the former U.S. Secretary of the Treasury, replaced him, leading the foundation until his death in 2000, when he was succeeded by James Piereson, the foundation's longtime executive director. Another executive director, Michael Joyce, influenced the foundation in its early years, before joining the Lynde & Harry Bradley Foundation, which became a significant force with many of the same goals as the Olin Foundation. Irving Kristol, the neoconservative writer and intellectual, was an important influence on all of these men.

One of the Olin Foundation's signal achievements was the establishment of law and economics centers at major colleges and universities. A brand-new discipline that brought empirical rigor and clear-eyed assessment to the understanding of governance and the solving of social problems, programs in law and economics gained firm footholds after the foundation started devoting more resources to that cause than any other. The law schools at the University of Chicago, Harvard, Stanford, Virginia, and Yale started law and economics centers in Olin's name.

In 1982, the Olin Foundation sponsored a seminal academic conference for law students and professors that gave rise to the Federalist Society, a membership organization of conservative and libertarian law students, lawyers, judges, and professors. The Federalist Society would go on to transform legal education and shape the federal judiciary.

Olin also became a backer of alternative campus newspapers at colleges where right-of-center perspectives of various sorts were missing, or even blocked, from public debate. The foundation also supported pioneering researchers, journalists, and public intellectuals in producing influential new arguments and books. These included Allan Bloom (author of *The Closing of the American Mind*), Linda Chavez (*Out of the Barrio*), Dinesh D'Souza (*Illiberal Education*), Milton Friedman (*Free to Choose*), Francis Fukuyama (*The End of History?*), Samuel Huntington (*The Clash of Civilizations*), Richard John Neuhaus (*The Naked Public Square*), and Michael Novak (*The Spirit of Democratic Capitalism*). Olin funding was often aimed more at generating constructive debate than in promoting particular points of view: Fukuyama and Huntington, for instance, were friendly rivals on vital questions about the nature of global conflict.

Organizations that relied on Olin support as they grew into important roles in American intellectual life and policy debates included the American Enterprise Institute, Center for Individual Rights, Heritage Foundation, Hoover Institution, Manhattan Institute, National Association of Scholars, *New Criterion*, The Philanthropy Roundtable, and many others. Olin research funding was crucial in launching new analyses that ended up driving consequential national reform movements in areas like school choice, welfare reform, and colorblind public policy.

Olin was also distinctive in how he organized his philanthropy. Before he died in 1982, he instructed his foundation to spend itself out of existence within a generation of his passing. Having observed the spectacle of the Ford Foundation turning against what many took to be the purposes of its founding family, Olin wanted to make sure his own foundation remained true to its mission. He believed a preordained lifespan was the best protection against wandering goals at a foundation, and a disconnection from the donor's intent.

Robust investment gains complicated Olin's objective of dispersing all of its funding relatively quickly. At the same time, this endowment growth and the determination to move all money out the door in a limited timespan gave the foundation the means to have an even larger effect during its operating years. This was magnified by a disciplined focus on doing a limited number of things very well in the realm of public policy, and a decision to support a limited number of the most effective entities, rather than dispersing grants far and wide.

By early in the twenty-first century, the Olin Foundation was issuing a series of large "termination grants" to proven recipients. In 2005, the foundation held its final board meeting, completed its last round of grantmaking decisions, and closed its doors.

↳ *John J. Miller*

Further reading

○ John J. Miller, *A Gift of Freedom: How the John M. Olin Foundation Changed America* (Encounter Books, 2006)

RAYMOND ORTEIG

Raymond Orteig was an early twentieth-century French-American hotelier, aviation enthusiast, and philanthropist. The scale of his charitable giving was not especially impressive, but Orteig's philanthropy was enormously consequential. He funded an innovative incentive prize that inspired Charles Lindbergh to make the first New York-to-Paris airplane flight. Decades later, it would directly inspire other incentive prizes, including the one that launched a new era of non-governmental manned space flight.

Born in 1870 in a shepherd community in the French Pyrenees, Orteig immigrated to the United States at the age of 12. He took a job as a bar porter in New York City, making $2 per week, and soon found work at the

Hotel Martin in Greenwich Village. Orteig worked his way up in the hotel, serving as waiter, head waiter, and hotel manager, and by 1902 he had saved up enough money to buy the hotel. He renamed it the Hotel Lafayette in honor of the Marquis de Lafayette, the young French nobleman who served as George Washington's aide-de-camp. Soon thereafter, he acquired a second property, the Brevoort Hotel in Greenwich Village.

Orteig's properties were jovial places, overseen by the short and bald bon vivant. They were particular favorites of French airmen who steamed over to the United States in the years after the First World War. Aviation was a young and risky field, and Orteig was captivated by the aviators' war stories. "He developed a serious passion for aviation, dreaming of the good that air travel could do and wanting to find a way to help progress along," write Peter Diamandis and Steven Kotler. In 1919—inspired by news of a nonstop flight from Newfoundland to Ireland and impassioned by the fellow-feeling among American and French flying aces—Orteig wrote to the Aero Club of America: "Gentlemen, as a stimulus to courageous aviators, I desire to offer, through the auspices and regulations of the Aero Club of America, a prize of $25,000 to the first aviator of any Allied country crossing the Atlantic in one flight from Paris to New York or New York to Paris, all other details in your care."

> This small businessman and aviation enthusiast donated the funds for a philanthropic prize that ushered in a new era of change.

The distance, 3,600 miles, was twice that of the longest previous nonstop flight. At first, Orteig's prize seemed impossible. After five years it remained unclaimed; Orteig renewed his offer. But the incentive prize spurred technological improvements, and aviators were determined to capture the purse. (Six men died in various failed attempts.)

On May 20, 1927, Charles Lindbergh took off from Roosevelt Field on Long Island in pursuit of the award. Some 33 hours later, he landed the *Spirit of St. Louis* at Paris's Le Bourget airfield. Orteig was vacationing in France and rushed immediately to Paris, where he met Lindbergh and arranged for the purse to be awarded. He later treasured the endorsed and canceled check as one of his proudest possessions.

To be sure, the idea of an incentive prize was not unprecedented. In 1714, the British Parliament created a Longitude Prize, to be awarded to anyone who devised a simple method by which ships at sea could determine their longitude within 60 nautical miles. But Orteig's was among the first incentive prizes offered by a private individual. And it encouraged enormous innovation. By some estimates, the purse sparked $16 of investments in new technologies for every dollar the giver had offered.

"The Orteig Prize captured the world's attention and ushered in an era of change," write Diamandis and Kotler. "A landscape of daredevils and barnstormers was transformed into one of pilots and passengers. In 18 months, the number of paying U.S. passengers grew thirtyfold.... The number of pilots in the United States tripled. The number of airplanes quadrupled."

"Orteig-inspired madness" is how historian Joe Jackson dubbed the 12 years of extraordinary aviation progress after Lindbergh won the Orteig Prize. Hawaii was reached by an airplane in 1927. The U.S.-to-Australia route was flown in 1928. Amelia Earhart became the first woman to fly solo across the Atlantic in 1932. Patents were awarded for jet engine designs, and rocket-fueled aviation was tested. Delta and American Airlines date to this era. In the summer of 1939, Pan Am launched the first regular passenger service from the U.S. across the Atlantic on its Boeing "flying boats."

Although Orteig himself flew regularly in the U.S., he never flew across the Atlantic. He made his annual summer sojourn to his native France by ship. Twenty years after he helped launched a new era in travel and innovation, the hotelier died in 1939.

Orteig's incentive prize, however, has outlived him in influence. His achievement was the direct inspiration for the X Prizes created by Peter Diamandis. The initial X Prize, funded by the Ansari family, offered $10 million to the first non-governmental team to launch a reusable three-person manned spacecraft into space twice within two weeks. With funding from Microsoft co-founder Paul Allen, Burt Rutan's SpaceShipOne took home the X Prize in 2004.

In the 1920s, Raymond Orteig's philanthropy opened the skies over the Atlantic. Nearly 80 years later, its echo opened the heavens to private spaceflight. Thus did the one-time porter inspire a new generation of humans to go aloft.

— *Evan Sparks*

Further reading

- Richard Bak, *The Big Jump: Lindbergh and the Great Atlantic Air Race* (John Wiley, 2011)
- Peter Diamandis and Steven Kotler, *Abundance: The Future Is Better Than You Think* (Free Press, 2012)
- Joe Jackson, *Atlantic Fever: Lindbergh, His Competitors, and the Race to Cross the Atlantic* (MacMillan, 2012)

DAVID PACKARD

David Packard was the co-founder of Hewlett-Packard, a pioneering business that accelerated America's computer revolution. He was also a prominent public servant, and a major funder of conservation efforts, public-policy think tanks, and his alma mater, Stanford University.

Packard was born in Pueblo, Colorado, in 1912. From a young age, he was fascinated by science. Relying on the *World Book Encyclopedia*, he dabbled in chemistry, cooking up his own homemade explosives—until he nearly blew off his left thumb. Young David then shifted to tinkering with homemade crystal-radio sets. By the time he was in high school, the six-foot-five Packard stood out for his athletic prowess—he lettered in football, basketball, and track—and his academic achievement.

In 1930, Packard began his freshman year at Stanford University. (During the lean years of the Great Depression, his father managed the quarterly tuition of $114 thanks to one of the era's few steady jobs: bankruptcy referee.) At Stanford, Packard had a remarkably rounded college career. He won three varsity letters in his first year. He studied engineering under Fred Terman, a relentless innovator whose research on vacuum tubes, circuits, and radios helped establish the field of electrical engineering. Under Terman's mentorship, Packard dropped basketball and track (but not football, he later explained, because of "peer pressure") and devoted most of his attention to his studies.

Packard excelled academically, and met his future business partner at Stanford, William Hewlett, another of Terman's students. He also met his future wife, Lucile Salter, while he was washing dishes at the Delta Gamma sorority. They married in 1938, forming a bond that lasted until her death in 1987, producing one son and three daughters. After graduation, Packard worked briefly for General Electric in Schenectady, New York, before returning to Stanford to earn a master's degree in electrical engineering in 1938.

Just as some American presidents were born in one-room log cabins, so too have some iconic American corporations been launched in one-car garages. One of the greatest of these is Hewlett-Packard, a pioneer in personal and business computers, and among the largest manufacturers of electronics in the world. It was founded in 1939 in Palo Alto, California, by Hewlett and Packard with an initial investment of $538. When the company incorporated in 1947, they tossed a coin to decide its name. Packard won the toss and put Hewlett's name first. It was that sort of partnership.

Having set up business in Packard's garage, Hewlett and Packard's first product was an innovative audio oscillator, a device for testing and synchronizing sound equipment. At the time, precision audio oscillators sold for over $200, but they introduced a temperature-dependent resistor that greatly improved stability. The two amateur history buffs decided to charge $54.40, after the 1844 Democratic rallying cry, "Fifty-four Forty or Fight!" Walt Disney bought eight of the oscillators for use in the production of *Fantasia*. The partners never looked back. In 2014, the company's net revenue was $111 billion, with 302,000 employees and an estimated 1 billion customers worldwide.

Hewlett concentrated on the product side of the business while Packard tended to the business side, where he ran a famously tight ship. (When Hewlett-Packard went public in 1961, several executives missed the ceremony at the New York Stock Exchange because they got lost on the subway on the way down from their midtown hotel. Their expense accounts didn't cover taxis, let alone limousines.) Packard stayed with the company he founded the rest of his life, except for two years (1969-1971) when he served as Deputy Secretary of Defense. He remained remarkably forward-looking throughout his business career; it was Packard who decided in 1986 to register the domain name HP.com, fully a decade before the Internet became commercially important.

> The Packards became generous givers, and then left the bulk of their $4 billion estate to philanthropy.

Packard's contributions to corporate America are well-known; his beneficence as a philanthropist, perhaps less so. That is unfortunate, not least because of the scale of his giving. He and his wife established the David and Lucile Packard Foundation, to which he left the bulk of his $4 billion estate. Moreover, the Packards were notable givers during their lifetimes.

Environmental conservation in general, and marine conservation in particular, was a lifelong concern for Packard. Perhaps the most conspicuous result of Packard's conservation giving is the Monterey Bay Aquarium, visited by 1.8 million people annually. Located on the site of an old California sardine cannery that had been featured in two of John Steinbeck's novels, it ranks among the world's largest aquariums. At the 1984 opening, Packard credited two of his daughters who studied marine biology—Nancy and Julie (Julie remains executive director of the aquarium)—with fanning his interest in the project.

Packard invested himself in the aquarium. Before beginning, he studied other successful models. "What we learned," he explained in a 1985 interview, "was that most aquariums are built on a fixed budget, and they made short cuts." Not so Packard. ("The result was that the aquarium cost us $40 million instead of $10 million," he added.) The aquarium has spectacular exhibits, including a live California kelp forest, made possible by pumps that circulate 2,000 gallons per minute of ocean water from Monterey Bay. Naturally, Packard designed the wave machine that keeps the kelp undulating. "My children thought we shouldn't charge admission so that poor people could come," he later said. "I said we weren't going to do it that way. If what we did was right, people will pay for it. If it wasn't right, we shouldn't have done it."

David Packard, who flourished so abundantly in the American capitalist system, was a firm believer in the power of free markets to enrich society as a whole. He served for years on the boards of the Hoover Institution, the Herbert Hoover Foundation, and the American Enterprise Institute. He was an enthusiastic patron of each, reported *Philanthropy* magazine in 2000, "donating his time, talents, and fortune to their success." When AEI hit financial trouble in the early 1980s, Packard "helped very significantly with his finances and his advice," according to former AEI president Christopher DeMuth. "He bailed us out. He was a hands-on trustee, a great man."

The third principal recipient of the Packard family's generosity was Stanford University. In 1986, David and Lucile Packard donated $40 million to found the Lucile Packard Children's Hospital located in Palo Alto, which opened in 1991, four years after her death. It is regarded as one of the best pediatric hospitals in the country, with a physician staff of 650. In 1996, it merged with the Stanford Medical Center.

Packard funded three professorships at his alma mater, in engineering, marine science, and literature. He also funded everything from sports facilities to the Terman Fellowships—named in honor of his old Stanford mentor to provide financial support to young science and engineering professors. In 1994, Packard partnered with Hewlett to donate $77 million to the school to build the David Packard Electrical Engineering Building next to the William Hewlett Teaching Center.

Altogether Packard and Hewlett, jointly and separately, donated more than $300 million to Stanford. As the university put it on his death, "Dave Packard, along with his wife, Lucile, and his partner, Bill Hewlett, have shaped and nurtured this university in ways that can only be compared to the founders, Jane and Leland Stanford."

"Everywhere I look I see the potential for growth, for discovery far greater than anything we have seen in the twentieth century," reflected David Packard in 1995, a year before he died. All mankind needed, he believed, was determination. "The state of change is proportional to the level of effort expended."

— *John Steele Gordon*

Further reading

○ *Philanthropy* magazine article, philanthropyroundtable.org/topic/excellence_in_philanthropy/the_new_packard

○ David Packard, *The HP Way: How Bill Hewlett and I Built Our Company* (HarperBusiness, 1995)

○ Christophe Lécuyer, *Making Silicon Valley: Innovation and the Growth of High Tech, 1930-1970* (MIT Press, 1996)

GEORGE PEABODY

George Peabody is often referred to as the "father of modern philanthropy." It is believed that Peabody gave away about $8 million of his $16 million fortune within his lifetime. Peabody's generosity was hailed as an example for his contemporaries, and later generations of philanthropists have continued to invoke it.

Peabody was born in 1795, the third of eight children in a working-poor family from Danvers (since renamed Peabody), Massachusetts. His family could only afford to give him four years of formal schooling; at age 11, he was sent to apprentice at a general store. In 1811, his father died, in debt, forcing the sale of the family home and many of its belongings. George and his brothers had to feed, house, and clothe their mother and sisters. "I have never forgotten," he once reflected, "and never can forget the great privations of my early years."

Peabody moved south to Washington, D.C., where he opened a dry-goods store in Georgetown. He served in the army during the War of 1812, where he met an older merchant named Elisha Riggs Sr. The two men hit it off, and Riggs offered to make Peabody, then 19 years old, a partner at his business, importing wholesale dry goods. The business flourished, and within three years, Peabody was worth $40,000, repaying his father's debts and providing a more comfortable life for his family.

In 1816, Peabody left D.C. and moved to Baltimore, where he spent the next two decades. Trusted for his fairness, Peabody prospered as a wholesale-goods merchant, and by 1827 was traveling to London to negotiate the sale of American cotton in Lancashire. In 1835, he established George Peabody & Co., a merchant bank offering securities in American enterprises—railroads, canals—to British and European investors.

His bank became one of the most important of his era, channeling much-needed British and European capital into promising ventures in the booming U.S. Given his rising stature among international bankers and London's unmatched centrality in the world of finance, Peabody moved to that city in 1837. Except for three visits back to the States, he remained in England for the rest of his life.

But there was never any mistaking his first loyalties. His Fourth of July parties were a highlight of the London social calendar. But Peabody's patriotism went deeper than that. He put his reputation on the line during the Panic of 1837, pledging creditors that the states he represented would not default on their loan obligations—even securing an emergency $8 million loan to save Maryland's credit. Peabody refused the $60,000 commission for his services. The Maryland state treasury, he insisted, needed to pay bondholders first. When several states did default, Peabody moved heaven and earth to persuade their legislatures to resume payment, with interest.

> Both in the scope of his giving and in the care and precision with which he targeted it, George Peabody was the "father of modern philanthropy."

George Peabody never quite escaped the marks of his boyhood poverty. He routinely worked ten-hour days, every day of the week, and during one 12-year stretch he never took off three consecutive days. He was frugal to the point of absurdity. His partner, Junius Morgan (father of J. Pierpont Morgan, who began his distinguished career in finance at the New York office of George Peabody), once found him standing in a drenching London rain. Morgan knew that Peabody had left the office 20 minutes earlier and stated, "Mr. Peabody, I thought you were going home." "Well, I am, Morgan," Peabody replied, "but there's only been a twopenny bus come along as yet and I am waiting for a penny one." At the time, Peabody had more than £1 million to his name, according to Ron Chernow.

In the early 1850s, Peabody's interests began to turn to philanthropy. For his Massachusetts hometown's 1852 centennial celebration he announced his plans to build the first Peabody Institute Library. The gift was followed by a number of similar benefactions throughout the United States. In 1857, he founded the Peabody Institute of Baltimore, which included a music conservatory, art gallery, lecture hall, and reference library. (It remains one of America's great music schools.) He built other Peabody Institute Libraries in Massachusetts, Vermont, and Washington, D.C. After a favorite nephew began teaching paleontology at

Yale, Peabody funded a museum of archaeology and ethnology at Harvard and a museum of natural history at Yale.

In 1862 Peabody wrote a letter to the *Times* of London announcing his intention to create an endowment, initially stacked with £150,000 of his money, to "ameliorate the condition of the poor and needy of this great metropolis, and to promote their comfort and happiness." The Peabody Donation Fund (since renamed the Peabody Trust) was chartered to build affordable housing for the workingmen of London. With gas lights, running water, subsidized rent, and smartly appointed dwellings, the resulting structures were vastly superior to the housing otherwise available to the laboring poor. Peabody ensured that tenants were deserving, demanding punctual rent payments, instituting a nighttime curfew and enforcing a morals code.

The gift was an instant sensation. Queen Victoria sent an adoring letter of thanks, enclosing a miniature portrait of herself and offering him a baronetcy or knighthood. (Peabody, a one-time infantryman who had borne arms against the British, declined the titles.) Peabody, proclaimed Prime Minister William Gladstone, "taught men how to use money, and how not to be its slave." He was the first American to be made Freeman of the City of London, and his statue was erected at the Royal Exchange. The gift "has repaid me for the care and anxiety of 50 years of commercial life." Peabody was so pleased with the results of his Donation Fund that, shortly before his death in 1869, he increased his total contribution to £500,000.

From 1866 to 1867, Peabody visited the United States and toured the American South. He was shocked by the war wreckage he found. Eager to help, he later announced the creation of the Peabody Education Fund, endowed with $2.1 million and charged with restoring primary and secondary education in West Virginia and 11 states of the former Confederacy. Peabody offered school seed grants to counties and districts, requiring local leaders to provide matching funds and charter the schools under state legislation. The Peabody Education Fund worked for 47 years, promoting and sustaining public schools and funding teacher-training institutes throughout the South.

Peabody's generosity endeared him to British and Americans alike, and at his death in 1869 he was honored on both sides of the Atlantic. A grave was prepared for him at Westminster Abbey—the first American to receive such honors—and it was made clear that the royal family wished to bury him in England. It was not to be. Peabody's dying words ("Danvers—Danvers! Don't forget!"), combined with the explicit instructions of his will, deprived London of his remains. Peabody was returned to his native land by a joint squadron of British and American naval vessels, where the flags of former enemies were matched at half-mast, reflecting two nations united in mourning, and in admiration.

☞ *Kari Barbic*

Further reading

○ Phebe Hanaford, *The Life of George Peabody* (B.B. Russell, 1870)

○ Muriel Hidy, *George Peabody: Merchant and Financier, 1829-1854* (Arno, 1978)

○ Franklin Parker, *George Peabody: A Biography* (Vanderbilt Press, 1995)

○ Robert Charles Winthrop, *Eulogy, Pronounced at the Funeral of George Peabody,* (John Wilson & Son, 1870)

THOMAS PERKINS

Thomas Perkins was a wealthy Boston merchant who became one of the great patrons of early nineteenth century Boston. He supported dozens of local causes and was a founder of the Massachusetts General Hospital, the Bunker Hill Monument, and the Boston Athenaeum. But he is perhaps best remembered as the benefactor of the Perkins Institution for the Blind, a school that revolutionized education for the physically handicapped.

Perkins was born in Boston in December 1764, the sixth of eight children to one of the colony's most successful wine merchants. Not long after his fifth birthday, young Thomas crouched inside his father's shop as the Boston Massacre raged outside. It marked the beginning of a turbulent time. Thomas's father died in 1773, forcing his mother, Elizabeth, to provide for the family. She opened her own merchant house, trading china, glass, and wine. She scratched together enough to send her three sons to preparatory school, hoping that they would all attend Harvard.

Thomas, however, "was strongly inclined by temperament to active life," according to a biographer. He apprenticed with Messrs. Shattuck, one of Boston's busiest counting houses. There he remained until he turned 21, at which point he joined a partnership with his two brothers, managing commerce between Boston and Santo Domingo. In February 1789, he sailed aboard the *Astraea* to the recently opened port of Canton, where he traded a cargo of cheese, lard, wine, and iron for tea and silk cloth. He threw himself into the maritime fur trade, acquiring sea otter skins from the Pacific Northwest and selling them in China. Perkins set up a trading house in Canton, from which he entered the highly profitable opium trade.

His commercial enterprises produced adventures. While fording a stream on the island of Java, Perkins saw a dozen crocodiles brush by his knees. He gambled on cock fights in Malaysia. Shortly after the Reign of Terror,

Perkins was in France, where James Monroe, Minister of the United States, asked him to perform a service for the nation. Would he, asked Monroe, smuggle the Marquis de Lafayette's son, George Washington Lafayette, to the United States? Perkins cheerfully did so, and was promptly invited to Mount Vernon where he was thanked by Washington himself.

After the turn of the nineteenth century Perkins began to spend less time abroad and more time managing his affairs from Boston. With his growing wealth came increasing civic responsibilities. He was named president of the Boston branch of the First Bank of the United States, elected to the Massachusetts State Senate, and made a colonel in the state militia. "Colonel Perkins," wrote Freeman Hunt, always took "a lively interest in all that concerned the welfare of the community in which he lived." He was an active supporter of the Mercantile Association of Young Men in Boston, the McLean Asylum for the Insane, and the Boston Museum of Fine Arts.

His first great philanthropic achievement was helping to found the Massachusetts General Hospital. In 1811, the Commonwealth granted a charter for the hospital that would take effect once the effort had raised $100,000. Perkins and his brother James each donated $5,000. By 1813, the full amount was raised

> **Perkins Institution for the Blind revolutionized education for the physically handicapped.**

and ground was broken. Perkins served on the board until 1827, including stints as president, vice president, and chairman.

Perkins was also a driving force behind the creation of the Bunker Hill Monument Association. In 1823, he hosted a breakfast at which William Ticknor suggested the memorial, and by June 1825 the Marquis de Lafayette laid the cornerstone. To haul granite from the quarry to barges on the Neponset, Perkins organized the Granite Railway, the first commercial railroad in the United States. Insufficient funds frequently interrupted construction, but Perkins guided the project until the capstone was erected in July 1842.

Perkins was not a founder of the Boston Athenaeum, but he supported it with funds and with items from his own collection. At two critical junctures, he offered donations that would allow the library and gallery to keep its doors open. In 1826, when $30,000 was needed, Perkins and his nephew each stepped forward with $8,000. Then, in 1853, after the Athenaeum incurred enormous expenses while building its current home at 10½ Beacon Street,

Perkins offered to retire whatever debt remained at the end of the year. His offer proved unnecessary (an unexpected bequest covered the shortfall) but to this day, a full-length portrait of Perkins adorns the Long Room in the ground floor entrance of the grateful Athenaeum.

Thomas Perkins may have had his biggest effect building up the Perkins School for the Blind. European schools for the blind fell into one of two camps: either vocational or academic. Under the leadership of Samuel Gridley Howe, the New England Asylum for the Blind, chartered in 1829 as the first such entity in the U.S., attempted to combine the two models: providing practical, real-world skills (weaving, pottery, and basket-making) while also cultivating the minds of the students (reading by "raised letters," as well as math, science, and literature). The concept was immediately popular, and the student body outgrew its space within a year.

Perkins, whose own eyesight was declining, took a special interest in the project. In 1833, he offered to donate his mansion on 17 Pearl Street, on one condition: that the school raise $50,000 within 30 days. The funds were collected, and the school moved into its new home, where it tripled its enrollment within six years. By 1839, it was clear that the school would need still more space. Perkins arranged the sale of the Pearl Street mansion and the purchase of the Mount Washington Hotel in South Boston, where the school remained for the next 75 years. Thankful for his sustained generosity, the school renamed itself the Perkins Institution for the Blind.

When Perkins died in 1854, a choir from the Perkins Institution sang the requiem. "Their high regard for his memory was seen," reported one newspaper, "in gleams of pleasure lighting their faces."

↳ *Christopher Levenick*

Further reading

○ Thomas Cary, *Memoir of Thomas Handasyd Perkins, Containing Extracts from His Diaries and Letters* (Little, Brown, 1856)

○ Freeman Hunt, *Lives of American Merchants* (Derby & Jackson, 1856)

○ Carl Seaburg, *Merchant Prince of Boston: Colonel T. H. Perkins* (Harvard, 1971)

J. HOWARD PEW

John Howard Pew was a successful oil entrepreneur who dedicated his philanthropy to serving the Presbyterian Church, funding higher education, and advancing the principles of a free society. Born into a devout family in 1882, the second son of the Sun Oil Company founder,

Howard graduated from Grove City College at age 18. He studied at MIT, then joined his father and older brother at Sun Oil.

Pew was a talented engineer. His father assigned him to find a use for the unwanted black residue from refining Texas crude. "The young scientist didn't disappoint his father," writes a historian of the Pew Charitable Trusts. "He developed a lubricating oil with an extremely low cooling point; it became an international success under the name Sun Red Stock. Howard's laboratory work also yielded the first commercially successful petroleum asphalt, called Hydrolene."

In 1912, Howard took over the company along with his younger brother after their father died. For 35 years, Howard presided over Sun's rise to national prominence in the oil business. Under his leadership, the firm vastly extended its interests, eventually including refineries, pipelines, oilfields, shipbuilding, and mining.

Pew had a natural instinct for anticipating current events. He prepared for the Depression's market crashes, and was proud that no Sun Oil employee was laid off or given a pay cut during the 1930s. Sensing another war in Europe, in 1933 Pew started to sell off Sun's investments on the Continent. In 1937, Pew opened the world's first large-scale, commercial catalytic cracking plant. During World War II, Sun's shipbuilding plants turned out 250 vessels—40 percent of America's tankers.

The Pews' conservative views were strengthened by the Supreme Court's 1911 decision to break up the Standard Oil Company under the Sherman Anti-Trust Act. "It reinforced their conviction that industry thrives best when markets and competition are free," writes one historian. Pew held free-market convictions throughout his life. The austere man would bristle, however, if anyone suggested that his beliefs were anything less than disinterested. He vigorously criticized the New Deal as a "government cartel" worse than any "private cartel," but he insisted that his "attack on the New Deal has not been prompted by materialistic considerations, but rather a desire to preserve in America an opportunity for coming generations." After the Second World War, Pew also opposed price controls, arguing that "free prices are the regulators of American industry."

To that end, Pew became involved in organizations that promoted free-market causes. He was a board member of the Foundation of Economic Education, led by Leonard Read (famous for his "I, Pencil" story that illustrates the working of the invisible hand). In joining FEE, Pew became part of the nexus of conservative and libertarian funders, organizations, and thinkers who helped to challenge the New Deal economic and political consensus. Pew didn't always agree with FEE's positions—he tussled with the board over FEE's anti-tariff perspective—but he found what biographer

Mary Sennholz has called "a remnant of kindred souls…who shared with him a great concern about the future of individual freedom and the private property order." Pew also supported emerging conservative think tanks, such as the Hoover Institution and the American Enterprise Institute.

Pew's philanthropy extended to other causes as well—in particular education and civic organizations. But his "most enduring object of philanthropy," as Sennholz puts it, was Grove City College, his alma mater. "I hardly remember a time when I did not know Grove City College," Pew reminisced. He joined its board in 1912, and served until his death— including four decades as chairman. Pew visited frequently, funded numerous projects on campus, and celebrated Grove City's conservative principles and reputation for independence. "To teach this appreciation of our liberty and the recognition of the forces that threaten it, will always be the foremost mission of this college," he said. Pew supported dozens of other colleges as well, especially a number of historically black universities.

> Pew helped fund organizations and thinkers who challenged the New Deal, built evangelical religious institutions, and taught the tradition of liberty on campuses.

After he left the helm of Sun Oil in 1947, Howard devoted more of his time and money to religious organizations. "In the years that followed World War II," writes historian Kim Phillips-Fein, "his most abiding preoccupation was rescuing the Protestant church in America from what he saw as the dangerous influence of liberal ministers."

A lifelong member of the mainline Presbyterian Church, Pew had a multi-pronged approach to his religious philanthropy. First, he participated in church debates, serving as president of the church's board of trustees and chair of the National Lay Committee, and opposing what he called "the same ideological mistake as was made by communism: that of attempting to change society by changing man's environment." Inspired by the Reformed doctrine that church councils should not take up secular causes, he fought church resolutions to endorse collective bargaining, promote birth control, and oppose capital punishment.

Pew also funded the then-emerging "parachurch" institutions of the evangelical movement. He gave millions to merge two seminaries to create Gordon-Conwell Theological Seminary, which is today actively evangelical and the largest seminary in the Northeast. He contributed $150,000 to launch *Christianity Today* magazine. He supported Billy Graham's ministry, the National Association of Evangelicals, and the International Congress on World Evangelization.

Finally, Pew sought to educate Christian ministers about the perils of left-wing politics, and encouraged church leaders to focus on mission and evangelizing. He helped to build up Spiritual Mobilization, which sought to counterbalance the New Deal surge toward centralization and redistribution of income. It involved business executives in lay church leadership and distributed books like F. A. Hayek's *The Road to Serfdom* to clergymen. Pew later helped to found (and contributed millions to) the Christian Freedom Foundation, which sent the *Christian Economics* newsletter twice a month to 180,000 ministers.

Pew did not achieve to his own satisfaction the goal of saving the Presbyterian Church from further decline. In his ecumenical work, however, he helped to create an evangelical infrastructure, from seminaries to publications, that would support new churches and soon eclipse the mainline in membership.

Pew and his wife, Helen, lived simply. They are said to have given 90 percent of their income away. In addition to the gifts they made during their lifetime, Pew and his brother and sisters contributed shares of Sun Oil to create the Pew Memorial Foundation, which would be dedicated to their ideals and in memory of their parents. In subsequent years, family members would establish separate funds under the umbrella of the family trust; the J. Howard Pew Freedom Trust was created in 1957. These together became known as the Pew Charitable Trusts. When Howard died in 1971, nearly all of his remaining $100 million was given to the Freedom Trust, which joined the $900 million (at the time) then held in the various other Pew trusts.

Pew gave a very specific mandate to his Freedom Trust:

> To acquaint the American people with the evils of bureaucracy and the vital need to maintain and preserve a limited form of government in the United States as intended by our forebears and expressed by them in the Constitution and the Bill of Rights—to point out the dangerous consequences that result from an exchange of our American priceless heritage of freedom and self-determination, for the false promises of socialism and a planned economy.... and to inform our people of the struggle, persecution, hardship, sacrifice and death by which freedom of the individual was won.
>
> To acquaint the American people with the values of a free market—the dangers of inflation—the need for a stable monetary

standard—the paralyzing effects of government controls on the lives and activities of people....

To promote recognition of the interdependence of Christianity and freedom and to support and expound the philosophy that we must first have faith in God before we can enjoy the blessings of liberty—for God is the author of liberty....

This charter was honored to the letter for the first few years after Pew's death, but starting in 1977 it was quickly eroded in pursuit of more conventional and left-leaning goals. Recently, the head of the Pew Charitable Trusts could only say that Howard "was a man of strong convictions and his successors on our board are following in his tradition by having strong convictions," adding that "times are different now and I don't think we really know how Howard Pew's views would have played out."

And so, despite his clear statement of philanthropic purposes, the funds Pew placed in trust are being applied to very different purposes.

⤙ Evan Sparks

Further reading

- Joel Gardner and Sue Rardin, *Sustaining the Legacy: A History of the Pew Charitable Trusts* (Pew Charitable Trusts, 2001)
- Mary Sennholz, editor, *Faith and Freedom: A Biographical Sketch of a Great American* (Grove City College, 1975)
- Martin Morse Wooster, *The Great Philanthropists and the Problem of "Donor Intent"* (Capital Research Center, 2007)

HENRY PHIPPS

Henry Phipps was a lifelong friend and business partner of Andrew Carnegie. The second-largest shareholder in Carnegie Steel, he had a brilliant mind for finance and accumulated one of the 100 largest fortunes in American history. With that wealth, Phipps built extensive public parks and conservatories throughout his hometown of Pittsburgh. He funded research into the treatment, prevention, and cure of tuberculosis, an effort which led him to create reduced-cost housing for the working poor. Perhaps most notably, he funded the creation of the country's first medical faculty in the field of psychiatry.

Born in 1839, Phipps grew up in Pittsburgh. "Harry," as he was universally called, dropped out of school at age 14, taking work as a jeweler's apprentice for $1.25 per week. At 17, he borrowed 25¢ from his brother and placed an ad in the *Pittsburg Dispatch*. It read: "A willing boy wishes work." Dilworth and Biddle, a company that made iron and railroad spikes, offered him a job as an errand boy.

"There was no holding back a boy like that," Andrew Carnegie later reflected in his autobiography. Phipps spent five years taking night courses in accounting, during which time he was made bookkeeper and not long after, partner. Thomas Miller, another childhood friend, lent Phipps $800 to invest in a new railroad equipment company, headed by Andrew Kloman. The partnership flourished and was soon investing in steel mills. In 1865, it caught the eye of Andrew Carnegie, who bought out Kloman and Phipps. It was then that Harry decided to work for his boyhood pal—a job he would hold for the next 36 years.

Phipps handled corporate finance—"he's my money-getter," Carnegie often said. Known for his calm demeanor, Phipps was a diplomat among and negotiator between increasingly fractious shareholders. (More than anyone else, Phipps ensured that Carnegie Steel held together until its merger into U.S. Steel.) When Carnegie and his partners sold the business in 1901, Phipps held 11 percent of the company's stock, second only to Carnegie's 58 percent. (Phipps's full statement to reporters: "Ain't Andy wonderful!") Phipps netted between $40 and $50 million from the sale—yet it would prove the basis for only part of his wealth. In 1907, he created a family office to oversee his fortune, which in time evolved into Bessemer Trust, now one of the nation's leading wealth managers.

Phipps dedicated the majority of his money to charity, although the full extent of his gifts will never be known. He refused all interview requests and chose to keep most of his gifts private. "Unlike Carnegie, Harry shunned all publicity about his personal life and philanthropies," notes his granddaughter.

Phipps began his efforts to beautify the city of Pittsburgh in the 1880s, donating to public parks, baths, playgrounds, and gardens. He is perhaps best remembered for creating the Phipps Conservatory in 1893, which remains to this day one of America's leading botanical gardens. In his dedication, Phipps made clear his desire to "erect something that will prove a source of instruction as well as pleasure to the people." In an unusual stipulation, he required that the conservatory be open on Sundays, so that workingmen and their families could visit on their day of rest. Local ministers denounced the proposal, but Phipps insisted on it—and ultimately won the argument.

"For my part," wrote Andrew Carnegie in *The Gospel of Wealth*, "I think Mr. Phipps put his money to better use in giving the working-men of Allegheny conservatories filled with beautiful flowers, orchids, and aquatic plants, which they, with their wives and children, can enjoy in their spare hours, and upon which they can feed their love for the beautiful, than if he had given his surplus money to furnish them with bread."

After the sale of Carnegie Steel, some of Phipps's first philanthropic projects involved improving the quality of health care for the poor. His first target: tuberculosis. In January 1903, he funded a new clinic in Philadelphia dedicated to the study, treatment, and prevention of tuberculosis. The institute, which eventually merged with the University of Pennsylvania, made special efforts to reach African Americans afflicted by the disease. Later that year, Phipps created another such institute in Baltimore, under the auspices of the Johns Hopkins Hospital. In both cases, reported the *New York Times*, "All money needed will be furnished by Mr. Phipps."

Once involved in the fight against tuberculosis, Phipps became increasingly interested in ways to improve housing for the urban working poor. In 1905, he donated $1 million to a new nonprofit to build homes for the poor in New York City. Now known as the Phipps Houses Group, this nonprofit has constructed over 6,000 apartments and for more than a century been among the city's leading affordable-housing developers.

Phipps's most enduring accomplishment may be his help in launching the academic discipline of psychiatry. In May 1908, while visiting the tuberculosis institute he had founded at the Johns Hopkins Hospital, he struck up a conversation with William Welch, dean of the medical faculty, who gave Phipps a copy of Clifford Beers's *A Mind That Found Itself.* A month later, Phipps sent Welch a letter, offering $825,000, plus $60,000 annually for a decade, to endow the Henry Phipps Psychiatric Clinic. "I understand that the building will be used both for treating and studying insanity," wrote Phipps, "and this study of dethroned minds by our finest physicians may result in great works." He remained committed to the school, funding it for the rest of his life, including a $1 million challenge grant in 1923 to improve faculty compensation and recruitment.

Phipps is one of the least-remembered great philanthropists of the early twentieth century. He sought no recognition for his philanthropy; he never endowed a foundation. But his charitable giving did real and lasting good, improving Pittsburgh civic life, exploring new ways to fight poverty, advancing medical research, providing health care to the poor, and inspiring other donors. Long before his death in 1930, he was widely admired for his decency and kindness. James Bridge, the muckraking author of a caustic account of Carnegie's rise, observed in a 1902 profile that Phipps's career "is without parallel for a man as successful as he has been: he never made an enemy, nor lost a friend."

~ *Martin Morse Wooster*

Further reading

○ Peggie Phipps Boegner and Richard Gachot, *Halcyon Days: An American Family Through Three Generations* (Harry Abrams, 1986)

○ James Bridge, *The Inside History of the Carnegie Steel Company: A Romance of Millions* (Aldine Book Company, 1903)

ENOCH PRATT

Enoch Pratt was one of nineteenth-century Maryland's most prominent businessmen. Today he is perhaps best remembered for creating a system of free lending libraries in Baltimore—a pioneering effort that set a model for his contemporaries, not least Andrew Carnegie.

Pratt was born in 1808 to a respectable middle-class family in Massachusetts, the second of eight children. His father was a successful businessman who left farming to manage a sawmill, a general store, and later a wholesale hardware business. Young Enoch learned to make nails at the little smithy in the Pratt's family kitchen.

After completing his education at Bridgewater Academy, Enoch announced himself ready for a life of business. "I suggest I am old enough to do considerable business," the 15-year-old wrote to a close family friend. "My school will be out in a fortnight and I do not want to stay at home." His friend helped young Enoch secure his first job: clerking at a wholesale hardware store. Pratt diligently saved his money, looking forward to the day when he could start his own business. At age 23, with just $150 to his name, Pratt opened a wholesale hardware business in Baltimore, the city he would call home for most of his life.

Pratt's iron business met with great success. As his fortune grew, Pratt expanded his portfolio, serving as vice president of the Philadelphia, Wilmington, & Baltimore Railroad; president of the National Farmers' and Planters' bank of Baltimore; and controlling stockholder in the Maryland Steamboat Company. Pratt matched success in business with domestic felicity. In 1837, he married Maria Hyde. It was a happy match, even though the couple was unable to have children of their own.

Pratt's philanthropy began with gifts to his church. A faithful Unitarian, he shouldered much of his church's financial burdens—paying off significant debts, buying a new organ, and remodeling the building. For more than 40 years, Pratt served as a church trustee, and on occasion as a delegate to national Unitarian conferences.

Much of Pratt's early philanthropy was similarly personal, escaping the notice of the larger public. It was a common practice, notes his biographer Richard Hart, for Pratt to come to the aid of hardworking young men "with money and good advice." He was patron to sculptor Edward Bartholomew, funding his study abroad under Italian master Ferrero. Pratt purchased many of Bartholomew's works and commissioned him to create busts and memorials throughout the city, perhaps most notably the statue of George Washington in Druid Hill Park, Baltimore's largest city park.

Later in life, Pratt became more focused on his philanthropy, with the majority of his gifts centered on the city of Baltimore. In 1870, he donated Cheltenham, a 752-acre tract of land in Prince George's county, to be used as a reform school for African-American boys. Pratt was president of the school's board for several years, and would regularly hire men who had been trained at Cheltenham to work on the grounds at his country home, Tivoli.

> Pratt created a superb free public library that became the finest in the country, inspiring other donors (including Andrew Carnegie) to likewise bring books and learning to everyday Americans.

Education was Pratt's great, lifelong interest—but, like many self-made men of his era, he did not equate education with schooling. He wanted to support those who wanted to learn, but he realized that few working people could afford to take the time to study in a formal, structured environment. For aspiring autodidacts, he found an elegant solution: the free lending library.

In 1865 Pratt expanded a school library in Massachusetts and opened it to all local citizens. He later came to believe that "a free circulating public library open to all citizens regardless of property or color" was the greatest need in his city of Baltimore. To address that need, in 1882, he offered the city his plan for a library with many local branches, plus a million-dollar endowment to operate it.

"For 15 years, I have studied the library question, and wondered what I could do with my money so that it would do the most good," he explained. "I soon made up my mind that I would not found a college—for a few rich. My library shall be for all, rich and poor without distinction of race or color, who, when properly accredited, can take out the books if they will handle them carefully and return them."

Pratt's funding established a central headquarters and four branches, and the interest on his endowment maintained the entire system. He remained an actively involved donor, took great pride in his libraries, and would frequently visit the branches. He personally escorted fellow philanthropist Andrew Carnegie on a tour of the central Baltimore library.

Andrew Carnegie took great interest in the Pratt library system, which became a model for his own program of building free lending libraries in Pittsburgh and beyond. "Many free libraries have been established in our country, but none that I know of with such wisdom as the Pratt Library in Baltimore," Carnegie wrote in *The Gospel of Wealth*. "By placing books within the reach of 37,000 people.... Mr. Pratt has done more for the genuine progress of the people than has been done by the contributions of all the millionaires and rich people to help those who cannot or will not help themselves."

Pratt's final gift to his adopted hometown was a $2 million bequest (of his remaining $2.5 million) to the Sheppard asylum, because he was so impressed with how that institution's trustees had handled their responsibilities. "They are the only board of trustees in Baltimore who have carried out exactly the directions of the founder," said Pratt. Pratt's bequest expanded the pioneering mental hospital and helped make it, now the Sheppard Pratt Health System, the largest mental-health institute in Maryland.

— *Kari Barbic*

Further reading
∘ Richard Hart, *Enoch Pratt: The Story of a Plain Man* (Enoch Pratt Free Library, 1935)

JOHN ROCKEFELLER SR.

After starting life in humble circumstances, John Rockefeller came to dominate the burgeoning petroleum industry by the time he was 40 years old. He became the richest man of his time, and indeed has a good claim to perhaps being the richest self-made man who ever lived.

He was equally distinguished as a philanthropist. A natural businessman with a strong moral sense and intense religious convictions, he dedicated unprecedented resources to charity. Within his lifetime, Rockefeller helped launch the field of biomedical research, funding scientific investigations that resulted in vaccines for things like meningitis and yellow fever. He revolutionized medical training in the United States and built China's first proper medical school. He championed the cause of public sanitation, creating schools of public health at Johns Hopkins and Harvard, and helped lead major international public health efforts against hookworm, malaria, yellow fever, and other maladies. He vigorously promoted the cause of education nationwide, without distinction of sex, race, or creed. He created the University of Chicago, virtually from scratch, and within a decade turned it into one of the world's leading universities.

Born in upstate New York in 1839, Rockefeller was the son of a strait-laced, deeply devout Baptist mother and a boisterous, fun-loving father who called himself a traveling salesman but was really a flimflam man. (Amid his many long business trips, Rockefeller's father would eventually contract a bigamous second marriage and have a second family while still returning periodically to his first.) The young Rockefeller, serious and somewhat humorless by nature, was much more influenced by his mother. A lifelong adherent of the northern Baptist church, he neither drank nor smoked.

As a boy, his family moved frequently. In 1853 they settled in Strongsville, Ohio, a suburb of rapidly expanding Cleveland. Rockefeller attended a local high school and took a ten-week course in bookkeeping. At age 16 he got his first job, keeping ledgers at a brokerage of fresh produce. From the very beginning of his work life, he gave 6 percent of his salary (which at first was a mere 50¢ per day) to charity. He was soon tithing to the Baptist church.

In 1859, Edwin Drake drilled the first oil well, in northwest Pennsylvania, and one of the world's greatest industries was born. That year Rockefeller and a partner opened a brokerage of their own, Rockefeller and Clark, that traded not only lettuces and tomatoes and other produce but petroleum products as well. Cleveland, with its proximity to the Pennsylvania oil fields and its excellent transportation network, quickly became the center of petroleum refining. In 1863, Rockefeller and partners opened their own refinery.

In 1865 Rockefeller bought out his partners and established a new firm with the chemist Samuel Andrews. Needing capital, he approached Stephen Harkness, who invested $100,000 and became a silent partner in the firm, requiring that his relative, Henry Flagler, be taken in as a partner to oversee the Harkness interests. Flagler proved an inspired choice, with organizational and creative business skills that neatly matched Rockefeller's careful money management.

In 1870, Flagler convinced Rockefeller to transform the partnership of Rockefeller, Andrews, and Flagler into a corporation named Standard Oil. Standard Oil expanded rapidly, both horizontally by buying up other oil refining companies, and vertically by acquiring oil wells and transportation routes and selling products at the retail level. Standard Oil pursued a monopoly position, using techniques—such as secret rebates from railroads and predatory pricing—that are today illegal, but were not then. It also invented the trust form of organization in order to circumvent out-of-date incorporation laws. It paid a fair price for the companies it wanted to acquire, often doling out Standard Oil stock and taking in useful executives. By 1880, Standard Oil controlled 90 percent of the oil business in America.

Rockefeller had a clear conscience about how he won his fortune. "God gave me the money," he often said. Believing that, he felt a profound obligation to put the money to good use. By the early 1880s, he was receiving thousands of letters a month asking for help. Rockefeller regularly gathered his family after breakfast to review the merits of the petitions. "Four fifths of these letters," Rockefeller noted years later, were "requests of money for personal use, with no other title to consideration than that the writer would be gratified to have it."

In these first years of large-scale philanthropy, Rockefeller favored a few causes close to his heart. He was the single most generous donor to the northern Baptist conventions, and he underwrote the work of missionaries and relief workers at home and abroad. He also took a deep interest in higher education for African Americans. In 1882, he began a series of gifts to the Atlanta Baptist Female Seminary, a struggling school for African-American women. As Rockefeller's contributions grew, the school took the maiden name of Rockefeller's wife: Spellman. Similar gifts were soon directed to two other black colleges—the Tuskegee Institute and Morehouse College.

> One of the richest men in history, with a strong moral sense and intense religious convictions, John Rockefeller dedicated unprecedented resources to charity and dramatically improved many social ills.

"About the year 1890 I was still following the haphazard fashion of giving here and there as appeals presented themselves. I investigated as I could, and worked myself almost to a nervous breakdown," Rockefeller noted in his 1909 memoir. "There was then forced upon me the necessity to organize and plan this department of our daily tasks on as distinct lines of progress as we did with our business affairs." It marked an important turning point in his career as a philanthropist.

Rockefeller made his fortune through canny consolidation, careful cost management, and economies of scale. Those instincts were reflected time and again in his charitable giving. Rather than make thousands of small, scattershot contributions, he preferred to make large donations to institutions that he believed had great promise. "The best philanthropy," he wrote, "is constantly in search of finalities—a search for a cause, an attempt to cure evils at their source."

Higher education was the first major beneficiary of Rockefeller's more focused philanthropic efforts. A project of lifelong interest to him was the creation of a distinguished Baptist university. Rockefeller considered several options before pairing with William Harper to establish the University of Chicago. In 1890, he made his first contribution—for $600,000—to the school. Over the rest of his life, he would give it a total of $35 million, making it possible for the upstart school to instantly rank among the world's leading institutions of higher learning. Rockefeller insisted that his name not be used anywhere on campus, even rejecting an image of a lamp on the university seal, lest it be taken as a suggestion of the influence of Standard Oil. The University of Chicago, he later said, was "the best investment I ever made."

At the urging of Frederick Gates, perhaps his most trusted philanthropic adviser, Rockefeller became increasingly devoted to medical research. In 1901, he funded the Rockefeller Medical Research Institute in New York City. Modeled on the Institut Pasteur in France and the Robert Koch Institute in Germany, it was the country's first biomedical institute, soon on a par with its European models. The results were dramatic. Within a decade, it created a vaccine for cerebrospinal meningitis and had supported the work of America's first winner of a Nobel Prize in medicine. Today, known as Rockefeller University, it is one of the leading biomedical research centers in the world. Twenty-four Nobel Prize winners have served on its faculty.

Like many wealthy industrialists of his era, Rockefeller was scandalized by the poverty and deprivation that still afflicted the American South nearly half a century after the conclusion of the Civil War. He created the General Education Board in 1902, charging it with a ranging mission that included improving rural education for both whites and blacks, modernizing agricultural practices, and improving public health, primarily through efforts to eradicate hookworm, which debilitated many Southerners and dragged down productivity of all sorts. The General Education Board helped establish hundreds of public high schools throughout the South, promoted institutions of higher education, and supported teacher-training efforts for African Americans.

Rockefeller's work to eliminate hookworm was part of a broader effort to improve public health generally. Starting in 1913, the smashing success against hookworm in the U.S. was exported globally. It was soon followed by similar efforts against malaria, scarlet fever, tuberculosis, and typhus, all under the auspices of the Rockefeller-funded International Health Commission. Rockefeller created the first school of public health at Johns Hopkins University in 1918, which he then duplicated at Harvard in 1921. In all, he spent $25 million introducing public-health programs at scores of universities across the globe. Rockefeller took a special interest in China (second only to the United States as a destination for his funding), and the China Medical Board he created can be credited with first introducing the country to modern medical practices.

Throughout the first decade of the twentieth century, Rockefeller was thinking seriously about founding a perpetual grantmaking foundation. By 1909, he had given away $158 million of personal funds to various causes. That year he donated 73,000 shares of Standard Oil, worth $50 million, as a first installment to establish what would become the Rockefeller Foundation. It was not the first such foundation, but it quickly became the largest. It was chartered by New York State in 1913 with a mission "to promote the well-being of mankind throughout the world."

The benefactions of the Rockefeller Foundation have been many and varied, from funding the research that led to the yellow fever vaccine, to the Montreal Neurological Institute, to a new building that holds five million books at Oxford's Bodleian Library. The foundation was a pioneer funder of the Green Revolution, which dramatically increased agricultural yields across the developing world, and may have saved as many as one billion lives.

As impressive as the legacy of the Rockefeller Foundation is, however, it is not clear that it has yet caught up with the accomplishments of its founding donor. John Rockefeller gave away approximately $540 million before his death in 1937 at the age of 97. With that money, he created two of the world's greatest research universities, helped pull the American South out of chronic poverty, educated legions of African Americans, jumpstarted medical research, and dramatically improved health around the globe. It is not surprising that his biographer Ron Chernow concluded that Rockefeller "must rank as the greatest philanthropist in American history."

↳ *John Steele Gordon*

Further reading

- Ron Chernow, *Titan: The Life of John D. Rockefeller, Sr.* (Random House, 1998)
- Raymond Fosdick, *The Story of the Rockefeller Foundation* (Transaction Publishers, 1989)
- John D. Rockefeller, *Random Reminiscences of Men and Events* (Doubleday, 1909)

JOHN ROCKEFELLER JR.

John Rockefeller Jr. was the only son and principal heir of the founder of Standard Oil. Much of the younger Rockefeller's working life was dedicated to philanthropy—first as an agent of his father and later with his own inherited funds. His principal philanthropic interests included conserving natural landscapes, preserving historical landmarks, collecting fine art, fostering international cooperation, and promoting the cause of Protestant Modernism.

Born in 1874, "Junior" (as he was known within the family) was earnest and devout, a dutiful son who labored conscientiously to reflect well on the family. After graduating from Brown, he went to work in his father's office, with unspecified responsibilities but an expectation that his time would be devoted to both business and philanthropy. He soon discovered he lacked his father's aptitude for profitmaking. After a nervous breakdown in 1904, Junior decided to devote himself almost exclusively to charitable giving.

Working alongside Frederick Gates, one of Rockefeller's key aides, Junior helped launch some of his father's most important philanthropic enterprises: the Rockefeller Institute for Medical Research (1901), the General Education Board (1903), the Sanitary Commission for the Eradication of Hookworm (1909), and the Rockefeller Foundation (1913). Junior won his father's respect with his hard work and commitment to the work he was given.

Junior rose to national prominence in 1915. The United Mine Workers had been striking against the Rockefeller-controlled Colorado Fuel and Iron, and in April 1914 the Colorado National Guard was sent in to keep order. A firefight broke out, in which two women and 11 children were killed. The "Ludlow Massacre" made John Rockefeller one of the most hated men in America. Junior stepped forward, reaching out to the union, speaking to the press, and testifying before the U.S. Commission on Industrial Relations. He charmed everyone. Even the *Masses*, a leading left-wing journal, called him "apparently frank," "gentle," and "Christianish."

Impressed by his son's leadership during the crisis, Senior began transferring his fortune to Junior. Between 1916 and 1922, Junior received gifts of approximately $450 million. By 1920, his net worth hovered around $500 million. This gave him independence in his charitable giving.

As a philanthropist in his own right, Junior remained famously self-effacing. In the late 1920s, for example, he decided to visit Versailles. He had recently contributed $2 million to the restoration of the palace and its grounds, but arrived at closing time, and the guards, not recognizing him, turned him away. He thanked them politely and returned to his hotel. This became "headline news in France," notes one biographer, "and no action on his part could have so endeared him to the French people."

The younger Rockefeller was an ardent conservationist, best remembered for his leadership in creating Grand Teton National Park in Wyoming and his contributions to Acadia National Park in Maine. In both cases, he bought tens of thousands of acres and donated them to the National Park Service; in Maine, he paid for the construction of 57 miles of auto-free "carriage roads," where visitors could enjoy the park's beauty at the speed of a horse instead of a car.

In all, it is estimated that Junior gave about $45 million to various conservation efforts, leading one expert to call him "the most generous philanthropist in the history of conservation." He put up $10.3 million to preserve parkland in northeastern New Jersey, donated funds to buy land and build a museum in Yosemite National Park, and underwrote the purchase of land for California's Humboldt Redwoods State Park. He helped create Shenandoah National Park, Mesa Verde National Park, and the Great Smoky Mountains National Park.

The same conservative impulse that inspired Junior's conservation efforts also animated his interest in historic preservation. In 1926, Junior visited Williamsburg, Virginia, then little more than William and Mary College surrounded by a few crumbling churches. Rockefeller began to restore the venerable town one building at a time, insisting on scrupulous historical accuracy, in what ultimately became a $60 million gift. It was a labor of love—"I really belong in Williamsburg," he once said. He later took up a similar effort to restore sections of the historic Hudson Valley.

Junior's conservation projects spanned the globe. He funded the restoration of Notre-Dame de Reims, a thirteenth-century French cathedral that was devastated by shellfire in World War I. When an earthquake destroyed the main library of Tokyo Imperial University (now Tokyo University), Junior paid for its reconstruction. Grants to the American School for Classical Studies helped archaeologists excavate the Ancient Agora of Athens. With a $2 million gift, he launched the Palestine Museum (now the Rockefeller Museum), the first institute in Jerusalem devoted to archaeological preservation.

Junior's taste in art was traditional, as evidenced by his close involvement in the creation of the Cloisters in New York City. In the 1920s, Junior began working with George Barnard, a sculptor who collected pieces from the great cathedrals of medieval France. Junior decided to combine Barnard's collection with the medieval works he had collected—most notably the seven "Hunt of the Unicorn" tapestries. To house one of the world's great collections of medieval art, Rockefeller funded the creation of a building that incorporates parts from five French cloistered abbeys, taken apart and shipped to northernmost Manhattan, where they were assembled between 1934 and 1938. Surrounding land was landscaped in styles recorded in medieval manuscripts and images.

Junior's wife, Abby Aldrich Rockefeller, had entirely different tastes in art. She fell in love with modern art quite early, and was given an allowance by her husband to pursue that interest. With those funds and some inheritance she acquired works by young, struggling artists. Later, she organized other donors and created New York's Museum of Modern Art. In 1934, Junior loosened the purse strings and allowed his wife to spend what she pleased on contemporary works. When she died in 1948, he honored her memory with gifts to the Museum of Modern Art that ultimately totaled over $6 million, despite his lifelong distaste for contemporary art.

> Lacking his father's aptitude for money-making, John Rockefeller Jr. devoted himself to guiding the most important charitable enterprises started by his father.

Junior also used his philanthropy to promote the cause of international harmony. He gave a library to the League of Nations, and later contributed the Manhattan real estate that allowed the United Nations building to be constructed there rather than abroad. He was a founder and major contributor to the Council on Foreign Relations. He funded dozens of International Houses, residential facilities on college campuses intended to enable graduate students from different countries to live together. He created the International Education Board and provided $28 million to fund graduate studies and institutions in 39 countries.

The largest component of Junior's philanthropy—totaling some $72 million altogether—was directed to churches and religious causes. Every year between 1919 and 1933, he was the largest single contributor to the Northern Baptist denomination, contributing as much as 13 percent of its annual budget. During the 1920s, as Modernist and Fundamentalist factions increasingly came into conflict, Junior sided squarely with the Modernists. His friend and family pastor was Harry Emerson Fosdick, a leading light among the Modernists; Fosdick's brother Raymond was a longtime Rockefeller employee (and Rockefeller Foundation president) and Junior's first biographer.

In 1922, Junior paid for the distribution of Fosdick's sermon "Should the Fundamentalists Win?" to every Protestant minister in the United States. He funded the nondenominational Riverside Church, contributing $32 million to its construction between 1925 and 1928. He supported the theologically liberal faculty at the University of Chicago Divinity School and gave millions to the Interchurch World Movement, an ecumenical effort to unite the Christian denominations.

Historians estimate that John Rockefeller Jr. gave away $537 million during his lifetime. Although one of the nation's most accomplished philanthropists, Junior always subordinated himself to his father. When the Virginia legislature formally honored him for the creation of historic Williamsburg, he was invited to deliver a few remarks. At one point, he looked up, departing from his prepared text. "How I wish my father were here," he said, his voice choking. "I am only the son."

↪ *Martin Morse Wooster*

Further reading

○ Raymond Fosdick, *John D. Rockefeller, Jr.: A Portrait* (Harper, 1956)
○ John Harr and Peter Johnson, *The Rockefeller Century* (Scribner, 1988)
○ Suzanne Loebl, *America's Medicis: The Rockefellers and Their Astounding Cultural Legacy* (Harper, 2010)

JULIUS ROSENWALD

Julius Rosenwald, who was born in 1862 while Abraham Lincoln was president, in a house just one block from the liberator's own home in Springfield, Illinois, eventually played his own towering part in reinforcing the unity of America, elevating its black citizenry, and moving the nation closer to fulfilling the promises of its founding.

A child of German immigrants, Rosenwald dropped out of high school after two years to apprentice with his uncles, who were major clothing manufacturers in New York City. By his 30th birthday he had achieved moderate success running his own business that made ready-to-wear men's suits. Then came his big break.

Richard Sears, a gifted advertising writer but chronically disorganized entrepreneur, had a tiger by the tail as he struggled to fill mail orders at his booming new company Sears, Roebuck. Julius got a chance to buy a quarter of the company, and soon he was imposing order on the shipping-room chaos.

Sears was the Amazon.com of its day, and Rosenwald had to take extraordinary measures to keep up with its growth. He put 7,000 laborers to work day and night building a huge warehouse. Special machines were made that could open letters at the rate of 27,000 per hour. A system of conveyor belts, pneumatic tubes, and color-coded tags shunted merchandise through the vast new plant. Henry Ford reportedly visited and absorbed ideas for his future assembly line. Management expert Peter Drucker later characterized Rosenwald as "the father…of the distribution revolution which has changed the world economy in the twentieth century and which is so vital a factor in economic growth."

When the dust settled around the end of 1908, Sears was one of the most popular enterprises in the country, with millions of customers and tens of thousands of employees, and Rosenwald was its president and a multimillionaire. With the company on an even keel, his attention turned rapidly toward philanthropy. Soon he was giving away money with at least as much gusto as he poured into earning it.

A deep root of Rosenwald's generosity was the fact that he was a secure and grounded individual, lacking in ego. In a 1916 article, young journalist B. C. Forbes (who founded his own business magazine the next year) profiled Rosenwald this way:

> The most notable thing about Julius Rosenwald is not any superhuman business ability, nor any phenomenal smartness in seeing and seizing mercantile opportunities…. *The greatest thing about Julius Rosenwald is not his business but himself, not what he has but what he is,* his character, his personality, his sincerity, his honesty, his democracy, his thoughtfulness, his charity of heart, his catholicity of sympathy, his consuming desire to help the less fortunate of his fellow creatures.

Religious motivations were an immediate spur for Rosenwald's philanthropy. His rabbi, Emil Hirsch, taught him that "property entails duties." Hirsch introduced Rosenwald to many people who inspired him to donate.

During the summer of 1910, Rosenwald read the autobiography of the great black educator Booker T. Washington, and was strongly affected. Within a year, Rosenwald and Washington were building a relationship that included visits to each other's homes. Rosenwald's first speech introducing the educator to Chicago's business leaders described Washington as "helping his own race to attain the high art of self-help and self-dependence" while simultaneously "helping the white race to learn that opportunity and obligation go hand in hand, and that there is no enduring superiority save that which comes as the result of serving."

In 1912, Rosenwald made a dramatic entry into large-scale philanthropy. He announced he would be celebrating his 50th birthday by giving away close to $700,000 (about $16 million in current dollars), and encouraged other wealthy individuals to support good causes of their own. "Give While You Live" was his slogan.

One of Rosenwald's birthday gifts was $25,000 to Washington's Tuskegee Institute. Washington shrewdly set aside part of it to launch a new experiment which he expected might interest his donor—a $2,100 effort to build new schools in parts of Alabama where little or no education was being offered to rural blacks. Washington documented progress on the schools with photos and careful accounting, including descriptions of the community enthusiasm the erection of the new schools created among locals of all races. Pride in the fresh facilities often overflowed into newly painted houses, improved roads, and expanded cooperation among residents.

Rosenwald was captivated. During this Jim Crow era, the educational offerings to African Americans, and many residents of the rural South in general, were miserably inadequate. Soon he and Washington were ramping up the program, eventually building schools all across the South over more than 20 years. There were correlated efforts to train teachers to serve in the new schools, and

> When government neglected its duties at the height of the Jim Crow era, Rosenwald's philanthropic grants built the schools where 27 percent of all black children in America got their education.

funds to provide libraries and workshops for students. These facilities would never have materialized absent this aggressive philanthropy, and they had both immediate and deeply enduring effects.

By 1932, the year Julius died, an astonishing 4,977 Rosenwald schools, and 380 complementary buildings, had been erected in every Southern locale with a significant black population. Fully 35 percent of all black children in the South (and 27 percent of black children period) were educated that year in a Rosenwald school. America would be a very different, and lesser, nation absent this philanthropic inspiration (which outflanked a scandalous dereliction of duty by a variety of governments).

In the rural-school program and all the rest of his giving, the *way* in which Rosenwald made his philanthropic investments was often as inspired as his underlying cause. For sheer canniness in donating resources, Julius Rosenwald may have been America's most innovative and influential donor ever.

In the school-building program, for instance, he insisted right from the beginning that his donation would only be made if it was matched by local residents (most of whom were poor blacks who skeptics said could never come up with adequate funds). He also craftily maneuvered local and state governments into participating, overcoming their historical dismissal of black education with the lure of outside manna.

These decisions reflected Rosenwald's disdain for unconditioned largesse, and his insistence that beneficiaries do their own large part in improving their lot. And despite their limited resources, thousands of rural black communities succeeded in pulling together the funds to match Rosenwald's gift. Poignant stories have been recorded of black laborers emptying bags of old coins, representing years of savings, to underwrite these schools. Sharecroppers set aside a "Rosenwald Patch" when they planted their cotton. Innumerable pie sales and fried chicken suppers were organized to raise matching funds. During construction, many black families donated materials or invested sweat equity via their labor. Local whites also contributed, encouraged by the uplift the new schools offered their towns.

Retrospective calculations show that, in the end, black families contributed slightly more than Rosenwald to the schools—16 percent of total costs, versus 15 percent from his fund. And leveraging the remainder from state and county education authorities was a game-changing triumph. Booker T. Washington credited Rosenwald with starting the entire program of state funding for black education in the South. And during this segregated era, that in turn initiated additional resources to improve substandard white schools.

Rosenwald was totally opposed to handouts, which he believed caused enervation and corruption of incentives. The only lasting help was self-help, he believed. He thus proclaimed that in his philanthropy he was looking for "opportunities for self-improvement, for education and recreation, for the acquisition of spiritual, moral, mental, and physical strength, that makes for manhood and self-reliance."

Rosenwald also pioneered other innovations in the mechanics of giving. Perhaps foremost, he urged that successful men and women should give not just of their money but of their time and expertise. When Rosenwald "became involved in a project, he did not merely accept the idea, write the checks, and hand the project over to someone else," notes biographer Peter Ascoli. Instead, he became deeply involved, contributing his wisdom, management expertise, and personality as well as his funds.

Rosenwald had well-developed and savvy ideas about use of the donor's name. He did not believe in giving anonymously, because he thought the visible support and credibility lent by a gift was often even more valuable to a receiving institution than the immediate cash. At the same time, he fought aggressively to keep his name from being affixed prominently to buildings and projects—not just out of his genuine humility, but in keeping with his idea that if a donor could get beneficiaries to take ownership of a project themselves and become emotionally invested in it, the undertaking is likelier to thrive and endure. "If no name is used it will belong to the people," was Rosenwald's encapsulation.

He also was a path-breaker in insisting on follow-up, evaluation, and accountability. He sent architects out to check on the construction of schools built with his money, demanded careful financial records, and followed outcomes. "Benevolence today has become altogether too huge an undertaking to be conducted otherwise than on business lines," he argued.

Rosenwald also combined business and philanthropy in novel ways, devising stock-purchase, profit-sharing, and health-and-welfare programs that benefited Sears employees. He created one of the first corporate foundations in history, the Sears, Roebuck Foundation, and built it to substantial size. To reduce the risk of bureaucracy and falling into complacent ruts, he was a trailblazer in encouraging term limits on trustees at foundations (six years in the case of his own fund).

Rosenwald was adamantly opposed to setting up foundations to exist forever, dribbling out only a small fraction of their money each year. He insisted this would lead inevitably to a focus on staff sinecures and the perpetuation of assets, rather than getting things done. Instead, he believed, foundations should urgently attack national problems with their best resources right now, use up their funds within a reasonable time, and leave future challenges to future donors. He insisted his own foundation should spend energetically so as to close up shop within 25 years of his death, and thus avoid the sclerosis he was already observing in permanent endowments.

One of Rosenwald's most unusual and bold philanthropic innovations was his willingness to pledge his own fortune (more than once) to protect Sears employees and even preserve the company during the periodic financial panics that wracked the U.S. in the early decades of the twentieth century. Most dramatically, when the sudden recession after World War I pushed Sears to the brink of bankruptcy, Rosenwald bailed out the firm while he was president by pledging $21 million of his personal wealth (the equivalent of $288 million today) in a combination of gifts and loans. This stunned Rosenwald's fellow business executives, and deeply impressed the country. Business writer C. W. Barron, who later fathered *Barron's* magazine, hailed the move as "business philanthropy."

Julius Rosenwald left a powerful imprint on numerous causes. He brought the inspirational science and technology museum to America by single-handedly funding the Museum of Science and Industry in Chicago. He gave many millions to Jewish interests, including saving thousands of victims of the Russian Revolution. He was a generous backer of black colleges. He funded the construction of 22 YMCA/YWCA community centers and urban dormitories for blacks during the segregated era. He was for many years the largest donor to the University of Chicago, located within a mile of his home, and spawned their medical school among many other worthy intellectual projects.

While Julius Rosenwald never possessed the assets of his contemporaries Rockefeller and Carnegie (in current dollars Rosenwald's total donations amounted to something under $2 billion) he got an enormous bang for his buck. This was due to his philanthropic vision and his determination to pump his fortune quickly into ameliorative projects rather than locking it up in permanent trusts.

In addition to changing the country, Rosenwald changed philanthropy. Together, this combination of the lives he directly transformed, and his many innovations in the practice and execution of giving which inspired other wealthy individuals to become more effective givers, set him apart. That he is largely unknown—thanks to his principles like keeping his name off projects and limiting the life of his foundation—is only a further tribute to his good motives.

Karl Zinsmeister

Further reading

○ Peter Ascoli, *Julius Rosenwald: The Man Who Built Sears, Roebuck and Advanced the Cause of Black Education in the American South* (Indiana University Press, 2006)

○ Joseph Hoereth, "Julius Rosenwald and the Rosenwald Fund: A Case in Non-Perpetual Philanthropy," Loyola University Chicago, 2007

○ Julius Rosenwald, "The Principles of Public Giving" (*Atlantic Monthly*, May 1929)

OLIVIA SAGE

Margaret Olivia Sage—Olivia to those who knew her—was the widow of Russell Sage, among the greatest Wall Street investors of the 1800s. When the 89-year-old financier died in 1906, he instantly made her one of the wealthiest women in the country. She in turn used her inheritance to become one of the nation's most notable philanthropists, a patroness of higher education for women, and a leading figure in the effort to apply social science to the root causes of large-scale social problems.

"One should remember," wrote Sage in her only published work, "that in America what is called 'blue blood' is distributed through both classes—with a preponderance of it, perhaps, among the unmoneyed class." It was a fact she was keenly aware of: though the Slocum and Sage families were both of distinguished stock, when she had married Russell Sage in 1869, at the age of 41, she left behind the life of a school teacher and governess struggling to support herself.

Sage was born in 1828 in Syracuse, New York, to Margaret and Joseph Slocum. Her father, a businessman who had benefited from the economic boom in central New York sparked by the Erie Canal, suffered tremendous losses in the Panic of 1837. Having received a private education to that point, Olivia was able to borrow money from an uncle to attend Troy Female Seminary, the first institution of higher learning for women. Her introduction to the school's founder, Emma Willard, would have a lifelong influence. Though Willard called suffragists "hyenas in petticoats," she was deeply committed to the cause of female education, and her school produced moral and cultural leaders who championed women's causes in many ways.

Upon her 1847 graduation from the Troy Female Seminary, Olivia praised "our distinguished inhabitants who spend their wealth in deeds of charity," giving evidence of the ideals she had acquired at the institution. But her family's worsening finances caused her to spend the next 22 years working hard, first as a teacher in Syracuse and then as a governess in Philadelphia.

In 1869, her fortunes seemed to change dramatically when Russell Sage made her an offer of marriage. He was a former Congressman and the partner of hated businessman Jay Gould. Sage was himself a tight-fisted miser, and 20 years earlier, he had swindled her father. But she accepted his proposal.

Though her married life was one of financial abundance, she was not able to pursue the charitable activity that she had admired even as a student. Russell Sage was notoriously stingy. A 1902 letter to the editor of the *New York Times* thanked the paper for the amusement it provided in chronicling his miserliness, seldom allowing "a week to pass without furnishing a new story about 'Uncle Russ,'" for instance, "how he permits his lawn grass to grow into hay for his horses." In the 37 years of their marriage, Russell and Olivia Sage were to make only three major donations: to the Troy Female Seminary, the Women's Hospital, and the American Seamen's Friend Society, totaling approximately $220,000. In the years after Russell's passing, however, Olivia made up for lost time.

Ruth Crocker, Sage's most recent biographer, refers to the period of her marriage as one of "performative philanthropy." In 1890, she helped to found and became the president of the Emma Willard Society, the alumni association of the Troy Female Seminary. In 1898 she made possible the publication of *Emma Willard and her pupils; or, Fifty years of Troy female seminary, 1822-1872.* She volunteered significant amounts of time working as a "lady manager" of the New York Women's Hospital. And by 1894 she was sponsoring women's suffrage meetings, motivated in part by the news that the governor of New York had vetoed the appointment of four women to Troy Female Seminary's board of trustees.

When Russell Sage died in 1906, he left a fortune of $75 million to his wife. She proceeded to give away approximately $45 million in the next dozen years before her own death in 1918. Her donations went to a wide variety of causes, the bulk of them in relatively small amounts. Much of her philanthropy was directed towards educational institutions—including large building and program grants to Syracuse University, Cornell, Princeton, and a founding grant for Russell Sage College—but she also invested significantly in the work of religious organizations and women's causes.

> Though her husband was a notorious miser, Olivia Sage used his money after his death to do much good in education and in studying social problems.

Olivia Sage is best remembered today for launching the Russell Sage Foundation for Social Betterment, which she endowed with $10 million in 1907. Her open-ended instructions were that "the income thereof [be] applied to the improvement of social and living conditions in the United States of America." The foundation gave modest amounts directly to poor people. Its much stronger focus was to employ experts in the emerging "social sciences" to study societal problems and devise systemic, "root causes" solutions.

The Russell Sage Foundation dramatically increased the influence of the social sciences in the nation's large foundations, and in America generally. Over many following decades it was a pioneer in encouraging the new tools of social science. In addition to supporting research and analysis, Russell Sage occasionally put social science into action in attempts to solve particular problems. For instance, as an experiment in municipal planning, it purchased a large expanse of land in Queens, now known as Forest Hills Gardens, to create a model suburb following the methods of the English garden-city movement. Olivia herself put $2.75 million into the project, with a hope that it would spur many similar projects where families of modest incomes could live comfortable lives near major cities.

In 1916, together with the head of the Troy Female Seminary (now known as the Emma Willard School) Olivia Sage founded Russell Sage College, a women's liberal arts college offering preparation for a variety of professions. Located in the buildings that the Emma Willard School had vacated six years earlier, it granted degrees under the auspices of the Willard School until it was granted its own charter in 1927.

When Olivia Sage died in 1918, a total of 19 educational institutions received equal allotments of approximately $800,000. Other organizations—including the Women's Board of Foreign Missions of the Presbyterian Church, the Emma Willard School, and the Metropolitan Museum of Art—received more than $1 million. The Russell Sage Foundation received a bequest of $5 million.

A "woman is responsible in proportion to the wealth and time at her command," she wrote in a 1905 *North American Review* article. "While one woman is working for bread and butter, the other must devote her time to the amelioration of the condition of her laboring sister. This is the moral law." And as soon as she had the independence to make her own choices, Olivia Sage followed those dictates of her conscience with obedient generosity.

— Monica Klem

Further reading

○ Ruth Crocker, *Mrs. Russell Sage: Women's Activism and Philanthropy in Gilded Age and Progressive Era America* (Indiana University Press, 2008)

○ David Hammack, *The Russell Sage Foundation: Social Research and Social Action in America, 1907-1947* (UPA Academic Editions, 1988)

○ Margaret Olivia Sage, "Opportunities and Responsibilities of Leisured Women" (*North American Review*, November 1905)

ELLEN SCRIPPS

Ellen Browning Scripps, whose fortune derived from the Scripps family's newspaper empire, is not well known outside of southern California, largely because she confined her extensive philanthropy to local causes. Indeed, when she was approached in 1914 and offered the opportunity to support an effort in Cleveland, Ohio, she declined with the simple response: "Charity begins at home."

She was born in London to James Scripps and his second wife in 1836. When she was seven years old, three years after her mother had died, the

Scripps family left England for the United States, where they settled in Illinois. Her father then married again and had five more children, bringing the number of his children to 13. Ellen was 19 years older than her youngest stepbrother, Edward Willis (known as E. W.), and had a particularly formative influence on him.

As a child, Ellen took full advantage of her father's library, and she continued her pursuit of knowledge longer than any of her siblings did. After spending two years teaching—and saving—she was able to enroll at Knox College in 1856. She spent three years at Knox before returning to teaching, but soon her brothers' increasing involvement in the newspaper business led her to work first as a copy editor and then as a columnist.

In 1873, when her brother James founded the *Detroit Evening News*, she invested her savings from teaching; when the paper was incorporated, she received a large number of shares. Consequently, she was able to provide assistance to E. W. when he founded *The Penny Press* in Cleveland, in 1878. Her investments in her brothers' businesses, which would expand steadily, provided her with financial independence. The Scripps family's successes led, however, to many difficulties. Ellen once wrote to E. W. that she wished she could be "where the air that I breathe will not be tainted, nor my ears polluted with the foul smell and sound of money, and the baseness of spirit it engenders."

It had occurred to Ellen that California might provide something like that respite. She had never visited the state before 1890, when she traveled to see her sister Annie who, in search of healing for rheumatoid arthritis, had established herself in a utopian community in Alameda. Her stepbrother Fred toured the state with her. They ended their trip in San Diego, which Ellen admired and which Fred was fascinated by, imagining it beneficial to his health and as offering him new financial beginnings. When they left California, Fred decided to buy a ranch there. His more successful sibling E. W. realized that he would have to finance Fred's project if it were ever to come to pass, so he went to San Diego to see it for himself.

By 1891, E. W. had purchased property and Fred had established himself in southern California. Within a few months, E. W. and Will, their wives, and their mother followed him, and they began construction on a house that was meant to be a home for the entire family. After the extended family had lived in the complex they called Miramar for a year, Ellen found herself discontentedly asking E. W., "Are there any two of us as a family who could live happily and contentedly together?" Shortly thereafter Will and Fred moved to properties of their own.

In 1896, Ellen bought land in La Jolla and had a house built on it, which she named South Moulton Villa after the street on which her family had lived in London. She rapidly became immersed in the life of the town, joining numerous clubs and going to lectures and concerts. In her conscious effort to enjoy the simplicity of life in the small town, she contributed to its becoming known as an active yet unpretentious place "where you could wear out your old clothes."

When George Scripps died in 1900, he left the bulk of his estate to his sister. Ellen wanted to use the money in a way that would honor him. In 1903, she and E. W. decided to assist William Ritter, a Berkeley biologist, in founding the Marine Biological Association of San Diego. Ellen gave it a sizable endowment, and the Scripps family provided its entire operating budget until it was taken over by the University of California at San Diego and renamed the Scripps Institution of Oceanography.

Ellen had been an early supporter of better education for women. In 1909, the bishop of the Episcopal diocese of Los Angeles approached her to ask for help in founding a college preparatory school for girls. She initially donated land for the Bishop's School and commissioned its first building; for years afterward, she remained one of its most important supporters. And in 1926, she endowed what would become Scripps College, a part of the Claremont Colleges, which she

> Believing that "charity begins at home," Ellen Scripps concentrated her giving in the San Diego area.

had helped to found. She also commissioned the La Jolla Women's Club's headquarters, the building that would become the La Jolla Community Center, and the country's first public playground.

In 1911, Ellen became a member of the Egypt Exploration Fund; she began providing support for its expeditions in 1919. (Her efforts resulted in the San Diego Museum's Ancient Egyptian collection.) She also worked to preserve the area that would become Torrey Pines State Natural Reserve, and helped finance the new headquarters of the San Diego Natural History Museum. In 1923, she gave the San Diego Zoo an aviary and an animal research hospital. And in 1922, she founded the Scripps Memorial Hospital and the Scripps Metabolic Clinic, prompted by dissatisfaction with the care she received for a broken leg.

Education was a central focus of Ellen Scripps's philanthropic work. From her youth until her death in 1932 at the age of 95, she saw herself primarily as an investor in human capital rather than as an almsgiver. The charity she launched "at home" in southern California fulfilled her sense of familial and civic duty to help persons and causes she believed would prove beneficial to all.

ɯ *Monica Klem*

Further reading

- Molly McClain, "The Scripps Family's San Diego Experiment" (*Journal of San Diego History,* Winter 2010)
- Charles Preece, *E. W. and Ellen Browning Scripps: An Unmatched Pair* (BookCrafters, 1990)
- Frances Hepner, *Ellen Browning Scripps: Her Life and Times* (San Diego State College, 1966)

WILLIAM SIMON

William Simon was a successful banker, public servant, and noted philanthropist. He was a bond trader and a pioneer of leveraged buyouts. He served as Secretary of the Treasury in the Nixon and Ford administrations, and led the U.S. Olympic Committee during the 1984 summer games. He gave generously of his own wealth and became a trustee of some of America's most influential philanthropic organizations.

Born in New Jersey in 1927, Simon volunteered for the Army and served as a private. After he was discharged, he attended Lafayette College. With graduation approaching, Simon was married and in debt, with one young son and another on the way. He camped out in the offices of Union Securities on Wall Street until he landed a $75-per-week job in the mailroom. Within two years, he made partner and was heading the firm's municipal bonds trading desk.

He moved to Salomon Brothers, where he became famous for his 16-hour days, standing beside his desk, guzzling gallons of ice water, and barking orders to his traders. He was a senior partner, member of the firm's executive committee, and sat on the board that oversaw federal mortgage giants Fannie Mae and Freddie Mac when, in 1973, he left Salomon to become chief deputy to George Shultz at the Treasury Department,

As Shultz's deputy and later as Secretary of the Treasury in the Ford administration, many of Simon's most cherished initiatives—tax reform, a balanced budget—would languish. In an ironic twist, the principled free-marketer was asked to head the government's price-control program for gasoline. He would later joke that he was the guy who "caused all the lines at gas stations."

After his government service, Simon returned to private life and found himself near-bankrupt. Inflation and losses in his blind trust had eviscerated his net worth. He quickly rebuilt his fortune, though, through a series of leveraged buyout deals. Most famously, with his partner Ray Chambers he purchased Gibson Greeting Cards for $80 million (all but $1 million of which they borrowed). They revitalized it, and took it public again for $290 million. In later years, Simon turned his attention to building a Pacific Rim merchant banking house with his sons, Bill and Peter.

From 1980 to 1984, Simon was president of the U.S. Olympic Committee. Under the leadership of Simon and Pete Ueberroth, the 1984 summer games in Los Angeles turned a profit of $225 million. These were the first profitable games since 1932.

At the time, U.S. Olympic athletes were struggling under confusing regulations governing their amateur status and what kind of resources they could use to train. Soviet-bloc countries skirted the rules by bringing their athletes onto state payrolls, an option unavailable to American athletes. Simon used a large part of the 1984 profits to create the U.S. Olympic Foundation, an elegant solution to the dilemma facing American Olympians. American athletes would no longer be handicapped because their government did not subsidize their training. Instead, private citizens would offer the funds that would ensure American Olympians could afford to prepare as needed. "It was really all Bill's doing," said hockey executive William Tutt.

Simon could be charming, but he was also—in the admiring words of Ed Feulner, head of the Heritage Foundation—a "mean, nasty, tough bond trader who took no BS from anyone." To an interviewer who suggested that he didn't suffer fools gladly, Simon barked, "Do you?" If his teenage sons slept late, he woke them up by dumping ice water over their heads.

But Simon had a softer side, which made his philanthropy deeply personal. Simon and his family often visited the homeless teens at Covenant House, playing games with them and working in the kitchen. Later in life, Simon became a eucharistic minister of the Catholic Church, taking Communion to the sick, lonely, and dying. He required all members of the board of his personal foundation to perform 150 hours per year of hands-on service to the poor.

Simon was also tapped to serve other philanthropists. John Olin asked him to lead his foundation after Simon left the Ford administration. Olin wanted his funds to be used to strengthen the American free-market system, and Simon was a natural ally. Under Simon's direction, Olin funded what Simon called "the counter-intelligentsia," the scholars and organizations who became the intellectual infrastructure of modern conservatism and libertarianism. Because Olin had a particular concern with the impact of law on public policy and culture, Simon also supported a host of academic programs that developed the law and economics movement at top-flight schools around the country, including Harvard, Chicago, Columbia, and Virginia.

Simon's commitment to Olin's donor intent was forged by Henry Ford II's departure from the board of the Ford Foundation in frustration at its direction in 1977—and by his own experience serving on the board of the John D. and Catherine T. MacArthur Foundation from 1979 to 1994. Catherine MacArthur had read his book *A Time for Truth* and wanted her foundation "to have the same mandate as the Olin Foundation." It was not to be: Catherine's stepson, Rod MacArthur, quickly steered the foundation his own way. New board members from academia and government were elected, and without a clear mandate in the foundation's incorporating documents, they picked causes they cared about—many of which Simon believed would have infuriated the MacArthurs. "As a result," Simon later said, "the MacArthur Foundation lost its ability to do what its founder wanted it to do."

Simon carried on Olin's program of research and organization-building through his own William E. Simon Foundation, which funds programs that support free markets, faith, and strong families. The foundation has striven to build the capacity of the poor and needy to help themselves, and promulgated its founder's support for one-on-one service. It has funded scholarship programs for poor children in Catholic schools, Bible literacy programs, retirement funds for priests and religious workers, mentoring programs, homes for runaway youth, and aid to victims of domestic violence.

> Simon required all members of the board of his personal foundation to perform 150 hours per year of hands-on service to the poor.

Simon died in 2000, and his foundation is in the process of spending itself out of existence, like Olin's before it. That was an easy choice for Bill Simon. He believed that the capitalist system produced, in his words, "the greatest prosperity, the highest standards of living, and most important, the greatest individual freedom ever known to man"—and would soon enough bring forward new wealth, new philanthropists, and new ideas for improving America.

☞ *Justin Torres*

Further reading

○ *Philanthropy* magazine article, philanthropyroundtable.org/topic/excellence_in_philanthropy/simon_says

○ William Simon, *A Time for Reflection: An Autobiography* (Regnery, 2004)

ROBERT SMITH

Robert Smith was a prominent real-estate developer in the Washington metro area, best known for leading the development of Crystal City in Arlington, Virginia. He was also a leading benefactor of prominent institutions in the national capital, with significant donations to the National Gallery of Art, the University of Maryland, and regional sites of historic importance like Mount Vernon, Montpelier, and Abraham Lincoln's summer cottage.

Born in 1928 to a family of newly immigrated Jews, Smith spent his earliest years in New York City. During the Second World War, his father, a homebuilder and property manager, moved the family to Washington, D.C. Robert Smith graduated from the University of Maryland in 1950, and immediately went to work for his father's company. He expanded the portfolio of the Charles E. Smith Company, adding commercial properties to its existing stock of residential properties.

In 1961, Smith inked what came to be his signature deal: a 99-year lease on 20 acres of rundown land near Washington National Airport. In exchange for 3 percent of gross profits, he had the rights to the land on which Crystal City was built. Six years later, his father retired, and Robert, with his brother-in-law Robert Kogod, took charge of the company. One successful deal followed another. Shortly before a 2002 merger, the Charles E. Smith Company managed over 15 million square feet of office space and more than 30,000 residential units in D.C., Maryland, Virginia, Florida, Chicago, and Boston.

In 1952, Smith married a painter named Clarice Chasen. She taught him to appreciate art, and helped assemble the couple's superb collection of Renaissance-era bronze sculpture. In 1972, they made their first major donation to the National Gallery of Art. They befriended Paul Mellon, son of the gallery's founder, Andrew Mellon. When Paul Mellon retired from the board, he asked that Smith replace him as a trustee. Smith accepted, and soon was leading a $123 million fundraising campaign; from 1993 to 2003, he served as president of the board. In 2008, the Smiths announced their intention to donate their entire collection to the National Gallery.

In the mid-1990s, the University of Maryland approached Smith about a business-school donation, and he asked for a concrete, multi-year strategy for raising the school's stature. He gave the business school a $15 million gift in 1997, and the Robert H. Smith School of Business has since shot up in the rankings—reaching the top 20 nationwide, and the top five among public schools. The Smiths later gave the University of Maryland another $15 million to complete the 318,000-square-foot Clarice Smith Performing

Arts Center. Another $30 million was offered in 2005, making the family the largest benefactor of public education in Maryland's history.

But their patronage of higher education extended beyond College Park: the Smiths were the lead donors to the Wilmer Institute at Johns Hopkins University, which is intended to become the nation's leading treatment and research center for eye diseases. At Hebrew University in Jerusalem, whose board Smith chaired from 1981 to 1985, they made major gifts for plant science and agricultural genetics research, and for expanding interdisciplinary research among those disciplines and animal sciences, biochemistry, nutrition, and environmental studies.

But Smith is perhaps best remembered for his leadership in preserving sites of historic interest. In the mid-1990s, he was asked to help fund an archaeological survey at Montpelier, the bucolic plantation home of James Madison. Smith had been reading biographies of the Founders, and felt a great respect for Madison, co-author of the *Federalist Papers*, driving intellect behind the Constitution, and 4th President of the United States. Smith helped fund the dig, and then led an effort to conserve 200 acres of old-growth forest on the property. He put up a $10 million challenge to increase the capacity of the Constitutional Village, a facility at Montpelier that hosts weeklong seminars on the Constitution.

> "One who has forgotten to be thankful has fallen asleep in the midst of life."

In 2000, Smith took on another preservation project: Mount Vernon. His donations helped build theaters and auditoriums, endowed a senior curator position, created a book-publishing fund, and redesigned Mount Vernon's website. He conceived and underwrote the "big tree program," in which 65 mature trees (some over 40 feet tall and weighing four tons) were planted to create a natural barrier between newly constructed facilities and the historic grounds. The trees are species that existed in eighteenth-century northern Virginia: elm, maple, tulip poplar, oak, beech, and American holly. Most recently, the Smiths played an instrumental role in preparing for construction of the Presidential library for George Washington.

Smith also took charge of restoring the Benjamin Franklin House in London, which opened on Ben Franklin's 300th birthday in 2006. It was at 36 Craven Street that Franklin served as deputy postmaster for the British colonies and befriended many of the most important political and intellectual leaders in the empire. Smith not only re-created the townhouse but funded a scholarship center to encourage research into Franklin.

When Abraham Lincoln's summer cottage in northern Washington, D.C., was reopened to the public in 2008, the Smiths had paid for more than $7 million of the $15 million restoration. At Monticello, they permanently endowed a center for Jefferson studies with $15 million. Smith was a major benefactor of Gettysburg National Military Park, and helped fund renovations at the New York Historical Society. The list goes on.

Arguably America's most important recent preserver of historic sites associated with the Founders, Smith explained his support as a token of his gratitude. "My family has had tremendous opportunities because we live in this free, democratic society, for which I am thankful," Smith said when President George W. Bush awarded him a National Humanities Medal. "One who has forgotten to be thankful has fallen asleep in the midst of life."

— Christopher Levenick

Further reading

○ *Philanthropy* magazine article, philanthropyroundtable.org/topic/excellence_in_ philanthropy/build_hold_give

○ David Smith, *Conversations with Papa Charlie: A Memory of Charles E. Smith* (Capital Books, 2000)

JAMES SMITHSON

James Smithson was a Briton who died in Italy in 1829 at the age of 75. Six years later, the primary beneficiary of Smithson's will died, and urgent letters were sent to Washington, D.C. It emerged that Smithson's estate, worth an estimated £100,000, had devolved "to the United States of America, to found at Washington, under the name of the Smithsonian Institution, an Establishment for the increase & diffusion of knowledge among men." It was the first time a private individual had made such a gift to the new nation, and added new contours to American philanthropy.

Smithson was born in 1754, the illegitimate son of Elizabeth Macie and Hugh Smithson, the first duke of Northumberland. During his years in Pembroke College at Oxford University, he became interested in the natural sciences, particularly chemistry. His research so impressed his colleagues and mentors that within a year of graduating from Oxford he was admitted as a fellow of the Royal Society of London.

Deprived of the right to his father's titles, Smithson set out to establish his name respectably and quickly gained the regard of his peers. Though he would call London home, he spent many years traveling the world to obtain samples of minerals and meteorites, study geography, and examine the mining and manufacturing processes.

Smithson's interests were broad: he investigated improved methods for making coffee and tea, wrote a paper on "Some improvements of lamps," and was said to have once held a small container to a woman's face in order to capture her tear, take it to his study, and analyze it. While doing much for his romantic reputation, the story has a note of plausibility; the majority of Smithson's work was dedicated to studying the chemical composition of compounds.

His methods were scrupulously careful, and he acknowledged the importance of detail in scientific work. At the end of a paper on the element fluorine he wrote that "measuring the importance of the subject by the magnitude of the object" might lead some people to "cast a supercilious look on this discussion; but the particle and the planet are subject to the same laws, and what is learned of the one will be known of the other." He advocated for publication of even marginal advances in scientific investigation, rather than withholding them on the assumption that they were insufficiently important.

> James Smithson's gift to a people and a country he did not know personally grew out of his interest in a "culture of improvement" and a belief that the U.S. would play an important role in future human progress.

It is not entirely clear how Smithson acquired his fortune. It seems to have been inherited, although biographers split on whether it resulted from a combination of inheritances from several relatives, or if it was Smithson's own careful investment of his mother's estate. In any case, by the time Smithson wrote his will in 1826 he was a wealthy man.

After providing an annuity for his servant, Smithson left his estate to a nephew, and in the event of his death to his children. But in the event Smithson's nephew had no children, the estate would transfer to the U.S. and the broad pursuit of knowledge.

Why America remains a mystery. Despite his world travels, Smithson had never visited the United States. He is not known to have been in regular communication with any Americans, and his papers—other than his will—never mention the U.S. The question of why Smithson chose to deed his estate to the citizens of a nation he seemingly had no connection to may never be satisfactorily answered. Heather Ewing, author of the most recent and comprehensive biography of Smithson, suggests that his donation reflected the late-eighteenth century's interest in a "culture of improvement," and a widespread belief that the United States would play an important role in advancing the arts and sciences.

A handwritten note later discovered among Smithson's papers suggests his decision was partly motivated by a bastard son's search for legitimacy, perhaps immortality. "The best blood of England flows in my veins," Smithson lamented, "but this avails me not." He hoped that his quests in the world of science might help his name "live in the memory of man when the titles of the Northumberlands and the Percys are extinct and forgotten."

Regardless of Smithson's motivation, the bequest flummoxed our government. President Andrew Jackson was unsure of the constitutional propriety of accepting the gift, and turned the matter over to Congress. Former President John Quincy Adams, then a Representative from Massachusetts, championed the gift as being consonant with "the spirit of the age." Senator John Calhoun of South Carolina vigorously disagreed, proclaiming it "beneath the dignity of the United States to receive gifts of this kind from anyone." Adams won that argument, and in 1836 Congress sent an envoy to London to secure the funds.

It took two more years of paperwork and promising that the stipulated institution would be built, but eventually our representative carried 11 boxes of gold coins back to the U.S. mint. The sovereigns were recast into $508,318 worth of hard currency—a sum equivalent to 1/66 of the federal budget. After nearly an additional decade of wrangling over what shape it should take, Congress formally established the Smithsonian Institution in 1846.

Since then, the Smithsonian has robustly achieved the ambitious goal set by its donor. The institution is today the world's largest museum complex, and a prominent center of research. James Smithson established a powerful precedent that individuals, acting voluntarily, can wield private gifts to achieve public benefits, even ones as grand as "the increase & diffusion of knowledge among men."

↦ *Monica Klem*

Further reading

○ Heather Ewing, *The Lost World of James Smithson: Science, Revolution, and the Birth of the Smithsonian* (Bloomsbury Publishing USA, 2007)

○ Nina Burleigh, *The Stranger and the Statesman: James Smithson, John Quincy Adams, and the Making of America's Greatest Museum: The Smithsonian* (Harper Collins, 2004)

○ William Rhees, "James Smithson and His Bequest," Smithsonian Miscellaneous Collections, Vol. XXI (Smithsonian Institution, 1881)

LELAND STANFORD

Leland Stanford built his railroad wealth in an era of rough-and-tumble politics and crony capitalism. He translated his riches into an institution that brought elite education west of the Rockies, became one of the world's most highly regarded universities, and incubated many of the twentieth century's technological triumphs.

Born in 1824 and raised in the Mohawk River valley near Albany, New York, A. Leland Stanford never used his given name of Amasa. He studied in the small town of Cazenovia, apprenticed at law in Albany, and went west in 1845 to open a legal practice in the new state of Wisconsin. Stanford spent seven years there, and married Jane Lathrop. But his firm faltered, and after a fire consumed his law office and library he turned his eyes farther west. In 1852, he followed his five brothers to California.

Stanford started off in ancillary businesses of the California Gold Rush, keeping a grocery store then a wholesale shop in Placer County. He participated in the founding of California's Republican Party, and was eventually elected governor in 1861. That same year, he became one of the four principal investors in the Central Pacific Railroad, which Congress authorized in 1862 to build the eastbound section of the first transcontinental railroad.

The transcontinental railroad was a remarkable feat of engineering, especially the Central Pacific's herculean efforts to carve tracks through the heights of the Sierra Nevada. Stanford, as president, enjoyed the triumph of driving the "golden spike" at Promontory Summit, Utah, in 1869 and for the rest of his life Stanford would remain one of California's best-known figures. From 1868 to 1890, he headed a second railroad, the Southern Pacific, which later merged with the Central Pacific. In 1885, he was elected to the U.S. Senate.

Political maneuvering made Stanford a very rich man. He participated in the worst practices of the Gilded Age: stock watering, kickbacks, rebates, bribes, collusion, monopoly. There is no acquitting Stanford on this front; his participation in such schemes is amply recorded in his letters.

Stanford is best remembered today, however, not for corruption but for a tribute to his only child. Leland DeWitt Stanford was born in 1868, and eventually came to call himself Leland Stanford Jr. On a trip to Europe in 1884, Leland Jr. died of typhoid fever. His parents were beside themselves. In their grief, the Stanfords pledged to themselves that "the children of California shall be our children."

What the children of California needed, they determined, was a modern university. They traveled through the East, visiting colleges along the

Atlantic seaboard. They learned about the practical education and applied sciences taught at new land-grant institutions like Cornell. And they were impressed by the modernizing curricular reforms taking place at many of the old, elite schools like Harvard.

In 1885, they founded the Leland Stanford Junior University. It would be private, coeducational, non-sectarian, and tuition-free. It would offer an education designed to "fit the graduate for some useful pursuit"—focusing on engineering, agriculture, and other practical disciplines in addition to the liberal arts and core sciences. It was consciously aimed to break higher education from its northeastern stranglehold, bringing a great university to the shores of the Pacific.

The Stanfords were intimately involved in virtually all aspects of planning the school. They located it on their stock farm in Palo Alto and hired Frederick Olmsted to lay out the grounds. For the design of the school they settled on a quadrangle of facilities made from local materials that reflected the nearby California landscape.

With total giving that would amount today to half a billion dollars, Stanford personally funded the operations of the university during its early years. When he died in 1893, his estate was frozen by federal lawsuits over loan repayments on Central Pacific construction funds. During the lawsuit's six years, Jane kept the university afloat via creative transfers of her personal living funds.

> There is no denying that corruption made Stanford rich. But grief later motivated him to use his ill-gotten lucre to benefit the children of California, and all Americans.

Stanford University immediately attracted excellent students; Herbert Hoover was in its first class. It opened professional schools in business, engineering, medicine, and law, and soon resoundingly achieved its founders' goal of making top-flight higher education a truly national rather than regional enterprise. Then in 1939, two Stanford alumni—Bill Hewlett and David Packard—opened an electronics business in their Palo Alto garage, spawning what is now called Silicon Valley, and turning Stanford University into ground zero for some of the most creative entrepreneurship of the digital age.

"Perhaps the greatest sum ever given by an individual for any purpose is the gift of Senator Stanford," wrote Andrew Carnegie in 1889, "who undertakes to establish upon the Pacific coast, where he amassed his enormous fortune, a complete university." Impressed by Stanford's skill and determination in bringing his gift to life, Carnegie simply concluded: "He is to be envied."

⮞ Evan Sparks

Further reading

○ Hubert Bancroft, *History of the Life of Leland Stanford: A Character Study* (Biobooks, 1952)
○ Bertha Berner, *Mrs. Leland Stanford: An Intimate Portrait* (Stanford, 1935)
○ Norman Tutorow, *Leland Stanford: Man of Many Careers* (Pacific Coast Publishers, 1971)

NATHAN STRAUS

Nathan Straus was one of the greatest retail merchants in American history, a co-owner of the Macy's and Abraham & Straus department-store chains. He used his fortune to help the poor in New York City, fund Jewish causes at home and abroad, and create safe milk at a time when milk was the leading killer of children. One of the most successful businessmen of his time, Straus gave away almost all of his money during his lifetime. For Straus, it was a point of principle. Invoking a Jewish proverb, he wrote in his will: "What you give for the cause of charity in health is gold, what you give in sickness is silver, and what you give in death is lead."

At the age of 18, Nathan Straus launched a glass and china import business with his brother and father. In 1874, L. Strauss & Son began to operate the china and glassware department at Macy & Co. Within a few years, they had the highest profits of any department and accounted for 18 percent of the total gross at Macy's. By 1898, the Straus family owned both Macy's and the Brooklyn store Abraham & Straus.

Nathan Straus had an instinct for merchandising. He was the first to offer depository accounts, against which customers could draw as they shopped. He was at the forefront of bargain sales, demonstrations, and store exhibitions. Perhaps most importantly he opened a lunch counter at Macy's—not to mention public restrooms—making shopping into something more than an errand. He helped turn it into a recreational activity, a way for middle-class women to spend part of a day.

All of this brought the Straus family great wealth. Nathan and his brothers were instilled with a sense of civic duty, and this was expressed by serving in public office. Nathan was Parks Commissioner of New York from 1889 to 1893, and was offered the Democratic nomination for mayor. (He declined.) Other times the brothers exercised civic leadership in a private capacity. During the Panic of

1893, for example, Straus saw firsthand the widespread human suffering. In New York City alone, over 39,000 families found their breadwinners without work. Thousands of homeless men wandered the streets, searching for work or food.

Nathan Straus did all he could to alleviate misery. As the terrible winter of 1893–94 blanketed the city, he provided 1.5 million buckets of coal to the poor. The following year, he supplied 2 million tickets for coal, food, and lodging at shelters he established. When coal was selling for 20¢ per pail, he supplied it at 5¢ to those who were poor, and gave away 2,000 tons for free to those who were desperate.

Straus undertook many other charitable initiatives. During the Spanish-American War, Rabbi Joseph Krauskopf alerted him of the need for pure water for the American troops in Santiago de Cuba. Straus sprang into action, buying a water distillation plant with a daily capacity of 20,000 gallons for the soldiers. In 1909, he led earthquake-relief efforts in Italy. When the Great War triggered widespread layoffs, he provided more than a million 1¢ meals for the unemployed. He paid for the construction of dozens of tuberculosis clinics from coast to coast—as well as a Catholic Church in Lakewood, New Jersey.

But the great philanthropic crusade of his life was providing safe milk for the nation's children. Before the Industrial Revolution, the overwhelming majority of babies were breast-fed. And most older children had access to fresh cow's milk because they lived on farms. But as the population moved increasingly to cities, the milk supply became a problem. Rich urbanites could keep a cow in their stables, but the less affluent had to depend on "swill milk." Produced by cows kept by brewers and distillers to eat up their agricultural waste, it was of the poorest quality imaginable.

> It is estimated that the efforts of Nathan Straus directly saved the lives of 445,800 children.

The railroads changed the situation in some ways, allowing fresh milk to be brought quickly to cities. It looked and tasted wholesome, but all too often it was not. Cows were milked by unwashed hands, and the milk was poured into unsterilized containers and transported long distances from farms to cities, without refrigeration. Along the way microorganisms multiplied quickly. Typhoid, diphtheria, and cholera can all be contracted from contaminated milk, even when there is no sign of spoilage. In New York in the 1850s, fewer than half all children born lived to see their fifth birthday, and bad milk was one of the biggest culprits.

Straus knew there was a scientific solution to this problem: pasteurization. He set to work both to provide pasteurized milk to needy children, and to have the process legally mandated for all milk sold. He set up milk stations in poor areas in New York City to give away pasteurized milk, and proof of the efficacy of his program was not long in coming. In 1891, fully 24 percent of babies born in New York City died in their first year. But of the 20,111 children fed on pasteurized milk supplied by Nathan Straus over a four-year period, only six died.

In 1898 Straus served as president of the city's Board of Health. He immediately donated pasteurization equipment to the city's orphan's asylum, located on what is now Roosevelt Island in the East River, which was run by the board. Straus established, at his own expense, 297 milk stations in 36 other cities. The national death rate for infants fell from 125 per thousand in 1891 to 16 in 1925. Altogether it is estimated that the efforts of Nathan Straus directly saved the lives of 445,800 children.

Straus's interest in eradicating disease and alleviating poverty extended beyond the shores of America. In 1912, he and his wife, Lina, traveled to Europe to attend the International Tuberculosis Conference in Rome. (His brother and sister-in-law went on the same trip, but sailed home aboard the *Titanic* and famously refused seats offered to them in the lifeboats.)

Before the conference, Nathan and Lina stopped in Palestine, which was ravaged at the time by disease and famine. The couple opened up a soup kitchen, and founded a health department there. Straus became active in the movement to create a Jewish state. He served as chair of the American Jewish Congress Committee and fought for the organization to adopt a stronger Zionist stance. The town of Natanya on the Mediterranean was named after him.

Straus returned to Palestine many times and his support would never waver—he gave over $1.5 million during the course of his life. He offered one of the first major gifts to Hadassah, the Zionist women's organization, for the support of a medical mission to Israel. He funded the construction of the Nathan and Lina Straus Health Center in Jerusalem, which he said was to be for all the inhabitants of the country, irrespective of race or creed. In 1927, after a great earthquake shook Palestine, Straus wired $25,000 to Jerusalem to help alleviate the suffering. At the age of 80, he served as the honorary chairman of the New York United Palestine Appeal, to which he donated $100,000. In 1931, Straus passed away at the age of 82, having expended most of his fortune on good causes.

"Candidly, as a Jew," Straus once reflected in the *Christian Herald*, "I have often felt that I owed this apology or explanation to my co-religionists, for the fact is that I have done a great deal more for Christians than I have for Jews. But when, as a Jew, the impulse has come to me to do more for my own people, the controlling thought has been that the God of all mankind does not draw any racial or religious lines in the distribution of his bounties."

‸ *Naomi Schaefer Riley*

Further reading

○ *Philanthropy* magazine article, philanthropyroundtable.org/topic/excellence_in_philanthropy/the_milk_man

○ June Hall McCash, *A Titanic Love Story: Ida and Isidor Straus* (Mercer University Press, 2012)

○ Lina Gutherz Straus, *Disease in milk: the remedy, pasteurization—the life work of Nathan Straus* (E. P. Dutton, 1917)

JOHN TEMPLETON

One of the world's most successful mutual fund managers, John Templeton eventually dedicated much of his money and energy to research into the overlap between two of his deepest fascinations: science and religion.

Born in 1912 in Winchester, a small town in rural Tennessee, Templeton was a straight-A student whose parents encouraged his healthy curiosity. They let him buy dynamite to dispose of backyard tree stumps, and gunpowder to manufacture his own fireworks. They took him on cross-country road trips in the early days of automobiles.

He studied at Yale and Oxford (the latter as a Rhodes Scholar), then took a job on Wall Street. His investing strategy was guided by the principles of thrift and positive thinking. "Bull markets are born on pessimism, grown on skepticism, mature on optimism, and die on euphoria," he said. "The time of maximum pessimism is the best time to buy, and the time of maximum optimism is the best time to sell." In 1939—on the eve of World War II, a time of maximum pessimism—Templeton purchased $100 worth of every publicly traded stock available to him that was trading for less than a dollar. He bought into 104 companies, only four of which never panned out. After an average holding period of four years, that portfolio had returned 400 percent. Templeton often mentioned that he wished he had held those particular stocks longer.

Templeton developed a methodical investment philosophy based on his own valuations of companies. "Templeton's basic formula is to divide the total value of a company by the number of shares the company has distributed," wrote biographer William Proctor. "This calculating will give you the true value of a company's stock, and if the market price is lower, it's a bargain." This method was used to operate the Templeton Growth Fund, opened in 1954. It was spectacularly successful, with the fund producing an annualized return of 14 percent over several decades. A $10,000 investment in 1954 would have been worth $2 million in 1992, when Templeton sold the fund.

Templeton attributed his success in part to his diligent research and in part to his relocation to the Bahamas in 1968, where he felt insulated from the groupthink on Wall Street. Templeton also attributed his success to the blessings of God, with whom he felt a closeness and unity. Throughout his life, Templeton was inspired by religious idealism.

As he grew financially successful, Templeton began to dabble in philanthropy. He built on his boyhood interests in science, philosophy, and religion. One of his first philanthropic initiatives was the Templeton Prize for Progress in Religion, which he created in 1972 out of the conviction that Alfred Nobel's prizes neglected metaphysical wisdom, and specifically the role of religion in progress. He offered a purse calculated to be larger than that of the Nobel Prizes, and stipulated that the award was to be ecumenical, with at least one judge from each of the five major religions "so that no child of God would feel excluded." To maximize attention to the winners, Templeton arranged for Prince Philip, the Duke of Edinburgh, to award the Templeton Prize at Buckingham Palace.

> Templeton believed that material, social, and religious progress were bound together.

The first honor was given to Mother Teresa of Calcutta, who six years later would win the Nobel Peace Prize. Other notable Templeton laureates have included Frère Roger, Cicely Saunders, Billy Graham, Aleksandr Solzhenitsyn, Stanley Jaki, Baba Amte, Charles Colson, Michael Novak, Freeman Dyson, and the Dalai Lama. Since 2000, laureates have tended to be philosophers, physicists, or biologists with insights that bear on religion.

Templeton believed that material, social, and religious progress were bound together, and that society advanced when these spheres moved together in unity. Templeton denied that there was any fundamental conflict between science and religion, and believed that each field has ground-breaking insights to share with the other. He wrote: "Is our human consciousness only a tiny manifestation of a vast creative consciousness that is often referred to by…names such as God, Allah, Spirit, Yahweh, Brahman, or the Creator? Has our human concept of this creative source been too small?…How can we learn to encourage progress and discovery in ways that tap the deep symphonies of divine creativity and involve us in God's purposes? Perhaps future generations will use scientific methods to speed up the search."

In 1987, Templeton established the John Templeton Foundation as a philanthropic vehicle for these inquiries. Through the foundation, he funded ventures ranging from an essay contest inviting youngsters to explore the spiritual principles of life, to an "honor roll" for character-building at universities, to a new college at Oxford University. Today the foundation has an endowment exceeding $2 billion, and funds research in four areas related to Templeton's "big questions": science (in particular math, physics, biology, psychology, and sociology), character development, free enterprise, and genetics. Speeding the pace of religious inquiry so that it might match the progress in science is a particular interest.

Templeton remained closely involved with the Templeton Prize and his foundation until his death in 2008 at age 95. He was married and widowed twice, and had three children, and as he aged he felt an urgency in his philanthropic work. "Evidence indicates that the rate of spiritual development is accelerating," he wrote. "Throughout the 200,000 years of our history as a species, there have been periods of gradual growth, followed by rapid development…. Now, a new vision of our place and purpose in the cosmos is unfolding. Possibly, we may be setting the stage for a giant leap forward in our spiritual understanding."

Templeton received many honors and awards during his lifetime, including a knighthood from Queen Elizabeth II. But the man known for his humility and belief in unity might well have preferred the Biblically inspired tribute offered by Princeton Theological Seminary: "There was a man sent from God whose name was John."

— Evan Sparks

Further reading

○ Robert Herrmann, *Sir John Templeton: Supporting Scientific Research for Spiritual Discoveries* (Templeton Press, 2004)

○ William Proctor, *The Templeton Touch* (Templeton Press, 2012)

JUDAH TOURO

Judah Touro was a leading merchant and philanthropist during the early days of our nation, known for benefactions throughout the country, but especially in Louisiana and Rhode Island. Born in 1775 in Newport, Rhode Island, Touro was the second son of Rabbi Isaac Touro, leader of Newport's synagogue.

Constructed in 1763, and now known as the Touro Synagogue due to the gifts and service of the Touro family, the Newport assembly was the recipient of a famous 1790 letter on religious liberty from George Washington. "The government of the United States," wrote Washington, "which gives to bigotry no sanction, to persecution no assistance, requires only that they who live under its protection should demean themselves as good citizens.... May the children of the stock of Abraham, who dwell in this land, continue to merit and enjoy the good will of the other inhabitants."

As a boy, Judah and his brother were apprenticed to their uncle, one of Boston's leading Jewish merchants. Judah fell in love with his cousin Catherine, but Judah's uncle disapproved. In 1801, his hopes of marriage firmly blocked, Judah left for the burgeoning port of New Orleans.

There, he opened a store handling consignments and shipments for colleagues in Boston. His timing was fortuitous. Touro established himself just before the Louisiana Purchase added New Orleans to the growing republic. The young man was ideally positioned to capitalize on the subsequent commercial boom. He traded in soap, candles, codfish, and other goods sent by his contacts in New England, and then invested his profits in ships and New Orleans real estate.

Touro's assets grew handsomely in value as the Crescent City expanded into one of America's preeminent urban centers. Within a decade, he was one of the wealthiest men in the entrepot. During the War of 1812, Touro volunteered as a private in the Louisiana Militia. He was seriously wounded in the Battle of New Orleans, and required more than a year to recover from injuries that his doctors initially assumed would be fatal.

Touro remained a devout Jew, although for most of his life he was without a synagogue. When he arrived in New Orleans, his co-religionists in the city could be counted on two hands; as late as 1826, there were no more than a few hundred Jews in all of Louisiana. In 1828, Touro supported the founding of New Orleans's first synagogue, which after some years divided into separate congregations in the Ashkenazi and Sephardic traditions. Touro, by then quite wealthy, gave generously to both congregations and attended the Sephardic gathering. (In 1881, the synagogues merged, and today the combined congregation is named for its benefactor.) Touro also created and funded numerous Jewish relief agencies and Hebrew schools in New Orleans.

Touro gave liberally and ecumenically. In 1824, he erected a free public library. He purchased a Christian church building and assumed its debts, while allowing the congregation to use the building rent-free in perpetuity. When a friend suggested the property might be valuable if sold for commercial purposes, Touro responded, "I am a friend to religion and I will not pull down the church to increase my means!" He founded a home for the poor, and during a yellow fever epidemic, he established a hospital. After his death, it became known as Touro Infirmary, and it remains the only nonprofit, faith-based community hospital in New Orleans. Influenced by the abolitionist views of his former Boston employer, he would also purchase slaves in order to manumit them.

> More than 200 years ago, this religious Jew started helping Americans of every religion and state of life, in multiple ways that continue to have positive effects today.

Touro's generosity also extended to his early hometowns of Newport and Boston. In 1840, he gave $10,000 anonymously to complete the long-languishing Bunker Hill Monument. (By nature somewhat bashful and retiring, he briefly considered withdrawing his gift when his anonymity was compromised.) At the dedication ceremonies in 1843, Daniel Webster, antebellum America's greatest orator, praised Touro and fellow funder Amos Lawrence in verse that is usually credited to Oliver Wendell Holmes:

> Amos and Judah! Venerated names!
> Patriarch and prophet press their equal claims.
> Like generous coursers running "neck to neck,"
> Each aids the work by giving it a check.
> Christian and Jews, they carry out one plan
> For though of different faith, each is in heart a man.

Touro died in 1854. In his will, he bequeathed $500,000 to institutions around the country—more than half of which went to non-Jewish causes. (As a percentage of GDP, these gifts would approximate $2 billion today.) The will includes Touro Synagogue and Touro Infirmary; various benevolent societies and hospitals; orphanages, almshouses, and asylums; libraries and schools; and relief for Jews overseas. According to one contemporary observer, "he gave ten times more than any Christian in the city to aid the cause of Christians in the land of Judaea."

He also gave thousands of dollars each to 23 Jewish congregations in 14 states—especially the Newport synagogue, where he endowed the cemetery in which he was laid to rest, the final surviving member of the Touro family line. "The last of his name," reads his tombstone, "he inscribed it in the Book of Philanthropy to be remembered forever."

↝ *Evan Sparks*

Further reading
○ Leon Huhner, *The Life of Judah Touro* (Jewish Publication Society of America, 1946)
○ Max Kohler, *Judah Touro, Merchant and Philanthropist* (American Jewish Society, 1905)

WILLIAM VOLKER

William Volker made his fortune manufacturing home furnishings, and dedicated the overwhelming majority of that fortune to charity. He gave generously to causes and institutions throughout his adopted hometown of Kansas City. To the best of his ability, he gave anonymously.

At one point, Volker partnered with Kansas City public officials, hoping to increase the effectiveness of his giving. To his horror, he discovered that city leaders saw charity not as a way to help people help themselves, but rather as a form of patronage that would help them retain power. The experience led Volker to a deeper appreciation for private initiative, and a desire to fund the study and promotion of classical liberalism.

Born near Hanover, Germany, in 1859, William Volker was taught early in life to work hard and love God. His father entrusted him with responsibility beyond his years, as when he charged the five-year-old boy with feeding the family's cows. His mother, pious and kind, provided religious instruction, and William read the Scriptures every day for the rest of his life. When he was 12 years old, war broke out between France and Prussia; fearing William would be conscripted, his family left Germany. They immigrated to the United States, settling in Chicago just days after the Great Fire of 1871.

Volker departed Chicago at age 23, having saved enough capital to start a small business in Kansas City, Missouri. William Volker & Company sold home furnishings—picture frames, window shades, moldings. After a few difficult years, the business thrived; it posted profits every year except for 1930-31. By 1906, at the age of 47, Volker was a self-made millionaire. He would have acquired his first million sooner had he not made it his lifelong practice to give away, by one estimate, about one-third of each year's income.

Early every morning after Volker arrived at work, he made himself available to employees, friends, and callers facing problems. He gave many thousands of small gifts to people with immediate needs—a pair of new dentures for an elevator operator, tuition for a hardworking college student. So personally involved was he that he wrote out every check himself, so that each gift could be kept confidential. While he tried to ascertain that there was a real need of assistance before offering aid, Volker would give a person the benefit of the doubt. He never wanted to risk denying help to someone in true need.

Deeply invested in the civic life of Kansas City, Volker supported scores of institutions and causes, building a research laboratory, diagnostic clinic, and nurse's residence at the Research Hospital, acquiring a collection of Chinese art for the Nelson-Atkins Museum—even purchasing two camels for the Swope Park Zoo. Perhaps his most visible contribution was to the University of Kansas City. Volker was the principal driver behind the creation of the school, donating 40 acres for the campus and endowing it with millions of dollars to fund the university's library, president's house, and science building.

Between 1908 and 1915, Volker worked closely with the city government. In 1908, he helped found the Kansas City Board of Pardons and Paroles, which oversaw the process of releasing prisoners. He made it a condition of parole that employment was arranged before release—"no job, no parole"—and that parolees agree to garnished wages, with the deducted funds deposited into a savings account. Impressed with the success of this program, he began to look for other ways to partner with local authorities.

In 1910, Volker led the creation of the Board of Public Welfare, the first municipal welfare department in the country. Excited about continuing his philanthropy through the new agency, Volker was surprised to learn that the city failed to adequately fund its commitments. He quietly contributed $50,000 to make up the difference. Almost immediately, local politicians—most notably, Tom Pendergast, the machine boss in Kansas City—began using the funds to further their partisan interests. After Volker retired in 1918, the board became a barely veiled political enterprise. The episode taught Volker, he later explained, that "political charity isn't charity." He concluded that "government must be restricted to those activities which can be entrusted to the worst citizens, not the best."

Volker returned to his extensive program of private philanthropy, which he continued until his death in 1947. When Friedrich von Hayek's *The Road to Serfdom* was published in 1944, Volker discovered a thinker who made sense of his experience. Disillusioned by government failures, he began funding scholars, writers, and teachers who could champion the cause of free enterprise, individual initiative, and limited government. He started supporting free-market and libertarian institutions, including the Foundation for Economic Education, the Institute for Humane Studies, and what became the Intercollegiate Studies Institute. He underwrote Hayek's salary at the University of Chicago, and paid a stipend that enabled Ludwig von Mises to teach at New York University.

Perhaps the most consequential check William Volker ever wrote was dated May 7, 1945. Made to Friedrich Hayek for $2,000, it underwrote the travel expenses for 17 American scholars to attend the first meeting of the Mont Pelerin Society. Volker did not live to see all of the Mont Pelerin Society's accomplishments, but with that small boost to a group of penurious writers and scholars, he helped launch an international network that distinguished itself in defending freedom in the West during the last half of the twentieth century.

> From disappointing experience, Volker concluded that government should "be restricted to those activities which can be entrusted to the worst citizens." For more idealistic and selfless improvement, society depended on personal generosity.

Mont Pelerin Society members periodically gather and debate to refine their ideas and encourage one another. Eight members eventually won the Nobel Prize in economics—four of whom, thanks to Volker, attended the first meeting. According to Nancy Hoplin and Ron Robinson, 22 of the 66 economic advisers to Ronald Reagan's 1980 presidential campaign were members. In Western Europe, three members of the Mont Pelerin Society became heads of state.

Closer to home, the people of Kansas City continue to honor Volker today. There is a Volker Elementary School, a Volker Memorial Fountain, and a Volker Boulevard. The University of Missouri-Kansas City Volker Campus is named for him, as is the Volker Neighborhood Association. This local outpouring, in the face of his diligent efforts to adhere to the Biblical precept that "alms...be in secret," is a testament to William Volker's remarkable generosity.

⊷ Monica Klem

Further reading

○ David Boutros, "William Volker and Company," Kansas City Public Library
   (July 2007)

○ Herbert Cornuelle, *Mr. Anonymous: The Story of William Volker* (Caxton Printers, 1951)

○ Nicole Hoplin and Ron Robinson, *Funding Fathers: The Unsung Heroes of the Conservative
   Movement* (Regnery, 2008)

MADAM C. J. WALKER

Madam C. J. Walker ranks among the greatest African-American philanthropists in history. When she died in 1919, Walker was widely eulogized as the first woman to become a self-made millionaire. The assumption may not have been correct; the estimated value of her remaining estate at the time of her death was $600,000 (about $8 million in today's dollars). Nonetheless, several generations of African Americans looked upon her as proof that dramatic economic success was possible for blacks as well as whites.

Born in 1867 as Sarah Breedlove, her first years were spent on the Louisiana plantation where her family had worked as slaves. She was the first in her family to be born free. Her parents died when she was a young child, leaving her to live with her sister. Ill treatment by her cruel brother-in-law motivated 14-year-old Sarah to leave the household and marry Moses McWilliams. Seven years later McWilliams died, and Sarah and her three-year-old daughter, Lelia, moved to St. Louis, where three of her brothers lived.

She took up work as a washerwoman. She remarried in 1894, and soon found herself supporting a drunkenly abusive and openly unfaithful husband. Determined to provide her daughter with a better life, she managed to send Lelia to Knoxville College in Tennessee. In 1903, she left her husband and took a job as a sales agent for Annie Pope-Turnbo, a St. Louis businesswoman who produced products that claimed to stimulate hair growth.

After two years, Sarah moved to Colorado. Her success as Pope-Turnbo's Denver sales agent suggested that she might begin selling hair products of her own. She created her own line of hair-care products, made specifically for African-American women. C. J. and her third husband, Charles Walker, spent a year traveling through the South, building the foundations of a mail-order business. By 1908, she had trained hundreds of sales agents. A visit to Indianapolis in 1910 convinced the Walkers that it would be a good location for a permanent headquarters.

An Indianapolis campaign to build a new YMCA recreation facility in a black neighborhood provided her first opportunity for public philanthropy. She explained her $1,000 gift saying, "If the association can save our boys, our girls will be saved, and that's what I am interested in." As her reputation for generosity grew, Walker was inundated with requests for help. Initially inclined to help individuals who showed a desire for self-improvement, the focus of her charitable giving gradually shifted away from individuals (due to a series of bad experiences) and toward organizations and causes instead.

In 1910, she created the Madam C. J. Walker Manufacturing Company of Indiana, putting up the necessary capital herself. (She had adopted "Madam" as a first name, to preclude being called "Auntie" by whites.) Walker traveled extensively, going as far as the Caribbean and Central America to increase the distribution of her products and train new agents. In 1916 she created the Madam C. J. Walker Benevolent Association, staffed by employees of her company, arguing that the beneficial publicity that flowed from charitable work was good for business.

> "I have built my own factory on my own ground…. Not for myself alone, but to do all the good I can for the uplift of my race."

Walker was devoted to improving the lives of African Americans. She was a major funder of anti-lynching programs run by the NAACP and the National Association of Colored Women. She led the effort to preserve the home of Frederick Douglass in the Anacostia neighborhood of Washington, D. C. When she passed away in 1919, Walker left the bulk of her estate to charity.

"I am a woman who came from the cotton fields of the South," summarized Walker in a speech to the National Negro Business League Convention a few years before her death. "From there I was promoted to the washtub. From there I was promoted to the cook kitchen. And from there I promoted myself into the business of manufacturing…. I have built my own factory on my own ground."

"I am in the business world, not for myself alone," she told Booker T. Washington in 1912, "but to do all the good I can for the uplift of my race." She worked toward that goal not only through her philanthropic activity, but by giving thousands of African-American women well-paying and dignified jobs as commissioned sales agents. As the *New York Post* acknowledged following her death, Walker's rags-to-riches life demonstrated that the American dream of personal success—and then sharing that success with one's fellows—applied to blacks as well as whites, and that talented and generous citizens of any color "may rise to the most distinctive heights of American achievement."

↳ *Monica Klem*

Further reading

○ Beverly Lowry, *Her Dream of Dreams: The Rise and Triumph of Madam C. J. Walker* (Vintage Books, 2003)

○ A'Lelia Bundles, *On Her Own Ground: The Life and Times of Madam C. J. Walker* (Washington Square Press, 2001)

JOHN WALTON

John Walton was a son of Walmart founder Sam Walton who used his multibillion-dollar inheritance to champion some of the most effective educational reforms of the last generation. Born and raised in Arkansas where his father owned a five-and-dime store, John attended the local public schools and then enrolled at the College of Wooster in Ohio. After two years he dropped out and joined the Army in 1966.

Walton qualified for the Special Forces, and served as a combat medic in Vietnam. His heroic efforts during fierce fighting in Laos won him a Silver Star for valor. He was once asked why he volunteered for the Green Berets. "I figured if you're going to do something," he said, "you should do it the best you can."

After his discharge from the service, Walton decided to strike out on his own. "He's the most independent of the bunch," his father later wrote. John tried his hand at crop dusting in Texas and Arizona. He launched a boat-building business in California. He joined the board of Walmart in 1992. Seven years later he founded True North Partners, a venture-capital fund that invested in high-technology companies.

Walton's philanthropy was principally focused on improving K-12 education in the United States. In 1983, he read *A Nation at Risk*, with its ominous warnings about the failings of public education. He circulated it among family members, prompting a number of discussions about ways to improve education. Sam Walton announced, "I'd like to see an all-out revolution in education."

In many ways, John Walton spent his life trying to bring that "all-out revolution" to schoolhouses. It was a more daunting task than he originally anticipated. "Our family followed the usual course of education giving," he explained in 2002. "You begin to support programs you hope will address the problems, and you see some improvement. But the improvements are transitory, lasting only as long as the heroes making them work are on the job. When the heroes go away, the programs become ineffective."

To create lasting change, Walton came to realize, the structure of the nation's public education would have to change. "If you look at it in terms of power," he explained, "you will 'follow the money.' The money in education comes from the top, filters its way down, and various interest groups and factions pull off their share into what they think is important. The customers at the bottom just take what they're given." Public schools would only improve, he believed, if "customers"—parents—had the power to leave ineffective schools and take the money with them.

In 1998, Walton and financier Ted Forstmann created the Children's Scholarship Fund. Each of the two donors pledged $50 million to underwrite scholarships that would enable low-income students to attend private schools. Their $100 million was able to fund 40,000 scholarships. In CSF's first season, an astonishing 1.2 million applications came in. Walton and Forstmann were right in guessing that low-income parents all over the country were eager to have better alternatives for their children's education, and would act if given any opening.

The initial donation was an experiment, and nothing was promised beyond a four-year period of support. But CSF's early results were so impressive—and the demand for its scholarships so intense—that the board and founders not only continued but greatly extended the program, which continues to flourish today. Through 2015, CSF has provided $645 million in scholarships to 152,000 low-income children. The great majority of CSF families are African-American, Latino, or recent immigrants. CSF serves a large number of single mothers, and grandparents who are raising their grandchildren.

Walton believed it was important to offer immediate help to children and parents who are struggling with failing public schools today. That was stage one. He also understood that it was necessary to change public education itself, to reduce the future ranks of ill-served kids.

Walton was an early backer of charter schools as an essential response to the long-term problem. As public schools that operate independent of district bureaucracies, charter schools enjoy a degree of autonomy in exchange for a measure of accountability. Recognizing the potential of charter-school successes to refute the defeatist notion that poverty and other factors make inner-city children unteachable, Walton drove his family's effort to seed effective charter schools across the country. Under his leadership, the Walton Family Foundation provided startup grants of $250,000 to hundreds of charter schools. Other support was offered to groups that organize and encourage charter-school growth, and cultivate and train administrators, principals, and teachers.

The Walton Family Foundation has watered those initial seeds by supporting venture-philanthropy groups like the NewSchools Venture Fund. Founded in 1998, NewSchools raises capital from a variety of donors and then invests it in promising charter-school networks so they can replicate their successful educational formulas in additional schools and fresh cities. This early funding for educational entrepreneurs has proven crucial in the expansion of impressive charter-school networks like KIPP, Uncommon Schools, Aspire Public Schools, Achievement First, and others, which collectively now operate hundreds of exemplary schools in scores of American cities.

John Walton further realized that large-scale school reform could not be accomplished without changing public policy. He founded the American Education Reform Foundation in 1991, which ultimately merged into today's American Federation for Children, which advocates for mechanisms that allow parents and children to choose schools matching their needs. As part of this public-policy work, Walton helped fund the legal defense of Cleveland's school voucher program, which in 2002 was constitutionally validated by the U.S. Supreme Court.

> John Walton believed public schools would only improve if "customers"—parents— had the power to leave ineffective schools and take the money with them.

John Walton died in a plane crash in 2005, when he was 58 years old. The year before, *Forbes* estimated his fortune at $18 billion. But such great wealth never seemed to affect him. Not long after a new charter school opened in San Diego, Walton made an unannounced visit, asking how he could be of service. The school's founder didn't recognize him, and told Walton that the bathrooms needed cleaning. Walton simply asked, "Where's the mop?" The fourth-wealthiest person in America then spent 25 minutes swabbing the floors, happy to help.

☞ *Naomi Schaefer Riley*

Further reading

○ *Philanthropy* magazine article, philanthropyroundtable.org/topic/excellence_in_ philanthropy/the_carnegie_of_school_choice

○ Sam Walton and John Huey, *Made in America: Sam Walton* (Doubleday, 1992)

○ "A Tribute to John Walton" (*Education Next*, Fall 2005)

GEORGE WASHINGTON

George Washington was well described as "first in war, first in peace, first in the hearts of his countrymen." What is much less known is that Washington was also first among the philanthropists of his generation. Throughout his life he was generous toward the poor; as he approached death he was revealed as the era's greatest patron of higher education.

The achievements of George Washington are without parallel in American history. Without his leadership, it is unlikely the Continental Army would have survived eight years of brutal war. Without his endorsement, the Constitution would probably never have been ratified. Without his guidance at innumerable points, our great experiment in republican government might have faltered. He was, in the elegant summation of one of his most perceptive biographers, the "indispensable man."

The brilliance of his public service sometimes blinds us to Washington's considerable achievements in private life. He was a self-made man who rose from relatively humble origins to acquire one of the largest fortunes in American history. Washington refused a salary even for his years as commander of the Continental Army. His wealth was all acquired in the private sector.

The basis of Washington's fortune was land. A surveyor in his youth, he had an eye for promising acreage, and owned property throughout Virginia, Maryland, Pennsylvania, Ohio, and Kentucky. This he collected by inheritance, purchase, and marriage—the widowed Martha Custis was the wealthiest woman in Virginia, and her marriage to Washington added some 17,000 acres to his holdings. Liquidity, however, was often a problem. Like many of his fellow planters, Washington was often poor-in-cash relative to his wealth of land.

Washington's early charitable giving reflected his upbringing in colonial Virginia. Life in the Northern Neck was built on reputation and hierarchy, British North America's closest approximation to the mores of the English country. Charitable giving was rarely institutional, but rather centered on a personal relationship between patrons and beneficiaries.

In 1769, for example, Washington offered his friend William Ramsay a sum of £25 annually so Ramsay's son could attend college at Princeton. "No other return is expected or wished for this offer than that you will accept it with the same freedom and good will with which it is made," he wrote, "and that you may not even consider it in the light of an obligation, or mention it as such; for be assured from me that it will never be known."

When Washington left Mount Vernon to assume command of the Continental Army, he left instructions to the groundskeeper that reflected a

Virginian's sense of liberality. "Let the Hospitality of the House, with respect to the poor, be kept up," he wrote. "Let no one go hungry away. If any of these kind of People should be in want of Corn, supply their necessities, provided it does not encourage them in idleness; and I have no objection to your giving my Money in Charity, to the Amount of forty or fifty Pounds a Year, when you think it well bestowed. What I mean, by having no objection, is, that it is my desire that it should be done."

Many biographers have observed that the Revolutionary War changed Washington's perspective. After eight years campaigning in the states of the mid-Atlantic and New England, his outlook became much more nationalistic. His politics and mores became closer to those of a Philadelphian than a Virginian.

This transition of his Revolutionary years was reflected, to some extent, in Washington's charitable giving. He grew more inclined to give as a donor than as a patron, to provide money for a cause rather than a cousin. While in New York and Philadelphia, President Washington made hundreds of gifts to churches and charities, many of which were offered under condition of anonymity and were only discovered after the publication of his papers.

> "No other return is expected or wished for this offer than that you will accept it with the same freedom and good will with which it is made."

"Washington," writes biographer Ron Chernow, "had particular sympathy for those imprisoned for debt, and gave generously to an organization—later called the Humane Society of the City of New York—that was formed to assist them." He often sent surplus food from the Presidential mansion to a nearby prison; when he made his Thanksgiving Day proclamation, Washington made a personal donation of beer and hot meals to persons imprisoned for debt. It was a rare instance in which he allowed his contribution to be made public, presumably because he thought it appropriate to set an example for the rest of the country.

Another favored cause for the childless Washington was the care and education of orphans. He contributed to orphanages in several states, but reserved his largest donations for the Alexandria Academy, established only a few miles from Mount Vernon.

In 1796, three years before he died, Washington offered a gift to Liberty Hall Academy of Lexington, Virginia: 100 shares of the James River and Kanawha Canal Company, worth at the time approximately $20,000. It was then the largest contribution to higher education in American history. Grateful for the gift, the school's trustees immediately renamed the college Washington Academy; today it is known as Washington and Lee University. By one estimate, roughly $12 of every current student's tuition is underwritten by the generosity of George Washington.

Generosity was an obligation to Washington. It was a virtue to be practiced constantly and liberally. "One thing more and I will close this letter," Washington once advised his step-grandson, George Washington Parke Custis, who was then attending college at Princeton. "Never let an indigent person ask, without receiving something, if you have the means; always recollecting in what light the widow's mite was viewed."

☞ *Christopher Levenick*

Further reading

○ James Flexner, *Washington: The Indispensable Man* (Little, Brown, 1974)

○ Leonard Helderman, *George Washington: Patron of Learning* (Century, 1932)

○ Writings of George Washington, etext.virginia.edu/washington/fitzpatrick

ISAIAH WILLIAMSON

Isaiah Williamson was the son of devout Pennsylvania Quakers, one of eight children, a farm boy who learned early on the value of industry, frugality, and honesty. At the age of 15, he apprenticed himself at a nearby country store. Within seven years, Williamson had saved $2,000—enough money to move to Philadelphia and open his own dry-goods business. By 1838, with assets worth about $2 million today, he retired, spending the next few years touring Europe.

But Williamson was unsuited for the life of a dilettante. He returned to Philadelphia, where he began investing his money in real estate and promising enterprises. By the 1880s he was known to be one of the wealthiest men in the commonwealth, with an estimated fortune of $20 million (approximately $500 million today). He was equally famous for his thrift, and was known throughout the city for making a meal of bread crusts, and keeping one suit for decades.

As he entered the last decades of his life, philanthropy engaged more and more of Williamson's attention. Determining the extent of his generosity is difficult, as virtually all of his donations were made in strict secrecy or under the pseudonym "Hez," but he is known to have handed off millions of dollars. Throughout the Delaware River basin he supported scores of asylums and orphanages, hospitals and benevolent societies, libraries, seminaries, colleges, and universities. As his close friend John Wanamaker—himself a philanthropist and entrepreneur as founder of the Wanamaker department store—wrote in the only book-length biography of Williamson: "He was invariably strongly moved to help the man who was trying to help himself, however humble the effort. But for mere beggars, low or high, he had little sympathy."

As early as the 1850s, Williamson had begun thinking of a plan for a school that would bear his name. As he told Wanamaker, "It was seeing boys, ragged and barefooted, playing or lounging about the streets, growing up with no education, no trade, no idea of usefulness, that caused me to think of founding a school where every boy could be taught some trade free of expense." In 1888, he unveiled his plan. "He had to be wheeled from his carriage in a rolling chair," wrote Wanamaker, "but his spirit was alert and joyful."

Williamson committed $2.1 million (roughly $50 million in present value) to the project for the purchase of a 211-acre site near Media, Pennsylvania, where the Williamson Free School of the Mechanical Trades would be opened in 1891.

> Williamson gave a huge gift for a school where poor boys would learn a trade, because "In this country, every able-bodied, healthy young man who has learned a good mechanical trade, and is truthful, honest, frugal, temperate, and industrious, is certain to succeed in life."

In considering admission to the school, "preference shall always be given to the poor," Williamson stipulated. To this day, the school recruits young men from the region's toughest areas, working closely with ministers, guidance counselors, coaches, and other mentors to find promising young men who would benefit from learning a trade. The school still provides a full scholarship for all of its students, not one penny of which comes from public sources. Programs are offered in carpentry, masonry, landscaping, machine tools, painting, and power-plant technology. All students are required to live on campus in supervised dormitories, attend a daily chapel service, and conform to the dress code.

"In this country," Williamson explained, "every able-bodied, healthy young man who has learned a good mechanical trade, and is truthful, honest, frugal, temperate, and industrious, is certain to succeed in life, and to become a useful and respected member of society." Isaiah Williamson did his part in keeping that wholesome pattern alive.

ᗌ Christopher Levenick

Further reading

○ *Philanthropy* magazine article, philanthropyroundtable.org/topic/excellence_in_ philanthropy/a_useful_and_respected_member_of_society

○ John Wanamaker, *Life of Isaiah V. Williamson* (J. B. Lippincott, 1928)

MAJOR ACHIEVEMENTS

—— *of* ——

AMERICAN PHILANTHROPY

1636-2015

In the pages following you will find nine carefully researched lists that
summarize major philanthropic achievements in America from our earliest
days to the present. They are grouped in nine categories, listed on the tabs
to the right. For quick location of any particular section, just fan this book's
pages to locate the tab of the topic you are seeking.

MEDICINE

EDUCATION

ARTS

NATURE

PROSPERITY

RELIGION

POLICY

OVERSEAS

LOCAL

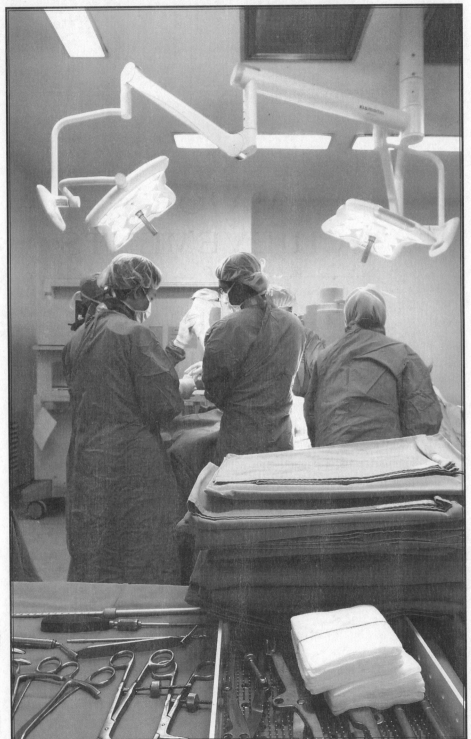

MAJOR ACHIEVEMENTS OF AMERICAN PHILANTHROPY
(1636-2015)

MEDICINE & HEALTH

edical philanthropy has a long history in the United States—from the founding of our first charity hospital in 1735 (by a common businessman acting in a remote frontier town that had only been in existence for 18 years) to the development of therapies that have saved hundreds of millions of lives. Charitable giving has been crucial in catalyzing many of the most far-reaching advances in medicine, such as penicillin, insulin, hookworm control, the polio vaccine, kidney transplants and dialysis, and much of today's success against cancer. Philanthropists established most of America's best medical schools and research institutes. They have endowed professorships, created labs, and built clinics. Philanthropy has been vital in carrying improved health measures out into communities—from the Rockefeller Foundation's heroic campaign against yellow fever right up to today's Gates Foundation battles against malaria, leprosy, polio, and other neglected diseases. With the last generation's explosion of private-industry research and government spending on health care, private philanthropy now comprises only a small portion of total funding for medical research and public health, yet because it tends to be flexible, risk-tolerant, fast-moving, and offered without the onerous red tape of government grants, philanthropic funding is especially prized by medical researchers, and continues to have a powerful impact on the field, as you will learn in the pages following.

― *Section research provided by Karl Zinsmeister and Cindy Tan*

CREATIVE APPROACH TO
DISEASE RESEARCH PAYS OFF

On the same day in August that he and three other Johns Hopkins University researchers published in *Science* their breakthrough explanation of the cause of ALS (also known as Lou Gehrig's Disease), Jonathan Ling did a Q&A session on Reddit. He said he wanted to set the record straight on whether the ALS Ice Bucket Challenge actually accomplished anything. The fundraising craze sponsored by the ALS Association raised $115 million for disease research in just six weeks in 2014 when it went viral on the Internet. It continued to raise tens of millions more in repeat donations that followed.

Ling recounted "reading a lot of stories about people complaining that the Ice Bucket Challenge was a waste and that scientists weren't using the money to do research, etc. I assure you that this is absolutely false." The surge of research funding from the ALS Association allowed his Johns Hopkins team to conduct high-risk, high-reward experiments that were crucial to their discovery, he reported.

It is hoped that lifesaving therapies based on the JHU findings could enter clinical trials within two or three years—and thanks to the money raised in the Ice Bucket Challenge, those expensive trials are already paid for. At any given time, about 30,000 people suffer from ALS, which kills most of its victims within a couple years of diagnosis. There is currently only one drug for treating the disease, and it quickly loses its effectiveness, extending a patient's life only three to six months.

Further reading

○ Jonathan Ling on Reddit, reddit.com/r/science/comments/3g4c7v/science_ama_series_ hi_im_jonathan_ling_a

○ *Washington Post* article, washingtonpost.com/news/to-your-health/wp/2015/08/19/ scientists-are-crediting-the-ice-bucket-challenge-for-breakthroughs-in-research

FUNDING THE SMALL AND THE LARGE OF
REGENERATIVE MEDICINE

Investors Louis Simpson and Kimberly Querrey are interested in the new medical specialty of regenerative medicine—which is developing ways to repair, replace, or regrow body tissues that are not functioning. Once a science-fiction dream, medical scientists are now discovering they can grow organs, skin, and other body parts to help victims of disease, accident, war, or genetic breakdown.

Between 2012 and 2014, the couple donated $25 million to establish an institute at Northwestern University that applies nanotechnology—the manipulation of matter at the molecular level—to regenerative medicine. One year later they added another $92 million to their gift to broaden their support for regenerative medicine. The gift allowed the university to break ground on a new biomedical research tower that will be completed in 2018. In addition to advancing fundamental understanding of how the body builds and repairs tissue, the Querrey/Simpson gift aims to speed development of drugs, fresh procedures, and clinical trials that will allow doctors at Northwestern to bring patients new solutions to cancer, burns, trauma, and degenerative diseases.

Further reading

○ *Chicago Tribune* report, chicagotribune.com/news/ct-northwestern-medicine-donation-20150305-story.html

---

2015

CORNELL BIOMEDICAL ENGINEERING SCHOOL

Cornell University is one of the strongest engineering schools in the country, but until 2015 did not offer an undergraduate degree in biomedical engineering. This despite the growing importance of that field, the fact that 60 percent of engineering students express interest in biological applications of engineering, and the existence of other Cornell entities that need expertise at the intersection of biology and engineering—the renowned vet school, the medical school, and Cornell Tech in New York City.

The Meinig family, who had previously given $25 million to Cornell to support research in the life sciences, filled that gap in 2015 when they doubled

◁ PhilAphorism

For U.S. scientific researchers, charitable donations are enormous engines of new opportunities, of starting in directions that wouldn't have been possible to fund by conventional sources. ☞ *Leroy Hood*

down on their previous bet with a $50 million gift. This donation spun Cornell's existing biomedical engineering department into an independent school of biomedical engineering. It allowed the launch of the undergraduate major in the fall of 2015. And it put into motion a wide array of new research and teaching in four areas: tissue engineering, biomechanics, biomaterials and drugs, and instruments and imaging.

Further reading

○ *Cornell Chronicle* announcement of new undergraduate major, news.cornell.edu/ stories/2015/06/biomedical-engineering-major-gets-green-light

PUTTING A $250M SHINE ON NYC'S HOSPITAL DISTRICT

On the east side of mid-Manhattan, close enough to each other to be the three bases in a game of stickball, stand a trio of formidable medical facilities: Rockefeller University, Memorial Sloan Kettering Cancer Center, and Weill Cornell medical school. On the very same day in 2015, the first two of those facilities announced they had received major philanthropic infusions.

Rockefeller got a pledge of $100 million from Henry and Marie-Josée Kravis to create a new medical laboratory. Meanwhile, MSK was promised $150 million by David Koch to erect an outpatient center. Both of these new buildings will stand hard by the East River, but they are otherwise sharply different: MSK's facility will be a giant people's clinic (treating 1,300 patients daily), while Rockefeller's will be a center for research by top academics. Koch's money will erect a 23-story skyscraper, while the Kravis funds will yield a two-story structure stretching three full blocks long.

Both gifts, however, address palpable needs. Since its founding by John Rockefeller in 1901, Rockefeller University has been our nation's foremost biomedical research institution. The labs being replaced with Kravis assistance date back to the 1950s, an eon in scientific time, so the new setup should play an important role in keeping Rockefeller strong in biological investigations.

The Koch cancer center, meanwhile, will be in heavy demand for treatment. In America, one out of every two men, and one out of three women, will be diagnosed with cancer in his or her lifetime. Cancer is an age-related disease, and with New York City's population over 65 rising fast to an estimated 1.4 million by 2030, there will be many new patients needing radiation, chemotherapy, surgery, and related help.

Further reading

○ *Wall Street Journal* summary report on the two projects, wsj.com/articles/major-donations-bolster-hospital-medical-research-1432094465

FIGHTING BACK AGAINST ALLERGIES

Allergies are both a common nuisance—with an estimated 60 million sufferers in the U.S.—and sometimes a mortal threat. The manifestations of allergic reaction include asthma, drug allergies, bee sting reactions, eczema, and food allergies. For unknown reasons, our rate of allergic problems is rising.

Sean Parker, who became wealthy at Facebook and is now an active philanthropist, understands this plague, having himself been hospitalized 14 times in the last four years for allergic trauma. Hoping to contribute to better understanding and cures for allergies, he offered $24 million in 2014 to establish a center for allergy research at Stanford University. Clinical trials began in 2015.

Further reading

○ *San Francisco Chronicle* reporting, sfgate.com/news/article/Sean-Parker-donates-25-million-to-Stanford-for-5961555.php

QUICK ACTION AGAINST EBOLA

Nearly 5,000 residents were killed when an epidemic of the dread disease Ebola swept west African countries in 2014. Philanthropists were among the quickest to understand the importance of nipping the epidemic before it spread.

Paul Allen, a major donor since retiring after co-founding Microsoft, had been watching Ebola for years. Back in 2009 he funded a project at Kansas State University to adapt an Ebola vaccine for use with wild apes. Perhaps a third of African gorillas and chimpanzees have been killed by the Ebola virus since the 1990s, and these infections give the virus easier pathways to humans. So it is perhaps not surprising that Allen led philanthropic responses to the 2014 outbreak of the disease, saying "I am committed to doing my part in tackling this crisis…to prevent it from becoming a global epidemic."

Allen offered $100 million of his own money to a mix of immediate and longer-term efforts to tamp down the virus. He helped convince other donors to contribute as well, including $50 million from the Gates Foundation, $25 million from Mark Zuckerberg, and other large and speedy gifts. The emergency operations director of the U.S. Centers for

Disease Control later attributed the successful control of the 2014 Ebola outbreak in West Africa "to the huge contribution made by Paul Allen." The almost instant speed with which Allen's foundation delivered the money made it possible to dispatch 500 emergency health responders and all of their equipment to Liberia and two other countries where the disease was ravaging thousands.

Further reading

○ *Seattle Times* reporting, seattletimes.com/seattle-news/billionaire-paul-allen-pledges-100-million-in-ebola-fight

○ West African reporting on the effects of Allen gift, liberianobserver.com/news/cdc-acknowledges-paul-allen-ebola-fight

SHOT IN THE ARM FOR PUBLIC HEALTH

Gerald Chan worked on a master's degree and then a doctorate at the School of Public Health at Harvard in the 1970s. After that he pursued medical research for a period. Eventually he entered the family business of real-estate development and founded his own investment fund.

Grateful for his education, and alarmed by growing international threats like Ebola, in 2014 Chan and his brother gave Harvard the largest single gift in its history—$350 million—to bolster the endowment of the university's public-health school. The money will be used for things like increased financial aid for the 1,000 students who are enrolled in the school at any given time, forgiving loans for graduates willing to work in underserved areas, improved faculty recruitment, and funding for early research projects. "While medical doctors give health benefits to individual patients, public health is a field that helps to give benefit to the whole population," Chan told the *Boston Globe* in announcing the family gift.

Chan's gift was just the latest and largest in a string of donations that have energized this field. Michael Bloomberg has provided major funding to build up the school of public health at Johns Hopkins University. In 2014, Michael Milken donated $40 million to the school of public health at George Washington University. In 2007 the Rollins family doubled the size of the public health facility at Emory University with a $50 million grant, and the Gillings family made a similar $50 million investment in the school at University of North Carolina at Chapel Hill. And Columbia's public health program was strengthened by one of the first large philanthropic infusions to this field, a $33 million gift in 1998 by Joseph Mailman.

MEDICINE

Further reading

○ *Boston Globe* report, bostonglobe.com/metro/2014/09/07/harvard-school-public-health-gets-largest-gift-university-history/YixNC3xkBfMtg3mrSmE6zJ/story.html

ANALYZING AN ARCHIVE OF TUMORS

Marie-Josée Kravis has served on the overseers' board at the Memorial Sloan Kettering Cancer Center for decades, and she heads the board of its research arm, the Sloan Kettering Institute. Her husband, financier Henry Kravis, was also interested enough in the Center to ask officials whether its long experience in the field could be combined with new advances in gene sequencing. The Kravises eventually offered $100 million to create a new center for molecular oncology at the New York City facility. Within a week of the public announcement, six new-generation gene-sequencing machines were being installed at the hospital. These will be used not only to analyze the tumors of 10,000 active patients each year, but also to explore the characteristics of "archived" tumors from more than a million patients who have been treated at MSK since 1980. The genetic qualities of each preserved tumor will then be compared with the archived records of that patient's care and his or her final treatment outcome. This cross-referencing of deep biological and clinical records could uncover important patterns previously undetected by physicians, and lead to new directions in treatment.

Further reading

○ Gift announcement, mskcc.org/pressroom/press/landmark-gift-100-million-marie-josee-and-henry-r-kravis-foundation-will-support-groundbreaking-approach-precisi

FIGHTING CANCER AT JOHNS HOPKINS

With its treatment of cancer patients expected to increase 35 percent or more over the next decade, Johns Hopkins needs a new building where treatments and consultation can be offered to the ailing. With a 2014 gift of $65 million, the foundation of Albert "Skip" Viragh provided, in one fell swoop, nearly all of the construction costs for a center scheduled to open in 2017. A Marylander who started a mutual fund and grew it into a $9 billion entity by creating leveraged index funds and other innovations, Viragh died of pancreatic cancer himself. His foundation previously gave Hopkins $20 million to establish a center for research and care for that disease. Its latest donation will relieve pressure on the medical facility's existing treatment center, which opened in 1999 thanks to a $20 million pledge from the Harry and Jeanette Weinberg Foundation.

Philanthropy has been the keystone on which Johns Hopkins has built its rise to the heights of cancer work. The Weinberg and future Viragh buildings are complemented by a facility located across the street that offers subsidized housing for patients and their families. It was funded by the Hackerman family (who also endowed a lab and oncology chair at the cancer facility). Umbrella funding over all of Hopkins's cancer work came from businessman Sidney Kimmel, who gave $150 million in 2001.

Cancer research, where Johns Hopkins has jumped to the top of the charts, has been particularly powered by donors. The university's state-of-the-art program for investigating cancer and teaching students is centered in the Bunting Blaustein Building, launched by twin $10 million gifts from each of those families. Another $20 million gift created the connected David Koch Research Building in 2006. Inside these structures labor teams led by Bert Vogelstein and Kenneth Kinzler, two cancer investigators with more citations in scientific papers over a recent ten-year period (50,000+) than any other researchers in the world. Their work was supercharged by a $20 million open-ended gift from the foundation of Daniel Ludwig (see 1971 entry), which they used to create the first genomic maps of cancer in 2006. Of the 75 cancers which had been genetically sequenced as of 2014, fully 68 were mapped at Hopkins. The combination of Ludwig and Kimmel funds also allowed the Hopkins center to lead in developing cancer screening tests, cancer vaccines, and therapies like bone-marrow transplants. In 2014, the Ludwig trustees made an additional $90 million grant to the Johns Hopkins Kimmel Cancer Center.

Like many other lab directors (see Eric Lander's remarks in 2012 entry on the Broad Institute, Charles Marmar's observations in the next entry below, and Leroy Hood's comments in 2000 entry on Systems Biology, 1986 DNA Sequencer entry, and 1982 Braun labs entry), the co-directors of the Ludwig

◄ PhilAphorism

No one would remember the Good Samaritan if he'd only had good intentions—he had money as well.　　　☞ *Margaret Thatcher*

Center at Hopkins have remarked on the outsized importance of philanthropic gifts in allowing laboratory breakthroughs that traditional research grants won't back. "The Ludwig bequests have revolutionized what we've been able to do," says Bert Vogelstein. "We've pursued some of the most important questions in cancer—not necessarily the most fundable questions."

When asked by a reporter, "Your discoveries have outpaced much larger laboratories. What is the key to this success?," Kenneth Kinzler answered: "Part of the reason we have been so successful and beaten huge groups is because of our Ludwig funding. It allows us to do what's important. Our focus is not decided by committee. We could do the most groundbreaking research without having to worry about where the next level of funding would come from.... We try to develop research projects that are not in the mainstream now."

Kinzler adds that, "Our current research programs focus on diagnostics for the early detection and prevention of cancers thanks, in large part, to Ludwig support. Compared with treatment research, early detection and prevention research is underfunded, but it can potentially make more of an impact on reducing cancer deaths. It takes a long time and a sustained effort to see the results of cancer prevention and early detection studies. Ludwig funding will enable us to carry this and many other research projects forward."

Further reading

○ *Baltimore Sun* report on Viragh gift, articles.baltimoresun.com/2014-05-06/business/bs-hs-hopkins-cancer-grant-20140506_1_skip-viragh-center-pancreatic-cancer-cancer-patients

○ Ken Kinzler interview, hopkinsmedicine.org/news/publications/promise_progress/special_commemorative_issue_of_promise__progress_the_ludwig_center_at_johns_hopkins/ken_kinzler_on_the_ludwig_center

○ Vogelstein and Kinzler on Ludwig bequests, hub.jhu.edu/gazette/2014/january-february/currents-ludwig-center-new-funding

2013

MAKING INVISIBLE BRAIN WOUNDS VISIBLE

One of the commonest injuries of the Iraq and Afghanistan wars, also a domestic concern thanks to auto and sports accidents, is brain injury. The resulting depression, irritability, and stress disorders can be almost impossible to document and measure, and thus hard to treat. A $17 million donation to New York University by financier Steven Cohen and his wife, Alexandra, aims to find out if brain injuries and mental health conditions can be assessed more concretely.

In a five-year study of 1,500 military veterans, NYU psychiatrist Charles Marmar and his lab will see if they can establish characteristic biomarkers of mental disruption. Hormone levels, blood chemistry, brain images, genetic clues, even voice patterns, will be assessed to see if any of these reliably signal disability or illness after a concussion. Just as certain blood proteins and brain shrinkages are now known to indicate Alzheimer's, the hope is that physical indicators can be established for syndromes like PTSD. That should improve diagnosis and treatment. "We want to elevate mental health to standard physical health," says Marmar.

Marmar told the audience at a 2014 Philanthropy Roundtable gathering that the speed, flexibility, and non-bureaucratic nature of private donations were crucial to getting his project off the ground. "I've been a National Institutes of Health researcher for decades, and to get an NIH grant from the government you essentially have to already have solved the problem in question." His business-experienced donors, however, were comfortable in undertaking highly speculative investigations, recognizing that huge benefits could result if the experiment succeeds.

Further reading

○ *New York Times* reporting, nytimes.com/2013/02/07/us/study-seeks-biomarkers-for-ptsd-and-traumatic-brain-injuries.html?_r=0

2013

REGENERATIVE MEDICINE IN SAN DIEGO

In addition to $800 million of medical donations to his native region of South Dakota, businessman Denny Sanford has been an important angel for medical research in San Diego—a national center for that work, and a second home for Sanford. He began by providing $70 million, in two chunks, to what is now known as the Sanford Burnham Prebys Medical Discovery Institute. His gifts sparked a subsequent $275 million donation offered anonymously, and then a $100 million gift from philanthropist Conrad Prebys.

Sanford Burnham Prebys has become one of a half-dozen bio-med powerhouses in San Diego, nearly all of them cooperating in a research alliance that Sanford established with a $30 million gift. The Consortium for Regenerative Medicine aims to accelerate practical therapies in its field by developing new drugs and treatment plans for patients. Sanford provided another complementary nudge in 2013 when he offered $100 million to consortium member University of California, San Diego to launch a stem-cell clinic in the region. Sanford has now provided $200 million to the hotbed of San Diego charities working to transform the promise of regenerative medicine into a practical, lifesaving reality.

Further reading

○ Sanford Consortium for Regenerative Medicine, sanfordconsortium.org

2013

TARGETING CANCER'S WEAK SPOTS IN OREGON

In 2008, Penny and Phil Knight (co-founder of Oregon-based Nike Sportswear) donated $100 million to the Oregon Health and Science University to create the Knight Cancer Institute. The university's prior cancer institute had grown to prominence and then hired one of the top cancer researchers in the world, Brian Druker, as its director in 2007. Druker launched the world's first drug to target a genetic weakness in a particular cancer when he developed Gleevec, which smothers myeloid leukemia by targeting an enzyme that triggers the disease. Gleevec has saved tens of thousands of lives since it burst onto the scene in 2001 and is credited with inspiring a whole train of similar potentially revolutionary drugs that zero in on specific cancer genes, thereby shutting down tumors without harming healthy surrounding tissue.

Armed with the $100 million Knight donation, Druker and his colleagues went on a hiring spree shortly after his arrival, attracting some of the brightest minds in the field to OHSU. In 2009, Druker received one of the Lasker Awards established by philanthropy to encourage top medical investigators (see 1945 entry).

Then in late 2013, the Knights announced they would donate an additional $500 million to OHSU if the university could raise the same sum from other donors within two years. (In between these two anti-cancer gifts, Penny and Phil Knight had donated $125 million to support cardiovascular medicine and research at OHSU.) If the university could meet its side of the challenge, its president concluded the day after the Knight's announcement, their cancer program would leap "from excellence to true preeminence." Thanks to many additional gifts, including one of $100 million given by Gertrude Boyle—the chairwoman of Columbia Sportswear, whose sister was a pioneering biologist and a cancer victim—the university announced in 2015 that it had collected sufficient donations to match the Knight pledge.

Further reading

○ News report in *The Oregonian*, oregonlive.com/portland/index.ssf/2013/09/phil_and_penny_knight_to_ohsu_1.html

○ OHSU website, ohsu.edu/xd/about/news_events/news/2013/09-21-nike-co-founder-issues-b.cfm

DEBT-FREE MEDICAL STUDENTS

Back in 2002, entertainment executive David Geffen donated $200 million without restriction to the medical school of UCLA, the single largest gift ever to a school of medicine. In 2012 he made an even more interesting donation to the school—a $100 million endowment to allow one fifth of each incoming class of medical students at UCLA thereafter to attend free of charge.

Geffen stipulated that the scholarships would be awarded by merit, allowing UCLA to attract some of the very best medical candidates in the country. And he included in the pool of students he would support those on a combined M.D./Ph.D. track—a path from which many medical-research breakthroughs emerge, though it is generally much less lucrative for the individual. The average newly minted doctor today leaves med school with a debt burden of about $200,000, which constrains subspecializations, regions of practice, and other career decisions.

Further reading

○ UCLA announcement, newsroom.ucla.edu/releases/100-million-david-geffen-
    scholarship-241543

ANTI-CANCER ENCYCLOPEDIA

Philanthropists Eli and Edythe Broad gave $100 million in 2003 to start a new type of biomedical research center that seeks to revolutionize clinical medicine by building deep understanding of the human genome among researchers. They later followed up with donations of an additional $600 million, for a total gift of $700 million. The Broad Institute is now an independent nonprofit run in collaboration among the Massachusetts Institute of Technology, Harvard University, and the Whitehead Institute. Drawing on some of the world's best academic researchers, the Broad Institute seeks to describe all the molecular components of life, to understand the molecular basis of disease, and to share this information widely.

Four hundred million of the Broad money was put into an endowment. This philanthropic kernel throws off $20 million of investment income every year that the institute can direct into whatever it wants, with no strings attached. "Unrestricted funds are gold, they're magic," states director Eric Lander. "We're able to say when we have a good idea, 'Let's start investing in it now rather than write a grant and start working on it two years from now after it wends its way through the NIH system."

In 2012, the institute announced one of its typically ambitious efforts: a public archive of the genetic aspects and chemical susceptibilities of 947 human cancer cell lines. Called the *Cancer Cell Line Encyclopedia*, this compendium of uncommon data on common afflictions will help scientists understand the disease, predict its course, and design therapies and drugs. The encyclopedia is a philanthropy/industry collaboration involving the Broad Institute, the Dana-Farber Cancer Institute, and research elements of the drug company Novartis.

Further reading

○ Story from the Broad Institute, broadinstitute.org/news/4048

○ *Harvard Gazette* announcement, news.harvard.edu/gazette/story/2012/03/writing-the-book-of-cancer-knowledge

○ Eric Lander quoted in *Philanthropy* magazine, philanthropyroundtable.org/topic/excellence_in_philanthropy/playing_the_long_game

2011

MALARIA VACCINE

Malaria remains one of the most intractable diseases in the developing world, killing one million people a year and damaging the economic productivity of many more. Large resources have already been poured into combatting the disease, yet a McKinsey study has noted that $11 billion more would be needed to end malaria deaths in the 30 worst-affected African countries. One promising alternative funded with support from the Bill & Melinda Gates Foundation is a vaccine. In 2011, the first-ever malaria vaccine was announced. It is still in trial stages, but so far seems to prevent severe symptoms in half of the individuals who receive it, while offering extra protection to infants and toddlers. While efficacy rates need to be improved before the vaccine is put into wide use, the initial findings have begun discussions about the long-dreamed-of possibility of widespread immunization in endemic countries.

In 2013, the Gates Foundation entered into an innovative pact with a consortium of investors and drug makers that will invest in bringing to market new therapies like a malaria vaccine, as well as drugs and technologies combating diseases like tuberculosis and HIV that also weigh heavily on poor countries. Gates's role will be to offset potential losses in the so-called Global Health Investment Fund. By eliminating some of the downside risk in the expensive business of developing new medicines, the foundation intends to stimulate more aggressive private investment.

Further reading

○ *New England Journal of Medicine* on vaccine trial results, nejm.org/doi/full/10.1056/ NEJMoa1102287

2011

TOP CANCER CENTER AND A MEDICAL EMPIRE IN HOUSTON

The M. D. Anderson Cancer Center lies at the heart of the remarkable Texas Medical Center, which has become by far the world's largest complex for healing the sick. The TMC, which CEO Richard Wainerdi describes as "probably the biggest confluence of philanthropy in the world," currently has more than 41 million square feet of office space. Every year the complex hosts 7.1 million patients, 350,000 surgeries, and 28,000 births. The first coronary bypass surgery in the U.S., the first heart transplant, and many other important medical innovations took place within the TMC. A wide range of top-flight hospitals and other medical facilities are now located in the center, which grew up around M. D. Anderson after it admitted its first patients in 1944.

The depth and power of Houston medical philanthropy can be seen in the capital campaign M. D. Anderson launched in 2006, with a goal of raising $1 billion in six years. The campaign was halted two years early when it passed the $1.2 billion mark. At that point more than 630,000 individuals had made gifts and a staggering 127 donors had given at least $1 million. In 2012, M. D. Anderson's regular annual philanthropic support totaled more than $190 million. In 2013, the center announced a $50 million gift from Texas philanthropist Lyda Hill toward a new $3 billion "Moon Shots Program" that aims to make fundamental research progress against killer cancers.

M. D. Anderson has applied this deep support to make itself a world leader. The hospital will serve its millionth patient within the decade. And in the *U.S. News & World Report* rankings it has been named the top cancer center in the U.S. for ten of the last 12 years. Other hospitals and treatment facilities within the Texas Medical Center have likewise benefited from private philanthropists—who made more than half a billion dollars of gifts to the wider complex in 2013 alone.

Further reading

○ *Philanthropy* magazine report on Houston medical philanthropy, philanthropyroundtable. org/topic/excellence_in_philanthropy/deep_in_the_heart_of_texas

○ M. D. Anderson release on results of 2006 capital campaign, mdanderson.org/gifts/donor-story-detail?DFID=UCM_PROD1-000944

DENTAL THERAPY

Tooth decay is the most common chronic childhood disease, with recent research suggesting it can lead to a wide variety of other health problems. Even though tooth decay is a preventable disease, many children face barriers that make it hard for them to obtain basic dental care. In particular, residents of isolated and rural communities, like Indian reservations, can be underserved. It's estimated that millions of Americans live in areas with a shortage of dentists and that the U.S. could use an additional 9,000 dental-care providers.

In response, the W. K. Kellogg Foundation established a new dental therapy program for children in 2010, starting in five states. The program promotes prevention and builds understanding of the importance of dental health. It funds mobile dental vans to reach rural and underserved areas, plus dental education, training for "dental therapists" who can substitute for dentists in underserved areas, and educational grants for underrepresented minorities to attend dental school. The Kellogg Foundation has drawn lessons from philanthropy-assisted community programs used to bring good dental care to remote parts of Alaska (funded by the Rasmuson and then Robert Wood Johnson Foundations—see 2006 entry on Local Achievements list) and is now a leader in addressing this widespread but highly avoidable problem.

Further reading

○ Kellogg Foundation, wkkf.org/what-we-support/healthy-kids/dental-therapy.aspx

⫷ PhilAphorism

There's no substitute for rolling up your sleeves and working with the people who can make a difference. They get the benefit of your participation and you gain a direct understanding of the real problems and potential solutions, which makes you a more informed giver.   ⟿ *Michael Milken*

2009

BRIDGING ELDERLY PATIENTS
FROM HOSPITAL TO HOME

Research has shown that one third of Medicare patients who leave a hospital will be readmitted within 90 days, and that a large portion of these rehospitalizations are unnecessary, due to things like patients not taking their medications properly. The costs of these elderly patients churning in and out of hospitals are high: unhappy patients, burdens on family members, and tens of billions of dollars in public health-care expenses. Studies in 2008 and 2006 estimated that patients unnecessarily returning to hospital within just the first 30 days cost a total of $49 billion.

To combat this, health-care providers at the University of Pennsylvania developed what they called the Transitional Care Model, which used nurses to train patients and caregivers in how to manage their medications and therapies and avoid future health issues, and then make sure in home visits that the instructions are being followed. This was not a program for long-term care, but strictly an effort to bridge between the hospital experience and the first months back at home. When the effort proved very successful, a program was launched to demonstrate the cost-effectiveness of this approach to insurers and health-care operators. This was done with financial support from five philanthropies: the Commonwealth Fund, the Jacob & Valeria Langeloth Foundation, the John Hartford Foundation, the Gordon and Betty Moore Foundation, and the California HealthCare Foundation.

Careful academic studies showed powerful results: improved health, greater patient and caregiver satisfaction, and a whopping 30 to 50 percent reduction in rehospitalizations, heading off unnecessary costs of nearly $5,000 per patient. When the program costs of $456 to $1,019 per patient are factored in, net savings came to approximately $4,000 per elderly participant. With this evidence in hand, health insurers began voluntarily integrating transitional care models into their coverage plans starting in 2009.

Further reading

○ Commonwealth Fund issue brief, commonwealthfund.org

○ About the Transitional Care Model, transitionalcare.info

○ Evaluation from the Coalition for Evidence-based Policy, evidencebasedprograms. org/1366-2/transitional-care-model-top-tier

KOCH CANCER INSTITUTE AT MIT

Industrialist David Koch is one of the most active medical philanthropists in American history. He currently sits on about a dozen hospital boards. He has provided $30 million for cancer research at Memorial Sloan Kettering and $150 million for its new cancer outpatient center (see 2015 entry), $20 million for a cancer center at Johns Hopkins, $25 million to M. D. Anderson Cancer Center, $15 million to New York-Presbyterian, and $25 million to the Hospital for Special Surgery in New York. He also supports Rockefeller University, Cold Spring Harbor Laboratory, and the Whitehead Institute. From 1998 to 2015, he donated about $600 million to support medical research and treatment.

His 2007 $100 million donation to the Massachusetts Institute of Technology created the David Koch Institute for Integrative Cancer Research—which aspires to energize the battle against cancer by drawing more engineers into the biological sciences. (Koch comes from a family of engineers.) The new facility opened in 2011, and its 650 investigators are working on projects like the one that uses nanoparticles to deliver chemical toxins directly and solely to a tumor instead of flooding the entire body with toxins as conventional chemotherapy does. The radical new therapy is now being tested, successfully, on patients suffering from advanced cancers.

Further reading

o Interview and profile in *Philanthropy* magazine, philanthropyroundtable.org/topic/
   excellence_in_philanthropy/the_team_builder

HEALING THE UPPER MIDWEST

The business triumphs of Denny Sanford allowed him to retire to Florida at age 45—but he was soon itchy and returned to the upper Midwest where he had spent his entire previous life. After further commercial successes, he started giving away money.

Having lost both of his parents to illness a few years after he was born, his philanthropic passion was medicine. He turned his attention to the Sioux Valley Hospitals and Health System, beginning with a $16 million gift for a children's hospital designed like a fairy castle. With his $400 million donation in 2007 (the largest single gift ever made to a U.S. health-care organization), the nonprofit was renamed Sanford Health.

Sanford Health now includes nearly three dozen hospitals and more than 140 clinics, centered on South and North Dakota but spread across eight states, making it one of the largest rural, not-for-profit health systems in the nation. After the latest in Denny Sanford's string of gifts to the health system—a $125 million donation made in 2014 that launched new efforts to tailor patient care using genetic information—his total contributions to Sanford Health exceeded $800 million.

In Fargo, Sanford Health is in the midst of one of the largest construction projects in the history of the Dakotas. The result will be a top-shelf medical facility filled with the best technology and some of the brightest medical experts in the country. It will bring a new level of care to the region, including a major trauma center, enhanced pediatric services, a heart center, an expanded cancer center, and new services in areas such as eating disorders and rehabilitation.

Sanford has also made massive medical-research donations in the San Diego area. (See 2013 entry.) A signatory of the Gates-Buffett Giving Pledge, Sanford says he aims to "die broke." That day comes a little closer with each subsequent gift, with Sanford's lifetime philanthropic giving having roared past the $1 billion mark in 2013.

Further reading

○ About Sanford Health, sanfordhealth.org/about

2007

TAMPING DOWN CHILDHOOD OBESITY

The Robert Wood Johnson Foundation, America's third-largest private grantmaker, with a strong focus on health issues, announced a half-billion-dollar commitment in 2007 to research how fast-rising childhood obesity could be slowed through improved diet and exercise. As their campaign wound down, child obesity wasn't rising fast any more; in fact it had begun to decline among younger children—from 14 percent of all two- to five-year-olds in 2004 to 8 percent in 2012. Buoyed by that progress, the foundation announced an additional $500 million commitment in 2015, bringing its total spending to a billion dollars. The next phase of the effort will emphasize educating parents on the advantages of a healthy diet, with a particular emphasis on poor and minority families, where obesity is commonest. More exercise, improved nutritional content in school lunches, calorie reduction in snacks and drinks, and similar efforts will be supported by foundation grants.

Further reading

○ 2015 announcement by Robert Wood Johnson Foundation, rwjf.org/en/library/articles-and-news/2015/02/rwjf_doubles_commitment_to_healthy_weight_for_children.html

APPLYING GENOMICS TO PEDIATRIC MEDICINE

When a hospital focused on children opened in San Diego in 1954, the city received it as a godsend as it suffered through another polio epidemic. The facility initially treated just 12 patients, and the hospital was gradually built up by a long string of donations. The biggest leap forward came in 2006, when hometown real-estate investor Ernest Rady donated $60 million, in addition to offering leadership on the hospital board. This soon turned the San Diego children's hospital into the largest such facility in California.

In 2014 Rady and his wife, Evelyn, presented an additional $120 million. This created an institute at the hospital that will apply genomics and other emerging medical knowledge to the treatment of its child patients, cementing its position as a prominent research and teaching institution as well as a saver of young lives.

Further reading

o 2014 gift announced, rchsd.org/about-us/newsroom/press-releases/rady-childrens-to-establish-pediatric-genomics-and-systems-medicine-institute

NOTHING BUT NETS CAMPAIGN

Sportswriter Rick Reilly first learned about malaria's toll in Africa from a *BBC* documentary. He was struck by the film's rhetorical question: "Did you know that every day 3,000 children in Africa die of malaria, needlessly?" Reilly was even more impressed by the ready availability and low cost of one easy solution: $10 bed nets treated with insecticide. Reilly dedicated his May 1, 2006 *Sports Illustrated* column not to sports, but to malaria. He exhorted his readers to donate ten lifesaving dollars. He arranged for contributions to be collected by the nonprofit Roll Back Malaria.

To his great surprise, the campaign collected nearly $1 million in its first week. Soon, celebrities and public figures lent their support to the campaign. Major League Soccer and the National Basketball Association became sponsors. The United Methodist Church and the Lutheran Church pledged to raise up to $100 million each. Corporate sponsors like Orkin Pest Control and Makita Tools joined in. The initiative soared primarily on a multitude of small donations from more than 70,000 individuals, averaging $60 each. Because Ted Turner's $1 billion donation covering all of the administrative costs of the United Nations

Foundation (which managed the Nothing But Nets funds), 100 percent of the giving went to mosquito nets (whose price dropped to $3 per net as production soared over the next several years).

While governments and international organizations have strived to eradicate malaria for years, Reilly's campaign raised public-awareness cheaply and at unprecedented speed. Nothing But Nets made possible the distribution of more than 6 million mosquito nets to vulnerable residents of Africa. "The effort primed the pump for the nearly simultaneous establishment of Malaria No More, a group that took the anti-malaria crusade to a larger scale. Founded in 2006 by financier Wesray Capital principal and philanthropist Raymond Chambers, this wider effort made malaria nets an international phenomenon. As of 2014, 427 million nets have been delivered to Africa, along with millions of treatments and diagnostics. Annual malaria deaths dropped by 350,000.

Further reading

○ Original Reilly column, sportsillustrated.cnn.com/2006/writers/rick_reilly/04/25/reilly0501/index.html

○ Origins of Ray Chambers involvement, givesmart.org/Give-Smart-Blog/April-2013/Ray-Chambers-Philanthropy-Malaria-Focus.aspx

2006

STARR FOUNDATION
BUILDS RESEARCH COLLABORATIVES

Financier Cornelius Vander Starr was an active but quiet philanthropist. His Starr Foundation, established in 1955, also maintains a low profile, though it has given away nearly $3 billion during its operating years, more than half of that in New York City. The group has a particular emphasis on fostering collaboration among successful civic institutions operating in the areas of medicine, education, public policy, and culture.

This longstanding strategy resulted in a burst of important medical grantmaking in 2005 to 2006. First a medical-research collaboration called the Tri-Institutional Stem Cell Initiative was announced—a $50 million grant to encourage the world-leading biomedical researchers at Rockefeller University, the cancer experts at Memorial Sloan Kettering, and the faculty at Cornell's Weill Medical College to cooperate in stem-cell work. (This initiative was renewed with an additional $50 million gift to the same three institutions in 2012.)

The second collaboration, launched in 2006, donated $100 million to the same three adjoining New York research organizations, plus two others, to create the Starr Cancer Consortium. (This new effort was likewise renewed in

2012, with an additional $55 million donation.) A third large Starr Foundation gift announced in 2006 sent $50 million to Rockefeller University to create a Fund for Collaborative Science. The Starr gift was paired with a $100 million pledge from David Rockefeller, $25 million given by investor Russell Carson, $15 million from financier Henry Kravis, a $25 million anonymous gift, and others.

Starr Foundation donations of more than $300 million have thus sped discoveries in basic biomedicine, and reinforced valuable cross-fertilization among the critical mass of research talent in the New York metro area.

Further reading

○ Starr Foundation news releases, starrfoundation.org/press.html

2005

MONTANA METH PROJECT

Early in the new millennium, Montana was one of the top ten states in methamphetamine usage. Fully 53 percent of kids in foster care were there because of meth, 50 percent of adults in prison had committed meth-related crimes, and the drug was costing the state tens of millions every year—not to mention human lives.

When Montana resident Tom Siebel learned of this, he wanted to do something about it. Siebel was a software developer who had made billions creating programs to manage customer relations. He began investing his own money to create the Montana Meth Project, which in 2005 launched the first of its memorable ad campaigns. The ads, ranging from billboards to television, show the effects of meth on the human body, relationships, and more—in graphic detail. The idea was to show teens (the target age group was 12-17) what they were getting into. The campaigns were based on extensive research about what kinds of communication and advertising had an effect on teenagers, and they were aired in such quantity that the project became the single largest advertiser in the state.

From 2005 to 2010, meth usage in Montana declined 63 percent according to the Montana Office of Public Instruction, a result of the public education done by the Meth Project, increased law enforcement, and state rehab programs. These results impressed Montana's neighbors enough that by 2012 there were spinoff programs, also aided by Siebel, in several other states. The Montana Meth Project has won more than 50 awards and was named the third most effective philanthropy in the world by *Barron's*.

Since 2000, the Thomas and Stacey Siebel Foundation has granted $230 million to various charitable causes, including more than $30 million to the Meth Project.

Further reading

◦ *Philanthropy* magazine on Siebel's anti-meth campaign, philanthropyroundtable.org/topic/
excellence_in_philanthropy/lassoing_montana_meth
◦ Montana Meth Project, montana.methproject.org
◦ PBS story, pbs.org/now/enterprisingideas/montana-meth-project.html

MEDICAL SCHOOL INFUSION

Charles Feeney has nothing named for him at the University of California, San Francisco School of Medicine, but he built much of the facility. His $100 million check written in 2015 to support faculty, students, and building projects brought his total giving to the medical school, which started in 2004, to $394 million. That is not Feeney's record in education giving—he has donated about a billion dollars in total to Cornell University—but it is the most any individual has donated to any campus of the University of California.

And Feeney's support has allowed the UCSF medical program to bloom. The school is now ranked as one of the finest in the country, and in 2014 led the list of U.S. medical schools winning biomedical research awards from the National Institutes of Health. UCSF's allied nursing, dentistry, and pharmacy schools were also top ranked that year in NIH grants.

Marc Benioff, founder of Salesforce.com, is another generous supporter of UCSF, having channeled $200 million to the children's hospitals affiliated with the university.

Further reading

◦ *San Francisco Chronicle* report on 2015 Feeney gift, sfgate.com/bayarea/article/Low-
profile-retail-titan-s-gift-to-UCSF-100-6088596.php

◅ PhilAphorism

I particularly dislike people saying, "I'm going to leave it in my will." What they're really saying is, "If I could live forever, I wouldn't give any of it away." ☞ *Jon Huntsman*

AGITATING FOR FASTER CURES

FasterCures, founded in 2003 with funding from the Sumner Redstone Charitable Foundation, Milken Family Foundation, and other donors, is a nonprofit that chips away at practical obstacles that slow medical progress. Its goal is to accelerate the movement of ideas from lab experiment to patient treatment, and its methods aim to link health researchers more closely with philanthropists, policymakers, and business investors. The organization's annual Partnering for Cures event has become an influential gathering of leaders from medical research, industry, foundations, and policy organizations. In 2007, FasterCures joined with the Robert Wood Johnson Foundation and the Bill & Melinda Gates Foundation to create a Philanthropy Advisory Service that guides donors to smart medical investments. In addition to counseling many private givers the group has influenced decisionmaking at the National Institutes of Health.

One result of FasterCures has been to heighten interest in so-called "orphan diseases" which affect too few victims to attract major interest from either pharmaceutical companies or government agencies. FasterCures and the Philanthropy Advisory Service both offer extensive support for disease-specific philanthropy—from compiling "disease landscape reports" that summarize the latest research efforts, to offering "investment opportunity landscapes" which identify key investigators and paths to treatment for a specific disease.

FasterCures benefited from some of the lessons learned by Michael Milken while funding his Prostate Cancer Foundation (see 1993 entry). A 2004 *Fortune* magazine cover story entitled "The Man Who Changed Medicine" summarized his approach:

> The Milken model, in a nutshell, is to stimulate research by drastically cutting the wait time for grant money, to flood the field with fast cash, to fund therapy-driven ideas rather than basic science, to hold researchers he funds accountable for results, and to demand collaboration across disciplines and among institutions, private industry, and academia.

"Of all the programs we've supported over the last generation," Milken concludes, "the biggest payoff…has come from the awards to young investigators." His organization funded Lawrence Einhorn, who went on to develop a highly successful chemotherapy regimen for testicular cancer, and

Charles Myers, subsequently chief of the clinical pharmacology branch of the National Cancer Institute. They supported Dennis Slamon, who discovered Herceptin, a major advance in the treatment of one type of breast cancer, and Owen Witte, whose subsequent work provided the basis for development of the cancer-inhibiting drug Gleevec. Milken backed Bert Vogelstein, who went on to conduct pathbreaking investigation on the p53 gene, whose mutant form is believed to be involved in more than half of human cancers.

Further reading

○ Story in *Philanthropy* magazine, philanthropyroundtable.org/topic/excellence_in_ philanthropy/the_accelerator

○ Philanthropy Advisory Service, fastercures.org/programs/philanthropy-advisory-service

2003

ALLEN INSTITUTE FOR BRAIN SCIENCE

Throughout the past decade or so, brain research has been a rising interest among philanthropists. Microsoft co-founder Paul Allen gave $200 million to establish a new Seattle-based nonprofit devoted to accelerating understanding of the human brain and its diseases. Among other projects, the Allen Institute for Brain Science produced interactive atlases of the mouse brain and the human brain, which have become staple tools for scientists worldwide.

In 2012, Allen pledged an additional $300 million to the institute, allowing it to increase its staff to 350 employees and to undertake deeper studies in three areas: how the brain processes information; what the basic structures of brain function are; and what goes wrong in brain cells to create neurological disorders. Freed of the need to repeatedly apply for federal grants, and working in teams more like an Internet firm or corporate lab, Institute researchers have made rapid progress in their chosen fields. When the federal government launched a $100 million human brain initiative in 2013, Allen Institute researchers provided shape to the plan.

Other donors have also made important contributions to neurological research. Patrick and Lore McGovern made one of the largest philanthropic gifts to a university when they donated $350 million to MIT in 2000 for creation of the McGovern Institute for Brain Research. Inventor Fred Kavli funded brain institutes at Columbia, Yale, Johns Hopkins, Rockefeller University, and the University of California. In 2013, property developer Mortimer Zuckerman donated $200 million to Columbia University to endow a new neuroscience institute whose "mission is both greater understanding of the human condition and the discovery of new cures for human suffering." The innovative Center for Brain Health of the University of Texas at Dallas has been built up with broad philanthropic support since its founding in 1999. And in 2015 the O'Donnell Foundation pledged $36 million to start a new Brain Institute at the University of Texas Southwestern Medical Center.

The Brain & Behavior Research Foundation is another philanthropically funded organization that has dramatically advanced neurology and psychiatry. In 1987, the group began offering grants and prizes to young researchers in the brain sciences. By directing more than $300 million to 3,300 scientists, the organization has become not only the world's leading private funder of mental-health research, but an important spur to innovation in the field— particularly by encouraging promising young investigators with its research grants, and recognizing neurological breakthroughs with its five lifetime-achievement prizes.

Further reading

○ Allen Institute for Brain Science, alleninstitute.org/about_us/founders.html

○ McGovern Institute, mcgovern.mit.edu/about-the-institute/history

○ Brain & Behavior Research Foundation, bbrfoundation.org/about/our-history

———————— 2003 ————————

FOUNDATION FOR INNOVATIVE NEW DIAGNOSTICS

One of the most effective ways to stem disease is early detection. Access to diagnostic tests remains a significant challenge for developing countries, in part because of the high cost of delivery and transport to remote areas. To

∾ PhilAphorism

"Your Giving Pledge has a loophole…permitting pledgees to simply name charities in their wills. Some billionaires hate giving large sums of money away while alive and instead set up family-controlled foundations to do it for them after death. And these foundations become, more often than not, bureaucracy-ridden sluggards."

☞ *Robert Wilson replying to Bill Gates's invitation to sign the Giving Pledge* address this problem the Foundation for Innovative New Diagnostics was launched in 2003 to develop urgently needed diagnostic tests for tropical diseases. The goal is to provide highly affordable point-of-care tests that will help control the spread of disease in endemic countries. This new organization and its work were made possible almost entirely by grants from the Bill & Melinda Gates Foundation, which considers fighting infectious disease in developing countries its first health priority.

Further reading

○ Information at World Health Organization, who.int/trypanosomiasis_african/partners/find/en/index.html

BOOSTING ELECTRONIC HEALTH RECORDS

Electronic health records that are consistent, interchangeable, and accessible by consumers and health professionals from anywhere will be essential to many future advances in health care, including medicine that is personalized to the patient, better quality control, and reduction of duplication and waste that inflates prices. It's estimated that electronic health records could save more than $100 billion in unnecessary medical costs.

Back in 2002, when universal electronic records were just starting to be discussed seriously, the Markle Foundation put up $2 million to launch Connecting for Health. The foundation acted as a neutral convener on this contentious topic, bringing together computer experts, medical professionals, insurers, government, and other interested parties—rejecting no one who wanted to participate. When the effort began to show promise, the Robert Wood Johnson Foundation became a partner and put additional millions into supporting regular exchanges of information among participants.

In 2003, Health and Human Services Secretary Tommy Thompson announced, with thanks to the Markle Foundation, that the standards produced out of the Connecting for Health meetings would be adopted by the federal government as it moved toward personal electronic health records. Duke University's philanthropy center concluded that the Markle Foundation's inclusive approach made it irreplaceable in this success. "The value added by Markle's participation has been widely recognized. As a private foundation, Markle was able to fill a key niche: that of the convener. No other entity, public or private, would have been able to conduct the discussions that led to the Connecting for Health standards."

Further reading

○ Duke University case study, cspcs.sanford.duke.edu/sites/default/files/descriptive/
connecting_for_health.pdf

2001

9/11 FUNDS AND SUBSEQUENT DISASTER GIVING

The attacks of September 11, 2001 prompted an unprecedented outpouring of American giving. The American Red Cross organized one of the nation's largest charity drives after 9/11, called the Liberty Fund. Americans donated more than $752 million to this fund to provide medical care and aid to survivors of the attacks and their families. Counting donations to other organizations, a total of more than $2.8 billion was offered to charitable causes after 9/11.

Researchers believe this historic outpouring set new standards for disaster relief and set the table for other massive surges of emergency giving by Americans in the years since—including $1.9 billion to the victims of 2004's Pacific tsunami, $1.5 billion in relief to Haiti after its 2010 earthquake, and a record $5.3 billion charitable outpouring in the immediate aftermath of Hurricane Katrina.

Further reading

○ "September 11: The Philanthropic Response," from the Foundation Center, foundationcenter.
org/gainknowledge/research/pdf/911book3.pdf
○ Discussion of 9/11 and other disaster giving, dcblog.foundationcenter.org/2011/09/
september-11-a-look-back.html

2000

SYSTEMS BIOLOGY IS CREATED

Systems biology is a new approach that studies complex interactions among networks of cells, tissues, and organisms, with the view that many aspects of biology and medicine cannot be understood except as interlinked phenomena. This often requires complicated measuring of simultaneous factors and then integration of the data using mathematical models. Another name often applied to this emerging discipline is quantitative biology. The deluge of data now being generated by automated gene sequencing, advanced imaging, and other technologies has overwhelmed the ability of biologists to make sense of it—so mathematicians, physicists, and statisticians are migrating into the field to help them draw useful inferences and models of complex life processes.

When government and commercial support for this new and highly speculative field proved impossible to come by in the early days, the seminal Institute for Systems Biology was established in 2000 as a nonprofit research organization supported by philanthropic funds. Individual donors like Bay Area financier Bill Bowes, whose William K. Bowes Jr. Foundation contributed $6 million, collectively offered $30 million to start the institute.

As it established scientific breakthroughs, this philanthropically launched organization (and its wider discipline) also began to attract hundreds of millions of dollars of venture capital. By 2012, ISB had spun off 17 separate for-profit companies. That same year, the Institute for Systems Biology was ranked as the fourth most successful scientific-research institute in the world (assessed by the impact of their published papers), and today there are 70 or 80 copycat institutes located across different parts of the globe.

"That's the kind of thing that a front-end investment by philanthropy can lead to," comments ISB founder Leroy Hood. "What I've always loved about philanthropy is it's money that has a potential to be flexible. It's money that can catalyze new ideas. It's money that lets you push the frontiers, follow the leading edge. Hard to do that at the National Institutes of Health. Today, if you haven't completed two thirds of your research, you're probably not going to get a NIH grant because everything is so competitive and so conservative. So a philanthropist who is willing to say 'Yes, I'll step in and help you find something new' is a jewel."

Hedge-fund founder James Simons has stepped up as a donor in just this way. In 2005 he funded the Simons Center for Systems Biology at Princeton. Three years later his foundation put additional millions of dollars into quantitative work at Rockefeller University, one of the foremost biological research institutions in the country. He also planted seeds that year at Cold Spring Harbor Laboratory, a birthplace of molecular biology. Those seeds entered full bloom in 2014 when James and Marilyn Simons donated $50 million to expand and institutionalize the Simons Center for Quantitative Biology at Cold Spring Harbor Lab.

◅ PhilAphorism

No one is useless in this world who lightens the burdens of another. ☞ *Charles Dickens*

Further reading

○ Bowes Foundation support for the Institute for Systems Biology, milliondollarlist.org/
donors/william-k-bowes-jr-foundation

○ *Philanthropy* magazine interview with Leroy Hood, philanthropyroundtable.org/topic/
philanthropic_freedom/interview_with_leroy_hood

○ Simons Foundation discussion of Systems Biology, simonsfoundation.org/features/
foundation-news/systems-biology

1999

HUNTSMAN CANCER INSTITUTE

Both of Jon Huntsman's parents died of cancer. In 1992, he was diagnosed with the disease himself—the first of his four separate personal battles with the killer. His stints in the hospital convinced him that better treatments, better research, and better institutional experiences for cancer patients were all sorely needed.

After inventing, at the company he founded, the clamshell container that cradled McDonald's Big Mac, Huntsman added many other commercial successes, so he had the resources to act on his dream. He brokered a deal with a big pharmaceutical company to split the $250 million cost of building a state-of-the-art cancer treatment and research center in Salt Lake City, to fill a void in the Rocky Mountain region. Then the company backed out at the last minute. Huntsman and his family decided to foot the entire bill.

A patient care center opened in 1999, followed by the new hospital in 2004. Today, the Huntsman Cancer Institute serves 60,000 patients every year and performs 3,000 surgeries. The treatment facilities are renowned for their peaceful beauty, comfort, family-friendliness, and attention to patient services. The institution now ranks in the 99th percentile in patient satisfaction. The six states of the Intermountain West region finally have the comprehensive cancer-treatment center they previously lacked.

In addition, the HCI conducts groundbreaking research on genetic cancer patterns that could change the way the disease is approached across the globe. One reason Huntsman placed his cancer institute in Utah is because the Mormon church has compiled meticulous genealogical records that can be cross-indexed with patient records to uncover patterns illuminating the genetic aspects of cancer. HCI now manages a database of 16 million people that links health records to genealogies—the largest such resource in the world. "It's an incredibly rich source of information that supports research on genetics, epidemiology, and public health," says Mary Beckerle, director of the Huntsman Cancer Institute.

Already, HCI researchers are credited with identifying more cancer-causing genes than any lab in the world, including the genes responsible for inherited breast, ovarian, and colon cancers, as well as melanoma and malignant paraganglioma. In late 2013 Huntsman announced he would make an additional $100 million donation to the institute, bringing his total giving to that organization to $450 million. Huntsman's lifetime charitable giving stood at $1.6 billion at the end of 2013, making him just one of 19 people in the world to have donated at least a billion dollars (there are about 1,200 living billionaires).

Further reading

○ *Philanthropy* magazine profile, philanthropyroundtable.org/topic/excellence_in_philanthropy/the_fearless_philanthropist

A FOUNDATION ACTS LIKE A VENTURE CAPITALIST, AND SCORES BIG

In the 1980s, researchers uncovered the genetic cause of cystic fibrosis. But by the late 1990s only incremental improvements in treatment were in place, despite decades of investments in researchers by the Cystic Fibrosis Foundation. Most sufferers of the disease continued to pass away by their 30s.

So in 1999, the foundation decided to shift gears. Instead of just funding academic researchers, it would put money directly into pharmaceutical companies, seeking to speed useful drugs and also to interest the industry in making its own larger investments in lifesaving treatment. The Cystic Fibrosis Foundation eventually poured $450 million into investments in a variety of small and large drug companies, an example of what is sometimes called "venture philanthropy."

These bets paid off in a big way. In 2012, a breakthrough drug developed with CFF funding was approved by the FDA. It treats underlying causes of the disease rather than symptoms. In 2015 an even more broadly effective drug was approved; it offers significant relief to half of all sufferers. These compounds may double the life expectancy of some patients.

In addition to catalyzing these clinical breakthroughs, the foundation recouped its investments. It sold its rights to future royalties from the drugs for $3.3 billion. These proceeds will allow the Cystic Fibrosis Foundation to maintain and expand existing patient support services while directing additional money into a "supercharged" scientific search for a long-term CF cure for all patients.

Further reading

○ *Washington Post* reporting, washingtonpost.com/national/health-science/in-hunt-for-new-treatments-nonprofits-are-acting-like-venture-capitalists/2015/07/02/c6094578-19b8-11e5-93b7-5eddc056ad8a_story.html

LINKING ENGINEERING AND MEDICINE

Former Stanford University professor of computer science James Clark established a clutch of successful business ventures: Silicon Graphics, Netscape, Healtheon, and myCFO. Feeling indebted to Stanford as the site where he incubated many of his ideas, he approached the university in 1996 and inquired about what he might give the university to express his gratitude. Thus was born the James H. Clark Center for Biomedical Engineering and Sciences, created with a $150 million contribution from the entrepreneur—then the single largest gift to Stanford since its founding, and the largest personal gift in higher education. The facility served as a bridge between Stanford's engineering departments and its medical school. The gift allowed the hiring of about 15 new faculty, the construction of a biomedical-engineering center and the purchase of extensive equipment to fill its labs, plus graduate student fellowships. Atlantic Philanthropies, the foundation created by businessman Charles Feeney, also contributed major funding to the center.

Further reading

○ 1999 Stanford announcement of the gift, news.stanford.edu/pr/99/991027Clark.html
○ Clark Center Web site, biox.stanford.edu/clark/index.html

IMMUNIZING THE DEVELOPING WORLD

Bill Gates has described how his perspective changed when he read a 1996 *New York Times* story about how hundreds of thousands of children in the developing world die every year from dehydration after they become infected with something called rotavirus. "That can't be right," Gates thought. "I read the news all the time. I read about plane crashes and freak accidents. Where is the news about these half-million kids dying?" At that time, Gates was "exclusively focused" on running his company, and the Bill & Melinda Gates Foundation was just getting launched. Very soon, though, the "number-one global health priority" of the organization was delivering vaccines to poor children throughout the world. And by 1998, Gates had retired from Microsoft to pour himself into his philanthropy full-time.

Then in 1999 Bill and Melinda Gates hosted a dinner at their home for experts and asked how momentum could be regained in vaccinating children overseas. By the end of the year the Gates Foundation had put $750 million on the table to launch a new Global Alliance for Vaccines and Immunization, now known as GAVI. The foundation subsequently made additional huge grants to expand the vaccine alliance, bringing the total Gates commitment to this cause to $2.5 billion.

With this burst of energy and funding, around three quarters of a billion children have been immunized against basic diseases since 2000, averting perhaps as many as 10 million deaths over a 15-year period. Working through the alliance and on its own, the Gates Foundation has been the prime driver in creating new vaccines—like ones for rotavirus, approved for widespread use in 2009, and pneumonia. In 2015 Gates announced a $50 million grant to Stanford University to set up a center to study how the immune system can be harnessed to develop future vaccines. The foundation has also greatly expanded access in poor countries to underutilized existing vaccines like those against hepatitis B, influenza type B, measles, and the five diseases blocked by the so-called pentavalent vaccine.

Further reading

○ About GAVI, gavialliance.org/about/mission/impact

1997

A CRUSADE AGAINST HUNTINGTON'S DISEASE

Huntington's disease is a genetic disorder that destroys portions of the brain involved in movement, thinking, and emotions, progressing over decades with ultimately fatal results. It strikes perhaps 30,000 persons in the U.S., and if one of your parents had it, you have a 50-50 chance of developing the disorder yourself. For years it was one of those afflictions that attracted relatively little research funding or attention outside of the families plagued by it. That changed in the mid-1990s, when a single donor began to pour large resources into a broad campaign against the disease.

Andrew Shechtel entered Johns Hopkins University at the precocious age of 16 and left three years later with degrees in math and political economy, then spent time at Harvard Business School and Wall Street before entering an investment firm focused on abstruse quantitative financial trades. He became a multibillionaire, and continues in the field, while also giving away several billion dollars.

His favorite cause is battling Huntington's Disease, to which he has donated at least $732 million directly since 2000, plus more indirectly via grants to allied organizations. In recent years, his annual spending of more than $100 million for an HD cure has exceeded the total efforts in this area of the massive National Institutes of Health (which devoted $55 million to Huntington's in 2013). With the charitable trust established by Shechtel containing $5 billion as of 2013, a good deal more spending can be expected.

The donor's gifts are primarily channeled through his CHDI Foundation, whose mission is to "bridge the translational gap that often exists between academic and industrial research" and "develop drugs that will slow the progression of Huntington's disease and provide meaningful clinical benefit to patients as quickly as possible." The organization's description of itself is businesslike: "Essentially, CDHI is a science-management organization.... Our science directors and project managers work closely with a network of more than 600 researchers...in the pursuit of novel therapies, providing strategic scientific direction and management. [Our] overall strategy is to de-risk therapeutic approaches [so] pharmaceutical company partners will view them as a good investment.... Our bottom line is ensuring the shortest possible time to getting effective therapeutics to HD patients."

Part of this involves encouraging scientists to take up work on Huntington's, by providing background knowledge, chemicals and supplies, animal models, and working protocols that can speed research. The nonprofit also has created its own large registry and observational study of families experiencing Huntington's disease. And it collaborates with a network of other advocacy organizations to support patients, family members, and clinicians.

Further reading

○ CDHI Foundation, chdifoundation.org/about-us

1997

ELLISON MEDICAL FOUNDATION

In the 1990s, Oracle software founder Lawrence Ellison developed a friendship with Nobel molecular biologist Joshua Lederberg of Rockefeller University. This led in 1997 to establishment of the Ellison Medical Foundation, with

∿ PhilAphorism

Don't just think, do.   ☞ *Horace*

Lederberg as lead scientific adviser. For 15 years, the foundation supported basic biomedical research, with a focus on understanding how organisms age, and how age-related diseases and debilities might be prevented. During that decade and a half, the foundation distributed $430 million of money donated by Ellison to 600 prominent or rising researchers. This financial surge advanced both the discipline of aging and the techniques of molecular biology (advanced versions of which are often required in age-related research).

Further reading

○ Ellison Medical Foundation, ellisonfoundation.org

VOLUNTEERS IN MEDICINE

In 1994, retired physician Jack McConnell, best-known as the developer of Tylenol while a researcher at Johnson & Johnson, had the idea of recruiting other retired doctors and nurses to serve, at no charge, the medical needs of poor people living in the area of Hilton Head, South Carolina. Soon, there followed a national organization dedicated to helping local volunteers start similar free clinics all across the U.S. Volunteers In Medicine, based in a small office in Burlington, Vermont and operating on a modest $250,000 annual budget, has provided the model and management guidance for 96 free clinics (and counting), in a riot of locations: Red Bank, New Jersey; Dunlap, Tennessee; Monroe, Michigan; Springfield, Oregon; inner-city Baltimore; Farmville, Virginia; Indio, California.

Much of the care is targeted toward those with chronic conditions—diabetes, hypertension, cardiovascular and gastro-intestinal problems—with the aim of preventing these long-term afflictions from debilitating their victims. Many clinics also provide vaccinations (especially for children) and dental services, which are not covered by public programs like Medicaid, but which have been increasingly shown to have consequential medical effects. Patients include a broad cross-section of immigrants and low-income persons who despite qualifying for Medicaid have difficulty actually getting access to medical care.

Without a central management structure or government funding, these valuable clinics have emerged via strong community support. The staff in Burlington have no mandate or goals for opening new clinics, and they don't own or operate any. They simply aid local "champions" who ask for their expert assistance. Before any local "champion" is allowed to use the VIM name in launching a clinic, he or she must first put together a committee that "represents various constituencies in the community—

people of influence, including within the medical community," as VIM director Amy Hamlin puts it.

The free labor of 11,000 medical professionals and associated volunteers drives these facilities, while donors cover building rents, lab charges, support staff, and medication costs. The end product is a half-million annual patient visits, worth tens of millions of dollars to the beneficiaries—all produced (as of 2011) at a modest per-visit philanthropic outlay of $316, including all medication and lab work.

Further reading

○ Directory of VIM clinics, volunteersinmedicine.org/vim-clinics

○ 2006 Social Entrepreneurship Award citation, manhattan-institute.org/pdf/SE2006.pdf

STOWERS INSTITUTE FOR MEDICAL RESEARCH

Jim Stowers founded Twentieth Century Mutual Funds at his kitchen table in 1958. A low-cost investment vehicle for small investors, the company began with initial capital of $107,000. By the time its creator died in 2014, the firm (renamed American Century Investments) was managing $141 billion in assets. In 1994, Stowers and his wife, Virginia, gave away 95 percent of their fortune. Both being cancer survivors, and Jim having grown up as the son and grandson of doctors, they donated $2 billion to endow a new top-flight medical-research facility in their hometown of Kansas City, Missouri. Experts pressed for the money to go to an existing organization, or at least one created in a major East- or West-Coast city, but the Stowers were determined to build something in their own region. The 550-employee institute focuses on basic science research, and has sparked growth of biological sciences of various sorts in Kansas and Missouri.

Further reading

○ *Kansas City Star* obituary, kansascity.com/2014/03/18/4898511/james-e-stowers-jr-founder-of.html

PROSTATE CANCER FOUNDATION

Business financier Michael Milken, a longtime anti-cancer donor, detected inefficient patterns in medical research similar to those he had worked against during his career in high finance. He discovered it tended to be established "safe" researchers who garnered grants even though many of these individuals were well beyond their years of peak creativity. Meanwhile, brilliant young unknowns with bold if risky ideas had great difficulty getting funding to test their theories. Milken also observed that grant paperwork absorbed large amounts of time for scientists who would be much better employed in their lab than at a desk filling out forms. He noticed that during basic research too little attention was paid to whether a new regimen had the potential to lead to better diagnostics or treatment. In all these areas, private donors were able to be much nimbler than federal grant agencies, and he made getting around such obstacles one priority of the Prostate Cancer Foundation he founded in 1993.

The PCF quickly became a leader on prostate cancer, having raised $500 million for medical research in less than two decades, which it used to fund more than 1,600 projects in 15 countries. One of PCF's first grants was to Judah Folkman, whose work on starving the blood supply to tumors had effects on many branches of cancer research. Early funding from the foundation also led to new treatments and drugs—including Zometa (for treating prostate cancer and other solid tumors), Provenge (an immunotherapy), and Jevtana (an enhanced chemotherapy). PCF-funded researchers made big strides in identifying various types of prostate cancer and creating treatments, and are now driving dozens of new drugs and therapies through clinical testing. Since the founding of the Prostate Cancer Foundation, the number of prostate deaths has fallen from 40,000 per year to below 30,000, despite a growing and aging population.

Michael Milken's medical giving now exceeds a billion dollars. The philanthropy model he pioneered, grafting business principles onto donating, is popularly called venture philanthropy. Its success in speeding the pace of innovation in research and treatment—and also in expanding public awareness of prostate cancer—has fed similar efforts from other funders and nonprofits—like the Susan Komen efforts against breast cancer, the Livestrong Foundation (testicular cancer), the Michael J. Fox Foundation (Parkinson's), and the Melanoma Alliance.

Further reading

○ Story in *Philanthropy* magazine, philanthropyroundtable.org/site/print/the_accelerator

○ *Genetic Engineering and Biotechnology News* article on venture philanthropy,genengnews. com/keywordsandtools/print/1/12978

1992

BILL GATES HELPS MASS-PRODUCE DNA ARRAYS

One of the first major philanthropic projects of Bill Gates, launched long before he shifted his gaze steadily to philanthropy, came back in 1992.

The University of Washington Medical School was trying to create the first-ever cross-disciplinary department of biology. Gates made the new department possible by putting up $12 million of his own money. He told the organizers, "I just want you to understand I am giving $12 million, but I'm in my acquisition phase, I'm not in my philanthropic phase, so don't expect any more." That offering was sufficient to launch what became not only a highly successful department but a blooming new discipline of molecular biotechnology.

Among other work, the team at Washington invented an inkjet device for creating DNA arrays that allowed tens of thousands of genes to be read at once. This instrument was soon commercialized and made available to other scientists, and transformed genomics, biology, and medicine. Given estimates by the Battelle Foundation that automated DNA sequencing and the human-genome project may have created in excess of $800 billion of value, this comparatively modest investment yielded potent returns. And philanthropy played a crucial role.

Further reading

○ *Philanthropy* magazine interview, philanthropyroundtable.org/topic/philanthropic_freedom/interview_with_leroy_hood

1991

PAINTING A TARGET ON AUTISM

In the early 1990s, an employee in an Atlanta Home Depot outlet had been missing work, then showing up sleepless and unkempt. Company co-founder Bernie Marcus took her aside and asked what was wrong. "Her child had this strange—well, I guess we called it a disability at first," say Marcus. "Nobody knew what it was. The child was not communicating. He would scream in pain and nobody knew why. Doctors didn't have the patience to work with him…. That's when I first saw how autism destroys families."

Marcus got involved. He learned that one out of every 88 kids has autism, versus one out of every 25,000 who have cancer, and yet cancer funding for children outstripped autism funding by a factor of 200 to one. Finding that "nobody was really doing a good job with this," Marcus decided to start an autism center himself. After much cajoling he arranged an affiliation with Emory University, and the operation opened with two psychologists working out of a pair of double-wide trailers. In addition to providing heavy financial subsidies every year, Marcus worked energetically to make "autism" a household word. He came up with the idea for Autism Speaks, and provided $25 million to launch the national advocacy organization, which has since raised more than $180 million for research, and expanded insurance coverage to behavioral treatments of autism.

By 2011, the Marcus Autism Center was treating 5,676 children annually. That same year, the center was able to hire away from Yale one of the foremost clinician-researchers in the field, Ami Klin. That spurred Marcus to make an additional $25 million gift (with $15 million more coming from the Joseph Whitehead Foundation) to support a major advance at the center. Dr. Klin and his team have developed eye-tracking technology that allows babies with autism to be identified in their first year, before symptoms develop. With treatment beginning early, instead of around age five when autism is generally recognized today, a child's development can be much improved. The new technique will undergo clinical trials at the center to gain FDA approval for use nationwide, with the aim of instituting universal childhood screening. Meanwhile, the Marcus Center is gearing up to treat more children as they are diagnosed, pledging to eliminate its current waiting list of 1,700 families.

The $90 million Bernie Marcus has invested has transformed autism from heartbreaking mystery to treatable condition. It has also made Atlanta and the Marcus Autism Center the leading organization for treatment and study in the world. In 2014, the city hosted more than 3,000 scientists from three dozen countries for the International Meeting for Autism Research.

Once this target had been painted on autism as an affliction that can be ameliorated, other donors became involved. The foundation of hedge-fund operator James Simons created a major Autism Research Initiative in 2003. It currently has an annual budget of about $60 million, with which it supports 175 investigators. In the last half-dozen years, Simons's center has granted more than $260 million to leading researchers.

Further reading

○ Profile in *Atlanta Business Chronicle,* bizjournals.com/atlanta/print-edition/2013/12/06/autism-research-gets-game-changing-boost.html?page=all

○ *Philanthropy* magazine, philanthropyroundtable.org/topic/excellence_in_philanthropy/building_america

○ Simons Foundation Autism Research Initiative, sfari.org/about-sfari

MIND-BODY LINKS UNCOVERED BY TEMPLETON

After noticing that the mental and physical health of many of his patients was deeply entwined with their spiritual state of mind, a Duke-trained M.D. named David Larson founded the National Institute for Healthcare Research in 1991 to systematically study how religious views and practice affect health. Throughout the next decade until Larson's sudden death in 2002, the John Templeton Foundation invested nearly $10 million in research and publication grants to allow NIHR to explore this uncharted territory.

In addition, the Templeton Foundation provided Duke University with a $9.8 million eight-year grant which created the Center for Spirituality, Theology, and Health at the Duke University Medical Center in 1998. The mission of CSTH was to "conduct research on the relationships between religion, spirituality, and health, to train others to do so, to interpret the research...and design future research." The center recruited a team of faculty from medicine, psychiatry, nursing, sociology, and other fields, and commenced an ambitious schedule of investigation and publishing. By 2012, the center had produced more than 200 peer-reviewed scientific articles on "relationships between religious involvement and a host of psychological and physical health outcomes." By that same time, ten other centers on health and spirituality had also taken root in the U.S., at places like the George Washington University Medical Center, Massachusetts General Hospital, and the Texas Medical Center, and four more had been founded in Canada and Europe.

Both medical education and medical practice have been affected by this new knowledge. As late as 2000, for instance, 92 percent of professional psychiatrists reported that while they encounter significant religious and spiritual issues in their practices, two thirds of them had had no serious training or research background in religious or spiritual issues. The number of medical schools offering courses on patient religious life could be counted on one hand when Templeton entered this field in the early '90s. By 2010, however, three quarters of U.S. medical schools had brought spirituality into their curricula, spurred not only by clearly demonstrated correlations between religious life and health but also by Templeton awards for medical schools and residency programs that innovated in this area. There is also now a David Larson Fellowship in Health and Spirituality, which is awarded to post-doctoral scholars annually by the Library of Congress.

⊸ PhilAphorism

Most people think that Americans are generous because we are rich. The truth is that we are rich, in significant part, because we are generous. ☞ *Claire Gaudiani*

"The amount of studies done since the year 2000" on spirituality and health "probably exceeds all the research in the 150 years prior to 2000," says Harold Koenig, associate professor of medicine and director of the Duke center. Christina Puchalski, director of George Washington University's Institute for Spirituality and Health, observes that including faith factors in medical treatment is part of a larger shift in medicine away from just thinking about disease, and taking account of wellness and "the inner life of the patient."

Further reading

○ About the Duke University Center for Spirituality, Theology, and Health, CSTH_Vision_ Mission_Accomplishments_and_Future.pdf

○ Some centers on religion and health, spirit-health.org/resources_detail.asp?q=55

1991

AARON DIAMOND FOUNDATION UNMASKS HIV'S WEAK SPOTS

In 1985 the Aaron Diamond Foundation was founded in New York City to honor the eponymous real-estate developer, who passed away suddenly of a heart attack in 1983, by his wife Irene. When Irene and Aaron decided to give most of their assets to their foundation, they committed to blasting its funds out intensively within about a decade of either's death, with the aim of making fast progress against targeted ills. When the funding of the foundation was all settled, one of the first places that Irene Diamond's gaze settled was the alarming new AIDS epidemic that was just beginning to ravage her hometown of New York City.

HIV had been identified as the cause of AIDS in 1983, and early hopes for a vaccine, treatment, or cure for the disease faded quickly. The Diamond Foundation and other New York City funders felt that "an effort was necessary to bring the city closer to its level of responsibility as the epicenter of the AIDS epidemic in the United States." So plans were laid for the Aaron Diamond AIDS Research Center, which opened in 1991 and immediately dove into high-level research under the direction of David Ho, a prominent microbiologist Irene Diamond selected to be director. By the time the foundation closed down at the end of 1996, it had invested $220 million and become the largest private supporter of AIDS research in the U.S.

The Diamond Center's scientific accomplishments are legion. ADARC did some of the most important basic research at the molecular level on what made the AIDS virus so tenacious. The center identified a gene mutation that confers immunity to HIV. Diamond clinicians championed anti-retroviral "cocktails" that by combining medications were able to suppress HIV infection to undetectable levels. Combination therapy is expensive, though, and HIV's ability to evade and adapt to immune defenses meant that a constant flow of improved and augmented cocktails was necessary, so ADARC researchers helped propel more than two dozen different drugs through the development pipeline. As a result, the death rate from HIV in America is now one fifth of what it was 20 years ago.

The center also did important work on prevention. Its major project in China, for instance, demonstrated that the rate of transmission of HIV from mothers to infants could be reduced from over 30 percent to less than 1 percent. Diamond researchers also pursued various HIV vaccination strategies right through the stage of clinical trials, including some work funded by the Gates Foundation using very innovative techniques.

Though never numbering more than about 75 researchers, its no-strings philanthropic funding gave the Diamond Center a nimbleness, speed, and tolerance for risk that allowed it to repeatedly precede and outperform government labs. By the time the Diamond funds were spent down, the center had developed a broad base of support. It remains the largest private AIDS research organization in the world, with a clinical relationship with Rockefeller University. In 1996, the year the Diamond Foundation closed, *Time* magazine selected ADARC's director as its Man of the Year, in recognition of the center research that saved millions of lives.

Further reading

○ Some major discoveries of ADARC, adarc.org/achievements_320.html
○ Diamond family strategy, *Philanthropy* magazine, philanthropyroundtable.org/topic/donor_intent/learning_from_the_sunset

───── 1990 ─────

TAKING ON THE TOP CAUSE OF PREVENTABLE DEATH

Each year more than 480,000 Americans die of tobacco use—the nation's largest cause of preventable death, accounting for about one out of every five U.S. deaths according to the Centers for Disease Control. About two thirds of smokers say they want to quit, but only about 5 percent succeed in a given year. In 1990, the new president of the Robert Wood Johnson Foundation, Steven Schroeder, aimed his organization squarely at reducing "the harmful effects, and the irresponsible use, of tobacco, alcohol, and drugs." As part of this, the foundation spent $700 million on a range of anti-tobacco programs during the next two decades. Programs were aimed especially at reducing youth smoking, publicizing the bad health effects of smoking and of secondhand smoke, and helping addicted smokers quit. (See 1991 entry on Public Policy list for other aspects of the campaign.)

Further reading

○ "The Tobacco Campaigns of the Robert Wood Johnson Foundation and Collaborators, 1991-2010,"rwjf.org/content/dam/farm/reports/evaluations/2011/rwjf70005

1990

FISHER HOUSES CREATED FOR FAMILIES OF HOSPITALIZED MILITARY

In 1990, New York City real-estate developer Zachary Fisher learned about a servicewoman who had recently received medical treatment at a military hospital. Her husband, unable to afford a hotel, spent the duration of her hospitalization sleeping in his car. Fisher was shocked to learn that the military made no provision for the families of hospitalized servicemembers and veterans—and decided to do something about it.

With an initial donation of $20 million to establish the Fisher House Foundation, Zachary and his wife Elizabeth began building "comfort homes" within walking distance of Veterans Affairs and military medical centers. These complexes were designed to provide free housing for families of military personnel and veterans who were hospitalized. At the time of Zachary's death in 2000, the Fisher House Foundation had built 26 houses at busy medical facilities, and there were 65 houses in operation by 2015.

As of 2015, the Fisher House Foundation has provided 6 million days of free lodging to the families of hospitalized servicemembers and veterans. In addition to saving those individuals a serious expense, the opportunity to commune with other families in similar stressful situations has proven invaluable for many beneficiaries.

With this enormously popular innovation under their belt, the Fisher family expanded their military-medical philanthropy. Between 2000 and 2012, their Intrepid Fallen Heroes Fund provided $120 million in support to wounded service members and their families, first through direct payments to the families of soldiers lost in war and later through the construction of new medical research and rehabilitation facilities for wounded military personnel. The Center for the Intrepid in San Antonio is focused on treatment of soldiers with amputations, burns, or loss of limb use. The National Intrepid Center of Excellence in Bethesda, Maryland, is focused on the care of brain injuries and psychological health and connects to satellite centers to bring advanced brain-injury care to other parts of the country.

Further reading

○ Zachary Fisher profile in Philanthropy Hall of Fame (see prior *Almanac* section)

○ Facts and figures on Fisher Houses, fisherhouse.org/assets/2877/fish_onepagefactsheet.pdf

LEADING A CHARGE
AGAINST PSYCHIATRIC DISORDERS

Ted Stanley has one of the longest histories in mental-health philanthropy. Back in the late-1980s the billionaire retailer founded the Stanley Medical Research Institute, which quickly became the biggest private backer in the U.S. of investigations into bipolar disorder and schizophrenia—diseases the director described as "massively underresearched" by government health agencies. Stanley ended up funding between a quarter and half of all research on those two maladies, to the tune of hundreds of millions of dollars in total.

Among other scientific contributions, this organization collected several hundred brains from persons suffering from various mental illnesses, which became the source for hundreds of thousands of tissue samples shipped to researchers making requests from all around the world. The Stanley Institute also supported scores of drug trials, seeking effective treatments via off-label uses of older medicines.

More recently, Stanley has underwritten mental-illness research at the Broad Institute of MIT and Harvard. His initial $100 million grant established a separate Center for Psychiatric Research. In 2014 he announced a huge $650 million gift to the Broad Institute, bringing his total giving to that group to $825 million. These funds will continue the work he launched there on uncovering the genetic roots of various psychiatric disorders.

Further reading

○ *Philanthropy* magazine on launch of Stanley Medical Research Initiative, philanthropyroundtable.org/topic/excellence_in_philanthropy/philanthropists_creating_cures

○ Boston Globe article on $650 million gift, bostonglobe.com/lifestyle/health-wellness/2014/07/21/broad-institute-receives-million-commitment-for-psychiatric-research/EkpKRskBV9tuTd09mLT39H/story.html

DEVELOPMENT OF THE
AUTOMATED DNA SEQUENCER

In the early 1980s, longtime Caltech biology professor Leroy Hood had conceptualized an instrument that would automate the slow, labor-intensive process of sequencing DNA. The tedious hand process, which required scientists to repeat multiple steps using hazardous radioactive elements, made it impossible to read any more than a tiny portion of any genetic string. Hood's new procedure substituted safe fluorescent dyes for the radioactive chemicals and used lasers and computers rather than human eyes to read the DNA patterns. Yet when he applied to the federal National Institutes of Health for grants to help his team create the planned machine, Hood reports that his grant proposals "got some of the worst scores the NIH had ever given. People said it was impossible, or they said 'Why do this? Grad students can do it more easily.'"

To get around this roadblock, Hood turned to what he called "a really interesting consortium of philanthropy and business." The philanthropy came from legendary donor Sol Price. The originator of the warehouse superstore concept that eventually produced Costco and Sam's Club, and an early creator of Real Estate Investment Trusts, Price poured himself into numerous charities after making his fortune in southern California.

"When the NIH funding didn't work out for the automated sequencer, I went to Sol, and he ended up giving me $200,000 a year for two or three years," says Hood, who describes Price as "really smart and flexible, and excited by innovation and new ideas.... He was a hard-nosed, critical guy who asked tough questions. But when he was done, he was satisfied, and he more or less gave me a blank check to spend as I felt needed. And that was enormously valuable." With the philanthropic money, Hood launched his work on the automated sequencer, and then went to the Monsanto Company and used Price's donation to leverage from the firm another $200,000-per-year for-profit investment.

By June 1986, Hood had his machine on the market. With continual improvements it was soon capable of sequencing 150 million DNA base pairs on a fully automated basis. Without this breakthrough, the sequencing of the human genome would not have been feasible. "The combination of philanthropy and industry really led to the conceptual and early-stage

◁ PhilAphorism

If you want to feel proud of yourself, you've got to do things you can be proud of.

         ☞ *Oseola McCarty*

development of the automated sequencer. Had it not been for those things, progress would have been delayed for an unknown period of time.... It was a critical catalytic moment, and philanthropy was there to push it forward."

Further reading

○ *Philanthropy* magazine interview with Leroy Hood, January 31, 2013, philanthropyroundtable.org/topic/philanthropic_freedom/interview_with_leroy_hood

○ Genomic history, genomenewsnetwork.org/resources/timeline/1986_Hood.php

1986

HEALTH SURVEYS AND PATIENT-CENTERED CARE

Harvey Picker had played an important role in commercializing X-rays and other forms of electronic imaging and became a significant donor with the money he made in the process. Making health care more humane became one particular interest. He wanted to encourage physicians and other professionals to treat patients as persons, not "imbeciles or inventory," and he would not be content with small changes. In 1986 he established the Picker Institute, devoted to seeing medical treatment "through the patient's eyes." The institute is credited with coining the phrase "patient-centered care," and promoting structural changes which would encourage it.

One Picker project to improve the quality of health care by more directly involving patients offered a grant to Beth Israel Hospital in Boston so they could conduct a survey of patients' perception of their treatment, in conjunction with the Louis Harris polling firm. The survey uncovered a lack of trust among patients, and inadequate communication which led to incorrect pain management and confusion among patients about their treatment regimens. Picker initiatives brought systematic surveying to other hospitals as well, hosted conferences on the prevalence of patient dissatisfaction, and instigated efforts to make medical care less impersonal and more patient-driven. The Picker patient-satisfaction surveys subsequently became a standard measure of patient care worldwide, and are credited with substantially improving the delivery of medical services.

Further reading

○ Harvey Picker obituary, smith.edu/news/2007-08/HarveyPickerObit.php

○ Case study, content.healthaffairs.org/content/17/1/236.full.pdf+html

1986

GUINEA WORM ERADICATION

Only one infectious disease has ever been eradicated: smallpox (gone as of 1980). Soon though, a second affliction will disappear, likely around 2018, when the Guinea worm becomes extinct. This will happen thanks largely to three philanthropic interventions: the leadership of the Carter Center, a nonprofit formed by former president Jimmy Carter and Emory University; the money of the Gates Foundation, which has donated more than $100 million to the effort while inspiring matching funds from many other givers; and the donated hours of hundreds of thousands of volunteers.

A parasite transmitted by eggs borne in drinking water, the worm is an affliction that has sickened millions in Asia and Africa for millennia (its signs can be found in ancient mummies). While rarely fatal, a Guinea worm can cause intense pain as it travels through the body. It usually migrates eventually to the feet or legs, where the worm chews its way through tissue and skin to exit the body, causing blistering pain that prevents victims from walking, secondary infections, and other miseries.

There is no known curative medicine or vaccine for Guinea worm. What is eliminating this horrific affliction today is not medicine or complex technology, but aggressive canvassing by volunteers. They give out simple hand-held filtering straws, teach villagers to use them whenever drinking water so as to avoid infection, add larvicide to central water sources, and scout the countryside for disease outbreaks.

When the current campaign against Guinea worm began in 1986, there were 3.5 million new cases of the disease every year, spread across 21 countries. In all of 2014, there were only 126 reported infections, in just four countries. In total, the Guinea worm eradication effort will have cost about $375 million.

Further reading

○ *New England Journal of Medicine* report, nejm.org/doi/full/10.1056/NEJMra1200391
○ Latest Centers for Disease Control report, cartercenter.org/resources/pdfs/news/health_publications/guinea_worm/wrap-up/232.pdf

——— 1983 ———

MARKEY TRUST LAUNCHES
BIOMEDICAL CAREERS

By the time Lucille Markey died in 1982, at age 85, she had seen a lot of death, sickness, and suffering, so she left her fortune (derived from her father-in-law's founding of the Calumet Baking Powder Company) to medical research. To get the biggest possible bang for her buck, Markey stipulated that her trust should push all of its money out the door over just a 15-year period. As a result of this concentrated burst, and some very sage leadership by those she put in charge, the Markey Trust became one of the most important forces in U.S. medical research from the mid-1980s through the time when it closed its doors for good in 1997, distributing more than $500 million in 200 grants.

An important part of the success of Markey's philanthropy was the flexibility it offered to investigators. Funding from NIH or NSF can rarely be used for preliminary investigations or risky science. Nor can it be used to recruit new scientists or graduate students or to build or equip a lab. Forget about shifting money from one year to another or one project to another, under a government grant, no matter how salutary the effects. And don't try to dramatically change research directions to follow new leads with government funding. The Markey grants, however, explicitly allowed these sorts of things in order to encourage innovation by recipients, and maximum efficiency. The trustees and experts who gave the Trust its marching orders in a series of intense meetings in 1984 emphasized several targets: support for young investigators with promise; trusting outstanding researchers with wide discretionary powers in using funds; supporting fields with the biggest upside; funding fields that are important but not popular; being willing to pay for the infrastructure (buildings, equipment, and people) necessary for great research, not just the end research.

In addition to being flexible, Markey was patient. One of the distinctive contributions of medical philanthropy has been to support top young researchers through the "valley of death" that extends from the end of their training until they are able to establish their reputations and begin winning grants from government science agencies. The Markey Scholars Awards are now considered exemplars for nurturing young talent in this way. The awards offered each recipient funding for five to seven years, plus money to establish his or her own lab. The 113 Markey awardees turned out to be extraordinarily successful and productive. Dr. Eric Lander is an example; during his fellowship he refined new concepts of gene mapping in the lab Markey supported, and today he heads the largest genome center in the world—the Broad Institute of MIT and Harvard.

The trust's savvy extended right to its shutdown. It produced a handbook on how to effectively spend a foundation right down to closure. And it paid the National Academy of Sciences to conduct a major assessment of its programs (published several years after the trust's shutdown) focused on two questions: Were its funds well spent? What can others learn from Markey's experience, both in terms of improving biomedical research and refining philanthropic practice? Academy investigators published five separate reports, and gave the trust brilliant grades for its influence on biomedical progress.

Further reading

○ Five National Academies Press books on the contributions of the Markey Trust (two published in 2004, three in 2006): nap.edu/catalog.php?record_id=11755

1982

KOMEN RACES TO CURE BREAST CANCER

In 1977 Susan Komen was diagnosed with breast cancer and her sister Nancy promised her she would help change the odds on that frightening disease, so more women would know how to discover it, fight it, and avoid its death sentence. Susan died in 1980 at age 36 and in 1982 Nancy Brinker founded the Susan G. Komen Breast Cancer Foundation, launching a global movement against breast cancer in the process. The foundation created successful public-awareness campaigns that increased early detection (including regularization of mammograms for women over 40) and sharply raised research budgets. From its first event in Dallas with 800 female runners, Komen's signature "Races for the Cure" now mobilize more than a million participants each year, and have invested $2.6 billion (as of 2015) in the foundation's education and research efforts. Since 1980, the five-year survival rate for women diagnosed with early-stage breast cancer has increased from 74 percent to 98 percent, and total breast-cancer mortality in the U.S. is down by more than a third.

Further reading

○ 2011 interview with Nancy Brinker in *Philanthropy* magazine, philanthropyroundtable.org/topic/excellence_in_philanthropy/racing_for_the_cure

○ About Komen, ww5.komen.org/AboutUs/AboutUs.html

1982

PUTTING GERIATRIC MEDICINE ON THE MAP

The number of elderly Americans is in the midst of doubling in less than one generation—to a total of more than 70 million. And they are heavy consumers of medical care. Though persons older than 65 account for only 13 percent of the population, they account for four out of every ten surgeries today and 44 percent of all visits to primary physicians. More than 40 percent of the elderly are currently taking five or more medications, and seniors with multiple chronic illnesses make an average of 37 annual visits to 14 different physicians, who write them 50 separate prescriptions.

With these stark realities in mind, starting in 1982 the John A. Hartford Foundation established a tight and disciplined focus on building the emerging field of geriatric medicine. A product of the A&P grocery fortune, the Hartford Foundation had been the largest funder of biomedical research in America during the mid-twentieth century decades prior to the growth of the National Institutes of Health. During this period the foundation underwrote many major medical innovations (see 1954 entry). The organization has proved equally savvy and influential in its latest focus on the health of the aged.

In the early '80s, Hartford set up many programs to build expertise in the new field of geriatrics, and offered multiple grants to recruit physicians into it. Among other efforts, money was provided to 13 medical schools to help them recruit and train faculty. The foundation then made 16 separate grants to pioneer the field of geriatric pharmacology, improving the safety and efficiency of drug-dispensing to the aged. Next, it funded efforts to develop geriatric subspecialties in fields like surgery, internal medicine, and primary care. To attract top researchers to medical problems associated with aging, the foundation devoted $39 million to establishing the now-prestigious Paul Beeson Awards.

Eventually, 28 Centers of Excellence were established with Hartford money at academic medical centers, deepening the quality of geriatric training. Major effort was also devoted to developing the profession of geriatric nursing. Soon after, a similar push funded the rise of geriatric social

ᕦ PhilAphorism

In the modern era, government has been seen as society's problem-solving agency, the place people go to address every conceivable need. This assumption of government omnipotence has warped the evolution of philanthropy. The principal function of a philanthropic group becomes interesting government in carrying out its goal, rather than being a problem-solving institution in its own right.

↩ *James Payne*

work, primarily by identifying leading scholars and funding them in faculty positions. Finally, Hartford was a strong leader in efforts to help frail elderly remain in their homes rather than being institutionalized.

From 1982 to 2012, the Hartford Foundation awarded 560 grants worth $451 million solely to improve health-care provision for the elderly—funding that experts say was unusually seminal. The foundation magnified its influence by allying itself with several other savvy donors working on geriatric care, including the Atlantic Philanthropies, the Robert Wood Johnson Foundation, the Donald W. Reynolds Foundation, and others.

The result? "With program after program, they changed the health-care system and improved health-care outcomes for older adults," states the director of the Johns Hopkins Geriatric Education Center, John Burton. The former dean of the University of Pennsylvania School of Nursing, Claire Fagin, makes a similar observation: "The contribution of the Hartford Foundation in putting geriatrics and gerontology on the map has been monumental. It is emblematic of what foundations should be doing in the sense of changing the field."

Further reading

○ *30 Years of Aging and Health*, 2012 Annual Report of the John A. Hartford Foundation, jhartfound.org/images/uploads/reports/temp_file_JAHF_2012AR4.pdf

1982

BATTLING SUBSTANCE ABUSE

For whatever reason, philanthropic activity in alcohol and drug treatment gets relatively little attention or public visibility. At the grassroots level, the most effective force for sobriety in the U.S. is Alcoholics Anonymous, the classic voluntary organization of the sort that has long kept American civil society healthy. But AA is powered by voluntarism and mutual collaboration, not by donated money.

There have, however, been some notable philanthropic successes in battling substance abuse. The philanthropy-supported Salvation Army does cost-effective, hands-on, faith-based work with difficult populations, persevering through the high relapse rates that afflict all treatment regimens and ultimately achieving success with many individuals. The nonprofit Hazelden Foundation, which started a twelve-step program for alcoholics in 1949, now operates a half-dozen campuses; in 2012, its 7,431 donors provided Hazelden with more than $10 million in gifts. The Betty Ford Center, founded in 1982 by the former First Lady with philanthropist Leonard Firestone, has served 90,000 patients as a high-visibility nonprofit supported by its own foundation, which raises several million dollars every year in donations. In 2013, Hazelden and the Ford Center announced a merger to create the largest nonprofit addiction-treatment organization in the U.S.

Another treatment center launched in 1982 by a political family is Marworth, donated by former Pennsylvania governor and U.S. ambassador to the United Nations William Scranton and his wife, Mary. Recognizing the dearth of residential substance-abuse treatment options in their area, they offered their magnificent family estate (located near the Pennsylvania city that bears their surname) to Geisinger Health Systems to become one of the country's leading alcohol and drug detoxification facilities. A nonprofit that grew out of philanthropist Abigail Geisinger's 1915 donation of a hospital (inspired by the Mayo Clinic), the Geisinger system is now one of the largest rural health-care networks in America, treating 2.6 million people in 44 Pennsylvania counties.

Since its establishment, Marworth has treated more than 40,000 patients— with a special focus on helping doctors and health-care workers as well as law-enforcement officials who are suffering from addiction. All services are rendered in the original stone mansion, "where the breathtaking exterior matches the interior—with colonial furnishings, paintings of the Revolutionary War, and leather and crochet-topped sturdy sofas and chairs," in the words of one rehab review. For years, William and Mary Scranton (he died in 2013) maintained a modest home at the foot of their erstwhile estate, from which they would periodically check in on the people being helped by their gift.

Philanthropists Mel and Betty Sembler founded Straight Inc., which treated 10,000 adolescents from 1976 to 1993 in a strict but effective program. They now support the policy, research, and advocacy work of the Drug Free America Foundation. Perhaps the most prominent advocacy group on this topic is the Partnership for a Drug Free America, which has long enjoyed major funding from the Robert Wood Johnson Foundation. And major donor Tom Siebel has put more than $30 million of his money into a highly focused and successful public campaign against methamphetamine use (see separate 2005 entry).

Further reading

○ *Philanthropy* magazine on anti-drug philanthropy, philanthropyroundtable.org/topic/ excellence_in_philanthropy/hope_for_the_addicted

1982

BRAUN LABS OPENS UP A NEW BIOLOGY

In the late 1970s, researchers at the California Institute of Technology were ramping up new investigations in human biology, talking about establishing a specialized cancer center, and doing all of this in an interdisciplinary, technology-heavy way. The university's scientists and administrators convinced John Braun to give a building that soon became an important center for new kinds of scientific collaboration. One researcher called it "a beautiful example of philanthropy encouraging innovation and creating new opportunities that didn't exist before." Funded by a large gift from the Carl F. Braun Trust (a philanthropy growing out of one of the world's leading engineering and construction companies), plus four other foundations, two companies, and four major individual donors, Braun Laboratories mixed researchers from the Caltech biology and chemistry faculties with some very advanced equipment and labs. The end result was to jump-start scientific work in recombinant DNA, monoclonal antibodies, and other early innovations in biotechnology. "We're talking about investigations of the fundamental structure and mechanisms of life itself," stated Caltech president Marvin Goldberger at the building's dedication.

Asked by *Philanthropy* magazine why the laboratory was so important, biologist Leroy Hood explained that "Federal funding has almost always focused on specific kinds of projects. It isn't focused on creating infrastructure—and it's the infrastructure that's so essential to making the house that really good people can work in. That was the point at Caltech with the Braun building. Suddenly we had 200,000 square feet into which we could bring all sorts of new people and things. And without that enabler we couldn't have made that jump. You don't get federal grants and contracts in general to build new buildings and create new visions and do those kinds of things. It's philanthropy that fuels these new opportunities and opens up innovation in exciting ways…. I think at really excellent places like MIT or Caltech or Harvard, new innovation almost always comes from philanthropy."

Further reading

○ *Caltech News* coverage of building dedication, caltechcampuspubs.library.caltech. edu/2414/1/1983_02_17_01.pdf

○ *Philanthropy* magazine interview with Leroy Hood, January 31, 2013, philanthropyroundtable.org/topic/philanthropic_freedom/interview_with_leroy_hood

1980

MAKE-A-WISH FOUNDATION

Starting with one terminally ill child in Arizona in 1980, a group of volunteers gradually grew the Make-A-Wish Foundation into a charity that helps thousands of children age 3 to 17 who have been certified by their doctor as facing a life-threatening illness to enjoy some experience they have dreamed of. The nonprofit is powered by many generous donors and over

32,000 volunteers—organized in 61 U.S. chapters, and now also 45 foreign countries. From 1980 to 2014 they gave the group the capacity to arrange 334,000 life experiences dreamed about by deeply sick children.

Further reading

○ Foundation website, worldwish.org

1979

NURSE-FAMILY PARTNERSHIP

Research has shown that unmarried, poor, and teenage mothers are much more prone to problems of infant mortality, neglect and abuse, fetal-alcohol and drug damage, accidental injury, household poisonings, impaired mental development due to understimulation, attachment disorders, and other maladies that wreak costly, often permanent damage on children. In 1979, the Robert Wood Johnson Foundation launched efforts to head off these sorts of problems before they take root. It supported a demonstration project in Elmira, New York, that used registered nurses to bring preventive health services right into the homes of young, low-income pregnant women and first-time mothers.

Careful follow-up studies conducted in Elmira and then Memphis, Tennessee, and Denver showed that the home visits resulted in better health and development for both children and mothers, and less subsequent abuse, crime, and school failure. For instance, child abuse and neglect injuries were reduced 20-50 percent. Subsequent births by the mothers during their teens or early twenties were reduced 10-20 percent.

Called the Nurse-Family Partnership, the Elmira program became the model for a national program of home visits. The organization was set up as a 501(c)(3) charity, and research, manuals, training, and documentation needed to duplicate the program with a high level of quality were funded not only by Robert Wood Johnson but also by donors like the Edna McConnell Clark, Gates, Kellogg, and Kresge foundations. As the Nurse-Family Partnership gradually spread across the country it regularly updated its services—for instance with efforts aimed at discouraging partner abuse. Sponsored by nonprofits, private organizations, or local agencies of government, it is now offered in 432 counties in 40 states. An estimated 860 registered nurses are active as home visitors and more than 22,000 mothers are counseled in any given year.

Further reading

○ Program synopsis, rwjf.org/content/rwjf/en/research-publications/find-rwjf-research/2008/08/nurse-family-partnership-program.html

○ History of the partnership, rwjf.org/en/blogs/human-capital-blog/2012/05/improving-on-success-why-the-nurse-family-partnership-model-is-a-work-in-progress.html

○ Evaluation from the Coalition for Evidence-based Policy, evidencebasedprograms. org/1366-2/nurse-family-partnership

1978

MERCY SHIPS

In 1978, Don and Deyon Stephens were serving in Europe with the evangelical missions group Youth With A Mission. Since a time when he had helped clean up after a deadly Caribbean hurricane, Don had dreamed of a hospital ship that could bring high-quality, sanitary medicine to poor port cities. When he learned that a retired Italian cruise ship was being sold for scrap value, he approached YWAM donors for financial support, recruited 175 volunteers, and borrowed a million dollars from a Swiss bank to take possession.

By 1981 they had rehabbed the ship into seaworthiness, and hundreds of volunteers had been recruited to man her hospital bay and cruising operations. Evangelical Christian donors supplied both the funds and the bodies. Mr. and Mrs. Stephens and their four children lived on the ship for the next ten years, organizing the crew of 400 dedicated volunteers as the ship visited a series of poor countries to offer complex surgeries, dental care, vision repair, and other medical assistance.

In 2003 Mercy Ships was spun off from YWAM as a separate charity. Today it operates a 367-bed hospital ship where 1,778 life-changing surgeries were carried out and 728 African health-care professionals were given technical training in 2014. The ship also provided 12,597 free dental treatments and 6,259 vision consultations.

⌁ PhilAphorism

Do all the good you can. By all the means you can. In all the ways you can. In all the places you can. At all the times you can. To all the people you can. As long as you ever can.   ⌁ *John Wesley*

All positions from surgeon to deckhand are filled by volunteers, some serving for as little as two weeks, some for many years. Every volunteer is required to pay all of his or her own expenses, so that all cash donations go directly into medical care. Shipboard volunteers are also important as blood donors.

From 1978 to 2014, Mercy Ships provided free medical aid to 2.5 million poor patients in 57 nations, and trained more than 40,000 local medical professionals to improve their expertise. The organization was sustained by $82 million of personal contributions and in-kind gifts from medical suppliers in 2014. A second ship that will have 458 working beds is on order and scheduled to go into service in 2018.

Further reading

○ 2014 Annual Report of Mercy Ships, mercyships.org/wp-content/uploads/2015/07/MSUS-AR-2014-Final-R1-lo-pps.pdf

1976

BIOMEDICAL ENGINEERING
WILLED INTO EXISTENCE

Uncas Whitaker had an unusual combination of expertises: He was both an engineer and a lawyer. Each came in handy as he expanded electronics parts maker AMP from a small New Jersey workshop to a company with 45,000 employees in 50 countries, and annual sales of nearly $6 billion. And he knew how to focus on one product (terminal connectors in the case of AMP) and become the best in the world at it.

Both of those traits showed up powerfully in the philanthropy he established at his death in 1975. He and his wife ultimately devoted more than $700 million to one cause: developing biomedical engineering as a legitimate and thriving field. To maximize their impact on this embryonic specialty, the trustees of the Whitaker Foundation decided to spend not just the interest on their bequest but the entire principal as well, sunsetting the foundation in 2006. By propelling the entirety of its funds out the door in three decades, and doggedly following a tight and savvy strategy, the Whitaker Foundation essentially invented biomedical engineering as a freestanding and highly productive discipline.

In the 1960s and '70s, there was very little engineering in medical research. The National Institutes of Health was focused on biology and regularly rejected proposals that involved lots of engineering, which it viewed as the domain of the National Science Foundation. Meanwhile, the NSF believed that engineering proposals with a heavy medical component should be brought to NIH. Most universities opposed moves toward a blending of the disciplines. So biomedical engineering languished until Uncas Whitaker filled the gap. A great believer in the ability of engineers to solve serious problems, he began with personal gifts to Harvard and Massachusetts Institute of Technology, which enabled Harvard medical students to simultaneously earn a medical engineering degree at MIT.

The Whitaker Foundation made its first research grant in 1976, to an M.D. who had invented a device to wean patients off heart-lung machines. The foundation went on to support a wide range of research at the crossroads of engineering and medicine. In addition to supporting direct research, the foundation set up programs to draw talented young investigators into the field. It offered universities funds to hire faculty. It paid for the development of curricula. It established internships at 33 universities that placed students in real-life work at companies. It paid for the construction of new classrooms, labs, and 13 entire buildings. It spawned several professional societies.

Together, these efforts institutionalized the field of biomedical engineering—it became the fastest-growing engineering specialty. Artificial hearts, lab-grown organs and skin, commonplace joint replacement, cochlear implants, laser surgery, new drug-delivery methods, image-guided surgery, and hundreds of other breakthroughs now dominate hospital suites.

Whitaker funding directly launched the careers of 1,500 biomedical engineers who invented more than 200 significant products or devices, started more than 100 companies, and accumulated 278 patents and 125 intellectual-property licenses. The foundation instigated the creation of many dozens of academic departments. In the early 1990s there were 22; now there are 80. "From a fledgling field to a mature discipline that has gained the recognition and respect of all," observed University of California professor of bioengineering and medicine Shu Chien, "the extent and rapidity of the development of a field by the effort of a single foundation is unprecedented."

Further reading

○ Whitaker Foundation history, bmesphotos.org/WhitakerArchives/glance/wfhistory.html

1975

SPINE, BRAIN, AND
NEUROLOGICAL HEALTH IN ATLANTA

After their son suffered serious neurological injury in a surfing accident, Alana and Harold Shepherd (who runs one of the largest construction companies in Georgia) decided to build up a medical facility in the southeastern U.S. that could treat future victims of spinal trauma. They began with six beds leased from a local hospital. In 1987, while he was still running the Home Depot company, Bernie Marcus became active on the board, helping raise $22 million for a major expansion. Then patients in a new field were taken on—those who had suffered brain injury.

Later, Bernie and Billi Marcus founded a program for patients being discharged by Shepherd after treatment of their trauma, designed to help them become self-supporting in their homes and work. When soldiers began returning from Iraq and Afghanistan with brain injuries, the Marcus Foundation funded another special program at the Shepherd Center to offer them intensive assistance. Major gifts from the Robert Woodruff Foundation and other donors also helped build the Shepherd Center into one of the leading hospitals in the country for rehabilitation of spinal cord and brain injuries, with additional expertise in other neurological areas like multiple sclerosis and Guillain-Barré syndrome.

The fruits of his giving to Shepherd and to autism (see 1991 entry) inspired Bernie Marcus, who grew up hoping to become a doctor, to make additional large gifts focused on research and treatment of neurological disorders. These include a $20 million gift to establish the Marcus Stroke and Neuroscience Center in Atlanta, and $25 million to create a neuroscience institute in Boca Raton, Florida, dedicated to the study and cure of Alzheimer's, Parkinson's, multiple sclerosis, and other disorders.

Further reading

○ Shepherd Center history, shepherd.org/about/history-and-mission

1974

THE HOSPICE MOVEMENT

Historically, hospices were institutions run by religious charities to offer short-term care to terminally ill patients too poor to afford alternatives. They began to be adapted to modern circumstances in the late-1940s, when British physician Ciceley Saunders, working in the suburbs of London, sought to bring more compassionate care to the dying, with a particular emphasis on relieving suffering. Saunders inspired a grassroots movement in the United States starting in the 1960s. A lecture Saunders delivered at Yale University inspired Florence Wald, dean of the school of nursing, to leave Yale and work at Saunders's hospice, St. Christopher's. Upon returning to the United States, Wald asked American foundations to support a feasibility study on opening a U.S. hospice.

An early grant from the Commonwealth Fund, then support from the van Ameringen and Ittleson Foundations, allowed Wald to establish the first such organization, in Branford, Connecticut, in 1974. It offered end-of-life care to 100 patients, in their homes and in its 44-bed facility. Abiding by the philosophy that patients need to be treated emotionally, spiritually, and physically, the hospice focused on providing comfort and dignity. It subsequently became a training facility for other hospices and paved the way for other such organizations to set up operations across the country.

The hospice movement was cemented nationally when the Robert Wood Johnson Foundation poured more than $170 million into efforts to improve end-of-life care. With 337 grants made between 1996 and 2006, the foundation sought to educate health-care professionals, improve institutions, and engage the public, all toward the end of better serving the dying. "Few foundations can say they built a field of medicine, but RWJF…built a very important field of medicine that hadn't existed before," summarized one expert observer. Today, there are an estimated 3,200 hospices providing palliative care across the United States.

Further reading

∘ The recent history of hospice, nationalhospicefoundation.org/i4a/pages/index.cfm?pageid=218

∘ "Improving Care at the End of Life" (Robert Wood Johnson Foundation, 2011), rwjf.org/content/dam/farm/reports/reports/2011/rwjf69582

∘ More hospice history, helpthehospices.org.uk/about-hospice-care/what-is-hospice-care/hospice-history/global-hospice-care

1974

RONALD MCDONALD HOUSES

When Fred Hill's three-year-old was fighting leukemia, he and his family passed hours and days sleeping in chairs and living off vending-machine food as they kept vigil with her in the hospital. Feeling there had to be a better way, he rallied friends to create a residential house where families of sick children could stay nearby while their loved ones were in treatment. Hill was a player on the Philadelphia Eagles football team, so he got lots of publicity for his efforts. This helped him connect with the regional manager of McDonald's Restaurants—which became a major funder. Thus was the concept of the Ronald McDonald House born.

Forty years after the creation of that first facility in Philadelphia there were 353 separate Houses and Ronald McDonald Family Rooms right within 196 hospitals, giving families places to sleep, eat, regroup, and meet other parents in similar situations. These are located at nearly all U.S. children's hospitals, and in 62 countries around the world. The families of 6 million children use them every year. Most houses charge visitors nothing, the maximum is $25 per day, and no family is turned away if they lack funds.

The charity running the houses is an independent and regionally decentralized 501(c)(3). It continues to be supported by the McDonald's Corporation to the tune of seven-figure annual donations, along with dozens of other corporate donors and small individual supporters. The group has also harnessed more than 300,000 volunteers.

Further reading

○ Ronald McDonald House Charities, rmhc.org/what-we-do

1974

TROPICAL DISEASE RESEARCH

In the early 1970s, the Edna McConnell Clark Foundation (whose namesake, heir to the Avon fortune, had recently doubled its endowment) was searching for candidates for its first international grants. They wanted a cause where needs were palpable, and measured progress was possible. Tropical diseases were getting relatively little attention from research scientists, drug developers, governments, and philanthropists. In the heavily regulated, litigious, and extremely expensive world of pharmaceutical research, the high risks of drug development and low opportunities for economic payback on maladies afflicting only very poor residents of the equatorial regions created serious obstacles to battling the parasitic diseases of the developing world. It

✺ PhilAphorism

Let no one be discouraged by the belief that there is nothing one person can do against the enormous array of the world's ills, misery, ignorance, and violence. Few will have the greatness to bend history, but each of us can work to change a small portion of events. And in the total of all those acts will be written the history of a generation. ✆ *Robert Kennedy*

was estimated in the mid-1970s that the poor-nation afflictions representing 90 percent of the global disease burden got only 10 percent of global health-research spending. Only about 1 percent of all drugs approved for human use worldwide were specifically for tropical diseases.

And so in 1974, the Clark Foundation committed itself to a program of tropical disease research. During the next 25 years, its small staff of three steered $90 million of grants into measures aimed at suppressing three particular chronic illnesses, each of which afflicts tens or hundreds of millions of people: schistosomiasis (snail fever), onchocerciasis (river blindness), and trachoma (a painful eye disease). The effort ended up being a partial success.

About half of the $32 million Clark spent against schistosomiasis went toward an unsuccessful effort to find a vaccine. But when the foundation exited "schisto" research in 1994 the field had been advanced considerably, and the baton was picked up by the Carter Center, the Gates Foundation, and others. Clark's work against river blindness followed a very similar course: progress in scientific understanding and public health counter-measures, accompanied by failure to find a vaccine. For trachoma, Clark spurred some of the first systematic research ever conducted on the disease, and birthed a promising public-health and drug-donation response. As of this writing, a new coalition has taken up the Clark mantle with the aim of eliminating blinding trachoma by 2020.

Further reading

o Duke University case study, cspcs.sanford.duke.edu/sites/default/files/EMClarkTDRfinal.pdf

1973

EMERGENCY MEDICAL SERVICES

In the early- to mid-1970s, much of the U.S. had no well-developed system for stabilizing victims of accidents, fires, crashes, crimes, and other traumas while rushing them to hospitals appropriately equipped to save them during critical early minutes. A panel of the National Academy of Sciences called accidental trauma "the neglected disease of modern society." The Robert Wood Johnson Foundation set sights on changing that with a $15 million initiative launched in 1973 called the Emergency Medical Services Program.

When it opened in December 1971, the $1.2 billion of assets at the Robert Wood Johnson Foundation (endowed by the man who turned his father's family business of Johnson & Johnson into a corporate behemoth) made it the second largest philanthropy in America. This allowed the foundation to undertake large and innovative projects. Its actions to catalyze a forward leap in our emergency medical services were one of its earliest initiatives, and also one of the most successful.

The foundation aimed to develop and standardize emergency services and spread them across the United States. At that point, emergency-room medicine was just beginning to develop as a specialty, EMS training was scanty to non-existent, and most ambulances were little more than hauling vehicles with sirens. RWJF sought to elevate the level of medical treatment offered by first responders, within transports headed to hospitals, and in emergency rooms themselves during the crucial early moments after a trauma arrives.

Participating hospitals developed sophisticated communications systems that linked them to newly trained paramedics in ambulances. Ambulances themselves were redesigned and fitted with essential medical equipment so that patients could be evaluated and given acute treatment before arriving at the hospital. And protocols were put into place at emergency rooms so that teams could pounce on victims with the right targeted care as soon as they arrived. When the Emergency Medical Services Program launched, there were only 12 reasonably organized paramedic units in the U.S. The foundation chose 44 grant recipients in 32 states, working with organizations ranging from fire departments to medical schools. Just four years later, at least 50 percent of the American population was within ten minutes of a paramedic unit. The RWJF efforts spurred parallel expansions funded by the U.S. Department of Health, Education, and Welfare, and together these enhancements saved many thousands of lives, eventually resulting in the 911 emergency-response system.

Further reading

○ Digby Diehl, "The Emergency Medical Services Program," in *To Improve Health and Health Care* (Robert Wood Johnson Foundation, 2000), Chapter Ten, PDF available at rwjf.org/content/dam/web-assets/2000/01/the-emergency-medical-services-program

1971

FOUNDATION FIGHTING BLINDNESS

To research methods of preventing, treating, or curing diseases like retinitis pigmentosa and macular degeneration—afflictions that impair or end vision for more than 10 million Americans—venture-capitalist Gordon Gund co-founded the nonprofit now known as the Foundation Fighting Blindness. The group has supported thousands of research studies by leading scientists, including clinical trials of very advanced technologies like bionic retinas and gene therapies. "The foundation, existing as an independent private entity, is able to very quickly fund young investigators and fund new and exciting projects," comments Dr. Donald Zack of the Wilmer Eye Institute at Johns Hopkins Medical School. As a result, it has "played a major role in getting a number of important projects off the ground which would not have happened without FFB support."

Since its creation, the foundation has raised more than $600 million to battle retinal diseases—a quarter of that donated by Gund himself (along with his relatives and businesses). In 2014 Gund announced he would match any donation to the foundation made over the next two years. He said his goal was to raise $100 million for the organization, but that his donation was not capped and that if others anted up he would provide matching funds even beyond a $50 million personal contribution.

Further reading

○ Foundation Fighting Blindness, blindness.org/index.php?option=com_
   content&view=article&id=65&Itemid=147

1971

A SUPERTANKER OF ANTI-CANCER FUNDING

Daniel Ludwig grew up on the shores of Lake Michigan near Ludwig's Pier, built by his grandfather in a little port, from which four of his uncles captained vessels plying the Great Lakes. So when his natural entrepreneurial instincts began to show themselves it's not surprising they took a nautical form. As a 9-year-old he paid $75 (which he'd earned selling popcorn and shining shoes) to buy a small sunken boat which he promptly salvaged and rented out. Bitten by the bug of commercial imagination, he left school after eighth grade and went to work. At age 19 he bought an old paddle steamer with $5,000 of borrowed money, and slowly built a shipping fleet around it. After World War II he started building tankers in Japan, using cheap local labor and a new technique he'd overseen which welded rather than riveted the ships together. Creating a series of ever-larger vessels, he pioneered the supertanker, and built his shipping firm into one of the largest in the world.

Ludwig branched out into mining, real estate, and other projects, and by 1976 he was one of only two billionaires in the U.S. Despite his wealth, he remained frugal: flying economy class, famously wearing the same plastic raincoat around Manhattan for years, walking to work, and owning only a 16-year-old Buick as a car when he died at age 95 in 1992.

Ludwig gave away nearly all of his money—and to a single entity, the Ludwig Institute for Cancer Research. Neither the donor nor any of his family members had ever been afflicted by cancer, yet he recognized the disease as a scourge of many innocent victims. Beginning slowly with endowed professorships and other support, the Institute delivered major gifts in 2006 to medical research arms at six institutions: Johns Hopkins, MIT, Harvard, Memorial Sloan Kettering Cancer Center, Stanford, and the University of Chicago.

In 2014, the Ludwig Institute for Cancer Research made its final big donation—offering $540 million to those same six academic cancer centers to endow different aspects of fundamental cancer research at each. (Prevention and early detection at Hopkins, metastasis at MIT, and so forth.) This brought Ludwig's total contributions to anti-cancer studies to a fighting total of $2.5 billion.

Further reading

○ Daniel Ludwig obituary in the *New York Times*, nytimes.com/1992/08/29/us/daniel-ludwig-billionaire-businessman-dies-at-95.html

○ About the Ludwig Institute for Cancer Research, ludwigcancerresearch.org/our-story/about-us/institute

1965

NURSE PRACTITIONERS AND PHYSICIAN ASSISTANTS

The increase of American population plus general affluence following World War II caused an acute shortage of doctors, especially in rural communities, and an escalation of medical costs. The University of Colorado responded by starting a program to train registered nurses into mid-level responsibilities as nurse practitioners. This pioneering effort was made possible by a $253,998 grant from the Commonwealth Fund.

By making nurse practitioners responsible for things like routine examinations, administering immunizations, and conducting basic tests, doctors were freed up for more complicated procedures and diagnoses. A particular specialty of nurse practitioners trained to work in schools emerged after an additional grant from the Commonwealth Fund. In 1976, funding from the Robert Wood Johnson Foundation helped standardize and improve the training of nurse practitioners, and the next year the foundation funded fellowships at nursing schools to expand the profession.

At about the same time as the Colorado experiment, faculty at the Duke University Department of Medicine were pushing for a new class of medical professional who could operate in the gap between nurses and doctors. Eventually a program was created that enrolled former military medics and gave them an intense two-year immersion in biological sciences and clinical medicine. This abbreviated version of medical school allowed the resulting "physician assistants" to perform many of the routine duties of a doctor, under direction of a supervising physician. Philanthropic grants from the Josiah Macy Jr. Foundation, the Carnegie Corporation, the Rockefeller Foundation, and the Commonwealth Fund supported this new initiative.

With additional funding from Commonwealth and Robert Wood Johnson, the Duke innovation was spread to other medical schools in the late '60s to mid '70s. Physician assistant programs were structured as B.S. degrees until the mid-1980s. Then a master of health sciences degree for P.A.s was established.

Physician assistants and nurse practitioners are now board-certified in nearly all states, and their numbers have roughly doubled over the last decade—to more than 91,000 P.A.s and 250,000 N.P.s as of 2014. These two new classes of care-provider have fundamentally changed the practice and economics of medicine. And strong philanthropic support was crucial in overcoming extensive resistance from the nursing establishment and initial reluctance in government to fund the new professions.

Further reading

○ Duke University case study, cspcs.sanford.duke.edu/sites/default/files/descriptive/nurse_practitioners_and_physician_assistants.pdf

ST. JUDE CHILDREN'S RESEARCH HOSPITAL

Located in Memphis, Tennessee, St. Jude Children's Hospital is internationally famous for its tight focus on treating and finding cures for catastrophic diseases of childhood—cancer especially. Nearly 8,000 young patients from all around the world are treated at the facility every year and no family ever pays St. Jude for anything.

From its beginning, St. Jude has conducted important research on childhood cancers that it shares with the profession. In a typical year, its staff will publish up to 800 articles in academic journals. Nobel Prize winner Peter Doherty conducts research on immunology at the hospital. It was the first institution to develop a cure for sickle-cell disease, via bone-marrow transplant. Protocols developed at St. Jude have helped push national survival rates for childhood cancers from less than 20 percent when the facility opened to 80 percent today.

The hospital is now America's second-largest health-care charity and fifteenth largest charity overall. Fully 75 percent of the $1.8 million per day that it costs to run the hospital comes from donations (typical hospitals derive 8-10 percent of their revenues from charitable giving); the rest comes from health-insurance reimbursements and research grants.

St. Jude was conceived by actor Danny Thomas as he prayed at a Catholic Church in Detroit while struggling in his young career. When he became a popular star he followed through, forming the fundraising arm that now raises more than $800 million every year for the hospital. The average gift is about $30.

Further reading

○ *Philanthropy* magazine profile, philanthropyroundtable.org/topic/excellence_in_philanthropy/millions_from_millions

○ St. Jude 2012 Annual Report, stjude.org/SJFile/annual-report-12.pdf

1954

KIDNEY TRANSPLANTS AND DIALYSIS

In 1940, an estimated $45 million was spent on biomedical research in the U.S., only $3 million of it from the federal government. World War II accelerated government health research, but as late as 1947 the entire budget for the National Institutes of Health was still only $8 million. Thus, the major force in funding biomedical research in the U.S., especially on the cutting edge, was private philanthropy. The most active foundation in this area was the John A. Hartford Foundation.

Brothers John and George Hartford created the behemoth A&P grocery chain, which became the largest retailer in the world. A&P was the first merchant to reach $1 billion in annual sales, which it hit in 1929. That very same year, John established the foundation that bears his name. After the brothers died in the 1950s, their combined contributions of A&P stock made the Hartford Foundation the fourth largest philanthropy in the country. Its trustees met and decided to focus their giving tightly on biomedical research, making the organization the largest supporter of clinical science in the U.S.

Between 1954 and 1979, the Hartford Foundation provided hospitals and medical centers with $175 million of research grants, equipment, and fellowships for scientists, catalyzing many of the era's important advances in medicine. During its peak spending years of 1962 to 1972, the foundation funded more biomedical research than all other major foundations combined. The products of this investment included kidney dialysis, successful kidney transplantation (and then leaps in other types of organ transplants), major improvements in understanding of immunology, development of the artificial heart, cryogenic surgery, many advances in cancer research, the groundwork for microneurosurgery, and more.

In 1954, Hartford gave Boston's Brigham Hospital a $300,000 grant that directly supported some of the world's first successful kidney transplants. These operations created worldwide attention and led to another $200,000 of Hartford support over the next few years. The foundation simultaneously underwrote pioneering work on organ transplantation by other researchers. Crucial investigations in immunology, aiming to avoid rejection of transplanted tissues, were also funded. In addition, the Hartford Foundation underwrote creation of professional organizations like the International Congress of Nephrology, the American Society of Nephrology, and the Transplantation Society.

Making the kidney-dialysis machine practical and affordable was another product of concentrated Hartford Foundation funding. The "artificial kidney" that existed in the beginning of the 1950s was huge, expensive, and destructive of patient blood vessels. In 1961, Hartford provided $250,000 to develop more efficient dialysis machines for use in the first outpatient clinic, in Seattle. A second center was subsequently created in Spokane, Washington. On January 8, 1962, the world's first out-of-hospital dialysis center treated its inaugural patient.

Other renal experts in Cleveland and Boston were simultaneously supported with six- and seven-figure grants from Hartford. The result? For the first time, the one-out-of-every-100,000 Americans whose kidneys had failed gained the prospect of escaping their death sentence.

Further reading

○ History of Hartford Foundation biomedical research by Judith Jacobson, *The Greatest Good* (Chester Jones Foundation, 1984), jhartfound.org/learning-center/wp-content/uploads/2013/04/GG_Intro.pdf

○ *Philanthropy* magazine reporting, philanthropyroundtable.org/topic/excellence_in_ philanthropy/frontiers_of_science

1953

HOWARD HUGHES MEDICAL INSTITUTE

In 1953, the eccentric billionaire Howard Hughes created a medical institute devoted to basic research, then gave it entire ownership of his Hughes Aircraft Company. The institute was intended to be a "steady operating organization with its own laboratories and not a general program of giving money away"—what the IRS has deemed a "medical-research organization" rather than a foundation. Business and legal battles prevented the institute from reaping much profit from the aeronautic company in its first few decades, but in 1985 General Motors bought Hughes Aircraft for $5.2 billion, and suddenly the Institute became the largest medical philanthropy in the country.

The Howard Hughes Medical Institute is focused on cell biology, genetics, immunology, neuroscience, and structural biology. It has long selected and employed Hughes Investigators who are left posted in labs across the country so they can benefit from wide cross-fertilization of ideas. In 2014 this investigator program supported about 350 scientists, along with their research teams, as they conducted experiments at more than 70 different universities, hospitals, or research centers. HHMI also runs a large program to support promising scientists at early stages of their career (a time when government grants are rarely forthcoming), as well as a program to support outstanding scientists working outside the U.S. (who again do not qualify for federal support).

Having become a driving force in U.S. biomedical research, the Howard Hughes Medical Institute launched a major new initiative in 2006 when it built a $300 million research campus of its own, called the Janelia Farm, on nearly 700 acres outside of Washington, D.C. There it employs over 400 people who do high-risk, long-term research in large interdisciplinary teams—with the idea that certain kinds of problems may be more easily solved by this more corporate style of investigation than by the traditional dispersed individual-researcher model that Hughes has long supported (and will continue to fund).

HHMI's endowment stands at $17 billion, and in its latest year it employed 2,883 individuals and spent nearly a billion dollars. Having provided more than $7 billion in direct support to scientists just since 2004, the organization is the largest private funder of academic medical research in the world.

And there is evidence that this philanthropy's flexible private grants have been much more effective than government counterparts. A study by the National Bureau of Economic Research, for instance, found that "investigators of the Howard Hughes Medical Institute, which tolerates early failure, rewards long-term success, and gives its appointees great freedom to experiment…. produce high-impact papers at a much higher rate than a control group of similarly accomplished NIH-funded scientists."

Further reading

○ Howard Hughes Medical Institute history, hhmi.org/about/history

○ National Bureau of Economic Research paper on HHMI's exceptional scientific fecundity, nber.org/papers/w15466

1952

ERADICATING POLIO

Polio is one of the most wounding viruses in history, and reached pandemic proportions in the early twentieth century. In America at that time it killed more people every year than any other communicable disease. Thousands of others were left living on iron lungs or hobbling about in leg braces.

For years, the Rockefeller Institute for Medical Research had funded basic investigations into the virological underpinnings of the malady, including hosting the work of Albert Sabin from 1935 onward. Millions of people all over the country donated money to the March of Dimes—formally known as the National Foundation for Infantile Paralysis—to wage battle against the disease. The foundation's annual budget soared from $3 million in 1940 to more than $50 million in 1953. That year, the foundation provided 25 times more funding for polio than the NIH. Its money went to science fellowships in virology, to direct research, to public information efforts, and to support for stricken families. Among many other things, the foundation funded the lab where the polio virus was first grown in non-neural tissue.

Eventually, this combination of rich-man's endowment with mass philanthropy—along with the timely action of a small private foundation— put a dagger in polio's heart. In 1948, Dr. Jonas Salk won a $35,000 grant from the Sarah Scaife Foundation that allowed him to equip a modern virus laboratory at the University of Pittsburgh to investigate the disease. He also received support from the March of Dimes and its millions of small donors, as did the parallel vaccine work of Albert Sabin. Two years later Scaife added to its initial risk capital with a follow-up grant to Salk.

In 1952, a particularly nasty polio epidemic broke out—more than 60,000 cases were registered in the U.S., and 3,000 people died. That same year, Salk announced a medical breakthrough. He had bravely immunized himself and his family with an experimental vaccine that worked. The Salk vaccine, the

ᴓ PhilAphorism

What do we live for, if it is not to make life less difficult for each other?

ᴓ *George Eliot*

world's first polio blocker, was soon deemed safe, thanks to field trials paid for by the March of Dimes, and went into production for use around the world in 1955. March funds were also responsible for distribution of free vaccine to many thousands of children.

Today, polio has nearly been eradicated across the globe. It remains endemic only in Nigeria, Pakistan, and Afghanistan. And other philanthropies have taken up the cudgel to drive the disease to a final extinction. In 1985, when there were still close to 400,000 international cases of polio every year, the Rotary International Foundation pledged $120 million to battle the affliction overseas, ultimately donating a billion dollars to the fight. In 2011, the Gates Foundation made complete eradication of polio one of its top priorities. India—which just a few years prior to benefitting from a Gates-led mobilization was described as the "most tenacious reservoir" of the paralyzing virus, with half the world's cases—recently celebrated its first year ever without a single case. The worldwide total was down to less than 250 cases in 2012, with the noose tightening.

Meanwhile, the March of Dimes, having effectively put itself out of work by beating polio, completely shifted its focus to premature birth and the prevention of birth defects.

Further reading

- *Philanthropy* magazine reporting, philanthropyroundtable.org/topic/excellence_in_ philanthropy/conquering_polio
- Claire Gaudiani, *The Greater Good* (Holt Publishing, 2004)
- Decades of medical philanthropy against polio, americanhistory.si.edu/polio/virusvaccine/ medphil.htm

1952

POPULATION-CONTROL MOVEMENT

As early as the 1920s, some notable philanthropists were strong backers of measures to reduce births among poor individuals. John Rockefeller Senior, Junior, and the Third were all strong supporters of the eugenics movement, as was George Eastman. But funding by elite philanthropists for population control, particularly abroad where growth was fastest, really ramped up starting in 1952.

At that time, John Rockefeller III created the Population Council, an influential information and lobbying group whose first administrator, appointed by Rockefeller, was Frederick Osborn, founder of the American Eugenics Society and trustee of the eugenics-promoting Pioneer Fund. Almost immediately after, the Ford Foundation made its first grant for population control, and by the late 1950s Ford was dispensing million-dollar grants to this cause. Throughout the Population Council's first 23 years, Ford provided $94 million. JDRIII had launched the Population Council with $100,000 from his personal fortune after his grandfather's foundation had rebuffed repeated entreaties to fund birth control for poor and overseas populations. But by 1963 the Rockefeller Foundation got into the game itself in a big way.

With America's two biggest foundations having paved the way, the government followed next into population control. In 1959, President Eisenhower had said he "could not imagine anything more emphatically a subject that is not a proper political or governmental activity." But after Dean Rusk (who ran the Rockefeller Foundation from 1952 to 1960) became President Lyndon Johnson's Secretary of State, John Rockefeller III pressed him to make birth control a federal cause. Johnson soon delivered the first characterization, in a speech to the nation, of population growth as a problem, and by 1965 there was an Office of Population within the U.S. Agency for International Development. In seven years its budget exploded from $10 million per year to $123 million.

Even as government support for population control mushroomed, select elite philanthropists continued to pour money into the crusade. The list of individual donors and foundations who devoted large funding to the cause includes not just Rockefeller, Ford, Eastman, and Osborn, but also Milbank, Mellon, MacArthur, Packard, Hewlett, Turner, Buffett, and Gates. They put their money into everything from the U.N. Fund for Population Activities, to research and distribution of new contraceptives, to establishment of activist organizations and academic centers at universities like Michigan, North Carolina, Johns Hopkins, Harvard, Princeton, and the University of Pennsylvania. Even after eugenics was completely discredited, and the "population bomb" had fizzled as an issue, America's large private donors were still putting on the order of $150 million per year into population-control grants in the early years of the new millennium.

Further reading

○ *Philanthropy* magazine reporting, philanthropyroundtable.org/topic/excellence_in_ philanthropy/the_world_population_crisis

○ Broad background from Villanova Environmental Law Journal, digitalcommons.law. villanova.edu/elj/vol11/iss1/4

1949

HEART CATHETERIZATION

Surgeries to alleviate congenital heart diseases began to advance rapidly in the 1940s and 1950s. Many of the techniques for detecting and diagnosing heart problems, however—life histories, physical examination, fluoroscopy, radiography, electrocardiography—remained comparatively underdeveloped or risky. This was holding back the revolution in cardiac care.

With funding from the Commonwealth Fund, Columbia University medical professor André Cournand and several colleagues pioneered various refinements in cardiac catheterization. This allowed oxygen levels and blood pressure to be safely tested right within the heart chambers, dramatically improving accurate diagnoses. These techniques were detailed in a 1949 book by Cournand and two others, which was in turn published by the Commonwealth Fund.

This work eventually yielded a 1956 Nobel Prize in medicine for the physicians supported by the fund. And the resulting clinical procedures turned cardiac catheterization into a routine diagnostic procedure. That allowed and supported tremendous advances in cardiac surgery—which over a 30-year period reduced U.S. deaths from heart disease by more than 50 percent.

Further reading

○ May 1951 paper in the *Bulletin of the New York Academy of Medicine* summarizing findings from Cournand's Commonwealth-funded research, ncbi.nlm.nih.gov/pmc/articles/PMC1930103/?page=1

KINSEY REPORTS

Most of the funding for *Sexual Behavior in the Human Male,* the controversial book on sexual practice published by insect biologist Alfred Kinsey in 1948, was funded by the Rockefeller Foundation. Kinsey received the first grant of $1,600 in 1941. By 1947 he was receiving $40,000 annually from the foundation, a large portion of their commitments in behavioral medicine.

Alan Gregg, who ran two important divisions of the Rockefeller Foundation, was a particularly enthusiastic supporter of Kinsey and wrote an introduction to his first book. Kinsey's claims, which were expanded by the 1953 publication of *Sexual Behavior in the Human Female,* radically transformed popular views of sex and laid the groundwork for the sexual revolution that followed.

Kinsey's research has since been substantially discredited. His interview samples heavily overrepresented prisoners, prostitutes, homosexuals, graduate students, and other subgroups that result in skewed estimates of many aspects of sexual activity. He included pedophiles in his group and published tables documenting extensive adult sexual contact with children, which he falsified as coming from many sources. He secretly encouraged and

recorded, in the attic of his own home, sexual interaction within his staff and between his staff and his family.

Kinsey's 1948 book became a popular seller, generating large royalties that dwarfed the Rockefeller Foundation's major grants. This would normally have led to a discontinuation of philanthropic support. In response to pleas from Kinsey, however, the foundation continued to fund him until 1954.

Further reading

∘ Rockefeller Foundation history, rockefeller100.org/biography/show/alan-gregg
∘ James Jones, *Alfred C. Kinsey: A Public/Private Life* (W. W. Norton, 1997)

SLOAN KETTERING INSTITUTE

General Motors vice president Charles Kettering is most famously known for his automotive inventions, such as the first electrical starter motor and leaded gasoline, and the 185 patents he held. Less understood are his contributions to medicine and science. An extraordinarily broad tinkerer, Kettering also developed several medical innovations, such as an incubator for premature infants, treatments for venereal disease, and magnetic diagnostic devices.

In addition, Kettering was a visionary philanthropist who devoted his wealth to funding projects that could be as productive as his contraptions. In 1945, he and Alfred Sloan, another General Motors vice president, established the Sloan Kettering Institute, the first private biomedical research center of its sort in the world. The center was built next to Memorial Hospital, an institution with its own long and impressive philanthropic history. Founded in 1884 as a specialized cancer hospital by a group that included Mr. and Mrs. John Astor, the hospital was moved in 1936 to its current location, on land donated by John Rockefeller Jr.

From its founding, the Sloan Kettering Institute aimed to harness the latest technology and research techniques to battle cancer. Matching the spirit of its founders, it held fast to the principle that advances in research always rest on "the creative genius of individual scientists." In 1980, the institute and the hospital were combined into a single entity and today the Memorial Sloan Kettering Cancer Center is one of the nation's leading biomedical research institutions and treatment facilities, treating more than 400 different subtypes of cancer with specialized regimens and advancing the state of the art via more than 120 research labs. In 2012, the first graduates matriculated from the center's new Ph.D. program in cancer biology.

Further reading

○ History of Sloan Kettering Institute and Memorial Hospital, mskcc.org/about/history-overview

○ Charles Kettering biography, mayoclinicproceedings.org/article/S0025-6196(12)00271-6/fulltext

1945

ALBERT LASKER AWARD
FOR BASIC MEDICAL RESEARCH

In 1942, pioneering advertising executive Albert Lasker and his wife, Mary, established a foundation to champion medical research. Their first major project (and the primary work of their foundation, still) was establishment of a prize to recognize and encourage leading biological research scientists. The Lasker Prize is perhaps the second most prestigious award a medical investigator can earn. Fully 83 Lasker laureates have gone on to win the Nobel Prize in medicine, including 31 in the past two decades. More recently, the foundation has established other prizes to recognize important achievements in clinical research, professional influence, and public service in medicine.

Further reading

○ Most recent award winners, laskerfoundation.org/awards/currentwinners.htm

1944

DNA UNCOVERED

In 1944, three scientists working at the Rockefeller Institute for Medical Research proved that it was the threadlike fibers of DNA, present in all cells, that were the chemical basis of heredity. This discovery was compared to the findings of Gregor Mendel and Charles Darwin in its scientific impact. It launched a new era in genetics.

◈ PhilAphorism

Men who leave their money to be distributed by others are pie-faced mutts. I want to see the action during my lifetime. ☞ *George Eastman*

This discovery was expanded and deepened by additional Rockefeller-funded work. Progress in X-ray imaging, for instance, and in understanding the nucleotides in DNA, was propelled by Rockefeller grants. New tools and understandings like these laid the groundwork for the 1953 discovery by James Watson and Francis Crick of the double helical structure of DNA (which won them the 1962 Nobel Prize in medicine). Indeed, the very Cambridge lab where Watson and Crick conducted their experiments owed its advanced state to the Rockefeller Foundation, according to researchers who worked there. Rockefeller grants funded many of the lab's assistants. They also made possible the purchase of X-ray diffraction equipment that was central to the mapping of DNA.

Decoding DNA was of course the keystone to understanding how cells are controlled and how they multiply and mutate. That kicked off the subsequent revolution in genetics, whose potential for changing medicine has yet to unfold in its most dramatic forms.

Further reading

○ George Beadle, "The Role of Foundations in the Development of Modern Biology," in *U.S. Philanthropic Foundations* (Harper & Row, 1967)

○ "When was DNA proved to be the chemical basis of heredity?," web.archive.org/web/20050404113820/http://www.rockefeller.edu/discovery/dna/index.php

PRODUCTION OF PENICILLIN

British scientist Alexander Fleming first uncovered the ability of mold to stem bacteria growth in 1928, but his finding drew little attention. It was Australian scientist Howard Florey and a team at Oxford University who revealed the therapeutic potential of mold-derived penicillin to squash bacterial infections and finally developed techniques for producing penicillin antibiotics. Florey's scientific training had been partly financed by the Rockefeller Foundation when it awarded him a Rockefeller Traveling Fellowship in 1925, which allowed him to work for a year in the lab of University of Pennsylvania pharmacologist Alfred Richards. Afterward, Florey finished his Ph.D. at Cambridge University.

Additional Rockefeller Foundation funding supported Florey's postdoctoral research at Oxford, from 1936 onward. Throughout a period of years, Rockefeller gave him about a half-million dollars in contemporary value, for research support, equipment, and supplies. With this crucial philanthropic help, Florey assembled a large team of a couple dozen investigators and technicians. By early 1940, they had zeroed in on penicillin as their special focus, first finding the compound to be both safe and effective in curbing bacteria in mice, then conducting their first human trials in early 1941.

It quickly became clear that penicillin had the potential to be one of the most important medical discoveries in history. For the first time, there existed a safe compound capable of killing the living bodily infections that gave deadly force to sepsis, pneumonia, diphtheria, meningitis, rheumatic fever, syphilis, scarlet fever, endocarditis, gonorrhea, and many other afflictions. The problem quickly became how to manufacture usable quantities of the miracle drug, which required laborious culturing and concentration.

In 1941, the Rockefeller Foundation brought Florey to the United States to make the case for a rapid mobilization to speed penicillin production. He convinced U.S. scientists of the import of his discovery, and with help from Alfred Richards, his Rockefeller Traveling Fellowship colleague, he enlisted assistance in fermenting and freeze-drying mass quantities of penicillin. Large-scale production soon began and by 1943 the new antibiotic was being used to treat wounded soldiers in North Africa. By the end of World War II, the drug had been produced widely enough to protect nearly all Allied troops. Penicillin and its successor antibiotics revolutionized medicine and saved literally hundreds of millions of lives. Florey and two other scientists were awarded the 1945 Nobel Prize in medicine.

Further reading

○ Rockefeller spending on Florey, philanthropyroundtable.org/topic/excellence_in_ philanthropy/rockefellers_other_pipeline

○ Chemical Heritage Foundation history, chemheritage.org/discover/online-resources/ chemistry-in-history/themes/pharmaceuticals/preventing-and-treating-infectious-diseases/florey-and-chain.aspx

——————— 1941 ———————

PAP SMEAR TEST

Cervical cancer was the deadliest form of cancer for women until physician George Papanicolau developed a highly effective method to detect the disease even before any symptoms were present. Papanicolau arrived at the Cornell Medical College from Greece in 1913. During the 1930s he found that vaginal smears, when placed under a microscope, could show the presence of cancerous cells. The medical establishment, though, dismissed the idea that cancer could be detected in individual cells. Papanicolau later wrote that "I found myself totally deprived of funds for continuation of my research.... At a moment when every hope had almost vanished, the Commonwealth Fund...stepped in."

Though it realized the grant was "highly speculative," Commonwealth offered him a research grant of $1,800 in 1941. Using smears from a broad sample of patients, Papanicolau quickly found that his method did indeed identify cellular abnormalities, even before the cells became fully cancerous. The discovery was momentous, amounting to a method of cancer detection even earlier than biopsy, and less difficult, intrusive, and expensive.

In 1943, the Commonwealth Fund itself published Papanicolau's findings in a groundbreaking study, *Diagnosis of Uterine Cancer by the Vaginal Smear*. The "Pap" test, named for its originator, continues to be the most effective and affordable way to detect cervical cancer today. It heads off thousands of deaths every year.

Further reading

○ Duke University case study, cspcs.sanford.duke.edu/content/support-development-pap-smear-test-commonwealth-fund-1941

○ commonwealthfund.org/From-the-President/2008/The-Commonwealth-Fund-at-90.aspx

1938

MARCH OF DIMES

The March of Dimes is one of the most popular and successful charity campaigns in American history. Founded in 1938 by polio victim Franklin Roosevelt as the National Foundation for Infantile Paralysis, the foundation existed to provide care for the afflicted and find a polio vaccine. Dubbed the March of Dimes by entertainer Eddie Cantor, the organization spurred Americans to give in a way that forever changed popular culture. Collection cans for the March of Dimes sat on diner countertops, at movie theaters, and in local schools.

In 1948, Jonas Salk's polio vaccine, substantially supported by the foundation (see 1952 entry), heralded one of the greatest public-health discoveries in American history. By that time, the campaign had raised $67 million, the equivalent of $536 million today. It was the largest amount of money raised by any health charity, or almost any other kind of nonprofit.

Having played a major role in eliminating the mass killer and crippler polio, the March of Dimes shifted its focus to birth defects and disorders associated with premature birth. It continues to be one of the largest charity fundraisers in the United States.

Further reading

○ *Forbes* magazine story on the evolution of the foundation, forbes.com/2008/11/19/march-dimes-revinvention-pf-charities08-cx_wb_1119dimes.html

YELLOW-FEVER VACCINE

Yellow fever, one of the most feared diseases in America, ravaged port towns and nearby communities throughout the eighteenth and nineteenth centuries. In addition to the human toll, international trade was often badly disrupted by its quarantines. While no medical consensus existed on the origins of yellow fever, many believed the disease originated in the tropics and was carried by ships involved in the slave trade in the West Indies or by transports returning soldiers from the Spanish-American War.

At one point President Grover Cleveland established a special commission to investigate possible causes and treatments of the disease; on both counts, no effective knowledge existed. Some scientists then believed that the disease was bacterial and that they had created the first "vaccines" against the malady. The commission declared them mistaken, that bacteria did not appear to be the cause but that the disease was transmitted by mosquitoes.

Meanwhile tens of thousands of Americans were dying in the early decades of the twentieth century. After the Panama Canal opened in 1912, exposing additional communities to the affliction, the Rockefeller Foundation launched an all-out three-decade campaign to eradicate the disease. In 1918, it sent a team to Ecuador to study potential causative agents. An initial claim that a

◈ PhilAphorism

We must be knit together in this work as one man, we must entertain each other in brotherly affection, we must be willing to abridge ourselves of our superfluities, for the supply of other's necessities.... We must delight in each other, make others' conditions our own... always having before our eyes our community as members of the same body.

☞ *John Winthrop at the founding of the Massachusetts Colony*

vaccine had been discovered by Rockefeller researchers was disproven in 1926. At that same time, the Rockefeller Foundation set up another research station in Nigeria. Scientists working amidst the tension of its dangerous environment learned how to use rhesus monkeys to test infection and immunity to the disease. But three of the lead researchers working for the foundation died in the process.

A little later, the Rockefeller Institute set up a lab in New York to continue its yellow-fever research using animals. Director Simon Flexner proceeded hesitantly, given the loss of life already experienced in the institute's work. Strict isolation policies were used to reduce the danger. Even still, many of the lab staff contracted the disease over the next two years, and a 1931 report from the institute noted that 32 cases of the disease acquired in eight labs had recently resulted in five deaths.

In 1931, Rockefeller Institute researcher Dr. Bruce Wilson volunteered to be injected with a new vaccine developed in mice. Held under strict isolation and supervision, he did not become ill and developed immunity. The vaccine required serum from already-immune humans, which meant it could not be produced in volume, but at least there was finally a means of protecting lab staff.

In 1937, foundation scientists finally announced a successful mass-producible vaccine. Between 1940 and 1947, the Rockefeller Foundation distributed more than 28 million doses of the vaccine. Lead researcher Max Theiler was awarded the Nobel Prize in medicine in 1951 for this work. The Rockefeller vaccine continues to be the most effective and affordable prevention strategy for yellow fever.

Further reading

○ Gordon Frierson, "The Yellow Fever Vaccine: A History," *Yale Journal of Biology and Medicine*, June 2010, ncbi.nlm.nih.gov/pmc/articles/PMC2892770/#R30

○ Rockefeller Foundation summary of program history, centennial.rockefellerfoundation.org/values/entry/solving-global-problems

1935

INVENTION OF HEALTH INSURANCE

Until almost 1930, health insurance to cover the risk of expensive hospitalization or doctor care did not exist in the United States. Families rolled the dice, and if a member became badly sick they could be saddled with frightening bills. North Carolina philanthropist George Hill, whose family had founded the first hospital in Durham, North Carolina, set out to solve this problem with Wilburt Davison, the founding dean of Duke University School of Medicine.

While he was in England as a Rhodes Scholar, Davison had observed voluntary, community-based prepayment plans that allowed individuals to pay moderate monthly fees in return for a promise of coverage if ever they needed hospitalization. Davison and Hill set out to establish such a plan in their home region, forming the Durham Hospital Care Association. It was forced to close, however, after the October 1929 stock-market crash.

Though the project folded, the idea spread. The very same month that the Durham association closed, Baylor University Medical School in Texas began a similar initiative that succeeded. Participants (Dallas schoolteachers were among the first to sign up) could prepay, at fifty cents per month, for 21 days of treatment at Baylor Hospital. In 1931, a citywide prepayment plan was created in Minneapolis-St. Paul, and then another in Newark, New Jersey.

Inspired by Baylor's great success, Davison and Hill retried their idea and opened another Hospital Care Association. Hill provided the money to get the nonprofit corporation operating. The Watts and Duke hospitals in Durham provided additional funding. And shortly after, the Duke Endowment made a $25,000 grant to establish a competing but similar voluntary prepayment plan, called the Hospital Saving Association. Eventually, the two entities merged into Blue Cross Blue Shield of North Carolina.

In 1940, less than 10 percent of the U.S. population had health insurance coverage. That grew to nearly 70 percent by 1955. Today, Blue Cross Blue Shield companies cover nearly one out of every three Americans, in every zip code in every state and Federal Territory. There are 37 independent, community-based, locally operated Blue Cross Blue Shield companies in the national federation.

Further reading

o Duke University case study, cspcs.sanford.duke.edu/content/predecessor-blue-cross-and-blue-shield-north-carolina-duke-endowment-1935

o *Encyclopedia of North Carolina*, ncpedia.org/blue-cross-and-blue-shield-north-ca

1933

A STANDARD NOMENCLATURE OF DISEASE

Before 1933, no standard reference existed in American medicine for describing and diagnosing illnesses. The New York Academy of Medicine convened the first conference on the nomenclature of disease in 1928 and the participating medical societies and institutions met year after year to try to hammer out a common terminology for medical practice. When they ran out of funds to support their effort they turned to the Harkness family's Commonwealth Fund, which became a major patron of the initiative.

Indeed, Commonwealth was the publisher of *A Standard Classified Nomenclature of Disease* when it was finally released in 1933. This reference offered the first industry standard, which not only aided clinical practice but also made compiling accurate health statistics possible for the first time. The Commonwealth Fund's nomenclature succeeded where others had failed to be accepted because it abides by a simple and logical classification scheme that helps physicians describe diseases uniformly, leading to more accurate diagnoses, and, in turn, more appropriate treatments. Within a few years of its arrival, nearly all major hospitals and medical schools in the United States and Canada were using the Commonwealth guide.

Further reading

○ George Baehr, "Purposes, Function and Use of Standard Classified Nomenclature of Disease," Bulletin of the New York Academy of Medicine, July 1940, ncbi.nlm.nih.gov/pmc/articles/PMC1911530/?page=1

——————— 1932 ———————

PUTTING PSYCHIATRY ON THE MAP

As early as 1914 the Rockefeller Foundation had dabbled in what was then called "mental hygiene," but in the 1930s the foundation became the driving force that built psychiatry into a serious academic discipline. In foundation reports, the expressed goal was "to find, to train, and to encourage first-rate [efforts at] correcting nervous disorders and mental behavior." This would "counter the economic losses" of personal breakdowns and institutionalizations, "integrate into standard medical curricula a neglected field of medicine," and "improve overall medical care by helping doctors understand connections between the body and mind."

In its first ten years, this effort poured $12 million of John Rockefeller's money into things like improving medical-school teaching, endowing university psychiatry departments, building research centers, and distributing fellowships to scientists working on mental health. By 1943, fully three quarters of all of the spending by Rockefeller's division of medical sciences

⌐ PhilAphorism

Let him that hath done the good office conceal it; let him that received it disclose it.

⌐ *Seneca*

was being funneled into psychiatry. Among other results, this established full-time departments of psychiatry in a large number of hospitals and medical schools, including at McGill, Chicago, Duke, Harvard, St. Louis, Tulane, Yale, Washington, and other places.

Further reading

° Rockefeller Foundation history, rockefeller100.org/exhibits/show/health/psychiatry

1931

DISCOVERY OF THE INFLUENZA VIRUS

When the influenza pandemic struck in 1918, most scientists and doctors believed it was caused by bacteria. Killing up to 100 million people worldwide, the pandemic was the deadliest in history. This drove many researchers to investigate and study influenza, searching for its cause and cure. A major breakthrough came in the early 1930s, when a young physician from Iowa, Richard Shope, turned his attention to swine influenza. While researching at the Rockefeller Institute for Medical Research, Shope took lung samples from infected Iowa pigs. He was able to isolate the rod-shaped bacterium that seemed always to correlate with their influenza. When the bacterium was injected into other pigs, though, it did not generate disease.

Forced to rethink, Shope referred back to some earlier research by Rockefeller Institute scientists Peter Olitsky and Frederick Gates and used their technique to finally isolate a *virus* that when injected into healthy hogs caused influenza. The bacterium which coincided with the flu in so many cases turned out to be an opportunistic follower-on which attacked subjects with a secondary infection after the virus had already weakened their defenses.

Shortly after Shope published his swine results, other scientists using his technique isolated the human flu virus. The path was opened to lifesaving flu vaccinations.

Further reading

° History from *The Journal of Experimental Medicine*, ncbi.nlm.nih.gov/pmc/articles/ PMC2118275

1927

RURAL HOSPITALS

When the Harkness family established the Commonwealth Fund in 1918, health care was one of their highest priorities. More than half of all counties in the United States lacked a hospital and overcrowding was a threat in many places that did have a facility. As early as 1919, Edward Harkness, the foundation's first president, expressed interest in building new hospitals. Fund officers eventually became convinced that hospitals in rural areas or predominantly black communities were particularly urgently needed. The fund decided to require recipient communities to raise one third of the construction costs themselves, and to cover all future hospital expenses—similar to what Andrew Carnegie had demanded to make sure each locality was invested in the libraries he built.

In 1927, the Commonwealth Fund built a pilot hospital, the Southside Community Hospital, in rural Farmville, Virginia. The $180,000 facility was charged with providing medical care regardless of economic status or background, with each patient paying what he was able to. During the next 20 years, the Commonwealth Fund established 15 more rural hospitals with $6.8 million in grants. The resulting facilities provided medical care to millions of people, and every one of the facilities is still operating today.

Further reading

∘ Harvey McGehee and Susan Abrams, *For the Welfare of Mankind: The Commonwealth Fund and American Medicine* (Johns Hopkins University Press, 1986)

1922

SHRINERS HOSPITALS FOR CHILDREN

In the first half of the twentieth century, polio created a heavy demand for orthopedic services for children. In response, the fraternal organization Shriners International placed a $2 yearly assessment on all of its members and opened a special hospital for children in Shreveport, Louisiana. Any child needing orthopedic care and lacking the wherewithal to pay for it would be admitted and treated with no charge. The organization continued opening free hospitals across the country until there were eventually 22 separate facilities. Orthopedic surgical techniques, therapies, and prosthetics developed in Shriners hospitals became standards around the world.

When vaccines and antibiotics pushed polio into sharp decline in the 1960s, the Shriners Hospitals began to focus on new specialties. Seeing that there were no burn facilities in the U.S. for children, four hospitals were dedicated to treating childhood burn victims. These are still the only hospitals focused wholly on pediatric burn care, and since their creation the survival rate for child burn victims has doubled and rehabilitation improvements have made much more normal lives possible. The Shriners also specialized in spinal-cord injuries, cleft palate correction, and orthopedic research (which is funded at about $40 million per year).

In 2011, in response to soaring health costs, the Shriners Hospitals that had always been 100 percent free began to bill insurance companies and to charge some families deductibles. All patients lacking means to pay, however, continue to be served free. Since their founding, nearly 1 million children have received care at Shriners Hospitals.

Further reading

○ Shriner Hospital locations, shrinershospitalsforchildren.org/locations

1922

DISCOVERY OF INSULIN

Though diabetes is one of the most common modern diseases, there was for generations no hope of recovering from it. One merely adopted a radically constricted diet. Or bodily decay and death advanced fairly quickly.

Hunting for something better, Nathaniel Potter applied to the new Carnegie Corporation of New York in 1916 for a grant to study diabetes patients as they underwent different clinical treatments. He received $7,500 annually from Carnegie, on the condition that he also raise $20,000 externally. Potter got Cottage Hospital in Santa Barbara, California, to build a laboratory for his research alongside their medical facility. When Potter died in 1919, William Sansum from the University of Chicago arrived to head the clinic in his stead.

At this same time, the Carnegie Corporation was also funding research in Canada to extract insulin from the pancreas of dogs. Scientists sought to convert the canine research into a possible injectable treatment for human beings. By 1922, insulin administered at Toronto General Hospital brought a diabetic child back to health—the first use of insulin to treat human beings. The Canadian work eventually led to a Nobel Prize for the lead researchers.

Because they were fellow Carnegie grant recipients, Sansum was corresponding with his Canadian counterparts throughout their experimenting. The Torontans offered detailed guidance in the hope Sansum would be able to improve the difficult process of extracting insulin. Soon, Sansum successfully extracted insulin at the Potter clinic, and made rapid progress at increasing its purity and strength. Four months after the Canadians, he became the first doctor to administer insulin to a patient in the United States.

Next, the Carnegie Foundation contributed additional funds to manufacture insulin injections on a large scale. Kits began to appear in drug stores by 1923. In the words of Duke University historians, "hundreds of thousands of patients near death from diabetes...subsequently recovered." In the years since, millions have had their lives saved or lengthened via insulin treatments.

Further reading

° Duke University case study, cspcs.sanford.duke.edu/content/development-insulin-treat-diabetes-carnegie-corporation-new-york-1916

° Sansum history, sansum.org/about/history

1915

GEORGE EASTMAN POPULARIZES
PREVENTIVE DENTAL CARE

By the time his company Eastman Kodak became a secure juggernaut in the early 1900s, George Eastman was one of the richest men in the world, but he had lost interest in accumulating wealth. He was gripped by a powerful desire to put his funds to work in the rest of society. Throughout the next couple decades he would give away more than any other American except John Rockefeller and Andrew Carnegie. In current dollars, his gifts totaled in the range of $2 billion.

Two of his most important efforts were medical. Having built extensive hospital complexes throughout his hometown of Rochester, New York, he single-handedly created the University of Rochester School of Medicine and Dentistry and shaped it according to the bold new scientific principles espoused by Abraham Flexner. The pairing of medicine and dentistry was quite intentional. Eastman recognized how painful and socially crippling oral illnesses and disabilities could be. And long before there was research proving this, he suspected that dental problems could lead to wider infections and degrade one's health generally.

Eastman was ahead of his time in emphasizing prevention in medicine, and especially in dentistry, where preventative care and the professional dental hygienists he promoted were nearly unknown in his day. After founding the Rochester Dental Dispensary in 1915, he went on to establish additional dental clinics serving children—not only throughout the U.S. but also across Europe. He persuaded other philanthropists like the Guggenheims in New York and Lord Riddell in London to subsidize dental facilities as well.

Children up to age 16 could visit any of Eastman's clinics at a cost to their indigent parents of a nickel per visit. In addition to work on their teeth, all children were checked for nose, throat, and mouth defects. Orthodontia was offered, and it thrilled Eastman that children not only had their appearances improved but also "improvements in speech were obtained." He pushed to bring hygienists into schools, encouraged the use of X-rays to diagnose dental health, and underwrote scientific training of dental interns.

"There is nothing I am more interested in than public health," Eastman told the governor of New York in 1922. The dental clinics were his very favorite projects, which brought him satisfaction to the end of his life. "Dollar for dollar, I got more from my investment" in them, Eastman told the *Saturday Evening Post*, "than from anything else to which I contributed." In the process, George Eastman did more to elevate modern dental health than perhaps any other giver ever.

Further reading

○ George Eastman profile in the Philanthropy Hall of Fame (see prior *Almanac* section)

○ Elizabeth Brayer, *George Eastman* (Johns Hopkins Press, 1996)

1915

HENRY FORD HOSPITAL

Henry Ford stood at the center of the manufacturing revolution after he established the Ford Motor Company in 1903. People flooded to Detroit in search of employment, and the swelling population meant rapidly growing health-care needs. In 1909, the Detroit General Hospital Association, of which Ford was the finance chairman, set out to build a new hospital for the working man. When support and funding for the project plummeted in 1914, construction on the new building halted.

At that point, Ford stepped in and assumed the outstanding debt and contracts for construction. In October 1915, Henry Ford Hospital opened with ten physicians, and an initial group of 48 patients. The hospital pioneered many new methods of operation, including employing the first closed staff of salaried physicians who worked exclusively for the hospital. It was also one of the first hospitals to use a standard fee schedule, and to offer private and semi-private rooms to patients instead of large wards.

The hospital continued to grow in succeeding decades and continued to innovate. It popularized the practice of adding iodine to kitchen salt to prevent endemic goiters. The Ford Hospital pioneered administration of purified heparin to treat vein clots. It developed the oxygen tent to assist respiration. In 1952, one of its doctors performed one of the world's first grafts of an aneurysm. Four years later, another performed the first successful open-heart surgery in Michigan. Today, the hospital is the flagship institution of the Henry Ford Health System.

Further reading

○ History of the Henry Ford hospital, henryford.com/body.cfm?id=47713

○ Innovations at the Henry Ford hospital, henryford.com/body_nologin.cfm?id=39485

○ Patricia Painter, *Henry Ford Hospital: The First 75 Years* (Henry Ford Health System, 1997)

SOCIAL-HYGIENE MOVEMENT

John Rockefeller Jr. poured himself into the philanthropic activities begun by his father, and is responsible for the creation or development of several signature Rockefeller organizations. These include the Rockefeller Institute for Medical Research, the General Education Board, and the Rockefeller Foundation. He was also a catalyst for the "social-hygiene movement" of the early twentieth century that targeted venereal disease and brought topics of sexuality to public consciousness.

Following his service in 1910 on a special grand jury investigating "white slavery" (prostitution) in New York City, Rockefeller established, largely with his own money, an independent organization he called the Bureau of Social Hygiene. His aim was to combat delinquency, crime, and sex trafficking. The bureau was active from 1911 to 1933, awarding education and research grants aimed at controlling prostitution, drug use, juvenile delinquency, and related social ills, plus the crimes and corruption that followed in their wake. For a period, the organization funded studies of the biological and social factors that influence human sexual conduct. Rockefeller provided five and a half million dollars to the bureau during its two decades of activity.

After Rockefeller attended a conference in Buffalo, New York, on the social problems of prostitution and attendant venereal disease, he funded the uniting of several organizations into the American Social Hygiene Association. The association resolved to control and treat diseases such as syphilis and gonorrhea through public education.

The association worked with the War Department to promote a very aggressive anti-venereal disease campaign within the U.S. military. It also helped to establish venereology as a branch of medicine and coordinated national efforts to treat patients, conduct medical studies, and develop school curricula on sexual health. In later years, the Rockefeller Foundation took over some of this work from the bureau and John Jr.'s personal giving.

Further reading

○ History of the BSH, Rockefeller Foundation archives, rockefeller100.org/exhibits/show/health/bureau-of-social-hygiene

○ ASHA records, special.lib.umn.edu/findaid/xml/sw0045.xml

AMERICAN CANCER SOCIETY

In the beginning of the twentieth century, a cancer diagnosis almost certainly meant death. Cancer was such a mortifying subject that doctors sometimes even kept confirmed diagnoses from their patients, and patients at times kept the news from their families. In May 1913, a group of physicians and businessmen met at the Harvard Club in New York City to address the cancer stigma and information blackout. They believed it was important to raise public awareness and reduce taboos if broader progress in fighting cancer was to be achieved.

Led by Dr. Clement Cleveland, the resulting group resolved to promote cancer awareness through an educational campaign of articles in popular magazines and professional journals. They also produced a monthly bulletin called "Campaign Notes." John Rockefeller Jr. provided the initial funds for the organization, which was named the American Society for the Control of Cancer. Rockefeller's support eventually led to additional funds from other wealthy donors in the New York area. In its early years, membership was kept low, never surpassing 2,000.

In 1936 Marjorie Illig, a field representative and leader of a women's public-health committee, suggested the group "wage war on cancer." The Women's Field Army wore khaki uniforms and successfully raised money and recruited volunteers. By 1938, the organization grew to ten times its initial size. It had become the premier voluntary health organization in the U.S. The organization continued to grow through small donations and was renamed the American Cancer Society in 1945. A $4 million fundraising campaign initiated a research program, and filled in gaps in the group's education and prevention efforts. Today, it remains the largest voluntary health organization in the world.

Further reading

○ Group history, cancer.org/aboutus/whoweare/our-history

1913

ROCKEFELLER'S MEDICAL GIVING SPROUTS 61 NOBEL PRIZES

John Rockefeller, the son of an itinerant seller of folk medicines, started pouring large sums from his Standard Oil fortune into medical research and treatment long before he founded the Rockefeller Foundation. The Rockefeller

⫇ PhilAphorism

The value of a man resides in what he gives.

☞ *Albert Einstein*

Institute for Medical Research (which grew into Rockefeller University—see 1901 entry) was America's first research institution in support of experimental medicine. After he set up his foundation, Rockefeller's money began to flow into many other institutions working to advance human health. Collectively, the Rockefeller investments in health gave perhaps the largest jolt to lifesaving and health improvement that any single source has ever exerted.

In 2013, *Philanthropy* magazine surveyed historical records and discovered that an astonishing 47 Nobel Prize winners working in the fields of medicine, biochemistry, and health received significant professional support from Rockefeller philanthropy before they earned their Nobels. Another 14 Nobel laureates were supported by a Rockefeller-founded entity some time after their award, allowing them to expand their research or to mentor a new generation of scientists.

The influence of Rockefeller funding peaked in the 1960s and '70s then declined. There were three Rockefeller-linked Nobelists up to 1929, then six in the 1930s, seven in the 1940s, and seven more in the '50s. There were 11 Rockefeller-related laureates in the 1960s and 13 more in the 1970s. Then came five in the '80s, four in the '90s, and three in the 2000s, with two in the 2010s as of this writing.

Just a few of the breakthroughs influenced by Rockefeller giving: Discovery of human blood types. Separate discoveries of Vitamin C and Vitamin K. Studies on polio that led to a vaccine. Evidence that viruses could cause cancer. Explanations of the working of the eye. Understanding the genetic structure of viruses. Mapping the chemistry of antibodies. Findings on RNA structure that paved the way for the biotech revolution. Discovering how retroviruses attack cells. And much more.

Further reading

○ *Philanthropy* magazine reporting, philanthropyroundtable.org/topic/excellence_in_philanthropy/rockefellers_other_pipeline

1910

MODERN AMERICAN MEDICAL EDUCATION

Andrew Carnegie did not have a strong personal interest in medicine. He believed in the power of education to promote wealth and well-being in society, though, so when the American Medical Association Council on Medical Education approached Carnegie in 1906 he was highly supportive of its efforts to restructure medical education in America. The Carnegie Foundation for the Advancement of Teaching became keenly interested in educator Abraham Flexner, who published a critique of American higher education in the same year. Henry Pritchett recruited Flexner to lead a study of medical education and present a report with recommendations.

Published in 1910, Flexner's book-length *Medical Education in the United States and Canada* set off a firestorm of controversy among educators and physicians. Though he praised a few medical schools, Flexner condemned the majority. He called for higher standards, more hands-on clinical work, more research. This prompted Robert Brookings, a wealthy merchant, to request a meeting with Flexner so they could plan a reconstruction of the medical school at Washington University. Yale also instituted changes recommended in the Flexner report. Other universities responded defensively.

The Rockefeller Foundation hired Flexner in 1913 to advise its General Education Board. The foundation then systematically funded reforms at several medical schools, including Washington University at St. Louis, Yale University, the University of Chicago, and Vanderbilt University. In 1923, the Rockefeller Foundation gave additional money to reform public medical schools in Iowa, Colorado, Oregon, Virginia, and Georgia. These efforts established a single high standard for medical education in the United States, and launched American medicine to international prominence, a prestige it continues to possess today.

Further reading

○ Steven Wheatley, *The Politics of Philanthropy: Abraham Flexner and Medical Education* (University of Wisconsin Press, 1998)

○ Short summary in American Academy for the Advancement of Science magazine, sciencemag.org/sciencecareers/2011/02/the-flexner-rep.html

1909

ELIMINATING HOOKWORM IN THE U.S.

When John Rockefeller announced that he intended to eliminate hookworm disease in the American South, it was an unheard of notion. Indeed, some of the intended beneficiaries were embarrassed and annoyed to have a spotlight shone on this aspect of their region. Yet in warm-weather sections of the U.S., endemic hookworm among the poor was a real problem. The parasite causes extreme anemia, fatigue, lowered cognitive function, and gastrointestinal distress by leaching vital nutrients and minerals from the host's body. The resulting lethargy creates economic as well as personal health problems.

Along came Rockefeller with $1 million (about $25 million in current dollars) and a savvy plan. In 1909, he created the Rockefeller Sanitary Commission to lead a public-health campaign. It worked to win the trust and support of local officials. It offered the public information on how to treat and avoid the disease. It sent field agents into infested states to demonstrate preventative hygiene. Because hookworm enters the bloodstream through the soles of the feet, wearing shoes and using sanitary latrines goes far toward preventing infection.

After a five-year campaign, hookworm disease was nearly eliminated in the South. This success led Rockefeller to create an International Health Commission in 1914 to launch similar campaigns in Mexico and Ceylon. Later Rockefeller's anti-hookworm effort served as the model for other campaigns against diseases like malaria, typhus, scarlet fever, and tuberculosis.

Further reading

○ Duke University case study, cspcs.sanford.duke.edu/content/curing-and-preventing-
disease-and-promoting-public-health-rockefeller-foundation-1909

1908

A MASS CRUSADE AGAINST TUBERCULOSIS

In the first decade of the twentieth century, tuberculosis accounted for about 11 percent of all U.S. deaths. About a quarter of all children were afflicted in cities like New York. Around the middle of that decade, a popular movement arose that convinced millions of small donors to give money to battle the disease. At Christmastime in 1908, a campaign was launched to sell, for pennies, "seals" that could be used to decorate letters, with all the money raised going to the National Association for the Study and Prevention of Tuberculosis, newly founded that same year. The holiday campaign raised $135,000 (the equivalent of several million dollars today). By 1916 this small-scale giving was bringing in more than a million dollars, and by the mid-1960s $26 million.

The mass givers were joined by a few wealthy philanthropists. The Russell Sage Foundation, for instance, which was founded in 1907, made tuberculosis one of its main targets during its early years. The Saranac Sanitarium in New York's Adirondack Mountains was one of several projects they helped bankroll. John Rockefeller and his charities eventually joined the fight.

But it was mostly small givers and volunteers who elevated the war on TB. Between 1904 and 1916 the number of TB clinics in the nation jumped from 18 to 1,324. The National Association for the Study and Prevention of Tuberculosis organized an "army" of 500,000 Americans at peak times of the year to raise funds for sanitariums, medical research, and relief for afflicted families and individuals. Eventually the development of antibiotics made tuberculosis a less pressing concern. The "people's philanthropy" launched against this frightening disease became the model, however, for subsequent popular crusades against polio, cancer, heart disease, and other medical scourges.

Further reading

○ Olivier Zunz, *Philanthropy in America* (Princeton University Press, 2011)

1906

PEKING UNION MEDICAL COLLEGE

The Peking Union Medical College was founded in 1906 by American and British missionary groups. It was a rare outpost of modern medicine in a nation with one of the highest mortality rates in the world. A decade later, John Rockefeller assumed financial responsibility for the school. A thorough renovation and expansion began in 1915.

The Peking Union Medical College became the Rockefeller Foundation's single largest expenditure—almost $45 million was poured into the institution. The effects were equally enormous. The college endured through many upheavals and today remains one of China's most prestigious institutes of higher education. It has served as the model for improving medical training in countries throughout the world.

Further reading

○ History from the China Medical Board, chinamedicalboard.org/centennial

1901

ROCKEFELLER UNIVERSITY

In 1901, John Rockefeller founded the first biomedical research institute in the United States. Although he discussed the idea for three years with his scientific adviser, Frederick Gates, it was the death of his three-year-old grandson from scarlet fever that jolted Rockefeller into action. At the time, infectious diseases like tuberculosis, diphtheria, and typhoid posed great threats to human health, and scarcely any organized research was under way to fight back.

Rockefeller initially committed $200,000 over ten years to construct the Rockefeller Institute for Medical Research, then added many millions more over the coming years. The organization, which was renamed Rockefeller University in 1965, produced some of the most important medical discoveries in history, including establishing that DNA is the chemical basis of heredity; discovering blood groups; finding new ways to freeze blood (which led to the creation of the first blood bank); explaining the structure of antibodies; Peyton Rous's discovery that cancer can be caused by a virus; proving the connection between cholesterol and heart disease; and so forth.

Many lifesaving drugs and therapies emerged from Rockefeller's walls, for instance: Simon Flexner's anti-meningitis serum; Hideyo Noguchi's treatments for syphilis and yellow fever; Louis Pearce's invention of drugs to treat African sleeping sickness; the use of methadone to manage heroin addiction; and developing anti-AIDS "cocktail" drugs. Fully 24 scientists associated with the institution have received the Nobel Prize, and 20 have been awarded the National Medal of Science. Considered one of the best research centers in the world, Rockefeller University has served as a model for many medical-research facilities elsewhere.

The organization has attracted support from many benefactors beyond its founder, right up to the current day. The Heilbrunn family, for instance, first became interested in the university's diabetes research, then supported cancer investigations, cellular research, and eventually a center for research nursing. New York City's Starr Foundation is another philanthropic entity that has donated hundreds of millions of dollars since 1992 to support RU's biomedical innovations.

Further reading

○ Duke University case study,cspcs.sanford.duke.edu/sites/default/files/descriptive/
rockefeller_university.pdf
○ Rockefeller University history, rockefeller.edu/about/history

───── 1893 ─────

JOHNS HOPKINS SCHOOL OF MEDICINE

Upon his death in 1873, Quaker merchant Johns Hopkins bequested $7 million to build a hospital and university. This sum was unprecedented at the time. He wished for the new institution to uphold a threefold mission. It should produce superior physicians, seek knowledge to advance medicine,

❧ PhilAphorism ───────────────

Charity is injurious unless it helps the
recipient to become independent of it.

☞ *John Rockefeller*

and administer free and excellent patient care. In 1889 the Johns Hopkins Hospital opened, followed by the Johns Hopkins School of Medicine four years later. The medical school became the premier educational institution in the country and single-handedly raised the level of medical education in the United States. It instituted rigorous standards for admission and developed a new scientific curriculum. When the Flexner Report came out in 1910 and lambasted most medical schools in the United States, Johns Hopkins was lifted up as an ideal institution. In addition to being the premier medical school for much of its existence, it was the first to admit women, the first to use rubber gloves during surgery, the discoverer of Vitamin D, the first to develop CPR, the first to succeed at "blue baby" surgery, uncoverer of the natural opiates in the brain, researcher of many of the building blocks of genetic engineering, and a leader in numerous other areas.

Further reading

○ Neil Grauer, *Leading the Way: A History of Johns Hopkins Medicine* (Johns Hopkins University Press, 2012)

○ History of Johns Hopkins medicine, hopkinsmedicine.org/about/history

○ JHU medical heritage, hopkinsortho.org/jhmi_history.html

1791

NEW YORK DISPENSARY

New York City clergyman John Rodgers was a classic charitable leader who honed his coalition-building skills as president of the Society for the Relief of Distressed Debtors, vice-chancellor of the University of New York, and founder of the Brick Church and its charity school. He needed all of those skills to open the second hospital in America ministering to the "laborious and industrious poor."

Philadelphia's creation of the nation's first major facility to distribute medical aid to the poor inspired deep interest (and some jealousy) in New York City. Squabbles among doctors, donors, and others, however, delayed action to replicate Philly's success. The *New York Daily Advertiser* ran several articles explaining the workings of the Philadelphia hospital. This persuaded citizens to offer financial contributions, and a cooperative plan finally emerged. The New York Dispensary quite consciously copied Philadelphia's pathbreaking institution—and ultimately had great success in improving the standard of medical care throughout New York.

Further reading

○ Dissertation covering dispensary history, deepblue.lib.umich.edu/handle/2027.42/60745

1786

A REVOLUTIONARY MEDICAL CLINIC

Benjamin Rush, physician and signer of the Declaration of Independence, opened a medical practice in Philadelphia in 1769. In 1786, he established the first free walk-in health clinic in the United States, the Philadelphia Dispensary. This organization also offered in-home visits for the poor who were too ill to leave their houses. An on-site apothecary compounded medicines of all sorts, which were offered to patients along with advice and therapies suggested by the dispensary's physicians. Urban dispensaries like this one in Philadelphia were staffed largely by volunteers, and for many generations were the primary means of providing health care to the urban poor throughout the United States.

Further reading

∘ Robert Bremner, *American Philanthropy* (University of Chicago Press, 1960)
∘ Charles Rosenberg, *Explaining Epidemics* (Cambridge University Press, 1992)

1751

RESCUING THE
"SICK POOR AND LUNATICKS"

At a time when Philadelphia was the fastest-growing city in America (and the second-largest English-speaking city in the British Empire), two city benefactors came together to create a hospital (an institution then coming into vogue in Europe). The institution was intended "to care for the sick poor of the Province and for the reception and care of lunaticks" who were then wandering the streets of the city of Brotherly Love. At a time when many medical institutions were designed simply to remove the ill from the community, the Pennsylvania Hospital aimed to restore them to active health, and toward this end it connected, from its very beginning, medical care and medical teaching.

Thomas Bond, who came up with the idea, was a London-trained physician. When he mentioned his aspiration to his friend Benjamin Franklin, Franklin offered a large personal donation and became a strong public advocate for the plan—offering the seemingly unreachable sum of 2,000 pounds, to be provided from his own pocket and those of friends he would solicit, if the Pennsylvania Assembly would match that amount. Franklin quickly exceeded his goal, and a charter was granted. Franklin remained a strong supporter to the end of his life, writing fundraising appeals, investing the hospital's endowment, purchasing modern equipment for it when he was in Europe, and continuing to give his own resources.

The seal of the new Pennsylvania Hospital was inscribed with an image of the Good Samaritan and the words "Take care of him and I will repay thee." Bond became a volunteer physician and manager, offering his professional services from the time of its creation until his death 33 years later. Bond also collaborated with Franklin in creating the educational institution that became the University of Pennsylvania, and beginning in 1766 he shared his own medical knowledge by conducting clinical lectures to students at the hospital. Dr. Bond thus became known as America's "father of clinical medicine." The Pennsylvania Hospital pioneered a number of other firsts—the first surgical amphitheater, the first hospital auxiliary, the first apothecary.

Pennsylvania Hospital's deepest influence, though, came in psychiatric care. In 1783 Benjamin Rush (whose own medical clinic is described in the 1786 entry above) joined the medical staff of Pennsylvania Hospital. Among other contributions at the hospital, Rush dramatically improved the treatment of the insane—who he recognized to be suffering from illness—to be deserving of respect, and to be responsive in some cases to treatment. From his work at Bond and Franklin's hospital, Rush later wrote the first psychiatric text produced in the U.S. He became known as the "father of American psychiatry."

Further reading

○ History from the University of Pennsylvania medical center, uphs.upenn.edu/paharc/features/creation.html

○ Biographical information on Thomas Bond, uphs.upenn.edu/paharc/timeline/1751/tline2.html

○ Background on Benjamin Rush, uphs.upenn.edu/paharc/timeline/1751/tline7.html

1735

A DYING SAILOR ENDOWS
THE FIRST U.S. CHARITY HOSPITAL

"Nothing being more certain than death, and nothing more uncertain than its hour...I bequeath...a hospital for the sick of the City of New Orleans, without anyone being able to change my purpose, and to secure the things necessary to succor the sick."

So stated the last will and testament of an ailing sailor named Jean Louis who had become a shipbuilder in the new French colony at the mouth of the Mississippi River. Having been founded just 18 years earlier, New Orleans was a ragged corner of civilization when Louis made his gift. By the city's mere nineteenth year, though, it was distinguished by a pioneering, philanthropically created facility offering free care for the sick.

With New Orleans being settled primarily by people recruited from jails, poorhouses, and urban streets, there was plenty of business for Charity Hospital. The facility "was noted as one of the most efficient and useful charities in the country, given that New Orleans was exposed to greater varieties of human misery, vice, disease, and want than virtually any other American town," states an official history. Among other maladies, the hospital treated record numbers of cases of venereal disease. In 1834 the Roman Catholic Sisters of Charity assumed control of the hospital, and they gradually built it into a "celebrated institution of healing in the city." The hospital was 269 years old (and located in its sixth building, a 2,680-bed landmark) when Hurricane Katrina struck. The facility closed and never reopened, though residents reluctant to let go of their beloved institution continue to argue for its revival.

Further reading

○ John Salvaggio, New Orleans' Charity Hospital (Louisiana State University Press, 1992)
○ History at the LSU Health Sciences Center website, mclno.org/MCLNO//Menu/ Hospital/History/CharitysBeginnings.aspx

EDUCATION

More philanthropic donations are channeled into education than to any other sector of American society except religion. That's been true since we were just a collection of settlements and not yet a nation. Our first college, donor-supported, was created in 1636—nearly as early as our first permanent towns. America's initial public schools for children, funded by private investors who wanted to make "New Amsterdam" attractive to additional residents, opened in the 1640s. American philanthropy created many of the greatest libraries in the world, beginning when we were a mere colony. From the seventeenth century right into the twenty-first, from preschool through independent research institutions, private giving has catalyzed many of our best educational innovations, deepened knowledge, and enhanced its sharing across our nation.

> ↳ *Section research provided by Karl Zinsmeister,*
> *Connor Ewing, Scott Walter, and Evan Sparks*

2015

DOUBLING WISCONSIN'S ENDOWED CHAIRS

John and Tashia Morgridge were high-school sweethearts in Wauwatosa, then attended the University of Wisconsin. John later led Cisco Systems from startup with 34 employees into one of the country's most successful tech companies. Back in 2007 they donated $175 million to provide scholarships that every year help about 1,000 low-income kids attend Wisconsin's state colleges. In 2015 the Morgridges challenged fellow Wisconsin alums to help them bolster their already well-regarded university by increasing the number of endowed chairs for faculty. Their call led to 1,000 donations totaling $125 million, which the Morgridges promptly matched. The resulting $250 million will boost the number of endowed professorships from 142 to 300, aiding recruitment of top instructors and researchers, and boosting the quality of academics campus-wide.

At about the same time, Albert and Nancy Nicholas made a $50 million donation to Wisconsin that is expected to be matched by other donors. This $100 million will go to student scholarships—creating 400 new annual support packages.

Further reading

○ *Milwaukee Journal Sentinel* reporting, jsonline.com/news/education/alumni-support-of-gift-to-uw-boosts-value-to-250-million-b99570300z1-325533431.html

2015

EDGY EDUCATION NEWS

With strong donor support, former CNN host Campbell Brown created a nonprofit news site in 2015 focused on reporting and analysis about public-school reform. "Less than half of our students can read or do math at grade-level, yet the education debate is dominated by misinformation and political spin," announced the Seventy Four, as the outlet calls itself in reference to the 74 million school-age children in the U.S. It promised to produce a stream of challenging fact-based journalism that would hold the education establishment accountable.

The publication launched with 13 employees, thanks to strong backing from Bloomberg Philanthropies, the Walton Family Foundation, Jonathan Sackler, and the Buck Foundation. Its website will not sell advertising, but instead rely entirely on philanthropic donations to fund operations. "Education is one of the most important issues facing this country—and it should be on the front page every day," stated Marc Sternberg of Walton's K-12 program, explaining his foundation's support.

Further reading

○ Website, the74million.org

FLEXIBLY INCUBATING NEW IDEAS AT CALTECH

Ron and Maxine Linde are long-time supporters of the California Institute of Technology, having trained there before building their own successful industrial firm. In 2015 they presented Caltech with an unusual present—a $50 million endowment that the college can use completely flexibly to advance promising initiatives of any sort in their early stages. Their money is earmarked not to a specific field, but to a process—early incubation of new ideas.

As soon as the idea being sprouted becomes established, it will be expected to turn to other funding, and the Linde endowment money will be redirected to some fresh unproven concept. This introduces a little of the method of the venture capitalist to university operations, and it encourages experimentation rather than bureaucracy and empire-building. "Our philosophy is to allow for flexibility, because you can't know the future," said Ron Linde. "Science is about exploring the unknown."

This brought the Linde's total giving to Caltech to more than $80 million.

Further reading

○ *Los Angeles Times* report, latimes.com/local/education/la-me-ln-caltech-donation-20150306-story.html

BUILDING REAL-WORLD LEADERSHIP
IN EVERY STUDENT

Experts say that most of the capacity to lead people is learned, not innate. And, typically, about 70 percent of what helps people become effective leaders is learned through experience rather than classrooms. This presents a challenge for educators.

Two veteran philanthropists have just taken up that challenge. John Doerr is a prominent venture capitalist in Silicon Valley whose philanthropy includes co-founding the NewSchools Venture Fund. His wife, Ann, is an electrical engineer and chair of the Khan Academy, a leading nonprofit in online education. Both are graduates of Rice University in Houston—where they have just established an institute that will help every student become a more effective leader.

Upon arrival as a freshman, each Rice student will be assessed for leadership skills, then given a custom plan combining classroom instruction, personal coaching, and hands-on experience in real-life roles that will hone his or her skills during each year on campus. The program will be directed by a former brigadier general in the U.S. Army who also taught leadership at West Point and the Yale School of Management, and it is funded by a $50 million gift from the Doerrs.

"Our nation and world need great teams and great leaders," said John Doerr in announcing the pledge. In almost all work today, the skills needed to put good ideas into action are "paramount," he insisted. Rice president David Leebron suggested that students would be attracted to this unconventional addition to the college-training process. "We expect students to say, 'yes, that's what I want from an education.'"

The Doerrs previously donated $15 million to build the leadership skills of engineers, a successful effort they are now expanding. Data will be collected on how Rice students change in leadership competence as a result of this unique collegewide program. The results will be used to identify the most effective practices, with an ultimate goal of expanding useful leader training to young people at other institutions as well.

Further reading

○ *Inside Higher Education* report, insidehighered.com/news/2015/05/14/rice-university-creates-new-leadership-institute

SCHOLARSHIPS FOR ENGINEERS

The School of Engineering at the University of Texas at Austin, one of the top-rated institutions of its kind, was strengthened further in 2014 by a gift from an alum who parlayed a Ph.D. in electrical engineering from the school into a quirky career. T. W. Whaley donated $35 million plus 700 claims to mineral rights. This will allow, in the first year alone, 34 promising students to learn engineering on scholarship.

Whaley had grown up as an orphan, been adopted, served in the Army, then gone to college. After completing graduate school he worked on production of the F-111 fighter, then was recruited by the CIA as an expert on antenna technology. He made his money by managing the family farm, which was not only a large agricultural operation but a beneficiary of oil and gas below the surface.

Oil and gas philanthropy was also important in building up the UT Austin engineering school in the first place. It was named the Cockrell School in 2007 in recognition of many years of gifts—totaling the equivalent of $220 million—from the petroleum earnings of the Cockrell family of Houston.

Further reading

○ University of Texas news, engr.utexas.edu/features/whaley-scholarship

2014

NEW ORLEANS SCHOOL DISTRICT GOES ALL-CHARTER

Before Hurricane Katrina, New Orleans public schools were the worst district in the second-lowest-performing state in the entire U.S. Fully 78 percent of NOLA students attended a school designated as "failing" by state standards. Then the storm wrecked 100 of the city's 127 schools. Rather than rebuild the dysfunctional and corrupt school district, local leaders decided to instead create the nation's most complete necklace of charter schools, then let them independently pursue a new set of higher common standards. Decision-making power was decentralized away from the old school-board bureaucracy and transferred to individual principals, teachers, and schoolhouses. Top charter operators from across the country were invited in to set up shop, and more than 40 different entities now operate charters in the city on a competitive basis. At the same time, school performance began to be monitored intensely, with the understanding that new schools given five-year operating charters would be shut down at the end of that period if their students were not succeeding.

This was bold new territory never before explored on a citywide basis, and education-reform donors leapt to help out. It is estimated that philanthropists have poured an average of $20 million per year into New

─୬ PhilAphorism ───────────────────────

If you want to do something for your children and show how much you love them, the single best thing—by far—is to support organizations that will create a better world for them and their children. ☞*Michael Bloomberg*

Orleans charter schooling over the past decade. In 2012, the Laura and John Arnold Foundation alone unveiled $40 million of support for high-quality schools and the organizations erecting them in New Orleans. In addition to writing checks, donors have set up oversight and assistance organizations, helped social entrepreneurs plan and build new schools, aided various training and support organizations in coming to the city to support the education upgrade, created a solid voucher program to give poor children access to private schools, and worked to give families as many choices as possible. In 2014, the Recovery School District (which runs all but five of the public schools in New Orleans) closed the last of its conventional schools and became the first in America to shift entirely to charter schools to educate its children. Much work remains to be done, but already the high-school graduation rate has climbed from 54 percent to 80 percent.

Further reading

○ Karl Zinsmeister, *From Promising to Proven* (The Philanthropy Roundtable, 2014)

2014

PROTECTING NYC CHARTER SCHOOLS
FROM POLITICAL OPPONENTS

New York City is home to one of the most successful charter-school expansions in the U.S., from its initial handful of students in the fall of 2000 to 95,000 enrollees at the start of the 2015 school year. In some poor neighborhoods a quarter of all youngsters were attending charter schools by that time, with powerful results. For instance, Success Academy Harlem 4, a school with 97 percent minority children, scored No. 1 in the state in math achievement by fifth graders. Stanford University research shows that, on average, New York City charter students absorb five months of extra learning per year in math, and one extra month in reading, compared with counterpart children in conventional schools.

Yet when Mayor Bill de Blasio took office in 2014 with strong support from unionized teachers, he made it clear that he intended to clip the wings of philanthropically supported charters. He announced almost immediately that he was canceling a $210 million construction fund important to the schools, ending space-sharing with them, and intended to charge them rent (unlike other public schools that have their buildings provided by the city).

Charter allies responded to these threats. Early on, thousands of families marched across the Brooklyn Bridge to demonstrate their concern. Advocates like the group Families for Excellent Schools, backed by the Broad, Walton, and Buck foundations and many individual donors, aired a series of advertisements spelling out the achievements of New York's charters and urging legislators to oppose de Blasio's crimps. Then on a freezing March 2014 day, 11,000 parents and children rallied in defense of charters in the state capital of Albany. (Donors helped pay for buses and such.) Telling them "Parents deserve a choice," New York governor Andrew Cuomo promised, "You are not alone. We will save charter schools." Nine days later, the state Senate passed a budget resolution containing several provisions that effectively annulled the new mayor's squeeze on charter schools.

Further reading

○ *New York Daily News* report, nydailynews.com/blogs/dailypolitics/nys-senate-propose-host-charter-school-initiatives-budget-plan-blog-entry-1.1733155

2013

PUTTING A BLOOMBERG ON THE HOPKINS ROSE

In 2013, data entrepreneur Michael Bloomberg made a $350 million gift to Johns Hopkins University. The large donation was structured to fund 2,600 scholarships for needy students, and to create 50 Bloomberg professorships with special cross-disciplinary expertise. This was only the latest in a 49-year string of offerings. One year after he graduated from Hopkins with an engineering degree, Bloomberg donated $5 to the college; his first million dollar gift came 20 years after leaving campus. With his 2013 investment Bloomberg's total giving to Johns Hopkins reached more than $1.1 billion. He also served as chairman of the university's board of trustees for six years, and has helped raised millions from other donors.

Further reading

○ Press release announcing 2013 gift, hub.jhu.edu/2013/01/26/bloomberg-gift

2013

BOSTON'S NO-LEMONS CHARTER SCHOOLS

By 2013, the charter schools in many U.S. cities were beginning to pile up remarkable achievement records, but the accomplishments of Boston's philanthropically supported charters were in a category by themselves. First, it's important to note that Boston charters enroll students who are almost indistinguishable from the students who attend conventional public schools in the city. In the latest school year, 84 percent of Boston's charter-school students were black or Hispanic, compared to 76 in the conventional system;

in both systems, seven out of ten students came from low-income families. Yet three top-tier studies released in 2013 demonstrated that the children in charters were getting much better educations.

A Stanford study found, stunningly, that charter students in Boston were learning at twice the rate of their peers in conventional schools—gaining, for every school year completed, an additional 13 months of progress in math, and an additional 12 months in reading. Charter schools were especially effective, the researchers showed, at pushing students above the "proficient" level and into the "advanced" ranking on the tough end-of-year exams administered by the state of Massachusetts.

A different study released that same year by an MIT economist and four fellow professors was a careful comparison of high-school students from charters to demographically matched counterparts in conventional schools. It found that the charter students were twice as likely to take A.P. classes (and scored higher on final exams), that they did much better in statewide tests ("with especially large effects on the likelihood of qualifying for a state-sponsored college scholarship"), that they ended up with composite SAT scores more than 100 points higher than non-charter kids, and that they were much likelier to attend a four-year college instead of a two-year college.

The final burst of high-quality charter-school research to ripple through the city in 2013 was an investigation funded by the Boston Foundation. It tracked very closely with the two results above, and added the detail that charter schools' "largest gains appear to be for students of color, and particularly large gains were found for English Language Learners."

But perhaps the most remarkable finding that year concerning Boston's charter schools was that not one of them was sub-standard. Fully 83 percent of Boston charters performed "significantly better" than neighboring schools, and the remaining 17 percent produced equivalent results. Zero percent performed below the norm.

Despite these stellar outcomes, Boston and the rest of Massachusetts are burdened with a cap on the number of charter schools permitted to exist. Even in districts where conventional schools are worst, a regulation imposed by charter opponents limits the proportion of students attending charters to a maximum of 18 percent of all public-school enrollees. In 2013 that blocked spectacularly successful inner-city institutions like the Edward Brooke Charter Schools, and others, from accommodating additional students languishing on lengthy waiting lists. The Massachusetts House voted in 2014 to raise the cap slightly, but opponents organized by the state teacher union knocked the measure down in the state Senate.

Further reading

∘ Stanford study, credo.stanford.edu/documents/MAReportFinal_000.pdf

∘ Boston Foundation study, tbf.org/~/media/TBFOrg/Files/Reports/Charter%20 School%20Demand%20and%20EffectivenessOctober2013.pdf

∘ MIT study, economics.mit.edu/files/8981

2013

RATING TEACHER COLLEGES

Until very recently there was no comprehensive review to assess U.S. teacher colleges, as other sectors and services are rated. That changed in 2013 when the National Council on Teacher Quality used philanthropic gifts to create a new annual assessment and guide. The 2014 second edition of *Teacher Prep Review*, produced in collaboration with experienced school ranker *U.S. News and World Report*, rated thousands of college programs that train the nation's elementary and secondary teachers, and found that low-rated teacher-prep efforts currently outnumber top-rated efforts by more than 8:1. Indeed, out of 1,668 teacher programs that were rated, only 26 for elementary-school teachers and 81 for secondary teachers earned NCTQ's highest marks. The report found that 23 states do not have a single college track that provides high-quality math training to teachers.

Further reading

∘ 2014 edition of *Teacher Prep Review*, nctq.org/dmsStage/Teacher_Prep_Review_ 2014_Report

2012

EASY ONLINE LEARNING

So-called "distance learning" has been available to disciplined students for generations, with instruction and degrees available by mail, television, even radio. The Internet, though, opened yawning opportunities for new forms of education that could be of a high quality yet much more accessible and lower in cost than traditional classroom education. The year 2012 was when Internet-based instruction developed some critical mass, as so-called MOOCs (massive open online courses) expanded beyond the confines of major universities and began to become widely available from specialized entities. Some of the leading ventures in online learning, like Coursera and Udacity, aspire to be profitmaking ventures; others like University of the People, EdX, and the Khan Academy are set up as not-for-profits. Donations from the Andrew Mellon, Hewlett, Gates, and MacArthur foundations, as well as donations from the philanthropic arms of companies like Google, helped launch entities of both sorts.

While several MOOCs quickly garnered millions of students, very low course-completion rates so far suggest that limited numbers of students will have the discipline and perseverance to work their way through free courses on their own. But for those who do (including many students in the developing world), online learning makes very high-level education accessible at little or no cost, without geographic barriers.

Further reading

○ *Philanthropy* magazine reporting on University of the People, philanthropyroundtable.org/topic/excellence_in_philanthropy/higher_ed_lower_costs

○ Sample EdX offerings in computer science, edx.org/course-list/allschools/computer-science/allcourses

○ *New York Times* story on accreditation of University of the People, nytimes.com/2014/02/14/education/free-online-university-receives-accreditation-in-time-for-graduating-class-of-7.html?_r=0

2012

CHOPPING THE PRICE OF COLLEGE TEXTBOOKS

College students shelled out an average of more than $1,200 each for books and supplies in the 2013-2014 school year, according to the College Board. In many basic subjects like introductory economics, biology, and statistics, a single textbook can cost up to $200. A new philanthropic product is now changing that. OpenStax College, established at Rice University with philanthropic funding from the Arnold, Hewlett, Gates, Maxfield, and 20 Million Minds foundations, creates open-source, peer-reviewed textbooks for today's most popular college classes and encourages professors to assign them so students can take advantage of their being free online and low-cost in print versions. Each title covers all the topics taught in a standard course, in the usual order, but professors who want to instruct somewhat differently can also customize the text to match their lessons. Thanks to a $6 million grant from the Laura and John Arnold Foundation in 2013, OpenStax is now in the midst of doubling its offerings, with new textbooks in pre-calculus, chemistry, U.S. history, and psychology on the way. The initial goal is offering free texts for the nation's 25 most-attended college courses. Creating each new textbook costs more than $500,000. But with strong donor support, and a distribution deal with the National Association of College Stores, OpenStax is on the way to its goal of supplying 10 million students with free or low-cost textbooks—saving them $750 million.

Further reading

○ About OpenStax, openstaxcollege.org/about

○ Rice University release, news.rice.edu/2013/05/02/openstax-college-doubles-down-on-free-textbooks

SILICON SCHOOLS FUND

Concerned that the prevailing "factory model" of education doesn't serve either students or teachers well, a group of reformers banded together in 2012 to encourage the personalization of schooling via computerized instruction blended with live tutoring from teachers meeting with small groups. With catalytic funding from philanthropist John Fisher, the group created a new way for donors to pool investments—called the Silicon Schools Fund—with the aim of providing the startup grants to found 25 new "blended-learning" schools in the Bay Area of California over a five-year period.

The fund assists school founders with initial planning and organization, and also supports entrepreneurs who can supply them with software, curricula, training, and other resources to help their students and teachers mesh online teaching with personal instruction. It then publicizes these schools as laboratories and models for the rest of the country. In addition to the Fisher family, ten other major givers joined as charter supporters of the $25 million effort, including Bruce and Martha Karsh, Sheryl Sandberg and David Goldberg, the Sobrato family, the Emerson Education Fund, the Schusterman and Schwab foundations, and others.

Further reading

○ News article at launch, edsurge.com/n/silicon-schools-fund-lands-12-million

○ Silicon Schools Fund, siliconschools.com/approach/overview

PROVIDING AN INTERNATIONAL YARDSTICK
TO MEASURE U.S. SCHOOLS

America's schools no longer compete just with each other; they must be measured against counterparts in other countries that are turning out inventors, workers, and citizens of the future. With this in mind, a donor-supported nonprofit called America Achieves has begun offering U.S. schools a chance to assess their students on today's top international exam—the OECD Test for Schools. In 2012, funding from Bloomberg Philanthropies, the Carnegie Corporation, and the Hewlett, Kern Family, Barrett, Stuart, and Rodel foundations made it possible for any U.S. school to participate in a pilot offering; 105 schools did. The results showed that most U.S. students now fall in the middle of the international pack in the amount of knowledge they have absorbed. Honest, fair, sobering results like this, some reformers believe, are essential if expectations for American schools are to be raised, and an accurate roadmap created of the sectors that are most potholed and dangerous.

With the 2012 experiment successfully completed, America Achieves and its donors are now making the OECD test available to any and every high school in the U.S. And schools that have had their student body assessed will have the opportunity to participate in a "Global Learning Network" where they can collaborate, learn from each other, and pull themselves up to international standards.

Further reading

○ Global Learning Network, americaachieves.org/oecd

○ Results from the 2012 U.S. debut of the OECD test, americaachieves.org/docs/OECD/ Middle-Class-Or-Middle-Of-Pack2.pdf

2011

CORNELL TECH

When New York City launched a competition to create a great technical college and business incubator from scratch on Roosevelt Island, right next to Manhattan, many of the world's leading universities leapt to submit proposals and funding plans. Cornell, Stanford, Columbia, and others jockeyed for approval to build a $2 billion campus. At the last moment, Cornell announced a $350 million philanthropic contribution—the largest in its history—to clinch the win. The donor turned out to be Chuck Feeney, a Cornell graduate whose total giving to the school thereby reached a billion dollars. "This is a once-in-a-lifetime opportunity to create economic and educational opportunity on a transformational scale," explained Feeney in a statement. Two years later, Irwin and Joan Jacobs, both also Cornell alums, made their own $133 million gift to what is now known as Cornell Tech. Then Michael Bloomberg donated $100 million, lauding the project's potential for diversifying his city's finance-heavy economy. In 2015, ground was broken for the first buildings of what could become a research and business juggernaut that does for New York what Stanford did for the Bay Area and MIT did for Boston.

Further reading

○ *Inside Higher Ed* reporting on competition, insidehighered.com/news/2011/12/20/ cornell-and-technions-win-new-york-competition-reflects-desire-grow-urban-ties#sthash. v61ydhvJ.dpbs

EDUCATION

PHILADELPHIA
SCHOOL PARTNERSHIP

Only 15 percent of eighth-grade public-school students in Philadelphia performed at grade level in 2009, one of the worst performances in the country. The city school district was bureaucratic, broke, and seemingly unable to reform itself, while local philanthropists were trying to rescue ill-served children by supporting the local charter schools and Catholic schools. Developer Mike O'Neill was one of these donors, simultaneously active in the group Business Leadership Organized for Catholic Schools while encouraging charter schools through his board service and donations to Mastery Charter Schools. His attitude, along with many other donors, was that any structure which produced good results for children should be supported.

In 2010, these pragmatic philanthropists and business leaders created the Philadelphia School Partnership. Their intention was to shift the local focus to the quality of instruction that children get, rather than what kind of school it takes place in. The Partnership announced it would raise $100 million from donors to create 35,000 "seats" in high-performing schools, without regard to whether the facility is district-run, charter, Catholic, or private—so long as it gets good results with primarily low-income children. The investment fund was set up to operate with demanding criteria, careful research, and all eyes on results, while remaining agnostic about school structure. The William Penn Foundation pledged $15 million to the effort, and a dozen givers offered at least a million dollars, including the Maguire and Walton family foundations and Jeff and Janine Yass, who exceeded $5 million.

The Philadelphia School Partnership also later became the local sponsor for Philadelphia's participation in the Gates Collaboration Compact, an effort to break down walls between different types of schools serving the same population of children (see 2012 entry on the Local Projects list). The Gates Foundation granted $2.5 million to the Philadelphia Great Schools Compact, to be used for things like training teachers, and building GreatPhillySchools.org, a website where parents can compare and select all types of schools from a single entry point. Philadelphia's Compact was the first to include Catholic schools.

Further reading

o Great Schools Fund, philaschoolpartnership.org/great-schools-fund

NEWARK'S SCHOOL STRUGGLE

The Newark, New Jersey, school district has the dual notoriety of being one of the most expensive in the country (with per-pupil spending of up to $24,000, and a ratio of one administrator for every six students) and one of the worst performing (where the high-school graduation rate is only 54 percent and more than 90 percent of graduates who attend the local community college require remedial classes). In 2010, Facebook founder Mark Zuckerberg donated $100 million to a major effort to transform the public schools of Newark. Other philanthropists chipped in with a nearly equal amount for the bipartisan crusade launched by Mayor Cory Booker and Governor Chris Christie.

By 2014, much of the philanthropic money had been committed. The largest portion was used to grease new labor arrangements—an agreement with the teacher union includes a more rigorous teacher-evaluation system to identify weak instructors and qualify top instructors for annual bonuses of up to $12,500. Unfortunately it is "balanced" by huge bones thrown to the union in the form of $31 million in undifferentiated "back pay" and a continuation of seniority-based layoff protections that make it extremely difficult to replace personnel. Beyond the pay-for-performance win, the Zuckerberg gift, four years down the road, has brought the Newark public schools 50 freshly chosen principals, several new primary schools and four new high schools, and around a dozen additional charter schools. The charters are the best-performing additions so far, but political resistance has limited them to a modest role in the overall reform, with less than 30 charters currently existing in the entire city.

Meanwhile the next steps in reducing the school district's dysfunction were supposed to be layoffs of 800 support staff and 1,000 teachers over three years, and some substantial student movement out of poor schools into others. These plans sparked "venomous" anger among reform opponents, and the 2014 election of Ras Baraka (principal of a

◁ PhilAphorism

No act of kindness, no matter how small, is ever wasted.   ☞ *Aesop*

low-performing high school and son of radical activist Amiri Baraka) as Newark mayor, on a platform promising to "take our schools back." So while Mark Zuckerberg and philanthropic colleagues brought educational change to Newark, it is very unclear whether that change will be enduring. Meanwhile, Zuckerberg announced in 2014 that he was making another large gift to public schools—this time $120 million to the Bay Area, where, after the Newark experience, he hoped to find "a place where we can engage more directly with the community."

Further reading

○ Reporting in the *New Yorker* magazine, newyorker.com/reporting/2014/05/19/140519fa_ fact_russakoff?currentPage=all

2010

COMMON CORE STATE STANDARDS

In 2008, a big effort to raise standards for English and math instruction and reduce the number of high-school graduates unprepared for college work was percolating through the National Governors Association and the Council of Chief State School Officers. Backers from the two groups asked Bill & Melinda Gates for help. They wanted to formulate intelligent, demanding benchmarks for what K-12 students should know, then advocate for their voluntary adoption by states, meanwhile building up the infrastructure of textbooks, teacher-training materials, new tests, and so forth that would be needed to help states meet such standards.

The Gates Foundation agreed to provide more than $200 million to help create what became known as the Common Core State Standards. Scores of other philanthropies also chipped in, including the Carnegie Corporation, the GE Foundation, the Helmsley Charitable Trust, the Broad, Hewlett, and Mott foundations, and local donors. The standards are not a course of study, but spell out competencies that each student should acquire at each grade level. For instance, the English standards emphasize nonfiction and expect students to use evidence to back up arguments they use in class. The math standards say students must learn differing ways to solve problems, and be able to explain how they got their answers. It is up to states and school districts to decide how best to teach and meet the standards.

Within two years of the Gates grant, 45 states had adopted the Common Core standards, and begun adjusting their course plans, instruction, and annual assessments. In August 2010, Kentucky became the first state to roll out new math and English curricula in its schools. Other regions followed. End of year testing in some states made it clear that many students currently fall well short of the capacities defined as necessary under the Common Core, which caused backlashes from teachers and some parents. Other opponents expressed fears that the Common Core would nationalize education and reduce state and local control of schools. This was exacerbated by heavy-handed efforts by the Obama administration to push school districts to adopt the standards, a departure from the voluntary, private, grassroots model that got the standards rolling. In 2014, states that had signed on to the Common Core began to pull back from the standards and tests, making it unclear how common the Common Core will eventually be.

Further reading

○ *Philanthropy* magazine article on rise of the standards, philanthropyroundtable.org/topic/ excellence_in_philanthropy/common_cores_uncommon_rise

A STATE MODEL FOR DEFENDING REFORM ON MULTIPLE FRONTS

Education reformers have learned over the past decade that philanthropic donations will often be much more effective if they are combined with political advocacy that supports innovation and defends new experiments from opposing interest groups. A pioneer in this area was John Kirtley, a major education donor who pulled together a 2010 grassroots rally of 5,600 Floridians to pass historic legislation offering families more educational choices. A Tampa venture-capitalist who had donated and raised millions to improve schooling for low-income families, Kirtley helped organize the demonstration in the state capital after realizing that a decade of funding charitable efforts was not enough, that he needed to coordinate his donations with legislative efforts and political advocacy.

Kirtley's charity Step Up for Students channels money directly to families for tuition and other school expenses. The donors, schools, and families involved in Step Up eventually discovered they needed to take their case directly to legislators, so Kirtley launched a parallel 501(c)(4) group that was able to handle political advocacy, and then a 527 political action committee to support election candidates willing to make tough votes in favor of reform. From 2002 to 2008, the 527 group invested about $5 million in various legislative races. Kirtley and his philanthropic allies also donated money directly to reformist candidates.

The culmination of this combined charitable, legislative, and political work came in 2010, when the Florida legislature cast historic bipartisan votes in favor of educational choice—immediately after Kirtley and fellow donors orchestrated the largest political gathering in state history. "If you want to achieve any real progress in education reform," Kirtley concluded, "you cannot just have a (c)(3) capability. You must also have advocacy and political capabilities. If your goal is to change K-12 policy, you're going to have to change K-12 laws. And if legislators refuse to change those laws, then you're going to have to change those legislators." This conclusion has become widely shared among school reformers across the nation.

Further reading

○ *Philanthropy* magazine article, philanthropyroundtable.org/topic/excellence_in_ philanthropy/they_shall_overcome

2010

COUNTER-BALANCING PROTECTORS
OF THE K-12 STATUS QUO

In 1996 a national group calling itself Stand for Children was founded as a broad, soup-to-nuts supporter of children's causes. Over a period of years the group shifted toward education as their focus, and then increasingly toward an understanding that protecting children's true educational interests would often require battling the forces of the status quo in education—which were much more interested in deflecting pressure from teachers, principals, and school administrations than in fixing urban schools. As it realized that more spending for public schools would have no effect unless the structure of public education was changed, Stand for Children created a 501(c)(4) public-advocacy wing to lobby for things like more rigorous teacher evaluations, performance-based teacher compensation, and improved parental choice. The group also established 527 political action committees devoted to electing pro-reform legislators and school-board members.

Around the same time this evolution was taking place, in 2010, Betsy DeVos and other education donors merged some groups to create the American Federation for Children. It has a similar mix of charitable, advocacy, and political branches, and a particular focus on school choice, charter-school authorization, and supporting vouchers and tax credits that help poor families send their children to private schools.

The very same year, Michelle Rhee founded the group StudentsFirst, with parallel (c)(3) charitable, (c)(4) advocacy, and 527 political-action wings—and a charge to act as a direct counterbalance to the power of teacher unions while advocating for increased school excellence and parental choice. The group raised more than $62 million in charitable donations in its first few years, and aims to rely indefinitely on a mix of philanthropy and dues offered by its 2 million grassroots members.

Other donor-supported reform groups mixing charitable and political work in these same sorts of way include Democrats for Education Reform, EdVoice, state chapters of the group 50CAN, and others.

Further reading

○ Karl Zinsmeister, *From Promising to Proven* (The Philanthropy Roundtable, 2014)

CHICAGO PRESCHOOL EXPERIMENT

A giant experiment is now taking place in Chicago to see what tools work best to improve the academic performance of underachieving inner-city children. Thanks to a $10 million grant from hedge-fund founder Ken Griffin, some of the enrolled families receive cash incentives to undergo yearlong parent training. Other families will have their children enrolled in a new preschool where it is the teachers who get special incentives if their students meet certain achievement levels. Additional experiments will make small payments to parents, children, or teachers if they meet narrower weekly goals.

All of the results of this careful field experiment will be carefully tracked by University of Chicago professor John List and colleagues, and compared to a control group of similar families who get no incentives. And the total 600 children involved will be followed by the investigators for decades—with attention paid to who graduates, who eventually gets jobs, who has trouble with the law, how much each person earns, etc. Because the lessons of this research will emerge only over a period of years, in steps, this kind of philanthropy requires patience. The findings, however, could eventually be pivotal in deciding how future educational dollars should be spent.

Further reading

○ *Chicago Maroon* article describing experiment and grant, home.uchicago.edu/~jlist/press/ Maroon_9_9_09.pdf

VALUE-ADDED TEACHING

For years, when disappointed observers noted how little was being learned by children in inner-city schools, the riposte from the public-school establishment would be "it's not the teaching, these kids are just too poor and disadvantaged in family background to do better." Then the "no-excuses" charter schools began to appear and get much better performance out of the very same children in the very same neighborhoods, making it clear that good teaching *could* make a big difference even with the neediest youngsters.

Reformers began to put serious effort into replacing today's conventional teacher assessments (which rate 90-98 percent of instructors as good or excellent even in cities where results are miserable) with more scientific and clear-eyed assessments. In 2009, the Bill & Melinda Gates Foundation unveiled $45 million of funding to pioneer and then spread rigorous new systems of teacher evaluation. Working carefully in several large school districts, researchers used a mix of testing, expert evaluations, videotaped assessments, and student and teacher surveys—applied to random assignments of different children with different teachers—to see which students moved up the learning ladder, and which didn't, and how that correlated with the teaching they received. Soon, reliable methods were developed that allow identification of effective teachers who improve student results, no matter where their students start out.

A central insight was that a teacher shouldn't be judged simply by where a child ends the year, because that will depend heavily on what happened to the youngster before he walked into the classroom. Rather, a teacher should be judged by how her students perform at the end of the school year compared to where they stood when they came to that instructor in September.

Having developed these new teacher assessments, Gates then distributed $290 million in four test cities to help them apply the new approaches. Public schools in Tampa, Memphis, and Pittsburgh, and a coalition of five charter networks in Los Angeles, were given grants to aid them in implementing the new measures of teacher effectiveness. This included offering extra training and support to teachers, and ultimately tying each teacher's tenure decision and compensation level to how effective she is. There is no use in sorting teachers into effective, middling, and ineffective piles, school reformers recognize, unless schools are willing to act to keep great teachers with merit pay and job protections, while offering weak performers compensatory training and ultimately showing them the door if they don't improve. Only this kind of accountability can put teaching on a more even footing with other professions like law and engineering that are honored socially and compensated economically because they have quality controls.

Thanks entirely to philanthropic mobilizations, a few cities like Washington, D.C., Houston, and Newark have begun to put reasonably sturdy value-added teacher assessments into effect. Half of a teacher's evaluation score in D.C. now comes from how much her students improve their standardized test scores after a year in her classroom. Other measures of increased student achievement, plus five classroom observations by principals and master teachers, are also used to grade teachers. Instructors in D.C. with a value-added score that shows them to be "highly effective" get a cash bonus of up to $27,000, and two "highly effective" ratings in a row lead to a raise in base salary of as much as $25,000. On the other hand, Washington teachers who get reviewed as "ineffective" are subject to dismissal, as are those rated "minimally effective" for two straight years, and those scoring for three years in a row at the middling level of "developing." During the first couple years of the new assessment system, 500 teachers with poor ratings were let go from the D.C. Public Schools, and a 2013 academic study showed the system is having clear positive effects in both retaining good teachers and easing out persistently ineffective ones.

D.C.'s program was pushed through only after a group of major philanthropists, including the Walton, Robertson, Arnold, and Broad foundations, put up $60 million of financial sweetener for teacher unions. The Newark union likewise demanded more than $30 million of philanthropic money for its priorities before agreeing to a pay-for-performance deal (which still retains many loopholes protecting underperforming teachers). The philanthropists who have subsidized these initial experiments are betting, however, that when the public sees the large jumps in school quality that result when rigorous value-added assessment is applied to teaching, it will be impossible for other cities to duck making their own tough-minded reforms, thereby bringing upgrades to public-school teaching in many places.

Further reading

○ Karl Zinsmeister, *From Promising to Proven* (The Philanthropy Roundtable, 2014)

2008

KHAN ACADEMY

In 2004, high-school-age cousins living 1,500 miles from his Boston home) were begging hedge-fund employee Sal Khan for help on their math homework. In response he began doing online tutoring, and then taping short instructive videos in a closet of his house, which he posted on YouTube for his family members to work their way through. Once public, anyone could look at them. Before long hundreds of thousands of people were. Khan has a gift for calmly and quickly getting to the nub of technical instruction, and then explaining problem-solving methods in clear, simple language. As the audience for his video lessons exploded, Khan decided to quit his job at the hedge fund and give himself a year to see if he could create "Khan Academy" as a viable educational nonprofit providing instruction on a wide range of topics.

A few months into the experiment, he was burning through $5,000 a month of personal savings to support his family, and feeling stressed. Then he received an unsolicited $10,000 donation from Ann Doerr, wife of prominent Silicon Valley venture capitalist and donor John Doerr. A friend's child had been helped by Khan Academy videos and she was intrigued. She and Khan met for lunch; she later gave him $100,000 to stay afloat. Two months after that meeting, Doerr sent Khan a text saying she was sitting in a session at the Aspen Ideas Festival and Bill Gates was lauding his online instructional videos in a speech. It turned out the Gates children were also improving their math skills with the free Khan videos. Barely a year after Khan quit his hedge-fund job, the Gates Foundation invested $1.5 million to expand operation of the Khan Academy, followed not long after by another $4 million donation. Google awarded $2 million to translate content into ten languages and create additional practice problem sets.

There are now efforts to fold Khan Academy materials directly into the instructional process at a few pilot schools. Khan Academy is being used by homeschoolers, by students seeking extra help, and by adults brushing up on old skills. Its instructional videos have been viewed more than 580 million times. The organization's self-described mission is "to provide a world-class education for anyone, anywhere, for free."

Further reading

○ Philanthropy Roundtable conversation with Sal Khan, philanthropyroundtable.org/ topic/K_12_education/blended_learning

○ Laura Vanderkam, *Blended Learning* (The Philanthropy Roundtable, 2013)

2008

HOUSTON CHARTER SCHOOL BLOOM

The nation's seventh-largest school district in Houston, Texas, has been plagued by the familiar problems of urban public education—

ᴧᴐ PhilAphorism

The proper aim of giving is to put the recipients in a state where they no longer need our gifts.

☞ *C. S. Lewis*

including four out of every ten students failing to graduate from high school within six years of starting ninth grade. To blaze a path to better results, a group of local donors plus a few national philanthropists made a massive commitment in 2008 to create tens of thousands of school seats in new high-performing charter schools. Two of the most effective charter operators in the U.S.—KIPP and YES Prep—were born in Houston, and they agreed to add dozens of new campuses between them, with the intention not only of providing excellent education to tens of thousands of children themselves but also of modeling and inspiring improvements in Houston's conventional public schools. Philanthropists backed this effort with more than $90 million of donations: $20 million from the Houston Endowment; $11 million from the Michael and Susan Dell Foundation; $10 million each from Jeff and Wendy Hines, John and Laura Arnold, and the Gates Foundation; $9 million from the Walton Family Foundation; $6 million from the Brown Foundation; $5 million from Don and Doris Fisher; $4 million from Jan and Dan Duncan. As of 2014, the Houston charter-school expansion was about half complete, with 22 KIPP schools open on their way to 42, and 13 YES Prep campuses in operation toward an eventual goal of 19. Already, one out of every five Houston schoolchildren attends a charter, with excellent results, and that ratio will increase as KIPP and YES create an additional 20,000 seats while other charter operators undertake their own expansions.

Further reading

○ Karl Zinsmeister, *From Promising to Proven* (The Philanthropy Roundtable, 2014)

○ YES Prep Houston plan, socialimpactexchange.org/sites/www.socialimpactexchange.org/
files/Yes%20Prep%20-%20Growth%20Plan.pdf

2008

BOOTH, AND OTHER, SCHOOLS OF BUSINESS

Business education has been an American specialty ever since Joseph Wharton's gift launched a special school at the University of Pennsylvania (see 1881 entry), and philanthropy remains the lifeblood of these institutions. The recent gift of $300 million to the University of Chicago graduate school of business is illustrative. David Booth and Rex Sinquefield, both Chicago MBAs, founded a money-management company and built it into a $300 billion fund. Booth had served as research assistant to Nobel-winning economist Eugene Fama at Chicago, and applied many academic techniques of analysis in building his firm. Wishing to express his gratitude to the university, Booth made his large donation to the business school right in the teeth of the economic turmoil of 2008, when universities were struggling with major endowment losses. Booth's gift was not only the biggest ever received by the University of Chicago, but also the fattest given to any business school. Renamed the Booth School, Chicago's program is now ranked among the top U.S. MBA programs.

Other major philanthropic gifts to business schools include the $200 million real-estate developer Stephen Ross gave to the University of Michigan, investor Robert King's $150 million donation to Stanford (to encourage entrepreneurship as a solution to poverty overseas), John and Marion Anderson's $142 million of support for UCLA's school of business (which allowed it to entirely cease dependence on state funds), real-estate investor Ernest Rady's $130 million to build up University of California, San Diego's MBA program, Nike founder Phil Knight's $105 million gift also to Stanford, and Henry Kravis's $100 million for the Columbia Business School. At least 25 gifts of $40 million or more have been made to graduate schools of business around the country over the latest decade and a half.

A philanthropist named Jeff Sandefer donated not only money but his full time to create a new MBA program called the Acton School of Business. It grants MBAs focused entirely on entrepreneurship, using an unconventional curriculum and school structure. Acton instructors are successful businessmen themselves, and there is no tenure. The program relies on actual business cases and hands-on experience. Instead of conventional courses in finance, marketing, accounting, etc., classes are on topics like "customers" and "raising money." Students have to sell items door-to-door, over the phone, and through a website, and they have to negotiate a real discounted sale with some merchant, or they cannot graduate. The first portion of academic work is done online, then candidates come to the campus and work intensively on a compressed schedule. This allows MBAs to be earned in one year, and, along with philanthropy donations and the fact that some top professors draw no salary and rely instead on their entrepreneurial income, allows MBAs to be acquired for about $50,000 instead of the typical price of two or three times that. Afterward, Acton graduates enter commerce much differently: while only about 5 percent of students at a conventional top MBA program start their own business right away, a quarter of Acton students do so within two months, and another quarter say they will soon.

Further reading

○ News report on Booth gift in the *Wall Street Journal,* online.wsj.com/news/articles/ SB122601317069606639

○ Partial list of large recent donations to business schools, poetsandquants.com/2012/10/13/largest-donors-to-business-schools/2

○ *Forbes* profile of Acton, forbes.com/sites/michaelnoer/2013/10/09/startup-school-an-mba-designed-for-entrepreneurs-not-i-bankers

2008

A NEW KIND OF TEACHER COLLEGE

Three of the nation's most accomplished creators of charter schools—Dave Levin of KIPP, Norman Atkins from Uncommon Schools, and Dacia Toll of Achievement First—found they were constantly short on great teachers. So they got together and resolved to build from scratch a dramatically different teacher college capable of turning smart, persistent young people into master educators. Within months of their first 2005 discussion, Levin, Atkins, and Toll had a business plan for the Relay Graduate School of Education. Then hedge-fund founder Larry Robbins made it real by pledging $10 million to get the program off the ground. Next, the Robin Hood Foundation, the high-octane New York City philanthropy founded by financier Paul Tudor Jones, raised an additional $20 million for the new college in one night in 2007. Relay opened its doors in 2008.

Relay's two-year course of study combines best practices unearthed by actual teachers practicing their craft at Uncommon Schools, KIPP, Achievement First, and other top charters. There are three distinctive qualities to the Relay curriculum: 1) Its strong preference for practical techniques proven to work with needy children, rather than educational theory. 2) Use of new technology: More than 40 percent of coursework is delivered online, and intensive video recording is done of each enrollee's classroom instruction, for later study and dissection. 3) A demand for measurable results: Fully half of the program's graduation credits are tied to measured student outcomes, and to receive a master's degree from Relay you must demonstrate that your pupils made at least a full year's worth of academic growth in one year of school time.

Relay was the first new graduate school of education to be founded in New York City in 80 years. By 2015 it had already been expanded to Chicago, Houston, Memphis, Newark, New Orleans, Philadelphia and Camden, and Wilmington. It was training more than 1,400 teachers and principals per year, with other campuses to come soon.

Further reading

○ *Philanthropy* magazine reporting, philanthropyroundtable.org/topic/excellence_in_ philanthropy/mediocrity_be_gone

○ Relay locations, relay.edu/campuses

TEACHING AMERICA'S HISTORY AND FOUNDING PRINCIPLES

Created in 2007, the Jack Miller Center for Teaching America's Founding Principles and History was a response to the low level of civics knowledge among American undergraduates. The center identifies academics who are expert or promising teachers of Western political philosophy and America's history and founding principles, and assists them—offering professional development, two-week seminars, research fellowships, lectures and special events, and other resources for scholars at all career levels, from professors to post-docs to graduate students. It operates job boards to connect proven scholars to departmental openings at top universities.

The center has also funded the establishment of 58 dedicated on-campus institutes where excellent research and teaching can gain a wider audience. These included the Thomas Jefferson Center for the Study of Core Texts and Ideas at the University of Texas at Austin, the Center for the Study of Representative Institutions at Yale, the American Democracy Forum at the University of Wisconsin-Madison, the Graduate Program in Constitutional Studies at the University of Notre Dame, and the Benjamin Franklin Project at MIT.

The center is funded by donations from Jack Miller, an entrepreneur who created an office-supply company that became a core of the Staples company, along with other individuals, businesses, and foundations. The center distributed $7 million in 2014, and has committed over $60 million since its 2007 founding. With more than 750 faculty partners on hundreds of college campuses, and rapid expansion continuing, the Jack Miller Center has emerged as the leader in promoting high-quality civics education at the collegiate and graduate levels.

Further reading

○ *Philanthropy* magazine reporting, philanthropyroundtable.org/topic/excellence_in_ philanthropy/bringing_civic_education_back_to_campus

○ 2014 Annual Report of the JMC, jackmillercenter.org/wp-content/ uploads/2015/06/2014-15-Annual-Report.pdf

NATIONAL MATH AND SCIENCE INITIATIVE

In 2007 a panel of business leaders and academics organized by the National Academy of Sciences published a report expressing alarm over the state of math and science education in the U.S. That same year, the National Math and Science Initiative was organized as a nonprofit to actually do something about the problem. Starting with an initial donation of $125 million from ExxonMobil, and evidence that Advanced Placement courses are the best way to prepare students for success in technical fields, NMSI set out to make A.P. classes mainstream. Organizers copied a program from Dallas (also created by concerned business donors) that had proven wildly successful at drawing new students and teachers into A.P. coursework and then helping them succeed. Before the model program was launched only 26 African-American students in the entire Dallas school district earned a passing score on an A.P. exam. Within a few years, over 1,100 did. Other groups of students flourished in similar ways.

NMSI set out to make A.P. success common across the country by relying on two techniques in particular: special supplemental summer training for math and science teachers, and financial incentives for both teachers and students. When a new school enters NMSI, program leaders conduct site visits to identify which teachers at the school best fit the program. Then they train the teachers over the summer, and mentor them throughout the school year. And at the end of the year teachers are given cash payments of $100 for every one of their students who passes an A.P. exam, plus a $1,000 bonus if a targeted number of students earn passing scores. Students likewise get a $100 cash reward if they pass the test.

All NMSI schools must allow every interested student the opportunity to take an A.P. class. "Teachers have to think differently about who is an A.P. kid," says a spokeswoman. In addition to carefully prepping the teachers and incentivizing instructors and students alike, NMSI offers students in the program extra study sessions outside of class hours. The nonprofit also offers longer-term curricular help to schools, bringing in specialists who advise on the best sequence of classes, starting back at sixth grade, to prepare students for A.P. success by the time they're in high school.

As of 2015, NMSI's A.P. initiative was used in 620 schools located in 26 states. Companies like ExxonMobil, Lockheed Martin, BAE Systems, Texas Instruments, and many others, plus institutions like the Carnegie Corporation, and Gates, Dell, Heinz, and Perot foundations, as well as individual donors, have made this possible by providing large contributions to both the national nonprofit and local schools that are implementing the program.

And results have been dramatic. In the average school participating in NMSI, the number of passing scores on math and science A.P. exams jumps 85 percent in the first year, and nearly triples by the end of year three. Though schools using NMSI's A.P. program are only 1.5 percent of the total schools in the U.S., they account for 7.4 percent of the country's overall increase in qualifying math, science, and English A.P. exam scores. As NMSI continues to expand rapidly, the lift it produces under our math and science wings will increasingly be felt nationally. The latest add-on to the program, thanks to $900,000 of initial funding from Lockheed Martin, extended NMSI to several dozen schools near military bases that serve military families. Almost immediately these schools saw their qualifying A.P. scores rise at nine times the national average.

NMSI has also led the national replication of a University of Texas program called UTeach that makes it easy for college students majoring in math and science fields to become teachers. The UTeach program now operates on 40 college campuses, and more than 7,000 collegians are enrolled. Five years after entering the teaching profession, eight out of ten UTeachers are still giving math and science lessons to children. By 2020, about 5 million students will have been influenced by a UTeach graduate.

Further reading

○ NMSI, nms.org/Home.aspx

○ Expansion to military schools, Thomas Meyer, *Serving Those Who Served* (The Philanthropy Roundtable, 2013)

○ Replication of UTeach, uteach-institute.org/replicating-uteach

2007

ODYSSEY SCHOLARSHIPS

The University of Chicago has long been known for its Common Core—a curriculum based on the foundational texts of Western civilization, like Homer's Greek epic *The Odyssey*. It was thus fitting that the financial-aid program designed to relieve tuition burdens on Chicago students, created in 2007 after an anonymous gift of $100 million, was called the Odyssey Endowment. The nameless donor (dubbed Homer) offered to immediately pay all annual costs so that the scholarships could be launched quickly, while requiring the university to raise matching funds sufficient to make the grants program a permanent endowment. The Odyssey Scholarships enable students whose family income falls below $60,000 per year to receive full rides. Those in the $60-75,000 range receive grants for half of their obligations. The gift was given, the donor wrote, "in the hopes that future generations of students will not be prevented from attending the college because of financial incapacity, and may graduate without the siren of debt distracting them from taking risks and fulfilling dreams." The

Odyssey program has led to increased matriculation of low- and moderate-income students.

Further reading

o Interview with anonymous donor, magazine.uchicago.edu/07910/features/epic_quest. shtml#homer

o *Chicago Tribune* news story, www-news.uchicago.edu/citations/07/070531.gift-ct.html

2006

NEW SCHOOLS FOR NEW ORLEANS

As school reformers surveyed the wreckage after Hurricane Katrina closed New Orleans schools for six months, they resolved to grab the opportunity to completely remake that city's disastrously failed education system. It soon became clear that a local nonprofit was needed to serve as an honest broker and advocate for dramatic change. With the backing of donors, an energetic organization called New Schools for New Orleans was created to serve as a kind of combined guide dog/watch dog.

Eight years later, the main New Orleans school district became the first in America to fully close down its conventional schools and replace them with a system of independent public charter schools from which parents can choose (see 2014 entry). New Schools for New Orleans helped make this possible by contributing to the city's still-unfolding schools revolution in three crucial ways: It helped establish or expand more than a quarter of the charter schools that now educate the city's children (students in NSNO-backed schools are now improving their growth scores at about twice the rate of students in other local schools). Second, NSNO has led the charge in improving the training of teachers and principals, supporting teaching fellowships and bringing in top national trainers like Match Teacher Coaching, the Relay Graduate School of Education, the Center for Transformative Teacher Training, and others. Third, NSNO has served as a fair but tough reviewer of school results, and a leader in assisting schools in raising their standards every year.

The results have been dramatic. New Orleans has closed about three quarters of the achievement lag by which it long trailed the rest of its state. In the process, NSNO has become a much-prized authority on school reform, and is now consulted regularly by educators from other cities attempting to turn around their own schools. In all of this NSNO has relied powerfully on philanthropic support, including $40 million of multiyear grants from the Laura and John Arnold Foundation and support from numerous other donors like the Robertson Foundation, Carnegie Corporation of New York,

Doris and Donald Fisher Fund, Michael and Susan Dell Foundation, W. K. Kellogg Foundation, and Gates Foundation.

Further reading

○ NSNO spending priorities, newschoolsforneworleans.org/our-investments

○ Announcement of Arnold Foundation investments, prnewswire.com/news-releases/ laura-and-john-arnold-foundation-announces-25-million-investment-to-support-high- performing-charter-schools-in-new-orleans-181182441.html

2006

THE MIND TRUST

Some of the most successful school-reform efforts today are driven by regional nonprofits with broad mandates to improve teaching, train principals, support school founders, and incubate launches of new charter schools (see adjoining entry on New Schools for New Orleans). Another highly successful example of such a leadership group is the Mind Trust of Indianapolis. By organizing philanthropic support, cultivating new school leaders, conducting research, and forging partnerships with organizations such as Teach For America, TNTP, College Summit, Project Lead the Way, and Stand for Children, the Mind Trust has dramatically improved the quality of education in Indianapolis and the wider Midwest. Its charter-school incubator offers $1 million grants to encourage the creation of excellent new schools, fostering both local startups and branches of top national networks like Rocketship, KIPP, and Phalen. Grants provided by the organization's Education Entrepreneurship Fellowship are drawing innovators into the field and creating new options for regional families. The Mind Trust's report "Creating Opportunity Schools" helped define the conversation not only regionally but also nationally on how to overhaul a creaky urban school district.

A spinoff of the group, CEE-Trust, is orchestrating similar efforts in other cities, using funding from the Carnegie Corporation and Joyce Foundation to link about three dozen inventive local foundations and nonprofits from across the country. Other major supporters of The Mind Trust include the Eli Lilly and Company, Walton Family, Gates, OneAmerica, and Richard Fairbanks foundations, and the Lilly Endowment. Individual donors and local businesses also helped the organization raise more than $35 million in its first several years, which in turn allowed the organization to aid 100,000 Indianapolis children.

Further reading

○ About the Mind Trust, themindtrust.org/our-history

BLENDED-LEARNING SCHOOLS

Marrying K-12 education with the technology revolution has been a slow and uneven process, with many dead ends. Halfway through the first decade of the new millennium, however, some educators with philanthropic backing began to figure out new ways of instructing that could increase quality and efficiency in some of the same ways that other fields have been dramatically upgraded by computerization. An emerging synthesis concentrates on freeing teachers and students to work together intensively on each child's blindspots by transferring to computer software much work that is either drill-based or best accomplished when personalized for each student.

One of the schools that pioneered this new mix of human and electronic learning was Rocketship Education. Founded in 2006 by a donor who had been both a teacher and a Silicon Valley entrepreneur, the school won financial backing from some prominent technology entrepreneurs like Netflix founder Reed Hastings (who donated $250,000 for each of the first eight schools opened), Facebook's Sheryl Sandberg and her husband Dave Goldberg of SurveyMonkey, and Arthur Rock, as well as philanthropic heavyweights like the NewSchools Venture Fund, the Charter School Growth Fund (which offered a $2.3 million grant in 2008 to expand the chain), and the Broad, Schwab, Dell, and Koret foundations.

Rocketship began with one San Jose school that integrated two hours of online learning into every day, relying on personalized-learning software that both instructs and tags problem areas identified via frequent quizzes, while teachers circulate through the learning lab to solve individual problems. By 2014 there were eight Rocketship schools in San Jose, serving more than 4,500 students (with 2,500 families on the waiting list).

Their results proved powerful: though 90 percent of the students came from low-income families, and 75 percent were English-language learners,

◈ PhilAphorism

I wanted to give my children enough money so that they would feel they could do anything, but not so much they could do nothing.

☞ *Warren Buffett*

fully 80 percent of Rocketeers scored at the "proficient" or "advanced" level on the California Standards Test (results otherwise seen only in schools located in California's ten most affluent districts). With funding from the Bradley Foundation and other philanthropists, Rocketship expanded beyond Silicon Valley to Milwaukee, then to Nashville, and will open a school in Washington, D.C., in 2016, with other locations to come.

Another early inventor of blended learning was the Arizona school Carpe Diem. It relies on personalized computer instruction supplemented with old-fashioned one-on-one and small-group teaching to help students when they reach sticking points in their online work. Its 300 sixth to twelfth graders begin their efforts at computer workstations, and when software programs identify areas where they are not understanding concepts, a master instructor swoops in for special tutoring. Thanks to donor support there were Carpe Diem schools operating by 2015 in Indiana, Ohio, Texas, and Arizona, with more planned.

In many other schools as well, impressive test results and heavy demand from families have turned blended learning into one of the more promising fields within the U.S. school-reform movement. Scores of donors are investing hundreds of millions of dollars to launch new blended schools, expand existing ones, fund software ventures, and found coordinating organizations.

Further reading

○ Laura Vanderkam, *Blended Learning* (The Philanthropy Roundtable, 2013)

2005

HELPING DISADVANTAGED HIGH SCHOOL STUDENTS LOVE THE CLASSICS

Walter Teagle, longtime president of Standard Oil (now ExxonMobil) graduated from Cornell University in 1899, served as a Cornell trustee for 30 years, and was an energetic advocate for "liberal education." He believed that lessons learned from the "great books" could give college students the perspective and confidence to succeed in life by thinking their way through changing conditions. His Teagle Foundation, established in 1944, has had a long history of supporting excellent traditional liberal-arts programming at fine universities. The foundation has long taken a special interest in its home community of New York City, and in young people who are the first in their family to attempt college. Combining these interests, the foundation launched in 2005 its College-Community Connections program to help New

York-area low-income and minority students grasp the advantages of high-quality liberal education. As its name implies, the program recruits community groups that have experience and credibility with disadvantaged high school students and links them to area colleges like Columbia, Cornell, Fordham, Drew, NYU, Skidmore, and Manhattan College that are willing to conduct special classes, often during the summer, to hook these young people on challenging reading and big-picture thinking.

For instance, one of Teagle's CCC grantees (with co-funding from the Jack Miller Center—see 2007 entry on teaching history) is a "Freedom and Citizenship" seminar that brings several dozen bright but poor high-school juniors or seniors to Columbia for an intensive three-week session where they read and discuss Aristotle, Hobbes, Locke, and other greats. Rather than offering skill training or test prep, as many college-track programs for underrepresented kids do, the CCC efforts try to fascinate students with the life of the mind so they will not only get into college but prosper and graduate once there. Participants also get paired with a Columbia undergraduate who mentors them during the subsequent year as they prepare to enter college.

Teagle has devoted many millions of dollars to this College-Community Connections effort. After interviewing several hundred students who participated in the program, professional evaluators described it as "highly effective" at helping disadvantaged high school students "learn about the academic rigors of college coursework and the social responsibilities of being a college student." With donor support, similar undertakings are operated by Scripps College for low-income girls in Los Angeles, by the University of Chicago for students from the Chicago public schools, and other colleges.

Further reading

○ Teagle Foundation CCC program, teaglefoundation.org/Grantmaking/College-Community-Connections

○ *New York Times* column on Columbia program, nytimes.com/2014/08/05/opinion/frank-bruni-plato-and-the-promise-of-college.html

2005

ARKANSAS DEPARTMENT OF EDUCATION REFORM

A criticism of the many schools of education in the United States is that they are much too wedded to the prevailing systems that have consistently underperformed. So it was a departure when the University of Arkansas established a new Department of Education Reform in 2005. The department's creation was made possible by a $10 million gift from the Windgate Charitable Foundation that was then matched by money from the Walton Family Foundation. These contributions prompted the university to kick in money of its own. Among the largest received by any school of education, these gifts were primarily used to endow six professorships, with additional funds set aside to fund future research and establish ten doctoral fellowships.

Throughout American history, one of the central challenges facing reformers has been overcoming the political interest groups that dominate public education. The new department at the University of Arkansas was organized with the aim of avoiding establishment pressure and conventional wisdom. In addition to seeking near-term improvements, the department is charged with forming independent education scholars and leaders for the future. In its early years, it has sponsored pioneering research into school choice, and reports on the performance of specific reforms throughout the United States, while touting international models for school excellence and diversity, and encouraging fresh thinking in areas like teacher assessment and accountability.

Further reading

○ Department of Education Reform, University of Arkansas, uaedreform.org

2005

CHARTER SCHOOL GROWTH FUND

In 2005, as it was becoming clear that charter schools could produce powerful results among previously ill-served students, funders turned to the imperative of increasing the number of these effective schools as fast as possible, without watering down quality. To kickstart replication of high-performing schools, John Walton and Don Fisher each committed $5 million of startup funding to create the Charter School Growth Fund. The fund would collect capital from large education donors, then channel the pooled money to carefully chosen operators who had demonstrated clearly that they could create effective schools.

Once the fund was in existence, more than 375 school operators applied for grants, but only 40 were selected, and large, multiyear investments of several million dollars were given to each. The beneficiaries included schools like Yes Prep, IDEA, Denver School of Science and Technology, and Rocketship, which have since grown into nationally renowned chains. Generally the fund invests in charter operators that are the top performers in their city. The money is not to be used to cover operating costs, but is specifically directed to gearing up management so the network has the capacity to open more schools. The fund offers expert business coaching as well as funding.

In addition to Walton's eventual $25 million and $17 million from Fisher, donors to the fund's first investment round of $87 million included the Bradley Foundation ($14 million) and other foundations like Kern, Dell, Gates, Broad, Casey, Anschutz, and Robertson. In 2010 the CSGF launched a fresh round of fundraising and collected more than $160 million from the likes of Reed Hastings and the Walton, Arnold, and Hyde family foundations. About the same time, the group began forming specialized sub-funds that focus on particular problems (its Facility Fund helps schools acquire buildings) or regions (special New Orleans, Tennessee, and Florida investment pools). By 2015 the Charter School Growth Fund had committed around a quarter of a billion dollars of philanthropic money to support the creation of a third of a million new seats for low-income and minority children around the country.

Further reading

○ Charter School Growth Fund donors, chartergrowthfund.org/invest-with-us/our-funders

○ Article in *Wells Fargo Conversations*, wfconversations.com/article_full/jumpstarting_schools/#.U2JBol6r8ds

NATIONAL ALLIANCE FOR PUBLIC CHARTER SCHOOLS

In the mid-2000s, state-level associations created to serve, improve, and defend charter schools were beginning to become very savvy and active in many parts of the country. A group of donors decide it would be helpful to school reformers, politicians, and families if a national association were created to serve as a clearinghouse of authoritative information, source of institutional guidance and assistance, and public spokesman. The Fisher, Walton, Annie Casey, and Gates foundations joined together to launch the National Alliance for Public Charter Schools. "If we don't have a major national program, the work of funders and grantees will be whittled away," explained donor Don Fisher. "Most Americans will never even be clear what a charter school is."

Today the NAPCS is a highly effective organization. It publishes the definitive statistics on charter-school numbers, policies, and performance. It maintains an up-to-date database of all of the charter-school laws now in effect. It researches the field and publishes regular reports on technical and operational topics. It holds national conferences. The alliance represents the interests of charter schools in the nation's capital, in the states, in courtrooms, and in the media. It does these things with annual funding from about ten large philanthropies.

Further reading

○ Data dashboard of the National Alliance for Public Charter Schools, dashboard.
publiccharters.org/dashboard/home

MATH FOR AMERICA

James Simons is a walking advertisement for the power of math. The former chairman of the mathematics department at the State University of New York at Stony Brook got an itch to try mathematical approaches to investing, founded a firm that helped usher in the new field of quantitative money management, and ended up with a $12 billion personal fortune. Simons has since given away more than a billion dollars, using some of that to establish a program to chip away at the gross shortage of teachers qualified to instruct students in higher-level math and science.

Math for America pays math and science majors who elect to become teachers an additional stipend beyond their scaled school-district salary. This stipend can total up to $100,000 spread over five years. The fellowship also provides opportunities for professional development, chances to network with other math teachers, and scholarships for candidates while they are students. The program began and remains largest in New York City, but operates now in seven locations, supporting more than a thousand teachers, and it is expanding.

Further reading

○ Math for America, mathforamerica.org

OPENING UNIVERSITY OFFERINGS TO THE WORLD

In 2001, the president of the Massachusetts Institute of Technology told the president of the Andrew W. Mellon Foundation that for $100 million his university could put every one of its courses online—reading lists, lecture videos, lecture notes, homework sets and solutions, exams. Online users would have no access to MIT faculty, and would not get academic credit, but the entire bounty of one of the world's great universities—more than 1,800 courses—would be available at no charge to the world's huddled intellects yearning to breathe free. The Mellon Foundation invited the William and Flora Hewlett Foundation to be their partner in paying for this gift to learners, and each organization put up an initial $5.5 million to launch a pilot program that put the first 50 MIT courses on line in 2002. By 2007 they had the entire MIT curriculum available on the Internet—every course in 33 different academic disciplines.

By 2014, several hundred additional new courses had been added, and more than 152 million individuals had sampled what MIT was calling its "OpenCourseWare." In addition, a new program allowed online students to pay a small fee and take exams that would qualify them for a special "MITx" credential showing they had successfully completed the course. As other universities like Johns Hopkins, Rice, Yale, Stanford, and Carnegie Mellon approached donors for help putting their offerings on line, additional foundations like MacArthur and Gates, plus numerous individual donors, as well as companies like Dow and Lockheed Martin, began to make grants to pay for the $10,000-$15,000 it costs to put an average course online.

In its first dozen years leading this philanthropic effort, the Hewlett Foundation alone spent approximately $150 million. It also provided invaluable leadership toward opening up the previously closed world of academe—for instance, overcoming faculty resistance against sharing of their "intellectual property" by building up the Creative Commons process for licensing fair uses of curricula and lectures. The Hewlett Foundation also provided funds to create the Open Education Consortium. This got more than 250 universities involved in putting free instructional material on the Internet, totaling about 15,000 courses in 20 different languages as of 2014.

Further reading

○ *Philanthropy* magazine reporting, philanthropyroundtable.org/topic/excellence_in_
  philanthropy/opening_up_the_university

○ Open Education Consortium, oeconsortium.org

2002

PULLING TALENTED LEADERS INTO EDUCATION

"We need to change public education from a tired, government monopoly to a high-performing public enterprise. To do that you need better people in management and governance," argues major education donor Eli Broad. With that goal in mind, Broad created two leadership-training programs: The Broad Residency in Urban Education, and the Broad Superintendents Academy. The residency picks 45 to 50 professionals with strong records outside education—often in finance, business, or law— and puts them through an intensive two-year program which prepares them to apply their high-level management and problem-solving skills to running schools. Most are placed in large public-school headquarters, the central offices of top charter-school networks, or city, state, or federal education departments. The Broad Academy is another highly selective leadership program that grooms each class of 10-15 individuals, over an 18-month period, to become superintendents of schools. These two efforts have launched a surge of talented reform-oriented leaders into public education. Among their several hundred alumni (about 90 percent of whom remain in education) are leaders like Chris Cerf (who became commissioner of education for the state of New Jersey), Chris Barbic (superintendent of Tennessee's statewide Achievement School District), John Deasy (Los Angeles United School District superintendent), Charlotte superintendent Heath Morrison, New Schools for New Orleans former CEO Neerav Kingsland, and Alex Hernandez of the Charter School Growth Fund.

Further reading

○ Broad Center for the Management of School Systems, broadcenter.org

2002

INSPIRED SCHOOLING

Seeing that "factory-style" public schools were having poor results, teacher Dan Scoggin went looking for an alternative. He became convinced that an emphasis on character development, linked to a demanding great-books curriculum, would help students feel their human value and potential, which would translate into academic achievement. Scoggin became the leader of a group of Phoenix, Arizona, residents who were determined to bring better schools to their city. Their goals were bigger than just improved test scores. They wanted to produce students capable of appreciating "the true, the good, and the beautiful"—while also being 100 percent qualified to attend college and otherwise achieve and contribute.

Taking advantage of Arizona's embrace of the charter-school concept, and a bevy of generous local donors, Scoggin's team founded the first Great Hearts Academy in 2002 as a free public charter school located in the Phoenix suburbs. Great Hearts employs teachers who are trained specifically in their academic field, rather than graduates of teacher schools. They require their pupils to read primary sources rather than textbooks, and they use Socratic-style discussion rather than lectures, and expect every child, not just the natural scholars, to participate and learn. All of which is easier said than done, of course, particularly given that charter schools are allotted about one-quarter less funding per student than conventional public schools.

Local donors large and small—like the Quayle family, fourth-generation Arizonans who gave $1.5 million in 2012—stepped forward to make Great Hearts possible. Philanthropy also covered crucial costs for expanding the Great Hearts model after it had demonstrated its power (95 percent of students, even those from difficult inner-city neighborhoods, go straight to four-year colleges). By 2015 there were 22 Great Hearts Academies in the Phoenix area, with several more in the works. The first academy outside of Arizona opened in San Antonio in 2014 and a dozen more schools located across Texas began the process of opening in the following years. Even with all of this growth, thousands of students remain on waiting lists for these schools. The network is planning additional expansion with major philanthropic support.

Further reading

○ Andy Smarick, *Closing America's High-achievement Gap* (The Philanthropy Roundtable, 2013)

2002

BROAD PRIZES

The $1 million Broad Prize, the largest K-12 education award in the country, was created in 2002 to reward urban public-school districts that "demonstrate the greatest overall performance and improvement in student achievement while reducing achievement gaps among low-income students and students of color." It is donated by the Edythe and Eli Broad Foundation. In 2012 the foundation established a parallel $250,000 prize to recognize the charter-school operator that best meets similar criteria. The ultimate aim of both prizes is to highlight school systems that others across the country might be able to learn from.

The charter-school prize offers many chart-topping candidates worth recognizing. The school-district prize, however, lost its luster when it was awarded to Houston city schools for a second time in 2013, without their possessing an especially proud achievement record, and when only two districts were named as finalists in 2014 (instead of the usual four to five), because the prize board found so few impressive records. The lack of impressive empirical results from conventional urban public school districts caused the foundation to "pause" that prize in 2015. Meanwhile, the charter-school prize continues to spotlight many highly effective operators.

Further reading

○ Prize website, broadprize.org

2001

EDUCATION

HEWLETT AND PACKARD FAMILIES
MAKE STANFORD A POWERHOUSE

In 2001, the William and Flora Hewlett Foundation made an historic announcement that it would be donating $400 million to Stanford University to reinforce its academic programs. This was just the most dramatic in a long series of grants from the Hewlett and Packard families, whose patriarchs had built one of the pioneering computer companies after graduating from Stanford. Way back in 1952, a brand-new engineering building was opened on the Palo Alto campus thanks to gifts from Bill Hewlett and David Packard. The men were the lead donors in nearly all of the capital campaigns the university conducted during their adult lifetimes. They funded faculty, fellowships, buildings, and scholarships. They drew in many other donors, particularly across Silicon Valley, who wanted to follow their philanthropic example.

Even before the 2001 gift announcement, the Hewlett and Packard families and their foundations had donated close to $400 million to Stanford, providing crucial support that in particular pushed the university's computer, engineering, and science programs to international preeminence. As one college official stated, "only Leland and Jane Stanford have played a larger role in Stanford's success."

Further reading

○ Announcement of Hewlett's 2001 gift, news.stanford.edu/news/2001/may9/gift-59.html

2001

LARGEST GIFT IN HISTORY TO A COLLEGE

In 2001, Gordon Moore, the co-founder of chip manufacturer Intel and author of many scientific papers and patents on semiconductors, gave the California Institute of Technology a massive $600 million gift to keep that institution, which he described as a "national treasure," on the forefront of science and tech research. The college announced that a portion of the gift would go to its endowment, but most would be spent for research projects and the hiring of new investigators. It became the largest donation ever to a single college or university. Moore has made many other gifts to Caltech as well, most recently $100 million in 2015 for a fund that will eventually provide fellowships for every Caltech graduate student. He also served on the university's board of trustees for decades.

Further reading

○ Caltech 2001 release, caltech.edu/content/caltech-receives-600-million-two-giftslargest-academic-donation-history

○ Caltech 2015 release, caltech.edu/news/100-million-gift-gordon-and-betty-moore-will-bolster-graduate-fellowships-47392

2000

NEW LEADERS FOR NEW SCHOOLS

In 2000, a group of students at the Harvard Business School became finalists in its annual business-plan contest with a proposal for a new organization to train principals. Later that same year, New Leaders for New Schools was launched as an operating nonprofit, and by 2015 the program will have offered high-quality training to 2,000 new principals. It recently set a goal to also train 1,000 sitting principals every year. The program is expensive—six figures per candidate per year. Foundation, individual, and corporate donors sustain the group with approximately $20 million of annual support, with recent top donors including the Boeing Company, the Roberts, Robertson, Gates, Schwab, and Hyde foundations, the Carnegie Corporation, and more than a hundred other givers. The program is now known simply as New Leaders.

Further reading

○ Laura Vanderkam, *Excellent Educators* (The Philanthropy Roundtable, 2014)

○ New Leaders 2014 donors, newleaders.org/support/philanthropic-partners

2000

DON FISHER TAKES KIPP NATIONWIDE

For education-reform advocates, the KIPP Schools are among the greatest successes of recent history. Started in 1994 by David Levin and Mike Feinberg, two teachers fresh from Teach For America stints, KIPP dramatically improves educational opportunities in urban areas by creating high-performing "no-excuses" charter schools in the most neglected neighborhoods of their cities. The schools rely on many innovations: carefully selected principals, a particular style of bright and dedicated teacher, more school time (including Saturday classes and a longer school year), strict rules on behavior, a culture of high expectations, contracts signed by students, parents, and teachers. Despite remarkable student results and growing reputation, in 2000 the KIPP portfolio consisted of just one school in Houston and another in the Bronx. That's when Don Fisher came along. The founder and longtime CEO of the Gap, Fisher closely examined KIPP's successes and was sufficiently impressed to give Levin and Feinberg $15 million, plus lots of intense guidance on organization and management, to take their model nationwide. An additional $20 million changed hands over the following four years. Fisher chaired the KIPP board for years.

Fisher and the KIPP leaders eventually decided that the training of principals would be the best way to accelerate the creation of excellent new schools. Today KIPP runs five renowned programs for building leadership skills in principals, assistant principals, and other leaders, plus a teacher leader program that prepares them to be grade-level head, department chair, or Saturday-school coordinator. The top two donor-endowed efforts are the Fisher Fellowship (which prepares individuals to open new KIPP schools) and the Miles Family Fellowship (which instructs leaders while they serve in existing KIPP schools).

KIPP's combination of intense staff training, high and uncompromising standards, and decentralized operational control allowed the network to mushroom from just two schools to a total of 183 campuses in 20 states plus D.C. by 2015, serving nearly 70,000 children. Most remarkably, it expanded in this way with no diminution of academic quality or student-performance results. Though the vast majority of its students are poor and from minority backgrounds, KIPP produces a 93 percent graduation rate and 83 percent college placement. Thousands of donors now support the KIPP schools, including dozens that make seven-figure annual donations—like the Walton, Arnold, Broad, Dell, Robertson, and Wallace foundations, and individuals like Thomas and Susan Dunn, Reed Hastings and Patty Quillin, and Arthur Rock and Toni Rembe in recent years.

But no philanthropists have contributed more to the success of KIPP than the Fisher family, which has now given about $80 million (and counting) to enhance and expand the network. And KIPP is just one of several places where Don Fisher germinated spectacular educational reforms; he was also a pioneer funder of Teach For America, the New Teacher Project, the Charter School Growth Fund, the California Charter Schools Association, the Black Alliance for Educational Options, StudentsFirst, the National Alliance for Public Charter Schools, and other landmark organizations. As his biography in the

◈ PhilAphorism

A large part of altruism…is grounded upon the fact that it is uncomfortable to have unhappy people about one. ↩ *H. L. Mencken*

Philanthropy Hall of Fame notes, Don Fisher "may have been the most consequential" funder of U.S. education reform in the modern era. "Fisher was among the very first to find and fund almost all of the most promising ideas and programs of the last 50 years. He seemed to have an uncanny knack for discovering effective people, which was coupled to a fierce independent streak that encouraged him to back them long before anyone else."

Further reading

○ Don Fisher profile in the Philanthropy Hall of Fame (see prior *Almanac* section)

○ Duke case study, cspcs.sanford.duke.edu/content/model-new-inner-city-school-kipp-academies-pisces-foundation-2000

○ Jay Mathews, *Work Hard, Be Nice* (Algonquin Books, 2009)

CENTER FOR RESEARCH ON EDUCATION OUTCOMES

Multi-year foundation funding totaling $1.25 million allowed the creation of the Center for Research on Education Outcomes at the University of Rochester in 1999. It was guided by one of the country's leading education economists, Eric Hanushek, and a distinguished advisory board. Later moved to Stanford University, it has become a leading source of reliable hard data on K-12 student performance and the cumulative effects of various school reforms. In particular, its studies of charter schools around the country quickly became the authoritative summaries of the strengths and weaknesses of the nation's fastest-growing alternatives to conventional public schools. An initial 2009 study spanning 16 states was followed by a 2013 26-state update (drawing on the records of a million and a half charter-school students), and by profiles of many particular regions. By providing a whole new level of detail and sophistication to understanding of the effects of charter schools, the CREDO studies have become the baseline evidence on charter results. Continuing updates on the mushrooming sector are planned, with recent support from the Walton Family Foundation and Pearson Learning Systems.

Further reading

○ CREDO at Stanford University, credo.stanford.edu

FREE TUITION AT MUSIC SCHOOL

Given his roaring success in business and private equity it was no surprise when Stephen Adams offered a large financial contribution to

Yale University. What *did* come as a surprise was the particular object of his support: the Yale School of Music. For most of his life, Adams possessed no special musical ability and very little interest in the field. But at the age of 55 he began playing piano, quite seriously, and quickly developed a love of the classical repertoire. On the occasion of his 40-year reunion, Adams decided to contribute $10 million to his alma mater's music program. And he wasn't done. As his knowledge of and passion for music continued to growth, so did his giving. In 2005 he gave an additional $100 million—which allowed the School of Music to cover the entire tuition cost of all of its students thenceforth.

In a field that matches extraordinary professional demands with very modest financial rewards, tuition-free music training was a breakthrough. The gift was initially given anonymously. "My wife and I are Christians and the Bible speaks of giving in secret," Adams said later, describing himself as devout. His benefaction only became known in 2008 when he revealed it offhandedly in an interview in hope of encouraging fellow members of the class of '59 to give generously for their 50-year reunion. The Adams Family Foundation has also made many other grants to support music education across the country, including substantial gifts to Westmont College.

Further reading

○ *Yale Daily News* coverage, yaledailynews.com/blog/2009/02/18/the-100-million-couple

1999

GATES MILLENNIUM SCHOLARS

Just before the turn of the millennium, the Bill & Melinda Gates Foundation put into operation a major college scholarship program for minority students, with an initial grant of a cool billion dollars that was later increased to $1.6 billion. Every year, the Millennium Scholars program selects 1,000 new African-American, Hispanic, Asian, or Native-American college prospects and offers them good-through-graduation scholarships (set at various levels to cover their need). These can be used at any college the student chooses. The program particularly aims to encourage minorities to enter scientific fields like computer science, math, public health, and engineering (where they are underrepresented), and any Millennium Scholar in good standing who finishes an undergraduate degree and wants to continue on to grad school in one of these technical fields will also have his or her graduate education paid for by Gates. In addition to financial aid, the program offers leadership development, mentoring, internships, and other resources to help students succeed—which collectively have yielded a rate of college graduation within six years of nearly 90 percent, more than double the average for all African Americans. Since its establishment, the Gates Millennium Scholars program has propelled more than 16,000 young Americans through their educational careers, and 28 percent have gone on to graduate school, half of them in the technical fields that Gates has particularly targeted.

Further reading

○ Gates Millennium Scholars Program, gmsp.org/publicweb/aboutus.aspx

LEADERSHIP AND CHARACTER EDUCATION
AT OUR MILITARY ACADEMIES

Character education has been a centerpiece of the training provided by America's military academies right from their foundings. The honor codes and leadership lessons expounded at West Point, Annapolis, and Colorado Springs have influenced many other schools as well. In recent decades, private donors have become increasingly active in reinforcing and enriching these offerings, with the intention of bolstering character strengths not only in the military but also in business and other sectors of civilian life.

In 1998, a $4 million endowment from Ross Perot, plus major support from the William E. Simon, John Olin, and Lynde and Harry Bradley foundations helped create at West Point the Simon Center for the Professional Military Ethic. The center leads all cadets through the academy's capstone course on officership, featuring repeated "dilemma-based exercises" that teach future military leaders how to balance high moral, legal, and practical responsibilities. The center also holds conferences where cadets, plus hundreds of students brought in from other colleges and universities, grapple with details of ethical decision-making, character development, and the maintenance of honor codes.

In 2011, philanthropist and former aircraft-manufacturing CEO Sandy McDonnell donated $5 million to the U.S. Air Force Academy to create its own Center for Character and Leadership Development. "The military academies are far ahead of almost all of the other universities in the emphasis they place on character-building," explained McDonnell at the time of his gift. "I hope universities all across the nation will emulate their programs for character development." The Harry and Jeanette Weinberg Foundation and Naval Academy graduate/NBA star/philanthropist David Robinson helped create similar programs at

Annapolis. Observing that "leadership is one of the scarcest resources in the world," former Procter & Gamble CEO Bob McDonald has given money to West Point for national conferences in character-building that train students from other colleges in methods that have produced good results at the U.S. Military Academy.

Further reading

○ *Philanthropy* magazine article, philanthropyroundtable.org/topic/excellence_in_ philanthropy/spartan_donors

1998

A WORLD-BEATING SCHOOL NETWORK

The first BASIS school was opened in 1998 with the intention of creating an open-admission public school that could produce results as good as the world's top-scoring schools in places like Shanghai, Finland, and South Korea. Founders Michael and Olga Block succeeded, then went on to build a string of similar schools using philanthropic funds. In each of them, BASIS administers a rigorous, Advanced Placement curriculum to all students, across the board. "We have been severely underestimating all kids," argue the Blocks. Science and math are a particular focus of BASIS schools—all students complete Algebra I by the end of their seventh-grade year, and in grade six students begin taking biology, chemistry, and physics as separate subjects. Also beginning in sixth grade, students are required to pass comprehensive exams in all core subjects in order to be promoted to the next grade.

This mirrors the demanding course schedule of many top-performing European and Asian schools. To make it work, BASIS negotiates an initial salary individually with each teacher, and offers performance-based financial incentives. Teachers of A.P. courses, for instance, earn an additional $100 for every student who makes a grade of four on the A.P. exam, and an additional $200 for every student who earns a five (the top score). Rather than traditional sick days, BASIS gives teachers a "wellness bonus" of $1,500. They lose a predetermined amount of that for each sick day taken.

The results of all of this are outstanding. The average BASIS student takes ten AP exams. Though only about one percent of the 1.5 million high-school seniors who take the PSAT test every year are selected as National Merit Scholar Finalists, more than 25 percent of all BASIS seniors earned that high achievement in 2012. International tests like the PISA exam show that BASIS students are competitive with the very best scholars anywhere in the world.

With support from donors like Craig Barrett, former CEO of the Intel Corporation, and his wife, Barbara, the network of BASIS charter schools is now undergoing expansion. It operates 18 schools as of 2015, with more in the works. In addition to its public charter schools the organization is experimenting with moderate-cost, high-performance private schools, opening prototypes in low-income neighborhoods in Brooklyn, the D.C. suburbs, and San Jose.

Further reading

○ Karl Zinsmeister, *From Promising to Proven* (The Philanthropy Roundtable, 2014)

○ BASIS charter schools, basisschools.org

○ BASIS private schools, basisindependent.com

1998

CHILDREN'S SCHOLARSHIP FUND

Ted Forstmann and John Walton were two of the country's most successful businessmen, but they'd never met until they donated $6 million to the Washington Scholarship Fund. That fund was set up to help low-income students in Washington, D.C., attend private and religious schools. (See 1997 entry on list of Public-Policy Achievements.)

After observing the powerful desire among parents in the nation's capital for educational opportunities beyond those offered in the public schools, the men decided to start a similar organization offering scholarships across the country. Each man contributed $50 million. The resulting fund would allow 40,000 children to attend better schools. The scholarships generally paid only partial tuition, though, so recipient families would have to make sacrifices to find the rest of the school fees.

When the Children's Scholarship Fund was announced, an astonishing 1.25 million applications were submitted. This roaring demand for educational opportunity prompted the men to expand CSF far beyond its initial scope. The organization set up local affiliates in major cities and secured long-term financial support from a host of fellow philanthropists.

From 1998 to 2014, the Children's Scholarship Fund awarded $677 million in private scholarships to about 160,000 low-income children, most of them from minority backgrounds. In addition to transforming those lives, the fund revealed the depth of hunger among parents across the country for alternatives to conventional public schools. This fed other elements of school reform.

Further reading

○ CSF history, scholarshipfund.org/about/history

○ *Philanthropy* magazine reporting, philanthropyroundtable.org/topic/excellence_in_philanthropy/the_carnegie_of_school_choiceFurther reading

NEWSCHOOLS VENTURE FUND

In the late 1990s, some Silicon Valley investors impressed by the ability of imaginative entrepreneurs to solve knotty problems in technology decided to see if they could apply some of that same creativity to reforming education. They set up a nonprofit organization modeled on venture-capital investing. Like a venture-capital firm it would pool money from a number of individuals and organizations, do careful research to find the most promising leaders in the target field (in this case, school improvement), then back these leaders with substantial sums of money. Instead of seeking a financial return, however, they would look for social impact.

In its first 15 years the NewSchools Venture Fund raised about $250 million from donors, then channeled that money into more than 100 nonprofit and for-profit organizations. Some of these were new schools: charter operators like Aspire, Alliance, Brooke, Match, North Star, Rocketship, and others. But the group also invests in social inventors who are creating new curricula, computer applications, or educational services. NSVF has built up three dozen education-technology firms whose products have reached 15 million students.

Online instructor Khan Academy, the school-reform advocacy group Families for Excellent Schools, D.C.'s superb authorizing board for charter schools, the GreatSchools Web rankings, principal-training organization New Leaders, the Relay Graduate School of Education, and many other reform groups have received money from the NewSchools Venture Fund. More than 7,500 teachers have been trained by recipients of its money. NSVF has special regional arms to support charter schools and other improvements in Boston, Oakland, and D.C. The latest roster of donors to the fund lists 39 individual givers, 45 foundations or donor-advised funds, and six companies or corporate foundations.

Further reading

○ NewSchools Venture Fund, newschools.org

AVE MARIA UNIVERSITY

Raised in an orphanage run by nuns, Tom Monaghan had a deep appreciation for Catholic education. After the 1997 sale of his stake in Domino's Pizza, the firm he founded and grew into a multibillion-dollar business, Monaghan turned his attention to philanthropy. He quickly zeroed in on the difficulty Catholic families told him they had in finding colleges that were both high-quality and faithful. And so in 1998 he founded Ave Maria College. Two years later he created the Ave Maria School of Law as a sister institution. Thanks to more than $500 million donated by Monaghan the schools grew quickly, and became permanently located in southwest Florida, with a current enrollment of 1,300 students. Broad philanthropic support is developing, with more than 10 patrons having given at least a million dollars, and over 100 making six-figure donations.

Further reading

○ *Philanthropy* magazine profile, philanthropyroundtable.org/topic/excellence_in_philanthropy/new_u

○ 2002 interview with Tom Monaghan, philanthropyroundtable.org/topic/excellence_in_philanthropy/opening_a_new_franchise

1997

PROJECT LEAD THE WAY

In 1986, a public-school teacher in upstate New York created a special high-school curriculum to encourage more of his students to study engineering. Within a few years he was not only attracting lots of kids to his hands-on classes in digital electronics and other subjects, but leaving them with valuable skills important in technology occupations. Within a few years he convinced the nearby Charitable Leadership Foundation to finance an expansion of the program. Thus was Project Lead the Way born with donated funds in 1997 across a network of 12 New York school districts. The next year it went national, as two New Hampshire schools joined. The first major corporate sponsor signed on in 1999, when Autodesk began to provide students with its world-leading computer-assisted-design software.

The program—which combines college-level technology concepts with exciting project-based learning (building a solar-powered car, creating fighting robots, using laser machine tools and print-jet manufacturing)— proceeded to grow explosively. By 2008, PLTW was being used in schools in all 50 states. The Kern Family Foundation gave the organization a $10 million gift in 2009 to allow further major expansion, and donated more than $26 million in total over the next several years. In 2013, Chevron made a $6 million donation. The program's many other donors include the Kauffman, Knight, and Conrad foundations, and companies like Lockheed Martin.

By 2015, more than 8,000 schools (now not only high schools but also middle and elementary campuses) were using PLTW curricula with 900,000 students. Project Lead the Way has become the nation's most successful provider of science, technology, engineering, and mathematics instruction for K-12 students.

In addition to the imaginative curriculum and the project-based orientation, highly competent teachers are the key to the program's success. Teachers who want to bring PLTW to their school must take an online skills assessment and then participate in weeks-long summer training to fill in their weak spots and hone their general technical understanding and teaching skills. The Rochester Institute of Technology has provided intensive teacher instruction for the program since 1998, and more that 10,000 teachers from across the U.S. have now been through the summer sessions.

At a time when the U.S. has a million unfilled technology jobs, engineering colleges, other educators, and employers have come to prize alumni from the PLTW courses—who score higher on math and tech tests, say they want to study engineering or computer science or other tech-related fields in seven cases out of ten, and drop out of university engineering programs at just one quarter the national rate of attrition. Clarkson University was one of the first high-quality tech schools to offer scholarships directly to PLTW students, and at some engineering schools today between 40 and 60 percent of the freshmen enrolled are project alums. Toyota and other employers are now also fast-tracking PLTW graduated into their technical training programs and skilled jobs.

Further reading

○ *Philanthropy* magazine article on the program's origins, philanthropyroundtable.org/topic/ excellence_in_philanthropy/building_tomorrows_engineers

○ Timeline, pltw.org/about-us/history/pltw-milestones

1997

REVOLVING FUNDS FOR BUILDING CHARTER SCHOOLS

The Charter Schools Development Corporation was founded in 1997 as a philanthropically funded nonprofit with a sole focus on addressing one of the most pressing obstacles to charter-school creation today: the difficulty of financing a campus. By offering direct loans, helping arrange commercial and public financing, providing loan guarantees, and other methods, the group has financed hundreds of school facilities, serving tens of thousands of students, in 26 states. The Daniels Fund and Kauffman Foundation, other donors, and private lenders have supplied millions of dollars of seed capital, much of which is recycled back to the CSDC in loan repayments, which then become available for offering to the next generation of schools. This successful model of paying for the buildings needed by new charter schools is now also employed energetically by other nonprofits in different regions of the U.S., like Civic Builders (which works in the New York area with support from the NewSchools Venture Fund, the Gates, Dell, and Casey foundations, and others), Pacific Charter School Development (supported by some of the same donors, as well as the Ahmanson, Broad, Walton, Weingart, and Parsons foundations), and Building Hope (which backs facilities in the D.C. area). The Charter School Growth Fund also operates a Revolving Facilities Loan pool.

A recent addition to the field combines nonprofit and for-profit operations. Charter-school backer Andre Agassi founded a venture in 2011 to build campuses for charter schools around the country. The Turner-Agassi Charter School Facilities Fund combined money from Agassi and Turner Capital with funds from the Ewing Marion Kauffman Foundation and investments from banks. They are now in the process of building half a billion dollars of charter-school infrastructure over a several-year period, creating new slots for 35,000 students on 45 campuses. The fund uses its own money and design/build expertise to erect structures, playgrounds, etc. as specified by the charter partner, delivering turn-key properties that the school then pays off by pledging up to 20 percent of its per-pupil reimbursements once it is fully up and operating.

Further reading

○ Karl Zinsmeister, *From Promising to Proven* (The Philanthropy Roundtable, 2014)

1997

OLIN COLLEGE OF ENGINEERING

Franklin Olin didn't finish school, but he was mechanically gifted and sufficiently studious that at age 22 he passed the entrance exam for Cornell University, where he studied engineering. He proved to be a natural entrepreneur, and when Olin died in 1951 his bequest made his foundation one of the largest in the nation. For years, the F. W. Olin Foundation supported science and engineering projects; then the trustees decided to create a brand-new college to offer students Franklin Olin-style twists on engineering. The Olin College of Engineering, chartered in Needham, Massachusetts, in 1997, particularly aimed to make its engineers more creative, more entrepreneurial, more interdisciplinary and comfortable working in teams, and equipped with better communications skills. All of these elements were lacking in traditional engineering training.

The foundation committed $200 million to start the fledgling school—at the time a record in higher education. It located Olin adjacent to Babson College, one of the nation's top-ranked entrepreneurship schools, and 25 percent of Olin students are simultaneously taking classes at Babson or nearby Wellesley College. To help produce a culture of change and innovation, faculty members are untenured. Only 16 percent of applying students are admitted, and 41 percent of alums go on to advanced study. Olin graduates soon ranked among the top winners of National Science Foundation graduate fellowships and Fulbright scholarships.

When it closed its doors for good in 2005, the Olin Foundation transferred the balance of its endowment—over $250 million—to the college. With a total of $460 million in gifts from its founder, the college gives all students a half-tuition scholarship. Olin's fresh approach to engineering has inspired wide interest and imitation. More than 50 universities send observers to the campus annually. Nine are now revising their programs along Olin's lines. At the University of Illinois at Urbana-Champaign, all engineering freshmen have begun following a program that borrows from Olin courses.

Could these changes have been triggered without creating a new privately funded model college? The college's founding president, Richard Miller, is doubtful. "The National Science Foundation spent around $100 million over 10 years to provoke this kind of change on large campuses in the 1990s. After five or six years, they ended it—concluding that its penetration into universities was disappointing…. I view Mr. Olin as a great example…. He was an entrepreneur, he was educated as an engineer, and he was motivated to do things to create opportunities for others. We are doing all that we know how to do to inspire the graduates of Olin to follow along that path."

Further reading

○ *Philanthropy* magazine article, philanthropyroundtable.org/topic/excellence_in_
   philanthropy/new_u

1997

THE NEW TEACHER PROJECT

Starting with the premise that nothing has a greater influence on a school's success than the quality of teachers, The New Teacher Project (later known simply as TNTP) was founded in 1997 by Michelle Rhee, and then run by her for ten years until she became school chief in the District of Columbia. The organization's original mission was to help large urban school districts recruit, train, and hire new teachers who could get classroom results, particularly in hard-to-fill specialties like special-ed and math. The group still does this, through its TNTP Academy, which has so far recommended to districts nearly 3,000 teacher hires. Over the years, TNTP has increasingly focused on drawing into the teaching profession talented candidates from nonconventional backgrounds.

In 2000, TNTP established its own teaching-fellows program to groom accomplished professionals and recent college graduates who aren't certified as educators but have subject knowledge and talents to help high-need students. The program is extremely selective—only 8 percent of all applicants make it to the classroom. Recruits are particularly steered into the hardest-to-fill jobs: about 40 percent of TNTP Teaching Fellows go into special education, 15 percent teach science, 12 percent teach math, and 10 percent work in bilingual education. More than 32,000 unusually effective teachers have come out of the fellows program since its creation. With the growth and dramatic success of charter schools over the last decade, increasing numbers of TNTP recruits have been placed in charters.

Both the charters schools and the conventional districts that TNTP works with pay the group a fee for providing them with a highly qualified teacher, and this revenue stream covers about 70 percent of the group's expenses. The remainder of its annual budget comes from philanthropists such as the Carnegie Corporation and the Gates, Walton, and Schwab foundations. One of the things that donor money has made possible is TNTP's increasing role in analyzing systemic problems in public schooling and prescribing solutions. In a series of influential reports over the last few years, like 2009's "The Widget Effect," TNTP has dispensed advice on evaluating, compensating, and keeping or replacing teachers.

Further reading

◦ TNTP, tntp.org

◦ Karl Zinsmeister, *From Promising to Proven* (The Philanthropy Roundtable, 2014)

1996

HOME LIBRARIES FROM AN ENTERTAINER

The philanthropy of country-music singer Dolly Parton (much of it anonymous) has aimed mostly to help her neighbors in the middle South raise their level of education, and boost the economy of the region. She has provided college scholarships in her home county since the 1970s, and through her Dollywood Foundation offers incentives to reduce high-school dropout rates in the area.

Then in 1996, Parton launched an even earlier intervention: her Imagination Library. The goal was to capture young hearts and minds and teach children to love reading from infancy. The mechanism: allow any child to build his or her own collection of books by kindergarten, at no cost to the family. The program sends a child one book per month, every month, from birth until his or her fifth birthday. Parton began the Imagination Library in her home county of Sevier in east Tennessee, and explained in a 2006 interview with the *Washington Post* that she wanted to give children something that had been rare in her family. "My mother was married when she was in the seventh grade, so a lot of my people didn't get a chance to get an education. Imagination Library was born out of my need to try to help people, knowing what a handicap it was with a lot of my relatives."

The program quickly became enormously popular, and Parton opened it beyond Tennessee in 2000, offering to replicate the library in any community willing to help support it financially. The service is now active in 1,600 locales, sending books to nearly 700,000 children every month. Every year now, the Imagination Library puts millions of books into the hands of preschool children in the United States, Canada, and the United Kingdom.

Further reading

○ *Philanthropy* magazine reporting, philanthropyroundtable.org/topic/excellence_in_ philanthropy/a_road_trip_across_philanthropic_america3

1994

TARGETING FIRST-GENERATION COLLEGE CANDIDATES

There are many students with high academic potential growing up in families that lack the means or confidence to steer their child toward a top college. Of the 30,000 low-income students who score at least 1300 on the SAT every year, only one out of five apply to even a single selective college. Over the last generation, a bevy of philanthropic organizations has grown up to identify these high-potential students, show them how to apply to elite institutions, and help them succeed once enrolled.

One of the older and larger examples is QuestBridge, founded in 1994 in the Bay Area as an outgrowth of one-to-one mentoring that a University of California, San Francisco medical student and his friends were offering to local low-income students. The program grew quickly and now offers a variety of summer programs, campus visits, application-counseling, and ultimately four-year full scholarships for students who are matched to 35 participating colleges like Stanford, Harvard, Emory, Rice, and Columbia. Yale, for instance, had about 200 QuestBridge scholars on campus in 2014, with plans to take even more in the future.

QuestBridge prepares about 3,000 students each year, mostly first-in-the-family-to-college, then matches the top 500 to an admission with a full scholarship at one of its partner colleges. "It's like a national admissions office" for capable students who would otherwise never show up on top campuses, summarizes Vassar College president Catharine Bond Hill.

Other nonprofit programs like Posse (see 1989 entry nearby), the Daniels Scholars, the Opportunity Network, and the Gates Millennium Scholars (see 1999 entry) provide similar services. There are also many programs run by specific colleges or companies that target students in their local area. Most of these combine counseling, summer boot camps, large scholarships, mentoring, and internships (made available by thousands of companies). Donors are legion, from the Daniels Fund to the Packard, Hewlett, George Roberts, Charles Hayden, and Hecksher foundations, among many others.

Further reading

◦ QuestBridge Home, questbridge.org

◦ Daniels Scholars Program, danielsfund.org/Scholarships/Index.asp

◦ Opportunity Network, opportunitynetwork.org/about-us/vision

1993

ANNENBERG CHALLENGE

In the early 1990s it was easier for well-meaning observers to assume that the failures in American public education might be undone with just a little more effort and spending within established educational channels. Publisher Walter Annenberg had an interest in national service, but little appetite for philosophical or political boat-rocking. When he offered a large sum of money and a challenge to the nation from the White House with President Clinton at his side in 1993, he assumed his $500 million plus a bit of goodwill and social engineering could nudge American public schooling into new effectiveness. At the time, and to this day, his grant was the largest ever to public education. After being matched by partner contributions the Annenberg Challenge came to $1.1 billion of special spending for the recipient public schools.

The challenge operated through 18 entities touching a total of 35 states. At each site, leadership groups distributed grants ranging from $1 million to $53 million, with additional public support often supplementing these funds. The Chicago program (which was run by Barack Obama, following a plan written by Bill Ayers) put $49 million into pet projects. The Boston program spent $10 million on a Boston Plan for Excellence that promised vaguely to improve educational practices in classrooms.

A lack of critical perspective and an unwillingness to take on the educational establishment's sacred cows, however, ultimately prevented the huge effort from yielding any measurable progress. The assessment study on the Chicago program, for instance, reported that "findings from large-scale survey analyses, longitudinal field research, and student achievement test score analyses reveal that...there is little evidence of an overall Annenberg school improvement effect. Any improvements were much like those occurring in demographically similar non-Annenberg schools." Indeed, classroom behavior and other measures were actually worse after the Annenberg experiments.

This costly disappointment motivated subsequent education-reform donors to be more demanding of hard measures on student progress, instead of simple tallies of inputs like additional spending and teachers. And it encouraged donors to focus on system change, rather than just pouring funds into more of the same in conventional public schools.

Further reading

○ Fordham Institute appraisal, edexcellence.net/sites/default/files/publication/pdfs/annenberg_6.pdf

1992

ROWAN UNIVERSITY

Started in 1923 as a two-year teacher's college in southern New Jersey, Rowan University is today home to 14,000 students, and one of only 56 institutions in the country granting full degrees in engineering, business, education, and medicine. Its unlikely rise was propelled by Henry Rowan's 1992 donation of $100 million—at that point the largest gift ever offered to a public college.

Having grown up amid the Depression, during which his family lost all of its money and his parents divorced, Rowan later recorded in his autobiography that his mother embedded within him "a doctrine of thrift and self-reliance" and "an inner drive that has no off switch." After service in World War II as a B-17 pilot he completed an electrical engineering degree at MIT, then started work at a big company that made metal-melting furnaces. Finding the managers unresponsive to his suggested improvements, he sold his family home, moved into a rental, and used the equity to start his own business, building its first furnace in his cellar and backyard.

Eventually Rowan's Inductotherm Industries became a multihundred-million dollar company, but he and his wife, Betty, continued to shop carefully, drive older American cars, and live simply. In the early 1990s, Glassboro

State College, an undistinguished school near Rowan's home, asked for a small contribution. He took a liking to some of the ambitious administrators and students and told them, "We should be teaching people how to build things, how to create real wealth, real jobs. Maybe we should be talking about industrial engineering, not business administration." He eventually offered the college $100 million on the condition that it establish an excellent engineering school. Glassboro obliged, and made a decision to change its name to Rowan University to boot. Thus began a meteoric rise that yielded a chemical-engineering program ranked third in the country (which feeds graduates to employers across the region), the first new medical school in New Jersey in more than a generation, and solid technical education in a range of fields.

"I give MIT a little every year for a scholarship program," Rowan explained later, but "MIT has billions of dollars stashed away," whereas in south Jersey his donation made a huge difference. "It turned out marvelously," Rowan concluded, while nonetheless keeping his business and philanthropic contributions in perspective: "We have 5,000 employees.... We've been averaging $200 million a year in sales in New Jersey. Over the years, we've probably paid out $3 billion in salaries and expenditures locally. That's worth far more to south Jersey than even $100 million to the college."

Further reading

o Profile in *Rowan* alumni magazine, rowanmagazine.com/assets/pdfs/1997/spring/henryrowan.pdf

o History of Rowan University, rowan.edu/open/subpages/about/history

1992

MATH AND SCIENCE FOR ALL

In 1992, three local college professors decided to try to improve high-school science and math in the New Orleans region. Enlisting business and civic supporters to their cause, they opened the New Orleans Center for Science and Math (known as SciHigh) as a half-day program that students from any area public school could access. Without any preselecting or testing of its students, the school is one of the few completely open science and math academies in the country.

The program's focus was underserved students, particularly African Americans. Its backers believed that most students could master high-level science, technology, engineering, and math if taught by knowledgeable and demanding teachers. Students quickly proved them right, and 12 successful years followed.

After Hurricane Katrina, the center reopened as a full-time charter school—the New Orleans Charter Science and Mathematics High School. Three quarters of its students are African-American, and a similar number qualify for free or reduced-price lunches. Fully 97 percent of these students pass the science section of the state exit exam in their first sitting, and 95 percent do so on the math section. The school offers ten A.P. classes (the most of any open-admission New Orleans school), and 80 percent of all seniors are enrolled in at least one. Its student body of 400 boasts a 93 percent graduation rate.

Further reading

○ SciHigh, noscihigh.org

1992

JSTOR MAKES GOOD RESEARCH ACCESSIBLE

For millions of college students across the world, the digital database of academic journal articles known as JSTOR (for "Journal STORage") is a central part of their educational experience. As pervasive as it has become in college research and coursework, however, JSTOR is a relatively recent creation, the offspring of a collaboration between a philanthropic foundation and a leading public university. Devised by William Bowen, then president of the Andrew Mellon Foundation and former president of Princeton University, the impetus for JSTOR was the seemingly endless expense of buying and shelving in college libraries hundreds of specialized journals. After attending a college board of trustees meeting in which he was presented with a $5 million pricetag for new facilities to store back-issues of scholarly journals, Bowen became convinced that there had to be a better way to provide access to the materials academic libraries need.

The Mellon Foundation enlisted the University of Michigan, where a smaller project had begun to enable universities to access scientific journals via an electronic database. The foundation's funding began with a $700,000 grant to develop the requisite software, followed by an additional $1.5 million for production. Over the five-year launch period, the Mellon Foundation provided $5.2 million for the project.

The foundation decided early on that JSTOR needed to be an independent organization, and it was launched as such in 1995. Two years later, after Bowen had negotiated licensing rights with an initial batch of journal publishers, and the team at Michigan had digitally archived the back issues, JSTOR went public. Almost immediately the database saved educational institutions hundreds of millions of dollars in library and storage costs. JSTOR has also made it possible for students in developing countries to have access to a wealth of knowledge that hitherto would have been beyond their financial reach. Recently, the organization began working with academic publishers on way to provide libraries with cheaper and wider access to books as well.

Further reading

○ Roger Schonfeld, *JSTOR: A History* (Princeton University Press, 2003)

PAT ROONEY AND EDUCATIONAL CHOICE

In 1991, insurance executive Patrick Rooney established the CHOICE Trust, a first-of-its-kind program to provide vouchers enabling low-income parents in Indianapolis to send their children to private or parochial schools. Families could qualify to have half the cost of tuition covered. Seeded by a gift from Rooney, the Trust was also supported by other philanthropic foundations and corporations. In the three days following its creation, the CHOICE program received over 600 applications, and 900 more poured in over ensuing months. The startling demand from Indianapolis parents led the trust to expand the number of vouchers it funded in its first year from 500 to 744. As the program continued to grow in size and popularity, it widened eligibility to include parents outside of Indianapolis, bringing educational choice to a greater proportion of Indiana families. Rooney's program is credited with inspiring the creation of similar voucher organizations across the country, with one estimate putting the number of successor groups at over 100. Since its founding, the trust has provided more than $20 million in tuition support for Indiana children.

Further reading

○ Rooney remembrance in *The American Spectator*, spectator.org/articles/42742/pat-rooney-rip

WALTON FAMILY FOUNDATION'S SUPPORT FOR CHARTER SCHOOLS

The Walton Family Foundation was founded in 1991, the same year that Minnesota passed the nation's first law establishing charter schools. The two innovations soon prospered in tandem, but only after some trial and error. After the foundation's early educational grants yielded disappointing results, John Walton concluded that empowering parents to choose among meaningful alternatives would be the best way to encourage excellent education. Schools would strive for the "business" of more parents, resulting in the long run in more successful institutions catering to a wider range of students. Under the status quo, he warned, "money in education comes

EDUCATION

from the top, filters its way down, and various interest groups and factions pull off their share into what they think is important. The customers at the bottom just take what they're given." If the customers are offered options, he believed, the incentives for educational improvement will be much stronger.

The foundation's grantmaking strategy was rebuilt around these convictions. A centerpiece was support for charter schools—which bring decentralized management to public education, and allow parents to select schools instead of being assigned to them. Since 1996 when its charter-school funding began, Walton has given grants to fully one out of every four charter-school startups in the U.S. The foundation has also been a crucial supporter of organizations that help charters find buildings, organizations that raise standards of charter-school performance, and organizations that monitor and enforce charter quality.

The Walton Foundation's focus on helping charters flourish—and on encouraging school choice generally, and bold educational reform as a whole—has made it the national leader in bringing excellence and choice to families in neighborhoods that have been poorly served by conventional schools. Walton's total giving to education reform exceeds a billion dollars, with the pace accelerating in the past few years, and the funding heavily focused on low-income and minority children.

Further reading

○ Duke case study, cspcs.sanford.duke.edu/sites/default/files/descriptive/charter_schools_
funding.pdf

○ *New York Times* report, nytimes.com/2014/04/26/us/a-walmart-fortune-spreading-
charter-schools.html

1990

TEACH FOR AMERICA

In 1989, a Princeton undergraduate named Wendy Kopp wrote a thesis proposing a new elite corps that would give teaching an urgency, prestige, and national mission similar to military or other service work. She suggested that with the right combination of challenges and stiff demands, thousands of recent graduates from America's very best colleges could be lured into teaching instead of jumping to law school or Wall Street or one of the high-paying professions where many of her peers traditionally headed. With $2.5 million of initial philanthropic backing (Ross Perot provided a crucial early gift of $500,000), Kopp managed to launch a working version of her idea the very next year, when 500 bright and earnest college graduates joined the first corps of Teach For America. By 2014, nearly 33,000 of the nation's best and brightest had signed on for a two-year TFA stint, instructing a total of more than 3 million children in some of our neediest schools.

TFA gets results. Its instructors "have a positive effect on high-school student test scores relative to non-TFA teachers," concluded an Urban Institute study in 2008, with this effect being "particularly strong in math and science." Mathematica Policy Research compared TFA teachers and other teachers in the same school, and found that randomly assigned students made about an extra month's worth of progress on math when they had a TFA instructor. In 2011, 90 percent of principals who work with TFA teachers expressed high levels of satisfaction with their work, with a majority saying their training made them more effective than graduates of conventional teacher colleges.

The ultimate compliment is that TFA instructors are prized. When the KIPP network was pioneering its highly successful school formula, about two thirds of the people they hired as school leaders were TFA alumni; even today a full third of KIPP teachers come out of TFA. In difficult inner-city neighborhoods that are hard to staff, conventional public schools also rely heavily on TFA teachers, particularly in areas like math and science, special ed, and bilingual instruction. More generally, much of the education reform movement today is being built by alumni of TFA.

Schools across the country would hire even more TFA corps members except that demand outstrips supply. This despite a doubling in the size of the program over the last five years—to a budget of over $250 million and more than 6,000 new incoming corps members annually. TFA has managed to grow rapidly without lowering its standards: in 2013 the program accepted only 11 percent of 57,000 applicants. Its cachet among talented young people is such that as much as 10-15 percent of the senior classes at colleges like Harvard, Spelman, Berkeley, and Yale have sought to enter the corps in some recent years. Looking at TFA's alumni from its inception, about 30 percent are still teaching, and two thirds are working in education full-time or pursuing further studies in the field. The 50,000 corps members and alumni have become a key constituency for elevating standards across many corners of the U.S. schooling system.

The philanthropic support that has powered TFA from the beginning has soared along with its enrollments. Don Fisher recognized in the early 1990s that a shortage of qualified reform-minded teachers could become a serious constraint on growth of the highly effective new charter schools that he and other donors were then sprouting across the country. So the Fisher Fund donated a total of $100 million to TFA during its first two decades. At TFA's twentieth anniversary, the Broad, Arnold, and

Robertson Foundations, plus Steve and Sue Mandel, each provided $25 million to a create a long-term endowment for the organization. Steady attacks from teacher unions and apologists for the educational status quo in inner cities have reduced student enrollments in recent years. But support from philanthropists remains robust—including $50 million from the Walton Foundation in 2015.

Further reading

○ Teach For America, teachforamerica.org/our-organization

○ *Philanthropy* magazine 2005 interview with Don Fisher, philanthropyroundtable.org/topic/excellence_in_philanthropy/mass-producing_excellence

1989

POSSE FOUNDATION

Posse has a simple mission: create social supports at top colleges to reduce dropout rates among students from poor urban neighborhoods. Although many elite colleges are anxious to have low-income and minority students on their campuses, they find it difficult to keep them in school. Even when provided with generous scholarship packages, students from these backgrounds often fail to complete their degrees. The missing supports, founder Debbie Bial realized, were social.

So Posse now works with universities to identify, in each of its ten operating cities, groups of ten high-potential high-school seniors who might not otherwise consider that top-flight university. Rather than bringing them in as isolated enrollees, Posse recruits them as a group (or posse) to undergo together eight months of training in teamwork, academics, and leadership before they enroll together at one of the foundation's partner universities—where each will be guaranteed a full scholarship. Once enrolled on campus, members of the posse continue to meet, offering each other support. They also receive weekly mentoring from Posse liaisons throughout their four years of undergraduate study. And as they approach graduation, Posse provides them with internship opportunities, an alumni network, and career counseling.

Multiple posses are pulled together in each city most years. As of 2015, Posse had sent 275 students to 53 top-tier colleges, secured $806 million in scholarships for those students, and graduated them at a rate of 90 percent. In recent years the foundation has added similar programs to help recently returned veterans succeed at elite colleges, and to support students majoring in demanding STEM fields (science, technology, engineering, or math). In addition to the tuition waivers contributed by the participating colleges,

Posse has been fueled by private donations—hundreds every year from smaller donors, as well as major gifts like the $60 million offered by the Ubben family.

Further reading

○ About Posse, possefoundation.org/about-posse

○ Thomas Meyer, *Serving Those Who Served* (The Philanthropy Roundtable, 2013)

1986

BRADLEY FOUNDATION
PUTS SCHOOL CHOICE ON THE MAP

Education policy doesn't change overnight; it must be nurtured until its moment arrives. The organization that did most to incubate America's expanded interest in school choice was the Lynde and Harry Bradley Foundation. In 1986, Bradley allocated $75,000 to fund the writing of an influential book by education scholars John Chubb and Terry Moe that laid out clear empirical data in support of increased parental options in schooling. After its publication, Bradley provided an additional $300,000 to distribute the book widely. In its home state, Bradley was also instrumental in founding the Wisconsin Policy Research Institute, a think-tank that concentrated on education policy in its early years. Bradley also provided other infrastructure that helped the state of Wisconsin create pioneering programs, beginning in 1990, that provided low-income parents with publicly funded vouchers they could use to send their children to private schools. In parallel, Bradley itself supported various privately funded scholarships for low-income students. These could be used not only at private but also at religious schools.

As interest in vouchers and better choices in schooling soared in Wisconsin, demand began to outstrip the capacity of private schools. So in 1995 the legislature also added religious schools to the options available to parents. A lawsuit was brought against the state program alleging that this was an unconstitutional establishment of religion. When an injunction against the vouchers threatened the academic careers of several thousand Milwaukee children already enrolled in voucher schools, the Bradley Foundation stepped in with a million dollars to fund their tuition while the legal maneuvering proceeded. Bradley also put up close to a million dollars over a period of years to defend the program in court. After long battling, this ultimately resulted in two landmark wins before the Wisconsin Supreme Court, upholding the choice program and allowing its extension to religious schools in 1998. In 2002 the U.S. Supreme Court concurred that school-choice programs are constitutional even if parents use them to send their children to religious schools.

The demand for private- and religious-school vouchers in Milwaukee, so great that there were again no slots left in participating schools by 2001, next spurred Bradley to offer a $20 million grant to increase the capacity of the participating schools. The resulting expansions allowed schools to accept additional students, and ensured that Milwaukee parents had not just theoretical educational choices for their children but real ones. By the 2015 school year, Milwaukee families could choose from either their local public school or one of 122 private and religious schools participating in the city's Parental Choice Program. Nearly 30,000 Milwaukee children attended one of the voucher schools. Counterpart programs had been created in Racine (20 schools) and statewide (98 more private and religious schools).

This great Milwaukee experiment powered by the Bradley Foundation was watched intently by advocates and opponents of school choice all across the country. It eventually spawned scores of other city and statewide scholarship programs. It also encouraged the formation of new public attitudes that allowed multiple forms of school choice, including the charter-school movement, to become mass phenomena.

Further reading

○ Wisconsin School Choice Programs, sms.dpi.wi.gov/choice_programs

○ John Miller, *How Two Foundations Reshaped America* (The Philanthropy Roundtable, 2003)

1984

HILLSDALE COLLEGE SHIFTS TO PRIVATE FUNDING

Founded in Michigan in 1844, Hillsdale College was built up in the early 1850s by hundreds of small private donations after professor and preacher Ransom Dunn rode more than 6,000 across the western frontier collecting funds to build a new hilltop campus. While eight out of ten American colleges founded before the Civil War would eventually close, this broad base of giving allowed Hillsdale to survive and prosper. Clear principles were central to Hillsdale's appeal to donors. It was the first American college to prohibit in its charter any discrimination based on race, religion, or sex. It was the second college in the U.S. to grant four-year liberal arts degrees to women. It was a force for the abolition of slavery. During the Civil War, 400 Hillsdale students fought for the Union, a higher level of participation than from any other western college.

In the 1970s Hillsdale refused on philosophical grounds to comply with demands from the U.S. Department of Health, Education, and Welfare that it count its student body by race. Courts ruled that because students brought federal student aid to the college, it must submit to any federal requirement. In response, Hillsdale announced that as of the 1984 school year it would withdraw from all forms of federal assistance. A few years later Grove City College took the same course for the same reason. In 2007, Hillsdale also stopped accepting funds from the state of Michigan, again to guard its independence of action.

To replace government aid and provide similar scholarship assistance to students, Hillsdale launched major efforts to raise private funds nationally. Today Hillsdale brings in approximately $50 million in donations every year, with private funding and investment income exceeding tuition and other revenues remitted by students, and zero reliance on public funds.

Further reading

○ Hillsdale brief history, hillsdale.edu/about/history

1982

EDUCATIONAL EXCELLENCE NETWORK

In 1982, a dozen or so education scholars devoted to high standards, choices for families, and accountability for schools and teachers met at Columbia Teachers College and resolved to assemble themselves into a kind of reform network. The Andrew Mellon and John Olin foundations provided initial funding, and the Educational Excellence Network crystallized as a kind of floating think tank that, over a period of decades, operated under the wing of a succession of nonprofits: first Columbia, then Vanderbilt University, next the Hudson Institute, and finally the Thomas Fordham Foundation. Many donors aroused by the underperformance of U.S. public schools eventually became supporters of what is now known as the Thomas Fordham Institute. These included foundations like Koret, Templeton, Joyce, Kauffman, Helmsley, Kern, Hume, Hertog, GE, CityBridge, Schwab, Carnegie, Searle, and Bloomberg. During its more than three decades of existence the network has produced or influenced many consequential research studies and conferences, from E. D. Hirsch's *Cultural Literacy*, to the book *What Do Our 17-Year-Olds Know?*, to much sharp and influential commentary posted on Fordham's website and blogs.

Further reading

○ Informal history of Educational Excellence Network, edexcellence.net/farewell-and-hello-again-finns-last-stand

○ Thomas Fordham Institute home, edexcellence.net

1981

KEEPING PHONICS IN THE READING MIX

For reasons that are hard to fathom, phonics (teaching children to understand the relationship between word sounds and various letters or groups of letters) became controversial with "progressives" at many teacher colleges about a generation ago. As a result, new readers today often never learn the relationship between words they hear and what they see on paper. The National Council on Teacher Quality reported in 2013 that only 18 percent of teacher-prep colleges offer all of the components of good reading programs, with phonics awareness being the main oversight.

A number of philanthropists have tried to compensate for this blind spot in teacher education. In 1997, for instance, David Packard committed tens of millions of dollars to develop and expand reading curricula that included phonetic tools, then absent from most of the instructional guidelines used in his home state of California. The donor who has perhaps been most enduring in resisting the abandonment of phonics instruction is Sandra Rose. Widow of New York City real-estate magnate Frederick Rose, and a major donor to educational causes generally, Rose founded the Reading Reform Foundation in 1981, and has since funded (along with other donors like the Leir and Skirball foundations) its work providing intensive training and classroom support to reading teachers in the New York metro region.

More than 20,000 teachers and principals have benefited from the foundation's assistance. Twice a week throughout the school year, 30 foundation employees and consultants offer expert assistance in New York City-area public schools. Training one teacher (which includes 120 hours of expert visits to her classroom over the course of a year) costs RRF $15,000, of which $12,000 is subsidized by foundation donors, while $3,000 is charged to the school.

In 2012, Rose and a co-author published a book outlining the foundation's successful phonics methods so they can be copied by other schools and organizations across the country. Rose also provided a $1.2 million grant to Manhattanville College in 2013 to establish a literacy institute that will instruct the nearly 800 students in its School of Education in practical integration of phonics into effective reading instruction.

Further reading

○ About the Reading Reform Foundation, readingreformny.org/about

○ Manhattanville College press release, mville.edu/news-a-events/press-releases/4863-12-million-gift-to-manhattanville-continues-sandra-priest-roses-history-of-giving-to-education.html

────────── 1981 ──────────

"I HAVE A DREAM" SCHOLARSHIPS

Eugene Lang attended the East Harlem elementary school P.S. 121 back in the 1930s. He went on to Swarthmore College on a scholarship, and then Columbia and Brooklyn Polytechnic for additional studies. His education helped him become wealthy running manufacturing businesses. After agreeing to speak to graduating sixth graders at P.S. 121 in 1981, he arrived intending to tell them that with enough hard work they could be as successful as he had been. Then just before he spoke the principal pointed out that, as a statistical matter, a majority of the students he would be addressing were unlikely to graduate from high school. Improvising his commencement speech on the spot, Lang told the 61 assembled sixth graders and their families that if they successfully completed high school, he would personally cover their college tuition costs. Invoking Martin Luther King Jr.'s "I Have a Dream" Speech, which he had seen delivered in 1963, Lang encouraged the students to aim high with the knowledge that financial obstacles would not obstruct their education.

When the high-school graduation date of the P.S. 121 "Dreamers" drew near, Lang's promise attracted wide public attention. He had hired a coordinator to support the children he addressed, and more than 80 percent eventually earned diplomas, with 32 children pursuing higher education, and almost all acquiring fulfilling jobs. To spread his promise beyond East Harlem, Lang established the "I Have a Dream" Foundation in 1986. It has provided tuition assistance to more than 15,000 students through 200 affiliates in 29 states. Lang's total gifts to education exceed $150 million. His experiences inspired many other philanthropic acts, including financier Paul Tudor Jones's creation in 1988 of the extraordinarily successful New York City charity known as the Robin Hood Foundation.

Further reading

○ *New York Times* report, nytimes.com/1985/10/19/nyregion/about-new-york-one-man-s-gift-college-for-52-in-harlem.html

○ History, "I Have a Dream" Foundation, ihaveadreamfoundation.org/html/history.htm

1974

OLIN BRINGS LAW AND ECONOMICS TO CAMPUS

Among the most significant intellectual revolutions of America's twentieth century is the so-called Law and Economics movement. Pioneered at the University of Chicago, this school of thought has injected market disciplines and knowledge into the making of legal and regulatory policy. In the process, notes distinguished legal scholar Michael McConnell, it "has profoundly affected the way we think and talk about law."

It is highly doubtful that the new scholarship would have taken root as it has absent the dedicated support of the John M. Olin Foundation. A scientist and successful business-builder, Olin viewed market mechanisms as important guarantors of both efficiency and equity. His foundation began funding scholarships to promote economic logic, then eventually concentrated on a methodical and focused effort to underwrite professors committed to a new synthesis of economic principles and jurisprudence, at some of the country's top colleges and universities. All told, Olin contributed about $50 million to support Law and Economics scholarship within law schools, and an additional $20 million to underwrite individual research and special programs.

One specialized Olin-funded program offered economics training for judges. By 2015 4,000 sitting judges had participated in these seminars, including a very large portion of all top federal jurists. A typical institute for judges might include 21 hours of lectures over a several-day period, plus about 500 pages of required reading on economic issues and their relevance in the courtroom. This has helped familiarize the judiciary with the complexities of economic regulation and related issues, and has had a remarkable influence in introducing high-level economic reasoning into legal decisionmaking in America.

Further reading

- John Miller, *How Two Foundations Reshaped America* (The Philanthropy Roundtable, 2003)
- Duke case study, cspcs.sanford.duke.edu/sites/default/files/descriptive/revolutionizing_legal_discourse.pdf
- Law and Economics Center at George Mason University, masonlec.org/about/history

CHILDREN'S TELEVISION WORKSHOP

By the time he endowed the Carnegie Corporation of New York in 1911, Andrew Carnegie had already given away some $43 million and started five charitable organizations. But he was 76 years old, and the day-to-day strain of managing his own philanthropy was getting to him. After consultation with friends, he gave $125 million to start a trust to distribute funds in his name. Additional sums were transferred upon his death.

One of the Carnegie Corporation's lasting achievements was in the area of children's television. In the 1960s, the trust began exploring whether television could be used as an instrument for education of the young. It allocated funds for TV producer Joan Clooney to explore, through interviews with medical and learning professionals, the possible viability of educational broadcasting. Her study suggested there was promise, but the multimillion-dollar costs of actually producing high-quality programming led Carnegie to seek out partners who could help it explore the idea further. The Ford Foundation eventually stepped forward to add $1.25 million to the Carnegie Corporation's 1968 grant of $1 million. This in turn opened the door to contributions from the Corporation for Public Broadcasting and the Office of Education. And with these joint resources, the Children's Television Workshop was established.

The Children's Television Workshop inaugurated a new way of planning and making television shows—combining creative work by writers and directors with educator expertise, and drawing on the results of more than a thousand studies and lab experiments on how children absorb knowledge. When the new CTW program "Sesame Street" premiered in 1969, the Educational Testing Service was given a contract to measure its effect on child viewers.

A string of studies showed that watching "Sesame Street" mildly increases letter recognition, vocabulary, and other elements of school readiness of preschoolers. 1994 research funded by the Markle Foundation, another loyal "Sesame" funder, found that some positive effects lasted through adolescence. (Meanwhile, passive cartoon watching and much other "children's programming" turns out to have negative cognitive effects on the very young.) Today, "Sesame Street" is the most widely viewed children's TV series in the world, and the winner of more than 100 Emmy Awards, showing that television can be fun for children while, at least, avoiding harming them.

Further reading

○ Brief review of literacy and numeracy effects, sesameworkshop.org/what-we-do/our-results/literacy-numeracy

○ Duke case study, cspcs.sanford.duke.edu/sites/default/files/descriptive/childrens_television_workshop.pdf

1966

CARNEGIE SEMINAR ON THE COLEMAN REPORT

In 1966, the federal government published a major investigation into the effectiveness of schools (and how that intersects with race) which

᠊ᠣ PhilAphorism

Community is a consequence. It results when people come together to accomplish things that are important to them and succeed. People who are uninvolved cannot feel this connection.

☞ *Richard Cornuelle*

came to be known as the Coleman Report. As soon as it was released the report was understood to be important, but at more than 700 pages, with 650,000 students in its sample, its specifics were not quickly absorbed. To make sure it wasn't ignored, Harvard professor Daniel Patrick Moynihan obtained a grant from the Carnegie Corporation of New York to convene a yearlong seminar to dissect and analyze the findings. The Harvard Faculty Seminar attracted 75 prominent scholars as regular attendees at its twice-monthly meetings, and resulted in a book and many papers which cemented Coleman's key insights. First among these were that home environment and peer influences are far more important than schools in determining educational outcomes, and that when it comes to schools, the quantity of money or other inputs pumped in has little correlation with results.

"Up until that time, very little attention was paid to student outcomes. It was all about inputs," says Eric Hanushek, a Stanford economist who was an important participant in the Harvard Seminar. The Harvard/Carnegie dissection of the Coleman Report drove home that schools must be judged by what their enrollees actually learn—as revealed in testing data—not by spending or class size. This new perspective fired the next wave of school reform—and recognition that school management is more important than physical resources, and that the only changes of consequence are those that produce measurably different outcomes.

Further reading

○ Frederick Mosteller and Daniel Moynihan, *On Equality of Educational Opportunity* (Random House, 1972)

────────── 1961 ──────────

A GIFT TEACHES DONORS
NOT TO WRITE BLANK CHECKS

In 1961, Charles and Marie Robertson anonymously gave Princeton University $35 million to create programs at its Woodrow Wilson School for Public Policy and International Affairs that would "strengthen the government of the United States and increase its ability and determination to defend and extend freedom throughout the world by improving the facilities for the training and education of young men and women for government service." At the time, it was the largest grant ever bestowed upon a single university, and by 2008 the donated assets were worth more than $900 million.

Within five years, the Robertsons were unhappy with Princeton. They did not like the direction or results at the Woodrow Wilson School, and had come to believe that Princeton accepted the donation without really intending to pursue its stated purposes. In 2002 the family brought suit, contending that the university had never been serious about honoring the Robertsons' goals, and instead spent the funds however it chose. Just before the case went to trial in 2009 the two parties reached a settlement which saw Princeton paying all the legal bills of the foundation while also returning about $50 million to the Robertson family. This case reinforced for donors, and also recipients, the importance of clearly spelling out the intent behind a gift—whenever possible with concrete and measurable results—and making sure that both parties are committed to the mission.

Further reading

○ Reporting on settlement in the *Chronicle of Philanthropy*, philanthropy.com/article/ PrincetonRobertson-Family/62967

○ Review of case in *Philanthropy* magazine, philanthropyroundtable.org/topic/donor_intent/ benefits_of_a_gift_gone_wrong

1959

FORD FOUNDATION AID FOR INNER-CITY SCHOOLS

During the 1960s (and after), many liberal reformers became convinced that the best way to improve social outcomes in areas like schooling, crime and safety, employment, and family structure was not to work on specific weaknesses of those sectors, but rather to "rebuild communities" broadly by redistributing income and political power and providing wholly new physical vessels like public housing projects, school campuses, and large "urban renewal" projects. According to this materialistic and utopian view, most of the problems visible in social life would heal and brighten when people were shifted into new structures and social forms engineered by technocrats, via root-and-branch "community redevelopment."

In 1959 the Ford Foundation launched one of the first major education reforms based on this view—its "Great Cities School Project," which aimed to turn the test cities of Boston, Oakland, New Haven, Philadelphia, and Washington, D.C. into laboratories for duplication elsewhere. Almost instantly, the staff decided they couldn't improve inner-city schools unless they first remade the inner city, so they created new "community action agencies" charged with funneling social-welfare aid in multiple forms into the test cities. Very soon the foundation decided that this too was insufficient. Even more comprehensive "urban renewal" was needed—which led to razing whole city blocks and construction of new "affordable housing" and "planned economic development" projects.

Jane Jacobs and other observers later pointed out that these enormously intrusive interventions only left poor people more disrupted and unsettled. Neither the Great Cities project nor other forms of "urban renewal" produced any positive outcomes or support from the populations affected, in spite of the large sums poured into these efforts by Ford, allied philanthropies, and various levels of government. (Spending in the first few years by the Ford Foundation alone exceeded $200 million in current dollars.)

Tragically, the Johnson administration, in its fervor to launch a "War on Poverty" in the early '60s, seized on Ford's model as the handiest available mechanism for trying to remake the world from Washington. The five Ford pilots, started as mere school-improvement plans, were taken over and funded by the federal government's new Office of Economic Opportunity as the first elements of its "Community Action Program." Bulldozing of old city blocks, social engineering, and gushing welfare spending spiraled across the country.

Ford Foundation president McGeorge Bundy and the Great Cities architects—who had designed their efforts from the beginning as an "adjunct to government"—felt vindicated, and certain that the much bigger hammer wielded by the feds would bring the success that had eluded them. In inner-city schools and neighborhoods, however, there were almost no positive results. Instead, social and educational indicators would spiral downward over the next three decades in the neighborhoods being "revitalized."

Further reading

○ Robert Halpern, *Rebuilding the Inner City* (Columbia University Press, 1995)

○ Essay on Ford in the Inner City, ucsc.edu/whorulesamerica/local/ford_foundation.html

1959

OLMSTED SCHOLARS PROGRAM

Even the quintessential government responsibility of national defense turns out to have elements where private giving can solve needs more effectively than state action. Retired general and successful businessman George Olmsted identified just such a niche. His service during World War II had required many delicate cultural judgments and political negotiations with allies and opponents in the China-Burma-India-Japan theaters. He was, for instance, given responsibility for making sure that as the Japanese surrender neared the commandants of their prisoner-of-war camps did not slaughter American prisoners as a face-saving action under Japan's *bushido* martial code. Olmsted's elaborate culture-based solution included parachuting teams of seven unarmed men into each camp, who informed the Japanese commanders by name that they would be held personally responsible for the safety of all prisoners.

After becoming wealthy building a string of insurance companies and banks after the war, Olmsted and his wife formed a charitable foundation to deepen the international savvy and judgment of military leaders so they could better navigate the kinds of dilemmas he faced in wartime. General Olmsted focused his trust tightly on funding intensive overseas immersions of active-duty military officers in two years of foreign language and culture training. The program was later expanded to also support shorter foreign-study immersions by cadets at U.S. military academies and future officers in the ROTC program.

To date, 601 active-duty officers have done full two-year stints in more than 50 countries as Olmsted Scholars, becoming deeply familiar with the people, history, and institutions of strategic countries like China, Egypt, Poland, Russia, and Turkey. These have included men and women like John Abizaid, who spent two years learning Arabic and Arab culture at the University of Jordan as a young officer and Olmsted Scholar—skills that he later drew upon heavily as CentCom commander during the Iraq war.

Further reading

○ *Philanthropy* magazine reporting, philanthropyroundtable.org/topic/excellence_in_
philanthropy/spartan_donors

1955

FORD FOUNDATION'S SPECIAL APPROPRIATION

In 1955 the Ford Foundation announced an extraordinary "special appropriation" of $560 million—the equivalent of more than $5 billion in 2015—the largest single investment in the history of philanthropy—to strengthen America's private colleges and hospitals. The foundation's stated aims were to bolster educational salaries, help private colleges compete with state-subsidized universities, and improve medical education and services. Over an 18-month period, checks were sent to every one of the 615 accredited private colleges in the U.S., with the amount determined by the size of their 1954-55 payroll, adding bonuses for colleges that could demonstrate they were "a leader in raising teacher salaries." The University of Pennsylvania, for instance, received a grant of $2.7 million ($24 million in 2014 dollars). Checks were also written to every one of the country's private, nonprofit hospitals, with the sum determined by the number of births and patient-days they recorded in 1954. Commenting on the sum effect of Ford's massive gift, the president of Yale University characterized it as a "trailblazing action giving new strength to American education."

Further reading

○ Dwight MacDonald, *The Ford Foundation* (Reynal, 1956)

○ Report in the *Daily Pennsylvanian*, library.upenn.edu/docs/kislak/
  dp/1955/1955_12_13.pdf

FORD BOLSTERS BUSINESS EDUCATION

In mid-twentieth-century America, business was already a popular college major, at both the undergraduate and graduate levels. Even with one out of seven students on campus specializing in some form of business education, however, the quality and rigor of these programs was often low. To upgrade the discipline, the Ford Foundation committed $35 million over a 12-year period to support research, fellowships, conferences, and faculty training. The foundation's grantmaking was driven by three objectives: to place business education on firmer academic footing, to bring it into line with the needs of the American economy, and to increase its efficiency. Ford was particularly effective in fostering high-quality business-administration programs at elite colleges, infusing them with perspectives from economics, statistics, and political science. These programs were then emulated elsewhere. A signal accomplishment of the initiative was the Gordon-Howell report, which was influential in pushing business schools to raise standards of admission and develop rigorous, interdisciplinary curricula. By reinforcing the training offered to men and women managing productive entities, these investments fattened the output of the American economy.

Further reading

○ Duke University case study, cspcs.sanford.duke.edu/sites/default/files/descriptive/
  program_to_strengthen_business_education.pdf

○ John Thelin, *A History of American Higher Education* (Johns Hopkins University Press, 2011)

AREA STUDIES PROGRAMS

New U.S. responsibilities on the global stage after World War II brought needs for expertise in many exotic regions. To fill knowledge gaps that were handicapping policymakers, business executives, and other American leaders, foundations like Rockefeller, Carnegie, and Ford took steps to expand intensive study of critical areas such as the Soviet Union, Asia, and the Middle East. In addition to raising general levels of understanding, this increased the supply of Americans with the language skills and cultural knowledge to make good commercial, diplomatic, and military judgments about such regions. Rockefeller and Carnegie focused primarily on funding universities—establishing academic centers to study Russia at Columbia and Harvard, for instance. Ford focused in the beginning on individuals, providing $35 million of fellowships to students and established scholars over two and a half decades. As individual experts began to populate these fields, Ford funded institutional structures as well, beginning in 1960 with $15 million of grants to further "area studies" work on places like the Soviet Union, Eastern Europe, East Asia, and the Middle East. In 1961, Ford allocated $21 million to build programs at Indiana, Northwestern, Michigan, Notre Dame, Yale, Princeton, Washington, and other universities. This strengthened Ford's reputation for leading the nation into timely new academic disciplines at moments of need.

Further reading

○ Duke case study, cspcs.sanford.duke.edu/sites/default/files/descriptive/area_studies_
  programs.pdf

1949

EARHART FELLOWSHIPS

Harry Earhart expanded the White Star Oil Company into a large enterprise during the automobile revolution, then established the Earhart and Relm foundations. In 1949, the Earhart Foundation focused on deepening national understanding of the role of free-market economics in creating American prosperity and liberty. It did so by supporting individual thinkers, researchers, and writers. In the 1970s, the foundation expanded its purview beyond economics to include intellectuals working in the humanities, recognizing their centrality to the preservation and persistence of American success. Over the years, the foundation awarded more than 2,500 Earhart Fellowships to graduate students, in the process showing remarkable success in identifying nascent talent. Early recipients of Earhart support include Friedrich Hayek, Milton Friedman, George Stigler, James Buchanan, and others. Ronald Coase, Gary Becker, Thomas Sowell, Leo Strauss, and Peter Bauer were also supported by the foundation at critical junctures. The Earhart Fellows include six individuals who went on to win the Nobel Prize in economics. The foundation also provided grants for important research projects, and kept seminal books in print, for instance supporting publication of the *Collected Works of Eric Voegelin*.

Further reading

○ Harry Earhart profile in the Philanthropy Hall of Fame (see prior *Almanac* section)

○ History of the Earhart Foundation, firstprinciplesjournal.com/articles.
  aspx?article=561&theme=amexp&page=3&loc=b&type=ctbf

1944

UNITED NEGRO COLLEGE FUND

Originally formed to establish a reliable flow of donations to America's historically black colleges and universities, the United Negro College Fund later took on the added mission of distributing individual scholarships to minority students attending any college. The most important early supporter of the UNCF was John Rockefeller Jr., who became chairman and sat on its board until his death in 1960. He contributed $5,250,000 to the fund during his lifetime. The fund's largest single gift was a $50-million donation made in 1990 by philanthropist Walter Annenberg. In 2014, industrialist Charles Koch offered a $25-million gift to support entrepreneurship programs. In addition to appealing to large donors, the fund began in the 1970s to direct broad fundraising appeals to black Americans, especially graduates of the historically black colleges, and this became another major source of annual funding. Today, the fund supports 37 member colleges, while also awarding 10,000 scholarships and internships to needy students attending 900 different institutions of higher education. The UNCF has added Native-American, Hispanic, and Asian students to its target audience, a shift accelerated when it was named administrator of the

◁ PhilAphorism

I have always believed that most large fortunes are made by men…who tumbled into a lucky opportunity. Hard work and attention to business are necessary, but they rarely result in achieving a large fortune. Do not be fooled into believing that because a man is rich, he is necessarily smart. There is ample proof to the contrary.

        ☞ *Julius Rosenwald*

Gates Millennium Scholars program (see 1999 entry). Since its founding, UNCF has raised more than $3.6 billion in private donations to help over 400,000 students receive college degrees.

Further reading

○ Marybeth Gasman, *Envisioning Black Colleges* (Johns Hopkins University Press, 2007)

○ UNCF history, uncf.org/sections/WhoWeAre/SS_AboutUs/aboutus.asp

○ Rockefeller archive, rockarch.org/bio/jdrjr.php

JOHN BOWLBY AND CHILD PSYCHOLOGY

The seminal research and theory explaining the development of young children was formulated by a British psychiatrist named John Bowlby, whose career was built largely on American philanthropy. In the 1920s, the new Commonwealth Fund of New York, endowed by the Harkness family of Standard Oil fortune, was investing heavily in child welfare (see 1918 entry) in the U.S., and also in Britain. With a very substantial grant they established the biggest facility in London for treating the social and mental disorders of children, called the London Child Guidance Clinic. In 1936, John Bowlby was appointed there as a child psychiatry fellow, where he developed understanding of how deeply a child's personality is shaped by family interactions during the first years of life (an insight now taken as commonplace, but only because Bowlby and colleagues demonstrated it uncontestably).

Bowlby and other social workers developed stellar reputations during World War II for work they did in aiding war-disturbed children. In response, Britain passed an Education Act in 1944 requiring establishment throughout the country of child-guidance clinics like the one created by the Commonwealth Fund. Bowlby was invited to take over the children's department of the Tavistock Clinic, where medical treatment was paid for by the government health service (characterized by Bowlby as "stable, rigid, limiting") but the pioneering research was paid for by private funding ("unstable but it could do what it liked," as the grateful Bowlby commented).

To support his research on the effects of maternal deprivation on children, Bowlby received a small grant from a British foundation that allowed him to hire a social worker who did many of the nursery observation that became the grist for Bowlby's studies. A short time later, Bowlby won a grant from the Josiah Macy Foundation, a New York donor then focused on treating traumatic shock and other war-related disorders. This gift allowed him to bring in Mary Ainsworth, another pioneer of child-development theory whose collaborations with Bowlby established much of the central understanding of the field. (The Macy Foundation was simultaneously supporting animal-behavior researchers who Bowlby drew upon while formulating his theories.)

Then in 1957, Bowlby won philanthropic support "on a very big scale," as he put it, from the Ford Foundation. This sustained Bowlby's research through his most productive years. It in turn led to a grant from what was known as the Foundations' Fund for Research in Psychiatry (a pooling of money from three U.S. donors leading this area: the Ford, Woods Kalb, and William Grant foundations).

Private donor support thus allowed Bowlby to pull together pathbreaking research and assemble it into coherent explanations of how young children develop, why secure family life is so important to their future happiness and educability, and what can go wrong when well-meaning social interventions overlook family attachments. Fifty years later, Bowlby's central elaborations of child psychology are still the reigning wisdom.

Further reading

○ Oral history with John Bowlby, beyondthecouch.org/1207/bowlby_int.htm

1924

DUKE UNIVERSITY

Though his success in business took him far beyond the borders of his native state, James Duke never truly left North Carolina. The longtime owner of Southern Power, and American Tobacco, Duke made clear his fondness for his home region when he donated $40 million to the Duke Endowment in 1924. All giving was to concentrate on educational institutions, hospitals, orphanages, and Methodist churches in North and South Carolina. The largest share, 46 percent of the endowment, was designated to support education, and of this, $6 million was set aside for the creation of "an institution to be known as Duke University" in honor of his father.

"Education, when conducted along sane and practical, as opposed to dogmatic and theoretical, lines, is, next to religion, the greatest civilizing influence," wrote Duke. While his endowment could have been used to start a new school, Duke offered Trinity College, of which he had been a longtime supporter, the option of expanding into the wider mission he envisioned. Trinity accepted, adding schools of law, medicine, and divinity, building a new campus, and changing its name. Less than one year later Duke gave the university an additional $7 million to finish its bold expansion.

Duke was a careful and attentive donor, who enjoyed details like laying out the university grounds, and who left clear instructions and documentation for his endowment on precisely how to hoped to assist his region of birth. Of his college he said, "I want it to become a great university." And today it is, standing as a top-tier institution alongside schools that have been developing two or three times longer.

Further reading

○ James Duke profile in the Philanthropy Hall of Fame (see prior *Almanac* section)

○ *Philanthropy* magazine profile, philanthropyroundtable.org/topic/donor_intent/duke_of_carolina

1923

INTERNATIONAL EDUCATION BOARD

Two decades after his father founded the General Education Board (see 1902 entry), John Rockefeller Jr. set out to expand the reach of the family's education philanthropy. Having been involved in the expansion of the GEB from its initial focus on African-American education in the South to nationwide educational reforms, Rockefeller was positioned to go one step further and begin funding education overseas—which he began to do in 1923 when he founded the International Education Board.

Unlike the GEB, the IEB not only funded institutions but also individual scholars. Focusing mainly on science and agriculture, the board provided hundreds of fellowships, along with grants to organizations in 39 different countries. Notable projects included the 200-inch Mount Palomar telescope, to which the board contributed $1.4 million, $283,000 to support Niels Bohr's physics research that eventually assisted the American atomic bomb, $357,000 to establish a mathematics faculty at Göttingen, and $3 million for the University of Chicago's Oriental Institute. In all, John Rockefeller Jr. contributed more than $21 million to the International Education Board during its 15 years. The IEB concluded its work in 1938, when its remaining capital, programs, and personnel were folded into other Rockefeller projects.

Further reading

○ Rockefeller Archive Center, rockarch.org/bio/jdrjr.php

1921

CARNEGIE ENHANCES LEGAL EDUCATION

Early in the twentieth century, rising demand for legal services led to a sharp increase in the number of lawyers, and a perceived decline in the professional standards of many of these newly minted practitioners. It was clear that reform of some kind was needed, but there was no clear leadership. Into this breach stepped the Carnegie Foundation for the Advancement of Teaching (whose origins are described in our 1905 entry).

The foundation had previously sparked a dramatic upgrade of medical education by sponsoring an influential critique known as the Flexner Report. That led to years of thoroughgoing reform, including $94 million of spending at 25 medical schools by John Rockefeller's General Education Board. (See details at the 1910 entry of our Medical Achievements list.)

Seeking to repeat this feat in legal education, the Carnegie Foundation for the Advancement of Teaching initiated two critiques of American law schools. These, along with promptings from Elihu Root, a prominent lawyer and Carnegie trustee, caused the American Bar Association to endorse higher standards of training. The ABA also partnered with the American Association of Law Schools to form the American Law Institute, which used $2.1 million of Carnegie funding to create accessible archives of the authoritative interpretations of U.S. law. ALI became the leading curator of court decisions and assisted in the development of the U.S. Uniform Commercial Code.

Further reading

o Duke case study, cspcs.sanford.duke.edu/sites/default/files/descriptive/reforming_the_
legal_profession.pdf

1918

JOHN STERLING'S GOLDEN BEQUEST TO YALE

By the time John Sterling graduated from Yale in 1864, the university had left an indelible mark on him. Upon his death in 1918, three quarters of the corporate lawyer's fortune—accruing to $29 million by 1931—was donated to Yale to establish "at least one enduring, useful and architecturally beautiful building." The gift came as a surprise to the university, which years earlier had tried to solicit a donation from Sterling and failed.

Arriving as it did in the teeth of the Great Depression, Sterling's bequest went a long way, ultimately producing not one but a whole set of cornerstone buildings on the Connecticut campus—including Sterling Memorial Library, Sterling Law Building, Sterling Hall of Medicine, Sterling Chemistry Laboratory, the Hall of Graduate Studies, and other dorms and classrooms. Sterling's donation also provided for "scholarships, fellowships, or lectureships; the endowment of new professorships, and the establishment of special funds for prizes." There are now more than two dozen Sterling Professors at Yale, including some of the world's leading authorities in the fields of law, political science, and literature. Today Yale honors its large donors with the title Sterling Fellow, thus reproducing the namesake's practice of formative private giving.

Further reading

○ Summary in Yale library history, web.library.yale.edu/building/sterling-library/history

○ Review of Sterling biography, digitalcommons.law.yale.edu/cgi/viewcontent. cgi?article=5711&context=fss_papers

1918

MENTAL HYGIENE FOR CHILDREN

A $10 million gift from Anna Harkness, the wife of one of John Rockefeller's Standard Oil partners and a great advocate of civic improvement and self-help, established the Commonwealth Fund in 1918. Under the leadership of her son Edward Harkness, the foundation promoted understanding of child psychology, and improved services and teaching for children. (See, for instance, nearby 1936 entry on John Bowlby.) Its Program for the Prevention of Delinquency sought to identify troubled children and offer assistance before they fell into trouble with the law. Through its integration of child psychiatry and social work into schools, and its discovery that parental education was a key component in reducing adolescent delinquency, the fund used the public education system to improve family well-being and American social life.

Further reading

○ History of medical issues in 1920s schooling, jstor.org/discover/10.2307/368156?uid=3739584 &uid=2129&uid=2&uid=70&uid=4&uid=3739256&sid=21104123400653

○ Commonwealth Fund Archive, rockarch.org/collections/nonrockorgs/commonwealth.php

1917

DESERT EDUCATOR

There are few institutions that generate more affection in the hearts of donors than excellent small colleges. And no college in America is smaller, nor really more excellent, than Deep Springs, an idiosyncratic place nestled a mile above sea level in the California mountains. At any one time, Deep Springs is home to two dozen of the smartest young men in America, who are attracted by its offer of two years of intense academic study, hard ranch work for 20 hours per week, and practical lessons in communal cooperation—all 100 percent free. Its graduates usually go on to complete their degrees at top universities, and more than half of all attendees have ended up with doctoral degrees.

All this is precisely as Lucien Nunn intended. Nunn pioneered long-distance transmission of alternating electrical current, then made his

EDUCATION

fortune building power plants for mines across the American west. As he expanded his operations, he felt a keen need for hardworking, skilled men of independence and integrity. In response, Nunn purchased Deep Springs Ranch and set up a school there that melds esoteric book learning, outdoor labor, self-governance, and a dose of desert spirituality.

Nunn's vision is now being argued over, however. Deep Springs is one of only four remaining men's liberal-arts colleges in the country, and a majority of the trustees recently voted to go co-ed. Dissenting trustees remain convinced that Nunn's donor intent was for Deep Springs to remain all-male and that their job as trustees is to protect that intent. "Neither trustees nor courts have the authority to change or ignore a trust provision simply because they think it isn't optimal or preferable, even if the preference is based on their passionate moral beliefs," trustee Kinch Hoekstra told the *Atlantic*. "The great thing about the legal protection of charitable trusts over time is that we don't all have a bunch of institutions in 2013 that are wholly determined by what trustees happen to think in 2013. That would lead to an appalling homogenization of our cultural, social, and educational landscape. Instead, people set up different projects in 1880, or 1938, or 1972, and those visions, sometimes gloriously out of step with how we currently think and sometimes maddeningly so, may continue to thrive."

Further reading

○ Deep Springs College, deepsprings.edu

1917

LINCOLN SCHOOL AT COLUMBIA

For three decades, the Lincoln School at Columbia University's Teachers College was at the vanguard of experimental education. Teachers College was the country's most influential center for teacher training, and the Lincoln School provided a laboratory for the development of curricula and educational practices that the college would later incorporate into its educational program. The school was established with money from John Rockefeller's General Education Board and sustained by additional philanthropic donations. Rockefeller was sufficiently convinced of the efficacy of the Lincoln School to educate his sons there. The purpose of the school was "to construct a fundamental curriculum which will be representative of the important activities, interests, and possibilities of modern life." Organized and led by some of the leading educational thinkers of the time, including former Harvard president Charles Eliot, the school was a potent institutionalization of new ideas in education. It operated independently until 1941, when it was combined with the Horace Mann School, another experimental facility with close ties to Teachers College, eventually closing in 1946.

Further reading

◦ 1922 descriptive booklet, archive.org/stream/cu31924013400605#page/n1/mode/2up

ROSENWALD SCHOOLS

For his fiftieth birthday in 1912, Julius Rosenwald, president of Sears, Roebuck & Company, donated $650,000 to a group of charities. One of the gifts was $25,000 to Booker T. Washington to help expand the school Washington led, the Tuskegee Institute. After completing his promised expansion, Washington reported to Rosenwald that $2,100 remained, and he proposed to the donor that this balance be used to build six schools for African Americans in the rural area surrounding the institute. He carefully documented progress on the schools with photos and letters from local residents. Once these were up and running, the impressed Rosenwald allocated another $30,000 for Tuskegee to construct 100 more schools throughout Alabama.

Rosenwald was a stickler for matched local contributions from the families who would benefit from the schools, and then for proof that each academy was well staffed and operating effectively. Washington was equally punctilious in demonstrating the schools' concrete results. As Rosenwald realized how bereft of educational options most black families in the South were, and how effective his spartan schools were in serving communities that had previously been neglected, he caught the fever.

Over less than 20 years, the Rosenwald school-building program erected 4,977 rural schools and 380 companion buildings in almost every Southern locale with a substantial black population, at a total cost of $28.4 million. A major portion of the money Julius Rosenwald gave away during his lifetime (approaching $2 billion in current dollars) went into his self-organized school-building effort. In the process he put a deep constructive imprint on American society: At the time of his death in 1932, the schools Rosenwald built were educating fully 35 percent of all black students in the American South, and 27 percent of black American children as a whole.

Further reading

◦ Julius Rosenwald profile in the Philanthropy Hall of Fame (see prior *Almanac* section)

GEORGE EASTMAN PUTS
MIT AND ROCHESTER ON THE MAP

As founder of the camera manufacturing and supply company Eastman

Kodak, and the inventor of many of the central processes of modern photography, George Eastman was well acquainted with the rocketing importance in modern life of technical expertise. In the early dog-eat-dog days during the birth of photography, Eastman had gone to a little commuter school known as Boston Tech to hire crucial engineers on several occasions. When his business boomed, he returned the favor by anonymously donating $20 million, beginning in 1912, to create today's Massachusetts Institute of Technology. He built the university an entirely new campus, where it now resides, and launched its transformation into the world-leading educational institution it is now.

In his hometown of Rochester, New York, Eastman was even more munificent in building up the University of Rochester. He donated $51 million to the institution during his lifetime, creating its medical school among many other things, in the process vaulting it into the top tier of scientific and technical universities. Eastman also did more than any other American to improve dental education and medicine, and to bring oral health care to everyday people.

In addition to these contributions to technical education, Eastman single-handedly built one of the top schools of music in the world (see the 1921 entry on our companion list of Arts achievements). And, inspired by Julius Rosenwald, he became the largest contributor in the U.S. to the education of African Americans during the 1920s.

Further reading

∘ George Eastman profile in the Philanthropy Hall of Fame (see prior *Almanac* section)

1909

MILTON HERSHEY SCHOOL

Chocolatier Milton Hershey didn't invent the candy bar, but he was the first to transform it from expensive delicacy to treat affordable by all, and in the process he became very wealthy. He and his sickly wife, Kitty, were unable to have children, so they decided to give their sweet fortune to orphans and

◅ PhilAphorism

A bone to the dog is not charity. Charity is the bone shared with the dog, when you are just as hungry as the dog. ☞ *Jack London*

other needy boys living in hardscrabble—something Milton understood well, after a peripatetic childhood and education that ended at fourth grade, due to a drinking father who left his family for long periods of time. In 1909, Hershey signed over to his new Hershey Industrial School a fully operating 486-acre farm that included the homestead where he had been born. In 1918 he went much further, placing all of his shares in the Hershey Chocolate Company in a trust whose sole purpose was to benefit the school. He kept the transfer secret until it was revealed in a 1923 interview with the *New York Times*, when he explained that "I have no heirs, so I have decided to make the orphan boys of the United States my heirs." To this day, the school retains controlling interest in the Fortune 500 Hershey Company, the Hersheypark entertainment complex, and other businesses.

Right up until Milton Hershey's death in 1945 (at which point his only assets were his home and its furnishings, having given away everything else while he was still alive) he remained intimately involved in the running of the school. He made sure his boys (and now girls too) received very practical upbringings, "a thorough common-school education, supplemented by instruction in the useful crafts." He had three goals for every graduate: a vocation, a love of God and man, and a sense of wholesome responsibility. "We do not intend to turn out a race of professors," he noted. Students had to build their own beds and chests in the school carpentry shop, and keep up with a host of chores, including twice-daily milking of the school's cows. The milking requirement for students continued until 1989, as the curriculum gradually shifted toward college preparation. Highly structured chores requirements remain, as does mandatory chapel time on Sunday. And to this day, active work in the school's agricultural, animal, and environmental centers (for example, a fish hatchery operated on the trout stream running through campus) are an important part of its efforts to promote initiative and responsibility.

Beyond this emphasis on individual commitment, discipline, and work, Hershey is renowned for creating an authentically personal, warm, and nurturing environment. Students live in groups of 10 to 12, two or three to a bedroom, in more than a hundred closely clustered houses overseen by a married couple with childrearing experience. A transitional living program places seniors in quasi-independent apartments, where they get help in buying and preparing their own food, setting their schedules, and running their own lives in preparation for college or self-support after graduation. More than three quarters of graduates now go on to four-year college, just shy of ten percent enter the work force or military, and the remainder attend technical or two-year college. With 1,900 pre-K to twelfth-grade students—

most with missing, deceased, or jailed parents and other disadvantages—today's Milton Hershey School is the largest boarding school in America, and its $11 billion endowment, larger than all but a few universities, allows it to offer its education (including large scholarships for college) and superb care (including things like intensive counseling, orthodontia, all food and clothing) entirely free to each child.

Further reading

○ Milton Hershey profile in the Philanthropy Hall of Fame (see prior *Almanac* section)

○ *Philanthropy* magazine article, philanthropyroundtable.org/topic/excellence_in_philanthropy/the_sweet_smell_of_success

○ *Washington Post* school profile, washingtonpost.com/wp-dyn/content/article/2008/10/24/AR2008102402383_4.html?sid=ST2008103003551

1907

COLLABORATING TO EDUCATE THE SEGREGATED

In the decades after the Civil War much effort was expended by philanthropists to remedy the educational disadvantages of African Americans. (See 1867, 1902, and 1912 entries.) In addition to the work of large donors like George Peabody, Julius Rosenwald, George Eastman, and John Rockefeller, many donors of more modest scope made energetic efforts to improve education in the South, particularly in rural areas, and especially for blacks lacking publicly funded schools.

What was eventually known as the Negro Rural Schools Fund was started by devout Quaker Anna Jeanes with one million dollars in 1907 to improve educational opportunities for rural African Americans. In a kind of proto-Peace Corps model, "Jeanes Industrial Teachers" traveled throughout poor counties to provide training to the teachers in black schools (usually African American women of modest education themselves). Promising teachers were often sent to Hampton University, Tuskegee Institute, and other colleges for additional learning. The roving "Jeanes Supervisors" simultaneously labored to improve curricula, and to organize community self-help efforts that allowed the purchase of school supplies and the meeting of teacher salaries.

The success of the Jeanes model inspired other philanthropies of about the same size to collaborate in expanding the program and bringing it to a wider area—eventually even to poor populations overseas. The Jeanes fund collaborated closely with the Phelps Stokes Fund, Virginia Randolph Fund, John Slater Fund, and others. Within a few decades there were hundreds of Jeanes teachers operating across the South. The Jeanes programs remained in place until school desegregation became a reality in the 1960s.

Further reading

○ University of South Carolina-Aiken research, usca.edu/aasc/jeanes.htm

FINANCIAL SECURITY FOR TEACHERS

In 1905, Andrew Carnegie established the Carnegie Foundation for the Advancement of Teaching with the express purpose of improving the financial security of instructors. Ultimately, the foundation also made other important contributions to higher education, like creation of the Educational Testing Service, which continues to be the nation's leading source of useful student exams. But economic enhancement of teaching remained a priority.

In 1907, Carnegie specifically prodded his foundation to investigate the possibility of providing insurance for faculty members. A few years later the foundation began to explore deeply how a practical system of pensions for professors might be created. Several reports later the foundation established the Teachers Insurance and Annuity Association, a private firm seeded with a $1 million grant from Carnegie. In the years following, TIAA received an additional $7 million of donations from Carnegie before it matured into a self-supporting company. A conservative investment strategy allowed it to not only survive but flourish during the Great Depression. Then when inflation made traditional annuities less attractive during the 1950s, the organization created innovative stock-savings accounts under its College Retirement Equities Fund umbrella.

TIAA-CREF's success and rapid growth allowed academics access to some of the best and most affordable financial services in the U.S. By 2014, TIAA-CREF managed more than $564 billion of teachers' assets, and served almost five million individuals.

Further reading

○ Who we are, tiaa-cref.org/public/about-us/who-we-are-at-tiaa-cref

◈ PhilAphorism

The ultimate achievement is how you feel about yourself. And giving your wealth away to have an impact for good does help with that.

☞ *Gerry Lenfest*

1903

EDUCATION

PROFESSIONALIZATION OF COLLEGE MANAGEMENT

John Rockefeller and Andrew Carnegie were not direct competitors in industry, but in a sense they were in their philanthropy. In many areas, however, they were in close agreement and exerted complementary influences. One such shared influence was in encouraging the professionalization of higher education.

In the Rockefeller-Carnegie era, philanthropic resources were extremely important to colleges and universities. For example, the assets commanded by Rockefeller's General Education Board in 1909—$53 million—were then equal to one fifth of the endowments at all American colleges and universities put together. Philanthropy also overshadowed annual public funding.

Rockefeller and Carnegie (along with compatriots like George Eastman, Mary Garrett, Leland Stanford, James Duke, and others) were thus well-positioned to encourage changes in the structure of higher ed. This happened in specific areas—like Rockefeller pulling medical education into the modern era, Garrett hastening coeducation at Johns Hopkins, and Carnegie improving professor pay and qualifications. It also happened in broad management.

Donor advocacy and funding required colleges to become much more businesslike by 1930. At leading private schools, nearly three quarters of trustees by that time were founders or managers of businesses. They brought with them a strong interest in improving efficiency, and expanding the customer base for college education. The academic professionalism and corporate organization that eventually propelled American higher education to the very top internationally is to a considerable degree the legacy of this philanthropy.

Further reading

○ John Thelin, *A History of American Higher Education* (Johns Hopkins University Press, 2011)

1902

GENERAL EDUCATION BOARD

John Rockefeller's philanthropy long predates his wealth. By the time he made millions he already had years of giving under his belt, mostly to religious and educational causes. Baptist colleges and the American Baptist Home Mission Society (with which he worked to found the University of Chicago) were among his first large-scale philanthropic interests. But Rockefeller was also very supportive of education for younger people.

In 1902 he endowed the General Education Board with an initial $1 million; almost $325 million of his money eventually flowed through its books. These were the largest gifts in the U.S. during their day. The GEB's earliest and longest focus was to build up the educational capital of the American South, which two decades after the end of the Civil War was still socially and economically depressed. The board first surveyed needs and then became a leader in promoting primary education for American blacks. By the board's second decade it had helped build or improve more than 1,600 new high schools across the southern states.

Many other successes followed. The GEB insisted that schools at all levels keep clear, open, and honest accounting books. It required colleges to raise their own funds to match GEB grants, seeding today's powerful campus fundraising operations. It spread knowledge of scientific agriculture in poor farming counties. It powered a methodical improvement of U.S. medical education (see 1910 entry on Medical list). It kept many colleges and schools from closing during the Depression.

More generally, the General Education Board helped usher in a new businesslike form of philanthropy. It brought expertise and spirit to the field that was energetic, creative, practical, and impatient for tangible results.

Further reading

○ GEB history, rockefeller100.org/exhibits/show/education/general_education_board

OPENING MEDICAL EDUCATION TO WOMEN, AND HIGHER STANDARDS

Born to the president of the Baltimore & Ohio Railroad, Mary Garrett inherited both wealth and a zeal for philanthropy from her father. He had been a trustee of Johns Hopkins University and close friends with both Johns Hopkins himself and George Peabody, two of the most prolific supporters of education in their era.

In 1887 Mary offered $35,000 to Hopkins to start a school of science, if they would make it coeducational. The university demurred. Later, when JHU was facing financial difficulties and having no luck launching a medical school, Garrett presented another proposal. She formed a committee to raise money for a medical school that would accept women. The group collected $100,000 in 1890, with Garrett contributing nearly half. That sum was offered to Hopkins president Daniel Gilman.

Gilman accepted the donation and its condition of female admission, but then pushed the women to raise additional money for an endowment to yield a truly top-tier medical school. When the half-million dollars of endowment that Gilman aspired for proved difficult to achieve, Garrett boldly wrote a check for more than $300,000 to push the effort over the finish line. But she gave the money with two additional conditions that turned out to be seminal in raising standards not only at Hopkins but at all medical schools: Every applicant would be required to have a bachelor's degree in science, and Hopkins must offer not just occupational training but a full graduate education culminating in a medical degree. After resistance from the school's trustees (these were remarkably rigorous standards for the day) the gift was agreed to. In 1893, Mary Garrett saw the Johns Hopkins School of Medicine open, with three women in the inaugural class and a stiff course of study that pushed medicine to the top of the professions.

Further reading

○ Kathleen Waters Sander, *Mary Elizabeth Garrett: Society and Philanthropy in the Gilded Age* (Johns Hopkins University Press, 2008)

○ Mary Garrett profile in the Philanthropy Hall of Fame (see prior *Almanac* section)

1890

UNIVERSITY OF CHICAGO

For decades a faithful Baptist, oilman John Rockefeller Sr. aspired to found a distinguished Baptist university. In 1890 he made his first contribution ($600,000) to establish the University of Chicago in league with the American Baptist Education Society. The university's land was in turn donated by Chicago department store magnate Marshall Field. Rockefeller would eventually give the new organization tens of millions of dollars, while insisting that his name not be used anywhere on campus. His collaborator William Harper, a young Biblical scholar from Yale, and UC's first president, oversaw a combination of English-style undergraduate college and German-style graduate research institute. With Harper's guidance and Rockefeller's unprecedented funding, the University of Chicago quickly became a national leader in higher education. Robert Hutchins, president from 1929 to 1951, put in place many of the innovations that the university became known for, including a core curriculum focused on classic works and original documents, an emphasis on discussion rather than lectures, interdisciplinary study, and comprehensive exams to measure progress. The core curriculum survived until the late-1990s when it was substantially modified to add "diversity." The University of Chicago was a founding member of the Big Ten Conference and the first to give its football coach, Amos Alonzo Stagg, academic tenure— until the college dropped football to concentrate on academics in 1939.

Rockefeller once described the University of Chicago as "the best investment I ever made."

Further reading

○ University history, uchicago.edu/about/history

1888

TOWARD COLLEGIALITY ON CAMPUS

The success of Standard Oil produced many fortunes and several great philanthropists—including Stephen Harkness. One of the company's first investors, he ultimately put much of his wealth toward charitable causes. His wife and their only son, Edward, continued and extended his habit of giving. (See, for instance, the 1918 entry on the influence of Harkness family money on child psychology.)

Edward Harkness was of the opinion that American undergraduates could benefit from greater collegiality, and some his most consequential personal philanthropy went to building residential colleges where students could live, study, and socialize on a more intimate scale than university-wide activities allowed. As a Yale alumnus he first approached his alma mater with the idea, but the school would not accept the gift because of uncertainty as to how it would be managed. Undeterred, Harkness shifted his offer to Harvard, where he found a sympathetic ear. His $13 million donation was used to construct an undergraduate "house" system, modeled on the example of the decentralized college system employed by Oxford and Cambridge. A few years later Harkness went back to Yale, which this time accepted the money and with it built a much-loved residential system of its own. Today, many other universities have copied these smaller-scale residential structures, believing as Edward Harkness did that close relationships are an invaluable part of a college education.

Further reading

○ 1908 description of the origins of college system, collegiateway.org/reading/seymour-1933

○ Edward Harkness profile in the Philanthropy Hall of Fame (see prior *Almanac* section)

1888

WILLIAMSON FREE SCHOOL
FOR MECHANICAL TRADES

Philadelphia merchant Isaiah Williamson was frugal and hardworking, and by the 1880s he was one of the wealthiest men in the commonwealth, with an estimated fortune of $20 million (about half a billion dollars today). He gave away millions, supporting asylums and orphanages, hospitals and benevolent societies, libraries and universities. He was "strongly moved to help the man who was trying to help himself," said his friend John Wanamaker. "But for mere beggars, low or high, he had little sympathy."

In 1888, Williamson founded "a school where every boy could be taught some trade free of expense," committing more than $2 million to the facility. To this day, the school recruits young men from Philadelphia's toughest areas, working closely with ministers, guidance counselors, and coaches to find promising individuals for whom learning an occupation could be the difference between success and happiness or misery in life. The school provides a full scholarship for all of its students, yet accepts no government money.

The school's formula was renewed and put on solid financial footing for the future by a 2008 campaign that raised $50 million—$20 million each coming from donors Henry Rowan and Gerry Lenfest. The school only enrolls about 275 men, and prides itself on instilling character that may have even greater value to the community in the long run than the economic skills imparted. Students must live on campus, where the workweek starts with a 6:45 a.m. inspection. Every student is expected to be properly groomed and freshly shaved, in a coat and tie, with shoes polished. (Violations earn an hour of landscaping duty on the weekend.) After breakfast and mandatory chapel, half the students head to class still in coat and tie, the other half don work gear and report to shops. After lunch, they switch.

Trades classes are physically and mentally taxing, and are matched with courses in effective business writing, accounting, entrepreneurship, business ethics, and public speaking that prepare many graduates for self-reliance and economic independence. The school has zero tolerance for alcohol and drugs, and the young men must be unmarried and childless. Each dorm has just one television, located in the common room. Every student rotates through landscaping and kitchen duties, and engages in off-campus community-service projects. Masons lay the stonework at veterans' memorials, while landscapers spruce up the grounds at retirement homes. Painters help local schools with set design, while carpenters build wheelchair ramps for state troopers disabled in the line of duty. "The goal is to create an identifiable Williamson Man," explains former school head (and space shuttle pilot) Guy Gardner. "We believe that Williamson men will be better fathers, husbands, employees, employers, neighbors, community leaders, and gentlemen."

Further reading

○ *Philanthropy* magazine article, philanthropyroundtable.org/topic/entrepreneurship/building_men

GIFTS TO PUBLIC UNIVERSITIES

Given the innumerable private colleges created, transformed, or sustained by private giving, it is easy to overlook the role philanthropy has played in the country's *public* universities. A large private gift aimed at encouraging the flourishing of the University of Michigan was received as early as 1887. A 1906 bequest of several million dollars enabled the University of Wisconsin to offer salaries twice as large as average to attract leading scholars. In 1929 the University of Virginia received an anonymous donation of $6 million that fueled scholarships and fellowships. Today, state colleges like the University of Virginia and the University of California, Berkeley actually receive more revenue from private gifts and endowment income than from state appropriations. Private giving is now crucial to the fundraising of most state universities across the country. Indeed, even our nation's federally funded military academies have come to count on donations to expand into important new areas or improve the quality of cadet life.

Further reading

○ Merle Nash & Roderick Curti, *Philanthropy in the Shaping of American Higher Education* (Rutgers University Press, 1965)

○ *Philanthropy* magazine article, philanthropyroundtable.org/topic/excellence_in_ philanthropy/spartan_donors

STANFORD UNIVERSITY

Within the circle of elite American schools to which it belongs, Stanford University is unique for being situated in the West. While that may not raise eyebrows today, there was a time when no one would think of equating America's grand early colleges with a comparative newcomer set up far from the nation's traditional centers of learning and culture. Railroad baron Leland Stanford created the university in 1885 as a memorial to his deceased son, and aimed from the beginning to "make it of the highest grade." He donated money and three of his California ranch properties for the campus, and devoted himself to improvement and expansion until his death in 1893. His widow, Jane, continued to nurture the institution, but tax and legal battles flowing from her husband's passing threatened to bankrupt both her and the university. At one point she journeyed to London to auction off her jewelry to secure the money necessary to keep the school open. In the end, Leland Stanford's stipulation that the school not sell the land he had given it resulted in a bonanza, as California's population boom drove up rents, bringing handsome financial returns to the university that enabled a rapid climb to high achievement.

Further reading

○ Leland Stanford profile in Philanthropy Hall of Fame (see prior *Almanac* entry)

GREAT LIBRARIES
FROM ENOCH PRATT—AND OTHERS

Enoch Pratt arrived in Baltimore from a Massachusetts farm with nothing but $150 in his pocket, but he was frugal and industrious and eventually thrived in a variety of businesses. In 1882 he offered to give the city of Baltimore a major circulating library for free public use, along with 32,000 books, plus four branch libraries in different quarters of the city, and an endowment of $1,058,333 for upkeep and future expansion. Once built, the Pratt almost immediately became one of the most heavily used libraries in the country, and it thrived over the century and a quarter since. Andrew Carnegie described it in *The Gospel of Wealth* as the best such institution in the country, and he cited Pratt as his exemplar for his own nationwide library program which he launched the year Pratt's main library opened. In fact, two decades after the initial opening of the Pratt Library, Carnegie donated a half-million dollars to Baltimore to allow the building of 20 additional branches—part of his wider campaign that paid for the erection of more than 2,500 libraries (see the 1881 Carnegie Library entry in our companion list of major achievements in Arts and Culture).

These were just two of the many American philanthropists who lifted American literacy and learning by donating important collections of books to the public. The grandfather of them all was Benjamin Franklin, who in

◈ PhilAphorism

If life happens to bless you with talent or treasure, you have a responsibility to use those gifts as well and as wisely as you possibly can.

☞ *Bill & Melinda Gates*

league with a group of friends incorporated the Library Company of Philadelphia, the first such entity in British North America, in 1731 (see separate entry following). In 1814, Thomas Jefferson offered his large and impossible-to-replicate library to Congress for official use after the British burned Washington. Judah Touro gave the American West its first public collection of books when he offered to put up the Touro Free Library in the city of New Orleans in 1824, and at his death he helped endow the famous Redwood Library in Newport, Rhode Island. John Jacob Astor gave $400,000 to New York in 1848 to establish a library, later combined with the $2 million library given by James Lenox, as well as a trust containing most of the wealth of Samuel Tilden, to form the New York Public Library. With a $50,000 gift and 30,000 books "of permanent value," financier Joshua Bates launched the Boston Public library, whose main reading room remains named for him.

These gifts transformed libraries, over the course of just a couple generations, from luxuries possessed by the wealthy to institutions of self-improvement available to all. Today there are more than 16,000 public libraries in the U.S., and they are visited a billion and a half times every year.

Further reading

○ Enoch Pratt Library history, prattlibrary.org/about/index.aspx?id=1604

○ Original Pratt documents, archive.org/stream/enochprattfreeli00enoc#page/14/mode/2up

1881

WHARTON SCHOOL AND ECONOMIC EDUCATION

Writing to the trustees of the University of Pennsylvania, Philadelphia metals manufacturer Joseph Wharton expressed disillusionment with the state of higher education. Citing his own experience in having to learn the ins and outs of business on the job, after leaving school at the age of sixteen, Wharton complained that there was no methodical training available for careers in commerce. He offered to begin to remedy this with a gift of $100,000 for the establishment of a "School of Finance and Economy." And so in 1881, the Wharton School at the University of Pennsylvania opened its doors—the first in the world of its kind.

In the coming years other donors followed Wharton's lead. John Rockefeller gave several million dollars in 1898 to found the College of Commerce and Administration at the University of Chicago. New York University's School of Commerce, Accounts, and Finance was started by a handful of New York businessmen who supplied not only funds but also instructional expertise. In 1900 the Amos Tuck School of Business

Administration at Dartmouth was born of a family benefaction. Banker-industrialist George Baker gave $5 million to start Harvard's graduate program in business administration. Like the philanthropists who preceded them in pushing scientific education into university curricula (notably Stephen Van Rensselaer—see 1824 entry), the donors to business education saw even before most academics did the need for new educational paradigms to meet the demands of an increasingly complex U.S. economy.

Further reading

○ Wharton School timeline, wharton.upenn.edu/about/wharton-history.cfm

1880

BRINGING TEACHER EDUCATION TO THE UNIVERSITY

Amid massive changes in Americans' educational needs in the late nineteenth century, the teaching profession came under scrutiny. Skilled educators were in short supply, and many observers were questioning how teachers were trained. Philanthropists undertook direct action. Perhaps the most significant act was Grace Dodge's decision in 1880 to establish the Kitchen Garden Association. Though initially created to teach domestic skills to New York's poor, several years later it would evolve into the New York College for the Training of Teachers, precursor to Teachers College at Columbia University. Dodge served as the first treasurer and provided crucial financial support. Teachers College took on a particular mission to properly educate the children of the poor, and it was influential. By 1900 one fourth of colleges and universities were providing some form of professional education for teachers, a fraction that rose as the twentieth century wore on.

Further reading

○ Grace Dodge papers, asteria.fivecolleges.edu/findaids/sophiasmith/mnsss295.html

○ Teachers College history, jstor.org/discover/10.2307/368780?uid=3739584&uid=2129&uid=2&uid=70&uid=4&uid=3739256&sid=21104157111313

1876

JOHNS HOPKINS UNIVERSITY

American colleges had undergone much growth and change by 1876, but that year might be thought of as the U.S. inauguration of the German university model—featuring academic independence, a high degree of structure, and an emphasis on research. Johns Hopkins, an enterprising Baltimore businessman, founded his university then with a $7 million grant and his selection of Daniel Gilman as president. The new institution's main departure was in putting priority on graduate research and education rather than undergraduate teaching. Hopkins' original vision included both a university and medical school, and Gilman subsequently attracted some of the leading medical minds and scientists in the country. Years later, Harvard president Charles Eliot confessed that his university's graduate school "did not thrive until the example of Johns Hopkins forced our faculty to put their strengths into the development of our instruction for graduates." The new university also became inextricably entwined with its patron's hometown. When the school fell on hard financial times, the people of Baltimore rallied to its aid. Twice before the end of the nineteenth century, the Baltimore business community saved the school after its railroad-heavy stock holdings bottomed out. And local giving extended far beyond financial emergencies. By 1902, new donations from Baltimoreans had surpassed the university's original endowment. Johns Hopkins now ranks as Maryland's largest employer.

Further reading

○ Johns Hopkins University history, webapps.jhu.edu/jhuniverse/featured/history

PEABODY'S RECONSTRUCTION SCHOOLS

After the Civil War, the American South was badly battered, and improving its economic and social prospects became a central part of repairing our national union. Religious groups were the first to offer aid, including schooling for children. Then philanthropists outside of church structures took up the cause of boosting educational opportunities for young Southerners of all stripes.

Baltimore banker George Peabody took the lead. Barely a year and a half after the bullets had stopped flying, in early 1867, Peabody established America's very first formal foundation, the Peabody Education Fund, with a gift of $2.1 million and a charge to raise the standard of schooling throughout the South without racial considerations. The fund ultimately distributed about $4 million across the region, building schools, training teachers, and offering scholarships for higher education. One of its lasting achievements was in creating a high-quality college for teachers at Vanderbilt University, which sprinkled instructors throughout the southern states for generations, right up to the present. The Peabody Fund was also important for inspiring others to take up the cause of upgrading the schooling available to everyday Southerners. A half dozen very active endowments, often working in close collaboration, eventually showered money, buildings, expertise, and encouragement on Southern education for several decades, strengthening and creating institutions at the primary, secondary, and college levels alike. (See 1907 entry.)

In addition to helping heal egregious regional sores, the Peabody Fund was a leader in what education historian John Thelin calls "long-distance philanthropy"—moving dollars out of the donor's home area to locations of special need. The fund was also the first U.S. philanthropy to focus on one social problem. And it was a pioneer in relying heavily on trustees to guide its giving, and in other operational aspects that later became common in modern philanthropy. George Peabody was thus a powerful influence not only on other givers in his place and time, like Enoch Pratt and Johns Hopkins, but also on later American philanthropists like Rockefeller, Carnegie, and Gates, all of whom have cited the generous and thoughtful Baltimorean as a model and inspiration, causing historians to refer to him as "the father of modern philanthropy."

Further reading

- J. Curry, *A Brief Sketch of George Peabody and a History of the Peabody Education Fund through Thirty Years* (Peabody Education Fund, 1898)
- George Peabody entry in Philanthropy Hall of Fame (see prior *Almanac* entry)
- John Thelin, *A History of American Higher Education* (Johns Hopkins University Press, 2011)

— 1861 —

MATTHEW VASSAR'S COLLEGE FOR WOMEN

Education philanthropy over the first century of American history was focused predominantly on young men. Then Matthew Vassar got it into his head to try something new. He resolved to use his fortune, accumulated from a self-made career in business, to establish "a college for young women which shall be to them what Yale and Harvard are to young men." Milo Jewett, a clergyman who had founded the Judson Female Institute in Alabama way back in 1839, encouraged Vassar, appealing "to his desire to serve mankind, his local pride, his Christian faith," according to historian Merle Curti. At an 1861 meeting of the new college's board of trustees, Vassar presented a tin box containing stock and bond certificates valued at $408,000, plus a deed to 200 acres near Poughkeepsie, New York. This gift, along with an additional $400,000 offered before his death, and continued support from the Vassar family, gave a powerful impetus to one of the world's first women's colleges offering a broad liberal education. Vassar's donation also marked a new era in college philanthropy generally—which had previously relied on subscriptions from many donors, and now shifted toward major gifts from individuals.

Further reading

○ Merle Nash and Roderick Curti, *Philanthropy in the Shaping of American Higher Education* (Rutgers University Press, 1965)

○ Vassar encyclopedia, vcencyclopedia.vassar.edu/matthew-vassar/matthew-vassar.html

1859

COOPER UNION FOR
THE ADVANCEMENT OF SCIENCE AND ART

Peter Cooper was born into a poor family, but even as a child he was inventing things—what may have been the world's first washing machine, an innovative mower, different ways of making gelatin, a steam locomotive, a new type of iron smelting, and so forth. He studied, experimented, apprenticed himself, even hired tutors for personal instruction, always self improving. By his later years Cooper was one of the richest men in the United States. Yet he lived simply, putting most of his wealth into helping others. He particularly hoped to see people develop talents that were latent within them. Having had only one year of formal schooling himself, he nursed a lifelong desire to help "the mass of struggling humanity" grab onto education. As a vehicle for supporting self-improvement of this sort he founded the Cooper Union for the Advancement of Science and Art in 1859, when he was 68.

The structure he erected to house the college was the first large building to be made of iron, an advance that greatly reduced the risk of fire and that was made possible by Cooper's own invention of superior I-beams. Cooper opened the institution to women, blacks, and the working classes. Its success was so immediate that a near-riot occurred at the launch, as New Yorkers swarmed to register. Cooper's son-in-law and business partner found it "incredible that there should be such a passion for learning among the toilers."

It was central to Cooper's vision that students should be able to attend at no cost, and thanks to his $600,000 founding gift and subsequent endowments, the college eventually offered full-tuition scholarships for all students. From his own personal experience Cooper knew that many students hoping to rise in society would face job and family demands that competed with their ability to study—so the school offered night classes, and kept its library open to all comers until 10 p.m. every evening.

In addition to providing technical skills that would boost prosperity (the engineering school remains one of the premier organizations in its field), Cooper wanted to foster artistic expression that could spark broader creativity. One early student was the sculptor Auguste Saint-Gaudens. Today, the schools of art and architecture at Cooper Union are among the most selective in the country, with alumni who have accumulated 18 Guggenheim fellowships, nine Chrysler Design Awards, and three Thomas Jefferson Awards for Public Architecture.

Further reading

○ Cooper Union founding documents, library.cooper.edu/archive/cooper_archives_page.html
○ Peter Cooper profile in Philanthropy Hall of Fame (see prior *Almanac* section)

WESTERN COLLEGES, EASTERN MONEY

A surprising number of colleges were founded in the early American West, but most struggled to find a financial footing. The periodic economic panics took a toll on educational philanthropy and even voided pledges undertaken during boom years. The successes of schools like Transylvania University and Western Reserve, though, attracted a stream of additional entries.

Congregationalists and Presbyterians wanting to support the expansion of Western colleges teamed up in 1843 to found the Society for the Promotion of Collegiate and Theological Education. The society maintained a rolling list of schools it supported, adding a new one in need whenever a school could be moved off the list after gaining a measure of financial security. Its board was based in the East, where each of the supported schools would send a fundraising agent who the society would help make appeals to local pastors and parishes. Money raised by the agents was put into a common fund and disbursed in previously agreed percentages.

By linking frontier schools with sympathetic religious congregations in the East, the society enabled colleges to weather the inherent challenges of starting new institutions in raw lands, and the difficulties of an unsteady economy. By the time of its merger with another organization in 1874, the society had raised more than a million dollars in small contributions to sustain 18 colleges throughout the West.

Further reading

○ First report of the Society, archive.org/details/annualreportofso1818441851soci

A COLLEGE AGAINST SLAVERY

Oberlin College was built on a strong opposition to slavery, and committed its intellectual resources to helping end the practice. When various financial downturns buffeted its home region in Ohio, Oberlin's moral mission helped the college find financial saviors. Founded in 1833 and opened to students of all races, as well as women, the college had brought Charles Finney and other prominent abolitionists onto its faculty. These principled hires attracted many donors, like New York businessman Arthur Tappan, who gave the school $17,000, plus funds to cover Finney's salary. Another group of New Yorkers committed more than $4,000 to fund eight professorships. The Financial Panic of 1837 almost scuttled Oberlin along with other colleges, but the school sent representatives to England, where $30,000 was collected from abolitionists in less than a year, putting the facility back on firm financial footing.

Further reading

○ 1839 text of appeal to Britons on behalf of Oberlin, oberlin.edu/external/EOG/Weld%20 Abolition%20Appeal/weld_appeal.htm

1831

EDUCATING THE ORPHANED

Born in France in 1750, Stephen Girard was a financier who immigrated to the United States nearly penniless and then made his name as a businessman and philanthropist of renown. By the time of his death in 1831 Girard was the wealthiest man in America, and he left almost all of his money to philanthropic causes. When a yellow-fever epidemic ravaged his adopted home city of Philadelphia he poured out personal funds to assist those in need, and personally nursed the sick. During the 1812 war with Britain he doctored the entire nation with crucial financial assistance.

His most lasting legacy came from several million dollars apportioned to establish and maintain a school in Philadelphia for "poor male white orphans," many of whom lost their fathers in coal mining. Generations of additional funding for the school would be provided by rents from Girard's real-estate holdings in and around Philadelphia, the sale of which he expressly prohibited. Having been largely cut out of its provisions, Girard's family contested the will, which after long controversy was finally upheld by the Supreme Court in a landmark case that secured respect in the law for the intentions of donors.

Girard College finally opened in 1848, offering an interesting and practical mix of types of education, just as spelled out in some detail by its patron. It continues today as an independent boarding school serving 550 boys and girls in grades 1-12 who come from low-income families missing a parent. All costs of attending the institution—approaching $50,000 per year—are covered by the school's endowment. And in a city where barely half of public-school students graduate, nearly all Girard students earn their high-school degree.

Further reading

○ Girard biography and school history, girardweb.com/girard/bookcover.htm

○ *Wall Street Journal* essay by alumnus, girardcollege.edu/page.cfm?p=863

WESTERN RESERVE UNIVERSITY

Western Reserve University, which sprang up in 1826 in a just-burgeoning section of Ohio, survived only through the sacrificial giving of frontier settlers. Western Reserve was not supported by a generous benefactor, as would become increasingly common in education philanthropy as the nineteenth century wore on. Rather, it was a broad base of farmers who committed their small contributions and, more often, their services to the fledgling educator. In one case a local man spent a whole winter hauling building materials to the school from a quarry that was ten miles away; in another, a farming family pledged an annual gift from the proceeds of their milk and egg sales, which they gave every year for a decade. This college built on grassroots philanthropy lives on today in its merged heir, Case Western Reserve University, a top independent research university located in Cleveland.

Further reading

○ Merle Nash and Roderick Curti, *Philanthropy in the Shaping of American Higher Education* (Rutgers University Press, 1965)

RENSSELAER SCHOOL
AND THE RISE OF SCIENTIFIC EDUCATION

Stephen Van Rensselaer was heir to one of the most valuable landholdings in the United States. Comprised of over a thousand farms, Rensselaer's New York estate and the requirements of its maintenance acquainted him with the need for efficiency and technical expertise in agriculture. Rensselaer had benefited from the best education his country had to offer, but in the years following his college graduation rapid economic development produced demands for practical skills not furnished by the classical curriculum provided by the leading American schools.

So Rensselaer turned his attention and his wealth to the promotion of more practical education. He funded the work of Amos Eaton, a prominent geologist and zoologist, and the relationship the men struck up laid the foundation for Eaton's request the following year that Rensselaer support a school centered on instruction in the sciences. Thus emerged the Rensselaer School in 1824, an institution dedicated to "the application of science to the common purposes of life." Stephen Van Rensselaer underwrote the college to the tune of $25,000 in its first decade. Under Eaton's supervision, it grew quickly and within a few years was responsible for educating a remarkable number of the nation's naturalists and engineers (for a period, a majority of all the engineers in the United States held a degree from the Rensselaer School). The college awarded the first civil-engineering degrees in the English-speaking world, offered the first courses in advanced agricultural studies, and led the shift from passive to hands-on learning in science education. The success of the Rensselaer model led to many other similar colleges, and the original continues to thrive in upstate New York as the Rensselaer Polytechnic Institute.

Further reading

○ RPI historical documents, rpi.edu/about/history.html

1805

NEW YORK FREE SCHOOL SOCIETY

In early nineteenth-century New York City, free primary education was largely the province of church-run charity schools. For families of means there was also the option of private schools maintained by individual teachers. While these two poles covered most of the city's children, some worried that certain poor youngsters were falling through the cracks. Thus in 1805 a group of residents led by Mayor DeWitt Clinton formed the New York Free School Society to establish schools open to all at no charge. The Society aimed both to educate and "to inculcate the sublime truths of religion and morality contained in the Holy Scriptures" in an ecumenical way. The New York legislature incorporated the group but did not provide funding, so the Society depended on subscriptions by individual members. Mayor Clinton provided an inaugural gift of $200, but most donations did not exceed $25. In this way the society raised $6,501 in its initial year and opened its first Free School. Gifts from Colonel Henry Rutgers, a member of the State Board of Regents, allowed a second school to open. In exchange for educating the children of the city almshouse, the group was given another building and money for its repair. By 1814, the combination of private philanthropy and public cooperation sustained almost 800 students in free schools established by the society, and the growth continued in subsequent decades.

Further reading

○ Emerson Palmer, *The New York Public School*, archive.org/stream/
newyorkpublicsch00palmrich/newyorkpublicsch00palmrich_djvu.txt

○ Sol Cohen (ed.), *Education in the United States: A Documentary History* (Greenwood, 1974)

WASHINGTON AND LEE UNIVERSITY

George Washington was not only "first in war, first in peace, first in the hearts of his countrymen." He was also first in philanthropic support for higher education in the young Republic, providing the largest gift the nation had ever seen for such purposes. This benefaction was typical of Washington, who had been a generous giver, and most often an anonymous giver, throughout his life. Even when departing his considerable estate to lead the Continental Army against the world's most powerful military, he left strict, detailed instructions of all the ways he expected his managers to continue the estate's assistance to the needy.

Washington's most consequential gift came in 1796 with a donation of one hundred shares of the James River and Kanawha Canal Company, valued at about $20,000, to Liberty Hall Academy located in Lexington, Virginia. The contribution, at the time the largest in American history, prompted the trustees to rename their school Washington Academy. It prospers today as Washington and Lee University.

Washington's early gift would be worth at least $20 million today, and it continues to underwrite a portion of each student's tuition. Like the other founders who encouraged higher education (Jefferson and Madison at the University of Virginia, Hamilton at Hamilton College, Franklin at today's University of Pennsylvania, etc.), Washington hoped education would deepen the attachment of Americans to the principles on which their young nation was founded. "If a nation expects to be ignorant and free," declared Jefferson, "it expects what never was and never will be."

Further reading

○ George Washington profile in the Philanthropy Hall of Fame (see prior *Almanac* section)

A UNIVERSITY ACROSS THE WOODS

In the early years of the American republic our population erupted over the heights of the Allegheny Mountains, starting the long national journey to the Pacific. Unlike their worldly possessions, the settlers of our frontier could not pack their schools for the move; they knew fresh educational institutions would have to be built from scratch. Persuading fellow Americans to donate to institutions of learning in the sparsely peopled Western territories would be a necessity. The first college west of the Alleghenies, established in 1780, was Kentucky's Transylvania University, and private donors came through generously on its behalf. By 1795, when the university was relocated to Lexington, it was a respected institution. Transylvania (Latin for "across the woods") educated 36 governors, 50 senators, and 101 congressmen, and its wide base of donors demonstrated the willingness of Americans to support fellow citizens working to improve themselves, even when they had no fraternal or geographic tie.

Further reading

○ Brief history, transy.edu/about/history.htm

1731

PHILADELPHIA
LIBRARY COMPANY

In the first half of the eighteenth century, American libraries were limited to small collections of books in private homes, or at colleges and seminaries, of which there were only a handful. Even middle-class people had very limited access to books. And the range of books seldom went beyond the core curriculum of theology and classics that dominated American higher education, many of them written in Latin rather than English. Thus when Philadelphia's Junto, a "club for mutual improvement" created by Benjamin Franklin, started a book service, it did more than create the first public library in North America. It charted a new course in general availability of reading materials.

The dues of Junto members were put toward the purchase of books. But those books were not kept exclusively for the private consumption of club members—the collection was also opened to the public. Books could be

᚛ PhilAphorism

God sends us the poor to try us…. And he that refuses them a little out of the great deal that God has given lays up poverty in store for his own posterity. ᚛ *William Penn*

picked out, returned, or exchanged any Saturday from 4–8 p.m. This created access to books that most Philadelphians would otherwise have no hope of ever seeing, much less an opportunity to read.

Junto subscriptions were thus supporting a new form of charity, one that resonated with Franklin's belief in the equalizing power of diffused knowledge. This circulating library's success inspired similar efforts in other American cities during the 1740s. In Philadelphia, the Library Company continues to operate today as a nonprofit lending library, much as it did in the 1700s.

Further reading

◦ The Library Company today, librarycompany.org/about/index.htm

◦ History, ushistory.org/franklin/philadelphia/library.htm

ENDOWED
COLLEGE CHAIRS

The endowed professorship—an educational post funded over a long period of time by the earnings from an initial gift—is among the signal accomplishments of U.S. educational philanthropy. The pervasiveness of the endowed chair in the U.S. today makes it easy to assume that the practice must be common everywhere. Actually the institution is rare outside of America, where it took root long before we were even a country.

Thomas Hollis, a wealthy merchant and Baptist from London, wanted to express his gratitude for the good treatment Baptists had received in Boston. So in 1721 he gave funds to Harvard University to found the Hollis Chair of Divinity with a salary of £80 per year for its occupant. The gift also included money to offset administrative expenses, to increase the size of the student body, and to support "ten scholars of good character, four of whom should be Baptists, if any such were there."

Hollis's gift was the largest Harvard had received from a single individual. Five years later he established another professorship, the chair of mathematics and experimental philosophy. All told, Hollis's gifts eventually topped £6,000, a staggering amount for the time.

The endowed professorship spread rapidly in the U.S. and became an increasingly popular way for donors to support institutions of higher education—undergirding the spectacular rise of American colleges and universities to their current position of international preeminence.

Further reading

◦ Nathan Wood, *History of the First Baptist Church of Boston* (Ayer, 1990)

1704

A SCHOOL FOR SLAVES

There were about 1,500 African-American slaves living in New York City at the beginning of the 1700s, nearly all illiterate and intellectually degraded. Elias Neau, a French Huguenot who had found asylum in New York after being persecuted, imprisoned, and driven out of his native France for his Protestant religion, was moved by his faith to aid slaves and native Americans in his new city. He asked the Church of England and the Society for the Propagation of the Gospel to support him in opening a school for these two neglected populations. They agreed.

In the beginning, Neau was only permitted to visit slaves from house to house at the end of their work day. Eventually he got permission to open a classroom on the upper floor of his home. His students would arrive, and all would kneel and pray Christian appeals which Neau taught them for the first time. Then Neau would instruct for about two hours. Students and teacher would sing a psalm to close and then pray again. On Sundays, students and teacher would meet again for instruction in the steeple of Trinity Church. In the afternoon the church rector would teach them, and baptize those he considered ready for that rite. By 1708, Neau had 200 black pupils.

In 1712 there was a slave riot in New York resulting in murders and fires, and Neau's school was criticized by outraged residents, though only one of his students had been involved. After a period of laying low, the school was again opened, protected by the church and encouraged by the governor. The faithful Neau continued to lead it until his death in 1722. Then a series of other missionaries, schoolmasters, and pastors extended his effort up to the era of independence. A 1764 report back to the funders of the school at the Society for the Propagation of the Gospel recorded that "not a single black" instructed and baptized through the school "had turned out badly or in any way disgraced his profession." This encouraged additional support for schools assisting African Americans and Indians in other places.

Further reading

○ James Anderson, *History of the Church of England in the Colonies* (Rivingtons, 1856)

1643

FIRST FUNDRAISING CAMPAIGN

Harvard University conducted what is considered to be America's first recorded fund drive when it launched an appeal in 1643 for donations to build up its new college. A gift from Ann Radcliffe allowed the establishment of its first scholarship fund. All told, the effort raised £500 and was deemed a "great success." The next year, four of the New England colonies recommended that each resident family contribute a peck of wheat or a shilling in cash to support the nascent college in their midst. For over a decade, these voluntary donations, known as the "college corne," supported Harvard's entire teaching staff, plus a dozen students.

This was a new development in higher education. Instead of relying on the crown or the church or the state, financial responsibility for training up the next generation of leaders and producers would be spread across a community, relying on private individuals willing to share their abundance. By 2014, 42 American colleges were in the midst of fundraising campaigns that had a goal of raising at least a billion in private donations—reflecting the extraordinary role of philanthropy in building and maintaining the excellence of college education and research in the U.S.

Further reading

o History at National Philanthropic Trust, nptrust.org/history-of-giving/timeline/1600s

1636

EARLY AMERICAN COLLEGES

Education philanthropy in the United States is much older than our country. The New College was founded in 1636 by the Massachusetts Bay Colony, and renamed in 1639 after a young minister from Charlestown named John Harvard left his library and half of his estate to the fledgling school upon his death. The ensuing century saw the rise of numerous privately supported schools that would train the religious, political, and commercial leaders of a nation striving towards independence: the College of William & Mary (1693), King William's School (1696, which evolved into St. John's College), Yale College (1701), King's College (1746, reopened after the Revolution as Columbia University), College of New Jersey (1747, eventually Princeton University), the Academy of Pennsylvania (1749, later known as the University of Pennsylvania). Beginning almost a century and a half before we existed as a nation, America's tradition of faithful education philanthropy dedicated to the common good helped establish the foundations for our success as the world's first modern democracy.

Further reading

o Harvard historical facts, harvard.edu/historical-facts

MAJOR ACHIEVEMENTS OF AMERICAN PHILANTHROPY
(1636-2015)

ARTS & CULTURE

espite its comparatively short history, the United States has become one of the most artistically and culturally rich societies in the world. It is largely private philanthropy that has done this. And unlike in some other nations, it continues to be philanthropy and audience support (rather than state funding) that creates and sustains most artistic activity today.

Consider symphony orchestras. Fully half of their income today comes from donations (33 percent from annual gifts, 16 percent from revenue off of endowments given previously). Paid concert revenue comes to 42 percent of their total income. Only 6 percent of symphony funds come from local, state, or federal governments.

The story is about the same for other creative fields. Nonprofit arts institutions in the U.S. as a whole currently get 45 percent of their budgets from donors. Eliminate philanthropy and our lives immediately become duller, flatter, darker, more silent.

Arrayed by year below you will find examples of some of philanthropy's significant contributions to our national artistic life: musical performance and creation, museums, architecture, historical preservation, arts education, libraries and the book arts, living history, poetry, TV and film, dance and theater, and more.

☞ *Section research provided by Karl Zinsmeister and Brian Brown*

2015

ART OF NATIVE AMERICA TO INDIANA

The Eiteljorg Museum was founded in 1989 by Indianapolis philanthropist and businessman Harrison Eiteljorg, and has quickly grown into one of the country's top repositories of high-quality Native American art and artifacts and Western paintings and sculpture. A 2002 gift by the family of George Gund added a new gallery stocked with 57 pieces of traditional Western art including paintings and bronzes by Frederic Remington and Charles Russell.

In 2015, the museum received as a bequest from Bud Adams—former NFL team owner and one of the country's highest profile businessmen of Native American heritage—a collection of more than 300 Indian cultural artifacts like beadwork, weavings, and pottery, plus almost 100 prominent paintings of the West by Remington, Thomas Moran, Albert Bierstadt, Charles Russell, N. C. Wyeth, and others. The gift solidified the museum's position as one of the great collections of art from and about the early American West.

Further reading

○ *Indianapolis Star* reporting, indystar.com/story/life/2015/09/17/tennesee-titans-owner-donated-historic-art-collection-eiteljorg-museum/72360178

2015

A NONPAREIL BOOK COLLECTION

William Scheide made a gusher of money in Western Pennsylvania's early oil industry. After he retired he pursued a passionate interest in book collecting. At his death, his son continued to build the collection, as did his grandson. The family eye was good, and the library came to include copies of each of the first six printed editions of the Bible (starting with the 1455 Gutenberg); many early Shakespeare folios; autographed scores and musical sketchbooks by Beethoven, Mozart, Schubert, and Wagner; original letters and speeches from Lincoln, Grant, and others during the Civil War; a manuscript of the Magna Carta; even Emily Dickinson's recipe for chocolate pudding (and you thought she was an ascetic!).

With the passing of the third generation of bookish Scheides, the library became the property of Princeton University, on whose campus the family even replicated the original Titusville room where the books were housed. Princeton president Christopher Eisgruber described the gift as "one of the greatest collections of rare books and manuscripts in the world today." The monetary value of the donation was placed at $300 million, the largest gift in Princeton's history.

Further reading

○ *Philadelphia Inquirer* report, articles.philly.com/2015-02-18/news/59236788_1_collection-firestone-library-princeton-university

STRINGING HOUSTON'S ART PEARLS

Houston's Museum of Fine Arts is a complex of multiple buildings, quite disparate, strewn across 14 acres: an original neoclassical structure, two Mies van der Rohe additions erected in the '50s and '70s, a 1986 sculpture garden, and a windowless tomb built in 2000. To link and unify all of this, the museum announced in 2015 that it would erect two connective buildings. These will accommodate the near doubling in two decades of objects owned by the museum, improve patron services, put parking underground, and rationalize the campus. The effort will cost $350 million, and an additional $100 million will be raised for an endowment to support the new facilities. Museum board chairman Rich Kinder and his wife, Nancy, donated $50 million to the effort, Kinder's investment partner Fayez Sarofim put up $70 million, 11 other donors provided $10 million gifts, and there were 40 additional gifts of at least a million dollars—all of this before the fundraising campaign was even complete.

Further reading

○ *Wall Street Journal* report, blogs.wsj.com/speakeasy/2015/01/14/houstons-museum-of-fine-arts-reveals-expansion-plans

ART FOR THE WEST

The Los Angeles County Museum of Art is the most popular art museum in the western U.S., with more than one million visitors annually. Local

◁ PhilAphorism

If you want happiness for a year, inherit a fortune. If you want happiness for a lifetime, help someone else. ↪ *Confucius*

leaders consider it important to their economy as well as to regional culture. In 2014, county supervisor Zev Yaroslavsky described the arts as "an economic engine" for Los Angeles, elaborating that the sector "employs more people than the defense industry does, something we could not say 25 years ago."

In 2014, Angeleno Jerry Perenchio—whose career in the entertainment business ranged from putting up the prizes for the first Ali-Frazier fight to building the Univision TV network—announced that upon his death he would be injecting some rocket fuel into L.A.'s economic engine. He pledged to donate 47 great works of European art to LACMA. Painstakingly collected over 50 years, these works by Cézanne, Degas, Monet, Picasso, and others are collectively valued at half a billion dollars, representing one of the largest art gifts ever made in the U.S.

Further reading

∘ *Los Angeles Times* interview with Perenchio at gift announcement, latimes.com/ entertainment/arts/museums/la-et-cm-lacma-donate-20141105-story.html#page=12014

2014

LAST OF THE MELLON PICTURES

When philanthropist Paul Mellon died in 1999, he bequeathed 110 major works of art to the National Gallery, the last in a very long string of art gifts from the Mellon family (see 1937 entry on Andrew Mellon). The donated pictures were to remain in the care of Paul Mellon's wife during her lifetime. She released some, but continued to enjoy others in her home. The final 62 works became property of the people of the United States when Rachel Mellon died in 2014. These include exceptional paintings by Winslow Homer, Claude Monet, Vincent van Gogh, and other masters. Because they were acquired for enjoyment in a family house, they are mostly intimate and cozy pieces. And they express collector appetites, eras, and viewpoints that may not be fashionable today. "These are not the works everyone else is acquiring and displaying," said a curator at the National Gallery at the announcement of the gift. This is an example of the way philanthropy adds diversity to institutions, by preserving individual idiosyncrasies and capturing perspectives that lie outside mainline trends. Some of the paintings went on display quickly; a 2016 exhibition was scheduled to present them *in toto*.

Further reading

∘ National Gallery of Art announcement, nga.gov/content/ngaweb/press/2014/mellon-bequest.html

ARTS

FOUNDATIONS RESCUE
DETROIT'S ACCUMULATED ART

In a development extraordinary in its intentions, its scope, and its emergency nature, 15 Michigan and national foundations announced that they would pool together $466 million of philanthropic funds to prevent works of art from the Detroit Institute of Arts from being sold off to cover pension shortfalls and other debts amid Detroit's municipal bankruptcy. The Ford Foundation, Kresge Foundation, Kellogg Foundation, and others pledged the funds to meet immediate demands from city retirees and shield the Detroit Institute so that it can be migrated from city ownership and control to an independent nonprofit trust, preventing the artworks accumulated at the museum over generations of giving from being liquidated and lost to the local viewing public. Donors also contributed to a separate $100 million the Detroit Institute of Arts committed to raise from private sources—including $10 million from the Andrew Mellon Foundation, $3 million from the J. Paul Getty Trust, and $26 million donated by the three Detroit automakers. In response to these private pledges, the state government offered to kick in $200 million. The philanthropic gifts came on top of existing heavy annual giving to the people of the greater Detroit area by most of the same foundations, for purposes ranging from education to policing to social uplift.

Further reading

○ *Detroit News* announcing initial pledge by ten foundations, detroitnews.com/
article/20140128/METRO01/301280087

○ *Philanthropy* magazine story describing wider role of foundations in keeping Detroit afloat, philanthropyroundtable.org/topic/excellence_in_philanthropy/philanthropy-keeps-the-lights-on-in-detroit

MAKING AN IMPRESSIONISM ON DENVER

The Denver Art Museum has been admired for its contemporary, Native American, and Western art. In 2006 the building gained a major Daniel Libeskind-designed expansion, thanks to a $20 million gift from longtime trustee Frederic Hamilton, who made his fortune in the oil business. "However, our museum is derelict in one significant area, and that is Impressionism," stated Hamilton. In early 2014, however, the benefactor filled that hole by promising to the museum his personal collection of 22 great Impressionist paintings, by the likes of Monet, Renoir, Pissarro, Manet, van Gogh, and Cézanne. These were described by Rusty Powell of the National Gallery of Art in Washington, D.C. as "an extraordinary grouping of works by the greatest artists of France. It would be a big deal for any museum to get." Valued at approximately $100 million, they will give Denver the biggest collection of Impressionist art in the Western U.S. when they transfer to the museum at Hamilton's passing. The city got a taste of what is to come when Hamilton lent the collection for a temporary exhibit in early 2014. The crowds that thronged to see the masterworks finalized Hamilton's decision to will them to the public institution instead of passing them on to his heirs, as he had originally intended.

Further reading

○ *Denver Post* news story, denverpost.com/entertainment/ci_24898646/denver-art-museum-acquire-its-first-van-gogh#

BOOSTING TRADITIONAL ARCHITECTURE

The architecture school at the University of Notre Dame is known, along with the University of Miami, as the finest in the U.S. for the study of classical architecture and traditional urbanism. That's why the Driehaus Prize (see 2003 entry) was based there. In 2013 Matthew Walsh, who runs his family construction company, the largest contractor in Chicago, announced that he and his wife, Joyce, would fund creation of a new School of Architecture building on the Notre Dame campus. They are simultaneously paying for the addition of two new programs—in historic preservation, and real-estate development—which will expand the program's enrollment. This was one of the largest gifts in the university's history, and aims to elevate the Notre Dame architecture school, which dates back to 1898, to the highest levels of the profession.

Further reading

○ School of Architecture announcement, architecture.nd.edu/news-and-events/news/43099-notre-dame-received-27-million-gift

SPACE FOR ARTS EDUCATION

The John F. Kennedy Center in Washington, D. C., is the nation's busiest single performing arts venue, hosting some 2,000 performances annually. For years it has been cramped by its lack of rehearsal space and classrooms. "We run the largest arts-education program in the country," says president Michael Kaiser. "We work with 11 million children a year ... but the building doesn't have a classroom in it." To address this, the Kennedy Center announced in 2013 an expansion that will add classrooms, rehearsal rooms, lecture space, some offices, gardens, and a stage floating on the Potomac River. The $100 million project will be entirely privately funded, centered on a $50 million gift (the largest in the Kennedy Center's history) from Washington-based financier David Rubenstein.

Rubenstein had previously donated $75 million to the Kennedy Center. He expressed hope that his latest donation will draw other donors to engage in what he calls "patriotic philanthropy." (See 2009 entry.) "The federal government today cannot afford to do many of the things it would have done before. I hope this will encourage other people to give to…organizations that have been helpful to our country."

Further reading

○ Expansion plan, kennedy-center.org/explorer/interactives/expansion

○ *Washington Post* report, washingtonpost.com/entertainment/kennedy-center-announces-plan-for-100-million-in-additions-to-campus/2013/01/29/ccd626be-69ac-11e2-95b3-272d604a10a3_print.html

2013

AN ART DONATION CUBED

Leonard Lauder, for many years CEO of the cosmetics firm Estée Lauder that was founded by his parents, became a disciplined and tightly focused collector of art as his wealth swelled in his forties. Eschewing the temptation to buy flashy works across a range of popular styles, he started scooping up one kind of creation: early Cubist works. "I liked the aesthetic," he told the *New York Times*, and during those years when Impressionism and post-Impressionism were much more fashionable, "a lot was still available, because nobody really wanted it." Lauder notes that "early on I decided this should be formed as a museum collection." He relied on expert guidance from Hunter College art historian Emily Braun, and "whenever I considered buying anything, I would step back and ask myself, does this make the cut?"

In 2013, the 80-year-old Lauder announced he was donating his melange of Cubist paintings, drawings, and sculptures to the Metropolitan Museum of Art in New York City. It totaled 78 works by just four artists, each represented in depth—Picasso, Braque, Léger, and Gris—and was valued at more than a billion dollars. Art experts characterized this as one of the most significant art donations ever, and described the group as single-handedly equaling or exceeding the very best collections of Cubism that major museums like New York's Museum of Modern Art, the Hermitage in St. Petersburg, or Paris's Pompidou Center had managed to accumulate over a century. "In one fell swoop this puts the Met at the forefront of early-twentieth-century art," asserted Metropolitan Museum director Thomas Campbell. "It is an unreproducible collection, something museum directors only dream about."

Further reading

○ Press release from the Metropolitan Museum of Art, metmuseum.org

○ *New York Times* report, nytimes.com/2013/04/10/arts/design/leonard-lauder-is-giving-his-cubist-collection-to-the-met.html

SAVING CONSECRATED GROUND

When John Nau was eight years old, his family visited a Civil War battlefield in Kentucky. Walking the contested land created a yearning in the boy and a fascination with history that never faded. He grew up to become CEO of the nation's largest Anheuser-Busch distributor, a major donor to the University of Virginia, a philanthropic leader in historic preservation, and one of the nation's most active donors to the protection of Civil War battlefields. He and his wife funded, for instance, the transformation of 90 acres of the Vicksburg siege site—where there were 20,000 American casualties—back to what they looked like at the time of the clash, allowing visitors to re-live the heat of the climactic battle. As a donor and volunteer with the Civil War Trust, Federal Advisory Council on Historic Preservation, National Park Foundation, Texas State Historical Association, Gilder-Lehrman Institute, and other groups, Nau has donated and raised many millions of dollars to protect all sorts of hallowed grounds across the nation.

Further reading

○ Award citation from the American Academy for Park and Recreation Administration, aapra.org/Pugsley/NauJohn.html

A PRIVATE PERFORMANCE HALL

When Kansas City's Municipal Auditorium (longtime home to the Philharmonic and other Kansas City cultural organs) was erected, it was paid for entirely by the federal government with New Deal money. That building's latest successor, opened in 2012, is the Kauffman Center for the Performing Arts. It was financed 100 percent from private sources.

The new arts center, which cost $366 million, had 25 donors who gave at least a million dollars. The heaviest support came via philanthropy from the Kauffman family. The Muriel Kauffman Foundation gave $80 million, and another $26 million was provided by the Ewing Kauffman Foundation. (These are the separate foundations of Ewing and Muriel Kauffman, a married couple who made their fortune in pharmaceutical and baseball investments.) An additional $25 million was donated by their daughter Julia.

Today the dramatically styled Kauffman Center is home to the Kansas City Symphony, Lyric Opera, and the Kansas City Ballet, along with many smaller and touring performers. A *New York Times* reviewer characterized the new facility as "one of the most enjoyable, exhilarating arts centers I've been to."

Further reading

○ Kauffman Center for the Performing Arts kauffmancenter.org

○ *New York Times* review, nytimes.com/2011/11/21/arts/music/kauffman-center-for-the-performing-arts-in-kansas-city-mo.html

A REVOLUTIONARY MUSEUM CHALLENGE

For more than a century, a priceless collection of relics of the American Revolution has been slowly gathering, waiting for an appropriate home.

> ⚛ PhilAphorism
>
> *It is a misconception that corporate or government support has ever provided the majority of arts funding. Each U.S. citizen pays about the cost of one postage stamp in taxes to support national arts. The real stars of arts giving are individual donors, who give more to arts than corporations and government entities combined.* ☞ *Beth Nathanson*

Included are the tent George Washington slept in during his war campaigning (carefully preserved by generations of admirers), works of art, manuscripts, weapons, and historical objects.

Late in 2012, a private donor campaign was kicked off to erect a new Museum of the American Revolution (a corner of U.S. culture that has been inexplicably under-explored in museums). The facility will be located just steps from Independence Hall and the Liberty Bell in the historic section of Philadelphia. It will open in 2017 to tell the tale of America's birth, and house artifacts like those mentioned above. Architect Robert Stern designed the building, which will occupy the site of the failed Independence Park Visitor's Center.

Catalyzing the creation of this new institution was a $40 million challenge grant—one of the largest matching offers ever made by a U.S. philanthropist. The donor was Philadelphia-area media mogul Gerry Lenfest, who has previously given generously to cultural causes. Paired with an additional $40 million from other private contributors, his gift will begin the creation of the new museum and 28,000 square feet of exhibit space filled with rare objects, images and films, and interpretive information describing the fiery invention of the American nation.

Further reading

○ Campaign for the American Revolution, americanrevolutioncenter.org

○ *Philadelphia Inquirer* news, articles.philly.com/2012-06-12/news/32175746_1_first-national-museum-new-history-museum-american-revolution-center

2012

KICKSTARTER EXCEEDS
THE NEA IN ARTS FUNDING

The federal government has never had a major role in arts funding in the U.S.—which is overwhelmingly supported by private patron spending and philanthropy. In 2014, total spending by all U.S. art nonprofits came to more than $60 billion. Sales of tickets and art works covered two thirds of those costs. Charitable giving covered another quarter (over $17 billion was donated to arts, culture, and humanities organizations in 2014). Meanwhile, the National Endowment for the Arts granted out $117 million in 2014. For perspective on how small this federal role is, consider that the nascent "crowdfunding" website Kickstarter surpassed the NEA in 2012 in the amount it passes on to arts creators. By 2015, Kickstarter was distributing several times as much annual funding to artists as the NEA. Indicators of

Kickstarter's new role in providing venture capital for the arts include the fact that works funded by its donors now regularly win Grammy and Academy awards, get exhibited at museums like the MoMa and Smithsonian, and perform in top venues like the Kennedy Center and Sundance Film Festival.

Further reading

○ *Giving USA* (Giving USA Foundation, 2015)

○ 2014 NEA Annual Report, arts.gov/sites/default/files/2014%20Annual%20Report.pdf

○ Spending statistics for Kickstarter, kickstarter.com/help/stats

2011

ARCHIMEDES PALIMPSEST

In 1998, an anonymous billionaire purchased a horribly preserved medieval prayer book at a Christie's auction for $2 million. The reason for the gaudy price? The battered volume also contained the most important scientific manuscript ever sold at auction. The book was a palimpsest—a text written on top of an older text (because parchment was once so precious that books no longer appreciated often had their pages washed or scraped clean, and then recycled into new books). Underneath the thirteenth-century prayers were the erased contents of seven ancient works, nearly all of them previously lost to civilization, including two hitherto unknown essays by the third-century B.C. Greek mathematical genius Archimedes.

Portions of the previous text were visible as ghostly shadows, and had been translated in the early 1900s. But after the anonymous donor purchased the palimpsest he deposited it at the Walters Art Museum in Baltimore, and donated additional funds, supplemented by gifts from the Selz and Stockman Family foundations, so that the manuscript could be studied, conserved, and then presented to the public. Curators proceeded to disassemble, clean, and analyze the work. Over a 12-year period, more than 80 experts contributed to this philanthropically funded effort, culminating in an X-ray scan at Stanford that detected residual iron atoms from the iron-based ink of the original texts. That allowed scholars to read large sections of previously hidden text.

In addition to previously unknown works of history, philosophy, and politics, there were two important treatises by Archimedes: *The Method of Mechanical Theorems*, which explores the concept of infinity and anticipates many of the techniques of calculus, and *Stomachion*, the earliest Western theorizing in mathematical combinations of a sort that are now central to modern computing.

The Stanford scan also discovered the name of the scribe who erased the Archimedes text and other ancient writings and transcribed the prayers on top: Johannes Myronas, who finished his work on April 14, 1229, in Jerusalem. The prayer book was apparently then used for centuries in the monastery at St. Sabbas in the Judean desert. All of this is fascinatingly documented in a layman's book, Internet postings, and a multi-volume work from Cambridge University Press that presents actual images of the processed pages with transcriptions—thanks to the anonymous donor who started the whole investigation, and his insistence that all findings and images be shared directly with interested scholars and members of the public.

Further reading

○ Description from the Walters Art Museum, thewalters.org/news/releases/pressdetail. aspx?e_id=279

○ *New York Times* story, nytimes.com/2011/10/17/arts/secrets-of-archimedes-at-walters-in-baltimore-review.html?pagewanted=all

○ Cambridge Press reproductions and academic discussion, cambridge.org/us/academic/subjects/classical-studies/classical-studies-general/archimedes-palimpsest-volume-1

2011

CRYSTAL BRIDGES MUSEUM OF AMERICAN ART

Only major centers like New York and Boston can support great museums. Such is the conventional wisdom, but Alice Walton didn't buy it. She had a vision of creating a superb American art museum in the center of the country, and inviting citizens to enjoy and learn from it in comfortable ways. As a successful banker, she had the savvy to guide the project. And she had the means. Alice's father Sam founded Walmart, and the family already owned an extensive American art collection deemed one of the finest in the country, including works by Durand, Sargent, Peale, and others—centuries of American masterpieces.

In 2011, the Crystal Bridges Museum of American Art opened in Bentonville, Arkansas (also the headquarters of Walmart). Named after a spring on the property, the museum boasts 120 acres, a library, a sculpture garden, an operating budget of $16 million, and an endowment of over $800 million. Defying the odds, Alice Walton's project received enthusiastic critical reviews for both its architecture and its collection. And thanks to Walmart sponsorship, admission is free. In its first full year of operation (2012), the museum attracted more than 600,000 visitors. Walton remains chairman of the board.

Further reading

○ *Philanthropy* magazine reporting, philanthropyroundtable.org/topic/excellence_in_
  philanthropy/wal_art

○ Crystal Bridges Museum of American Art, crystalbridges.org

○ Alice Walton biography, alicewalton.org

2009

ARTS

HISTORY PHILANTHROPY

Washington-area financier David Rubenstein, who has a passion for U.S. history, has focused his philanthropy in the national capital region. The goal of many of his gifts, he has said, "is to remind people of American history.... People know so little about our history.... That's really why I try to do this."

Many of Rubenstein's efforts involve rehabilitation of patriotic sites. Take Arlington House. When Robert E. Lee sided with his state instead of his nation and took command of the Confederate army, the U.S. seized his family estate. It was located on a hill overlooking the nation's capital from the south bank of the Potomac. Lee's residence—which was modeled on the Temple of Hephaestus in Athens and built as a tribute to his relative George Washington—was turned into a military headquarters. The grounds became the home of several thousand liberated slaves. Then, in the third year of the war, the property was turned into a burying ground for men killed in the fight to preserve the Union. We now know it as Arlington Cemetery.

The residence, Arlington House, was designated a memorial to Robert E. Lee in 1925 and put under the protection of the National Park Service. But by 2014 it was tattered. To improve the experience of the 650,000 people who visit each year, David Rubenstein pledged $12.4 million to the National Park Foundation for restoration of the house and museum, the landscape, and the historic slave quarters.

A year later, Rubenstein made a $5.4 million donation to refurbish a more recent war memorial: the Iwo Jima sculpture which remembers the sacrifices of World War II marines. Then just days later came more spit and polish: a $10 million gift to the private foundation that maintains Thomas Jefferson's Monticello residence for public visits. That donation will help restore outbuildings, roads, and landscaping to return the property to its appearance as Jefferson knew it.

Previously, Rubenstein provided $7.5 million to repair the Washington Monument after it was damaged in an earthquake, $10 million toward a new library at George Washington's Mount Vernon estate, and a share of the $30 million pledged by a group of local philanthropists to expand the

National Gallery of Art. Rubenstein is known for buying historic documents and lending them to educational institutions or museums. One of the 17 remaining copies of the 715-year-old Magna Carta, which he purchased, is now on display in the National Archives.

From 2009 to 2015, Rubenstein's giving to landmarks and historic sites in the national capital region totaled $75 million.

Further reading

○ *Washington Post* report on Arlington gift, washingtonpost.com/local/
   robert-e-lees-arlington-mansion-gets-12-million-donation-from-david-
   rubenstein/2014/07/17/4981b686-0d0a-11e4-8341-b8072b1e7348_story.html

○ *Washington Post* report on Monticello gift, washingtonpost.com/local/philanthropists-
   latest-gift-10-million-to-jeffersons-monticello-plantation/2015/05/01/97e36c9c-ee8d-
   11e4-8abc-d6aa3bad79dd_story.html

2008

LINCOLN'S COTTAGE

It is little known that for fully a quarter of his presidency, Abraham Lincoln didn't live in the White House. He and his family chose to reside at a cottage on the grounds of a home for retired soldiers in northern Washington, D.C. At that time this was a rural area, and amid the pressure of the Civil War, their sorrow over losing their 12-year-old son Willie, and the fact that the White House was a wide-open bedlam where the President could be besieged by public petitioners at any time of day or night, the Lincolns found the quiet green oasis a place of peace and comfort. They slept there just days after their first inauguration, and on the night before the President was killed. Lincoln made some of his most momentous decisions there, including formulating the Emancipation Proclamation, and he read the Bible, poetry, and Shakespeare on its breezy porch. One historian described the Soldiers' Home cottage as "The only place we are certain Lincoln was happy during his Presidency."

✒ PhilAphorism

I believe the power to make money is a gift from God...to be developed and used to the best of our ability for the good of mankind.

☞ John Rockefeller

After being largely forgotten for generations, the cottage was preserved and opened to the public by a private nonprofit, the National Trust for Historic Preservation. Funds were raised to restore the building and interpret it for visitors, with real-estate developer and philanthropist Robert Smith being the primary donor. United Technologies Corporation provided $1 million and technical expertise to help create the nearby visitor center. Matthew and Ellen Simmons, Save America's Treasures, and many other foundations and individuals also contributed. Lincoln's Cottage opened for fascinating public tours in 2008.

Further reading

○ President Lincoln's Cottage at the Soldiers' Home, lincolncottage.org

A BROAD INFUSION OF
MODERN ART IN LOS ANGELES

Eli and Edythe Broad's foundations have assets of some $2.4 billion. Lifelong philanthropists, one of their major areas of focus has been art, and specifically, increasing access to contemporary art. Their own two collections, obtained over four decades, include nearly 2,000 works; they have donated 8,000 more pieces to nearly 500 museums worldwide. Their home region, the Los Angeles area, has benefited most from their art philanthropy. In 2006, the couple made a $23 million gift to build an incubator for artists at the University of California, Los Angeles. In 2008, the Broads offered a $30 million challenge grant to revitalize the Museum of Contemporary Art in Los Angeles. That same year they gave $60 million to build the Broad Contemporary Art Museum. And in 2013 they are scheduled to open their definitive museum, simply called The Broad, in downtown Los Angeles. They have also funded concert halls, revitalizations of public spaces, and served on countless museum boards.

Further reading

○ The Broad Foundation, broadartfoundation.org

○ Marjorie Garber, *Patronizing the Arts* (Princeton University Press, 2008)

CLASSICAL MUSIC POPULARIZED IN SAN FRANCISCO

The San Francisco Symphony was the first orchestra to feature radio broadcasts—in 1926, funded by local philanthropists. Almost 80 years later, in 2005, another generation of philanthropists (Evelyn and Walter Haas Jr.)

offered a $10 million grant to bring San Francisco's classical music to the Internet, television, home video, and local schools, through a program called Keeping Score. The result of this long pattern of philanthropically supported audience cultivation far afield of their home area, argues Terry Teachout of the *Wall Street Journal,* was "to turn the San Francisco Symphony into the most adventurous, audience-friendly orchestra in America." By 2015, the symphony had won 11 Grammy awards, and was playing for 600,000 fans every year.

The San Francisco Opera has similarly benefited from popularizing technology funded by philanthropy. The Koret Foundation purchased equipment that allowed the opera to record productions for showing in movie theaters nationwide, to beam free live simulcasts to parks and public spaces, and to create DVDs for public schools. Living donors John and Cynthia Gunn made a record $40 million grant that allowed the commissioning of new operas. And Dede Wilsey offered $5 million to modernize the business office, saving the opera $1.5 million every year in administrative costs.

Together, gifts like these have put classical music on a much more solid footing in San Francisco than in most other places.

Further reading

○ History of the San Francisco Symphony, sfsymphony.org/About-Us/Mission-History.aspx

○ About Keeping Score, keepingscore.org/about

○ *San Francisco Business Times* report, bizjournals.com/sanfrancisco/print-edition/2011/10/21/bay-area-philanthropy-arts-dance-to.html?page=all

2003

DRIEHAUS PRIZE IN ARCHITECTURE

Self-made Chicago financier Richard Driehaus argues that "Americans deserve better buildings.... Architecture should be of human scale, representational form, and individual expression that reflects a community's architectural heritage." He believes that relatively few contemporary buildings offer the "delight, proportion, and harmony" that good classical architecture provided in the past. So he created a major annual cash prize to encourage architects to do better.

Until then, the most prominent annual architecture award was the $100,000 Pritzker Prize, which generally went to ideological modernists, without much regard to how much fondness their buildings generated among the residents who had to live with them. Driehaus wanted to create incentives for architects to concentrate on traditional forms of architecture—which continue to be loved by ordinary citizens as much as they are neglected by many elites.

In 2003, Driehaus partnered with the University of Notre Dame's architecture school (a hotbed of neoclassicism) to establish the $200,000 Driehaus prize. It is given each year to "a living architect whose work embodies the highest ideals of traditional and classical architecture in contemporary society, and creates a positive cultural, environmental, and artistic impact." Its first recipient was Leon Krier, who designed the model town of Poundbury in England. Other winners have included neoclassicists like the husband-and-wife team of Andres Duany and Elizabeth Plater-Zyberk, Allen Greenberg, England's Quinlan Terry, and Egypt's Abdel-Wahed El-Wakil. Postmodern architects Robert Stern and Michael Graves, who have demonstrated fluency in classical motifs, have also won the award.

"The prize thus represents a partial counterbalance to the rejection of classical forms by elite architecture that prevailed for much of the last century," writes James Panero. In the process it has encouraged a fresh look at traditional modes of building and styling, and encouraged a whole new generation of designers to respect the forms created through centuries of urban evolution.

Further reading

○ *Philanthropy* magazine reporting, philanthropyroundtable.org/topic/excellence_in_philanthropy/from_driehaus_to_our_house

○ *Atlantic Cities* report, citylab.com/design/2012/02/should-cities-future-look-more-past/1094/

○ Richard Driehaus Prize at the University of Notre Dame, architecture.nd.edu

―――――――― 2002 ――――――――

RUTH LILLY, PATRONESS OF POETRY

Ruth Lilly was a poet herself. She had grown up wealthy, but that wasn't an advantage as she tried to express herself through verse. For years she sent samples to *Poetry* magazine using the pseudonym Guernsey Van Riper, but nobody was ever quite impressed enough to print what she wrote. That didn't dampen her love for the medium, or her belief in the magazine that had printed most of the great American poets since its founding in 1912. Over time, the Indianapolis resident's interest turned less toward her own poetry and more toward promoting poetry as such.

In 1986, she established the Ruth Lilly Poetry Prize, a $100,000 award to honor the lifetime accomplishments of living American poets. In 1989, she funded the Ruth Lilly Poetry Fellowships, $15,000 awards given to young up-and-coming poets to encourage their further study and writing of poetry. And in 2002, at age 87, she made her biggest splash, giving $100 million to *Poetry* magazine's publisher, the Poetry Foundation. In the words of the *Los Angeles Times*, this transformed the organization "from the most highly regarded but also perennially penniless American poetry journal into the world's largest foundation for verse." The endowment allowed the foundation to expand the fellowships from one winner per year to five, to pay printed poets more than the paltry $2 per line it had been able to afford in the past, and to offer funding to deserving writers. This changed the landscape of American poetry, at least at the highest levels, offering a path in which success could actually pay. Lilly, who also gave $120 million to the nonprofit Americans for the Arts, died in 2009.

Further reading

- *Los Angeles Times* report, sfgate.com/news/article/Poetry-magazine-gets-100-million-from-poet-it-2752418.php
- Ruth Lilly Poetry Prize and Fellowships, poetryfoundation.org
- Marjorie Garber, *Patronizing the Arts* (Princeton University Press, 2008)

2001

DORIS DUKE FOUNDATION INVESTS IN NEW ARTISTS

The Doris Duke Charitable Foundation has been a groundbreaker in the growing field of direct philanthropic support to artists—ranging from open-ended gifts to commissioning of specific works. Founded in 1996 in large part to improve the quality of people's lives through arts and culture, DDCF has already given more than $218 million to the arts, and has made two major investments in the lives of performing artists.

The first, in partnership with the Surdna Foundation, began in 2001. The idea was to pair budding performers with more experienced ones in a long-term mentorship program. After conducting research to establish the structure of the program, the Talented Students in the Arts Initiative invited applications from performing-arts schools that allowed aspiring artists to work with professionals. The applications required the institutions to demonstrate program excellence, matching funding, and a commitment to nurturing new artists.

In the first year, four arts high schools and five training institutions received grants totaling between $1 million and $1.6 million. All told, the program disbursed about $16 million in three- to five-year commitments, and strengthened programs like the Jacob's Pillow Dance Festival in New England and the Cleveland School for the Arts. (The latter, for example, was able to send 20 more students to camps and internships with established professionals each year.)

Ten years after the start of the Talented Students in the Arts Initiative, Duke Foundation president Ed Henry announced a second kind of investment in performing-arts talent. Over 10 years, $50 million would be allocated to provide multiyear fellowships of up to $275,000 to performing artists in jazz, theater, and contemporary dance. These grants represented the largest cash allocations to performing artists in history, and would allow the foundation to support up to 200 artists. The fellowships would be initiated by an anonymous peer-review panel—no applications would be accepted—and they would be an investment in the artist and his work, not a grant to create a specific project. The foundation collaborated on this project with the Creative Capital Foundation, which itself has been a pioneer in venture-philanthropy for artists since its founding in 1999. The first Doris Duke Artists were announced in 2012, the centennial of Duke's birth.

Further reading

° Duke University case study, cspcs.sanford.duke.edu/sites/default/files/descriptive/talented_students_in_the_arts.pdf

° Doris Duke Performing Artist Awards, ddpaa.org

° Creative Capital Foundation, creative-capital.org

2000

SEE-THE-GOOD TV

Brigham Young University has developed a reputation within the entertainment industry for its ability to turn out well-trained graduates with technical and storytelling skills, middle-American values, and solid work habits—making them prized hires in fields like movie animation. (See 1999 item nearby.) The latest area of growth and achievement is in television.

BYUtv is a major enterprise at the university, with a budget of $40 million per year, some of it coming from institutional support or commercial sponsorship, but most of it philanthropically funded. Fully 350 students work half time in the production studios, which also have 100 full-time employees. The most valuable "output" of the operation is thus not actually its programming, but the fully trained students who leap from BYU's Utah campus to Hollywood, Manhattan, Nashville, and other centers of entertainment production.

Thanks to donor support, the BYU studios now feature state-of-the-art digital equipment. With it, the department produces some 1,200 hours of television per year, which it distributes free all around the world via Internet streaming, cable distribution, and broadcast. And the organization has a special mission: to help people see the good in the world, via high-quality, wholesome, entertaining programing that entire families and people of all faiths and backgrounds can enjoy.

Both the "wholesome" and the "entertaining" parts of that equation are important. "You want your kids to eat broccoli, and they want to eat pizza," analogizes Scott Swofford, the director of content at BYU Broadcasting. "We're making broccoli pizza. The balance for us is if there's too much broccoli and edifying and uplifting and faith-based content, then no one's going to eat the pizza."

So BYUtv has shows on American history, on the charitable spirit, on family life, on holidays—but all of it works hard to be amusing. As often as not, it succeeds. The sketch-comedy show "Studio C," for instance, has drawn 40 million online views in just a few seasons. The Cold War drama "Granite Flats" is produced at a cost of $1 million per episode—about a third the cost of a typical network drama—yet is winning accolades. In recent years, BYUtv programs have won more than two dozen regional Emmy awards.

Further reading

○ Website of BYU Broadcasting, byutv.org

1999

IRA FULTON FEEDS
THE DIGITAL IMAGINATION

Ira Fulton's mother taught him to give generously from the time he was a child in Arizona. Her hamburger stand never turned anyone away, even if customers couldn't pay. "They're hungry," his mother explained simply. Fulton didn't have much money himself growing up, nor in his first years of marriage. What he did have was a tremendous work ethic (inspired by his Mormon faith) and a lively imagination. Diligently working one job after another, he eventually struck out on his own. He started a computer company. He helped remake a dying clothing retailer into a big moneymaker. He got into homebuilding.

By then he was wealthy, and wanted to leave his mark on the world through his giving spirit. He had already donated tens of millions to his alma mater, Arizona State, and to Brigham Young University. But where many wealthy people interested in art focus on museums or symphonies, Ira's vivid imagination kept him closer to young fields and young creators. He donated a supercomputer to BYU in 1999, and four more in the years that followed. In 2003, he funded the creation of BYU's computer-animation program. The program promptly turned out some of the star animators involved in films like *I, Robot* and *Star Wars*. One of the unique features of BYU's curriculum is that it doesn't just teach the students how to do animation, it trains them in the business environment of movie studios and how to work in teams to create commercial films.

Ultimately, Fulton would give over $80 million to the school. Today, BYU's Center for Animation produces about 25 animators per year, and is considered one of the best programs of its sort in the world. Pixar and Dreamworks assign employee mentors for the animation students and recruit graduates heavily. Having recognized the influence of digital animation within American popular culture—and particularly its significance to children and family life, Ira Fulton used a few savvy gifts to place the center of gravity for training new practitioners in a particularly family-friendly place, thereby changing the industry and our country.

Further reading

○ *Philanthropy* magazine report, philanthropyroundtable.org/topic/excellence_in_ philanthropy/joy_story

○ BYU Center for Animation, animation.byu.edu

○ *BYU Magazine* profile, magazine.byu.edu/article/ira-fulton-full-of-surprises/

1999

$60 MILLION FOR SAN DIEGO ART

Rea Axline had southern California written all over him. He had graduated from Caltech in 1931, and then figured out how to coat metal alloys onto other metal objects—reaping a fortune when World War II turned that capability into a goldmine.

Rea's wife, Lela, had an equally strong SoCal signature, except she was an artist rather than an inventor. She garnered critical acclaim for her abstract painting during the 1950s—and also loved teaching and helping other people appreciate what she did. When the Axlines turned to philanthropy, both of their occupations profited, as did their home city of San Diego, where they

◈ PhilAphorism

It is one of the most beautiful compensations of life that no man can sincerely try to help another without helping himself.

☞ *Ralph Waldo Emerson*

ARTS

focused their giving. They supported hospitals, the local zoological society, Rea's alma mater Caltech, and the local art museums.

It was after their deaths (Rea in 1992, Lela at the end of 1998) that their greatest contributions became known. One was a multimillion-dollar bequest to Caltech. The other was a pair of $30-million bequests: to the San Diego Museum of Art, and to San Diego's Museum of Contemporary Art. In each case, the sum was the largest gift the museum had received. The Museum of Art's endowment prior to the gift had been $47 million; the MCA's, only $4 million. The MCA was consequently able to expand into two new buildings in 2007, and the Museum of Art undertook a major renovation of its art school.

Further reading

○ *Los Angeles Times* report, articles.latimes.com/1999/jan/12/entertainment/ca-62616
○ *Los Angeles Times* obituary, articles.latimes.com/1992-11-03/local/me-1118_1_san-diego
○ Museum of Contemporary Art, San Diego, mcasd.org
○ San Diego Museum of Art, sdmart.org

1995

PRESERVATION OF COPLAND HOUSE

Aaron Copland meant a lot to a lot of people. So it's no surprise that when he died in 1990 the preservationists got to work. One of America's most distinctive composers, Copland wrote ballets, symphonies, movie scores, and jazz. He won the Presidential Medal of Freedom in 1964, the Pulitzer Prize in composition in 1945, an Academy Award for musical score in 1950, and many other honors. His home in Cortlandt Manor, New York, was simple and unspectacular—a prairie-style house with unobtrusive rooms that echoed to the sounds of his piano for 30 years—but it reflected its historically significant resident artist.

When Copland died in 1990, there were plans to sell the house. But a group of local citizens banded together to preserve it as a museum. Incorporated in 1995, the group conducted an effective grassroots fundraising campaign, raising $150,000 to restore the home. Today, it is owned by the town of Cortlandt and leased (virtually for free) to the Copland Heritage Association. Unlike some preserved artist residences, Copland House is not just a shrine. The Aaron Copland Awards, established in 1998, provide fellowships for six to eight emerging composers to live and work in the building, drawing their inspiration from its chambers for months at a time. The house also has a resident repertory ensemble, called Music from Copland House, which has won national acclaim for its performances. Various education programs based at the home also keep community members and enthusiasts entertained and educated. And in 2009, the Copland House and Westchester County established a new creative center for American music, bringing more resident composers to the area to learn and create.

In 2008, the Copland House was designated a National Historic Landmark. It is the only classical-music-related landmark to receive the distinction.

Further reading

○ Copland House, coplandhouse.org

○ Howard Pollack, *Aaron Copland: The Life and Work of an Uncommon Man* (University of Illinois Press, 2000)

1994

KNIGHT FOUNDATION EXPERIMENTS IN SAVING ORCHESTRAS

Creed Black was concerned. President of the John S. and James L. Knight Foundation, which conducts arts philanthropy in the 26 cities in which the Knight brothers owned newspapers, Black had noticed an increase in S.O.S. calls from struggling orchestras in its communities.

Recognizing that last-ditch cash infusions were rarely the way to save an orchestra, Black proposed a longer-term investment. With help from Oberlin College, he gathered a group of arts experts from Knight cities. Some of the experts thought there wasn't a long-term problem at all. Others suggested the problem was that concert halls were too stuffy. In the end, they created a Magic of Music program that had the goal of reversing the decline in audiences, and strengthening the relationship between audience and orchestra.

This was executed in two five-year phases, beginning in 1994 and concluding in 2004. In phase one, $5.4 million of grants supported fresh multiyear projects from ten orchestras. In phase two, $7 million supported 13 orchestras, some of whom had been involved in phase one, some new. Based on what the program's leadership learned in the first program, phase two introduced tighter goals, useful audience research, technical assistance, and better evaluation. Along the way, Knight commissioned two independent studies—one researched how Americans relate to classical music and local orchestras, the other analyzed the Magic of Music program itself.

By the end of these programs, orchestras and art philanthropists nationwide had far better knowledge about audience behavior (including

ARTS

the people who weren't coming to performances). A host of long-held assumptions was debunked. A working consortium of orchestras shared information on grants, programs, publications, and more.

Thanks to the Magic of Music program, orchestras knew that classical music wasn't dead, and they had long lists of what did and didn't work to cultivate audiences. Meanwhile, music philanthropists learned that technical assistance and research could be as important as dollars. From 2004 onward, lovers of classical music knew much more about how to keep symphonies alive.

Further reading

○ Thomas Wolf, "Magic of Music Final Report" (Knight Foundation, 2006), knightfoundation.org/publications/magic-music-final-report-search-shining-eyes

○ Knight Foundation press release, knightfoundation.org/press-room/press-release/new-knight-publication-examines-change/

1993

SAVING THE JOFFREY BALLET

When philanthropist Patricia Kennedy invited rock artist Prince to join her at the Joffrey Ballet in 1991, she didn't think the shy star would say yes.

Prince was renting a mansion from her at the time, and had a reputation as a recluse. He surprised her by agreeing, and after seeing his first ballet, went home in excitement to write dance music. The Joffrey had been founded in 1956, and moved from New York to Los Angeles in 1982, staggering under $1 million in debt and in danger of folding. Kennedy had long been one of its biggest supporters, and she gave extensively to keep the wolf from the door. Her introduction of a popular artist to formal art, however, may have been the biggest gift she ever gave the company.

As the Joffrey's finances continued to spiral downward, Kennedy suggested that the company use Prince's music in a ballet. A few months and a few conversations later, Prince had offered the company unprecedented access to his music, which allowed the Joffrey in 1993 to produce the first-ever rock ballet, entitled *Billboard*. In seemingly no time the work caught fire, winning a vast, new, younger audience that would fill its seats for a generation. By 1995 the company had made a permanent home in Chicago, and today bills itself as the "mavericks of American dance."

Thanks in large part to the visibility generated by Kennedy's tenant, the Joffrey is also known as America's company of firsts: the first ballet troupe to perform at the White House, the first to appear on television, the first on the cover of *Time* magazine, the first to have a major movie based on it (*The Company*, 2003), and, of course, the first to perform a rock-and-roll ballet.

Further reading

- The Joffrey Ballet history, joffrey.org/company/history
- *Hamptons* magazine profile, hamptons.com/The-Arts/Performing-Arts/16502/ Philanthropist-And-First-Lady-Of-The-Joffrey.html#.VjesE7erRpg
- *Chicago Tribune* report, articles.chicagotribune.com/1993-03-14/ entertainment/9303180252_1_joffrey-ballet-artistic-director-gerald-arpino-joffrey-board-member

$1 BILLION ANNENBERG ART COLLECTION DONATED TO THE METROPOLITAN MUSEUM

Walter Annenberg spent his life building a media empire, launching *Seventeen* and *TV Guide* magazines, and starting or buying one television station or cable company after another. By the mid-twentieth century he was making sizable charitable donations, and by the 1980s he had turned almost full time to philanthropy. While his roughly $2 billion in cash for education, research, broadcasting, and other areas included many notable milestones, perhaps his most stunning single gift came in the arts realm.

Annenberg had already been influential in lobbying to get the Barnes Collection in Philadelphia's suburbs opened to the public. He later tried unsuccessfully to start a center for art education through television. Then in 1991, he pledged his personal collection of 53 Impressionist and Post-Impressionist masterpieces to the Metropolitan Museum of Art. The collection was valued at $1 billion at the time. When the gift was announced, the *New York Times* suggested that the "Annenberg collection

---

♂ PhilAphorism

Neither the individual nor the race is improved by almsgiving. The best means of benefiting the community is to place within its reach the ladders upon which the aspiring can rise.

⊷Andrew Carnegie

...may be acclaimed in due time as the most important single gift to have been given to the Metropolitan Museum since 1929."

Further reading

◦ Waldemar Nielsen, *Inside American Philanthropy* (University of Oklahoma Press, 1996)

◦ *New York Times* report, nytimes.com/1991/03/12/arts/annenberg-picks-met-for-1-billion-gift.html?pagewanted=all

CARNEGIE HALL IS RESCUED, AND REORIENTED

Carnegie Hall is an American treasure—its history, its architecture, and its magnificent acoustics make it the gold standard for American music halls even a century and a quarter after its opening. It is also a masterpiece of philanthropy, having been created in 1891 for the enjoyment of the American public as a gift from Andrew Carnegie, who paid the entire bill for its creation and whose family owned the hall until 1925. Over the decades, thousands of concerts by the world's greatest artists have taken place in the facility, and the New York Philharmonic was in residence from 1892 to 1962.

By the early 1980s, though, the hall was in serious disrepair. Having rarely turned a profit in 90 years of existence, the facility required an estimated $30 million in fixes, and was in danger of being demolished. Then James Wolfensohn, an investment banker with a passion for music, led an ambitious effort to not only raise the money for restoration but also revamp the hall's business practices to ensure a long life. Wolfensohn overhauled the concert schedule and modernized the hall's marketing. He donated a million dollars of his own and roped other prominent New Yorkers into joining the effort. They raised $80 million, broadened the base of annual contributors from under 800 to over 9,000, and set the hall on a secure financial footing for the first time in decades.

The very earliest effort to meld commerce and art to keep Carnegie Hall flush had been when Andrew Carnegie himself added towers to the original auditorium to provide practice studios that could be rented to musicians. This both addressed a shortage of practice space in the city and gave the hall some regular cash flow. In 2014, a major donor-funded renovation of these practice spaces was unveiled. Fully rebuilt, enlarged, and sound-proofed, the rooms have allowed the facility to greatly expand its teaching, student performances, children's programming, master classes for artists, and chamber music activity, while making rehearsing more efficient for all sizes of ensembles.

During the construction, a roof garden was also added, the backstage areas of the hall were redone, all 450 windows were restored, and the exterior of the building was floodlit for the first time. The $230 million project made the hall more visible and useable, and the new spaces are also being rented, as planned, for receptions, weddings, and celebrations, adding another source of steady revenue to support the facility's arts programming. This further solidification of the future of the musical capital of the nation was supported by major donors like Joan and Sanford Weill ($35 million), Judith and Burton Resnick ($10 million), Lily Safra ($6 million), and others.

Further reading

○ Waldemar Nielsen, *Inside American Philanthropy* (University of Oklahoma Press, 1996)

○ New Carnegie Hall education wing, carnegiehall.org/uploadedFiles/Resources_and_ Components/PDF/Press/PressKit1415_StudioTowers_0122.pdf

1987

A NEW GENERATION DISCOVERS JAZZ AT LINCOLN CENTER

Many of the performing-arts organizations based in New York City's philanthropically supported Lincoln Center perform outside the metropolitan area during the summer. To help fill the gap in concerts, Lincoln Center managers launched a new program in 1987 to stage a series of jazz performances at the Center in the warm-weather months. By 1991, Jazz at Lincoln Center had become an official department devoted to year-round support and performance of America's original music. Under the direction of Wynton Marsalis, a resident orchestra was assembled and sent on regular national tours. The program received generous support from a range of donors, foundations, and companies, including a $20 million gift from investor Robert Appel in 2014.

Donor support also allowed numerous jazz-education initiatives to be created. These include not only instruction for local school children, but also a remarkable national festival that supports jazz in high school bands around America. The "Essentially Ellington" program sends full sets of classic jazz music, specially selected for each year, to any interested high-school music program in the U.S. Additional training materials, recordings, workshops, and on-site coaching are also offered to teachers and students who delve into the music. Up to a dozen regional festivals are held around the country, giving local high-school ensembles access to expert critiques and instruction. Toward the end of the year, jazz bands that have prepared that year's selected songs for concert are invited to send recordings to the "Essentially Ellington" staff, and the top entrants are invited to Lincoln Center. There they get additional workshops and mentoring from jazz masters, and then play in a climactic concert, along with Wynton Marsalis. Competition winners and runners-up are honored. Repeated every year since 1996, the "Essentially Ellington" festival has engrained the great jazz standards and techniques in a whole new generation of American youngsters.

Further reading

○ JALC history, jazz.org/history/

○ The "Essentially Ellington" program, academy.jazz.org/ee/

1987

NATIONAL MUSEUM OF WOMEN IN THE ARTS

On a trip to Europe, Wallace and Wilhelmina Holladay fell in love with some paintings by seventeenth-century Flemish artist Clara Peeters. When they returned home, they were disappointed to find they couldn't find Peeters in any of the major art textbooks.

Around this same time, in the early 1960s, the Holladays decided to focus their art collecting on women in the arts. After a couple of decades their collection had grown large enough that Wilhelmina started thinking about displaying it. Her initial idea was to donate it to some museum, but Nancy Hanks, chairwoman of the National Endowment for the Arts, convinced her to start a museum of her own with the Holladay collection as its core.

By 1981, Wilhelmina's energies had gotten enough people on board for the National Museum of Women in the Arts to open in temporary offices, with most of the 500 pieces of art remaining at the Holladays' home (open for tours). By 1983, Wilhelmina had completed a tenacious capital campaign and raised enough money to purchase and renovate an 80,000-square-foot building near the White House. All in all, $17 million was raised, and the museum opened in its new home in 1987. The museum's unusually active membership spans all 50 states, and the collection now includes approximately

⌐ PhilAphorism

If you would help another man, you must do so in minute particulars. ☞ *William Blake*

3,000 works dating back to the Renaissance. Wilhelmina received the 2006 National Medal of Arts from President George W. Bush.

Further reading

○ National Museum of Women in the Arts history, nmwa.org/about/our-history

○ Wilhelmina Cole Holladay, *A Museum of Their Own* (Abbeville Books, 2008)

MOSES ASCH AND
AMERICAN FOLK MUSIC

Moses Asch originally co-founded Folkways Records in 1948 in an ambitious attempt to record and document "the entire world of sound." At the time, this meant everything from music of all sorts to poetry and historical recordings. His tiny staff recorded over 2,000 albums in 38 years, capturing some of the most important artists and writers of the day, including Woody Guthrie, Ella Jenkins, Pete Seeger, and W. E. B. DuBois.

The idea wasn't to make money, and they didn't stop offering something if it wasn't selling. "Would you take the letter 'q' out of the dictionary because it was used less than the other letters?" Asch liked to ask. Near the end of his life, in the 1980s, Asch was looking for a way to preserve his recordings for future generations.

He found Ralph Rinzler at the Smithsonian, who was running the institution's folk festival. Asch offered to donate the collection on one condition: that the Smithsonian uphold his commitment to keeping the sounds of American folk music alive. Asch died before the deal could be completed, but in 1987 it was finalized and a new nonprofit, Smithsonian Folkways, was launched. Smithsonian Folkways has subsequently added 375 more recordings, and in 2005 made much of the collection available online—with the help of a grant from the Rockefeller Foundation.

Further reading

○ Smithsonian Folkways, folkways.si.edu

○ Smithsonian Center for Folklife and Cultural Heritage, folklife.si.edu

○ Richard Carlin, *Worlds of Sound* (HarperCollins Publishers, 2008)

THE POLLOCK-KRASNER FOUNDATION

Jackson Pollock was one of the most significant painters of the twentieth-century, but his family's legacy goes far beyond his paintings. By the early 1980s, with Pollock long dead and his wife, Lee Krasner, ailing, their wealth (largely consisting of both spouses' works) was valued at approximately $20 million. Krasner opted in 1985 to donate those assets to create a foundation, not to promote her art or her husband's, but to support "worthy and needy visual artists" around the world. The Pollock-Krasner Foundation became the first successful foundation established by an artist, for artists, and is known for its smart, personal, flexible, fast philanthropy. It has to work that way, because unlike most art-loving groups, it focuses on providing emergency financial assistance to artists.

The foundation has been known to pay rent, provide health care or mental help, and meet a variety of other needs for talented artists. It supports dozens of artists each year, with grants varying in size and purpose based on the artist's skill and need. It funds only visual artists who work in the categories of painting, sculpture, and installation (e.g. no computer or video artists), but has no requirements in terms of style. The foundation also operates the Lee Krasner Awards, which are by nomination only and recognize an artist's lifetime achievements. As of 2012, the Pollock-Krasner Foundation has made over 3,500 grants totaling $54 million to artists in 72 countries, and artists have credited its assistance for rescuing them from everything from poverty to creative blocks to suicide.

Further reading

○ Waldemar Nielsen, *Inside American Philanthropy* (University of Oklahoma Press, 1996)

○ Pollock-Krasner Foundation, pkf.org

1982

STATUE OF LIBERTY-ELLIS ISLAND FOUNDATION

The Statue of Liberty may be the best known monument in the world, and the adjoining Ellis Island immigration halls are among America's most historic sites. Both venues have been restored and revamped for mass visitation entirely by private philanthropy. In 1982, as the centennial of the statue approached, President Ronald Reagan appointed Lee Iacocca, then chairman of Chrysler Corporation, to lead a private-sector effort to fund restoration and preservation; the Statue of Liberty-Ellis Island Foundation was born. Almost 1,000 laborers soon went to work, and the internal structure of the statue was rebuilt, the deteriorated torch replaced, an elevator installed, and a public exhibit created in the pedestal base. The preserved monument reopened to the public on July Fourth weekend, 1986. The foundation then went to work saving the badly deteriorated Ellis Island structures where millions of American families first touched U.S. soil. Five buildings were saved and turned into informative exhibits, and the island opened to visitors in 1990, two years ahead of schedule. In 1993, the foundation created a permanent endowment to fund enhancements of the two sites for years to come; so far, more than 200 projects have been carried out with endowment proceeds. The American people have now contributed more than $600 million in voluntary contributions to the Statue of Liberty-Ellis Island Foundation, allowing all this work to be done without any government funds. Since opening in 1990, the Ellis Island Immigration Museum has welcomed 40 million visitors, and the Statue of Liberty hosts 4 million guests every year.

Further reading
○ Statue of Liberty-Ellis Island Foundation, statueofliberty.org/Foundation.html

THE NEW CRITERION

The founding of *The New Criterion* is a case study in how foundation philanthropy has changed. Two art critics, Hilton Kramer and Samuel Lipman, wanted to start a conservative journal that focused on intellectual criticism. As Kramer put it, they wanted a publication that would "identify and uphold a standard of quality, and speak plainly and vigorously about the problems that beset the life of the arts and the life of the mind in our society."

Kramer was an intellectual heavyweight who eventually became the chief art critic at the *New York Times*, and Lipman was a pianist who served as the long-time music critic at *Commentary*. Both carried weight in critical circles, but the linchpin of their publication's launch was Michael Joyce, executive director of the John M. Olin Foundation. Joyce was sold on the pair's idea before he'd seen a single grant application, business plan, or funders list; he thought the strength of the editors would carry the project. He contacted Richard Larry at the Sarah Scaife Foundation and Leslie Lenkowsky of the Smith Richardson Foundation, and each of the three organizations agreed to commit $100,000 per year for the first three years.

Almost before they'd begun, Kramer and Lipman had the funding they

◁ PhilAphorism

It is by spending oneself that one becomes rich.
☞ *Sarah Bernhardt*

needed to get started. In the years that followed, Joyce would hold up *The New Criterion* as a paragon for conservative philanthropy—relying on reputations and relationships, rather than red tape, to quickly translate a fresh idea into reality. The strength of the project idea, not the needs of the funders, had driven the project. *The New Criterion* remains a small but significant intellectual force today, influencing conservative and liberal intellectuals alike, leading the London *Telegraph* to tag it "America's leading review of the arts and intellectual life."

Further reading

- *The New Criterion*, newcriterion.com
- Hudson Institute report, hudson.org/research/8919-conservative-philanthropy-and-the-larger-view
- *New York Times* Hilton Kramer obituary, nytimes.com/2012/03/28/arts/design/hilton-kramer-critic-who-championed-modernism-dies-at-84.html
- *The New Criterion* Samuel Lipman obituary, newcriterion.com/articles.cfm/Samuel-Lipman--1934-1994-5070

1981

SUNDANCE INSTITUTE

In 1981, the actor Robert Redford gathered a group of his friends and colleagues in the Utah mountains to think through ways of encouraging high-quality independent filmmaking in the U.S. Later that spring, ten younger filmmakers were invited to the first Filmmakers/Directors Lab sponsored by a new nonprofit calling itself the Sundance Institute. In the remote natural setting, the participants were given opportunities to develop original film projects with guidance from experienced writers and directors, while getting advanced training in practical areas like editing and storytelling.

Since that time, Sundance's Feature Film Program has supported more than 300 additional feature films, and 500 films have been supported by the institute's Documentary Film Program. In 1984 a Theatre Program was added, which has since supported the development of more than 200 plays. The institute also took over a pre-existing film festival staged in Park City, Utah, and turned the January event into the nation's most important festival for presenting independent movies. Festival features have included productions like *Reservoir Dogs, Hedwig and the Angry Inch, American Splendor, An Inconvenient Truth, Little Miss Sunshine,* and *Beasts of the Southern Wild.* Many significant filmmakers, like Steven Soderbergh and Quentin Tarantino, received their first prominence at Sundance.

All of this is heavily supported by philanthropy. Contributions to the institute totaled $20 million in 2014. Ticket and fee income, meanwhile, came to under $15 million. Donors thus carry most of the group's expense load. They range from small individual contributors to foundations like Annenberg, Ford, and Gates.

Further reading

○ Sundance Institute history, sundance.org/about/us

ARTS

YOUNGARTS

Ted Arison knew something about building small chances into big successes. He had grown Carnival Cruise Lines from a single ship into the largest and most profitable cruise line in the world (by far, with revenues of over $2 billion a year). When he took up art philanthropy, he founded the YoungArts program and the National Foundation for Advancement in the Arts. Rather than focus on the display or creation of art, Arison wanted to start an organization that focused on young artists themselves, building them up with encouragement and support. Since Florida hosted several of Carnival's major hubs, Arison opted to locate the program in Miami, a city he believed was in need of a stronger arts presence.

Since its founding, YoungArts has supported the careers of thousands of budding artists through education programs, financial support, awards, and more. One of its programs, YoungArts Week, brings 150 of the nation's best young artists to Miami for a week each year, providing them with encouragement, training, and networking opportunities with their peers and with established artists.

Further reading

○ National YoungArts Foundation history, youngarts.org/about-youngarts-0

○ YoungArts Week, miami.com/youngarts-week-article

○ *New York Times* Ted Arison obituary, nytimes.com/1999/10/02/business/ted-arison-carnival-founder-dies-at-75.html

SPOLETO FESTIVAL USA

Gian Carlo Menotti was a Pulitzer Prize-winning, Italian-American composer who had a passion for introducing popular audiences to opera. In 1958, he had founded the Festival of Two Worlds in Spoleto, Italy, a festival that drew hundreds of thousands of people to see and hear music, theater, and dance performances. In the 1970s, he decided he wanted to bring the same experience to America, and got other composers and music-lovers on board. A search led them to Charleston, South Carolina, as the perfect city in terms of setting and amenities.

The first Spoleto Festival USA in 1977 was a success, and Charleston became its permanent home. Since then, the festival has become a 17-day phenomenon, with more than 700 events attended by up to 80,000 people. It has become one of the world's leading music festivals, presenting more than 200 world or American premieres, and hosting budding artists who later become acclaimed, like Joshua Bell, Renée Flemming, and Yo-Yo Ma.

Philanthropy has made the festival possible from the beginning. Today, ticket sales provide half of the event's revenue, and an equal amount (more than $3 million per year) comes from donations large and small. Major gifts come from a pool of more than 600 annual donors. Private giving is likewise central to the physical plant that hosts the musical and theatrical performances. The city-owned auditorium which is the festival's largest venue recently got a $142-million renovation with exactly half paid for privately.

Further reading

○ About the festival, spoletousa.org/about/program-history-2/

1974

HIRSHHORN MUSEUM
OF CONTEMPORARY ART

Joseph Hirshhorn's parents brought him to America from Latvia in 1907, as an eight-year-old. When he reached 13, he dropped out of school to get a job, and by 15 he was working on Wall Street. He saved $255 and used it to become a teenage stockbroker. He had a knack for making money, and used it to start collecting art, beginning with two small works by Albrecht Durer he purchased at age 18.

By the 1940s, he had become rich thanks to some mining investments, and had begun to quietly accumulate a substantial collection of modern sculpture. He made friends with many living artists. After he loaned some pieces to the Guggenheim Museum in 1962, galleries began to vie for his collection.

Particularly aggressive in courting Hirshhorn was Smithsonian president Dillon Ripley, who offered a location on the National Mall. The museum opened in 1974, in an unfortunate new building designed by Gordon Bunshaft. The structure became "known around Washington as the bunker or gas tank, lacking only gun emplacements or an Exxon sign," wrote Ada Louise Huxtable of the *New York Times*. She described the structure as "born-dead, neo-penitentiary modern…not so much aggressive or overpowering as merely leaden."

Hirshhorn's collecting impulse, however, was not dead. He kept acquiring, and left another large bequest upon his death in 1981. Today, the museum houses over 12,000 works.

Further reading

○ Waldemar Nielsen, *Inside American Philanthropy* (University of Oklahoma Press, 1996)

○ Hirshhorn Museum description of founding donor Joseph Hirshhorn, hirshhorn.si.edu/collection/history-of-the-hirshhorn/#detail=/bio/the-founding-donor/&collection=history-of-the-hirshhorn

SANTA FE CHAMBER MUSIC FESTIVAL

Featuring cellist Pablo Casals as honorary president, the inaugural Santa Fe Chamber Music Festival launched in 1973, with 14 artists performing a handful of Sunday concerts. Today, its six-week season in July and August brings thousands of people to the Sangre de Cristo Mountains to partake of more than 80 musical events staged in auditoriums around the city. Since 1980 the festival has also commissioned more than 50 works from contemporary composers, adding significantly to the modern chamber-music repertoire. And the festival supports a strong year-round music-education series for K–8 school children in the Santa Fe area.

Americans all across the country who've never had a chance to attend the festival have also been soothed and aroused by music from Santa Fe. Since 1981, hundreds of festival performances have been broadcast nationally by the WFMT radio network. From its inception, the festival has relied heavily on hundreds of private donors. In a typical recent year, ticket sales brought in $538,000, while voluntary contributions totaled $1,150,000.

Further reading

○ About the festival, santafechambermusic.com/about/vision-mission-history/

WORTHY ART AT THE KIMBELL MUSEUM

Kay and Velma Kimbell were among Texas's first major art collectors, and it all happened virtually by accident. They attended a 1935 exhibit of paintings at Fort Worth's downtown library, and bought one of the works. The exhibit's organizer, Bertram Newhouse of New York, told them Texas needed more great art, and that they should start collecting. They did. Kay was a bit of an Anglophile, so their initial purchases focused on eighteenth-century British art, but they quickly branched out.

When Kay died in 1964, the entire family fortune was given to the Kimbell Art Foundation, with instructions to create a first-class art museum in Fort Worth. The project was begun in 1966, beginning with the Kimbell's own collection of some 350 items, ranging from antiquity to the present. Since the collection was so diverse, there was no question of focusing on a particular era or art form; the organizing criteria was simply that the collections must be of the "highest aesthetic quality."

The building itself met that same criteria. Designed by Louis Kahn and completed in 1972, it won numerous awards and is admired for creating one of the fine interiors of the twentieth century. The museum expanded in 2013.

Further reading

○ Kimbell Art Museum, kimbellart.org/about/history

WOLF TRAP NATIONAL PARK FOR PERFORMING ARTS

"You have many parks for recreation, but you have nothing in the performing arts," Catherine Filene Shouse told the U.S. Secretary of the Interior. "Do you want Wolf Trap?" Heiress to the Filene's department-store fortune, Shouse was offering her family's farm located just outside Washington, D.C. Soon, Congress accepted the gift of 100 acres of land plus funds to build a 6,800-seat open-air theater, and in 1971 the venue opened just in time to capitalize on the massive expansion of Washington's Virginia suburbs. Ten years later Shouse donated additional lands and money to create an indoor theater, made by connecting two eighteenth-century barns moved from upstate New York, so the park could host performances year-round. Wolf Trap is run by a private nonprofit foundation set up to program its music and dramatic events, handle marketing, develop educational programs, and raise philanthropic funds so ticket prices can be kept affordable. The National Park Service owns and maintains the grounds and buildings. Still the nation's only national park dedicated to the performing arts, Wolf Trap has become a favorite cultural venue in the national capital region.

Further reading

○ Wolf Trap Foundation, wolftrap.org/Learn_About_Wolf_Trap.aspx

MASTERPIECE THEATRE

In 1967, a 26-part BBC adaptation of "The Forsyte Saga," John Galsworthy's book series following an upper-middle-class British family, premiered on American television. Stanford Calderwood, president of the Boston PBS station WGBH, loved the idea of regularly putting classic dramas on TV, and asked the BBC about a deal to allow his station to play more such British-produced shows. Talks went on, but money, as it so often is, was the problem. Calderwood explored several ideas for the show's format and funding, and eventually found himself standing before Herb Schmertz of Mobil (later ExxonMobil).

Schmertz, a savvy intellectual, handled Mobil's corporate gifts. Calderwood asked him if he had seen "The Forsyte Saga" and Schmertz said he had loved it. Calderwood asked if Mobil would consider funding similar BBC programming via a modest investment of $375,000. Schmertz was interested enough to find out what Calderwood was talking about, and eventually able to get the go-ahead from Mobil's chairman.

In 1971, Masterpiece Theatre aired its first show ("The First Churchills"). Over the years, the series presented many beloved programs, bringing works of classic and recent literature to U.S. television—many of them unknown to American popular audiences. Notables included "Jeeves and Wooster," "Upstairs/Downstairs," "Wives and Daughters," "I, Claudius," and "Downton Abbey." Over a 32-year period, Mobil/ExxonMobil would give $250 million in support of Masterpiece Theatre, ending its sponsorship in 2004. The series was supported by PBS viewer donors until 2011, when Franklin Templeton Investments became the next of several corporations to become sponsors.

Further reading

○ *Los Angeles Times* reporting, articles.latimes.com/2002/dec/14/nation/na-pbs14

1968

BUSINESS COMMITTEE FOR THE ARTS

Esquire magazine began giving annual Business in the Arts awards in 1966. A year later, David Rockefeller launched a national task force of CEOs dedicated to increasing arts philanthropy. In 1968, the two programs were

 PhilAphorism

I resolved to stop accumulating and begin the infinitely more serious and difficult task of wise distribution.   ɛ *Andrew Carnegie*

combined into one project to recognize firms making significant contributions to the American arts.

Rockefeller believed that modern corporations had a major role to play in patronizing culture, filling the place that rich individuals occupied in Renaissance Europe. He hoped that the awards would play a role in encouraging corporations to step up. One of the earliest winners, the department store Abraham and Strauss, was honored in 1968 for funding revitalization of the Brooklyn Academy of Music. In later years, IBM, Polaroid, and other companies were celebrated for sponsoring museums, performances, telecasts of art events, and more.

In 2008, the Business Committee for the Arts merged operations with Americans for the Arts to form the largest-ever private-sector advocacy organization for the arts. By that time, the business community's art philanthropy had grown from an estimated $22 million in 1967 to over $3 billion in 2006.

Further reading

○ Marjorie Garber, *Patronizing the Arts* (Princeton University Press, 2008)

○ Americans for the Arts press release, americansforthearts.org/sites/default/files/pdf/ news/press-releases/2008/10/AFTA-and-Business-Committee-for-the-Arts-Merge-Operations.pdf

1968

NEW YORK MUSIC AND THE MARY FLAGLER CARY CHARITABLE TRUST

When Mary Flagler Cary inherited a great deal of money from her wealthy parents, there was no doubt but that she would use much of it for the flourishing of music. Her father, Standard Oil investor Henry Flagler, had been president of the New York Philharmonic, her family's rich music collection would be valued in 2005 at $100 million, and artists and musicians had been around the house for her entire life. When Mary died in 1967, she left a $72 million charitable trust focused on two purposes: New York City musical organizations, and national and local groups devoted to nature conservation. There was one catch: the trust must be depleted within 50 years.

Nearly a third of the trust's gifts went to music. There was a focus on all five of New York City's boroughs, and on many gifts to small organizations rather than big gifts to large entities. The trust made grants in performance, modern music, and music education, funding small orchestras and opera companies, ensembles, youth symphonies, and the like. The Cary Trust wound down by 2009 as methodically as it had operated, at the end making big gifts and setting up endowments so that its grantees would not be left in the lurch. In its lifetime, the Cary Trust distributed over $330 million.

Further reading

○ Heidi Waleson, *A Trust Fulfilled: Four Decades of Grantmaking by the Mary Flagler Cary Charitable Trust* (The Mary Flagler Cary Charitable Trust, 2009)

1966

AVERY BRUNDAGE
BRINGS ASIAN ART TO THE U.S.

Avery Brundage is perhaps best known for his involvement with the Olympic movement—he was a track-and-field competitor at the 1912 Stockholm games, and led the International Olympic Committee from 1952 to 1972. He grew up penniless, after his father abandoned the family, and was once described by *Sports Illustrated* as "the kind of man whom Horatio Alger had canonized—the American urchin, tattered and deprived, who rose to thrive in the company of kings and millionaires." After his sporting career, Brundage made a fortune in construction, developing commercial buildings in fast-growing early-twentieth-century Chicago. During the Depression he would sometimes take an ownership interest in properties in lieu of cash payment—which paid off handsomely after World War II.

Brundage used a big part of his wealth to accumulate a collection of Asian art that *Life* called "one of the largest and most important in private hands in this country." Its works spanned the continent, coming from not only Japan, Korea, and China, but also Southeast Asia, India, Tibet, and Persia. They included jades from the neolithic period to the modern era, as well as hundreds of bronzes, and an eclectic mix of ceramics, scrolls, paintings, prints, and textiles.

In the 1950s, Brundage offered to donate his treasures to the city of San Francisco. His unabashed goal was to help "the Bay Area become one of the world's greatest centers of Oriental culture." The new Asian Art Museum opened in 1966, with Brundage's collection at the core. By the time he died in 1975, Brundage had given 7,700 artworks to the museum, and prodded it to increasing heights in public presentation and scholarly authority. Since then, other philanthropists have opened great collections of Asian art to the public—for instance, the Sackler and Freer Galleries in Washington D.C., and the Crow Museum in Dallas. Asian art is thus no longer uncommon in the U.S. Yet America's preeminent repository of creations from across the Pacific remains the one gathered by the urchin from Chicago.

ARTS

Further reading

° San Francisco Asian Art Museum, asianart.org/about/history

1966

A DELICIOUS COLLECTION
DONATED BY CAMPBELL

John Dorrance and William Murphy, chairman and president of Campbell Soup Company, had soup in their blood. Dorrance was the son of the founder of Campbell's, and Murphy had worked there for nearly three decades. Not content with just making soup, the men wanted to showcase the fanciest crocks in which people served it. In 1966 they began collecting soup tureens and servers, and eventually founded a museum in Camden, New Jersey, to house hundreds of exquisite objects. In their enthusiasm, the men pulled together items of great and eclectic beauty: china, metalwork, and glass items, some of them dating back to the early 1700s.

During the 1990s, Campbell's leadership decided its collection needed better care than they were able to provide. They found a willing partner in Winterthur, the lavish museum of American decorative arts located on the du Pont estate in Delaware. Winterthur already housed an impressive collection of nearly 100,000 art objects, and in 1997 added the 300-piece Campbell donation to a specially designed gallery. The collection is one of Winterthur's most popular attractions.

Further reading

° Campbell Collection of Soup Tureens at Winterthur, winterthur.org/?p=557

° *Washington Post* reporting, washingtonpost.com/archive/lifestyle/home-garden//1996/03/28/soups-on-at-winterthur/966091e6-8a25-4f22-a839-332a1e4fba20/

1966

IMA HOGG AND THE HOUSTON ARTS SCENE

Unlike some philanthropists, Ima Hogg's first challenge wasn't getting rich—it was getting around her comical name. The daughter of the governor of Texas was part of a high-powered family, and never lacked for stature or money, especially when oil was discovered under the family land she had inherited. From a young age, she played a major role in her father's political and business affairs, and when she became an heiress in 1906 she turned her wealth to philanthropic purposes.

While she is perhaps best known for her work in mental health, she had an equally powerful interest in the arts. She had been a musician herself, having studied in New York, Berlin, and Vienna. She was a key figure in the creation of the Houston Symphony (which played its first concert in 1913). She outdid herself in 1966, though, when she gave her plantation home to the Houston Museum of Fine Arts, including its magnificent main building, sprawling gardens, and impressive collection of American furnishings. The property, Bayou Bend, is now the museum's American decorative arts center, and houses "one of the finest showcases of American furnishings, silver, ceramics, and paintings in the world." It draws thousands of visitors each year.

Further reading

○ Museum of Fine Arts Houston, mfah.org

○ Virginia Bernhard, *Ima Hogg: The Governor's Daughter* (Texas Monthly Press, 1984)

1966

PRESERVATION OF OLANA

When renowned Hudson River School painter Frederic Church bought his Olana property in 1860, he originally lived there in a small cottage. Following extensive travels in Europe and the Middle East, he and his wife Isabel had a grand house built. It would be "Persian, adapted to the Occident," as Church described it. The family moved into the building in 1872 and stocked it with thousands of items from great world civilizations—tapestries, paintings, sculptures, etc.—along with Church's own wall stencils, room colors, and furniture and textile designs. Church simultaneously shaped the landscape around the house, considered by some to be among his most beautiful creations.

The property remained a project for the rest of the artist's life; he had it more or less the way he wanted it by 1891, nine years before his death. When he passed away in 1900, the home stayed in the family, preserved by the fierce efforts of his daughter-in-law Sally. When she died in 1964 her nephew opted to auction off the property. Art historian David Huntingdon begged for time to raise funds to buy the house outright. He formed Olana Preservation and convinced some of the biggest names in the art and philanthropy worlds,

◈ PhilAphorism

Whoever sows sparingly will also reap sparingly, and whoever sows bountifully will also reap bountifully. ☞ *St. Paul*

ARTS

including Lincoln Kirstein and Henry Hope Reed, to lend their support. The group was able to buy the 250-acre property, the house, and the furnishings in 1966. It is open today as a historic site and art museum, one of the most popular tourist sites in upstate New York. Even Church's original cottage remains much as he left it.

Further reading

○ Olana Historic Site, olana.org

SAVING FRANK LLOYD WRIGHT MASTERPIECES

Architectural legend Frank Lloyd Wright designed the house known as Fallingwater for the Edgar Kaufmann family in 1936. The Kaufmanns owned a department store in Pittsburgh. The challenge they gave Wright: build them a house next to a waterfall on their remote property in the mountains far outside Pittsburgh. Wright upped the ante, saying the house should be meshed with the waterfall instead of just looking upon it. He produced an architectural marvel that doesn't appear to be grounded in the earth at all; it hovers over the cascade, and the water's sound is part of the home. The 5,300 square-foot structure was completed in 1939 for just over $150,000. It made the cover of *Time* magazine.

It remained the family's vacation home until 1963, when Kaufmann's son, recognizing the home's artistic and architectural significance, donated it to the Western Pennsylvania Conservancy. The nonprofit opened it as a museum in 1964; the only Wright-designed building to be open to the public with its original furnishings and artwork. In 1988, 1995, and 2002, major repairs were conducted due to structural problems. The museum remains open to the public and sees about 150,000 visitors per year (4.5 million since opening).

Several other Frank Lloyd Wright masterpieces have also been saved over the last generation by the intervention of generous donors and public-spirited volunteers. Wright's own favorite design, the Darwin Martin House near Buffalo, New York, was rescued by the Martin House Restoration Corporation, a nonprofit founded in 1992 to bring the deteriorated site back to its former glory. Many individual and corporate donors collaborated to purchase the several buildings on the site, undertake exterior renovations and re-creation of removed structures, and launch interior renovations—eventually to include restoration or re-make of all of Wright's original custom furniture for the home.

Further reading

○ Fallingwater museum, fallingwater.org

○ Martin House complex, darwinmartinhouse.org

1962

VAN CLIBURN INTERNATIONAL
PIANO COMPETITION

Harvey Lavan Cliburn, better known simply as Van Cliburn, shocked the world in 1958 when he traveled to the Soviet Union and won the International Tchaikovsky Competition in Moscow at a peak of the Cold War. Cliburn was in debt and unable to afford the trip, but a $1,000 grant from the Martha Baird Rockefeller Fund for Music program made his participation, and ultimate triumph, possible. The acclaimed pianist subsequently played for Reagan and Gorbachev at the White House, for the New York Philharmonic's 100th anniversary, and at other momentous occasions. Nearly as popular in the Soviet Union as in America, he became a performing ambassador for the universality of classical music in a divided world.

In his honor, certain of his friends and some music teachers in Fort Worth, Texas, raised funds to create the Van Cliburn International Piano Competition in 1962. Held every four years as a kind of Olympiad for young pianists, the competition awards large cash prizes and three years of concert management services to its champions. Since its inception as the funder and organizer of the competition, the Van Cliburn Foundation has sought to bring the highest-quality music to audiences around the world.

Thanks to support from corporations and foundations, the organizers have also been able to broadcast the competitions, stream them live on the Internet, and produce documentaries behind the scenes. In addition, in 1999, the foundation launched an international piano competition for outstanding amateurs over age 35. The Van Cliburn prize has become one of the most sought-after competition awards in all of music.

Further reading

○ The Cliburn Competition, cliburn.org

○ *New York Times* feature, query.nytimes.com/gst/fullpage.
   html?res=9E0CE0DD133FF931A25755C0A9679D8B63&pagewanted=all

1962

CREATING, AND RE-CREATING, LINCOLN CENTER

Lincoln Square in Manhattan was badly blighted in 1955. An informal committee that met to discuss what to do with it quickly elected John Rockefeller III as chairman. Rockefeller and his entire family became convinced that what the area—and New York City generally—really needed was a musical center. So he began raising funds to build one. Altogether, Rockefeller would raise nearly half of the $185 million used for the project, with various Rockefeller foundations and family members contributing heavily. The first building was 1962's Philharmonic Hall, renamed Avery Fisher Hall in 1973 after a donor, and then David Geffen Hall after a renovating donor. The New York State Theater followed in 1964, and the Metropolitan Opera House opened in 1966. The Lincoln Center for the Performing Arts was incorporated as home of the New York Philharmonic, Juilliard School, Metropolitan Opera, New York City Ballet, and dozens of other performing-arts organizations.

Philanthropy played as impressive a role in later expansions of Lincoln Center as it had in the founding. By the 1980s, the center had run out of space, and between nervous neighbors, inflexible zoning codes, and high costs, expansion in its crowded neighborhood was a long shot. Frederick Rose was a successful real-estate developer who served on the center's board. He loved music, and frequently entertained his fellow members on the piano after board meetings. Rose also loved making things happen, and volunteered to pick a team of lawyers, architects, and consultants who could overcome the barriers to expansion.

Rose handled negotiations with property owners and the city, and raised $100 million, including giving more than $15 million himself. By 1991, an impressive array of new facilities was complete, including the 31-story Rose Building that allowed the center's performing tenants new room. This work was completed remarkably quickly and efficiently. In a further 2004 expansion, Frederick Rose Hall was named in honor of the man who gave not just money but expertise to achieve what others could not.

By the turn of the millennium, the State Theater of New York, one of the center's original buildings, was showing its age. David Koch, one of the wealthiest businessmen in America and a major philanthropist, had been attending ballets and concerts at the theater since it was built. Inspired by financier Stephen Schwarzman's recently announced $100-million donation to the New York Public Library, Koch offered to donate $100 million to renovate and maintain the State Theater. The project was completed on schedule in 2009.

Then in 2015, the cycle of modernizing improvements began again. Entertainment mogul David Geffen announced he was donating $100 million to help renovate the symphony hall. The New York Philharmonic's home had long since been surpassed in acoustic quality, and the new construction, scheduled to begin in 2019, will solve that.

Further reading

○ *Real Estate Weekly* Frederick Rose obituary, thefreelibrary.com/
  Frederick+P.+Rose+dies+at+75.-a057386597
○ David Koch Theatre, davidhkochtheater.com
○ *New York Times* report, nytimes.com/2015/03/05/arts/david-geffen-captures-naming-
  rights-to-avery-fisher-hall-with-donation.html

1961

REVIVAL OF NEW ORLEANS JAZZ

Art and music lovers Allan and Sandra Jaffe were driving back home to Philadelphia from a Mexico City honeymoon when they decided to make a stop in New Orleans to listen to jazz musicians in the beautiful French Quarter. Sandra later related, "When I heard the music for the first time, it felt like a total transformation. We found this whole new world…the music was just so wonderful."

They decided to stay in New Orleans for a few more days in order to hear the (mostly elderly) musicians again. Then they stayed a little longer. Then the owner of the art gallery hosting the musicians, Larry Borenstein, told them the building was for sale. Worried that this could mean the end of the fading New Orleans style of traditional jazz music, the Jaffes never left the city. They started renting the premises in June, and in September 1961 opened it as Preservation Hall, dedicated to preserving and deepening New Orleans jazz.

Allan went around town rounding up musicians, and Sandra employed her journalist skills to market the offerings. What started as a few performances per week eventually turned into one of the most respected jazz music series in the country. They quickly added a touring band, which began to travel the nation in 1963. A 501(c)(3) foundation was created to maintain a jazz archives and offer young players in New Orleans lessons with jazz masters. Now directed by the Jaffes' son Ben, the hall has been credited with saving New Orleans jazz.

Further reading

○ Preservation Hall, preservationhall.com
○ Jaffe history in *Patches* magazine, preshall.blogspot.com/2011/01/sandra-jaffe-interview-
  in-harcum.html

1957

HIDDEN GEMS: COMMUNITY MUSEUMS

Some of America's best art and history isn't found in big cities or major institutions. It's located in places where formative events took place. Many of these community museums were created by local donors who weren't trying to make names for themselves on the national stage, yet embodied true excellence.

In the Adirondack wilderness of upstate New York, for instance, civic-minded donors and residents pooled their resources to create the Adirondack Museum in 1957, which now houses more than 30,000 objects, 10,000 books, and 70,000 photographs that document the region's rich culture, art, and history. A bit to the north in Ogdensburg, New York, the boyhood home of Frederic Remington houses a deep collection of his paintings, sketches, sculptures, and personal memorabilia, all created and sustained by generous local friends (see 1923 entry). And to the south, the Fenimore Art Museum in Cooperstown, New York, displays in its bucolic small-town setting more than two dozen portraits by John Singer Sargent, among other treasures.

In 1971, a conservancy started by concerned local citizens and many generous foundations and individual donors resulted in the Brandywine River Museum in Chadds Ford, Pennsylvania. It houses a beautiful collection of American paintings and sketches by locally rooted artists like Andrew Wyeth, Howard Pyle, and N. C. Wyeth, and offers tours of the nearby studios of some of these great artists. Further down the Brandywine Valley lies the Winterthur Museum, Garden, and Library. Henry du Pont's rural estate is now one of the greatest decorative arts museums in the country.

A sequence of bequests from the Speed family and other local philanthropists have made the Speed Art Museum in Louisville, Kentucky, both a very fine national gallery and a great regional museum. Vermont's Shelburne Museum, created by philanthropist Electra Havemeyer Webb, combines glorious Americana and folk art with astonishing Impressionist pieces and other international glories. The Wolfsonian in Miami presents the spectacular decorative-arts collection of founding donor Mitchell Wolfson.

◈ PhilAphorism

Some writers have so confounded society with government as to leave little or no distinction between them; whereas they are not only different, but have different origins. ◈ *Thomas Paine*

In 1985 William Morris III endowed the Morris Museum of Art in Augusta, Georgia, as a rich repository of Southern painting.

In other communities all across America, local philanthropy has created, underwritten, and sustained hundreds of other similarly superb institutions. These educate and edify nearby residents on art, culture, and history, and in the process enrich and anchor local identities.

1956

TO CREATE A
MOCKINGBIRD

When Harper Lee decided to try to make it as a writer, she relocated (like many before her and since) to New York City. When she got there she found (like many before her and since) that she was so preoccupied with paying her rent—by working at an airline office and bookstore—that she had little time left over to focus on her writing. Fortunately, some attentive and generous acquaintances figured this out and changed the course of U.S. literature with some very personal philanthropy.

Lee spent Christmas 1956 with her close friends Michael and Joy Brown and their two young boys. Michael was a Broadway lyricist, and the year before his musical *House of Flowers* starring Pearl Bailey and Diahann Carroll had been a hit, so the family was enjoying a burst of unanticipated prosperity. Toward the end of their gift exchange that holiday, the Browns handed Lee an envelope. Inside was a note that said: "You have one year off from your job to write whatever you please. Merry Christmas."

Harper Lee later explained: "They'd saved some money and thought it was high time they did something about me.... Whether I ever sold a line was immaterial. They wanted to give me a full, fair chance to learn my craft, free from the harassments of a regular job. Would I please accept their gift?... What made them think anything would come of this? They didn't have that kind of money to throw away.... I went to the window, stunned by the day's miracle.... A full, fair chance for a new life...*Our faith in you* was really all I had heard them say. I would do my best not to fail them."

During that gift year, Harper Lee wrote *To Kill a Mockingbird*. It won the Pulitzer Prize in 1960 and became one of the most influential American books of all time.

Further reading

○ Harper Lee's autobiographical account, web.archive.org/web/20070701015651/www.chebucto.ns.ca/culture/HarperLee/christmas.html

1954

COLUMBUS DISCOVERS MODERN ARCHITECTURE

Columbus, Indiana, a town of 44,000 people about an hour south of Indianapolis, is one of the world's greatest troves of contemporary architecture. It is ranked by the American Institute of Architects as the sixth most architecturally innovative American city—behind only Chicago, New York, Washington, Boston, and San Francisco. The city is home to dozens of notable buildings, sculptures, and landmarks, including a public library by I. M. Pei; Eliel Saarinen's First Christian Church; North Christian Church and Irwin Union Bank designed by Eliel's son Eero; a downtown shopping center by Cesar Pelli; Harry Weese's First Baptist Church; and a firehouse by Robert Venturi. Other architects and artists who have designed projects in Columbus include Henry Moore, Richard Meier, Kevin Roche, and Gunnar Birkets.

What brought these architectural giants to little Columbus was private philanthropy. Irwin Miller, chairman of the Columbus-based Cummins Engine Company, was an architecture enthusiast. In 1942, he commissioned a new design for his home church from Eliel Saarinen. The church became an instant landmark, and Miller saw a role for philanthropy in beautifying his hometown and raising its worldwide profile. He became a major patron of civic architecture in 1954 when he struck an innovative deal with the people of Columbus: any time a new public building was needed, Cummins would pay the commission for any first-rate architect selected from its own list.

Miller expanded his program to cover both municipal structures and private buildings with public purposes, such as churches, banks, and malls. And his own house, designed by Eero Saarinen, is a National Historic Landmark. "By the 1960s," Radley Balko has written, "Columbus had become a world-renowned magnet for privately financed modernist design." Miller's vision continues today: architectural grantmaking in Columbus and its surrounding area remains a central interest of the charitable arm of Cummins Inc.

Further reading

○ *Reason* magazine report, reason.com/archives/2009/09/30/when-columbus-discovered-moder

○ Miller House and Garden, Indianapolis Museum of Art, imamuseum.org

1954

GETTY MUSEUM

"Twentieth-century barbarians cannot be transformed into cultured, civilized human beings until they acquire an appreciation and love for art," pronounced the cranky J. Paul Getty. Born in 1892, the immensely wealthy oilman spent much of his time in Europe, and collected predominantly European art created prior to 1900. Unlike many great art philanthropists, he was less interested in the creators of his day than in the great artists who had already claimed their place in history. These were precisely the kinds of artists he felt residents of his native southern California did not adequately appreciate. It should not be surprising, then, that Getty bucked several trends when he decided to start a museum in Los Angeles.

His approach mixed elitism and populism in the same ways that many nineteenth-century museums did. He firmly believed he had acquired truly excellent art that could be appreciated by all, and just as firmly believed that most ordinary people would need to be taught to understand it. He didn't house the art in one of the bleak modernist buildings of the sort that were popular in his time. Starting in 1954, Getty displayed items in a wing of his own house that was open to the public without charge. When he decided to expand the exhibit to a proper museum, he built a handsome Roman-style villa on the same Malibu grounds, reminiscent of the buildings that would have housed art in the Mediterranean region during the classical era.

Getty thought a structure that looked like it was designed to house great and beautiful things would attract people to see what was inside. He spent $17 million to make the villa appealing. It opened in 1974.

The Getty Museum was further expanded in 1982, after the founder's death, on a new campus in the Brentwood section of Los Angeles—where Getty's other European and American art is housed, along with the $1.2 billion Getty Trust's extensive research facilities. All the museums remain free and open to any barbarians seeking to be edified.

Further reading

- *Philanthropy* magazine analysis, philanthropyroundtable.org/topic/excellence_in_ philanthropy/the_getty
- The J. Paul Getty Museum, getty.edu/about/getty/index.html
- Getty obituary in *New York Times*, nytimes.com/learning/general/onthisday/bday/ 1215.html

CULTURAL KINGMAKER AT THE FORD FOUNDATION

Sometimes the most significant successes of even the biggest foundations come down to one person.

By the 1960s, the Ford Foundation was the largest entity making grants to the arts in the U.S. The man who had made most of that happen was McNeill Lowry. Under Lowry's leadership, the foundation expended millions in arts funding, became the first foundation to support dance, and offered lifelines to scores of individual creators. The amounts were small by Ford standards, but huge to the organizations and individuals who received them. In 1957, $105,000 produced an entire year of performances by the New York City Opera. In 1963, eight major ballet companies were bolstered with $7.7 million, because Lowry had decided dance was underfunded.

Lowry's influence was particularly crucial in locating the individual artists the foundation funded. Lowry, who started running Ford's arts and humanities program in 1957 and became a vice president in 1964, had the final say on who got the money and who didn't. This practically made him America's kingmaker in the 1950s and '60s when it came to cultural production.

With individualized grantmaking, a savvy personal touch was needed more than a rigorous application process. An example: novelist James Baldwin was in his mid-thirties and struggling financially in 1959, when he was having difficulty finishing *Another Country*. He exchanged letters with Lowry on his literary ambitions for the novel. Very shortly after, Baldwin received word that he'd been awarded a two-year, $12,000 fellowship from Ford. He completed *Another Country* and published it in 1962, thanking Lowry in an impassioned note saying that the book might have been torn up and abandoned absent the timely grant.

Playwright Tom Stoppard was another writer who received a Ford grant at a crucial time. His fellowship allowed him to spend five months in a Berlin writer's studio where he wrote the first draft of *Rosencrantz and Guildenstern Are Dead*. The play made Stoppard's career, and won a Tony award.

McNeill Lowry retired in 1974, perhaps the most influential figure of his generation in arts philanthropy.

Further reading

- *New York Times* reporting, nytimes.com/2012/04/09/arts/ford-foundation-records-move-to-rockefeller-archive-center.html?rref=collection%2Ftimestopic%2FBaldwin%2C%20James&action=click&contentCollection=timestopics&region=stream&module=stream_unit&version=latest&contentPlacement=6&pgtype=collection

- Lowry obituary in *New York Times*, nytimes.com/1993/06/07/obituaries/w-mcneil-lowry-is-dead-patron-of-the-arts-was-80.html

1951

CORNING MUSEUM OF GLASS

A classic example of a corporation doing philanthropy that only it could carry out, the Corning Museum of Glass was very unlike most corporate museums. It was opened in 1951 by Corning Glass Works (later known as Corning Incorporated), and located in the Finger Lakes region of upstate New York. While many corporate museums are centered on the company, the Corning Museum focuses on a product—glass—in all of its many historic, artistic, and technological incarnations.

And calling this facility a museum is a bit like calling Yankee Stadium a field. Its mission is to preserve and expand the world's knowledge about glass. It opened with an impressive display of 2,000 glass products and descriptions, housed in an international-style glass building designed by Wallace Harrison. But it is also a research library, an auditorium, a science hall with information about glass technology, and an artisan workshop with opportunities to watch actual glassmaking.

After several expansions and renovations, the museum today features more than 50,000 objects created over 35 centuries. These include ancient glass pieces from 1500 B.C., scientific and industrial uses of glass, contemporary art glass from around the world, hot glass demonstrations, and today's most comprehensive store selling objects and books related to glass. After its latest $64 million expansion, in 2015, the spectacular museum is able to handle half a million visitors every year.

Further reading

○ Corning Museum of Glass, cmog.org/about

FORD AND CARNEGIE
CREATE PUBLIC BROADCASTING

The Ford Foundation inaugurated public broadcasting with a 1951 grant that developed programming to air in a few cities the next year, as National Education Television. Over the following decade and a half, Ford paid for the development of additional new styles of TV, and for the gradual weaving together of nonprofit stations from different regions into a nascent system.

In 1964, the president of the Carnegie Corporation, John Gardner, was pitched on the idea of turning these emerging educational television efforts into a publicly funded network. His foundation earmarked $500,000 to create the Carnegie Commission on Educational Television the next year. It studied how Americans used their televisions, and made recommendations on how the technology could spread learning. The commission included prominent figures like author Ralph Ellison, pianist Rudolph Serkin, and a number of businessmen and academics.

The Carnegie Commission's report, published in 1967, called for the establishment of a corporation to guide public television, with a mix of public and private funding. It made headlines, sold 50,000 copies within a few days, and was mentioned by President Lyndon Johnson in his State of the Union address. In November of 1967, Carnegie's central suggestion became reality with the passage of the Public Broadcasting Act.

During the formative years from 1968 to 1972, while the Corporation for Public Broadcasting and PBS were just finding their way, it was primarily the Ford Foundation that kept educational television developing toward something practical. Ford shoveled more than $90 million into public TV in those few years alone. Over its 50 years as godparent, the Ford Foundation provided more than $435 million to raise public broadcasting to maturity—underwriting new arts programming like adaptations of classic literature, filmed live performances, music, and children's shows. The Carnegie Corporation was also a steady supporter.

Further reading

○ *Report of the Carnegie Commission on Educational Television*, http://current.org/1967/01/carnegie-i/

○ Paul Saettler, *The Evolution of American Educational Technology* (Information Age, 2000)

------------------- (1949) -------------------

ASPEN MUSIC FESTIVAL AND SCHOOL

Walter Paepcke made his fortune as a corporate executive in Chicago in the first half of the twentieth century before launching a career in philanthropy. The town of Aspen, Colorado, owes its international identity to Paepcke.

⅋ PhilAphorism

It is not our part to master all the tides of the world, but to do what is in us for the succor of those years wherein we are set, uprooting the evil in the fields that we know, so that those who live after may have clean earth to till. What weather they shall have is not ours to rule.

☞ *J. R. R. Tolkien*

Organizations he endowed to support the arts and debates over ideas and public policy have turned Aspen into a cultural brand.

Paepcke and his wife, Elizabeth, were originally drawn to Aspen by their love of nature. As a trustee of the University of Chicago and a sometime participant in its Great Books program established by Mortimer Adler, Walter was an advocate of classical learning. In 1949, the Paepckes staged a celebration of the German writer Goethe that drew many prominent artists and humanitarians to their small adopted alpine town. They subsequently established the Aspen Music Festival and School in 1949, created the Aspen Institute (a major politics and education nonprofit), and built the Aspen Skiing Company during the 1950s.

The early Aspen events united nature, art, music, and ideas, and set a template for subsequent celebrations of the arts and intellect. The Aspen Institute has become one of the nation's most important venues for consideration of ideas and public policy, with a campus in Maryland as well as Colorado. And the Aspen summer music festival and school now presents more than 350 classical music events each summer—performances, seminars, and master classes. The festival attracts 100,000 annual visitors, and music students and masters from all over the world come to perform, learn, and be rejuvenated—with two thirds of the students receiving financial aid thanks to generous donors.

Further reading

○ Aspen Institute, aspeninstitute.org

○ Aspen Music Festival and School, aspenmusicfestival.com

1948

NEW YORK CITY BALLET

Until the 1930s, American ballet dancers had to rely on touring foreigners for teaching. Heir, cultural impresario, and donor Lincoln Kirstein, who came from a wealthy family of clothing retailers, dreamed of an American ballet school that would allow young dancers to learn from the greatest masters. In 1933, he invited Russian veteran George Balanchine to come to New York and help him start the school as the choreographer. In 1934, students were enrolled, and performances by various offshoots began. But financial struggles and the Second World War postponed any prominent success by the company.

After the war, Kirstein promised to have the best ballet company in America within three years. In 1948 the New York City Ballet was formed out of his school, and it was a triumph. It remains the largest dance company in America, with over 90 performers and a repertoire of 150 works. The associated School of American Ballet enrolls around 350 students from around the world and has become, true to Kirstein's vision, the gold standard for American ballet instruction.

Further reading

○ New York City Ballet, nycballet.com

○ School of American Ballet, sab.org

OLD STURBRIDGE VILLAGE, PLIMOTH PLANTATION

Albert Wells was an executive in the thriving American Optical Company of Southbridge, Massachusetts, built up by his father. In 1926, A. B. (as he was called) went antique hunting with some friends, and quickly became a thoroughgoing collector of old New England artifacts. Anything from a bowl to a plow could catch his interest, and his collection grew quickly.

By the 1930s, there was no room left in the house he'd been using as a museum, and a family meeting was held to decide what to do with their New England antiques. Historical preservation was coming into vogue at the time. Other wealthy Americans were beginning to gather together pieces of the past that were threatened by the rapid scramble of change underway in the 1920s and '30s. But when A. B. proposed a multi-building museum, his son stunned him with an even more ambitious idea: recreate an entire nineteenth-century village. Don't just erect buildings, but set costumed staff to work at what villagers would have been doing—living history. A. B. bought the idea, and work began. The family asked major landscape architect Arthur Shurcliff to help them design the premises, and by 1946 they had dirt rural roads, barns, shops, and homes. Period farmers were cropping, craftsmen were creating. Old Sturbridge Village was a functioning microcosm, and open to visitors. The village grew into a thriving historical attraction of nearly 60 buildings.

Across the state of Massachusetts, Henry Hornblower II was undertaking a similar labor of love. A Bostonian who had made his money in finance, he'd always enjoyed history, and the story of the Pilgrims' seventeenth-century plantation at Plymouth especially fascinated him. He was particularly interested in the complex relationship the English settlers had with the Wampanoag Indians who lived nearby. He had studied archaeology and history at Harvard, and later financed several archaeological digs in the area, seeking historical artifacts.

Then Hornblower got a really bold idea: to recreate the Plymouth settlement as a living-history museum. He believed full immersion was the most powerful way to educate Americans about their important historical moment in the 1620s, and set about convincing others. In addition to his own money, his first outside donation of $20,000 came from his father. Hornblower managed to get "Plimoth Plantation" launched as a nonprofit in 1947, with two model cottages from the period. It grew steadily, with the addition of a replica *Mayflower* in 1957, an entire English village in 1959, the Wampanoag village in 1973, and a visitor center in 1987, two years after Hornblower's death.

Today, with seven decades of living history under their belts, Old Sturbridge Village and Plimoth Plantation—each incorporating pioneering standards of historical accuracy that were far ahead of their time—remain beloved cultural attractions in New England.

Further reading

○ Old Sturbridge Village, osv.org/about-us

○ Plimoth Plantation, plimoth.org/about-us

1943

TAMING WESTERN ART

Thomas Gilcrease, whose parents had Creek ancestry and whose first wife was Osage, grew up on Indian lands within present-day Oklahoma. Oil was eventually discovered under 160 acres he had been allotted as a tribe member. He proved an astute businessman, and built his own substantial oil company.

At a time of scant appreciation for art coming out of the American West, Gilcrease began acquiring paintings, sculptures, historical documents, Indian handcraft, contemporary Indian art, and archaeological items (many from digs he financed himself) associated with his home region. In 1943 he opened the first version of the Gilcrease Museum, focused on Western art, at his oil company's headquarters. In 1949 he built a grand villa for displaying the growing collection on his estate near Tulsa. He eventually conveyed the museum to the city of Tulsa, along with oil revenue to maintain it— buildings, contents, and 23 acres of grounds landscaped thematically with plants important to different Western peoples and time periods.

The Gilcrease Museum represents one of the largest and richest collections of fine art, artifacts, archives, and flora associated with the American West. It helped give legitimacy to its field, and inspired other collectors of Western art and culture.

Amon Carter was a classic self-made Texan. He was born in a log cabin 65 miles from Fort Worth in 1893, and raised with no access to the arts and high culture, but a series of sales and advertising jobs eventually led him to majority ownership of the *Fort Worth Star-Telegram* and several radio and TV stations. Carter was also an early evangelist for the oil and gas industry. After drilling 90 dry holes himself he eventually discovered a large reservoir he sold to Shell Oil in 1947 for $17 million. These funds became the basis of the Amon Carter Foundation.

Carter became an energetic booster of Fort Worth, and of the West in general. One of his best friends was comic Will Rogers, with whom he shared a passion for American pioneer history. He began to collect Western art aggressively, and when he died in 1955, his will provided for a major Western art museum that opened in 1961 with an impressive array of Frederic Remington's art, and an almost complete collection of Charles Russell sculptures. It also holds one of the great collations of American photography.

Sid Richardson was another Texan who made a million dollars in oil in 1919-20, lost most of it, then struck it rich (again in oil) in 1933. He gave generously to churches, hospitals, and schools in his home region, and developed an appreciation for the art of the West after he took up ranching in the 1930s. In 1982 his Sid Richardson Foundation opened an art museum to display his collection, free to the public, in downtown Fort Worth.

One of the finest museums in this genre is the American Museum of Western Art, created by Denver billionaire Philip Anschutz. It is surely the most comprehensive. Its Anschutz Collection begins with expeditionary art created by the West's first explorers, includes examples from the Hudson River and Rocky Mountain painting schools, the Taos and Santa Fe schools, Regionalist painters, New Deal art, right up to works of Cubism and Abstract Expressionism with Western links. All are

◦ϑ PhilAphorism

Men have committed murder for jealousy's sake, and anger's sake, and hatred's sake, and selfishness' sake, and spiritual pride's sake; but no man that ever I heard of ever committed a diabolical murder for sweet charity's sake.

✦—*Herman Melville*

housed in the historic Navarre Building across from the Brown Palace in downtown Denver.

- Thomas Gilcrease Museum, gilcrease.utulsa.edu
- Amon Carter Museum, cartermuseum.org
- Sid Richardson Museum, sidrichardsonmuseum.org
- Anschutz Collection at the American Museum of Western Art, anschutzcollection.org

ARTS

HISTORIC HUDSON VALLEY

John Rockefeller Jr. was an ardent antiquarian and historic preservationist (as indicated by the money and energy he poured into recreating Colonial Williamsburg—see 1927 entry). These interests extended to the area around his home in Westchester County, north of New York City, which has a rich history and architectural and artistic heritage. In 1940 Rockefeller acquired an eighteenth-century Dutch-English farm and restored it for public visitation to offer a glimpse into life in a northern colonial manor house. In 1945 Rockefeller bought and opened to the public Sunnyside, the romantic, rambling Hudson-Riverside home of America's first internationally prominent writer, Washington Irving, creator of the Sleepy Hollow legends. A few years later Rockefeller purchased the nearby colonial home of a prominent Dutch family to save it from destruction. Later, other historic properties were added—including the Rockefellers' own family home for four generations, Kykuit, along with its spectacular art and gardens. All of these sites are managed by the nonprofit Historic Hudson Valley with an acute eye toward historical accuracy and public enjoyment and education.

Further reading

- Origins of Historic Hudson Valley, hudsonvalley.org/about/history

RARE BOOKS MADE ACCESSIBLE BY BERG AND ROSENWALD

In the 1940s, donors established two major collections of rare books at America's most significant libraries. In 1940, Albert Berg, a New York surgeon from a Hungarian immigrant family, donated a very special 3,500-volume collection to the New York Public Library. A lifelong bachelor, Berg had assembled the books in concert with his older brother Henry—also a bachelor physician in New York City.

The brothers Berg filled the East 73rd Street rowhouse they shared with their unmatched collection, which included heavy representation from Dickens (Albert's favorite author since his boyhood job as a page at the Cooper Union library), Thackeray (Henry's favorite writer), Walter Scott, Goldsmith, Lord Byron, Robert Louis Stevenson, Kipling, and Nathaniel Hawthorne. Among their rarest objects were a first edition of Spenser's *Faerie Queene*, Shakespeare's second folio, a first edition of Milton's *Poems*, and a "perfect copy" of a 1786 edition of Burns's *Poems*. Berg also acquired for the New York Public Library collections put together by publisher W. T. H. Howe and RCA founder Owen Young. These added more than 30,000 items to the Berg collection, including a copy of "The Raven" inscribed by Poe to Elizabeth Barrett Browning, and John Keats's final letter to Fanny Brawne.

Another great book lover who was determined to make his collection available to others was Lessing Rosenwald, who served from 1932 to 1939 as chairman of the Sears, Roebuck company that his father Julius Rosenwald had built up. After retiring, Lessing devoted himself to collecting rare printed objects, gathering together an exceptional trove of items in the ensuing decades. His assemblage of works by William Blake is the finest outside of Britain. Prized books from England's great printer William Caxton, illuminated manuscripts from the medieval and Renaissance periods, and a superb assortment of fifteenth- and sixteenth-century woodcut books are among his treasures.

Rosenwald opened his home, published facsimile versions, and took other measures to make sure that experts and the public could have access to the items he purchased. In 1943, he began a series of gifts of books to the Library of Congress. These culminated shortly after his death in 1979, when his remaining volumes were donated to the library's Rare Book and Special Collections Division.

The approximately 3,000 books donated by Lessing Rosenwald continue to rank among the most valued and heavily used rare books in the Library of Congress collection. One highly visible gift is the Giant Bible of Mainz, which Rosenwald presented to the nation in 1952, one year after acquiring it from a private European collection. It is one of the last hand-written and illuminated Bibles, created at almost exactly the same time, and perhaps in the same city, as the first Gutenberg Bible produced with moving type. Rosenwald's Giant Bible is permanently displayed directly across from one of the first Gutenberg Bibles in the main building of the Library of Congress.

Further reading

○ The Berg Collection at the New York Public Library, nypl.org/about/divisions/berg-collection-english-and-american-literature

○ The Rosenwald Collection at the Library of Congress, loc.gov/rr/rarebook/coll/211.html

TEX MET: BROADCASTING
THE METROPOLITAN OPERA

The Metropolitan Opera had been founded in 1883 by a group of wealthy New York City businessmen who wanted to run their own theater. From its inception it attracted top talent, but frequent changes in management and America's rapidly shifting artistic appetites made for a tumultuous life as a for-profit enterprise. By 1966, when the opera signed on as a constituent of the brand-new Rockefeller-propelled Lincoln Center arts center, it had already been transformed by philanthropic intervention into a national artistic and educational force.

The opera had experimented with radio broadcasts in the 1920s, but the Great Depression made funding difficult to come by. Then in 1940 Texaco stepped in to sponsor nationwide Saturday radio broadcasts of opera performances. For 63 landmark years these concerts were anxiously anticipated in communities across America. They continue to this day with different corporate donors. The Met eventually expanded into television, satellite radio, HD television, movie-theater broadcasts, and Internet streaming. But it was the Texaco radio partnership that kicked it all off and turned the Met into a national icon.

Further reading

○ Metropolitan Opera, metopera.org/About/The-Met/

THE CLOISTERS

One of the most unusual museums in New York City, or anywhere in America, is The Cloisters, a branch of the Metropolitan Museum of Art located in far northern Manhattan. The structure is a unified assemblage of pieces of five separate medieval monasteries that were moved from France to the United States. The site is surrounded by elaborate gardens built precisely as described in medieval manuscripts, and housed inside are several thousand priceless objects created during the Middle Ages, including tapestries, manuscripts, stained glass, metalwork, liturgical objects, ivory sculptures, and furniture.

The Cloisters is the product of one generous man: John Rockefeller Jr., who drove the idea, and its execution, and provided nearly all of the resources. It began when Rockefeller purchased for the Met the remarkable collection of medieval art assembled by George Barnard. It soon became clear some special place would be needed to display the objects. So Rockefeller spent $6 million to acquire a large stretch of land and create a park overlooking the Hudson River in upper Manhattan (including portions of New Jersey on the opposite shore to protect the views). He donated the park to the city, and situated The Cloisters at its heart. The philanthropist hired architect Charles Collens to create a unified design that incorporated elements from the five cloistered abbeys (dating from the twelfth to fifteenth centuries), after they had been taken apart, stone by stone, and transported to the U.S.

The complex amalgamation and rebuilding, then landscaping and decorating, took place during the 1930s and cost Rockefeller $16 million in Depression-era currency. To cap the undertaking, Rockefeller donated works from his own collection, including the famous "Hunt of the Unicorn" Netherlandish tapestries. He also provided an endowment that allows the institution to continue to acquire objects illustrating the many remarkable qualities of life in medieval Europe.

Further reading

○ History of the Cloisters Museum and Gardens, metmuseum.org/about-the-museum/ history-of-the-museum/the-cloisters-museum-and-gardens

1937

ANDREW MELLON AND
THE NATIONAL GALLERY OF ART

Under the influence of his friend Henry Frick, Pittsburgh banker Andrew Mellon had begun collecting art in the 1910s. During years of great instability in Europe, he acquired a remarkable number of masterpieces, including at one point a group of Rembrandts, Van Dycks, and Botticellis from Josef Stalin himself. Mellon donated the paintings to his own foundation, with the stated intent of starting a national museum. In 1934 he hired architect John Russell Pope (with whom Mellon had already worked on construction of the National Archives) to design a museum building located in Washington, D.C.

Mellon died in 1937, leaving his art collection to the United States as promised. His foundation funded the creation of what is now known as the West Building of the National Gallery of Art, and President Franklin Roosevelt accepted the finished museum in 1941. Mellon had hoped that his donation would inspire others to make similar gifts, and his hope was rewarded in the following years. Many prominent donors gave large collections to the museum, including Samuel and Rush Kress, Joseph Widener, Chester

Dale, Lessing Rosenwald, Edgar William, Bernice Chrysler Garbisch, and Mellon's own daughter, Ailsa Mellon Bruce.

Mellon's impact on the National Gallery of Art extended long after his death, as the Andrew Mellon Foundation continued its support of the museum. In 1978, a second building (the East Building) was completed, funded by the foundation and several of Mellon's descendants. The new building focused on special exhibits, offices, and facilities for conservation. In 1999, an outdoor sculpture garden was added on the west side of the original building (funded by the Morris and Gwendolyn Cafritz Foundation).

Together, the museums offer one of the largest and broadest collections of world art anywhere. Today's Andrew W. Mellon Foundation, given its current structure by Mellon's two children, donates about $240 million a year, with art restoration and the development of junior and senior museum staff among its leading areas of interest.

Further reading

○ National Gallery of Art history, nga.gov/content/ngaweb/about.html

○ Olivier Zunz, *Philanthropy in America: A History*, (Princeton University Press, 2012)

THE GUGGENHEIM

Solomon Guggenheim was born into a wealthy mining family, and expanded his fortune through his own mining ventures. He turned primarily to philanthropy after the First World War. The Solomon R. Guggenheim Foundation was launched in 1937 "to promote the understanding and appreciation of art, architecture, and other manifestations of visual culture, primarily of the modern and contemporary periods, and to collect, conserve, and study the art of our time." It opened its first museum in 1939, showcasing samples of Guggenheim's

---

◅ PhilAphorism

A man there was,
though some did count him mad,
the more he cast away,
the more he had.

☞ *John Bunyan*

unusual collection. The foundation consistently promoted Solomon's interest in the current, the abstract, and the unusual, even in its buildings.

Frank Lloyd Wright was commissioned to design a larger home for the museum in 1943. New York City's Guggenheim Museum opened in 1959. A spiraling cylinder, the building is one of the most iconic of modern structures.

The collection continued to grow through the '50s and '60s, and during the 1970s Peggy Guggenheim (Solomon's niece) added her own considerable collection of abstract and Surrealist art. Upon Peggy's death in 1978, the foundation began to expand to sites around the world—Venice; Bilbao, Spain; and Abu Dhabi have permanent bases, the latter two in flamboyant buildings designed by Frank Gehry. Today, the collective aggregate of what is colloquially known as The Guggenheim represents one of the most formidable assemblages of modern art and architecture in the world.

Further reading

○ The Guggenheim, guggenheim.org

CREATING A CULTURAL VILLAGE

Members of the Clark family, heirs to much of the Singer Sewing Company fortune, have resided in the bucolic village of Cooperstown, New York, since the mid-1800s. When the Depression damaged the area's prosperity, Stephen Clark and other representatives of the Clark Foundation (founded in 1931) sought to revive local business and tourism by creating a baseball museum. In 1936, the Baseball Hall of Fame announced its inaugural class of five members: Ty Cobb, Babe Ruth, Honus Wagner, Christy Mathewson, and Walter Johnson.

The hall went on to become a classic of American culture, and the progenitor of many other museums. It attracts 300,000 visitors a year, has an $11-million annual budget, and employs 100 full-time staff in a village of a little more than 2,000 people. The current chairman of the board of directors of the National Baseball Hall of Fame and Museum is Jane Clark, who is also president of the Clark Foundation.

In the decades before and after the founding of the Hall of Fame, Clark relatives and foundation members were also instrumental in building up other cultural institutions in the Cooperstown area—including the historic Farmers' Museum, the Fenimore Art Museum, the New York State Historical Association, and the Glimmerglass Opera. The foundation also spends millions in the Cooperstown region on annual scholarships for children, village beautification, land preservation, local sports, the regional hospital, and the historic Otesaga and Cooper inns.

With half a billion dollars in assets, and nearly $20 million of annual giving, the Clark Foundation has funded many projects. In its support for the various cultural complexes in Cooperstown, however, the family has created an entire community of museums and art, and a true center of Americana.

Further reading

○ *Palm Beach Post* profile of Jane Clark, palmbeachpost.com/news/spots/baseball/jane-forbes-clark-a-powerhouse-behind-the-baseball/nL8c9

○ Founding of the Baseball Hall of Fame, baseballhall.org/media-info/museum-history

ARTS

CENTURIES OF ART SHOWN
FOR CHARITY IN BALTIMORE

William Walters and later his son Henry made a great deal of money in railroads, and beginning in the 1860s poured much of it into collecting art in Europe. In 1874, William decided to share his bounty with the public. Every April and May starting in 1878 he began opening his house to visitors each Wednesday, charging a 50-cent admission fee which he donated to the Baltimore Association for the Improvement in the Condition of the Poor. These openings became eagerly anticipated events in his hometown of Baltimore.

When William died in 1894 he bequeathed his collection to Henry, who greatly expanded it, including purchase of the entire contents of a palace in Rome that contained more than 1,700 pieces including classical antiquities, early Italian paintings, and Renaissance and Baroque art. Henry created a complex of buildings in downtown Baltimore to display all the Walters' art, and opened it to the public in 1909. When he died in 1931 he bequeathed the institution and its contents to the city for "benefit of the public."

The Walters Art Museum opened its doors for the first time as a public institution in late 1934. Today, the collection has grown to more than 35,000 objects, from ancient Egyptian mummy masks and medieval armor to Asian sculpture and European paintings. It is a beloved Baltimore institution.

Further reading

○ William Johnston, *William and Henry Walters, The Reticent Collectors* (Johns Hopkins University Press, 1999)

○ Walters Art Museum, thewalters.org

SAVING NEGRO SPIRITUALS

Edward "Ned" McIlhenny, who ran the Louisiana Tabasco-sauce company founded by his father, racked up some major accomplishments as a preserver of rare birds and plants (see 1892 item on our list of achievements in Nature philanthropy). A man of very wide interests and a willingness to study and devote resources to causes that interested him, McIlhenny also helped save another endangered species: the Negro spiritual.

McIlhenny had grown up with an African-American nanny who took him to her church every week during the decade or two after the Civil War—where he often heard mesmerizing songs that he came to love. Later in life he realized this music was disappearing. When he took up his preservation project in his late fifties, he could remember only about 30 tunes, and just one or two verses of each. So he began visiting old acquaintances, and located two elderly residents of the area who could remember the songs in detail. McIlhenny enlisted the help of a New Orleans musicologist and they set to work in 1930 writing down the lyrics and melodies of 125 spirituals.

They took great pains to notate the tunes and phrasings exactly as presented. The songs were performed again and again over many days so notes and words could be transposed to paper, and "no air was considered finished until it was sung back to the original singers and approval given as to its correctness," writes McIlhenny in his introduction to the collection. Being music that was handed down orally, often by illiterate performers, many of these songs had never before been committed to print. Others were recorded in detail for the first time.

Only four of the spirituals in McIlhenny's 325-page book are known in the same form in other songbooks. Fully 80 songs are wholly different from any other printed source, and half again as many are different in part. Musicologists have thus described the book, titled *Befo' de War Spirituals* and published in 1933, as "a real treasure." It preserved for history many elements of slave music and culture that would otherwise have been forgotten.

Further reading

○ Google books bibliography, books.google.com/books/about/Befo_de_War_Spirituals. html?id=byMl3kc1eqUC

○ *American Music* analysis, jstor.org/stable/3051938

1933

BRINGING THE SCIENCE MUSEUM TO AMERICA

One of the favorite places that Chicago philanthropist Julius Rosenwald ever visited with his family was the Deutsches Museum in Munich—which (then as now) was the world's foremost exhibit of technology and science. The inspired Rosenwald resolved to give America its first great science museum, replete with a full-size re-created mine, huge machines, and clever interactive exhibits. To bring the project to fruition during the 1920s and '30s he pledged $3 million of his own money (ultimately increased to $5 million).

Even more crucial than Rosenwald's inspiration and funding was his steely determination and executive resolve—every ounce of which was required to translate his dream into reality in the face of municipal incompetence, cost overruns, staff disputes, neighborhood resistance, engineering disasters, and myriad other roadblocks. Yet Rosenwald fiercely rebuffed every effort to place his name on the museum, reasoning that the people of Chicago would be more likely to feel they "owned" the institution—and thus be willing to expend effort to keep it healthy and fresh over the decades ahead—if the institution was simply identified with the city, not its main patron.

Rosenwald seems to have calculated right, as the Museum of Science and Industry in Chicago has continued to be updated and improved in dramatic ways. Today it remains the largest science museum in the Western Hemisphere, and the second most popular cultural attraction in its home city.

Further reading

○ Peter Ascoli, *Julius Rosenwald: The Man Who Built Sears, Roebuck and Advanced the Cause of Black Education in the American South* (Indiana University Press, 2006)

○ Museum of Science and Industry, msichicago.org/about-the-museum

1932

FOLGER SHAKESPEARE LIBRARY

In 1879, Henry Folger was a senior at Amherst College, which he attended with financial aid from generous private individuals. That year he attended a lecture on Shakespeare given by Ralph Waldo Emerson. It sparked a lifelong fascination. His wife, Emily, came to share the bug, eventually writing a master's thesis on the Bard.

Starting as a clerk, Folger built a career in the oil industry. He ended up as president of the firm eventually known as Mobil Oil. A few years out of college, Henry bought his first Shakespeare facsimile text for $1.25. During his working years, he and Emily built up the world's largest collection of Shakespeare materials, including rare antique folios and supporting publications of all sorts.

When Henry retired in 1928, the couple devoted their full energies to planning the library that would house their collection. Henry died unexpectedly in 1930, just after the 1929 stock crash wiped out most of his fortune. Nonetheless, in 1932 Emily offered the elaborate library, along with several millions of dollars in endowment, as a gift to the nation—planting it in Washington, D.C., adjoining the Library of Congress.

Thanks to the Folgers' support, the library was able to steadily expand its holdings to become the premier center for Shakespeare studies and resources outside of England. Its exhibitions, lectures, and publications, plus Folger Theatre productions, early-music concerts, and poetry and fiction readings, make it one of the cultural gems of our nation's capital.

Further reading

○ Folger Library, folger.edu/about

SEVERANCE HALL

The Cleveland Orchestra, today one of the top symphonies in America, had humble beginnings. It was founded in 1918 by a group of local citizens led by Adella Prentiss Hughes, a Cleveland pianist. It began its existence as a traveling orchestra, performing throughout the eastern U.S., because scheduling conflicts and an inadequate facility prevented it from performing often in the city's Masonic Auditorium.

In the 1920s, John Severance, president of the orchestra's board, offered more than a million dollars toward the construction of a building to permanently house the orchestra. The project was of particular interest to his wife, Elisabeth, and when she died in 1928, Severance poured himself into the project in her honor. He ended up giving nearly $3 million of the total $7-million cost. Severance built a whole series of industrial companies and distributed his wealth liberally to bolster not only the orchestra but also the Cleveland Museum of Art, several universities, and a medical school and hospital in Korea.

The orchestra's new home was designed to be compatible with the traditional architecture surrounding its site in Cleveland's beautiful University Circle area. Severance Hall was built with a Georgian exterior, and incorporated a variety of more modern styles inside. When it opened and the Cleveland Orchestra gave its first concert to rave reviews in February 1931, it was one of the most advanced concert facilities in America. As the facility aged, it had its acoustics upgraded in 1958 (at the demand of music director George Szell, who brought the orchestra to prominence). The hall later underwent a two-year, $36-million restoration that ended in 2000. By then, the Cleveland Orchestra had become one of the top orchestras in the country, beloved not only regionally but across the globe thanks to recordings and broadcast performances. And Severance Hall, which put the ensemble on its path to prominence, is commonly considered one of the most beautiful concert halls in the country.

Further reading

○ Severance Hall history, clevelandorchestra.com/Plan-Your-Visit/Severance-Hall/Building-History/

○ *Cleveland Plain-Dealer* family history, cleveland.com/arts/index.ssf/2001/02/the_severances_one_familys_leg.html

1930

SAVING GEORGE WASHINGTON'S BIRTHPLACE

In the 1920s, a group of public-spirited women became interested in preserving the lands where George Washington had been born, and erecting a Tidewater plantation house similar to the one the Washington family had occupied until it burned in 1779. The Wakefield National Memorial Association pieced together land that was donated and purchased around the home site, then interested John Rockefeller Jr. in cementing the property with a larger land acquisition. Rockefeller bought 273 acres of the old Wakefield plantation and signed it over to the U.S. government in 1930 at about the same time the Association transferred its 100 acres. Almost 400 acres of land was designated as George Washington Birthplace National Monument, and the Wakefield National Memorial Association was given permission to erect an eighteenth-century-style brick home. Furnished with period artifacts and appropriately landscaped, the home was opened to visitors in 1931, a few months before the 200th anniversary of Washington's birth.

Further reading

○ History of the monument, cr.nps.gov/history/online_books/hh/26/index.htm.

PhilAphorism

Rich men are neither better nor worse than all other humans. They contribute to greatness or mediocrity, strength of character or weakness in exactly the same proportion as persons in all other walks of life do.　☞ *Julius Rosenwald*

1929

MUSEUM OF MODERN ART

Abby Aldrich Rockefeller, wife of John Rockefeller Jr., fell in love with Modern art quite early. Though her husband had entirely different tastes, and indeed actively disliked most Modern art, he offered his wife an allowance to pursue her different artistic interests. With those funds and some inheritance, she acquired works by many young, struggling artists.

Eventually, Abby and her friends Lilly Bliss and Mary Sullivan decided that a separate museum devoted wholly to Modern art was needed. They co-created New York City's Museum of Modern Art late in 1929 and opened it in a small rented building. The museum moved three times into progressively larger, temporary quarters. Seeing his wife's enthusiasm, John Rockefeller Jr. allowed her to spend what she pleased on contemporary works. In 1939 the MoMA moved into the building it occupies today.

When Abby died in 1948, her husband honored her memory with gifts to the Museum of Modern Art that ultimately totaled over $6 million. Today the MoMA collection includes 150,000 paintings, sculptures, prints, photos, and other objects. It owns 22,000 films. It has expanded many times and occupies many buildings.

Further reading

○ Suzanne Loebl, *America's Medicis: The Rockefellers and Their Astounding Cultural Legacy* (Harper, 2010)

○ Museum of Modern Art, moma.org/about/history

1929

PRESERVATION OF MYSTIC SEAPORT

Mystic Seaport, in Mystic, Connecticut, had been an active seaport since the 1600s—filled with ships either being built or sailing in and out on merchant business. Between the late-eighteenth and early-twentieth centuries, its yards built more than 600 sailing vessels.

By the 1920s, the port was fading fast. In 1929, three Mystic residents took it upon themselves to preserve their town's vibrant past. Lawyer Carl Cutter, industrialist Edward Bradley, and doctor Charles Stillman formed the Marine Historical Association (known today as Mystic Seaport), and rapidly filled a one-building museum with donated photos, books, and maritime artifacts. Then in 1941 the men managed to purchase the

Charles W. Morgan, the last remaining U.S. wooden whaleship. Buildings followed, and the recreated Mystic Seaport began.

In the 1970s, the du Pont family got involved as donors, and the entire shipyard was recreated. By the 1990s, Mystic had become the nation's leading maritime museum. In 1998, it built an eighteenth-century schooner from scratch, with an educational program surrounding the building process. Mystic is still growing, thanks to a $35-million expansion and renovation effort. Scholars have access to its impressive archives and 300,000 visitors come each year to see the 40 acres of 500 boats, one million photographs, and two million artifacts.

Further reading

○ Mystic Seaport, mysticseaport.org/about

BLACK CREATIVITY AND THE JULIUS ROSENWALD FUND

Philanthropic giant Julius Rosenwald (president of Sears, Roebuck) started the Julius Rosenwald Fund in 1917 "for the well-being of mankind," but devoted much of its philanthropic power to improving the welfare of black Americans. The fund's directors operated with a sense of urgency, as Rosenwald had directed that the fund be liquidated within 25 years of his death. When the fund was reorganized in 1929 it was one of the largest philanthropies in the country.

One of the fund's several high-profile achievements was a fellowship program that supported artists, writers, and historians, most of them black, to take year-long breaks to further their education or pursue projects. The fund's list of recipients includes most of the greatest names in African-American art and literature in the 1930s and '40s: Jacob Lawrence, Marian Anderson, Zora Neale Hurston, Langston Hughes, Ralph Bunche, John Hope Franklin, Franklin Frazier, W. E. B. DuBois, and others. Ralph Ellison wrote *The Invisible Man* on a Rosenwald fellowship. When the fund closed in 1948 as Rosenwald had instructed, it had provided fellowships to nearly 600 black artists.

Further reading

○ Peter Ascoli, "Julius Rosenwald Fund" in Dwight Burlingame (ed.), *Philanthropy in America* (ABC-CLIO, 2004)

○ Joseph Hoereth, "Julius Rosenwald and the Rosenwald Fund: A Case in Non-Perpetual Philanthropy," in ecommons. luc.edu/curl_pubs/17

1929

SAMUEL KRESS SPRINKLES
GREAT ART ACROSS AMERICA

Samuel Kress realized his philanthropic dreams by bringing great art to Main Street. He started with one five-and-dime shop in 1896, which he expanded to 264 stores by the 1930s. While he was stocking his outlets with attractive retail goods, Kress also "envisioned his stores as works of public art that would contribute to the cityscape," according to one observer. To distinguish his stores from competitors Woolworth and Kresge, he hired on-staff architects to design landmark buildings—from Gothic revival to Art Deco—that helped to beautify and unite American downtowns. Many former Kress stores are now listed on the National Register of Historic Places.

But Kress's greatest philanthropic achievement was the creation and disposition of the Kress Collection, comprised of more than 3,000 works of European art, mostly Italian Renaissance paintings and sculptures. (By comparison, Andrew Mellon's founding gift to the National Gallery of Art included less than 200 pieces.) Kress's collection included masterworks by Giotto, Botticelli, Fra Angelico, Duccio, Filippo Lippi, Raphael, Titian, Tintoretto, Veronese, Bernini, and Tiepolo, as well as non-Italian artists such as Dürer, Holbein, Cranach, El Greco, Rubens, and Goya. During the Great Depression, Kress toured 50 of his greatest pictures through 24 American cities, and he made many gifts to regional art museums. He was intrigued by Andrew Mellon's invitation to other collectors, when founding the National Gallery of Art, to donate their artworks. Kress became one of the first to respond to Mellon's challenge. He made a gift of nearly 400 pieces—enough to stock 34 galleries—to the National Gallery.

After World War II, Kress had an opportunity to distribute his benefactions more broadly. He (who died in the midst of this project, in 1955) and his foundation donated a total of 700 Old Master paintings to 18 regional museums across the United States—most in cities where Kress had a retail presence, and predominantly in the South and the West. Thanks to Samuel Kress, art museums in Birmingham, El Paso, Denver, Houston, Memphis, Tucson, Tulsa, and other medium-sized cities enjoy high-quality cores in their collections. Kress's collection was ultimately divided among 90 institutions in 33 states. By foregoing the creation of a single spectacular museum, Kress elected not to receive the eternal fame that often accompanies such acts. Instead his gifts spread a rich legacy of artistic appreciation among millions of Americans living in communities all across our heartland.

Further reading
- About the Kress & Company buildings, nbm.org/exhibitions-collections/collections/kress-collection.html
- The Kress Legacy, kressfoundation.org/about/kress_legacy/

1927

REVIVAL OF COLONIAL WILLIAMSBURG

ARTS

In the mid 1920s, Abby Aldrich Rockefeller and her husband, John Rockefeller Jr., were contacted by Dr. W. A. R. Goodwin, an instructor at the College of William & Mary in Williamsburg, Virginia. Goodwin was also the rector of Williamsburg's historic Bruton Parish Church, and had spearheaded a campaign to restore the building for its 300th anniversary. Goodwin was disturbed by the loss of historic structures in the area, and proposed a restoration of all of Williamsburg similar to what had been done with the church. The town was full of historic colonial-era buildings that were deteriorating and in some cases endangered.

The Rockefellers initially weren't interested. Nor was Henry Ford. After seeing the parish church during a visit to Williamsburg, however, the Rockefellers agreed to start a modest restoration project of a few buildings. Work began in 1926. The project quickly expanded to eventually include 85 percent of the original town. Keeping their plans secret in order to hold prices down, the Rockefellers and Goodwin quietly bought property after property, eventually revealing their intentions at town meetings in 1928 (to some disquiet).

Ultimately, 720 non-colonial buildings were demolished, and today's Williamsburg is comprised of about 500 buildings, 88 of which are original. Some of the most significant buildings, like the capitol and the governor's mansion, had been destroyed and had to be re-created. The initial project was completed in the 1930s with the addition of retail shops.

Among its many other exhibits and cultural features, Colonial Williamsburg is home to the Abby Aldrich Rockefeller Folk Art Museum. Built on the personal collection of Mrs. Rockefeller, the institution has grown dramatically over the years. It is today the nation's leading center for preservation and display of craftwork by self-taught artists.

The Rockefellers remained personally involved and invested in the preservation and operation of Williamsburg until their deaths. Colonial Williamsburg operates today as a private foundation, subsequently supported by many major donors, notably Lila and DeWitt Wallace (founders of *Reader's Digest*), and thousands of annual supporters. More than 100 million visitors have immersed themselves in Colonial Williamsburg since 1932.

Further reading

○ Colonial Williamsburg restoration, history.org/Foundation/general/introhis.cfm

○ "The Far-visioned Generosity of Mr. Rockefeller," history.org/foundation/journal/Winter00_01/vision.cfm

1926

GEORGE EASTMAN DEBUTS MARTHA GRAHAM

At a time when film was often viewed as crude and vulgar entertainment, George Eastman was adamant that it could become a respectable art form. Between the projection of movie reels at his Eastman Theater in Rochester, New York, snatches of ballet or operatic music were often presented to the audience.

In 1925, an avant-garde dancer who had broken with classical ballet, named Martha Graham, was hired to train dancers for these interlude performances. Mr. Eastman was generous with her, and she had wide opportunities to develop her new art. Graham created entirely novel techniques for her Rochester students, and presented them not only locally but also in an April 1926 performance in New York City where she and three of her acolytes danced 18 numbers. A month later, a work created by Graham called the "Flute of Krishna" was itself turned into a 12-minute film in the Eastman School's Kodak studio.

Martha Graham then returned to Manhattan and went on to create much of the aesthetic and physical language of modern dance. She would be remembered as one of the most influential American artists ever.

Further reading

○ Elizabeth Brayer, *George Eastman: A Biography*, (University of Rochester Press, 2006)

1926

SPENCER AND KATRINA TRASK'S YADDO

Manhattan financier Spencer Trask was one of Thomas Edison's principal backers, and provided money that supported development of the light bulb,

◆ PhilAphorism

The charitable give out the door, and God puts it back through the window.

☞ Traditional proverb

telephone, phonograph, trolley car, electric grid, and motor car. He also gave a propulsive shove to America's twentieth-century artistic and literary output by establishing one of the country's most productive artistic retreats.

In 1881, Trask and his wife—poet, novelist, and playwright Katrina Nichols Trask—bought an estate in the resort town of Saratoga Springs, New York, which their youngest daughter nicknamed "Yaddo." A series of tragedies struck the Trasks, and by 1900 all four of their children had died at young ages, two taken by diphtheria, two by other early maladies. The heartbroken, heirless Trasks decided to turn Yaddo into an artist colony, following a vision by the bereft Katrina of "generations of talented men and women yet unborn walking the lawns of Yaddo, 'creating, creating, creating.'"

With the additional support of the Trasks' friend and business partner George Foster Peabody, the first artists took up residence at Yaddo in 1926. Since then, more than 5,500 artists have nurtured their creativity there, including 67 Pulitzer Prize winners, 61 National Book Award winners, 108 Rome Prize winners, and one Nobel laureate (Saul Bellow). Yaddo's additional luminaries include John Cheever, Aaron Copland, Jonathan Franzen, James MacPherson, Flannery O'Connor, Sylvia Plath, Philip Roth, Alice Walker, Eudora Welty, Leonard Bernstein, and William Carlos Williams.

Today, Yaddo continues to rely on private philanthropic support. One third of its funding comes from gifts from its alumni artists, reflecting their views of the institution's efficacy and importance. The "permanent home" that Spencer Trask sought to create for "authors, painters, sculptors, musicians, and other artists" to do "good and earnest work" has lived long. The procreativity denied to him and his wife resulted instead in a bloom of creativity benefiting all Americans.

Further reading

○ Yaddo, yaddo.org/yaddo/history.shtml

1925

BARNES COLLECTION

Albert Barnes had been raised in one of Philadelphia's poorest neighborhoods, with experiences to match. Fistfights, not painting, dominated his childhood. Ferocious determination became one of his most characteristic traits.

His academic performance earned him a scholarship to the University of Pennsylvania, and he emerged a physician. He went into business manufacturing pharmaceuticals, and by age 35, in 1908, was worth $24 million in 2015 dollars. Gradually, as his business consumed less of his energy, he turned to art. His mother had taught him to appreciate it as a child, and now that he had money and leisure time, he threw himself into collecting as aggressively as he had into entrepreneurship.

Barnes enlisted high-school friend William Glackens, a painter, as his art buyer, and quickly became known in contemporary art circles. Right through the Great Depression he employed his business savvy to buy magnificent works for far less than their market value, taking them off the hands of the formerly rich who could no longer afford the pieces. His collection includes more than 40 works by Matisse, 60 by Picasso, and no fewer than 180 by Renoir. Yet Barnes never paid more than $100,000 for a painting. His trove of more than 2,500 works is currently valued at an astonishing $30 billion (the approximate worth of the entire Bill & Melinda Gates Foundation).

Barnes then became intensely involved in interpreting his collection to the world and erecting a building to house it. When a Philadelphia exhibit of a few of his works was panned by local critics, Barnes furiously withdrew his art from the city. Rather than let the Philadelphia Museum of Art touch it, he opened the Barnes Collection as its own institution in suburban Merion, Pennsylvania, in 1925—and not merely as a museum, but as an educational center designed to help adults and children understand and appreciate art (as he believed the Philly elite were unable to). As much as for the remarkable quality of the works, the collection became famous for Barnes's detailed and iconoclastic requirements on how the art should be displayed for popular edification—by color, shape, craft, or similarity of effect, rather than chronology or other traditional criteria.

Barnes died in 1950; the last stewards of his collection who had known him were gone by the 1980s; soon one after another of his highly specific instructions for the disposition of his collection were being violated. In 2012, the whole lot was moved to a purpose-built museum in downtown Philadelphia, bringing one of the most impressive art collections in the world to a city its collector had pulled away from.

Further reading

○ *Philanthropy* magazine reporting, philanthropyroundtable.org/topic/donor_intent/outsmarting_albert_barnes

○ Howard Greenfeld, *The Devil and Dr. Barnes* (Penguin Publishing, 1995)

1924

MORGAN LIBRARY

In 1890, when his father died and left him the family's London banking house and millions of dollars, J. Pierpont Morgan began collecting on a grand scale. Over the next three decades he spent $60 million (nearly a billion dollars today) on books and art. "Morgan's collecting tastes could only be described as encyclopedic—what he amassed in such a short period encompassed virtually the full range of artistic and human achievement in Western civilization, from antiquity to modern times," explains today's Morgan Library and Museum.

Morgan's scholarly nephew and a young librarian he hired helped guide him through many extraordinarily savvy purchases. Initially he kept, and displayed, his manuscripts and artwork at his homes. Eventually he outgrew those quarters, and so he asked the architect Charles McKim to design "a gem" of a building next to his home in New York City, for publicly displaying his gathered objects.

When Morgan died in 1913, up to three quarters of his enormous net worth was tied up in his book and art collection. He left the disposition of these objects to his son, Jack, with the requirement that the objects be "permanently available for the instruction and pleasure of the American people."

Jack was forced to sell some objects to pay taxes. Others were donated to the Metropolitan Museum of Art in New York, and the Wadsworth Atheneum in Hartford. Morgan's collections of books, manuscripts, and drawings, however, remained intact and became the core of the Morgan library when it opened in 1924 as a public institution, with its own board, private endowment, and one of the world's most impressive set of documents.

Further reading

o Morgan Library history, themorgan.org/about/history-of-the-morgan

1923

WEST BY NORTHEAST TO THE FREDERIC REMINGTON ART MUSEUM

The beloved painter, sculptor, and illustrator Frederic Remington was the progenitor of America's famed school of cowboy art. Remington was not a westerner, however, but an upstate New Yorker, born and buried in the far north country near the U.S.-Canada border, where he gloried in the local hunting, fishing, swimming, camping, and horse riding. His widow Eva was from the same area, and when she returned to Ogdensburg, New York, after her husband's death, she brought his personal collection of paintings, sketches, bronzes, western artifacts, and private memorabilia with her, along with Frederic's papers and effects. She tried to offer the Indian-related items to the Smithsonian Institution in Washington, but reversed course when she learned that the museum would break up the firearms, clothing, saddles, and other items into separate displays.

Thus did one of America's great troves of Western art end up in the custody of the Ogdensburg Library in 1915, within a revolver shot of Canada. Local businessmen and philanthropists John Howard and George Hall offered the library $100,000 to erect a proper building to house the treasures, and these two patrons eventually provided the means to have the collection installed in the 1810 home where Eva lived out the end of her life, suitably renovated and opened to the public in 1923. In the years since, locals have continued to generously support the beloved museum, allowing it to add many additional items, and to expand into a second building.

Today, the "benefactors and supporters" page of the Remington Museum's annual report lists ten full pages of area boosters—hundreds of individual donors plus regional businesses like the Heritage Clock Shop, the Busy Corner Café, and the North Country Savings Bank. Along with an active mix of teas, raffles, BBQs, and replica sales, these local angels sustain a top-flight art collection in a rural New York locale that remains nearly as wild today as it was during the formative years when Frederic Remington rambled its woods and streams.

Further reading

○ John Howard's history of the Remington Art Memorial, fredericremington.org/photos/custom/history_of_ogdensburg.pdf

○ About the museum, fredericremington.org/the-museums-c5.php

EASTMAN SCHOOL OF MUSIC

George Eastman had raised himself from poverty to wealth by founding Eastman Kodak, pioneering much of the science and art of photography, and building his company to world dominance through a combination of inventiveness and enormous stamina. His creation of the Eastman School of Music at the University of Rochester required much the same combination of traits.

Eastman had adored music since childhood. In fact, music was such an important part of his life that when he built himself a mansion (finished in 1905), he had a large organ installed in the music room and paid his own organist to wake him with the instrument every morning, then serenade him with fugues and toccatas until Eastman had finished breakfast. By the mid-1910s, Eastman had decided his native Rochester needed a high-level conservatory. "Without the presence of a large body of people who understand music and get enjoyment out of it, any attempt to develop the musical resources of any city is doomed to failure," he pronounced.

Eastman wanted to create a music school that included not just international-level training for university students, but also major community elements and preparatory training for children and adults—an unconventional notion at the time. He also aspired to celebrate high music and popular music alike, and to resist practices that reduce the audience for classical music. In 1918, he presented his ideas to University of Rochester president Rush Rhees. It soon became clear that Eastman would have to shoulder almost the entire burden of making the project happen. So he put his legendary ingenuity and determination to work and overcame one objection after another.

Starting from scratch would be difficult, so Eastman bought the property and practice of the existing D. K. G. Institute of Musical Art. He then purchased more land around it and closely supervised every detail of the design of a campus and magnificent main building, insisting that it include one of the most glorious auditoriums ever built for music, dance, and film screenings—the 3,100-seat Eastman Theater. Ground was broken in 1920, and the school (with 32 instructors) opened to 104 students in 1921. Buildings and students were added with the passing of years.

Today, 500 undergraduate and 400 graduate students are enrolled in the collegiate division of the school. They are taught by almost 100 faculty members, whose numbers have included seven Pulitzer winners and numerous Grammy awardees. Eastman's vision for community education and engagement is alive and well; the Community Music School enrolls around 1,000 students (children and adults) each year. Eastman alumni now fill important roles, from musician to conductor to manager, at many of the world's greatest musical entities, and the Eastman School's graduate program is regularly ranked first in the nation.

Further reading

- Elizabeth Brayer, *George Eastman: A Biography* (Johns Hopkins University Press, 1996)
- Eastman School of Music, esm.rochester.edu/90th
- George Eastman Papers, rbscp.lib.rochester.edu/864

1921

AMERICA'S FIRST MODERN ART MUSEUM

Duncan Phillips was the son of a Pittsburgh businessman, and had a passion for art along with family economic means. In 1914, six years after his graduation from Yale, he published his first book, *The Enchantment of Art.* He then managed to talk his parents into giving him a "collecting allowance," so he could start assembling works he admired.

He and his mother were shattered by the death of Duncan's father in 1917. They channeled their grief into the founding of a memorial to the senior Phillips: America's first museum dedicated to modern art. The Phillips Collection, said Duncan, should be "an intimate museum combined with an experiment station." The cadre of artists whose work was gathered included Degas, van Gogh, Matisse, Picasso, and many more.

The museum opened in 1921, originally located in the Phillips' home in D.C.'s Dupont Circle neighborhood, which the family eventually vacated to make its full space available for art. Phillips worked with his wife to extend and organize the collection, and continually built friendships with living artists. He remained involved in directing the museum until his death in 1966. It has grown through building expansions in 1989 and 2006, and remains one of the finest privately owned museums in America.

Further reading

∘ The Phillips Collection, phillipscollection.org

HUNTINGTON LIBRARY

The Huntington Library is one of the world's great cultural, research, and educational centers. It was founded by Henry Huntington, an upstate New Yorker who came to California and built rail lines, and eventually served on 60 corporate boards. Huntington's railroad building helped drive the explosive growth of the Los Angeles area, and his library gave the raw new city a great institution of research, art, and scholarship.

During his lifetime, Huntington amassed one of the finest private libraries in the world, established a splendid art collection, and created a stunning array of botanical gardens. At the age of 60 he retired to focus on his collections and the landscaping of his 600-acre ranch. Huntington's wife, Arabella, was herself one of the most important art connoisseurs of her generation, and highly influential in the development of the collection now displayed in their former mansion. It includes many masterpieces, and the botanical garden of 120 acres features more than a dozen different specialized gardens, including the Desert Garden, the Japanese Garden, the Rose Garden, the Chinese Garden, and subtropical, herb, jungle, and palm gardens.

The library has on display some of the finest rare books and manuscripts of Anglo-American civilization, and includes about 6 million items in total, including a Gutenberg Bible on vellum, the double-elephant folio edition of Audubon's Birds of America, and a superlative collection of the early editions of Shakespeare's works. The Huntington is also among the nation's most important centers for the study of the American West, including the pioneer experience, the Gold Rush, and the development of southern California. Much important research has been conducted in the library.

In 1919, Henry and Arabella Huntington transferred their San Marino home and collections to a nonprofit educational trust. The Huntington Library, Art Collections, and Botanical Gardens now host more than 500,000 visitors each year. An extensive education program serves about 12,000 school children annually.

Further reading

○ About the Huntington, huntington.org/WebAssets/Template/content.aspx?id=56

ARTS

1919

FRICK COLLECTION

Henry Clay Frick was a Pittsburgh industrial magnate who made his money in coal and steel. He built an impressive mansion in New York City that was designed, from its earliest planning, so that it could serve as an art museum after he died.

At his death in 1919, Frick bequeathed the house and most of his art collection to establish a gallery for "encouraging and developing the study of the fine arts." His gifts included sculptures, prints, furniture, silver, rugs, Chinese porcelains, and more. The Frick Collection was both diverse and impressively deep. Its 131 paintings formed its core; there were eighteenth-century English portraits, van Dykes, Vermeers, and Rembrandts.

Along with his art, Frick left an endowment of $15 million for operation and upkeep. After his wife died in 1931, the home was transformed into the museum he had ordered. Thanks to investment growth of the endowment the collection was gradually expanded, and by 1995 it had grown to more than 1,100 paintings. Today it is considered one of the finest small collections in the world.

Further reading

○ The Frick Collection, frick.org/collection/history

1917

JOSEPH PULITZER CELEBRATES LETTERS AND ARTS

At Joseph Pulitzer's death, the self-made Hungarian immigrant who built the *St. Louis Post-Dispatch* and later the *New York World* into hugely successful newspapers left $2 million to Columbia University to found the Columbia School of Journalism and create (with one quarter of the bequest) the Pulitzer Prizes.

Pulitzer explained in his will that he hoped to attract into the writing professions individuals "of character and ability, also to help those already engaged in the profession to acquire the highest moral and intellectual training."

First awarded in 1917 by an advisory board he created for the purpose, the prizes aimed to encourage excellence in both journalism (four awards) and literature (with prizes for best American novels, plays, histories, and biographies). Prizes for poetry, music composition, and photography were introduced later. Winners are announced in April of each year.

Further reading

○ Joseph Pulitzer biography, pulitzer.org/biography

○ Pulitzer Prize history, pulitzer.org/history of prizes

1917

GODMOTHER OF THE HARLEM RENAISSANCE

Charlotte Mason was a wealthy white widow who in the 1920s thought black art had a spirituality and "primitive energy" that nothing else mustered. She was a controversial figure even then, bearing the classic marks of the old-style patron: demanding loyalty from her artists, meddling with their work, and holding a very specific vision of what Negro art should and shouldn't be. One of her bemused artists wondered if she realized he'd been born in the Bronx and not the Sudan. As one might imagine, some of her artistic relationships didn't end well. Langston Hughes, for example, relied on her for support from 1926 to 1930 (at $150 a month), but broke with her in 1930 over her efforts to control his work. (He later tried to reconcile.)

Yet in other ways, Mason was different from the original Renaissance patrons. For one thing, she stayed out of the public eye. For another, she was truly devoted to the art; her meddling was usually due less to her desire to make the art fit her whims than to her determination that the art should be authentic.

Whatever her quirks, Mason's energy, passion, and major financial involvement earned her her favorite title: "godmother." Many of the Harlem Renaissance artists and writers could not have accomplished what they did without her support. Among the individuals whose artistic creativity she supported were Alain Locke, Aaron Douglas, and Zora Neale Hurston.

Further reading

○ Marjorie Garber, *Patronizing the Arts* (Princeton University Press, 2008)

○ Charlotte Mason biography entry, artsedge.kennedy-center.org/interactives/harlem/ faces/charlotte_mason.html

MUSEUM OF THE AMERICAN INDIAN

George Heye (pronounced "hi") was raised in a wealthy home in New York City, and despite finishing college with an electrical-engineering degree in 1896, opted in 1901 to start an investment-banking firm. The considerable amount of money he eventually earned from this successful venture funded what had become his real passion: Heye was fascinated by Native American customs and handcraft. We don't know the origins of his interest, but he was soon traveling all over the country looking for artifacts. By car, train, or boat, Heye would end up in the most remote places, dig up or buy whatever he could, and send it back to New York. He even bankrolled archaeological digs in Central America. In just a few years, he amassed over a million Native American items; the largest collection ever assembled by a single person.

Heye established the Museum of the American Indian in 1916 in New York to display his collection. After he died in 1957 the museum's fortunes rose and fell until 1989, when by an act of Congress a National Museum of the American Indian was added to the Smithsonian Institution. Heye's collection became it's backbone. The materials he gathered now span three facilities—the George Gustav Heye Center in Manhattan, which opened in 1994, the main National Museum of the American Indian located on the National Mall in Washington, D.C., since 2004, and the Cultural Resources Center in Suitland, Maryland, which houses the museum's conservation and curatorial work.

Further reading

○ National Museum of the American Indian, nmai.si.edu

○ *Smithsonian* magazine profile of Heye, smithsonianmag.com/history/a-passionate-collector-33794183/?no-ist

◅ PhilAphorism

The foundation is an instrument forged by citizens who transfer profit from the commercial sector and put it directly to work as risk capital for the general betterment of the society.

☞ *Richard Cornuelle*

LOEB CLASSICAL LIBRARY

A book from the Loeb Classical Library is instantly recognizable. Each of the 518 hardbound volumes is uniformly sized and sports a minimalist cover—red for works in Latin and green for those in Greek. Inside is a layout that has not changed in 100 years of publication. On every left-hand page runs the original text, with a near-literal English translation running on the right-hand page.

The books preserve and popularize an enormous body of ancient wisdom: early dramas, novels, and poetry, histories by the likes of Herodotus and Josephus, scores of works from philosophers like Aristotle and Seneca, works of mathematics, Greek and Roman political speeches, biographies, and early Christian texts.

The series is a pure product of philanthropy. James Loeb was a son of the founder of one of America's earliest investment banks. He worked for the family business until illness forced his early retirement, then dedicated himself to a life of quiet scholarship and giving. Loeb was lead funder of what would eventually become the Juilliard School (see entry dated 1905). He sponsored psychiatric research, charitable hospitals, and convalescent homes. And he personally financed the translation, production, and publication of the Loeb Classical Library.

When he left Harvard money in his will to complete the series, Loeb directed that profits from sales of the books should be put toward scholarships in the classics. To this day, the library's proceeds support Harvard graduate students. The Loeb Library also inspired three similar large efforts to present great literatures in a consistent high-quality format: a series of crucial works from the Renaissance, a medieval library, and a trove of the classical literature of India. These also relied on philanthropy.

Further reading

○ *Philanthropy* magazine report, http://www.philanthropyroundtable.org/topic/higher_education/ex_libris_philanthropy

PRESERVING FORT TICONDEROGA

The scene (during the French and Indian War) of the bloodiest battle in America until the time of the Civil War, Fort Ticonderoga on the New York shore of Lake Champlain went on to become one of the most important historical sites in the birth of America. Several crucial U.S. victories in our Revolutionary War were centered on Ticonderoga, including Ethan Allen's seizure of the fort's cannons, which were then used to drive the British out of Boston, Benedict Arnold's heroic Battle of Valcour, and the seminal British defeat at Saratoga in 1777.

In 1820, the crumbling fort and its 546-acre grounds were acquired by New York City merchant William Pell, a wealthy importer of mahogany and marble, for $6,008. Thus began his family's almost single-handed preservation of the historical battleground. In the early 1900s, Pell's great-grandson Stephen Pell proposed a thorough rebuilding of the fort, and asked his father-in-law Robert Thompson to finance the construction. A Naval Academy graduate who earned a fortune in copper and nickel mines (and later became chairman of the American Olympic Committee), Thompson replied, "Have it done, and send the bill to me." He pledged $500,000 to the project, which commenced in 1909.

Stephen Pell and his wife assembled the museum's collection of weaponry, historical documents, and accoutrements of all sorts, and in 1931 established the private Fort Ticonderoga Association to maintain the site as a national shrine open to the public. Many visitors assume it must be a national park, but it is instead a product of philanthropy. Leading military historian Eliot Cohen describes the current privately preserved site as "a standard setter in terms of reconstruction and presentation."

Further reading

∘ Fort Ticonderoga, fortticonderoga.org
∘ Eliot Cohen, *Conquered Into Liberty* (The Free Press, 2011)

MACDOWELL ARTIST COLONY

Tucked into the woods surrounding the quiet town of Peterborough, New Hampshire, there is a powerhouse of explosive creativity. The MacDowell Colony was founded in 1907 by the composer Edward MacDowell and his wife Marian to foster "enduring works of the imagination." It attracts and supports 250 promising American artists every year, both the famous and the unknown, in fields from architecture to theater to music composition. A MacDowell residency, which may last from two weeks to two months, allows the artist to focus on a project without distraction, while drawing inspiration from the beautiful New England environs.

Edward MacDowell, an inaugural member of the American Academy of Arts and Letters, realized toward the end of his life that the tranquility of his New Hampshire summer home had enabled him to compose many of his best

ARTS

pieces. As he was dying, Marian hoped to extend his legacy by offering the same opportunity to other artists. With the support of Andrew Carnegie, J. Pierpont Morgan, Grover Cleveland, and others, she converted the property into a retreat, with (ultimately) 32 individual studios scattered through the 450-acre forest, and a common dining area and library. Among the signature features of the colony are the lunches delivered silently to artists' doorsteps in picnic baskets every day, and the tablets inside the studios inscribed by everyone who has worked there before. The Colony was designated a National Historic Landmark in 1962.

In the century since its founding, MacDowell Colony has not only supported more than 6,000 artists, but inspired similar colonies across the nation and the world. Dozens of the works created at MacDowell have gone on to win a Pulitzer Prize or similar award, including Aaron Copland's *Appalachian Spring*, Michael Chabon's *The Adventures of Kavalier & Clay*, and Thornton Wilder's *Our Town* (which was modeled on nearby Peterborough, setting "the village against the largest dimensions of time and space," Wilder wrote, in an attempt "to find a value above all price for the smallest events of our daily life").

Further reading

○ History of MacDowell Colony, macdowellcolony.org/about-History.html

JULLIARD SCHOOL

Frank Damrosch was born into music. His father was a conductor and his mother a singer; his godfather was composer Franz Liszt. The household moved from Germany to America when he was young, and he stuck to the family trade. His efforts to teach music to the poor in New York earned him, in 1897, the position of head of music education for New York City's public schools.

Musical ignorance was common in America's schools at the time, and the best musicians had to either come from Europe (as he had), or study there. Damrosch firmly believed American musicians should not have to go abroad to become masters. He wanted to create a conservatory that rivaled the great European music schools.

Money remained the problem until he met banker James Loeb—who agreed to finance a conservatory in memory of his mother, Betty. It was originally known as the Institute of Musical Art, and opened in 1905. Thanks to Loeb's generosity the school was freed from pressure to please tuition-paying students, and instead focused on inculcating demanding standards of musical art.

In 1919, a rich textile merchant named Augustus Juilliard (who led the board overseeing New York's Metropolitan Opera) made the largest bequest ever for the advancement of music. A sum ultimately totaling $12.5 million was used to create the Juilliard Graduate School. Just a few years later, in 1926, the two superb training academies built by these donors merged to form the Juilliard School of Music.

The Juilliard School is today one of the world's leading conservatories, and supports instruction in dance and drama as well as music. Juilliard continues to benefit from powerful support by many of America's most devoted philanthropists, most recently hedge-fund billionaire Bruce Kovner. In the late 1960s, Kovner left a Ph.D. program at Harvard, felled by writer's block, and took up driving taxis, working on political campaigns, and studying the keyboard at Juilliard. The school made a mark on him, and he later became long-serving chairman of its board, not to mention its most generous giver. In 2006, he donated a priceless collection of manuscripts to the school (original sheet music by Beethoven, Bach, Mozart, and many others). In 2009, he began supporting the school's Historical Performance Program, which encourages authentic presentations of music created from 1600 to the early 1800s. In 2012, Kovner donated $20 million to fully fund the program—providing total scholarships for all students. In early 2013 he offered $5 million to the Juilliard drama program. And at the end of 2013 he gave $60 million, the largest gift in the school's history, to allow 52 of the music conservatory's most accomplished students to be given full-ride scholarships every year.

Further reading

○ Juilliard School history, juilliard.edu/about/brief-history

○ Augustus Juilliard's initial bequest announced in the *New York Times*, query.nytimes.com/mem/archive-free/pdf?res=FB0F12FD3F5E157A93C5AB178DD85F4D8185F9

○ *New York Times* reports 2013 Kovner gift, artsbeat.blogs.nytimes.com/2013/10/09/60-million-gift-to-establish-fellowships-at-juilliard

1903

ISABELLA STEWART GARDNER MUSEUM

As one of America's foremost female patrons of the arts, Isabella Stewart Gardner was determined to open a museum that would be available "for the education and enrichment of the public forever." Her father had made a great deal of money as a trader, and she spent the 1880s and '90s rapidly collecting art, antiques, jewelry, and rare manuscripts. She and her husband, Jack, traveled extensively through Europe, the Middle East, and Asia, snapping up objects wherever they went.

In 1898, Isabella bought a plot of land on the Fenway, former marshland in Boston. She worked with architect Willard Sears to design and build a mansion large enough to house a museum, yet imbued with the intimacy, light, and warmth of a Venetian palazzo. In 1903 Gardner's museum was launched with thousands of pieces of American, European, and Asian art, a million-dollar bequest, and the blissful new building to house it all. It opened to the public amidst a fanfare of Baroque and classical music played by musicians from the Boston Symphony Orchestra, another institution supported by Gardner.

This musical opening was no anomaly. Gardner wanted her intimate space to be a home for music and dance as well as the visual arts. Choreographer Ruth St. Denis, renowned soprano Nellie Melba, and many other performers lent their talents to the museum.

The art collection, though, was the greatest achievement. Gardner owned works by scores of masters including Titian, Rembrandt, Michelangelo, Raphael, Botticelli, Manet, Degas, Whistler, and Sargent. An infamous 1990 heist resulted in the theft of 13 paintings valued at up to $500 million. They remain lost. Yet Isabella Gardner's museum continues to thrive, the rich personality she injected into it through its building, location, displays, room uses, and combinations of art remaining the hallmark of the institution today.

Further reading

○ Gardner Museum, gardnermuseum.org

1895

CARNEGIE CULTURES PITTSBURGH

Like so many other great philanthropists, Andrew Carnegie was raised poor. He started work at age nine and steadily progressed upward, making it big in railroads, oil, mining, steelmaking, and more. By 1901, when he sold his last business to J. P. Morgan and dedicated his life to philanthropy, his business was worth $480 million (in 1901 dollars).

Carnegie insisted that giving a beggar a dollar was destructive. Investing in things that would help the beggar pull himself up, however, was help worth offering. So it's hardly surprising that much of his money went to the causes of education and self-improvement.

Carnegie's native Pittsburgh was an industrial region that lacked the intellectual and cultural amenities he thought distinguished great cities from the merely good. So in the 1890s he commenced to provide Pittsburghers with a string of great facilities. During the decade he built an art museum, a natural history museum (one of the largest in the nation), a grand music hall, and the central branch of the Carnegie libraries in Pittsburgh. The four structures sprawl across a contiguous four-block portion of the city's Oakland neighborhood. Carnegie being Carnegie, the sandstone buildings themselves were works of art.

Carnegie's goal at his Museum of Art was to collect and encourage "the Old Masters of tomorrow." In this sense, it was America's first major gallery devoted to modern art—which at the time meant painters like Winslow Homer and James McNeil Whistler.

Further reading

○ Waldemar Nielsen, *Inside American Philanthropy* (University of Oklahoma Press, 1996)

○ S. N. D. North (ed.), *A Manual of the Public Benefactions of Andrew Carnegie* (Google eBook: The Carnegie Endowment for International Peace, 1919)

CARNEGIE'S LIBRARIES, AND OTHERS

Waldemar Nielsen called Andrew Carnegie "an extremist in every sense." When Carnegie gave, he really gave.

And the man who had started life as a poor immigrant considered libraries the single most valuable gift that could be given to a city. He had relevant family history. His father had helped build a little collection of library books back home in Scotland. And in Allegheny, Pennsylvania, the young Carnegie had delighted in his access to a generous patron's personal library. The avid reader had dreamed of giving the same free access to other working boys some day.

In 1881, Carnegie offered Pittsburgh Mayor Robert Lyon $250,000 for a public library building, if the city would fill it with books and maintain it. Lyon pulled together the necessary support. Carnegie, though, was just beginning. He later informed the city leadership that Pittsburgh had grown in size and significance and needed more libraries. He gave an additional $1 million to create eight branch libraries, with the condition that a board of trustees be appointed to see that they operated well. (Henry Frick, of later Frick Art Collection fame, was the first treasurer of the board.)

Nearly 100 architects vied to design Carnegie's buildings, which ended up being high achievements in themselves. The main library was three stories in a

◁ PhilAphorism

No one need wait a single moment to improve the world. ✍ Anne Frank

modified Italian Renaissance style, trimmed in bronze and decorated with references to the great creators whose stories could be found inside (Bach, Galileo, etc.). The branch libraries were built soon after in similarly rich style.

This story would be repeated over and over across the country. By the time of Carnegie's death in 1919, 2,800 requests for libraries had come in from around the U.S. Carnegie demanded the cities prove both their need and their ability to sustain the libraries, but few localities were refused. Most of the collaborations were roaring successes. During his lifetime Carnegie gifted $60 million to build and support more than 2,500 libraries. At one time, more than half the libraries in the United States were products of Carnegie's munificence. Nearly a century later, more than 90 percent of his buildings still existed, and nearly two thirds were still in active use as libraries.

While the scale of Carnegie's gift is without precedent, other American donors have also created marvelous libraries for public use. In 1857, Baltimore merchant George Peabody donated hundreds of thousands of dollars to create a combination art gallery/music school/library "which is to be maintained for the free use of all persons who desire to consult it." The stunning "cathedral of books" remains open to use by the general public. A brilliantly conceived chain of public libraries was later given to Baltimore by Enoch Pratt (an inspiration to Carnegie).

Splendid libraries combining books with art, historic maps, and other rarities were created and eventually given to the public by Henry Huntington, J. P. Morgan, and J. Paul Getty. And in our own day, great libraries continue to be given to America—like the $100 million George Washington library opened in 2013 at Mount Vernon with major support from the Smith family, the Donald Reynolds Foundation, Karen Wright, David Rubenstein, the Mars family, and other donors.

Further reading

o S. N. D. North (ed.), *A Manual of the Public Benefactions of Andrew Carnegie* (Google eBook: The Carnegie Endowment for International Peace, 1919)

o Duke University case study, cspcs.sanford.duke.edu/content/carnegie-public-libraries-americas-communities-andrew-carnegie-and-carnegie-corporation-new-

1879

ART INSTITUTE OF CHICAGO

After the Great Chicago Fire in 1871, the city's art scene was devastated. It was Chicago philanthropists who rebuilt it. One notable funder was Charles Hutchinson, who founded the Art Institute of Chicago.

Hutchinson's father had made and lost fortunes in determined pursuit of money. The younger Hutchinson was a savvy businessman himself (he was running a bank before he was 30, and was president of the Board of Trade by 34), but he also had a civic drive. He said everyone should put as much into a city as he gets out of it.

His philanthropy started early. Having watched his father's own example, he thought Chicago was becoming too materialistic. The fire, and the renewed interest in culture that it created, presented him with an opportunity to put a spotlight on creations of the human spirit that might counterbalance runaway materialism. At age 28, Hutchinson led a drive to start the Art Institute. It opened in 1879, and moved to its permanent home in 1883. He used his business connections to build the organization, convincing family friends to donate or bequeath their private collections to the institute. Determined to influence all types of Chicagoans, he insisted that admittance to the museum be free three days a week. The institute also housed an art school—one which would produce great artists like Georgia O'Keefe. A research library was added in 1901, and a modern wing in 2009. In between those dates, the institution grew into one of the premier fine-art museums and schools in the country, housing a permanent collection of more than 300,000 works.

Further reading

○ Art Institute of Chicago, artic.edu

○ PBS profile, pbs.org/wgbh/amex/chicago/peopleevents/p_hutchinson.html

1874

CORCORAN GALLERY OF ART

William Corcoran was a D.C. native, having been born in Georgetown in 1798. He started his first business by age 19, lost it in an economic downturn by age 27, and was running another by 33. In 1837, he got into the stock market, and quickly became wealthy, then began collecting art.

Soon his art collection was so good, he felt obliged to open his house twice a week to visitors eager to see it. As he became active in philanthropy in the 1850s, he decided to construct a building specifically to house his art, and work commenced in 1859 on a property that is now the Smithsonian's Renwick Gallery across from the White House. Corcoran, a Southern sympathizer who retired to Europe to wait out the Civil War, returned after the war to finish the museum, and leave it (and its collection, valued at $100,000 in 1865 dollars) to a board of trustees.

The Corcoran Gallery officially opened in 1874. Unlike the other museums in the District of Columbia, the Corcoran was particularly committed to art education (and remains so to this day). Corcoran gave a further donation in 1878 specifically to establish a college of art and design, which is fully integrated with the museum. From the start, per Corcoran's instructions, the gallery charged a small entrance fee most of the time but followed his tradition of opening for free two days per week.

In 1897 the Corcoran moved to a large new Beaux-Arts gallery built to house both its burgeoning collection and the college. Additional artworks contributed by other private donors necessitated further expansions. With more than 17,000 pieces of art, and the only accredited school of art and design in Washington, D.C., (offering undergraduate and graduate degrees as well as youth classes and extensive continuing education), the Corcoran operated for decades as a rare privately funded museum competing with the free National Gallery of Art and Smithsonian branches.

Then in 2014 that all changed. After years of indecisiveness by its board, the Corcoran announced that it was donating most of its art collection to the National Gallery. The Corcoran art school and building, meanwhile, would be taken over by George Washington University.

Further reading

○ National Gallery announces initial accessioning of Corcoran works, nga.gov/content/ ngaweb/press/2015/nga-corcoran-announcements.html

1870

METROPOLITAN
MUSEUM OF ART

On July 4, 1866, a number of well-to-do Americans in Paris are celebrating Independence Day with a fancy dinner. The group includes Mr. Bigelow, the American ambassador; Mr. Fox, assistant secretary of war; and

---

⌇ PhilAphorism

Let your heart feel for the afflictions and distresses of every one, and let your hand give in proportion to your purse. It is not every one who asks that deserves charity; all, however, are worthy of the inquiry, or the deserving may suffer.   ☞ *George Washington*

---

several prominent pastors and businessmen. Lawyer and philanthropist John Jay has been invited to address the group, and, to their surprise, Jay uses the occasion to propose the founding of a "national institution and gallery of art" in New York.

Several men in the audience liked the idea, and they soon asked the Union League Club of New York (of which Jay was president) to take the lead in organizing the worthy endeavor. The club's art committee concluded in 1869 that both the state and federal governments would be "utterly incompetent" to fund or lead such an institution. They also cautioned, though, against putting such a complex project in the hands of one powerful individual. Instead, a large private committee was appointed, and in 1870 the Metropolitan Museum of Art was incorporated and its first officers appointed, with railroad tycoon John Johnson selected as president.

Johnson was an aficionado of ancient art, and indeed was in Egypt when the committee cabled asking him to come back to New York and take the lead. He donated a Roman sarcophagus and most of his own art collection to the institution, and insisted that as one of the largest cities in the world, New York should have a museum to match, with a collection spanning the whole history of world art. Initial fundraising was difficult, and much of the launch goal of $250,000 was covered by Johnson himself, along with William Blodgett, who got the museum's collection started with audacious acquisitions of two major European art collections that were endangered due to war between France and Prussia. The city of New York agreed to provide a building on Fifth Avenue, and in 1872 the museum opened.

Johnson and the museum's board made clear their seriousness in the early years, as they rapidly acquired works from ancient Rome and major European artists. By the time of Johnson's retirement in 1889, the museum was already among the best in the world. It moved to its current location in the early 1900s, and today, after more than a century of devoted support from legions of philanthropists, the museum houses more than two million objects.

While the building is still owned and partially supported by the city, the museum remains fiercely privately operated, and centered on philanthropy. A private corporation of just under a thousand benefactors owns the nonprofit, which has an endowment of over $2 billion and raises more than a hundred million dollars every year in fresh donations. The admission fees of 5 million annual visitors cover more than a seventh of the operations budget.

Further reading

○ Metropolitan Museum of Art, metmuseum.org

○ Winifred Howe and Henry Kent, *A History of the Metropolitan Museum of Art*
(Gillis Press, 1913)

PRESERVATION
OF MOUNT VERNON

Mount Vernon was the legacy of one great man. Preserving it was the work of many great women.

The Mount Vernon estate had been in George Washington's family since 1674. Our first President grew up there, and managed the classic Federal-style house and large surrounding farm after inheriting it in the mid-1750s. He toiled hard and much improved both the home and the estate.

After Washington's death in 1799, though, the property started to go downhill. His descendants didn't have his management skills, endurance, or success. By 1853 they had given up on the place.

Some outsiders were unwilling to see Mount Vernon go to wrack and ruin. Ann Cunningham, a South Carolinian who had grown up on a plantation herself, was shocked and saddened when she saw the state of Mount Vernon during a family sail up the Potomac River. If America's men could not keep this founder's home in repair, she thought, perhaps the women of his country could succeed.

Cunningham sent a letter to a Charleston newspaper in 1853, appealing to the women of the South to save the estate. In 1854 she founded the Mount Vernon Ladies' Association. By 1858, despite tensions along the Potomac just prior to the Civil War, she had raised enough money to try to buy the house. John Washington (the President's great-grandnephew) refused. Undeterred, Cunningham met with his wife, and promptly completed a sale for $200,000. Thousands of Americans donated to fund the purchase price, and the association took possession of the nearly empty home in February 1860.

Resisting suggestions to turn the estate into a memorial park, Cunningham wanted to restore and preserve it as it had been in Washington's day (an unusual idea at the time). With an impressive campaign of fundraising and publicity, the ladies' association was able to raise large sums of money, jumpstarting America's historic preservation movement. Over time, as restoration techniques have improved and the collection of furniture and décor has grown, the Mount Vernon Ladies'

Association has been able to very closely re-create the house's appearance in 1799, the year Washington died.

Today, the association remains a case study in effective grassroots conservation. It still manages the estate, as a 501(c)(3) nonprofit governed by a board of regents (all women) from almost 30 states, without any funds from federal, state, or local governments. It employs 500 staff and 400 volunteers, raises and manages an annual budget of $45 million, and has domain over approximately 500 of the original 8,000 acres of the plantation. Mount Vernon is the most popular historic estate in the country, hosting an average of one million guests per year—and over 80 million since it was opened to the public.

In 2012, a new National Library for the Study of George Washington opened on the Mount Vernon grounds, funded by private donors including the Donald W. Reynolds Foundation—which has committed $69 million in recent years for projects at Mount Vernon, including a museum and education center in addition to the new library.

Further reading

○ Mount Vernon, mountvernon.org

○ National Building Museum exhibit in 2003, nbm.org/exhibitions-collections/exhibitions/mount-vernon.html?referrer=https://www.google.com/

○ Ann Cunningham biography, nwhm.org/education-resources/biography/biographies/ann-pamela-cunningham/

1846

SMITHSONIAN INSTITUTION

James Smithson was a British scientist with no obvious connection to the United States. He had no family in the New World, had never visited, and had built his successful professional life entirely in Europe as a chemist and geologist. It came as a surprise, therefore, when in 1836 President Andrew Jackson informed Congress that Smithson had bequeathed half a million dollars to the government of the United States.

Smithson had inherited the money from his aristocrat mother, and in the absence of an heir he left instructions to build, "at Washington, under the name of the Smithsonian Institution, an establishment for the increase and diffusion of knowledge." Smithson was active in the Royal Society of London, and had close friends who were interested in the education of the lower classes. But why he planted his learned benevolence in America, we don't know.

ARTS

Whatever the reason, Congress accepted the bequest, and after nearly a decade of wrangling, established the institution in 1846. The Smithsonian would operate independently, being governed by a board of regents and a secretary, and would be a relatively unique hybrid of museum and research institution. The phrase "national university" was frequently used, although the debate over what precisely that meant was heated. Ultimately, an act of Congress allowed for the creation of a building that would house an art gallery, a lecture hall, a library, two laboratories, and a science museum. Renowned architect James Renwick was commissioned to design the building, which still stands on the National Mall today. Over time, further philanthropy allowed for the creation of additional buildings, museums, libraries, laboratories, art and science collections, and programs for popular education and elite investigation.

Today, the Smithsonian is the world's largest complex of the type, comprised of 19 art, science, and history museums, the National Zoo, and nine research facilities. Many donors have followed Smithson's lead and enriched the art and scientific collections, and physical campus of the organization. Yet more than 200 works from Smithson's personal library still sit in the heart of the institution.

Further reading

○ Smithsonian history, si.edu/About/History

○ Library exhibition on origins, sil.si.edu/Exhibitions/Smithson-to-Smithsonian

1842

WADSWORTH ATHENEUM

An atheneum, in nineteenth-century parlance, was a cultural institution broadly devoted to art, books, science, history, and other fields, often broadly combined in a mix of library, gallery, scientific rooms, and lecture spaces.

Hartford, Connecticut, resident Daniel Wadsworth was a relative of painter John Trumbull, friend of landscapist Thomas Cole, amateur painter and architect himself, and one of the first important American patrons of the arts. He originally hoped to give his city "a Gallery of Fine Arts," but was persuaded instead to create a broader Wadsworth Atheneum. In addition to its art gallery, it originally housed the Connecticut Historical Society, the forerunner of the Hartford Public Library, and a Natural History Society.

The institution officially opened in 1844, making it the oldest public museum of art and culture in the U.S. Like many philanthropic creations it was built up, broadened, and deepened by generations of succeeding donors.

Watkinsons, Goodwins, Colts, Averys, Sumners, and other donor families added whole new elements to the museum. Hartford native J. P. Morgan gave the Morgan Memorial, and in 1917 his son J. P. Morgan Jr. donated many ancient, Renaissance, and seventeenth-century items from his father's personal holdings.

The Morgans later purchased for the Atheneum a preeminent collection of Pilgrim furniture and decorations. This was fitting given that Wadsworth's ancestors were some of the first Pilgrim settlers in Connecticut. (Daniel's father, Jeremiah, generated the family's wealth—as a trader, manufacturer, banker, and insurer.)

The Atheneum has been a remarkably catholic center of culture. It hosted the first performance of Russian choreographer George Balanchine's American dance company. It organized the first surrealist exhibit in the U.S. It premiered an opera by Gertrude Stein and Virgil Thomson. In addition to housing 50,000 works of art, the Atheneum continues to present dramas, dance performances, literary lectures, historical exhibits, textile shows, concerts, storytelling and poetry readings, films, and other cultural events. And matching the museum's many distinct nooks and divisions are extraordinarily deep boards of donors, hundreds strong, who guide and support each branch.

Further reading

○ Wadsworth Atheneum history, thewadsworth.org/about/history

1836

PRESERVATION
OF MONTICELLO

Thomas Jefferson sometimes argued that the earth belonged to the living and that each generation owed little to those before or after it. At times he lived his own life that way. Fortunately his heirs had different views.

When Jefferson died in 1826, he left over $100,000 in debts, badly encumbering the next generation of his family. They were forced to sell most of his eclectic collection of furniture and artwork, hundreds of acres of his estate, and, in 1831, his beloved home itself, Monticello. Jefferson had designed Monticello with his own hands; he called it his "essay in architecture," and it was full of the Greek, French, and Roman influences that had shaped his political philosophy. Franklin Roosevelt would later say he had never seen a historic home that was such a perfect expression of the personality of its builder.

It was an aspect of Jefferson's legacy that would ultimately save the historic house. Uriah Levy was the first Jew to serve a career as an officer in the United States Navy, and he had gone on to a successful career in real-estate speculation. A passionate believer in the freedom of religion that America had offered his family, he was grateful to Jefferson for the role he had played in extending that landmark liberty.

After his acquaintance the Marquis de Lafayette inquired about Jefferson's home, Levy found that it was in disrepair. In 1836 he bought and restored it as a tribute to its creator. Upon Uriah's death his family lost control of the estate, and the house again deteriorated. The not-accidentally named Jefferson Levy, Uriah's nephew, regained possession in 1879. The younger Levy was also a successful speculator, and a three-term New York congressman. He put hundreds of thousands of dollars into restoring the house to its former glory.

In all, the Levy family owned the home for nearly 90 years—far longer than Jefferson himself. They eventually transferred the structure to the Thomas Jefferson Foundation to preserve it indefinitely. Since 1923 the private nonprofit foundation has operated the home as a museum, historic site, and research center—a testament to the way generations should honor those who come before and after.

Further reading

○ Marc Leepson, *Saving Monticello: The Levy Family's Epic Quest to Rescue the House that Jefferson Built* (University of Virginia Press, 2003)

○ Thomas Jefferson's Monticello, monticello.org

1815

RE-FOUNDING
THE LIBRARY OF CONGRESS

The Library of Congress was established by an official act in 1800 as a modest reference library for America's legislators, and composed primarily of law books. The collection was destroyed in August 1814 when the British army captured Washington and burned the Capitol building. Former President Thomas Jefferson then offered his extensive personal book collection as a replacement. This historic in-kind donation (for which Jefferson was later paid) changed the course of America's library.

Jefferson's nearly 6,500 books represented one of the finest collections anywhere. They included (in his words) "everything which related to America, and indeed whatever was rare and valuable in every science." Jefferson had long been a collector of manuscripts, artwork, experimental logs, machinery, and other products of the human intellect that he viewed as having significance. If he wasn't studying something, he was combining eclectic pieces of existing knowledge to create insights of his own—fresh ideas, new architecture, technical inventions, and expository writing. A longtime proponent of a national university, Jefferson believed strongly in the importance of an educated citizenry.

So when he reconstituted the Library of Congress through his personal gift to the nation, Jefferson didn't have a mere reference collection in mind. "There is in fact no subject," he argued, "to which a Member of Congress may not have occasion to refer." And there was no backtracking at the Library once Jefferson had placed his magnificently diverse works at the core of the collection. Today, the library houses 144 million items—books, maps, works of art—that touch on virtually every aspect of human inquiry.

In 1999, a million-dollar gift from philanthropists Jerry and Gene Jones allowed the library to largely re-create Jefferson's original assemblage of books—pulling together the surviving volumes from numerous specialized sections, and purchasing matched period books wherever one of his original volumes had disappeared or been destroyed. The resulting library is now exhibited in a single room, and may be browsed in a spiral bookcase by visitors, much as it would have been experienced by its donor. This visiting room is in the magnificent main structure of the Library of Congress—which is called, appropriately, the Thomas Jefferson Building.

Further reading

○ History of the Library of Congress, loc.gov/loc/legacy

PENNSYLVANIA ACADEMY OF THE FINE ARTS

The oldest art museum and art school in America was built up through many decades of private support, particularly from Philadelphia business leaders. With George Clymer—a revered Pennsylvania merchant and banker who had been a primary financer of the American Revolution—as the lead monetary backer, and artists Charles Willson Peale, William Rush, and Rembrandt Peale providing the inspiration, the Pennsylvania Academy of the Fine Arts was founded in 1805. A small clutch of talented painters had by then become established in America, but a desperate shortage of art schools and museums meant that most had to go to Europe to develop their craft.

Soon after its launch, the Pennsylvania Academy began to benefit from repeated acts of private largesse. In 1811, wealthy local merchant William Bingham donated Gilbert Stuart's beloved *George Washington (Lansdowne*

Portrait). That same year, Napoleon Bonaparte contributed 24 books of European etchings. In 1813 a large gift of paintings, casts, books, and engravings (probably the most important art collection then owned by an American) was given to the academy by philanthropist Allen Smith. Many other masterpieces, particularly by American artists, were donated over following decades.

The academy had a financial crisis in the 1830s, from which it was rescued by public contributions. By mid-century it was the major force in American art. Thomas Eakins, who had been a student at the Academy, returned to teach, and became the director in 1882, installing an original curriculum that mostly remains today—two years learning the fundamentals of drawing, painting, and sculpture (with an emphasis on anatomy, dissection of natural subjects, and extensive sketching of the nude), followed by two years of guided independent study. Other prominent artists like William Merritt Chase, Mary Cassatt, and Alexander Calder were also tied to the academy, as were great donors like Joseph Harrison and Albert Barnes. The academy continues to operate today as one of the country's most august artistic nonprofits.

Further reading

○ About the Academy, pafa.org/About/32

MAJOR ACHIEVEMENTS OF AMERICAN PHILANTHROPY
(1636-2015)

NATURE, ANIMALS, AND PARKS

Many of America's most iconic natural attractions are the products of philanthropy. Hundreds of national parks, urban green spaces, zoos and aquariums, wildlife protections, gardens and arboretums have been created or bolstered by private givers. The Rockefeller family alone established or enlarged parks like Grand Teton, Great Smoky Mountains, Virgin Islands, Yosemite, Big Bend, Rocky Mountain, Acadia, Olympic, Grand Canyon, Glacier, Haleakala, Redwood, Lassen Volcanic, Mesa Verde, Shenandoah, Antietam, Big Hole, Fort Donelson, various state parks, the Marsh-Billings farm, the Blue Ridge Parkway, numerous historic sites and monuments, and local parks. Small donors and grassroots philanthropic efforts have been even more important, helping save creatures like the peregrine falcon, swift fox, wild turkey, wolf, bluebird, whooping crane, and numerous fish, creating outdoor oases for everyday citizens to enjoy, conserving rare trees and plants, uncovering fresh solutions to ecological dilemmas, and pushing the boundaries of natural science through private support research.

Section research provided by Karl Zinsmeister,
Brian Brown, Evan Sparks, and Justin Torres

A GOLDEN AGE FOR PARKS

"Throughout much of the country, this is a golden age for signature urban parks. From Boston to Houston, New York to San Francisco, Atlanta to Pittsburgh, St. Louis to Detroit, beautiful old destination parks are being renewed and some great new ones are being created." That's the conclusion of a 2015 report from the Trust for Public Land, which looks closely at the use of private, donor-powered conservancies to manage public parks. The report finds that since the first experiment in 1980—the Central Park Conservancy which has since raised more than $700 million to burnish that New York City treasure—roughly half of all major cities now rely on at least one nonprofit to manage and fund crucial parks. A majority of these have been created just since 2000.

Further reading

○ Trust for Public Land Study, tpl.org/sites/default/files/files_upload/ccpe-Parks-Conservancy-Report.pdf

HEALING HORNED OWLS AND BREEDING BUGS

Oracle software chief Larry Ellison has long shown philanthropic interest in wildlife. Now he is taking an active role in sustaining threatened animals. He is making a major donation, estimated in the range of $55 million, to create a center near San Jose, California, that will rehabilitate about 8,500 injured creatures annually, and also operate an advanced breeding and rehabilitation facility focused on local species—particularly on unflashy reptiles, amphibians, and insects. It is hoped, for instance, that Ellison's breeding program can have a role in rebuilding the population of Lange's metalmark butterfly, down to an estimated 45 individuals at last count. U.S. Fish and Wildlife officials say they would welcome the help of a donor-organized effort that might someday allow the creature to be removed from the endangered species list.

Further reading

○ *San Jose Mercury News* report, mercurynews.com/saratoga/ci_27336567/saratoga-cutting-edge-wildlife-facility-works-courtesy-oracles

NATURAL-HISTORY EDUCATION

Over a 20-year period, investor Richard Gilder donated more than $125 million to the American Museum of Natural History in New York City. He also devoted much time and brainpower—for instance in spearheading the museum's expansion of its Hayden Planetarium into the more ambitious Rose Center for Earth and Space (described in a nearby 1999 entry). His most interesting gift, however, may have been the one that established the Richard Gilder Graduate School right within the museum—where scientists can now earn Ph.D.s in biology, and teachers can complete master's degrees in science instruction. Building on this unusual pedagogical capacity within the museum, Gilder announced his latest and largest gift in 2014: $50 million to kick off a six-story addition that will particularly provide space for the museum's growing education programs. The new wing will also accommodate additional research by staff, and help the museum cope with its jump in visitors: from 3 million annually during the 1990s to 5 million per year in 2015.

Further reading

○ *New York Times* report, nytimes.com/2014/12/11/arts/design/american-museum-of-natural-history-plans-an-addition.html

NATURE

2014

A PARK ON THE WATER

The Hudson River Park Trust is a nonprofit charged with converting four miles of abandoned piers and industrial lots strung along the lower west side of Manhattan into nature spaces and entertainment venues. In 2014, the trust proposed one dramatically different park that had emerged from its discussions with philanthropists Barry Diller and Diane von Furstenberg. Asked to contribute funds for a simple pier rebuilding along the decayed Hudson waterfront around 13th Street, Diller urged something more ambitious. He hired a prominent architect to design an

∽ PhilAphorism

If you combine all the spectral rays into a single beam, you get white light; and if you combine all the virtues into a single beam you get charity.

☞ *Austin O'Malley*

undulating wooded and grassy area that hovers above the river on 300 mushroom-shaped concrete columns. The suspended island would be reached by two gangways, and would feature open amphitheaters where a range of ambitious live performances would be scheduled.

In addition to offering these ideas and promising a $113 million donation to build the park, Diller recruited top theater and entertainment impresarios to advise on the cultural programming, and created an independent foundation to take responsibility for carrying it out. This being New York City, some activists were politically and environmentally annoyed by the notion of a privately funded park, requiring piers driven into a river. Lawsuits were launched in 2015 to try to stop the project. The proposal, however, enjoyed wide endorsement from New York leaders.

Further reading

○ Web reporting on park design details, ny.curbed.com/archives/2015/06/04/new_renderings_details_revealed_for_pier55_floating_park.php

2014

$350 MILLION FOR A CITY PARK IN TULSA

Tulsa, Oklahoma, offers a good example of how local philanthropy enriches American lives. This small city has generous individual donors and independent foundations along with a community foundation endowed with $3.8 billion in assets. Now a new donor-funded park is taking shape along the Arkansas River that runs through town, placing a fresh green crown on Tulsa's head. In the summer of 2014 local oilman and banker George Kaiser made a $350 million gift—the largest for a public park in U.S. history—to create what will be known as "A Gathering Place." The park will wind through the heart of the city and total nearly 100 acres when complete.

Drawing on suggestions collected in public meetings, it will connect four riverside sites into a cohesive recreation area with amenities like bike trails, boating, tennis courts, open lawns and gardens, playgrounds, a skate park, water features, and public meeting spaces. The Kaiser Foundation donated most of the land, as well as design, engineering, and construction plans, plus $50 million to operate and maintain the park once it is open. Supplementing Kaiser's $200 million were funds from other private donors, companies, and foundations like those created by the Chapman, Schusterman, Murphy, and Helmerich families. The local government will own the property, but a private conservancy established by the Kaiser Foundation will manage and program it, following the philanthropic model which has been so successful in other parts of the country.

Further reading

○ *Tulsa World* reporting, tulsaworld.com/homepage4/george-kaiser-foundation-makes-record-donation-to-river-parks-for/article_d1865fb1-003c-5414-9fb7-eaf86857f4ca.html

2013

CARVING OUT NEW URBAN OASES

Much of Houston was built on marshland, and the hundreds of miles of natural streams and man-made ditches that drain the area were converted in many places to simple storm channels, lined with concrete and pared of trees and vegetation. Local citizens began to realize that these waterways could serve multiple purposes as recreation areas, non-motorized travel corridors, and beautifiers of the city, without impairing their role in watershed management.

The Houston Parks Board, a private nonprofit that has been improving local green space since 1976, developed an ambitious plan to turn 1,500 acres of utilitarian drainage channels into a citywide necklace of parks and trails. Nine different bayous touching scores of neighborhoods would be cleaned, landscaped, planted, and linked together via 150 miles of new or improved trails. The board would take responsibility for raising $115 million of donated private money, to be matched with $100 million from the city of Houston, and after construction is complete the nonprofit will manage a total of 4,000 acres of new and existing bayou parklands. This will give Houston the largest system of public off-street paths in the nation, and it is estimated that six out of every ten city residents will live within a mile and a half of a bayou park or trail.

Launching this dramatic project was a $50 million gift from local residents Rich and Nancy Kinder—one of the largest voluntary offerings ever for public greenspace in the U.S. Other givers include the Houston Endowment, the Wortham, Fondren, and Brown foundations, and many individual donors. The Kinders had previous experience at underwriting public parks with their donations, (see our 2010 entry describing their revival of Buffalo Bayou Park) and back in 2004 the Kinders provided $10 million to another nonprofit conservancy to create a brand-new permanent green space and public park near their city's convention center. The new Discovery Green was carved out of 12 underused acres in the middle of downtown. Nancy Kinder served as founding chairwoman of the organization that created and now privately manages the intensively used park—which hosts 400 concerts, festivals, exercise classes, child play groups, pet gatherings, and other events every year, attracting more than a million people.

NATURE

This and other philanthropic ventures in a number of cities that created popular new parks out of vacant lots, forlorn waterways, abandoned subway trestles, and other overlooked areas have inspired a new wave of donors to build great urban parks using similar private conservancy models. In 2012, for instance, a park opened in Dallas on more than five acres of land created "out of thin air" by decking over a recessed expressway that cuts through the arts district. As in other cases, this project was catalyzed by donor funds, created and managed by a private nonprofit, and enjoyed immediate popularity and heavy use.

Further reading

○ Houston Parks board fact sheet on Bayou Greenways 2020, houstonparksboard.org/ assets/Fact_Sheet_for_Bayou_Greenways_2020_FINAL.pdf

LARGEST CASH GIFT TO NATIONAL PARKS

More than 70 of our national parks have established cooperating nonprofit membership associations to help them raise donated funds for park improvements. In 2013, one of these linked nonprofits—the Golden Gate National Parks Conservancy—received the largest-ever cash gift made to a U.S. national park. The S. D. Bechtel Jr. Foundation, founded by the owner of the Bechtel construction and engineering firm, offered $25 million to create a new natural space on the top of a roadway that tunnels across the Presidio, the historic and highly scenic open area overlooking the Golden Gate Bridge, San Francisco Bay, and the Pacific Ocean, which used to be a military post. The funds will also support programming at the Presidio for local youths. A focus of Stephen Bechtel's philanthropy elsewhere has been Scouting. (See 2013 entry on his gift for the Summit.)

Further reading

○ Conservancy gift announcement, parksconservancy.org/assets/about/pdfs/sd-bechtel-jr-foundation.pdf

LUFKIN PRIZE

Wall Street investor Dan Lufkin grew up in small-town New York, studied at Yale as a naval reservist, joined the Marines, and then earned his MBA at Harvard Business School in 1957. He and two classmates established an investment firm that focused on small fast-growing firms rather than blue-chip companies. Starting with $240,000 in 1960, Donaldson, Lufkin & Jenrette grew over the next 11 years to a net worth exceeding $50 million, and then expanded further.

In 1970 Lufkin approached Tom Meskill, a Republican candidate for governor of Connecticut, with ideas for a new Department of Environmental Protection. The subsequently elected governor appointed Lufkin as the department's first commissioner. A serious problem in the civil service, Lufkin later noted, is that "you can't get rid of people who are really doing nothing. With the Department of Environmental Protection, we had a new department.... As a result, all the people we brought were there on merit, not tenure." His experience in state government led Lufkin to publish *Many Sovereign States* in 1975, a defense of devolving resources and sovereignty to individual states.

After Lufkin returned to finance, he continued to take an interest in conservation and the outdoors. Riding horses and raising dairy cows, horses, and cattle, were passions, and he was inducted into the Cutting Horse Association's Hall of Fame. He donated to the National Audubon Society, Nature Conservancy, National Park Foundation, Environmental Defense Fund, Conservation Fund, American Farmland Trust, and Atlantic Salmon Federation. With an endowment from Lufkin's family and friends, the National Audubon Society created the Dan Lufkin Prize for Environmental Leadership in 2013. The initial recipients of the $100,000 cash prize for innovators in conservation were Dr. George Archibald in 2013, co-founder of the International Crane Foundation, land trust pioneer Patrick Noonan in 2014, and Spencer Beebe, an expert in integrating economic and ecological well-being, in 2015. All men in Lufkin's mold, with an interest in finding ways of conserving nature without damaging human prosperity.

Further reading

○ Detailed Lufkin biography, hbs.edu/entrepreneurs/pdf/danlufkin.pdf

○ About the Lufkin Prize, audubon.org/dan-w-lufkin-prize-environmental-leadership

2013

HIGH-ADVENTURE HAVEN FOR BOYS

The Boy Scouts of America had a problem. Fort A. P. Hill in Virginia had for nearly two decades been home to the Scouts' national jamboree, which draws 45,000 boys and up to 300,000 friends and family from across the country. But throwing up the temporary infrastructure needed for the quadrennial jamborees cost the Scouts as much as $16 million each time, and the Scout leadership realized they needed a more permanent fix. That solution came in

NATURE

the form of a 10,600-acre site in the Allegheny Mountains of West Virginia, near the wild New River Gorge. (The deep gorge is cut by the only river that rises east of the Appalachians yet manages to find a slot through the mountains and reach the Ohio River Valley.) The location was perfect: 70 percent of Scouts would be within a 10-hour drive of the site, and it would provide not only a jamboree location but also an eastern "high adventure" base to supplement Scouting's famous Philmont ranch in the West. The site is surrounded by more than 70,000 acres of federal recreation land that Scouts may explore.

The BSA has long relied on generous giving, but acquiring and developing the West Virginia property was an extraordinary philanthropic lift. Starting in 2009, a long string of individual donors plus some corporations lined up with more than $300 million of quiet gifts. Stephen Bechtel donated $50 million. Walter Scott gave $25 million. Mike Goodrich funded creation of a man-made lake. Consol Energy offered $15 million. Most of the lead donors to the Summit are Eagle Scouts.

A major amount of "terraforming" was needed to create useable sites on the rugged topography. Camping areas and bike trails had to be built. The large lake was dammed. A 9,000-square-foot warehouse was needed on the grounds. A landmark pedestrian bridge was designed to cross the gorge dividing the eastern and western halves of the property.

In addition to hosting jamborees, this spectacular facility, known as the Summit, will allow 88,000 Scouts each year to enjoy whitewater rafting, hiking, mountain biking, climbing and rappelling, swimming, fishing, and shooting sports. The Summit is projected to host 1.5 million Scouts within its first decade; by comparison, Philmont took 70 years to reach 1 million visitors.

Further reading

○ Summit Bechtel Reserve in the New River Gorge, summitblog.org/programs/about/the-new-river-gorge/

2012

A PARK ON THE FREEWAY

As in lots of cities that get transected by highways, when the Woodall Rodgers Freeway was slashed through downtown Dallas as eight lanes of submerged concrete, the surrounding neighborhoods were damaged. But few observers anticipated how strongly the area would re-blossom after three large blocks of the freeway were roofed over and turned into the Klyde Warren Park. Named for the son of lead donor Kelcy Warren, the five-acre site was turned into a busy mix of lawn, dog park, playgrounds, food trucks, and performance areas. The free public park has a packed daily schedule of events, concerts, workouts, and meet-ups—all privately managed by the Woodall Rodgers Park Foundation, which led creation of the oasis, and raised $55 million of private donations for its construction.

Further reading

○ *D Magazine* retrospective on creation of the park, dmagazine.com/publications/d-magazine/2012/special-report-the-park/the-woodall-rodgers-park-strong-foundation

ROLLING RESTORATION OF SMITHSONIAN'S NATURAL HISTORY MUSEUM

The Smithsonian Institution was a product of philanthropy (a bequest from James Smithson), and about 30 percent of its budget continues to come from private donations (which play a particularly large role in expansions and new initiatives). A major refresh of its National Museum of Natural History began in the late 1990s, sparking the largest gift to the museum to that point from Ken Behring, who rose from harsh poverty to riches by selling cars and then developing real estate. He donated $20 million to spearhead a massive renovation of Natural History's ground floor, resulting in, among other things, a new Hall of Mammals which opened in 2003. (Behring later donated $80 million to revitalize the National Museum of American History, making him the Smithsonian's largest private donor.)

The Museum of Natural History continued its upgrade with a subsequent $15 million gift from philanthropist David Koch, creating the David Koch Hall of Human Origins. Then in 2012 Koch donated an additional $35 million which will be used to remake the museum's dinosaur hall, its most visited area. One of the highest priorities of museum officials, the dinosaur-hall funding will provide fresh displays and specimens, and allow obsolete interpretations to be updated with the newest information from the fast-changing science of dinosaur paleontology.

Further reading

○ *Smithsonian* magazine, smithsonianmag.com/science-nature/New_Hall_on_the_Mall.html

○ *Philanthropy* Interview with Ken Behring, philanthropyroundtable.org/topic/economic_opportunity/interview_with_ken_behring

○ *Washington Post* article announcing Koch gift, washingtonpost.com/lifestyle/style/david-koch-donates-35-million-to-national-museum-of-natural-history-for-dinosaur-hall/2012/05/03/gIQAIjT3yT_story.html

NATURE

PUTTING THE BAYOU BACK IN BAYOU CITY

The city of Houston was founded on Buffalo Bayou, which runs from the surrounding prairie through downtown to the port lands. A 158-acre park hugging its banks has long been a Houston icon and destination for residents seeking a bit of green or some exercise. But the public park suffered years of neglect and underperformance. The Buffalo Bayou Partnership was established as a nonprofit in 1986 to make better use of Houston's most significant natural resource. In 2010, the Kinder Foundation, the family charity established by gas pipeline titan Rich Kinder and his wife, Nancy, offered the nonprofit a $30 million grant to catalyze major improvements at the park. After fundraising completed in 2015, a $56 million project was begun to restore the land surrounding the waterway to a more natural and healthy state, build trails and pedestrian bridges, improve lighting and amenities, and otherwise make the park more attractive for users.

The Kinders have provided funds to preserve and upgrade other public parks in Houston as well, including Hermann Park, home to the city zoo and other important institutions, and Emancipation Park, an historic site first purchased by freed slaves. In addition to this work reviving existing parks, the Kinders have been leaders in creating brand-new parks in their home city (see 2013 entry).

Further reading

○ Buffalo Bayou Partnership, buffalobayou.org

SAVING AMERICA'S MUSTANGS

Wild horses, or mustangs, have roamed free in the American West since the days of the Spanish conquistadors. Because they have almost no natural

---

~∂ PhilAphorism

Never respect men merely for their riches, but rather for their philanthropy; we do not value the sun for its height, but for its use.

☞ *Gamaliel Bailey*

predators today, they multiply rapidly and threaten to overgraze the areas where they live on protected federal land in ten Western states. The U.S. Bureau of Land Management keeps the herds at about 27,000 horses by regularly rounding up extra animals. Historically, about 60 percent of these surplus horses have been purchased at auction for adoption. Passage of the American Horse Slaughter Prevention Act in 2005 banned the killing of leftover horses. Since then, nearly 50,000 mustangs have accumulated in corrals and pastures where the federal government nows pays something like $70 million a year to feed them.

In response, Madeleine Pickens and her husband Boone Pickens purchased two ranches in northeastern Nevada, along with their grazing rights on adjoining public land, and proposed to use this land, fully fenced, as a preserve where culled horses could be allowed to run free. All males would be gelded to prevent the herds from reproducing, and visitors would be invited to camp on the lands and view the wild animals with guides. The BLM would pay fees to the 501(c)(3) preserve at substantially lower levels than their existing costs of warehousing the animals. No agreement has been concluded with the BLM, but in 2015 a portion of the ranch was opened as a tourist destination where Americans can learn about the horses Pickens considers national treasures.

Further reading

○ Mustang Monument eco-ranch, mustangmonument.com

○ Prospectus to BLM, blm.gov/pgdata/etc/medialib/blm/wo/Communications_
Directorate/public_affairs.Par.76646.File.dat/SAM_pospectus.pdf

2007

LARGEST PARK IN CHESTER COUNTY, AT NO PUBLIC COST

Chester County, one of the three original counties established in Pennsylvania by William Penn, lies west of Philadelphia, and is home to about half a million people. It is a beautiful region made famous by Wyeth-family paintings of scenes along the Brandywine valley that snakes through the area. Two decades ago, Gerry and Marguerite Lenfest, Philadelphia natives who have given away $1.2 billion of the fortune he earned in cable television, bought 500 acres of open land in the county and had a house designed for the site. "I went out to see it," Lenfest told *Philanthropy* magazine. "The hole was dug and the rebar was being put in. I asked the architect, 'How big is that house?' And he said: '16,000 square feet.' I thought for a moment, and I said, 'You know what, fill up the hole.'" With their children grown, that seemed like too much home, Lenfest explained. He and his wife decided to instead give away the property for public use. They kept their residence in the same house they bought in 1966 for $35,000.

The Lenfests donated the Chester County land, which had a market value of about $32 million, to the Natural Lands Trust, a local nonprofit that has helped private-property owners protect 128,000 acres since its founding in 1953. They also donated $5 million to create an endowment for the property, helped the group acquire an adjoining farm, and in 2012 paid for erection of a public lodge. Their gifts were combined with another plot owned by the county to create the 1,263-acre ChesLen Preserve—a privately owned nature center fully open to public access at no charge. It offers eight miles of unpaved tails, canoeing on two miles of the West Branch of Brandywine Creek, horseback riding, and birdwatching, and is one of the largest parks in southeast Pennsylvania. All created at no cost to taxpayers.

Further reading

○ *Philadelphia Inquirer* story, articles.philly.com/2007-03-16/news/25237088_1_gerry-lenfest-natural-lands-trust-public-park

○ ChesLen Preserve, natlands.org/preserves-to-visit/list-of-preserves/cheslen-preserve

2007

DINOSAUR HALL
AT THE MUSEUM OF THE ROCKIES

The world's greatest collection of dinosaur fossils is not located at the Smithsonian, or Field, or British museums, not in New York or Oxford or Boston. It is housed in Bozeman, Montana, at the Museum of the Rockies. The MOR possesses more T. Rex specimens (13) than any other institution, including the world's largest T. Rex skull. Its curators excavated and conserved the second-most-complete T. Rex skeleton in existence; they were the first to discover soft tissue and proteins in dinosaur bones 67 million years old; the first to document an ovulating female dinosaur; and leaders in finding and categorizing baby and juvenile dinosaurs. The Museum of the Rockies has pioneered new understanding of the growth rates and behavior of dinosaurs, and has launched many fresh hypotheses, such as that tyrannosaurs were scavengers rather than predators, and that dinosaurs nurtured offspring in colonies rather than leaving them to their own devices like modern reptiles.

The museum is associated with Montana State University, but is an independent nonprofit, and heavily reliant upon private philanthropy in developing the dinosaur collections it is famous for. Prominent national donors like Tom Siebel, Catherine Reynolds, George Lucas, Nathan Myhrvold,

Ted Turner, and Klein Gilhousen have paid for excavations, subsidized research, and funded the creation of a spectacular museum exhibition that opened in 2007: the Siebel Dinosaur Complex. "This is my dream dinosaur hall," explained MOR curator of paleontology Jack Horner, the world's most prominent dinosaur expert, who designed the exhibits paid for by Siebel and others. The *Bozeman Daily Chronicle* reported on the opening of the complex: "Horner said almost all of the money supporting the museum's paleontology comes from private donations. Winning grants from agencies like the National Science Foundation is fine, he said, but they always ask, 'Can you do it with less?' Private donors, on the other hand, tend to ask, 'Are you sure it's enough?'"

Further reading

○ Story on hall opening, bozemandailychronicle.com/news/article_0500402d-8705-5ab1-a000-76efcecf58d5.html?mode=print

2007

GARDEN IN A QUARRY

Andrew Hodges developed oil and gas fields in Louisiana, then became interested in the cutover timberlands of northwest Louisiana, from which all the virgin longleaf pine trees had been harvested, and the land abandoned. In the 1930s he purchased 107,000 acres of clear-cut and had thousands of pine seedlings planted there, earning himself the title "Father of Forestry" in the region. In the midst of this land was an abandoned stone quarry. Hodges and his wife Nina were attracted to its romantic setting, and built themselves a residence there and began planting gardens amidst the rock of the quarry terraces. They created a large man-made lake, and became obsessed with beautifying the picturesque location. In 1957 they opened the property for public garden visits, hiking, fishing, horse riding, and camping, with a nonprofit organization overseeing operations. In 2007, the Hodges Foundation donated 948 lushly landscaped acres, including the unusual stone-quarry gardens and 225-acre lake, to become the newest Louisiana state park—Hodges Gardens.

Further reading

○ History at Friends of Hodges Gardens, hodgesgardens.net/pages/history

2007

TRANSFORMING PARKS
IN MEMPHIS, ATLANTA, AND BEYOND

Shelby Farms is a huge oasis (4,500 acres, or five times the size of Central

Park in New York) inside Tennessee's largest city. For most of its life it has been a hodgepodge of raw land and developed areas sprawling without much coherence. Then in 2007 the county awarded a management contract for the park to a new nonprofit conservancy headed by Barbara Hyde, a major Memphis philanthropist married to AutoZone founder Pitt Hyde. The volunteer board created a master plan for developing the park, and in 2008 the Hydes provided a $20 million donation to launch the initiative. Ideas for improvements were solicited from the many neighborhoods adjoining the park, and top designers were brought in to plan a lake, creation of an amphitheater and boathouse, extensive new trails, the planting of one million trees plus other landscaping, and many new amenities. A dramatic playground, new pedestrian bridges, and other enhancements were completed quickly, and park attendance has already tripled since the private conservancy took over. The fundraising campaign hit its goal of $70 million in 2015.

One model for this effort was a similar rejuvenation of a keystone urban park in Atlanta, where a $73 million expansion and renovation of Piedmont Park, the city's most heavily used green space, attracted donations from the Robert W. Woodruff Foundation ($10 million), the Arthur Blank Family Foundation ($5 million), and many others. The City of Atlanta had to commit only $5 million of public funds. In Atlanta as in Memphis, the key element was establishment of a private nonprofit conservancy to manage the effort.

As urban parks expert Guy Hagstette told *Philanthropy* magazine, the key to building an effective park conservancy is giving the conservancy both fundraising and management power. American cities are dotted with so-called conservancies that are really just fundraising vehicles for city parks departments, without any design or operations power. "That's just business as usual," warns Peter Harnik of the Trust for Public Land. Conservancies with independent authority can accomplish projects faster, with better results—which both deepens donor confidence and dramatically improves the experiences of park users.

Further reading

- *Philanthropy* magazine article on park donors, philanthropyroundtable.org/topic/ excellence_in_philanthropy/philanthropy_on_the_green
- Master plan for Shelby Farms Park, shelbyfarmspark.org/masterplan
- Piedmont Park Conservancy, piedmontpark.org/conservancy/mission.html

2007

TRUST FOR THE NATIONAL MALL

After opening his commercial real estate firm in the nation's capital in 1974, John "Chip" Akridge developed more than 11 million square feet of office space. Disturbed by the increasingly degraded state of the National Mall, Akridge established the nonprofit Trust for the National Mall in 2007 to assist the National Park Service in its maintenance of this heavily used public space (more than 25 million annual visits). He donated $250,000 of his own money to start the project and helped raise millions more. In addition to helping with immediate needs, the Trust sparked a new National Mall Plan which details ambitious improvements that will take place over a period of decades. Trust chairman Akridge announced a $350 million private fundraising effort to pay for these renovations of the nation's front yard, and donated the first $1 million himself in 2012.

Further reading

○ Trust for the National Mall mission, nationalmall.org/about-trust/mission

2005

A NOAH'S ARK IN THE SUNSHINE STATE

Brad Kelley—a college dropout whose discount cigarette empire made him a billionaire—brews his own bourbon, never uses e-mail, sometimes wears a kilt, and owns more land than there are acres in the whole state of Rhode Island. Astonishingly, none of these are the most eccentric thing about him. That honor undoubtedly goes to Rum Creek Ranch, Kelley's 40,000-acre spread in southwest Florida where he breeds endangered animals. Kelley's foray into animal conservation started with rare strains of cattle. That led to the acquisition, over 2004 and 2005, of some 40,000 acres in DeSoto County, for a reported $50 million. Kelley now propagates many exotic species on that land, including tapirs, anoas (a three-foot-tall Indonesian buffalo), hippos, rhinos, bongos (an African mountain antelope featuring psychedelic white-yellow stripes and huge tapered horns), bentang (wild cattle), and others. Many of these animals had been reduced to just a handful of breeding pairs; Kelley's goal is to work with zoos and conservation groups to reintroduce them in sustainable numbers within their native habitats.

Further reading

○ *Wall Street Journal* interview, online.wsj.com/news/articles/SB10000872396390444799904578050541251702834

2005

ACRES ACROSS AMERICA

In an example of what is called "cooperative conservation," Walmart made a ten-year, $35 million commitment, in partnership with the National Fish

NATURE

and Wildlife Foundation, to conserve at least one acre of wildlife habitat for every acre the company developed as a store site. The first grant bought more than 300,000 acres in Maine. Thousands of acres of rare blue oak in the Sierra foothills, tallgrass prairie in Colorado, land adjoining the Appalachian Trail, and a redwood forest in California have also been preserved. In 2011 and 2012 the program branched into urban conservation as well, funding fish ladders, wetland restorations, and other projects in Bridgeport, Chicago, San Diego, and other cities. By 2015, the program had helped conserve more than 900,000 acres in 31 states.

Further reading

○ National Fish and Wildlife Foundation, nfwf.org/acresforamerica/Pages/home.aspx

○ Walmart Acres for America, corporate.walmart.com/global-responsibility/environment-sustainability/acres-for-america

WORLD'S LARGEST AQUARIUM

Not surprisingly for the man who brought the big-box store to the hardware business, when Bernie Marcus decided that Atlanta needed an aquarium, he wanted it to be *large*. And he got his wish: the Georgia Aquarium is the grandest in the world. Marcus was the co-founder of Home Depot, and after he decided to give a present to the Atlantans who made his stores successful by shopping at and staffing them, he went seeking something accessible that all kinds of people could enjoy. He ultimately gave $250 million to build and stock the giant fish tank, which opened in 2005. The facility recently hosted its 20-millionth visitor.

The centerpiece exhibit is an acrylic enclosure holding 6.3 million gallons of sea water and four whale sharks that many biologists did not believe could be successfully transported (by boat, truck, and plane) from Taiwan. The aquarium is also host to one of only two captured sets of great hammerhead sharks, and the only four manta rays displayed in a U.S. aquarium. There are dolphins, Japanese spider crabs, black-footed penguins, and a new exhibit of

⌇ PhilAphorism

Not what we give, but what we share,
for the gift without the giver is bare.
⌖ James Russell Lowell

sea otters. The facility is also home to the Correll Center for Aquatic Animal Health, the world's only integration of an aquarium and veterinarian teaching hospital. It uses 10,000 square feet to produce some of the leading research on conservation of sea creatures.

Further reading

○ About the aquarium, georgiaaquarium.org/members-and-donors/about-us.aspx

○ Marcus profile in *Philanthropy*, philanthropyroundtable.org/topic/excellence_in_ philanthropy/building_america

2005

MAINE NORTH WOODS

In the mid-1970s, Roxanne Quimby relocated to rural Maine to live close to the earth, without electricity or running water. A decade later, she partnered with beekeeper Burt Shavitz and began making beeswax candles, polishes, and eventually the lip balm that turned Burt's Bees into a multimillion-dollar personal-care company. In 2000, Quimby started buying up land in Maine's north woods, near Mount Katahdin, with some of her profits. She accelerated the process after she sold Burt's Bees for hundreds of millions of dollars (she had previously bought out Burt). Quimby now controls 120,000 acres of woodland wilderness, and is seeking to donate most of it as a national park.

Quimby's desire to catalyze a park has proved controversial. A liberal environmentalist, she closed access to land she purchased, banned hunting and fishing, tore up roads and bridges, and stopped snowmobiling. This sparked a loud outcry from locals, who were allowed easy access to the land for personal enjoyment by the paper companies that were the previous proprietors. In addition to the curtailed recreational use of this vast swath of land, many residents of the Maine woods fear losing forestry jobs and development opportunities if land becomes locked up in a national park. In response to the backlash, Quimby and her son, Lucas St. Clair, have been reopening some of their holdings to recreational use. Whether Congress will designate a Maine park that Quimby can seed with her land remains to be seen.

Further reading

○ News story, pressherald.com/news/roxanne-quimbys-son-offers-new-hope-for-national-park-plan_2013-09-15.html?pagenum=full

2005

GREAT RIVERS PARTNERSHIP

Caterpillar Inc. headquarters overlooks the Illinois River, which inspired their

NATURE

Great Rivers Partnership with the Nature Conservancy. The corporation's foundation donated $12 million to the conservancy in 2005 to start the program, which aims to help "conserve and restore the world's great river systems." The effort brings together scientists, navigators, landholders, government officials, business representatives, and residents to improve the health and function of large river systems. The Great Rivers Partnership began by improving stretches of the Mississippi River—which provides drinking water to 18 million people, is vital to farmers and industries, and affects 60 percent of North America's bird species and many fish and animals. The partnership then used what it learned in its Mississippi work to assist management of two other important rivers: the Upper Yangtze in China, and Brazil's Parana River. Kicked off by Caterpillar's initial investment, the conservancy raised $60 million in private funding for the program over five years.

Further reading

○ Nature Conservancy report, conservationgateway.org/Files/Pages/great-rivers-partnership-.aspx

2005

YOSEMITE FALLS RESTORATION

At 2,565 feet, Yosemite Falls is the highest waterfall in North America, and one of the icons of the national park that encloses it. By the early 2000s, though, the falls were blighted by an ugly bridge, asphalt paths, and a polluted parking lot. In 2003, a private capital campaign was launched to raise $12.5 million to revitalize the visitor experience in the area. Bay Area landscape architect Lawrence Halprin was hired to head up the design, with private donations raised by the Yosemite Fund covering three quarters of the cost. Fully 14,500 individual donors contributed to the effort, and construction was complete a speedy two years after the goal was first announced. The new Lower Yosemite Falls area included re-vegetated areas, natural-looking paths and bridges, 52 acres of habitat restoration, new restrooms, educational exhibits, trail maps, a bus stop, and more. This was just one of more than 300 projects, expending $55 million, that have been privately funded by what is now known as the Yosemite Conservancy. Similar donor funds have sprung up at other parks, and the overarching National Park Foundation now privately raises and grants more than $31 million annually.

Further reading

○ Projects of the Yosemite Conservancy, yosemiteconservancy.org/map

○ Evolution of philanthropy in the National Park system, nps.gov/partnerships/evolvphiltpy5.htm

DONOR-CREATED
PUBLIC PARKS IN LOUISVILLE

Native son David Jones co-founded Humana Inc. in Louisville, Kentucky, and built it into one of America's largest private health-care companies. Along the way he participated in many initiatives to improve his home city, but none bigger than the Parklands—a project to create nearly 4,000 acres of brand-new parks in Louisville and then operate them permanently with no public money. Starting in 2004, Jones took responsibility for raising $71 million of private donations; his family provided about $15 million themselves, and he made 100 personal visits and countless calls to raise the remaining funds from 550 individuals, foundations, and companies. His son, Dan Jones, took direction of the nonprofit charged with acquiring land and then designing and building the facilities, including 100 miles of hiking, biking, and paddling trails, playgrounds, a scenic drive, and numerous buildings. The same nonprofit will operate and maintain the facilities (which began to open in 2011, and were two thirds complete in 2015). The Jones family also contributed a large portion of a separate $60 million endowment that the nonprofit will use to meet the annual expenses of operating and maintaining the five major new greenspaces. The Parklands "will always be a donor-supported park," notes Dan Jones, fully open to the public, but run without any taxpayer support.

Further reading

○ The Parklands, theparklands.org

SAVING FISHERIES THROUGH CATCH SHARING

Concerned about the decline of the world's fish population and the abysmal failures of existing government interventions to solve the problem, Barrett Walker decided to use market-based techniques and funding from his family's Walker Foundation to take on the issue. He started a chain reaction of philanthropy that in less than ten years transformed solutions to overfishing.

Previously, government regulations had simply capped the total number of fish that could be caught, or the number of days that fishing was allowed. These encouraged a survival-of-the-fittest rush each year to garner as big a haul as possible before the caps set in, which led to safety problems and overfishing. Encouraged by experiments in Alaska and overseas, Walker

NATURE

decided to promote catch sharing—which makes fishermen shareholders in each year's total allowable catch (which is set by scientists based on fish populations). Shares can be traded, and grow in value as the allowable catch increases thanks to improved fish reproduction and sustainability. Walker started working in 2003 with the Bradley and Koch foundations to improve understanding of the subject. In 2006, Microsoft co-founder Paul Allen made a $5 million research grant to the University of California, Santa Barbara to research the effectiveness of catch sharing. The study concluded that it could stop and even reverse the decline of fisheries. The Allen Family Foundation then provided money to allow the California Fisheries Fund to plan a transition to such a system.

The Gordon and Betty Moore Foundation, a multibillion-dollar entity established by the ex-Intel CEO with a focus on water and marine life and a particular interest in "aligning economic incentives with conservation goals" in fishery management, then donated funds to test an onboard video system that allowed fishermen to monitor their catches efficiently. It was so successful the foundation followed up with a 2007 grant to New England fishermen. Catch sharing was implemented in 2010 in New England, and in 2011 for Pacific trawl groundfishing. In 2012, the Moore Foundation made a $2.7 million grant to assess the New England and Pacific systems so operations could be refined.

Further reading

○ UC Santa Barbara study, ia.ucsb.edu/pa/display.aspx?pkey=1845

○ Origins of catch-sharing described in *Philanthropy* magazine, philanthropyroundtable.org/site/print/taking_stock_of_the_seas

2000

PAYING FOR LYNX HABITAT AT LOOMIS FOREST

The Canada lynx was added to the U.S. endangered species list in 2000. One of the five areas of "critical habitat" for the animal was Loomis State Forest in Washington, where up to half of the cats in that state were thought to live. Most of that forest was trust land managed by the state, with the proceeds from timber sales going to schools to pay for the education of local children. In 1998 the state of Washington offered to end timber sales on the land if conservationists could raise sufficient funds—within one year—to compensate the schools for loss of this lumbering revenue. A local campaign was launched to raise $13 million in donations from private individuals and foundations. Just as the campaign reached its goal, via 3,500 donations large and small, the estimate of the fair market value of the lumber in the forest increased to $16.5 million. Seattle philanthropist Paul Allen then stepped forward to contribute the extra amount. The proceeds upon closing went directly into the school trust fund to benefit education, and the state redesignated the forest as a natural resource conservation area, allowing it to be managed as a wild area to benefit the lynx rather than for timbering.

Further reading

○ Conservation Northwest, conservationnw.org/what-we-do/forests/loomis-forest

○ Tom Butler, *Wildlands Philanthropy: The Great American Tradition* (Earth Aware, 2008)

2000

T. REX CLIFFHANGER

Though he lacks academic credentials, Jack Horner has revolutionized paleontology with the help of a gaggle of independent-minded donors. After flunking out of college seven times then serving a tour of duty in Vietnam, Horner sweet-talked his way into a technician's job at a natural history museum. He soon began a string of spectacular finds in dinosaur fossil beds that eventually propelled him to leadership of America's most productive dinosaur research program. Along the way, his work has been powered by about $12 million of private donations from enthusiastic givers who were not bothered by Horner's unconventional path into his field.

One highlight came in 2000, when one of Horner's crews discovered a T. Rex footbone jutting from the steep face of a cliff. Soon an epic excavation was under way, quickly funded by Microsoft chief technology officer Nathan Myhrvold. Once the remarkably intact specimen had been hacked out and encased in a plaster jacket, the only way to carry it off from the cliff was with a helicopter. Enter improvising donor number two: philanthropist and pilot Terry Kohler, who lent his whirlybird, flew it himself, and gave Horner hundreds of thousands of dollars to analyze his fossils.

To pull off the air-evacuation of the 3,000-pound specimen it had been necessary to break one of the creature's massive femurs. Horner used this "problem" as an opportunity and asked one of his students to study the inside of the bone. Shockingly, she found the remains of soft tissue preserved inside the 68-million-year-old fossil—revealing blood vessels and bone matrix reminiscent of what is found in an ostrich, and suggesting the T. Rex was a female.

Horner reports he has relied much more on private philanthropy than on government science-funding bureaucracies because donors are more willing to support unusual approaches, to move quickly and flexibly, to stick passionately with work that is slow to yield results, and understand

NATURE

imaginative breakthroughs. "Frankly, my donors are more engaged than the government is," he told *Philanthropy* magazine. "They want to see the project succeed."

Further reading

○ *Philanthropy* magazine reporting, philanthropyroundtable.org/topic/excellence_in_ philanthropy/the_dinosaur_discoverer

CREATION OF THE HIGH LINE

When freight trains ran at ground level through the industrial portions of Manhattan there were so many accidents that eventually a massive effort was made to elevate the rail line on trestles. The project, which opened to trains in 1934, cost $2 billion in current dollars, and was built so solidly that the structures were still there long after the freight stopped running in 1980. Hardy grasses and trees had grown up amidst the remaining elevated trackways, snaking for more than a mile through lower Manhattan, and offering unexpected views of the city. Officials were making plans to demolish these sections when Friends of the High Line was formed as a nonprofit in 1999, by two neighborhood residents, to advocate for preservation and reuse of the open rail-bed as a snaking linear park. The group developed popular momentum, began to raise funds to pay for its dream, and garnered its first million-dollar donation in 2006 (from the married couple of Barry Diller and Diane von Furstenberg). In 2009 the first of three major sections of elevated park opened to the public. Phase two debuted in 2011, with a third section launching in 2014. The nonprofit has a contract with the city giving it responsibility for maintenance and operation of the park, and it has raised more than $100 million of private money to design, create, and run the operation. Diller and von Furstenberg have donated more than $35 million, and other foundations, individuals, and corporations have made large gifts as well. The unconventional open space has proven wildly popular, attracting 4.4 million visitors per year and sparking an estimated $2 billion of private development in formerly industrial sections of New York.

Further reading

○ High Line history, thehighline.org/about/high-line-history

GORGES STATE PARK

When Duke Energy started selling most of its landholdings in the 1990s, conservationists took an interest. One section alone where the Piedmont hills meet the Blue Ridge Mountains in North Carolina is home to 46 endangered species of plants. By 1999, deals were brokered that transferred 40,000 acres in South Carolina to state wildlife management areas, and 10,000 acres of the Jocassee Gorges to North Carolina park authorities (thanks to leadership from the Nature Conservancy and funding from the Richard King Mellon Foundation—see 1988 entry). Of this latter section, 7,200 acres became Gorges State Park, the only North Carolina state park west of Asheville. After an additional decade of private fundraising, headed up by an all-volunteer board of community advisers, a $3.6 million visitor center opened to accommodate people who came to gaze upon the many waterfalls and temperate rainforest, which hosts one of the greatest concentrations of rare plant species in the eastern United States.

Further reading

○ Gorges State Park, ncparks.gov/Visit/parks/gorg/main.php

ROSE CENTER FOR EARTH AND SPACE

Sometimes the vision and management direction a philanthropist offers to a project can be as valuable as his money. Financier Richard Gilder was a longtime member of the board of directors for the American Museum of Natural History in New York, and served on its planetarium committee. By 1992, annual attendance at the venerable Hayden Planetarium had dropped by more than 20 percent in a decade, and the facility was showing its age. Museum leaders originally planned a modest upgrade that would cost $15 million. Gilder urged starting over, and called not just for a new planetarium and exhibits but also a high-powered research center (Gilder eventually convinced astrophysicist Neil deGrasse Tyson to be the first

NATURE

◆ PhilAphorism

Every right implies a responsibility;
every opportunity, an obligation;
every possession, a duty.

☞ *John Rockefeller Jr.*

director). The grand $210 million project attracted donations, including one for $20 million from builder and philanthropist Frederick Rose. Gilder contributed significantly himself. In just a few years, the modest planetarium had become the Rose Center for Earth and Space, with multiple theaters, halls, and exhibits.

Further reading

○ American Museum of Natural History, amnh.org/exhibitions/permanent-exhibitions/ rose-center-for-earth-and-space/

1995

KENTUCKY'S LARGEST OLD-GROWTH FOREST

In the 1920s, Grover Blanton purchased 2,300 acres of forested land on Pine Mountain in Harlan County, Kentucky. It was one of the few ancient forests left in the state, full of huge oaks and other rare trees towering 100 feet or more. These were the same trees seen by American pioneers passing through the Cumberland Gap in the 1700s, and the Blanton family faithfully maintained and protected the forest for another 73 years. In 1995, the Kentucky Natural Lands Trust was founded with the aspiration of courting enough donors to acquire the Blanton Forest. Keen to protect what they saw as their regional treasure, local residents by the hundreds contributed to the campaign. Eventually, an anonymous $500,000 gift and another $500,000 from the James Graham Brown Foundation in Louisville raised the group's kitty to the level needed to buy the land. The first purchase was made in 1995, and a second in 2001, and the 3,000-acre Blanton Forest State Nature Preserve was dedicated. With this success in hand, the Kentucky Natural Lands Trust went on to use additional land purchases, easements, and conservation partnerships to protect other acreage surrounding the state's largest old-growth forest.

Further reading

○ Kentucky Natural Lands Trust, knlt.org/blanton.html

1995

SWIFT FOX REVIVAL

The swift fox is the smallest of North America's wild canids, weighing only 4 to 6 pounds, or not much more than an average house cat. Historically, the animal ranged from the northern Great Plains to Texas, but by 1990 it was gone from 90 percent of its historic U.S. territory. In 1994 the U.S. Fish and Wildlife Service ruled that listing the swift fox as endangered was warranted, but the designation was suspended while a conservation team considered recovery strategies. Various state, tribal, and private groups swung into action. Philanthropic efforts to rehabilitate shortgrass and mixed-grass prairies on private land (under the auspices of the Nature Conservancy, American Prairie Foundation, and other nonprofits) added habitat congenial to the foxes. A number of community programs were launched to reintroduce foxes to land where they were absent. For instance, a grant from the Sand County Foundation's Bradley Fund for the Environment paid for relocation of several hundred foxes from Canada to the Blackfeet Indian Reservation in Montana. University of Montana research showed the project was a success, and as a direct result the swift fox in Montana was removed as a candidate for threatened status. The cumulative result of these efforts was to allow the little foxes to make a comeback. In the United States, the swift fox has now returned to more than 40 percent of its historic range. In 2001, federal authorities removed the species from consideration for protection under the Endangered Species Act.

Further reading

○ University of Montana study of Blackfeet Reservation reintroduction, bradley.scf2014. mhwebstaging.com/wp-content/uploads/sites/3/2013/11/ausband_foresman_2007.pdf

○ Bradley Fund for the Environment summary, bradleyfund.org/success-stories-2

1995

ARC OF APPALACHIA PRESERVES

The Arc of Appalachia isn't a government park, and it's not run by professionals, but it's one of the more ambitious land-preservation efforts of recent years. Nancy Stranahan and Larry Henry had worked in the Ohio state parks system before starting a bakery in the 1980s after tiring of bureaucracy. Their love of nature led them to start buying abandoned land in Ohio to "re-wild" it. They opened their first park, Highlands Nature Sanctuary, in 1995. By 2004 they had sold their bakery to focus on managing 38 pieces of land, totaling 1,600 acres, that they had acquired with support from individual givers and foundations. They let native deciduous forests re-grow on the acreage, and built visitor centers from which the public could enjoy the forests. By 2014, their Arc of Appalachia nonprofit had raised over $10 million, 75 percent from individuals and the rest from foundation grants, and was operating 14 nature preserves across Ohio supported entirely by donations.

Further reading

○ Arc of Appalachia Preserves, arcofappalachia.org/arc/what-we-do.html

FRED MEIJER AND RAILS-TO-TRAILS

At 14, Fred Meijer joined the new grocery store business of his parents, immigrants from Holland, and in 1962 he started building what would become known as superstores. By the time Meijer was finished he had 200 retail outlets and the fifteenth-largest private company in the nation. As he became a major donor in his home region of Michigan, one of his interests was to get Americans outdoors more often. So he provided steady funding for creation of the first rail-to-trail projects in his state.

In 1994, Meijer purchased a 42-mile stretch of abandoned CSX Railroad corridor and began converting it into a "linear park" open to the public. He also provided a Midwest Michigan Rail Trail Endowment Fund to cover future maintenance. The old trackbed threads voyagers through fields, woods, and small towns in the heart of Michigan farm country and one of America's major potato-growing regions, where Fred Meijer grew up on his family dairy farm. The Fred Meijer Heartland Trail, completed in 2011, will eventually be part of a larger trail system stretching 125 miles—making it the fifth-largest continuous rail-trail in the nation.

During his lifetime, Fred Meijer donated about $10 million to rails-to-trails work. The Meijer Foundation remains an important funder of right-of-way acquisitions and construction costs. The Rails-to-Trails Conservancy, which today has 150,000 members and a hand in 20,000 miles of pathways nationwide, has honored Fred Meijer as one of the pioneers of the rail-trail movement.

Further reading

○ Description of the Meijer Heartland trail, traillink.com/trail/fred-meijer-heartland-trail.aspx

DISNEY WILDERNESS PRESERVE

In Florida, management of water is crucial to human residents, agriculture, and wildlife. The rain that falls on the savannahs in the center of the state fills the Kissimmee River, which drains into Lake Okechobee, which in turn supplies the Everglades "river of grass," as well as providing drinking water for about 40 percent of Floridians. In the 1930s, ranchers began to dig drainage ditches which converted thousands of acres of central Florida wetland into pasture. Fresh water that had gone to the Everglades was increasingly diverted to canals dumping into the sea on the east and west coasts. The Kissimmee and Okechobee suffered; the Everglades retreated; and the tracts south of Orlando that had previously acted as sponges absorbing billions of gallons of water during Florida's rainy season, then slowly filtering it south, were now impermeable hard grassland or, increasingly, urban development. Complicated engineering to restore the health of Florida's hydrological system turned out to be extremely expensive, so regulators, developers, and nature nonprofits began to jointly seek more natural solutions.

A partnership between the Disney Company and the Nature Conservancy suggested that plugging the drainage ditches on the cattle ranches in central Florida and restoring their degraded but reclaimable wetlands could be a comparatively simple and effective contribution. So to legally mitigate for filling in 550 acres of marsh near Lake Buena Vista (already surrounded by development) in order to build housing for Disney World, Disney bought an 8,500 acre cattle ranch along the Kissimmee River that was slated to experience suburban development, then donated it, along with millions of dollars, to the Nature Conservancy so the nonprofit could restore the land to wetland and native habitat. Three years later, the Orlando airport authority donated an adjoining 3,000 acres to the Nature Conservancy for similar restoration, to compensate for 736 acres of wetland eliminated to expand the airfield.

The 11,500 total acres then had their drainage closed. Introduced plants and trees were removed, controlled burns were begun, and native plantings were made. A decade and a half after these land swaps, the former cattle ranch had been restored to its primeval state, and its wetland filtering was improving the quality and quantity of water in the Everglades watershed. Red-cockaded woodpeckers were reintroduced to the preserve's restored longleaf pines, hundreds of pairs of endangered wood storks bred among the bald cypress rimming Russell Lake, and the largest concentrations of bald eagles and sandhill cranes in the region took up residence.

Disney donated a total of $45 million over 20 years to create the Disney Wilderness Preserve. With its success, easements began to be purchased from other cattle ranches in the same watershed and donated to the Nature Conservancy and other nonprofits so that additional historic wetlands could be naturally rehydrated, while pasturing continued nearby. One of the largest wetland restorations in history is now under way, creating a decentralized "dispersed storage" solution to aid Florida's water problems. Home to 1,000 species of plants and animals, the Disney Wilderness Preserve is also open to the public for recreational use.

Further reading

○ Nature Conservancy description, nature.org/ourinitiatives/regions/northamerica/ unitedstates/florida/placesweprotect/the-disney-wilderness-preserve.xml

1992

A NATIONAL PARK FOR VERMONT

Vermont's first national park, described at its opening as "an entirely new kind… one where the human stories and the natural history are intertwined," was a gift of Laurance Rockefeller and his wife, Mary. In 1992 they paved the way for the Marsh-Billings-Rockefeller National Historic Park by donating a pristine antique farm with a rich American history, one of the first managed forests in the U.S., and a mansion house with a rich collection of nature paintings by Thomas Cole, Albert Bierstadt, Asher Durand, and others. The gift was collectively valued at $21 million, and transferred with a $7.5 million endowment in addition.

The park operates in partnership with the nonprofit Woodstock Foundation, which manages the Billings Farm and Museum. The Billings Farm was a product of earlier philanthropy, established in 1871 by native Vermonter Frederick Billings after he made his fortune during the San Francisco Gold Rush. He built a model herd of Jersey cows and experimented with advanced agricultural processes, which he then showcased for others. While operating as a museum of rural heritage, the farm also remains a working dairy—every year producing prized Jersey breeding cows along with thousands of pounds of milk that is used to make Cabot cheese.

The Woodstock Foundation also owns the for-profit Woodstock Inn and Resort, likewise gifted by the Rockefellers, whose earnings are used to benefit the work of the foundation. Together, these institutions give thousands of annual visitors a detailed picture of New England nature, traditional agricultural work, and three generations of American history.

Further reading
◦ History of the property, webhost.bridgew.edu/jhayesboh/marsh-billings.htm
◦ Park listing, nps.gov/mabi/historyculture/index.htm

1991

FORT WORTH ZOO

When the Fort Worth Zoo was owned and operated by the city, money was scarce, facilities were outdated, and attendance was dropping. In 1991, the middling public facility was almost forced to close due to lack of funds. Then Ramona Bass, a local animal lover from a wealthy family, suggested moving control of the zoo to a nonprofit association. More substantively, Bass suggested a new mission for the zoo. Frustrated by increasingly negative zoo narratives of people versus planet—a zero-sum game where one side prospers only at the expense of the other—she envisioned a facility that recognized shared interests between humans and animals, and "strengthened the bond between humans and the environment by promoting responsible stewardship of wildlife."

Bass recruited impressive support from individuals and local businesses, built an unusually diverse board that included people like wildlife experts at corporations and professors of agriculture, and was able to create innovative programming that visitors could find nowhere else. The new zoo was simultaneously pro-animal and pro-human, with striking new displays that highlight harmonious co-existence, rather than walling off wildlife. (Their black bears, for instance, were placed in a facsimile of an abandoned lumbering camp, emphasizing recovery and intelligent adaptation.) Even the logo for the section of the zoo on Texas wildlife—a human hand print overlapping a coyote track—emphasizes mutual prosperity.

Since its transfer from public management, the association-run zoo has raised more than $20 million in private funding and opened 16 new permanent exhibits and facilities. Attendance has doubled, and the Fort Worth Zoo is now rated near the top in the U.S.

Further reading

○ Fort Worth Zoo, fortworthzoo.org/about-us/history

○ *D Magazine* feature, dmagazine.com/publications/d-magazine/2000/october/perspective-why-dallas-matters

NATURE

1990

CIVIL WAR LAND PURCHASES

The Richard King Mellon Foundation has been one of the nation's most active conservers of American land over the last generation. (See separate 1988 entry.) Protecting Civil War battlefields has been one of their priorities. In 1998, for instance, the foundation purchased the land where Stonewall Jackson made his

✍ PhilAphorism

Let no one go hungry away. If any of these kind of people should be in want of corn, supply their necessities, provided it does not encourage them in idleness. ☞ *George Washington*

famous flank attack at Chancellorsville, being mortally wounded in the process. The tract was donated to Spotsylvania County, with an historic easement being simultaneously given to the Fredericksburg and Spotsylvania National Military Park. The foundation's investment of $10.5 million in Civil War land purchases in 1990 was one of the largest gifts given to create a park up to that time, and preserved acreage at the Antietam, Gettysburg, Fredericksburg, and Petersburg battlefields plus the Shenandoah National Park.

Further reading

○ News story on 1998 purchase, news.google.com/newspapers?nid=2472&-
  dat=19981120&id=uPAyAAAAIBAJ&sjid=oggGAAAAIBAJ&pg=4866,4646072&hl=en

1990

ANDORRA FOREST

Jim and Mary Faulkner began purchasing timberlands in New Hampshire in 1937, and over time assembled what is now the Andorra Forest—11,500 acres strong, and productively used and enjoyed in many ways. Several generations of the Faulkner family have now managed the property as a sustainable "tree farm," aiming to maximize four benefits of the land according to the longstanding Tree Farm System: wood production, water quality, recreation, and wildlife.

Agriculture that ended in the late-1800s and a forest fire that swept through in the 1940s created some small pastures within the forest where Highland beef cattle are raised, and open sections where 50 acres of wild highbush blueberries now grow. Controlled burns and brush hogging are used to keep the blueberries from being overgrown, and for a small fee the public is allowed to come in and pick the wild bushes in late summer. For decades, the forest was mostly managed by weeding and thinning trees, but now that much of the timber is reaching maturity, sustainable silviculture practices are followed to harvest commercial hardwood and softwood lumber selectively every winter, when the ground is hard. Thinnings and canopy openings are also undertaken to encourage tree regeneration and wildlife habitat in particular areas.

The entire 11,500 acres is open to the public for recreational use. There is a nine-mile stretch of through-hiking trail crossing the property, plus many local trails used by showshoers, skiers, and walkers. Snowmobiling is the only motorized use allowed. Wildlife studies are conducted on the property in conjunction with partners like Antioch University and the Audubon Society. In 1990 the family donated a conservation easement for the entire property to the Society for the Protection of New Hampshire Forests, making it one of the largest private forests in the eastern U.S. with such an easement. In 1991, the family designated 2,685 acres of the property as the Wildcat Hollow wilderness area, to preserve it (including the first known moose breeding grounds in southwestern New Hampshire) as animal habitat, managed on a "forever wild" basis.

Further reading

○ Andorra Forest easement, conservationregistry.org/projects/129579

1989

REVIVING THE BISON BY EATING IT

On the list of Americans who own the most land, media mogul Ted Turner has been No. 1 or No. 2 for much of the last couple decades. His two-million acres (more than three times the size of the entire state of Rhode Island) are primarily ranches in the western U.S. To put these lands to work, Turner has become the world's largest fosterer of bison. One out of every nine bison living today wanders on his land. Largely on his own, Turner has created a thriving national market for bison meat, sold at groceries like Whole Foods and at his Ted's Montana Grill restaurant chain. Bison is lower in fat and cholesterol and higher in protein than beef, and the hardy animals require much less husbandry. And keeping them afield has been a highly effective way of maintaining scenic Western lands in fruitful use.

Turner also opens his ranches every year to hunters willing to pay approximately $12,000 each to stalk trophy elk, and he has a fishing program on some properties too. Along with his environmental businesses, Turner's philanthropy has frequently focused on balancing economic usages of nature with conservation (as in his giving to the Greater Yellowstone Coalition). It is estimated that Turner has so far spent more than $1.5 billion on nature philanthropy. In 1997 he created the Turner Endangered Species Fund to protect imperiled species and habitat on his own land, and to "bring the role of private lands to the forefront of ecological conservation." Its current projects focus on nine creatures: Aplomado falcon, black-footed ferret, Bolson tortoise, Chiricahua leopard frog, Mexican wolf, prairie dogs, red-cockaded woodpecker, Rio Grande cutthroat trout, and Westslope cutthroat trout.

Further reading

○ Turner Endangered Species Fund, tesf.org

○ Ted Turner Enterprises, tedturner.com

1989

ATLANTA BOTANICAL GARDEN FUQUA CENTERS

Atlanta had no botanical garden until 1973 when a group of civic-minded residents gathered and offered up the resources for launching a private nonprofit to create and run a garden adjoining the city's popular Piedmont Park. Atlantan J. B. Fuqua became the main donor. Fuqua had grown up exceedingly poor then made his fortune in radio stations and manufacturing, going on to become a major philanthropist—giving about $40 million, for instance, to create the Fuqua School of Business at Duke University.

Fuqua provided $8.5 million to the Atlanta Botanical Garden to create a main pavilion named in honor of his wife, plus a specialized structure for orchids. The Dorothy Chapman Fuqua Conservatory, opened in 1989, offers indoor exhibits of tropical flora, desert plants, and other living things. The adjoining Fuqua Orchid Center, which debuted in 2002, displays the largest and rarest orchid collection in the United States. In addition to its tropical orchid house the Fuqua Center offers a unique High Elevation House that uses customized air-handling technology to propagate and display orchids normally found only at elevations of 6,000-10,000 feet near the equator, in the Andes Cloud Forest. The 30-acre Atlanta Botanical Garden also offers an unusual elevated trail, the $55 million donor-funded Kendeda Canopy Walk, which allows visitors to stroll 40-feet off the ground amidst mature trees, the only feature of its kind in an American botanical garden.

Further reading

○ Collections in the Fuqua Conservatory, atlantabotanicalgarden.org/our-gardens/plant-collections#block-views-nodequeue_2-block

○ High Elevation House, atlantabotanicalgarden.org/plan-your-visit/locations/high-elevation-house

1988

AMERICAN LAND CONSERVATION PROGRAM

The Richard King Mellon Foundation established its American Land Conservation Program in the late 1980s and then spent more than $400 million to conserve 190 different pieces of land—like 375,000 acres in the

֍ PhilAphorism

You take nothing with you that you gained—only what you gave away.

☞ *Francis of Assisi*

Sheldon National Wildlife Refuge in Nevada, and 37,000 acres adjacent to the Alaska Peninsula National Wildlife Refuge. The Mellon Foundation donated $10 million to the Nature Conservancy purchase which created Gorges State Park in North Carolina (see 1999 entry). All told, the $2 billion foundation has funded the conservation of more than two million acres of American land, located in all 50 states.

Further reading

○ *From Sea to Shining Sea: Richard King Mellon Foundation American Land Conservation Program 1988-2002* (Mellon Foundation, 2002)

1987

KOHLERS FLY TO THE AID OF ENDANGERED SWANS AND CRANES

Wisconsin industrialist Terry Kohler and his wife Mary are both nature lovers and pilots, so when their governor and friend Tommy Thompson called them to ask if they would help the state Department of Natural Resources with a project to reintroduce the endangered trumpeter swan to the eastern U.S., they quickly agreed. They flew their company's business jet to Alaska and picked up a clutch of eggs removed from the nests of remaining wild trumpeters (the largest waterfowl on earth, with a wingspan exceeding eight feet). These were whisked to the Milwaukee County Zoo for a captive breeding program, and the deed was repeated every spring for years, eventually resulting in the successful reintroduction of trumpeter swans to the midwestern flyway. After being absent for a century, there are now more than 5,000 of these huge native birds migrating in this central corridor.

The year after their first trumpeter-egg trip, the president of the International Crane Foundation asked them to undertake a similar trip to bring down precious whooping crane eggs from a different part of Alaska for a similar captive-breeding program. Whoopers were down to just two dozen birds in existence at one point, and this effort increased their numbers to several hundred, though many risks to the bird remain. Released captive-raised birds had to be taught to migrate from the refuges in Wisconsin where they were reintroduced—which was eventually done, at Terry Kohler's suggestion, by leading them south with ultra-light airplanes. Kohler also created special controlled-temperature incubators in which substantial numbers of crane and trumpeter swan eggs could be safely flown long distances.

Other private donors were also crucial to these programs. The cost of rearing and releasing one whooping crane is estimated to be more than $100,000, all told. A majority of the budget of crucial groups like the

Trumpeter Swan Recovery Project and the Whooping Crane Eastern Partnership has come from donations. In Louisiana, where the latest important efforts to preserve whoopers are centered, the state Department of Wildlife and Fisheries has requested several million dollars from private individuals and companies to support a 15-year project.

In addition to offering in-kind assistance in the form of many hundreds of hours of jet, propeller plane, and helicopter transport and aerial surveying over three decades, the Kohlers also became major donors to the International Crane Foundation, Operation Migration, the Whooping Crane Conservation Association (which buys critical habitat, among other contributions), and other avian conservation groups. They contributed as well to efforts to protect the threatened Siberian crane. While transporting eggs around the globe, one of Kohler's planes became the first private jet to cross Russia after the fall of the Soviet Union.

Further reading

○ David Sakrison, *Chasing the Ghost Birds* (International Crane Foundation, 2007)

○ *Philanthropy* magazine interview, philanthropyroundtable.org/topic/excellence_in_philanthropyinterview_with_terry_and_mary_kohler

1987

USING ECONOMIC INCENTIVES TO SUSTAIN PREDATORS

When wolves were first reintroduced to the greater Yellowstone region, Hank Fischer, the regional director of Defenders of Wildlife, set up a meeting with 20 local livestock producers to discuss their concerns over the new presence of predators. "It's easy to be a wolf lover. It doesn't cost anything," stated one rancher. "It's the people who own livestock who end up paying for wolves." That got Fischer and his organization thinking, and by 1987 Defenders had devised a wolf compensation fund to pay livestock owners the market value of animals killed by wolves. "It's not our intent for this restoration to occur at the expense of livestock producers. Our goal is to have wolf supporters take responsibility for the wolf's indiscretions," explained Fischer. Over the next 23 years the fund paid out more than $1.4 million for animal losses, using private funds donated for the purpose. Another fund was established to reward ranchers willing to allow wolves to breed on their property. Defenders established a Livestock Producer's Advisory Council to keep communication open and routinely adapt its programs to changing conditions.

In 1997, Defenders of Wildlife assumed responsibility for a similar program to compensate local residents for losses due to grizzly bears. In

2000, the Bailey Wildlife Foundation make a large contribution that allowed expansion of the wolf and grizzly compensation trusts that had previously been funded through small donations, including creation of a Proactive Carnivore Conservation Fund that helps local landowners avoid wolf and grizzly conflicts in the first place—by buying them electric fencing, for instance. A major project was launched in Idaho to give sheep ranchers tools (like guard dogs, fencing, and range riders) to avoid predator losses in the Sawtooth Wilderness. More than a million dollars of philanthropic money has been spent on these preventive measures. Both the loss-compensation fund and the preventive assistance were later extended to southwestern states when wolves started appearing in that area.

In 2011, the Defenders compensation fund for wolves came to an end after the western states established their own state-wide mechanisms to pay for animal losses to wild predators (which Defenders helped set up and initially fund with donated private money). The nonprofit continues to fund conflict-prevention programs across the West, and it still operates the Grizzly Compensation Trust. In 2010 the organization, along with other charities like the Conservancy of Southwest Florida, launched pilot programs to compensate Floridians who lose animals due to the revival of the Florida panther—which is in the midst of rebounding from as few as 12-20 animals left in the wild to 100-200 today. By taking the economic sting out of predator recovery, these efforts are easing the coexistence of wildlife and nearby residents.

Further reading

○ PERC report, perc.org/articles/who-pays-wolves

1984

MONTEREY BAY AQUARIUM

Silicon Valley pioneer David Packard had two daughters who studied marine biology, and they saw to it that an aquarium celebrating and studying the marine life of Monterey Bay became a reality. The Packards gave a one-time personal gift of $55 million for construction, with the condition that the aquarium be economically self-sustaining after opening. An old cannery in Pacific Grove was selected as the site, and Julie Packard became executive director. Displays focus on the species existing in the Pacific waters just outside the facility's doors. Strong local support for the aquarium has translated into 45 percent of residents of the Monterey Peninsula becoming members—the core of more than 107,000 enrollees, the largest aquarium membership in the world. Today, the Monterey Bay Aquarium attracts more than 2 million visitors each year, and has a $65 million annual budget.

NATURE

Further reading

○ Monterey Bay Aquarium, montereybayaquarium.org

1983

IMPROVING WATER QUALITY
WITH MARKET INCENTIVES

In 1983, a group of flyfishers calling themselves Oregon Trout started working for new water laws that would allow fishermen to buy a right to water and then keep it in a stream. Traditional water law was premised on the idea that if flowing water reaches your property first, you get first rights, but that to keep your rights you must use the water or the next guy can step up. This, of course, destroys incentives for conservation. In 1987 the group got Oregon law amended. Then in 1993, funding from the Northwest Area Foundation allowed creation of the Oregon Water Trust to apply various additional market mechanisms to water conservation. The trust buys water rights to maintain stream flows, or offers other users economic incentives to improve the efficiency of their usage or leave water in streams rather than consume it. This benefits fish and other downstream users who would otherwise come up short.

By 2002, the trust was operating in six major watersheds and completing 80 projects a year in 60 different streams. In 2009, it merged with Oregon Trout to become the Freshwater Trust. In 2012 the trust started a multiyear experiment in water-quality trading, signing a contract with the city of Medford to help it meet expensive water-quality requirements by undertaking cost-effective streambank restorations. The successes of this group in Oregon have spawned similar organizations in other states across the country.

Further reading

○ Water-quality trading, thefreshwatertrust.org/fixing-rivers/water-quality-trading/

1982

LAND TRUSTS TAKE OFF

Land trusts, or conservancies, are private nonprofits that protect land directly by owning it. Though their roots go back to the 1890s, in the latest generation land trusts have become one of the fastest growing and most successful elements of environmental conservation in the U.S. The grandaddy of land trusts is the Nature Conservancy (see 1951 entry), but there are others operating on a national level, like the American Farmland

Trust, the Wetlands America Trust affiliated with Ducks Unlimited (see 1930 entry), the Appalachian Trail Conservancy, and trusts with specialized missions like the National Trust for Historic Preservation, and the Civil War Trust.

In 1982 the Land Trust Alliance, a 501(c)(3), was created to help trusts consult and coordinate with each other. In addition, the Alliance conducts periodic censuses of the field. The latest census, funded by ExxonMobil Corporation and documenting groups in existence as of 2010, shows explosive growth over the latest decade of this voluntary mechanism for conserving the outdoors. Land trusts had 4,986,093 dues-paying members as of 2010, plus 347,000 volunteers, and they were conserving 47 million acres (a leap upward from 24 million acres in 2000). Their lands were either purchased with donated money, or protected by conservation easements offered by owners. There were 1,723 different land trusts active across the United States, a majority of them staffed as all-volunteer efforts, and all but a dozen or so locally operated rather than national.

Land trusts are nonconfrontational and apolitical, relying on voluntary transactions by willing landowners. In this they differ from "land-advocacy" groups (for instance, the Wilderness Society and Sierra Club) that primarily lobby the government or litigate to regulate or purchase land. In the words of former Sierra Club director Michael Fischer, land trusts use love of the land, not anger at its despoliation, as their principal motivating force.

Further reading

○ 2010 National Land Trust Census, landtrustalliance.org/land-trusts/land-trust-census

○ Richard Brewer, *Conservancy: The Land Trust Movement in America* (University Press of New England, 2003)

1980

CENTRAL PARK CONSERVANCY

Starting in the 1960s, Central Park began a long decline. Once emerald lawns were trampled to bare dirt. Ineffective policing and homeless policies allowed

ℵ PhilAphorism

It is more difficult to give money away intelligently than to earn it in the first place.
☞ *Andrew Carnegie*

vagrants and gangs to take over. Graffiti was everywhere. New York's 1970s fiscal crisis and restrictive public-employee union rules cut routine maintenance, and the park's landmarks were neglected and vandalized. Many thought the park was beyond rescue. Along came Richard Gilder, the founder of a brokerage firm and a leading philanthropist in New York City. "I could see the dreadful condition of the park." To do something—*anything*—Gilder teamed up with hedge-fund titan George Soros. "This was my first attempt at philanthropy," Soros later remembered. "Our outlook on life is quite different. He's a libertarian, and I'm much more of a government-interference type. Nevertheless, we got on very well." A 1976 study the two men commissioned called for a private board and modern management to revive the park. In 1978, newly elected Mayor Ed Koch took an interest in this citizen activism and the nonprofit Central Park Conservancy was born in 1980 to improve a public asset with private organization and resources. Its central insight, according to director Elizabeth Rogers, was that "You don't throw money at the problem, you throw management."

The Central Park Conservancy resodded the Sheep Meadow and rebuilt crumbling Belvedere Castle. With each successful project, the public could see that the conservancy was working, and the nonprofit gradually took the reins from the city parks department, raising hundreds of millions of dollars in citizen donations (crowned by a 2013 gift of $100 million from financier John Paulson). Since 1998 the conservancy has had a long-term contract with the city to manage the park. Central Park currently attracts 40 million visitors annually, up from 12 million in the early 1980s, and crime has fallen by more than 90 percent. The conservancy now provides 85 percent of the park's $45 million budget, and employs 90 percent of the park's maintenance staff. Private money and private management have made Central Park a jewel, and created a model that spread quickly to other places. "Dick Gilder made it possible for citizens to get involved in the life of public parks," says Adrian Benepe of the Trust for Public Land.

The successes of the Central Park Conservancy inspired dozens of similar efforts in other cities across the country. Piedmont Park in Atlanta, St. Louis's Forest Park, Shelby Farms in Memphis, and strings of parks in Pittsburgh, Louisville, Buffalo, and other places were modeled directly on the Central Park example, not to mention spinoffs launched in New York City itself to create the High Line and improve Battery, Prospect, and other parks. Ironically, the original conservancy is now threatened by the desire of New York mayor Bill de Blasio to siphon resources out of the independent conservancies and redirect them to other locations under city control.

Further reading
○ About the Central Park Conservancy, centralparknyc.org/about

○ *Philanthropy* magazine, philanthropyroundtable.org/topic/excellence_in_philanthropy/
philanthropy_on_the_green

1980

FREE-MARKET ENVIRONMENTALISM

As far back as the 1930s, pioneer conservationists like Aldo Leopold argued that in a country like the U.S. built around private property and markets, it is important to find ways to harness those mechanisms to work productively for environmental quality. In 1980, a group of economists trained in the Chicago school of economics founded the Bozeman, Montana, organization now known as the Property and Environment Research Center. "We asked ourselves: If markets can produce bread and cars and make them available for everyone, why can't they produce environmental protection?" says PERC president Terry Anderson, who also teaches at Stanford University. "Most Americans operate under the assumption that if we have economic growth, we destroy the environment, and if we preserve the environment we destroy economic growth. We at PERC don't see that conflict." PERC accepts no government money and little corporate funding, relying on private giving for its annual support. The organization's 1991 book *Free Market Environmentalism* helped spark new thinking on how property rights and economic incentives can be used to encourage individuals to be better stewards of land, water, animals, and other natural resources.

Since this beginning, groups like the Environmental Defense Fund, which hired the first Ph.D. economist to work full-time at an environmental organization, have become adept at employing economic tools for ecological benefit. In 1995 EDF launched the "safe-harbor" mechanism that allows economic use of private land where endangered species are present, so long as a certain level of habitat protection is provided. Market-based approaches have also been folded into acid-rain regulation, efforts to restrain packaging waste, fishing regulation based on catch shares (see 2003 entry), Western water law, pollution auctions, and other places.

Further reading

○ *Philanthropy* magazine reporting, philanthropyroundtable.org/topic/excellence_in_
philanthropy/soaring_high

1978

CITIZEN-LED BLUEBIRD RECOVERY

The bluebird, an American favorite, faced disaster when the non-native house sparrow took over much of its habitat. Both birds are cavity nesters, and the sparrows will often kill bluebirds and destroy their eggs to occupy desirable spots. In 1976, bluebird enthusiast Larry Zeleny published a book entitled *The Bluebird: How You Can Help Its Fight For Survival*, and the next year he placed an article in *National Geographic* pointing out that despite their precipitous population decline there was hope for bluebirds if only everyday landowners would take a few simple measures: put out nesting boxes with entry holes just 1½" in diameter (small enough to exclude most sparrows), and then provide a little monitoring and regular maintenance. "There is not much the average person can do to help the bald eagle or the whooping crane, but an individual can help the bluebird," summarized ornithologist Chandler Robbins.

In 1978 bluebird lovers spontaneously organized themselves into the North American Bluebird Society, followed shortly after by 15 active state-level societies. The next year, *Parade* magazine printed a story for its 15 million readers called "You Can Hear the Bluebird's Song Again." As a result, the society received 80,000 letters requesting a copy of its brochure on how to help bluebirds. It took volunteers three months to get all those requests answered, but soon memberships were flooding in, and nesting boxes were popping up in fields and orchards across the country. The NABS history notes that "no tax money has ever been sought by the society. Funding for programs and operational expenses has come from dues, donations, and profits from the sale of bluebird-related items, along with corporate grants, awards from private foundations, and bequests." These philanthropic efforts have had great success. To take an example from one representative state: a 1979 bird census found just 22 bluebirds in Minnesota; today the state population is estimated at 25,000.

Further reading

○ North American Bluebird Society history, nabluebirdsociety.org/Main/nabs%20history.htm

---

1978

EARLY USE OF CONSERVATION EASEMENTS IN MONTANA

Montana Land Reliance was founded in 1978 by Barbara Rusmore and

⌇ PhilAphorism

The best recreation is to do good.

⌇ *William Penn*

Christina Torgrimson, who wanted to preserve Montana's beautiful outdoor scenery and "provide permanent protection for private lands that are significant for agricultural production, forest resources, fish and wildlife habitat, and open space." The John Hay Whitney Foundation provided a startup grant, and the group made the most of its resources by becoming one of the aggressive early users of the then-brand-new concept of "conservation easements"—which protect land without requiring it to be purchased from the owner.

Easements can be purchased with money provided by donors (for far less than the cost of buying the land), or gifted by public-spirited landowners. In either case the property remains on the tax rolls, while the owner gets a partial credit. Easements are extremely flexible. On a working farm an easement might forbid housing subdivisions, but allow any desired agricultural structures to be built. An easement on property containing a rare plant or animal might sign away all development rights on the areas it occupies. Conservation easements can be applied to just a portion of a property, or all of it. Each agreement is crafted to meet the particular needs of the landowner while respecting the conservation goal for that land.

Land Reliance didn't buy up land and then sell it to the government, like some land trusts. Rusmore and Torgrimson wanted the preserved plots to remain in private hands—which helped win over local landowners who were skeptical of government involvement in their areas, and local officials who didn't want too much land leaving the tax rolls. Relying 100 percent on easements as their conservation tool, MLR soon built a strong base of support from Montana landowners.

Wheat farms and ranches had historic as well as farming and ecological value that made them one focus of the group. MLR also put a great deal of effort into encouraging stewardship of the private property surrounding Yellowstone National Park and Glacier National Park—land which is important to wildlife, tourism, and state beauty. Today, Montana Land Reliance is a model statewide land trust, and the voluntary conservation easements the nonprofit has acquired from private landowners protect 907,425 acres of ecologically, agriculturally, and historically important land, plus 1,577 miles of stream frontage. These include nearly 500,000 acres of elk habitat, 10,000 acres of wetlands, the watersheds supporting Montana's now-thriving trout fishery, and more.

Further reading

∘ Montana Land Reliance, mtlandreliance.org/achieve.htm

NATURE

YAWKEY WILDIFE CENTER

Almost exactly midway between Myrtle Beach and Charleston in South Carolina is a 24,000-acre beachfront refuge and resting spot considered one of the best in North America—but for transient birds rather than humans. The Yawkey Wildlife Center is a mix of marsh, pine forest, and beach that supports 200 species of birds, rivaling almost any spot in North America for its variety and rarity of migrating and resident species. An unusual number of raptors—hawks, ospreys, peregrine falcons, golden and bald eagles—frequent the area to nest, feed, or recuperate during migration. The undisturbed beaches provide protected feeding and resting areas for the brown pelican, least terns, the threatened piping plover, and many other sea birds, as well as excellent egg-laying locations for the threatened loggerhead turtle. The endangered red-cockaded woodpecker also inhabits the longleaf pine uplands of the preserve.

Considered a major gift to U.S. wildlife conservation, the center was willed to the people of the state of South Carolina in 1976, along with an endowment to support its upkeep and improvement, by the late Tom Yawkey, longtime owner of the Boston Red Sox. He had hunted and fished the land throughout his life, but in the middle of the twentieth century he became concerned that the waterfowl population was declining. Yawkey stopped hunting the birds and started manipulating the marshes on his property to produce more of their main food sources. It worked. Today a quarter of a million birds live on the property every spring.

Further reading

○ South Carolina Department of Natural Resources, dnr.sc.gov/mlands/managedland?p_
   id=64

GUADALUPE MOUNTAINS NATIONAL PARK

In 1918 Wallace Pratt became the first geologist to work for Humble Oil (forerunner to ExxonMobil). He and several colleagues created scientific ways to find oil with less guesswork, and he eventually became known as America's most distinguished petroleum scientist. In 1921, Pratt was in Texas purchasing land leases for Humble. Exploring McKittrick Canyon near Pecos he saw streams, stunning waterfalls, and grand trees, and understood why the locals had told him it was the most beautiful place in the state. The ranch enveloping the canyon was useless for oil, but when it later came up for sale, Pratt and some partners bought it because of the land's natural beauty and history (it was the historic refuge of the Mescalero Apaches and other residents going back thousands of years).

By 1930 Pratt had bought out his partners. Meanwhile, local judge and oil man J. C. Hunter had been purchasing surrounding lands, creating the 70,000-acre Guadalupe Mountain Ranch where he raised sheep and goats. He too appreciated the area's beauty, and he protected fragile habitats and supported efforts to create a park in the region. After Hunter died his son kept buying land and pushing for park status, as did Pratt.

In 1945 Pratt moved his residence to the McKittrick Canyon land, where he studied its geology—it was a fossilized reef. In 1959, Pratt offered his land to the National Park Service. Several years later the Hunter lands were added to the property, and in 1972 the Guadalupe Mountains National Park, the core of which was the McKittrick Canyon property, opened to the public.

Further reading

∘ Guadalupe Mountains National Park, nps.gov/gumo/historyculture/people.htm

1971

SAVING THE WINGED CHEETAH

The peregrine falcon is the fastest creature on earth. When it spots prey with its piercing eyesight, it shrieks down out of the sky at more than 200 miles an hour. Yet in 1970, the U.S. peregrine falcon was nearly as dead as the dodo. In the lower 48 states there were only 39 known breeding pairs left. The bird's recovery since then is one of the dramatic ecological success stories of our times, and philanthropy is a star player.

Once measures had been taken to curb overuse of pesticides that were weakening falcon eggshells, the government launched efforts to repopulate the bird. They failed. Enter Tom Cade. When Cornell University offered him a job at its famed ornithological lab, he agreed—on condition that it support his efforts to test ideas for restoring the peregrine. A $125,000 grant from IBM was earmarked for the purpose. Then other donations began pouring in, including many small ones from individuals who, like Cade, had taken up the sport of falconry.

Instead of trying to breed captured birds, as the government had, Cade's philanthropic project hand-reared hatchlings and kept them in captivity for use as breeders, starting in 1971. Within a few years, the Cornell group was releasing into the wild the first of 4,000 young birds, and discovering how to keep them alive until they learned to hunt on their own. The researchers

NATURE

concluded, counterintuitively, that one of the best places for artificially incubated peregrines to make the leap back into the wild was the downtown regions of major cities. Skyscrapers and bridges served as cliff-like roosting and nesting places, free from the owls and eagles that were devouring juvenile falcons released into the wilderness. Urban pigeons were ideal food sources for the young hunters.

Since 1984, the Peregrine Fund has been located on a bluff near Boise, Idaho. Throughout its history, it has been supported by thousands of private donations that cover operating costs, plus an endowment given by donors such as Lee Bass, Roy Disney, Julie Wrigley, and Hank Paulson. Thanks to its efforts, a creature that was nearly extinct now breeds naturally and thrives in at least 40 states across the U.S. The peregrine falcon was removed from the endangered species list in 1999. More recently, the Peregrine Fund has produced chicks to help restore the California condor to the Grand Canyon, the Aplomado falcon to the Southwest, the Harpy eagle to Central America, and many other birds to their respective homelands.

Further reading

○ *Philanthropy* magazine, philanthropyroundtable.org/topic/excellence_in_philanthropy/a_road_trip_across_philanthropic_america5

1970

ORDWAY PRAIRIE PRESERVES

Katharine Ordway's father took a struggling company called Minnesota Mining and Manufacturing and turned it into 3M. She eventually inherited part of his fortune, and used it to buy and protect swathes of the subtly lovely prairies of the American Midwest, which she loved for their beautiful wildflowers and connection to the state's pioneer history. Ordway started in 1970 in her own backyard of Minnesota. Working with the Nature Conservancy, she assembled several thousand acres of Minnesota prairie into the Ordway, Wahpeton, Chippewa, and Santee preserves. Next, Ordway financed purchases of exemplary sections of remaining prairie in other parts of the Great Plains—in South Dakota, in Missouri, and in Kansas where she bought the large, pristine Konza prairie. The vast majority of the Konza reserve, in the Flint Hills of the eastern part of the state, is steeply sloped grassland with shallow soils unsuitable for cultivation, so it has never been plowed and retains its native characteristics, making it one of the largest remaining undisturbed tallgrass prairies in North America.

After her death in 1979, Ordway left her remaining money to a foundation with instructions to the family members and allies she put in charge to expend all the funds quickly. The foundation spent more than $40 million in less than five years to buy additional prairie land, including 54,000 acres in the Niobara Valley of Nebraska. These prairie lands are actively managed (as most wild lands need to be today). The Ordway and Konza preserves, for instance, are regularly burned (as would have happened naturally in the times before wildfires were suppressed) to prevent the grassland from growing into forest. Ordway's collective gifts made her one of America's most important private conservationists.

Further reading

○ Nature Conservancy Ordway profile, nature.org/ourinitiatives/regions/northamerica/ unitedstates/minnesota/explore/mn-hero-katharine-ordway.xml

1969

FRANCIS BEIDLER FOREST SANCTUARY

Francis Beidler was a Chicago businessman who owned the Santee River Cypress Company. By 1905 he had stopped timbering in swamps he possessed near Charleston, South Carolina, having decided it wasn't cost-effective to pull logs out of the inaccessible waterlogged lands. In addition, one of those tracts, the Four Holes Swamp, was full of ancient trees as much as 1,000 years old, making it one of the few areas in the state that remained just as it had been when the original European settlers arrived. It was against Beidler's historic and conserving instincts to cut this forest, and his descendants also decided not to. Indeed, they fought heated battles with the federal government, which wanted to use the land during FDR's administration.

In the 1960s, the Nature Conservancy and the Audubon Society joined together and launched a campaign that raised $1.5 million in donations to buy 3,400 acres of the Four Holes Swamp, which they renamed the Francis Beidler Forest. In 2003, the two organizations combined forces again to expand the tract. Today, it is the world's biggest virgin cypress-tupelo swamp forest—a 12,500-acre National Natural Landmark that harbors, among other things, one of the oldest bald cypress trees in the world.

Further reading

○ Nature Conservancy, nature.org/ourinitiatives/regions/northamerica/unitedstates/ southcarolina/placesweprotect/francis-beidler-forest.xml

1963

HENRY DOORLY ZOO

The Omaha Zoo was a sleepy little city-run affair, like hundreds of others, when in 1963 the widow of the publisher of the local newspaper gave $750,000 to improve the facilities as a memorial to her husband Henry Doorly. Within two years a nonprofit society had organized itself to plan, expand, operate, and maintain the zoo in the future. The Doorly gift sparked a steady string of additional major gifts—from Claire Hubbard, Ernst Lied, Eugene Eppley, Edward Owen, Bill and Berniece Grewcock, Walter and Suzanne Scott, and others. The result is a triumph of philanthropy. Measured as a combination of animals, species, and acreage, the Doorly Zoo has grown into the largest in the world, and, more importantly, one of the most beloved. It features the world's largest indoor desert, largest indoor swamp, and largest nocturnal exhibit, plus the nation's largest indoor rainforest—all richly stocked with plants and animals easily accessible to visitors. It also hosts the largest cat complex in North America, and dramatic orangutan and gorilla living spaces. Users of the popular TripAdvisor website have rated the Henry Doorly as America's best zoo.

Further reading

○ Zoo exhibits, omahazoo.com/exhibits

1958

KENTUCKY'S FLORACLIFF

Mary Wharton completed a doctorate in botany at the University of Michigan, then moved to Kentucky to put her knowledge to work near her family home. She led the Georgetown College biology department for almost 30 years, wrote several books on Kentucky plants, and even discovered several new species. But perhaps her finest achievement was in personally assembling a nature sanctuary in Fayette County, which she called Floracliff and built up through numerous purchases over the course of her life, starting in 1958. The property includes Elk Lick Falls, a 61-foot waterfall that is one of the largest surface deposits in the U.S. of travertine (a form of limestone made by mineral springs). It also hosts wildflowers, rare plants, and trees hundreds of years old. By the time Wharton was finished, Floracliff included nearly 300 acres and had a nonprofit to oversee it, and she left an $800,000 endowment when she died in 1991. In 1996 Floracliff became a Kentucky state nature preserve. Six years later one of Wharton's Georgetown College colleagues left a bequest to add a nature center, which was finished in 2010.

Further reading

○ Floracliff, floracliff.org/about.html

1956

VIRGIN ISLANDS NATIONAL PARK

In the 1940s, Laurance Rockefeller, grandson of the famous scion, began exploring the Caribbean islands with his wife, Mary, in their boat *Dauntless*. St. John was one of three islands the United States had purchased from Denmark during World War I to preclude a German submarine base there. The Rockefellers found it lovely and undeveloped. Laurance began buying acreage with two goals in mind: to establish a resort hotel in Caneel Bay as a business proposition, and to purchase land he could eventually donate for a national park. He acquired most of the island, about 5,000 acres, using the same nonprofit entity his father employed to buy private land for transfer to the Grand Teton park (see 1949 entry), and eventually donated this territory to the nation. In 1956, on the very same day they opened for business their Caneel Bay resort, designed to blend into the landscape on the western edge of the island, Laurance and Mary attended the dedication of Virgin Islands National Park, covering most of the rest of St. John.

Further reading

○ Tom Butler, *Wildlands Philanthropy: The Great American Tradition* (Earth Aware, 2008)

1954

HUMANE SOCIETY OF THE UNITED STATES

In the half-century or so after the civil war, a "humane" movement grew up which encouraged kindness to animals, compassion for humans, and a reverence for life. Albert Schweitzer's 1952 Nobel Prize was a culmination of this popular thinking. Two years after that ceremony, the Humane Society of the U.S. was formed specifically to reduce cruelty to animals. The organization's first priority was humane slaughtering of food animals. The

ᗏ PhilAphorism

Giving frees us from the familiar territory of our own needs by opening our mind to the unexplained worlds occupied by the needs of others. ☞ *Barbara Bush*

founding principles of the society "do not consider the utilization of animals for food to be either immoral or inappropriate," explained a former head of the group, but the organization "opposes and seeks to prevent all use or exploitation of animals that causes pain, suffering, or fear." Supported entirely by member donations and philanthropic gifts, the Humane Society of the United States is today the largest animal protection organization in the country, with a $174 million budget.

Further reading

○ Humane Society of the United States, humanesociety.org/about

○ Bernard Unti, *Protecting All Animals* (Humane Society of the United States, 2004)

1951

THE NATURE CONSERVANCY

The Nature Conservancy has more than 1 million contributing members and is the largest environmental charity in the U.S. measured by revenue (nearly a billion dollars in 2015, mostly donations of land or cash) and assets. In addition to working with private owners to protect land in all 50 states it has also expanded to more than 35 countries overseas. The group is the national leader in popularizing conservation easements, debt-for-nature swaps, land trusts, and other voluntary and market-based techniques for preserving land. The conservancy's success and expansion, which has put more than 120 million acres under long-term protection, stems from four factors: A commitment to practical, non-confrontational solutions. A rooting of actions in good science (the group employs hundreds of staff scientists). Creative and flexible management of lands under its protection (in some cases permitting timbering, mining, or gas and oil drilling). And assiduous, productive partnering with land owners, indigenous communities, businesses, governments, and fellow nonprofits.

Further reading

○ Nature Conservancy annual reports, nature.org/about-us/our-accountability/annual-report/index.htm

1951

JOHN OLIN LAUNCHES
SCIENTIFIC GAME MANAGEMENT

In the 1940s and '50s, as sporting game like deer, waterfowl, and turkeys became rare amid post-war hunting and building booms, John Olin had an idea. Wildlife could be replenished through scientific improvement of habitat, stocking of creatures bred in captivity, and relocation of seed animals captured elsewhere. And this needn't wait on state action—it could be done right away by private landowners. Both government wildlife agencies and hunters were dubious, thinking such efforts sounded artificial, and unlikely to make much difference. But Olin was not only a passionate lover of hunting himself but also a determined man with extensive personal resources. He had built a range of Olin enterprises into a juggernaut with 40,000 employees and strong revenues, and after years of financial support for his alma mater Cornell University he enjoyed excellent connections to research expertise. Olin was also a scientist himself, with deep experience as an investigator and a couple dozen U.S. patents to his name. In addition, Olin had funded early studies on private husbandry of land and wildlife conducted by Aldo Leopold, the nation's first professor of game management at the University of Wisconsin, who bought 120 acres of played-out land on the Wisconsin River floodplain in 1935 to test his ideas on building a conservation ethic among property owners (spelled out in his 1949 classic *A Sand County Almanac*).

In 1951 Olin launched his own bold conservation experiment. He purchased a farm along the Mississippi River and converted its 522 acres to food and cover plants favored by game birds. He hired a staff of trained conservationists to manage his new "preserve," and installed a breeder and trainer of field dogs on the property. Soon his "Nilo Farms" (and companion private reserves he established in Georgia and elsewhere) were teeming with wildlife, and his Labrador retrievers and other sporting dogs were winning national field trials and sending their prize offspring around the country to generate new lines of hunting companions. "In less than a decade the Cornell-Nilo relationship has been reversed," wrote *Sports Illustrated* in a cover story on this success. "Where once the university assisted John Olin in setting up his program, Olin is now assisting Cornell with valuable research and experimentation undertaken at Nilo."

Actively managed game preserves exploded in popularity, soon numbering in the thousands as they were established in both private and public formats all across the country—most of them patterned after Nilo Farms. And wild game of all sorts made tremendous comebacks.

Further reading

○ *Sports Illustrated* story, si.com/vault/cover/1958/11/17

1950

BERNHEIM ARBORETUM

Isaac Bernheim was a German immigrant to Kentucky who went to work as a peddler and eventually became a wealthy distiller. Grateful for his good fortune, he gave Bernheim Arboretum as a gift to the people of his beloved adopted state in 1929. His will stipulated that "said 14,000 acres be used for a park...to be developed and forever maintained...for the people of Kentucky, and their friends, as a place to further their love of the beautiful in nature...and as a means of strengthening their love and devotion to their state and country." Bernheim died in 1945, and five years later his forest was opened to the public. It presently includes a research station, a visitor center, and many ecological education programs and nature studies.

Further reading

○ Bernheim Arboretum, bernheim.org/general-info/history

CEMENTING GRAND TETON NATIONAL PARK

Almost from the time that Yellowstone was established as our first national park, there was interest in extending its boundaries south to include the toothy Grand Teton peaks and the lovely valley and lakes that lay at their feet. But the valley had economic uses that made it harder to set aside than the surrounding mountain regions. So when Congress designated a Grand Teton National Park in 1929, the boundary stopped at the foot of the peaks. John Rockefeller Jr. had visited the Teton valley several times, including in 1924 with three of his sons and in 1926 with his wife. He noted not only that the mountains "are seen at their best from the Jackson Hole valley," but that the valley "is the natural and necessary feeding place for the game which inhabits Yellowstone Park and the surrounding regions." Rockefeller was disappointed to find power lines and ramshackle buildings springing up in the beautiful area along the foot of the mountains, so he empowered local agents to begin buying up property (anonymously) from willing sellers in the valley. He spent $18 million to purchase and maintain tens of thousands of acres which he finally donated to the Park Service in 1949. A newly expanded 310,000 acre Grand Teton National Park was signed into law in 1950, encompassing all the large alpine lakes and crucial parts of the Snake River valley.

In 2008, a final 1,100 acres of Rockefeller-owned land bordering Phelps Lake was opened to the public. The pristine Laurance Rockefeller Preserve includes an impressive visitor center and hiking-trail network funded by more than $20 million of donations from this third generation of the philanthropic family. Park officials estimate the Phelps Lake land alone to be worth $160 million, making this one of the most valuable gifts in the history of our park system.

Further reading

o Tom Butler, *Wildlands Philanthropy: The Great American Tradition* (Earth Aware, 2008)
o Laurance Rockefeller Preserve, nps.gov/partnerships/snapshots_grandteton.htm

1947

MELLON PARKLANDS

Out of the bank he established in Pittsburgh in 1869, Thomas Mellon left behind both a fortune and a string of descendants who variously increased those funds and gave them away to a wide range of philanthropic projects—prominently including land conservation. Among their other accomplishments in nature giving, former National Park Service historian Barry Mackintosh has noted that, "after the Rockefellers, the Mellon family has contributed most generously to the growth of the national park system." For instance, various Mellon family foundations funded shoreline surveys along our Great Lakes and sea coasts, over a period of decades starting in 1947. These led to the creation of several national seashores and lakeshores. Mellon money purchased much of the land for the Cape Hatteras and Cumberland Island National Seashores. It funded acquisition of the Hampton National Historic Site in Maryland. And family members helped preserve Rocky Mountain National Park and Redwood National Park. They also landscaped Lafayette Park across from the White House.

Further reading

o Philanthropy and the national parks, nps.gov/history/history/hisnps/NPSHistory/philanthropy.HTM

1937

APPALACHIAN TRAIL

In 1921, an article was published in the *Journal of the American Institute of Architects* proposing a series of trail-connected camps along the Appalachian Mountains. Very soon, volunteer crews of hikers were constructing a first segment of the proposed New England-to-Georgia footpath on their own, starting in Harriman-Bear Mountain State Park in New York. A small core of about 200 activists began to select and blaze routes, set standards, establish more than 30 local clubs to oversee local segments, negotiate with private landowners and government agencies over rights of way, and publish maps and guidebooks. By 1937 a continuous

NATURE

Appalachian Trail was open, running through 2,000 miles of wild land from Georgia's Mount Oglethorpe to Mount Katahdin in central Maine. Not until the end of the 1960s did the overseeing nonprofit have any paid employees. To this day, local volunteers continue to handle most of the club duties and trail upkeep.

Further reading

○ History of the Appalachian Trail Conservancy, appalachiantrail.org/about-the-trail/history

○ Brian King, *The Appalachian Trail: Celebrating America's Hiking Trail* (The Appalachian Trail Conservancy, 2012)

1934

HAWK MOUNTAIN

Hawk Mountain is regularly mistaken for a public park, whereas it's actually a classic example of a concerned citizen taking action on her own. A series of ridges in the eastern Appalachians of Pennsylvania, Hawk Mountain enjoys thermal currents that draw thousands of migrating birds every year, particularly raptors. But in the early 1930s it became a shooting range, as the Pennsylvania Game Commission began paying $5 for every goshawk killed, in an attempt to protect chicken farmers. Bounty shooters killed hundreds of hawks as they passed lookouts at eye-level in great concentrated streams. Philanthropist Rosalie Edge saw photos of the carnage, tried in frustration to find allies who would help stop it, and eventually acquired most of the mountain herself in 1934. She forbade bounty hunting on her 1,400 acres. Edge brought in wardens and opened Hawk Mountain to the public the next year as a bird-watcher's paradise. The world's first refuge for birds of prey, Hawk Mountain today remains the oldest and largest member-supported raptor-conservation organization in the world. It now extends over 2,600 acres, and visitors travel from far away to see its wonders. In addition to its bird viewing there

◁ PhilAphorism

A bit of fragrance always clings to the hand that gives roses. If you are generous, you will gain everything.

☞ *Confucius*

are trails, a garden, a visitor center, a facility for conservation training, and a multimillion-dollar research program on raptors.

Further reading

○ Hawk Mountain, hawkmountain.org/who-we-are/history/page.aspx?id=387

○ Maurice Broun, *Hawks Aloft: The Story of Hawk Mountain* (Stackpole Books, 1977)

MOUNT KATAHDIN AND BAXTER STATE PARK

Mount Katahdin, at 5,269 feet, is the highest peak in Maine and the terminus of the Appalachian Trail. The surrounding area features hundreds of lakes, streams, and waterfalls, wildlife are abundant, and prominent features of Ice Age glaciation are on display. While he was governor of Maine from 1921 to 1925, Percival Baxter tried to persuade legislators to conserve Katahdin. He failed. After leaving office, Baxter put his money where his mouth was—buying the peak and 6,000 surrounding acres in 1930, then making them a gift to the people of his state. Over the next 32 years he continued to purchase additional parcels, assembling what is now a state park of 210,000 acres, containing 40 peaks besides Katahdin. Baxter also left a trust fund of $7 million to ensure there would be money to manage the park properly without pressing on Maine taxpayers. Today about 75 percent of the Baxter State Park operates as a wildlife sanctuary, 53,000 acres are open to hunting and trapping, there are 215 miles of popular trails, and ten campgrounds. Baxter designated 30,000 acres to be managed as a showplace for timbering and sound commercial forestry. What the state refused to do, private initiative accomplished to great public benefit. In Baxter's words, "Buildings crumble, monuments decay, wealth vanishes. But Katahdin in all its glory forever shall remain the mountain of the people of Maine."

Further reading

○ History of the park, baxterstateparkauthority.com/about/history.htm

HUNTER-LED WILDLIFE RECOVERIES

Experience from the last 85 years shows that people who stalk and harvest animals are often the best at saving them. The Dust Bowl droughts of the 1930s decimated North American populations of ducks and other waterfowl. Federal wildlife refuges and the recycling of "duck stamp" revenues back into habitat maintenance proved inadequate. A history entitled *The Ducks Came Back* describes how much this disturbed sportsmen: "Hunters all over the United States were putting their fowling pieces in mothballs or attempting to sell them.... It just isn't worthwhile to go duck hunting these days—having to get up early in the morning or sit out in hard weather for a shot or two all day. I wouldn't want my son to pursue a sport that I love so well that has sunk to such a low level." Attendees at the American Game Association conference in 1935 bandied about a desperate proposal to ban all duck hunting for one year.

Instead, sportsmen went to work. That same year, the first international wild duck census was conducted by the More Game Birds in America Foundation, which had been formed in 1930 to rally hunters behind efforts to restore habitat. In 1937, the work of More Game Birds evolved into the new group Ducks Unlimited. The organization launched hundreds of thousands of dollars worth of marsh and breeding-ground restorations, and created popular publications, local chapters, and regular meetings to unite wildfowlers from across the U.S., Canada, and Mexico behind voluntary conservation efforts. Today, Ducks Unlimited is the world's largest and most effective private waterfowl conservation organization, with 750,000 dues-paying members and partnerships with landowners, companies, agencies, scientific organizations, and private individuals that have allowed it to directly conserve 13.1 million acres of habitat, while influencing the management of another 100 million acres. One of its advantages over government agencies is its ability to work simultaneously in the three countries of North America, each of which is important in the lifecycle of migrating birds.

There are many other so-called "hook and bullet" conservation groups backed by hunters and fishermen that have been instrumental in saving and reviving wildlife in similar ways. The recovery of the wild turkey, which nearly disappeared from America, was funded by millions of dollars of donations and fees paid by hunters. For instance, the National Wild Turkey Federation and its partners have spent more than $412 million since the group's founding in 1973 to conserve more than 17 million acres of turkey habitat, powering the recovery of this iconic bird to almost all of its historic range. A remnant of just 30,000 creatures has now grown to more than 7 million wild turkeys—marking one of the greatest wildlife recoveries in American history. Quail, grouse, pheasants, songbirds, and deer have benefitted in parallel as the 250,000-member group has planted cover and food, transplanted birds, consulted with farmers and corporations, hired scientists, and otherwise spent donated funds to make lands more animal-friendly. (See 1951 entry on John Olin for more on this topic.)

Further reading

◦ Timeline for Ducks Unlimited, ducks.org/about-du?timeline=1

◦ About the National Wild Turkey Federation, nwtf.org/about_us

1930

WOODS HOLE OCEANOGRAPHIC INSTITUTION

In the early 1920s, Wickliffe Rose of the Rockefeller Foundation began conversations with the director of the U.S. Marine Biological Laboratory about the need for better understanding of the oceans. They launched a committee which eventually proposed creating a well-equipped institution on the U.S. east coast to conduct oceanographic research. The Rockefeller Foundation provided $1 million for construction, boats, equipment, and upkeep of a center located at Woods Hole, Massachusetts, along with a $1-million endowment, and $500,000 for ten years of summertime operating expenses.

By the early 2000s, there were over 1,000 researchers, ships' crew, and support staff employed at Woods Hole, and philanthropy continued to be relied on to launch extensions of the federal facility's programs. When fish ecologist Simon Thorrold developed doubts about the common way of reducing overfishing of depleted species—establishing large Marine Protected Areas where harvesting is banned until the fish population grows back—he and his colleagues developed a way to tag fish with harmless chemical signatures so the population dynamics and migrations of fish could be studied in detail. Woods Hole approached the David and Lucille Packard Foundation, which had been associated with marine philanthropy since their founding of the Monterey Bay Aquarium (see 1984 entry), with a request to fund the project. The Packard Foundation provided a half-million dollars starting in 2007. Woods Hole's new Fish Ecology Laboratory was born.

Further reading

○ Origins of Woods Hole Oceanographic Institution, whoi.edu/main/history-legacy

○ Thorrold research, philanthropyroundtable.org/site/print/briefly_noted10

1928

GREAT SMOKY MOUNTAINS

John Rockefeller Jr. had already catalyzed creation of a national park at Acadia in Maine, and set events in motion for another at Grand Teton in Wyoming, when in 1928 he offered $5 million (about half the total needed) to purchase land for the Great Smoky Mountains National Park that now straddles the North Carolina-Tennessee border. With additional contributions from the two states, the cities of Asheville and Knoxville, $2 million from the federal government, and contributions from thousands of private citizens, 6,600 separate plots were painstakingly assembled, and about a decade later the National Park opened. Today it includes 700 miles of fishable streams, 800 miles of trails including a long section of the Appalachian Trail, abundant wildlife, magnificent trees like a yellow buckeye more than 19 feet in circumference, and artifacts of pioneer life. It is America's most visited national park, with more than 9 million annual guests.

Further reading

○ Michael Frome, *Strangers in High Places: The Story of Great Smoky Mountains National Park* (University of Tennessee Press, 1966)

1919

ACADIA NATIONAL PARK

Maine's Acadia National Park mixes ocean, forest, and mountains in combinations of legendary beauty. It is a product of the tenacity of one George Dorr, a Bostonian with an inherited textile fortune who began acquiring land in the area after establishing a home on Mount Desert Island (on which most of the park is located). In 1901, Dorr was contacted by Charles Eliot, the president of Harvard, whose son had started the first land trust in America a decade earlier (see 1890 entry). Eliot was promoting another private land trust, to protect this scenic section of Maine coast. Dorr soon found himself at the head of the Hancock County Trustees of Public Reservations. He donated tracts of his own land, and tirelessly encouraged his neighbors to donate others. In 1908, he and another trustee bought the summit of Cadillac Mountain. By 1913, the "reservation" totaled over 5,000 acres. (Dorr meanwhile had to battle attempts by the state government to hamstring his group by revoking its nonprofit status.) In 1919 the property became Lafayette National Park—the first in the East, and the first created from privately donated lands. Dorr continued to expand and improve the park, which was renamed Acadia in 1929. Dorr's friend and neighbor John Rockefeller Jr. donated 10,700 acres to the property, and spent $3.5 million of his own money to create an immaculate network of 45 miles of horse-drawn carriage road, including 17 granite bridges, that shows the island at its best. It is still used today for hiking and biking. Acadia National Park currently covers 47,000 acres, and more than 2 million Americans enjoy its rugged beauty every year.

Further reading

○ PBS profile, pbs.org/nationalparks/parks/acadia/

○ George Dorr, *The Story of Acadia National Park* (Acadia Publishing, 1985)

STEPHEN MATHER BUILDS
THE NATIONAL PARK SERVICE

Stephen Mather was the first director of the National Park Service, but he was much more than a bureaucrat. His abilities as a manager and his personal donations as a private citizen were his greatest contributions to nature conservation, not least in creating the Park Service itself. An outdoorsman from an early age, Mather always found time to climb mountains and hike canyons no matter how busy he got as a businessman (he made a fortune selling borax) or philanthropist. He was not only interested in protecting scenic resources and natural areas, but devoted to encouraging new transportation methods that would allow Americans to reach and enjoy them. By 1915, he had gotten a group together to buy the Tioga Road to Yosemite for $15,500 and donate it to Yosemite National Park. In 1915, Mather accepted a position as assistant secretary of the interior in Washington, D.C., and when the National Park Service was created in 1917 he was appointed its first director.

Mather wished to have the parks supported by avid users. This led him to focus on access and programming. In 1916 he convinced several railroad companies to join him in donating $48,000 to publicize the national parks. He got automobile companies to "democratize" parks by supporting the construction of roads to get a broader cross-section of Americans into them. He spent thousands from his own pocket to improve park access, and created the first visitor centers, including providing $25,000 of personal funds to build the Rangers' Club at Yosemite. Mather pushed for "nature study" and interpretation programs that would attract citizens to their parks, and invited in concessioners who could provide basic comforts. He also led and paid for trips to parks by influential people, and supplied material to the press which generated 1,050 magazine articles on parklands from 1917 to 1919 alone.

Mather continued to buy acreage and donate it to the parks, and convinced wealthy friends to do likewise. He took on talented staff and paid them himself, and professionalized the park ranger corps into one of the most competent parts of the federal work force. With this impressive start, the National Park Service went on to attract an estimated $48 billion in private preservation investment from 1916 to the present.

Further reading
○ National Park Service profile, cr.nps.gov/history/online_books/sontag/mather.htm

○ Mather biographical information, hpdfhost.focus.nps.gov/docs/NHLS/Text/66000877.pdf

○ Horace Albright, Marian Schenck, *Creating the National Park Service: The Missing Years* (University of Oklahoma Press, 1999)

CAMEL'S HUMP STATE PARK

Joseph Battell was a Vermont newspaper publisher, and promoter of the Morgan horse. His creation of the American Morgan Horse Registry and donation of his horse farm to the national breeding program for Morgans helped save the breed. Battell was also an avid land buyer, and when he died in 1915 he left more than 30,000 acres of forest and farm to Middlebury College, of which he was a trustee. The college established a summer writers' school within the Victorian buildings at the heart of the property (which it continues to operate to this day), and sold most of the surrounding land to the U.S. Forest Service. Contrary to Battell's hope that the tract could be preserved as "a specimen of the original Vermont forest," the college and Forest Service saw no responsible way to maintain the property without some commercial logging.

In 1911, Battell made a separate gift to the State Forester of about 1,000 acres of wild land surrounding the third highest peak in Vermont—Camel's Hump, which offers one of the most distinctive rocky profiles in New England and tops out at 4,083 feet. Apart from its popular hiking trails, this mountain land was left undisturbed until 1969, when it was turned into a state park with a forest reserve to surround it—now totaling 20,000 acres. The area includes a section kept in a

◆ PhilAphorism

When you find your battery of hope, excitement, and even idealistic naiveté so drained that you don't let an applicant finish a presentation without pointing out why it can't be done, it's time you departed for another profession. Philanthropy builds on the hope of rising generations; it lights fires rather than snuffs them out.   ☞ *Paul Ylvisaker*

primitive state to protect rare alpine plants and wilderness settings. A second portion is managed for timber production, wildlife and hunting, hiking, Nordic skiing, and snowmobiling. A third piece includes farms and some seasonal and permanent homes. Camel's Hump is the only peak in Vermont of 4,000 feet or more that doesn't have an adjoining ski resort.

Further reading

○ Vermont State Parks, vtstateparks.com/htm/camelshump.htm

○ Tom Butler, *Wildlands Philanthropy: The Great American Tradition* (Earth Aware, 2008)

1908

MUIR WOODS NATIONAL MONUMENT

The oldest surviving California sequoias are thousands of years old. Sheathed by the fogs that roll in daily from the Pacific, they reach hundreds of feet in height. Ancient specimens once grew in many northern California coastal valleys, but during the 1800s most were logged off. Having lived as a boy in Marin County, William Kent knew and loved the redwoods, and after returning to the area after making money in real estate and livestock in Chicago, he and his wife decided to buy 611 acres of one of the last uncut stands of old-growth sequoia in the Bay Area in 1905. Though located just a dozen miles north of San Francisco, the patch along Redwood Creek was hard to reach and so had been left untouched. They paid $45,000, much of it borrowed. Soon a Sausalito water company had designs on Kent's land, which it intended to flood and use as a reservoir. It planned to wield condemnation by eminent domain to get the land, and since much of San Francisco had just burned in the fires following the 1906 earthquake, the chances of a water company winning favor in court seemed good.

In an attempt to protect the redwoods, the Kents mailed the deed for 295 acres of their land to the secretary of the interior, asking that President Roosevelt declare the donated tract a national monument, and name it Muir Woods, for conservationist John Muir. A fan of redwoods and an admirer of the Kents' generosity, and their selflessness in refusing to have the gift named after themselves, Roosevelt acted as requested in 1908. Muir Woods became the first national protected area donated by private individuals. The Kents donated more land to the monument in 1921. Today, Muir Woods National Monument covers 554 acres, adjacent to 6,000 acres of state-protected land, and hosts more than 800,000 visitors each year.

Further reading

○ People behind the Muir Woods National Monument, nps.gov/muwo/historyculture/people.htm

NATURE

1907

GRAND CANYON OF THE EAST

Central New Yorker William Letchworth made a fortune in the iron business, then retired at age 48 to a property he had purchased in the spectacular deep gorge carved by the Genesee River as it snakes its way north to Lake Ontario near Rochester, New York. His retirement was a busy one—he poured himself into good works as president of the New York State Board of Charities. Letchworth inspected and reformed hundreds of orphan asylums, juvenile reformatories, and poor-houses. He then toured, at his own expense, model facilities in the U.S. and Europe for housing the insane, epileptics, and poor children, and wrote two definitive books on these subjects that were later used to establish new hospitals and homes offering a better standard of care. Eventually he served as president of the National Conference of Charities and Correction, and the National Association for the Study of Epilepsy.

A Quaker raised to value not only hard work, self-improvement, and charity but also nature, Letchworth poured himself into improving his property in the Genesee gorge. He then allowed unfettered access to tourists drawn by the waterfalls and rugged scenery (immortalized by painter Thomas Cole among others) in what is still referred to as the Grand Canyon of the East. Late in Letchworth's life, there were moves afoot to dam the Genesee River to power mills and factories. To preserve the rare beauty of the area he donated his thousand acres to create a state park in 1907. Today Letchworth remains one of the most visited state parks in the eastern U.S.

Further reading

○ Letchworth history, letchworthparkhistory.com/glimpse1.html

1906

PIERRE DU PONT CREATES LONGWOOD GARDENS

In 1798, the twin grandsons of a Quaker who was farming 400 acres in the far southeastern corner of Pennsylvania developed an interest in natural history; they began planting a collection of trees that eventually included specimens from throughout the U.S. and overseas. The grove, which grew to 15 acres, became a popular spot for picnics and family reunions. Generations later the family lost interest in the arboretum and new owners were at the point of contracting with a lumber company to remove the trees when successful industrialist Pierre du Pont purchased the land in 1906 to preserve its botanical richness and create an outdoor sanctuary for enjoyment.

"I have recently experienced what I would formerly have diagnosed as an attack of insanity," du Pont wrote to a friend soon after. "I have purchased a small farm. I expect to have a good deal of enjoyment in restoring its former condition and making it a place where I can entertain my friends." Without fixed plans, he gradually added gardens, an open-air theater, then a vast greenhouse, and large buildings for music and entertaining. He began hosting elaborate garden parties, and created illuminated fountains that shot 10,000 gallons of water per minute as high as 130 feet.

Du Pont eventually gave a great deal of thought to the future of his gardens, and in 1937 began the Longwood Foundation to maintain them for long-term public enjoyment and education. At his death in 1954 he left the foundation with a sizable endowment, a solid board of trustees, and a long tradition of offering visitors rare beauty. The gardens have continued to grow, and with an annual budget of nearly $50 million and a staff of 1,300 employees, students, and volunteers, has become one of the world's great gardens.

Further reading

○ History of Longwood Gardens, longwoodgardens.org/history

○ Tim Richardson, *Great Gardens of America* (Francis Lincoln, 2009)

NATURE

——— 1903 ———

SCRIPPS INSTITUTION OF OCEANOGRAPHY

Ellen Scripps, whose fortune derived from the Scripps family's newspaper empire, generously supported a range of charitable causes across southern California. She donated the land and first building for a Catholic college-prep school for girls, and supported it financially for years. She endowed what would become Scripps College, a part of the Claremont Colleges that she had helped to found. She commissioned a women's club headquarters and community center, and the country's first public playground, in La Jolla. She funded Egyptian explorations that resulted in the San Diego Museum's Ancient Egyptian collection. She founded the Scripps Memorial Hospital and the Scripps Metabolic Clinic.

Nature philanthropy was one of Ellen Scripps's favorite causes. She helped preserve the area that would become Torrey Pines State Natural Reserve. She was a financer of the new headquarters of the San Diego Natural History Museum. She gave the San Diego Zoo an aviary and an animal research hospital. And in 1903, she underwrote the founding of the Marine Biological Association of San Diego. Ellen gave it a sizable endowment, and the Scripps family provided its entire operating budget for a decade until it was taken over by the University of California, San Diego and renamed the Scripps Institution of Oceanography—which is today one of the oldest, largest, and most important centers in the world for research, education, and public service on the oceans, earth, and atmosphere.

Further reading

○ History of the Scripps Institution of Oceanography, scripps.ucsd.edu/about/history

1892

FROM SNOWY EGRETS TO JUNGLE GARDENS

Just after the Civil War, E. A. "Ned" McIlhenny was born on Louisiana's Avery Island—a 2,500 acre dome surrounded by marsh, swamp, and bayou. His family had operated a sugar plantation thereon, but the war put an end to that, so McIlhenny's father built a new business on the island selling hot pepper sauce—which he and his successors popularized as "Tabasco." The firm (which is still family owned and operates from Avery Island) was run by Ned for most of his adult life, but Ned is best remembered as a remarkable amateur naturalist. Homeschooled and given free run of the surrounding watery lands, he was sometimes out in nature for days at a time.

Alarmed at the disappearance of the charismatic snowy egret from the region, Ned set up a rookery and refuge near his house in 1892, when he was 20. To quote from his book *Bird City*, "I went into the swamps in search of nests of the snowy herons to get some young so that I could try to save these beautiful birds from being exterminated by the hunters who killed them for their feathers with which to decorate ladies' hats. After several days' search I found two nests, each containing four young. The eight birds were not yet old enough to fly and, storing them in the pockets of my hunting coat, I brought them to the cage I had built." After rearing the hatchlings in protective captivity he released them in the fall to join their fellow fliers migrating across the Gulf of Mexico. But the following spring they returned, with others of their species. The numbers of egrets breeding in the protection of Avery Island grew every year, helping save the snowy and American egrets from extinction. Today, thousands of water birds still migrate to the private sanctuary near the Tabasco factory.

McIlhenny went on to lead a fascinating life, which included many other contributions to naturalism. He became an Arctic explorer, and collected bird and mammal specimens that are still held in museums (while also helping save, via his hunting skills, more than 200 sailors marooned in Alaska by early-arriving ice). He conducted original research on the habits of many creatures, writing books on the wild turkey, egrets, and the alligator that became standard references. He published heavily in ornithological journals, and banded an astonishing 189,298 birds during his lifetime. He also trained himself in botany—translating from French to English the classic 13-volume iconography of camellias, becoming a pioneer planter and taxonomizer of bamboo, and earning international recognition for his work culturing camellias, azaleas, and irises. He created a 170-acre experimental garden on Avery Island, packed it with interesting plant specimens, and in 1935 opened it to the public as Jungle Gardens, which is still operated as a park by the family, and can be visited in its glory for a modest private admission fee.

In the first two decades of the twentieth century, McIlhenny approached major American philanthropists with a proposal to create a string of wildlife refuges along the Louisiana coast. Under his guidance, Charles Ward, Olivia Sage and her foundation, John Rockefeller and his foundation, and others made purchases of marshland totaling 175,000 acres to provide protected winter habitat for upward of a million waterfowl. Back on Avery Island, meanwhile, McIlhenny took pains to preserve the area's pristine beauty and continue its role as a wildlife refuge even when oil was discovered on the property in 1942. He resolved to demonstrate that energy production and nature could responsibly coexist, and succeeded. Informed by this example, gas and oil production was also allowed a decade later by no less than the Audubon Society at their Paul Rainey Bird Sanctuary in Louisiana.

Further reading

○ McIlhenny biography contained within an article on his bamboo studies, lgcc-abs.org/DF/
  McIlhenny_History.pdf

1890

TRUSTEES OF RESERVATIONS

During the later nineteenth century, Charles Eliot was a young man working as a landscape architect in Boston. His father was president of Harvard and

◁ PhilAphorism

Philanthropic leaders genially speak of complementing government, not competing with it—as if monopoly were good and competition destructive—thus unwittingly conspiring against the public interest.

☞ *Richard Cornuelle*

would be instrumental in founding what would become Acadia National Park. Eliot himself had more local ambitions. But these local efforts set a hugely important, quintessentially American, precedent for private conservation that would eventually spread all across the nation.

During Eliot's day, New England didn't get much attention from conservationists. Conserving was something one did to big patches of wilderness in the West, not an undertaking for the long-settled Atlantic states. It was clear to Eliot, though, that the time was coming soon when a majority of the U.S. population would be living packed into cities. He thought it important to make special efforts to help citizens access clean, healthful, beautiful outdoor areas close at hand, where they could gain relief from urban pressures.

In 1890, Eliot wrote a letter to the publication *Garden and Forest* suggesting that an association should be created to acquire "reservations"—lands "which possess uncommon beauty" where New Englanders could experience rural refreshment. "As Boston's lovers of art united to form the Art Museum, so her lovers of Nature should now rally to preserve for themselves and all the people as many as possible of these scenes of natural beauty which, by great good fortune, still exist near their doors." Eliot researched precedents in the form of historical societies and village improvement groups, and then persuaded the Appalachian Mountain Club (see 1876 entry) to invite enthusiasts from around the state to a meeting in Boston. About a hundred interested souls showed up, including influential leading citizens.

The gathering resolved to form a voluntary group "capable of acquiring and holding for the benefit of the public beautiful and historic places in Massachusetts." The Trustees of Public Reservations was soon up and running as America's first conservation land trust (the "public" was dropped in 1954 to make clearer that it is a privately run organization). The founders began raising donations, and by 1891 they had already been offered their first reserve, a lovely 20-acre parcel with a stream and old woods in Stoneham (which has since grown into a 2,575-acre section of the Boston metro park system). Today the Trustees of Reservations still operates as a thriving, member-supported nonprofit, overseeing 70 miles of coastline, 270 miles of trails, 12,292 acres of natural habitat, and numerous historic sites, gardens, woods, and landscapes. And it has inspired the blossoming of other land trusts across the U.S. (See 1982 summary.)

Further reading

○ Richard Brewer, *Conservancy: The Land Trust Movement in America* (Dartmouth, 2004)

○ The Trustees of Reservations, thetrustees.org/about-us/history

APPALACHIAN MOUNTAIN CLUB

In 1876, Edward Pickering, professor of physics at the Massachusetts Institute of Technology, convened on MIT's Boston campus a gathering of 34 men with a shared interest in mountain exploration and the outdoors. Some of the attendees wanted to form a "New England Geographical Society," but rather than create "one more learned society," the attendees decided to create "a vigorous, full-blooded, ardent club" that would support actual outdoor adventuring by building paths and huts available for general use. By 1906 the Appalachian Mountain Club had more than a thousand members and managed more than 100 miles of trails and many cabins. Its success inspired John Muir and some professors from the University of California, Berkeley and Stanford University to found the Sierra Club in 1892, though that organization soon veered in a different direction as a mass-membership political group, rather than an operating entity.

Today the Appalachian Mountain Club is still focused on enabling the active enjoyment of the outdoors. Its 100,000 members, 16,000 volunteers, and many loyal donors maintain over 1,800 miles of forest trails plus hundreds of shelters, working through 12 local chapters stretching along the East Coast. In 2003 the club took another bold step into direct conservation by raising private money to buy and permanently protect a 37,000-acre tract bordering the Appalachian Trail in Maine. Six years later the organization bought an adjacent 29,500-acre block, thus creating a large continuous corridor of conservation lands stretching north to Baxter State Park and Mount Katahdin (described in a 1930 entry). These major purchases were inspired by concern over the decline of the timber industry in Maine, which had traditionally allowed generous public use of its lands while keeping them in a wild state.

The AMC launched its "Maine Woods Initiative" to demonstrate creative ways to combine four productive uses of wild lands: recreation, conservation, sustainable forestry, and community partnerships. On their purchased lands, ecological and local economic needs are pursued simultaneously by mixing various forms or outdoor recreation, timber harvesting, and new nature-based tourism that aims to create jobs and provide the club with revenues. On this land the club currently maintains an 80-mile network of trails, three full-service lodges with private cabins in the traditional Maine sporting-camp tradition, and access for hunting and fishing, paddling, skiing, snowmobiling, and other uses.

Further reading

○ Club history, outdoors.org/lodging/huts/125thanniversary/amc-huts-history.cfm

○ Fact sheet, including details on the Maine Woods Initiative, outdoors.org/pdf/
upload/2013_AMC_Fact_Sheet.pdf

1866

ASPCA BIRTHS THE ANIMAL WELFARE MOVEMENT

Henry Bergh operated the shipbuilding business founded in New York City
by his father, and retired early with a substantial fortune. An abolitionist,
his friendship with William Seward won him an appointment as part of the
American delegation to Russia during the Civil War. While in St. Petersburg
Bergh came upon a Russian mercilessly beating his fallen cart horse;
disturbed, he tried to intervene. Later, on his way back to the U.S., Bergh
stopped in London to meet with the president of the Royal Society for the
Prevention of Cruelty to Animals. Shortly after his return to New York he
began to solicit friends with a plan to found a U.S. counterpart. He won a
public charter in 1866, put a good deal of his own money into launching
the organization, and became the first president of the first animal-welfare
organization in the country: the American Society for the Prevention of
Cruelty to Animals.

Bergh engaged public opinion, and frequently put himself in harm's way
to stop acts of cruelty himself. His debates with P. T. Barnum on humane
conditions for show animals led to a friendship; Barnum helped form an
SPCA branch in Bridgeport, Connecticut, and was eventually a pallbearer
at Bergh's funeral. The success of the New York City group spurred the
formation of local SPCA chapters in Buffalo, Philadelphia, Boston, and then
many other cities. In 1874 Bergh became involved in a case of abuse of a
foster child that resulted in creation of a parallel Society for the Prevention
of Cruelty to Children. A broad "humane" movement, nudged further by
horror at the violence of the Civil War, spread across the U.S., with Henry
Bergh's loyal financial support and steady enlistment of friends helping it
along the way.

Further reading

○ Biography of Henry Bergh, learningtogive.org/papers/paper357.html
○ Essay at New York Historical Society, blog.nyhistory.org/henry-bergh-angel-in-top-hat-
or-the-great-meddler

1856

HENRY SHAW'S ST. LOUIS PARKS

Henry Shaw came to America as a teenager, the son of a man who was looking for new markets for his family's English steel business. The family set up a hardware store in a little village called St. Louis. By the time he was 40, Henry was able to retire a rich man. It was when he revisited the beautiful open gardens of England in 1851 that he found a new purpose. He recalled that St. Louis—indeed all of America—then had no public gardens, and few public parks. Returning to the by-now bustling city where he had made his fortune, Henry commenced building the Missouri Botanical Garden in 1856.

The idea of a public horticultural reserve funded by an enterprising private citizen captivated plant experts like St. Louisan George Englemann and Asa Gray of Harvard, the nation's foremost botanist. They began accumulating plants to contribute to Shaw's project. In 1859, the Botanical Garden opened to the public.

Yet its benefactor wasn't finished. Since all of the city's extant parks were small, he approached municipal leaders about possibly donating a large public park. He envisioned a glorious, sprawling place where all residents could enjoy the outdoors. It took some legislative wrangling at the state level, but Shaw eventually donated his own property to create Tower Grove Park—277 acres of land covered with 20,000 trees. It opened in 1870.

Shaw later published botanical tracts, endowed the School of Botany at Washington University, and opened schools, hospitals, and other contributions to his home city. His botanical garden is now a National Historic Landmark, and the oldest and one of the greatest of its type in the U.S. It offers nearly 80 acres of garden oasis in the heart of the city, numerous impressive collections of rare flowers, and centers for research and education.

Further reading

- Missouri Botanical Gardens, missouribotanicalgarden.org/about/additional-information/our-mission-history.aspx
- Tower Grove Park, towergrovepark.org/index.php/history/henry-shaw.html

NATURE

MAJOR ACHIEVEMENTS OF AMERICAN PHILANTHROPY
(1636-2015)

PROSPERITY

ighting poverty is one of the oldest charitable imperatives. This in turn often requires battling syndromes that lead to poverty—like family breakdown, alcohol and drug abuse, or economic obstructions. Philanthropists often act to make their fellow citizens more prosperous, and to spread economic flourishing broadly among all Americans. Private donors were helping Indians, African-Americans, ethnic minorities, refugees, and women become educated and productive many decades before government agencies got in the act.

Donors have often been motivated in this work by religious impulses. Many entries on the list that follows could just as easily have been filed on our roster of Major Achievements in Religious Philanthropy. Likewise, many charities that might have been included here because of their success in spreading prosperity among Americans—like the Salvation Army, Habitat for Humanity, Goodwill Industries, etc.—are featured instead on our Religious Philanthropy list.

On top of efforts to extend economic success to widening circles of citizens, interventions that encourage economic flourishing generally have been almost as popular among philanthropists. Many donors believe that expanding our economic pie over the long run is the very best way to ensure that everyone eventually earns a generous slice. Gifts to economic research and the hard sciences, for example, are usually made in this hope of increasing general prosperity. Nearly a third of the funds available for science research at America's top 50 universities currently come from private donations. Top lab directors like Eric Lander and Leroy Hood have energetically explained how important philanthropy is as a form of risk capital that lets scientists explore unconventional, unusually hard, or very early-stage problems. Many technical breakthroughs that later bear economic fruit in abundance are powered by donations. Even defense-related innovations like artificial intelligence, rocketry, and radar that we think of as classic government responsibilities have been powered primarily by philanthropy in their early stages—as you are about to read.

> ☛ *Section research provided by Karl Zinsmeister,*
> *Scott Walter, Jo Kwong, and Thomas Meyer*

JAILING EFFICIENTLY—AND LESS OFTEN

Deciding which arrestees to keep in jail while they await trial is one of the more difficult and arbitrary tasks facing judges. Under-incarcerate arrestees and they may disappear, endanger witnesses or victims, or commit additional crimes that harm the community. Over-hold arrestees and you may cause innocent parties or minor offenders to lose their jobs, have a hard time preparing their defense, or endure unnecessary stress while locked up awaiting trial.

In 2015, the Laura and John Arnold Foundation rolled out a new tool to make this judgment easier, fairer, and more efficient. The tool was developed by studying the actual results of 1.5 million cases across the country, and it allows judges to enter the charge, criminal history, and age of the arrestee, then get a scientific, real-life assessment of the wisdom of either holding him or letting him remain at home until trial. This avoids subjective unfairness, jailing's potentially toxic effects on people's lives, and unnecessary taxpayer expense for housing inmates.

During the past 20 years the average stay for a jail inmate has grown from 14 days to more than three weeks. Pilot tests of the new Arnold tool show that it will reduce jail populations by about 20 percent. The foundation has offered to provide the tool for free to any city, county, or state that would like to have it available. In 2015 it was introduced in 29 jurisdictions—including three large cities (Chicago, Charlotte, and Phoenix) and three entire states (Arizona, Kentucky, and New Jersey).

Both local jail and federal prison populations have peaked—jail numbers started declining in 2008, and prison levels topped out in 2013. But a number of philanthropies have expressed interest in further speeding deincarceration. The John and Catherine MacArthur Foundation announced in 2015 that it was dedicating $75 million to help local jurisdictions find ways to reduce jail populations. It granted $150,000 to 16 counties, three cities, and one state to help them develop ideas for reducing jailing, with follow-up grants of up to $2 million promised so half of them can put their plans into action. The foundation also funded academic research on alternatives to sending people to jail.

Further reading

○ Arnold Foundation announcement, arnoldfoundation.org/more-than-20-cities-and-states-adopt-risk-assessment-tool-to-help-judges-decide-which-defendants-to-detain-prior-to-trial

○ MacArthur Foundation announcement, macfound.org/press/press-releases/macarthur-announces-20-jurisdictions-receive-funding-reduce-jail-use

2015

ENGINEERING IMPROVEMENTS AT HARVARD

In hard meritocracies like engineering and computer science, either you can solve a problem or you can't—there is no credit for having a glitzy credential or a fancy label on your stationery. Harvard and other top universities that are not used to being also-rans have found over the past decade that their engineering, computer science, and applied science schools have fallen behind leading institutions like Carnegie Mellon, MIT, Cornell, and Stanford. In these fields where change is blindingly fast, improvement must be constant or one will be lapped by the rest of the field.

Back in 1996, Microsoft executives Steve Ballmer and Bill Gates gave Harvard $25 million for a new engineering building that they hoped would lift Harvard toward the upper tier in computing and engineering. But just from 2007 to 2014, undergraduate enrollment in engineering at Harvard tripled. By 2010, the facility provided by Ballmer and Gates was overcrowded and dated.

As the fastest-growing major at Harvard, computer science has particularly outstripped the university's ability to keep up. So in 2014 Ballmer came back to his alma mater with a gift (rumored to be approximately $60 million) to increase the school's computer-science faculty from 24 to 36 professors. This 50 percent expansion will allow a similar increase in student studies.

Just a few months later, in 2015, financier John Paulson emphatically put his own imprint on this effort to improve Harvard's engineering programs. He provided $400 million—the university's largest gift ever—to endow its school of engineering and applied sciences. This

PROSPERITY

will allow the engineers to leap to an entirely new campus in Allston, Massachusetts, across the Charles River from Harvard Yard, where they will occupy advanced new facilities next to the university's innovation lab and business school. With engineers, entrepreneurs, and innovators placed together in an enterprise zone stocked with powerful tools, it is hoped that much useful scientific invention will follow.

Further reading

- Paulson gift reported in *Harvard Gazette*, news.harvard.edu/gazette/story/2015/06/ harvard-receives-its-largest-gift
- Ballmer gift reported in *Harvard Crimson*, thecrimson.com/article/2014/11/13/ballmer-computer-science-gift

2014

COMPUTING PROMOTED TO THE MAJOR LEAGUE OF SCIENTIFIC PRIZES

The Turing Award is the highest prize in computer science. Since first being awarded in 1966 it has grown in importance along with its field. In 2007, it began to include a cash award of $250,000, thanks to corporate donations from Google and Intel. In 2014 Google sharply increased its support so the prize could be quadrupled to $1 million. That approximately matches the Nobel award, and puts Turing in the major league of scientific honors and incentives.

Further reading

- *New York Times* report, bits.blogs.nytimes.com/2014/11/13/google-lifts-the-turing-award-into-nobel-territory/?_r=0

2014

ALLEN INVENTS NEW METHODS FOR NEW SCIENCE PUZZLES

Human cells are complicated machines, and scientists have recently gathered lots of detail about their sub-elements. But "nobody studies how these entities function as complex systems, and how they interact to determine cellular behaviors. Instead, people focus on just a small, manageable part," says biologist Rick Horwitz. This is mostly because of the way academic labs are structured (to support deep dives on narrow slices of a problem) and the way government research money is distributed (only to very tightly defined projects, not for exhaustive, boundary-breaking macro-examinations).

To understand the astonishing ways that cells transform themselves, signal each other, migrate, and take various kinds of "action," however, microstudies of proteins and genes and chemicals are not enough. One must watch the whole sprawling "movie" of what the cell does over time, and identify patterns. That essentially is what former Microsoft co-founder and current multibillion-dollar philanthropist Paul Allen created a new cell-science institute to accomplish. He donated $100 million to start the work, and personally recruited Rick Horwitz from the University of Virginia to direct the effort.

The institute's 70 researchers will work as one interdisciplinary team rather than as independent investigators. They will use induced pluripotent stem cells—a new creation that allows a common skin cell, for instance, to be converted into a stem cell after scientists use chemicals and other stimulations to turn off certain genetic switches. A stem cell is capable of growing into any other more specialized cell (bone, muscle, blood, etc.), depending on what the body needs. By taking long, complete sequences of microscope images of those stem cells transforming themselves into more specialized cells, the Allen Institute scientists believe they will gather tremendous amounts of big-picture information about cellular machinery.

The institute will advance the field by releasing to all interested researchers both the original "movies" and any conclusions the Allen investigators draw from them. This is a classic example of unconventional, highly speculative science that is almost never funded through traditional university and government channels, yet can be a forte of philanthropy.

Further reading

○ Announcement of creation of the institute, alleninstitutecellscience.org/press/press-release/paul-g-allen-give-100-million-create-cell-science-institute

2014

SUPPORTING DRUG DISCOVERY AS AN ECONOMIC ENGINE

The so-called Research Triangle in North Carolina is one of the nation's centers for biological research, and pharmaceutical innovation in particular. And Fred Eshelman is one of the whirlwinds at the center of North Carolina pharma, having founded and built to huge success there two different drug-research firms. A graduate of the University of North Carolina School of Pharmacy, Eshelman started donating to his alma mater in 2003 and gave a total of $38 million over a decade.

In 2014 Eshelman noted that "in the past ten years the school has generated more than 130 patents and created 15 spinoff companies. Their success demonstrates the power and the future of drug discovery in academia, and it's a future that I am eager and proud to support." With that, he announced a new mega-gift: $100 million to create within the pharmacy school a center explicitly focused on creating valuable drug products that will "fuel innovation, create jobs, and spur economic development in the state."

In addition to bulking up his region's economic productivity, the Eshelman donations helped build the UNC School of Pharmacy into one of the largest and highest rated educational facilities of its sort, with about 750 students enrolled in one of its degree programs at any given time.

Further reading

○ Announcement of $100 million gift, pharmacy.unc.edu/news/schoolnews/100-million-eshelman-gift-to-fund-innovation-center-is-largest-ever-to-a-pharmacy-school

2013

BETTING ON CROSS-FERTILIZATION

Graduate school is typically a monkish undertaking, in which many participants become comparatively isolated from peers during their deep dive into a chosen academic subject. To balance this a bit, investor Charles Munger helped fund graduate-student housing at Stanford which ganged students into four-bedroom apartments in hopes that the communal interactions coming from living together would overflow into useful professional sharing. This was a success.

Munger then gave the University of Michigan the largest gift in its history—about $110 million worth of Berkshire Hathaway stock—to go even further in this direction. With his 2013 donation, Michigan built a 632-bedroom apartment building that houses graduate students in an innovative way. Every student has a soundproof bedroom and study area and a private bath, but these

◈ PhilAphorism

The spirit of community will be revived as we succeed in devising ways to reinvolve people in solving the perplexing problems they see about them, not just in talking about them, and certainly not in petitioning government to solve them. ☞ *Richard Cornuelle*

are grouped as seven-bedroom flats sharing extremely large and comfortable living rooms and kitchens. "Almost every occupant has to share an apartment with six others," notes Munger. The idea is to give grad students (who come from 113 countries at Michigan) easier opportunities to build relationships with fellow scholars, with the expectation that this will not only be pleasant but also encourage useful informal exchange of ideas.

Munger made a similar investment in the co-location of thinkers at the Kavli Institute for Theoretical Physics at the University of California, Santa Barbara. A creation of physicist-turned-businessman Fred Kavli, who donated hundreds of millions to science philanthropy before his death in 2013, the institute brings together top physicists from around the world for professional discussion outside of any teaching or research responsibilities. "Away from day-to-day responsibilities they are in a different mental state," says director Lars Bildsten. "They're more willing to wander intellectually."

Physics is famously a field where insights can bubble up from insights in everyday life, or casual conversations with peers, and Kavli encourages this in its daily programming. However, there was no physical counterpart in the way the visitors were housed. Until 2014—when Munger pledged $65 million to build a permanent residence hall where it will be easy for visiting physicists to mingle informally after hours.

Further reading

○ Munger Residences at the University of Michigan, mungerresidences.org

○ *New York Times* report on Kavli Institute gift, dealbook.nytimes.com/2014/10/24/a-billionaires-65-million-gift-to-theoretical-physics

2012

SKILLED JOBS AND VETS, BROUGHT TOGETHER

"We need to look into this," said GE chairman Jeff Immelt in 2012. He was bothered by the elevated rates of unemployment among young men and women just leaving the U.S. military. He knew many of them had valuable technical skills. He also knew that his company and many others were finding it hard to hire skilled workers—fully 82 percent of manufacturers now say they can't find adequate employees for all of their skilled production positions. Over the next decade, it is projected that America will have 2.6 million jobs for which there will be a shortage of workers with the necessary talents.

Mixing corporate philanthropy with corporate business-interest, GE thus launched its "Get Skills to Work Initiative." The assignment was to unkink the talent pipeline so that a social problem (unemployed veterans) could be fixed at the same time as an economic problem (trained labor shortages). GE began at its aviation business in Cincinnati, and other corporations in the area were invited to join in—including Alcoa, Lockheed Martin, and Boeing, plus nearly 30 of GE's regional suppliers. The Manufacturing Institute, a nonprofit dedicated to improving U.S. factories, was brought in to connect veterans to the areas where these companies would be hiring in the near future.

A host of companies were subsequently recruited into the Get Skills to Work Coalition, which aims to take 100,000 veterans with useful technical abilities and certify them for civilian work, placing many of them immediately in jobs. Where needed skills are not already present among vets, training paths are being established between community colleges and manufacturers. Vets are being recruited to take part through social media and at a dedicated website.

Further reading

○ Get Skills to Work portal for veterans, getskillstowork.org

○ Thomas Meyer, *Serving Those Who Served* (The Philanthropy Roundtable, 2013)

2012

PAY-FOR-PERFORMANCE SOCIAL INVESTING

In 2010, a new method of solving social problems was proposed in Britain. It called for putting up philanthropic or private investment funds to create programs that could head off bad future outcomes that would carry social costs. If the interventions were successful in avoiding future problems, then some of the public money that consequently didn't have to be spent on things like law enforcement or welfare programs would be shared with the program funders. This is called "pay-for-performance" social investing (or sometimes described misleadingly as a "social-impact bond"). If proven and refined over time, this could become a way for not only donors but also for-profit investors to apply the power of capitalism to the amelioration of social problems in efficient ways.

Not long after the debut of this idea in Britain, American social entrepreneurs and philanthropists imported it to the U.S. and began much more extensive testing of the concept. In 2012, Goldman Sachs put up $10 million to offer nonprofit services to New York City juvenile delinquents exiting Rikers Island prison, aiming to avoid future lockups by offering them help in finishing their education, finding jobs, and managing their lives. Bloomberg Philanthropies provided a financial guarantee of the invested funds.

While that project was not successful, other pay-for-performance experiments are currently being set up around the U.S. These include a Utah effort, using money from United Way of Salt Lake, Goldman Sachs, and philanthropist J. B. Pritzker to reduce spending on special-ed and other remedial schooling later in life by educating children in high-quality preschools. It was the first pay-for-performance test to pay off for its investors, though there is disagreement on how successful it was because the effort failed to include a control group against whom outcomes could be compared. There are efforts in Massachusetts to get chronically homeless individuals off the street, and to reduce recidivism among young released convicts. In California, the James Irvine Foundation and REDF (see 1997 entry) joined in an effort to reduce joblessness, and another pilot was launched to try to cut the social costs of treating children with asthma by managing the problem earlier. In 2014, 15 states were in the process of testing pay-for-performance ventures in collaboration with philanthropists and corporate social investors.

Further reading

○ Recent activity, socialfinanceus.org/social-impact-financing/social-impact-bonds/history-sib-market/united-states

2012

SPEEDING SAFE SHALE-GAS PRODUCTION

In 2012, two major philanthropists—oil-and-gas pioneer George Mitchell and Wall Street entrepreneur Michael Bloomberg—announced a joint effort by their foundations to encourage safe and efficient production of natural gas via shale fracking. They proposed to head off problems through "common-sense" state rules and voluntary adoption of best practices by the industry. The two foundations put up millions of dollars for efforts to improve fracking by minimizing water concerns, reducing methane leaks, optimizing well construction, disclosing chemical usage, and reducing local impacts on roads, land, and communities.

In 2013, a related collaboration of philanthropic organizations, oil and gas companies, and environmental groups established a Center for Sustainable Shale Development. It set 15 voluntary standards for improving shale-gas production in the Appalachian region, and encourages drilling companies to earn certificates of operational excellence by meeting criteria monitored by an independent auditor. It is working with states to encourage sensible rules that will avoid environmental problems which could damage public support for hydraulic fracturing. The significance of these philanthropic assists can be seen against the fact that fracking has become one of the most consequential economic, environmental, and national-security innovations of our time—turning the U.S. into the world's largest gas producer in 2010, and the world's largest oil producer in 2013.

PROSPERITY

Further reading

○ *Washington Post* op-ed by Bloomberg and Mitchell announcing initiative, washingtonpost.com/opinions/fracking-is-too-important-to-foul-up/2012/08/23/ d320e6ee-ea0e-11e1-a80b-9f898562d010_story.html

2012

MAPPING KILLER ASTEROIDS

The B612 Foundation was founded by an ex-NASA astronaut to study ways of deflecting or destroying asteroids with the potential to be dangerous if they strike Earth. Eventually, the nonprofit reached the conclusion that it was coming at the problem from the wrong end—because no one knows the location of every space rock big enough to do damage, and neither NASA nor any other government agency had a plan to map all of the asteroids that could endanger humans. So in 2012 the foundation shifted its mission: It would partner with space-imaging leader Ball Aerospace to design and launch its own space-based infrared telescope capable of scanning the solar system and identifying all objects whose size and orbit made them threats. Once that was done, deflection would be realistic.

The private spacecraft planned to do the job is priced at $450 million (about half what the government was going to spend in a failed project). Funding is being sought from hundreds of private donors, including leaders of major Silicon Valley companies, philanthropies like the William Bowes Foundation and Google.org, plus corporate matching funds from firms like Microsoft and Google. The project received a fresh boost in 2013 when a previously unknown meteor exploded over Russia and injured more than 1,200 people.

Further reading

○ Interview with director of B612 Foundation, spacenews.com/article/features/35102profile-edward-lu-chief-executive-b612-foundation

○ About the Sentinel mission, sentinelmission.org

2011

VENTURE FOR AMERICA

"Smart people should be building things," says Andrew Yang. He believes far too many graduates of top colleges currently follow the crowd into finance and law and consulting, and that more of them should become entrepreneurs, manufacturers, and businesspeople who create tangible products and jobs for others. In 2011 Yang recruited a long roster of donors to launch a

501(c)(3) inspired by Teach For America. Venture for America, like TFA, now attracts some of the nation's best and brightest young graduates, accepting only about 15 percent of applicants, training them, then plunging them into practical work and problem-solving. VFA members are sent not to cities that are already entrepreneurial hotspots but rather to locales that are struggling or have the advantage of being low-cost for new businessmakers—like Detroit, Cleveland, Baltimore, Las Vegas, New Orleans, St. Louis, and San Antonio. In addition to introducing the young to business as a creative act, and invigorating struggling communities, VFA aims to "restore the culture of achievement" in the U.S. by supporting those who take economic risks in hopes of achieving common good and future rewards.

Individual donors like Zappos CEO Tony Hsieh ($1 million pledge), Quicken Loans founder Dan Gilbert ($1.5 million), Graham Weston of Rackspace in San Antonio, and LinkedIn co-founder Reid Hoffman are supporters, as are numerous philanthropies like the PricewaterhouseCoopers Foundation, the Abell Foundation, and the Blackstone Charitable Foundation. In its first four years VFA placed 318 fellows at 150 small companies in 15 cities. Another 111 high-ranked college graduates entered the program as its class of 2015. Yang's goal is for the companies that VFA fellows are reinforcing to create 100,000 new jobs by 2025.

Further reading

○ About Venture for America, ventureforamerica.org/about

○ *Philanthropy* magazine article on Venture for America, philanthropyroundtable.org/topic/excellence_in_philanthropy/a_new_way_to_serve

2009

HELPING COMMUNITY-COLLEGE STUDENTS COMPLETE DEGREES

Since the mid-twentieth century, community colleges scattered all across

⌐ PhilAphorism

The world is moving so fast these days that the one who says it can't be done is generally interrupted by someone doing it.

⌐ *Harry Fosdick*

America have filled an important role in training workers to fill positions in their regional economies (see also the 1960 entry later in this section). In the twenty-first century, philanthropic support for community colleges continues to be strong.

For instance, the Gates Foundation made a $17 million grant in 2009 to strengthen remedial programs and student retention at 15 community colleges. In 2010, the foundation unveiled a $35 million investment to increase course-completion and graduation rates. "These are the schools that enroll the majority of low-income students," said Melinda Gates in announcing the effort. "Community colleges have untapped potential for getting students the credentials they need to earn a living wage." The Gates Foundation has allotted nearly half a billion dollars for spending in this area during the next two decades.

Bill & Melinda Gates have many philanthropic colleagues in this work. The Bernard Osher Foundation, for example, announced a $70 million grant in 2008 to bolster community colleges in California. Noting that only about half of the students who enroll in two-year colleges today end up with a degree, the Lumina Foundation made a $75 million commitment, to which the Gates Foundation and other donors made supplemental pledges, to launch a ten-year effort to improve the community-college experience. They partnered with dozens of colleges to research students' reasons for dropping out, reduce that rate, and strengthen the institutions. Since 2011 there has been a national prize, funded by the Lumina, Joyce, and Kresge foundations and Bank of America, administered by the Aspen Institute, which awards $1 million every second year to community colleges that have done the most to increase learning, graduation rates, and the hiring and earning levels of their students.

Further reading

○ Summary reporting on Gates funding, diverseeducation.com/article/59973

2008

SCIENCE PRIZES AND RESEARCH INSTITUTES

Fred Kavli intimately understood how scientific understanding could create economic bounty—he had earned hundreds of millions of dollars applying his knowledge of physics to make precision sensors for manufacturers. So when he established the Kavli Foundation in 2000 he used it to fund theoretical physics, astrophysics, nanoscience, and neuroscience at 17 research institutes around the world, seeding each with at least $8 million, which he asked each recipient to match. "It is unrestricted funds, which is indispensable in discovery science," noted the foundation president. In 2008 Kavli added prizes to his science philanthropy. Every other year, three prizes are awarded, each carrying a million-dollar purse. In total, the Kavli Foundation has now funneled a quarter of a billion dollars into basic scientific investigations, confident that this will yield long-term benefits as rich as those that accrued to physicist-turned-businessman Fred Kavli himself.

Further reading

○ About the Kavli Prize, kavlifoundation.org/about-kavli-prize

○ *New York Times* obituary for Fred Kavli, nytimes.com/2013/11/25/us/fred-kavli-benefactor-of-science-prizes-dies-at-86.html?_r=0

2007

STRENGTHENING CHARACTER THROUGH SPORTS

David Weekley was involved in character-building activities as a youth through Boy Scouts and church groups. After his success as a major home builder he decided to devote 50 percent of his income and his time to philanthropy, and character development was a key concern. It "is every bit as critical as economic aid or health care or education reform," he told *Philanthropy*. Weekley was a longtime funder of Scouting, which reaches 20 or 25 percent of young people; sports, however, reaches around 75 percent. "I'm not personally a sports enthusiast but the country has become more focused athletically and more and more kids are involved," said Weekley. So he set out looking for a charitable partner who could help children and their coaches build wholesome and productive values through athletics.

Weekley discovered there was no national organization doing this well, but his gaze eventually settled on a small northern California group called the Positive Coaching Alliance. Founded in 1998 and operating at just a handful of regional locations when Weekley discovered it, PCA trains parents in positive sportsmanship, teaches coaches how to offer constructive life lessons to their charges, and helps athletes become better teammates and citizens. Weekley offered the group grants to expand first to his hometown of Houston, and then to the rest of Texas, Boston, Chicago, and dozens of other cities. Believing that decentralized leadership and local boards "are critical" to grassroots success, Weekley worked with the group's leaders to develop a model that would allow many other cities to start their own chapters. PCA also built strong links to existing groups like Little League baseball, Pop Warner football, and the Amateur Athletic Union.

Within a few years, 5 million young athletes had been touched by the PCA, and numerous other philanthropists had gotten involved, including the S. D. Bechtel Jr. Foundation, which gave the group a $2 million grant in 2012. "There's no reason that in 10-15 years PCA can't become like the Boy Scouts or

PROSPERITY

YMCA in every major city in the country," says Weekley. "The need for character development, given the breakdown of the family and other challenges we face in our society, is not going away, and PCA has the potential to have a major impact."

Further reading

∘ PCA interview with David Weekley, positivecoach.org/our-story/our-supporters/
  david-weekley

CLEARING MINEFIELDS FOR PEANUTS

Even in the hungriest countries, fear of landmines left behind after nasty guerrilla conflicts causes much valuable farmland to be abandoned, just because the acreage cannot be cleared of hidden dangers in a cost-effective manner. National governments and international bureaus have tried. They hire men in bomb-suits to painstakingly sweep land with handheld metal detectors. Each metallic strike must be carefully dug up to find out if it's a booby trap or a bobby pin. A civil servant can clear about a bedroom-size plot per day using that method. Meanwhile buried explosives continue to maim innocent people every year.

As a boy, Bart Weetjens kept rats as pets. As an adult, he became interested in their powerful scent-detection abilities, and how that might be put to good use for humanity. He founded a charity that trains rats to detect TNT and raises money to deploy the animals to minefields across the globe. His so-called Hero Rats don't false-alert on bobby pins, shell casings, or empty sardine cans—they zero in solely on high explosives. As a result, a rat and its handler can clear 20 bedroom-size plots of land per day rather than just one. And ordinary people can go to websites like GlobalGiving.org to "adopt" a Hero Rat for an $84 annual donation. (The rats get paid in bananas and peanuts.)

The rats have also been trained to detect tuberculosis in human sputum by scent. This is much faster, cheaper, and (in developing nations) more accurate than traditional microscope diagnoses. This may open new avenues for finding and eliminating tuberculosis in poor countries, where it kills 1.7 million people every year.

Further reading

∘ Skoll Foundation social entrepreneur award citation, skollfoundation.org/entrepreneur/
  bart-weetjens

HELPING PEOPLE WHO ARE READY TO CHANGE

Real-estate developer Bill Butler, who describes philanthropy as "central to my purpose in life," spearheaded establishment of the Life Learning Center in 2006. It has gone on to become one of the most successful nonprofits in the country at helping struggling people heal and get jobs so they can support themselves in independence and dignity. Forty percent of the people who come to the center have a criminal record. Many have had family or substance-abuse problems. Fifteen percent dropped out of high school, 35 percent earned a high-school diploma or GED, 25 percent have some college coursework, and 25 percent actually hold some college degree (showing that education alone does not guarantee life success). The center has a highly structured curriculum that runs for 16 weeks. They want to deal with the whole person—intellectually, emotionally, physically, and spiritually—and nurture a commitment to long-term change. The training culminates with an employment-readiness component.

"The Life Learning Center is for the person who is ready to do something drastically different in all aspects of life," says Butler. "The attitude we look for is 'I don't just need food or transitional housing. I need to change what I'm doing so that everything improves.' The center strengthens individuals so they are ready for real and lasting change, and we only admit candidates who are willing and able to commit. One must rise above a state of mind, or addiction, or illness that prevents success. Programs are most effective where there is both an economic platform and a love-centered environment that provides support."

The Life Learning Center does not accept government dollars, but it is generously supported by Butler and a range of philanthropists and businesses in northern Kentucky and southwest Ohio. In 2014, the group opened a new $3.2 million facility with expanded classrooms, computer labs, partner-agency offices, a child-care center, a 221-seat lecture hall, a fitness center, a cafeteria, a commercial training kitchen, a credit union, room for future on-site medical services, and more. The LLC's growth and success with difficult populations have made it a national model. Sixty-two percent of its candidates are employed by the time they finish their program. One-on-one life coaching continues beyond completion of the curriculum, and people can stop back in at any point, especially if they hit a stumbling block in their work or personal life.

Further reading

○ Interview with founder, philanthropyroundtable.org/topic/economic_opportunity/when_they_want_to_start_over

○ Life Learning Center, nkyllc.org

PROSPERITY

CREATING AN ECOSYSTEM OF AID
FOR SERVICEMEMBERS

Three years into the Iraq and Afghanistan wars, hedge-fund co-founder David Gelbaum walked into the California Community Foundation, put $105 million into a fund, and asked that it be funneled to troops and their families in ways that would help them cope with family separations, recover from injuries incurred in battle, or make successful transitions into civilian life after their military service. He later added another $138 million, and a few stipulations: He wanted all the money sent out the door within three years. He wanted it to go to direct service, not studies or institution-building. And he wanted to do it all anonymously (which he managed to achieve for several years).

$243 million is a lot of money to spend that quickly, particularly in veterans philanthropy, which at that point was a new and very lightly trafficked field. Gelbaum and his staff began by allying themselves with the blue-chip player in this arena—the foundation run by the Fisher family, which blazed the trail for veterans giving, starting two decades previous (see 1990 entry on our list of achievements in Medical philanthropy). Gelbaum's fund gave $43 million to various projects launched by the Fishers. This led to three large accomplishments: It provided lead funding for the Center for the Intrepid, a groundbreaking rehabilitation center in San Antonio for military amputees and burn victims. It helped create the National Intrepid Center of Excellence, which researches, diagnoses, and treats traumatic stress and brain injuries. And it paid for the construction of eight new Fisher Houses (home-like no-cost housing for family members who are caring for injured servicemembers as they recover at medical centers).

The rest of Gelbaum's money was distributed in scores of smaller grants. Some went to existing local organizations that offer veterans job training,

⌁ PhilAphorism

I can testify that it is nearly always easier to make $1,000,000 honestly than to dispose of it wisely. ⌕ *Julius Rosenwald*

counseling, and economic assistance. Some went to new ventures like the educational TV programs made by the creators of "Sesame Street" to help children adjust to the deployment of their military parents. One gift built up a group called TAPS (Tragedy Assistance for Survivors) that provides emotional support to grieving family members after a wartime loss.

Some of the money was also redistributed to other community foundations around the country serving areas with lots of military families. Foundations in Texas and Florida, for instance, each received $45 million to distribute for pressing war-related needs in their home regions. The Dallas Foundation used one allocation to set up some well-used mental-health counseling for families living around Fort Hood.

David Gelbaum's gift was the largest single philanthropic measure benefiting those who served in the U.S. military after the 9/11 attacks. It opened entirely new doors to a population in need. As a result there is now a whole ecosystem of charities serving members of the military, their families, and veterans.

Further reading

○ Thomas Meyer, *Serving Those Who Served* (The Philanthropy Roundtable, 2013)

2006

SANFORD UNDERGROUND RESEARCH FACILITY

Astronomical observations demonstrate that as much as a quarter of the universe is made up of some material which is invisible to conventional measurements. The gravitational effects of this invisible matter can be seen, even though the material itself cannot currently be detected. Until someone figures out how to observe, measure, and categorize what is currently referred to as dark matter, many of today's most pressing uncertainties in physics and cosmology will remain unexplained.

Given the importance of this quest, it is interesting to note that today's best research on dark matter is being carried out only because of the intervention of a private donor. The Homestake gold mine in South Dakota, which extends nearly a mile underground, is a perfect location for a dark-matter detector, because the overlaying rock shelters any instruments placed in the mine from false signals created by the cosmic radiation that surrounds us on the surface of the Earth. After the mine closed in 2003, various government agencies hoped to create a permanent physics lab in the underground site, but failed to find funding. In swooped philanthropist Denny Sanford, a Dakotan who made his fortune in

PROSPERITY

banking and has given away more than a billion dollars. He put up $70 million to secure the site, pump water out of the shafts, and create the Sanford Underground Research Facility. This sparked the state of South Dakota to commit additional funds, and the U.S. Department of Energy to underwrite the cost of science experiments on the premises.

The first such experiment, known as the Large Underground Xenon detector, went into operation in 2013 and soon excited physicists by ruling out one favored theory on the nature of dark matter. The sensitivity of the detector was then increased for additional runs. A second important experiment under way at Sanford, called the Majorana Demonstrator, is searching to explain differences between matter and anti-matter, which could rewrite today's standard theory of physics. In 2014 Congress funded a third major particle-physics experiment to be conducted in the Sanford Lab. It will involve beaming a string of neutrinos right through the earth from Illinois to South Dakota to test the behavior of the particles and clear up some mysteries fundamental to the origins of the universe.

Further reading

○ About the Sanford Underground Research Facility, sanfordlab.org/about/deep-science-frontier-physics

2005

NUTRITION RESEARCH
HUB IN NORTH CAROLINA

A site near the geographic center of North Carolina that housed one of the world's largest textile mills until it went bankrupt in 2003 has since had $781 million of donated money poured into it by David Murdock. Murdock made a fortune in real estate and then bought Dole Foods, the world's largest producer of fruits and vegetables. Having both a professional stake and a deep personal fascination in nutrition, Murdock set up his own research institute to study issues at the intersection of food, agriculture, and human health. Then he invited eight North Carolina universities and numerous private corporations with nutritional interests to establish their own labs on the 350-acre campus. The curative and prophylactic effects of plant foods and healthy diets are a particular focus. Approximately 600 scientific investigators and support staff currently work on the campus, and Murdock has funded dozens of specific studies.

Further reading

○ Murdock Research Institute, dhmri.org/about-dhmri

WORLD'S MOST POWERFUL TELESCOPE

The most influential tool in astronomy and astrophysics over the last generation has been the Hubble Space Telescope. In 2014, construction began on a new instrument, to be located atop Mauna Kea in Hawaii, that will provide images 12 times sharper than Hubble's. The Thirty Meter Telescope will have nine times the light-collecting power of the largest existing telescopes, and its new "adaptive optics"—making constant minute mirror adjustments to counteract turbulence in the earth's atmosphere—will allow it to create images as sharp as those taken in space where there is no atmosphere to deflect incoming light. The potent instrument will initially be used to understand the formation of stars and planets and the evolution of galaxies, and is expected to have revolutionary effects on cosmology and fundamental physics.

The Thirty Meter Telescope is likely to work often in tandem with the James Webb Space Telescope—the successor to Hubble now being built by NASA for launch sometime between 2018 and 2020. The Webb telescope may locate targets that will then be studied in detail by the powerful spectrometers in the TMT. Interestingly, the Webb is a government-run, publicly funded project that currently is nine years late, with an expense overrun of four times the original plan, yielding a total cost of $9 billion. Meanwhile the TMT is a collaboration among U.S. universities and overseas science organizations, funded by private philanthropy, and its total cost will be about $1.2 billion by the time it opens its "eye" eight years from the construction launch.

The trailblazing funder enabling the Thirty Meter Telescope is the Gordon and Betty Moore Foundation. Endowed by the co-founder of Intel Corporation, the Moore Foundation has poured approximately $850 million into basic scientific research in recent years, in areas ranging from marine biology to physics to plant science. The Moores provided a seminal early investment of $50 million in 2003 to design the Thirty Meter Telescope, then pledged an additional $200 million in 2007 to complete the planning and initiate construction. By the end of 2013, Moore's full quarter-billion dollar pledge had been delivered to project leaders at the California Institute of Technology and the University of California. Both universities launched campaigns to raise matching millions from other private donors, thus powering this landmark project almost entirely with philanthropic money.

There will never be as much instrument time on large telescopes as astronomers would like for conducting experiments, so a similar project—

PROSPERITY

the Giant Magellan Telescope backed by a different group of universities and philanthropists—has been nearly as avidly supported. Oil and gas pioneer George Mitchell, father of the "fracking" process and a major science donor (see 2002 entry), gave $35 million to the Magellan project before his death in 2013. His donations through Texas A&M University starting in 2004 not only launched the telescope from concept to construction project, but also spurred major financial and scientific partners like the University of Texas at Austin, Harvard, and the University of Arizona to sign on as well.

In 2014, the University of Arizona announced that entrepreneur Richard Caris had made a $20 million donation to Magellan. That same year, site preparation began. Initial operation of the telescope, which will have a lens 82 feet across, is expected in 2020.

Further reading

○ Thirty Meter Telescope consortium home, tmt.org

○ Program archive at the Gordon and Betty Moore Foundation, moore.org/programs/
science/thirty-meter-telescope

○ Giant Magellan Telescope at the Mitchell Foundation, cgmf.org/p/magellan-telescope.html

2002

BUILDING BASIC SCIENCE

Texan George Mitchell spent his work days peering downward, deep into the earth, where he was one of the most successful men of his generation at finding valuable oil and gas, especially by the method of hydraulic fracturing that he largely invented. As a philanthropist, though, he often gazed at the heavens, where he loved to support astronomy and other basic sciences. Mitchell had considered becoming a physicist before majoring in petroleum engineering, and by the time he passed away in 2013 he had donated an estimated $360 million to major scientific efforts—like construction of the Giant Magellan Telescope (see 2003 item), and his 2002 creation of a "fundamental physics and astronomy" program at Texas A&M University. The $100 million he gave to A&M also endowed 13 academic chairs—several in physics, others in astronomy, three in marine sciences. He built the campus physics building and other structures, and endowed fellowships, lectures, and meetings related to astronomy and physics. Mitchell's giving during the last decade of his life has been described as one of the greatest philanthropic campaigns in support of basic science ever.

Further reading

○ Mitchell Foundation physics and astronomy projects, cgmf.org/p/physics.html

○ *Houston Chronicle* story, houstonchronicle.com/news/nation-world/article/Money-made-
in-oil-Mitchell-dreamed-of-the-stars-4704432.php

=== 2001 ===

BATTLING POVERTY VIA FAMILY SUPPORT AND ECONOMIC INCENTIVES

Mauricio Miller's bio states that more than two decades of working in social services left him "disenchanted with the social sector's approach to fighting poverty" and wanting to try something new—encouraging low-income households to rely on families and neighbors and good financial habits to "create security…rather than assuring jobs and stability to the social workers and government bureaucrats who seek to help them."

The nonprofit Miller set up, the Family Independence Initiative, did detailed research on the successes of immigrants who thrived after arriving very poor. It found they used mutual family support and disciplined saving to move into the middle class. Miller's group then created models to help other poor people learn from these successes. Instead of dispatching professionals from the helping occupations to educate struggling individuals, the Family Independence Initiative encourages the poor to connect themselves to relatives and neighbors and establish new daily disciplines learned from them, including saving money and focusing on stronger family bonds.

The initiative provides a series of small cash incentive awards to reinforce constructive behavior—making payments to families of several hundred dollars when they achieve goals like raising a child's grades, completing a skills-training class, or saving money. Over two years, families following this course increased their savings by 240 percent on average, increased their earnings by 23 percent, and created or expanded 33 percent more small businesses. Almost 80 percent of children reported an improvement in grades, and families reduced their dependence on government subsidies, improved their health, and otherwise made progress. The success of this unusual anti-poverty model has attracted several million dollars of philanthropic support in recent years from donors like the Boston, Kresge, Levi Strauss, MacArthur, and Eos foundations.

Further reading

○ 2013 news report on the FII, america.aljazeera.com/articles/2013/10/1/a-springboard-outofpoverty.html

○ *Chronicle of Philanthropy* story, philanthropy.com/article/A-Veteran-Antipoverty-Activist/65101

PROSPERITY

LIFTING RISKY CASES
INTO THE WORK FORCE

Gerald Chertavian co-founded one of England's fastest-growing companies while living there in the early 1990s, then cashed out in 1999 at age 34 to devote the rest of his career to social entrepreneurship. He'd long participated in Big Brothers Big Sisters, and the troubles faced by his original Little Brother in a bad New York City neighborhood fed his concern about the human talent going to waste among poor children. In 2000 Chertavian devoted $500,000 to founding Year Up, his effort to help low-income, urban young adults. Enrollees must be ages 18-24 with a high-school diploma or GED, and "at-risk but not high-risk"—that is, not use drugs or have committed violent crime. Many are Spanish-speaking; their average high-school GPA is 1.9 and their average SAT is 780. The one-year program combines classroom training, college credit, and "behavior management."

After two interviews and signing of an agreement that includes immediate expulsion for drug use and a lower stipend for being even one minute late to class, those accepted receive six months of training (mostly for computer-related jobs) before beginning a six-month internship at a corporate partner. Their "high-expectation, high-support" training also addresses social and emotional development, time management, personal finance, writing skills, conflict resolution, and even current affairs, so they will be at home in a corporate environment. They receive staff advisement on personal as well as professional issues, and are assigned a mentor from the business community. Students receive a weekly stipend of roughly $200, paid by the corporate partners, who also help Year Up itself defray roughly $2,000 out of the $11,000 annual cost per student.

In 2007 the philanthropic arm of Microsoft granted Year Up a multiyear $10 million grant that helped spread the program across the country. Current supporters of the program include more than 80 foundations, companies, and individual donors.

While government-funded job-training programs typically see no more than 50 to 55 percent of their graduates continuing in work after graduation, 84 percent of Year Up alumni are either working or attending college full time four months after graduation. Starting salaries average $30,000 per year, and a 2011 outside study found this was 30 percent more than a control group earned. "These are the most exciting evaluation results we've seen in youth employment in 20 or 30 years," the study's author remarked, "the first to show a really substantial earnings gain."

By 2014, Year Up was serving over 2,000 students at 11 sites nationwide, and 91 percent of its 250-plus corporate and government partners say they would recommend the program. Chertavian launched a new program, the Professional Training Corps, modeled after college ROTC, in 2011. Based at community colleges, PTC helps at-risk young adults find jobs to support themselves while earning their associate's degree. Chertavian aims to expand PTC to serve 100,000 students per year.

Further reading

○ Gerald Chertavian, *A Year Up* (Viking, 2012)

○ Site visit, philanthropyroundtable.org/topic/economic_opportunity/year_up_in_boston

2000

SENDING DIAMONDS IN THE ROUGH TO COLLEGE

Bill Daniels completed a couple years of junior college before serving as a fighter pilot in World War II, but never returned to campus or received a degree. He subsequently worked in the insurance business, as a roughneck in oil fields, as a short-order cook, and as a bellhop. He recognized business potential when he saw early cable-TV systems in the West, and he eventually built a large cable empire. But he understood that some people bloom late, and he never lost his sympathy for underdogs. So when he died, Daniels left $1.1 billion to establish a charitable fund to help residents of the Western states where he spent most of his life, with a special mandate to provide "second chances" to people in need.

◈ PhilAphorism

Different philanthropists have different views about what makes society better off. One of the things that I think is wonderful about the non-accountability of philanthropy is that it allows for multiple versions of what makes society better off. The U.S. is unique in supporting those multiple versions of the good.

☞ *Paul Brest*

PROSPERITY

The largest part of his money is dedicated to offering college scholarships to "diamonds in the rough"—young people who show grit and determination despite having been "knocked down a time or two." In the population targeted by the Daniels Fund, only about a fifth of young people go to college. Many of the applicants lack strong academic credentials, but a process of recommendations and interviews allows the fund to identify a pool who are hungry for opportunity, able to lead, and willing to work. The program covers not only tuition, room, and board but also transportation, health care, and a computer. Students are required to hold a paying job for a few hours each week during the academic year, and they participate in special workshops on ethics, civics, business principles, leadership, critical thinking, patriotism, etiquette, and other topics.

In 2014, 244 Daniels Scholars were selected from four Western states. This brought the cumulative total of students who have been awarded scholarships to 3,006. More recently, the Daniels Fund launched its "Boundless Opportunity" scholarships, targeted at adults heading to college, GED recipients, youths coming out of foster care or reformatories, returning military, and other nontraditional populations.

The success of the Daniels Scholarship Program has inspired other efforts to assist students who might otherwise be overlooked. Fellow Denver residents Tim and Bernie Marquez donated $50 million in 2007 (which other donors supplemented with an additional $28 million of private giving) to fuel the Denver Scholarship Foundation. Echoing Bill Daniels, Tim Marquez explains that "we look for the hidden jewels, kids who maybe haven't worked so hard because they didn't think they could go to college, or who felt they had no reason to try. They are not in the top 10-15 percent of their class, but have natural abilities." The Marquezes will support not only college attendance but also trade schools, community college classes, and studies to become accredited as an auto mechanic, child-care provider, or other trained worker. As Bernie Marquez puts it, "Whatever students choose to do beyond high school to further their education, we will help them do that."

Further reading

○ Overview of Daniels Scholarship Program, danielsfund.org/Scholarships/Scholars/Index. asp#hide1

○ *Philanthropy* magazine article on Denver Scholarship Program, philanthropyroundtable. org/topic/excellence_in_philanthropy/donating_a_motive_to_strive

REINFORCING VOCATIONAL EDUCATION

Former Intel co-founder Andrew Grove wanted to overturn the common

assumption among educators, parents, and students that technical education is for less intelligent people. So he funded vocational-training scholarships at community colleges and nonprofit training groups. The value of the scholarships ranges from $500 to $5,000 per year, and "the people for whom we provide support are not those who intend to transfer to four-year universities," as Grove puts it. These recipients intend to go right to work in a practical career.

Grove's aim, in addition to helping individuals, was to raise the American estimate of vocational education to the level of respect it receives in European countries. In Germany there is a tradition of skilled apprenticeships that serve as rungs on the ladder into the middle class, and Grove believes the U.S. could benefit from similar mechanisms. He believes philanthropy must play a significant role in this, because government and market forces are not excelling at the task.

Over two decades, Grove distributed more than 100 scholarships per year. Then in 2005 he took more concentrated action to bolster technical education, announcing a $26 million donation to the City College, New York City's low-cost institution of higher ed, to invigorate its school of engineering. This gift also provided for successive cohorts of Grove Scholars.

Further reading

○ Interview with Andy Grove, *Philanthropy*, philanthropyroundtable.org/topic/ entrepreneurship/interview_with_andrew_grove

○ Stanford report, csi.gsb.stanford.edu/grove-scholars-program-putting-rungs-back-on-the_ladder

1997

JOBS FOR PEOPLE WITH IMPEDIMENTS

George Roberts was co-founder of the pioneering private-equity firm Kohlberg Kravis Roberts & Co., and when he entered philanthropy he brought the mindset of an investor expecting returns, only this time measured in lives changed rather than dollars accumulated. His most inventive work has been in battling poverty, and his focus there has been consistent from the beginning: work (rather than social work) is the best anti-poverty strategy.

Today it is not unusual for successful business people to orient their philanthropy toward market-based solutions to social problems, but Roberts was a pioneer of such efforts. When he gave a million dollars to a nonprofit so it could set up a cabinetmaking shop where minorities could be trained, he insisted the organization take out a bank loan to cover the other half of the project's costs—because their commitment to the bank would keep them focused on running the operation like a business rather than a giveaway.

In 1997, after several years of supporting nonprofits that tried to help homeless people get jobs, Roberts created REDF (the Roberts Enterprise Development Fund), a so-called venture philanthropy that supports groups with "equity-like grants and business assistance" so they can start sheltered businesses where "people facing the greatest barriers to work"—convicts, school dropouts, the mentally ill, alcoholics, etc. who would otherwise be living on government assistance or charity—can get a foot on the employment ladder. The groups REDF funds are expected to be business-like in their work, and to find revenue streams that can be reinvested into training and services for their employees.

Here are examples of some social enterprises that have recently been in REDF's portfolio:

∘ Chrysalis runs a maintenance and property-management service for buildings in the Skid Row section of Los Angeles, as well as street-cleaning crews who contract with merchants in the Fashion District.
∘ Community Housing Partnership has a growing business providing lobby services to landlords in San Francisco.
∘ The social enterprise 360 Solutions provides pest-control in southern California towns.
∘ The Center for Employment Opportunities has maintenance contracts that keep its workers busy in several cities.

In 2004, REDF converted itself from a family foundation into an independent nonprofit so other donors could participate and expand its footprint and methods. The Roberts Foundation continues to be its biggest contributor with millions in annual contributions, but donors like the Kellogg and Weingart foundations now also fund the group.

From 1997 to 2015, REDF has supported 50 social enterprises that have employed more than 8,700 people with little previous success in the workforce. These individuals earned more than $140 million, and three quarters still held their jobs two years after starting. REDF's goal is to expand enough to help create an additional 2,500 jobs in the near future.

Further reading

∘ List of social enterprises currently and previously supported by REDF, redf.org/what-we-do/investF

1997

VIOLENCE-FREE ZONES

In the 1980s, Sister Falakah Fattah and her husband, David, used the House of Umoja, a neighborhood group they founded, to help Philadelphia's gangs negotiate truces and reduce violence. Robert Woodson of the Center for Neighborhood Enterprise (CNE), an "intermediary" that helps local nonprofits, documented the principles involved and prepared manuals, training programs, and other resources that could be used to set up similar "violence-free zones" in other strife-torn neighborhoods. The key to the system is to find young adults who grew up locally and overcame the same challenges that still face students in troubled neighborhoods. CNE puts these "youth advisers" through background checks (no abuse or sexual crimes) and drug, alcohol, and health testing, then trains them in identifying, mediating, and solving various types of conflicts. Once trained, the advisers are hired by local nonprofits and spend their days at schools focusing on the most troublesome students. The same students who lead disruption can, with coaching by advisers they respect, learn to turn their leadership skills in more productive directions.

In 1997, CNE and local sponsor the Alliance of Concerned Men, along with advisers they trained, negotiated a peace agreement in Washington, D.C., between two warring groups at the Benning Terrace public-housing development, where dozens of youths had been killed. The murders ended completely. Other locales where violence-free zones have been funded by private donors like the Bradley and Marcus Foundations and public agencies include Milwaukee, Atlanta, Baltimore, Dallas, Richmond, and Prince George's County in Maryland. Tracking studies done at Baylor University and elsewhere have found clear drops in attacks, increases in school attendance, and other positive effects from these interventions.

Further reading

○ Description at the Center for Neighborhood Enterprise, cneonline.org/reducing-youth-violence-the-violence-free-zone

○ Manhattan Institute Social Entrepreneurship Award, 2008, manhattan-institute.org/pdf/SE2008.pdf

○ 2010 Baylor Case study of Milwaukee program, baylorisr.org/wp-content/uploads/case_milwaukee_revised.pdf

1997

FINDING TECHNIQUES THAT STRENGTHEN FAMILIES

A group of Chattanooga, Tennessee, businessmen led by Hugh Maclellan, the chairman of his family's foundation, sat down in 1997 to confront the hard facts about collapsing families in their city, and the resulting multigenerational poverty. Their city had a divorce rate 50 percent higher than the already elevated national average, and the fifth highest unwed birth rate among U.S. cities. With funding from Maclellan and other local groups and individuals they launched an effort called First Things First to link religious congregations, private social-service groups, and public agencies to help regional residents build stronger marriages and be good parents. The organization worked with churches to widen premarital preparation. It launched parenting classes for fathers and mothers. It created media campaigns to publicize the advantages of family intactness for children and adults. It went into city schools, and it set up "lunch-and-learn" seminars inside workplaces.

First Things First trained mental-health professionals on how to help marriages in danger of divorce. It partnered with hospitals to provide Boot Camp for New Dads, and helped programs like Early Head Start incorporate fathering material into their curricula. It assisted the county divorce court in a divorce mediation project—couples with minor children must now take a class where they learn about the effects of divorce on children and then develop a post-divorce parenting plan. Judges find that these two requirements often dissuade couples from divorcing at all, and that those who do are now far less likely to revisit the courts over custody and child support.

Within nine years the locality had seen a 28 percent drop in divorce filings. Teen out-of-wedlock pregnancies decreased 23 percent. These rates have since fallen further.

Sometimes informed and inspired by the success of First Things First and sometimes acting on their own, numerous other cities and funders launched similar efforts in other places. From Families Northwest in Washington and Oregon, to Healthy Marriages Grand Rapids, to special efforts targeting black families in Baltimore, new initiatives in areas like marriage preparation, pre-divorce intervention, parenting education, and fatherhood reinforcement have sprung up regionally and nationally. Major funders have included the WinShape Foundation (funded by the Cathy family), Terry and Mary Kohler (who have given more than $5 million in this area), the Annie E. Casey Foundation, the DeVos family, the Johnson Foundation, and others. A National Healthy Marriage Resource Center has arisen to coordinate efforts by such groups.

Further reading

○ William Doherty, *Reviving Marriage in America* (The Philanthropy Roundtable, 2007)

○ *Philanthropy* magazine interview with Terry and Mary Kohler, philanthropyroundtable. org/topic/excellence_in_philanthropy/interview_with_terry_and_mary_kohler

○ National Healthy Marriage Resource Center, healthymarriageinfo.org/about/index.aspx

LAUNCH OF NON-GOVERNMENTAL
SPACE TRANSPORT

Until recently, anyone hoping to slip the surly bonds of Earth needed to talk to a federal bureaucrat; there was no such thing as a private or nonprofit space effort. That began to change in 1996, when a group of donors led by entrepreneur Peter Diamandis announced they had formed the X Prize Foundation to reward the first non-governmental team that could successfully send a three-passenger vehicle at least 100 kilometers into space twice within two weeks. The prize money was set at $10 million thanks to gifts from the Ansari family. The inspiration for the effort was the Orteig Prize—a $25,000 bounty offered in 1919 by a French hotel owner to the first aviator who could fly nonstop between Paris and New York City. Nine teams spent several hundred thousand dollars hoping to win the Orteig Prize, which was eventually claimed by Charles Lindbergh. (See 1919 entry.)

The X Prize had a similar effect. More than two dozen teams invested over $100 million in pursuit of the reward (and the companies created for the competition later received more than a billion dollars in additional private investment). A group bankrolled by philanthropist and Microsoft co-founder Paul Allen was first to meet the requirements in 2004. That success inspired the X Prize Foundation to subsequently offer other prizes for achievements in rocketry, 100-mile-per-gallon vehicles, techniques for cleaning up oil spills, and other causes. Currently active is a $20 million X Prize for any private team that successfully lands a rover on the moon.

The deepest benefit of the Ansari X Prize was to dramatically accelerate non-governmental work on space transport. In 2012, one of the ventures formed amidst the excitement over the Ansari X Prize—the SpaceX organization funded by entrepreneur and philanthropist Elon Musk—became the first private entity to deliver a cargo payload to the International Space Station. With NASA experiencing serious design failures, cost overruns, and bureaucratic sclerosis, the SpaceX Falcon rocket and Dragon capsule have become crucial elements in U.S. plans for spaceflight over the next generation. And many other individuals, like Amazon founder Jeff Bezos and entrepreneur Richard Branson, are also using personal wealth to subsidize creation of spacecraft that may become important in the future.

Further reading

○ Ansari X Prize, space.xprize.org/ansari-x-prize

○ SpaceX, spacex.com/about

PROSPERITY

○ *Philanthropy* magazine article on the X Prize, philanthropyroundtable.org/topic/ excellence_in_philanthropy/extraordinary_feats_of_an_x-man

1996

ADVANCING WORK
AS A CURE TO POVERTY

When Dave Phillips reached his mid-50s as managing director of a large accounting firm, he retired early and joined his wife Liane in attacking poverty in his home town of Cincinnati, Ohio. In 1996 they launched a nonprofit called Cincinnati Works, built on a carefully researched model of the most effective ways to move people from poverty into work and then self-sufficiency free of public assistance. In addition to providing its "members" with practical things like job training, child care, and transportation help, CW offers specialty services to individuals with difficult backgrounds—including behavioral counseling, legal advocacy, mentoring, chaplain services, and an anti-violence program. A study by the University of Cincinnati concluded that being a CW member reduced an individual's probability of felony indictment by almost 50 percent.

CW starts members in a required class which teaches work ethics, problem solving, personal budgeting, life values, self-confidence, employer expectations, and the techniques of applying and interviewing for jobs. "Soft skills and the overall culture of poverty is a big part of the challenge," states president Peggy Zink. Then the nonprofit offers intensive job-search and placement help. After a member lands a job, CW staff stay in touch with both the worker and the employer for at least one year to help ensure job

◁ PhilAphorism

Speeches by businessmen on social responsibility…may gain them kudos in the short run. But it helps to strengthen the already too prevalent view that the pursuit of profits is wicked.… There is one and only one social responsibility of business—to…engage in open and free competition without deception or fraud.

✒ *Milton Friedman*

retention. "One Job, One Year" and "Call Before You Quit" blare posters in the group headquarters.

The fourth step in the CW process is advancement. Once the member has held the same job for a year, staffers create a plan to improve skills, education, or behavior such that the member can increase his or her earning power, with the goal being 200 percent of the poverty level, with health benefits. Between 70 and 80 percent of Cincinnati Works members retain their job for at least a year (much better than government job-training programs) and the average hourly pay of members is two dollars higher than the state minimum wage.

In addition to helping the jobless and underemployed, Cincinnati Works has been lauded by the *Harvard Business Review* for providing employers with a valuable source of stable entry-level workers—reducing the job turnover of some companies by half. And CW's services are provided entirely free to both individuals and employers. The privately funded nonprofit relies on 106 volunteers plus donors who cover the salaries of 27 employees. The program has been studied widely and replicated in Texas, Kentucky, Indiana, Ohio, and other places.

Further reading

○ Cincinnati Works model, cincinnatiworks.org/index.php?option=com_
content&view=article&id=30&Itemid=35

○ *Harvard Business Review* assessment, hbr.org/2006/12/tapping-a-risky-labor-pool/ar/1

1994

FOSTERING COMPLEX MATH AND SCIENCE

James Simons was a mathematician before he earned billions operating a hedge fund, and since he and his wife Marilyn established their charitable foundation in 1994 their philanthropy has focused on advancing mathematics and science research. Particular interests include physics, autism, genetic puzzles, quantitative biology (see 2000 entry on our list of achievements in Medicine), cosmology, esoteric math, and math education (see 2004 entry describing Math for America on the Education achievements list). Simons raised $13 million to allow completion of a major experiment on the particle accelerator of Brookhaven Lab after budget problems threatened an early shutdown. The Simons Foundation created a popular math museum in New York City, and a world science festival. Over a several-year period, Simons has donated more than $105 million to Stony Brook University to build up its math and physics departments. His foundation has so far given more than a billion dollars to scientific causes.

PROSPERITY

Further reading
○ *New York Times* profile, nytimes.com/2014/07/08/science/a-billionaire-mathematicians-
   life-of-ferocious-curiosity.html

FINANCIAL SERVICES
FOR LOW-INCOME WORKERS

Recognizing that low-income workers in Manhattan were having trouble budgeting, saving, and staying out of debt, a former New York City school teacher raised $85,000 from donors including Atlantic Philanthropies to create the organization now known as Neighborhood Trust to provide financial services to residents in need. Most of these were immigrants, but one quarter of all American families who earn less than $25,000 per year have no bank account. These people end up relying on payday check cashers, high-interest lenders, and other unproductive channels outside the banking system. The typical client who initially came into the Neighborhood Trust program earned $18,000 per year, had less than a high-school education, and no banking relationship. He had average household debt of $14,000, poor credit scores, and was on track to spend $40,000 in his lifetime for exploitative check-cashing and credit services. Improving the financial knowledge and health of households like these helps stave off many social dysfunctions and work problems that flare up when families fall into insolvency.

The new organization began by offering financial counseling and courses teaching basic money management in Spanish and English. In 1997 a credit union was opened that quickly had thousands of account-holders at two branches—60 percent of whom had never previously had a bank account, and 75 percent of whom had never used a credit card. (Two thirds had used loan sharks, however.) The credit union also made small loans to this population to allow the establishment of businesses like livery cabs and family day-care services. As they proved themselves, clients were migrated to larger commercial banks.

In 2012, grants from the Robin Hood Foundation, the Harry and Jeanette Weinberg Foundation, and other donors helped create two new programs: The "Employer Solution" builds partnerships with companies that hire many low-income workers and embeds its services in their human resources departments so that, for instance, employees get their paychecks electronically deposited, and payroll savings becomes easy. Workers are offered no-cost meetings with financial advisers who help them prepare budgets, plan for emergencies, set goals, save money, and eliminate debt. The "Trust Card Program" is a second initiative that helps people who have run up credit-card backlogs pay these off by entering into a structured program offering personalized information, limits on household spending, and personal contracts pledging rapid pay-down of debt.

In its Upper Manhattan service area, 6,000 working families now rely on Neighborhood Trust to solve money problems and help them work their way up the economic ladder. Within months, most achieve substantial debt reductions, increased savings, and improved credit scores. Scores of donors have helped the program expand, including, in addition to Atlantic, the Robin Hood, Weinberg, and Altman foundations, the Carson Family Charitable Trust, a number of New York bank philanthropies, and many individual donors.

Further reading

○ Neighborhood Trust, neighborhoodtrust.org/our-approach

IMPROVING PUBLIC UNDERSTANDING OF TECHNOLOGY

Alfred Sloan, son of a machinist, finished an electrical engineering degree at MIT in three years, graduating as the youngest member of his class. He later presided over the rise of General Motors into the world's biggest auto manufacturer. So it is appropriate that his Alfred P. Sloan Foundation is focused on technology and science. In addition to funding for basic research and efforts to improve the teaching of science and math—areas where many other foundations are also active—Sloan has one unusual program that aims to help everyday Americans understand and appreciate technical achievements. One of its major undertakings is an effort to expand "Public Understanding of Science, Technology, & Economics." Since 1993 it has supported more than 100 top authors as they researched and wrote a large span of science books that "aim to reach a wide, lay audience." These have included works like physicist Freeman Dyson's *Disturbing the Universe*, the personal reflections of biologist Francis Crick in *What Mad Pursuit*, *Astronomer by Chance* by Bernard Lovell, fractal-geometry creator Benoit Mandelbrot's memoir, and analyses of scientific issues by writers like Jared Diamond, Kai Bird, and Richard Rhodes. In addition to supporting books, the program encourages plays, films, and radio and TV programming that open doors to wider understanding of science.

Further reading

○ Sloan's "public-understanding" program, sloan.org/major-program-areas/public-understanding-of-science-technology-economics

PROSPERITY

BEATING HOMELESSNESS IN CHICAGO

After Tom Owens retired from his successful career as an IT entrepreneur, inspiration from Mother Teresa led him to pour his energy and money into helping poor and homeless people become self-sufficient in his hometown of Chicago. He visited dozens of shelters, halfway houses, addiction groups, and job-training centers, studying what made some effective and others not. After some disappointing false starts he began to bottle lightning in 1995. He established a nonprofit named CARA that successfully mixed several services.

First comes serious assessment of each person's needs. Then those accepted into the program undergo tough-minded life-skills training—typically four to six months of all-day classes—that builds competence and confidence in individuals who often lack both. Workshop topics include vital practical skills like conflict management, relationship-building, forgiveness, and anger control. Participants are required to start each day by speaking into a microphone to their group, which fosters public-speaking skills and self-esteem. This all grows out of studies showing that employment success is founded not just on economic skills but on psychological and spiritual abilities as well. CARA uses a variety of rituals and repetition to encourage good habits, elevate constructive role models, and reinforce a culture of work and independence.

Next, the organization puts graduates into its powerful job-placement network, which connects them to dozens of area employers who have learned to trust CARA referrals and hire them in substantial numbers. The toughest cases go to work in CARA's own in-house enterprises (providing building and outdoor maintenance, for instance). Last, there is long-term follow-up that helps graduates hold onto their jobs and progress up the pay and responsibility ladder over time.

Following this system, CARA has placed into permanent employment more than 3,600 individuals who had been snarled in homelessness and other serious problems. The one-year job retention rate for CARA participants is 25 percentage points higher than the national average for entry-level jobs, despite the challenges of this particular population (for instance, the fact that 45 percent arrive with criminal records). In 2014, CARA graduates placed in permanent jobs earned $6.2 million and paid $2 million in taxes. Because they were working rather than drawing on welfare programs or being incarcerated, it is estimated that society saved $6.5 million that would otherwise have been spent managing them. And while 70 percent of the individuals who enter the program come in homeless, at 12 months, nine out of ten are in permanent housing.

Further reading

○ About CARA, thecaraprogram.org/about

○ Interview with founder Tom Owens, philanthropyroundtable.org/topic/economic_opportunity/from_homeless_to_employed

ADVANCING THE SCIENCE OF BUSINESS-BUILDING

Ewing Kauffman was a congenital entrepreneur. After two years in his first corporate job he quit in disgust, vowing he would never again work for anyone else. He started his own firm in his basement and didn't look back. He became wealthy enough to create the Ewing Marion Kauffman Foundation with a multibillion-dollar endowment, making it one of the larger grantmakers in the U.S. Its mission is "to help individuals attain economic independence by advancing educational achievement and entrepreneurial success, consistent with the aspirations of our founder."

The foundation has conducted much research to advance "the science of entrepreneurship." Its signature effort FastTrac is a practical training, networking, and mentoring program that helps men and women with ideas launch new businesses. More than 350,000 individuals have taken the course over the last two decades. In the words of former Kauffman president Carl Schramm, "every time we help an entrepreneur take the risk of starting a business, we strengthen the American economy."

Further reading

○ Foundation profile in *Philanthropy* magazine, philanthropyroundtable.org/topic/excellence_in_philanthropy/ewing_marion_kauffman_foundation

◈ PhilAphorism

My theme for philanthropy is the same approach I used with technology: to find a need and fill it.

☞ *An Wang*

FUNDING A HARLEM REBOUND

The Harlem Children's Zone is a massive effort to bring 97 square blocks of the poorest neighborhoods in northern Manhattan to a positive "tipping point." Beginning in 1989 the Edna McConnell Clark Foundation began to pour money into the expansion of pilot programs that meshed health, parenting, and early-childhood services. Its $34 million investment allowed the "zone" to quadruple in size. Another angel for the program is Stanley Druckenmiller, a hedge-fund founder and philanthropist who was a college friend of HCZ leader Geoffrey Canada. In 2006 Druckenmiller gave the program $25 million, and between 2009 and 2011 he gave twice that much more. Druckenmiller also convinced the Robin Hood Foundation, a major New York City anti-poverty crusader, to get involved in supporting the Harlem Children's Zone to the tune of multimillions of dollars over the years.

The HCZ program starts with "Baby College"—a series of classes for parents of children under age four. The organization also offers all-day pre-kindergarten, and extended-day schooling for older children is available at its Promise Academy charter schools. Health care, recreation, anti-violence programs, and other social services are also provided. And when students reach college age there are programs to help them get onto campus and stay long enough to earn a degree.

The schools and companion services are funded by a combination of large-scale philanthropy and government grants, with philanthropy providing about seven out of ten dollars during the buildup of the program. About 10,000 youth and 8,000 adults are now served by the effort, which has contributed to the transformation of Harlem from dangerous and economically languishing to one of New York's fastest rising neighborhoods. The HCZ health and social-service "wraparounds" add heavy expense to the program and get mixed reviews. The clear stars of the Harlem Children's Zone are the charter schools, which produce results—measured in test scores, graduation rates, and college-attendance levels—much superior to those achieved in other schools in Harlem.

Further reading

○ Broad assessment of HCZ, heritage.org/research/reports/2013/03/assessing-the-harlem-childrens-zone

○ Harlem Children's Zone history, hcz.org/about-us/history

HOMES FOR PHILLY'S HOMELESS

Among the ten largest cities in the U.S., the one with the highest poverty rate is Philadelphia, at 26 percent. Yet Philly has one of the lowest rates of homeless people per capita. That paradox can be explained to a considerable degree by the success of Project HOME, the Philadelphia charity that has helped get close to 9,000 people off the streets, in the process becoming one of the nation's most influential and admired organizations for battling homelessness.

The organization was launched with a $100,000 check from the Connelly Foundation, after three daughters of foundation creator John Connelly went to visit a "feisty" nun and a newly minted MBA who they had been told were planning an attack on homelessness in their mutual hometown. Sister Mary Scullion and Joan Dawson went on to build an efficient and business-like charity with 370 employees, 650 volunteers, and a reputation for getting things done. Project HOME has recently collected some of the largest donations ever made to an organization aiding the homeless: $30 million from Philadelphians John and Leigh Middleton. Singer and philanthropist Jon Bon Jovi has also made multimillion-dollar contributions to the group, helping finance the latest of its 15 residential centers, which feature 55 efficiency apartments with support services in the areas of recovery, health care, education, and employment.

Further reading

○ Project HOME programs, projecthome.org/our-work

FIGHTING POVERTY WITH DATA

In the wake of the stock market crash of 1987, a group of New York City hedge-fund savants led by Paul Tudor Jones came together to plan for what they anticipated would be a widespread economic meltdown. They created a nonprofit that would alleviate poverty in their home city using rigorous data tools. Although their gloomy expectations for the U.S. economy did not come to pass, the Robin Hood Foundation's analytical method emerged as a potent new philanthropic model—wielding cost-benefit studies, analyses of return on dollars spent, and other business techniques to improve social outcomes.

In addition to new ways of doling out money, Robin Hood pioneered new ways of collecting it from donors. Its annual gala has turned into a spectacular fundraiser, setting its latest record for single-event donations by raking in $101 million on one May 2015 evening. These successes have

PROSPERITY

allowed Robin Hood to disburse more than $2 billion of poverty-fighting aid from 1988 to 2015. The foundation claims an average social return of $15 for every dollar in grants.

In 2015, the foundation announced a new venture to make charities more business-like. Its LeaderLink program will take finance professionals looking for a second career and train them to assume management positions at nonprofits.

Further reading

○ Robin Hood Foundation, robinhood.org

1987

GUIDING POOR KIDS TO BUSINESS

Steve Mariotti owned an import-export business in New York when he was mugged by a gang of teenagers in 1981. He wondered what made young people act like that and decided to find the answer by selling his business and becoming a public-school teacher. He asked to work in "the worst schools in the worst neighborhoods," and then he asked for "the troubled kids." He believed teaching these children how to start a business would give them "a vision" that would motivate them to stay in school and learn. His first class was part of the typing department at Jane Addams Vocational High School in the South Bronx. In January 1987, the principal asked him to make it an all-day program for 16 of the most troubled students: "Try to save one student," she told him. It worked much better than that.

The following year, *New York Times* reporters were shocked by the successes of students to whom Mariotti was teaching business, like Howard Stubbs, a 17-year-old who helped his mother expand a hot-dog stand into a six-cart operation. Mariotti wasn't surprised: "The best entrepreneurs have had trouble in a structured environment." In August, he and a colleague hand-wrote fundraising appeals to the entire *Forbes* 400 list. Ray Chambers, chairman of the private-equity firm Wesray Capital, called him at school and became his first donor, providing $200,000 in seed money to establish what became the Network for Teaching Entrepreneurship. The organization received additional financial lifelines from Chambers and the JM Foundation when expansion of the operation caused cash-flow struggles. After it launched programs to train teachers, the group began to grow exponentially.

By 2015, NFTE had 11 offices serving 18 states, plus licensed operations in Europe, Asia, the Middle East, and Africa. The group has trained more than 500,000 young people in how to start and succeed in their own business. The eleventh edition of its curriculum, *Entrepreneurship: Owning Your Future,* won the 2010 Distinguished Achievement Award of the Association of Education Publishers for best high-school math curriculum. Research by scholars at Harvard, Brandeis, and the Koch Foundation shows that alumni are far more likely than control groups to have started a business, attended college, and increased their business knowledge.

Among hundreds of individuals, foundations, and companies that now support NFTE, to the tune of $18 million per year, leading recent funders have included the Diana Davis Spencer Foundation, MasterCard, Ernst & Young, and the Seedlings Foundation.

Further reading

○ Early *New York Times* story, nytimes.com/1988/03/13/nyregion/problem-youths-learn-how-to-succeed-in-business.html

○ *New York Times* story 25 years after NFTE's startup, boss.blogs.nytimes.com/2012/05/15/a-youth-entrepreneurship-program-goes-international

1985

TRAINING THE HOMELESS
TO DO FOR THEMSELVES

In the early 1980s when New York City was at an economic and social nadir, winter cold killed several homeless people. In response, donors launched the Doe Fund, named for one of the women who froze to death, known only as "Mama Doe." A single principle served as its lodestar: the homeless have "the potential to be contributing members of society."

The fund employs one simple means—work—to help the homeless, the formerly incarcerated, and other strugglers achieve self-sufficiency. Not just the money but the daily structure and sense of accomplishment that work provides can have magical effects that extend far beyond the help offered by free welfare services. The Doe Fund prepares residents of its shelters for

PROSPERITY

❧ PhilAphorism

Earlier in this century, philanthropy often flowed from the wills of dead industrialists. In recent decades, it's as likely to have come from a very alive business leader. ☞ *Michael Milken*

outside employment by first requiring that they work in its own enterprises. For instance, some prepare meals and learn cooking skills at the fund's dormitories around the city. Its most famous in-house business is a contract to clean over 150 miles of New York streets.

The in-house businesses employing the homeless yield multiple benefits: The lives of the workers become much more orderly. Neighborhoods are cleaned up. And the nonprofit gains a steady revenue stream ($25 million in 2014) to pay for its services.

Other support comes from individuals and foundations who share the nonprofit's philosophy that "work works," and that special training for ex-offenders, substance abusers, school dropouts, and those suffering from mental or physical disabilities is crucial if the "demoralizing burden" of chronic unemployment is to be overcome. The fund's "men in blue" are overwhelmingly minorities, nearly three quarters of them have a criminal record, and 85 percent have been substance abusers. Yet more than 60 percent of those who enter Doe's "Ready, Willing & Able" training program graduate into independent life and employment. A 2010 Harvard study found ex-cons who graduated from the program were 60 percent less likely to have a felony conviction three years after leaving prison.

The Doe Fund has expanded into multiple locations, programs, and businesses, with an annual budget of $48 million in 2014. One graduate, a multiple felon now pursuing a college degree, highlights the fund's guiding principle: "This was the first time that I was told what I could do for myself."

Further reading

○ Doe Fund award citation, manhattan-institute.org/pdf/SE2008.pdf

○ Harvard evaluation of "Ready, Willing & Able,'" prisonstudiesproject.org/wp-content/uploads/2011/07/RWA_evaluation.pdf

1985

HELPING IMMIGRANT FAMILIES FLOURISH

Sister Jennie Lechtenberg was a Catholic-school teacher who took a sabbatical to tutor low-achieving first- and second-graders in a poor Los Angeles barrio. Seeing that children whose parents lacked literacy skills struggled the most, she started an English class for the mothers and fathers. Two years later, in 1985, she formalized her swelling effort into the PUENTE Learning Center.

While serving on an education commission Lechtenberg met venture capitalist (and later L.A. mayor) Richard Riordan, who provided her school with a computer lab. Soon her classes for preschoolers, after-school children, and adults were bursting again. She took Riordan to see a potential building spot in the neighborhood, and he agreed to provide $2.1 million to buy it. PUENTE erected a high-tech building whose architecture aims to reflect not only the technology within but also the dignity of the people it serves—which explains why the neighborhood never allows it to be defaced with graffiti.

After the 1992 Rodney King riots, PUENTE was asked by the ARCO Foundation to set up a second campus in south central L.A. Double-wide-trailer classrooms were eventually replaced with another impressive building. English classes were offered on computers that also taught typing, providing a dual competency. Instruction in public speaking and in computer programming could also be taken.

The Annie E. Casey Foundation studied the effect of PUENTE's preschool-readiness program and kindergarten charter school and found that "all of the students who entered preschool or kindergarten speaking little or no English ended the year functionally bilingual." And 100 percent of their parents were either in adult classes or volunteering for PUENTE. Similarly, PUENTE's high-school tutorials and SAT preparation course were found to yield above-average rates of high-school graduation, and boosts in SAT scores of as much as 240 points.

PUENTE also sees its multigenerational approach as a way to strengthen families, which are weakened when parents command less English than their children or can't adequately support the family. Recently, PUENTE has responded to neighborhood needs by offering programs for unemployed and underemployed veterans. Many tens of thousands of southern California immigrants have now been eased into successful lives by the center.

Further reading

○ *Philanthropy* reporting, philanthropyroundtable.org/topic/excellence_in_philanthropy/ assimilating_the_new_american_immigrant

○ PUENTE Learning Center, Puente.org

1985

KECK OBSERVATORY

The scientific telescopes that dethroned the Rockefeller-funded Hale reflector as the largest in the world (see 1928 entry) were also paid for by a private donor. In the mid-1980s the W. M. Keck Foundation (created by oilman William Keck) invested a total of $144 million to create two telescopes with 33-foot diameters, placed on the Mauna Kea mountaintop in Hawaii. The first imaging at the Keck Observatory began in 1993. These two devices have brought many profound scientific discoveries. They have helped train a generation of scientists. And their very creation required groundbreaking

PROSPERITY

new technologies (including advances in "active optics" that constantly shift the mirror to compensate for distortions that would compromise image sharpness) that have been spun off into other industrial uses.

Further reading

○ W. M. Keck Observatory, keckobservatory.org

1984

JOB TRAINING FOR HARD CASES

Two Manhattan banker/donors disturbed by a chronic lack of employment among many inner-city residents. An East Harlem ex-convict and drug addict who got clean and then earned a master's degree from Columbia University. Put them together, and an unusual job-training program built on (very) tough love is born. It's called STRIVE, and it is highly effective among difficult populations. One third of STRIVE clients are former prisoners, about a third have no high-school diploma or GED, yet two thirds of its graduates are placed in jobs, at pay averaging 150 percent of their state minimum wage, and more than 70 percent of these stick in their new employment—all figures that shatter typical results from government job programs. Meanwhile the average cost per job placement for STRIVE is less than $2,000, while the U.S. Department of Labor's Job Corps program, which serves similar persons, costs almost *eight times* as much, even though only 20 percent of its graduates were employed after six months.

One big difference, *City Journal*'s Kay Hymowitz has noted, is that STRIVE builds "the all-important 'soft skills'"—respect, punctuality, initiative, honesty, reliability—and in an determinedly no-nonsense way. Uncooperative attitudes and excuses for failure are broken down by the STRIVE instructors, all of whom have themselves triumphed over corrosive street habits. The result of their strict demands, in-your-face intensity, and follow-up and support (graduates are monitored for at least two years after graduation and assisted as needed) is creation of a new "understanding of the manners and values of an alien mainstream work world."

STRIVE's successes have allowed it to spread to more than two dozen cities. Over 50,000 tough clients have been trained under its auspices. Since its founding, STRIVE has enjoyed philanthropic support from donors like the Clark, Abell, and Annie E. Casey foundations. The Harry & Jeanette Weinberg Foundation has been a stalwart backer from early on, and current donors include Walmart, the Blackstone Group, and the Rudin Foundation. Each chapter is mostly funded by local philanthropists.

Further reading

○ David Bass, *Clearing Obstacles to Work* (The Philanthropy Roundtable, 2015)

○ Program profile in *City Journal*, city-journal.org/html/7_1_a1.html

TURNING ADDICTS INTO WORKERS

Bob Coté was clutching a vodka bottle one night when he saw three of his drinking buddies passed out on the street with urine stains on their trousers. Standing in Denver's Skid Row, he realized he was only a step away from joining them; so he poured his bottle into the gutter and decided to spend the rest of his life helping save fellow addicts. The 6-foot-3 former Golden Gloves boxer started Step 13. His rehabilitation center applied three simple rules: 1) No drinking or drugs. The organization devotes thousands of dollars per year to testing, and requires residents to take Antabuse, a medicine that causes nausea if alcohol is consumed. 2) Get a job. Step 13 has placed thousands of residents in dozens of local businesses, as well as in its own three in-house enterprises, which include a busy car-detailing operation. 3) Your bunk is your property. Residents must pay a modest weekly amount for their stay, keep their area clean, cook their meals, do their dishes, and otherwise live up to civilized standards.

As residents progress, they move from a bunk in the basement to a room with a door, then to an upstairs studio apartment with a lock. Many shelters for homeless alcoholics and addicts ask nothing of their residents but limit their stays to prevent long-term dependence. Step 13, by contrast, expects a lot, including rent and employment, but has no time limit at all. The average stay is a year or more as residents shake off their destructive addictions. The program's veterans produce "constructive envy" in newcomers, spurring them to believe that they too can turn their lives around.

The shelter offers high-quality dental and vision care to clients who have often gotten little attention in these areas. Volunteer doctors use equipment donated by philanthropies to provide checkups and corrections. Roughly 35 percent of the men who reside at Step 13 walk away from alcohol and drugs, a significantly better success rate than local government-run shelters. (Step 13 refuses all government funding.) Moral support and spiritual counseling is a big part of the program. Coté, who died in 2013, maintained that "without the chapel, my success rate would drop in half. Even once you get a job and a home, you still need a purpose."

Colorado billionaire Philip Anschutz was one of Step 13's early backers. He walked uninvited into the shelter in its young days and wrote a check. A

PROSPERITY

decade later it was Anschutz who provided a few hundred thousand dollars to help Coté buy the shelter's property after Step 13 lost its rental lease.

Further reading

○ Profile in *The American Enterprise*, unz.org/Pub/AmEnterprise-2002oct-00020

○ Step 13 website, step13.org/index.php/en

1975

ADDICTS SUPPORT THEMSELVES IN GROUP LIVING

If any group of unfortunates would seem to need outside, professional assistance, it would be substance abusers. Yet the Oxford-House movement has produced an amazing story of self-help. In over 1,600 homes in 45 U.S. states, plus a few foreign countries, groups of recovering substance abusers support each other in sobriety.

The first house was established in Silver Spring, Maryland, in 1975 by a recovering alcoholic. The halfway house in which that man was living was about to close for financial reasons, so he and the other residents took over the lease and chose a group name to honor the Oxford Group, a religious organization that influenced the founders of Alcoholics Anonymous. The Oxford-House movement teaches three primary rules: do not use drugs or alcohol or be disruptive, run the house democratically, and pay your share of rent, utilities, and other expenses. Weekly business meetings are held so every resident knows the house's financial status, and officers (treasurer, chore coordinator) are elected on a rotating basis. Residents are encouraged to attend A.A. or N.A. meetings.

No one is ever forced to leave an Oxford House unless a majority of his peers vote to dismiss him for violating the rules. Those who leave in good standing are encouraged to become associate members and offer friendship to new members. Each house is to be self-supporting, though financially secure houses may, with the central office's approval, provide new or needy houses with a loan for up to one year. In 1988, Congress encouraged states to set up a revolving fund to grant loans for a new house's first-month rent and security deposit, to be repaid within two years, with those proceeds used to start additional houses. These funds have allowed dramatic expansion of Oxford Houses.

Researchers from DePaul University who have studied the movement over many years find the average stay is about 175 days, and recovery rates without relapse are over 80 percent. In 1989, Oxford World Services was established to help experienced residents teach others how to open and maintain houses.

Further reading

○ History, oxfordhouse.org/userfiles/file/oxford_house_history.php

○ Leonard Jason, Bradley Olson, Karen Foli, *Rescued Lives: The Oxford House Approach to Substance Abuse* (Routledge, 2008)

SETTLING A MILLION VIETNAMESE REFUGEES

After the fall of South Vietnam, two million people poured out of that country plus Laos and Cambodia, many of them taking desperate risks in fear of their lives, often leaving with nothing but their clothing. Half of those refugees have settled in the U.S. (which has historically sheltered as many displaced persons as all other countries combined). The first wave of "boat people" arrived in 1975, and the Indochina Migration and Refugee Act that was passed in 1975 relied on local voluntarism and small-scale philanthropy to make sure their resettlement was successful. It was mostly churches and some local community organizations that organized food, clothing, and apartments for families as they arrived across the U.S. Each arriving household was paired with one or more volunteer sponsor families, who helped with language and cultural navigation, guided work searches, assisted with driving lessons or procurement of a used car, and provided friendship and support. Many families and churches donated furniture and linens, and groceries for initial weeks and months. This resettlement was not only the largest refugee influx in U.S. history, but one of our most successful. Vietnamese Americans are employed, own homes, and become citizens at a rate higher than most other immigrant groups, partly thanks to the intimate person-to-person charity that was employed to welcome the new arrivals.

Further reading

○ Profile of Vietnamese immigrants, migrationpolicy.org/article/vietnamese-immigrants-united-states

MARRIAGE ENCOUNTER

In 1967, a program developed by a young Catholic priest in Spain to help married couples create a deeper and more honest relationship was presented as a weekend conference to seven couples and a few priests meeting at the University of Notre Dame. Almost immediately, the program now known as Marriage Encounter began to spread rapidly across the United States, and within quite different religious traditions. The weekends are open to all ages, and people of any (or no) faith. Alumni of the program lead most presentations, and follow-up conversations by couples are conducted privately in their own rooms.

The only cost for participants, who are housed and fed for the weekend as well as presented with ideas to discuss, is a $50-$100 registration fee. The approximately $600 per-couple cost has always been covered by donations—from groups like the New Hope Foundation, local churches, or in freewill gifts from participating couples who have been impressed by the program's value. The best testimony to the effectiveness of this effort is the fact that with scant institutional structure it has spontaneously spread throughout the U.S. and more than 90 foreign countries, and into a variant that helps engaged couples.

Further reading

○ Background on Marriage Encounter, encounter.org/about

1960

CULTIVATING
COMMUNITY COLLEGES

In 1947, as the post-WWII boom in higher education was taking off, the President's Commission on Higher Education urged the spread of community colleges to serve students of diverse abilities and interests for minimal cost. Then in 1960, the W. K. Kellogg Foundation initiated an even larger wave of expansion. Declaring community colleges and the practical occupational training they offer to be one of its top priorities, Kellogg made over $50 million in direct grants to community colleges between 1959 and 2001. In addition, the foundation worked with 12 universities—including Stanford, UC Berkeley, UCLA, Michigan, and UT Austin—to establish and fund centers to train two-year college leaders. These Kellogg Junior College Leadership Programs graduated hundreds of future deans and presidents, and became the centerpiece of Kellogg's success in this area. The '60s saw the opening of 457 community colleges across the U.S. (an increase of more than 100 percent). This allowed an enormous expansion of educational opportunity as the Baby Boomers reached college age. While less than 2 percent of college freshmen in 1920 were in two-year colleges, by the 1980s these schools served half of America's collegians.

Further reading

○ George Vaughan, *The Community College Story* (Community College Press, 2006)

○ Arthur Cohen and Florence Brawer, *The American Community College* (Jossey-Bass, 2008)

1958

SAVING TRADITIONAL CITY NEIGHBORHOODS

American cities were just beginning to fall apart in the middle of the twentieth century—a process accelerated by many of the technocratic efforts undertaken to "improve" them, like "urban renewal," public housing, rent control, freeway construction, and architectural "modernism"—when a unknown scholar named Jane Jacobs came along and shouted "Stop!" A diminutive woman with a sharp pen and a beady eye for the way human nature and the physical world really interlink, Jacobs convinced the Rockefeller Foundation to fund her research and writing on the subtle factors that make city neighborhoods safe, efficient, and enjoyable, and how easily these evolved traits can be snuffed out by social engineers. Her resulting 1961 book, *The Life and Death of Great American Cities*, became a classic that transformed views of architecture, city planning, and government administration. It helped birth a rebellion against modern design and planning, discredited the machine aesthetic, championed a return to human-scale buildings, accelerated historic preservation, and revived traditional architecture and traditional understandings of what makes a city thrive. It continues to echo loudly today in the offices of those who build and regulate cities, and American urban areas are now again growing rather than collapsing.

Further reading

○ Rockefeller and Jacobs, rockefellerfoundation.org/our-work/current-work/new-york-city/
jane-jacobs-medal

1957

SCIENCE FOR THE NATION IN TIME OF NEED

John Hertz was an immigrant to Chicago, from Slovakia, who made a good deal of money by creating transportation firms, including the car rental company bearing his name. During the Cold War he worried over the security of his adopted country and so established a foundation whose main work has been to support scientific exploration by young minds, especially in applied areas that can strengthen the U.S. economically and militarily.

From 1963 to 2015, the Hertz Foundation gave away $200 million to provide graduate education to 1,169 competitively selected fellows. In addition to $250,000 of stipend and tuition payments, the fellows gain extraordinary freedom to pursue their research ideas without funding limits or restrictions on subject matter. In return, John Hertz asked them to sign a pledge that they would "give back to the country in time of great need."

PROSPERITY

Hertz fellows have so far included two Nobel winners, a Fields Medal recipient, a National Medal of Science awardee, more than 200 company founders, the registrants of over 3,000 patents, heads of universities, and senior military leaders.

Further reading

○ 2015 Hertz Fellowship recipients, hertzfoundation.org/dx/newsevents/pressrelease. aspx?d=248

ARTIFICIAL INTELLIGENCE

In its first half-century of existence, the Rockefeller Foundation was a powerful supporter of basic research in the sciences, medicine, and technology—driving many breakthroughs that increased economic prosperity and human happiness. One nascent field where the foundation invested was machine intelligence. Rockefeller's 1955 grant to mathematics professor and cognitive scientist John McCarthy initiated a vast and valuable new area of knowledge.

The $7,500 award funded a summer research group at Dartmouth College to investigate the theory that machines could be programmed to mimic features of human intelligence. It was in his proposal to the Rockefeller Foundation that McCarthy first coined the term "artificial intelligence." The conference ended up being attended by nearly all of the early leading lights of machine learning, and would come to be regarded as the birth event of artificial intelligence.

While the group, which also included scientists from Bell Labs, Harvard, and IBM, did not create intelligent computers in the span of one summer, they definitively established a new and consequential field of research, with leading scientists adopting McCarthy's term and main concepts. McCarthy went on to found the MIT Artificial Intelligence group in 1959 and the Stanford AI Laboratory in 1962, and artificial intelligence was established as a fully fledged course of academic study.

⌐ PhilAphorism

As the furnace purifies the silver, so does charity rid wealth of its dross.

↜ William Downey

Further reading

○ History, rockefeller100.org/exhibits/show/natural_sciences/computer-science

○ 20-page proposal from John McCarthy to Rockefeller Foundation, rockefeller100.org/items/show/3807

1952

HIGHWAY SAFETY BREAKTHROUGH

John Dorr was an industrial chemist whose inventiveness allowed him to build a successful company, and then a charitable foundation which he eventually focused on practical solutions to everyday problems. One of his concerns was that when visibility became poor due to weather, and drivers were forced to hug the center stripe to make sure they stayed on the road, collisions became inevitable. If stripes could also be painted on the outer edge of every lane it would be easier for drivers to keep to the road without veering so close to oncoming traffic.

Dorr pressed the highway commissioner in his home state of Connecticut to test his idea, eventually getting New York and Connecticut to paint a right-hand stripe on a stretch of busy parkway. It immediately showed positive effects, but the highway bureaucracies continued to balk, arguing that it would cost $150 per mile to stripe all roads that way, and questioning the return. To answer this, the Dorr Foundation paid for an independent four-state study, which showed that additional lane-striping produced a 37 percent reduction in deaths and injuries. The foundation turned itself into a clearinghouse for studies on this topic, pressed safety groups and highway departments, and eventually was able to shame and cajol states into making right-side road-striping a standard practice, saving thousands of lives.

Further reading

○ Duke University case study, cspcs.sanford.duke.edu/sites/default/files/descriptive/preventing_crashes_on_americas_highways.pdf

1948

COUNTING, AND COMFORTING, DISADVANTAGED CHILDREN

Jim Casey and his siblings lost their father when they were young, and were raised on very little income by their mother. To contribute to the family's support, Jim launched a delivery service in Seattle in 1907. It grew into one of the largest companies in the nation—UPS. With some of his eventual

PROSPERITY

proceeds, he created the Annie E. Casey Foundation in 1948, named for his mother, and aimed at helping kids weather difficult times, both through direct help and by advocating for expansion of public social-welfare programs.

Jim kept enlarging the foundation, and when he died in 1983 left a major bequest. One of Casey's signature efforts has been Kids Count, a center for dispensing detailed data on child and family well-being to help policymakers and organizations identify needs, track trends, and measure successes. The foundation has also become involved in debates about crime, race, health-care programs, economic development, welfare spending, and other topics.

Today it is one of the largest private foundations in America, with assets of $2.9 billion in 2013. It provided $184 million in grants that year, in pursuit of its mission of "fostering public policies, human services, and community supports that more effectively meet the needs of vulnerable children and families."

Further reading

∘ Kids Count Data Center, datacenter.kidscount.org

1940

LOOMIS LABORATORY CREATES RADAR

Finding himself bored in the practice of law as a young man, Alfred Loomis returned to an earlier interest in scientific experimentation—befriending internationally prominent experimenters and conducting quite advanced investigations in garages and basements. Concluding that he needed a fortune to finance his deep scientific interests, the restless genius launched an investment firm with his brother-in-law. Soon he was wealthy enough to build a state-of-the-art lab near his home, in Tuxedo Park, New York, where he installed advanced machinery superior to what was available at major universities, plus housing for visiting scientists, and a support staff.

Concluding in 1928 that stock prices were unsustainable, Loomis converted all of his firm's assets to cash before the crash of 1929. He then purchased collapsed stocks at bargain prices, and made an additional $50 million in the first years of the Great Depression (the equivalent of more than $700 million today). In the early '30s he was one of the richest men in America, and as influential on Wall Street as J. P. Morgan and John Rockefeller.

At age 45 Loomis retired from finance to put his full time and energy into his scientific research. Working with top scientists including Nobel winners, Loomis made many valuable discoveries in physics, biology, and scientific instrumentation—in areas ranging from brain-wave measurement to his invention of the global long-range navigation system that preceded and birthed GPS navigation. While visiting Berlin in 1938, Loomis was unsettled by the popularity of Hitler and the advanced state of German weaponry. After his return he provided funding to Ernest Lawrence for development of the cyclotron. Loomis likewise provided funding for Enrico Fermi and other investigators to explore the budding field of nuclear fission.

Then, in 1940, Loomis doubled the size of his personal laboratory and focused it on a brand-new field with profound military implications: radio-wave detection of moving objects. By early 1941 he had a working prototype radar set. When the U.S. entered World War II, Loomis was put in charge of the nation's crucial effort to beat the Germans to military use of radar. He hand-picked scientists and used all of his entrepreneurial and finance skills, along with timely personal donations, to prevent military bureaucracy from slowing their work. By mid-1943 nearly 6,000 radar sets had been delivered to the Army and Navy and thousands more were on the way. Radar is considered to have won the war by neutralizing the German U-boat, bomber, and rocket threats, while giving Allied airplanes and ships in Europe and Asia remarkable new defensive and targeting powers.

One scientist described Loomis's laboratory as "the greatest cooperative research establishment in the history of the world." Nobelist Lawrence later stated, "If Alfred Loomis had not existed, radar development would have been retarded greatly, at an enormous cost in American lives…. He used his wealth very effectively…. He exercised his tact and diplomacy to overcome all obstacles…. He steers a mathematically straight course and succeeds in having his own way by force of logic and of being right." Loomis's organization was next copied for the secret Manhattan Project, and many of Loomis's scientists were transferred to work on development of the world's first atomic weapons. President Roosevelt subsequently lauded Loomis for doing more to win World War II than any civilian except Winston Churchill.

After the war, Loomis continued to financially support, and personally toil on, important scientific projects. He showed a lifelong gift for identifying men capable of transforming their fields. Alfred Loomis also produced a great-grandson who became a pioneer of the Internet—Netflix founder Reed Hastings, who similarly applied the riches from smashing business triumphs to highly influential philanthropy, namely the creation of charter schools. (See 2000, 2005, and 2006 entries on our companion list of achievements in Education philanthropy.)

Further reading

○ Alfred Loomis entry in the Philanthropy Hall of Fame (see prior *Almanac* section)

○ Biographical essay, ncbi.nlm.nih.gov/pmc/articles/PMC2900993

○ Jennet Conant, *Tuxedo Park: A Wall Street Tycoon and the Secret Palace of Science That Changed the Course of World War II* (Simon & Schuster, 2003)

1936

BUILDING UP THE BOYS CLUBS

Herbert Hoover, now remembered mainly as a President, was both a wealthy businessman and a prominent humanitarian and donor. Orphaned at an early age, he had a lifelong devotion to children's causes. In 1936 he became chairman of the Boys Clubs of America, and he devoted time, treasure, and organizational expertise to turn it into one of the country's largest charities by the time of his death a quarter-century later. He added hundreds of clubs to help city youths at risk of delinquency, offering them, in the words of one observer, "a place to play checkers and learn a trade, swim in a pool, and steal nothing more harmful than second base." Today, Boys and Girls Clubs serve over four million children in over 4,000 autonomous local clubs that head off gang membership, crime, drug use, and violence by means of proven formulas: supportive adults, challenging activities, and a place where young people feel they belong.

Further reading

○ Boys & Girls Clubs profile, bgca.org/whatwedo/Pages/WhatWeDo.aspx
○ Herbert Hoover profile in the Philanthropy Hall of Fame (see prior *Almanac* section)

1933

SAVING EUROPEAN INTELLECTUALS

As fascism swept Europe, scholars, artists, scientists, and religious leaders began to come under serious official pressure. In Germany, and later the countries that Germany overran, some were discharged from their positions for political reasons. In 1933 the Rockefeller Foundation set up a Special Research Aid Fund for Deposed Scholars charged with relocating these deposed intellectuals to universities in the U.S., Canada, England, France, or the Netherlands, so their minds would not be lost to the cause of human accomplishment. In addition to

∿ PhilAphorism

The greatest use of life is to spend it for something that will outlast it.

☞ *William James*

helping the scholar flee with his family, the foundation typically paid half of his salary, for a time, at the new institution where he was placed.

By the end of the '30s this effort had moved 214 deposed scholars (people like physicist Leo Szilard and novelist Thomas Mann) into new positions. In 1940, with German soldiers in Paris, it became clear that if Hitler prevailed in Europe, many individuals from disfavored races, religions, occupations, or political backgrounds would be in danger, especially if they were what the foundation described as "persons with capacity for independent leadership." So that year, the foundation added an additional Emergency Program for European Scholars that even more aggressively whisked individuals out of Germany and conquered countries, mostly to the U.S.

The Rockefeller leadership knew they couldn't carry out a mass refugee rescue in the middle of a war, so they focused on saving gifted thinkers in their productive years who held promise of producing breakthroughs that could benefit all people. Two foundation officers were permanently stationed in Europe to aid the endangered, and they showed great inventiveness in moving their charges to safety. Among those protected were twelve future or past Nobel Prize winners. As the war wound on, officials at the foundation realized they were making life and death decisions, which they found wrenching, and many began diverting other foundation funds, and even using their own money, to complete some of the relocations.

Further reading

- ○ Program summaries, rockefeller100.org/exhibits/show/peace-and-conflict/refugee-scholar-program
- ○ Archived information at the Rockefeller Foundation, rockarch.org/collections/rf/refugee.php

1933

INVENTING MOLECULAR BIOLOGY

By the early 1930s, the Rockefeller Foundation had dramatically accelerated the fields of chemistry and physics through its grants. In 1932 the foundation hired mathematician Warren Weaver to create programs in other branches of science that would be equally productive. Weaver became convinced that "movement of really heroic dimensions" could be sparked in the field of biology, but that this would require bringing the new, precise tools of laboratory exploration into the life sciences, which were at that point lagging other fields. In 1933 Warren and the Rockefeller Foundation launched a large effort to find investigators around the globe with first-rate technical lab skills and convince them to tackle biological studies that could help unlock the mysteries of life.

PROSPERITY

In the beginning, Weaver called this the study of "vital essences." Then he renamed it "experimental biology." As new instruments and tools began to open up the smallest units of life, Weaver finally coined the term "molecular biology" for this new field. It stuck.

By visiting labs across the U.S. and Europe and then using fellowships and grants to cajole the best minds to transfer the techniques of chemistry and physics to the study of living things, the Rockefeller staff sparked many of the most prominent triumphs of mid-century science. Investigations done with Rockefeller funding included Linus Pauling's work on the DNA helix and on chemical bonds, the Beadle-Tatum research on how genes govern metabolic processes, Dorothy Hodgkin's X-ray crystallography, Norbert Wiener's research on biofeedback, Albert Kuhn's developmental biology, Boris Ephrussi's studies on regulation of embryo development, and multiple-researcher work on photosynthesis, the function of vitamins, the effects of radiation on cancers, and so on.

Rockefeller's molecular biology program ran until 1951. At that point the desired insights and techniques were being aggressively pursued in industry and public research, so the foundation shut down its pioneering instigations and shifted its natural-science efforts toward agriculture, where it saw need for practical solutions that could end hunger.

Further reading

○ Information from the Rockefeller archives, rockefeller100.org/exhibits/show/natural_sciences/molecular-biology

○ Rationalization of new program at its launch by Warren Weaver, rockefeller100.org/files/original/95d66f29291e79a7fe9424e6b4bc15e7.pdf

○ George Beadle, "The Role of Foundations in the Development of Modern Biology," in *U.S. Philanthropic Foundations* (Harper & Row, 1967)

1932

MAKING BOOKS TALK FOR THE BLIND

For most of history, the enormous repository of human knowledge represented by books was out of reach for the blind. Only a small percentage of persons with vision loss have ever mastered braille. So when it came to accessing literature, history, practical information, and everything else contained between hard covers, the blind were, literally, in the dark.

In 1932 two donors—the Carnegie Corporation, and Ada Moore, a generous patron of libraries and art—gave $15,000 to the American Foundation for the Blind to fund a crash program to bring books to the sightless in a practical audio form. Both donors followed up with additional grants, totaling $20,000 from each of them. With these funds the AFB went to work to see if a brand-new patent for what was being called a "long-playing record," or LP, might work. LPs were much larger and slower-spinning than the 78-rpm records that existed then, and thus played more than four times as long on each side, making them practical for extended readings from books.

The foundation experimented with making discs out of various materials, seeking one durable enough to stand up to shipping from house to house among blind subscribers. It eventually settled on vinyl. The AFB also had to build players for the records, creating one that was electric and one that was hand-cranked, and struggled to make them cheap enough for mass purchase. This philanthropic product-development effort succeeded, and in 1934 "Talking Books" began to be shipped around the country, bringing literature to blind Americans everywhere, leaving them wide-eyed with wonder.

The LP record funded by Carnegie and Moore was enjoyed exclusively by the blind for the first 14 years of its existence, until CBS turned it into a popular medium for playing music among the general public in 1948. And while convalescing from a heart attack in 1955, President Eisenhower, not blind but bedridden, asked to use Talking Books and a Talking-Book machine. Audiobooks for the general public took a step forward. Thus did a charitable product for the sightless gradually become a big part of American pop culture.

Carnegie, meanwhile, developed a wider interest in bringing information to the blind. It made subsequent grants to develop a braille typewriter, new flexible records, and bibliographies of available recorded books. It also funded research on how to use Talking Books to educate blind children.

Further reading

○ Extract on development of the talking book from Frances Koestler, *A Social History of Blindness in the United States*, afb.org/unseen/book.asp?ch=Koe-10

○ Talking Book exhibit at the AFB, afb.org/talkingbook/home.asp

1930

LAUNCHING ROCKETRY

Robert Goddard was the world's greatest genius in rocketry, which only existed in science fiction when he penned his first articles about it in high school. After he earned a doctorate in physics at Clark University in 1911, his rocketry research expenses overwhelmed his salary, and he began fundraising. Goddard received scant financial backing and little interest from government or his fellow scientists, and the media (especially the *New York Times*) attacked his ideas so mercilessly he shunned publicity. In 1929, though, he was befriended by famed aviator Charles Lindbergh, who persuaded philanthropist Daniel Guggenheim to provide Goddard with a $100,000 grant. For the next 11 years, the Guggenheim family were Goddard's primary supporters, providing the salary, research funds, and materials with which Goddard created his many breakthroughs in rocket and jet propulsion.

Freed by these donations from the demands of fundraising or teaching, Goddard made bold progress on a range of problems and set the stage for the jet and rocket revolutions—and space exploration, including the multistage boosters that allowed the U.S. to be the first nation to land men on the moon. Subsequent Guggenheim-funded labs eventually yielded the Mars lander, and probes which traveled to Jupiter, Saturn, and beyond. "Today," notes historian Claire Gaudiani, "all rockets and planes depend on some of Goddard's 300 separate aeronautical inventions." Indeed, the federal government (which had largely ignored Goddard's work) agreed after his death to pay his widow and his philanthropic patrons at the Guggenheim Foundation $1 million for infringing on the master scientist's 214 patents during World War II.

Further reading

○ Claire Gaudiani, *The Greater Good* (Times Books, 2003)

○ Milton Lehman, *The Life of Robert H. Goddard* (Farrar Straus Giroux, 1963)

200-INCH TELESCOPE

The pioneering U.S.-based telescopes used by scientists to make fundamental scientific discoveries have been products of private philanthropy. The first modern mega-telescope was the 60-inch reflector, at that point the world's biggest, built on Mount Wilson in California with a 1904 grant from the Carnegie Institution. This historic instrument allowed measurement of the size of our galaxy, and plotting of the position of our solar system within it. Carnegie also funded the 100-inch telescope that went into use on Mount Wilson a decade later. Edwin Hubble used it to show that there are many galaxies, and that the universe is continuing to expand.

In 1928, $6 million of Rockefeller funding (at that point the largest single grant they had ever awarded) paid for construction of the 200-inch Hale telescope on Mount Palomar. After years of work, the original mirror proved impossible to manufacture. Corning Glass of upstate New York was called in to create an enormous blank using their new Pyrex product, which was eventually transported across the country, polished, and finally opened to the heavens two decades after the initial Rockefeller gift. The Hale telescope was the world's largest for 45 years (1948-1993), and is still a workhorse of modern astronomy, used nightly for a wide range of studies.

Further reading

○ Rockefeller Foundation reflection on Hale funding, rockefellerfoundation.org/blog/philanthropy-go-partner-risk

○ History at Caltech, astro.caltech.edu/palomar/history.html

1925

REVERSING THE RHODES SCHOLARSHIP

The philanthropic foundation set up by the Harkness family with Standard Oil earnings was called the Commonwealth Fund. In 1925 Edward Harkness—one of the most active and most effective donors of the first half of the twentieth century—decided to create a kind of mirror image of the Rhodes Scholarships. Cecil Rhodes paid for promising Americans to go to Britain for advanced study. The Commonwealth Fund Scholarships reciprocated that, bringing bright Britons to U.S. universities for a meeting of minds. They did that successfully for the next 72 years (though they were renamed Harkness Fellowships in 1961). Many Harkness fellows went on to prominent success, like *Sunday Times* editor Harold Evans, composer Peter Maxwell Davies, architect Rem Koolhaas, and London School of Economics director Howard Davies. Some became Americans, such as physicist Freeman Dyson and journalists Andrew Sullivan and Alastair Cooke. In 1997 the Harkness Fellowships were narrowed into study awards for health-care specialists only.

Further reading

○ Harkness Fellowship alumni 1925-1997, commonwealthfund.org/grants-and-fellowships/fellowships/harkness-fellowships/harkness-fellowship-alumni

PROSPERITY

⚛ PhilAphorism

Philanthropists enjoy…the freedom to experiment and take risks—risks that business and government entities cannot, or will not, accept. In fact, philanthropy has served as society's "risk capital" for more than a century.

☞ *Tom Tierney and Joel Fleishman*

1925

ENABLING AERONAUTICS AND
COMMERCIAL AVIATION

Harry Guggenheim served as one of America's first naval pilots in the First World War. By 1925 he had interested his father, Daniel—the multimillionaire mining industrialist and philanthropist—in donating a half-million dollars to New York University to establish the nation's earliest school of aeronautics. The family later established additional schools of aeronautical engineering at MIT, Caltech, Stanford, Harvard, Syracuse, Georgia Tech, the universities of Michigan and Washington, and other campuses.

Before commercial air travel existed, Harry Guggenheim established a Safe Aircraft Competition with $150,000 in prizes to spur innovation in ways of flying through fog, snow, rain and other adverse conditions. As a result, Jimmy Doolittle flew the first instrument-only flight in 1929, taking off, cruising, and landing a plane from a cockpit with its glass completely covered. The Guggenheims also bankrolled weather tracking and reporting services essential to flyers, and development of the first gyroscope compass. They made the equipment loans that allowed the first regularly scheduled commercial airline to set up operations in the U.S. They popularized air travel by touring famous aviators like Charles Lindbergh and the pilot who flew Commodore Byrd to the North Pole to scores of cities across the U.S.

The Guggenheims funded Theodore von Kármán, who invented the wind tunnel and designed an early helicopter and the DC-3. Right up into the 1960s, by which time nearly all of America's senior aerospace engineers were graduates of Guggenheim-sponsored schools, they continued to endow professorships and establish additional research and development centers to make flying safer, more efficient, and more widespread. Aeronautics became a huge element in the U.S. economy and national defense.

Further reading

◦ Entry in Aviation Hall of Fame, nationalaviation.org/guggenheim-harry-frank/

◦ Claire Gaudiani, *The Greater Good* (Times Books, 2003)

1920

ECONOMIC RESEARCH

The same philanthropic impulse that produced a slew of private scientific organizations in the 1920s to improve American governance (see 1919 entry on Public-Policy list) also created new expertise to help keep the government honest and informed on the economic front. The National Bureau of Economic Research was created in 1920 with $35,000 provided by the Commonwealth Fund. It was erected as a "private, nonprofit, nonpartisan research organization dedicated to promoting a greater understanding of how the economy works," with its independence guaranteed by a diverse board of economists, businessmen, and workplace experts. The Carnegie Corporation kicked in an additional $95,000 during 1921 and 1922. Today the bureau continues to do valuable work—officially designating the beginning and end of every national recession, for instance, and producing a rich diet of economic papers and books on timely topics. A third of the U.S. economists who have won the Nobel Prize have put in a stint as a researcher at NBER, and 13 alumni have chaired the President's Council of Economic Advisers.

It wasn't just foundations that strove to improve economic knowledge in the U.S. during the tumultuous early decades of the twentieth century. Individual donors like Alfred Cowles also got involved. Cowles was an investment adviser in Denver who decided to direct some of his wealth into supporting the most quantitatively gifted economists of his day, in the hope they could improve understanding of what was really happening in the American economy. Eventually he and some U.S. and European economists he had taken under his wing decided to make a systematic effort to encourage the application of advanced mathematics and statistics to the budding field of economics. Their Econometric Society was born in 1931, along with its research journal *Econometrica*—both funded by Cowles. The Guggenheim and Rockefeller foundations later chipped in as well, and scholars fueled by these donated funds earned nine Nobel Prizes in subsequent years.

Further reading

○ Joel Fleishman, *The Foundation* (Public Affairs, 2007)

○ Claire Gaudiani, *The Greater Good* (Times Books, 2003)

SPEEDING FLIGHT

Raymond Orteig was a French immigrant to New York City who started as a hotel porter at age 12 and worked his way up to owning hotels. Impressed by the good that regularized air travel could do for international understanding, economic growth, and human exploration, Orteig created one of the first great philanthropic prizes in 1919. He donated $25,000 to be awarded to any aviator and team of engineers who succeeded in flying nonstop between New York and Paris.

That distance was twice as far as anyone had managed to stay airborne to date, but Orteig's challenge spurred continual technological improvements. Six men died in various failed attempts over an eight-year period. Then in 1927, Charles Lindbergh lifted off from a Long Island airfield, buzzed across the gray Atlantic chop for 33 hours, and touched down outside Paris. Orteig happened to be vacationing in France and rushed to hand the pilot his check. It was estimated that Orteig's $25,000 gift sparked 16 times that much investment in new technology, speeding America into the skies.

Further reading

○ Richard Bak, *The Big Jump* (John Wiley, 2011)

○ Raymond Orteig entry in the Philanthropy Hall of Fame (see prior *Almanac* entry)

1918

ANDREW CARNEGIE POPULARIZES PENSIONS

Andrew Carnegie believed strongly that helping programs work best when beneficiaries make contributions to their own well-being, so starting in 1918 he provided millions of dollars to set up the Teachers Insurance and Annuity Association, and charged it with managing retirement funds put aside by professors themselves and their schools. During its first two decades, the fund was given free office space and had all of its administrative expenses paid by Carnegie. TIAA-CREF grew so large by 1937 that the foundation spun it off as an independent company.

Today, not only colleges but also many think tanks, community foundations, and other nonprofits rely on the company to manage their retirement plans. More broadly, Carnegie's example helped make retirement saving a common expectation among millions of middle-class workers in professions of all sorts.

Further reading

○ Duke University case study, cspcs.sanford.duke.edu/sites/default/files/descriptive/tiaa-cref.pdf

○ Ellen Lagemann, *Private Power for the Public Good: A History of the Carnegie Foundation for the Advancement of Teaching* (Wesleyan, 1988)

1915

BIRTH OF CRYPTOLOGY

George Fabyan was a classic entrepreneurial philanthropist—curious, quirky, full of passionate interests, deeply respectful of inventive thinking, distrustful of conventional wisdom and bureaucracy. Fabyan was a great believer in science, and with proceeds from his textile business he set up one of America's early private research labs, Riverbank Laboratories, on his estate near Chicago. Becoming interested in genetics and plant growth, he brought in a promising Cornell student to study, among other things, the effects of moonlight on wheat maturation. William Friedman went on the payroll in 1915.

Fabyan was also fascinated by secret messages and cryptography, and soon Friedman was as well. Before long, Friedman and his wife were running the Riverbank Lab Department of Codes and Ciphers, and publishing a series of papers that established much of the mathematical basis for cryptanalysis. When World War I broke out, the U.S. military asked Riverbank Laboratories to train its personnel in the use of codes. Friedman became the principal instructor, and eventually an officer in the Army's cryptography unit. Throughout the war, George Fabyan's private lab was the center for all U.S. military code-making and -breaking.

William Friedman eventually ran signals intelligence for the Army. He headed the group that famously broke the Japanese diplomatic codes—one of the great technical breakthroughs of World War II. He helped create for America the most secure cipher machine used in the Second World War. The organization Friedman established evolved into today's National Security Agency, the preeminent coding, surveillance, and information-security entity. The young geneticist who George Fabyan recruited into the world of ciphers is today described by the NSA as "the father of American cryptology."

Further reading

○ Friedman entry in NSA Cryptologic Almanac, nsa.gov/about/cryptologic_heritage/
center_crypt_history/almanac/#article2

1914

THE COMMUNITY FOUNDATION

From modest beginnings, Frederick Goff rose as a lawyer at John Rockefeller's Standard Oil, then became president of the Cleveland Trust Company, where he experimented with theories on improving philanthropy. He invented "living trusts" that encouraged donors to give during their lifetime rather than just in bequests, and helped the city launch what became its community chest and United Way campaigns, to make giving easier and more common.

In 1914 Goff launched his most dramatic innovation: the nation's first community foundation. Only about a dozen foundations of any kind existed at that time, and his Cleveland Foundation was quite novel in pooling the donations of many small givers into a common fund of real heft. During the years when the foundation was slowly building enough capital to permit giving, Goff personally covered expenses, which included surveys of recreation areas, schools, and other community assets which might benefit from enhancement. During the century since he launched the organization, the Cleveland Foundation has channeled $1.7 billion worth of gifts into local charitable causes.

This example inspired civic leaders in other places to copy the effort, so that small donors in their area could have easy ways to exercise their philanthropic impulses. Many large private foundations—including Ford, Mott, Wallace-Reader's Digest, Kellogg, Packard, Irvine, Lilly, Kresge, Packard, and Knight—eventually made it a part of their mission to seed new community foundations. By handling grants, record-keeping, and investing, community foundations allow modest-income Americans to give money in efficient and lasting ways. Today there are more than 730 community foundations in the U.S., and an equal number of these distinctly American inventions have been established in other countries.

Further reading

○ Cleveland Foundation's first 25 years, clevelandfoundation.org/wp-content/
uploads/2013/08/Cleveland-Foundation-1939-First-25-Years.pdf

○ Nathaniel Howard, *Trust for All Time: The Story of the Cleveland Foundation and the Community Trust Movement* (Cleveland Foundation, 1963)

1910

SCOUTING IMPROVES BOYS AND GIRLS

Founded in 1910 as part of an international movement, the Boy Scouts of America enrolled 2.4 million youth members in 2014, reached another 422,000 children receiving character education from the organization, and enjoyed nearly a million adult volunteers—making it one of the largest nonprofits in the U.S. The group's mission is to train boys in responsible citizenship, character development, self-reliance, and individual hardiness.

At the beginning of the twentieth century, prominent Americans were concerned that the migration of our population from farms to cities was reducing the physical activity, communal identity, religious development, and social health of children. Some leaders worried that independence and patriotism were not being reinforced among the young. Former President Theodore Roosevelt complained about a decline in American manhood. Partly to address concerns like these, the Boy Scouts were founded with strong support from observers across the political and social spectrum. The BSA became one of just a small number of charitable organizations to be granted a Congressional charter.

The organization is supported by fees and donor pledges. In 2014, contributions and bequests totaled $59 million, and the organization's endowment from previous gifts generated additional earnings of $35 million. The Boy Scouts partner with churches, fraternal clubs, PTAs, and other organizations that donate meeting space and basic oversight. The BSA provides leader training, activities, camping programs, insurance, and various forms of professional support.

Since the group's birth, more than 110 million Americans have been members of the Boy Scouts. Two years after the organization's creation a counterpart with similar aims for girls was founded. Girls Scouts of the USA currently enrolls 2 million girls and 800,000 adult volunteers.

Further reading

○ Annual Report of Boy Scouts of America, scoutingnewsroom.org/about-the-bsa/annual-reports/

○ Annual Report of Girl Scouts of the USA, girlscouts.org/who_we_are/facts/annual_report.asp

1908

FRANKLIN INSTITUTE
OF TECHNOLOGY

Benjamin Franklin is most often thought of in connection to his adopted city of Philadelphia, but he was raised in Boston, and remembered his birth city at his death. His will included a provision providing that a thousand English pounds from his estate (about $60,000 in current funds) be invested for a hundred years and then gradually released to the city of Boston, with a particular aim of aiding "young workmen." (An identical provision was made for the city of Philadelphia.) In 1908, Boston decided to use the money accumulated in its account (which ultimately totaled millions of dollars), supplemented with an additional donation from Andrew Carnegie, to create a technical school called the Benjamin Franklin Institute of Technology. Inspired by Franklin's maxim that good workmen make good citizens, it is now one of the oldest industrial training schools in the country, offering job-oriented education (mostly two-year associate degrees) to a student body with a large representation of low-income students and minorities.

Further reading

○ School history, bfit.edu/The-College/About-the-College/Benjamin-Franklin-s-Legacy

PROSPERITY

1907

CREATING BUSINESS PHILANTHROPY

During the period when Julius Rosenwald was building Sears, Roebuck into the nation's biggest retailer, he was also pioneering many novel combinations of business and philanthropy. In 1907, just after selling its first public stock, the firm advanced $90,000 to older employees at Rosenwald's impetus to help them buy shares so they could participate in the company's success. At the same time, the company created a savings bank for employees that paid 5 percent interest.

The formal launch of the Sears, Roebuck Employees' Savings and Profit Sharing Plan occurred in July 1916, and it was immediately the largest such plan in the country for including workers in the prosperity of their company. Participation was voluntary and open to any employee with three or more years seniority; enrollment required a deposit of 5 percent of salary. The company in turn added to the fund 5 percent of its net annual earnings. An employee was fully vested in the plan after ten years of service, at which point he could withdraw the full amount of his contributions plus the company's. No other offering at the time came close to matching the Sears plan in generosity, which Rosenwald believed spurred both workers' productivity and their habits of thrift.

Rosenwald also created one of the first corporate foundations in history, the Sears, Roebuck Foundation, and built it to substantial size. But his most unusual and bold philanthropic innovation was his willingness to pledge his own fortune (more than once) to protect Sears employees and even preserve the company during the periodic financial panics that wracked the U.S. in the early decades of the twentieth century. Most dramatically, when the sudden recession after World War I pushed Sears to the brink of bankruptcy, Rosenwald bailed out the firm by pledging $21 million of his personal wealth (the equivalent of $288 million today) in a combination of gifts and loans. This stunned Rosenwald's fellow business executives, and deeply impressed the country. Business writer C. W. Barron, who later fathered *Barron's* magazine, hailed the move as "business philanthropy."

Further reading

○ Julius Rosenwald profile in the Philanthropy Hall of Fame (see prior *Almanac* section)

○ Peter Ascoli, *Julius Rosenwald: The Man Who Built Sears, Roebuck and Advanced the Cause of Black Education in the American South* (Indiana University Press, 2006)

1907

SAGE SOCIAL SCIENCE

When upstate New York financier and railroad builder Russell Sage died in 1906, he left his fortune to his wife, Olivia, who the very next year poured $10 million into a foundation in her husband's honor, charging it to "take up the larger and more difficult problems" and then "aid in their solution." One of the very first general-purpose foundations in the country, the Russell Sage Foundation took a diagnostic approach to social ills, aiming "to understand and alleviate the conditions that cause [problems], rather than providing direct assistance." When Mrs. Sage directed the construction of a headquarters in New York City, it was decorated with carved panels in which Service was flanked by Study and Counsel. The Russell Sage Foundation created some of the first scientific surveys of living conditions, of opinion, of health, of school performance. It investigated problems in housing, loan-sharking, working conditions, and early childhood education, funding the first White House Conference on Children in 1909. It financed the development of Forest Hills Gardens to create a model of town design for working-class urbanites.

The foundation's deepest influence was in professionalizing the social sciences, and raising standards in many professions that feed into that discipline—like social work, nursing, demography, and law. The pioneering social worker and child-welfare expert Mary Richmond was a long-time employee of the foundation, and published classic works that injected into her field important elements of science, psychology, and morals, careful measurement, and understanding of the influence of a person's social environment. Out of her experiences, she counseled caseworkers to first look at individual behavior and family structure, then consider close influences like schools, churches, and jobs. Only after that should they look to the wider community and government for a problem's origins or solutions.

In addition to focusing on child welfare and inventing modern social work, the Russell Sage Foundation strove over a period of decades to make other professionals more effective, in fields like medicine, mental health, economics, and statistics. Olivia Sage, who had been a teacher for 20 years before marrying, was a strong supporter of education, and gave generously from her personal funds to support Syracuse University, where she propelled a teacher college, along with many other schools. In 1916 she founded Russell Sage College for the education of women. The Russell Sage Foundation, meanwhile, eventually focused on the improvement of philanthropy itself, providing crucial support that created the Foundation Center and the

PROSPERITY

Foundation Directory, two of today's vital resources for making private giving intelligible and accessible.

Further reading

○ Olivia Sage entry in the Philanthropy Hall of Fame (see prior *Almanac* section)

○ 100-year history of Russell Sage Foundation, russellsage.org/sites/all/files/u137/Brief-History.pdf

PIONEERING WORKER BONUSES
AND PROFIT-SHARING

George Eastman had no wife or children and believed in giving while living. One of the world's richest men, he gave away more money ($2 billion in current dollars) than anyone of his era except John Rockefeller and Andrew Carnegie, yet his personal giving and even his face were little known in his day because of his predilection for anonymous gifts.

He could not hide, however, his extraordinary generosity to what he always called his "fellow employees" at Kodak. In 1899, the company Eastman had created dominated the photography market and had great success with a stock offering. Eastman decided to give $178,000 of his personal profit to his nearly 3,000 employees worldwide in one of corporate history's first bonuses. Each person's check was calculated using a formula based on salary, position, and time at Kodak, and it came with a note: "This is a personal matter with Mr. Eastman and he requests that you not consider it as a gift but as extra pay for good work."

For decades to come, Eastman continued to reward employees generously. In 1911, he created a safety committee to study accident prevention. The same year, long prior to workmen's compensations laws, he used $1 million to create a benefit, accident, and pension fund for employees, 50 years before most firms evolved sick pay, disability benefits, pension, and hospital

◌ PhilAphorism

The best way of doing good to the poor is not making them easy in poverty, but leading or driving them out of it.

☞ *Benjamin Franklin*

benefit plans. The following year, Kodak employees received their first wage dividend, a profit-sharing program that continued for the life of the company. Every employee began receiving a 2 percent dividend on his wages of the past five years.

In 1919 Eastman provided his biggest gift to fellow employees. He donated back to the company 10,000 shares of common stock, a third of his personal holdings, so that employees could buy these at just 17 percent of market value. He also had the company set aside a matching amount of unissued, company-held stock so employee sales could continue in the future. In addition, the million-dollar proceeds to the company from selling this stock were channeled into the company's Welfare Fund, which was administered by the newly established Kodak Employees Association. They used it, among other things, to help employees buy homes. Though long suspicious that pensions encouraged improvidence, by the late 1920s Eastman changed his mind and set up his final gift for employees—a retirement annuity, life insurance, and disability benefits.

Further reading

○ George Eastman profile in the Philanthropy Hall of Fame (see prior *Almanac* section)

○ Elizabeth Brayer, *George Eastman: A Biography* (University of Rochester Press, 2006)

○ 1920 issue of *The Kodak Magazine* describing company benefits, books.google.com/books?id=bs8WAAAAYAAJ&pg=PA10&lpg=PA10&dq=kodak+magazine+1920+company+benefits&source=bl&ots=8cT8oJGRvp&sig=FmldOzQyb7GViJGouGe_Ng-CjgE&hl=en&sa=X&ved=0CCMQ6AEwAWoVChMI__Xwis-DyQIVSJUeCh1JUAYX-#v=onepage&q=kodak%20magazine%201920%20company%20benefits&f=false

1892

MILLIONS OF LIVES SAVED
BY PASTEURIZED MILK

Nathan Straus is little remembered today, though he is one of the most effective philanthropists in American history. He immigrated from Bavaria with his family as a small child in 1854. Following a typical path for many Jews of the era, the family pursued retailing, eventually coming to New York City. Nathan entered the family's china and glassware business at 18, and in 1874 the family began operating the china and glassware departments of the Macy's department store. The Straus family's departments were so profitable that the family became partners with R. H. Macy's heirs in both the Macy's and Abraham & Straus stores, before taking over both concerns entirely. And still the family made gains, bringing numerous innovations to retailing that fueled Macy's expansion. In 1902 the store became New York's largest, and the family one of the city's wealthiest. But their philanthropy had become prominent years before.

Nathan and his wife gave away the great bulk of their fortune during their lives, spreading their charity widely. Their efforts included everything from providing clean water to soldiers in the Spanish-American War, to constructing dozens of tuberculosis clinics across America, to building a health center in Jerusalem to aid persons of all races and creeds, to building a Catholic Church in New Jersey.

The Strauses would have their greatest effect on human flourishing by crusading for pasteurized milk. It began as concern for their own six children. Like many affluent families, the Strauses kept cows to supply their home with milk, but one of the beasts abruptly died and was discovered to have tuberculosis. Recalling that Louis Pasteur's method of heating milk killed most dangerous germs, Straus decided his children would drink only pasteurized milk. At the same time, he embarked on reforms to help poor children obtain safe milk. He established milk stations in poor neighborhoods to give away the pasteurized product and prove its value. "In 1891 fully 24 percent of babies born in New York City died before their first birthday. But of the 20,111 children fed on pasteurized milk supplied by Nathan Straus over a four-year period, only six died," notes historian John Steele Gordon.

Straus donated pasteurization equipment to the city's orphan asylum, an institution so gruesome that its children suffered a death rate four times worse than that of children in general. Forty-four percent of the children there died in 1897. The following year, with Straus's milk the only change, the rate dropped to 20 percent.

Straus's philanthropic crusade saw him provide support for 297 milk stations in 36 cities, which dispensed more than 24 million glasses and bottles of milk over a quarter-century. Gordon reports that the U.S. infant mortality rate dropped from 125.1 per thousand in 1891 to 15.8 in 1925. Straus directly saved an estimated 445,800 children's lives, and his crusade for mandatory pasteurization indirectly saved millions more lives.

Further reading

○ *Philanthropy* magazine article, philanthropyroundtable.org/topic/excellence_in_philanthropy/the_milk_man

○ Lina Straus, *Disease in Milk: The Remedy, Pasteurization—The Life Work of Nathan Straus* (E. P. Dutton, 1917)

○ Master's thesis, *Philanthropic Life of the Merchant and Humanitarian Nathan Straus*, preserve.lehigh.edu/etd/197/

SETTLING THE POOR

In 1889, Jane Addams and Ellen Starr opened Hull House in Chicago, the nation's first and most influential "settlement house"—a movement that aimed to link successful citizens to the poor, especially immigrants, in relationships of support, mentoring, and friendship. At first, Addams operated Hull House from her inheritance. Later, she received contributions from individuals such as Anita Blaine, Louise Bowen, Mary Smith, and other donors.

By 1907, Hull House had grown to 13 buildings covering most of a city block, with gym, theater, art gallery, boys' club, cafeteria, residence for working women, libraries, and more; it served thousands of people each week. Among other efforts, Addams ran a labor bureau at Hull House to help residents find jobs, and opened a bank to encourage saving. By 1920, nearly 500 settlement houses existed nationally, and they played an important role in helping America assimilate millions of new arrivals during our decades of heaviest immigration.

Over the years, Addams shifted away from direct instruction and assistance to the poor, and increasingly focused on influencing public policies. She began to question the practice of "middle-class moralists" who urged on the lower classes "the specialized virtues of thrift, industry, and sobriety." Historian Joel Schwartz describes this shift as "tragic" because it "discouraged poor people from practicing precisely the behaviors that are most likely to allow them to escape their poverty." As dependency and the welfare state grew, the personal service to the poor that settlement houses had provided declined, and Hull House, after decades of powerful service, finally shut its doors.

Further reading

○ Jane Addams, *Twenty Years at Hull-House* (Empire, 2013)

○ Jean Bethke Elshtain (ed.), *The Jane Addams Reader* (Basic Books, 2001)

RESCUING REFUGEES

In the last decades of the nineteenth century, anti-Semitic riots in Russia and Eastern Europe killed many Jews, and caused hundreds of thousands of Jewish families to leave or be expelled from their homes. Many of these ended up on ships to the U.S., with meager resources and little help. In response, Jews in America banded together to form aid societies to help their immigrant brethren and relatives settle and prosper in America. The largest and oldest of these groups is the Hebrew Immigrant Aid Society, whose roots go back to 1881 in New York City.

Nearly all of the early Jewish refugees arrived at Ellis Island. Some of them were severely malnourished because there was no kosher food available on their steamships. Others had lost all their property in pogroms. Most spoke no English, and all needed jobs. HIAS set up its own office at Ellis Island which provided translators, kosher food, and assistance toward becoming a legal entrant to the U.S. HIAS lent new arrivals money for their landing fees, or for railroad tickets that would take them to relatives in other places. The large numbers of Jewish immigrants who stayed in New York City were offered language classes, instruction in occupations like dressmaking, and, later, civic training that would allow the refugees to become U.S. citizens. Funding came from successful Jews who sponsored and donated funds.

The outbreak of World War I caused a new surge of refugees—140,000 Jews arrived in the first year of the war alone. The Russian Revolution killed about 50,000 more Jews and generated many additional refugees, some of whom made it to the U.S. During World War II, HIAS helped settle more Jewish refugees, and after the war the charity relocated a third of a million of Europe's scattered and battered Jews. Later, the Hebrew Immigrant Aid Society helped co-religionists uprooted from Hungary, Egypt, and Cuba during upheavals and attacks of the 1950s, and assisted more than 400,000 Soviet Jews who immigrated to the U.S. in the later years of the Cold War.

The Hebrew Bible has 36 different injunctions calling on believers to help strangers, and with most Jews now safely consolidated in the U.S. or Israel, HIAS has shifted much of its effort to assisting threatened refugees of other religions and ethnicities. The organization has foreign offices that help reunite families, resettle those in danger, and integrate the displaced into receiving countries, whether the U.S. or some other land. It is estimated that the Hebrew Immigrant Aid Society has aided nearly 4.5 million people in its century and a quarter of charitable operations.

Further reading

○ Hebrew Immigrant Aid Society, hias.org/history

CREATION OF THE AMERICAN RED CROSS

Clara Barton became famous as the "angel of the battlefield" during the Civil War. Afterward she raised significant sums from the public for other good works, such as efforts to account for missing soldiers. Exhausted by all this, she went to Switzerland to recuperate. There she met the founders of the new International Red Cross.

After returning to America, Barton organized an American version with a twist—the U.S. group would not only assist in wartime, but also help with peacetime disasters. She incorporated the American Association of the Red Cross in 1881. When a terrible fire left thousands of Michiganders homeless that year, Barton quickly raised $2,500 and a large supply of volunteers and donated goods, then raced to relieve the victims. Other early interventions in prominent crises included an 1893 hurricane that left 30,000 Georgians in need, and the group's first wartime effort during the Spanish-American War of 1898. World War I brought tremendous growth to the Red Cross, with local chapters jumping from 107 to 3,864, and membership growing from the tens of thousands to the tens of millions. The Red Cross remains one of America's ten largest charities.

Further reading

○ Martin Morse Wooster, *By Their Bootstraps: The Lives of Twelve Gilded Age Social Entrepreneurs* (Manhattan Institute, 2002)

○ Clara Barton, *The Red Cross in Peace and War* (American Historical Press, 1910)

STEERING THE U.S. BETWEEN DEPENDENCE AND NEGLECT

In the post-Civil War years, America's cities and the popularity of Social Darwinism both grew. The increasing anonymity of city life perhaps made it easier for Social Darwinists to assume that all poor persons were doomed, and that charity toward them would thus be useless. Buffalo clergyman Stephen Gurteen rejected this fatalism and founded the Charity Organization Society in Buffalo in 1877. He argued against both the Social Darwinists' indifference to the poor, and the failures of previous sentimental approaches to aiding the poor—which indiscriminately handed out relief that made givers feel good but undermined the character and independence of the receiver. Gurteen consciously emulated London's Charity Organization Society, founded by hard-headed social reformer Octavia Hill, and Paris's Society of St. Vincent de Paul.

Five years later, Josephine Lowell founded another branch of the Charity Organization Society in New York City. She too attacked both callous indifference to the poor, and indiscriminate aid that "fails to save the recipient" because "no man can receive as a gift what he should earn

PROSPERITY

by his own labor without a moral deterioration." In her work Lowell used volunteers to "supply the precious element of human sympathy and tender personal interest which must often be lacking where the care [is] the means of livelihood of overtaxed officials."

Both Gurteen and Lowell used work tests with the able-bodied poor, requiring tasks like wood chopping from men and sewing from women as a condition for aid. In addition to sustenance their organizations provided no-interest loans, job banks, and advice in home management. By 1894, historian Marvin Olasky reports, Gurteen's group "was providing 6,286 days of work to men with families and 11,589 days of work to homeless men," and the Charity Organization Society system had "caught on across the country." Denver's COS, established in 1887, is the precursor to the United Way.

Further reading

- Marvin Olasky, *The Tragedy of American Compassion* (Regnery, 1992)
- Josephine Lowell, *Public Relief and Private Charity* (G.P. Putnam's Sons, 1884), archive.org/ details/publicreliefpriv00loweuoft
- Stephen Humphreys Gurteen, *A Handbook of Charity Organization* (self-published, 1882), archive.org/details/ahandbokcharity00gurtgoog

VOLUNTARY ORGANIZATIONS PIONEER LIFE INSURANCE

Along with medical benefits and aid for orphaned children (see 1842 entry), another important socioeconomic protection provided to American workers by voluntary organizations was life insurance. For instance, the fraternal group known as the Ancient Order of United Workmen was founded in 1868 and offered life insurance to help attract members. It guaranteed a death benefit of $1,000, later increased to $2,000, which was funded by a $1 assessment on every member of the group. Membership expanded rapidly and by early in the twentieth century nearly half a million brothers were protecting each others' families with life-insurance coverage. Hundreds of other fraternal organizations followed suit, and by 1908 the top 200 lodges had paid out more than $1 billion in death benefits. At that point, voluntary fraternal life-insurance societies had 8.5 million members, and they provided more protection than all commercial policies put together.

Further reading

- David Beito, *From Mutual Aid to the Welfare State* (University of North Carolina, 2000)

PRIVATE DONATIONS TO SETTLE FREED SLAVES

At the end of the Civil War, Congress created the Bureau of Refugees, Freedmen, and Abandoned Lands to resettle former slaves on empty plots, and otherwise help African Americans uprooted by the conflict. Though it was a poorly managed bureaucracy, the organization nonetheless carried out many crucial tasks—thanks primarily to its private donors. Though federal funding was only $1 million, Northern aid societies, wealthy individuals, black small donors from both the North and the South, and groups like the American Missionary Association collected the modern equivalent of several hundred million dollars for use by the Freedmen's Bureau. These donations were used in many lifesaving and constructive ways. For instance, they helped reunite separated families, and purchased emergency rations. The donated funds supported 2,700 schools and 3,700 teachers where 150,000 illiterate black children learned to read and write over a five-year period. The giving underwrote legal assistance, helped slaves marry, encouraged the liberated to contract out their labor, and paid the salaries of agents who protected the newly freed from vengeful mobs.

Further reading
◦ Kathleen McCarthy, *American Creed* (University of Chicago, 2003)

1861

SANITARY COMMISSION SAVES LIVES
IN THE CIVIL WAR

Once the Civil War began, charitable groups rushed to aid soldiers. The U.S. Sanitary Commission, a private relief agency founded in 1861 by a Unitarian minister, became nationally important. The Lincoln administration officially

⌁ PhilAphorism

The highest use of capital is to make money do more for the betterment of life.

☞ *Henry Ford*

PROSPERITY

recognized the group, but many government officials were unhelpful or worse. The USSC plowed on regardless, preventing disease in camps and hospitals by providing expert advice on drainage, ventilation, and medical procedures. It created a hospital directory that allowed families to track their wounded and dead. Its critiques helped spur a much-needed reorganization of the federal Medical Bureau, and it provided vast amounts of food, medical supplies, and clothing to soldiers and to prisoners on both sides of the war. It later helped soldiers and kin negotiate the military bureaucracy to secure pensions and back pay.

The decentralized organization of the Sanitary Commission—it was composed of more than 7,000 local aid societies—often allowed it to provide supplies more quickly than the government could. By the time it disbanded the year after the war's end, the USSC had raised $7 million in cash and $15 million of in-kind donations, provided over 1 million nights' lodgings, and collected over $2.5 million in soldiers' wages. Most of its volunteers were women, including novelist Louisa May Alcott, and a nurse named Clara Barton, who would later found the American Red Cross. In addition to raising medical standards and giving the field of public health a boost, the USSC received high praise from contemporary political observers such as the British statesman Gladstone. Philosopher John Stuart Mill lauded "the spontaneous self-devotion and organizing genius of a people, altogether independent of government."

Further reading

○ Charles Stillé, *History of the United States Sanitary Commission* (Lippincott, 1866), play. google.com/store/books/details?id=7OYzY-J_hjEC&rdid=book-7OYzY-J_hjEC&rdot=1

○ William Maxwell, *Lincoln's Fifth Wheel: The Political History of the United States Sanitary Commission* (Longmans, 1956), ourstory.info/library/1-roots/Maxwell/wheelTC.html

EDUCATION FOR THE DEAF

In 1856, Amos Kendall, who had made his fortune helping Samuel Morse commercialize his telegraph patents, was touched by the plight of several deaf and blind children in the nation's capital. A neighbor had discovered the children cruelly neglected in a "school" for disabled children run by a con man who displayed them to raise money for himself. Kendall went to court to be appointed their guardian, and began teaching them himself. Then he donated two acres for housing and educating the children and got Congress to incorporate the Columbia Institution for the Instruction of the Deaf and Dumb and Blind. The first superintendent was Edward Gallaudet, whose father had founded and run one of North America's first schools for the hard-of-hearing in 1817 (now the American School for the Deaf). Both Gallaudets pioneered the use of sign language for instruction. In 1864 a collegiate department was created—North America's first institution of higher education for the deaf. When Amos Kendall died, the government purchased the remainder of his estate to keep the school together. Later the pre-college part was renamed the Kendall School, and the higher-education division became Gallaudet College.

Further reading

○ Edward Gallaudet, *History of the College for the Deaf: 1857-1907* (Gallaudet College Press, 1983)

○ History at Gallaudet website, gallaudet.edu/kdes/about_/history.html

1853

CONNECTING ORPHANS TO FAMILIES

Congregationalist minister Charles Loring Brace was emphatic that the thousands of miserable homeless children roaming the streets of nineteenth-century New York had the "same capacities" and the same importance "as the little ones in our own homes." That was an essential part of his Christian creed. But Brace also believed that "habits of life and the inner forces which form character" ultimately drive success and happiness, so it is important for unformed children to be given both love and good examples. He didn't like traditional orphanages, which he thought fostered passivity and dependence, so in 1853 Brace founded the Children's Aid Society and began helping boys and girls leave the streets and enter lodging houses that required small payments from the children to remind them of their capacity to support themselves. The society offered workshops and industrial schools that taught trade skills.

Brace eventually came to the view that the "orphan trains" the society established later were the best long-term solution to abandonment. These transported tens of thousands of children to permanent new homes across the country, especially on the frontier. A precursor to the modern foster-care system, the placements had economic value to the receiving family as well as security and emotional value to the child. Successful results varied from mutual economic support to full-blown substitute-family bonds. These out-placements were a great improvement on traditional indentured servitude because either the child or the host family could end the arrangement at any time. To help ensure the children's proper treatment, the Children's Aid Society used local community leaders to guide and supervise placements.

Because his appeals to New York's wealthy found willing ears, Brace was able to build his aid work to a very large scale. The Astors, Dodges, and

PROSPERITY

Roosevelts all made regular and generous donations, but there was also a wide and faithful base of small-scale supporters who sustained the society's work with gifts of money, clothing, supplies, and volunteer time.

A 1917 CAS annual report noted that the program's alumni included two governors, two district attorneys, two sheriffs, two mayors, a justice of the Supreme Court, two college professors, 24 clergymen, and 97 teachers. Though its mission has changed, the society still exists as one of America's largest child-welfare agencies. It created the first PTA, first visiting nurse service, first free school-lunch program, first free dental clinics, and first day schools for handicapped children.

Further reading

○ Stephen O'Connor, *Orphan Trains: The Story of Charles Loring Brace and the Children He Saved and Failed* (University of Chicago Press, 2004)

○ Children's Aid Society website, childrensaidsociety.org

1843

FIGHTING POVERTY IN A PERSONAL WAY

When the Panic of 1837 caused widespread economic dislocation, charitable organizations in America's growing cities experienced sharply increased demand for their services. Many Christian philanthropists became concerned that the mushrooming charities sometimes did not distinguish between the "worthy poor" and the merely idle. In response, a group of New York donors decided to emulate the personalized anti-poverty program of Glasgow clergyman Thomas Chalmers.

Their organization, called the Association for Improving the Conditions of the Poor, launched in 1843. The group disdained "gratuitous charity" that lumped the poor together without considering their individual needs, strengths, and weaknesses. They believed that person-to-person spiritual and moral aid would be, in the long run, more important than material assistance in turning around the fortunes of many households.

The donors first divided their city into manageable districts, to enable the one-on-one relationships between assisters and assisted that keep charity humane, differentiated, and efficient. They put an emphasis on willingness to work, and were willing to withdraw assistance if it seemed to be enervating the recipient. They relied heavily on the judgments and due diligence of volunteers, church members, and donor merchants. Recipients of aid were counseled, helped to plan ways of rebuilding their lives and their relationships, and urged to end destructive habits.

The society also worked to improve the physical surroundings in which the poor lived. It got landlords to repair plumbing, sanitation, and heating. It created inexpensive public baths for women and children.

Robert Hartley, the AICP's secretary for more than 30 years, described the causes of poverty as "chiefly moral," and thus "whatever subsidiary appliances may be used—they admit only moral remedies." The AICP's approach was influential across our young republic. AICP-inspired organizations popped up in Baltimore, Boston, Chicago, Philadelphia, St. Louis, and other major cities. The Baltimore Association, for instance, had 2,000 volunteers making 8,227 visits to 4,025 families as of 1891. "It worked," concluded scholar Marvin Olasky after studying the organization. "The crucial understanding was simple but profound: people got by when other people took a personal interest in them."

Further reading

○ Marvin Olasky, *The Tragedy of American Compassion* (Regnery, 1992)

1842

FRATERNAL LODGES SUPPLY HEALTH BENEFITS

During the century prior to the outbreak of World War II, the most important sources of sick benefits and health insurance in the U.S. were fraternal charities. The Independent Order of Odd Fellows was a leading example. In 1819, the first U.S. branch of the British Odd Fellows lodge opened in Baltimore. Throughout the following decade the fraternal group spread across four states, and attracted more than 6,000 members drawn from all economic classes. In 1842 the American lodges formed their own fraternal order, the IOOF.

Like dozens of other fraternal organizations at that time, the Odd Fellows offered financial support to members who fell sick, and the IOOF made these offerings much more uniform and predictable. Any member who became too ill to work could claim a weekly stipend ranging between $3 and $6, paid by his fellow lodge members. Most other lodges referred to these mutual benefits as charitable relief, but the Odd Fellows called them benefits and treated them as "every Brother's right, and paid to every one when sick, whether he be high or low, rich or poor." There was accountability, however: payments were withheld in cases of habitual drunkenness, adultery, or anti-social behavior.

From 1830 to 1877, IOOF membership soared from 3,000 to 465,000. It and other fraternal orders dispensed many millions of dollars in sick benefits (as well as funeral benefits) to their participants. Lodges also provided charitable aid to thousands of orphans of deceased members. These valuable benefits were supported by a broad base of voluntary contributors—at least one third of all U.S.

PROSPERITY

adult males age 20 or older belonged to one or more of the voluntary fraternal organizations in the early decades of the twentieth century.

Further reading

○ David Beito, *From Mutual Aid to the Welfare State* (University of North Carolina, 2000)

1841

PURIFYING THE AIR OF AMERICAN BUSINESS

In the aftermath of the religious revival known as the "Second Great Awakening," a web of evangelical Christian charities called the "Benevolent Empire" mobilized across America. Lewis Tappan was a major donor to this Protestant reform movement, which created scores of groups like the American Bible Society, American Missionary Association, American Anti-Slavery Society, and American Tract Society.

Tappan's dealings with officers in these organizations, along with his many business contacts, gave him keen insight into the character of the men leading America. Recognizing that there were economic ramifications to honesty, trustworthiness, and other aspects of character, Tappan created the nation's first credit-rating business—the Mercantile Agency—in 1841. Agents across the states, many of them attorneys (including Abraham Lincoln), reported to the agency on the sobriety and payment histories of small entrepreneurs. Subscribers to the agency paid to be able to check the backgrounds of these businessmen as they sought credit—which in such a vast, fast-growing, and mobile country, where cash was often scarce, was crucial to commerce.

By 1846 Tappan had over 700 agents and his financial reports were earning $15,000 a year, which he used to continue his large donations to religious and anti-slavery causes (see 1830 entry on our list of Religious philanthropy). But inventing credit ratings wasn't just a way for Tappan to fund his philosophical goals—he believed his ingenious agency, which became today's Dun & Bradstreet, was itself an important boost to the nation's morals: "It checks knavery, and purifies the mercantile air." Historians agree

✦ PhilAphorism

It's better to tell your money where to go than to ask where it went.

☞ *Farmer's Gazette*

that Tappan's innovation, which "blended business and moral agendas," was critical to the development of the American economy. As Ronald Walters observes, it gave "economic preference to virtue."

Further reading

○ Kathleen McCarthy, *American Creed: Philanthropy and the Rise of Civil Society* (University of Chicago Press, 2005)

○ Bertram Wyatt-Brown, *Lewis Tappan and the Evangelical War Against Slavery* (LSU Press, 1997)

BUILDING THE
UNDERGROUND RAILWAY

To agitate against slavery and "create a fund to aid colored persons in distress," a group of abolitionists established the Vigilant Association in Philadelphia in 1837. The association had a secret arm, the Vigilant Committee, that raised money to assist runaway slaves by giving them shelter, food, clothes, medical care, transportation, and legal assistance while they were in or passing through Pennsylvania. Because aiding fugitive slaves was illegal and dangerous, this had to be done entirely privately and apart from the courts or other apparatuses of government. To fund this work, members of the association were asked to pay dues of 75 cents annually, and a member of the committee was designated to conduct fundraising among non-members on a confidential basis so as to protect donors from reprisals by slave owners. (Gerrit Smith was a major donor.) Just the same, mobs sometimes threatened contributors. Over a period of three decades, though, the organization and sister groups in New York City, Albany, Syracuse, Rochester, and Boston erected many of the procedures and stopping places of the Underground Railroad that ultimately channeled thousands of escapees to freedom in Canada and other northern locations.

Further reading

○ Historical Society of Pennsylvania, www2.hsp.org/collections/manuscripts/v/vigilant1121.htm

=== 1837 ===

INITIATING BLACK COLLEGES

America's 106 historically black colleges played a major role in improving the status and social contributions of our black citizens. The very first of these, Pennsylvania's Cheyney University, was launched by the philanthropy of Quaker Richard Humphreys. At his death he bequeathed $10,000 and asked

13 of his fellow Quakers to use it to "instruct the descendants of the African race in school learning, in the various branches of the mechanic arts, trades, and agriculture, in order to prepare and fit and qualify them to act as teachers." The school opened in Philadelphia offering a classical higher education for free.

Further reading

○ History, cheyney.edu/about-cheyney-university/documents/RichardHumphreys_
   QuakerPhilanthropist.pdf

───────────── 1829 ─────────────

EDUCATING THE BLIND

America's first school for the disabled sprang from a cocktail combining a Boston Brahmin with two quite different visionaries. John Fisher first envisioned a school for the blind after visiting Paris, where the National Institution for Blind Youth inspired him. Having helped found Massachusetts General Hospital, he was able to persuade the state legislature in 1829 to incorporate the New England Asylum for the Blind and award it $6,000. As headmaster, Dr. Fisher chose fellow visionary and Harvard Medical School alum Samuel Gridley Howe, who was as fiery as Fisher was quiet. Howe studied European schools for the blind and returned convinced they were wrong to separate students into two different tracks—to receive either industrial training or academic education. He combined curricula so students could gain "both the ability to think and the skills to support themselves." He also stressed physical exercise and manners.

The school quickly showed progress but outran its funds and outgrew its rooms in the house of Howe's father. Enter trustee Thomas Perkins—an aristocratic millionaire trader whose own eyes were failing. Perkins donated his mansion to be used by students on condition the school raise matching funds. Six years later, continued expansion required even more space, and Perkins let his mansion be sold to purchase new facilities. In tribute, the school became the Perkins Institution for the Blind. Its most famous alumnae are Helen Keller and her teacher, Anne Sullivan. Dr. Howe went on to pioneer the Braille system, and helped replicate across the nation many schools similar to the Boston original. Today Perkins is active in 67 countries, thanks in part to tens of millions in Hilton Foundation support.

Further reading

○ Kimberly French, *Perkins School for the Blind* (Arcadia Publishing, 2004)

○ History from Perkins Museum website, perkinsmuseum.org/section.php?id=186

○ Perkins School today, perkins.org

○ Thomas Perkins profile in the Philanthropy Hall of Fame (see prior *Almanac* section)

A REFUGE FOR
JUVENILE DELINQUENTS

Until 1825, it was standard practice to lock up delinquent children with adult criminals. As a *New York Times* report put it, this often served only to make the youthful offenders "adepts in vice" by the time they were discharged from prison. To address this problem, a group of concerned citizens in New York, primarily Quakers, formed the Society for the Prevention of Pauperism and Crime. The 1823 report they commissioned suggested that young petty offenders needed their own system of adjudication, counseling, and incarceration. They proposed a "House of Refuge" that pioneered the concept of juvenile reformatories.

The society took up a subscription that raised $20,000 (philanthropist Thomas Eddy was one prominent giver), and these donations were used to renovate a donated military arsenal and set it up to receive and redirect underage offenders. The organization changed its name to the Society for the Reformation of Juvenile Delinquents, and assumed management of the House of Refuge. It operated as a privately managed facility to which statewide courts could commit juveniles. The facility received not only those who had already committed crimes but also young people who were vagrant and destitute and deemed by authorities to be on a path to delinquency. Within ten years 1,678 inmates resided there, spending their days in supervised labor.

"Typically, male inmates produced brushes, cane chairs, brass nails, and shoes. The female inmates made uniforms, worked in the laundry, and performed other domestic work," according to state archives. Both sexes received instruction in literacy and religion, and they could be bound into apprenticeships with outside employers who promised to supervise them. The boys tended to be sent to farms, the girls to homes in need of domestic laborers. The system drew considerable praise over time. In the 1830s and 1840s, such visitors as Alexis de Tocqueville, Frances Trollope, and Charles Dickens cited it favorably. By 1840, this successful example had been copied in 25 other cities, and the desirability of a separate track for administering justice to juveniles had been established.

Further reading

○ 1860 *New York Times* article, nytimes.com/1860/01/23/news/our-city-charities-the-new-york-house-of-refuge-for-juvenile-delinquents.html

○ History in *Stanford Law Review*, jthomasniu.org/class/589/Readings/juvjust-hist2.pdf

1819

A BANK FOR MODEST-INCOME WORKERS

Born in 1758, Thomas Eddy was a paragon of entrepreneurial ingenuity in both business and philanthropy. The scrappy Quaker founded the first mutual insurance company in New York City, helped devise the Erie Canal, pioneered prison reform (see 1825 entry), and much more. But most observers agree his greatest philanthropic achievement was the founding of the Savings Bank of New York. Eddy admired similar institutions in Boston and Philadelphia, which helped the working poor by providing a safe place to deposit small savings, and by paying interest that helped the poor accumulate wealth. Historian Kathleen McCarthy notes that the bank "was designed as a philanthropic venture in its techniques, as well as its aims." Directors like Eddy volunteered their time; no paid staff were engaged. And profits were channeled to pay interest to depositors rather than dividends to investors.

When the state legislature resisted incorporating the proposed bank, the Society for the Prevention of Pauperism, an earlier Eddy endeavor, launched the Bank as its own project. Just a half-decade after opening, it was serving 9,000 depositors who had entrusted it with $1.4 million in funds. The bank further helped working Americans by investing much of its capital in the Erie Canal, which, as McCarthy put it, "provided the backbone for the market revolution by helping to speed the movement of money and goods across the hinterland."

Further reading

○ Alan Olmstead, *New York City Mutual Savings Banks: 1819-1861* (U. of North Carolina, 1976)

○ Thomas Eddy entry in the Philanthropy Hall of Fame (see prior *Almanac* entry)

1812

A PRIVATELY WON WAR

When the War of 1812 broke out, the U.S. Navy possessed a total of seven frigates and less than a dozen other seagoing ships. The British Navy at that same moment numbered a thousand warships—including 175 double-gundeck "ships of the line," of which the United States had none. The comparison by firepower was even starker: the U.S. Navy carried 450 cannons; the Royal Navy 27,800.

So how did America avoid being obliterated by the English juggernaut? Individually funded, decentralized warfighting—in the form of privateers. Typical records of the day from Marblehead, Massachusetts, showed that 900 local men volunteered for service during the 1812 conflict—120 of them in the Navy, 57 as soldiers, and 726 as privateersmen. Not long after hostilities were declared, there were 517 private corsairs defending the U.S. "Let every individual contribute his mite, in the best way he can to distress and harass the enemy, and compel him to peace," urged Thomas Jefferson in 1812.

These small privateers proved enormously effective—providing the lion's share of military punishment during the three-year struggle. Over the course of the War of 1812, the U.S. Navy captured or sunk about 300 enemy ships. Privateers captured or sunk around 2,000. Maritime insurance for British traders became three times more expensive than when all of Europe was at war in the Napoleonic era.

"Privateers contributed more than the regular navy to bring about a disposition for peace in the British classes most responsible for the war," concluded Henry Adams in his history of this era. The American merchants and ordinary sailors who organized themselves into fighting units ultimately got everything they hoped for: no more impressment of U.S. seamen, a restoration of free trading, and deep respect for the ability of America's small colonies— weak of government but strong of civil society—to defend their interests.

Further reading

- Michael Rutstein, *The Privateering Stroke* (SchoonerFame.com, 2012)
- Theodore Roosevelt, *The Naval War of 1812* (G. P. Putnam, 1882)

1806

AN ORPHANAGE FOR NEW YORK

The New York Orphan Asylum Society was established in 1806 by a group of concerned women. (These included the recently widowed Mrs. Alexander Hamilton, who was then caring for six children whose mothers and fathers had died.) The women raised private funds and received a donation of land so that children would not have to resort to the local government-run almshouse. In 1807 the cornerstone was laid for a permanent orphanage in Greenwich Village. As they grew up, boys were apprenticed to mechanics or farmers, while girls either entered trades like hatmaking or became servants in private homes. The society cared for more than the children's material well-being: "They must have religious instruction, moral example, and habits of industry inculcated on their minds," stated one contemporary maxim. Staying afloat during its early decades through bequests and skilled investing, the society and its successor organizations have now served at-risk children and their families for more than 200 years.

Further reading

○ Joanna Mathews, *A Short History of the Orphan Asylum Society* (A.D.F. Randolph & Co., 1893)

SERVING ELDERLY SAILORS IN AMERICA'S FIRST SECULAR CHARITY

Robert Randall, a founder of the Chamber of Commerce and heir to a maritime fortune, signed a remarkable will that left his property as a bequest to establish America's first secular charity—benefiting aged sailors. It took decades to defend the will against family members trying to break it, but by then the original estate was producing enormous rental income. Once the legal challenges were fended off the trustees purchased a 130-acre farm on Staten Island overlooking the sea and erected a main building and two dormitories, leaving other land for farming that would provide the sailors' food. The complex known as Snug Harbor grew quickly until by century's end over 55 major buildings served 1,000 retired seamen. They enjoyed hospitals, churches, and a music hall in an operation that presaged modern-day elder care. From the start, the harbor served sailors of any race, religion, or background.

In 1976 the trustees moved the retirement home to a new facility in North Carolina. The endowment now assists elderly individuals who served at least ten years at sea with "living needs" that public programs don't cover. The original campus and Greek Revival buildings are a historic landmark district and city park now considered the "crown jewel" of Staten Island.

Further reading

○ Gerald Barry, *The Sailors' Snug Harbor: A History, 1801-2001* (Fordham University Press, 2000)
○ Snug Harbor Trust, thesailorssnugharbor.org

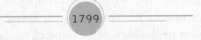

FIGHTING SHIPS BY SUBSCRIPTION

In the late 1700s, when the newborn U.S. was exchanging blows with Barbary pirates and fighting repeated engagements against revolutionary France, private donors joined together to build fighting ships for the nation. Boston, Baltimore, Salem, New York, Philadelphia, and other towns took up subscriptions. Salem, for instance (with a population of less than 10,000 but a proud seafaring tradition), built the famous 32-gun frigate *Essex*, which wrought repeated retribution on behalf of its nation over two decades following its 1799 launch. In donations ranging from $10 given by Edmund Gale to $10,000 each from Elias Derby and William Gray, citizens of Salem contributed a total of $74,700 to create their warship for the common defense.

The donors didn't just provide cash; they honed the weapon. Subscribers met at the Salem courthouse and voted on the exact kind of vessel they would build. Residents who couldn't donate funds were asked to supply building materials. This newspaper advertisement ran in the *Salem Gazette*:

> True lovers of the liberty of your country, step forth and give your assistance in building the frigate to oppose French insolence and piracy. Let every man in possession of a white oak tree…hurry down the timber to Salem…to maintain your rights upon the seas and make the name of American respected among the nations of the world. Your largest and longest trees are wanted.

Later, locals selected the captain who would command the ship when she was presented to the U.S. Navy three months after being launched.

Further reading

○ Frances Robotti and James Vescovi, *The USS Essex and the Birth of the American Navy* (Adams Media, 1999)

----- 1797 -----

A CHARITY BY WOMEN FOR WOMEN

In 1797, devoted Presbyterian Isabella Graham and future nun Elizabeth Seton founded the Society for the Relief of Poor Widows with Small Children in order to provide food and financial assistance to needy widows in New York City. It was one of the first private charitable organizations in the country, and its work bore many marks of the faith and devotion of its two founders. Subscribers were recruited to make regular donations. Volunteers provided physical resources like food and coal, plus moral encouragement, to women and children in difficult

⚘ PhilAphorism

Leisure is time for doing something useful.

☞ Benjamin Franklin

straits. In its first year, the society assisted 98 widows and 223 children. By 1800, that had increased to 152 widows and 420 children.

A hallmark of the society's work was caution in the distribution of aid. The volunteers took great pains to determine the special needs and situation of all recipients, and how they might best be lifted up. They looked for alcohol problems, and located relatives who could be helpful. To keep families out of the almshouse the society sought to match women with jobs, started its own program providing sewing work that allowed widows to earn regular income, and distributed spinning wheels and cloth. The society also operated schools for fatherless children, and hired some of the mothers to run schools across the city.

Further reading

○ Society history, povertyhistory.org/era/early_ny#isabella-grham-and-the-society-for-the-relief-of-poor-widows

○ Graham biography, b-womeninamericanhistory18.blogspot.com/2012/02/charity-worker-isabella-marshall-graham.html

MANUMISSION IN NEW YORK

Kidnapping black residents (both free and slave) and selling them into bondage in other places was common enough in 1785 to inspire some of New York City's most influential citizens and wealthiest donors to join together and fight back. Individuals like Alexander Hamilton, George Clinton, and John Jay organized not only to battle kidnappings but also to protect slaves generally, to preserve the rights of free blacks, and ultimately to "liberate" slaves and ban the ownership of one human by another. They eventually helped push through the 1799 law that established manumission across New York State, and sped the 1808 law that abolished the trade in slaves.

Prior to that, in 1787, the New York Manumission Society created the New York African Free School. Members donated and raised funds to pay for teachers, supplies, and a series of buildings. The school began with 40 students, many of them children of slaves. By 1820 there were 500 students enrolled, several teachers, and two substantial buildings, all paid for by donors.

The school day ran from 9 to 12, broke for lunch, then resumed from 2 to 5. Instruction was provided not only in academic subjects but also in practical occupational skills like mapmaking, ship navigation, and sewing. Both boys and girls could attend. Graduates became visible in a variety of fields. Alumnus Ira Aldridge became one of the most famous African-American actors of the nineteenth century, known for his Shakespearean roles and other performances. Another school product, James McCune Smith, was the first black American to earn a medical degree and to run a pharmacy.

Further reading

○ Information at New York Historical Society, nyhistory.org/web/africanfreeschool/history/ manumission-society.html

FINANCING OUR REVOLUTION

The war that created America depended heavily on private action and philanthropy. In present terms, it cost billions of dollars to equip Washington's Continental Army, arm our new Navy, and fund the deliberations of Congress. Financiers Robert Morris and Haym Salomon borrowed or raised for their country nearly all of the necessary money, working for free, battling for low interest rates, and repeatedly donating their own funds.

The unsung Salomon, for instance, gave money over and over to help key members of the Continental Congress come to Philadelphia to deliberate. He personally bought vital supplies, and used his connections to get the best possible terms for the nation as it borrowed funds in turbulent money markets. When Washington trapped British General Cornwallis near Yorktown but lacked the means to move and supply his army for the final battle of the Revolution, he cried "Send for Haym Salomon"—who quickly scratched together $20,000 under great pressure.

Having joined the Sons of Liberty early on, Salomon was twice imprisoned by the British as a spy. The second time he escaped on the day before his execution. He gave his own money to many men he considered unrecognized heroes of the war, like senior Army surgeon Bodo Otto, who had bankrupted himself buying medical supplies for his soldier patients.

Salomon was an active philanthropist in several sectors before he died at age 44 of tuberculosis (contracted while he was in prison). And his repeated contributions in wartime left his widow and four children penniless, because the hundreds of thousands of dollars of Continental debt he bought with his own fortune were worth only about 10 cents on the dollar at the time of his passing.

Robert Morris, who personally bought much of the ammunition used by Washington's army, was likewise damaged financially by his giving and his work without pay during the Revolution. James Swan, a financier who was wounded twice at Bunker Hill, then rose to command the Massachusetts militia, sold millions of acres of western land he owned to pay the military expenses of Massachusetts soldiers and equip several privateers to operate against the British. He later assumed the U.S. debt to France run up during the Revolution.

Further reading

○ Revolutionary War Archives history, revolutionarywararchives.org/salomon.html

CHARITY FOR STATE-SIDE BRITONS

Englishmen living in New York City founded a group in 1770, named the St. George's Society, for Britain's patron saint, to provide relief to any of their fellow countrymen who fell into distress. Over the years, the organization offered help to the needy in many forms: a bag of coal or pile of wood during the cold months, a winter coat, payment of a hospital stay, even ship fare to return to England for someone whose dreams had not panned out. The society continues to operate today as one of New York's oldest charities, offering scholarships, medical assistance, monthly stipends, even interment in one of the nonprofit's cemetery plots.

Further reading

○ Charles Bowring, et al., *A History of St. George's Society of New York from 1770 to 1913* (New York: Federal Printing Company, 1913)

○ St. George's Society web history, stgeorgessociety.org/history.html

IMPROVING THE ALMSHOUSE

In 1766, a group of Quaker merchants formed the Committee to Alleviate the Miseries of the Poor and won a charter to take over operation of Philadelphia's miserable almshouse from the city government. They combined private donations, public poor-relief funds, and income earned by the inmates to make improvements. The operation was moved into better facilities, and its name was changed to the more hopeful Philadelphia Bettering House.

◌ PhilAphorism

Nothing contributes more to make men polite and civilized than true and genuine charity.

◌ Wellins Calcott

To teach skills and self-improvement, the new operators set up residents in useful work picking oakum, cobbling shoes, and producing cloth and nails. This pioneering effort made the house (though never a cheery place) a more humane effort to care for the unfortunate at a time when, as one historian of social relief puts it, "most public action…depended upon private energy and private funds."

Further reading

○ Charles Lawrence, *History of the Philadelphia Almshouses and Hospitals* (Charles Lawrence, 1905)

BEN FRANKLIN ADVANCES LEARNING

In 1743, Benjamin Franklin brought into being an idea originally hatched by his friend John Bartram, one of the colonies' most distinguished naturalists. Their joint vision was a "society to be formed of Virtuosi or ingenious Men residing in the several Colonies, to be called the American Philosophical Society." Members would correspond among themselves and with international peers, especially in other British colonies, to share discoveries that could benefit the empire or "Mankind in general." Franklin's intent was to focus on ways to improve practical things like animal husbandry, mining, beer brewing, mapmaking, and the like.

Some years after getting it off the ground, Franklin grew disappointed in the society, and it became inactive. Then in the 1760s younger members keen to strengthen America's economy reinvigorated the group. They created six committees, divided by subject matter, and earned international acclaim when they charted the Transit of Venus from the Philadelphia State House yard in 1769. They also plotted possible canal routes which decades later would be used by diggers.

Another moribund period occurred during the American Revolution. The Society was re-energized in 1785, though, after Franklin returned from his ambassadorship in Paris. His European connections strengthened the group, as did his proposal—which he generously supported with a contribution and a loan—to build a headquarters.

Philosophical Hall still stands, and the society's roughly 1,000 American and international members oversee its library of nearly 200,000 volumes and over 6 million manuscripts, including Franklin's personal books, the journals of Lewis and Clark, and Darwin's letters. Its membership over the centuries makes the society's influence clear, beginning with individuals like George Washington and Thomas Jefferson (who was simultaneously president of the society and

President of the United States), and continuing through the Marquis de Lafayette, Baron von Steuben, Tadeusz Kościuszko, Louis Pasteur, Charles Darwin, John James Audubon, Thomas Edison, Linus Pauling, and Robert Frost. The society continues to award the nation's oldest scientific prize, the Magellanic Premium, and also runs several grant and fellowship programs for scholars.

Further reading

○ Jonathan Lyons, *The Society for Useful Knowledge: How Benjamin Franklin and Friends Brought the Enlightenment to America* (Bloomsbury, 2013)

○ American Philosophical Society, AmPhilSoc.org

○ Benjamin Franklin profile in the Philanthropy Hall of Fame (see prior *Almanac* section)

1727

FRANKLIN'S NETWORK FOR GOOD

In 1727, just 21 years old and cut off from his own family, Ben Franklin began his first experiment in voluntary association, thereby helping deepen America's most distinctive characteristic. He called together a circle of 12 "Leather-Apron Men" into what he later described as "a club of mutual improvement." One member was an affluent gentleman, but the rest like Franklin worked with their hands in such trades as glazier, cobbler, bartender, clerk, and cabinetmaker. Called "Junto," after the Spanish word for "meeting," the club "was distinguished by its novel blend of self-help and civic aims, and by the relatively humble status of its members," observes historian Kathleen McCarthy. Historian Gordon Wood notes that the Junto refuted the then-common notion that "servile" men could not engage in public service.

Meeting Friday evenings for dinner and discussion, the Junto followed rules drawn up by Franklin that required discussion of academic questions but also practical topics, such as how they could assist each other's success, and what could be done to help the community at large. The group proved fertile in both dimensions. It lent Franklin, for instance, the money he needed to set up as editor of the *Gazette*. It also gave birth to such community projects as the Library Company of Philadelphia, one of America's first public book collections (see 1737 entry on list of achievements in Education philanthropy). It spawned the colonies' first learned group, the American Philosophical Society (see 1743 entry). It produced the city's first volunteer fire brigade.

The Junto met for more than three decades. Instead of enlarging its original circle Franklin urged each member to start his own group. This bequeathed a template for building in Philadelphia and other parts of America the communal linkages and trust that enable individuals to work together in ways that help both themselves and the larger society. After the Junto set up its fire company, Franklin similarly encouraged others to copy the effort and bring it to new places. He also birthed the first tax incentive for philanthropy when he persuaded town officials to offer property tax abatement to persons who participated in volunteer fire companies.

Further reading

○ Benjamin Franklin profile in the Philanthropy Hall of Fame (see prior *Almanac* section)

○ Benjamin Franklin, *The Autobiography of Benjamin Franklin*, etext.lib.virginia.edu/toc/modeng/public/Fra2Aut.html

THE CONTINENT'S FIRST ETHNIC CHARITY

When 28 "Scottish men" signed the "Laws, Rules, and Order of the Poor Boxes Society" in Boston on January 6, 1657, they formed one of America's first charities, and one that still exists in its fourth century. Their Scots' Charitable Society aimed at relieving fellow countrymen who were struggling in America, particularly those who had been captured by Oliver Cromwell in battles in 1650 and 1651 and sold as indentured servants to labor in iron works and other production facilities in the American colonies. Some of these Scots fell into bad straits after their indentures expired.

The Scots' Charitable Society prefigured many future American philanthropic efforts that built their benevolence on a foundation of ethnic ties. Within a few years the society faced mismanagement and declining membership, but a reorganization in 1684 turned matters around with reforms like the careful investment of assets, and financial controls (a lockbox that required two keys). The group also suffered a crisis during the Revolutionary War because of divided political loyalties, but it has never wavered from its aim of serving the poor and having a minimum of administrative expenses. It currently focuses on "providing academic scholarships and limited financial support for individuals and families in need."

Further reading

○ *The Constitution and By-Laws of the Scots' Charitable Society of Boston* (John Wilson and Son, 1878), books.google.com/books reader?id=bRkXAAAAYAAJ&printsec =frontcover&output=reader&pg=GBS.PA9

○ Short history, scots-charitable.org/about

PROSPERITY

RELIGION

A merica's major faiths put great emphasis on charitable giving. Christians are taught to look out for those with the least, to be good stewards, to tithe, or donate ten percent of their income. Jews have the obligation of *tzedakah*, and Muslims the duty of *zakat*. In all cases the motivation is to improve the well-being of others, to share bounty with fellow creatures of God, to express devotion. Religious giving is a pillar of belief and conformity with divine intentions, and a means of expanding the community of faith and bringing enlightenment to new corners.

Religiously motivated generosity combines with American wealth and cultural norms to create potent charitable flows in the U.S., especially compared to other nations. In 2014 Americans donated $115 billion to religion-related causes. That was 33 percent of all charitable giving and proportionately twice as big as the next favorite cause, education. The deep religious convictions of Americans are a leading reason that we give at a rate two to ten times higher than other developed nations.

In addition to supporting good works at home, there is a 200-year tradition of U.S. Christians sending donations overseas. This is actually an original aspect of the faith: Christian witness has always moved restlessly toward the weak and unwanted—from ancient Jerusalem to forsaken Greece, then Italy and north Africa during their pagan centuries, next to Dark Ages Europe, eventually over to frontier America, and now across the developing world.

Interest among U.S. Christians in carrying good works and the Gospel to people in poor lands has clearly risen in recent years. Today's developing world is thought to be where needs are most urgent, where people are most receptive, where opportunities for improving both external and internal life are most open. This migration of mission work is one reason the number of Christians in Latin America, Asia, and Africa is currently rising ten times faster than population growth. A milestone was passed within the last few years: the majority of the globe's Christians now live in the less-developed world. As said by one evangelical we quote below, poor countries "are where God is really working" right now.

God is also at work—in partnership with millions of faithful givers— in a great many communities across America. All of this is abundantly documented in the religious philanthropy that follows.

‚ Section research provided by Karl Zinsmeister,
Connor Ewing, Evan Sparks, and Liz Essley Whyte

2015

A RECORD FOR CATHOLIC-SCHOOL SCHOLARSHIPS

In September 2015, the Inner-city Scholarship Fund run by the Archdiocese of New York announced the largest-ever U.S. gift to Catholic schooling. Christine and Stephen Schwarzman gave a record $40 million to an endowment that will provide 2,900 New York City children per year with scholarships. The Schwarzmans started contributing money in 2001 to this cause. "We've met so many impressive young women and men who have benefited greatly from the values provided by a Catholic-school education," stated Christine, who also serves as a trustee of the Inner-city Scholarship Fund. The fund combines contributions from New York business leaders and church donors, and provided tuition assistance to nearly 7,000 Catholic-school students in 2015, prior to the Schwarzman gift. The church has pledged to match the Schwarzman gift, and to raise an additional $45 million from other donors to increase the fund's scholarship endowment by $125 million in total.

Further reading
o Andy Smarick and Kelly Robson, *Catholic School Renaissance: A Wise Giver's Guide to Strengthening a National Asset* (The Philanthropy Roundtable, 2015)

A FUND TO SEED NEW CATHOLIC SCHOOLS

B. J. Cassin has taken the venture-capital model that made him wealthy and applied it to his Catholic-schooling philanthropy. He was a key funder in building Chicago's acclaimed Cristo Rey Jesuit High School from a single site in 2000 to a network of 30 schools in 20 states today, with more on the way. These Catholic schools now serve 10,000 low-income students each year, with excellent educational results (in 2014, every single Cristo Rey graduate was accepted to college), an acclaimed program for placing every student in a work-study job at one of 2,000 partner businesses, affordable tuition, and a sustainable economic model. (See 2000 entry describing Cristo Rey schools in detail on our companion list of achievements in Education.)

Now Cassin is seeking to amplify this success. He is part of a group of Catholics seeking new models for financing religious schools, whose enrollments as a proportion of the entire U.S. student body have declined by a third over the past half century. He and two colleagues have launched a philanthropic venture called the Drexel Fund that will invest in carefully selected academies, education entrepreneurs, and school networks with the intention of "transforming" and expanding faith-based schooling. The fund will raise $85 million from a variety of wealthy individuals and use it as venture capital to create tens of thousands of new seats in excellent, sustainable schools—most of them Catholic, but also including other religious orientations and some secular private schools.

"There are a lot of interesting new models in faith-based and especially Catholic schools, but we don't have a platform to replicate the most successful ones," Cassin says. "That's where the idea of Drexel came from." It seeks to do for religious schools what the NewSchools Venture Fund and the Charter School Growth Fund have done for charters: provide capital to scale up successful existing institutions and start promising new networks. Cassin gave $1 million in seed money and recruited several other donors, allowing the effort to launch in six states where tax credits or vouchers also help parents afford religious and private schools— Arizona, Florida, Indiana, Louisiana, Ohio, and Wisconsin.

By 2024, Drexel's funders aim to create 125 new schools, grow six to eight school networks, and cultivate 40 new school entrepreneurs. And if all goes according to plan, no more than 15 percent of a Drexel-supported network's budget will come from philanthropy once it is fully functional.

Further reading

○ *Philanthropy* magazine reporting, philanthropyroundtable.org/topic/excellence_in_
philanthropy/stronger_together

MUSEUM OF THE BIBLE

In 2015, a $400 million construction project was launched by the Green family to create a highly visible, philanthropically created Museum of the Bible in Washington, D.C. Located three blocks from the National Mall and U.S. Capitol, the building will house the Green Collection of Biblical Artifacts (see 2011 entry), attractions like a reconstruction of first-century Nazareth and specialized films, a 500-seat performing-arts theater, and a large scholarly wing with a reference library, artifact research labs, and academic conference center. A flight simulator will allow guests to soar over Washington, then swoop down and read the Biblical inscriptions that adorn so many of its landmarks. Textured bronze panels at street level, custom stained-glass work, and a 200-foot LED-panel ceiling will display artistic interpretations of Biblical themes.

"The Bible has had a huge impact on our world today—from culture and politics, to social and moral justice, to literature, art and music, and more," explains philanthropist Steve Green, chairman of the Museum of the Bible, and president of Hobby Lobby, which his family founded and owns privately. "Our family has a passion for the Bible and we are excited to be part of a museum dedicated to sharing its impact, history, and narrative with the world." The museum is on track to open in 2017.

Further reading

○ Steve Green interviewed in *Philanthropy*, philanthropyroundtable.org/topic/excellence_in_
philanthropy/interview_with_steve_green

○ *Architectural Record* on the museum design, archrecord.construction.com/
news/2015/02/150220-Hobby-Lobby-Owners-Break-Ground-on-Bible-Museum.asp?WT.
mc_id=rss_archrecord

POLIN MUSEUM

There are facilities across the U.S. and the globe that remember the World War II genocide against Jews. But great museums celebrating the rich history and contemporary vigor of Jewish life are rare. A group of American donors led by San Francisco businessman Tad Taube and the Koret Foundation set out to remedy that.

The group focused their efforts on the country that had the largest Jewish community in the world at the onset of the twentieth century—Poland. They donated $30 million ($20 million of it committed by Taube) to create a series of exhibits that include a replication of a seventh-century synagogue, dozens of films, and a trove of historical documents and artifacts. The government of Poland erected an $80 million building to house the exhibition, which opened in late 2014.

The museum aims to undo some of the erasures of Jewish existence carried out during the Nazi period—when Jewish cemeteries were bulldozed, synagogues destroyed, and books and official records burned. "I want to improve the Jews' image of themselves. And I want to see the world abandon its attempt to make Jews the victims," says Taube in explaining his gifts that celebrate the strength and endurance of Jewish community traditions.

Further reading

○ *Philanthropy* article on the Polin Museum, philanthropyroundtable.org/topic/excellence_in_philanthropy/a_tribute_to_life

AN ILLUMINATED BIBLE FOR THE COMPUTER AGE

The Saint John's Bible, commissioned by the Benedictine fathers of Saint John's Abbey in Collegeville, Minnesota, and funded by 1,500 donors, is a completely handwritten and hand-illuminated Bible. It is a glorious seven-volume work of art, each volume stretching two feet tall by three feet wide when open, and weighing 35 pounds. The text and images were inked with hand-ground pigments and platinum- and gold-leaf on pages made of calf-skin vellum.

Theologians selected passages for large-scale illustration. Computers scaled images and plotted line breaks. All calligraphy and illumination was crafted by hand in a scriptorium—*Smithsonian* magazine described the end product as "one of the extraordinary artistic undertakings of our time." Goose,

RELIGION

❧ PhilAphorism

Charity is the great channel through which the mercy of God is passed on to mankind. It is the virtue that unites men and inspires their noblest efforts. ☞ *Conrad Hilton*

turkey, and swan quills were used for lettering. Mineral pigments were mixed with egg yolks and water to paint pages in vivid hues that will endure for centuries, as in medieval illuminated manuscripts.

Production extended over two decades and cost $8 million. To bring the Bible to a wide audience, trade books reproducing the seven volumes in a smaller format are being sold. The original work is touring churches, museums, and libraries around the world for in-person viewing of what Pope Benedict XVI called "a great work of art…a work for eternity."

Further reading

∘ The Saint John's Bible, saintjohnsbible.org/process

2011

GREEN COLLECTION

David Green founded Hobby Lobby and built it into a nationwide arts-and-crafts chain. From its Sunday closures to its debt-free policy, Hobby Lobby runs on consciously Biblical principles. This fascination with the Bible extends to the Green family's philanthropy. Starting in 2009, the family began collecting what quickly became the world's largest private collection of Biblical artifacts. The more than 40,000 items acquired by the Greens include an unpublished fragment of Genesis from the Dead Sea Scrolls, the *Codex Climaci Rescriptus* (which contains the earliest known manuscript of the New Testament in Palestinian Aramaic), many rare cuneiform tablets, the Roseberry Rolle (a translation of Psalms into Middle English that predates John Wycliffe's famous English Bible by 40 years), and more than 1,000 different versions of the Jewish Torah.

At the 400th anniversary of the King James Bible in 2011, the Greens launched their collection on a world tour, sending the artifacts to the Vatican, New York, and other cities until they settle into a permanent home at the new Museum of the Bible in Washington, D.C. That facility is being constructed by the Green family—see nearby 2015 entry.

Further reading

∘ *Philanthropy* article, philanthropyroundtable.org/topic/excellence_in_philanthropy/ illuminated_giving

∘ *New York Times* report, nytimes.com/2010/06/12/business/12bibles.html?_ r=2&pagewanted=all

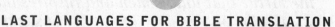

2008

LAST LANGUAGES FOR BIBLE TRANSLATION

About 6,900 languages are currently in use across the globe. Only a few hundred of these have a complete translation of the Christian Scripture; another 2,300 have a partial translation. There are 2,200 languages into which the Bible is currently being translated (often a laborious process—an alphabet or grammar sometimes has to first be created because the language is spoken but not written). That leaves more than 1,900 tongues for which no Bible translation has even been started; these have around 200 million native speakers.

Wycliffe Bible Translators was founded in 1942 by Cameron Townsend, who discovered while serving as a missionary in Guatemala that many of the people he was working with didn't understand Spanish; they spoke Cakchiquel, in which no Bible text was available. Since then, Wycliffe and other nonprofits have made great progress in translations. University of Notre Dame professor Mark Noll describes the creation of Wycliffe Bible Translators as "one of the great Christian events of the century," and "a turning point symbolizing the movement of Christianity from the northern hemisphere to the southern." It has also been found that Bible literacy often becomes an entryway to multiple forms of progress for isolated peoples, not only in reading and writing but in bettering public health, agricultural improvements, human rights, and economic development.

However, it was a huge task that Wycliffe took on. By 1999 the group was launching Bible translations at the rate of 20 new languages per year; at that pace it would have required an additional century and a quarter to reach all remaining populations. So Wycliffe committed to a breakthrough: It promised to raise a billion dollars of donated money and use that to hire additional linguists and deploy new techniques to fast-track translations. Soon, the so-called Last Languages Campaign was launching 109 new versions of Scripture each year. The goal is to have a translation at least begun in every language under the sun within 17 years of the campaign's 2008 commencement.

In short order the Last Languages Campaign had raised $235 million, including one anonymous $50 million gift. Today Wycliffe employs nearly 6,000 translators, linguists, aviators, and supporting humanitarian workers and teachers. Along with Biblical literacy, its teams now bring water purification systems, AIDs education, and other assistance to 90 poor countries.

Further reading

○ *Christian Post* reporting, christianpost.com/news/wycliffe-raises-250-million-for-last-2000-bible-translations-47680

○ Wycliffe timeline on Bible translations over the centuries, wycliffe.org/about

2008

ENCOURAGING MUSLIM GIVING

Approximately a quarter of the world's population is Muslim, and their faith's *zakat* requirements enjoin them to share a portion of their annual income with the less fortunate. Much of this giving traditionally has been done in secret, spontaneously, or without any system. After years of giving to medical charities, victims of the 2005 Pakistan earthquake, and other causes, Chicago physician Tariq Cheema decided to form a group to make Muslim giving easier, more strategic, and more open. He also recognized that it is now important for donors to Islamic charities to make certain their gifts will not support advocates of violence.

Cheema and collaborators launched the first World Congress of Muslim Philanthropists in Istanbul in 2008. Wealthy Muslim donors, foundations, companies, and charities gathered to share best practices, create multi-donor pooled funds for battling poverty, and encourage others in their faith to become generous givers to causes that are accountable and effective.

Further reading

○ WCMP website, thewcmp.org/home

○ *Chronicle of Philanthropy* report on WCMP founding, philanthropy.com/article/New-Group-Meets-to-Promote/163185

2008

NEW LEADERS FOR CATHOLIC SCHOOLS

Minnesota businessman Jack Remick and his wife, Mary Ann, are long-time supporters of the Alliance for Catholic Education, an extraordinarily successful program created at the University of Notre Dame to train teachers for needy Catholic schools. (See 1993 item on companion list of Education achievements.) In 2008, a gift from the Remicks allowed the Alliance to create an additional program for training principals to lead Catholic schools. ACE founder Timothy Scully reports that his organization is going to particularly zero in over the next decade "on forming principals and superintendents. School leaders establish the culture of high expectations; they hire the teachers. That's why we are going to focus on the principal."

Scully argues that "thoughtful philanthropists can have their greatest leverage on Catholic education by investing in leadership programs," and that this will in turn change American inner cities. "Evidence shows that Catholic schools form citizens who are two and a half times more likely to graduate from college, who have high expectations, who are more tolerant, who are more generous. Those are the kinds of schools we need."

In 2014 the Remicks donated $10 million to double the endowment of the ACE principal-training program. By then, approximately 250 of the program's graduates were already leading Catholic schools across 41 states.

Further reading
○ Q&A with Timothy Scully, philanthropyroundtable.org/topic/excellence_in_philanthropy/ qa_with_timothy_scully

GIVING IT ALL

Alan Barnhart is an evangelical Christian, and when he and his brother Eric decided to go into business together in 1986 (they were in their mid-20s), Alan studied the Bible to see what it said about moneymaking. Wherever he turned he found warnings that money can be dangerous. "I read all these verses and I thought, 'I want to be good in business, and I'm competitive. But I don't want to make a lot of money if doing so would damage my life. And I could see where it really could." So the two young men did something very unusual. When they launched their new crane and rigging company, they vowed to cap their income at the level of the middle-class fellow members of their Sunday-school class in Memphis, Tennessee, and channel much of their company's profits to charity. In their first year of business they donated $50,000—more than Alan's salary.

Nearly 30 years later, the two men run a company with $250 million of annual revenue, but they have stuck to their decision on salaries and profits and have given away about $100 million. Half of the money made each year by Barnhart Crane & Rigging is reinvested in the company; the other half goes to charity. There is no corporate foundation or bureaucracy—committees of employees and their spouses meet regularly to decide where to donate. Currently most of the funds are sent to development projects and Christian ministries in poor countries in Africa, the Middle East, India, and southeast Asia. Employee Joye Allen says that's where she and her co-workers see the largest needs. "That's where God is really working."

In 2007, the Barnharts decided to go even further: They moved the entire company into a charitable trust owned by the National Christian

RELIGION

◄ PhilAphorism

Each man should give what he has decided in his heart to give, not reluctantly or under compulsion, for God loves a cheerful giver.

☞ *St. Paul*

Foundation. NCF has developed a specialty at helping entrepreneurs donate still-operating businesses, and they set up a structure which allows Alan and Eric to continue to run the firm. This retains the for-profit power of the enterprise and its skilled managers, while guaranteeing that all of the wealth generated by the company, either in annual earnings or increased valuation, ultimately goes to charitable good. Alan's wife, Katherine, says the donors get something out of the bargain too: "Giving feeds our soul. Giving has us looking outward...to serve the God that we love."

Alan views it as a bonus that this arrangement prevents his children from growing up wealthy. "There are great benefits to a kid to hear the word 'no,' and the theology of the Rolling Stones: 'You don't always get what you want,'" he says. "I taught them the joy of giving early," adds Katherine. "I taught them the joy of contentment."

Further reading

○ *Philanthropy* magazine profile, philanthropyroundtable.org/topic/donor_intent/giving_it_all1

2006

CREATING MORE, AND BETTER, FOSTER FAMILIES

Religious donors have worked productively with churches over the past decade to get needy children adopted into permanent families, as the 2005 entry below catalogues. In addition, where children are not candidates for adoption, donors and believers have united in some remarkable ways to improve the availability and quality of foster care. Most children whose family lives become disrupted remain legally connected to their parents; they merely go temporarily into state care. On average, they spend about five months outside their natural home while authorities work to stabilize the parents. It is much better for most children if they pass this time with a foster family rather than in an institution. But in many places there are not enough foster families to go around, especially not enough good ones.

Social entrepreneur Bill Hancock and philanthropist Rick Jackson (both of whom are devoted Christians who grew up in disrupted families) went to work on this problem, starting in 2006. They knew that, historically, church members tended to be the most patient and effective foster parents, and reasoned that a church congregation could be a valuable support to any fosterer if volunteers were trained and organized to help. Jackson, who had created 25 companies as a health-care entrepreneur, provided strategic advice and offered to fund the effort single-handedly for five years.

Hancock researched where children in need of fostering in their home state of Georgia were coming from, then started visiting churches in those neighborhoods to see if couples in the congregations could be aided and encouraged to take on local children in need of sheltering. Organizing circles of church members who will help the families that volunteer to foster or adopt turned out to be crucial. Individuals who can't commit to full-blown fostering can at least offer respite care, babysitting help, assistance with food and clothing, emotional support, and other backup that makes the church programs work.

The Jackson/Hancock nonprofit, now known as FaithBridge Foster Care, has been enormously successful. The foster families recruited from churches by FaithBridge methodically draw on support from their congregations, and 96 percent stay with fostering. These couples have already served hundreds of children across a growing number of Georgia counties. The nonprofit spends about $3,600 per case, which compares to an annual cost of $90,000 (and far worse social outcomes) for a child housed in an institution.

The organization now has satellite operations in two other Georgia cities, in Florida, in New York, and in Arkansas. FaithBridge estimates that its model of improved fostering can easily be duplicated in 17 metro areas where three quarters of the nation's demand for foster care is currently located.

Further reading

○ FaithBridge Foster Care, faithbridgefostercare.org

○ *Philanthropy* magazine reporting, philanthropyroundtable.org/topic/excellence_in_ philanthropy/making_forever_families

2005

RELIGION

MOVING UNPROTECTED CHILDREN INTO FOREVER FAMILIES

Among evangelical Christians, the adoption of unprotected youngsters, both domestic and foreign, has become a charitable passion in recent years. When Colorado pastor Robert Gelinas discovered in late 2004 that there were hundreds of children in his home state who were legally available for adoption but had no one willing to take them, he urged fellow Christians to "make sure there are no children waiting for homes." He and other Coloradans launched Project 1.27 to train couples and congregation support teams to adopt or foster children languishing under state institutional supervision. Over the next few years, hundreds of children who had been waiting for adoption were scooped up by families guided by the program.

Taking its name from James 1:27 ("look after orphans and widows in their distress"), Project 1.27 is not an adoption agency, but rather educates parents on the legal, financial, and emotional issues involved in adoption and fostering. Participants pay a nominal $100 administrative fee; all other expenses of being trained and legally certified are covered by donors. It costs the organization an average of $5,000 to help a family adopt one child. That compares to $50,000 of annual cost to the government to maintain one child in the foster-care system.

Families recruited from affiliated churches are given 36 hours of training over a period of several weeks. Church leaders and members of the local community are also trained to help, because the organization believes families taking on needy children require the support of friends and neighbors. The organization shepherds volunteer families through the required paperwork, helps church leaders establish parent-support groups and adoption resources within their congregations, and advocates for parents throughout their engagement with the foster-care system.

Project 1.27 expanded beyond Colorado in 2014 and 2015 to Arizona, D.C., New York, Wisconsin, and Florida, and opened collaborations with eight similar organizations operating across the country. The group relies mostly on volunteers, and receives financial support from many small donors who give monthly, sponsor one child, or offer annual gifts. Pastor Gelinas, who has himself adopted five children with his wife, tells audiences that if "people of faith step up…it is possible that a foster-care system can be emptied."

Further reading

○ The Project 1.27 network, project127.com/1-27-network/current-1-27-ministries

○ *Orange County Register* background on church adoptions, ocregister.com/articles/children-248143-care-orange.html

2004

BOSTON JEWISH DAY SCHOOLS

According to the latest census conducted by the AVI CHAI Foundation, total enrollments in U.S. Jewish day schools increased from 184,000 children in 1998 to 255,000 in 2013, as many parents sought to strengthen the Jewish identity of their children in the course of educating them. In Boston, three anonymous families made a major gift of $45 million in 2004 to improve the 14 Jewish day schools operating in that metro area. Over the previous 15 years, the number of day-school students in greater Boston had more than doubled, and this grant aimed to improve teaching, curriculum, and educational excellence.

The grant inspired a smaller subsequent grant from Boston's Ruderman Family Foundation to improve the quality of instruction and care for special-needs students at these same schools. This allowed placement of a dedicated staff of 12 special educators at 12 of the region's Jewish day schools.

Further reading

○ *Boston Globe* reporting, boston.com/news/education/k_12/articles/2004/10/10/jewish_day_schools_given_45m_gift?pg=full

○ AVI CHAI 2014 census, avichai.org/knowledge_base/a-census-of-jewish-day-schools-in-the-united-states-2013-14-2014

FAITH ANGLE FORUM

From the Middle East to social issues, religion is a huge influence on current events and news today. In addition, faith is a big part of personal life for most Americans: According to the Pew Research Center, 56 percent of Americans say that religion is "very important" to them, while another 26 percent say it's "somewhat important."

Yet for many or most reporters, religion is a foreign land. "I was practically born and raised in the news business, and know firsthand that newsrooms are exceedingly secular places," says veteran journalist Carl Cannon. Religion expert Michael Cromartie recounts how he once mentioned the Book of Ephesians while providing a reporter with information for a story that touched on faith; the reporter asked him for the name of the author and the publisher.

To help fill some of this unhealthy knowledge gap, Cromartie and Luis Lugo, who worked within the Pew Charitable Trusts, discussed how it might be possible to "educate the press on religion." In 1999 they began staging lunchtime seminars in D.C., a common practice in the nation's capital. Cromartie eventually proposed getting the journalists out of Washington and "away from their deadlines, to actually have a reflective two days with serious scholars."

Pew provided funding, and in 2002 a weekend conference, now hosted semiannually near Miami, was launched. It is known as the Faith Angle Forum, and features presenters like megachurch pastors Tim Keller and Rick Warren, Pakistani ambassador Husain Haqqani, National Institutes of Health director and Christian Francis Collins, and an expert on Mormonism during Mitt Romney's Presidential run. Every invitation-only conference is

RELIGION

ᔄ PhilAphorism

As the purse is emptied the heart is filled.

☞ *Victor Hugo*

limited to about 20 reporters, columnists, or producers, including some of the most influential correspondents in the country.

The gatherings cost about $150,000 each to produce. Pew footed most of the costs for the first ten years. Additional funders like the John Templeton Foundation, Pierre Omidyar's Democracy Fund, the Gloria Dei Foundation, and the Lynde and Harry Bradley Foundation have contributed in recent years.

Further reading

○ Faith Angle Forum, eppc.org/programs/the-faith-angle-forum

○ *Philanthropy* magazine reporting, philanthropyroundtable.org/topic/excellence_in_ philanthropy/building_religion_iq_in_reporters

RECONCILIATION AND ECONOMIC PROGRESS

The Christian-led national reconciliation taking place in the east African nation of Rwanda after its horrendous genocide some years earlier has attracted many generous Christian donors, including Dale Dawson. A serial entrepreneur looking for his next challenge, Dawson was visited by an Anglican bishop from Rwanda raising donations for his war-torn country. The cleric challenged him. "Rwanda doesn't have a vibrant economy," said Bishop John Rucyahana, donations will help only fleetingly. "You're a businessman. Why don't you build businesses in Rwanda?"

Captivated by the bishop's charge, Dawson investigated a Christian overseas-development nonprofit called Opportunity International. The investment banker in him was quickly impressed by Opportunity's carefully developed microlending model. Soon Dawson was not only making his own multimillion dollar donations but also serving as a spokesman and fundraiser for the group. Among other projects, Dawson eventually spearheaded the creation of a popular bank that quickly became Rwanda's most important financial institution (see 2007 entry in our companion list of Overseas achievements).

As his interest in faith-based solutions in Africa grew, Dawson first joined a few other donors in building schools in Rwanda for genocide orphans and other needy children. Their church-linked group Bridge2Rwanda kept creating schools. And then it established a scholars program that paid for promising Rwandans to attend colleges abroad. Soon, Dawson was spending half of his time in the country.

Dawson and colleagues subsequently expanded Bridge2Rwanda into economic development projects. These included a coffee exporter, an egg farm, a shoe distributor, a feed mill, and an entity providing financial services to foreign companies operating in the country. A think tank to educate people across Africa on the merits of market enterprise was launched by B2R in 2010.

Further reading

o *Philanthropy* magazine profile of Dale Dawson, philanthropyroundtable.org/topic/ excellence_in_philanthropy/lending_a_hand

o About Bridge2Rwanda, bridge2rwanda.org/about

2002

CHRISTIAN UNION

The successful Campus Crusade model for religious work on college campuses (see 1951 entry) asks missionaries to raise their own funds and moves them from institution to institution. The Christian Union is distinctive in raising funds tied to particular schools. When donors contribute to Christian outreach at a specific college, the funding stays there. Christian Union is also unusual in its focus on bringing the evangelical message to a particular type of setting—the predominantly secular world of the Ivy League. Founder Matt Bennett, a Cornell alumnus, recognized that graduates from these selective schools will end up as "leaders in so many places in society," and "we need people who have the values of Jesus Christ" in those slots. So the Christian Union now operates on the campuses of Princeton, Columbia, Cornell, Yale, Harvard, Dartmouth, Brown, and the University of Pennsylvania.

While the group seeks to find, create, and encourage believers, its primary focus is on Christian leadership development. Instructors take eight to ten students through a book of the Bible each semester, seeking lessons for living. They also provide two specialty courses: one for freshmen on sex and spirituality, another for seniors on vocations. The group offers one-on-one mentoring, a weekly lecture series, book giveaways, and conferences as well.

At Princeton, the Christian Union now attracts 500 students per year to at least one of its programs. That's about 10 percent of undergraduates, making it one of the more successful student groups on campus. The Harvard chapter attracts 200 participants.

Though most of the students already are believers when they become involved with the Christian Union, students experience religious conversion through the group every year. Student demand on its campuses is outstripping fundraising, despite an annual budget of about $6 million. Many of the union's hundreds of donors are Ivy League alums who wish they had had access to such a program when they were in school. Others simply agree

RELIGION

with Bennett that "if we want to see the nation change for the better, people who are in leadership in culturally influential institutions have to have the right values. That's why we do what we do."

Further reading

○ Christian Union's description of its focus on leaders, christianunion.org/about/why-leaders

○ *Philanthropy* magazine reporting, philanthropyroundtable.org/topic/excellence_in_ philanthropy/campus_crusades

LDS PERPETUAL EDUCATION FUND

The Perpetual Education Fund, created in 2001 to provide loans for schooling to needy Mormon students, is a 150-year echo of one of the very first efforts at mutual aid set up by the Church of Jesus Christ of Latter-day Saints. It is modeled on an earlier LDS revolving charitable pool called the Perpetual Emigration Fund (see 1849 entry). While the Emigration Fund was established to help isolated Mormons move to the church's new heartland in Utah, today's Education Fund offers church members living in any part of the globe financial assistance to train and educate themselves.

Loans can be used for technical, vocational, or professional education, and can include tuition, training materials, books, and licensing fees. To qualify for a loan, students must go through a process similar to the selection process for missions service, including getting a bishop's certification of church involvement. The fund is supported by donations from fellow Mormons and loan repayments from previous beneficiaries. The program now operates in 63 countries. Around 100,000 students, mostly young adults in poor nations, have so far financed their studies using the PEF.

◈ PhilAphorism

When you give to the needy, do not announce it with trumpets, as the hypocrites do in the synagogues and on the streets, to be honored by others.... Your Father, who sees what is done in secret, will reward you.

☞ *Jesus*

Further reading

○ Program description, lds.org/topics/pef-self-reliance/perpetual-education-fund?lang=eng

2000

MELDING WORK AND HIGH SCHOOL VIA CRISTO REY

For years, venture capitalist B. J. Cassin gave scholarships to inner-city kids; then he wanted to help on a wider scale. In 2000 he and his daughter visited Chicago to investigate a new kind of Catholic high school. The Cristo Rey Jesuit High School not only provided low-income children with an excellent, values-rich education, it also offered a new financial model, after the loss of low-cost teaching by nuns wrecked the finances of most inner-city Catholic schools. Cristo Rey designed into its high school a corporate work-study program that has all students working entry-level jobs at firms like JPMorgan Chase or Pricewaterhouse Coopers. Four students share one full-time position. Each student works one day per week, then takes a full schedule of classes compressed into the remaining four days. The students thus acquire business familiarity, skills, and mettle that give them a foot in the door to white-collar professions. And the firms pay the school for the work received—which covers two thirds of the school's expenses.

Cassin donated $12 million to expand Cristo Rey into a network of schools applying this shared work/learn structure. He also dedicated a large chunk of time to chairing the network. Each potential school first undergoes a nine- to 12-month feasibility survey, and those that pass are then given a half-million-dollar seed grant over three years, with additional start-up costs covered by local donors. In 2003, the Bill & Melinda Gates Foundation was so impressed it began multimillion-dollar contributions to seed the creation of even more schools. Donors in particular cities, like David Weekley and others in Houston, have also paid for new schools.

A Gates official noted early on that the work-study component is especially valuable for Cristo Rey's low-income students. Their "sense of confidence and efficacy" is striking, he observed. "They appreciate being treated as adults and given real responsibility. They also recognize they're gaining valuable work experience and learning a lot of things they wouldn't learn at school."

By 2015, 9,000 students attended the Cristo Rey network's 30 schools in 19 states and D.C. They worked in more than 2,000 different partner businesses. Among the network's graduates from the past five years, 90 percent have enrolled in college and persisted into their sophomore year—twice the rate of peers from the same socioeconomic background.

RELIGION

Further reading

○ Andy Smarick and Kelly Robson, *Catholic School Renaissance: A Wise Giver's Guide to Strengthening a National Asset* (The Philanthropy Roundtable, 2015)

○ Cristo Rey work-study program, CristoReyNetwork.org/page.cfm?p=372

GENEROUS GIVING

The Maclellans of Chattanooga, Tennessee, have long been sacrificial givers to Christian causes, with family members having years ago increased their charitable "tithes" to as high as 70 percent of their annual income. The Maclellan Family Foundations make grants to more than 200 ministries and charities every year, with a special focus on faith-based solutions to serious social problems, in the U.S. and around the world. They methodically support Christian education within a 500-mile radius of their headquarters in Chattanooga. They have been generous funders of national and international groups, like Campus Crusade for Christ, that bring the evangelical message to young people and other seekers. Their grants have trained Christian and nonprofit leaders in China to grapple with local concerns in an effective way. And the Maclellans were crucial early backers of a pathbreaking program called First Things First, which strengthens marriage and parental bonds with children.

In 2000, the Maclellan Foundation launched a parallel organization called Generous Giving specifically to educate and inspire wealthy Christians to share more of their bounty. Noting that the fraction of household income donated to charity has not risen since the 1930s, despite the large jump in living standards since then, Generous Giving aims to help more people "experience the joy of generosity and excel in the grace of giving." The group sponsors an annual two-day "Celebration of Generosity" attended by about 400 living religious donors who participate in teaching, storytelling, worship, and interaction with peers. Smaller "Journey of Generosity" retreats are intimate 24-hour gatherings hosted by a couple or individual or organization, where the small group explores how generosity can change one's life. Generous Giving held more than 150 of these meetings in 2014.

There is no soliciting or agenda at GG meetings; the emphasis is on conversation with Christian peers about the satisfactions of sharing resources effectively. President Todd Harper reports that uncertain donors often come in with a mindset of "I ought to give," and leave with the view that "I get to give!" The gatherings are credited with having a transformative effect on many wealthy participants.

Further reading

◦ Generous Giving, generousgiving.org

◦ Maclellan Foundation profile in *Philanthropy*, philanthropyroundtable.org/topic/excellence_
in_philanthropy/maclellan_foundation

1999

BIRTHRIGHT ISRAEL

Birthright Israel was founded in 1999 to send young Jews on a fully paid ten-day trip to Israel so they can explore Judaism and understand their personal connections to the Jewish homeland. It was the brainchild of philanthropists Charles Bronfman and Michael Steinhardt, who put up $8 million apiece and recruited 15 other partners to contribute $5 million each to get things started. Today, the program has a broad base of 25,000 individual donors who make it possible for about 51,000 souls to travel to the Jewish homeland each year. (Sheldon and Miriam Adelson have been the single biggest donors, giving $250 million to the organization since 2007.)

To date, Birthright has brought to Israel over 400,000 young Jews from more than 66 countries, most of them for the first time. The organization is thus strengthening Jewish faith and identity. In a 2012 study of long-term effects, Brandeis University researchers found that 90 percent of Birthright participants reported feeling "closer to Israel," and trip-goers were somewhat more likely to marry someone Jewish and to place importance on raising a family in Judaism.

Steinhardt warns that Birthright is just a starting point, not a panacea for lost religious identity. He cautions that "the ten days of Birthright Israel cannot fully offset the appallingly poor Jewish education most of its participants were subjected to." Nonetheless, the philanthropic footprint of the program is impressive: A 2013 Pew Research study found that 44 percent of American Jews under 30 have now visited Israel, and about half of them did so courtesy of Birthright.

Further reading

◦ About the trips, birthrightisrael.com/visitingisrael/Pages/About-the-Trip.aspx

◦ *Philanthropy* magazine reporting, philanthropyroundtable.org/topic/excellence_in_
philanthropy/nonprofit_spotlight

1999

JUBILEE SCHOOLS

When he became Catholic bishop of Memphis, Tennessee, says Terry

RELIGION

Steib, "I was shocked that our schools were closing. I thought, 'That's not the church's way.'" In 1999 he announced that the slide would be reversed: Eight previously shuttered Catholic schools would be reopened to serve children in the greatest need—those living in the poor urban neighborhoods of Memphis. They were to be called the Jubilee Schools, in honor of the forthcoming millennium of 2000, a year of mercy for the poor within Catholicism. An anonymous non-Catholic donor called and offered a $15 million gift to back the brave plan; from that point on the project was popularly known as the Miracle in Memphis. The diocese had the first school reopened, and 20 children registered, within three weeks. Today more than 1,200 students attend eight reopened schools. Tuition is on a sliding scale, and minimal for poor families—thanks to the $60 million Memphis residents and groups like the Poplar and Hyde Family foundations donated to reconstruct and endow the schools, and the fact that operating costs per pupil are held down (to half of what neighboring public schools cost). Fully 90 percent of the children attending Jubilee Schools live below the poverty level, and 81 percent are non-Catholic. Yet the Catholic high schools of Memphis ultimately graduate nearly 100 percent of their students.

Further reading

∘ Article in *Catholic Education*, digitalcommons.lmu.edu/cgi/viewcontent.
  cgi?article=1662&context=ce

∘ *Philanthropy* magazine coverage, philanthropyroundtable.org/topic/k_12_education/
  an_episcopalian_an_atheist_and_a_jew_walk_into_a_catholic_school

REBUILDING CHRISTIANITY
BEHIND THE IRON CURTAIN

As the harvest of a century of religious persecution, only 2 percent of Russians now attend church weekly; 7 percent attend at least once a month. To help rebuild the faith, a group of American Christian philanthropists decided to launch an American-style Christian liberal-arts college. The Russian-American Christian University opened its doors in Moscow in 1996, offering business and social work as its first two majors. The mission, explains Howard Dahl, the owner of a North Dakota manufacturing firm who donates three quarters of his income to charity, and a founding member of the college's board of directors, was to produce students who would come out of their education "bilingual, computer literate, with a deep sense of the value of a liberal-arts education, and a strong Christian faith." An early slogan was "Character, Competence, and Christian Worldview."

Along with Dahl and other individual donors, the Lynde and Harry Bradley Foundation was a supporter. The college produced several hundred graduates before running into political and government opposition, a refusal of state accreditation, and heavy taxes which forced it to close its undergraduate program in 2010. The school of social work was spun off to the Russian Orthodox Church and a few programs continue under the rubric of the Russian-American Institute.

Howard Dahl also helped build up Lithuania Christian College, one of the only other private, faith-based liberal-arts colleges in the territories of the former Soviet Union. He and his wife have also funded social and fraternal groups working to re-establish Christian practice in former Soviet lands, including a thriving youth organization in south Russia connected to Young Life.

Further reading

◦ Howard Dahl interview in *Philanthropy* magazine, philanthropyroundtable.org/topic/ excellence_in_philanthropy/interview_with_howard_dahl

◦ Interview with the college president, eastwestreport.org/35-english/e-18-2/278-moscow- s-russian-american-institute-instilling-character-competence-and-christian-worldview

1993

ALLIANCE FOR CATHOLIC EDUCATION

In the early 1990s, the Reverend Tim Scully and other leaders at the University of Notre Dame decided that if Catholic elementary and secondary schools were going to survive and prosper in the future they would need help from Catholic colleges. In 1993 Scully founded the Alliance for Catholic Education, which recruits and trains about 90 new top-ranked college graduates each year to serve as teachers for two years in an underresourced Catholic school. During summers, the 180 active ACE

RELIGION

❧ PhilAphorism

I feel called to help individuals, to love each human being. I never think in terms of crowds in general but in terms of persons. Were I to think about crowds, I would never begin anything.

☞ *Mother Teresa*

participants undergo intensive training and study on the Notre Dame campus, and at the end of their two-year teaching commitment more than 90 percent emerge with a no-cost master's degree in education. During their two years as a classroom instructor they live with other ACE students in group houses provided by their local Catholic diocese—which allows sharing of work experience and knowledge, along with emotional support and spiritual growth. Fully 82 percent of ACE graduates continue to serve as educators after their two-year commitment is up, and 75 percent are still working in education five years out.

The Alliance for Catholic Education has been built on the support of the University of Notre Dame and myriad individual donors like Chicago investor John Jordan, who designated the program as one of the beneficiaries of the $150 million he has given the university in recent years. In the cities where it sends its teachers, ACE also encourages donors to support local schools. An example would be the $1 million Ralph and Trish Nagel donated to Catholic schools in their hometown of Denver, where in many of the classrooms 90 percent of the children live at the poverty level. The most enduring supporters of ACE have been Minnesota businessman Jack Remick and his wife, Mary Ann, whose latest gift of many was a 2014 donation of $10 million. (See 2008 entry.)

ACE has sent more than 1,300 teachers to serve in high-need schools throughout the United States. The group has recently added to its offerings professional and consulting services to help strengthen local Catholic schools. The Alliance's success has inspired 12 other Catholic colleges to launch similar teacher-training programs, which under the umbrella of the University Consortium for Catholic Education annually instruct and send forth 400 much-needed teachers.

Further reading

○ Brief ACE history, ace.nd.edu/about/history

○ Release on Jack and Mary Ann Remick gifts, insideindianabusiness.com/newsitem. asp?ID=65115

==== 1993 ====

BOLSTERING LUTHERAN TRADITION

After graduating from college in 1949, Marvin Schwan went to work with the family dairy and dramatically expanded it over a period of decades into a huge food-service company. At the end of his life, Schwan created a nearly billion-dollar foundation by giving it two thirds of his company in 1993. The foundation, like Schwan himself, has maintained a low profile throughout its existence. But it has operated as a bulwark of traditional Lutheranism in America.

Schwan instructed his foundation trustees to support seven Lutheran organizations, including five evangelical organizations and two colleges. These groups have received hundreds of millions of dollars in donations from the foundation in the years since. The churches, missions, and schools of the conservative Lutheran faith have thus been strengthened and perpetuated into the future.

Further reading

○ Facts about the Schwan Foundation, faqs.org/tax-exempt/MO/Marvin-M-Schwan-Charitable-Foundation.html#b

TIKVAH FUND

Zalman Bernstein served in the U.S. Navy, acquired an education in economics, and then brazened his way onto Wall Street—first talking his way into an entry-level job and eventually founding his own brokerage firm on boldly unconventional practices. He made a fortune, and later in life devoted himself to Orthodox Judaism. Bernstein eventually gave most of his money to three different foundations intended to help Jewish religious practice flourish in the modern age. The Tikvah Fund, created in 1992, was the smallest but perhaps the most influential because it focused, under the direction of Roger Hertog (a business associate of Bernstein and himself a savvy philanthropist), on advancing intellectual excellence within traditional Judaism and bringing this wisdom to Jewish leaders.

The Tikvah Center in Manhattan offers one- to three-week institutes on Jewish thought and history, two- to three-day workshops for busy professionals, and summer fellowships for college and high-school students. Tikvah also sponsors public lectures and events. And the fund subsidizes publications: the quarterly *Jewish Review of Books*, the monthly *Mosaic*, the Library of Jewish Ideas book series, and others. Tikvah was also important in the creation of Shalem College, Israel's first Ivy League-style liberal arts college with a core curriculum.

Further reading

○ Tikvah Fund, tikvahfund.org/about

SISTERS OF LIFE

After Catholic Archbishop of New York John O'Connor returned from a tour of the Dachau concentration camp, he penned an article for the archdiocese newspaper mulling how easily humans can lapse into disregard for life, and envisioning a new burst of pro-life activism. In June of 1991, eight women committed themselves to this mission, forming a new religious order called the Sisters of Life. To the three traditional vows of Catholic nuns, the sisters added a fourth: "to protect and enhance the sacredness of human life."

The Sisters of Life focus on caring for women with troubled pregnancies. At their mission house in Manhattan, they welcome women to live with them, providing a safe place offering sustenance, care, and counseling while they carry their children to term and get their upbringing well-launched. The nascent order relied on donations of funds and supplies—particularly from members of the Sisters of Life Guild, individuals who donate at least $1,000 a year. An outpouring of funding allowed the sisters to provide residential care for mothers and newborns for up to a year after birth.

Subsequently, additional convents where these services could be offered to mothers in distress were opened across New York City, and then outside the city. At a time when other Catholic orders were shrinking dramatically, the Sisters of Life have grown to 80 nuns. In 2007, the archbishop of Toronto invited the sisters to establish their first international mission in Canada. (See 1968 entry for information on the rise of other pro-life religious charities.)

Further reading

○ Reporting at AmericanCatholic.org, americancatholic.org/Messenger/Jan2010/Feature1.asp

○ About the Sisters of Life, sistersoflife.org/about-the-sisters-of-life

1990

MANNA FROM HEAVEN

Seven members of the First Presbyterian Church in Philadelphia joined together in 1990 to provide meals for individuals and families afflicted by the new and scary AIDS epidemic. The goal was not only to help sustain

---

◄ PhilAphorism

If your aims as a donor are modest, you can accomplish an awful lot. When your aims become elevated beyond a reasonable level, you not only don't accomplish much, but you can cause a great deal of damage. ✐ *Irving Kristol*

---

those who were ill, but to help them feel less isolated from the church's care. Soon scores of volunteers were involved and MANNA (the Metropolitan Area Neighborhood Nutrition Alliance) was delivering thousands of meals and nutritional counseling from a commercial kitchen and a fleet of trucks.

After delivering more than 2 million meals, MANNA expanded its mission to help feed other area residents stressed by life-threatening illnesses like cancer, renal disease, cardiac disease, and diabetes. The average recipient is now 61 years old and has a household income of $10,188. All meals (65,000 per month) and counseling are delivered free of charge. MANNA annually receives donations of more than $1.6 million, and volunteer labor worth a half-million dollars. By its twenty-fifth anniversary, the group had delivered 8 million meals and was a good exemplar of hundreds of other church-initiated and -staffed feeding programs in existence across the U.S.

Further reading

○ History of MANNA, mannapa.org/history

SYNTHESIZING RELIGION AND DEMOCRATIC CAPITALISM

Bursts of philanthropic support helped create important new centers of religious intellectual dynamism in the 1980s and 1990s. The venerable Jewish magazine *Commentary* expanded its circulation during the 1980s and became a prominent advocate for liberty abroad. Lutheran and then Catholic pastor Richard Neuhaus became an increasingly influential advocate for traditional religious understandings of social issues, and in 1990 founded the acclaimed ecumenical religious journal *First Things*. That same year, the Reverend Robert Sirico co-founded the Acton Institute, a new research organ promoting the complementarity of economic freedom and religious practice. Around the same time, Catholic intellectual George Weigel was publishing defenses of democratic capitalism and creating his definitive biography celebrating Pope John Paul II's role in the collapse of communism. Along with Michael Novak's work reconciling capitalism and religion (see 1978 entry), these energetic new scholars, groups, and journals—all donor-supported—generated fresh public understanding of the role of spiritual faith in maintaining the health of Western society.

Further reading

○ *First Things* journal, firstthings.com

○ *Commentary* magazine, commentarymagazine.com

○ Acton Institute, acton.org

○ George Weigel, *Witness to Hope: The Biography of Pope John Paul II* (Harper Collins, 1999)

MILKEN ARCHIVE OF JEWISH MUSIC

Music plays an important part in nearly all religious traditions. But sacred music is not necessarily self-preserving. Dedication and foresight are sometimes needed to ensure that musical traditions will be around for future generations to experience. Inspired by his "own interest in music, and deep abiding commitment to synagogue life," philanthropist Lowell Milken created the Milken Archive of Jewish Music to catalogue and preserve the diversity of sacred and secular music linked to "the American Jewish experience."

Since its founding in 1990, Milken has committed more than $30 million to the archive, which now includes impressive collections of written and recorded music, oral history, and historical artifacts. In addition to saving existing works, the archive has commissioned new recordings, by artists ranging from Dave Brubeck to the Vienna Boys Choir. In partnership with the Naxos classical music label, the Milken Archive of Jewish Music has released a 50-disc series that documents the span of Jewish music.

Further reading

○ Milken Archive of Jewish Music, milkenarchive.org
○ Catalogue of Naxos recordings, naxos.com/series/milken_archive_of_american_jewish_ music.htm

STEPUP MINISTRY ENCOURAGES WORK

White Memorial Presbyterian in Raleigh, North Carolina wanted to help house families who were homeless or at risk of becoming homeless. Eventually, that mission transformed into a jobs-training approach. The effort was initially funded by the church budget and the generosity of several congregation members. Soon the ministry was incorporated as a multi-denominational nonprofit supported by several churches, and eventually also by individuals, the John William Pope Foundation, and other donors.

A major 2004 grant from the White Memorial Community Fund laid the foundation for StepUp Ministry's current two-pronged approach: life-skills training and job-skills workshops. The job-skills portion begins with a weeklong classroom-instruction period where students learn the ins and outs of finding and maintaining employment. The life-skills training extends over a full year and is designed to help participants stabilize their living patterns so they can hold jobs for the long haul.

Careful attention to practical details helps the programs succeed. For instance, the job-skills classes are held in a different location each day because the ministry found this reminds participants that getting to a job site can take time and requires planning and consulting maps or bus schedules in advance.

A more fundamental secret to StepUp's success is that it reinforces family interdependence. When a father or mother requests assistance, StepUp requires that the children also be enrolled in complementary programs. The whole family is ministered to. "Four out of five African-American males are not living with their children and the birth mom. Dealing with that fracture and helping to restore families is critical," says president Steve Swayne.

By using careful tracking mechanisms, StepUp is able to demonstrate impressive results. The ministry made 326 job placements in 2014, with 67 percent of the new workers being ex-offenders, 38 percent homeless, and 31 percent recovering substance abusers. This was accomplished on an operating budget of $1.6 million.

The ministry recently expanded to Greensboro, where it made 181 job placements in 2013. It next aims to replicate its programs in Durham and other parts of North Carolina. StepUp and programs like it created in other parts of the country—like Houston's WorkFaith Connection which placed more than 3,500 graduates in jobs between 2007 and 2015—are emblematic of hundreds of local efforts by churches and faith-driven nonprofits to improve the economic status of the poor.

Further reading

○ About StepUp Ministry, stepupministry.org/about-stepup/history

○ David Bass, *Clearing Obstacles to Work: A Wise Giver's Guide to Fostering Self-Reliance* (The Philanthropy Roundtable, 2015)

1988

RALPH BEESON'S ORTHODOX PHILANTHROPY

Ralph Beeson was legendarily cheap when it came to his own needs. Once, when given some new corduroys, the insurance executive turned them down on account of already owning a pair. At his modest house just south of Birmingham he often chose not to operate the air conditioning during brutal Alabama summers, saying it "costs a fortune to run that thing." But just down the hill from his home, he had a view of Samford University—to which he was nothing but generous.

As a 29-year-old life-insurance salesman, Beeson had poured his savings into the stock of his company, Liberty National, just after the crash of 1929. The bet paid off handsomely, and he cashed in for $100 million in the 1980s.

RELIGION

From that windfall, he gave $70 million to create a new divinity school at Samford as a tribute to his father. Knowing that its future clergy would mostly hold low-paying jobs after graduation, Ralph went to great lengths to ensure that the seminary would be affordable. As a result, tuition is held to just a fraction of what comparable schools charge, even though the student body is capped at 180 to maximize teaching quality.

Beeson aimed for much more than just affordability, though. He told the founding dean, "Now, Timothy, I want you to keep things orthodox down there." Moreover, "I want you to train pastors who can preach." Thanks to the donor's clear guidance, a quarter-century after his death the school remains richly evangelical, and known for turning out excellent sermonizers.

Methodist by upbringing, Beeson was married to a Baptist and became Presbyterian—so his divinity school, though located at a Baptist university, welcomes all Christian faiths. That same eclecticism is on display in the school's architectural centerpiece—the beautiful Hodges Chapel. It combines classical Palladian and colonial American designs, pairs the cruciform footprint of a Catholic cathedral with a traditionally placed Protestant pulpit, and employs Renaissance-inspired art to celebrate Christian historical figures. Only in America does one find this kind of generous religious mix.

Upon his death in 1990, Beeson also left $39 million to Asbury Theological Seminary, a prominent evangelical graduate school in Kentucky. That gift doubled Asbury's endowment and funded the creation of new academic programs and seminary buildings. Though the two recipients of Beeson's beneficence have differences, they are united in their commitment to Christian theological education that is orthodox but ecumenical, and consistently excellent.

Further reading

○ Reporting in the *American Spectator*, spectator.org/articles/41731/welcome-beeson

○ History at FaithandLeadership.com, faithandleadership.com/jason-byassee-argument-stone

1986

SPONSORING LOW-INCOME
CHILDREN IN CATHOLIC SCHOOLS

When Catholic schools serving poor children in New York City were in danger of shutting down for lack of tuition-paying capacity on the part of parents, banker and longtime donor Peter Flanigan sprang into action. He established a Patrons Program that encouraged contributions to financially stressed inner-city Catholic elementary schools. And he set up Student Sponsor Partners to connect donors directly with at-risk kids who needed mentors and financial sponsors in order to attend Catholic schools.

In the first year of Student Sponsor Partners, Flanigan and 44 other men and women backed 45 students. Within a few years the program was serving 1,000 students annually. In 2001, supporter David Dunn began giving $500,000 per year, then $750,000 per year to support students, and in 2008 SSP received its first million-dollar gifts.

In 2014, more than 1,400 children attended 25 Catholic schools around New York City thanks to Student Sponsor Partners. Fully 85 percent of SSP students graduate from high school, compared to 61 percent of their peers in public schools, and 93 percent of graduates go on to college (versus 50 percent of NYC public high school grads). The Student Sponsor Partners program has now been copied in nine other cities, including Boston, Chicago, San Francisco, and Washington, D.C.

Further reading

○ Student Sponsor Partners, sspnyc.org

1985

LDS CHARITIES

Since its early days, the Mormon church has run highly effective relief societies and special programs to aid the needy within its fold. (See this list's 1936 and 2001 entries for descriptions of some large-scale efforts that attend to the welfare and educational needs of fellow church members.) In 1985, LDS Charities was set up to methodically offer humanitarian services to people of other religions across the globe.

That year, the church collected a special "fast-offering" (where congregants skip meals and donate what they would have spent on themselves) and earmarked it to help famine victims in Ethiopia. When officials traveled to that country to decide how best to use the $6 million raised, they found staggering need. A second fast-offering of about the same size was collected later in the year, and that led to a gradual institutionalization of overseas humanitarian work.

RELIGION

PhilAphorism

What we do for ourselves dies with us. What we do for others and the world remains and is immortal.   ☞ *Albert Pine*

Today, members of the Church of Jesus Christ of Latter-day Saints may designate their gifts for developing-world aid in a variety of ways. The church covers all administration and overhead so that every penny given to LDS Charities goes to direct services and care. Since 1985, more than a billion and a half dollars have been donated, helping 30 million people in 179 countries without regard to religion or culture. In addition to disaster relief and emergency services, favored projects include long-term initiatives in clean water, food production, immunization, and vision care.

Further reading

○ Background on the founding of LDS Charities, lds.org/church/news/viewpoint-1985-fast-marked-beginning-of-lds-charities?lang=eng

○ 2014 Annual Report of LDS Charities, ldscharities.org/pages/2014-annual-report?lang=eng

1984

LEADERSHIP NETWORK
HELPS BUILD MEGACHURCHES

When Angelus Temple opened in Los Angeles in 1923 with seating for 5,300, the megachurch was born. An evangelical Christian congregation led by a charismatic pastor, committed to welcoming new believers, Bible-based but lacking conventional denominational boundaries, the new church drew huge crowds. Lakewood Church, founded in Houston in 1959, was another early example of the type. It was theologically conservative, racially inclusive, and popular from the start. By 1979 Lakewood was attracting more than 5,000 people to its services; today it is America's largest church, with average weekly attendance of 43,000. (Megachurches are among the most integrated institutions in the U.S., averaging a 20-percent-minority mix of congregants, while Lakewood is 40 percent white, 30 percent black, 30 percent Hispanic.)

Megachurches are conventionally defined as those attended by at least 2,000 congregants per week. There are now 1,300 such churches in the U.S. (up from just 50 in 1970), housing about a tenth of all U.S. churchgoers, and they are continuing to expand in both size and influence. They include prominent institutions like the Willow Creek Church led by Bill Hybels, the Saddleback Church under Rick Warren, the McLean Bible Church founded by Lon Solomon, and the Potter's House pastored by T. D. Jakes.

This vast expansion was driven not just by congregational donors but also by broader philanthropy. Bob Buford built a large network of cable television stations, but he was also a devoted Christian and in his mid-50s felt strongly drawn into the world of nonprofits and church-building. Buford had become close friends with famed management theorist Peter Drucker, who viewed America's vigorous civil society of churches, charities, and helping organizations like the Salvation Army as secrets to the country's success, and vital buffers between private interests and the state. Together they discussed what became the Leadership Network—a group devoted to helping the pastors of fast-growing churches thrive even more. Leaders of new churches with a thousand members or above would be brought together with similar peers so they could learn from each other, and be taught essentials of excellent management and oversight.

Bill Hybels and Rick Warren were just two of many church founders who benefited from Leadership Network training and resources as they grew their congregations to over 20,000 members. Bob Buford also joined with philanthropist Phil Anschutz to finance the Burning Bush Fund, which concentrated on planting new churches and cultivating new leaders to open churches. Pastors like Tim Keller, Larry Osborne, and Greg Surratt were aided by the fund as they built thriving, multi-campus evangelical churches. In a 1998 *Forbes* interview, Peter Drucker characterized megachurches as "surely the most important social phenomenon in American society in the last 30 years."

Further reading

○ *Forbes* reporting on Buford, Drucker, and Warren, forbes.com/sites/ richkarlgaard/2014/03/26/peter-drucker-and-me

○ *Christianity Today* background, christianitytoday.com/edstetzer/2014/april/catalyst-that-fostered-movement.html

1982

RELIGION

NATIONAL CHRISTIAN FOUNDATION

In 2014, the National Christian Foundation was the fifteenth largest charity in America. It handed out $859 million during the year, and received more charitable contributions than groups like the American Cancer Society, Harvard University, and Habitat for Humanity. The foundation continues to grow dramatically, as it has since its 1982 creation.

The brainchild of three evangelical financial professionals, NCF was established to "simplify the process of giving, multiply the results, and glorify the Lord." The founders created one of the first donor-advised funds designed specifically for Christian givers. They also focused on making it easier to donate non-monetary gifts—like an operating business—which most philanthropic organizations find too complex to handle. They are now national leaders in this work.

By streamlining the philanthropic process, connecting Christian donors with the wisdom and charitable choices of other givers, providing up-to-the-minute advice on Christian nonprofits, and offering definitive handling of complicated donations, the National Christian Foundation has become not only one of the most important religious philanthropies in the U.S. but one of the most innovative philanthropic organizations of any sort. Its grants to religious charities now exceed a billion dollars a year, and in 2015 reached a total of $6 billion since the organization's founding.

Further reading

◦ National Christian Foundation, nationalchristian.com/home

◦ *Philanthropy* magazine reporting, philanthropyroundtable.org/topic/excellence_in_ philanthropy/alms_alchemy

1981

HEALTH-CARE SHARING MINISTRIES

Hundreds of thousands of American families currently have no medical insurance yet know that their health-care needs are covered. They have joined one of the four major "health-care sharing ministries" now operating across the U.S., the earliest of which was formed in 1981. These religious nonprofits allow their members to share the costs of each other's medical needs, without the commercial mechanisms of insurance. Inspired by ancient Christian practices of burden sharing and mutual aid, each of these groups requires enrollees to make a profession of Christian faith, and to avoid smoking, alcohol abuse, and other practices they deem incompatible with faithful Christian living. These requirements cement the personal commitment, communal feeling, unity, and trust that have allowed these voluntary networks to thrive.

The lifestyle pledges also help contain expenses, as does the prudence with which members seek care, knowing that fellow believers will be asked to share all bills. The monthly costs of health-care sharing ministries tend to be half or less of what comparable commercial insurance would require. Each ministry operates differently, but all involve a considerable degree of personal contact and mutual support. People send notes and prayers along with the checks they mail to families in health crises, which participants cite as one of the great satisfactions of their voluntary pooling of medical needs.

These ministries have proven quite practical, flexible, and effective, with billions of dollars of reimbursements having taken place since their creation. When the Affordable Care Act was written in 2009, with penalties for parties lacking insurance, health-care sharing ministries were granted an exemption. The organizations have experienced record enrollments in the years since.

Further reading

○ *Philanthropy* magazine reporting, philanthropyroundtable.org/topic/philanthropic_
freedom/sharing_health1

INSTITUTE ON RELIGION & DEMOCRACY

Around the time that the Cold War abroad and culture wars at home reached their peak after the election of Ronald Reagan, some worshippers in mainline denominations became distressed by politicization of church statements and policies. One flash point was open support among some church officials for Marxist causes, including undemocratic and illiberal rebel groups in Latin America. A drift into left-wing social policies and "liberation theology" was another trend that set off alarms. In response, some members of the United Methodist Church along with other concerned Christians raised funds, created a board of directors, and launched the Institute on Religion & Democracy as a membership organization in 1981.

As one of the group's leaders put it, "We believe the church should be the church, proclaiming the Gospel, discipling believers, assisting the needy, and teaching broad principles for a better society without becoming narrowly political. Our unity as Christians is based on our faith in Jesus Christ, not positions on secular legislation." In the words of founding board member and prominent theologian Thomas Oden, "we are not presuming to create new doctrine but hold firmly to apostolic teaching in ways pertinent to current circumstances." Funding has come from membership dues, church contributions, individual donors, and grants from foundations like the John M. Olin Foundation, Smith Richardson Foundation, and the Lynde and Harry Bradley Foundation.

The IRD has promoted renewal of an energetic Christian orthodoxy— within the Methodist, Presbyterian, and Episcopal churches in particular. It has also closely monitored the National Council of Churches, the National Association of Evangelicals, and other ecumenical groups, reinforcing theology that is "orthodox, reliable, stable, beautiful, familiar, and glorious."

⁊ PhilAphorism ──────────────────

The man who dies rich dies disgraced.

⮩ *Andrew Carnegie*

RELIGION

Religious liberty in foreign lands has always been an important issue for the group, and continues to be today.

Further reading

○ Institute on Religion & Democracy, theird.org

1978

MICHAEL NOVAK SYNTHESIZES
CATHOLICISM AND CAPITALISM

Michael Novak wrote a Vietnam protest book, worked for Eugene McCarthy, Robert Kennedy, George McGovern, and Sargent Shriver, nearly became a priest, and launched a new program for the Rockefeller Foundation supporting scholarship in the humanities. Then in 1976 he published, in *Harper's Magazine,* an early story worrying over the deterioration of the family. Thus began a theological journey from left to right (Novak later defined a conservative as "a progressive with three teenage children") that ultimately had national and international political consequences.

In 1978 Novak became a researcher at the American Enterprise Institute, where he was supported year after year by the John M. Olin Foundation—in what subsequent AEI president Christopher DeMuth called "a pretty high-risk investment, a brilliant bet. At that time almost everybody, including its defenders, viewed capitalism as useful for fueling progress and high levels of material welfare, but essentially amoral and selfish at its root. Nobody did more to uncover the ethical attributes of the free-market system than Michael Novak, and he did this entirely on year-to-year philanthropic support." In 1982, Novak's book *The Spirit of Democratic Capitalism* injected a new moral and spiritual dimension into our understanding of economics. The work was widely translated, and helped inspire rebellion against Marxist economics in Latin America and behind the Berlin Wall.

In 1983, Novak led a group of 100 influential Catholics through new thinking on the morality of nuclear weapons, and their publication of a lengthy letter bolstered the move toward missile defense. Novak made the case for moral pressure on the Soviet Union based on human-rights concerns, and he was eventually appointed as a human-rights ambassador of the U.S. government. In more than 45 books and other voluminous writing, he applied religious principles and moral arguments to scores of other public controversies: welfare reform, environmental conservation, liberation theology, and arms control. His analysis of the linkages between economic freedom and moral and political freedom influenced Pope John Paul II's important encyclical on economics, *Centesimus Annus,* which defended private property rights and voluntary associations, and refuted state socialism.

Further reading

◦ Novak biography, michaelnovak.net/biography

◦ DeMuth on Novak, Karl Zinsmeister and John Miller, *Agenda Setting: A Wise Giver's Guide to Influencing Public Policy* (The Philanthropy Roundtable, 2015)

1976

HABITAT FOR HUMANITY

"What the poor need is not charity but capital, not caseworkers but co-workers." So declared Millard and Linda Fuller in the letter that launched their new group Habitat for Humanity in 1976. Millard had become a millionaire by age 29, but his workaholism nearly destroyed their marriage. As part of their healing the couple joined Koinonia Farm, a small interracial Christian community outside Americus, Georgia, and there they conceived the idea for "partnership housing." After a stint as overseas missionaries, the Fullers began to put their vision into practice.

Habitat for Humanity has grown to have more than 1,400 local affiliates across America and the globe. Its housing program uses volunteer labor and donations (large and small) of money and material to build and rehabilitate homes with "partner families" who are in need. Local affiliates select the families, who then invest hundreds of hours of "sweat equity" in their own home. The families also provide a down payment and monthly mortgage payment. These family contributions make the house "their own," but the volunteer labor, donated materials, no-interest mortgages, and no-profit sale combine to bring ownership within reach of people who would otherwise have no chance of possessing their own residence.

Many of the families Habitat works with need some counseling and nurturing as well, which the organization provides. The result is a very low default rate, and families tend to increase their education and incomes after earning their home, while their children tend to become healthier and do better in school. "We are openly and unashamedly a Christian program," Fuller proclaimed in the early years, and the program retains its Christian roots today. It refuses any government funds that would limit its ability to proclaim its faith-based mission. At the same time, it is thoroughly ecumenical in the persons it helps and the volunteers it recruits.

And Habitat for Humanity doesn't just help the poor: as Fuller told *Philanthropy* magazine, wealthy people "can have a poverty of spirit…and when we put them out on a Habitat work site they literally weep, because

RELIGION

they feel like their lives are meaning something." By 2012, Habitat had placed over 4 million people in more than 800,000 families into homes of their own.

Further reading

○ *Philanthropy* interview with Millard Fuller, philanthropyroundtable.org/topic/excellence_in_philanthropy/millard_fuller_give_that_man_a_hammer

○ Millard Fuller, *The Theology of the Hammer* (Smyth & Helwys, 1994)

CHRISTIAN STUDY CENTERS ON CAMPUSES

When Daryl Richman arrived at the University of Virginia in 1968 he encountered students who had little experience of church but hungered to understand the intellectual traditions of Christianity. Some of these pursued studies at places like the L'Abri Fellowship that evangelical theologian Francis Schaeffer created in Switzerland. Soon there was interest in having a somewhat similar gathering place at UVA where Christian intellectual life, lectures, and fellowship would be supported. In 1976, with financial help from townspeople and faculty, the Center for Christian Study bought a house on the edge of campus and began to host events.

The group expanded, and soon inspired similar entities on other campuses in California, Minnesota, Connecticut, and elsewhere. In 2009 an informal network of these groups formed themselves into the nonprofit Consortium of Christian Study Centers. By 2015 the consortium had 19 member centers at colleges across the country, where students wrestled to connect Christian beliefs with their classroom work and with challenges in the world around them. An annual budget of about $300,000 provided by donors allowed the organization to incubate new campus affiliates, advise their growth, and help them find staff and speakers. "This is a movement," says director Drew Trotter.

⊸ PhilAphorism

Many persons have a wrong idea of what constitutes true happiness. It is not attained through self-gratification, but through fidelity to a worthy purpose.

☞ *Helen Keller*

Some of these study centers have become quite advanced in their offerings. For instance, the Chesterton House at Cornell now provides not only stimulating talks, study groups, and social events, but also opportunities to take classes in theology and Biblical studies and get Cornell credit. Thanks to dual million-dollar gifts from the parents of one student, Chesterton House is establishing residential units—jokingly referred to by the director as "crosses between a fraternity and a monastery"—for both men and women.

Further reading

◦ Membership map for the Consortium of Campus Study Centers, studycentersonline.org/membership/map

◦ *Philanthropy* magazine reporting, philanthropyroundtable.org/topic/excellence_in_philanthropy/campus_crusades

1976

PRISON FELLOWSHIP

In 1976, ministering to prisoners was "an unfashionable, underrated, underfunded, Christian activity with no national or international leadership," observes a Chuck Colson biographer. Notorious as President Nixon's "hatchet man," Colson had a religious conversion shortly before entering prison for obstruction of justice, and after serving his time he founded Prison Fellowship to battle the reality that two thirds of all prisoners released back into society returned to committing crimes. His group, which combined a message of repentance and reconciliation under God with strong advocacy for prisoners' interests, grew tremendously.

Colson himself donated $77,000 of the first-year budget of $85,000, and $240,000 of the second year's $440,000. For the rest of his life he continued to donate all the speaking fees and book royalties he earned, plus his $1 million honorarium upon being awarded the Templeton Prize. Almost from the beginning Prison Fellowship also received significant funding from Art DeMoss, the evangelistic founder of the Liberty Life Insurance Company (who posted bail for ex-Black Panther Eldridge Cleaver after his conversion). Other significant donors have included Phil and Nancy Anschutz, Richard and Helen DeVos, and Thomas and Sandra Usher.

Prison Fellowship's ministry now attracts 50,000 volunteers, and has expanded to include helping the families of prisoners, improving prison conditions, aiding crime victims in new ways, training volunteers to work in prisons, and reconciling victims and victimizers. One area of special effectiveness is efforts to help prisoners when they re-enter society and are most vulnerable. The ministry has been replicated in many other countries.

RELIGION

Sociologists like Byron Johnson have documented the group's effects in lowering recidivism, and in preventing crime by heading the children of criminals away from illegal activity.

Further reading

○ Jonathan Aitken, *Charles W. Colson: A Life Redeemed* (WaterBrook Press, 2005)

○ Resources from Prison Fellowship, prisonfellowship.org/resources/training-resources

1973

NORTH AMERICAN ISLAMIC TRUST

The growth of America's Muslim population (which rose from less than a million a generation ago to 3.5 million in 2015) has created demand for many more mosques and Islamic schools in the U.S. To help meet this need, a donor-funded endowment known as the North American Islamic Trust was created in 1973 to finance mosque construction for new congregations. A 2000 study found that over a quarter of all U.S. mosques had by then been funded by NAIT, and many more have been financed since. To ensure their perpetual use for Islamic purposes, NAIT now holds title to more than 300 Islamic centers in 42 states.

The trust also established a publishing arm to produce the texts needed for Islamic worship. In addition, NAIT created *sharia*-compliant mutual funds and business investments where congregations can build endowments to support Muslim religious and community life in the future.

There is controversy around NAIT. Some of the founders of the trust were members of the Muslim Brotherhood, which is banned or watched closely by police in many countries due to a history of militancy. With extensive funding from Saudi Arabia, the trust sometimes supports Wahhabist strains of Islam that can become extremist. During the past decade, leaders of NAIT-owned mosques in Florida and New York have been convicted of supporting terrorist activity.

Further reading

○ North American Islamic Trust, nait.net

1972

TEMPLETON PRIZE

"How little we know, how eager to learn." That was the motto that guided John Templeton through much of his success as an investor, and that animated much of his philanthropy. Religion is one of the areas where Templeton believed man has the most to discover. Concerned that modern intellectual life often neglects metaphysical wisdom, and particularly the role of religion in undergirding human advancement, he created the Templeton Prize for Progress in Religion in 1972, with a purse (currently around $1.6 million) engineered to be larger than the Nobel awards.

The Templeton Prize honors a living person who "has made an exceptional contribution to affirming life's spiritual dimension, whether through insight, discovery, or practical works." It aims to identify "entrepreneurs of the spirit" who expand our vision of human purpose and ultimate reality. The prize celebrates no particular faith tradition or notion of God, but rather many diverse manifestations of the divine. Templeton stipulated that there would be at least one judge from each of the five major religions "so that no child of God would feel excluded."

The first recipient was Mother Teresa of Calcutta, who six years later would win the Nobel Peace Prize. Other Templeton laureates have included religious leaders like Billy Graham, Baba Amte, Charles Colson, and the Dalai Lama, philosophers and theologians such as Aleksandr Solzhenitsyn, Michael Novak, and Charles Taylor, and scientists including Freeman Dyson, Stanley Jaki, and Martin Rees.

Further reading

○ Prize information, templeton.org/signature-programs/templeton-prize

○ John Templeton profile in the Philanthropy Hall of Fame (see prior *Almanac* section)

1970

SAMARITAN'S PURSE

RELIGION

Bob Pierce was an evangelist in China when he met some Christian women who were living as missionaries among lepers. In 1970, their devotion inspired him to create a new nondenominational ministry that would support evangelical Christians providing spiritual and physical aid to hurting people around the world. He called the group Samaritan's Purse, echoing the Biblical example of the Good Samaritan. It soon developed a specialty in getting assistance to victims of war, poverty, natural disaster, disease, and famine in some of the neediest corners of the globe. (Pierce had previously founded the Christian overseas charity World Vision—see 1950 entry.)

Billy Graham's son Franklin was a bit of a prodigal, but during a period when he was drifting abroad he connected with Bob Pierce and his group. Franklin Graham was powerfully moved by their mission, and after Pierce died of leukemia, Graham became president of Samaritan's Purse in 1979. He proved to be a formidable fundraiser, and led the charity through a period of explosive growth.

Today, Samaritan's Purse raises more than $500 million every year to feed

African children, provide medical care to cyclone victims, offer HIV treatment in countries like Peru, donate Christmas gift boxes to the dispossessed, and otherwise deliver physical aid and spiritual hope. The group has a particular reputation for operating without bureaucracy or corruption, and for eschewing red tape in ways that allow its planes and aid workers to arrive first and get things done when poor people are hurting. It has been named many times as one of today's most efficient religious charities.

Further reading

○ 2014 ministry report, static.samaritanspurse.org.s3.amazonaws.com/pdfs/2014_SP_ Ministry_Report.pdf

1968

COVENANT HOUSE

In 1968, two Catholic priests, Bruce Ritter and James Fitzgibbon, resigned from comfortable professional college work and moved into a tenement building in New York City's East Village to establish a ministry for helping runaway teenagers and other troubled youths. They called their home Covenant House, and their effectiveness in providing a mix of counseling and practical shelter, food, and safety services to vulnerable youngsters drew many clients and volunteers. The organization was incorporated in 1972 and set out to acquire additional properties, first in midtown New York, and then across the country. The group developed a specialty in rescuing sexually exploited teenagers, and added to its homelessness services drug counseling, physical and mental-health programs, foster-care transitions, and other assistance.

Originally, much of the group's funding came from contracts with New York City agencies, but disagreements with city officials over how facilities should be run led Covenant House to decide most of its funding should come from private donations instead of government. Catholic philanthropists like Peter Grace and Bill Simon became loyal donors. Simon started volunteering in the group's homes, often with his children, starting in the 1970s. When grown, his children later became important donors and volunteers at Covenant House chapters.

In 1990, charismatic founder Bruce Ritter became embroiled in a sexual scandal and resigned. Donations collapsed and the organization was in peril. Aggressive intervention by the board of directors, with help from Cardinal O'Connor, resulted in a thorough investigation and airing of all findings, changes in staff and internal governance, and a stern new director in the person of Sister Mary Rose McGeady. The organization stabilized, and donations recovered. Today Covenant House shelters and otherwise serves 62,000 youths per year, in 21 locations, relying on $100 million of annual contributions.

Further reading

○ *Philanthropy* magazine history, philanthropyroundtable.org/topic/excellence_in_ philanthropy/when_founders_fall

PREGNANCY RESOURCE CENTERS

Religious charities like the Salvation Army, Jewish Maternity Homes, Catholic Charities, and others have long offered assistance to women facing unexpected pregnancies. As sexual experimentation and abortion rates soared during the 1960s, concerned Christians and churches established a new wave of modern centers to help individuals facing pregnancy crises. The first examples opened in California in 1968, and in 1971 many of these nonprofits organized themselves into the first national network of such groups, now known as Heartbeat International (which publishes an online directory of pregnancy resource centers that is searchable by zip code and service needed). Three other large associations currently help local PRCs improve and coordinate their offerings: Care Net, Birthright, and the National Institute of Family and Life Advocates.

Today there are about 2,500 pregnancy resource centers in operation, offering various levels of services including pregnancy testing, sonograms, obstetrical care, counseling, financial assistance, clothing and food banks, nutrition guidance, childbirth classes, midwife services, lactation consultation, child psychology classes, and other social work. All aim to offer alternatives to

RELIGION

◈ PhilAphorism

Gain all you can without harm to mind or body, your own or your neighbor's, by honest industry and by common sense. Save all you can to keep yourself, as well as your children from prodigal desires.... And, finally, as God placed you here not as a proprietor, but a steward, give all you can. ☞ *John Wesley*

abortion, and adoption assistance is available for mothers who seek it. More than 70,000 volunteers, including volunteer physicians and nurses, plus $200 million of annual donated funding, allow PRCs to serve about 2.3 million clients every year. Most services are free to the users. More than 20 states provide some funding for the centers, as has the federal government sporadically, but 80 percent of all centers are completely reliant on private support, and more than 90 percent of the total annual revenue of the nation's pregnancy resource centers comes from individual donations, often raised through churches.

Special philanthropic campaigns have been launched to equip pregnancy resource centers with ultrasound machines that can be used to confirm pregnancies, detect dangerous ectopic conceptions, and determine if the fetus is viable and how far along it is in development. The Knights of Columbus, the National Institute of Family and Life Advocates, Focus on the Family, and the Southern Baptist Convention have donated substantial funding to purchase hundreds of ultrasound machines for centers, and fund training and personnel that will allow more centers to add higher-level medical services to their counseling and social work offerings. As of 2010, a majority of PRCs (54 percent) were offering ultrasound services.

Further reading

○ Family Research Council national survey and report on PRCs, downloads.frc.org/EF/ EF12A47.pdf

○ Worldwide directory of pregnancy resource centers, heartbeatinternational.org/ worldwide-directory

1966

SAVING ADDICTS, AND OTHER FAITH-BASED SOCIAL WORK

Growing up as a poor Mexican-American, Freddie Garcia despised Anglo society, joined a gang, and ended up a heroin addict with a live-in girlfriend and two children. After numerous federal- and state-funded rehab programs failed to change his life, he tried Teen Challenge, a religious program, even though he couldn't imagine how "Jesus, whom I can't see, feel, or touch" could succeed where so many credentialed experts had failed. But the program dramatically altered Garcia's life in 1965. He married his children's mother, and together they felt called to minister to street addicts. They opened their tiny San Antonio home to anyone in bad straits, and soon it was overflowing with desperate cases. Garcia then opened a church focused on helping addicts receiving treatment, along with graduates of rehab who needed continuing support. The ministry used the recovering addicts to help current ones.

The couple spread their ministry throughout Texas and far beyond. Garcia died in 2009, and his son Jubal now runs the fellowship, which has helped more than 14,000 men and women leave drugs and alcohol behind. More than 70 satellite centers operate in New Mexico, Texas, California, Colorado, Puerto Rico, and some Latin American countries.

A major step in the ministry's growth occurred in 2005, when the Center for Neighborhood Enterprise helped Garcia raise funds for a multibuilding home campus in San Antonio. An anonymous donor provided $1 million and challenged the group to raise the rest. Local San Antonio businessmen led by Jack Willome and Bill Lyons pulled together pledges for the needed funds, and the new Victory Home was completely paid for when it opened.

Victory Fellowship is also known for being pressured by the Texas Commission on Alcohol and Drug Abuse, which demanded in 1992 that the ministry employ medical specialists or close. After a media outcry, the commission backed down, but in 1995 it attacked another faith-based rehab program in San Antonio. That led newly elected Governor George W. Bush to introduce legislation that changed regulations to allow faith-based programs—an innovation he later continued as President.

Further reading

∘ Freddie and Ninfa Garcia, *Outcry in the Barrio* (Freddie Garcia Ministries, 1987)

∘ *Charisma* magazine reporting, charismamag.com/blogs/199-j15/features/christian-compassion/409-when-god-came-to-the-barrio

PEW BUILDS THE EVANGELICAL PARACHURCH

Longtime Sun Oil president and Pennsylvania philanthropist Howard Pew had a multipronged approach to his religious philanthropy. He served as president of the board of trustees and chair of the National Lay Committee of the Presbyterian Church (of which he was a lifelong member), using both his time and his contributions to bolster its traditional theology. But Pew also funded the then-emerging "parachurch" institutions of the evangelical movement. He contributed $150,000 to launch Carl Henry's *Christianity Today* magazine in 1956. He gave millions to merge two seminaries into Gordon-Conwell Theological Seminary, which remains evangelical and is the largest facility training pastors in the northeast. He supported the Billy Graham Evangelistic Association, the National Association of Evangelicals, and the International Congress on World Evangelization. Pew sought to keep left-wing politics out of Christian ministry, and encouraged church leaders to focus on mission and new disciples.

Pew helped to build Spiritual Mobilization, a group which involved business executives in church leadership. He later was instrumental in the Christian Freedom Foundation, which sent a "Christian Economics" newsletter twice a month to 180,000 ministers. Pew did not achieve to his own satisfaction his goal of saving his church from loss of relevance and public support. As it drifted to the left during the '80s, '90s, and '00s, the Presbyterian Church (USA) shrunk from 3.1 million members to 1.9 million. In his other giving, however, Pew helped to create an evangelical infrastructure that now supports many fast-growing churches in the U.S.

Further reading

○ Howard Pew profile in the Philanthropy Hall of Fame (see prior *Almanac* section)

○ Kim Phillips-Fein, *Invisible Hands* (W. W. Norton, 2009)

FELLOWSHIP OF CHRISTIAN ATHLETES

Don McClanen was a 29-year-old basketball coach at a small Oklahoma college nursing a big idea. It would be good for young athletes and good for America if some of today's obsession with sports was redirected into higher purposes. To turn his idea into reality, he sent out letters to pro athletes whom he knew to be Christian and got a few to sign on. His challenge was funding.

In 1954, McClanen met with Branch Rickey, the legendary baseball manager who drafted Jackie Robinson, invented the minor-league farm system, and won four World Series. Rickey was also a devout Methodist who had never played on a Sunday. After a five-hour meeting, Rickey pledged to raise $10,000. "This thing has the potential for changing the youth scene in America in a decade," he said. Among the early supporters Rickey recruited was Pittsburgh oilman Paul Benedum. From those beginnings, the Fellowship of Christian Athletes grew rapidly, offering national camps, programs for youth and adults, and ministries and Bible studies (called "huddles") on campuses. In 2014, FCA reached nearly 10,000 coaches and

⊸ PhilAphorism

Too often, a vast collection of possessions ends up possessing its owner.

☞ *Warren Buffett*

450,000 student-athletes at nearly 12,000 sites nationwide. The group raised $101 million in donations that year for its missions.

Further reading

○ FCA annual reports, fca.org/about-fellowship-of-christian-athletes/ministryreport

○ "A League of God's Own," *Sojourners*, 2009

GIANT MAINZ BIBLE

At the very same time Johannes Gutenberg was creating his historic first printed Bible, and perhaps in the very same town, one of the last great handwritten and illustrated Bibles was being inked near Mainz, Germany. It is even possible, say experts, that this written Bible was a direct influence on the size, shape, and design of Gutenberg's initial edition. In any case, the Giant Mainz Bible represents a culmination of centuries of Christian tradition that kept Biblical knowledge alive only through laborious scribe work. Penning and illustrating the Mainz Bible took its artist 15 months of intensive labor, ending in 1453.

One of America's major book collectors—Lessing Rosenwald, son of the great philanthropist Julius Rosenwald and an important donor is his own right—acquired this beautiful and historic copy of the Scriptures. In 1952, he gave it, along with other important books, to the Library of Congress. The Giant Mainz Bible is considered one of the prizes of the Library's collection, and is on constant display in the original Library building, just outside the entrance to its main reading room.

Further reading

○ Library of Congress description, loc.gov/exhibits/bibles/the-giant-bible-of-mainz.html

RELIGION

RELIGIOUS FELLOWSHIP ON CAMPUS

Campus Crusade for Christ (more recently known as Cru) is one of the largest evangelical organizations in the world, ministering not only to 64,000 college students but also to members of the military, sports teams, politicians, and others via offshoot organizations. Similar groups like the Navigators and InterVarsity Christian Fellowship also minister to college students with opportunities for Christian learning, small-group intimacy, Bible study, fellowship, and social fun. These nonprofits are all supported entirely by philanthropy, and collectively they touch hundreds of thousands of young Americans every year.

These successful evangelical Protestant groups have more recently inspired other faith branches to create campus networks of their own. FOCUS, the Fellowship of Catholic University Students, is modeled on Campus Crusade, using recent college graduates as two-year missionaries who help students wrestle with questions of faith. From its first branch formed at Benedictine College in Kansas in 1998, the FOCUS network exploded to 99 chapters in 35 states by 2014. Some of these chapters constitute the largest student group on their campus.

Judaism has had its own growth spurt on campuses. Most colleges have for years had a branch of Hillel, the organization for Jewish students founded in 1923. But the rapid growth of the last generation has been driven by the group Chabad on Campus, which teaches Jewish orthodoxy, pride in Judaism, and "active goodness and kindness," as its president puts it. Private-equity founder and philanthropist George Rohr provided seed funding which helped Chabad mushroom from about 30 centers in the mid-1990s to 250 now. British donor David Slager helped fund the creation of 26 new centers across Europe in recent years. Mark Gottlieb of the Tikvah Fund, another donor, describes Chabad as "a bulwark" against the encroachments on religion "that many college campuses foster."

Further reading

○ *Philanthropy* magazine reporting, philanthropyroundtable.org/topic/excellence_in_
philanthropy/campus_crusades

1950

BILLY GRAHAM EVANGELISTIC ASSOCIATION

Billy Graham was one of the most influential men of the twentieth century, but in his early years Graham owed his success to two wealthy newsmen: William Randolph Hearst and Henry Luce. In 1947, Hearst instructed his newpapers to promote the Los Angeles rallies held by the 29-year-old evangelist. Hearst's favorable coverage led to positive support from *Time* and *Life* publisher Luce, who had grown up as a Presbyterian "missionary kid" in Taiwan.

Financially, Graham's ministry was built on grassroots giving. Offerings received at the rallies would be used to support local evangelistic groups and to organize future editions of the popular crusades. Throughout his career Graham depended on everyday giving from Christians rather than big philanthropy.

In his memoir *Just As I Am*, Graham recounts a story from early in his career, when he was approached by a man who at the time was among the richest in the country. The man offered to underwrite the evangelist's crusades. Graham thanked the donor but told him, "We are getting about fifteen to twenty thousand letters a week. Most of those letters will have a little money in them, maybe $1, maybe $5. But every one of those letters is saying, 'We're praying for you.' If they know there's a rich man underwriting my work, they'll stop praying, and my work will take a nosedive. So I can't accept it."

Further reading

○ Billy Graham, *Just As I Am* (Harper Collins Publishers, 1999)

○ Billy Graham archive at Wheaton College, wheaton.edu/bgc/archives/bg.html

WORLD VISION

Bob Pierce was a Baptist minister helping the group Youth for Christ hold evangelical rallies in China, where the depth of misery he witnessed among the poor had a powerful effect on him. When a Western missionary teacher brought a battered and abandoned child to him and challenged him to care for the youngster, he gave the woman, Tena Hoelkedoer, his last five dollars and promised to send the same amount each month for the child's care. This was the seed of the child sponsorship model that became the heart of the charitable efforts of World Vision—the group Pierce founded in 1950 to relieve child poverty in Asia.

The original emphasis was on buying food and protection for children in orphanages in China. The effort spread to Indonesia, Thailand, India, and eventually to almost 100 countries. (And two decades later, Pierce founded another important Christian overseas charity, Samaritan's Purse—see 1970 entry.)

Pierce filmed short movies to help Americans understand the penury of children abroad. His films also helped evangelicals understand how the communist revolution in China was causing problems in that country. He is considered a pathbreaker in popularizing the social-action movie. World Vision still relies on short videos of children it aids to connect them to small donors.

Today, World Vision describes itself as "a Christian humanitarian organization dedicated to working with children, families, and their communities worldwide...as a demonstration of God's unconditional love for all people." The organization retains a focus on individual child sponsorship, while offering aid in many forms. In 2014, the group raised $600 million in private contributions.

Further reading

○ Bob Pierce history, worldvision.ca/aboutus/Pages/History.aspx

○ World Vision mission, worldvision.org/about-us/who-we-are

WEYERHAEUSER'S STEWARDSHIP

Dave Weyerhaeuser, an executive of Weyerhaeuser Timber Company, created a family trust in 1947 to "contribute to the propagation of the Christian Gospel by evangelical and missionary work." With it, he supported the growth of numerous evangelical organizations, including Young Life, InterVarsity Christian Fellowship, the Moody Bible Institute, the National Association of Evangelicals, and Fuller Theological Seminary. He also gave generously to overseas work: Mission Aviation Fellowship, Wycliffe Bible Translators, the China Inland Mission, Food for the Hungry, and World Vision.

Weyerhaeuser considered it Biblically sound to do his giving anonymously, and declined all offers to have his name attached to any projects. He focused on making general operating grants. He also gave generously of his time, serving on more than 60 boards of Christian organizations. By the time of his death in 1999, Dave Weyerhaeuser had given more than $100 million to religious causes, making him one of the century's most significant Christian donors.

Further reading

o Biography at Weyerhaeuser's foundation, stewardshipfdn.org/applying-for-funding/ submitting-an-applicationproposal/our-founder

CATHOLIC RELIEF SERVICES AND THE RASKOB FAMILY

The Second World War reduced much of Europe to a shadow of its former glory. Cities and villages across the continent were destroyed, churches lay in ruins, millions of people were uprooted from their homes. While the U.S. government would eventually take the lead in rebuilding Europe with the Marshall Plan, that would not commence until 1947. America's Catholic bishops were ahead of their government in the relief business. In 1943 they formed War Relief Services to address the widespread devastation and aid in the resettlement of refugees. By 1955 that organization had become Catholic Relief Services and expanded its reach into Africa, Asia, and Latin America.

In the early years, support for CRS work came from grassroots giving via parish offerings. As the organization grew, Catholic philanthropists began to offer larger gifts as well. John and Helena Raskob, for instance, became early and strong supporters. John had made a fortune handling finance at DuPont and then General Motors, and later used his earnings to build the Empire State Building.

The Raskob Foundation today involves more than 100 family members and has given more than $150 million to Catholic entities working at home and abroad. A typical CRS project funded recently by Raskob trained Afghan women in embroidery skills so they can support themselves while living in refugee camps.

Further reading

○ Raskob Foundation for Catholic Activities, rfca.org/AboutUs/History/tabid/57/Default.aspx

○ Catholic Relief Services history, crs.org/about/history

YOUNG LIFE

When he was in seminary, a local minister challenged Jim Rayburn to consider the local high school his parish and figure out ways of connecting with kids who had no interest in church. In 1941, Rayburn and four other recently minted pastors created a new organization, Young Life, to run clubs where students could learn that faith in God can be both fun and life-changing. The idea spread across Texas, and then the U.S., and eventually to 95 countries.

Special ministries to children with disabilities, middle-schoolers, rural students, military children, and multicultural urban students were added to the original formula. Energetic summer camps were also established. Today, about 60,000 adult volunteers lead close to 7,000 local Young Life chapters that are funded by hundreds of thousands of donors. The organization had $311 million of revenue in 2014.

Young Life is on a path to reach 2 million children annually by the year 2016.

Further reading

○ About Young Life, younglife.org/About/Pages/default.aspx

JEWISH FEDERATIONS OF NORTH AMERICA

With the need for financial aid to European Jews becoming urgent in the late 1930s, three of the most prominent Jewish charities came together to form the United Jewish Appeal for Refugees and Overseas Needs (UJA). By joining forces, the three groups were able to raise nearly $2 billion between UJA's founding in 1939 and 1967.

Right after World War II, UJA focused its efforts on evacuating Holocaust survivors; in 1947 alone, 25,000 refugees were resettled in the United States. With the founding of the State of Israel in 1948, endangered Jews were more often brought to Israel, along with funding to strengthen the fledgling nation. When the Six Day War threatened Israel, UJA raised $308 million for relief. Six

RELIGION

years later, with the onset of the Yom Kippur War, the organization mustered $100 million before the first week of hostilities concluded. And when the Soviet Union crumbled in the late 1980s, the group removed Russian Jews to Israel, raising $900 million in 1990 alone to provide 800,000 Jews with safe passage.

In 1999 another merger of Jewish charities folded the UJA into what is now the Jewish Federations of North America. The JFNA provides money and organizational assistance to the more than 150 local Jewish Federation chapters spread across the United States and Canada. These local federations have raised and disbursed funds since 1895, when the first chapter was organized in Boston. Collectively, these partners raise more than $3 billion every year and distribute it for social welfare, education, and religious services.

Further reading

○ About the JFNA, jewishfederations.org/about-us.aspx

SEALANTIC FUND

John Rockefeller Jr. started the Sealantic Fund in 1938 to provide additional support to some of the causes he was funding personally, especially in support of liberal Protestantism. It began with an initial endowment of $23 million. Protestant theological education was its main emphasis.

Among other places, Sealantic grants went to Harvard Divinity School, New York City's Interchurch Center, Union Theological Seminary, and the Interdenominational Theological Center. Sealantic partnered with the American Theological Library Association to develop religious libraries. To strengthen liberal seminaries and divinity schools, the fund promised them gifts if they would raise matching dollars.

In 1973, 13 years after the death of "Junior" Rockefeller, the Sealantic Fund was merged into the Rockefeller Brothers Fund.

Further reading

○ Account of the founding of the Interchurch Center, interchurch-center.org/history.html

LILLY ENDOWMENT

With assets of $10 billion and annual giving of around $350 million, the Lilly Endowment is one of the largest foundations in America. It was founded in 1937 when three members of the Lilly family donated stock in the Eli Lilly pharmaceutical company. Along with education, and development of its home city of Indianapolis and home state of Indiana, "deepening and enriching the religious lives of American Christians" is the other major charge of the endowment.

Enhancing the quality of ministry in the U.S. is a primary focus of its grantmaking. This involves recruiting and training top candidates, and stimulating existing ministers in pursuit of "pastoral excellence." Strengthening religious education, congregational life, faith formation, and public understanding of religion are also interests of Lilly's.

Further reading

○ Lilly's Insights into Religion, religioninsights.org

○ Lilly's Resources for American Christianity, resourcingchristianity.org

1936

LDS WELFARE SYSTEM

From the time of their baptism at age eight, members of the Church of Jesus Christ of Latter-day Saints are encouraged to tithe. The church also asks the able-bodied to fast for two consecutive meals on one Sunday every month and donate what would have been spent to help the needy. These disciplines have made Mormons America's biggest givers.

Among other effects, this giving has allowed their church hierarchy to build the most robust welfare system in the country. From its nineteenth-century beginnings, the LDS church has had a tradition of creating storehouses that provide food for the hungry. This system was expanded and refined amidst the hardships of the Great Depression, when it proved highly effective in rescuing people from want.

Wherever the church has congregations there is a facility where groceries, clothing, furniture, and other staples are available to any person who receives a slip from his or her bishop certifying need. The church has developed a network of its own farms, ranches, dairies, canneries, and other food processing and storage facilities to produce goods, and a central storehouse of roughly 600,000 square feet now serves five regional storehouses which

RELIGION

◈ PhilAphorism

A man wrapped up in himself makes a very small bundle.

☞ *Benjamin Franklin*

redistribute to more than 200 smaller local storehouses. The church also operates 40 thrift stores.

Church officials broker employment between those who need jobs and those who have work to offer. And counseling and help navigating service providers is available to those with marital or health problems. The church focuses on its members, but also assists others outside of its congregations, including large numbers overseas.

The principle of mutual aid governs all interventions. "The real long-term objective of the welfare plan is the building of character in the members of the church—givers and receivers," explains an official. "The aim of the church is to help the people to help themselves. Work is to be enthroned as the ruling principle of the lives of our church membership."

As a current LDS leader told *Philanthropy*, when serving the needy today, there is a growing tendency to "wait for experts with specialized knowledge to solve specific problems. When we do this, we deprive our neighbor of the service we could render. And we deprive ourselves of the opportunity to serve."

Further reading

◦ *Philanthropy* magazine reporting, philanthropyroundtable.org/topic/excellence_in_ philanthropy/a_welfare_system_that_works

◦ Historical memoir in *The American Enterprise*, unz.org/Pub/AmEnterprise-1995sep-00031

◦ Glenn Rudd, *Pure Religion: The Story of Church Welfare Since 1930* (Church of Jesus Christ of Latter-day Saints, 1995)

1933

CATHOLIC WORKER MOVEMENT

Dorothy Day was working as a reporter for socialist publications in New York City when the faith and commitment of her three Catholic roommates made an impression on her. In 1927 she converted to Roman Catholicism herself. After reporting on a Hunger March in 1932, Day went to Washington's Shrine of the Immaculate Conception to pray. She later wrote that she "offered up a special prayer...which came with tears and anguish, that some way would open up for me to use what talents I possessed...for the poor."

The next morning, she met Peter Maurin, a Franciscan who encouraged her to bring attention to Catholic social thought and offer uniquely Catholic solutions to social ills. Captivated by the suggestion, Day financed the production and publication of a newspaper she called the *Catholic Worker*, whose first edition appeared in 1933. In the pages of the *Worker*, Day offered her unique synthesis of Catholic social thought. Her religious-political vision resonated in that era, and the paper was an instant success.

Soon Day was not just describing but acting. She opened two houses in New York for the destitute and the difficult, where those offering assistance and those needing assistance lived together in simple circumstances as equals. These establishments were partially funded by the wages of those who lived there, plus financial and in-kind donations from donors across the city.

Today there are 217 Catholic Worker communities located throughout North America and Europe. Each serves a particular neighborhood in its own way. More than three decades after Day's death, her vision is still alive as a Christian social movement.

Further reading

◦ Dorothy Day biography, learningtogive.org/papers/paper86.html

◦ Catholic Worker Movement perspective, catholicworker.org/dorothyday/ddbiographytext. cfm?Number=72

CAPUCHIN SOUP KITCHEN

Capuchin friars first came to Detroit to work among the poor in 1883. With the arrival of the Great Depression they established a feeding program that was avidly received. Generations later, the Capuchin Soup Kitchen still operates, offering more than 2,000 free nutritious hot meals every day at two sites to anyone desiring to eat. The city's Capuchins also operate a house that offers substance-abuse treatment to indigent men, a bakery that employs recovering addicts and the formerly incarcerated, a children's program, an emergency shelter, and services that distribute 30,000 articles of clothing and 300,000 pounds of groceries to poor families every month. The Capuchin Soup Kitchen receives no government funds, relying as it has for 85 years on donations, plus earnings from the bakery.

Further reading

◦ History of the Capuchin Soup Kitchen, cskdetroit.org/about_us/history

PERSHING AND THE NATIONAL CATHEDRAL

The construction of Washington National Cathedral atop the highest point in the District of Columbia was a grand epic. Located on land set apart by Pierre L'Enfant for a "great church for national purposes," its creation stretched from a congressional charter in 1893 to the placement of the final carved stone in 1990. The nation's second-largest cathedral, it was described by George Will in 1978 as "the last pure Gothic work the world will see built."

RELIGION

The building was erected as donated funds became available. The foundation was laid in the 1900s, the nave was completed in the 1970s, and the west towers were finished in 1990. The work was supported by thousands of Episcopalians and other Christians from across the country.

A big financial impetus to the project was the intervention of retired World War I hero General John Pershing, when he became president of the National Cathedral Association during the 1920s. Pershing raised funds tirelessly, squiring donors around the in-progress facilities and even taping a nationwide movie-reel appeal in 1930. At a 1928 fundraiser he argued that "the capital of the nation is the strategic point at which to make a demonstration of our common Christianity. To try to build a worthy nation without God is impossible. I welcome you tonight, therefore, not only as friends, but as co-workers in an enterprise which seems to me of vital importance to the future of our country—the hastening of the day when it can no longer be said that in…the capital of the United States, there is no adequate expression of the religious faith of the people."

The National Cathedral has hosted many services of national significance. These have included the national prayer service following the 9/11 attacks, and funerals for former Presidents Dwight Eisenhower, Ronald Reagan, and Gerald Ford. It is a popular site in Washington, and often a symbol of national unity in times of trouble.

Further reading

○ Cathedral history, nationalcathedral.org/about/history.shtml

○ John Perry, *Pershing: Commander of the Great War* (Thomas Nelson, 2011)

— 1924 —

JAMES DUKE AND THE METHODIST CHURCH

"I am going to give a good part of what I make to the Lord," said tobacco and hydroelectricity entrepreneur James Duke, "but I can make better interest for Him by keeping it while I live." Duke exaggerated a bit—he was involved in philanthropy during his lifetime—but he did labor to build up a large private fortune that could be entrusted to religious and other social purposes after

✒ PhilAphorism

Charity is the note that resolves the discord.

☞ *Austin O'Malley*

his passing. In 1924, less than a year before he died, Duke created the Duke Endowment and dedicated it to supporting Carolina hospitals, Carolina orphans, four Carolina universities (especially the future Duke University), and the Methodist church.

"If I amount to anything in this world," he would say, "I owe it to my daddy and the Methodist church." Duke instructed the endowment to give 12 percent of its annual payout to Methodist causes—10 percent for the construction and maintenance of rural Methodist churches in North Carolina, and 2 percent for the support of "worn-out" Methodist clergymen and their widows (a common enough risk in the days of Methodist circuit ministry). Duke's funding allowed Methodist churches to invest in upgraded facilities to meet their communities' needs, and it provided security in retirement for ministers and their family members who had often known privation during their careers.

Since 1924, the Duke Endowment has distributed nearly $150 million to Methodist causes in North Carolina and the result has been the steady growth of Methodism in the state. Today, North Carolina's two United Methodist regional groups rank third and eighth in membership size among the nation's 60 counterparts, with a total of approximately 1,900 churches and 530,000 members in the state.

Further reading

○ Rural Church program at the Duke Endowment, dukeendowment.org/program-areas/ rural-church

○ James Duke history in *Philanthropy* magazine, philanthropyroundtable.org/topic/donor_ intent/duke_of_carolina

1922

JUNIOR ROCKEFELLER PROMOTES LIBERAL PROTESTANTISM

In the early twentieth century, orthodox and liberal forms of Protestantism were competing for public favor. At the helm of the liberal ship was Harry Fosdick, whose views included denial of the divinity of Jesus. His 1922 sermon "Shall the Fundamentalists Win?" was a stinging critique of traditional Christian theology.

John Rockefeller Jr. had long been supportive of liberal religious causes, and as early as 1912 he was trying to recruit Fosdick away from his post at New York City's First Presbyterian Church. When "Shall the Fundamentalists Win?" was published, Junior provided the funds to distribute copies to every Protestant clergyman in the country, solidifying Fosdick as a leader among

RELIGION

theological progressives. Then Junior made a big offer: he would build a great new interdenominational church on New York City's upper west side if Fosdick would preside. The pastor accepted, and Junior donated $10 million to erect a grand Gothic cathedral in Morningside Heights that became known as the Riverside Church. The first services were held in 1930, and Riverside became what its donor intended: a bastion of modern liberal Protestantism.

Further reading

○ Peter Paris, et al., *History of The Riverside Church in the City of New York* (NYU Press, 2004)

1917

AMERICAN FRIENDS SERVICE COMMITTEE

When the United States entered World War I in 1917, the prospect of a military draft troubled American Quakers who were religiously principled pacifists. To support conscientious objectors and find alternative ways that they could serve the nation amidst the national mobilization, they formed the American Friends Service Committee. Quakers drove ambulances, did medical duty, and served stateside.

Long known for their philanthropy, the Quaker churches also sent volunteers to Europe to aid civilians disrupted by the fighting. And at the conclusion of the war Herbert Hoover asked the AFSC to help distribute food in Germany. The Friends took similar roles during World War II, and the Quakers were awarded the Nobel Peace Prize in 1947 in recognition of AFSC's service and donations across Europe during the three decades of warring.

The group has become extensively involved in "peace and social justice" advocacy over the decades. Private contributions and bequests have always fueled the organization, and continued to make up 99 percent of its 2014 budget of $32 million.

Further reading

○ AFSC 2014 Annual Report, afsc.org/document/afsc-annual-report-2014-0

1915

EARLY FUNDRAISING
FOR ENDANGERED JEWS

When many Jews were endangered amid the turmoil of World War I, a committee was formed with the goal of raising $5 million. The American Jewish Relief Committee for Sufferers of the War announced that four anonymous donors had each pledged $100,000 to launch the campaign, if another $600,000 could be raised in New York in a single event. Requests for tickets to the December 1915 gathering at Carnegie Hall soon tripled the number of available seats, and more than 3,000 people congregated outside the hall in the hope of being admitted at the last minute. There were addresses by the Episcopal bishop of New York, the president of the Central Conference of Rabbis, and speakers describing the plight of Jews caught between war and pogroms abroad.

Then people began walking to the stage one by one to drop off donations. In addition to cash there were slips of paper pledging one-time or monthly gifts. Others, the *New York Times* reported, left rings, necklaces, and earrings. When the event ended well after midnight the gifts exceeded $1 million, and the campaign was off to a roaring start. Julius Rosenwald, head of Sears, Roebuck & Company, subsequently donated a million dollars, and others like Jacob Schiff, Nathan Straus, and Felix Warburg made similar large gifts. Most remarkable was the breadth of giving. An estimated 3 million Americans made a donation to this cause at some time during the war.

The funds were used to aid to Jewish refugees, and to finance relocation of families to safer countries. This campaign demonstrated the commitment of American Jews to their brethren abroad. It was a tie that would be tested repeatedly over the course of the twentieth century.

Further reading

○ *New York Times* account, query.nytimes.com/mem/archive-free/
  pdf?res=9C0CE0D61239E333A25751C2A9649D946496D6CF
○ Albert Lucas, "American Jewish Relief in the World War," *Annals of the American Academy of
  Political and Social Science*, Vol. 79, 1918

1911

MAKING GROUP HOMES WORK

In twenty-first-century America, orphanages might seem like relics of the past. Because research in human attachment has taught us that children need close and lasting human connections, when those with disrupted lives need new homes, every effort is now made to place them in families rather than institutions. Sometimes, however, this isn't feasible—due to shortages of foster or adoptive parents, or behavioral issues and special needs beyond what most substitute parents are equipped to handle.

The default option is to send such youngsters to state-run group homes. Many of these are miserable places. Thanks to private philanthropy, though, a number of high-quality residential homes and schools exist across the country as alternatives for children with severe challenges. One of the most iconic is a Christian residential school called Crossnore.

Crossnore was founded by Mary Sloop and her husband, Eustace, two young physicians anxious to serve as medical missionaries. In 1911 they moved to an impoverished mountain county in North Carolina and began offering medical, educational, and economic aid to local children. Their project gradually evolved into a boarding school for orphans and other needy children. Adjoining the school, the Sloops set up a weaving workshop and a working farm where the children could learn skills and personal disciplines. This, along with resources donated and raised by the Sloops, allowed the school to be largely self-supporting.

Crossnore currently houses about 100 kids at any one time, ages one to 21, who have been severely neglected or abused, and whose needs aren't met by the foster-care system or public schools. They live in cottages, supervised by couples, and attend classes and intensive activities that promote healing, faith, and self-improvement. The school has its own K-12 charter school that is also open to children from the surrounding community, a special program to help residents ages 17 to 21 transition gradually to independent living, and a scholarship program that pays tuition of alumni who go to college. There is also a special effort to assist the adoption of Crossnore kids into families.

Impressed by the good results achieved with difficult children at this facility, a loyal cadre of Christian donors has provided financial support over more than a century. A recent capital campaign raised $20 million for the school's private endowment. Similar facilities in other states include the Alabama Baptist Children's Homes & Family Ministries; Hope Village for Children in Meridian, Mississippi; Safe Harbor Boys Home of Jacksonville, Florida; the Hendrick Home for Children in Abilene, Texas; and 11 homes operated across the country by Youth Villages.

Further reading

○ Crossnore School, crossnoreschool.org

○ *North Carolina Encyclopedia* entry on Mary Sloop, ncpedia.org/biography/sloop-mary

1910

CATHOLIC CHARITIES

The president of Catholic University in Washington, D.C., invited Catholic clergy and laity to gather on his campus in 1910 to launch Catholic Charities. Local parishes had been doing charitable work right from their beginnings—

there were more than 800 Catholic social services organizations nationwide around the turn of the twentieth century. Some Catholics, however, felt there needed to be a more centralized anti-poverty effort.

Today about 170 social service efforts across the U.S. are supported by Catholic Charities, serving several million people each year. The 501(c)(3) coordinating body, Catholic Charities USA, raised $24 million in contributions and grants in 2013. Linked to its origins in the nation's capital, and its continued headquartering there, Catholic Charities has also involved itself extensively in political debates right from its beginning. It organized letter-writing campaigns on behalf of New Deal legislation, for instance, and led pushes for various forms of public housing. In the 1960s, the group tilted further toward advocacy of government activism. Today, about two thirds of Catholic Charities' annual spending comes from government sources (more than half a billion dollars of federal grants alone).

Further reading

○ CCUSA, catholiccharitiesusa.org

○ Critique of the swing to government funding, city-journal.org/html/10_1_how_catholic_charities.html

GETTING THE WORD OUT

In 1898, two traveling businessmen found themselves sharing a room in an overbooked Wisconsin hotel. On discovering that they were both Christians, they studied the Bible together and knelt in prayer. Encouraged by their fellowship, a year later these businessmen met with another friend in Janesville, Wisconsin, and formed a ministry for traveling businessmen. Calling themselves the Gideons—after the Old Testament judge who did whatever God called him to—they came up with an additional strategy for reaching their fellow travelers: placing a Bible in every hotel room in America. With the philanthropic support of their members and members' home churches, the Bible

RELIGION

⤳ PhilAphorism

Cast your bread upon the waters,
for after many days you will find it again.

☞ *Ecclesiastes*

project launched in 1908 became the Gideons' signature outreach. Today, with 290,000 members in 190 countries, the Gideons have distributed 1.7 billion Bibles, stocking most hotels in the U.S. and many other countries.

Further reading

○ About the Gideons, gideons.org/?HP=USA&sc_lang=en

1905

GOODWILL INDUSTRIES

Edgar Helms was a Cornell grad and ordained Methodist minister hunkered down in a South Boston outpost in 1902 fighting some of the city's worst poverty. His building was collapsing, the nation was in a depression, and his church lacked funds. A staff member suggested they repair and sell the used clothes often received as donations. Helms realized clothes donations were easier to collect than monetary ones and that a market existed for cleaned and repaired clothes. But he was even more attracted by the fact that the process would provide what his congregation most needed: employment.

In 1905, Helms incorporated the first branch of what became Goodwill Industries. Helms differed from many poverty-fighters of his day. Some focused on single problems like drunkenness among the poor. Others bypassed direct service to poor persons in favor of lobbying government for reforms of housing, medical care, and wages. Helms insisted that what the poor most needed was work that would make them self-reliant and self-respecting. "You can't help a man by doubting him. When he tells us he wants work, we assume that he does," Helms explained, stressing that the poor need "a chance, not a charity."

In 1915, Helms's innovative program spread to Brooklyn. Then, in 1919, the Methodist church provided several hundred thousand dollars of seed money that helped Goodwill expand across America, Canada, and abroad. By the mid-1930s Goodwill Industries had 100 branches in the U.S., and others in foreign countries. During the Great Depression Goodwill narrowed its focus to employment of men and women with disabilities, a specialty it has preserved to this day.

The founder's most important legacy may be the decentralized structure of his organization. The 165 local Goodwill branches can assist each other and request advice and aid from the world headquarters, but each is autonomous in policy and funding—a stark contrast to centralized nonprofits like the Red Cross and Catholic Charities. The central office's budget is dwarfed by those of branches in cities like Milwaukee and Houston. Yet the movement is vast: nearly $5 billion in worldwide revenues; over 3,000 stores in the

U.S., Canada, and 13 other countries; and workforce training provided to 26 million persons in a great variety of fields. The central office's current CEO, Jim Gibbons, echoes Helms's original principle: "We believe work is the mechanism by which people gain financial and personal independence."

Further reading

○ Goodwill timeline, goodwill.org/wp-content/uploads/2011/01/First_100_Years_Timeline.pdf

○ *Philanthropy* magazine profile, philanthropyroundtable.org/topic/excellence_in_ philanthropy/goodwill_industries

○ Beatrice Plumb, *The Goodwill Man: Edgar J. Helms* (Denison & Co., 1965)

ANDREW CARNEGIE, ORGAN DONOR

By the beginning of the twentieth century the organ had become an important animator of worship in American churches. Andrew Carnegie turned up the volume by donating nearly 7,700 organs to churches worldwide (4,100 of those in the U.S.), starting in 1902. Carnegie, only a sporadic churchgoer himself, considered fine music a devotional experience, and quoted Confucius' line: "O Music, sacred tongue of God, I hear thee calling, and I come." His organ-funding program was very methodical. Churches applying to his foundation had to contribute half of the funds, and they had to select an organ that was suited to the size of their worship hall. It was an ecumenical program— Baptist, Presbyterian, Methodist, Congregational, Lutheran, and Episcopal congregations alike received instruments. This highly personal initiative by one of America's seminal donors transformed American church life.

Further reading

○ Account at Estey Organ archive, esteyorgan.com/carnegie.htm

○ Peter Krass, *Carnegie* (Wiley, 2002)

A COOKBOOK HELPS AMERICANIZE JEWS

While working as a truant officer in Milwaukee in the 1890s, Lizzie Kander discovered that the home conditions of Russian immigrant families were "deplorable...threatening the moral and physical health of the people." Believing that women were the keys to household success and acculturation, she devoted herself to a variety of self-funded initiatives to teach cleanliness, child education, good nutrition, household skills, and economically useful trades like sewing to Russian women. By 1900 she was deeply involved in running a settlement house that assimilated Jewish immigrants using funds

RELIGION

donated by Milwaukee businessmen. When additional money was needed, Kander compiled a 174-page cookbook-cum-housekeeping-guide to sell as a fundraiser. The board of directors would not pay the $18 needed to print the book, so she paid for production by selling ads. It became known as the *Settlement Cook Book* and eventually sold two million copies—thereby funding the mainstreaming of Jewish immigrants in the upper Midwest, and many other charitable causes, for 75 years.

Further reading

○ 1901 edition of the *Settlement Cook Book* with background information, digital.lib.msu.edu/ projects/cookbooks/html/books/book_52.cfm

1892

CATHEDRAL OF ST. JOHN THE DIVINE

Wall Street banker J. P. Morgan was a devoted Episcopalian. He was an officer of his local church. He served on a national committee charged with revising the Book of Common Prayer (much of which he knew by heart). As an adult, he set aside three full weeks every third year to meet with theologians and discuss faith. And he quietly underwrote the salaries of scores of Manhattan clergy.

He was also the principal funder behind the construction of the Cathedral of St. John the Divine in upper Manhattan, one of the largest stone churches in the world. In 1892 alone, the year construction began, Morgan donated the current equivalent of $13 million to underwrite construction of an Episcopal edifice that could compare with the Catholic St. Patrick's Cathedral begun a dozen years earlier in midtown. The massive church—covering much of a city block, with interior ceiling heights of 124 feet—is constructed in traditional stone-on-stone style without steel or modern supports, in a riotous Gothic/Byzantine/Romanesque style. Its rose window is made of 10,000 pieces of glass assembled in traditional medieval fashion. Ellis Island opened the year construction began, so the cathedral includes seven chapels designed in seven distinct national styles to represent the seven largest immigrant groups then flooding into the U.S.

In the 1920s, Franklin Roosevelt headed a campaign to raise $10 million in private donations (the equivalent of $134 million today) for the next stage of construction. This allowed building to continue even through the Depression. Work was stopped by World War II, however, and the cathedral, though heavily used, remains incomplete in many of its elements—sparking its nickname, St. John the Unfinished.

Among many remarkable elements of Christian iconography on the building are a series of stone carvings reflecting apocalyptic scenes from the Book of Revelation, which was authored by the cathedral's namesake, the apostle John. Interpretations by the modern stonecarvers include scenes of New York City being engulfed by a tidal wave, the Brooklyn Bridge cracking in two, and the World Trade Center towers and Chrysler building teetering. Even as a work in progress, this wholly donor-funded cathedral represents one of the most monumental Christian edifices in the world.

Further reading

◦ General history, legacy.fordham.edu/halsall/medny/stjohn2.html

1891

KATHARINE DREXEL DEVOTES HER FORTUNE TO INDIANS AND BLACKS

Katharine Drexel was born in 1858 into one of America's wealthiest families—the namesake founders of Drexel University and the Drexel Burnham Lambert investment firm. Her parents were of French Catholic extraction, and devout and deeply charitable. The family opened its grand home to hundreds of poor Philadelphians twice a week, providing food, clothing, and rent money. This was only part of the family's annual giving, which was roughly equivalent to $11 million today.

Katharine felt a calling to religious life as early as 14, and it intensified during a trip through the American West, where she was troubled by the poverty of Native Americans. After her father died in 1885, the young woman took her multimillion-dollar inheritance and began funding schools and missions for New Mexican Indians. During an audience in 1887 with Pope Leo XIII she urged that more missionaries be sent to help Native Americans. The Pope replied, "Why not, my child, become a missionary yourself?" In 1889 Katharine bade farewell to Philadelphia high society and became a nun with the Sisters of Mercy.

Two years later, Drexel founded her own order, the Sisters of the Blessed Sacrament, and made a special vow not to "undertake any work which would lead to the neglect or abandonment of the Indian or Colored races." She converted her family estate into a home for African-American orphans, using it also to train young novices before they departed as missionaries to the western U.S. Drexel developed a network of 145 missions, 12 schools for Native Americans, and 50 schools for African Americans throughout the South and West. Staffed by laypersons and often attached to a local church, the schools offered religious instruction and vocational training. Students did not have to be Catholic to enroll.

In 1915, Drexel provided a $750,000 grant that allowed the sisters to found Xavier University in New Orleans—the only historically black Catholic college

RELIGION

in the United States (and one that, among other educational contributions, has produced a quarter of the black pharmacists in America over the last century). Katharine led the Sisters of the Blessed Sacrament until 1938. During her lifetime she is estimated to have given away half a billion dollars in present-day funds to support her order. She was canonized by Pope John Paul II in 2000.

Further reading

○ Katharine Drexel profile in the Philanthropy Hall of Fame (see prior *Almanac* section)

○ Ellen Tarry, *Saint Katharine Drexel: Friend of the Oppressed* (Farrar Strauss, 1958)

1889

NETTIE MCCORMICK BOLSTERS RELIGIOUS SCHOOLS

Cyrus McCormick, the inventor of important farm machinery, was a generous religious philanthropist, giving away at least $550,000 in the second half of the nineteenth century to religious organizations—mostly the Presbyterian church, seminaries, and other schools. His wife, Nettie, raised in a devout Methodist and devotedly philanthropic home, outlived her husband by 39 years and became an even more prolific giver to religious causes on her own, starting in 1889. She felt strongly that she was accountable to God for how she used the money entrusted to her, and sought gifts that had a crisp moral purpose, a spiritual or educational benefit, and a chance of helping recipients better themselves.

Nettie gave away millions of dollars. Orphanages, schools, colleges, hospitals, and relief agencies all benefited from her endowments. She took a strong interest in schools like Tusculum College, the Moody Bible Institute, and Princeton University in the U.S. And her large gifts made several Christian colleges and hospitals possible overseas, including Alborz College in Tehran, and a theological seminary in Korea. It has been estimated that McCormick was the lead funder of at least 46 schools, and possibly more.

Further reading

○ Nettie McCormick profile in the Philanthropy Hall of Fame (see prior *Almanac* section)

1884

JACOB SCHIFF'S PHILANTHROPY

Jacob Schiff was born in Germany in 1847, the son of a prominent rabbinical family. Over the objections of his father, he traveled to New York City in 1865 to work a brief stint as a broker. Eventually he settled in the U.S. and took a position at the prominent banking firm of Kuhn, Loeb, and Company. By the close of the nineteenth century Schiff was one of the richest and most prominent men in the country. He channeled much of his wealth into Jewish causes like Hebrew Union College, Jewish Theological Seminary, and the American Jewish Relief Committee.

Indeed, Schiff supported nearly every major Jewish charity of his day. He was a major lifelong funder of the Henry Street Settlement that did so much to reduce immigrant squalor in New York City's Lower East Side. Amid rising pogroms in Russia and elsewhere he financed Zionist organizations and efforts to relocate European Jews to safety in Palestine. He also aided many non-Jewish causes. He funded the Montefiore Hospital in New York for decades, served as its president, and visited the hospital weekly. Throughout his philanthropic career Jacob Schiff resisted public recognition. When he saw plans for a plaque on the Jewish Theological Seminary building he immediately crossed out his name.

Further reading

o Biography, jewishvirtuallibrary.org/jsource/biography/schiff.html

───────── 1884 ─────────

EXPANSION OF CATHOLIC SCHOOLING

The first Catholic school in America was opened in St. Augustine, Florida, in 1606. In New Orleans, the Ursuline Academy opened in 1727 and is still operating today as the oldest Catholic school in the U.S. Other U.S. faith-based schools have roots nearly as deep. The first Jewish day school opened in New York City four decades before the American Revolution. The oldest Quaker school in the world, currently known as the William Penn Charter School, was established in Philadelphia in 1689.

But Catholic schools are the largest element in faith-based schooling today—representing about one out of every three religious schools operating in the U.S. They grew up primarily after the Civil War, as immigration from Catholic countries created demand for facilities where education could coexist with spiritual training and Catholic culture. After several efforts to secure government funding for religious education failed, the American Catholic bishops met in Baltimore in 1884 and decided that all parishes should establish schools themselves for the children of congregants. (The same council passed the resolution that led to the creation of the Catholic University of America.) Thus began many decades of grassroots philanthropy to establish, construct, and maintain parochial schools.

Financed by religious subsidies plus modest tuition payments from parents, Catholic schools exploded from only about 200 in the first half

RELIGION

of the 1800s to 5,000 by the year 1900, and 13,500 schools educating 5.6 million children at their peak in 1965. Catholic schools have since receded to 6,600 and an enrollment of 2 million, but philanthropists are working to maintain and revive them, particularly in poor urban neighborhoods where they offer the only decent education to local children (now mostly minorities, and not Catholic).

With backing from donors, new networks, economic models, management structures, and funding methods are now being energetically experimented with, all aiming to secure Catholic education as an option for families in future generations. New York City's Catholic schools currently receive as much in large philanthropic donations as they do in aid from the archdiocese.

Further reading

- Andy Smarick and Kelly Robson, *Catholic School Renaissance: A Wise Giver's Guide to Strengthening a National Asset* (The Philanthropy Roundtable, 2015)
- *New York Times* report on 1884 Plenary Council, query.nytimes.com/mem/archive-free/pdf?res=FA0A16FB3F5B10738DDDAE0894D9415B8484F0D3
- White House report on urban faith-based schools, www2.ed.gov/admins/comm/choice/faithbased/index.html

1880

SALVATION ARMY MARCHES TO AMERICA

Methodist minister William Booth and his wife, Catherine, founded the Salvation Army in London in 1865 to help prostitutes, drunks and drug addicts, and the poor—using his "three S's" approach: "first, soup; second, soap; and finally, salvation." Some observers were put off by the flamboyance of the "Sallies," with their brass bands and bright uniforms and their direct engagement with the lower classes. But they achieved

◁ PhilAphorism

When the crumbs are swept from our table, we think it generous to let the dogs eat them; as if that were charity which permits others to have what we cannot keep.

☞ *Henry Ward Beecher*

great success, and then strong support from the public in dollars and volunteer hours.

In 1880, the Salvation Army arrived in the U.S. with its flags flying (emblazoned "Blood and Fire"). Fascinated reporters were told that the arriving officers were part of an "army of men and women mostly belonging to the working class" who had been saved from immorality and wasted human potential. They immediately strode into saloons, brothels, and slums, engaging the most desperate residents, and established what became one of America's largest and best-run charities.

In less than a decade this combination church and social movement created a citywide service network. By 1900, reports historian Marvin Olasky, the Army had 20,000 American volunteers, its employment bureaus placed 4,800 persons a month into jobs, and it operated 141 relief operations including 52 shelters, 14 homes for women facing crisis pregnancies, and two children's homes. The Army's massive disaster relief after the 1900 Galveston hurricane and the 1906 San Francisco earthquake further enhanced its reputation. Disaster relief continues to be offered— Army workers and volunteers gave more than 900,000 hours of service after Hurricane Katrina.

Today, the Salvation Army's several thousand uniformed officers oversee 7,600 centers and a multibillion-dollar budget serving tens of millions of Americans. Its lean, decentralized management system pays officers the minimum wage and raises and spends all money locally. Management expert Peter Drucker called it "by far the most effective organization in the U.S."—nonprofit or for-profit. "No one even comes close with respect to clarity of mission, ability to innovate, measurable results, dedication, and putting money to maximum use," he concluded. *Forbes* calculated that if the Army's employees and volunteers in 126 countries were paid market wages, it would be one of the world's largest companies.

In 2003, McDonald's heiress Joan Kroc left more than $1.5 billion to the Army, the largest philanthropic gift ever given to one charity. A recent National Commander in the U.S. explained its unchanging view on helping the needy: "You can't divorce individual responsibility from the societal ills that create poverty. Low-income persons begin to see their own self-worth as they take responsibility for themselves."

Further reading

∘ Diane Winston, *Red-hot and Righteous: The Urban Religion of the Salvation Army* (Harvard University Press, 1999)

∘ *Philanthropy* magazine interview with National Commander, philanthropyroundtable.org/ site/print/venture_capitalists_of_the_streets

RELIGION

SEVENTH-DAY ADVENTISTS
CREATE HEALTH FOOD

During the nineteenth century there was much experimentation in the U.S. at combining religious observance with new dietary practices. Seventh-day Adventism had a significant effect in this area through its Battle Creek Sanitarium. The church follows the food codes prescribed in Leviticus, and recommends vegetarianism to adherents, while banning alcohol and tobacco. Seventh-day Adventists put these principles into practice at their Battle Creek Sanitarium in Michigan, funded by the donations of congregants.

Under the direction of physician John Kellogg, the Adventist church created what amounted to an early health spa, where a low-fat diet rich in whole grains, fiber, and nuts was served, along with something new: flaked cereals. Both Kellogg's younger brother, W. K., and sanitarium visitor C. W. Post picked up on this innovation and created companies offering the convenience and nutrition of flaked cereals to the general public—ventures which created a large industry.

In addition to controlled diet and lots of exercise, John Kellogg offered many exotic health treatments like cold-air exercise, hydrotherapy, water-and-yogurt enemas, and odd sexual regimens. The sanitarium became a popular spot, generating national interest in health and wellness and attracting famous patients like Mary Lincoln, William Taft, Henry Ford, and Amelia Earhart. It went into decline during the Depression.

Further reading

◦ Battle Creek Sanitarium history, heritagebattlecreek.org/index.php?option=com_content&view=article&id=95&Itemid=73

◦ Brian Wilson, *Dr. John Harvey Kellogg and the Religion of Biologic Living* (Indiana University Press, 2014)

SPIRITUAL GROWTH
ON CHAUTAUQUA LAKE

The Chautauqua Institution is a quintessentially American organization where citizens have been trooping for a century and a half to fire their spirits and refine their souls. Founded in 1874 by a Methodist minister and an inventor/philanthropist named Lewis Miller, Chautauqua's original purpose was to educate and train Sunday-school teachers from around the nation so they could more effectively instruct and minister to their charges back home. The original assemblies were in tents pitched thickly along Chautauqua Lake in western New York. Over time, the grounds grew into a seasonal village of beautiful little cottages, outdoor lecture spaces, numerous chapels, several theaters, and recreation areas. The grounds are now listed as a National Historic Landmark.

A century and a half after its start, Americans continue to flock to Chautauqua for religious inspiration, opportunities to improve their minds, and chances to develop their creative talents. All day long, there are lectures, Bible studies, art classes, concerts, dance performances, sports activities, singalongs, and study groups of all sorts. Every evening there is lively conversation around dinner tables and on packed front porches.

The Chautauqua Literary and Scientific Circle, which was founded to promote independent learning, particularly among those unable to attend formal schools, is the oldest book club in the United States. The institution has had its own permanent summer orchestra, theater, opera, ballet, and fine-arts programs for decades. Many religious denominations operate houses on the grounds where learning, conversation, fraternity, and daily worship are shared. Much of the instruction at Chautauqua is self-guided, and the animating purpose behind spending a week or a summer at Chautauqua has always been to improve oneself. This earnest do-it-yourself learning caused Teddy Roosevelt to describe the Chautauqua gatherings as "the most American thing in America."

By the turn of the twentieth century, this upstate New York phenomenon had became so popular and influential it spawned several hundred other "daughter Chautauquas" in locales across the country. The word thus entered the American lexicon to describe any assembly where Americans come together with the goal of re-forming themselves into better people.

Further reading

∘ Chautauqua Institution history, ciweb.org/about-us/about-chautauqua/our-history

TEMPERANCE MOVEMENT

The anti-alcohol movement, which was rooted in America's Protestant churches, powered by philanthropy and female volunteers, and ultimately a powerful political force, was an organic response to a real problem. During the first half of the 1800s, the average American over age 15 drank almost seven gallons of pure alcohol per year. That's three times modern U.S. consumption levels.

It was primarily men who abused alcohol. The effects included vicious fighting (eye gouging was popular), the dissipation of wages, and domestic violence. It was often women and children who were particularly victimized by drinking.

So not surprisingly, the temperance movement was primarily driven by women, specifically religious women. It sought, first, to moderate alcohol use. Then came an emphasis on helping drinkers lean on each other to resist the temptation to drink. Finally, the temperance movement sought local, state, and national laws prohibiting alcohol.

Amid even greater horrors, temperance became less visible and urgent during the Civil War. But after the war, the arrival of waves of immigrants from Ireland, Germany, and Italy brought spikes in alcohol consumption and production that reinflamed many Americans, led by Methodist and Baptist clergy. Starting in upstate New York in 1873, thousands of distraught wives and mothers organized themselves into the Women's Christian Temperance Union and became a potent social force. Local laws began to regulate and restrict alcohol consumption, and nearly every school in America used a WCTU anti-alcohol educational curriculum. Concomitant drives to clean up slums, protect children, and secure women's rights often led to overlapping support for controls on alcohol.

The WCTU was joined in its anti-alcohol work by the Anti-Saloon League. The ASL also worked very closely with churches, and enjoyed many small funders, but in addition it attracted funding from major philanthropists like Henry Ford, Andrew Carnegie, and John Rockefeller Jr. When the creation of the income tax in 1913 made the federal government less dependent upon liquor taxes, the campaign for prohibition shifted into high gear. In 1920, production and consumption of alcohol became illegal nationwide.

Enforcing the ban would prove chimerical. Alcohol consumption, however, would never return to its nineteenth-century levels. And some modern philanthropists (like the Robert Wood Johnson Foundation, which is also a leader of America's anti-smoking effort) continue to support efforts to moderate alcohol consumption.

Further reading

○ Women's Christian Temperance Union background, wctu.org/earlyhistory.html

○ Anti-Saloon League background, westervillelibrary.org/antisaloon-history-saloon

○ PBS history of prohibition, pbs.org/kenburns/prohibition/roots-of-prohibition

1864

BAPTIST COLLEGES BOLSTERED BY ROCKEFELLER

From childhood, John Rockefeller was a devout Baptist. Even before he made his fortune with Standard Oil he consistently tithed 10 percent of his income to religious causes. Starting around 1864 he exhibited a particular interest in supporting Baptist colleges.

He began by giving $5 to a school in Gambier, Ohio. That was followed by a $500 donation to another Ohio Baptist facility, Denison University. Denison had received $22,000 more from Rockefeller by 1882.

In 1884, Rockefeller covered the nearly $5,000 debt of the Atlanta Baptist Female Seminary, which out of gratitude took the maiden name of its donor's wife and renamed itself Spelman Seminary. That same year, he gave $25,000 to the African-American Baptist seminary in Richmond, Virginia. And when Northern Baptist officials created a separate society to support higher education, Rockefeller pledged $100,000 to launch it in 1888.

The American Baptist Education Society ultimately received more than $800,000 from John Rockefeller between 1890 and 1914. Among other causes, Rockefeller and the Society partnered to create a flagship Baptist university for the country: the University of Chicago. In today's dollars, Rockefeller's giving to the University of Chicago during its first 20 years comes to about $35 million.

Further reading

○ Rockefeller and the American Baptist Education Society, rockarch.org/publications/resrep/rose1.pdf

RELIGION

UNITED STATES CHRISTIAN COMMISSION IN THE CIVIL WAR

The carnage at the First Battle of Bull Run (just a preview of the destruction to come in our Civil War) stirred the hearts of many Americans. Among those summoned to action were members of the Young Men's Christian Association. At their 1861 convention they created the United States Christian Commission to provide war relief. Unlike the U.S. Sanitary Commission, another private aid organization that raised $25 million to

⌐ **PhilAphorism**

As I give, I get.

☞ *Mary McLeod Bethune*

succor war victims (see 1861 entry on Prosperity list), the USCC would not separate physical from spiritual assistance.

The USCC organized 5,000 volunteers to serve in military camps and on battlefields. It also collected $6 million worth of goods and supplies, which it distributed to those in need. The group brought Christian love and comfort to many thousands of soldiers, spurring spiritual revivals in numerous encampments.

Among the USCC's most dedicated supporters was inventor Matthias Baldwin, owner of the Baldwin Locomotive Company. Baldwin was already providing crucial support to the Union cause by supplying the army with trains—for which he ultimately lost nearly all of his Southern customers. In addition, he donated 10 percent of his company's profits to the USCC during the war. Support from Baldwin, Philadelphia merchant George Stuart, and other contributors enabled the USCC to construct permanent chapels alongside army forts, to offer reading rooms and literature, to provide medical care to the wounded and dying, and to turn its attention late in the war to literacy training among black soldiers.

Further reading

◦ *New York Times* background on USCC revivalism, opinionator.blogs.nytimes.com/2011/12/22/onward-christian-soldiers

1854

JUDAH TOURO, FRIEND TO RELIGION

New England merchant Judah Touro set up shop in New Orleans in 1801, and he profited handsomely from the growth of the Crescent City and eventual addition of Louisiana to the United States. This allowed him to become one of the most prolific religious philanthropists of his day.

Although he was without a synagogue for most of his life, Touro remained a devout Jew. When he arrived in New Orleans, his co-religionists in the city could be counted on two hands, and as late as 1826 there were no more than a few hundred Jews in all of Louisiana. In 1828, Touro financed the founding of New Orleans' first synagogue. When it divided into separate Ashkenazi and Sephardic congregations after some years, he gave generously to both groups, while attending the Sephardic gathering. (In 1881 the synagogues merged back together, and today the combined congregation is named for its benefactor.)

Touro also created and funded numerous Jewish relief agencies and Hebrew schools in New Orleans. He gave liberally to Christians, too. At one point he purchased an imperiled Christian church building and assumed its debts, allowing the congregation to use the building rent-free in perpetuity.

When a colleague suggested the property might be valuable if sold for commercial purposes, Touro responded, "I am a friend to religion and I will not pull down the church to increase my means!")

Touro died in 1854. In his will, he bequeathed $500,000 to institutions around the country—more than half of them non-Jewish. (As a percentage of GDP, those gifts would approximate billions of dollars today.) His last testament included crucial support for the historic Touro Synagogue in Newport (see 1763 entry) and the Touro Infirmary in New Orleans. He also bequeathed to various benevolent societies, hospitals, orphanages, almshouses, asylums, libraries, schools, and relief efforts for Jews and Christians overseas, especially in Palestine. Touro's gifts of thousands of dollars each to 23 Jewish congregations in 14 states made him one of his era's greatest benefactors of his faith.

Further reading

○ Judah Touro profile in the Philanthropy Hall of Fame (see prior *Almanac* section)

○ Leon Huhner, *The Life of Judah Touro* (Jewish Publication Society of America, 1946)

○ Max Kohler, *Judah Touro, Merchant and Philanthropist* (American Jewish Society, 1905)

JEWISH COMMUNITY CENTERS

In 1854, the first Hebrew Young Men's Literary Association opened its doors in Baltimore to serve Jewish immigrants. Other branches soon opened in additional cities, serving as libraries, cultural centers, settlement houses, and social hubs. Amidst heavy Jewish immigration around the end of the century, the HYMLAs became important in acculturating new arrivals, teaching them English, and coaching them in American civic responsibilities.

When World War I broke out, the group raised money, established rules, and recruited rabbis to serve Jewish soldiers. Contributions of more than $6 million from Jewish philanthropists like Jacob Schiff and many others allowed distribution of prayer shawls, mezuzahs, calendars, and scrolls. The group had to work to overcome divisions among Judaism's orthodox, conservative, and reform factions, and even produced a prayer book that could be shared by soldiers from different branches.

Credibility earned in this process allowed the association to absorb other Jewish fraternal organizations and take responsibility for building community centers, children's camps, and other communal facilities for Jews across the country. Jewish community centers became rallying points for Hebrew education, cultural and sports events, and Jewish celebrations. Today, the JCC Association is the successor organization, with responsibility for more than 350 community centers and camps.

RELIGION

Further reading

◦ JCCA, jcca.org/about-jcc-association

1851

YMCA COMES TO AMERICA

In the late 1840s, Thomas Sullivan had retired after a long career as a sea captain, but he continued to sail as a marine missionary. While in London, he admired a place called the Young Men's Christian Association where men and boys, far from home, could get a clean and safe place to stay, find fellowship, and be taught the Christian gospel. Inspired to provide a "home away from home" for young American seamen on leave, Sullivan brought the YMCA to Boston, opening the first U.S. branch of the organization in 1851 at the Old South Church. As it grew, the Y added educational programs and a gymnasium to its original offerings of overnight lodging, socializing, and prayer and Bible-study meetings.

Prominent evangelist Dwight Moody worked for the YMCA for many years in the later 1800s and expanded its missions work. Evangelist John Mott did likewise in the first half of the 1900s, steering the Y into war relief and assistance to foreign needy as a supplement to its domestic mission. Mott was awarded the Nobel Peace Prize in 1946 for leading the YMCA's international humanitarian efforts.

With the growth of additional branches across the country, the YMCA became a haven for young people arriving in cities looking for work after leaving rural farms, and later for travelers during the tumultuous decades of the world wars and Great Depression. The Y also helped make basketball and volleyball popular sports, and YMCA summer camps introduced many children to the great outdoors. The organization eventually became a cultural touchstone for suburban Americans. In the process, however, the Y lost its explicitly Christian orientation. Today, YMCA chapters serve 21 million Americans per year at 2,700 sites.

Further reading

◦ History of the YMCA movement, home.gwi.net/~bathymca/yhistory.htm

1849

PERPETUAL EMIGRATION FUND

Established in 1849 by the Church of Jesus Christ of Latter-day Saints, the Perpetual Emigration Fund distributed loans that enabled more than 30,000 Mormons to settle in the American West. Supported by church donations, private contributions, and repayments that were then distributed again on a revolving basis, the loans made it possible for converts from across the world to relocate themselves into the company of fellow believers in the burgeoning LDS heartland in Utah. Many of these immigrants came from the Midwest, the previous center of the Mormon diaspora, while others arrived from overseas, with transportation for many being organized out of Liverpool, England.

Once relocated, those assisted by the PEF would begin paying back their loans, thus enabling the settlement of yet more church members. In this way, a nascent church was able to consolidate and expand its embryonic and oft-threatened community despite very limited finances. In 1880, on the occasion of the LDS Church's fiftieth anniversary, a Jubilee Year was declared and half of all debts to the PEF, totaling $337,000, were forgiven.

Further reading

∘ Background, historytogo.utah.gov/utah_chapters/pioneers_and_cowboys/
  perpetualemigratingfundcompany.html

SOCIETY OF ST. VINCENT DE PAUL

Throughout much of America's early history, Catholic philanthropy was characterized by its decentralization. Nearly all giving originated in and was disbursed by individual parishes, often through religious orders supported by the congregation. One of the first efforts to provide services on a wider level than the parish began when the Society of St. Vincent de Paul was imported to St. Louis, Missouri, to provide relief for the poor, 12 years after it had been founded in Paris. The group has provided many charitable services during its history, from running homeless shelters to prison ministry to providing emergency aid after disasters. The emphasis has always been on person-to-person care, modeled on the interactions of Christ with his followers. As one of the organization's later presidents put it, "the Society has two aims: to do a great deal of spiritual good to its members through the exercise of charity, and to do a little spiritual good to a few poor families in the name of Jesus."

Further reading

∘ Society history, svdpusa.org/About-Us/History

RELIGIOUS COLLEGES COME (AND GO) IN WAVES

A majority of America's private colleges and universities were founded with a distinct religious affiliation and aim. Yale was created by Puritan clergymen. Harvard was named for a Christian minister. Baptists launched Colgate and the University of Chicago. Duke and Syracuse University grew out of Methodism. Princeton was a Presbyterian project. Georgetown was started by Jesuits. Many institutions of higher education like these, however, have now surrendered or lost their religious foundation. (Andrew Carnegie actually accelerated this by insisting that only secular institutions could participate in the important fund he set up to pay for pensions to professors, which became today's TIAA-CREF company.)

Yet other colleges have maintained a coherent faith angle, keeping religious orientation as a countercultural centerpiece of their teaching, their wider mission, and their campus identity. Notre Dame has proclaimed a clear Catholic mission since its founding in 1842. Baylor University has clung to its Baptist heritage since its birth in 1845. Wheaton College in Illinois and Calvin College in Michigan have built strong orthodox Protestant identities over a century and a half. Brigham Young University, created in 1876, remains a citadel of Mormonism. Yeshiva University fills a similar role for orthodox Jews, dating back to 1886.

Universities with unabashed religious identities continue to be formed in the U.S. Some of them have grown rapidly into established educational institutions, thanks to powerful philanthropic backing. Oral Roberts (1963), Liberty (1971), and Ave Maria (1998) universities are examples in the last generation.

Further reading

∘ William Ringenberg, *The Christian College* (Baker, 2006)

1827

EVANGELICAL DO-GOODING BY THE TAPPAN BROTHERS

Arthur and Lewis Tappan first imbibed their evangelical Protestant beliefs at the Northampton, Massachusetts, church where Jonathan Edwards had preached. They were apprenticed to Boston merchants and soon began a

 PhilAphorism

When we do any good to others, we do as much, or more, good to ourselves.

☞ *Benjamin Whichcote*

lifetime of keen business dealings, but never lost their religious fervor. Lewis dabbled in Unitarianism for a while, but in 1827 Arthur drew him back to Christianity and the Congregational church.

As they made money, the brothers poured large sums into a wide range of religious and social causes. Most famously these included their brave leadership in the movement to abolish slavery and improve the lot of freedmen. (See 1833, 1841, and 1846 entries on our list of achievements in Public Policy.)

But, sparked by their Christian convictions, the Tappans were also active in many other causes. They subsidized the Sunday School movement, supplied Bibles and other resources for new churches in the West, and funded religiously infused colleges. They defended Christian Cherokees against forced removal by the federal government. Before the Civil War they shipped Bibles to slaves, and after the war they backed schools and colleges charged with increasing literacy and prosperity among African Americans. And the Tappan brothers subsidized many missionaries who brought the Gospel, education, and health care to poor countries abroad.

Further reading

○ Bertram Wyatt-Brown, *Lewis Tappan and the Evangelical War Against Slavery* (LSU Press, 1997)

1816

AMERICAN COLONIZATION SOCIETY

In the early nineteenth century, American philanthropists desperately sought peaceful solutions to the horrid dilemmas of slavery. One proposal involved buying the freedom of slaves and repatriating them to western Africa. The American Colonization Society was founded in 1816 to promote this idea. It was presented as having dual benefits: restoring blacks to their rightful freedom, while introducing Christianity, the beginnings of literacy, and economic improvements to desperately poor countries as the liberated returned to the lands of their ancestry.

The ACS became a mass movement, with numerous local auxiliaries. It was collecting annual membership revenues of $15,000 by its tenth year. The society attracted support from American leaders like John Marshall, Andrew Jackson, Daniel Webster, James Madison, and Henry Clay, for a variety of motives.

The ACS drew criticism from African-American civil-society organizations like the African Methodist Episcopal Church. It was also opposed by slave owners, and by some abolitionists. Yet under President James Monroe the ACS became an official partner of the U.S. government in establishing the colony that is now the nation of Liberia—where 13,000 black freedmen were ultimately settled, using a mix of privately donated and federal funds.

RELIGION

Further reading

○ Kathleen McCarthy, *American Creed: Philanthropy and the Rise of Civil Society* (University of Chicago Press, 2003)

1810

AMERICAN BOARD OF COMMISSIONERS FOR FOREIGN MISSIONS

The ABCFM was founded during the Second Great Awakening by several students from Williams College, with the intention of helping to spread Christianity worldwide. The organization was supported by individual donations and financial apportionments from the Congregationalist, Presbyterian, and Dutch Reformed denominations. It sent its first missionaries to British India in 1812, and added missions to Ceylon, China, Singapore, Siam, Greece, Cyprus, Turkey, Palestine, Syria, Persia, western Africa, southern Africa, and the Sandwich Islands.

All missionaries were ordained, trained individuals, often from colleges like Middlebury, Amherst, and Williams where evangelical feeling then burned brightly. Many of them translated the Bible into new, sometimes previously unwritten, languages. They built schools and health facilities. Lots ended up advising local governments. More than 1,230 missionaries were sent afield in the organization's first 50 years, almost always in married couples.

The ABCFM also developed a strong emphasis on missions to American Indians. They first ministered to Cherokees in Tennessee, and then followed displaced southeastern tribes to Michigan, Wisconsin, the Dakotas, Minnesota, and Oregon. During Indian uprisings, missionaries attended to Indians in jail or sent on exile. They produced Bibles, dictionaries, and schoolbooks in Dakota and Ojibwe when there were no print versions of these languages. They trained indigenous preachers and leaders.

Another religiously driven, philanthropically funded missionary society that had major effects on America and overseas countries during the nineteenth century was the American Missionary Association. For more information on that group, see the 1846 entry on our companion list of achievements in Public-Policy Reform.

Further reading

○ Dissertation on the formation of the ABCFM, maxfieldbooks.com/abcfm.html

○ Brief history, christianity.com/church/church-history/timeline/1801-1900/american-missions-11630355.html

CATHOLIC SCHOOLS LAUNCHED
BY THE SISTERS OF CHARITY

Elizabeth Seton was raised an observant Episcopalian in New York, but after she was widowed at age 29, with five young children while living in Italy, she was exposed to a tender Roman Catholicism that had an effect on her. She returned to the U.S. and converted two years later, then became a nun in 1809. Soon Seton and a few other nuns started America's first sisterhood, the Sisters of Charity.

A wealthy Catholic donor named Samuel Cooper gave the church $10,000 and 269 acres near Emmitsburg, Maryland, to establish a home for the order. He continued to support its work for many years. A school for girls was launched—one of the first in the U.S. catering to needy children, and the foundation from which a vast network of American Catholic schools would soon grow. Seton taught, trained teachers, wrote textbooks, and later pioneered a new business model: admit some students whose parents could pay in order to subsidize students whose parents could not.

A whole string of other charitable entities developed simultaneously, including projects to aid the elderly and to help the poor find work. After assuming control of a Philadelphia orphanage in 1814, the Sisters of Charity began opening other orphanages. Then came hospitals, old-age homes, and settlement houses, all across the rapidly growing country.

Today the order has 1,246 sisters working in charitable establishments across the U.S. and South America. They run schools, nurseries, medical facilities, homes for the aged, and services for visiting the poor in their homes. In 1975, a century and a half after she died, Elizabeth Seton became the first native-born American to be canonized by the Catholic Church.

Further reading

◦ Biography of Seton, emmitsburg.net/setonshrine/index.htm

◦ History of the order, famvin.org/wiki/Sisters_of_Charity_of_Saint_Joseph

◦ Joseph Dirvin, *Mrs. Seton: Foundress of the American Sisters of Charity* (Farrar, Straus & Giroux, 1975)

BIBLE SOCIETIES

Early American Christian philanthropists placed great importance on sharing the Bible through various associations—preeminent among them

RELIGION

the New York Bible Society and the American Bible Society. The founders of the NYBS in 1809 included Henry Rutgers (namesake of Rutgers University), William Colgate (founder of what became Colgate-Palmolive), and Thomas Eddy (the first commissioner of the Erie Canal). Their ambitions quickly grew beyond New York—they funded a translation of the Bible into Bengali by missionary William Carey. By 1815, the NYBS had distributed 10,000 Bibles; by 1909, 4.9 million; and by 1990, 300 million in over 400 languages. Today known as Biblica, the society also holds the copyright on the New International Version, today's bestselling English translation of the Bible.

With help from the NYBS, another group of Christian donors launched the American Bible Society in 1816. This second collaborative undertook four national surveys to ascertain where Bibles were most in need. It also created translations—its first being a Delaware Indian version of the epistles of John, another being the first Bible in braille. The ABS began the country's long and continuing tradition of distributing Scripture to members of the armed services when it supplied Bibles to the crew of the USS *John Adams*. Almost 450,000 Bibles were distributed by the American Bible Society in its first decade, a remarkable figure given the difficulties of manufacturing and the state of roads and trade in the early 1800s.

Generations of American philanthropists have supported both of these organizations. Sometimes they have done so on a very large scale, like the Russell Sage Foundation's $500,000 gift to the ABS in 1908.

Further reading

○ About Biblica, biblica.com/en-us/about-usABS historical timeline, americanbible.org/about/history

○ Kathleen McCarthy, *American Creed: Philanthropy and the Rise of Civil Society* (University of Chicago Press, 2003)

1807

ANDOVER THEOLOGICAL SEMINARY

The oldest graduate school of theology in the U.S. (and oldest graduate school of any sort, for that matter) is the Andover Theological Seminary. It was Boston merchant Samuel Abbot who provided most of the initial financing for the new institution. The widow and son of the founder of Phillips Academy, Phoebe and John Phillips, also made important contributions when they constructed two buildings on the campus of Phillips Academy to house the theological students and administrators and get the seminary launched.

Many prominent American pastors, scholars, and theologians came out of Andover, including leaders of numerous other seminaries and colleges.

Further reading

○ About Andover, ants.edu/about

1804

BUILDING EVANGELICALISM

As Unitarianism started to become fashionable in New England, a group of Boston Congregationalist parishioners joined together in 1804 to form a "Religious Improvement Society" that would reinforce traditional Christian understandings of the Bible, prayer, and the trinitarian God. This grew into an energetic and fast-growing congregation, whose members soon contributed $100,000 to build a meetinghouse: the Park Street Church. Over the next two centuries the church would pioneer many new elements of Christian outreach, and build and then keep alive an evangelical spirit in the oldest part of America.

Park Street became a hub of the abolitionist movement. Harriet Beecher Stowe's brother Edward was pastor there in the 1820s, and William Lloyd Garrison gave his first major anti-slavery address in the sanctuary in 1829. He rejected the idea of African colonization, and urged emancipation instead, saying, "I call upon the churches of the living God to lead in this great enterprise."

Park Street Church was also a hub for the religious arts. Boston's Handel and Haydn Society (America's second-oldest musical organization) was formed there in 1815. The church's organist Lowell Mason composed the standard settings of hymns like "Joy to the World" and "Nearer, My God, to Thee." Many of today's congregational singing patterns began at this church.

Park Street also became a leader in Christian foreign missions. It sponsored the first American missionaries to the Hawaiian islands and several other overseas locations. It continues to send out missionaries today, concentrating on locations where Christianity is unknown. It funds its own Bible translation and church-planting efforts, and provides health, schooling, and economic services in poor lands.

In the mid-twentieth century Park Street Church was influential in the formation of the modern evangelical movement. It took part in Billy Graham's crusades, helped create the National Association of Evangelicals, and contributed to the formation of Gordon-Conwell and Fuller seminaries.

Park Street currently has a thriving congregation of about 2,000. Its present charitable outreach activities include the City Mission Society that it co-founded, America's first prison ministry, an inner-city school for

RELIGION

minority children called Boston Trinity Academy, homeless ministries, a crisis pregnancy center, an Animal Rescue League, and language training for immigrants. Park Street Congregational Church may have had a greater impact on American history than any other single U.S. congregation.

Further reading

◦ Garth Rosell, *Boston's Historic Park Street Church: The Story of an Evangelical Landmark* (Kregel Publishing, 2009)

◦ Park Street Church today, parkstreet.org

CHARLESTON'S HEBREW ORPHAN SOCIETY

When America was born as a nation, Charleston, South Carolina, had the largest Jewish population in the U.S. The city had been the main receiving point for Sephardic refugees for more than a century. Many of Charleston's Jews were merchants, and amid a burst of post-Revolution prosperity they wanted to share their good fortune with others.

In 1784 they formed the oldest Jewish charitable society in the United States, which led in 1801 to the creation of a dedicated group "for the purpose of relieving widows, educating, clothing, and maintaining orphans and children of indigent parents." The constitution of the Hebrew Orphan Society cited the good fortune of Jews living "in the United States of America, where freedom and equal rights, religious, civil and political, are liberally extended to them," and stated that the aim of the society's charity was to "qualify" recipients to exercise "those blessings and advantages to which they are entitled" as they "freely assume an equal station in this favored land."

Orphans were mostly placed in private homes and provided with money, clothes, and education by society members, though for several decades before the Civil War a group home and school for orphans was also operated. Today the society still exists, and funds medical needs in Charleston, gives grants to schools and nonprofits, and awards ten to 20 annual college scholarships.

Further reading

◦ History, jhssc.org/JHSSC_Hebrew_Orphan_Society.html

REBECCA GRATZ

At the tender age of 20, Rebecca Gratz founded the Female Association for the Relief of Women and Children in Reduced Circumstances, an 1801 charitable organization that assisted victims of the American Revolution. Several years later she was a principal contributor to the establishment of the Orphan Society of Philadelphia. While the society was a Christian organization and Gratz was a devout Jew, she served as one of three original board members and gave of her family fortune. When a fire destroyed the society's building, Gratz led the fundraising campaign to build a new one. Gratz was equally active in Jewish causes. She was a founding member of the Female Hebrew Benevolent Society in 1819, which continues two hundred years later in its mission of aiding Jewish women in financial crisis. Gratz also helped start the Hebrew Sunday school and laid the groundwork for Philadelphia's Jewish Foster Home and Orphan Asylum.

Further reading

○ Detailed history of Gratz and her charitable works, jwa.org/womenofvalor/gratz

SUNDAY SCHOOLS SPREAD LITERACY AND CONSTRUCTIVE BEHAVIOR

When the Sunday School movement began to spread across America in the 1790s and early 1800s as part of the Second Great Awakening, these gatherings were the only places were many poor children had a chance to learn to read. Christian philanthropists wanted to both acquaint youngsters with the Scriptures and free them from a life of illiteracy. The Bible was the textbook, and all the requirements of reading and writing— alphabetic instruction, word sounds, penmanship—were assiduously taught in church classes. Millions of children became literate by copying out Biblical passages. The appetite for Bibles, language primers, and religious instructional materials in turn stimulated the growth of publishing houses and other aids to reading.

Christian morality and virtues were inculcated by the Sunday School movement. And pupils often graduated to become Sunday School teachers—providing a leadership opportunity the poor rarely enjoyed in other parts of their lives. Every state had Sunday Schools by 1826, and the percentage of New York children attending Sunday School was double the enrollment of the public schools in 1829. By the mid-nineteenth century, Sunday School attendance was a near-universal aspect of American childhood; parents who were not regular churchgoers often insisted that their children attend. Even Marxist atheists observing from abroad credited the Sunday School movement with being important in elevating the working classes in the U.S.

RELIGION

With Sunday Schools dramatically increasing the overall U.S. literacy rate, the U.S. ended up at the top of international lists in this area. Literacy in turn "sparked an avalanche of organizational activity" that fed American prosperity. Historians argue that the learning and personal habits spread by charitable Sunday Schooling improved social conditions, fueled commercial prowess, and revved the nation's economic metabolism.

Further reading

○ Anne Boylan, *Sunday School: Formation of an American Institution 1790-1880* (Yale University Press, 1990)

BENEZET AND THE QUAKERS AID THE FORGOTTEN

Anthony Benezet immigrated from France to North America with hopes of becoming a successful merchant. When he fell on hard times instead, he sought support from the Society of Friends, whose worship circles he had joined upon his arrival in Philadelphia. Soon Benezet began teaching at the Friends' English School. In 1754 he founded the first school in Pennsylvania that offered girls more than an elementary-level education.

Later he made an even more unconventional decision for his day—he would offer classes for poor blacks during the evening. After several years, he secured Quaker financing to start the Negro School at Philadelphia in 1770. Amid his religious and occupational devotion to educating blacks, Benezet began producing written materials arguing that slavery was inconsistent with Christian beliefs. This eventually led him to found the Society for the Relief of Free Negroes Unlawfully Held in Bondage. Benjamin Franklin and Benjamin Rush would later reorganize the group in 1784 as the Pennsylvania Abolition Society.

Like numerous Quakers who would follow in his steps, Benezet's work at aiding forgotten populations was motivated by a desire to improve the condition of men and women of all sorts. "Though I am joined in Church fellowship with the people called Quakers, yet my heart is united in true gospel fellowship with the willing in God's Israel," he wrote. "Let their distinguishing name or sect be as it may."

Further reading

○ Benezet biography, abolition.e2bn.org/people_27.html

CALIFORNIA'S MISSIONS

For nearly a century starting in 1768, Spanish priests (mostly Franciscans) founded and operated 21 missions across California to bring Catholicism and European-style development to the far coast of North America. The missions introduced to the region not only Christianity but schools and medical facilities, European crops and animals plus cropping and husbandry techniques, water works, and art and architecture that is still admired. These missionaries established much of the initial pathbreaking, population settlement, and place naming of our most important state. The Catholic church financed the initial mission settlements, which then undertook various kinds of economic activity in an effort to support themselves and the Indians seeking aid at their walls. Few of the missions ever became wholly self-sufficient, though, so supplementary funding came from a private religious endowment known as the Pious Fund of the Californias. It was built from voluntary donations by Mexican families and churches. This represented one of the most significant charitable ventures in early American history.

Further reading

○ Remarks on Spanish missions at 2013 Annual Meeting of The Philanthropy Roundtable, philanthropyroundtable.org/general/a_leading_role_for_philanthropy

A SHRINE TO RELIGIOUS LIBERTY

As the oldest extant Jewish house of worship in America, dating from 1763, Touro Synagogue in Newport, Rhode Island, would be famous under any circumstances. But Touro's place in history was cemented when George Washington visited Newport to drum up support for passage of the Bill of Rights. The warden of the synagogue sent Washington a welcoming message, and, in return, the newly ensconced head of state penned a 340-word response.

In his note, Washington unveiled a glimmering vision of a nation where citizens of all faiths abide together under a government that "gives to bigotry no sanction, to persecution no assistance." Closing with imagery straight from the Old Testament, he expressed his wish that "the children of the stock of Abraham who dwell in this land continue to merit and enjoy the goodwill of the other inhabitants—while every one shall sit in safety under his own vine and fig tree and there shall be none to make him afraid." The father of his country was well aware that Americans would not overlook his gesture towards this small, frequently persecuted minority, and his letter became a seminal document in the history of American religious freedom, cited by judges, politicians, and philosophers.

RELIGION

Supporters of the Touro Synagogue have sustained the facility for two and a half centuries. The name comes from two sons of an early prayer leader who made a series of gifts over several decades to maintain and expand the worship hall and its grounds (in the process establishing themselves among the first great American philanthropists). Abraham Touro bequeathed large funds to maintain the building and the street it sits on, after having previously built a wall around the adjoining Jewish cemetery. His brother, Judah Touro, gave several gifts of his own, plus a large grant in his will to preserve the facility (amidst many other donations he made to Jewish and non-Jewish charities around the U.S.—see 1854 entry).

In a nice twist of philanthropic genealogy, it was yet another descendant of the Touro family—financier John Loeb—who funded the new visitor's center built next to the synagogue in 2009. The exhibit-filled building is a shrine to religious liberty and to George Washington. The associated George Washington Institute for Religious Freedom extends the mission of the Touro Synagogue, reinforcing respect for faith among the next generation of Americans.

Further reading

∘ History of the Touro Synagogue, tourosynagogue.org/history-learning/synagogue-history

1740

A GREAT AWAKENING OF MASS PHILANTHROPY

In the first half of the 1700s, a crucial religious revival swept the American colonies. In addition to setting the stage for a political revolution based on the sovereignty of the individual, it sparked a vital transformation of American philanthropy. The so-called Great Awakening highlighted the importance of each person's direct connection to God, unmediated by church or other institutions, and in the process fueled desires within the colonial population to live life as Christ would want, taking personal responsibility for the goodness of one's behavior. This inevitably fueled charitable generosity and made it a mass phenomenon, even among the poor. "Of all the conversions wrought by the Great Awakening certainly the most remarkable was the transformation of do-goodism from a predominantly upper- and middle-class activity…into a broadly shared, genuinely popular avocation," wrote historian Robert Bremner.

One of the strongest drivers of this new understanding of the importance of individual charity was George Whitefield, a charismatic 25-year-old Methodist preacher who set out in 1739 on a series of evangelizing tours that brought him into contact with thousands of everyday colonials stretched across a wide frontier. He excited his audiences with his vision of an intensely personal relationship with Christ and urged them to live out their internal convictions via generosity to fellow men. Whitefield took up collections at his meetings for many good causes: relief of victims of disaster (of which there were many in this raw land), assistance to keep debtors out of prison, funds to buy books for the hard-pressed new educational institutions of the colonies—Harvard, Dartmouth, the University of Pennsylvania.

Whitefield's personal top charitable priority was an orphanage he founded in impoverished Georgia in 1740. It was modeled on an institution created by the German clergyman and philanthropist August Francke, and Whitefield labored to build it up over three decades. It never met his expectations, but as he described the effort during his seven preaching tours across the America, his charity became for many of his listeners a template for how a serious Christian might offer up money and energy to assist the abandoned, the ill, the poor, and victims of sickness, fire, or other misfortune. Individual humanitarian action became a distinctive mark of the American character.

Further reading
○ Robert Bremner, *American Philanthropy* (University of Chicago Press, 1960)

1727

URSULINE SCHOOL, HOSPITAL, AND ORPHANAGE IN NEW ORLEANS

When 11 Ursuline nuns arrived in New Orleans in 1727—at which point the French colonial city was a raw settlement just nine years old—they established a school for girls. It educated not just European children but also slaves, Native Americans, and free girls of color. It continues to operate today, the oldest Catholic school in America. The Ursulines also created a hospital, which nursed 30-40 patients at any given moment, in a place and time when other medical attention was virtually nonexistent.

In 1729 the nuns set up an orphanage (originally to take care of children who survived the Indian massacre of settlers at Fort Rosalie that year). Over a period of years it fed, cared for, and trained up hundreds of children who had no other protectors or resource. The nuns were supported by the French and New World church, and by donations from merchants and residents.

Further reading
○ James Zacharie, *New Orleans Guide* (Hansell, 1893)

RELIGION

1681

QUAKER PRISON REFORM

Quakers showed deep philanthropic conviction from their earliest days in America. They gave generously of both money and time to scores of causes—building schools, aiding the sick, donating to the poor, registering early opposition to slavery. Prison reform was one of their earliest crusades.

William Penn had been imprisoned several times in the Tower of London for his religious beliefs. (He wrote his Christian classic *No Cross, No Crown* while locked up.) So when King Charles II handed over to Penn, as repayment for a debt the king owed Penn's father, the land that now makes up Pennsylvania and Delaware (one of the largest individual land grants in history), Penn was determined that his new colony would take a very different approach to imprisonment.

In 1681 he spelled out that in Pennsylvania "all prisoners shall be bailable... unless for capital offences, where the proof is evident, or the presumption great." At a time when prisoners had to pay for their food, and for small services like having their irons unlocked so they could appear in court, Penn stipulated that "all prisons shall be free as to fees, food, and lodging." Penn limited the death penalty to the crimes of murder and treason—at a time when English law doled out capital punishment for more than 200 different crimes. He also insisted that instead of being dungeons, prisons should be workhouses, aimed at rehabilitation, with inmates taught a trade that could allow them to earn an honest living once released. In his lockups, men finished and shaped wood, and women spun yarn. Penn intended that in these new measures "an example may be set up to the nations as...a holy experiment."

Quakers continued to put energy and money into prison reform for centuries. Dismayed by the nineteenth-century convention of locking 30 to 40 inmates together in large rooms, the Quakers pushed to have hardened criminals separated from novices, debtors from the violent, women from men, and so forth. They were instrumental in establishing separate channels to handle juvenile delinquents. (See 1825 entry on companion list of achievements building Prosperity.)

In 1829 Quakers opened a famous prison in Philadelphia that housed every resident in a strict solitary confinement meant to encourage penitence. The concept became influential worldwide. This innovation was taken to an extreme—the isolation and silence could also sometimes encourage mental illness—but the shift to small cells, more humane treatment, and rehabilitative efforts became the new norm in America and other countries.

Further reading

◦ Quaker history, fcnl.org/issues/justice/quakers_know_prisons
◦ Quaker history, archstreetfriends.org/exhibit/p078.html

PUBLIC-POLICY REFORM

onating money to modify public thinking and government policy has now taken its place next to service-centered giving as a constructive branch of philanthropy. Grants that aim to reform society's rules are sometimes controversial, but less so than in times past. Many donors now view public-policy reform as a necessary adjunct to their efforts to improve lives directly. From school choice to creation of think tanks of all stripes, from tort reform to gay advocacy, donors have become involved in many efforts to shape opinion and law.

This is perhaps inevitable given the mushrooming presence of government in our lives. In 1930, just 12 percent of U.S. GDP was consumed by government; by 2012 that tripled to 36 percent. Unless and until that expansion of the state reverses, it is unrealistic to expect the philanthropic sector to stop trying to have a say in public policies.

Sometimes it is not enough to pay for a scholarship; one must change laws so that high-quality schools exist for scholarship recipients to take advantage of. Sometimes it's not enough to build a house of worship; one must erect guardrails that protect the ability of its citizens to practice their faith freely.

Because public-policy philanthropy has only become common recently, this list has more entries dating from the latest generation, compared to our other lists of U.S. philanthropic action. And since one man's good deed is another man's calamity when it comes to giving with political implications, we have included policy advocacy of all sorts on this list.

Not all public policies split into "Left" vs. "Right" variants, but for those that do, the reality is that much more philanthropic money has been deployed leftward than rightward. Detailed quantification in the book *The New Leviathan* showed that 122 major foundations with total assets of $105 billion provided $8.8 billion of funding for liberal causes in 2010. That same year, 82 foundations with total assets of $10 billion provided $0.8 billion for conservative causes. In other words: there is eleven times as much foundation money going into public-policy philanthropy that aims left as aims right. (Individual donors are more evenly split, though still predominantly on the left.) The *Washington Post* once observed that the Ford Foundation alone has given more to liberal causes in one year than donor Richard Scaife (sometimes called the Daddy Warbucks of the Right) gave to conservative causes in 40 years.

Whatever your aspirations for American governance and society, tracking the deeds of previous public-policy donors—summarized below—will help you find the best ways to succeed.

Section research provided by Karl Zinsmeister and John Miller

2015

GESTATING AN IRAN DEAL

President Obama's 2015 decision to end sanctions on Iran in return for promises of increased nuclear accountability did not emerge on its own. It grew directly out of years of quiet activity by the Rockefeller Brothers Fund. After the 9/11 attacks demonstrated that al-Qaeda had become the most urgent Islamic threat, the fund began to convene meetings to explore the possibility of some U.S.-Iran rapprochement. Its Iran Project, given $4.3 million, funded a group of former U.S. diplomats to develop a relationship with Mohammad Javad Zarif and other Iranian officials, and begin to get them engaged with influential Americans. Zarif is now Iran's chief nuclear negotiator and the godfather of the Iran-Obama plan. The Rockefeller Brothers Fund also paid for most of a $4 million campaign launched in 2010 by the Ploughshares Fund, a San Francisco-based peace group, to build support among liberal think tanks and activists for pressure on behalf of an Iran deal.

Further reading

○ Bloomberg reporting, bloomberg.com/politics/articles/2015-07-02/how-freelance-diplomacy-bankrolled-by-rockefellers-has-paved-the-way-for-an-iran-deal

2015

BUILDING U.S. INTEREST IN ISRAEL

John Boruchin was born in Poland, and lost most of his family to death camps during World War II. He immigrated to the United States, carved out a career building homes in California, and gradually accumulated a large fortune. At his death he left $100 million to endow a new center devoted to shaping public understanding of Israel in America. The Boruchin Israel Education Advocacy Center, which will be managed by the Jewish National Fund, will run student and faculty exchanges between the U.S. and Israel, organize campus seminars, sponsor young professionals on visits to the Jewish state, run a speaker's bureau, and otherwise advocate for close ties between the U.S. and Israel.

John Boruchin was an admirer of Ze'ev Jabotinsky—a Russian Jewish journalist and organizer who warned in the decades before the Holocaust that Jews in many countries were "living on the edge of the volcano" and needed a safe sanctuary in their Middle-Eastern homeland, where he proposed creation of a democratic state of Israel. In 2015, amid attacks on Jews in Europe, and the rise of boycott-Israel movements on U.S. campuses, the chairman of the new policy organization created by Boruchin suggested that his gift "comes at a critical period in history, as Israel and world Jewry face serious challenges with rising anti-Israel sentiment and anti-Semitism. This center is needed now more than ever."

Further reading

o Jewish National Fund press release on Boruchin bequest, jnf.org/about-jnf/100-million-jnf-boruchin.html"

2015

INDEPENDENCE PROJECT FOR VETERANS

With almost predictable regularity over recent years, the Department of Veterans Affairs has become embroiled in repeated scandals combining inadequate service and out-of-control backlogs. A root of the problem is an explosion in the number of former servicemembers who are now defined as disabled. Eleven percent of all World War II veterans received disability payments. Among those who served in Vietnam, 16 percent got checks. But among the men and women who served after the 9/11 attacks, a whopping 45 percent have already applied for disability compensation after leaving the service, a ratio that will increase as this cohort ages.

POLICY

Not only do close to a majority of former servicemembers now call themselves disabled, but under what has come to be known as the "disability-compensation escalator," those on the rolls tend to ratchet up their official degree of disability every few years. Recipients can claim additional disabilities at any time, and it is very common for someone who goes on the books at "30 percent disabled" to later be re-rated at 40 percent, then 60 percent, etc.

The vastly increased recourse to disability support and the constant upward drift of benefits combine to create terrible disincentives against work and independence. This hurts participants in many ways. Veterans who work not only have much higher income than those on the dole, they are also more likely to recover from their afflictions, have better mental health, much bigger social networks, deeper self-esteem, and more stable family lives. So the disability "aid" increasingly pumped out by the federal government correlates with more joblessness and less wealth, health, and happiness among veterans.

On top of these ill-effects for vets, the existing system is bad news for taxpayers. The cost of the veterans disability program more than tripled from 2000 to 2015, to an annual total of $65 billion, and is still rising fast. The budget of the Department of Veterans Affairs is now ballooning more rapidly than any other major department of the federal government.

Despite all this, efforts to create a more humane and effective system for assisting wounded warriors have failed in Congress. There are simply too many interest groups with a stake in the status quo. To get around this public-policy gridlock, donors launched a bold effort in 2015 to find a better way of operating. Their privately funded experiment will turn disability benefits on their head—instead of trickling a lifelong stream of small monthly checks to vets that keep them in low-income dependency, the program will make heavy upfront investments in veterans with mild to moderate injuries so they can acquire the skills for their dream jobs, start businesses or trades, and otherwise upgrade their lives to the point where they can support themselves in dignity. A wide variety of medical, technical, motivational, and economic incentives will be offered to each volunteer participant. In return they must commit themselves to stepping away from the disability dole and working toward self-reliance instead. In preliminary focus groups, 80-90 percent of disabled veterans leapt to take this deal.

The Independence Project was launched with a million-dollar grant from the Anschutz family of Colorado, $4.1 million of funding from the John and Laura Arnold Foundation, another million-dollar grant from the Daniels Fund, $10 million from the Diana Davis Spencer Foundation, support from the Milbank, Wilf, Morgridge, and Bradley foundations, and investments from other individual donors and foundations that were in process as this book went to print. The program will allow a careful scientific test of the revised approach with a group of disabled vets. When results accumulate, the philanthropic backers will use the research findings for a public-education and policy-reform campaign aimed at remaking the major Veterans Affairs disability programs in this healthier and more fiscally sustainable form.

Further reading

○ *Philanthropy* magazine story, philanthropyroundtable.org/topic/veterans/labeled_disabled

○ Brief video encapsulation of problem at Philanthropy Roundtable annual meeting, philanthropyroundtable.org/topic/veterans/beyond_the_uniform

○ *Philanthropy* magazine article sketching early vision of forthcoming program, philanthropyroundtable.org/topic/excellence_in_philanthropy/real_opportunities_for_veterans

HELPING TRANSITIONS TO FREEDOM

"When I was working with the Slovaks, I realized there are no books written, no roadmap, for a country to transition from an authoritarian government to a free society. Studying countries that have made the successful transition to democracy gives us an opportunity to help nations that are in the process. We're talking about people having the opportunity to come out from under the thumb of authoritarian rule, and with that freedom to have a better life for themselves and their children, as well as freedom from fear of their government, their police, and even their neighbors."

Those were the words of Ron Weiser on announcing his $25 million gift in 2014 to the University of Michigan's Weiser Center for Emerging Democracies, following an earlier $10 million founding gift. After founding a national real-estate investment firm, Weiser served as U.S. ambassador to Slovakia from 2001 to 2004. His academic center aims to "assure and extend freedom and democracy" by encouraging and supporting movement away from oppressive government in Eurasian countries.

POLICY

⚘ PhilAphorism

If you want to lift yourself up, lift up someone else.

☞ Booker T. Washington

Further reading

○ Weiser Center for Emerging Democracies, ii.umich.edu/wce

○ Announcement of 2014 gift, leadersandbest.umich.edu/comm/news/weisers-50-million-gift

2014

KEEPING THE LIGHTS ON IN DETROIT

Detroit may be America's most ill-governed, and saddest, city. That's the public's verdict: The city's population plummeted from 1.9 million in 1950 to just 680,000 in 2014, just after Detroit filed the nation's largest-ever municipal bankruptcy, estimating that it was $20 billion in debt.

Private philanthropies have tried for years to stanch the worst of Detroit's bleeding. The only streetlights that work in midtown are the ones paid for by the Hudson-Webber Foundation. In 2013, the Kresge Foundation and some partners donated 100 police cars to the city (where the average response time to a 911 call is 58 minutes). These and other donors poured at least $628 million into the city between 2007 and 2011, particularly hoping to soften life for children and other innocent victims of the misgovernance, and to spark a bit of private-sector economic activity.

Then in late 2014, a coalition of 15 foundations—both local and national—plus some corporate and individual donors pledged $466 million to shore up the city's insolvent pension system and transfer the Detroit Institute of Arts from city to nonprofit ownership, so that its great works and building wouldn't have to be sold for cash. This philanthropic help was the key to negotiation of a grand bargain of concessions, cuts, and contributions that allowed the city to emerge from bankruptcy. Whether Detroit will ever become a healthy community again remains to be seen, but the donors who had been protecting city residents for decades at least gave the city and the state breathing space to create more responsible and sustainable public policies.

Further reading

○ *Philanthropy* magazine reporting, philanthropyroundtable.org/topic/excellence_in_philanthropy/philanthropy_keeps_the_lights_on_in_detroit

○ *Detroit News* report on first payments, detroitnews.com/story/news/local/wayne-county/2014/12/11/first-payment-made-toward-detroits-grand-bargain/20240369/

2014

$50 MILLION FOR GUN CONTROL

Though he is no longer mayor of New York City, Michael Bloomberg continues to nudge public policy—these days as a donor. In 2014 he put up $50 million to create an educational nonprofit (with separate lobbying and campaign-donation arms) to push for stricter gun control. To put that in perspective, $50 million is about two and a half times what the National Rifle Association spent that same year to campaign for gun-owner rights.

In the run-up to the 2014 election, Bloomberg's groups surveyed candidates on gun issues, and bought millions of dollars of TV issue ads. The allied political action committee made campaign donations to selected candidates at the state and federal levels. *Ad Age* calculated that Bloomberg's money allowed gun-control groups to outspend gun-owner groups by 7:1 on television advertising.

Even still, gun controllers didn't do well in the 2014 election. Bloomberg is swimming against inhospitable policy currents. According to the Pew Research Center, public support for gun control deteriorated steadily over the last two decades. When asked "Is it more important to control gun ownership or protect the right of Americans to own guns?" the public flipped from favoring gun control 57-34 percent in 1993, to favoring gun-ownership rights 52-46 percent in 2014. A sharp drop in the rate of murder committed with firearms between 1993 and 2011—from 6.6 victims to 3.2 victims per 100,000 population—corresponds with a large rise in gun ownership during that same period. Americans owned 310 million firearms in 2009, up from 192 million in 1994.

Further reading

o *Washington Post* analysis, washingtonpost.com/blogs/wonkblog/wp/2014/04/16/can-michael-bloomberg-really-build-a-gun-control-lobby-bigger-than-the-nra

o Congressional Research Service study of gun ownership vs. murder rates, fas.org/sgp/crs/misc/RL32842.pdf

2014

BOOSTING POLICY INSTRUCTION
AT U. CHICAGO

POLICY

The national rankings of top graduate schools in public policy have held pretty steady for some years, centered on Syracuse University's Maxwell School, the Kennedy School at Harvard, Indiana University, University of Georgia, and the Woodrow Wilson School at Princeton. Recent philanthropic gifts aim to move another entity up that list. The University of Chicago's Harris School of Public Policy is a relative newcomer established in 1988 (thanks to leadership and an endowment gift from businessman Irving Harris). It enrolled 410 graduate students in 2014, and is particularly known for its quantitative training. In 2014, DeVry University co-founder Dennis Keller donated $20 million, and the family of Irving Harris gave another $12.5 million, to build a new home for the graduate school. This will allow expansions into leadership training, with the goal of anointing more trailblazers in public policy.

Further reading

○ *Chicago Tribune* reporting on gifts, carrollcountytimes.com/news/ct-university-chicago-harris-school-met-20141105,0,5224617.story

A $250 MILLION MEDIA EXPERIMENT

Pierre Omidyar, the billionaire founder of eBay, first pursued an interest in media operations that promote "good government" when he funded a digital "newspaper" devoted to investigative reporting, public policy, and politics in his home state of Hawaii. His appetite whetted, Omidyar considered buying the *Washington Post* before fellow tech-tycoon and donor Jeff Bezos did so for $250 million in 2013. Instead, Omidyar decided to devote the same pile of money—$250 million—to create his own muckraking publications from scratch. In 2014 he unveiled his first venture: the *Intercept,* an online magazine devoted to "adversarial journalism on national security, criminal justice" and related topics. It was formed around a trio of hard-left reporter-commentators: Jeremy Scahill of the *Nation,* filmmaker Laura Poitras, and Glenn Greenwald, who led publication of the Edward Snowden leaks.

Omidyar's next publication was to be a scathing forum called *Racket* that would "attack Wall Street and the corporate world." Before the venture even published its first story, however, the attacker-in-chief hired by Omidyar to run the publication clashed with his bosses and was accused of sexual harassment by an underling. The venture collapsed and it was announced that the staff hired to run it would be let go.

◌ PhilAphorism

In America, communities existed before governments. There were many groups of people with a common sense of purpose and a feeling of duty to one another before there were political institutions.

☞ *Daniel Boorstin*

Two years after Omidyar's announcement that he was going to loose on the world a whole stable of digital news sites "that will cover topics ranging from entertainment and sports to business and the economy," the only fully functioning element was the *Intercept*, and the founding donor was at war with many of the journalistic crusaders he hoped to lead into society-altering news coverage. The effectiveness of this investment is thus in doubt. Its sheer size, however, and the interest it has sparked among other donors and a press corps obsessed with new media, guarantee that it will be looked back upon as a milestone in public-policy philanthropy, whether of a positive or negative sort.

Further reading

○ *Philanthropy* magazine reporting, philanthropyroundtable.org/topic/excellence_in_
philanthropy/investigative_philanthropy

○ Description of the collapse of *Racket* published by the *Intercept*, firstlook.org/
theintercept/2014/10/30/inside-story-matt-taibbis-departure-first-look-media

2014

SUING FOR REFORM

Philanthropists have been funding lawsuits as a way to improve public policies for more than a century. Booker T. Washington secretly financed the *Giles v. Harris* case back in 1903, and throughout the rest of his life paid for other litigation aimed at undoing racial disenfranchisement (see details in 1903 entry).

In this same spirit, Silicon Valley entrepreneur David Welch spent several million dollars between 2011 and 2014 building a court case that California's teacher-tenure laws—which grant permanent employment after just 18 months on the job, make it nearly impossible to fire even the most terrible teachers, and require school districts to lay teachers off based on seniority rather than competence—deprive students of the right to be educated as guaranteed by the state constitution.

Welch and his wife first tried traditional education philanthropy, giving money to bring new teaching methods and technology into schools. They soon realized that in many public schools, incompetent teachers made necessary educational improvements impossible. So in 2011 they founded a group called Students Matter and gathered facts about the forces blocking school reform.

Eventually David Welch found nine students who said their education suffered after they were stuck in classrooms with poor teachers. He hired a top-flight legal team to help them assemble a court case. He was also savvy enough to fund an accompanying public-relations campaign to fend off the massive counterattack by teacher unions that predictably followed.

POLICY

In 2014 a judge of the Los Angeles Superior Court ruled that "there are a significant number of grossly ineffective teachers currently active in California classrooms" and that this causes thousands of students to fall years behind in math and reading. "The evidence is compelling. Indeed, it shocks the conscience," wrote Judge Rolf Treu in his *Vergara v. State of California* decision striking down seniority-based job protections for unionized teachers.

The state appealed, a process that could take three years. Almost immediately, however, other philanthropists and education reformers began to consider similar donor-funded lawsuits in states like New York, Connecticut, New Jersey, New Mexico, Oregon, and elsewhere, aiming to eliminate rigid teacher tenure.

Welch's funding is part of a longer tradition of public-interest law philanthropy on behalf of educational improvement. Donor-funded groups like the Institute for Justice and the Goldwater Institute have litigated over many years to protect school choice, educational tax credits, charter schools, and other elements of school reform.

Further reading

○ *Philanthropy* magazine reporting, philanthropyroundtable.org/topic/k_12_education/suing_for_reform

○ Sponsor of *Vergara* case, studentsmatter.org

○ Institute for Justice educational litigation, ij.org/cases/schoolchoice

2013

SUPREME ASSISTANCE

The Searle Freedom Trust was founded in 1998 by Dan Searle with proceeds from the sale of the G. D. Searle pharmaceutical company. The foundation has been a major funder of university professors, supporting career development and detailed, esoteric, long-term research with the goal of bolstering academics working outside of reigning liberal orthodoxies. The trust has also been underwriting online higher education as a way to make college instruction less monolithic.

More recently, Searle has influenced public policy via support for important litigation. "Our biggest victories lately have come in the legal arena," says president Kim Dennis. "There have been numerous Supreme Court decisions that we helped to fund. These produced decisions in policy arenas as diverse as voting rights, environmental regulation, education, and health care."

"Of course these things can all be changed by one heart attack on the Supreme Court," notes Dennis. "But there are also state courts. There's a lot you can do in litigation."

Further reading

○ *Shelby County v. Holder* opinion, supremecourt.gov/opinions/12pdf/12-96_6k47.pdf

○ *Fisher v. University of Texas* opinion, supremecourtreview.com/case/11-345

○ *King v. Burwell* docket, supremecourt.gov/search.aspx?filename=/docketfiles/14-114.htm

2013

A BIT OF DIVERSITY
IN THE FACULTY LOUNGE

The University of Colorado at Boulder is famous as a citadel of "progressivism," for which it is sometimes referred to as the "Berkeley of the Rockies." All faculty members, for instance, are encouraged to put a prepared statement in their initial class materials telling students they are free to choose a different gender pronoun for themselves if that would make them feel more comfortable.

In the hope of introducing missing perspectives into the university's teaching, and broadening political discussion on campus, a group of Boulder-area donors including local banker Earl Wright and former Boulder mayor Bob Greenlee proposed to fund within the political-science department a new position in Conservative Thought and Policy. After more than 20 area donors raised a million dollars, a three-year pilot program was set up to bring a series of visiting scholars to campus on annual rotations.

Political scientist Steven Hayward, CU-Boulder's first Visiting Scholar of Conservative Thought and Policy, taught four classes during the 2013-2014 school year: two on Constitutional law, one on free-market environmentalism, and another on American political thought. In addition to teaching, he organized debates and guest lectures that brought center-right scholars to campus. In 2014, the second visiting scholar arrived—Hillsdale College historian Bradley Birzer. The third visiting scholar, economic historian Brian Domitrovic, arrived on campus in 2015.

Further reading

○ CU-Boulder FAQ on program, artsandsciences.colorado.edu/ctp/faq/

2011

AVOIDING MELTDOWNS
OF PUBLIC PENSIONS

The public-pension gap—the retiree and health benefits that have been promised to government workers but not funded—is the single gravest economic threat to the U.S. today. That is the position of the Laura and

POLICY

John Arnold Foundation. It's a strong claim, but there are scary numbers behind it: unfunded state and local promises to civil servants now total a breathtaking $2 trillion.

There are ways out of that deep, deep hole—switching from defined-benefit to defined-contribution pensions (as almost all private companies did decades ago), asking public workers to make co-contributions and co-payments. But these reforms are politically difficult. To make them easier, the Arnold Foundation has offered its services around the country as a kind of *pro bono* think tank—helping states and cities calculate exactly how much they've overpromised, and then advising them on ways to stem their flood of red ink. The foundation offered important technical and communications help that allowed Rhode Island to pass the first major pension reform, heading off a Detroit-like disaster from taking place on the state level. Laura and John Arnold complemented that assistance with personal contributions in support of political leaders and groups fighting for pension reform.

Working with the Pew Center on the States, Arnold then offered research and other help to additional locales with runaway pension costs. Kentucky, San Jose, San Diego, Utah, and other jurisdictions acted. Many others are still scrambling, often with Arnold Foundation aid. In its first three years working on this subject, the foundation spent about $11 million to help formulate more sustainable pension policies, with much additional policy assistance to come. Election contributions to officeholders backing reform (from the Arnolds as individuals) came on top of that funding and protected the project from being undermined by political opposition.

Further reading

○ *Philanthropy* magazine reporting, philanthropyroundtable.org/topic/excellence_in_
philanthropy/solving_the_2_trillion_problem

2011

DON'T ASK, DON'T TELL

In 1987, the J. Roderick MacArthur Foundation awarded a group called Alternatives to Militarism the first known grant to challenge military regulations on homosexual behavior. The topic worked its way into politics, and during the 1992 Presidential race Bill Clinton said he would be willing to sign an executive order permitting homosexuality in the armed forces. The compromise that eventually resulted, known as the "don't ask, don't tell" policy, went into effect in 1993.

Almost immediately, gay activists and their philanthropic supporters went to work to overturn all remaining strictures. The Servicemembers

Legal Defense Network was created in 1993 and fueled by more than $7 million in foundation grants. It provided counsel to troops who ran afoul of the ban on open homosexual behavior, ran media campaigns against the rule, and organized the first legislative efforts to go beyond it. Similar work was carried out by other nonprofits operating with donations earmarked for this cause. The American Civil Liberties Union, Lambda Legal, the Gay and Lesbian Alliance Against Defamation, the Center for American Progress and others "played a critical role in mobilizing grassroots support, taking on early legal battles, monitoring media debates, and publishing position papers," according to the *Chronicle of Philanthropy*.

The most dogged and focused efforts on this front were carried out by the Center for the Study of Sexual Minorities in the Military, which changed its name to the Palm Center after receiving a $1 million contribution from the Michael Palm Foundation in 2006. The center produced a steady stream of papers criticizing "don't ask, don't tell" and circulated them through academe and the media. Their work was central to the 2011 establishment of a new policy protecting overt homosexuality in the military. Since overturning "don't ask," the Palm Center's main project has been to end strictures on transgender service and sex changes among military personnel.

Grants of more than $12 million were used to undo "don't ask, don't tell," with the Evelyn and Walter Haas Fund and the Wells Fargo, Gill, and Arcus foundations being other lead donors. Three quarters of that money was offered as super-flexible general operating funding. More than 20 donors supported the organizations leading the charge for at least five years in a row, with many of them loyally providing funds every year for over a decade.

Further reading

○ *Chronicle of Philanthropy* reporting, philanthropy.com/article/Philanthropys-Military/128431

○ Analysis by Palm Center director, *How We Won: Progressive Lessons from the Repeal of "Don't Ask, Don't Tell,"* howwewon.com

POLICY

⚘ PhilAphorism

I cannot think of a more personally rewarding and appropriate use of wealth than to give while one is living.... Interventions have greater value and impact today than if they are delayed.

☞ *Charles Feeney*

KOCH PROGRAMS FOR STUDENTS

The Charles Koch Institute was founded in 2011 by the billionaire industrialist to run educational programs that give students and professionals a deeper understanding of markets and politics. Its main work in influencing future generations is done through four programs.

The yearlong Koch Associate Program places young people in full-time jobs at public-policy organizations in the Washington, D.C., area while providing a full day each week of classroom training. The Koch Internship Program is a similar venture that works with college students for just one semester. The Koch Fellows Program is much the same but places students in organizations across the country. And the Institute's Liberty@Work effort offers Web-based professional training based on a similar economics-and-politics curriculum. More than 3,000 alumni of these programs had graduated into permanent careers by the end of 2015, and about 350 additional individuals are trained every year.

Further reading

○ Charles Koch Institute, charleskochinstitute.org/educational-programs

A NEW TOP DOG IN PUBLIC-POLICY FUNDING

Hedge funder Thomas Steyer made lots of money developing new coal mines in Asia. More recently, he decided fossil fuels are evil, and developed a taste for policy fights on this subject. In 2010 Steyer personally launched and funded a $25 million campaign to defeat a voter proposition in California that would have suspended the state's global-warming law (which requires a statewide reduction of greenhouse gases to 1990 levels) until the state unemployment rate fell below 5.5 percent (it was then above 12 percent). The year before, Steyer had given $40 million to Stanford to bankroll a climate and energy center, and the year after he pledged $25 million to Yale for a similar environmental center.

By the time the next election rolled around in 2012, Steyer had funded a California voter proposition of his own. This one would raise about a billion dollars of taxes and steer much of the money into "clean energy" spending. Steyer poured tens of millions of dollars into getting the referendum passed. Next, he started funding and appearing in a series of 90-second ads attacking the Keystone XL pipeline; they were instrumental in stalling that project.

The philanthropist has recently been a strong supporter of the Energy Foundation (see 1991 entry).

In 2013, Steyer stepped out as America's No. 1 public policy and politics donor on the left. He spent $11 million to help elect Terry McAuliffe as governor of Virginia, millions more on the Democrat primaries in Massachusetts, and then invited a couple dozen other top liberal donors to one of his vacation homes to announce his creation of NextGen Climate—his own politics and policy organization focused on global-warming activism. He donated $50 million to the group and asked others for matches so they could seat 2014 candidates favoring global-warming controls. In the end, Steyer poured around $73 million into various 2014 campaign races. For the 2016 election season Steyer reoriented NextGen almost completely away from policy formation and toward political efforts on climate issues.

Steyer has become the largest funder not only of climate causes, but also of the Democratic Party and of the left-wing Democracy Alliance (see 2005 entry). According to the Center for Public Integrity, he gave more than any other political donor in the U.S. in 2014. After the election, his chief strategist told the *New York Times* that "Steyer's spending was a down payment on a multiyear strategy aimed at ensuring that climate change stays at the center of the political debate."

Further reading

○ *Chronicle of Philanthropy* summary, philanthropy.com/article/How-Thomas-Steyer-Uses-Charity/146595

2010

FRACKING GETS DRILLED

Drilling horizontally into shale and then cracking it by pumping in water under high pressure—a process known as "fracking"—has had stunning effects on U.S. oil and gas production, turning the U.S. into the world's leading producer of natural gas and cutting our oil imports sufficiently to crash the world price of oil. The contributions of fracking include more than a million jobs, over $110 billion of GDP, and a reduction in pollution and carbon emissions (due to substitution of gas for coal in electricity production) that has actually pushed U.S. emissions well below our level of the previous ten years, despite population and economic growth.

Even with these dramatic benefits, fracking became a controversial process in recent years, and much of that is due to the effort of a foundation in upstate New York that supports left-wing media, and activist and environmental groups. In 2010 the Park Foundation approached a Cornell University

POLICY

marine ecologist about writing an academic article making the case that shale gas is a dangerous, polluting product. They gave him a $35,000 grant, and when his paper came out a year later scientists from across the ideological spectrum with geology and energy expertise were sharply critical. But a *New York Times* reporter leapt on the article and turned its negative view of natural gas into a cause célèbre, spawning hundreds of spinoff stories.

This was just one of hundreds of interventions in the fracking debate by Park over the last few years. The foundation also offered scores of small grants to activist groups and publications to support anti-fracking articles, conferences, rallies, and legislative campaigns. The *Gasland* films attacking fracking were also funded by Park. By carefully targeting about $3 million per year to a mix of sympathetic academics, ideological publications, and pressure groups, this one medium-sized foundation was able to make a large impression on public policy.

Indeed, this effort was sufficient to get fracking banned in Park's methane-rich home state of New York, and to stimulate similar bans or moratoriums in Maryland, Vermont, a number of U.S. cities and towns, and even locations abroad where the energetic advocacy campaign against shale gas and oil managed to alarm public opinion.

Further reading

○ *Philanthropy* magazine reporting, philanthropyroundtable.org/topic/excellence_in_ philanthropy/gas_heat

2010

EXPOSING TOP STUDENTS TO THE CLASSICS

Retired investor Roger Hertog has made it a centerpiece of his philanthropy to create first-rate intellectual seminars that can inspire an interest in politics among top students who are likely to be involved in setting national policies in the future. His Hertog Foundation describes itself as "an educational philanthropy whose mission is to bring the very best ideas in defense of Western civilization to a new generation of intellectual and political leaders." It operates a half-dozen different seminars toward this end.

The Hertog Political Studies Program brings college students to Washington for six weeks of classes on political theory and practice. The foundation's Economic Policy Studies Program is a two-week immersion in the politics and finances of the welfare state. The War Studies Program is a similar session on military and foreign policy. Various Advanced Institutes tutor students and young professionals in specialized areas like Lincoln's political thought or the lessons of the Iraq war. An American History Scholars program is designed for high-school students.

Each of these programs is taught by prominent scholars hired by the foundation. The Hertog Foundation also supports special seminars at Macaulay College and Columbia University to inspire talented students to become engaged citizens acquainted with the best of classic political thinking. The ultimate effects of this work will be felt as graduates of Hertog classes enter positions of influence in government, academe, and other fields.

Further reading

○ Syllabi and lecture videos for Hertog Political Studies Programs, hertogfoundation. org/resources

2010

$27 MILLION TO PASS OBAMACARE

In the summer of 2008, the three largest unions of government employees and a collection of left-wing organizations including ACORN, MoveOn.org, the Center for American Progress, Alliance for a Just Society, and USAction announced the creation of Health Care for America Now—a political pressure group with a single goal: to pass the Affordable Care Act, popularly known as Obamacare. The group had a $40 million budget, primarily to be used for political ads and organizing. At their launch event that July they unveiled their initial $1.5 million ad purchase. "We began the campaign by attacking the insurance industry as the chief villain in the story," the group summarized in its online history. "This message mobilized the progressive base and moved people in the 'middle'."

It was Atlantic Philanthropies, the foundation created by Duty Free Shoppers Group co-founder Chuck Feeney, that made all of this activity possible. Atlantic launched the Health Care for America Now coalition with a 2007 grant, and put a total of $26.5 million into the cause over a two-year period. This direct intervention in political action was made easier by the fact that Atlantic is headquartered in Bermuda, freeing it from the federal prohibition on lobbying by U.S. foundations.

In the end, the Affordable Care Act passed without a single vote to spare in the U.S. Senate. Absent the investment by Atlantic Philanthropies, noted the *Huffington Post* and other observers, it is unlikely the legislation would have taken effect. And the Atlantic-financed campaign didn't end with passage of the legislation.

"Once the bill became law," explains HCAN's online history, the group "fought back hard against the ACA-attacks in a myriad of ways. Working with unions like AFSCME and SEIU and our field partners, HCAN broadened its

POLICY

'which side are you on' organizing around Obamacare to protecting Medicare and Medicaid and calling for wealthy Americans and big corporations to pay their fair share in taxes." Once it exhausted its funds, HCAN finally closed down as an organization.

Further reading

○ HCAN history, healthcareforamericanow.org/about-us/mission-history

○ Profile of Atlantic Philanthropies then-director Gara LaMarche in Chapter 3, *Agenda Setting: A Wise Giver's Guide to Influencing Public Policy* (The Philanthropy Roundtable, 2015)

PAINTING NORTH CAROLINA REDDER

While working for the governor of North Carolina in the 1980s, Art Pope became frustrated by a lack of organizations able to supply well-developed ideas for conservative political reform. After leaving government, he decided to do something about it. Over the next three decades he used his family foundation to donate more than $60 million (earned through the family's privately owned chain of discount stores) to build a robust network of think tanks and advocacy groups in North Carolina. In the process, he turned North Carolina into a swing state where conservative ideas and policymakers are able to match liberal ideas and politicians.

◈ PhilAphorism

Governments don't really like organizations which are outside their control. There is much talk today in the voluntary sector of a "compact" with the state. This could turn out to be the sort of compact which the oysters had with the Walrus and the Carpenter: it ends up with one party getting eaten by the other.

☞ *Robert Whelan*

First, Pope created the John Locke Foundation in 1990. The Raleigh center has become one of the most influential state-based free-market think tanks in the country. Legislators now routinely look to the group for alternative state budgets and suggestions on changing taxes. In 2007, its work helped voters around the state defeat a series of county-level tax-hike initiatives. In 2010, former Democratic governor Mike Easley was convicted on federal corruption charges, in part due to the investigative work of the *Carolina Journal*, published by JLF.

With an annual budget of about $3.5 million, the think tank now has a variety of donors, but the John William Pope Foundation (named for Art's father) has remained its major underwriter. Art Pope has also funded the Civitas Institute (which promotes grassroots activism), the North Carolina Institute for Constitutional Law (which litigates), and the Pope Center for Higher Education Policy (which monitors colleges and universities in the state). Left-of-center policy groups still outnumber right-of-center groups by two or three to one in North Carolina, but Pope has created a real competition of ideas in the state.

This new public-policy infrastructure gradually helped change the climate for political reform in North Carolina. In the 2010 elections, voters flipped both the state Senate and House from Democrat to Republican control—the first time since 1870 that a Republican majority had existed in both chambers. In the 2012 elections, voters also picked a Republican governor for the first time in 20 years, and elected three new Republicans to Congress, shifting their state's representation in the U.S. House from 7-6 D to 9-4 R.

Art Pope took a leave from the foundation to become the new governor's budget director, and the state government enacted a burst of dramatic reforms over the next two years—flattening and cutting taxes, reducing the growth rate of the state budget, and reforming education. In the 2014 elections, this new political alignment was largely ratified by North Carolina voters, and the incumbent Democrat U.S. senator was defeated by a Republican.

Further reading

○ *Washington Post* 2014 article, washingtonpost.com/politics/in-nc-conservative-donor-art-pope-sits-at-heart-of-government-he-helped-transform/2014/07/19/eece18ec-0d22-11e4-b8e5-d0de80767fc2_story.html

○ Profile of Art Pope in Chapter 9, *Agenda Setting: A Wise Giver's Guide to Influencing Public Policy* (The Philanthropy Roundtable, 2015)

2009

REFOCUSING GOVERNANCE IN WISCONSIN

Back in 1987 the Milwaukee-based Lynde and Harry Bradley Foundation

POLICY

provided a $2.8 million startup grant to launch the Wisconsin Policy Research Institute, a think tank focused on the economic and social health of its home state. The institute published a steady stream of research reports on education problems, the business environment, state pension imbalances, and other concerns.

Then in 2009 and 2010, WPRI rang alarms over runaway government-employee costs and a state budget deficit heading past $3.6 billion. At that time, Democrats controlled both houses of the state legislature as well as the governorship. The 2010 election, though, swept in a Republican governor and flipped control of both the Assembly and state Senate.

Anticipating this power shift, the Bradley Foundation had given the Wisconsin Policy Research Institute a million-dollar grant in 2009 (on top of its normal $400,000 in annual support) to produce a special policy document entitled *Refocus Wisconsin*. "We saw how much the Reagan administration relied on the Heritage Foundation and how much Mayor Rudy Giuliani relied on the Manhattan Institute in New York City," said Bradley president Michael Grebe. "We wanted to support a project that provided a similar level of policy assistance to our own governor and lawmakers." The 154-page publication offered information and policy recommendations on budgeting, taxes, public pensions, and education. The Wisconsin Institute for Law and Liberty and the MacIver Institute, also Bradley grant recipients, offered additional ideas for improving governance in their home state.

When Governor Scott Walker and the new legislative class took office in 2011, they enacted a Budget Repair Bill that dramatically reformed state government—requiring public employees to contribute to their pensions for the first time, trimming the power of public-employee unions (whose membership dropped by half after state and local employees including public-school teachers were allowed to opt out), establishing controls on medical costs, and so forth. After protests, work refusals, legislators going fugitive, and a recall vote on the governor (which he won with a larger percentage of the vote than in his initial election), the reforms stuck, and immediately became an influence on other states.

In his capacity as a private citizen, not a foundation CEO, Grebe chaired Governor Walker's re-election campaign in 2014. Walker was returned to office, and the GOP majorities in both state houses were enlarged.

Further reading

o "Refocus Wisconsin" report, wpri.org/WPRI-Files/Special-Reports/Reports-Documents/WPRI_Refocus_Digest_FNL_090710.pdf

PAINTING COLORADO BLUER

In 2004, Colorado was a solidly Republican state: the governor, both U.S. Senators, and five of seven House members belonged to the GOP, and President George W. Bush won the state's nine electoral votes. By the end of the 2008 elections, everything had reversed: the governor, both U.S. Senators, and five of seven House members were Democrats, and Barack Obama carried the state. National political trends explained some of this transformation. The rest was the work of four liberal philanthropists who set out to remake Colorado through a mix of public-policy giving and campaign donations—software entrepreneur Tim Gill, venture capitalist Rutt Bridges, Internet businessman Jared Polis, and heiress Pat Stryker.

In 1999, Bridges founded the Bighorn Center for Public Policy, a think tank that swiftly altered state campaign-finance rules. The liberal Bell Policy Center was established immediately after. Then came a Colorado version of the national MoveOn.org pressure group, called ProgressNowAction.org. Colorado Media Matters was created in 2006 to influence state reporters and editorial writers. A litigation group, Colorado Ethics Watch, was set up the same year, along with an online newspaper called the Colorado Independent and several blogs like ColoradoPols.com and SquareState.net, all oriented to promoting progressive policies and investigating and criticizing opponents. A new academy to train liberal activists, the Center for Progressive Leadership Colorado, was also funded.

The Denver Post characterized the mechanics of the nonprofits set up by the "Four Millionaires" and their allies this way:

> A liberal group with a nonpartisan name like Colorado First puts out a list of polluters and demands official action. A Republican running for Colorado office is on the list. Paid liberal bloggers chatter. An online liberal publication with a newspaper-like name writes an article about the candidate and his company polluting Colorado's streams. A liberal advocacy group puts out a news release, citing the group and the pollution, which sound reputable to an ordinary voter. They mass e-mail the release and attach a catchy phrase to it like "Dirty Doug." At some point, the mainstream media checks out the allegations.

In the 2004, 2006, and 2008 elections, the Four Millionaires spent more than $20 million trying to tip Colorado from Republican to Democrat via a mix of political attack ads during election season and long-term funding for what political analyst Fred Barnes described as "a vast infrastructure of liberal organizations that produces an anti-Republican, anti-conservative echo chamber in politics and the media." They were wildly successful: After 2008, Democrats controlled not only all of the national offices described in the first paragraph above, but also the governor's mansion and both chambers of the state legislature. By 2012, according to the *Denver Post*, liberal Super PAC contributions exceeded conservative ones at a rate of 150:1.

Observing this triumph—which became known as the Colorado Model—other donors launched or intensified similar efforts in other "purple" swing states. The Coors Foundation also worked to help Colorado conservatives learn from the progressives' success, and in the deep-red 2014 election, Republicans finally reclaimed one of the two U.S. Senate seats in Colorado. But the other Senate seat and three of the seven House seats remained with Democrats. The incumbent Democrat governor won a tight re-election. Republicans narrowly took control of the state Senate, and they pared down Democrat control of the state Assembly from 37-28 to 34-31. Colorado was purple again. But the Gill/Bridges/Polis/Stryker nonprofit infrastructure remains in place.

Further reading

○ Rob Witwer and Adam Schrager, *The Blueprint: How Democrats Won Colorado* (Speaker's Corner, 2010)

○ *Denver Post* analysis, denverpost.com/ci_20148556/spending-by-super-pacs-colorado-is-dominion-democrats

○ Fred Barnes analysis, weeklystandard.com/Content/Public/Articles/000/000/015/316nfdzw.asp

2008

ADVOCATING FOR GENERATIONAL FAIRNESS IN FISCAL POLICY

Pete Peterson became a billionaire as co-founder of the Blackstone investment firm, but he was the son of poor Greek immigrants and never lost his distaste for profligacy and waste. He watched horrified as the federal budget went from a slight surplus in 1960 to a deficit of 2.6 percent of GDP at the end of the 1970s, and 4.1 percent of GDP (that's $680 billion) as of 2013. Since 2008 Peterson has put more than a billion dollars of his own money into educating policymakers and the public on the dangers of that kind of fiscal imbalance. He warns that "on our current course, our children will not do as well as we have. For years, I have been saying that the American government, and America itself, has to change its spending and borrowing policies."

The Peterson Foundation sponsors conferences, reports, debates, films, and television ads on the dangers of massive federal debt. In 2010 it launched a series of annual fiscal summits for national political leaders. The latest versions included Bill Clinton, Michael Bloomberg, Chris Christie, Nancy Pelosi, Alan Greenspan, and others. In 2011, and then again in 2012 and 2015, the foundation funded several think tanks, positioned on both the left and the right, to create plans that would eliminate federal deficits. These were then promoted to lawmakers.

This is somewhat unusual territory for philanthropy, but recently one other donor has become active on the same topic. Hedge-fund founder Stanley Druckenmiller began speaking actively to college students in 2013, warning that out-of-control entitlement spending threatened to degrade the standard of living of their generation.

Further reading

○ *Philanthropy* magazine reporting, philanthropyroundtable.org/topic/economic_ opportunity/economia

2008

CAUSE-ORIENTED JOURNALISM

Take one scoop of donors looking for new ways to affect public opinion and government policy, mix with three scoops of mainstream journalism bleeding red ink in the face of new Internet-based competition, and you get a layer-cake of donor-funded reporting operations. The granddaddy of these creations is ProPublica, founded by hyperactive liberal donors Herb and Marion Sandler to be a twenty-first-century muckraker, with a special focus on topics like gun control, civil rights, health care, fracking, campaign-finance limits, labor laws, the climate change, Guantanamo, and other policy hot buttons. With more than $35 million of checks written by the Sandlers, ProPublica quickly hired a deep stable of reporters and editors and started churning out heavily researched exposés. The organization posts articles on its own website and lets newspapers run them for free. The operation quickly became a favorite of the journalistic establishment, and was awarded the first Pulitzer Prize for investigative reporting given to an online publication. It now receives support from large foundations like Ford, MacArthur, Annie E. Casey, and Hewlett.

Many local variants of ProPublica, and a few national ones, followed with their own angel funders. These range from the Texas Tribune, funded by Democratic Party donors in that state, to the MinnPost, launched by four

POLICY

public-minded families in Minneapolis, to the Honolulu Civil Beat financed by eBay founder Pierre Omidyar. Watchdog.org, a project of the Franklin Center, was established as a miniature version of ProPublica digging from the right in 29 states as of 2015, and the American Media Institute is struggling to launch itself as another investigative reporting operation positioned on the right side of the political spectrum.

All of these are digital-only publications to contain costs, and they all depend on philanthropic support—primarily annual operating grants, supplemented by small donations from readers. All have demonstrated some ability to influence local or national debates on policy and politics.

Further reading

○ *Philanthropy* magazine reporting, philanthropyroundtable.org/topic/excellence_in_
philanthropy/investigative_philanthropy

2007

DESIGNED TO WIN CLIMATE-POLICY FIGHTS

"Left unattended, human-induced climate change could overshadow all our other efforts to cure diseases, reduce poverty, prevent warfare and preserve biodiversity. Global, collective action is paramount.... How can philanthropists turn the tide against global warming?"

Those were some of the opening sentences of a 2007 report that the Hewlett, Packard, Doris Duke, Energy, Oak, and Joyce foundations commissioned in hopes of finding ways to *"win* in the battle against climate change." These donors had long been activists on the global-warming issue, and the study they paid for, called *Design to Win*, laid out a strategy for blocking coal-fired power plants and other producers of carbon dioxide in the short term, then creating new policies in the longer term to drastically reduce energy use and greenhouse gas emissions. The report called on climate-concerned philanthropists to increase their giving in this area from the existing $177 million annually to $660 million annually.

The very next year, an activist organization called ClimateWorks emerged out of this. The Hewlett Foundation pledged $100 million per year for five years to get it launched, and the Packard Foundation kicked in $40 million to $60 million per year. The Packard and Hewlett foundations are the two largest philanthropic funders of global-warming activism in the world, having between them granted more than a billion dollars over the most recent decade just to their two favorite recipients—ClimateWorks and the Energy Foundation.

These two megadonors were joined in setting up ClimateWorks by the McKnight, Ford, Rockefeller, Kresge, Moore, and other foundations, and the KR, MacArthur, and Oak foundations are now big backers. ClimateWorks channels their donated money to affiliated organizations, and presses for strong new government policies and environmental controls. IRS filings show that ClimateWorks collected $170 million from donors in 2012. The group's official goal is to slash emissions of carbon dioxide and other greenhouse gases by 50 percent by the year 2030.

Further reading

○ *Design to Win* report on climate-change philanthropy, climateworks.org/imo/media/doc/ design_to_win_final_8_31_07.pdf

2007

ED IN '08

A year and a half before the Presidential election, the foundations of Bill Gates and Eli Broad—which together had already given more than $2 billion to various education-reform causes—announced a $60 million effort to make education a central issue in the political debate. Under the tagline "ED in '08," their campaign launched elaborate communications efforts, celebrity endorsements, fancy campaign paraphernalia, petitions, swing-state advertising, other media efforts, and meetings with candidates and staff.

Despite being what the *New York Times* described as "one of the most expensive single-issue initiatives ever in a Presidential race," this effort produced no significant increase in the political salience of educational issues. Both parties adopted their usual platform planks on schools, and over the course of the Presidential debates 20 education-related questions were posed to the candidates—not significantly different from previous election cycles. By the time they had spent $25 million, the Gates and Broad foundations announced that no further money would be put into the initiative.

Reflecting on the aborted project shortly after the election, Bill Gates observed that "most of what we were causing people to do was mouth platitudes." Fuzzy, generalized efforts to influence policy while dancing around controversial details may not be worth the effort, many observers and donors concluded.

Further reading

○ *New York Times* story on campaign's launch, nytimes.com/2007/04/25/ education/25schools.html?_r=0

○ Bill Gates reflects on ED in '08 in *Education Week*, blogs.edweek.org/edweek/ campaign-k-12//11/bill_gates_on_ed_in_08_mouthin.html

POLICY

2006

NUDGING STATES LEFT

A year after a group of liberal donors set up the Democracy Alliance, the same forces joined together to establish the Committee on States in 2006. Just as the Democracy Alliance (see 2005 entry) is a conduit for steering donor money to approved left-wing national political organizations, the Committee on States is a conduit for steering money to left-wing political organizations working on the state level. In every state where it operates, the group recruits major donors and recommends places to send money. The funds pay for political data and analysis, grassroots organizing, opposition research, fundraising, and messaging. The goal is to elect officeholders who will enact liberal policies and be in a position to influence the redrawing of election districts in the states after the 2020 census.

The committee is a nonprofit 501(c)(4) advocacy organization. Under IRS rules, such groups can advocate for public policies without limitation, can urge particular votes on issues, and can depict candidates in positive or negative ways, but must not make active electioneering their primary purpose. Donations to a (c)(4) are not tax-deductible, but the Committee on States has set up a parallel 501(c)(3) whose more research-related work does allow supporters to deduct their giving.

During the 2014 election cycle the committee coordinated about $50 million of donations made in 20 different states—including $9 million of

ᴥ PhilAphorism

It is calculated that a certain amount of revenue is lost to the government because a private college is tax exempt. The logic is that all of society's wealth really belongs to the government and that the government should therefore be able to determine how wealth exempted from taxation should be used. This implication is incipiently totalitarian.

☞ *Peter Berger and Richard Neuhaus*

spending in Wisconsin, $7 million each in North Carolina and Minnesota, and $6 million each in Colorado and Florida. The group hopes to create donor networks in seven more states for the next election. The intent is to establish durable political machines in each place, and the Committee on States aims to increase spending to $100 million per year by 2020.

Liberal philanthropists are funding not only this electoral organizing but also efforts to link liberal officeholders in affinity groups, and supply them with ideas and legislative ammunition. The Public Leadership Institute has established a Progressive Leaders Network that connects 13,000 left-leaning city, county, and state officials. A new group called the State Innovation Exchange was kicked off in 2014 by the donors of the Democracy Alliance. That organization plans to raise $10 million a year in donations "to boost progressive state lawmakers and their causes—partly by drafting model legislation…while also using bare-knuckle tactics like opposition research and video tracking to derail Republicans and their initiatives," according to *Politico.*

Further reading

○ *Mother Jones* reporting, motherjones.com/politics/2014/11/committee-on-states-democracy-alliance-redistricting-2020

○ Public Leadership Institute scorecards of legislative results, publicleadershipinstitute.org/tracking

○ *Politico* reporting, politico.com/story/2014/11/democrats-create-an-alec-killer-112733.html

2006

INTELLIGENCE SQUARED DEBATES

Robert Rosenkranz made a fortune in insurance and investing, and when he began to give money away his first interest was in efforts to improve public policy and governance. He supported the Federalist Society and Manhattan Institute. He funded Rosenkranz Hall to house Yale University's political science department and international relations program.

But Rosenkranz mourned the disappearance of respectful, meaty, intelligent public debate, seemingly squeezed out by the rise of personal, partisan, and emotional political wrangling on Internet and media outlets. Then during a trip to London in 2005 he took in a high-quality Oxford-style debate organized by a new group called Intelligence Squared. He purchased the rights for an American version of Intelligence Squared, hired a former *Nightline* producer to orchestrate, and debuted the first debates before live New York City audiences in 2006. Rosenkranz immersed himself in the process—choosing many of the topics, suggesting sparring partners on opposite sides of

POLICY

important public questions, and delivering opening remarks that framed the issues being argued over.

The Intelligence Squared U.S. debates quickly became popular, both as live events and as media and Internet phenomena—most of them are aired over NPR, streamed and posted as videos on the Web, and offered as podcasts. Not only the audience but also website visitors are given a chance to vote their own position on the debate topic, both before it takes place and right after. The statistical change in opinion as a result of the back-and-forth on stage is used to judge who won the argument.

As of 2015 there had been about 120 jousts, on hot topics in public policy like "Too many kids go to college," "A booming China spells trouble for America," "Global warming is not a crisis," and "FDA caution is hazardous to our health." Many constructive and enjoyable discussions, along with several awards for best public-affairs programming, have resulted from the mix of top-flight thinkers and lively controversialists arguing within a fair and scrupulously structured discussion format. Rosenkranz remains a central funder of the effort, but other philanthropists like Paul Singer and Gerry Ohrstrom, plus foundations like Rupe, Sackler, and Bradley, have also provided grants to keep the smart arguments flowing.

Further reading

∘ Rosenkranz profiled in *Philanthropy* magazine, philanthropyroundtable.org/topic/excellence_in_philanthropy/resolved

∘ Origins of Intelligence Squared, philanthropyroundtable.org/topic/excellence_in_philanthropy/intelligence_squared

2006

STRYKER ROILS MICHIGAN POLITICS

Jon Stryker, the billionaire heir to the Stryker medical-instruments fortune, set up the Arcus Foundation in 2000. It almost immediately became a national force for lawmaking and electioneering on behalf of gay rights, thanks to $78 million of targeted donations to gay groups in just its first ten years.

Stryker also used his giving to change the political calculus in his home state of Michigan. At the same time he and his sister, Pat, were using their inherited billions to help flip Colorado into the political blue column (see 2008 entry), he was carrying out a similar game plan on the Great Lakes. He employed philanthropic donations plus $5 million of PAC spending to help flip the Michigan State House from Republican to Democrat control, and to help Jennifer Granholm defeat Dick DeVos in the governor's race.

Further reading

○ *Inside Philanthropy* scorecard, insidephilanthropy.com/home/2014/10/7/the-marriage-equality-hall-of-fame-8-funders-who-helped-make.html

2005

DEMOCRACY ALLIANCE

Rob Stein had worked for the Democratic National Committee, the Clinton-Gore campaign and administration, and a private-equity firm. Then he set out on a new task: to convince wealthy liberal donors to pay for political infrastructure that would beat conservatives in policy and electoral contests. He put together a PowerPoint cautionary, traveled the country, and in 2005 kicked off a new group: the Democracy Alliance.

The philanthropic and political giving club invites to its closed-door meetings individuals who have donated at least $200,000 to one of its favored activist organizations. It has about 100 members, who have included major donors like George Soros, Tim Gill, Chris Hughes, Patricia Stryker, and Tom Steyer, plus the leaders of unions that command large political funds like NEA, AFT, and SEIU. The alliance doesn't collect money itself but rather encourages and coordinates donations to political groups it selects and endorses—21 "core" groups plus 180 other organizations designated to fill a role on its "Progressive Infrastructure Map." These include operations like the Center for American Progress, Media Matters, the Center on Budget and Policy Priorities, and a variety of electioneering groups (America Votes, Catalist, Emily's List, Organizing for Action, etc.).

Beneficiaries of Democracy Alliance funding include a wide mix of groups: There are 501(c)(3) nonprofits (for which donations are tax-deductible and public) that must mostly steer clear of lobbying and politics. There are also 501(c)(4) social-welfare groups who can lobby and advocate for public policies, and get involved in modest amounts of electioneering (donations to them are not deductible, but are anonymous). And there are 527 Political Action Committees and SuperPACs, both of which give directly to political candidates (with donations being publicly disclosed and non-tax-deductible).

Donations earmarked through the Democracy Alliance total about $70 million per year. Including funds raised from other sources, just the 21 core groups in the Democracy Alliance portfolio set in motion $374 million of spending to boost liberal policy causes and political candidates in the 2014 midterm election, according to *Politico*. In private meetings held after the 2014 conservative wave, the alliance formulated a giving plan with four

POLICY

goals: Increase funding for liberal groups. Motivate progressives. Persuade independents. Divide the right and reduce its funding.

Further reading

○ *New York Times* reporting, nytimes.com/2014/11/14/us/politics/shaking-off-midterm-drubbing-liberal-donors-look-6-years-ahead.html?_r=0

SKOLL PIONEERS "FILMANTHROPY"

Movies with a political message are hardly a new phenomenon, but never before has a donor made social change via film the main focus of his philanthropic investing. In 2004, eBay co-founder Jeffrey Skoll founded Participant Media, into which he poured "hundreds of millions of dollars...with much more to follow," understanding that "everything I put into Participant, I don't expect to get back." The company began to produce films with a liberal-activist tilt, paired with accompanying media campaigns aimed at translating public sentiment stirred up by the films into legislation or other political action.

By 2015 Skoll's venture had produced more than 65 films, convinced stars like Matt Damon, Gwyneth Paltrow, Tom Hanks, Julia Roberts, Benedict Cumberbatch, and George Clooney to take roles for far less than their normal fees, and charmed Hollywood into more than 30 Oscar nominations. The movies included titles like *An Inconvenient Truth* (which won Al Gore his Nobel Peace Prize for climate-change alarmism), *Citizen Four* (extolling Edward Snowden's national security leak), *Food, Inc.* (attacking modern farming), *Good Night, and Good Luck* (skewering McCarthyism), *Syriana* (big oil threatens the world), *Charlie Wilson's War* (right-wing Americans planted the seeds of al-Qaeda), *The Help* (on mistreatment of African-American domestic workers), and many others. Corporate abuses, violence against women, gay rights, and environmental and union causes are other favorite topics of the studio. One of the studio's early films, *Waiting for Superman*, drew acclaim from school reformers on all parts of the political spectrum.

Each Participant movie is launched with a companion "social action campaign" (coordinated by a separate division) that prompts consumers to take some political or economic action, promotes the film for use in school, holds special screenings for legislators and journalists, and so forth. Participant has even teamed up with the Gates and Knight foundations to fund work at University of Southern California's Annenberg School for Communication and Journalism that aims to create reliable measures of whether, and how, entertainment can spur citizens to become social activists.

Though none have made a commitment to "filmanthropy" on the scale of Jeff Skoll, other philanthropists have funded moviemaking in an attempt to influence cultural and political trends. These have included AOL founder Ted Leonsis, backer of a website for short documentaries known as SnagFilms, and businessman Philip Anschutz, who financed major movies like the *Narnia* series, and others based on classic children's books, in order to encourage popular entertainment that is more friendly to families raising youngsters.

Further reading

○ *Philanthropy* magazine feature article, philanthropyroundtable.org/topic/excellence_in_ philanthropy/changing_the_world_through_storytelling

2003

REMAKING THE THINK TANK INTO A POLITICAL WAR ROOM

As they prepared for the 2004 presidential election and beyond, a small group of liberal donors led by bankers Herb and Marion Sandler concluded that the Left needed a new kind of think tank that would combine public-policy research with political activism. Joined by real-estate magnate Steve Bing, insurance mogul Peter Lewis, and investor George Soros, they bankrolled the Center for American Progress, to be directed by Clinton-administration operative John Podesta. They were motivated by a sense among many liberals that Republicans benefited from an infrastructure of conservative think tanks, and that Democrats enjoyed nothing similar. The Brookings Institution, numerous academic centers at universities, and many liberal advocacy organizations existed, but these funders did not consider them as effective as groups like the Heritage Foundation, Cato Institute, and American Enterprise Institute. A series of reports from the left-wing National Committee for Responsive Philanthropy on how the right-leaning think tanks had been built by donors was also influential in sparking wealthy liberals to act.

Podesta's idea was to create a nonprofit organization that would have a traditional think-tank arm (a research group eligible for tax-deductible donations), as well as a legislative advocacy arm (not eligible for tax-deductible donations). This combination of 501(c)(3) and 501(c)(4) was an innovation for large-scale research institutions. "With the Center for American Progress, Podesta was trying to create something new," wrote journalist Byron York, "a think tank that doubled as a campaign war room." Podesta himself described CAP as "a think tank on steroids."

The donors did not achieve their immediate objective of electing a Democrat to the Presidency in 2004, but CAP became an aggressive part

POLICY

of the left-wing political machine. Its "communications" department became its largest office, and dispatching the organization's employees for "rapid response" media attacks on conservative arguments or proponents became the central function of the group. Its influence on the political discourse aided Democratic triumphs in the 2006 congressional elections, and Barack Obama's victories in 2008 and 2012.

CAP attempts to hide its financial information as much as possible. By 2014, though, the group's budget was more than $45 million. Copying Podesta's model, the Heritage Foundation launched its own 501(c)(4) group seven years after the creation of CAP.

Further reading

○ Byron York, *The Vast Left Wing Conspiracy*, (Crown Forum, 2005)

○ *New York Times* analysis, nytimes.com//11/07/us/politics/07podesta.html

○ "Devaluing the Think Tank," *National Affairs*, nationalaffairs.com/publications/detail/devaluing-the-think-tank

OPEN SOCIETY OPENS DOOR TO GAY MARRIAGE

Among many other public-policy causes, the Open Society Foundations funded by financial speculator George Soros have been leading donors to gay rights. Their Lesbian, Gay, Bisexual, Transgender, and Intersex program gives $5-10 million per year to upwards of 70 advocacy groups. Their most consequential grants in this area may have come between the years of 2000 and 2005, when they invested millions in political and legal efforts to promote gay marriage. They were among the first significant funders of two of the groups that led this campaign: Freedom to Marry, and the Civil Marriage Collaborative. In 2004, Massachusetts became the first state to establish gay marriage, and from then on activist funders like the Gill and Overbrook foundations and the Evelyn and Walter Haas Fund piled onto the cause. Open Society, however, was a pioneer.

Further reading

○ *Inside Philanthropy* scorecard, insidephilanthropy.com/home/2014/10/7/the-marriage-equality-hall-of-fame-8-funders-who-helped-make.html

A DONOR-ADVISED FUND FOR
CONSERVATIVE POLICY REFORM

Twenty-three years after the Tides Foundation invented the funding collective for public-policy causes (see 1976 entry), liberty-minded donors created a counterpart organization. Called DonorsTrust, it helps philanthropists create donor-advised funds that encourage "limited government, personal responsibility, and free enterprise." The entity was founded in 1999, just as donor-advised funds were taking off as funding mechanisms for all sorts of charitable purposes.

Since opening its doors in northern Virginia, DonorsTrust has channeled $850 million toward causes favored by its donors. Philanthropists attracted to DonorsTrust run the full spectrum of the Right, from libertarians to conservative traditionalists. The beneficiaries of their grants range widely— economic-research organizations, religious groups, hawkish foreign-policy advocates, outfits working to reduce imprisonment rates, you name it. Grants also go to hospitals, schools, camps, and other causes not related to public policy.

Like the Tides Foundation, notes co-founder Kim Dennis, DonorsTrust was inspired by the creativity of its donors to eventually expand beyond just administering donor-advised funds. The group can now also help incubate new charities and projects. And as with Tides, part of the power of DonorsTrust is that it helps philanthropists magnify the effect of their donations by bundling them together with funds from other likeminded contributors.

To make sure that donations go to the purposes philanthropists actually intend (rather than causes favored by administrators acting after the donor is out of the picture—a problem at many foundations), DonorsTrust recommends that accounts should "sunset" (be fully spent) while givers are still around to help set priorities. As a "fail-safe" to preserve donor intent, the organization allows no perpetual trusts. "Only the original donor can name successor advisers, and accounts should be closed 20 years after a donor's death," explained then-president Whitney Ball.

Further reading

○ About DonorsTrust, donorstrust.org/AboutUs/MissionPrinciples.aspx
○ *National Review* essay on DonorsTrust and Tides Foundation, nationalreview.com/article/388705/dark-money-bill-zeiser

POLICY

❧ PhilAphorism

No person was ever honored for what he received. Honor has been the reward for what he gave.

☞ *Calvin Coolidge*

MOVING ON TO INTERNET POLITICS

Unhappy at the prospect of Bill Clinton's impeachment, software entrepreneurs Joan Blades and Wes Boyd set up an online petition that soon grew into a major force for mobilizing liberal donors and voters via the Internet. The MoveOn.org website became a hub for communication and fundraising for left-wing causes, including environmental controls, liberal social issues, and opposition to the war on terror. The group has used a 501(c)(4) advocacy arm, a Political Action Committee, a 527 political fund, hundreds of Internet petitions, and other mechanisms to influence policies and politics with its donations. The group's growth was accelerated by multimillion-dollar gifts during the 2004 election cycle from Linda Pritzker, George Soros, Peter Lewis, and other large patrons. It also accumulated many small donors and volunteer activists and claimed 8 million participants as of 2015. In its first decade-and-a-half of existence, MoveOn raised and spent close to $100 million to promote favored policies.

Further reading

○ MoveOn website, front.moveon.org/about/#.VjuAD7TmZXA

NUDGING CONGRESS BY
FUNDING SCHOOL CHOICE IN D.C.

Investor Theodore Forstmann and Walmart heir John Walton were disappointed by waffling in Congress in the mid-1990s over a school-choice pilot program. There were proposals, enthusiastically backed by local residents, to help Washington, D.C., families trapped in miserable public schools place their children in private or parochial alternatives, but the plans were going nowhere. The Congressional indecision "was a joke," Forstmann concluded. "So we said, 'Okay, we'll do it. Let's get this program going and see if it works.'"

Forstmann and Walton joined forces in 1997 to donate $6 million to the Washington Scholarship Fund. The fund was a roaring success, with low-income families in the nation's capital lining up several deep for every available scholarship. (This inspired Walton and Forstmann to collaborate in 1998 on a national version of their project: the Children's Scholarship Fund, which they launched with contributions of $50 million each. For more information on this and other private philanthropy advancing school choice, charter schooling, and other innovations in school reform, see the companion list of achievements in Education giving.)

Because all of this happened right in Congress's backyard, the philanthropic effort influenced politics and national opinion. In 2004, legislation finally passed creating the D.C. Opportunity Scholarship Program, the first federally funded school voucher program in the U.S. As of 2015 it provides scholarships of $8,000-$12,000 to low-income families so they can send their children to private or religious schools of their choice, benefiting more than 5,000 children.

Further reading

○ Reporting in *Philanthropy* magazine, philanthropyroundtable.org/topic/excellence_in_
philanthropy/education_reform_goes_private

○ 2012 *New York Times* reporting upon renewal of federal program, thecaucus.blogs.nytimes.
com/2012/06/18/much-debated-scholarship-program-for-d-c-students-is-renewed

A NEW WAY
TO FIGHT CRIME

In 1982, social scientists George Kelling and James Q. Wilson published an article arguing that speedy public reaction to petty disorders like a broken window could head off more serious crimes—which often spike when perpetrators get the sense that no one is paying attention. With support from the Olin Foundation and other donors, this argument was developed further at the Manhattan Institute (where Kelling became a senior fellow), and then empirical studies showed the theory to be accurate.

One of those listening was Rudolph Giuliani. When he became New York City mayor in 1994 he and police commissioner William Bratton rolled out a radically different policing style, cracking down on small crimes like subway fare jumping and aggressive panhandling, pushing officers out onto streets, and using detailed crime data to allocate police resources and hold precinct commanders accountable. Within five years, major crimes in New York were cut in half (homicides dropped by two thirds), and those declines continued for years thereafter. The new policing techniques were copied in many other cities, and the safety and savor of urban life in America was dramatically changed for the better.

Further reading

○ Manhattan Institute work on "broken windows" policing, manhattan-institute.org/html/
critical_acclaim-fixing_broken.htm

POLICY

1994

SOROS DECLARES WAR ON THE WAR ON DRUGS

When Arizona and California became the first states to approve the "medical" use of marijuana in 1996, it was currency speculator George Soros who, as the *New York Times* put it, "almost singlehandedly" made these victories possible. He made million-dollar donations on behalf of ballot referenda and other organizing efforts.

With the door cracked open by "medical marijuana," Soros continued to contribute several million dollars every year to promote wider drug legalizations. He backed organizations like the 501(c)(3) nonprofit Drug Policy Alliance and its political-campaign arm, Drug Policy Action. These organizations first expanded legalization of medical marijuana to 20 states, then pushed through open-ended sanctionings of recreational use of marijuana products—first in Colorado and Washington state, followed by Alaska, Oregon, and D.C.

From 1994 to 2014, George Soros poured at least $80 million into efforts to undo drug prohibitions, prompting Joseph Califano of Columbia University's National Center on Addiction and Substance Abuse to label him the "Daddy Warbucks of drug legalization." Nearly matching Soros in funding the relaxation of drug laws was Peter Lewis, former chairman of Progressive Insurance and an active pot smoker himself. In the decades before his death in 2013, Lewis donated up to $60 million for the cause of legalization. Between them, Soros and Lewis provided more than two thirds of the funding for the groups that drove marijuana legalization in states like Colorado and Washington.

Further reading

○ Reporting in *Philanthropy* magazine, philanthropyroundtable.org/topic/excellence_in_ philanthropy/drug_donors

○ 1996 *New York Times* report, nytimes.com/1996/12/17/us/with-big-money-and-brash-ideas-a-billionaire-redefines-charity.html

ᴧᴦ PhilAphorism

The political maturity of a country is measured by what citizens willingly do for themselves and one another.

☞ *Frank Prochaska*

TUG-OF-WAR OVER CAMPAIGN FINANCE

In the decade between 1994 and 2004, philanthropists proclaiming the importance of "taking the money out of politics" spent more than $140 million on politics. Eight liberal foundations supplied 88 percent of this funding that sought to restrict paid speech in political campaigns, with the Pew Charitable Trusts alone spending more than $40 million. Grants went to organizations such as the Center for Responsive Politics, the Center for Public Integrity, Democracy 21, and the League of Women Voters Education Fund. Large grants also went to liberal media organizations like NPR and the *American Prospect* to pay for stories on campaign-finance reform.

"The idea was to create an impression that a mass movement was afoot—that everywhere [members of Congress] looked, in academic institutions, in the business community, in religious groups, in ethnic groups, everywhere, people were talking about reform," explained former Pew program officer Sean Treglia at an academic conference after campaign-finance reform had already passed Congress. He added that he "always encouraged the grantees never to mention Pew" because the disclosure would clash with an image of grassroots activism.

Whatever the motives and tactics, the results were clear: In 2002, the so-called McCain-Feingold campaign reform act, a sweeping measure that regulated both dollars and words in political campaigns, was passed into law. Almost immediately, however, this legislative victory turned into a legal rout. Judges repeatedly trimmed the law's limits on what campaigns, corporations, and labor unions could do and say. The biggest blow came in 2010, with the *Citizens United* ruling in which the U.S. Supreme Court found that the First Amendment to the Constitution prohibits government from restricting independent political expenditures by nonprofits, corporations, labor unions, and other associations.

The Pew Charitable Trusts halted its philanthropy in this area in 2008, and the philanthropic enthusiasts for throttling campaign spending gradually recognized that they had reached an impasse.

Further reading

○ *New York Post* reporting on Treglia presentation, rhsager.com/blog/index.php/buying-reform

TIM GILL PUTS BIG MONEY INTO GAY RIGHTS

In 1994, Tim Gill, founder of the software company Quark, set up his Gill Foundation with a fierce focus on changing public policies and officeholders to advance gay rights. A decade later he established a political-action arm focused directly on influencing elections, and formulated a specific plan to legalize gay marriage within ten years. Gill subsequently devoted more than $300 million of personal and foundation gifts to these causes, to great effect.

Gill's gay-marriage goals were largely achieved within his ten-year time frame. And his donations also helped swell AIDS funding, create new hate-crime categories, defeat a Constitutional amendment to define marriage in traditional ways, repeal the military's prohibitions on overt homosexuality, undo religious-freedom protections in federal and state laws, and promote the Employment Non-Discrimination Act legislation making sexual orientation and gender identity protected categories in labor law. "Normalizing LGBT people in the eyes of the public" has been at the heart of his effort.

Gill made a special push to turn his home state of Colorado into a model. Working with three wealthy colleagues, he set out to establish a cautionary for policymakers in other places by defeating political candidates viewed as hostile to gay causes. The heavily funded effort succeeded at flipping Colorado politics for a period of years (see 2008 entry), a success that public-policy donors in other states subsequently worked to copy.

In 2014 it was reported that Gill will spend at least $25 million over the next few years to remake policies and attitudes in Southern and Western states into forms more friendly to gay rights. This funding will help nonprofit groups like the Human Rights Campaign and the ACLU bring in new staff for major initiatives to shift law and culture in culturally conservative states.

Further reading

○ *New York Times* article, nytimes.com/2014/04/28/us/politics/gay-rights-push-shifts-its-focus-south-and-west.html?smid=tw-share&_r=0

DICK WEEKLEY TRIMS LAWSUITS IN TEXAS

Houston real-estate developer Dick Weekley worried that runaway litigation costs in trial-lawyer-friendly Texas were imperiling the state's business environment. So in 1994 he and several allies founded a nonprofit called

Texans for Lawsuit Reform. The group's mission statement called lawsuit abuse "the No. 1 threat to Texas's economic future."

At first, Weekley contributed his time to the project. Before long, he was contributing his money and raising additional funds from other Texans. Within two years, TLR had convinced the state legislature to put some limits on punitive-damage awards. As the organization pushed for more changes and helped finance the campaigns of like-minded political candidates, it attracted a mass following. In 2014, TLR had more than 16,000 individual supporters, representing 1,266 different trades and professions, from 857 towns across the state. "Membership continues to grow because Texans recognize that a small, powerful group of plaintiff lawyers are abusing the system for financial gain, resulting in harm to consumers and the Texas economy," said Weekley. "Other groups have raised more money," wrote *Texas Monthly* in 2011, "but none have been so singleminded in their pursuit of an ideological goal."

TLR's biggest breakthroughs came in 2003. To supplement its research and educational work, the organization had added a political-action arm, TLR PAC, to fund candidates. The PAC's donations played a key role in the 2002 Republican takeover of the Texas House of Representatives (which Democrats had controlled since Reconstruction). A flood of reforms followed in the next legislative year. Lawmakers overhauled the rules on medical-malpractice lawsuits, for example, adopting a cap on non-economic damages.

By 2008, TLR could take credit for almost two dozen important reforms, and Texas had transformed itself from lawsuit mecca to leader in legal moderation. An economic analysis calculated that 8.5 percent of the state's economic growth since 1995 was due to lawsuit reform. It credited lawsuit reform with bringing 499,000 new jobs, a 21 percent reduction in medical liability insurance costs, and health insurance coverage for 430,000 formerly uninsured Texans. After raising more than $100 million from donors in its first 20 years, TLR continues to pursue adjustments to the state civil-justice system in each legislative session.

Further reading

○ "New group hopes to quell lawsuit abuse," *Houston Chronicle*, August 30, 1994

○ The Perryman Group, "Texas Turnaround: The Impact of Lawsuit Reform on Economic Activity in the Lone Star State," April 2008

POLICY

―――――― 1993 ――――――

SCUTTLING HILLARYCARE WITH FAXED MEMOS

Shortly after Bill Clinton's election, Republican operative Bill Kristol raised $1.3 million from conservative foundations and New York donors to fund a nonprofit activist organization to resist nationalized health care. Clinton had promised a health-care overhaul as a signature effort, and tasked First Lady Hillary Clinton and top aides to come up with a proposal. Their solution, critics noted, would have had the government take direction of one seventh of the American economy.

Kristol and a few donor-financed assistants were among the chief organizers of opposition to the plan. They drafted strategy memos and broadcast them to politicians and journalists via fax machines (then a cutting-edge technology). At a time when polls indicated wide support for a new health-care law, the organization insisted that "there is no health-care crisis." Eventually, rising public opposition forced the White House to abandon its massive reform, and set the stage for Republican domination of the 1994 elections—which broke the Democrats' grip on Congress for the first time in decades.

From this success sprouted the Project for the New American Century, which continued the strategy of faxed memos but in the service of a hawkish foreign policy, and then creation of the *Weekly Standard*, a conservative magazine launched in 1995 with Kristol as editor.

Further reading

○ Nina Easton, *Gang of Five: Leaders at the Center of the Conservative Crusade* (Simon & Schuster, 2000)

○ Haynes Johnson and David Broder, *The System: The American Way of Politics at the Breaking Point* (Little, Brown, 1996)

1991

ENERGY FOUNDATION

Three large foundations—Rockefeller, MacArthur, and the Pew Charitable Trusts—pledged a combined $20 million in 1991 to found a new organization devoted to political-campaign-style efforts to change U.S. energy policy: reducing energy use, promoting renewable sources, and (most recently) pushing the U.S. economy away from "yesterday's fossil-fuel technologies" via proposed government caps and taxes. The Energy Foundation is the resulting conduit. It collects money from large givers, then re-grants it to groups scrambling to change policy. The original donors were eventually joined by the Packard, Hewlett, and McKnight foundations, and a few wealthy donors like Jeff Skoll, Tom Steyer, Julian Robertson, and James Simons.

The Energy Foundation was influential in convincing around three dozen states to set controversial regulations requiring utilities to generate a minimum fraction of their electric power from renewable or alternative sources, passing on the increased costs to their customers. The EF also helped convince regulators in California to require that one out of every six cars purchased in the state by 2025 be a zero-emission electric plug-in. The foundation then helped export the California standard to a dozen other states.

The Energy Foundation now funnels approximately $80 million per year from its supporting philanthropists to about 500 different action groups.

Further reading

○ Duke University case study, cspcs.sanford.duke.edu/sites/default/files/descriptive/ energy_foundation.pdf

BACKSCRATCHING PHILANTHROPY SOWS HAVOC

Charitable donations aimed at influencing policy can occasionally lead to disaster, particularly if they are entangled with taxpayer money. That's the lesson of Fannie Mae and Freddie Mac, so-called government-sponsored enterprises created by Congress to lubricate the housing market. The two agencies were allowed to operate almost like corporations—including in setting up foundation arms and making large donations to nonprofits, even though they were neither real private companies nor real philanthropists.

Fannie Mae had become insolvent during the 1980s, and government officials were exploring ways of ending the government privileges (like loose capital standards) that kept it and Freddie Mac afloat. In 1988, the White House Commission on Privatization called for an end to "all federal benefits and backing for Fannie and Freddie." In the 1990 reconciliation act, the Congressional Budget Office was asked to study the financial risks to taxpayers created by these government-sheltered housing subsidizers.

To fight back, Fannie Mae hired the political operator who had run Walter Mondale's presidential campaign. When Jim Johnson became CEO in 1991, two of his first ventures were to 1) allocate $10 billion for low-income people to borrow money to buy houses, and 2) establish a string of "partnership offices" in congressional districts across the U.S. where Fannie Mae would distribute grants to local nonprofits and win allies. As a Fannie Mae executive told *New York Times* reporter Gretchen Morgenson, "the partnership offices gave us an enormous advantage when Congress was debating further regulations. We were able to call… upon all our partners in the cities where we had these offices and say you have to weigh in. Write to Congress."

Johnson put $350 million into Fannie Mae's foundation and started making hundred-thousand-dollar gifts to scores of advocacy groups and

POLICY

nonprofits. In the words of the *Times* reporter, Fannie's CEO made the foundation "a powerhouse in charitable giving that targeted organizations associated with favored politicians, or located in their areas." For instance, a nonprofit founded by the mother of Barney Frank (who became chairman of the House Financial Services Committee) was twice given an "Award of Excellence" by Fannie Mae.

In addition to myriad local nonprofits, national activist groups like ACORN, the National Council of La Raza, and the National Low Income Housing Coalition were showered with grants and attention. Poverty and minority advocates were charmed when Johnson announced in 1994 that Fannie Mae would spend $1 trillion on "affordable housing" over the next seven years. When the bills aimed at reining in reckless mortgage underwriting finally came up in Congress, Fannie and Freddie literally wrote much of the language, according to the *New York Times*. Not only was privatization of the agencies fended off, but so were stricter operating standards.

Fannie and Freddie's share of the mortgage market soared from 5 percent in 1990 to ten times that much in 2008. And at that point the entire U.S. housing market melted down, made toxic by mortgages pumped into non-creditworthy households. The economic trauma caused by the subprime-mortgage mess damaged family incomes and national prosperity for years thereafter.

Further reading

○ Gretchen Morgenson and Joshua Rosner, *Reckless Endangerment* (St. Martin's Press, 2011)

○ Heritage Foundation research report, heritage.org/research/reports/2013/11/fannie-and-freddie-what-record-of-success#_ftn25

○ *Philanthropy Daily* analysis, philanthropydaily.com/a-public-private-disaster

INSTITUTE FOR JUSTICE

In 1991, former Reagan administration lawyer Chip Mellor approached philanthropist Charles Koch with an idea for a "national law firm on liberty" that he would co-found with litigator Clint Bolick. Koch pledged up to $500,000 per year for three years. The Institute for Justice never needed this full amount, though. It quickly raised additional funds from other sources, especially as it began accepting and winning cases.

IJ rapidly became one of the leading firms pursuing "public interest" cases in the courts, usually for no fee, by aggressively litigating in four areas: economic rights, private-property protection, school choice, and free speech. It has taken numerous cases all the way to the U.S. Supreme Court. In *Zelman v. Simmons-Harris* (2002), for instance, the high court endorsed public funding of private-school vouchers. In *Kelo v. City of New London* (2005) the justices rejected IJ's call to forbid use of eminent domain for economic development, but a public backlash stirred up by the case and harnessed by IJ resulted in 44 states passing laws that restrict eminent domain—highlighting the success of IJ's model combining good lawyering with strategic research, media savvy, and political activism.

The organization's second donor, retired investor Robert Wilson, helped fuel it to new heights when, after years of making annual gifts of $35,000 and promising more only "when the time is right," he issued a challenge grant in 2008. Over a period of five years, he donated $15 million on the condition that IJ raise $2 of additional new contributions for every $1 he donated. This $45 million total infusion allowed the organization to expand significantly and become one of the nation's leading litigants for liberty. In 2014, futures trader and longtime IJ supporter William Dunn revived the 1:2 challenge with an offer to give IJ $5 million if the organization would raise $10 million to match it.

In 2010, IJ launched an initiative to challenge civil forfeiture, which allows law-enforcement officials to permanently seize private property including homes, cars, and cash even if the owners haven't been charged or convicted of a crime. Applying its trademark mix of research, cutting-edge litigation, media campaigning, and legislative advocacy, IJ set out to end or limit the practice. Its research report, "Policing for Profit: The Abuse of Civil Asset Forfeiture Laws" graded every state forfeiture law and found that only three states received a B or higher. The institute simultaneously launched litigation in Georgia, Massachusetts, and Philadelphia, and lawsuits against the federal government as well, challenging currency seizures.

Early in 2015, the U.S. Department of Justice announced it was suspending its program for sharing proceeds of civil forfeitures with police departments, and would review how it uses the law. At the same time, legislation was introduced in the House and Senate to rein in civil-forfeiture practices.

POLICY

⏴ PhilAphorism

The true friend of the people should see that they be not too poor, for extreme poverty lowers the character of the democracy.

☞ *Aristotle*

By this time, the Institute for Justice had more than 80 employees (about half of them lawyers), five state offices in addition to its headquarters, and a clinic at the University of Chicago where small businesses can get legal help. Individual donors supplied 85 percent of the institute's $19 million budget in 2014.

Further reading

○ *Wall Street Journal* profile of Chip Mellor, online.wsj.com/news/articles/ SB10001424052970203513604577144902274972614?mod=ITP_opinion_0&mg= reno64-wsj

○ About the Institute for Justice, ij.org/about-ij-ij-at-a-glance

CAMPAIGNING AGAINST TOBACCO

The Robert Wood Johnson Foundation began a long-term public crusade against tobacco use in 1991. Moving far beyond traditional medical efforts and using all the levers of public-policy advocacy, the group invested more than $700 million of its own funds and recruited allies to contribute more. This massive philanthropic investment hastened many changes in law and policy that damped smoking: the Synar Amendment requiring states to prohibit the sale of tobacco to minors, public-health warnings against secondhand smoke, smoking bans on airplanes and in public spaces, bans on tobacco advertising, and agreements with Hollywood to stop glamorizing smoking in movies and TV. Starting in 1998, the Master Settlement Agreement transferred billions of dollars from cigarette companies to state governments to settle suits over the public costs of treating smoking-related illness.

In 1996, Johnson joined the American Cancer Society, American Heart Association, American Medical Association, and others in launching the National Center for Tobacco-Free Kids. The foundation put $84 million into that effort over the next 11 years.

The foundation pushed hard for higher cigarette taxes to suppress use. "Raising tobacco taxes is our No. 1 strategy," said one collaborating activist. "The tobacco industry…can't repeal the laws of economics." RWJ devoted $99 million to its SmokeLess States program. When the campaign was over, more than 30 states had increased cigarette taxes and six had approved indoor-air laws that proscribed smoking in workplaces and restaurants. The federal government doubled cigarette excise taxes in 2009.

It's not clear what would have happened to tobacco use absent this intervention led by the Robert Wood Johnson Foundation. The decline in smoking in the U.S. has actually been quite steady since the first U.S. Surgeon

General report warning of tobacco's dangers appeared in the mid-1960s. In any case, the fraction of active cigarette smokers in America fell from 27 percent in 1994 to 17 percent in 2014, and it is estimated that more than 8 million lives have been saved as a result of reduced tobacco use—which proceeded faster and further in the U.S. than in most other countries.

Further reading

○ Anti-tobacco efforts of R. W. Johnson Foundation, rwjf.org/en/research-publications/find-rwjf-research/2011/04/the-tobacco-campaigns-.html

NEW APPROACH TO RACE DISCRIMINATION

During the 1980s, scholars such as Thomas Sowell developed intellectual arguments against the racial preferences advocated by the civil-rights establishment. By the end of the decade, conservative foundations were ready to translate these new ideas into law and policy. In 1988, attorneys Michael Greve and Michael McDonald persuaded the Bradley, Olin, and Smith Richardson foundations to provide seed money to start the Center for Individual Rights, which filed suit against public universities over their use of racial quotas and preferences to shape their student bodies. The center won *Hopwood v. Texas* in federal court in 1996, marking the first victory against color-coded admissions. In 2003, a pair of CIR-driven cases involving the University of Michigan went to the Supreme Court, which accepted the constitutionality of race-based admissions for particular purposes, establishing a stalemate in use of racial preferences.

A range of donor-backed organizations now argues both in courts of law and in the court of public opinion for limits on race-conscious policies. The California Civil Rights Initiative, approved by California voters in 1996, banned the use of race in that state's public employment, contracting, and college admissions. Ward Connerly of the American Civil Rights Institute led the campaign on its behalf, and later became involved in similarly successful efforts in Arizona, Michigan, Washington, and elsewhere. For other recent philanthropically supported cases see 2013 entry on "Supreme Assistance."

Further reading

○ Steven Teles, *The Rise of the Conservative Legal Movement* (Princeton University Press, 2008)

A THINK TANK FOR FAMILY REINFORCEMENT

When Michigan auto-parts executive Edgar Prince visited Christian radio

POLICY

personality James Dobson in Colorado in 1988, he learned that Dobson was trying to raise $1 million to jumpstart the Family Research Council, a small and languishing think tank. Prince immediately pledged the full amount, a contribution that allowed Gary Bauer to join FRC as its president. This launched a phase of rapid growth for FRC, giving religious conservatives and Americans concerned with family breakdown an institutional voice they previously lacked in Washington public-policy circles. By the late 1990s, the FRC had grown into a major organization, with a budget of $14 million, 120 employees, and its own building in the nation's capital. The organization played a role in Supreme Court confirmation battles, passage of child tax credits, the ban on partial-birth abortion, and many other issue debates.

Further reading

○ Family Research Council history, frc.org/historymission

1988

PEW WARMS TO CLIMATE CHANGE

In 1988, the Pew Charitable Trusts, whose resources derive from Sun Oil, offered a $120,000 gift to the University of California at Santa Barbara to study "the impact of climate change on northern temperate forest reserves." Since then, climate change has been a major priority of Pew, one of the largest and most powerful philanthropies in the country.

In 1998, for instance, Pew put up $12 million to launch the Pew Center on Global Climate Change. It produced nearly 100 reports, had witnesses testify before Congress 30 times, and worked to influence regional and international talks on setting new climate and energy policies. The organization is now known as the Center for Climate and Energy Solutions, and continues its work with an annual budget of around $4 million and support from the Hewlett, Rockefeller Brothers, Energy, and Alcoa foundations.

In 2002, Pew converted itself from private foundation to public charity, so it could not only provide funds for public-policy causes but also lobby and raise funds from others on their behalf, putting "an emphasis on action." In 2007, for instance, it played a major role in launching the U.S. Climate Action Partnership, a group wholly focused on lobbying for government controls on greenhouse gases. The Pew Charitable Trusts currently spend about $300 million every year, with a strong focus on influencing public policy.

Further reading

○ 2004 Capital Research Center analysis, capitalresearch.org/wp-content/uploads/2013/01/FW0113.pdf

○ Center for Climate and Energy Solutions public-policy activity, c2es.org/about/history

ORGANIZING SCHOOL CHOICE

One of the first major initiatives of the Lynde and Harry Bradley Foundation was to bring school choice to its home city of Milwaukee. In so doing, it both revolutionized local schooling and created a powerful demonstration project for the rest of the country. This required policy and political alliances with black community activists in Milwaukee and the administration of Republican governor Tommy Thompson, who were jointly developing legislation that would allow low-income children trapped in poor public schools to attend private and parochial schools. A small program was launched and grew steadily in size and strength. During the 1990s it survived repeated legal assaults and political challenges, becoming the country's longest-living and most-watched private school-choice program in the United States. (See 1986 entry on our companion Education list.) By the 2014-15 academic year, more than 26,000 students were attending 113 schools under the Milwaukee Parental Choice Program.

Milwaukee's successes inspired similar voucher and school-choice programs in Florida, Pennsylvania, Arizona, Ohio, Indiana, and other states. Research on student performance indicates that school choice improves high-school graduation rates, college admittance, and college persistence. While participants typically enter their choice schools one to two years behind grade level, achievement test results at choice schools are equal to or higher than at public schools. Voucher programs save taxpayer dollars (the Milwaukee program reduced state spending by $52 million in 2011) and encourage public schools to improve by applying competitive pressure.

The Milwaukee program came under renewed pressure in 2011 when the ACLU and Disability Rights Wisconsin filed a complaint alleging that the private schools that parents were choosing for their children were not following disability law. In 2013 the Obama administration's Department of Justice Civil Rights Division sent the Wisconsin education superintendent a letter pressing the ACLU's arguments, and threatening that "the United States reserves its right to pursue enforcement through other means." The Wisconsin Institute for Law & Liberty, a public-interest law firm partly funded by the Bradley and Kern foundations, defended the program.

Further reading

○ 2012 comprehensive review of Milwaukee program, uaedreform.org/downloads/2012/02/report-36-the-comprehensive-longitudinal-evaluation-of-the-milwaukee-parental-choice-program.pdf

POLICY

○ Wisconsin Institute for Law & Liberty analysis of U.S. Department of Justice letter, will-law.org/home/WILL-Blog/2013/08/28/WILL-RESPONDS-TO-US-DOJ

1986

CREATING STATE THINK TANKS

Thomas Roe, founder of the construction-supply firm Builder Marts, was an active public-policy donor until his death in 2000. When he expressed an interest in the "New Federalism" proposed by Ronald Reagan, which would allow states to solve their own problems as an alternative to standardized programs from Washington, Reagan challenged him to "do something about it." Roe decided that supporting market-oriented think tanks in every state would help. In 1986 he founded the South Carolina Policy Council in his native place.

Simultaneously, activists favoring decentralized and limited government started similar policy centers in other states—like the Independence Institute in Colorado, and the Mackinac Center in Michigan. With Roe's encouragement and financial support these organizations began to collaborate and learn from each other. In 1992, they organized the State Policy Network, a consortium of free-market think tanks focused on improving public policy in state capitals rather than via federal legislation in D.C.

Roe served as SPN's founding chairman and its major financial backer. At its launch, SPN had a dozen think tanks as members; by 2014 it numbered 64 think tanks representing all 50 states, with combined budgets exceeding $80 million. In addition to the traditional think-tank work of policy analysis, they are increasingly becoming involved in new ventures like nonprofit journalism and public-interest litigation.

Further reading

○ Thomas Roe history, capitalresearch.org/wp-content/uploads/May-2007-Foundation-Watch.pdf

○ Directory of SPN state think tanks, spn.org/docLib/20120501_Map2012.pdf

1986

ACLU LGBT PROJECT

Since establishing its LGBT Project in 1986 (to expand lesbian, gay, bisexual, and transgender rights), the American Civil Liberties Union has received about $20 million of earmarked donations to support that work. Lawsuits brought by the organization have upended numerous public policies at both the state and national level. ACLU litigation was crucial, for instance, in eventually undermining voter initiatives passed in California (barring same-sex marriage) and Colorado (barring the granting of protected status to homosexuals), effectively blocking popular verdicts on these issues. In 1997 an ACLU suit in New Jersey established the first right of gay couples to adopt children. ACLU lawsuits in scores of states were vital in gradually creating a right to same-sex marriage. And it was an ACLU case that invalidated the Defense of Marriage Act that had been passed by Congress and signed by President Clinton. The organization's LGBT Project continues to have strong effects on law, policy, and public opinion in all of these areas, along with a growing advocacy for individuals who decide to change their sex—helping them in child custody, college housing, military service, health-insurance, public-restroom usage, and other disputes.

Further reading

○ ACLU LGBT Project, aclu.org/lgbt-rights

1986

SPARKING WELFARE REFORM

In 1986, the Lynde and Harry Bradley Foundation built an intellectual

 PhilAphorism

There are only four things you can do with your money. You can give it to the government. You can spend it. You can give it to your kids, to their detriment. My three sons understand this. I never want to deprive them of the wonderful feeling of making it on their own. I don't think you do your kids a favor by leaving them a lot of money, or letting them think they're working with a net.

And the fourth thing you can do with your money is create something good with it. I think it's incumbent on everybody with any amount of funds at all to start thinking like that.

☞ *James Kimsey*

POLICY

coalition for welfare reform. Its $300,000 grant assembled top conservative and liberal social scientists to see if agreement could be found on ways to reduce the destructive effects of welfare programs on family structure, work rates, crime levels, and other social factors. Members of the new group on both sides of the political divide made concessions, and a final report entitled "The New Consensus on Family and Welfare" was drafted under the leadership of Michael Novak.

The conservatives acknowledged that government has a role to play in the alleviation of suffering. The liberals admitted that welfare programs often produce dysfunctional levels of dependency. The report sketched the outlines of revised programs, with work requirements and supports that would be healthier for U.S. society. This new synthesis proved to be the kernel of the welfare-reform compromise that was eventually debated and passed into law during the Clinton administration.

Another bit of seminal philanthropy was the 1982 funding from the Olin Foundation that helped Charles Murray write his influential critique of the existing welfare state, *Losing Ground.* Olin grants also supported two books by Lawrence Mead that made the case for work requirements in return for cash payments. The Bradley Foundation sped welfare reform as well by paying for the research that led to Marvin Olasky's book *The Tragedy of American Compassion*—which uncovered the forgotten but highly effective religious-based charity of the nineteenth century, reviving interest in faith-based social work.

The most direct way Bradley advanced welfare reform, though, was by helping set a successful template in their home state of Wisconsin. The foundation established the Wisconsin Policy Research Institute to take some of the fresh theory being generated by national scholars and reformers and translate it into practical new policies that could improve the lot of the poor in Milwaukee and the rest of the state.

This activity emboldened Wisconsin Governor Tommy Thompson to launch demonstration projects overhauling welfare in a couple of Wisconsin counties. Soon these experiments were expanded to the entire state. Instead of handing out welfare checks as automatic entitlements, the state began to require certain constructive behaviors from recipients, such as finding employment or pursuing an education, while offering them help with child care, transportation, and other practical barriers to work. When he needed additional scholarly help in designing these reforms, and encountered resistance from academics at the University of Wisconsin, Thompson turned to the Hudson Institute, also supported by Bradley (and Olin).

These late-1980s experiments resulted in dramatic reductions in welfare dependency across Wisconsin, rising work rates, and improved child welfare. That in turn inspired the federal welfare-reform legislation signed into law by President Clinton in 1996, which quickly cut national welfare caseloads in half, chopped poverty rates, and brought other healthy results. By using its home state of Wisconsin as a "laboratory of democracy," the Bradley Foundation proved that smart local philanthropy could yield powerful national results.

Further reading

○ First-hand account on creating the *New Consensus* report, firstthings.com/web-exclusives/2006/08/bill-clinton-and-welfare-refor

○ Lawrence Mead, *Government Matters: Welfare Reform in Wisconsin* (Princeton University Press, 2005)

1985

MINTING NEW DEMOCRATS

Following President Ronald Reagan's landslide re-election in 1984, moderate Democrats sought ways to push their party away from doctrinaire liberalism and toward the political center. Party loyalist Al From organized wealthy benefactors in a series of private retreats, then tapped them for donations with which to found the Democratic Leadership Council—dedicated to supporting more moderate so-called "New Democrats." The DLC functioned as an alternative and rival to the Democratic National Committee, causing controversy within party ranks but also preparing the way for future victories.

In 1989, the DLC formed a nonprofit research arm, the Progressive Policy Institute, to operate as a think tank for centrist Democrats. Wall Street magnate Michael Steinhardt served as PPI's board chairman, pledging hundreds of thousands of dollars to the organization. By 1992, this "pint-sized think tank" with a budget of just $700,000 had become the primary idea-generator for Bill Clinton's campaign for President. Once in the White House, Clinton staffed his administration with numerous alumni of the Democratic Leadership Council and the Progressive Policy Institute, looking to them for ideas on trade promotion, welfare reform, and streamlining government. By 2001, the DLC and PPI had a combined budget of $7 million.

With the resurgence of liberalism inside the Democratic party during the first decade of the twenty-first century, the DLC and PPI struggled to remain relevant. In 2011 the DLC formally dissolved and donated its archive to the Clinton Foundation. The Progressive Policy Institute continues to seek policies it views as centrist and sensible.

POLICY

Further reading

○ Kenneth Baer, *Reinventing Democrats* (University of Kansas Press, 2000)

○ Critical review in *American Prospect*, prospect.org/article/how-dlc-does-it

KOCH BROTHERS TAKE UP ADVOCACY

From the mid-'70s to mid-'80s, brothers Charles and David Koch contributed to public-policy philanthropy mainly by building the Cato Institute, Mercatus Center, and other research organizations capable of formulating detailed critiques of national problems (see 1977 and 1980 entries). In 1984 the Koch brothers took a step toward more direct advocacy. They provided about a million dollars a year to help launch Citizens for a Sound Economy, which quickly attracted additional funding from other foundation and business donors. The group distributed studies, analysis, polling, and other information to promote a vision of "less government, lower taxes, and less regulation." It attracted prominent staff like former U.S. Office of Management and Budget director James Miller, economist Larry Kudlow, and retired Congressman Dick Armey. The group rescued the Tax Foundation, since 1937 an invaluable collator of tax data.

In 2004, Citizens for a Sound Economy restructured into two new organizations: FreedomWorks (which over the next few years organized several million activists interested in individual liberty and limited government) and Americans for Prosperity (which built a similar following, including 2 million members, 35 state chapters, and financial support from 100,000 contributors) in order to "educate citizens about economic policy and mobilize those citizens as advocates in the public-policy process." Both groups were important in building the organizational and intellectual resources of the so-called Tea Party movement as an alternative channel for activism by libertarians and conservatives frustrated with the Republican party establishment.

Over a period of decades, the Koch brothers contributed more than $200 million to three dozen or so advocacy organizations focused on free-market reforms. (Meanwhile they have been only light contributors to political candidates.) In 2003 the Kochs also started convening semi-annual free-enterprise seminars where other donors interested in public policies were invited to discuss topics like budget control, health care, climate change, tax reduction, and respect for Constitutional limits on government, and then encouraged to contribute to advocacy groups promoting market-oriented solutions to such problems. The first seminars included less than 20 people, but donor participation gradually grew, and over a decade several hundred million dollars were donated by attendees to organizations active in public-policy debates. The last Koch seminar of 2015 was attended by about 450 donors, with the goal of encouraging $889 million in annual donations to groups active in policy and political advocacy.

Further reading

○ Brian Doherty, *Radicals for Capitalism* (PublicAffairs, 2008)

○ Charles Koch description of his policy philanthropy, online.wsj.com/news/articles/SB1000 14240527023039783045794758605150021286

RELIGION IN PUBLIC LIFE

Richard Neuhaus, a Catholic priest who had been an anti-war activist in the 1960s, took a look at the rise of the Religious Right in the 1970s and found himself in democratic sympathy. The gatekeepers of culture, he concluded, had largely banished from public discourse any serious expression of religion—the most important element in the life of many Americans. He predicted "a deepening crisis of legitimacy if the courts persist in systematically ruling out of order the moral traditions in which Western law has developed, and which bear for the overwhelming majority of the American people a living sense of right and wrong."

Neuhaus began to deepen these ideas with funding from the Lilly Endowment. He received grants from the Bradley and Olin foundations to write a book he ultimately titled *The Naked Public Square*, which came out in 1984. Both his title and his thesis went mainline, and even commentators who "subscribed to exaggerated notions of church-state separation," as Neuhaus put it, began to acknowledge that America is harmed when all moral calculus is stripped from public discussion and policy. With continuing donor support, Neuhaus subsequently published the influential journal *First Things*, which deepened and extended this understanding of religion's healthy role in public life.

Further reading

○ *Philanthropy* magazine essay, philanthropyroundtable.org/topic/excellence_in_ philanthropy/eight_books_that_changed_america

BIRTH OF THE
FEDERALIST SOCIETY

The Institute for Educational Affairs, a group backed by the Olin, Earhart,

POLICY

JM, Scaife, and Smith Richardson foundations, provided a grant of $15,000 in 1982 to underwrite a legal conference on federalism put on by law students with an interest in conservative politics. Speakers at the forum, which took place at Yale, included future Supreme Court Justice Antonin Scalia and federal appeals judge Robert Bork. Using the successful conference as a springboard, several of the organizers—including future Senator and energy secretary Spencer Abraham and future Congressman David McIntosh—decided to form a national group with student-run local chapters, calling it the Federalist Society for Law and Public Policy.

Strong interest among students, and additional foundation support, allowed the group to grow rapidly. By the 1990s the Federalist Society had become one of the most influential legal groups in the country. On appointments to the federal judiciary, its influence arguably surpassed even the American Bar Association.

In 2015, the Federalist Society had chapters at every accredited law school in the United States, 10,000 student members, 60,000 members of its Lawyers Division, and a budget of around $16 million. Inspired by its success, several philanthropists have tried to adapt its model to business schools (the Adam Smith Society), medical schools (the Benjamin Rush Society), and schools where students are trained in foreign policy (the Alexander Hamilton Society).

Further reading

○ About the Federalist Society, fed-soc.org/aboutus

1981

GIVE PEACE A GRANT

Coincident with the election of President Ronald Reagan, a "nuclear freeze" movement sprang up to oppose research and development of nuclear technology, advocate for disarmament, criticize American "belligerence," resist a general U.S. defense buildup, and vehemently oppose the placement of missiles in Europe to balance Soviet missile growth. In 1981 the movement went public with its first rally and garnered endorsements from pacifist, religious, and union groups. Referenda declaring "nuclear-free zones" were placed on ballots in many cities. The "freeze" agitation peaked in a large 1982 gathering in New York City during a U.N. special session on disarmament, and culminated with inclusion of freeze rhetoric in the Democratic Party platform during the 1984 race for President.

At the heart of these efforts were a handful of major donors, and a new philanthropic entity. From 1974 to 1982 three foundations—Ford, the

Rockefeller Brothers Fund, and Rockefeller Family Fund—spent about $7 million to build up anti-nuclear groups. Then in 1981, the Ploughshares Fund was started by an ACLU San Francisco board member who argued that "the threat of nuclear war overshadows everything else." The fund was established specifically to coordinate donations to disarmament and peace groups, and guide creation of their strategies.

Ploughshares has since channeled more than $100 million to peace groups, making it the largest philanthropy on this topic. It still exists today, its $11 million of 2014 income coming from about 2,000 individuals plus foundations like the Carnegie Corporation, the Compton, Ford, MacArthur, Turner, Rockefeller, and Hewlett foundations, and the Open Society Institute. It re-grants roughly half of its revenue to peace groups, and does some of its own programming with the rest.

Joan Kroc, heiress to the McDonald's fortune, also became a passionate nuclear disarmer in the 1980s. In 1985 she spent millions on advocacy, including ads in major publications calling for disarmament. She also reprinted and publicly distributed the book *Missile Envy* by Helen Caldicott. Kroc endowed two major academic centers for "peace studies"—the Kroc Institute for International Peace Studies at the University of Notre Dame, and a similar institute at the University of San Diego.

Further reading

○ 2014 annual report of Ploughshares Fund, ploughshares.org/sites/default/files/ resources/2014%20Ploughshares%20Annual%20Report.pdf

———— 1981 ————

NEW EFFORTS TO OPEN MINDS ON CAMPUS

Philanthropists bothered by the conformity of liberal orthodoxy on college campuses have long supported outposts where alternative views could be offered to a new generation of young students. The founding of the

POLICY

~ PhilAphorism

Do what you can, with what you have, where you are.

☞ *Theodore Roosevelt*

Intercollegiate Studies Institute in 1953 was an early effort to reintroduce students to the deep Western values behind America's founding. Many other such efforts followed.

In 1981, the John M. Olin Foundation awarded $50,000 to professor Allan Bloom at the University of Chicago to seed a new center for exploring political philosophy and democracy. In addition to funding a series of lectures, conferences, and fellowships, this support allowed Bloom to write a pathbreaking book warning of the perils of cultural relativism and declining intellectual standards on campus. *The Closing of the American Mind* became an unlikely bestseller in 1987, occupying the top spot on the *New York Times* bestseller list for four months with withering criticisms of modern universities for dismissing great books and timeless truths in favor of trendy ideology.

The bestseller *Illiberal Education* by Dinesh D'Souza, which extended this argument and popularized the term "political correctness," was also produced with support from Olin. Olin likewise funded a series of faculty fellowships that nurtured unconventional young scholars like John DiIulio, Frederick Kagan, and John Yoo. Other donors sponsored similar initiatives to open higher ed to points of view differing from the liberal conventions that dominate campuses. The group ACTA was founded in 1995 to mobilize trustee and alumni donors.

The James Madison Program in American Ideals and Institutions at Princeton University was founded by professor Robert George in 2000 with startup funding from the Olin and Bradley foundations, then donations from Princeton alumni, followed by other campus-specific groups. With financial support from a range of donors, the Intercollegiate Studies Institute, the Fund for American Studies, the Institute for Humane Studies, and similar organizations run summer programs, reading groups, websites, and special networks that aim to round out student educations with ideas, scholars, and philosophical perspectives not otherwise represented on most college campuses. The National Association of Scholars is a similar effort to support dissenting professors; funded by donors since 1987, it has 3,000 members, holds conferences, and publishes a quarterly journal. The Veritas Fund for Higher Education is a more recent creation that allows donors to fund professors who teach America's founding principles and history.

Another venture to improve civics knowledge among American undergraduates is the Jack Miller Center. It has established 58 on-campus institutes dedicated to study of our classic national texts, with funding from the entrepreneur who helped create the Staples company. As of 2015, he and other donors had committed over $60 million to the undertaking.

Further reading

○ *New York Times* reporting, nytimes.com//09/22/education/22conservative.
   html?pagewanted=print&_r=0

○ *Philanthropy* magazine description of Madison program, philanthropyroundtable.org/
   topic/excellence_in_philanthropy/a_new_birth_of_civic_education_on_campus

AUSTRIAN ECONOMICS
ALONG THE POTOMAC

A center devoted to market-based economics and philosophy, called the Austrian Economics Program, was established at Rutgers University in the late-1970s with a grant from philanthropist Charles Koch. It was promptly squeezed by a hiring freeze. The president of George Mason University, just across the Potomac from Washington, D.C., invited the program to relocate to his campus in 1980. There, it eventually became known as the Mercatus Center (mercatus is Latin for "marketplace"), and with steady donations from the Charles Koch Charitable Foundation it grew into a very active academic hub and economic think tank.

More generally, a stream of Koch support that eventually totaled tens of millions of dollars was crucial in turning the George Mason economics department into one of the best in the nation. Two GMU economists have been awarded Nobel prizes: James Buchanan in 1986 and Vernon Smith in 2002. Public-choice theory and other concepts used to assess government policies today have been honed at the northern Virginia institution.

In 1985, George Mason University also became home to the Institute for Humane Studies, another quietly influential product of long-term Koch support. With online instructional materials, lectures, debates, seminars, and scholarships that help students pursue further studies, IHS now trains hundreds of thousands of students in principles of liberty and economic success. Over 1,700 of its alumni have become professors, and they will teach an estimated 10 million students over their careers. Some will also shape public policy through their research.

The Charles Koch Foundation has greatly expanded its giving to higher education over the last decade. "Currently we're fortunate to support over 350 programs, and over 250 colleges and universities across the country," says John Hardin, director of university relations at the foundation. Grants underwrite everything from guest lectures by leading scholars to special student seminars, from course-development assistance for faculty to student research fellowships.

POLICY

Further reading

○ About the Mercatus Center, mercatus.org/content/about

○ Institute for Humane Studies support for professors, supportihs.org/professors

HUMAN RIGHTS CAMPAIGN

The Human Rights Campaign began its life in 1980 as a PAC—a mechanism for funneling campaign donations to elect gay-friendly politicians. In 1982 the organization distributed $140,000 to 118 congressional candidates. Four decades later, HRC was the largest gay-advocacy group in the country, and electoral campaigning was still a huge part of its purpose. In the 2012 Presidential campaign year, HRC raised or contributed more than $20 million to influence referenda on same-sex marriage, elect pro-gay members of Congress, and re-elect Barack Obama.

In 1995, when HRC was a $6 million organization with both 501(c)(3) advocacy and 501(c)(4) political action arms, it reorganized— adding new family projects and work projects, and expanding all research, communications, and public-relations efforts. The nonprofit grew rapidly into a $57 million-per-year operation by 2014. Major donors now supply 22 percent of its income; smaller individual contributions total 38 percent; bequests come to 5 percent; and investments, merchandise, and special events provide a quarter of the group's revenue.

The Human Rights Campaign operates a sophisticated and effective lobbying effort in Washington, D.C. It recruits attorneys from major law firms to provide pro bono litigation services. And it has worked hard to make allies among other activist groups on the political left so it can later call in chits for its priorities.

HRC has also assiduously cultivated the entertainment industry. Producers, writers, actors, musicians, and others have been honored at

∿ PhilAphorism

At the head of any new undertaking where in France you would find the government, or in England some great lord, in the United States you are sure to find an association.

☞ *Alexis de Tocqueville*

dinners, given awards, and involved in marketing efforts. This has yielded not only many celebrity endorsements and financial contributions, but also television story lines that have brought gay-friendly ideas and characters into the living rooms of everyday Americans over two decades—which the organization has found invaluable to its political and policy advocacy.

Further reading

○ Independent Sector case study, independentsector.org/uploads/advocacystudy/IS-BeyondtheCause-HRC.pdf

PUTTING MILTON FRIEDMAN ON PBS

After the liberal economist John Galbraith filmed *The Age of Uncertainty*, a television series for the BBC, several American philanthropists and corporations looked for a way to even the ideological balance sheet. They turned to Nobel Prize-winning economist Milton Friedman, who guided viewers through economic successes and failures around the globe, including their social effects, in a ten-part television series that appeared on PBS in 1980. The Sarah Scaife Foundation led the way, with a grant of $500,000. The John M. Olin Foundation contributed $250,000, Getty Oil Company $330,000, and the Reader's Digest Association $300,000. Other supporters included the Lilly Endowment, and the National Federation of Independent Business.

The show made a vigorous intellectual case for capitalism and was a smashing popular success. A book co-authored by Milton's wife, Rose, and published as a companion to the television series hit the bestseller lists in the United States and abroad. In the wake of his *Free to Choose* series and book, Friedman was perhaps the most popular and influential economist on the planet.

Further reading

○ Video archive, freetochoose.tv/broadcast.php?series=ftc80
○ Milton and Rose Friedman, *Free to Choose: A Personal Statement* (Harcourt Brace Jovanovich, 1980)

POLICY

MOTHERS AGAINST DRUNK DRIVING

In 1980, the mother of a 13-year-old California girl who was killed by a repeat drunk driver founded a nonprofit to fight back. Mothers Against Drunk Driving helped set the drinking age at 21 in all states, promoted tougher sanctions and the deployment of new technology against impaired driving, and rated states on DUI enforcement. In the first five years of the group's existence, annual traffic deaths related to alcohol were reduced by 20 percent—representing 6,000 lives saved. By 2015, alcohol-related deaths had been roughly cut in half, a total saving of about 300,000 lives.

Even still, alcohol-related crashes remain the most frequently committed violent crime in the U.S. On average, one American is killed by a drunk driver every 40 minutes. Economic losses exceed $114 billion per year.

In the 1990s MADD began to receive significant amounts of money from the federal government. The organization grew into a large bureaucracy, spending $20 million on annual staff salaries by 2009.

Further reading

○ History of Mothers Against Drunk Driving, madd.org/about-us/mission

1980

STARTING THE PRESSES FOR CONSERVATIVE STUDENT JOURNALISTS

In 1980, Irving Kristol encouraged donors to support a new conservative student publication at the University of Chicago. Before long, the John M. Olin Foundation and other donors were building the Collegiate Network, a consortium of conservative and libertarian student publications that voiced an alternative to conventional wisdom on campus and trained a generation of writers and editors. Since 1995 the Collegiate Network has been administered by the Intercollegiate Studies Institute.

Thanks to donor support that paid for printing costs, most of the country's top colleges and universities had a conservative student publication by the 1990s. Many prominent writers emerged from these publications, including Pulitzer-winner Joseph Rago (*Dartmouth Review*), ABC News correspondent Jonathan Karl (*Vassar Spectator*), *New York Times* columnist Ross Douthat (*Harvard Salient*), commentator Ann Coulter (*Cornell Review*), *National Review* editor Rich Lowry (*Virginia Advocate*), blogger Michelle Malkin (*Oberlin Forum*), author and Silicon Valley investor Peter Thiel (*Stanford Review*), author Dinesh D'Souza and radio host Laura Ingraham (both *Dartmouth Review*), and many others. "If everything we have done since was stripped away, leaving only the Collegiate Network as our legacy," said longtime Olin Foundation head James Pierson in 2004, "we would still proudly say our work yielded enormous success."

Further reading

○ The Collegiate Network, collegiatenetwork.org

QUESTIONING STATISM
IN MANHATTAN AND ELSEWHERE

While visiting the U.S. after World War II, entrepreneur Antony Fisher was impressed by the work of agriculturalists at Cornell University who were transforming chicken farming from a cottage industry into an efficient modern process. When he went back to Britain he set up similar operations growing chickens on a large scale, which altered Britain's diet and made Fisher a wealthy man. With some of the first profits from this business he set out to feed new thinking in his home country.

Discouraged to see centralizing economic policies sweep Britain after a war that had been fought to preserve freedom, Fisher visited free-market thinker Friedrich Hayek and told him he was considering entering politics. Hayek argued that the better course would be help change the intellectual currents running in the direction of socialism. In response, Fisher founded London's Institute of Educational Affairs, one of the world's early think tanks, which produced new ideas and experts that subsequently redirected both British and American politics. In recognition of Fisher's achievement, Nobel economist Milton Friedman wrote that "the U-turn in British policy executed by Margaret Thatcher owes more to him than any other individual."

Though business reversals later cost Fisher his fortune, he kept raising money for additional think tanks—this time in North America. In New York he was the progenitor, in 1978, of today's Manhattan Institute, which quickly shaped national debate by supporting landmark books on supply-side economics (*Wealth and Poverty* by George Gilder) and welfare reform (*Losing Ground* by Charles Murray). In the 1990s, New York City Mayor Rudy Giuliani looked to the Manhattan Institute for crucial ideas on law enforcement and other subjects.

Fisher was also behind the launch of the Pacific Research Institute in San Francisco, the National Center for Policy Analysis in Dallas, and the Fraser Institute in Vancouver. He created the Atlas Economic Research Foundation, which raises capital to launch new free-market groups in parts of the world that have inadequate experience in capitalism. Atlas has seeded more than 400 market-oriented organizations in over 80 countries.

By funding fresh ideas, and thinking of change in terms of decades rather than months, Antony Fisher helped create an international backlash against statism during the second half of the twentieth century.

POLICY

Further reading

○ Gerald Frost, *Antony Fisher: Champion of Liberty* (Profile Books, 2002)

○ Tom Wolfe on the birth of the Manhattan Institute, manhattan-institute.org/
turningintellect/chapter1.html

MACARTHUR'S MONEY MOVES LEFT

Shortly before businessman John MacArthur died, as one of the two or three wealthiest men in America, the insurance and real-estate magnate created a foundation. He was a selfish and misanthropic man, however, and gave little thought to how its board would execute the philanthropy carried out in his name. "You people, after I'm dead, will have to learn how to spend it," he told his lawyer. MacArthur's son from the first of his two marriages, Rod, eventually launched a pitched battle for control of the trust, and won. Ever since, the John D. and Catherine T. MacArthur Foundation has been one of America's largest funders of left-of-center public causes.

The foundation is perhaps best known for its "genius grants," which are no-strings-attached fellowships that pay $500,000 over five years, typically to artists, scientists, and political activists. Yet that makes up only a small portion of MacArthur's overall giving. During the days of the Soviet Union, the foundation was a major financier of the arms-control movement, pouring money into groups such as the Arms Control Association, the Center for Defense Information, the Federation of American Scientists, and the Union of Concerned Scientists. Other prominent recipients of MacArthur support include the American Civil Liberties Union, the Brookings Institution, the Carnegie Endowment for International Peace, the NAACP, and Planned Parenthood. In 2014, the foundation held assets exceeding $6.3 billion.

Further reading

○ Nancy Kriplen, *The Eccentric Billionaire: John D. MacArthur* (Amacom, 2008)

∿ PhilAphorism ————————————————————————————————

Benevolence today has become altogether too huge an undertaking to be conducted otherwise than on business lines.

☞ *Julius Rosenwald*

1978

A POPULAR TAX REVOLT

In a 1978 referendum, nearly two thirds of California voters approved Proposition 13, which lowered and capped the state's property taxes and heralded the coming of a nationwide "tax revolt" that helped sweep Ronald Reagan into office in 1980. Behind the success of Proposition 13 stood thousands of grassroots philanthropists. The sponsor organization, the United Organization of Taxpayers, relied on 50,000 small donors who offered up $440,000 and an estimated one million hours of volunteer time to get the measure on the ballot.

The *New York Times* described the measure's passage as "the beginning of a tax revolt—a modern Boston Tea Party." During the two years following, California property and sales taxes were cut by more than $4 billion. In 1980 the tax revolt moved to Washington. Reagan cut tax rates sharply during his first year in office, and chopped the top income tax rate down to 28 percent in 1986.

Further reading

○ Alvin Rabushka and Pauline Ryan, *The Tax Revolt* (Hoover Institution, 1982)

1977

IMPROVING IDEOLOGICAL
DIVERSITY AMONG REPORTERS

Decades of research have shown that the large majority of working journalists define themselves as political liberals. Conservatives who consider this a problem have made efforts, with donor support, to train young journalists who are more open to including conservative perspectives in their stories. The oldest of these programs is the National Journalism Center, which since 1977 has offered budding reporters the chance to intern with media outlets in Washington, D.C., while attending journalism classes taught by experienced professionals, many of them alumni of the program. Now operating under the sponsorship of Young America's Foundation, NJC has put 2,000 beginning practitioners through its 12-week internship program.

The newest effort to introduce more political balance into journalism is the Student Free Press Association, launched in 2010 to give conservative-leaning campus journalists a national website where they can release their work, as well as paid fellowships with publishers of political journalism. And back in 1994 the Phillips Foundation launched

POLICY

the Robert Novak Journalism Fellowship, awarding about $7 million over the next two decades to 130 young reporters in the form of $25,000 part-time or $50,000 full-time fellowships, giving them a year to produce a deeply researched story. In 2013 the program was transferred to the Fund for American Studies.

A fourth program for nurturing conservative or libertarian journalists is the Buckley Journalism Fellowship. Since 2009 it has installed one or two top young writers per year at *National Review*, the leading conservative politics magazine. The $75,000 cost for each fellow is covered by donations.

Further reading

○ *Philanthropy* magazine reporting, philanthropyroundtable.org/topic/excellence_in_ philanthropy/new_balance

1977

RISE OF THE CATO INSTITUTE

When businessman Charles Koch learned that Libertarian Party leader Ed Crane was thinking about leaving politics, he asked what it would take to keep him involved. Crane suggested that libertarianism needed a think tank: a public-policy organization that would join political debates with deep research and a crisp point of view. Koch agreed to fund its launch.

The Cato Institute—named for *Cato's Letters*, a set of eighteenth-century essays on freedom—opened its doors in San Francisco in 1977. It published newsletters and policy reports and provided radio commentaries. In 1981 it moved to Washington, D.C. Over the next three decades Cato grew rapidly into one of the country's prominent policy-forming organizations. It is best known for championing free-market policy reforms like Social Security privatization, school choice, and free trade, along with libertarian causes like open-borders immigration, drug legalization, and a dovish foreign policy.

From their founding days, Charles and David Koch's accumulated gifts to the Cato Institute come to about $30 million. The institute raised a total of $400 million during that period, from tens of thousands of donors. In 2015, Cato had 124 staffers and revenue exceeding $37 million (86 percent of that from individual donors).

Further reading

○ Brian Doherty, *Radicals for Capitalism: A Freewheeling History of the Modern American Libertarian Movement* (PublicAffairs, 2007)

○ Cato Institute annual reports, cato.org/about/annualreports

1976

A DONOR-ADVISED FUND
FOR LIBERAL POLICY REFORM

Campus protestor and student activist Drummond Pike took a position in 1970 at a youth group funded by the Ford Foundation. There he met philanthropists looking for ways to use their money to alter public policy. In 1976, Pike and Jane Bagley Lehman, heir to the Reynolds tobacco fortune, co-created the Tides Foundation to bankroll left-wing groups and causes.

Tides pioneered the use of donor-advised funds for public-policy purposes, allowing wealthy liberals to fund social change. An early coup was helping Hollywood producer Norman Lear create People for the American Way, one of the leading left-activist groups of the 1980s. Tides also helped establish the National Network of Grantmakers to unite "progressive" donors. (Later, Pike went on to serve as treasurer of the Democracy Alliance—see 2005 entry.)

Today the Tides Foundation manages 373 donor-advised funds averaging several hundred thousand dollars each. Through them, the foundation distributes around $100 million every year to promote causes like "global warming, AIDS treatment and prevention, and economic disparity," to quote its website. The San Francisco-based organization also operates the Tides Center, created in 1996, to sponsor nascent "social justice" nonprofits, offering them technical, administrative, financial, human-resources, and public-relations services while guiding their activism, and connecting them with donors willing to fund their projects. This and other Tides subgroups spend about as much again as the foundation, making Tides as a whole an approximately $200 million-per-year operation.

Further reading

○ Tides Foundation history, tides.org/about/history

1974

LINKING LAW AND ECONOMICS

The area where John Olin invested more donated resources than any other—the Law and Economics movement—was a matter of abiding personal interest for the philanthropist. Olin became persuaded that studying the interplay between laws and economic behavior was an important new academic discipline that could have potent implications for governance and public policy. Hoping to nudge America's dominant lawyer class toward a more sophisticated understanding of markets

POLICY

and economic discipline, Olin's foundation made its first grant for Law and Economics training in 1974—awarding $100,000 to a center run by Henry Manne at the University of Miami. It sponsored fellowships allowing students with graduate degrees in economics to receive legal training, and staged educational seminars introducing judges to important economic concepts.

Much more Olin funding would follow during the next two decades. The original Law and Economics Center migrated from Miami to Emory University and finally to George Mason University. And additional centers were endowed by the foundation at many top law schools, including Chicago, Harvard, Stanford, Virginia, Michigan, Columbia, Cornell, and Yale. By the time the Olin Foundation closed in 2005, it had spent more than $68 million to root the Law and Economics movement on campuses and in courthouses.

Olin's efforts began bearing rich fruit as early as the 1980s, as economic understanding and reasoning became much more visible within American jurisprudence. Judges and legislators paid greater attention to incentive effects, to regulatory costs, and to the benefits of competition. Most every year, beginning in 1985, there was at least one Olin Fellow from a Law and Economics center represented among the clerks selected for the U.S. Supreme Court. Legal scholar Bruce Ackerman described the Law and Economics movement as "the most important thing in legal education since the birth of Harvard Law School."

Further reading

º John Miller, *A Gift of Freedom: How the John M. Olin Foundation Changed America* (Encounter Books, 2006)

1973

FILER COMMISSION DEFENDS PRIVATE GIVING

Public debate over the Tax Reform Act of 1969 stirred up some basic questions about and criticisms of the role of private philanthropy in America. Several public figures decided it would be a good idea to examine and address some of these controversies with a blue-ribbon commission. It was a suggestion from John Rockefeller III that sparked creation of the panel, and his family provided $200,000 to organize and fund its investigation. More than 700 other individuals and organizations also helped underwrite the Commission on Private Philanthropy and Public Needs.

Rockefeller invited Aetna Insurance chairman John Filer to lead the commission of two dozen prominent Americans, and it became popularly known as the Filer Commission. The group commissioned 85 studies and convened many meetings over a two-year period. In 1975 it issued a 240-page report full of data and recommendations.

The commission described a "third sector," distinct from government and business, that plays a unique role in American life. "Private support is a fundamental underpinning for hundreds of thousands of institutions and organizations," said the report. "It is the ingredient that keeps private nonprofit organizations alive and private, keeps them from withering away or becoming mere adjuncts of government." The commission defended tax deductibility of contributions made to charity and suggested self-policing and consistent rules to protect the integrity and positive social effects of independent giving.

At a time of rumblings against independent giving, the Filer Commission's work is credited with heading off possible political intrusions into philanthropy—thus protecting the right of Americans to direct their money into private solutions to public problems.

Further reading

○ Report of the Filer Commission, archives.iupui.edu/bitstream/handle/2450/889/giving.pdf?sequence=1

○ Eleanor Brilliant, *Private Charity and Public Inquiry: A History of the Filer and Peterson Commissions* (Indiana University Press, 2000)

⌁ PhilAphorism

We are the most individualistic country on the face of the earth... and yet this individualistic society is still one of the most communitarian and undoubtedly the most philanthropic on the face of the earth. How can the most individualistic of societies also be the most philanthropic? Because of another great American tradition: that every individual is worthy, and no one is trapped by their circumstance. ☞ *Condoleezza Rice*

POLICY

1972

FEMINIST FLURRY FROM THE FORD FOUNDATION

In 1972, Ford Foundation president McGeorge Bundy pledged "to investigate grantmaking possibilities in the area of women's rights and opportunities." Between that moment and the end of the 1970s, dedicated women's programs accounted for more than one out of every 20 dollars the foundation spent.

At first, the Ford Foundation moved to create special programs within organizations it already supported. So the Women's Rights Project was promoted at the American Civil Liberties Union. The Minority Women's Employment Program was funded at the NAACP Legal and Educational Defense Fund, and the Chicana Rights Project got money at the Mexican American Legal Defense and Educational Fund.

The most influential of these was the ACLU project, co-founded in 1972 by Ruth Bader Ginsburg. Ginsburg's strategy was to file lawsuits based on a new reading of the Fourteenth Amendment's equal protection clause, leading the courts to wipe out gender distinctions in everything from employment rules to family law. In 1993, Ginsburg became a justice of the U.S. Supreme Court.

In 1980, Ford's trustees turned up the flow of money even further, committing the foundation to spending more than 10 percent of its resources on explicit women's causes. In addition to paying for various legal challenges, the foundation put money into supporting abortion, research on sex stereotypes, and increasing female leadership at unions. By 1986, Ford had spent $70 million in these areas, and women constituted a majority of its professional staff. "Ford's early funding for women's organizations and women's issues," philanthropic consultant Mary Ellen Capek concluded, "lent credibility" to feminist organizations.

Further reading

○ *Washington Post* description of Ginsburg's work, washingtonpost.com/wp-dyn/content/article/2007/08/23/AR2007082300903_pf.html

○ Duke University case study, cspcs.sanford.duke.edu/sites/default/files/descriptive/rights_and_opportunities_of_women.pdf

1972

JOE COORS BREWS UP
THE HERITAGE FOUNDATION

After backing Ronald Reagan's Presidential bid in 1968, beer magnate Joseph Coors concluded that an intellectual infrastructure for shaping public policies was just as important as good candidates. Liberals already had a policy infrastructure in universities and organizations like the Brookings Institution. Coors decided that conservatives needed think tanks of their own—so in 1972 he wrote a $250,000 check to begin the Heritage Foundation. Other philanthropists like the Samuel Roberts Noble Foundation and Richard Mellon Scaife joined the cause, but the Coors cash was catalytic, and also consistent. Coors continued to invest in the Heritage Foundation over many years, including a $300,000 gift in 1980 that allowed it to move to improved offices.

As Ronald Reagan finally took office in 1981, the Heritage Foundation issued *Mandate for Leadership*, a book of nearly 1,100 pages that became a policy blueprint for his administration. The think tank became active in virtually every area of government action, from welfare transfers to national defense. It eventually grew into the biggest and at times most influential think tank on the right.

Coors was also a principal backer of the Free Congress Foundation (a D.C. think tank focused on social issues), the Mountain States Legal Foundation (a public-interest law firm), and the Independence Institute (a Colorado-based free-market think tank). Yet Heritage remained his largest legacy. "There wouldn't be a Heritage Foundation without Joe Coors," said longtime Heritage president Edwin Feulner. In 2014, the organization spent $78 million, 75 percent of it raised from individual donations.

Further reading

○ Nicole Hoplin and Ron Robinson, *Funding Fathers* (Regnery, 2008)

○ Lee Edwards, *The Power of Ideas: The Heritage Foundation at 25 Years* (Jameson Books, 1997)

AN EXPLOSION OF GIVING
FOR GAY ADVOCACY

In 1970, RESIST, a Massachusetts-based funder that had supported draft resistance and opposition to the Vietnam War, awarded what is believed to be the first foundation grant to a gay and lesbian organization. The precise amount given to the Gay Liberation Front, a short-lived political group, is lost to history, but the gift marked the birth of a new field of philanthropy. As recently as 1986, giving to gay and lesbian causes was still tiny ($772,000 that year) but it proceeded to grow explosively—to $11 million in 1998, $49 million in 2004, and $129 million in 2013.

During the 1980s, the overwhelming majority of gay philanthropy involved health services, in response to the spread of HIV and AIDS. First

POLICY

there was donor funding for direct medical care at clinics. Then came a giant advocacy push for more government spending—which rose meteorically from $8 million (1982) to $30 billion (2014) at the federal level alone.

With radical groups like ACT UP and Queer Nation using protests to gain political traction, discrimination and "human rights" issues soon moved to the fore. Philanthropic giving became increasingly oriented toward public policy. Groups like the National LGBTQ Task Force (organizing), GLAAD (advocacy), PFLAG (support groups), Lambda Legal (litigation), and Human Rights Campaign (advocacy and lobbying) began to rake in tens of millions of dollars in contributions. During the decade starting in 2004, promotion of gay marriage became a dominant issue, with nonprofits like Freedom to Marry receiving multimillions for action campaigns.

In 2013, more than half of all philanthropic donations to gay causes came either from foundations wholly focused on gay issues (37 percent) or anonymous givers (12 percent). Of the remaining gifts, 44 percent came from multi-issue foundations, and 7 percent from corporations. The top funders that year (after the $17 million given anonymously) were the Arcus ($17 million), Ford ($15 million), Gill ($8 million), and Haas ($6 million) foundations.

The vast portion of this philanthropy is directed toward advocacy, litigation, media campaigns, political organizing, and other policy-related work. Only 11 percent of gay-related giving from 1970 to 2010 went for direct services to gay populations.

In the past decade, about 800 institutions and thousands of individual donors have given nearly a billion dollars to gay causes. With more than nine tenths of gay-oriented giving having emerged within the last decade and a half, this new field is likely to continue to mushroom in the future.

ᵇ PhilAphorism

The more government takes the place of associations, the more will individuals lose the idea of forming associations and need the government to come to their help. That is a vicious circle of cause and effect.

ᵇ*Alexis de Tocqueville*

Further reading

- 2013 tracking report for gay philanthropy, lgbtfunders.org/files/2013_Tracking_Report.pdf
- *Forty Years of LBGTQ Philanthropy 1970-2010*, lgbtfunders.org/files/40years_lgbtqphilanthrophy.pdf

1970

ENVIRONMENTAL LAWSUITS

Environmental conservation was a part of the Ford Foundation's program as early as 1952, when it provided seed money to Resources for the Future to conduct economic research on nature issues. Over the years, Ford dedicated tens of millions of dollars to RFF. In the 1960s, however, the foundation's focus shifted.

Ford had been experimenting with shaping public policy by sponsoring litigation from public-interest law firms like the NAACP Legal Defense and Educational Fund (see 1967 and 1969 entries). Now it sought to apply this lawsuit model to the new environmental movement. One of its initial grants supplied $100,000 to the Rachel Carson Fund of the Audubon Society to sue for restrictions on the use of DDT for mosquito control.

In 1970, the question of whether groups dedicated to filing environmental lawsuits should quality as tax-exempt was resolved in favor of the activists, and the Ford Foundation began a period of vigorous financial support. A grant of $410,000 launched the Natural Resources Defense Council, and by 1977 that group had received $2.6 million of Ford money—which it used to sue the Army Corps of Engineers over dams, push for the expansion of the Clean Air Act, and block oil drilling in the Arctic National Wildlife Refuge. By 2014, NRDC was raising $129 million per year.

The Ford Foundation also helped launch the Environmental Defense Fund ($994,000 in grants between 1971 and 1977), the Sierra Club Legal Defense Fund ($603,000 over the same period), and the Southern California Center for Law in the Public Interest ($1.6 million). These donations built a network of legal institutions that allowed environmental activists to become involved in countless lawsuits and regulatory disputes. Litigation is now one of the most influential tools by which the environmental movement changes society.

Further reading

- Robert Mitchell, *From Conservation to Environmental Movement: The Development of the Modern Environmental Lobbies* (Resources for the Future, 1985)
- Duke University case study, cspcs.sanford.duke.edu/sites/default/files/descriptive/environmental_public_interest_law_centers.pdf

POLICY

1969

ETHNIC-RIGHTS LAWSUITS

Upon deciding to make a major push for black rights during the 1960s, the Ford Foundation started funding the NAACP Legal Defense and Educational Fund (see 1967 entry). It quickly expanded that effort by setting up similar organizations to launch lawsuits on behalf of other minority groups. (This went beyond lawsuits alone. Ford also funded groups like the Mexican American Youth Organization, a militant arm of the Chicano movement that preached separatism, disseminated revolutionary literature, sponsored visits to Cuba, and registered voters.)

One ethnic litigator receiving Ford Foundation money was the Mexican American Legal Defense and Educational Fund. MALDEF received its first Ford grant in 1969: $2.2 million of startup sponsorship. By 1973, MALDEF had attracted additional donors, but the Ford Foundation still supplied about half of its budget. The group plunged into voting-rights battles, guaranteeing the creation of Hispanic-majority jurisdictions around the country. In 1982, it won a Supreme Court ruling that public schools must open their doors to illegal aliens. The organization filed lawsuits on affirmative action, immigrant rights, and election redistricting. It had a budget of more than $6 million in 2013.

The Native American Rights Fund was also bankrolled by Ford, starting with a pilot grant of $155,000 in 1970, another $95,000 the next year, and a three-year grant of $1.2 million in 1972. NARF had grown into a $9.4 million-per-year organization by 2013.

The Ford Foundation also supported the creation of the Puerto Rican Legal Defense and Education Fund in 1972. Many of its lawsuits focused on language rights. Today the group is known as LatinoJustice, with a budget just under $3 million. It frequently works in conjunction with NAACP-LDF and MALDEF.

Between 1967 and 1975, the Ford Foundation spent $18 million specifically to create and build up civil-rights litigation groups; their lawsuits redirected many aspects of American public policy and social practice in ensuing years.

Further reading

○ Robert McKay, *Nine for Equality Under Law: Civil Rights Litigation* (Ford Foundation, 1977)

○ Duke University case study, cspcs.sanford.duke.edu/sites/default/files/descriptive/civil_rights_litigation.pdf

1968

CARNEGIE PUSHES A "G.I. BILL" FOR THE POOR

In 1967, the Carnegie Corporation announced formation of the Carnegie Commission on Higher Education, headed by Clark Kerr, who had just been fired as president of the University of California for failing to overcome campus unrest. The commission was promised at least five years of funding and the effort ended up running for a full dozen years, with the foundation devoting about $12 million to its work.

Between 1967 and 1979 this initiative churned out 37 policy reports and 137 research and technical reports. The most consequential result was a push for greater federal responsibility for higher education. "One of the most urgent national priorities for higher education," insisted a 1968 clarion call, "is the removal of financial barriers for all youth." The recommendations were characterized as a "G.I. bill" for the poor.

Members of Congress duly proposed legislation based on the Carnegie suggestions. Within a few years, the federal government had established an elaborate apparatus of grants and loans for college students. Today, Pell Grants are probably the best-known element of the system. In 2014, nearly 9 million students received about $30 billion in federal Pell Grants.

Further reading

○ Retrospective on the Carnegie Commission and Council on Higher Education, cshe.berkeley.edu/sites/default/files/shared/publications/docs/ROP.Douglass. Carnegie.14.05.pdf

○ Ellen Lagemann, *The Politics of Knowledge: The Carnegie Corporation, Philanthropy, and Public Policy* (Wesleyan University Press, 1989)

1967

RACE-RIGHTS LAWSUITS

In 1967, the Ford Foundation decided to become a major funder of the civil-rights movement. By 1970 it was spending 40 percent of its grantmaking on minorities. Much of the money went to advocating for new government policies or spending aimed at economic enrichment of minorities. Another important slice went to litigation for civil-rights causes.

The foundation started with a 1967 grant of $1 million to the NAACP Legal Defense and Educational Fund. This organization had been involved in the 1954 desegregation suit *Brown v. Board of Education* and many other cases since its establishment in 1940. With Ford as a backer, the NAACP-

POLICY

LDF ratcheted up the lawsuits, and migrated from a commitment to equal opportunity and toward an embrace of equal results.

In 1971, the LDF's *Griggs v. Duke Power* case established the principle of disparate impact—which held that even policies of colorblind neutrality would be considered discriminatory if they produced uneven racial outcomes. The NAACP-LDF went on to become a major promoter of racial preferences in public employment, contracting, and education.

The organization also functioned as an incubator of politicians and advocates. Obama Attorney General Eric Holder, Massachusetts Governor Deval Patrick, Harvard Law School professor Lani Guinier and others worked for the NAACP-LDF. In 2014 it had a budget of about $16 million.

Further reading

○ Richard Magat, *The Ford Foundation at Work* (Plenum Press, 1979)

1966

FORD INVENTS ADVOCACY PHILANTHROPY

From the time of the Gilded Age—when many political and journalistic careers were built by taking shots at robber barons—wealthy donors and large foundations tended to be skittish about taking up controversial political causes. It wasn't until the 1960s that public-policy philanthropy became popular, and the individual who did the most to light that fire was Ford Foundation president McGeorge Bundy. Having moved into his post directly from the Johnson White House, it was a short step for Bundy to plunge his new employer into racial issues, ethnic politics, environmental lawsuits, poverty policy, and feminist litigation.

The foundation didn't lobby directly, but formulated ideas and promoted strategies that would lead to legislation, regulations, and court cases advancing liberal policies like affirmative action, disarmament, and welfare transfers. Litigation by new "public-interest" legal groups was a special focus. (For some details, see the five Ford-related entries on this list between 1967 and 1972.)

The Council for Public Interest Law—which was created by the Ford Foundation specifically to help coordinate legal activism on the left—surveyed 86 groups pushing "public-interest law" in 1975. It found that 70 percent of them had popped up from 1969-1974, when Ford was seeding this oyster bed. These groups reported receiving $61 million from donors during that five-year period, with more than half of that total coming from Ford itself. Fully 589 salaried attorneys were then employed by these 86 groups, which have since grown into even more potent policy-shapers like the Natural Resources Defense Council and the Center for Law and Social Policy.

Bundy viewed this effort as an extension of earlier policy-related maneuvering by Ford. In the 1950s and '60s, Ford funding powered much of the urban renewal movement—which demolished slums, built new government-run subsidized housing, and launched an array of social programs for residents. Ford programs were picked up directly by Lyndon Johnson as germs of his "Great Society" expansion of welfare spending and social activism.

But the aggressiveness with which Bundy moved into advocacy philanthropy (including paying for enormous amounts of litigation) produced lots of friction and political backlash. Ford's 1968 funding for radical community school boards in New York City, for instance, was a spectacular failure that inflamed race relations in that metro area for an entire generation. Resentment over what was viewed as the Ford Foundation's over-aggressive involvement in political questions spurred heavier regulation of foundations in the 1970s, and new controversy about whether charitable donations should even be tax deductible.

Further reading

○ *Philanthropy* magazine essay, philanthropyroundtable.org/topic/excellence_in_ philanthropy/foundations_and_public_policy

MAKING A CASE FOR GOVERNMENT ARTS SPENDING

Founded by businessman Edward Filene in 1919, the Twentieth Century Fund (rechristened the Century Fund in 1999) shaped the course of arts philanthropy by sponsoring the work of Princeton University economists William Baumol and William Bowen. In a 1965 academic paper, they described a phenomenon that has earned the nickname "Baumol's cost disease." A society's rising wealth threatens its artistry, they argued, because the wages of artists increase but not their productivity. "The output per man-hour of the violist playing a Schubert quartet in a standard concert hall is relatively fixed." To continue flourishing, the professors contended, the art world would require subsidies from the government.

Baumol and Bowen turned their Twentieth Century Fund work into a 1966 book, *The Performing Arts: The Economic Dilemma*, that became a kind of bible for advocates of public spending on the arts. A few other philanthropists were promoting a similar line: The Rockefeller Brothers Fund underwrote a study led by Nancy Hanks (who subsequently became the second chairman of the National Endowment for the Arts) that also pressed for federal funding of the arts.

The NEA had just been set up by the federal government in 1965. Its initial appropriation of a mere $3 million immediately spiked upward. The endowment's budget reached $175 million in 1992. Its involvement in political controversies later reduced its annual funding, but in 2014, the NEA received more than $146 million in federal support.

Further reading

° Baumol and Bowen 1965 paper, pages.stern.nyu.edu/~wbaumol/
  OnThePerformingArtsTheAnatomyOfTheirEcoProbs.pdf

° Abridged version of Rockefeller/Hanks Report, images.library.wisc.edu/Arts/EFacs/
  ArtsSoc/ArtsSocv03i3/reference/arts.artssocv03i3.rockefeller.pdf

1964

BUFFETT BILLIONS FOR ABORTION

The biographer of billionaire investor and donor Warren Buffett describes him as having "a Malthusian dread" of population growth among the poor. In 1964 he set up an Omaha foundation centered on stopping that growth, both domestically and abroad, and to this day, the *New York Times* summarizes, "most of the foundation's spending goes to abortion and contraception." Buffett and his first wife put several billion dollars into the foundation, making it the third largest in the country as of 2015. He heads it along with his children, and both its domestic and international programs are directed by veteran abortion activists. (For other causes, Buffett channels his money through the Bill & Melinda Gates Foundation.)

Buffett has put time and energy as well as money into this issue. He and his investment partner and fellow donor Charlie Munger were quite involved in *People v. Belous*, a 1969 case paving the way for abortion in California on privacy grounds, which was cited during the *Roe v. Wade* debate. After abortion was allowed in California but still illegal in most states, Buffet and Munger set up a "church" which they dubbed the "Ecumenical Fellowship," and used it as a kind of underground railroad to transport women to Los Angeles and other cities for quick abortions. The Buffett Foundation has even promoted the partial-birth method of abortion (in which a later-term child is partially delivered but dismembered before emerging from the birth canal). The foundation financed early lawsuits and legal work to overturn bans on partial-birth abortion. These went all the way to the U.S. Supreme Court before a federal ban ultimately was upheld.

After examining his foundation's IRS filings, the Media Research Center reported that Buffett's grants to abortion groups just from 1989 to 2012 (with the tax returns from 1997 to 2000 missing) totaled at least $1.3 billion. And the Buffett Foundation's spending in this area was accelerating rapidly as the 2000s unfolded. Beneficiaries of Buffett's giving include Planned Parenthood ($300 million), NARAL, National Abortion Federation, Catholics for a Free Choice, Abortion Access Project, Population Council, Marie Stopes International, Center for Reproductive Rights, and dozens of other such advocates.

Buffett Foundation donations were instrumental in creating the abortion drug RU-486 and pushing it through clinical trials. The family foundation has funded many programs that teach clinicians how to perform abortions. And it has given hundreds of millions of dollars—more than any other foundation in existence—to groups providing contraception, sterilization, and abortion to poor women overseas.

Further reading

○ *Inside Philanthropy* on Buffett Foundation, insidephilanthropy.com/home/2014/2/4/whos-who-at-the-secretive-susan-thompson-buffett-foundation.html

○ *New York Times* magazine touches on Buffett funding for abortion, nytimes.com/2010/07/18/magazine/18abortion-t.html?pagewanted=all

○ 2014 Media Research Center calculation of total giving, mrc.org/articles/warren-buffett-billion-dollar-king-abortion

○ Bloomberg reporting, bloomberg.com/news/articles/2015-07-30/warren-buffett-s-family-secretly-funded-a-birth-control-revolution

1964

A REPORT CARD FOR SCHOOLS

As policymakers began to focus on improving the performance of public schools, they felt the need for accurate ways to track student achievement. In 1963, U.S. Commissioner of Education Francis Keppel turned to the Carnegie Corporation for help. The foundation immediately sponsored a pair of conferences, and in 1964 created the Exploratory Committee on Assessing the Progress of Education.

Carnegie rapidly disbursed more than $2.4 million to develop a set of standard tests that would allow U.S. educational performance to be reliably measured and assessed over time. Carnegie's grants led to the National Assessment of Educational Progress, now known as "the nation's report card." The NAEP tests are taken by American students every two years, and have become "the largest nationally representative and continuing assessment of what America's students know and can do in various subject areas." If educators, policymakers, media, and the public are to gauge the improvement or decline of American schools—accurately, across eras, without ax-grinding or wishful thinking—there has to be a consistent, widely accepted yardstick.

POLICY

NAEP is that accountability device, and it has been essential to the rise of the educational excellence movement over the last 30 years.

In the 1980s, additional important refinements of the NAEP testing regimen were made with philanthropic support from the Lyle Spencer Foundation. In NAEP's early days, education bureaucrats worried about unflattering comparisons got state-by-state data collections and comparisons banned. A panel headed by Spencer's Thomas James and Tennessee governor Lamar Alexander managed to have that prohibition removed, and since then, state comparisons have become a powerful force for motivating higher educational standards in places that are lagging.

Further reading

- History of NAEP's creation, nagb.org/content/nagb/assets/documents/ publications/95222.pdf

- Ellen Lagemann, *The Politics of Knowledge: The Carnegie Corporation, Philanthropy, and Public Policy* (Wesleyan University Press, 1989)

1962

DISARMAMENT LOBBIES

The arms control and disarmament movement is a product of philanthropy. The earliest influential donor was Andrew Carnegie, an internationalist and pacifist who felt sure that war could be banished through stronger international laws and group efforts for peace. (See 1910 entry about the Carnegie Endowment for International Peace.)

Another longstanding donor-supported organization with a focus on disarmament is the Council for a Livable World. Founded in 1962 as a 501(c)(4) advocacy organization, the nonprofit is active in lobbying against military

∿ PhilAphorism

Donors represent a private version of the legislative process—a deliberative process that selects goals, sets values, and allocates resources.... an alternative vehicle for getting things done.

☞ *Paul Ylvisaker*

spending and in favor of dovish defense policies. It was a major backer of the nuclear-freeze movement (see 1981 entry), and has throughout its history been heavily involved in steering giving to candidates for political office who are devoted to disarmament. The organization has a special fund that earmarks campaign donations, and a separate PeacePAC.

In 1980 the council spun off a sister organization, the Center for Arms Control and Non-Proliferation. It promotes pacific positions on homeland security, defense budgets, and weapons development, and urges accommodation to the nuclear-weapons programs of Iran and North Korea. The center is largely supported by individual donors.

Another prominent voice for disarmament is the Arms Control Association. It was established in 1971 by the Carnegie Endowment for International Peace as part of its effort to modernize the pacifist message. The association continues to receive Carnegie funding, as well as grants from funders like the Ford, MacArthur, Mott, and Hewlett foundations, and the Ploughshares Fund.

Further reading

○ Council for a Livable World history, livableworld.org/who/legacy

1960

PUTTING BAIL ON
A SCIENTIFIC FOOTING

When Louis Schweitzer heard that a thousand boys had languished in a Brooklyn prison for at least ten months without trial, he was astonished and disappointed. Schweitzer, an immigrant from Ukraine who had thrived in the United States, thought of the Eighth Amendment in the U.S. Constitution's Bill of Rights with its prohibition on "excessive bail." The boys were not necessarily guilty, but they were too poor to pay an appearance bond.

Schweitzer engaged the services of Herb Sturz, a young journalist who had written on the Bill of Rights, to examine the problem. This was the birth of the Vera Foundation. Its first effort was called the Manhattan Bail Project.

With a seed grant of $95,000 from Schweitzer, then $25,000 in each of the next two years, Sturz examined the backgrounds of thousands of defendants, trying to determine which ones posed flight risks (and therefore required incarceration) and which ones could be released with reasonable confidence that they would show up for trial. Factors like work history, family structure, previous criminal history, military service, and so forth were tested in various weightings. With the cooperation of New York City mayor Robert Wagner, which Schweitzer procured, a three-year experiment was run where more than 3,500 accused people were released without bail, based on the

POLICY

recommendations of Vera. Only about 60 of them failed to appear at trial for reasons within their control.

Based on these results, New York courts overhauled their bail procedures, informed by the Bail Project algorithms. In 1966, crediting the influence of the Vera Foundation's work, President Lyndon Johnson signed the Bail Reform Act. Vera eventually turned its attention to other areas, spinning off a series of nonprofit groups involved with employment, drug addiction, immigration, and victim services. Now known as the Vera Institute for Justice, the group is a $31 million-per-year organization that studies criminal-justice policy and supports demonstration projects. At this point only one third of the Institute's funding comes from private donations, the rest is now provided by federal or state governments.

Further reading

○ Sam Roberts, *A Kind of Genius: Herb Sturz and Society's Toughest Problems* (PublicAffairs, 2009)

1960

PIERRE GOODRICH AND THE LIBERTY FUND

Pierre Goodrich was a successful Indianapolis businessman; as son of a former governor he had a deep interest in public affairs; and he loved to read the great classic books. Convinced that a commitment to human liberty and moral goodness needed to be nurtured anew in each generation, he established the Liberty Fund in 1960. Its mission, he wrote, was to contribute "to the preservation, restoration, and development of individual liberty through investigation, research, and educational activity." When Goodrich died in 1973 he left most of his estate to the fund; further bequests from his widow gave it assets of about $300 million.

Through most of the 1970s the Liberty Fund was a grantmaking foundation. In 1979, it transformed itself into an operating foundation that sponsors its own programs. By 2014, it had hosted about 3,500 small, invitation-only conferences for scholars and students on topics such as "Liberty and Markets in the Writings of Adam Smith" and "Shakespeare's Conception of Political Liberty." It has published more than 300 new editions of classic books, such as *Democracy in America* by Alexis de Tocqueville and *Human Action: A Treatise on Economics* by Ludwig von Mises. In addition to the conferences and books, the Liberty Fund maintains a free online library of important writing on freedom, dating back hundreds of years, and including 459 authors writing in a wide range of fields.

Further reading

○ Dane Starbuck, *The Goodriches: An American Family* (Liberty Fund, 2001)

○ David Lasater and Leslie Lenkowsky, "Pierre Goodrich," in *Notable American Philanthropists* (Greenwood Press, 2002)

1959

LAW SCHOOL CLINICS
INSTITUTIONALIZE POLITICAL ACTIVISM

Beginning in 1959, the Ford Foundation gradually established a network of law-school-based legal clinics that became a powerful tool of liberalism. Many professors resisted the effort at first, because the clinics are expensive to operate and can distract students from their academic training. As the Ford Foundation poured millions of dollars into the efforts during the 1960s, however, faculty opposition collapsed. The number of law schools allowing students course credit for clinical work leapt from just 12 in 1968 to 125 in 1972 (out of a total of 147 law schools in the country).

From the start, the agenda was much more than offering useful vocational training to students. The goal favorably cited in a contemporary Ford Foundation report was to "reinforce the social consciousness of certain law students and professors through confrontation with injustice and misery." The clinics, which were openly built on political activism, would also be a tool for changing the cities where they operated. The one at Columbia University Law School pledged to use the law to fight "poverty, racism, inequality, and political tyranny."

Many Ford-funded, student-fueled clinics opened across the country, and over time they were remarkably successful at pushing liberal policies. Among many other achievements, Ford-funded clinics forced New Jersey to fund abortions, compelled Princeton University's eating clubs to admit women, and put the public schools of Berkeley, California, under judicial control in order to take over the disciplining of black and Hispanic students.

Further reading

- *City Journal* reporting in 2006, city-journal.org/html/16_1_law_schools.html
- Steven Teles, *The Rise of the Conservative Legal Movement: The Battle for Control of the Law* (Princeton University Press,)

1958

PASTOR ROBINSON BLAZES
A PATH FOR THE PEACE CORPS

Drawing on the long American tradition of religious missionary work abroad, Harlem minister James Robinson founded Operation Crossroads Africa with donated money in 1958. Several trips to Africa had convinced him of the need for an interracial service program that would assist poor Africans on a people-to-people basis outside of political considerations. During the summer of 1958, about 60 American students traveled to Cameroon, Ghana, Liberia, Nigeria, and Sierra Leone, where they built schools, assisted with manual labor, and formed friendships with the locals. They each collected donations and put in money out of their own pockets to fund this work.

The Crossroads service model and its philanthropic projects were an inspiration for the Peace Corps. "This group and this effort really were the progenitors of the Peace Corps," said President Kennedy in 1962. Weak management has slowed the program in recent decades, but more than 11,000 volunteers have served in Operation Crossroads Africa since the nonprofit's creation, and about 50 students still go abroad to work on village projects each summer.

Further reading

○ Damon Freeman, "James Robinson," in *Notable American Philanthropists* (Greenwood Press, 2002)

○ Gerard Rice, *The Bold Experiment: JFK's Peace Corps* (University of Notre Dame Press, 1985)

1957

SPAWNING BIRTH CONTROL

Katharine McCormick had grown up in a prominent Chicago family, struggled through eight difficult years to become the second woman to graduate from MIT, then married the emotionally disturbed youngest son of Cyrus McCormick (reaper of the International Harvester fortune). Their marriage was probably never consummated, and her husband soon spiraled into horrifying mental illness and decades of institutionalization. Katharine poured her energies into the nascent women's movement. She became an officer of the National American Woman Suffrage Association, was heavily involved in organizing and funding the campaign to ratify the Nineteenth Amendment to the Constitution, and became vice president of the League of Women Voters after ratification.

When her mother died in 1937, Katharine inherited $10 million, and the death of her husband in 1947 left her additional tens of millions. It took five years to conclude family battles and pay inheritance taxes, but once the estate was settled Katharine was rich. She asked Margaret Sanger (the founder of what would become Planned Parenthood and a friend made through suffrage politics) for advice on where she might make a difference with her money.

Sanger had long dreamed of a means of preventing pregnancy that would be as easy as taking an aspirin, so in 1953 she introduced McCormick to a scientist she thought might be able to pull off such a creation. Gregory Pincus was a brilliant biologist but so unobservant of conventional ethical scruples that he had been fired by Harvard and was scraping by in a small lab of his own in Worcester, Massachusetts. At their first meeting, McCormick wrote a check to Pincus for $40,000. She funded him steadily thereafter at $150,000-$180,000 per year—eventually investing more than $2 million in his quest to develop a daily birth-control pill.

McCormick was the sole and entire funder of this work. In today's dollars her contributions come to approximately $20 million. And she was involved in more than just funding. She brushed off suggestions from Sanger and others that she support broad basic research, and spread her contributions across many labs. McCormick wasn't seeking scientific advance; she wanted a consumer product available as soon as possible. She eventually moved from California to Massachusetts to monitor development of the pill and pushed constantly for the researchers to speed the drug trials.

At a time when 30 states still had laws on the books that nominally forbade the sale of contraceptives, the philanthropist and her scientists were intentionally obscure about much of their work. Live trials were conducted on women without their consent or even knowledge. And the drugs had been tested on only about 60 women, for a year or less, when Pincus announced publicly that they had a working birth-control pill. He did this to generate public pressure for FDA approval, which followed quickly in 1957.

The pill was subsequently credited with kicking off the Sexual Revolution and sparking dramatic changes in family life, economic behavior, and social order. Katharine McCormick's indispensable impetus in bankrolling creation of the pill has often been overlooked, but she herself reveled in her accomplishment—even getting a prescription, as a matron in her 80s, so she could buy some of the first birth control in her local pharmacy. Not because she needed it, but because she wanted it.

Further reading

○ PBS film, pbs.org/wgbh/amex/pill/peopleevents/p_mccormick.html

○ Jonathan Eig, *The Birth of the Pill* (Norton, 2014)

AEI GUARDS FREE ENTERPRISE

Founded in 1938 by a group of businessmen aiming to strengthen "free, competitive enterprise," the American Enterprise Association had been only mildly effective when William Baroody arrived in 1954, quitting a comfortable job at the U.S. Chamber of Commerce to do so. Within a generation, he

POLICY

transformed the think tank—renamed the American Enterprise Institute—into one of the great conservative forces in Washington, rallying corporate and philanthropic dollars to make it happen.

Libertarian economist Milton Friedman became an AEI academic adviser, and conservative intellectuals like Irving Kristol, Arthur Burns, Antonin Scalia, Herb Stein, and Michael Novak began long associations with the think tank. At a dinner honoring Baroody's twentieth anniversary at AEI, President Richard Nixon sent a message that praised him for breaking liberalism's "virtual monopoly in the field of ideas." By the time of Ronald Reagan's election, AEI had a budget of $8 million and a stable of innovative thinkers. It helped fill the new administration with personnel like Jeane Kirkpatrick, an AEI foreign-policy expert who became Reagan's ambassador to the United Nations.

AEI's finances sagged in the 1980s, but new president Christopher DeMuth revived donations and lifted the organization to another peak during his 22 years at the helm. He built around scholars and fellows like James Q. Wilson, Charles Murray, Lynne Cheney, Glenn Hubbard, Leon Kass, Robert Bork, Michael Barone, John Bolton, Newt Gingrich, Christina Sommers, and Arthur Brooks. He attracted a large paid circulation for the institute's monthly current-affairs magazine *The American Enterprise*. AEI researchers led policy in many areas: a group convened by Michael Novak set groundwork for the 1994 welfare reform; Frederick Kagan helped the Bush Administration develop the successful troop surge in Iraq; Peter Wallison gave advance warnings of the looming mortgage crisis, and the government role in causing it.

Economist Arthur Brooks became AEI's president in 2009. He greatly expanded the institute's communications capacities, continued to add scholars, became a nationally popular speaker, book writer, and commentator himself at newspapers like the *New York Times* and *Wall Street Journal*, and

ᕍ PhilAphorism

To get the best long-term results the foundation should not only provide grants to help competent men do their best work, but should also seek to increase the supply of competent men.

ᕬ *1949 Ford Foundation report*

demonstrated a flair for fundraising. Gifts of $100 million allowed the group to renovate an historic building on Washington's "Think Tank Row" into its new headquarters. In 2014, AEI raised $41 million, 41 percent of that donated by individuals, 34 percent coming from foundations, and 19 percent contributed by corporations.

Further reading

○ AEI 2014 Annual Report, aei.org/wp-content/uploads/2014/12/2014-Annual-Report-.pdf

ROCKEFELLER III
BIRTHS THE POPULATION COUNCIL

When global population passed 2½ billion in the early 1950s (it is now more than 7 billion), John Rockefeller III was among those convinced that catastrophe was on the way. He believed his family foundation bore some of the responsibility for rising numbers—because its health programs had reduced death rates in poor countries. So he convened a panel of experts for advice on blunting population growth. They called attention to the cultural, religious, and political sensitivities that would complicate any intervention into matters of sex and fertility, and the Rockefeller Foundation refused to adopt "overpopulation" as an area of interest.

John III, however, was adamant. With a personal grant of $100,000 he founded a new group called the Population Council, and followed that soon after with a $1.25 million donation. Soon, the Rockefeller Brothers Fund joined the cause. Before long, the Ford Foundation pitched in $600,000, followed by a $1.4 million Ford grant later in the 1950s. (Ford continues to be a significant donor to the council today.) Eventually the Rockefeller Foundation itself became a major donor. Foundations like Mellon, Hewlett, Packard, and Gates became involved later, and the Population Council now operates in scores of countries, spending $87 million in 2014.

From its beginning, the Population Council was associated with eugenics. Its first president, Frederick Osborn, was a founding member of the American Eugenics Society. Eugenics and alarm about population growth were entwined for decades, and there has been no shortage of wealthy philanthropists willing to spend money to reduce births among poor families in other countries.

This topic has always generated controversy. In 1959, reacting to a proposal for U.S. government funding for fertility control in other countries, President Dwight Eisenhower declared that he "could not imagine anything more emphatically a subject that is not a proper political or governmental activity." But by 1965 President Lyndon Johnson was asserting that "five dollars invested

POLICY

in population control is worth a hundred dollars invested in economic growth."

Coercive measures controlling family size in China, India, and other countries led to protests and suspensions of international funding on several occasions. Even amid backlashes against eugenics, coercive fertility control, and population alarmism, donors ranging from the MacArthur and Scaife foundations to Ted Turner and Warren Buffett have made large donations to a cause they viewed as a crisis. And government agencies like the World Bank, United Nations, and the U.S. Agency for International Development have also been heavily committed to reducing births in foreign countries. Fully 69 percent of the Population Council's $75 million of grant revenue in 2014 came from governments.

Further reading

○ Peter Collier and David Horowitz, *The Rockefellers: An American Dynasty* (Holt, Rinehart, and Winston 1976)

○ Matthew Connelly, *Fatal Misconception: The Struggle to Control World Population* (Harvard University Press, 2008)

1950

PHILANTHROPISTS VS. COMMUNISM

During America's Cold War with the Soviet Union, many philanthropists hoped that the confrontation could be settled peacefully through a competition of ideas rather than with weapons. In the end, it was. Early on, the big foundations—Carnegie, Ford, and Rockefeller—spent tens of millions of dollars creating new "area studies" programs at universities to churn out experts with the language, cultural, and historical skills needed for diplomacy, analysis, popular communications, and intelligence-gathering in communist countries. (See 1952 item on our companion list of achievements in Education.)

Many foundations battled Marxist ideas in partnership with the Central Intelligence Agency. The initial meeting of the Congress for Cultural Freedom, a group of anti-communist liberals, was held in Berlin in 1950, sponsored by a mix of philanthropic money and CIA grants. "Friends, freedom has seized the offensive!" declared Arthur Koestler, author of the influential book *Darkness at Noon* and a CCF organizer.

The CCF would thrive over two decades, growing to employ 280 staffers and operating in 35 countries, making the positive case for cultural and economic liberalism. The goal was not only to confront the Soviet Union, but also to fend off communism in countries like Greece and Turkey, and to balance the communist parties that actively vied for influence in elections in France, Italy, and other western European nations. The CCF published a number of anti-communist magazines, including *Encounter*, a well-read London-based literary journal founded by poet Stephen Spender and intellectual Irving Kristol, whose contributors included individuals like Albert Camus, George Kennan, Isaiah Berlin, Vladimir Nabokov, Arthur Koestler, Jorge Luis Borges, and V. S. Naipaul.

More than a hundred U.S. foundations worked with the CIA in funding such causes early in the Cold War, out of patriotic duty and alarm over the spread of totalitarianism. When parts of the American press began to criticize these efforts in the later 1960s, CIA funds dried up and foundations began to refuse to cooperate, especially as liberals abandoned anti-communism during the Vietnam War. Much of the intellectual capital that allowed the West to successfully resist the spread of communist governance, however, was built up during the opening stages of the Cold War by this quiet partnership between philanthropists and intelligence analysts.

Further reading

○ Peter Coleman, *The Liberal Conspiracy: The Congress for Cultural Freedom and the Struggle for the Mind of Postwar Europe* (Free Press, 1989)

○ Frances Saunders, *The Cultural Cold War: The CIA and the World of Arts and Letters* (New Press, 1999)

○ *Philanthropy* magazine history, philanthropyroundtable.org/topic/excellence_in_philanthropy/victory

VOLKER BOLSTERS ECONOMIC LIBERTY

William Volker was a millionaire by age 47, and could have been so earlier had he not begun each workday by meeting with anyone who asked and writing checks to help many of them, giving away perhaps one third of his income. He had been powerfully impressed as a young boy when his German-immigrant family arrived in Chicago shortly after the Great Fire and saw "a vast spontaneous system of relief supported by charitable persons." When he grew up he did his part to keep such neighborly assistance alive. "Mr. Anonymous" was a devout Christian and very active in the civic life of his adopted Kansas City, Missouri.

In 1910, Volker helped the Kansas City government create the nation's first municipal welfare department. He was soon disillusioned, however, by political manipulation of the funds. "Political charity isn't charity," Volker concluded. Later in his life Volker discovered the free-market thinker Friedrich Hayek, whose analysis of the ways government is often kidnapped by special interests helped Volker make sense of his experience.

POLICY

When Hayek, amid Western Europe's flirtation with Marxism, was trying to organize a meeting of free-market economists in Mont Pelerin, Switzerland, he worried that no Americans would attend due to the high cost of travel. Volker's foundation came to the rescue with a check that allowed 17 Americans to fly across the ocean for the 1947 gathering. The American attendees included Milton Friedman, Henry Hazlitt, Leonard Read, George Stigler, and Ludwig von Mises (who was not an American but was teaching in New York). The Mont Pelerin Society, as the resulting group came to be called, went on to become a leading hub of free-market thinking. Eight of its members have won the Nobel Prize in economics. Many others have held important government posts in the U.S. and elsewhere.

Under the influence of Volker's nephew and business partner, Harold Luhnow, the Volker Fund continued to play a role in the re-emergence of free-market thinking during the twentieth century. At a time when few other philanthropists showed any interest, it supported organizations that made the case for liberty in the Western cultural tradition.

In 1956, the Volker Fund sponsored a series of lectures by Milton Friedman that evolved into his seminal book *Capitalism and Freedom.* "This series of conferences stands out as among the most stimulating intellectual experiences of my life," wrote Friedman in the preface. The Volker Fund also underwrote the fellowship that allowed Friedrich Hayek to teach at the University of Chicago for many years (which helped cement that campus as a center of classical liberalism and home for subsequent scholars like Milton Friedman, George Stigler, Ronald Coase, Gary Becker, Eugene Fama, Robert Fogel, Lars Hansen, and Robert Lucas—all winners of Nobel Prizes in economics), as well as grants that supported Ludwig von Mises at New York University.

Further reading

○ Herbert Cornuelle, *"Mr. Anonymous": The Story of William Volker* (Caxton Printers, 1951)

○ R. M. Hartwell, *A History of the Mont Pelerin Society* (Liberty Fund, 1995)

1946

ROCKEFELLER KEEPS THE U.N. IN THE U.S.

When the United Nations was created in 1945, after the trauma of World War II, it lacked a home. The organization initially met in cramped quarters at Manhattan's Hunter College and on Long Island. The inadequate arrangements forced the new body to look for permanent accommodations in other cities or overseas. Switzerland was a possibility. Hours before a final decision was due, John Rockefeller Jr. swooped in with an irresistible offer:

He would buy 17 acres along the East River in Manhattan and donate it to the international organization. The U.N. quickly accepted the multimillion-dollar gift.

Rockefeller was motivated by a hope that the U.N. could help avert future catastrophes like the previous world wars, and that having the organization in the United States made it less likely that it would stray into mistaken or irrelevant policies. He also saw practical benefits: New York City would enjoy economic benefits, American diplomats would have easy access to counterparts in a convenient location, and U.S. intelligence could keep an eye on foreign officials.

Further reading

○ Raymond Fosdick, *John D. Rockefeller Jr.: A Portrait* (Harper & Brothers, 1956)

○ Peter Collier and David Horowitz, *The Rockefellers: An American Dynasty* (Holt, Rinehart, and Winston, 1976)

1946

RAND CORPORATION

There was recognition after World War II that one of the important factors allowing the U.S. to win the war was an unprecedented mobilization of scientific and industrial resources by a combination of private companies, philanthropists, and government. (See, for instance, 1940 item on the creation of radar on our list of Prosperity achievements.) In 1946 the U.S. Army launched an effort to institutionalize such cooperative research free from government bureaucracy, calling it Project RAND (for research and development). In 1948, the Ford Foundation provided a $1 million interest-free loan, plus a guarantee on a private bank loan, to allow the organization to become an independent nonprofit called the RAND Corporation. This was the first of many grants from Ford to RAND.

National-security issues dominated RAND's initial research agenda. Its first report, involving satellites, was issued a decade before *Sputnik*. The group's experts subsequently formulated nuclear strategies, proposed new weapons, and started fresh fields like terrorism studies and systems analysis (which aims to improve organizational decision-making). RAND's early research on computers helped develop the Internet, and its researchers sped magnetic-core memory, video recording, and other technologies.

The nonprofit gradually evolved into a broad "think tank" (one of the first progenitors of such organizations). Today, RAND remains active on military topics but also studies everything from obesity to educational accountability. In 2014, it had revenues of $270 million, with about half coming from the

POLICY

Pentagon and most of the rest from non-military government agencies. Roughly 10 percent came from philanthropic contributions.

Further reading

○ RAND history from *Invention & Technology*, rand.org/pubs/reprints/RP1396.html

○ Alex Abella, *Soldiers of Reason: The RAND Corporation and the Rise of the American Empire* (Harcourt, 2009)

1936

LAYING THE INTELLECTUAL FOUNDATION FOR RACIAL EQUALITY

In 1935, the board of the Carnegie Corporation expressed interest in "Negro problems" in the United States, and the extent to which they could be reduced through education. This led to a decision to commission a study of the issue. For reasons of objectivity, the foundation sought a European scholar to conduct the work, settling in 1936 on Swedish economist Gunnar Myrdal, who had spent 1929 and 1930 in the U.S. as a Rockefeller Foundation Fellow, and who later went on to win the Nobel Prize in economics. The Carnegie Corporation arranged a two-month tour of the South for Myrdal, guided by a knowledgeable official of Rockefeller's General Education Board. They gave Myrdal $300,000 of funding, with which he commissioned 40 research memoranda from experts on different aspects of race issues. Beyond this, the foundation gave Myrdal wide latitude for his investigation.

 PhilAphorism

Society is produced by our wants, and government by our wickedness. The former promotes our happiness positively by uniting our affections, the latter negatively by restraining our vices. The one encourages intercourse, the other creates distinctions. The first is a patron, the last a punisher.

Thomas Paine

Drawing from the research papers and his own observations during his Southern tour, Myrdal wrote a 1,500-page book called *An American Dilemma*, which the Carnegie Corporation published in 1944. The book took a basically positive view of the potential of black Americans and the ability of U.S. society to transform itself to accommodate them as productive and equal citizens, and strongly influenced the public view of race relations. It sold over 100,000 copies, and its second edition published in 1965 influenced the civil-rights activism of that time. The study was cited in five different Supreme Court opinions, including the *Brown v. Board of Education* case that ushered in full racial integration.

Further reading

○ Gunnar Myrdal, *An America Dilemma: The Negro Problem and American Democracy* (Harper & Row, 1944)

BUILDING THE ACLU

Charles Garland, age 21, told the executor of his father's estate that he would not accept the inheritance left to him because it came from "a system which starves thousands." When they saw press reports describing this decision, radical activists Upton Sinclair and Roger Baldwin urged Charles to accept the money and devote it to left-wing political causes. Baldwin, who had just founded the American Civil Liberties Union, managed to persuade the young man. Garland used his father's money to establish the American Fund for Public Service, commonly known as the Garland Fund, in 1921.

A board was appointed whose members included the prominent socialist Norman Thomas and Benjamin Gitlow, a founding member of the Communist Party USA. Garland attached few requirements, letting the trustees decide how to disburse the money. The fund resolved not to support political parties or religious organizations, preferring radical journalism, labor unions, and Marxist causes.

The ACLU turned out to be the fund's most consequential grantee. Garland money was crucial in helping the ACLU grow into an influential policy organization promoting free speech, secularism, gay rights, and other liberal causes. By 2015, annual spending by the ACLU topped $134 million.

The Garland Fund dissolved in 1941 after spending all of its assets.

Further reading

○ Gloria Samson, *The American Fund for Public Service: Charles Garland and Radical Philanthropy, 1922-1941* (Greenwood Press, 1996)

○ Merle Curti, "Subsidizing Radicalism: The American Fund for Public Service, 1921-41," *Social Service Review* (September 1959)

POLICY

HOOVER INSTITUTION

Fresh from leading humanitarian relief efforts during World War I, future President Herbert Hoover founded the Hoover Institution on War, Revolution, and Peace at Stanford University in 1919. His goal was to create an archive on the Great War so that future generations would learn its lessons. With an initial gift of $50,000, Hoover funded scholars to travel to Europe so they could hunt down relevant historical documents and bring them back to Stanford. The Hoover Institution soon focused on other aspects of twentieth-century history— most notably the Russian Revolution and the development of the Soviet Union. Hoover encouraged ambitious scholarship and publication, with an eye toward warning Americans about the dangers of communism.

Following his one term as President (1929-1933), Hoover returned to his namesake organization. He eventually came into conflict with the increasingly liberal faculty at Stanford, and in 1959 wrested control of the Hoover Institution from the professors, ensuring its independence while maintaining a link to the university. His statement to the Stanford trustees that year outlines the mission of his organization:

> This Institution supports the Constitution of the United States... and its method of representative government. Both our social and economic systems are based on private enterprise from which springs initiative and ingenuity.... Ours is a system where the Federal Government should undertake no governmental, social or economic action, except where local government, or the people, cannot undertake it for themselves.... This Institution is...to recall man's endeavors to make and preserve peace, and to sustain for America the safeguards of the American way of life.

Major donors to the Hoover Institution in its early decades included Alfred Sloan Jr., Jeremiah Milbank, and the Lilly family. Over time, the organization grew into an important think tank. Its experts provided public-policy advice to Ronald Reagan when he was governor of California. Top-flight scholars took up residence—like Robert Conquest, Milton Friedman, and Thomas Sowell.

Even as it became an important policy generator, the institution remained true to its historical mission, providing a home for the papers of Friedrich Hayek, for Hoover himself outside of his years in national government (those records are at his Presidential library in Iowa), and for rich archives in areas like communism, war and peace, intelligence, business and commerce, and more.

The Hoover Institution's budget was $47 million in 2014, with 59 percent of its income coming as philanthropic gifts, and 39 percent more deriving from earnings on its endowment of several hundred million dollars.

Further reading

○ George Nash, *Herbert Hoover and Stanford University* (Hoover Institution Press, 1988)

1919

PRIVATE SCHOLARLY
INSTITUTES TO GUIDE GOVERNMENT

In its early years, Andrew Carnegie's main foundation, the Carnegie Corporation, had a Republican board that was anxious to improve the quality of American governance without increasing the size of government. Toward this end, the corporation began to make grants creating independent advisory groups that aimed to elevate the quality of information available to government officials. Beginning in 1919, Carnegie and allied funders set up a whole series of private research institutes and scientific councils that, as historian Ellen Lagemann puts it, "would be accessible to the federal government but not controlled by it." The aim was to encourage an "associative state," where experts supported by private philanthropy could improve the policymaking process and help solve national problems while preserving America's traditionally limited sphere of government action.

Carnegie and Rockefeller funds led this effort by establishing the National Research Council during World War I. It was tasked with helping solve important military problems by serving as a "department of invention and development." Drawing on numerous scientists, the council brought the government many military advances, including nascent sonar systems for detecting submarines, intelligence tests used to classify army recruits, and range finders for airplanes. In 1919 the Carnegie Corporation donated $5 million to make the National Research Council a permanent adviser to government, under the wing of a revived National Academy of Sciences. A headquarters building and a permanent endowment were created with the Carnegie money, and today the NRC conducts hundreds of studies every year to guide and improve federal operations.

Other donors followed this with similar efforts to capitalize private think tanks and advisory organizations with the aim of refining government policies and enhancing the performance of public agencies.

POLICY

Thanks to philanthropic money from Ford, Russell Sage, Rockefeller, Eastman, Rosenwald, and many others, independent organizations like the RAND Corporation, the Social Science Research Council, and the American Council of Learned Societies began to appear, elevating governance via better information.

Further reading

○ Ellen Lagemann, *The Politics of Knowledge: The Carnegie Corporation, Philanthropy, and Public Policy* (Wesleyan University Press, 1989)

1916

BROOKINGS INSTITUTION

Robert Brookings made a lot of money in St. Louis manufacturing and selling housewares, then devoted much of his fortune and energy to building up Washington University and other institutions in his home city. At the start of World War I he agreed to serve as co-chairman of the War Industries Board, where he became the link between hundreds of private companies and a federal government trying to organize emergency war production. The experience convinced him that federal policymakers needed better economic data and better informed civil servants.

So in 1916 Brookings organized the Institute for Government Research, the first private organization aimed at bringing a factual and scientific approach to policymaking and governance. Other donors to the effort included J. P. Morgan and John Rockefeller, and companies like Fulton Cutting and Cleveland Dodge. Brookings also established the Institute of Economics in 1922 and a graduate school in 1924.

In 1927 the three organizations merged, becoming the Brookings Institution, which is generally regarded as the first think tank. Brookings researchers later contributed to the Marshall Plan, establishment of the United Nations, creation of the Congressional Budget Office, and many other national efforts. Employees of the Brookings Institution often

‹» PhilAphorism

Where charity keeps pace with gain, industry is blessed.

☞ *William Penn*

moved back and forth between government posts and their perches at the think tank.

Although normally associated with mainstream liberalism, the Brookings Institution has also contributed to causes associated with conservatism. These include welfare reform, school choice, tax reform, and regulatory rationalization. A University of Pennsylvania survey has named the Brookings Institution the world's leading think tank.

Further reading

○ Hermann Hagedorn, *Brookings: A Biography* (Macmillan, 1936)

MOTHERS' PENSIONS

Early in the twentieth century, concerns about poor children led a rag-tag alliance of progressive politicians, early feminists, and dissident philanthropists to promote what they called mothers' pensions—direct government aid to impoverished mothers of minor-age children. Mainstream organizations such as the Russell Sage Foundation and the National Conference of Charities and Corrections opposed the initiative, fearing that public relief would encourage dependency, invite political corruption, and deflate private anti-poverty efforts that involved extensive personal contact and behavioral counseling.

A group of Jewish philanthropists, led by Hannah Einstein of the United Hebrew Charities, dissented from these concerns within the charitable establishment, however. They pushed for direct government payments, and some activists like Jane Addams joined them. In 1911, Illinois passed the first statewide program of mothers' pensions. Thanks to continuing pressure on legislatures, 40 states had approved their own versions by 1920.

Funding proved more difficult. Most of the programs focused on widows with children, as opposed to unmarried women, because they were regarded with the most sympathy. Critics also complained that the pensions were too stingy. The mothers' pension movement cast a long shadow, though—providing the model for the Aid to Families with Dependent Children welfare payments created in 1935 as part of the Social Security Act, and establishing a precedent for the subsequent rise of a dense system of federal payments to individuals lacking income.

POLICY

Further reading

○ Theda Skocpol, *Protecting Soldiers and Mothers: The Political Origins of Social Policy in the United States* (Harvard University Press, 1992)

○ *Social Service Review* history of mothers' pension movement, jstor.org/stable/30021515

CARNEGIE ENDOWMENT
FOR INTERNATIONAL PEACE

"To hasten the abolition of war, the foulest blot upon our civilization." That was the utopian aim when Andrew Carnegie handed over a $10 million startup grant in 1910 to create the Carnegie Endowment for International Peace. The charter written by the optimistic Carnegie actually made plans for what the organization should do next after it ended armed conflict: "When the establishment of universal peace is attained, the donor provides that the revenue shall be devoted to the banishment of the next most degrading evil or evils, the suppression of which would most advance the progress, elevation, and happiness of man."

Pacifists dominated Carnegie's initial board, and rosy hopes abounded. In the 1920s, the endowment pushed for the adoption of the Kellogg-Briand Pact, whose signatories foreswore the use of war to resolve conflicts. Nicholas Butler, president of the Carnegie Endowment for International Peace actually won the Nobel Peace Prize in 1931 for his promotion of Kellogg-Briand. The pact's real-world effect, however, was nil: Its signatories included Nazi Germany, imperial Japan, and the Soviet Union.

Disappointed in its efforts to ban war, the endowment turned its attention in the 1950s and '60s to promoting the United Nations and training young foreign-service officers from newly independent countries. In the 1970s, in what the organization called a "second founding," the endowment moved from New York to Washington, D.C., and began to focus on influencing U.S. foreign policy. It launched the Arms Control Association to advocate for disarmament, and took control of *Foreign Policy* magazine, a voice for liberalism in international affairs.

Additional think tanks have been spun off of the endowment, including the Henry Stimson Center (a similar group promoting liberal security policies), the Institute for International Economics (now the Peterson Institute), and the Migration Policy Institute. In 2007, the endowment announced plans to become "the world's first global think tank," opening offices in Moscow, Beijing, Beirut, and Brussels. All of this has been possible because the group maintains an endowment of more than $300 million, thanks to Andrew Carnegie's original investments.

Further reading

○ Joseph Wall, *Andrew Carnegie* (Oxford University Press, 1970)

○ Centennial history, issuu.com/carnegie_endowment/docs/centennial_essaybook?e=0

1903

BOOKER T. WASHINGTON'S
SECRET LITIGATION DONATIONS

Born into slavery, Booker T. Washington went on to become the best-known African American of his generation, primarily as the leader of the Tuskegee Institute, which prepared thousands of black students for skilled occupations. Washington was a prolific fundraiser and received support from Northern industrialists who admired his self-help philosophy and his practical organizing skills. Among his "sainted philanthropists" were Andrew Carnegie, Collis Huntington, John Rockefeller, Julius Rosenwald, and Jacob Schiff.

Some critics, however, particularly modern ones, have complained that Washington's reluctance to stir up social conflict was too accommodating. Long after he died in 1915, though, historians discovered that Washington had another non-public face. He was also a philanthropist himself, secretly making personal donations to fund legal challenges to Jim Crow laws.

Washington quietly supported the *Giles* cases of 1903 and 1904 that took on black disenfranchisement. They went all the way to the Supreme Court before ultimately failing in their claims for black voting rights. In the *Rogers* case of 1904, Washington supported a winning argument. The Supreme Court ordered the retrial of a convicted black man because qualified blacks had been deliberately kept off the jury.

Major legal and political advances for black Americans would not arrive until decades later, but the modest gains of Booker T. Washington's hidden philanthropy gave him and others solace. He credited the *Rogers* decision, for example, with giving "the colored people a hopefulness that means a great deal."

Further reading

○ Louis Harlan, "The Secret Life of Booker T. Washington" (*Journal of Southern History*, August 1971)

1902

ROCKEFELLER SENDS
THE SOUTH TO HIGH SCHOOL

When John Rockefeller put up a million dollars to create the General Education Board, his mission was to improve public education in the Southern states—particularly high schools. In many places (rural towns, black districts) public high schools didn't even exist, and where they did they were usually inadequate. State law actually prevented Georgia from using public dollars for secondary education.

POLICY

In addition to devoting millions of its own dollars to building up decent high schools (see 1902 entry on our Education list), the GEB created a strategy aimed at getting governments to meet their educational responsibilities. In particular, the GEB asked state universities to appoint professors of secondary education onto their faculties, paying for their salaries and expenses with Rockefeller money. Once in place, these specialized educators often pressed legislators and the public on the importance of improving high schools.

With remarkable speed, these state-college professors were able to build convincing cases, overcome local resistance, and convince lawmakers to pass enabling statutes. In the case of Georgia it required an amendment to the state constitution. After securing successes at the state level, the GEB-backed education professors began encouraging local communities to improve their schools. They promoted bond proposals to finance local construction of schools. They pushed for a longer academic year. They suggested improved curricula.

Across the South, the GEB transformed attitudes toward secondary education, and for the first time high schools became widely available to ordinary Southerners.

Further reading

○ Duke University case study, cspcs.sanford.duke.edu/sites/default/files/descriptive/ general_education_board_support.pdf

1895

JANE ADDAMS PUSHES SOCIAL REFORM

In 1895, with the help of private philanthropy, Jane Addams published *Hull House Maps and Papers*, a collection of articles calling public attention to the Chicago housing and working conditions that her Hull House organization aimed to alleviate. Addams's original mission was to defeat poverty and encourage assimilation through education, services, and counsel supplied by successful members of the community. Over the years, she shifted toward more collective and impersonal action. She pushed for legislation on housing regulations, law-enforcement issues, factory inspections, child labor, women's suffrage, worker's compensation, prostitution, international pacifism, and other topics. She took high-profile roles in the Progressive Party, the Women's International League for Peace and Freedom, and the founding of the American Civil Liberties Union.

Further reading

○ Jean Bethke Elshtain, *Jane Addams and the Dream of American Democracy* (Perseus Books, 2002)

JOHN MUIR GUIDES
THE SIERRA CLUB TO ACTIVISM

A difficult upbringing under a fanatical father turned John Muir into a loner and wanderer who spent long stretches isolated from other people in remote places. Once he had formulated his own quasi-religious gospel of nature, however, he recognized that he needed to enlist other people, and ideally government, in his crusades against exploitation of natural areas. So in 1892 he and some likeminded activists founded the Sierra Club. He was president for 24 years, until his death.

One of the Sierra Club's founding goals—"to explore, enjoy, and render accessible the mountain regions of the Pacific Coast"—echoed the purpose of the Appalachian Mountain Club started on America's opposite coast 16 years earlier. (See 1876 entry on the Roundtable's list of philanthropic achievements in Nature.) But the Sierra Club's third goal became its distinguishing characteristic: "To enlist the support and cooperation of the people and government in preserving the forests and other natural features of the Sierra Nevada." Rather than becoming an operating entity aimed at the enjoyment of land, the Sierra Club turned into a protectionist group focused on lobbying.

Sustained in its early years by small donations, the group eventually reached a dominant financial and political position amid the growth of the environmental movement. Muir's popular writings on nature continued to attract followers long after his death in 1914. And in recent decades new generations of activists have been inspired by the radicalism of his previously unpublished work, which includes rejections of people-centric policy, capitalism, nationalism, and Christianity. The Sierra Club is now a large national organization at the center of environmental politics, with a budget exceeding $104 million as of 2013.

Further reading

○ Donald Worster, *A Passion for Nature: The Life of John Muir* (Oxford University Press, 2011)

○ Franklin Rosemont, "Radical Environmentalism," in *Encyclopedia of the American Left*

POLICY

ADDING ACTIVE RESISTANCE TO ABOLITIONISM

The long, hard campaign to ban slavery was the first, and still largest, triumph of public-policy philanthropy in the U.S. When it began in earnest in the 1830s, private donations from hundreds of thousands of Americans were used for everything from dogged journalism, literature creation, and tract distribution, to the creation of schools for slaves and former slaves, to special events like the *Amistad* trial (see 1841 entry). From the beginning there were also acts of civil disobedience—as by the volunteers and financial donors who aided furtive transport of escaped slaves to northern states or Canada via the Underground Railway.

As decades passed, some abolitionists edged closer to active, physical resistance. Gerrit Smith's family had partnered with John Jacob Astor in the fur trade and became the largest landowners in New York state. But Gerrit lived simply so that he could give most of his money to favorite causes, primarily his passion for eliminating slavery. Smith donated to every kind of anti-slavery effort. He was the main funder of Frederick Douglass's newspapering. He paid large sums to buy the freedom of slaves and whole slave families. He supported the building of schools. He gave money and land to create a village of new freedmen surrounding his own home in central New York state.

Smith was not a vindictive man, as shown by the fact that he also bailed Jefferson Davis out of jail after the Civil War, and argued against criminal prosecutions of Southerners in order to hasten national healing. In the decades of stalemate before the war, however, Smith became frustrated with mainstream efforts to change public law on slavery. In 1848 he met for the first time with John Brown, who was countenancing lawbreaking.

In 1850, Smith organized and underwrote the Cazenovia Convention that urged Americans to disobey and nullify the Fugitive Slave Law. Its resolution, written by Smith, called on slaves to use all means necessary to escape, including stealing and force, was written by Smith. Over the next decade, Smith brought John Brown to his home for meetings several additional times, and he secretly began to finance Brown's running of guns into Kansas, and then his attack on the federal arsenal at Harper's Ferry. "I can see no other way," he said.

These violent acts of resistance were an exception to Smith's mostly pacific philanthropy, and they led him to a nervous breakdown. But they were part of his indefatigable use of his personal fortune to end legal slavery, and of course the Harper's Ferry attack ultimately sparked the Civil War. Gerrit Smith's abolitionist philanthropy totaled about a billion dollars of donations, in current value. There is no question that this giving accelerated the most important national policy change that our nation is ever likely to undergo.

Further reading

∘ Gerrit Smith entry in National Abolition Hall of Fame,
  nationalabolitionhalloffameandmuseum.org/gsmith.html

AMERICAN MISSIONARY ASSOCIATION

Led by a mix of evangelical pastors and funded by Lewis Tappan and other public-minded philanthropists, the American Missionary Association was created in upstate New York in 1846. It promulgated Christian principles, opposed slavery, educated blacks, and promoted racial equality. By linking eastern abolitionists with those in Ohio, Illinois, and other parts of what was then "the West," the group exerted an important influence on American politics and culture.

The association supported missions for runaway slaves in Canada and for liberated slaves in Jamaica. It paid teacher salaries for schools serving African Americans in border states. It helped American Indians, Chinese immigrants in California, and the poor in Hawaii, Sierra Leone, Thailand, Egypt, and other overseas locations. The AMA helped anti-slavery ministers plant hundreds of new churches across the Midwest.

In the lead-up to the Civil War, Lewis Tappan and other AMA leaders denounced the Democratic Party as pro-slavery, and nurtured anti-slavery political parties that eventually coalesced in the birth of the Republicans. During the Civil War itself, the AMA fielded a corps of missionaries and teachers that followed in the wake of the Army. They seized every opportunity to educate, comfort, and evangelize.

After the war, the AMA aided freedmen, and founded schools. The association also chartered eight colleges that became the core of what are now referred to as America's historically black colleges and universities. By 1888, 7,000 teachers trained by the American Missionary Association were instructing hundreds of thousands of pupils in Southern states.

Further reading

○ Bertram Wyatt-Brown, *Lewis Tappan and the Evangelical War Against Slavery* (Louisiana State University, 1997)

○ Historical notes, amistadresearchcenter.org/archon/?p=creators/creator&id=27

POLICY

AMISTAD DECISION

In 1839, a group of Africans captured by Spanish slavers and then sold into bondage in Cuba rose against the crew of the ship transporting them. They eventually came to shore on Long Island, where they were put on trial for murdering a crewmember. Abolitionist financier Lewis Tappan immediately recognized this as a potential teaching moment for public understanding of slavery.

Tappan collected donations from some fellow abolitionists and set off for Connecticut, where the 36 Africans were locked up. The defendants were clothed and fed by Tappan and questioned with the aid of interpreters he brought in. Tappan subsequently retained respected lawyers to represent their interests, and hired Yale students to tutor them in English, American manners, and Christianity.

After criminal charges were dismissed, the case was referred to civil trial. Lewis Tappan initiated a suit charging the Spanish ship owners with assault and false imprisonment of the Africans, which got the Spaniards arrested. The case became a national and international cause célèbre, drawing large crowds and banner headlines.

The courtroom struggle eventually reached its final appeal before the U.S. Supreme Court, and Tappan convinced former President John Quincy Adams to join the all-star legal team. Ultimately, though five of its nine justices were Southerners who either owned or had owned slaves, the court ruled that the Africans were kidnap victims, not property, with a right to defend themselves. They were declared wholly free.

Lewis Tappan had almost single-handedly financed and organized the defense. He attended every day in court. He engineered much of the publicity and reporting that transfixed many Americans in sympathy with the Africans. Some months later he helped finance the excursion which returned the Africans to their native lands. Hundreds of donors moved by the *Amistad* trial also contributed funds, which were used to supply the returnees and help them resettle. Abolitionism had turned a corner toward a wide popular following.

Further reading

○ Trial archive at the University of Missouri-Kansas City, law2.umkc.edu/faculty/projects/ ftrials/amistad/amistd.htm

1833

AMERICAN ANTI-SLAVERY SOCIETY

The powerful religious and moral revival in America during the early 1800s, known as the Second Great Awakening, spawned an outpouring of voluntary giving and the creation of many new charitable societies aimed at spreading Christianity and reducing social ills like drunkenness, violence, and slavery.

One of the most consequential of these new charities was the American Anti-Slavery Society. It was established in 1833 with financing from major philanthropists Arthur and Lewis Tappan and Gerrit Smith, along with many small donors mobilized by an army of religious female fundraisers. Within two years the society had 200 local chapters, and there were 1,350 by 1838, mobilizing an estimated 250,000 members. Given the controversial cause, historian Kathleen McCarthy calls this "a stunning level of recruitment, accounting for almost 2 percent of the national population within the scant space of five years in an era of primitive communications." As a fraction of the national population, the society was larger than today's Boy Scouts, National Rifle Association, National Wildlife Federation, or Chamber of Commerce.

In the process, abolitionism became a national crusade. Advocates presented the following arguments for reform: No one has the right to buy and sell other human beings. Husbands and wives should be legally married and protected from involuntary separation. Parents should maintain control of their children. It is wrong for slaveowners to be able to severely punish a slave without trial. Laws prohibiting the education of slaves must be repealed. Planters should pay wages to field hands instead of buying slaves.

In the summer of 1834, slavery apologists reacted violently to this new opposition. During a riot in New York City, leading AAS donor Arthur Tappan escaped with his life only by barricading himself and his friends in one of the family stores well supplied with guns. The home of his brother Lewis Tappan was sacked that same evening, with all of his family possessions pulled into the street and burned while some leading citizens looked on passively.

Despite their narrow escapes, the Tappan brothers were undeterred. Lewis left his house unrepaired, to serve, he said, as a "silent anti-slavery preacher to the crowds who will flock to see it." More substantively, the Tappan brothers decided to flood the U.S. with anti-slavery mailings over the next year. They founded and subsidized several important magazines to popularize anti-slavery arguments, including the high-circulation *Emancipator*, the children's magazine the *Slave's Friend*, the *Record* illustrated with woodcuts, William Lloyd Garrison's the *Liberator*, and the journal *Human Rights*.

These publications and other abolitionist tracts and papers were flurried across the country by the American Anti-Slavery Society. The campaign was powered by $30,000 of donations. It targeted ministers, local legislators, businessmen, and judges, using moral suasion to make the case against enslavement. The society's publications committee, headed by Lewis Tappan, mailed over a million pieces in the course of ten months, harnessing new technologies like steam-powered presses plus the religious enthusiasms of thousands of volunteers to mobilize public opinion.

As McCarthy notes, defenders of slavery had "kept the leavening potential of civil society in check...watchfully curbing any trend which might contribute to the development of alternative, independent power bases." So the enemies of abolition struck back against this civil

POLICY

information campaign. In his 1835 message to Congress, President Andrew Jackson called for a national censorship law to shut down mailing of these politically "incendiary" writings. He encouraged his postmaster general to suppress the deliveries or at least look the other way while local postmasters did, and in many places abolitionist tracts were pulled out of the mail and subscribers were exposed and threatened.

Arthur and Lewis Tappan and other philanthropists subsidizing the effort were subject to additional violence. Lewis was mailed a slave's ear, a hangman's rope, and many written threats. An offer of $50,000 was made for delivery of his head to New Orleans. A Virginia grand jury indicted him and other members of the American Anti-Slavery Society. As his only weapon, Lewis carried a copy of the New Testament in his breast pocket.

These thuggish reactions helped turn public opinion against slavery, especially among Northern churchgoers, and fueled the rapid spread of AAS chapters described above. The Tappans, meanwhile, continued their dogged efforts to change national policy on this issue. See their contributions, for instance, in the nearby 1841 entry on the *Amistad* decision, and the 1846 entry on the American Missionary Association. Combining abundant generosity with personal passion and a genius for organizing and public relations, the Tappan brothers made giant contributions to the most consequential public-policy reform in the history of the United States.

Further reading

◦ Kathleen McCarthy, *American Creed: Philanthropy and the Rise of Civil Society* (University of Chicago Press, 2003)

◦ University of Missouri-KC monograph on Lewis Tappan, law2.umkc.edu/faculty/projects/ftrials/trialheroes/Tappanessay.html

◦ Lewis Tappan, *The Life of Arthur Tappan* (Hurd and Houghton, 1871)

OVERSEAS

For more than two centuries, Americans have sought to be helpful to fellow human beings beyond their own borders. They have carried literacy, knowledge, and technology to remote places, battled medical suffering, and alleviated poverty and misery of all sorts. From the first Christian missionaries in the nineteenth century, to the bold overseas projects of Rockefeller and Carnegie, to the 8 million lives saved in the developing world by the Gates Foundation in just its first two decades of existence, to the disaster assistance and many relief organizations powered by small gifts from millions of citizens, Americans have built a record as the most charitable of neighbors.

It's a powerful but little understood fact that our private giving actually dwarfs the official humanitarian aid sent overseas by the U.S. government. The latest calculations from the indispensable Index of Global Philanthropy and Remittances show that $39 billion of private philanthropy was invested in developing countries in 2011, while individual Americans (mostly immigrants) sent an additional $100 billion abroad to support relatives and friends in foreign lands. Meanwhile, official development assistance from the U.S. government that year totaled $31 billion.

And it isn't just the quantity of aid that matters, but also the quality. From creating new lifesaving vaccines to constructing major universities, from promoting property rights to battling terrorism and nuclear proliferation in fresh ways, American philanthropists are pursuing many inventive initiatives overseas. Not only the content but also the forms of giving are being rapidly refined—with for-profit mechanisms, e-giving, entrepreneurial methods, and other new means reshaping the efficiency and effectiveness of philanthropy in lands where bureaucracy and corruption are constant risks.

The cases that follow are representative examples of what has been achieved around the globe by more than two centuries of American donating. Many additional examples of overseas philanthropy in specific areas like medicine and religion can be found on our companion Major Achievement lists devoted to those topics.

⤙ Section research provided by Karl Zinsmeister,
Christopher Levenick, Evan Sparks, Adam Sawyer, and John Murdock

2015

GATES DOUBLES SPENDING AGAINST HUNGER

In 2015, Melinda Gates announced that the foundation she and her husband steer would double its investments against hunger in the developing world. "Malnutrition is the underlying cause of nearly half of all under-five child deaths," she noted, promising that the Gates Foundation would spend $776 million over the next six years to help change that. Malnutrition is now concentrated in a small number of countries where Gates will focus its efforts—India, Ethiopia, Nigeria, Bangladesh, and Burkina Faso. Emphasis will be placed on improving the nutrition of women and girls as soon as they become pregnant, educating mothers on infant feeding, encouraging breastfeeding, increasing sanitation to reduce energy-sapping infections, fortifying purchased foods with nutrients known to be underconsumed, and focusing on keeping children fed from birth to age two, when neurological development and other crucial growth is most rapid.

Further reading

○ News report, trust.org/item/20150603143702-53fbj/?source=fiOtherNews2

○ Gates Foundation nutrition strategy, gatesfoundation.org/What-We-Do/Global-Development/Nutrition

2015

GLOBAL STUDIES AT NORTHWESTERN

Roberta Buffett Elliott, the sister of Warren Buffett who has profited from his meteoric investment returns, is an alumna of Northwestern University.

By funding the Buffett Center for International and Comparative Studies there she has supported academic work on overseas poverty, migration, understanding of world religions, tropical medicine, and democratic governance in the developing world. In 2015 she made a $100 million gift to expand Northwestern's center into a full-blown institute. It will hire professors focused on international subjects, fund new research, provide up to $20 million in scholarships to bring overseas students to Northwestern to earn degrees, and otherwise expand international study and exchange.

Further reading

○ Announcement in institute newsletter, buffett.northwestern.edu/documents/ newsletters/2015-Buffett-Spring-Newsletter.pdf

A CHINESE RHODES SCHOLARSHIP

Stephen Schwarzman, co-founder of the Blackstone investment company, has focused his giving on learning. In the U.S. he is a long-time supporter of Catholic schools in New York City, and gave a $100 million donation to rejuvenate the New York Public Library. In 2014 he announced a major overseas foray into education philanthropy: the Schwarzman Scholars, a program modeled on the Rhodes scholarship, with an even bigger endowment.

Every year, the program will unite 200 top young college graduates from leading countries around the world. They will study together at Tsinghua University in Beijing, the alma mater for many of China's elites. The large role that China will inevitably play in future global developments demands deeper personal ties and more mutual understanding among the next generation of Chinese and Western leaders, argues Schwarzman.

To supplement his $100 million gift, Schwarzman raised another $200 million in private matching funds toward the project. The first students enroll in 2016.

Further reading

○ Interview with Stephen Schwarzman in *Philanthropy*, philanthropyroundtable.org/topic/ donor_intent/endowing_a_new_chinese_rhodes

BOLSTERING SCIENCE IN ISRAEL

U.S. philanthropists Sheldon and Miriam Adelson made two large gifts in 2014 to bolster the sciences in Israel. They offered $25 million to the school

OVERSEAS

of health sciences at Ariel University to allow it to open a full program in medical science. And they donated $16.4 million to SpaceIL for its project which aims to land the first Israeli craft on the moon.

SpaceIL, which is also supported by the Schusterman Family Foundation and other U.S. donors, is participating in the latest competition sponsored by the X Prize Foundation: the Google Lunar prize. This offers a $20 million award to the first team that lands a privately funded operating robot on the moon, an effort to speed affordable access to the moon by encouraging private entrepreneurs and donors to get involved.

Other major U.S. donors to Israel include Bernie Marcus, Haim Saban, John Paulson, Charles Bronfman, Morton Mandel, Michael Steinhardt, and the Weinberg Foundation. Overall, it is estimated that about $2.7 billion is now donated annually to various causes in Israel by diaspora Jews, with the largest portion of that coming from the U.S.

Further reading

○ *Jerusalem Post* report on Ariel University gift, jpost.com/Jewish-World/Jewish-Features/
   Sheldon-Adelson-pledges-25m-to-Ariel-University-360480

○ *Haaretz* report on SpaceIL gift, haaretz.com/life/science-medicine/1.584852

2014

BOOSTING ART IN HONG KONG

Robert Miller, co-founder of Duty Free Shoppers, is a long-time supporter of the arts in Hong Kong. In 2014 he and his wife, Chantal, made the largest gift ever for that purpose when they donated $12.9 million to support artists in the port city. Their gift to the Asia Society Hong Kong Center will be used to commission new works, underwrite performances, and maintain galleries. The Millers previously donated $3 million to restore an important Hong Kong theater.

◁ PhilAphorism

Any good that I can do or any kindness that I can show to any human being, let me do it now. Let me not defer or neglect it, for I shall not pass this way again. ☞ *Mahatma Gandhi*

Further reading

○ Asia Society announcement, asiasociety.org/files/uploads/402files/ASHK_%20Miller%20
   Donation%20release_Eng_final.pdf

2014

PRESERVING JEWISH HISTORY
IN TEL AVIV AND VENICE

Beit Hatfutsot, the museum of Jewish history and culture located at Tel
Aviv University, first opened in 1978. It needed an overhaul to bring its
story up to date, so in 2014 two American donors pledged $5 million
each to create a new wing and freshen the exhibits. The gifts came from
Alfred Moses and from Milton and Tamar Maltz. The Maltzs are serial
progenitors of museums, having been involved in creating the Maltz
Museum of Jewish Heritage in Cleveland, the Rock and Roll Hall of Fame,
and the International Spy Museum in D.C. This joint $10 million donation
will allow creation of a new Great Hall of Synagogues and a new core
exhibition to open in 2017.

At about the same time, a group of U.S. philanthropists led by designer
Diane von Furstenberg and real-estate investor Joseph Sitt announced they
were donating $12 million to restore the Jewish Museum in Venice and the
five remarkable small synagogues in the surrounding Jewish neighborhood.
The project was planned so it would be complete in 2016—the 500th
anniversary of the declaration by the Republic of Venice that the city's Jews
must live in the one-block enclosed area that remains home to much of the
Venetian Jewish community, as well as the museum and synagogues.

Further reading

○ Beit Hatfutsot gift announcement, bh.org.il/new-museum/beit-hatfutsot-receives-a-10-
   million-contribution

○ *New York Times* report on Venice restoration, artsbeat.blogs.nytimes.com/2014/11/11/
   jewish-museum-and-synagogues-in-venice-to-undergo-12-million-restoration/?_r=0

2013

OVERSEAS GIVING BY U.S. CHURCHGOERS

American Christians have actively donated to charitable work overseas for
more than 200 years. And there is evidence that the level of foreign donations
by U.S. Christians has risen briskly during the past decade.

In 2011, American churches contributed $14 billion to relief and
development abroad. (This totals both direct mission work and giving to

OVERSEAS

other aid groups.) That religious giving compares to $5 billion sent overseas that same year by foundations, $7 billion from secular relief organizations, and $8 billion donated internationally by U.S. corporations. The $14 billion in religious overseas philanthropy also compares impressively to the $31 billion of official development aid handed out by the federal government in 2011.

One indicator of the sharp rise in overseas giving by U.S. churchgoers is the *Mission Handbook* compiled by the Billy Graham Center. It cumulates the budgets of prominent Protestant groups that are providing international aid—like World Vision, Compassion International, Heifer International, and Opportunity International. Between the years of 1992 and 2008, those budgets more than doubled (in constant, inflation-adjusted dollars).

Further reading

○ *Philanthropy* magazine reporting, philanthropyroundtable.org/topic/excellence_in_
philanthropy/unto_the_nations

○ The 2013 *Index of Global Philanthropy and Remittances*, hudson.org/content/
researchattachments/attachment/1229/2013_indexof_global_philanthropyand_
remittances.pdf

○ Linda Weber, editor, *Mission Handbook* (Billy Graham Center, 2010)

2012

CLEAN WATER TO DRINK

Philanthropists Lynn and Foster Friess began supporting the nonprofit Water Missions International in 2005, after a tsunami created a health crisis in south Asia. They have since visited the group's projects in Haiti and Malawi, and supported other efforts in the 49 countries where WMI builds safe water and sanitation systems for poor residents or victims of natural disasters. In 2012, the Friesses gave the group its largest contribution ever, $1 million, and printed and distributed 20,000 copies of a book of photos of people aided by WMI, to encourage other givers to become involved. Since its founding in 2001, Water Missions International has brought healthy water to more than 2 million persons.

Other donor-supported groups focused on bringing drinkable water and healthy sanitation to poor countries include the Water Project, Water.org, charity:water, Water is Life, PureMadi, Miya, Three Avocados, and the Water Center at Columbia University. Social businesses created and incubated with philanthropic funds are also becoming active in sanitation and drinking water—for instance, Water Health International, and Sanergy, both of which approach villagers and slum dwellers as customers rather than donees.

Further reading

○ Press release on 2012 gift, watermissions.org/Websites/watermissions/images/FF_
Release_SC.pdf

2011

MOBILE PAYMENTS IN POOR COUNTRIES

At present, 2.5 billion people in developing countries have no access to formal financial institutions like banks. They must rely on cash, tin-can savings, and other unsafe and inconvenient methods of managing their family finances. This also drags down national economic growth. Since its creation in 2004 by the founder of eBay, the Omidyar Network has made multimillion dollar donations to overcome that lack of financial infrastructure.

Almost 2 billion of those 2.5 billion people lacking banking services do, fortunately, have access to a mobile phone. Omidyar and other U.S. donors have thus made it a focus of their overseas work to support and expand methods of bill-paying and saving via mobile phone. In developing countries, platforms like MPeso and GCash now have millions of users of their reliable systems of financial exchange. Poor people rely on phone transactions to pay the school bills of their children, buy supplies for their small businesses, and purchase medical care.

With a $2 million grant in 2011, the Omidyar Network was one of the founders of Mobile Money for the Unbanked—a support group for firms providing financial services by cell phone that helps them connect to additional customers, encourages interoperability, and resists regulatory barriers by governments. Omidyar also supports efforts to bring other life-enhancing services and products to people in the developing world via their mobile phones.

Further reading

○ Mobile Money for the Unbanked, gsma.com/mobilefordevelopment/programmes/mobile-
money-for-the-unbanked
○ Omidyar MMU history, omidyar.com/investees/gsma-mobile-money-unbanked

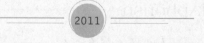

2011

OVERSEAS

COLLABORATING FOR A BIGGER BANG

"We had become a de-facto co-funder group: We were funding a lot of the same poverty-fighting organizations, had similar philosophies, and liked each other's company." That's what a group of 12 funders with a special focus on the needs of the poor in developing countries discovered back in 2011. So they created an informal alliance they named Big Bang Philanthropy. The group is collegial, with a minimum of rules beyond the simple requirement of spending at least $1 million annually overseas, and having a desire to compare notes and collaborate with similar peers. The current 12 members donate more than $60 million per year to battle international poverty. They don't pool their money, but there is heavy overlap in their funding decisions, and they share much useful information. The David Weekley, Segal, Mulago, and Peery Foundations are included among the members.

Further reading

○ *Stanford Social Innovation Review* report, ssireview.org/blog/entry/big_bang_
philanthropyphilanthropyroundtable.org/topic/excellence_in_philanthropy/making_
forever_families

RADIOS AGAINST GENOCIDE

Ever since he learned details of the Holocaust as an eighth grader, John Montgomery has been haunted by the idea of genocide, and determined to do his part to prevent it in the future. As the Houston investment firm that Montgomery helped found began to thrive, he and his wife and their Bridgeway Foundation (which receives 50 percent of the after-tax profits of his firm) became generous givers to poor people around the globe, with a particular emphasis on sub-Saharan Africa. And the central priority of Montgomery's philanthropy is overcoming genocidal dangers, a cause to which he has devoted tens of millions of dollars.

Montgomery has supported Rwandan widows and funded the healing of wounds from that country's tribal terrors. More recently, 90 percent of his resources were focused on the Democratic Republic of the Congo, Central African Republic, and South Sudan—areas where the murderous warlord Joseph Kony and his LRA terror group had rampaged for years, killing thousands and abducting children to serve as soldiers or sex slaves.

⨀ PhilAphorism

Help your brother's boat across, and your own will reach the shore.

☞ *Hindu proverb*

In addition to funding groups that publicize LRA violence (which helps generate international backlash), Montgomery became directly involved in stopping killings. In 2010 he suggested that imperiled villagers could be warned of impending attacks if a radio network were built in the remote region, so residents could flee before fighters arrived. Montgomery and Bridgeway equipped tribal chiefs in the area with radio transmitters, receivers, and towers, so information on the movements of Kony's men could be quickly shared.

Thereafter, when militants approached villages, locals faded into the forest, saving many lives and avoiding the kidnapping of their children. The radio network also yielded intelligence which helped authorities track Kony, forcing him to be more reclusive. Rebel commanders began to defect and be killed. The U.S. detailed 100 soldiers to the area, and the LRA threat receded.

"There is a spiritual aspect to this to me," Montgomery told *Philanthropy* magazine, "a life calling. There are people dying."

Further reading

○ *Philanthropy* magazine profile of John Montgomery, philanthropyroundtable.org/topic/ excellence_in_philanthropy/stopping_the_slaughter

○ Bridgeway Foundation, bridgewayfoundation.org/index.php

2010

PREEMPTING NUCLEAR ENRICHMENT

Philanthropist Warren Buffett is an adviser to the Nuclear Threat Initiative, a nonprofit led by former Senator Sam Nunn that seeks to reduce threats from atomic weapons. Working through the NTI, Buffett announced a $50 million pledge in 2010 toward the construction of the world's first nuclear fuel bank—which would guarantee countries a supply of uranium to operate their nuclear power plants. This would allow the more than 30 countries considering building their first nuclear power plant to proceed without setting up their own uranium enrichment facilities. Enrichment facilities, once in place, can be used to create not just electricity-generating fuel but also bomb-grade fuel, worsening the dangers of nuclear proliferation. Buffett's contribution represented the single largest philanthropic gift in the worldwide effort to slow nuclear proliferation. And it bore fruit in April 2015, when Kazakhstan signed an agreement with the International Atomic Energy Agency establishing the low-grade uranium fuel bank on its territory.

Further reading

○ *New York Times* essay on fuel bank by Sam Nunn, nytimes.com/2014/07/12/opinion/ open-a-nuclear-fuel-bank.html?_r=0

OVERSEAS

2010

GIVING PLEDGE SPREADS PHILANTHROPY ABROAD

The twentieth century has witnessed an explosion in the number of billionaires. Under the leadership of Bill Gates, a group of billionaires announced a "Giving Pledge" in 2010, through which the signee promises to give away at least half of his or her wealth to charitable causes. The first 40 pledgers committed an estimated $125 billion to charity in this way. A year and a half later, 81 billionaires had made the commitment. By 2015, 137 individuals or couples had signed the Giving Pledge, representing many hundreds of billions of dollars of donations.

In addition to lining up Americans, Bill Gates and Warren Buffett have visited China, India, Saudi Arabia, and other countries to encourage moguls there to consider American-style philanthropy. Their initial 2010 meeting in China yielded zero signatures, and commitments from other countries have been sporadic, but the first Indian signee came on board, along with the first African pledger. As of 2015, the individuals who had taken the Giving Pledge came from a dozen countries, evidence that U.S.-style long-term giving is gradually spreading abroad.

Further reading

◦ The Giving Pledge, givingpledge.org

◦ *Atlantic* analysis of overseas organizing, theatlantic.com/business/archive/2014/05/how-us-philanthropy-is-inspiring-foreigners-to-give/370889

2010

AMERICAN MISSIONARIES

Having done so for two centuries, America still dispatches more missionaries overseas each year than any other nation. Research by the Center for the Study of Global Christianity found that the U.S. sent 127,000 missionaries abroad in 2010, as many as the next six top-sending countries (Brazil, France, Spain, Italy, South Korea, U.K.) *combined*. U.S. givers are also by far the largest source of funding for missions, donating several billion dollars for overseas ministry every year (a figure that is growing fast). These days, about a thousand U.S. agencies with a religious mission carry out relief work overseas, according to the *Mission Handbook*.

In the 1960s, the argument that mission work is "imperialistic" burst forth. There are also counterviews. In a 2008 London *Times* essay, journalist

Matthew Parris described himself as "a confirmed atheist" but argued that "I've become convinced of the enormous contribution that Christian evangelism makes in Africa: sharply distinct from the work of secular non-governmental organizations, government projects, and international aid efforts.... Christianity changes people's hearts. It brings a spiritual transformation. The rebirth is real. The change is good.... Those who want Africa to walk tall amid twenty-first-century global competition must not kid themselves that providing the material means or even the knowhow that accompanies what we call development will make the change. A whole belief system must first be supplanted.... Removing Christian evangelism from the African equation may leave the continent at the mercy of a malign fusion of Nike, the witch doctor, the mobile phone, and the machete."

Further reading

○ 2013 study by Gordon-Conwell Theological Seminary, gordonconwell.com/netcommunity/CSGCResources/ChristianityinitsGlobalContext.pdf

○ Linda Weber, *Mission Handbook: U.S. and Canadian Protestant Ministries Overseas* (Billy Graham Center, 2010)

2010

PROMOTING GOOD GOVERNMENT ABROAD

Investor and U.S. immigrant Len Blavatnik made a major gift to Oxford University in 2010 to establish a brand new School of Government at the nearly 1,000-year-old college. The primary aim of his $117 million donation is to prepare students from all over the world to be more productive leaders in public service. The first students enrolled in 2012, and the master's class of 2014 included 75 students from 48 different countries. The school places a heavy emphasis on development economics, and almost instantly became one of the most selective graduate programs at Oxford. A dramatic new headquarters building on the Oxford campus debuted in 2015.

Further reading

○ Information on Blavatnik, bsg.ox.ac.uk/about/leonard-blavatnik

2009

ROBERTSON ADOPTS NEW ZEALAND

U.S. hedge-fund pioneer Julian Robertson developed a deep affection for New Zealand after taking a sabbatical there with his family in 1978. He subsequently developed a few real-estate properties, and owns personal retreats in the country.

OVERSEAS

He has also expressed his attachment through a series of philanthropic gifts. In 2009 Robertson pledged to the Auckland Art Gallery 15 modern artworks by Cezanne, Matisse, Mondrian, Picasso, and others, valued at more than $100 million—the largest gift ever made to an art gallery in Asia or Australia. In 2012 he made a $12 million gift to the Rhodes Scholarship program to add three annual awards for students from New Zealand. And, in 2012, he gave $5.3 million to create the New Zealand Antarctic Research Institute.

Further reading

○ *Forbes* profile, forbes.com/sites/annabel/2012/10/22/julian-robertsons-empire-down-under/2

ROAD SAFETY IN POOR COUNTRIES

Public health has been a hallmark of Michael Bloomberg's philanthropy. In 2007, the Bloomberg Family Foundation donated $9 million for pilot programs promoting motorcycle helmet use in Vietnam and Mexico. The effort quickly recorded 20 percent reductions in both countries in head-injury fatalities. Following this success, Bloomberg established a standing program within his foundation to improve road safety broadly in poorer countries. More than $250 million has so far been donated to efforts to chip away at the 1.2 million annual deaths from traffic accidents across the globe—making the foundation the world's leading advocate for road safety.

Further reading

○ Bloomberg program site, bloomberg.org/program/public-health/road-safety

A PEOPLE'S BANK IN RWANDA

In 2002, investment banker and entrepreneur Dale Dawson became interested in efforts to rebuild the war-torn east African nation of Rwanda. (See 2002 entry on our companion list of achievements in Religious philanthropy.) As Dawson began to spend half his time on charitable projects in Rwanda, he noticed that residents were in desperate need of places where they could safely save money, and where small-business creators could go for loans. He and the Christian nonprofit Opportunity International made plans to create such a bank, then joined with other faith-based partners to launch the Urwego Opportunity Bank in 2007. It operates as a business, but the founders reinvest all earnings back into the enterprise.

This microbank became a phenomenal success, soon growing to eight branches across the countryside, 225 employees, and 40,000 outstanding loans, in an average amount of $300. Only 1 percent of their loans become overdue by 30 days or more. The faith-inspired bank also offers small entrepreneurs insurance, safe money-transfer services, and financial education.

When Urwego opened, 95 percent of Rwandans had zero experience with a bank. Now 120,000 clients have savings accounts, in an average amount of about $60. To work around illiteracy, all accounts are tied to fingerprints. When small savers go to a teller window and press a digit on a reader pad, their account info pops open. The bank has helped Rwanda become one of the freest and fastest-growing economies in Africa.

Further reading

○ *Philanthropy* magazine profile philanthropyroundtable.org/topic/excellence_in_ philanthropy/lending_a_hand

○ Urwego Opportunity Bank of Rwanda, uob.rw

BOLSTERING
PROPERTY RIGHTS

The Omidyar Network, the philanthropy created by eBay founder Pierre Omidyar and his wife, Pam, is organized around five major initiatives. One is property rights. This dates back to 2007, when the Omidyars read Hernando de Soto's book *The Mystery of Capital.* That seminal book explains both why insecure property rights are such a serious problem in the developing world, and how establishing private ownership can be a giant boon to economic growth and prosperity. (See 1989 entry.)

The Omidyars have taken this insight to heart. "A significant proportion of the world's population," their foundation notes, "has weak or nonexistent protections for their property and resources. This leaves people vulnerable to wrongful eviction and forced displacement—and it disempowers them and prevents them from engaging in the formal economy. Without formal recognition and protection of their property, people are unable to have ownership of goods, start and run a business, or be protected when buying, selling, and trading." Extensive multiyear grantmaking by the Omidyar Network now helps poor residents of developing countries establish ownership of land and businesses, as the essential foundation for future prosperity.

Further reading

○ *Philanthropy* magazine background story, philanthropyroundtable.org/topic/excellence_ in_philanthropy/home_land_security

○ Omidyar Network initiative in property rights, omidyar.com/initiatives/property-rights

OVERSEAS

BLOOMBERG CAMPAIGN AGAINST TOBACCO

It is estimated that tobacco use could kill a billion people globally during this century. One of the major initiatives of Bloomberg Philanthropies since 2007 has been an effort to create greater awareness overseas of tobacco risks, reducing consumption. The foundation promotes several strategies: tracking tobacco use, creating smoke-free public places, launching community programs to help people quit smoking, posting warnings on tobacco's health effects, banning advertising, and raising taxes on tobacco. The foundation invested more than $600 million in these efforts as of 2015.

Further reading

○ Bloomberg international tobacco initiative, bloomberg.org/program/public-health/ tobacco-control/#overview

2006

EXTENDING THE GREEN REVOLUTION TO AFRICA

Three quarters of the world's poorest people gain their income and their food by farming small plots about the size of a football field. The Green Revolution (see 1943 entry) dramatically improved life for small farmers in Asia and Latin America. But for a variety of reasons the Green Revolution never rooted deeply in Africa. As a result, about 70 percent of Africans struggle with unproductive soil, plant diseases, pests, and weather problems.

In 2006 the Bill & Melinda Gates Foundation began a concentrated effort to import the lessons and techniques of the Green Revolution to sub-Saharan Africa. They invested more than $2 billion in this effort

∿ PhilAphorism

To give away money is an easy matter and in any man's power. But to decide to whom to give it and how large and when, and for what purpose and how, is neither in every man's power nor an easy matter. ☞ *Aristotle*

just in their first eight years. Part of the initiative involves research and development seeking plant varieties that will have increased yields, better resistance to pests and weather stress, and enhanced nutritive value. Extensive resources also go into spreading information on effective farming techniques, expanding the access of small farmers to markets where they can sell their produce, and veterinary labors to upgrade the health and productivity of livestock.

Further reading

○ Overview of Gates agricultural development strategy, gatesfoundation.org/What-We-Do/ Global-Development/Agricultural-Development

2006

SOROS OVERSEAS SPENDING

Since 1979, when he began his philanthropy, George Soros has donated large sums to international causes—more than $8 billion by 2015, with additional hundreds of millions being sent overseas with each passing year. His sharpest focal point, and the scene of his most effective work, was Eastern Europe amid the withering of communism (see 1984, 1991, and 1993 entries on this list). Soros's other overseas giving has been a much more mixed bag.

For instance, in 2006 he donated $50 million as lead funder of the Millennium Villages Project, trumpeted by economist Jeffrey Sachs as the solution to poverty in Africa. In 2011 Soros promised the project another $27 million, and consideration of $20 million more beyond that, to "scale up" the effort. By 2015, extensive reporting, World Bank research, and other evidence made it clear that the five-year plans created by the MVP architects crashed into so many unanticipated cultural and economic obstacles that the Millennium Villages were not noticeably more successful than counterparts where no investment took place. Indeed they are actually *less* successful by some measures like child mortality.

Further reading

○ Nina Munk, *The Idealist* (Doubleday, 2013)

○ World Bank analysis of child mortality, blogs.worldbank.org/impactevaluations/the-millennium-villages-project-impacts-on-child-mortality

2003

OVERSEAS

PRIVATE SCHOOLS IN POOR COUNTRIES

Officially, education in most poor countries is provided by the government at no charge to parents. But in practice, these state-run schools are often terrible—with teachers appointed by nepotism rather than skill, who don't show up, or require bribes—yielding miserable student results. In Nigeria, Africa's largest country, 5 million elementary-age children don't even have a school available to them at all.

In every land, though, parents are ambitious for their offspring, and seek out workarounds when offered lousy education. James Tooley, who was a teacher in Africa before he became a professor of education at Britain's Newcastle University, began to hear about extremely low-cost private schools springing up in slums across the developing world. Though government officials denied that such schools existed, or that they were anything but exploitative if they did, Tooley decided to investigate for himself. In 2003, the John Templeton Foundation awarded him nearly $800,000 for in-depth research, and he set off to Old City Hyderabad in India, Makoko, Nigeria, and many other such shantytowns.

Tooley discovered a vast ecosystem of bare-bones private schools that charge parents $2 to $6 per month (about 5-10 percent of the salary of the poorest workers). These administer a heavily scripted curriculum, using energetic instructors hired from the same slum where the school is located, and generally produce test results so much better than the available government school that parents line up to enroll their children. "The fees make school and parent accountable to each other. The state schools lack that accountability," reports U.S. philanthropist Steve Beck, who has been funding the expansion of such academies in Nairobi, Kenya.

Fully half of all schoolchildren in impoverished districts of south India turned out to be enrolled in low-cost private schools. In Hyderabad it was 65 percent. In the slums of Accra, Ghana it was 64 percent. In Lagos, Nigeria, 75 percent were in private schools. Across low-income districts of China, India, and Africa the results were the same.

In every single region Tooley studied, students from the super-cheap private schools significantly outscored their counterparts in government schools (after careful adjustment for demographic differences, IQ, and so forth) on both math and language skills. The private-school teachers were much more likely to actually be teaching when unannounced school visits were made, and the private schools were better equipped with toilets and drinking water. After accumulating test results from 24,000 children, Tooley concluded that academic results were dramatically better for the children attending private schools. To top it all off, all of this was achieved at just a fraction of the cost of the ineffective government schools.

When this research won a development prize in 2006, philanthropists realized they could accelerate and extend the successes of these low-cost private schools by offering loans or grants for expansion. The Orient

Global Education Fund put up $100 million in 2007. Other philanthropies (Opportunity International, the IDP Foundation, Edify, etc.) began to provide microloans of $500 to $2,000 so educational entrepreneurs could open branches or install latrines or buy land for building.

Donors like Steve Beck, David Weekley, and many others have put $100 million of launch money into for-profit schools like Bridge International Academies. After starting in a Nairobi slum in 2009, Bridge now educates about 100,000 African children. It has been opening as many as 150 schools in a year, and is now popping up two private "schools in a box" every week across Africa and Asia.

Further reading

○ *Philanthropy* magazine reporting, philanthropyroundtable.org/topic/excellence_in_philanthropy/an_invisible_hand_up

○ Summary of Tooley research, ft.com/intl/cms/s/0/379b98c4-4670-11db-ac52-0000779e2340.html#axzz3cfPkrtz7

○ Detailed Tooley whitepaper, object.cato.org/sites/cato.org/files/pubs/pdf/tooley.pdf

2001

ACCELERATING MICROFINANCE

The arrival of microfinance—offering small loans to poor people so they can start businesses that help support their families—is one of the most important developments in overseas philanthropy over the past generation or two. (See 1976 entry.) As the wildly successful results of the first microloan experiments became clear, certain donors decided to make sure this new tool was understood, valued, and spread to as many poor communities overseas as possible.

The Seattle-based nonprofit Unitus—created by four successful and generous businessmen with roots in the Church of Jesus Christ of Latter-day Saints—was a leader. When Unitus launched their project to accelerate the spread of microfinance in 2001, the sector was dominated by very small and not especially efficient operations that were growing only slowly. By bringing new capital, management systems, and leaders into the field, Unitus strove to bring new microbanking options to hundreds of thousands of poor householders. In particular, Unitus aimed to turn microfinance into an attractive and self-supporting business so that for-profit firms would flood the field and greatly expand the number of loans made.

The initiative was successful in all of this. It set up partnerships with 22 organizations in underserved countries like Indonesia, Brazil, Mexico, Kenya, and India. These partners, as a group, grew in size by more than

OVERSEAS

100 percent per year for many years, eventually serving 12 million families. In 2010, Unitus announced that with microfinance having matured and become a professionally run, market-oriented business in many countries, it was ending its ten-year acceleration effort.

Further reading

○ Unitus microfinance acceleration project, unituslabs.org/projects/historical-projects/ microfinance-acceleration

FORD'S INTERNATIONAL FELLOWS

Drawing from its long history of supporting international scholars, the Ford Foundation launched a freestanding International Fellowships Program with a $280 million grant in 2001—the largest single gift ever allotted by Ford—and operated the program through 2013. It provided study stipends to community leaders from regions of the world with little access to higher education, particularly targeting minorities and less successful populations, and "prioritizing social commitment" over academic potential.

More than 4,300 individuals from 22 countries in Africa, the Middle East, Asia, Russia, and Latin America won fellowships. One third of them pursued degrees in the United States or Canada, another third studied in Europe, and the final third enrolled in institutions in their home regions. After completing their education, most participants returned to their homes to work. When last surveyed, 46 percent of alumni were living in their home community, an additional 36 percent were living in their home country, and 18 percent were living in a different country. The Ford International Fellowships Program was intended as a demonstration project to widen college access. The foundation's total spending on the program over its 13-year life came to $355 million.

Further reading

○ Ford IFP outcomes, fordifp.net/AboutIFP/Outcomes.aspx

CLEAN WATER THANKS TO COKE

The world's largest beverage company, Coca-Cola, has since the early 1990s made investments in water supply and sanitation one of the top priorities of its philanthropic arm, the Coca-Cola Foundation. In 2009, for instance, the foundation offered a $30 million grant to the Replenish Africa Initiative (RAIN), aimed at bringing clean drinking water and sanitation to two million Africans over a five-year period. The foundation was created in 1984 when the company made a commitment to give away, every year, 1 percent of its prior year's operating income. In 2013, Coca-Cola donated $143 million, across 122 countries.

Further reading

○ Coca-Cola Foundation, coca-colacompany.com/our-company/the-coca-cola-foundation

GATES CAMBRIDGE SCHOLARSHIPS

In 2000, the Bill & Melinda Gates Foundation created the Gates Cambridge Trust with a $210 million endowment. This program brings college graduates to England's Cambridge University for two or three years of post-graduate study, under an all-expenses-paid structure similar to Oxford's Rhodes Scholarships. About 200 Gates scholars are in residence at Cambridge at any given time, and since the program's founding they have come from almost 100 different countries. Recipients are selected by "academic excellence, leadership ability, and commitment to improving the lives of others." That last criterion, says the program, is "fundamental and sets this program apart from others of its kind."

Further reading

○ Gates Cambridge Scholarship, gatescambridge.org

GORDON MOORE'S ANDES-AMAZON INITIATIVE

A signature international effort of the $6 billion Gordon and Betty Moore Foundation is the Andes-Amazon Initiative. The Amazon River basin stretching from the Andes mountains to the south Atlantic holds one fifth of the world's liquid fresh water. It also contains the globe's highest diversity of birds and primates, one third of all freshwater fish species, and

◈ PhilAphorism

I'm not doing my philanthropic work out of any kind of guilt. I'm doing it because I can afford to do it, and I believe in it.

☞ *George Soros*

OVERSEAS

more than 60,000 plant species. To support this biological trove the Moore Foundation has invested more than $150 million in forest conservation and an additional $70 million in other forms of conservation. Moore's efforts have helped restore a forested area about four times the size of California, while establishing sustainable business partnerships to mitigate local environmental degradation.

Further reading

○ Moore Foundation Andes-Amazon Initiative, moore.org/programs/environmental-conservation/andes-amazon-initiative

BUILDING CIVIL SOCIETY AFTER COMMUNISM

In 2000, six U.S. foundations joined together to form the Trust for Civil Society in Central and Eastern Europe. Its charge was to help build up the fragile elements of civil society in countries emerging from decades of communist rule. The foundations invested $66 million in Bulgaria, the Czech Republic, Hungary, Poland, Romania, Slovakia, and Slovenia to strengthen service organizations, journalism, watchdog groups, think tanks, and other private organizations and charities that could help sustain democratic governance. The trust completed its grantmaking at the end of 2012. By then its target countries were holding regular elections and integrating with other European nations to the west.

Further reading

○ 2001-2012 Report of the Trust, scribd.com/doc/137522875/CEE-Trust-Report-2001-2012#scribd

BOLSTERING AFRICAN UNIVERSITIES

In sub-Saharan Africa, only 4 percent of the college-age population got a chance to enroll at a university when the Partnership for Higher Education in Africa kicked off. Believing that more college training was essential to progress in the poorest continent, the presidents of four U.S. foundations (Rockefeller, Ford, MacArthur, and the Carnegie Corporation) joined together in 2000 in a $100 million commitment to bolster African universities. They were later joined by the Hewlett, Andrew Mellon, and Kresge foundations and the effort was extended from five to ten years. Institutions in nine different African countries were helped to build up their faculties, develop new degree programs, improve facilities, and create long-term financing mechanisms. Over the course of the ten-year effort these donors poured a total of $440 million into African universities, substantially improving their functioning and visibility.

Further reading

○ *Accomplishments of the PHEA 2000-2010*, foundation-partnership.org/pubs/pdf/ accomplishments.pdf

○ PHEA home, foundation-partnership.org

1999

SUSTAINABLE ENERGY IN CHINA

Concerned over the energy and environmental impact of China's breakneck industrial expansion, the David and Lucile Packard Foundation provided $22.2 million in 1999 to create the China Sustainable Energy Program. CSEP makes grants inside China for research, training, and policy formation to improve energy efficiency and reduce air pollution in the country. Universities, commercial firms, industry groups, and policy organizations can be eligible for support, and as of 2015, 1,560 projects had been funded at more than 440 different organizations. The program also holds workshops in China for entrepreneurs and public officials on topics like efficient transportation, improving electric utilities, appliance efficiency, green buildings, and so forth.

In 2002, the William and Flora Hewlett Foundation became a funding partner with a contribution of $2 million directed at transportation initiatives. Other donors have joined as well, and cumulative grantmaking in China has exceeded $200 million. The effort is now known as Energy Foundation China.

Further reading

○ Duke University case study, cspcs.sanford.duke.edu/sites/default/files/descriptive/china_ sustainable_energy_program.pdf

○ Energy Foundation China, efchina.org

1996

FAIR STANDARDS TO FUEL TRADE

Recognizing how easily foreign aid can encourage corruption and dependency in poor countries, an alternative movement has grown up which emphasizes international trade as a means of helping farmers, small manufacturers, and residents of developing countries. Paul Rice spent years organizing coffee farmers into cooperatives where they could improve their quality control and maximize their pricing leverage. In 1996 he founded the nonprofit now known as Fair Trade USA. With donations from scores of foundations, hundreds of individuals, and

OVERSEAS

many corporations, the organization has become the largest third-party certifier of products produced and sold on terms that are generous to overseas workers. The group puts its stamp of approval on items like coffee, cocoa, produce, nuts, sugar, apparel, stitched sports balls, and many more—a total of 12,000 products exported from 70 countries. The nonprofit estimates that consumers who prefer certified products currently deliver an annual premium of about $40 million to producers in poor countries, and that figure is rising every year.

Further reading

∘ 2013 *Almanac* of Fair Trade USA, fairtradeusa.org/sites/default/files/2013-Fair_Trade_USA-Almanac.pdf

MASSIVE GIFTS TO GLOBAL HEALTH FROM THE GATES FAMILY

Bill Gates often explains in interviews how he decided to become a philanthropist: He was "exclusively focused" on Microsoft in the mid-1990s when his attention was captured by an article about how rotavirus kills half a million children per year by severe diarrhea. That mostly unreported misery seemed cruel and unnecessary, and inspired him to form his foundation in 1994 with an initial stock gift of $94 million. From the beginning his efforts were particularly devoted to improving health in poor countries overseas, because "every life has equal value."

In 2008, Gates left Microsoft and became a full-time philanthropist. From its inception through 2014, his foundation gave away $34 billion, most of it for health-related work. Just in 2014, the $3.9 billion distributed by the Gates Foundation in direct grants included the following major health investments:

∘ Eradicating polio, $442 million
∘ Agricultural development, $442 million
∘ Vaccinating people in poor countries, $327 million
∘ Battling HIV/AIDS, $223 million
∘ Battling malaria, $201 million
∘ Battling tuberculosis, $145 million
∘ Improving maternal and child health, $135 million
∘ Battling enteric and diarrheal diseases, $100 million
∘ Battling pneumonia, $100 million
∘ Battling neglected diseases, $100 million
∘ Improving sanitation and water hygiene, $96 million

In a typical year, the Gates Foundation spends about as much as the World Health Organization on global health. It has been estimated that Gates directly saved 8 million lives in its first two decades, and headed off untold human misery, via its attacks on infectious diseases.

Further reading

○ 2014 *Annual Report of the Gates Foundation,* gatesfoundation.org/Who-We-Are/Resources-and-Media/Annual-Reports/Annual-Report-2014

○ Infographic on lives saved by Gates philanthropy, businessinsider.com/infographic-is-bill-gates-better-than-batman-2012-1

SAVING BOSNIANS AND SERBS

In 1992, Serbian forces encircled the city of Sarajevo in Bosnia. Their siege lasted until 1995 and killed more than 10,000 people, most of them unarmed civilians out on the street to find food and water. Aware of the city's desperate condition thanks to the foundations he had set up across Eastern Europe to encourage the transformation of societies away from communism (see 1984 entry), philanthropist George Soros put up $50 million of emergency aid at a time when almost no other agency or person was helping, and asked his foundation staff to determine the most effective ways to save lives and alleviate suffering with the money. They consulted with nonprofits like Refugees International and the International Rescue Committee and brought into the tortured city Fred Cuny, an engineer who had founded his own charitable agency called Intertect Relief and Reconstruction. The fearless 240-pound Texan had deep experience in humanitarian disasters, and was famous for his view that no crisis was too overwhelming to handle.

Cuny decided the best way to help residents survive would be to restore water, gas, and electric service. After arranging that his transport planes would be on the ground only for minutes, to avoid being machine gunned, he flew in iron piping to restore the main gas lines. But only about 10 percent of

◈ PhilAphorism

Every man goes down to his death bearing in his hands only that which he has given away.

☞ *Persian proverb*

OVERSEAS

households were connected to gas at that time, so Cuny bought miles of small plastic piping and Soros's foundation enlisted 15,000 city residents to dig trenches to connect homes to the gas mains. Soon 60 percent of families had service. Cuny then designed a small gas-burning room heater that could be manufactured in Sarajevo and could be turned on its side to cook meals. These efforts rescued thousands of people from freezing and starving in the bitter Bosnian winters.

Because a large portion of the people killed by Serbian snipers were standing at wells drawing water, Cuny simultaneously used Soros money to restore municipal water service. He designed a 200-meter-long filtration system and had it manufactured in Texas, then flown into the city in pieces. He assembled it in an old road tunnel leading to the Miljacka River, where it was protected from shelling by the siege forces, and created a whole new piped water supply for the city. The Soros donation also increased local electric supplies by 30 percent, provided seeds with which residents could create gardens to feed themselves, and otherwise saved lives and reduced misery. Author Anna Porter concludes that the money Soros gifted to Bosnia "may have saved more lives than the combined efforts of the world leaders and United Nations."

Soros's Open Society Foundations also provided humanitarian assistance to Serbians on the other side of the civil war with Bosnia. International sanctions were clapped on Serbia's government during the conflict, which had the undesirable side effect of preventing everyday Serbs from having access to lifesaving drugs and other medical supplies. Negotiating a humanitarian waiver with the U.S. Department of the Treasury, the Open Society Foundations purchased millions of dollars of U.S. pharmaceutical supplies and distributed them across Serbia.

Further reading

° Anna Porter, *Buying a Better World: George Soros and Billionaire Philanthropy* (Dundurn Press, 2015)

° Open Society Foundations Balkans war projects, opensocietyfoundations.org/voices/ helping-balkans-survive-decade-war

1991

CENTRAL EUROPEAN UNIVERSITY

After the Berlin Wall fell, George Soros decided to found the first American-style university in Eastern Europe to help encourage the democratic transition of the region. The school, which offers only graduate degrees, opened in Budapest, Hungary, in 1991 with a charter from the State University of New

York and full U.S. accreditation. Instruction is provided in English to 1,381 students from 93 countries, about half of them on a full scholarship. Thanks to the $880 million Soros provided to endow the university (instantly making it one of the wealthiest in the world), it is highly competitive. Its MBA, political science, and legal degrees are rated as some of the best in Europe. George Soros was chairman the CEU board for a decade and a half, and remains a trustee.

Further reading

○ CEU facts and figures, ceu.edu/about/facts-figures

○ *Financial Times* 2011 reporting, ft.com/cms/s/0/b43b0572-fe68-11df-845b-00144feab49a.html#axzz3bq4H1A51

REINVENTING DEVELOPMENT ECONOMICS

In 1981 a Peruvian economist named Hernando de Soto formed a nonprofit in his country called the Institute for Liberty and Democracy. He had become convinced that a lack of property rights was the ultimate problem dragging down economic production in most poor countries, not traditional bugaboos like the legacy of colonialism or exploitation by rich countries. His 1989 book, *The Other Path*, demonstrated that many of the world's poor were forced to earn most of the income in the black market because entrepreneurship and private property were discriminated against by blockheaded governments.

By the late 1980s, private land-titling, recognition of small underground businesses, and other market-based reforms initiated by the ILD were being implemented across Peru, with dramatically positive results. This caught the attention of American donors like the Smith Richardson Foundation, Lilly Endowment, Omidyar Network, and John Templeton Foundation. They began to support the ILD and help it export its insights and practical reforms to dozens of other poor countries. They funded research, books, films, and other methods of spreading the message on the power of secure private ownership to bolster economic output.

De Soto's work brought him into conflict with the violent Marxist group in Peru known as the Shining Path, which targeted the economist for death. Among its other contributions to his work, Smith Richardson paid for protection for de Soto. "The foundation is an old and loyal friend which, when the ILD was being bombed and shot at during the early 1990s, provided us with a bullet-proof vehicle, thus enabling us to continue with our work," wrote de Soto in the acknowledgments to his 2000 book, *The Mystery of Capital*. De Soto is today considered one of the

OVERSEAS

most important and influential analysts of developing-world poverty.

Further reading

○ The work of the ILD, ild.org.pe/index.php/es/introduction

○ PBS interview with Hernando de Soto, pbs.org/wgbh/commandingheights/shared/
minitextlo/int_hernandodesoto.html

A COOL BILLION
AFTER ARMENIA'S EARTHQUAKE

Late in 1988, a devastating earthquake struck Armenia, followed by months of aftershocks, killing more than 25,000 people and injuring 15,000 more. Factories and utilities were destroyed; roads and railways were wrecked. There were many American gifts of aid in the aftermath, but none as big as what Kirk Kerkorian delivered. The investor, a child of Armenian immigrants to the U.S., put up a billion dollars to help rebuild his ancestral homeland, repairing 261 miles of highway, constructing 3,700 new apartments, and rehabilitating countless homes, among other contributions. In 2005, Armenian president Robert Kocharian awarded his country's highest honor to Kerkorian as thanks for this help.

Another donor who was vital to Armenia's recovery was Jon Huntsman. One of the most generous Americans of his generation in his proportionate giving, Huntsman was moved by the suffering after the earthquake, and went to visit the country. It turned out to be the first of 46 trips he and his family made to Armenia after he adopted that land as a personal cause. In addition to immediate relief aid, Huntsman set up factories and businesses to supply

⁓ PhilAphorism

The best philanthropy is not just about giving money but giving leadership. The best philanthropists bring the gifts that made them successful—the drive, the determination, the refusal to accept that something can't be done if it needs to be—into their philanthropy.

↪ *Tony Blair*

building materials. He provided money to reconstruct schools and hospitals. He also provided scholarships which allowed Armenian college students to study in the U.S. In the 25 years after the earthquake Huntsman devoted about $50 million to Armenia, which not only helped it recover from the earthquake trauma but also allowed its business environment to develop faster than many of the other nations that were spun into freedom after the dissolution of the Soviet Union. "Many individuals rendered huge aid to Armenia after the 1988 earthquake, but Jon Huntsman is one of those who have continued aid and even increased it," summarized president Kocharian.

Further reading

○ Kerkorian obituary in the *Chronicle of Philanthropy*, philanthropy.com/article/ Obituary-Kirk-Kerkorian/230933

○ Armenian-American report after Huntsman award ceremony, asbarez.com/40044/ jon-huntsman-arrives-in-armenia

1987

DONATING DRUGS TO STOP DREADFUL DISEASES

Private corporations have been key partners in certain philanthropic causes— particularly battles against diseases. Most of the major pharmaceutical companies now have charitable arms through which they give away free or heavily discounted drugs for use with poor populations, especially overseas. Billions of dollars worth of goods are donated in this way every year (see Chart 22 in this book's Statistics section).

An example is the drug Mectizan. The firm Merck & Co. discovered that it was highly effective in treating onchocerciasis, commonly known as "river blindness," a disease of low-income tropical countries that causes agonizing itching of the eyes and eventual loss of sight. In 1987 Merck created the first disease-specific drug-donation program in the world with an offer to supply the drug to any person needing it for as long as required. Administered once annually, Mectizan halts development of the infection, with minimal side effects.

In 1998 Merck announced it would be donating the same drug for use against another devastating developing-world plague—lymphatic filariasis, often called elephantiasis, a profoundly disfiguring syndrome caused by a parasitic worm. To stem elephantiasis, Mectizan is administered along with another drug donated by the GlaxoSmithKline pharmaceutical company. The two companies established a partnership to supply their life-changing compounds across Africa, in parts of Latin America, and in Yemen. By administering 140 million doses per year, the firms have made elimination of

OVERSEAS

both of these diseases foreseeable within current lifetimes.

A second example of a major overseas drug donation program is Pfizer's provision of Zithromax to stop trachoma, another infectious eye disease that causes blindness, currently afflicting 41 million people, particularly children. In its advanced stages a person's eyelashes turn inward and scrape the cornea, an excruciating condition. Pfizer set a goal of eliminating blinding trachoma by 2020, and has so far donated more than 250 Zithromax doses in dozens of countries. Pfizer and the Edna McConnell Clark Foundation jointly set up a nonprofit to carry out the treatments internationally. The Gates Foundation, Lions Clubs, and other private donors have become financial partners.

Further reading

○ Mectizan Donation Program, mectizan.org/about

○ Zithromax donation, pfizer.com/responsibility/global_health/international_trachoma_initiative

PARTNERS IN HEALTH

Ophelia Dahl, daughter of the late writer Roald Dahl, volunteered at an eye clinic in Haiti in the mid-1980s, where she met a medical student named Paul Farmer. A few years later, they and a few friends also interested in providing medical care to the destitute formed Partners In Health, a donor-supported organization which provides high-quality health services in Haiti and other poor countries. In 1993, the MacArthur Foundation awarded Farmer a MacArthur Fellowship, whose cash award helped expand Partners In Health. PIH was a pioneer in battling AIDS in Haiti. And in 2013 the group opened a major new hospital in Haiti, which not only provides extensive care but also trains medical residents.

Further reading

○ Partners In Health website, pih.org

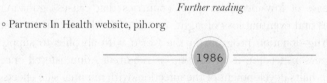

MOBILIZING AFRICAN AID

In 1986, the Christian charity World Vision invited popular rock musician Paul Hewson, better known as Bono, to visit some of their aid sites in Ethiopia. Moved by what he saw, he began a long involvement in African philanthropy. In 2002 he founded a charity that rang alarms over the AIDS epidemic ravaging the continent. He encouraged donors, companies, and governments to become involved, saying, "You can't run businesses if 10 percent of employees are dying." He helped convince all of those sectors to become involved in the subsequent decade's massive effort to use donated resources to reduce transmission of the HIV virus, treat its victims, and search for cures.

Further reading

○ Paul Hewson's charity, one.org/us/about

ERADICATING POLIO

In 1985, the fraternal organization Rotary International began a major project to battle polio. Since then, Rotarians have contributed more than $850 million plus hundreds of thousands of volunteer hours to eliminate the disease. The goal soon became global eradication of the polio virus by around 2018.

In 2008, the Bill & Melinda Gates Foundation started contributing hundreds of millions of dollars to Rotary's efforts. With support from other donors and a few international agencies, a final mass-immunization effort was launched. It has reduced the number of children paralyzed by polio from more than a thousand a day back when Rotary's effort began to much less than one case per day at present. Today, only two or three countries still harbor the wild polio virus, and a concerted effort is under way to render it extinct as soon as possible—which would end a scourge than has plagued humanity since at least the time of the Egyptian pharaohs.

Further reading

○ Rotary "End Polio Now" program, endpolio.org

ARCHAEOLOGY GOES DONOR-FUNDED

Archaeology was born thanks to private funding and passion. Then came a nationalistic phase where governments began to heavily regulate digs, and to fund them. In the past two or three decades, however, government

Მ PhilAphorism

Do not give, as many rich men do, like a hen that lays her egg and then cackles.

☞ *Henry Ward Beecher*

OVERSEAS

funding in most places has fallen far short of what archaeologists hoped for. Private donors have filled the gap. Of the thousands of major digs around the world, more than half of the funding for American-led excavations now comes from private individuals and foundations, reported Jim Wiseman, president of the Archaeological Institute of America, in 2006.

Financier Leon Levy and his wife, Shelby White, were major donors to this effort. Every year since 1985 they have supported a massive dig at Ashkelon, Israel, one of the most important ancient seaports in the eastern Mediterranean, with a history extending from the Bronze Age to the Crusaders. Most years, Shelby White participates in the digs herself, along with students of the Harvard professors overseeing the project. White is also paying for the crucial publications analyzing what has been found at the site—an eventual ten-volume set. In addition, White gave $200 million to New York University in 2006 to establish an Institute for the Study of the Ancient World that supports scholarship in archaeology and anthropology dating to ancient times.

Another New York financier who has funded important overseas digs, and the follow-up scholarship needed to make sense of them, is Roger Hertog. Starting in 2005 he provided several hundred thousand dollars to make possible a four-year excavation in Jerusalem which discovered, using clues from the Bible, what is thought to be King David's palace. Hertog described his support as "venture philanthropy—you have the opportunity for intellectual speculation, to fund something that is a work of great consequence." In this case, showing "that the Bible reflects Jewish history." Roger and Susan Hertog are also donating the resources for the Temple Mount Excavations Publication Project, a multi-volume work of scholarship sharing the findings of archaeologist Benjamin Mazar's historic digs in the epicenter of Jerusalem.

Other enthusiastic donors like Leon Reinhart, Artemis Joukowsky, the Packard Foundation, and Charles Williams have likewise funded academics investigating the physical remains of Mayan, Inca, Greek, Nabataean, Roman, and other civilizations.

Further reading

○ *Philanthropy* magazine interview with Shelby White, philanthropyroundtable.org/topic/ excellence_in_philanthropy/words_from_a_leading_culture_philanthropist

○ *Wall Street Journal* reporting, wsj.com/articles/SB114746911548351719

1984

OPENING FORMER COMMUNIST SOCIETIES

Born in Hungary in 1930, George Soros endured Nazi occupation as a child and then communist oppression under Stalin. In 1947, he escaped to London and attended the London School of Economics, where Karl Popper's *The Open Society and Its Enemies* shaped his thinking. After his work as a financier made him one of the wealthiest men in the world, he took up philanthropy on a large scale, beginning in 1979.

Soros's initial philanthropic crusade aimed at bringing down communism in Eastern Europe. In 1984, he created Hungary's first foundation. It funded cultural exchanges with the West, supported individual scholars, underwrote youth groups, and encouraged independent journals—all of this in the face of resistance by the government. It distributed copying machines across the country to overcome censorship and circulate alternate points of view. Aid was provided to improve the lives of stunted social groups like Eastern Europe's Roma people (gypsies). The region's first major new private university was created in Budapest (see nearby 1991 entry).

Open Society Foundations similar to the one in Hungary were created across the East-bloc countries, funded by hundreds of millions of dollars from Soros. These were eventually important in introducing a generation of opinion-makers in communist lands to democracy and Western views. The Solidarity movement, for instance, received Soros support when it was still illegal and underground, as did Russian dissident Andrei Sakharov. By some estimates, one out of ten members of the first post-communist Parliament in Hungary had some connection to Soros philanthropy.

At the fall of the Soviet Union, Soros dramatically expanded his philanthropy in Eastern Europe. He poured hundreds of millions of dollars into Russia— more than the U.S. government in many years—in an attempt to encourage privatization of industries and liberalization of the economy. When anti-capitalist hardliners blocked free-market reforms, he eventually dropped most of his assistance there. Soros likewise shut down his three-year-old Chinese foundation in 1989 upon learning that instead of promoting tolerance of dissent and democratic governance, it was controlled by the Beijing security apparatus.

Further reading

○ *Atlantic* analysis, theatlantic.com/magazine/archive/1993/07/finance-the-unifying-theme/305148

○ Duke University case study, cspcs.sanford.duke.edu/sites/default/files/descriptive/open_society_institute.pdf

1982

TURNING PEASANTS INTO LANDOWNERS

In 1982, Seattle lawyer and philanthropist Chi-Dooh "Skip" Li heard a guest speaker at his church suggest that helping poor Latin Americans buy

OVERSEAS

the land that they were farming might be the best solution to the unrest and insurrections then sweeping that region. Li went to Guatemala to do some research and returned home convinced that rural people would always be vulnerable, economically and politically, until they owned their own land. He began to formulate a plan for a new nonprofit called Agros that would allow private donors to acquire farms, stabilize the title and pay off taxes, and then sell the plots to the low-income tenants through many small payments.

The first project in Guatemala survived guerrilla war and eventually thrived, and in 1995 a ceremony was held to transfer title to the residents. The process was then repeated in other villages in Guatemala, Nicaragua, El Salvador, Mexico, and Honduras. Gradually, the effort added health services, agricultural training, help in selling produce, and other features, but the focus continued to be private ownership of the land, and the great stimulus to productivity and good citizenship that this provides. As of 2015, 10,000 people in 42 Latin American communities directly benefited from Agros. A third of those participants had already completed payment and earned full title to their own land, and the rest were on course to do the same.

Further reading

○ *Philanthropy* magazine reporting, philanthropyroundtable.org/topic/excellence_in_
philanthropy/the_power_of_ownership

○ Chih-Do Li, *Buy This Land* (CreateSpace, 2012)

1976

FORD LAUNCHES MICROFINANCE

When economist Muhammad Yunus returned to his native Bangladesh after studying in the U.S. as a Fulbright Scholar, he bored into the problem of South Asian poverty that then seemed so intractable. He eventually concluded that lack of access to capital was a major reason everyday people in his country were poor. He experimented with small loans ($27), and learned that they could spur an efflorescence of business activity.

Local commercial banks would not back Yunus's idea of awarding small loans for business purposes to people without regular employment or collateral. The Ford Foundation had supported his academic research starting in 1976, so Yunus approached its office in Dhaka about the possibility of an $800,000 grant to help him roll out his microcredit operation. Ford approved the proposal in 1981. Additional donations followed Ford's lead, and funds began to be lent, repaid, and then re-lent on short cycles at Yunus's new

Grameen ("Countryside") Bank. Very soon, it had disbursed a cumulative total of more than $13 million, in tiny doses, to small business creators. The microbank eventually offered billions in loans, and achieved astonishingly high recovery rates of more than 98 percent.

By the time Muhammad Yunus and the Grameen Bank shared the Nobel Peace Prize in 2006—"for their efforts to create economic and social development from below"—tens of millions of poor people in scores of developing countries had become active capitalists and seen their lives transformed by microfinance. In places where government agencies and commercial lenders saw only want and risk, philanthropists demonstrated that they could spark extraordinarily productive behavior among the poorest citizens on the globe.

Further reading

○ Muhammad Yunus, *Banker to the Poor: Micro-lending and the Battle Against World Poverty* (PublicAffairs, 2007)

○ History at Harvard Hauser Center, hks.harvard.edu/var/ezp_site/storage/fckeditor/file/pdfs/centers-programs/centers/hauser/publications/working_papers/workingpaper_44.pdf

1974

NEW URGENCY AGAINST TROPICAL DISEASES

In the early 1970s, the Edna McConnell Clark Foundation was searching for worthy candidates for its first international grants. The foundation's namesake, heir to the Avon fortune, had recently doubled its endowment. Now Clark wanted a cause where the needs were palpable and clear progress possible.

Tropical diseases were then getting relatively little attention from research scientists, drug developers, governments, and philanthropists. In the heavily regulated, litigious, and extremely expensive world of pharmaceutical research,

OVERSEAS

⌁ PhilAphorism

We make a living by what we get, we make a life by what we give.

☞ *Winston Churchill*

the high risks of drug development and low opportunities for economic payback on maladies afflicting only very poor residents of the equatorial regions created serious obstacles to battling the parasitic diseases of the developing world. It was estimated in the mid-1970s that the poor-nation afflictions representing 90 percent of the global disease burden got only 10 percent of global health-research spending. Only about 1 percent of all drugs approved for human use worldwide were specifically for tropical diseases.

And so in 1974, the Clark Foundation committed itself to a program of tropical disease research. Over the next 25 years, a small staff of three steered $90 million of grants into measures aimed at suppressing three particular chronic illnesses, each of which afflicts tens or hundreds of millions of people: schistosomiasis (snail fever), onchocerciasis (river blindness), and trachoma (a painful eye disease).

Of the $32 million Clark spent against schistosomiasis from 1974 to 1994 (with the foundation providing a third of the total spent globally to research that disease), an effort to find a vaccine consumed about half of the funding yet ended without success. However, the field had been advanced considerably when the foundation exited "schisto" research in 1994, and the baton was picked up by the Carter Center, the Gates Foundation, and others. Clark's work against river blindness followed a very similar course: failure to find a vaccine, but major progress in scientific understanding and public health countermeasures. For trachoma, Clark spurred some of the first systematic research ever conducted on the disease, and the foundation's mantle was taken up by a promising drug-donation effort that aims to eliminate blinding trachoma by 2020. (See 1987 entry on this list for details.)

Further reading

○ Duke University case study, cspcs.sanford.duke.edu/sites/default/files/EMClarkTDRfinal.pdf

1962

FORD BOOSTS MARKET DEMOCRACY IN LATIN AMERICA

In the first two decades of its existence, the Ford Foundation was a conventional family philanthropy that mostly limited its donations to local projects in the Detroit region. As the Cold War between communism and market democracies became serious in the 1950s, however, Henry Ford II initiated an effort to redirect the foundation. It was decided that the foundation should take on national and international responsibilities to "advance democracy" in poor countries where pre-modern economics and communist politics threatened stability and progress.

Alarmed at the spread of totalitarianism, Ford launched overseas programs to build up universities, promote the values of individual liberty and market economics, create cultural and scholarly exchange programs, subsidize open media in other countries, and so forth. Ford opened offices in Latin America, Asia, the Middle East, Europe, and Africa, and launched what would cumulate to tens of billions of dollars of overseas grantmaking over the next half century. During the 1950s and 1960s, the overseas spending of the Ford Foundation grew to be larger than any other private organization, and larger than initiatives run by the United Nations.

About a hundred other American foundations also funded overseas work as a contribution to the Cold War. Many worked with the State Department and the CIA on joint projects, like funding intellectuals and artists to make the moral case for democratic capitalism. The Rockefeller Foundation even explained its heavy funding of the Green Revolution (see 1943 entry) partly on the grounds that increased food security was "a valuable weapon in the struggle to contain communist expansion."

In 1962, as the Kennedy Administration worked to contain the spread of Marxism, Ford launched its first programs in Latin America. "The crisis in the world today requires that democracy do more than restate its principles and ideals; they must be translated into action," read a 1962 statement from Ford's board of trustees. A billion dollars in donations to universities, agriculture programs, and other efforts followed. In Chile, for instance, Ford offered $10 million in 1965 to strengthen the University of Chile and the Catholic University of Chile and to create an exchange program to bring Chilean academics to the U.S. for training. The goal was to infuse modern concepts of economic development and individual rights into Latin American higher education as alternatives to radicalism.

These sorts of efforts had clear effects. One historian writes that as a result of Ford's grants to Chilean faculty and curriculum, "Santiago probably had a higher concentration of intellectual talent in the social sciences than any other capital in Latin America." One dramatic result: A group of economists at the Catholic University of Chile who had been funded by Ford became known as the "Chicago Boys" because they absorbed ideas on economic liberalization and development at the University of Chicago. These intellectuals became crucial in turning Chile into a free-market paragon, one of the fastest growing economies on the globe, and, after a period of instability, a great democratic success.

Further reading

○ Jacquelyn Holmes, *From Modernization and Development to Neoliberal Democracy: A History of the Ford Foundation in Latin America* (Bates College Honors Thesis, 2013)

OVERSEAS

AVERTING MILLIONS OF DEATHS BY STARVATION

When the Rockefeller Foundation decided to extend the Green Revolution (see 1943 entry) to Asia and Africa, it went looking for philanthropic partners for the huge venture. To that point, the Ford Foundation had never funded agriculture or scientific research, but excited by Rockefeller's breakthroughs it began supporting such work in 1956. Then in 1962 Ford made a large grant to join forces with Rockefeller in opening the International Rice Research Station in the Philippines. Agriculture research stations in three other nations soon followed.

Over the years, weather- and disease-resistant varieties of many staple crops were developed at these stations. Poor farmers were introduced to chemical fertilizers and other modern farming techniques. And food shortages began to disappear all across the world. In India and Pakistan, wheat yields doubled by 1980 and nearly doubled again by 2000. Life in China and other parts of the east was similarly transformed by high-yield, stress-resistant rice. Nations previously described as "basket cases" were now able to feed themselves without strain.

During its 50-year leadership of the Green Revolution, the Rockefeller Foundation invested $600 million in the effort. Ford and other foundations donated hundreds of millions more. Rockefeller employee Norman Borlaug was awarded the Nobel Peace Prize in 1970.

Overall, the philanthropically led transfer of hybrid crops and modern farming techniques to the developing world is estimated to have saved up to a billion humans from painful death by starvation.

Further reading

○ Nobel citation for Borlaug, nobelprize.org/nobel_prizes/peace/laureates/1970/borlaug-bio.html

○ Borlaug interview in *Philanthropy* magazine, philanthropyroundtable.org/topic/excellence_in_philanthropy/mouths_wide_open

A LIFE SERVING THE POOR IN HAITI

W. L. Mellon, grandnephew of business titan Andrew Mellon, grew up in privileged circumstances in Pittsburgh, dropped out of college to work in the family bank, and endured an unsuccessful society marriage. Adrift and seeking a more meaningful life, he read reports on the devoted missionary work of Dr. Albert Schweitzer in Africa. He wrote asking how he might do something similarly useful, and received a long handwritten letter back from Schweitzer encouraging him to take up medical mission work.

"Larry" Mellon promptly uprooted himself and went back to college to complete first an undergraduate degree and then an M.D. at Tulane University. Upon receiving his medical degree in 1954 at age 44 he set off for Haiti. Two years later he opened a brand new hospital there, named for his idol Albert Schweitzer, which he equipped to the level of an American counterpart using family money. Dr. Mellon practiced medicine and also became active in community development—building roads, water supply, and attending to other desperate needs in the rural Artibonite Valley where he now lived with 150,000 Haitians.

With continuing support from American philanthropists including the Mellon family, the Gates Foundation, and others, the Albert Schweitzer Hospital still provides lifesaving services in the most unhealthy and impoverished nation in the Western Hemisphere. It is the only hospital serving a current population of 350,000. From the beginning, the Mellons invested in medical training for Haitians so that local people could assume positions at the hospital, and today 98 percent of its employees are Haitians. Due to the nation's gross misgovernance, the hospital must provide its own infrastructure—producing all of its electricity, water, and transport linkages itself.

Further reading

∘ Hospital history, hashaiti.org/about/originsmission

∘ Biographical profile, ncbi.nlm.nih.gov/pmc/articles/PMC1447782

1944

HEIFER INTERNATIONAL

A Midwestern farmer named Dan West was ladling out milk to youngsters on a Church of the Brethren relief mission when he realized, "these children don't need a cup, they need a cow." The Christian nonprofit that grew out of this idea shipped its first group of 17 heifers to Puerto Rico in 1944. The idea of giving malnourished and poor people long-term sources of food and economic means to support themselves, instead of just short-term relief, caught on.

Today, Heifer International ships not only cows but goats, chickens, pigs, llamas, fish, honeybees, seeds, irrigation pumps, and more, plus extensive agricultural training and husbandry instruction. This helps poor farmers both to feed themselves and to produce food products (and animal offspring) they can sell to support themselves. "The goal of every Heifer project is to help families achieve self-reliance," the group reports. "We do this by providing them the tools they need to sustain themselves."

All of this is funded almost exclusively by thousands of small donors. In 2014 Heifer International raised $102 million in contributions. This allows the group to operate in 30 countries, where every year it helps about 2 million families become producers. Since the group's founding it has assisted 23 million poor families in Asia, Africa, and the Americas.

Further reading

○ Heifer International, heifer.org

1943

GREEN REVOLUTION

In the early 1940s, disease was destroying half of the wheat harvest in Mexico, and the country's farmers (like many others in the developing world) were unable to produce enough food to meet demand in their own country. The trustees of the Rockefeller Foundation became interested in the problem, which they considered a logical extension of their existing large efforts in international public health and the biological sciences.

In 1943, the Rockefeller Foundation gave $20,000 for an initial survey of Mexican agriculture; the following year they spent $192,800 to construct and equip a research lab in the country. In 1944 they hired DuPont scientist Norman Borlaug and others to staff a new initiative to improve agriculture in the developing world. Entirely new varieties of wheat, corn, and potatoes were created. Farmers were taught to fertilize and irrigate. Soon, crop production rocketed upwards in Mexico (per acre yields for wheat *quadrupled*), and the country became a net exporter of food.

In 1954, when stem rust devastated American wheat production, Borlaug's research was modified to rescue American agriculture as well. But the most dramatic effects came when the so-called Green Revolution spread across the developing world, saving hundreds of millions of lives and transforming global economics. (See companion 1962 and 2006 entries.)

Further reading

○ Rockefeller Foundation agriculture work, rockefeller100.org/exhibits/show/agriculture
○ Duke University case study on Green Revolution, cspcs.sanford.duke.edu/sites/default/
  files/descriptive/green_revolution.pdf

1928

ALUMINUM-CLAD ASIAN EDUCATION

Charles Hall, a son of overseas missionaries, worked in a shed behind his family home in Oberlin, Ohio, to develop a smelting process that eventually reduced the cost of aluminum to just a two-hundredth of its previous price. He eventually founded the ALCOA company and became quite wealthy. In his will he left nearly all of his money to charity.

Hall shared the Protestant missionary zeal for promoting education in the less Christianized regions of the world, and stipulated that a third of his funds (about $235 million in current dollars) should be used to promote college education in Asia. The trustees of his estate eventually created an independent charitable trust closely connected to Harvard University and affiliated with China's Yenching University. The Harvard-Yenching Institute developed the Department of East Asian Languages and Civilizations at Harvard, created an Asian-language library, launched a *Journal of Asiatic Studies,* helped Yenching University expand its teaching of humanities, and built up five other colleges in China plus one in India.

More recently, the institute has supported Asian students and faculty with fellowships and sent American scholars overseas to study Asian culture at Asian universities. Hall's institute has supported major translation projects, funded conferences, and published new works in China, Vietnam, and other countries. It has endured for most of a century as one of the premier academic organizations established with a single donation.

Further reading

○ Harvard-Yenching Institute background, harvard-yenching.org/history

1919

INVENTING INTERNATIONAL EXCHANGE PROGRAMS

International exchanges of scholars and leaders—which have had a large role in fostering peace, freedom, and economic liberalism across the globe—were invented by American philanthropic organizations. One early exchange program was the Roosevelt Partnership linking Harvard University and the University of Berlin, which was established with a $50,000 gift from James Speyer in 1905. Philanthropically supported exchanges were formed at the University of Wisconsin in 1911 and at Cornell University in 1913.

The Rockefeller Foundation and the Carnegie Corporation both sponsored early international exchanges, academic fellowships, and organizations promoting cross-cultural understanding. In 1919 Carnegie established the Institute of International Education. Today it is the largest student and faculty exchange program in the world, administering almost 700 programs on behalf of thousands of donors. Between 1918 and 1934,

OVERSEAS

the Rockefeller Foundation spent $15 million on scholarly exchanges between overseas nations and the U.S. Many other Rockefeller ventures in this area followed, for instance the Asian Cultural Program created in 1967 specifically to build wider linkages and understanding between the U.S. and the Orient.

Finally recognizing the value of exchanges as a form of public diplomacy, the U.S. government started supporting international visits and study after World War II. Today a wide mix of private, public, and dual-funded exchanges exist, involving a panoply of countries. If anything, philanthropic innovation in this area has accelerated over the past two decades. A few examples follow.

The Freeman Foundation, created from the fortune of Mansfield Freeman, who was both a co-founder of the AIG insurance company and a longtime resident of Asia and a China scholar, has donated millions of dollars since 1994 to support academic exchanges with Asian countries. From 2001 to 2013 the Ford Foundation spent $355 million to provide higher education to 4,300 leaders from poor countries, mostly at Western universities, through its International Fellowships Program (see 2001 entry). The Bill & Melinda Gates Foundation has already devoted $210 million to its Gates Cambridge Scholars program which brings people from around the world together for graduate study (see 2000 entry). The Open Society Foundations pour large sums every year into educational and cultural exchanges benefiting persons living in countries with "repressive governance." Financier Stephen Schwarzmann recently pulled together $300 million to create a program that unites at China's Tsinghua University 200 top college graduates from China and Western countries (see 2014 entry). The aim of many of these efforts is to build mutual understanding among national leaders of the next generation.

Further reading

○ Database of the Institute of International Education listing scholarship opportunities, fundingusstudy.org/home.asp

◁ PhilAphorism

Charity is a universal remedy against discord, and a holy cement for mankind.

☞ *William Penn*

AIDING ARMENIANS
AFTER GENOCIDE

As part of a jihad launched by Muslim authorities in Ottoman Turkey to exterminate Christian minorities, up to 1.5 million Armenian Christians were destroyed, starting in 1915, through systematic killings, forced relocations into the desert, and starvation. Hundreds of thousands of others were forcibly expelled and became refugees. At the time, the U.S. government did little, but everyday Americans, missionaries, and philanthropists appalled by the atrocities quickly sprang to offer both immediate relief and long-term rebuilding aid to Armenians.

James Barton, the secretary of the American Board of Commissioners for Foreign Missions (one of the leading Christian missionary groups in the U.S.—see 1810 entry on our list of Religious achievements), had been a missionary in the Near East and was alarmed by initial reports out of Armenia. He quickly convened a meeting of New York businessmen and religious leaders. The host, mining mogul Cleveland Dodge, had a daughter in school in Constantinople and a son at the American University of Beirut and instantly understood the import of the genocide. Barton and Dodge formed the American Committee for Armenian and Syrian Relief in 1915, which subsequently raised over $100 million in donations through public rallies, church collections, and contributions from charitable foundations and private individuals. By the end of the 1920s, a total of $120 million in voluntary donations had been offered up by Americans. (Adjusted for inflation that is more than $1.6 billion in 2015 dollars.)

Missionaries in the region were used to distribute food, clothing, and other aid purchased with the donated funds. From 1915 to 1930, the committee saved over a million refugees and took responsibility for 130,000 orphans. Simultaneously, nearly 1,000 Americans volunteered to go to the region to build orphanages and assist refugees. Thousands more cared for dislocated Armenians when they made their way to the U.S.

The committee for Armenian relief still exists today, having evolved into the Near East Foundation, a charity which aids economic development in the Levant and Africa, in partnership with Syracuse University.

Further reading

○ History of the Near East Foundation, neareast.org/who-we-are

OVERSEAS

BIRTHING MODERN MEDICINE IN CHINA

In 1863, John Rockefeller introduced kerosene to China as part of the expansion of his thriving oil business. To lend a practical boost to its romantic marketing slogan "oil for the lamps of China," Standard Oil donated more than 8 million kerosene lights to residents of China, then built a commercial and cultural relationship that formed a foundation for Sino-American relations into the next century. In addition to weaving strong business connections, Rockefeller became a major philanthropic donor in China.

Rockefeller's gifts to the Chinese for education and medical care were unprecedented. After an expert commission reported that China's need for medical modernization was "great beyond any anticipation," the Rockefeller Foundation established its China Medical Commission in 1914. The first task was to visit hospitals throughout the country and study the health of the nation's population and the quality of medical practice. Then the commission set out to help make improvements, at a time when China had the highest mortality rate in the world.

One recommendation was to build up a potent medical school in China's capital. The Rockefeller Foundation assumed all financial responsibility for the Peking Union Medical College, which had been created in 1906 by six Christian missionary societies. Steady effort transformed the college into an advanced institution, subsequently known as "the cradle of modern medicine in China." One journalist described PUMC after Rockefeller's beneficence as "an airplane college in a wheelbarrow country."

In 1928, Rockefeller provided an endowment and set up a freestanding China Medical Board to continue this work as an independent American foundation. With the arrival of the communist government, the board withdrew from China and the Peking medical school in 1950. In 1980, the CMB was invited to return to China, where it has expanded its support of medical education and research to more than a dozen universities.

Further reading

∘ China Medical Board, chinamedicalboard.org/centennial

RESCUING JEWS AMID WORLD WAR

When World War I broke out in 1914, about 60,000 Jews were living in Palestine under the rule of the Turks (who sided with Germany).

The outbreak of hostilities left these Jews, many of them recent immigrants from Europe who depended upon assistance from Jews in other countries, isolated and destitute. When U.S. ambassador to Turkey Henry Morgenthau discovered their misery he sent an urgent telegram to Jewish philanthropist Jacob Schiff in New York City: "Palestinian Jews facing terrible crisis...belligerent countries stopping their assistance... serious destruction threatens thriving colonies...$50,000 needed." The U.S. ambassador, in other words, was begging private donors to rescue this vulnerable population.

Three U.S. Jewish charities quickly set up what they called the Joint Distribution Committee to raise the necessary money from individuals, synagogues, and community philanthropies, then dispatch it abroad. As World War I dragged on, and pogroms in Russia flared up and other threats appeared, the JDC found plenty to do. Between 1914 and 1925 the committee collected $59 million and sent it overseas to aid besieged foreign Jews in a variety of lands. When World War II arrived, the group began operating secretly in Nazi-occupied Europe, helping hundreds of thousands of Jews to emigrate, smuggling aid into prison camps, and financing the Warsaw ghetto uprising. After the war, the committee mobilized to sustain surviving Jews in refugee camps, to relocate many to Israel or other havens, and to provide emergency aid during the difficult early years of the Israeli state.

The American Jewish Joint Distribution Committee still operates today as a thriving nonprofit. In 2013 it spent $336 million to aid poor and threatened Jews overseas. Fully 44 percent of that was spent in the former Soviet republics, and 35 percent in Israel.

Further reading

∘ Archives of the JDC, archives.jdc.org/history-of-jdc/?s=archivestopnav

∘ 2014 Annual Report of the JDC, support.jdc.org/site/DocServer/annual_report_2014_update_100dpi.pdf

1913

BUILDING A PALACE FOR PEACE

Andrew Carnegie was deeply utopian on the question of international peace. (See the 1910 entry on our list of achievements in Public-Policy philanthropy.) He was enthralled by the declarations and treaties promising world amity that flowed out of the conventions held in 1899 and then 1907 in The Hague, Holland's capital. Carnegie was asked to build a "temple" to peace at the Hague, and ultimately provided $1.5

OVERSEAS

million to erect the "Peace Palace" that opened in 1913. In the strife-filled century since its construction, the ornate administrative building has been home base for many high-minded organizations. It currently houses the International Court of Justice, the Permanent Court of Arbitration, the Hague Academy of International Law, and the Peace Palace Library.

Further reading

∘ Peace Palace, vredespaleis.nl/?tl=1

ROCKEFELLER PIONEERS PUBLIC HEALTH IN FOREIGN LANDS

The Rockefeller Foundation was at the center of the global effort to control diseases in the first half of the twentieth century. That was its very goal when the foundation established the International Health Commission—the first philanthropic organization dedicated to that cause—with a $25,000 gift in 1913. The smashing success of Rockefeller's initiative to control hookworm in the American South had encouraged the foundation trustees to extend new health efforts beyond the borders of the U.S. Many of the structures and procedures that worked against hookworm were copied for the IHC. In this fashion, Rockefeller created many of the practices and protocols that became the new discipline of "public health."

Hookworm was a major cause of high mortality among blacks in the West Indies, so Rockefeller's trustees directed many of their first international grants to the Caribbean and Latin America. Throughout, the intention was to train and equip medical professionals in each country so they could sustain public-health improvements after the foundation departed. The international hookworm program quickly began to succeed as its U.S. predecessor had, so the commission next initiated campaigns against deadly yellow fever in 1914, and malaria ("the heaviest handicap on the welfare and economic efficiency of the human race") in 1915. The board used pilot projects against both diseases in the U.S. to inform its treatment and research agendas overseas.

All three of these initial programs made great strides in meliorating cruel epidemics. In time, the entity eventually renamed as the International Health Division of the Rockefeller Foundation was operating in more than 80 foreign countries. Rockefeller thereby became hugely influential on the ways that world health plagues were attacked in the future.

Further reading

∘ 100 years of the International Health Division, rockefeller100.org/exhibits/show/health/ international-health-division

CARNEGIE BOLSTERS SCOTTISH UNIVERSITIES

Andrew Carnegie, one of the fathers of modern philanthropy, was born in Scotland. When industrialization crippled his father's handloom business, the Carnegie family emigrated to America in search of a better future. Andrew emphatically found that future, starting in a mill job at age 13 and controlling 20 percent of U.S. iron and steel production by the time he was in his 50s.

When Carnegie devoted himself entirely to philanthropy after retiring in 1901, he made provisions for the people and communities of Scotland as well as for Americans. Among other actions, he created the Carnegie Trust for the Universities of Scotland with an unprecedented gift of $10 million. The Scottish universities of Aberdeen, Edinburgh, Glasgow, and St. Andrews were to use funds from the trust to expand their scientific research capabilities, and build libraries, academic facilities, and residences.

Carnegie later created additional trusts in the United Kingdom to underwrite worthy projects in education and culture. These still rank among the largest grant-giving organizations in that country. And Carnegie's legendary library-building program extended beyond U.S. borders to the British Isles—where he funded the construction of 660 public libraries.

Further reading

○ Current activities of the Carnegie Trust, carnegie-trust.org/about/about-the-carnegie-trust/what-we-do.html

◃ PhilAphorism

To say that private foundations exist only on the sufferance of government is to promote the untenable premise that government is the whole of society, that the citizen and all his institutions are creatures of the state, not the other way around.

☞ *Richard Cornuelle*

OVERSEAS

1901

MISSIONS TO THE PHILIPPINES

The American missionary movement reached its peak influence in the late 1800s, when thousands of Christians funded by donors and churches back home were in service overseas. After the U.S. annexed the Philippines in 1898 as a consequence of the Spanish-American War, leaders of the Presbyterian, Baptist, and Methodist churches met in New York to discuss how they could best aid the indigenous populations of those islands. The Spaniards had imposed Catholicism as a state religion, and as that was ended U.S. missionaries in the Philippines created an Evangelical Union in 1901 to allocate regions of responsibility to specific denominations and mission groups. More than 200 Protestant groups were active in the islands at one point. Most of the population remained Catholic, but Protestant missionaries founded many of the schools, universities, and hospitals in the country, and cultivated a new generation of leaders, including many who ultimately led the nationalist movement that brought the Philippines independence in 1946.

Further reading

○ Religious philanthropy in the Philippines, asia.isp.msu.edu/wbwoa/southeast_asia/philippines/religion.htm

1873

FATHER DAMIEN REDEEMS
THE LEPERS OF HAWAII

Through human history, leprosy has been one of the most supremely feared diseases, sometimes known as "the death before death." When the affliction reached the Hawaiian Islands, every victim was forced to relocate to a remote and completely wild peninsula where he or she was dumped with some seeds and a few tools and ever thereafter cut off from the outside world. Many of these quarantined persons were starving, filthy, and living in squalid huts made of nothing but branches when a Catholic priest named Joseph Damien de Veuster volunteered to serve the eight-year-old leper colony in 1873. He provided medical care, pressed lepers to plant gardens, built public structures, rescued orphans, fought off anti-social residents, and saw to it that people who died were properly buried (1,600 funerals and handmade animal-proof coffins in his first six years).

Damien energetically dispatched fundraising letters that pulled in the donations that funded his improvements, first from church parishioners, then from citizens who read his accounts in newspapers, eventually from the Hawaiian royal family, and from people in many lands inspired by his story. He also attracted other volunteer priests and nuns from America. At the age of 49, Father Damien died of complications from leprosy.

Further reading

○ Biography of Father Damien, workersforjesus.com/fatherdamien.htm

FIRST MODERN COLLEGE IN CHINA

Calvin Mateer and his wife Julia were missionaries sent to China by the Presbyterian Church in 1864. They were charged with opening a free school for boys in what is today Shandong province. They set to work as soon as they arrived and, despite significant obstacles, planted China's first Christian school for children. They and their funders back in the States provided the students with food, clothing, medical care, and supplies, in addition to an education. Both Christians and non-Christians were welcomed, and the school filled quickly.

Calvin used his language skills to produce and translate many Chinese materials for instruction and use in missions. He was the first American to publish primers on the Chinese language. And he presided over translation of the Bible into Mandarin. He and his wife gradually expanded their Tengchow School with financial support from the American Board of Commissioners for Foreign Missions, and summoned additional missionaries.

Eventually, the Mateers added college-level instruction, establishing Tengchow College as the first modern institution of higher education in China. They particularly emphasized science, and taught classes themselves in astronomy and mathematics. Their students played an important role across north China as teachers in early schools. Tengchow College grew into what is today Shandong University, a major national institution with more than 50,000 students.

Further reading

○ Short Mateer biography, bu.edu/missiology/missionary-biography/l-m/mateer-calvin-wilson-1836-1908

○ Full Mateer biography, archive.org/details/calvinwilsonmate00fish

AMERICAN COLLEGES ABROAD

The growing popularity of overseas missions spurred significant private giving by Americans in the later 1800s. These gifts exported American-

OVERSEAS

965

style schools, colleges, hospitals, and public works overseas, and sustained the many thousands of missionaries who manned these projects. The first American-style overseas college created in this way was Robert College, set up in Istanbul in 1863. It was named for New York philanthropist Christopher Robert, who poured $600,000 into it, and run by missionary Cyrus Hamlin. Other New York donors like the Dodge and Huntington families also supported the school, allowing it to add degrees and serve both male and female students, a groundbreaking practice at that time and place.

With organizing help from groups like the American Board of Commissioners for Foreign Missions, other similar institutions followed—like Syrian Protestant College founded in 1866 with a substantial endowment provided by U.S. donors. Its medical school was planned from the beginning to be one of its central features. It is now known as the American University of Beirut. These institutions produced many important alumni over the years.

Further reading

◦ History of the American University of Beirut, aub.edu.lb/main/about/Pages/history.aspx

1862

PEABODY BATTLES LONDON SLUMS

American trader and large-scale philanthropist George Peabody relocated to London—from which much of his business originated—in mid-life. He was moved by the plight of that city's poor, and over the years mulled various schemes for helping everyday families, including a water purification plant that would pipe pure drinking water to public fountains, and various forms of education aid. He finally settled on a plan to address the problem that was then most urgent in London—the horrendous slums into which many families crowded unhealthily.

With a gift of $2.5 million in 1862, Peabody created the Peabody Donation Fund. He appointed American and English trustees, and charged the charity with creating decent housing for "the labouring poor." The first block opened in 1864, a handsome building with every two apartments sharing their own full bathroom. Many additional model properties followed. The charity still operates today as a housing and urban regeneration charity, now known as the Peabody Trust, and owns 27,000 properties that it rents at moderate rates. It also offers assisted living for people needing help, and various efforts to promote home ownership and healthy living.

Further reading

◦ Peabody Trust, peabody.org.uk/about-us/our-story

RESPONDING TO
THE GREAT FAMINE OF IRELAND

Potato blight ravaged crops all across Europe in the 1840s, but in 1846 three quarters of Ireland's harvest was lost, leading to massive hunger and rampant disease. Amid shocking government incompetence, from a population of eight million a million people perished, and another million or so fled to the United States, Great Britain, and Canada. When it became evident that state authorities were not going to fend off the starvation, the Quakers in Dublin sent out a call for philanthropic action in November 1846. This, along with harrowing reports like those of starving dogs clawing up shallow graves and consuming the dead, got heavy play in U.S. newspapers. The result was more American giving for the Great Famine in Ireland than to any other cause in the first half of the nineteenth century. Donations poured in not just from Irish immigrants but from Protestants, Jews, Quakers, African Americans, and citizens of all stripes, mostly in small amounts but large numbers.

American aid "evoked a great national response in Ireland," notes historian Merle Curti, and "encouraged emigrants and would-be emigrants to think of America as a place of refuge, as offering a chance to share in an abundant society. The Irish relief campaign also fixed fairly well the main pattern of American giving for the relief of a disaster abroad."

Further reading

○ Merle Curti, *American Philanthropy Abroad* (Rutgers University Press, 1963)

○ Historical essay, irishamerica.com/2009/08/international-relief-efforts-during-the-famine

SUPPORT FOR GREEK INDEPENDENCE

The 1821 outbreak of the Greek War of Independence from the Ottoman Turks stirred deep sympathies among Americans, for whom the struggle for liberty and democracy in a fabled land recalled their own revolution not so long before. A May 1821 letter to John Quincy Adams by one of the Greek leaders sought American support as "friends, co-patriots and brothers, because you are fair, philanthropic, and brave." While the American government insisted on a position of neutrality during the war, local civic groups encouraged giving. Volunteers traveled to Greece—like Dr. Samuel Gridley Howe, who after completing his degree at Harvard Medical School served as chief surgeon of the nascent Greek Navy. Howe and many other

OVERSEAS

such American volunteers spoke at fundraising gatherings in cities like Albany, Boston, New York, and Philadelphia. West Point cadets raised $515, while Yale and Rutgers students raised $500 and $177, respectively. Many modest donations were bundled together and dispatched across the globe, the first American effort to provide emergency relief to a foreign people.

Further reading

◦ Merle Curti, *American Philanthropy Abroad* (Rutgers University Press, 1963)

◦ Historical essay, helleniccomserve.com/greek_war_for_independence.html

1820

PIONEER MISSIONS TO HAWAII

The first Christian missionaries to land in Hawaii (then known as the Sandwich Islands) were funded by donations to the American Board of Commissioners for Foreign Missions. A group of men, women, and children from Massachusetts—a mix of Presbyterians, Congregationalists, and Dutch Reformists—arrived to begin their service after spending a grueling 164 days at sea. They began building schools and churches, provided medical care that was avidly appreciated by natives, taught farming, home building, and sewing, established the first written form of the Hawaiian language, and printed materials in the native tongue, including classic Hawaiian tales.

The ruling families of Hawaii began to send their children to mission schools, and to convert to Christianity in the 1820s and 1830s. An 1839 Edict of Toleration from King Kamehameha III established religious liberty in the islands.

When whalers began to frequent Hawaiian ports in the 1820s, the missionaries intervened to protect natives from exploitation, weathering threats for their trouble. The missionaries also agitated against native practices like widespread infanticide and occasional human sacrifice. Every few years, ships brought additional small groups of missionary families; some became permanent residents while others rotated home. The actions of the American missionaries were crucial in linking Hawaii to the U.S. and eventual statehood.

Further reading

◦ Orramel and Ann Gulick, *The Pilgrims of Hawaii* (Revell, 1918)

1810

A BOARD TO FUND AMERICAN MISSIONARIES

Americans became interested in foreign missions in the early nineteenth century when the Second Great Awakening revitalized evangelical activity.

As church membership swelled, many Americans were inspired by the activities of the London Missionary Society. Interdenominational groups were formed to support missionaries serving, first, among American Indians and on the Western frontier, and then overseas.

Young people powered much of the missions movement. On a summer evening in 1806, five students from Williams College met in a grove to discuss the theology of spreading Christianity. When thunder clapped overhead they took refuge under a haystack. Later in their meeting they resolved to devote themselves to pursuing missionary work abroad, and what is now called the Haystack Prayer Meeting led to creation of a society that prepared students for overseas missions.

The American Board of Commissioners for Foreign Missions, created in 1810 out of the effort of these students, was America's first charitable agency focused on needy persons in other lands. The group's first fundraising appeal produced $1,000, and a $30,000 bequest from the widow of a wealthy Massachusetts merchant allowed the board to plan its first mission to India, which commenced in 1812. Popular support and individual donations for U.S. foreign missions grew steadily over the coming years and decades.

In its first 50 years of existence, the board sent more than 1,250 mission parties overseas. The hard-laboring young women and men it funded brought more than Christianity to the people they encountered. They served as schoolteachers, builders, health-care providers, farming instructors, translators, and human-rights advocates. They were often the first Americans many foreigners met, and helped form lasting friendly relations with the residents of many foreign lands.

Further reading

○ Timeline of events in the first 125 years of the ABCFM, globalministries.org/resources/ mission-study/abcfm/abcfm-in-history.html

OVERSEAS

MAJOR ACHIEVEMENTS OF AMERICAN PHILANTHROPY
(1636-2015)

LOCAL PROJECTS

Fantom: I despise a narrow field. O for the reign of universal benevolence. I want to make all mankind good and happy.

Goodman: Dear me! Sure that must be a wholesale sort of a job. Had you not better try your hand at a town or neighborhood first?

Fantom: Sir, I have a plan in my head for relieving the miseries of the whole world…. I would alter all the laws, and put an end to all the wars…. This is what I call doing things on a grand scale….

Goodman: One must begin to love somewhere; and I think it is as natural to love one's own family, and to do good in one's own neighborhood…. If every man in every family, village, and county did the same, why then all the schemes would be met, and the end of one village or town where I was doing good would be the beginning of another village where somebody else was doing good….

Fantom: Sir, a man of large views will be on the watch for great occasions to prove his benevolence.

Goodman: Yes, sir; but if they are so distant that he cannot reach them, or so vast that he cannot grasp them, he may let a thousand little, snug, kind, good actions slip through his fingers in the meanwhile. And so between the great thing that he cannot do and the little ones that he will not do, life passes, and nothing will be done.

McGuffey's Reader, 1844

LOCAL

971

"When I became serious about philanthropy, it was easiest to determine the needs in my own community. When you start working in your own community, there are a lot of positives. You've already got relationships. The programs you support are accessible and visible. You can go see them, talk with them, get a feel for them. And you get lots of affirmation. There are many reasons why people give locally."

      ❧ David Weekley, Philanthropy, *Winter 2009*

As a simple matter of fact, more donors agree with the rhetorical Mr. Goodman and the very real Mr. Weekley (winner of the 2015 William E. Simon Prize for Philanthropic Leadership) than with the more abstract and grandiose Mr. Fantom. A recent study out of Indiana University's Lilly Family School of Philanthropy showed that of all gifts of a million dollars or more made during the years 2000-2011, two thirds went to organizations in the same region as the giver. If you add in all the gifts of less than a million dollars, the proportion of American philanthropy that takes place locally is overwhelming.

In addition, a great many of the most effective charities in America— Goodwill, the Boy Scouts, the Salvation Army, Habitat for Humanity, the Union Gospel Missions, KIPP schools, and many more—provide their local affiliates with a powerful degree of operational autonomy. When donors give to these groups built out of decentralized chapters they are effectively supporting a neighborhood or regional group more than a national entity.

By definition, most local, small-scale giving is not visible to outsiders, so it's easy to miss. The cases we present below are merely examples—a kind of tip of the U.S. iceberg. Our intent is simply to remind everyone interested in philanthropy that, each day in this country, scads of close-to-home acts of support take place. It's easy to think that these local philanthropies are too small, too uncoordinated, too limited to generate "fundamental change." But piece together a scholarship program here and an inspiring museum there, a rural dental program in this town and an "Alice's Integrity Loan Fund" in another, and soon you see the outlines of a living, thousand-armed mechanism that responds to millions of local needs and longings, marshaling tens of billions of dollars. And every one of our hometowns is made more livable, richer, safer, and more interesting by the gifts rained down by this organic process of sharing bounty among neighbors.

      ❧ *Section research provided by Karl Zinsmeister,*
      Brian Brown, Caitrin Keiper, and Bill Kauffman

SAFETY AND A NEW LIFE FOR WOMEN IN CRISIS (DALLAS-FORT WORTH)

Lisa Rose and 11 other women in north Texas began meeting weekly to discuss their faith and how they could apply it to help "women in crisis" in their area. This eventually evolved into a nonprofit that zeroed in on a wrenching problem: There were not enough spots in the region where women and children could find help when fleeing abusers. And those that existed only allowed residence for 30 days, which was not enough time for most women to line up alternate housing and jobs and get their life back on track (which is why the abused typically return to their abusers several times before leaving for good).

The donors and organizers behind Rose's nonprofit developed a vision of "a supportive living community where women and their children in crisis can discover a new path for permanent change." They decided to offer a wide range of recuperative services—initially food, clothing, housing, and medical care, then counseling, life-skills mentoring, childcare, and education, and finally help with job placement and life on their own. It would be a faith-based program infused with Christian love and guidance, and it would be entirely privately funded, without government money.

Rose's husband Matt is chairman of the BNSF Railway and became involved in raising $28 million for the project. He eventually acquired 61 acres of land and helped the group build a freestanding community of 96 apartments, a general store, and a clothing boutique, between Dallas and Fort Worth. The Gatehouse opened in 2015. In addition to Lisa and Matt Rose, other major endowers of the program were Mark and April Anthony and the Walton Family Foundation. Large contributions were also provided by the Rees-Jones, Sid Richardson, Amon Carter, Mabee, and Washington foundations, and donors like the Perot, Rowling, Corman, and Albritton families.

Further reading

○ The Gatehouse, gatehousegrapevine.com

CALIFORNIA TECHIES FIND PHILANTHROPY (SILICON VALLEY)

Despite the enormous amount of money sloshing through Silicon Valley, and

LOCAL

the high-profile giving of families like the Packards, Hewletts, and Moores, our tech heartland has traditionally been a comparatively low-donating area. Until just the last few years, the community foundation covering Silicon Valley (San Mateo and Santa Clara counties) trailed well behind community foundations in places like Tulsa and Kansas City in total benefactions. That began to change in recent years, and by 2014 the Silicon Valley Community Foundation became the largest in the nation.

Most of the SVCF's recent expansion is thanks to Facebook founder Mark Zuckerberg and his wife, Priscilla Chan. In 2012 they placed in their donor-advised fund 18 million Facebook shares that were then valued at $500 million, and worth about a billion dollars a year later. Late in 2013 they gave another 18 million shares. The $100 million the couple had earlier pledged to Newark school reform was also channeled through the foundation, pushing their total personal boost to foundation assets to more than $2 billion. There have been a few other megadonors to the Silicon Valley Community Foundation as well, like former eBay head Jeff Skoll, who has given about $500 million. GoPro founder Nick Woodman and his wife, Jill, gave another to the SVCF when they donated shares worth $500 million in late 2014.

Of course most giving in Silicon Valley, as everywhere else in America, is made through direct donations, not through any community-foundation structure. Whatever form the donating takes, though, there is clear evidence that typical residents of Silicon Valley give far less to charity, especially on an income-adjusted basis, than Americans in most other places. (See "Who Gives Most to Charity" near the end of this book.)

The Silicon Valley Community Foundation is also a less home-oriented version than most counterparts across the nation, with a comparatively high proportion of its funds being directed to national or international causes. Nonetheless, a slight majority of its spending is done in the counties where it is based. It funnels about 40 percent of its grants into education. Health care, economic security, and immigrant integration are other significant priorities.

Further reading

◦ Foundation Center totals for giving by community foundations, foundationcenter.org/findfunders/topfunders/top25giving.html

2014

AN ART TROVE FOR HIS HOMETOWN (ST. LOUIS)

Charles Spink was a St. Louis institution. He was publisher of the locally based

Sporting News, a national weekly considered the "bible" of baseball reporting, and his wife Edie was mayor for 20 years of the inner suburb of Ladue where they lived. The couple had a passion for collecting Asian art, which they focused on in considerable measure because it was an area where their city's art museum was weak. Charles and Edie consulted with the St. Louis Art Museum throughout the time they collected, and loaned many pieces to the gallery as they purchased them. When Edie died, the 215 pieces she and her husband had accumulated—ceramics, jade, metalwork, works in lacquer, wood, and glass, with one jade piece being 5,000 years old—were bequeathed by the couple to their local museum.

In addition, the Spinks gave their hometown 10 paintings by American artists. These include a Rembrandt Peale portrait of George Washington, four Wyeth watercolors, and two works by Norman Rockwell: "Thanksgiving" and "Hot Stove League." The cumulative value of the Spink donation to their community was conservatively estimated at $50 million.

Further reading

○ *St. Louis Post-Dispatch* report, stltoday.com/entertainment/couple-donates-works-worth-at-least-million-to-st-louis/article_cb558144-e93f-5e62-ad59-416216be9042.html

2013

REMEMBERING THE OUTER BOROUGHS (NEW YORK CITY)

In March of 2013, health-care entrepreneur Donald Rubin and his wife, Shelley, donated $500,000 to the Bronx Museum of the Arts to expand and extend its free admission policy. In May, the couple gave another $500,000 to the Queens Museum of Art. And in September they presented $300,000 to the Socrates Sculpture Park, hard by Manhattan's Upper East Side—except that it's on the opposite shore of the East River, in Queens, on a former landfill site. "I haven't seen anybody else do this 'we-believe-in-the-rest-of-the-city' tour," said Queens Museum of Art director Tom Finkelpearl. "They're definitely not cookie-cutter philanthropists."

The Rubins do have some counterparts, however. For instance, Alan and Stuart Suna, brothers who co-own the TV production facility in Queens where shows like "The Sopranos" were shot. They have been loyal donors to museums, parks, and theaters in their unglamorous borough. "We're Queens guys," Alan told the *New York Times*. "Our business is in Queens, and Queens is always getting short shrift, so we're there to help."

Compared to Manhattan, four times as many New Yorkers live in Queens, the Bronx, Brooklyn, and Staten Island.

LOCAL

Further reading

○ *New York Times* reporting, nytimes.com/2013/10/09/arts/design/these-donors-will-take-anything-but-manhattan.html?_r=0

2012

GATES PUSHES SCHOOLS TO COOPERATE
(BOSTON, DENVER, HARTFORD, PHILADELPHIA, ETC.)

With the aim of encouraging cooperation between school districts and charter schools for the good of local children, the Bill & Melinda Gates Foundation announced a $25 million investment in seven lead cities in 2012. Their "Collaboration Compacts" require operators of different kinds of schools, local leaders, and community members to hammer out citywide agreements for sharing ideas, buildings, teacher training, school sign-up websites, assessment tests, and other resources between conventional district schools and charter schools. The Compacts in Philadelphia and Boston also fold the Catholic archdiocese schools into the mix.

The highest aim of the Compacts is to make it easy for families to find good options in their neighborhood. The idea is that authorities shouldn't care what sector a child gets instructed in, so long as the youngster and his family are well served. In addition to the seven cities that divided this $25 million grant, Gates is offering financial support and leadership in other cities to encourage additional experimentation with Compacts.

Further reading

○ Karl Zinsmeister, *From Promising to Proven* (The Philanthropy Roundtable, 2014)

○ Press release for $25 million Gates donation, gatesfoundation.org/media-center/press-releases/2012/12/gates-foundation-invests-nearly-25-million-in-seven-cities

2012

POLISHING JEWELS OF COLUMBUS
(OHIO)

Leslie Wexner lived the immigrant dream. Born in Dayton of Russian parents, he majored in business at Ohio State University. He continued on to law school before deciding business was much more interesting. He dropped out, got a $5,000 loan from an aunt, and started a young women's sportswear store in 1963. It eventually grew into Limited Brands, which owns Victoria's Secret, Bath and Body Works, and other popular companies.

Wexner believed Ohio State University had a lot to do with his success. "Attending this university changed my life," he said flatly. He made his first donation, $5, three years after getting his degree. In 1989, he gave $25 million to create the Wexner Center, a "research laboratory for all the arts" that university president Gordon Gee called "one of the crown jewels of Ohio State." Wexner subsequently gave the center $50 million more, plus a $42 million Picasso painting.

In 2011, the Wexners pledged $100 million to expand Ohio State's hospital, which serves a wide region while also training doctors (and where all four of the Wexner children were born). That brought the family's total giving to the university to $200 million. Wexner also put in 16 years of service on the school's board of trustees, while his wife was active on the medical-center board.

Further reading

○ Wexner Center for the Arts, wexarts.org/about/history

○ *Columbus Dispatch* reporting, dispatch.com/content/stories/local/2012/02/11/ohio-state-honors-wexners-devotion.html

2012

FINGER LAKES MUSICAL THEATER FESTIVAL (AUBURN)

The Finger Lakes Musical Theater Festival, which unfolds during summers in the small city of Auburn in the heart of New York state, is one of the largest musical-theater producing organizations in the country, serving 60,000 patrons in just its third year. It grew out of the success of the local Merry-Go-Round Playhouse, which had expanded into a $5 million summer operation with a companion youth-theater program that serves 125,000 students during the school year. The festival operated at three area theaters in its first years, providing Broadway, off-Broadway, and experimental shows in appropriate venues.

Creation of the Finger Lakes Musical Theater Festival has been fueled by millions of dollars of support from the local Emerson, Stardust, Schwartz Family, and Allyn foundations, along with individual donors. With a mission of using the arts to generate economic growth across the region, the festival and its philanthropic backers have long-term plans to build an additional theater in the heart of Auburn, and to collaborate with the local community college in expanding theater education for students. The festival is already collaborating with the many local wineries and hospitality businesses across the scenic Finger Lakes region to expand cultural tourism.

Further reading

○ Finger Lakes Musical Theater Festival, fingerlakesmtf.com

LOCAL

2011

BRISK DISASTER RELIEF
(ALABAMA AND MISSOURI)

Jessie duPont's foundation, located in Florida, hadn't devoted much energy to neighboring Alabama until more than 60 tornadoes struck the state on a single day in 2011, killing 248 people and devastating a 1,100-mile-long, 20-mile-wide stretch of property. Americans always respond generously to disasters, and the initial outpouring from individuals and foundations had been strong. But after the crisis passed, the tough work of rebuilding remained. That was when the duPont Fund stepped in with helpful strategy and smart grantmaking.

On her death in 1970, duPont left behind the $42 million Jessie Ball duPont Religious, Charitable, and Educational Fund. Investment growth brought its assets to more than $250 million, allowing it to distribute $12-18 million a year to causes Mrs. duPont had backed for years. In the years leading up to the tornadoes, that included about $1 million of grants in Alabama for housing and education in rural areas, and to help jumpstart a community foundation serving the poorest communities of the state.

After surveying the tornado wreckage, duPont started a special fund focused exclusively on Alabama's long-term recovery. It co-hosted a conference, 90 days after the storm, that mixed community leaders and non-local experts to plan solutions. Then it began to distribute support to scores of organizations to overcome specific sticking points. The fund became increasingly sophisticated, and eventually published a manual, "Creating Order from Chaos: Roles for Philanthropy in Disaster Planning and Response," to help other donors give intelligently when they swoop in to assist after calamities.

Just a month after these southeastern storms, a smaller but even more intense tornado tore through Joplin, Missouri, killing 161 people and destroying 4,000 homes in a town of 50,175 people. A massive outpouring of voluntary assistance was central to the immediate coping and long-term recovery of Joplin. At least 182,044 volunteers descended on the city from all over America, and over the next months and years they put in more than 1.5 million hours of service.

In the first weeks after the disaster, volunteers removed half of all of the storm debris (749 different groups organized by churches, colleges, and other sponsors pulled out 1.5 million cubic yards of mess). The Joplin YMCA provided free daycare for a year for survivors busy rebuilding.

Habitat for Humanity quickly built 95 new homes at no charge. Samaritan's Purse brought in 6,400 volunteers to tarp houses that lost their roofs, and otherwise protect the damaged property of low-income survivors. Local churches became focal points of the recovery.

The Margaret Cargill, Greater Kansas City Community, and Tulsa Community foundations supported families, offered legal assistance, and bought school supplies. Businesses like Walmart, Home Depot, Walgreens, Proctor & Gamble, Stanley, Chick-fil-A, and hundreds of others also made extraordinary contributions, donating millions to charitable groups, offering groups of employees as volunteers, providing crucial supplies, and rebuilding needed retail facilities on a crash basis. Local banks worked with customers to pause and restructure mortgage and loan payments.

Further reading

○ duPont Fund recovery conference, dupontfund.org/convening-helps-alabama-leaders-build-relationships-to-aid-tornado-recovery

○ "Creating Order from Chaos" report, dupontfund.org/wp-content/uploads/2012/05/duPont-Disaster-Relief-Guide.pdf

○ Analysis of Joplin recovery, independent.org/pdf/tir/tir_18_02_01_smith.pdf

2011

LOANS WITH INTEGRITY (LANCASTER COUNTY)

When Alice Dittman was president of Cornhusker Bank, she often found herself wishing she could give out more loans than she did. Sometimes the business idea looked good, but the credit history wasn't there. So in 2011, soon after she retired, she decided to start where her previous job had left off.

Dittman donated $1 million to start Alice's Integrity Loan Fund, a microfinance program to help entrepreneurs, especially minorities and

◈ PhilAphorism

Never doubt that a small group of thoughtful, committed citizens can change the world. Indeed, it is the only thing that ever has.

☞ Margaret Mead

LOCAL

women, get their businesses started. Unlike with traditional loans, getting a loan from Alice's Integrity starts with assessment of the moral character of the applicant. According to the official criteria, "Alice's Integrity Loan Fund weights the criteria differently than a regular financial institution would—placing the greatest value on Character and minimizing the need for Capital. It is the fund's intent to encourage responsible use of credit and work with borrowers who wish to honor their word and keep their reputation sound."

Loans of up to $5,000 are given out at 3.25 percent fixed interest, for a maximum term of 36 months. If that is repaid, applications for $10,000 loans will be considered. The loans can be used only to start or expand a business. Recipients don't just get money; they also receive mandatory training and mentoring from retired executives and the Nebraska Business Development Center. Unlike some of the more famously successful microfinance initiatives, which tended to be international, Dittman's effort is entirely local—only residents of Lancaster County, Nebraska are eligible.

Further reading

○ Alice's Integrity Loan Fund, cdr-nebraska.org/site/financial-products/alices-integrity-loan-fund

AVIATION SCHOOL
(GRAND RAPIDS)

Dick DeVos is a businessman and former member of the Michigan State Board of Education who is keen to give families choices in the schools their children attend. He is also a jet-rated pilot. He connected these interests by founding the West Michigan Aviation Academy as a public charter school. It opened in 2010 on the grounds of the Grand Rapids airport with 80 freshmen. By 2015 there were 500 students enrolled, with room to grow. Along with its college-prep curriculum WMAA offers several aviation-related tracks: flight, engineering, aviation maintenance, and aviation business. "We try to introduce an aviation concept into everything we teach," explains DeVos. Reading or writing assignments may be connected to flying; math problems are often presented in terms of the practical realities of navigation.

"We're in the process of acquiring a plane and offering full flight capabilities so that individuals could graduate with their pilot's license if that's their interest." The school offers a gliding program during the summer. A number of retired pilots in Grand Rapids volunteer as flight instructors. There is a radio-controlled aircraft club.

As president of the board, DeVos was involved with the school on a daily basis, and he and his wife, Betsy, donated about $5 million to get it launched. WMAA is an example of the specialized schools the charter movement is making possible—there are schools that are arts oriented, trades based, sports focused, environmentally driven, that teach in two languages, that emphasize science instruction. This particular school's combination of academics, character training, technical instruction, and hands-on opportunities in aviation exists in no other public or private school in the U.S.

Further reading

○ West Michigan Aviation Academy, westmichiganaviation.org/about

ARTPRIZE (MICHIGAN)

Rick DeVos, grandson of the founder of Amway (and son of Dick and Betsy DeVos), wanted to boost the arts in western Michigan. He initially explored the idea of a film festival, but concluded his hometown would have nothing unique to offer in that crowded field. Instead, he settled on a more unorthodox idea: a citywide art contest.

Borrowing ideas from science contents that have offered large cash prizes for the best inventions, DeVos established clear and simple rules. And he added his own twist by turning his entire city into the gallery where entries would be displayed (in public locations all across Grand Rapids). Then he got really unconventional: Everyday people would be the judges, selecting winners by popular vote.

DeVos's goal wasn't high art, it was to build interest in creativity within his region. He succeeded. By its second year the contest attracted 1,700 artists and 400,000 votes from Michiganders and others visiting from all over the world. The Dick and Betsy DeVos Family Foundation kicks in about a million and a half dollars every year to defray the festival's cost of about $3 million per annum.

Further reading

○ ArtPrize 2014 annual report, artprizeannualreport.org

○ *Philanthropy* magazine reporting, philanthropyroundtable.org/topic/excellence_in_ philanthropy/contesting_art

○ *Wall Street Journal* analysis, magazine.wsj.com/hunter/donate/critical-mass

OUTDOOR THERAPY (BOZEMAN)

"Bozeman is the Holy Grail of fly fishing." So says Tom O'Connor

LOCAL

of Warriors and Quiet Waters, a Montana-based charity that takes service-injured veterans on weeklong trips to learn the sport and spend time in nature. For many participants, the trip is a short vacation from an intensive and lengthy recovery at a military hospital. They are housed in a log cabin outside of town, fed by local "moms," outfitted with all the gear they'll need from the last remaining U.S. manufacturer of fishing clothing, taught and led by professional fishing guides, and joined in casting along blue-ribbon streams by local companions. As O'Connor explains, "We decided when we started that we were going to do this right."

Since its inception in 2007, more than 470 servicemembers have gone through the program in groups of six. The progression remains the same with each cohort—initial apprehension followed by deep relaxation. So striking is the change from Day One to Day Six that O'Connor's wife often "can tell by looking at the photos which day of the week it is." Several attendees have enjoyed the program so much that they moved out to Bozeman to attend college at Montana State after completing their recovery.

The program has also added skiing and horseback programs. Remarkably, most of the donations that support each attendee (at a total cost of $4,300) come from small local donors—the million-dollar organization's median donation is $110. It is broad support, not major wealth, that keeps Warriors and Quiet Waters in business. Speaking of one local supporter, O'Connor says, "I know I can count on a little old lady at the retirement home to send us $25 per month."

Further reading

○ Warriors and Quiet Waters, warriorsandquietwaters.org/about

2006

BOOSTING BOY SCOUT COUNCILS (PHOENIX, LEBANON, PARKERSBURG)

With 288 separate councils operating across the country with a great deal of autonomy, most philanthropic support for the Boy Scouts of America is local support. There have been important national gifts, like the 1939 donation by oil man and philanthropist Waite Phillips of 125,000 acres of mountain range in New Mexico to create the beloved Philmont Scout Ranch. Also the donations by Stephen Bechtel and others that recently carved out a counterpart high-adventure wilderness property in West Virginia (see 2013 entry on our list of Nature achievements). But the lifeblood of Scouting is community giving.

This starts with volunteers: Nearly one million adults volunteered in local councils across the U.S. in 2015, with the average volunteer giving his

Scout unit hundreds of hours of time per year. Millions more Americans wrote checks to their local Scout council. And it isn't just the legions of small donors who focus on their home communities; major donors frequently also funnel gifts to localities they have special connections to. Ed and Jeanne Arnold, for instance, who had been loyal contributors to the BSA initiatives (giving $10 million, for instance, to help troops across the country attract more Hispanic boys into Scouting), donated $1 million in 2006 to bolster Boy Scout councils in three specific areas where they have family roots: Lebanon, Pennsylvania; Parkersburg, West Virginia; and Phoenix, Arizona.

A local Scouting experience has been important to many boys and men. Fully 181 U.S. astronauts were Scouts, including 11 of the 12 who walked on the moon. Six U.S. Presidents were Scouts, as were 18 sitting governors as of 2014, and 191 members of the 113th Congress. More than a third of the cadets at West Point have been involved in Scouting, and one out of six were Eagle Scouts.

Further reading

◦ Scouting fact sheet, scouting.org/About/FactSheets/ScoutingFacts.aspx

◦ *Philanthropy* magazine reporting, philanthropyroundtable.org/topic/excellence_in_philanthropy/a_century_of_scouting

───────── 2006 ─────────

TAKING THE ACHE OUT OF BUSH LIFE (ALASKA)

The people served by the Rasmuson Foundation are different. Many reside in very small and isolated towns. Transportation is often poor, weather

☙ PhilAphorism

Historically, Americans did not raise funds by appealing to donors' guilt, or by urging them to "give back" to society. Instead, they appealed to their fellow citizens' ideals and aspirations, their religious principles, and their desire to create.

☞ *Adam Meyerson*

LOCAL

frequently fierce. Because they are thinly scattered across the Union's largest state, it can be difficult to provide philanthropic services to Alaskans.

But these challenges have always defined Rasmuson's work, so the foundation has gotten good at coping. Founded in 1955 with an initial $3,000 gift from Jenny Rasmuson, the foundation was created to honor her husband, a Swedish immigrant who built the Bank of Alaska into a powerful financial enterprise. When their son bequeathed the foundation much of his personal fortune of $400 million in 2000, the task became easier.

With assets of $650 million and annual grants of $22 million in 2014, Rasmuson has disbursed more than $280 million across its state since 1955. The foundation has a hand in most current philanthropy in Alaska, and pays particular attention to small things that can improve the quality of life for ordinary people. A prime example: dentistry. People with normal access to oral care forget how miserable life can become when a tooth erupts and a dentist is nowhere to be found.

In 2006, Rasmuson gave a $1 million grant to the Alaska Native Tribal Health Consortium to train special dental-health aides who live in or fly into remote Alaskan villages. The aides provide preventive and palliative care, and improve the oral health of people residing in areas that can't keep a dentist in business. Rasmuson's innovation has brought life-changing dental assistance to more than 35,000 rural Alaskans. Other funders have been inspired to export the resoundingly successful program to sufferers in different parts of the U.S.

Further reading

○ *Anchorage Daily News* 2003 history of Rasmuson Foundation, rasmuson.org/index. php?switch=viewpage&pageid=48#top

○ Alaskan Native Tribal Health Consortium, anthc.org/chs/chap/dhs

2005

NEW MUSIC IN MIZZOU (MISSOURI)

Rex Sinquefield had taken himself from a Missouri orphanage in 1951 to leadership of a major investment firm in 1981. He developed some of the first index funds, and his company, Dimensional Fund Advisors, managed $376 billion in assets as of 2015. Throughout his rise, Sinquefield remained intensely interested in his home state—where he retired in 2005. He became active in Missouri politics, and he and his wife, Jeanne, operated the Sinquefield Charitable Foundation. With Jeanne being a musician (string bass) and a firm believer in the value of the arts to education, they began funding the University of Missouri's School of Music.

An annual $50,000 in Sinquefield funding started a project called Creating Original Music. It was a program of camps and competitions for a variety of ages that promoted composition of new music statewide. In 2009, an additional $1 million gift started a spinoff project, the Mizzou New Music Initiative. This incubated the composition and performance of new music via scholarships, a summer music festival, an annual prize, a new-music ensemble, and more. And in 2015 the Sinquefields donated $10 million to construct a new building for the School of Music. The Mizzou New Music Initiative is "intended to position the University of Missouri School of Music as a leading center in the areas of composition and new music."

Further reading

○ Mizzou New Music Initiative, mizzounewmusic.missouri.edu/introduction.html

○ University of Missouri 2009 news release, munews.missouri.edu/news-releases/2009/0309-sinquefield-gift.php

2005

ENTREPRENEUR HIGH
(PROVIDENCE AND NEWPORT)

Rhode Island resident Bill Daugherty was wealthy by the age of 40. While in business school he came up with an idea for an online media and search company, then built it and sold it for $500 million. He started looking around his small state for ways to use his money philanthropically. He didn't just want to write checks or sit in board meetings—as a successful business owner he had more to offer than money, and he wanted to get involved.

At last, in 2005, a neighbor introduced him to a social entrepreneur who thought the same way. Dennis Littky was co-founder of the Met Schools in Providence, an alternative academic program oriented toward career and technical skills, funded by CVS Pharmacy founder Stanley Goldstein. Littky's schools were built on the latest research about how kids learn, but he was missing something he wanted: an entrepreneurial element to the curriculum. The two men connected, and Daugherty designed a new program for the schools called Entrepreneurship 360.

The program gave students an inside look at how to start a business. Daugherty did more than create it and fund it—he spent two mornings a week mentoring the students, in keeping with the Met Schools' philosophy that adult nurturing is crucial to child development. The program led to successful businesses started by kids graduating from high school, and a freestanding Center for Entrepreneurship on the school campus in

LOCAL

Providence, the only standalone business incubator for high-school students in the country. The Entrepreneurship 360 curriculum remains an integral part of the Met coursework, now taught in their six Rhode Island high schools and exported to 36 other alternative schools in 16 cities nationwide.

Further reading

○ Met Schools, metcenter.org/entrepreneur-360-e-360-history-and-leadership

CADE MUSEUM FOR CREATIVITY AND INVENTION (GAINESVILLE)

James Cade was a creator. Best-known for Gatorade, he also invented the first shock-dissipating football helmet, a diet-changing method for treating autism, and many other things. On the side, he was a poet, writer, and art collector.

He was also a loyal Floridian. The professor of medicine at the University of Florida named his legendary sports drink after the Florida Gators, its first major users. When he turned to philanthropy, Florida was also his center of attention. He and his wife, Mary, helped found the Community Foundation of North Central Florida, and funded the Fisher House in Gainesville for the families of wounded veterans.

When Cade became concerned about America's declining performance in science and math, he decided to give the Gainesville area an organization that would help redraw the link between technical skills and creative abundance. In 2004, three years before his death, he and his family created the Cade Museum Foundation with an endowment to cover most operating costs of a museum dedicated to promoting creativity. Exhibits were planned. A temporary facility was created for school visits and other purposes. Fundraising is now under

⚘ PhilAphorism

When I talk to young people who seem destined for great success, I tell them…concentrate on your family and getting rich (which I found very hard work). Don't forget that those who don't make money never become philanthropists.

☞ *Robert Wilson*

way for costs of a dramatic $9 million building to be erected in Gainesville's central park.

Further reading

○ Cade Museum for Creativity and Invention, cademuseum.org

2003

VIDEO MEDICINE IN THE DESERT
(NEW MEXICO)

There aren't enough medical specialists available to treat some illnesses, particularly in rural areas. Telemedicine, however, allows primary physicians and nurses in more remote locations to bring in specialists to consult with their patients via video. In a state like New Mexico—with a population of 2 million spread over 120,000 square miles, and just one academic health center to serve them all—this offers big enhancements of basic primary care.

Project ECHO is a philanthropically supported telemedicine initiative that aims to radically and inexpensively expand the availability of expert care to rural New Mexicans. The mechanism is simple: Local family doctors join weekly videoconferences with a panel of specialists, where they present their patients' cases and receive advice on what treatments to pursue.

The program began with a focus on improving care for hepatitis C, a serious health problem in New Mexico. It has since developed a capacity to address many chronic conditions. The latest addition is mental-health services offered by video link, with major support from the GE Foundation and the Robert Wood Johnson Foundation.

Further reading

○ University of New Mexico website, echo.unm.edu/about-echo

2003

DECENTRALIZED GIVING AT EL POMAR
(COLORADO)

Spencer Penrose went west in 1892 to seek his fortune, and found it in copper mines, then went on to build important institutions across his adopted home state of Colorado, like the Broadmoor hotel and the Pikes Peak highway. Upon their deaths, he and his wife, Julie, left most of their money to the Colorado Springs foundation they established to benefit their region, known as El Pomar. By 2003, the foundation's endowment had grown to over $500 million.

At that point, the El Pomar board established a major new mechanism to draw on local knowledge and make sure that their grants included

LOCAL

priorities important to each of the communities across their state. They divided their state into sub-regions (currently 11 in number), and created in each one a council of local community leaders. Every regional council includes one member of the El Pomar board, plus residents from the locality: businessmen, college presidents, elected officials, newspaper publishers, nonprofit leaders, and so forth. Each regional board has the authority to distribute a few hundred thousand dollars of grants themselves, in addition to advising the mother foundation on what in their area would be most useful to support on a larger scale.

The councils allow a better sense of what Colorado's counties and smaller towns need to improve their quality of life. They help El Pomar identify the best operators and innovators, particularly in rural areas that might otherwise get overlooked. And they encourage the transfer of good ideas from one place to another. As of 2014, the regional councils had helped El Pomar distribute $10 million of highly focused aid.

Further reading

o El Pomar Foundation, elpomar.org/what-we-do/regional-partnerships

o *Philanthropy* magazine profile, philanthropyroundtable.org/topic/excellence_in_ philanthropy/el_pomar_foundation

ENTREPRENEURS ADOPT CLASSES
(DISTRICT OF COLUMBIA)

The Network for Teaching Entrepreneurship has been showing high schoolers how to lift themselves out of poverty by creating their own businesses since 1987. But the organization added a new twist when its Washington, D.C., branch started getting real business owners involved. Successful entrepreneurs in the area were asked to adopt a class. This meant providing the $10,000 in funding it took to put a typical group of 20 to 30 students through a semester of training on how to start a businesses, including supplies, field trips, and cash prizes for actually launching an enterprise. It also required the business owners to provide mentorship—meeting with their adopted class to provide real-world perspective and help the students refine their business ideas. Twelve D.C.-area entrepreneurs took on the challenge in the program's first year, critiquing business plans, coaching students on how to manage employees, and providing the kind of practical guidance that only people who have done something themselves can offer.

The innovation in D.C. was such a success that it was quickly expanded to other cities. NFTE has now helped more than 500,000 students from low-income communities understand the demands and satisfactions of business creation. (See 1987 entry on our companion list of philanthropic achievements encouraging Prosperity.)

Further reading

○ *Philanthropy* reporting, philanthropyroundtable.org/topic/excellence_in_philanthropy/ great_local_grants_adopt-a-class

○ Network for Teaching Entrepreneurship, nfte.com/get-involved/support/adopt

WINGED HISTORY
(VIRGINIA)

As they glide into Washington's Dulles Airport, air travelers pass an enormous hangar complex. Beneath its gently curved roof lies one of the world's greatest collections of aviation treasures. The man who built that complex is a Hungarian immigrant to the U.S. named Steven Udvar-Hazy. In 1973 he co-founded a company that purchases aircraft and leases them to commercial carriers. His firm eventually owned 1,000 planes and counted most of the world's major airlines among its customers.

As Udvar-Hazy was growing his business, the Smithsonian's National Air and Space Museum had a growth problem of its own. Its facility on Washington's National Mall could not accommodate its fast-expanding collection. Udvar-Hazy stepped forward with a $65 million gift to build a museum annex adjacent to Dulles Airport, where aircraft joining the collection, even very large specimens, could simply be flown in and taxied over to the exhibition space, saving millions of dollars that would otherwise have to be spent on disassembling, trucking, and reassembling large display craft. The largest construction project in Smithsonian history, the Udvar-Hazy Center is also the only Smithsonian facility to be constructed entirely with private funds.

Opened in 2003, the Udvar-Hazy Center quickly became the most visited museum in Virginia, hosting more than a million guests every year. It is home to hundreds of important artifacts, including the *Enola Gay*, the B-29 that dropped the atomic bomb on Hiroshima; space shuttle *Discovery*; a *Gemini* capsule; a Concorde; an SR-71 Blackbird; the prototype for the first commercially successful jetliner, the Boeing 707; a Dassault Falcon that was FedEx's first jet; and the GlobalFlyer, the first craft to circumnavigate the world nonstop without refueling. Multimedia offerings and a tower from which visitors can observe movements at Dulles and learn about air traffic control complement the collection. Says

LOCAL

989

Udvar-Hazy: "I know this museum will impart to millions of children the same love for aviation that I have."

Further reading

○ About the Udvar-Hazy Center, airandspace.si.edu/about/history/udvar-hazy-center.cfm

2002

CHARITABLE FOOD DISTRIBUTION INITIATIVE (NEVADA, OKLAHOMA, ARKANSAS)

The Donald Reynolds Foundation has made some high-profile national gifts like the one to Washington's National Portrait Gallery that created the Donald W. Reynolds Center for American Art and Portraiture, and the $38 million grant to the Mount Vernon Ladies' Association that spurred creation of a great library devoted to the study of George Washington at his Mount Vernon estate. The foundation has longstanding interests in health care, journalism, and Nevada colleges that reflect its founder's passions.

But it has also put a special emphasis on serving its home region. A deep and innovative effort to improve local food banks has been an important part of this. Unlike much charitable food support, Reynolds's efforts were focused on helping groups get their supplies to people who most need it via improved distribution. Its 2002 Charitable Food Distribution Initiative awarded grants to food banks in Nevada, Oklahoma, and Arkansas (the three states where Reynolds made most of his money in the newspaper business) so they could plan and build better distribution networks. The foundation then launched further efforts to make these food banks more efficient. The initiative granted a total of $69 million over a decade, much of it to build new or expanded facilities for more effective distribution to families whose access to food is "insecure."

Further reading

○ Grants by the Reynolds Charitable Food Distribution Initiative, dwreynolds.org/Grants/
  Web%20-%20CF.pdf

2001

A NEW MUSEUM FOR A NEW SOUTH (CHARLOTTE)

The Levine Museum of the New South in Charlotte has a tricky mission: to faithfully tell the story of the American Southeast since 1865. It's a period that brought the region Reconstruction, Jim Crow, the civil-rights movement, an economic boom, waves of northern and then international immigration, and tumultuous change. The museum opened in its 40,000-square-foot space in the city's recently revitalized First Ward in 2001, with a permanent exhibition called "Cotton Fields to Skyscrapers: Charlotte and the Carolina Piedmont in the New South," plus a range of special exhibitions. This and subsequent enhancements were made possible by $5 million of support from Leon Levine, who opened a store called Family Dollar in Charlotte in 1959 and expanded it into a company with 7,600 outlets in 45 states.

"We want to help build the quality of life here," Levine says of his hometown of Charlotte. Levine tells us that in his philanthropy as in his businesses, he has sought to provide useful services and fill gaps in people's lives. Selling household items at low cost allowed families to have things they might not otherwise be able to afford. The museum has gone beyond recording the region's history and attempted to strengthen its surrounding community by hosting educational events tied to important current issues— like a discussion of problems in the city's education system, and a bus tour of Charlotte's neighborhoods.

Further reading

○ Latest Levine challenge grant, museumofthenewsouth.org/support/the-levine-challenge-grant

FRIST CENTER FOR THE VISUAL ARTS (NASHVILLE)

Thomas Frist Sr. was a founder of modern hospital systems. He and his son built the Nashville-based Hospital Corporation of America, which numbered 165 hospitals and 115 surgery centers as of 2015. They also built a charitable arm which became known as the Frist Foundation in 1997. It is dedicated to improving the quality of life in Nashville, with a particular interest in funding the visual arts.

The Frist Center for the Visual Arts opened in 2001 with 24,000 feet of space in the city's old central post office. Rather than having a permanent

---

⌐◊ PhilAphorism

If you can't feed a hundred people,
then feed just one.

☞ *Mother Teresa*

LOCAL

collection, the center was built to host visiting exhibitions, which flow through the building every couple months, on average. Much of the $10 million granted annually by the Frist Foundation is operating support for this Visual Arts center. The foundation's other priority in Nashville has been to build up the charitable infrastructure. It has created and sustained a community foundation, a volunteer center, management consulting services for local nonprofits, and annual grants to nonprofits to improve their technology.

Further reading

○ Frist Center for the Visual Arts, fristcenter.org

RESPECTABLE EDUCATION
(LAS VEGAS)

Andre Agassi grew up in Las Vegas, spending the first 15 years of his life there before heading to a tennis academy in Florida to begin one of the most storied careers in professional tennis. But his heart never left home. At age 24, in the meaty middle of his playing career, Agassi formed a foundation with the aim of helping underprivileged kids in his hometown. After briefly running an after-school program, it founded a Boys & Girls club, and the following year built a shelter and educational center for abused children. "But then a light bulb went off," Agassi explains. "We realized we were sticking band-aids on real issues."

Agassi decided that to help kids lastingly, they needed education. So he built his own charter school and focused his foundation on its success. He planted his flag in West Las Vegas, the city's most depressed neighborhood, about nine miles from the glitzy Strip. The Andre Agassi College Preparatory Academy opened in 2001 and now spans grades K-12, with more than 1,100 students. Their campus was built with $40 million of private money raised by Agassi. Tuition at the charter school is free, and students are chosen by lottery (though Agassi convinced regulators to allow him to give admissions preference to children who live within a two-mile radius of the school). School days are two hours longer than at other Las Vegas public schools, and the school year is ten days longer. There is no tenure for teachers. The school is centered on Agassi's detailed "code of respect."

Further reading

○ Andre Agassi Prep, agassiprep.net

LARGEST GIFT FOR LITERACY
(MISSISSIPPI)

After selling his company Netscape, Jim Barksdale and his wife, Sally, gave the largest gift ever to improve literacy—$100 million—to start the Barksdale Reading Institute in 2000 in the state of Mississippi, where 700,000 adults couldn't read at a high-school level. The institute works with public schools and universities to improve teaching of reading and increase the literacy levels of Mississippi students in grades K-3. Finding cost-efficient progress elusive within conventional schools, the BRI in 2010 added a "principal project" which places new highly qualified principals in chronically underperforming schools, giving them wide authority over personnel, curriculum, discipline, grading, etc., and a mandate to improve reading instruction with special teaching and testing. Barksdale's latest gift, creating the Mississippi Principal Corps at the University of Mississippi, builds upon this approach by producing an annual cohort of specially trained reform-minded principals. A 2012 gift by the Robert Hearin Support Foundation reinforced the program.

Further reading

○ Chester Finn and Kelly Amis, *Making it Count: A Guide to High-Impact Education Philanthropy* (Thomas Fordham Foundation, 2001)

○ News report on the shift to Principal Project, hechingerreport.org/content/in-mississippi-private-money-and-strong-principals-boost-struggling-schools_11189

BANKING ON THE PALMETTO STATE
(SOUTH CAROLINA)

Darla Moore was the highest-paid woman in banking. Then she married multimillionaire investor Richard Rainwater in 1991. Working together, they tripled his fortune to $1.5 billion by 1998.

That same year, Moore gave $25 million to her alma mater, the University of South Carolina (which renamed its business school after her). That gift was followed by an additional $45 million to the Moore School of Business in 2004, and $5 million to the school's aerospace center. She also gave $10 million to Clemson University in her father's name, and founded the Charleston Parks Conservancy and the Palmetto Institute (a think tank focused on expanding the state economy).

LOCAL

Further reading
○ Darla Moore School of Business, mooreschool.sc.edu/about/darlamoore.aspx

BUBBLE-UP ECONOMICS (TEXAS)

Students can get a refreshing lesson in free enterprise at, of all places, the Dr. Pepper Museum in Waco, Texas. The man who built the Dr. Pepper brand after starting his career driving trucks had a dream of educating the public on the many creative nuances and social benefits of creating a successful business. He proposed to do this by using soft drinks—the embodiment of an industry built on fun and fancy rather than necessity—as a model. In 1997, the museum created the W. W. Clements Free Enterprise Institute to bring his dream to life.

"Advertising and Marketing Kid Style" is one of three day-long programs put on for Texas school children by the Clements Institute. Students first tour the museum's exhibits—which include a replica of an old corner drugstore and a section of bottling equipment—to get acquainted with the principal product and the soft-drink industry in general. Then they get a crash course in entrepreneurship, with hands-on training that leads them to create their own product, logo, and marketing campaign, including a video commercial. Staff members judge the finished products and marketing materials. This gives students a taste of market competition and of the hard work it takes to succeed as an entrepreneur.

Further reading
○ Free Enterprise Institute, drpeppermuseum.com/FEI/Free-Enterprise-Institute.aspx

HEALTH CARE FOR THE NEEDY (ORLANDO)

The pastor of St. Luke's United Methodist Church in Orlando, William Barnes, asked his congregation to create a volunteer medical clinic to serve immigrants, itinerant agricultural workers, homeless persons, seasonal tourism employees lacking health insurance, and other needy locals. Within six months, the church had opened a clinic where volunteer doctors, nurses, and helpers were seeing patients at no charge. Central Floridians began to drive long distances to visit Shepherd's Hope, so other churches joined as partners, and in 2015 there were five Shepherd's Hope clinics operating in greater Orlando, seeing low-income patients from one to four days per week.

Every clinic relies on three sponsors. Churches are the primary providers of volunteer doctors, nurses, therapists, and other assisting persons, who are motivated to serve by their faith commitment. The church also is expected to provide an advisory committee to oversee the center, to appoint a volunteer director and fill other positions, and to supply several thousand dollars for expenses. A facility partner provides space in a building. And a hospital partner offers donated pharmaceuticals, diagnostic tests, and other specialty services. When uninsured persons get sick they often show up at emergency rooms which are expensive to operate, so hospitals have economic as well as humanitarian incentives to assist Shepherd's Hope.

The other crucial support to these clinics is philanthropic donations. The Dr. Phillips, Edyth Bush, Robert Wood Johnson, Magruder, Friends, Komen, and Eckerd Family foundations were crucial in the early years of setting up the clinics. The organization gets no direct government funding. The state removed a crucial obstacle to the clinics' success, however, by passing a law that grants immunity from malpractice suits to any health-care professional who volunteers in a program serving low-income patients. Shepherd's Hope has provided more than 160,000 free medical consultations since opening.

Further reading

○ Organization website, ShepherdsHope.org

○ The Philanthropy Roundtable talk, philanthropyroundtable.org/site/print/annual_
meeting_highlights_great_local_grants

1996

A DONOR-ASSISTED URBAN TURNAROUND
(NEW YORK CITY)

Beneath its sometimes rude exterior, New York City is actually a generous town. A study by the Center on Wealth and Philanthropy concludes that,

PhilAphorism

There are eight levels of charity…. The highest is when you strengthen a man's hand until he need no longer be dependent upon others.

Maimonides

LOCAL

adjusted in the center's own way for the cost of living, high-income households in the New York metropolitan area give more to charity than in any other city—on average, nearly 9 percent of their disposable income. This dates way back. For instance, when a collection of businessmen decided after the Civil War that the city needed to add some polish to its industrial vigor, they quickly provided funds for what became the Metropolitan Museum of Art. Today, local cultural institutions supported by philanthropic giving are some of the most important elements in making New York what it is.

What happens, though, when it's not a museum that needs help, but the culture of the city itself? By the end of the 1970s, New York City was broke, the Bronx was burning, crime and drug abuse were spiking, essential agencies seemed ungovernable, and racial tension was literally murderous. Dystopia lurked around every corner.

Once again, private philanthropy stepped in. Nonprofit "business improvement districts" were created to provide basic street services where the city government was falling down. Philanthropically supported research organizations like the Manhattan Institute spewed new ideas on how to tame and revive the metropolis. Donor-funded researchers like Charles Murray, Lawrence Mead, the Working Seminar on Poverty, and others churned out fresh ideas that, within a decade, led to new laws undoing the excesses of what Bill Clinton criticized as "welfare as we know it."

Idea-based philanthropy similarly helped spread the "broken-windows" understanding that tolerating petty offenses and visual blight will quickly lead to bigger crimes. Acting on this new insight eventually pushed New York City crime down to less than a fifth of its 1990 peak. As urban war zones stopped smoking, Habitat for Humanity and other housing charities built blocks and blocks of single-family homes ringed by carefully tended lawns in places like the Bronx, where just a few years before, arson-scorched empty towers had seemed likely to molder forever.

As the gravest emergencies were gradually solved, smart philanthropists improved other aspects of the city's quality of life, often by challenging prevailing assumptions. Richard Gilder and allied donors (capped by a $100 million gift from John Paulson) formed the privately funded Central Park Conservancy to resuscitate the worn fields, dangerous thickets, and dilapidated structures of the city's crown jewel open space. Stephen Schwarzman led a rehabilitation of the New York Public Library, Roger Hertog revived the New York Historical Society, and David Koch and cadres of other donors revitalized important institutions like Lincoln Center and the Metropolitan Museum. Robert Rosenkranz established a brainy live debate series in the city called "Intelligence Squared." Another group of donors created the High Line, which attracts 4.4 million annual visitors and is estimated to have sparked $2 billion of surrounding real-estate development. Sandy Weill, the Kraus family, and others funded an explosion of enhancements to the city's hospitals.

A city where ugliness, dysfunction, and danger had become the norm was once again made livable. And private giving sparked many of the turnarounds.

Further reading

∘ *City Journal* on recent private gifts, city-journal.org/2014/24_3_nyc-private-wealth.html

PRITZKER PRIZES
(CHICAGO)

Nicholas Pritzker came to America from Russia in 1881 at the age of 10. He taught himself English, got a law degree, and went into business. His sons built on the family holdings, and in 1957 they bought a hotel near Los Angeles—which they subsequently expanded into the Hyatt hotel chain. In addition to many national philanthropic achievements like the Pritzker Architecture Prize, the Pritzkers have placed many philanthropic crowns on the head of their Chicago motherland.

In 1996, Robert Pritzker made a $60 million challenge grant that revitalized Chicago's Illinois Institute of Technology. The family backed the Pritzker School of Medicine at the University of Chicago, the Pritzker Institute of Biomedical Science and Engineering at Illinois Tech, Pritzker College Prep charter school, and the Jay Pritzker Pavilion at Millennium Park. The Pritzker Military Library, the A. N. Pritzker Elementary School, the Pritzker Family Children's Zoo, the Pritzker Legal Research Center at Northwestern University, the University of Chicago's Urban Education Institute, and other institutions are also their handiwork.

Further reading

∘ Robert Pritzker obituary, nytimes.com/2011/10/31/business/robert-a-pritzker-dies-at-85-family-conglomerate-included-hyatt.html

RECLAIMING A CITY
(HARTFORD)

Starting in the 1950s, the city of Hartford slowly tumbled from being one of the wealthiest cities in America to becoming one of the poorest. The city

LOCAL

hit bottom in the mid-1990s when several key industries closed, moved, or cut staff. The population was shrinking and crime was roaring. Hartford's leading citizens and organizations decided to act.

The Hartford Foundation for Public Giving began advocating for a plan to develop the city's neglected riverfront and make it a centerpiece of revitalization. The foundation provided $1 million over four years to fuel the effort. Individual donors, businesses, and governments then joined in.

Meanwhile, the president of Hartford's Trinity College, Evan Dobelle, decided to fight the deterioration of the neighborhood around his college. In 1996, he announced a $175 million initiative with investment from the college endowment to encourage more owner-occupied housing, and to improve schools, nonprofits, and performing arts in the area. The Kellogg Foundation and others added funding. Dobelle would go on to champion similar investments by nonprofit universities aimed at shoring up single-family living in college towns across New England.

By 1998, almost 500,000 people a year were frequenting Hartford's riverfront. $1.5 billion in further investment was being directed into the area. Hartford was on its way to being a liveable city again.

Further reading

○ *Philanthropy* magazine reporting, philanthropyroundtable.org/site/print/building_a_better_city

─────────── 1995 ───────────

MEIJER GARDENS AND SCULPTURE PARK (GRAND RAPIDS)

In 1962, when Fred Meijer was working in the grocery business started by his Dutch immigrant parents, he developed the concept of the retail superstore. Three decades later he was at the head of one of the largest private companies in America, with more than 200 huge outlets combining grocery and discount items. He was also by then a major philanthropist in his home region of Grand Rapids, Michigan.

Even when his parents were pouring everything into their small business and had little spending money, Meijer remembered that his parents made art and culture experiences for their children a priority. "I had piano lessons, clarinet lessons, and violin lessons. I was encouraged to sing in choirs. No matter how hard up we were, things like that came as a part of life." In 1995, Meijer gave the Grand Rapids public a gift of art in nature: the Frederik Meijer Gardens and Sculpture Park. It is a high mix of 158 acres of horticultural and lakefront beauty with more than 100 pieces of large outdoor art created by prominent modern sculptors. The nonprofit attracts over 600,000 visitors annually. Thanks to Meijer's gifts plus the contributions of 23,000 members from the surrounding community, it is comfortably endowed to provide years of rich programming organized by its 200 staff members and 800 volunteers.

Further reading

○ About the gardens, meijergardens.org/about

FARESTART (SEATTLE)

Chef and entrepreneur David Lee floundered around for several years when he set out to help feed, and then employ, some of Seattle's homeless. Then in 1994 he received a grant from the local Medina Foundation (which had been giving away about $4 million a year since its founding by philanthropist Norton Clapp in 1947) so that Lee could rebuild his kitchen. The efficient new setup allowed his nonprofit to begin to thrive as a working restaurant and catering service that employed the homeless. Soon, 60 percent of its operating budget was coming from sales and 90 percent of its trainees were employed after they graduated from the program (with 70 percent still employed a year later, both extraordinary rates for this population).

The program expanded over time. With funding from Medina, a café was started at Antioch College. Top chefs from all over Seattle began to donate their time. Today, FareStart trains 800 struggling individuals per year. In 2011 it launched an effort to bring its formula to organizations in other cities, and now dozens of similar nonprofit operations are loosely linked through its Catalyst Kitchens network.

Further reading

○ FareStart, farestart.org
○ *Philanthropy* magazine reporting from 1999, philanthropyroundtable.org/topic/excellence_in_philanthropy/great_grants_farestart_seattle

⌁ PhilAphorism

Many people are alienated by faceless bureaucracy and what they see as an erosion of participatory democracy. Consequently, there has been a revival of interest in charitable service.

☞ *Frank Prochaska*

LOCAL

TRANSFORMING HIS CITY'S WORST NEIGHBORHOOD (ATLANTA)

After reading a newspaper report that just a few sections of New York City supplied 70 percent of the entire state's criminals, Atlanta real-estate developer and philanthropist Tom Cousins asked Atlanta's chief of police about his own city's crime patterns. He learned that just two or three neighborhoods generated most of Atlanta's offenses, the worst being East Lake, dominated by a government housing project in which 90 percent of the residents had been victims of a felony. "I decided right then," Cousins told *Philanthropy* magazine, "East Lake was going to be our target."

Cousins realized his years of quiet giving to anti-poverty causes must change to public engagement. We'd "given a lot of money," he explained, "but we had not given ourselves." Cousins and his family and friends started to work with local residents and a new city housing official on a plan to tear down the housing project and build mixed-income housing under the control of a new charity. It wasn't easy to reach an agreement, but eventually the existing 650-unit project was replaced with a 542-apartment complex that leases half of its units at market rates and half for government housing vouchers. The new foundation in charge would have authority to change the dysfunctional culture of the old project—for instance, by requiring residents of working age to either work or enroll in a program that will help them find work, or else leave.

The foundation also took over the nearby East Lake Country Club, which had once been among the city's finest but was nearly bankrupt by 1993. Cousins invested in the facility but required new members to donate $200,000 to the foundation overseeing the area housing upgrade. He also directed all future club profits to the foundation. Now the club hosts the PGA Tour Championship each year, buoying the neighborhood.

Cousins also built the Charles Drew Charter School to educate area children. It replaced the neighborhood's disastrous elementary school.

A few numbers tell the story of East Lake's transformation: violent crime dropped 95 percent. The fraction of adults on welfare tumbled from 59 percent to 5 percent. Where once only 5 percent of local fifth graders met state math standards, by 2007, 78 percent did, and 80 percent of eighth-graders met or exceeded state reading standards. The median home value jumped from $46,000 in 1996 to $212,000 in 2004. One neighborhood activist says simply, "We tore down hell and built heaven."

In 2009, the East Lake Foundation established a new nonprofit to spread the lessons of East Lake. Now known as Purpose Built Communities, it helps unfold similar efforts in other cities across the country.

Further reading

○ *Philanthropy* magazine reporting, philanthropyroundtable.org/topic/excellence_in_ philanthropy/a_civic_hole-in-one

○ Wilson Center webcast, wilsoncenter.org/event/creating-communities-hope-and-opportunity-the-revitalization-east-lake

○ Purpose Built Communities, PurposeBuiltCommunities.org

1993

ADOPTING A WHOLE NEIGHBORHOOD
(TANGELO PARK)

Just a quarter of a mile from the tourist centers of Orlando, Florida, sat a squalid neighborhood plagued with drug problems and lousy schooling. Harris Rosen, who had made his fortune building and operating hotels in the area, decided to personally do something about this. He developed and funded a simple approach to improving the lives of local families.

First, Rosen created a string of good quality, small, home-based preschools across the neighborhood—by offering to renovate space in residents' houses and provide all operating funds if they would become trained as teachers. All two-, three-, and four-year-old children in the low-income neighborhood may attend these schools free of charge. Then Rosen offered an incentive at the other end of the childhood spectrum: a full scholarship, including books and travel, for any neighborhood resident who graduated from high school and got accepted into a Florida two- or four-year public college or vocational program. Support was recruited from other philanthropies and civic groups in the neighborhood like the Tangelo Park Baptist Church, the local YMCA, and the area schools.

The results are impressive. The neighborhood's elementary school has earned "A" ratings on the Florida standardized annual exam for five of the past seven years—one of only two or three low-income schools in the state to earn the top rating. High-school graduation rates, which were below 50 percent when the program started, are now close to 100 percent. More than half of neighborhood youngsters go to college. Crime rates are down, property values have tripled, and new families are moving into the neighborhood. As of 2015, Harris Rosen had injected $11 million of his money into improving Tangelo Park, and he continues to spend about $500,000 per year on his program.

LOCAL

Further reading

○ About the program, tangeloparkprogram.com/about/tangelo-park-program
○ Interview with Harris Rosen, philanthropyroundtable.org/topic/economic_opportunity/ the_tangelo_park_model_for_transforming_a_troubled_neighborhood

1991

YOUTH ENTREPRENEURS
(KANSAS AND MISSOURI)

Charles Koch is known for distilling the rules that make free markets work, and applying them to both his business endeavors and his philanthropy. He began this in his hometown of Wichita, where he became CEO of Koch Industries at age 32 and expanded the company 2,800-fold to $115 billion in revenues and 100,000 employees as of 2014.

As he looked around Wichita in the late 1980s, Koch saw few people who knew how to run companies in ways that would both maximize their value and benefit American society. He decided to start a nonprofit that would teach young people those things.

He founded Youth Entrepreneurs with his wife, Liz, in 1991. It was open to any high-school student, but targeted at-risk youth. It started out as an eight-week program at Wichita High School North that was later expanded into a two-semester course. It teaches the basics of entrepreneurship through hands-on experience as well as classroom training. The students write business plans, are encouraged to use them to launch businesses, and get not only academic credit but chances to do internships at local businesses, to be mentored, to win scholarships, and to get venture-capital funding. The program was offered in 41 high schools across Kansas and Missouri as of 2015.

The program graduates more than a thousand students every year. Compared to their peers, its alums demonstrate better business skills and are more likely to pursue higher education (by 58 percent to 32 percent).

Further reading

○ Youth Entrepreneurs, youthentrepreneurs.org/about
○ *Philanthropy* magazine profile of Charles Koch, philanthropyroundtable.org/site/print/ market_based_man

1987

MATCHING LOCAL HEALTH-CARE SOLUTIONS
(49 STATES)

The Robert Wood Johnson Foundation, established by the head of Johnson &

Johnson, has a special interest in health care and is one of America's largest foundations. Big national foundations rarely consider grants to small local projects, and when they do it is typically in a top-down fashion, recruiting locals to execute one of their national projects. But in 1987, RWJF inaugurated a new program, eventually known as Local Funding Partnerships, which gave grants in the $50,000–$500,000 range to local organizations who come with their own ideas on what problem to attack, and how to do it. "The best ideas for solving pressing community problems," explains the foundation, "come from members of the communities themselves." Local funders were required to provide a dollar-for-dollar match to each grant.

The program was instantly popular and highly competitive, with just 6 percent of the hundreds of annual proposals winning awards. Some sample projects that were funded: Preventing teen pregnancies among Hmong refugees in Minnesota (1988). Providing support services to frail elderly so they can remain in their homes in Maryland (1989). Creating dental care for people with AIDS in Texas (1992). A Los Angeles program to combat teenage obesity (1998). An effort to reduce emergency-room visits by homeless adults in Georgia (1999). A satellite clinic in Ohio for Amish children with rare genetic disorders (2002).

In addition to money, RWJF offered expertise and managerial guidance to its local grant winners. In 2013, the last annual meeting of the Local Funding Partnerships program was held. By then, pairing grants from a national donor with local ideas and local matching funding had become a philanthropic commonplace, and many of the experimental health interventions tried through the program were accepted practices.

A total of 369 grants in 49 states were given during the 25-year life of the Local Funding Partnerships program. A 2002 outside evaluation found that fully 75 percent of the experimental projects launched by the partnership turned into sustained and successful health-care programs.

Further reading

∘ History of the Local Funding Partnerships, lifp.org/html/aboutus/history.html

1987

FINANCIAL LITERACY FOR YOUNG AMERICANS (COLORADO)

In 1984, Bill Daniels read an article in the Denver newspaper about a fifth-grade class that couldn't get funding to start a business. A successful cable-TV entrepreneur, Daniels decided there ought to be opportunities for young people to learn about money and business. Daniels decided to

LOCAL

open a bank for children—a real bank, state-chartered, FDIC-insured, offering a full range of services.

It took a good deal of struggle to win over government regulators lacking Daniels' vision. In 1987, though, he finally opened Denver's Young Americans Bank. The world's only institution of its sort, it only accepts new customers who are 21 and under, offering them savings and checking accounts, loans, credit cards, and ATM cards—as well as instruction in their optimal use, money management classes, classes on entrepreneurship, and financial summer camps. Since its creation, the bank has served 70,000 customers.

In 1990, Daniels added Young AmeriTowne to provide students with hands-on experience in business and civics. Today his nonprofit has four branches spread across Colorado that have given half a million young people practical instruction on the American economic system.

Further reading

○ Young Americans Center for Financial Education, yacenter.org/about-us

FROM STATE TO LOCAL
(MINNESOTA)

William and Maude McKnight established the McKnight Foundation in 1953, after William had helped build the 3M Company. As the foundation has grown into one of the largest in the country, with more than $2 billion in assets, it has remained focused on its own state of Minnesota. And in the mid-1980s the McKnight Foundation became even more rooted when under the leadership of the founders' daughter Virginia McKnight Binger it decided to take a strongly community-based approach to philanthropy.

As the state economy underwent major changes, the McKnight team believed decisions needed to be better informed by residents closest to local needs. The foundation particularly wanted to improve the quality and quantity of rural philanthropy beyond the state's dominant Minneapolis-St. Paul core. So in 1986, the McKnight Foundation launched six independent regional foundations ranged across the 80 counties of its state.

Each foundation focuses on improvement and growth of its particular region, and its priorities in areas like economic development, education, community building, and families, youth, and seniors are set by leaders living in those regions. To date, the McKnight Foundation has invested $237 million in these foundations to help them carry out their local priorities. These so-called Minnesota Initiative Foundations function as regional spark plugs—a blend of economic development corporation and community foundation, and are nationally recognized for the strength and impact of their work.

Further reading

○ Minnesota Initiative Foundations, mcknight.org/grant-programs/mn

1982

GABRIEL HOMES
(VIRGINIA)

Gabriel Homes, a nonprofit launched by Catholics in northern Virginia, was a pioneer in helping people with mental disabilities. It was started by local residents who saw appropriate housing as the most pressing need in accommodating mentally disabled persons in their community. The organization opened its first group home in 1985, housing several developmentally disabled adults in ways that allowed them chances for independence, for work, and for shared social life. The costs of the residents' medical care remained a problem, however, until the Arlington Health Foundation (a local trust with $350 million in assets) made a 1998 grant that allowed Gabriel Homes to hire three part-time health-care staff. By 2008, Gabriel Homes had expanded to seven homes, the number it maintains today.

Further reading

○ Gabriel Homes, gabrielhomes.org/About/Background.asp

1954

ELEVATING HOME CITY AND STATE
(LOUISVILLE)

"Do things that will promote the well-being of the citizens of the city of Louisville and the state of Kentucky. Kentucky has long been thought of as a

⌐ PhilAphorism

What I did was help myself by learning to help others. You only keep what you have by giving it away.

☞ *Sean MacMillen,
on why he led a nonprofit for veterans*

LOCAL

backward state and projects which the Trustees should undertake are those which will correct this impression, so that Kentucky and Louisville will be recognized nationally."

That was the gist of the directive that lumberman and real-estate developer James Graham Brown left for his foundation before he died as the richest man in Kentucky. His trust has followed through. Hardly a major project has been completed in Louisville over the past half century without the foundation's involvement. It helped create the Louisville Zoo, Louisville Waterfront Park, the James Graham Brown Cancer Center at the University of Louisville, and the Kentucky Derby Museum. It has funded many improvements to local universities, including a current program that supports ten students every year at the University of Louisville or Centre College in the hope of making them "lifelong ambassadors" for the region.

The Louisville area is now thriving, with more than a million residents, growing industries, and booming tourism. The James Graham Brown Foundation remains the largest philanthropy in the state, and has awarded more than 3,000 grants totaling over half a billion dollars.

Further reading

○ James Graham Brown Foundation, jgbf.org/about-the-foundation

1951

MOREHEAD, CAIN, AND LEVINE MINT SCHOLARS (NORTH CAROLINA)

The Morehead-Cain Scholarship is a prestigious merit-based award that attracts top students to the University of North Carolina at Chapel Hill by paying not only all tuition and board, but also all supplies and expenses, plus a generous stipend for travel or study every summer. It was created by the Morehead Foundation in 1951, and renewed by the Cain Foundation in 2007 with a fresh $100 million endowment. Its alumni include many high achievers.

In 2009, Charlotte philanthropist Leon Levine, founder of the Family Dollar stores, decided to create a similar merit scholarship for the University of North Carolina at Charlotte. Like its model, the Levine Scholarship offers full tuition and board plus subsidized travel and internships. "But we put a little extra spice in ours," notes Levine.

During one of their summers, the Levine scholars work in a local nonprofit. And then they are given $8,000 to start their own charitable project. Levine sees this as a triple win: Getting some philanthropic good done, and conditioning top students to think about charitable problem-solving. And to top it off, "by the time they graduate, we will have the potential of keeping them in Charlotte. That could be a bonus for the entire community."

"It seems like every time Charlotte needs a pick-me-up, the Levines are there," former mayor Anthony Foxx once told the *New York Times*.

Further reading

○ Morehead-Cain Scholarship, moreheadcain.org

○ Levine Scholarship, levinescholars.uncc.edu

OLD SALEM (WINSTON-SALEM)

In 1766, missionaries of the Moravians, a Protestant group mostly living in what is now the Czech Republic, arrived to establish a settlement in the North Carolina wilderness. The Moravians were a serious, religious, industrious, musical people, and they built a thriving community which became a center of trade and culture. It eventually spawned the current North Carolina city of Winston-Salem, which grew up around its original core.

Most of the city's old Moravian center never got knocked down, and in 1950 a group of local volunteers and donors came together and decided to preserve the interesting wooden and brick architecture, the original church, the burial ground (where remains were interred separately by sex rather than in family units), the wooden bridge, and the many unusual gardens. The historic adjoining Salem Academy was included, a new museum of Southern decorative arts was created, and "living history" interpretation was launched to run period businesses like the tavern, bakery, and candy shop, and to demonstrate traditional crafts. Today the museum has more than 200 employees, thriving retail elements, a book publishing house, a research center, numerous gardens, and a bustling business renting its historic spaces for business and social events. The nonprofit is almost entirely privately funded—a combination of $8 million of its own annual revenue and about $2 million per year of individual contributions and foundation grants.

Further reading

○ Old Salem workshops, oldsalem.org/learn/museum-classes

A GONZO MEMORIAL TO CRAZY HORSE (SOUTH DAKOTA)

Crazy Horse famously refused to be photographed, and after he died in U.S.

LOCAL

Army custody in 1877 his burial place was kept secret. So what would he make of a 560-foot-tall memorial to him and his people?

For 65 years, Thunderbird Mountain in the Black Hills has been slowly transforming into an epic tribute to the Lakota fighting chief. Korczak Ziolkowski, a sculptor who cut his teeth as an assistant on nearby Mount Rushmore, began blasting away sections of the mountain in 1948. Ziolkowski continued the laborious work until his death in 1982. Since then his widow, Ruth, has directed the project with the help of seven of their ten children. In 1998, they completed Crazy Horse's face. Since then they have been excavating his horse one high-explosive gouge at a time. "Go slowly so you do it right," was Korczak's parting wisdom to Ruth.

The nonprofit project—the world's largest mountain carving—has been funded entirely by philanthropic gifts and admission fees. Ziolkowski turned down millions in government funds because of his commitment to "individual initiative and private enterprise," according to the memorial's foundation. It's a good guess that Crazy Horse, a fellow skeptic of U.S. government involvement in people's lives, would have approved.

Further reading

○ Crazy Horse Memorial, crazyhorsememorial.org

SOIL STEWARD (OKLAHOMA)

Back before there was a state of Oklahoma, Lloyd Noble was born in the town of Ardmore, then part of the Chickasaw Nation. After stints teaching in rural schools and studying at the University of Oklahoma, he and a partner bought a drilling rig. In 1926 they struck gold—or its Sooner liquid equivalent—in the famed Seminole oil field. By the 1930s he was a very wealthy man.

It was Noble's view that his home state's long-term welfare depended more than anything else on healthy land—something that the Dust Bowl disasters showed should not be taken for granted. In 1945, he created the Samuel Roberts

～ PhilAphorism

It is prodigious the quantity of good that may be done by one man, if he will make a business of it.
☞ *Benjamin Franklin*

Noble Foundation (named after his father) to help Oklahoma's farmers be good stewards of their soil. While the foundation has funded universities and think tanks extensively, its most important work has always taken place within 100 miles of its home in Ardmore. The foundation employs agricultural consultants who work with more than 1,700 local farmers to provide them with research, information, and new techniques in agronomy, plant biology, and related subjects. Roughly a quarter of the foundation's 360 employees have Ph.D.s, and it has led ambitious projects like the development of a new kind of sustainable perennial forage grass for livestock.

The Noble Foundation has also awarded more than $300 million in scholarships for young Oklahomans and grants to local charities, generally in ways that link back to the field of agriculture. Overall, the foundation has spent a billion dollars on its charitable activities, and been one of the best friends Oklahoma farmers and ranchers could ever have.

As a footnote (though to Sooner fans, football is anything but a footnote), Lloyd Noble is also the man who revived Oklahoma's pigskin program in the mid-1940s. Once described as "the most charitable and influential regent Oklahoma University had ever seen," his benefactions ranged from paying bonuses out of his own pocket to top-flight professors, to luring coach Bud Wilkinson to Norman.

Further reading

○ Entry on Lloyd Noble in the Encyclopedia of Oklahoma History & Culture, okhistory.org/publications/enc/entry.php?entry=NO004

○ Samuel Roberts Noble Foundation history, noble.org/about/history

1940

A FORESTER SPROUTS RESEARCH (OREGON)

Edmund Hayes owned small woodlands and sawmills in Oregon, and was a leader in finding newly efficient and effective ways to manage timberland. He started purchasing already-cut forestland and second-growth timber. "We Grow Trees" became his company motto at a time when replanting was thought to be nature's responsibility. By the end of Hayes's career, putting in seedlings after cutting timber had become routine, and loggers were learning to profit from second-growth cuttings on land they would often own themselves and manage to maximize multiple uses. Today, forestry science has gone even further in finding new value and efficiencies in woodlands management, including selective logging and multiple overlapping uses of the same acreage.

Hayes eventually became a board member of Weyerhaeuser lumber company and also one of the more generous philanthropists in Oregon.

LOCAL

He was the first chair of the Keep Oregon Green Association, a pioneering forest-fire prevention nonprofit. He funded studies of early Oregon history, medical research, libraries, and churches.

After his death, his family endowed a Hayes professorship at Oregon State University's College of Forestry that continues today to generate fresh ideas on "silviculture alternatives." The latest Hayes professor is using insights from the new field of complexity science to better understand the confluences of hundreds of factors that allow a forest to thrive and produce timber, wildlife habitat, clean water, and other valuable goods all at the same time. Believing that "Oregon will always need diverse and productive forests and the wood products that come from them," the Hayes family donors have emphasized the same mix of practicality and bold new ideas that characterized the philanthropic and business career of their father.

Further reading

∘ Keep Oregon Green Association history, keeporegongreen.org/in%20the%20 beginning.html

∘ "Hayes Family Endows a Professorship in Silviculture" (*Focus on Forestry*, Spring 2001)

1937

LILLY BUILDS CIVIL SOCIETY (INDIANA)

Eli Lilly made his fortune in pharmaceuticals, with a company he founded in 1876. In 1937, three members of his family, son J. K. Lilly and grandsons Eli and J. K. Jr., founded Lilly Endowment with gifts of stock in the company. The men were grateful to the region where their business had prospered, and their foundation has remained deeply committed to Indiana ever since, with about 70 percent of its annual grants staying in the state. Community development, education, and religion have been its major focuses.

The Lilly family believed that strong church communities were essential to a healthy society, and their foundation has consistently funded religious research, ministerial training, even specific congregations. In its secular funding there has been an emphasis on the infrastructure of civil society—everything from library restoration to vehicles for fire companies. Raising the educational level of Indianans has been a preoccupation of the endowment in recent years. Its efforts are a major reason that Indiana is currently considered one of the nation's leading states in educational experimentation and reform.

The foundation has not shied away from general operating support grants, as many foundations do. And its longtime advocacy of self-sufficient communities has led the number of community foundations inside Indiana to grow from fewer than a dozen to more than 80. In 2014 the endowment's assets totaled $10 billion and it disbursed $344 million.

Further reading

○ Lilly Endowment, lillyendowment.org/theendowment.html

○ *Philanthropy* magazine reporting, philanthropyroundtable.org/site/print/when_charity_ begins_at_home

1931

MARQUEE DONORS OF LAFAYETTE
(PENNSYLVANIA AND NEW JERSEY)

Fred Kirby was one of the founders of the F. W. Woolworth Company (predecessor to today's Foot Locker). He revolutionized retail in America, introducing affordable fixed pricing across his 96 stores, which he merged into Woolworth's in 1911 to create one of the biggest retailers in the nation. He got involved in philanthropy in 1931 via his F. M. Kirby Foundation, which has since been a force for social good in Pennsylvania and New Jersey (as well as a supporter of national organizations that reinforce free enterprise and individual liberty). The foundation's nearly half-billion dollars of grantmaking over the years has built up colleges like Lafayette, churches, homeless shelters, YMCAs, and medical research facilities across its region.

Further reading

○ Kirby biographical information, explorepahistory.com/hmarker.php?markerId=1-A-324

1924

DUKE OF THE CAROLINAS
(NORTH AND SOUTH CAROLINA)

James Duke was entirely committed to concentrating his philanthropy in the area where he grew up and then made good. In 1874, when he was 18, his parents opened a small tobacco factory in Durham, North Carolina. The market was tough, and Duke eventually convinced his family to start larger-scale machine production to outproduce the competition. By the early 1900s, he had built a global tobacco empire. Then he turned his attention to the brand new and booming industry of rural electrification. He wanted to use the waterways of the western Carolinas to provide inexpensive hydropower that could attract industry and speed economic growth in his poor region. His business vision for the Carolinas had a philanthropic component itself, as he was determined to build his home region into something great.

LOCAL

In 1924, he took up philanthropy directly by starting the Duke Endowment. He tightly focused his foundation on specific areas. First was Methodism, which he credited with building the character and work ethic that made him successful. Duke stipulated that 12 percent of his endowment's expenditures would go to support the denomination's rural churches and their clergy. (Methodism flourished in the Carolinas thereafter—see 1924 entry on our list of achievements in Religious philanthropy.)

As someone who had lost his mother at an early age, Duke sympathized with the ill and the orphaned. Ten percent of his money would go to children who lost their parents, and 32 percent to hospitals. (North Carolina's growth in hospital beds per capita was almost twice that of comparable states after the endowment went into action.)

The remaining 46 percent of spending from his endowment, Duke spelled out, would go to four Carolina universities. Among other effects, this support transformed Durham's small Trinity College into today's high-ranked Duke University.

His strong localist bent, and precise expression of his philanthropic desires, separated Duke from many of the other major philanthropists of his time. He was keen not to have his life's creation spent on projects unpalatable to him. And he believed that by focusing his giving on the Carolinas he could do more good than would be accomplished by spreading his dollars thinly. It is hard to argue with his logic given how much success his universities, his Methodist church, and his social projects have had in his designated region in the decades since he adopted them.

Further reading

○ *Philanthropy* magazine history, philanthropyroundtable.org/topic/donor_intent/duke_of_carolina

○ Duke Endowment, dukeendowment.org

1914

WORLD'S FIRST COMMUNITY FOUNDATION (CLEVELAND)

As a lawyer and banker, Frederick Goff had seen charitable gifts go awry because there was no one to follow through after a generous gift. So he started talking to his fellow Clevelanders about the desirability of forming a joint "community chest" that could help generous residents make sure their donations really did good. Ultimately, he talked area leaders into forming a single permanent endowment, composed of various subfunds, to be managed in perpetuity. Local donors could leave their fortunes to this fund and know that the money would be used for "such charitable purposes as will best make for the mental, moral, and physical improvement of the inhabitants of Cleveland" for years down the road.

The Cleveland Foundation, the world's first community foundation, was launched in 1914. Since then it has grown to $2.2 billion, and has distributed over $1 billion in grants around the region—including $98 million in 2014. More generally, their idea of a community foundation caught on famously, and today there are more than 730 similar local charitable pools containing tens of billions of dollars in assets and distributing several billion dollars in their home areas every single year. The idea has even spread to scores of other countries. It all started 100 years ago on the banks of Lake Erie.

Further reading

○ Cleveland Foundation, clevelandfoundation.org/about/quick-facts

○ Waldemar Nielsen, *Inside American Philanthropy* (University of Oklahoma Press, 1996)

1909

GRANDADDY OF CHARITY MARATHONS (BOSTON)

In the early years of the twentieth century, Italians were one of the largest immigrant groups in America. So when a tremendous earthquake rocked southern Italy and Sicily in 1908 and killed 100,000 people, Americans leapt to mobilize relief. One of the most significant charitable efforts was centered in Boston, where would-be helpers launched what is now one of the grand philanthropic traditions in our country.

Marathon road races were all the rage in America a century ago, partly due to Johnny Hayes's gold medal for the U.S. in the 1908 Olympic Games. So when the *Boston American* went looking for a vehicle to raise money for earthquake relief, the decision was quickly made to organize a charity event around a marathon. The newspaper publicized a January 9, 1909 contest managed by the local amateur athletic association, and Boston businesses covered the costs. It was announced that all proceeds from admission to the grounds where the finish could be viewed would be devoted to the victims in Italy.

Despite freezing temperatures, 108 runners participated, and thousands of spectators turned out. Hundreds of thousands of dollars were raised (the exact figure is not known). In 1909 currency that was an eye-popping result. The Boston Marathon thus became the first in a long history of charity marathons held all across the United States, which collectively now raise close to $2 billion annually.

LOCAL

Even as the phenomenon spread to other cities, interest has never waned in the cradle of the concept. In 1989 (the year the charity mechanism for the Boston race was formalized into its current structure), 5,000 runners participated in the Boston Marathon; by 2015 that was up to 30,251. The latest year's charitable haul was $38.4 million, with those funds going to a few dozen local charities ranging from the Dana-Farber Cancer Institute, to the Girl Scouts of Eastern Massachusetts, to Boston Children's Hospital.

Further reading

○ *Boston Globe* article, boston.com/sports/marathon/articles/2012/04/10/charity_for_
  boston_marathon_began_at_home_in_1909/
○ Boston Athletic Association, baa.org/about.aspx
○ 2014 fundraising record, bostonglobe.com/metro/2014/07/01/organizers-say-marathon-
  runners-raised-record-amount-for-charity-million/L1iRwlttF8zQtwwqUnDmoK/story.html

KAMEHAMEHA SCHOOLS
(HAWAII)

Bernice Pauahi Bishop, a daughter of Hawaiian royalty, was offered the throne of her Pacific land in 1872 but refused it, preferring to pursue good works through her private means and devout Christian faith. She inherited ancestral land that eventually made her the largest property owner in the islands, and her husband, Charles, was very successful in business. They both put much of their energy and wealth into helping others, and drew up wills to make sure their estates would also eventually be devoted to worthy causes.

With the lion's share of her bequest, Bernice established the Kamehameha Schools to provide native Hawaiians with "a good education…and also instruction in morals and in such useful knowledge as may tend to make good and industrious men and women." After her death from breast cancer Charles set to work making her schools a reality. A boys' facility opened in 1887, following by a girls' counterpart. Today the Kamehameha Schools remain the state's largest private landowner, controlling 365,000 acres. The organization's total endowment of $9 billion makes it one of the best-financed charities in the nation, allowing it to educate more than 7,000 children every year at almost no charge to their families.

Further reading

○ Bernice Pauahi Bishop profile in the Philanthropy Hall of Fame (see prior *Almanac* entry)
○ Bernice Bishop's will, ksbe.edu/about_us/about_pauahi/will

═══ESSENTIAL═══
BOOKS & ARTICLES
ON PHILANTHROPY

As a shortcut to the very best that has been said and written on philanthropy,
we've compiled the crucial literature—from recent essays to classic books.
To give you a quick sense of longer works we've included many brief extracts,
reviews, and links to fuller-text versions. For ease of browsing, we've sorted
the readings into 11 general themes, each listed on a table of contents
you'll find on the page following.

READINGS BY TOPIC

STRATEGIES FOR GIVING

"Gain, Save, Give" by John Wesley
In his 1744 sermon, "The Use of Money," John Wesley, clergyman and founder of Methodism, gives three "plain rules" for the stewardship of wealth. This is classic Protestant ethic on work, thrift, and charity. An excerpt:

"The love of money," we know, "is the root of all evil"—but not the thing itself. The fault does not lie in the money, but in them that use it. It may be used ill: and what may not? But it may likewise be used well....

In the hands of His children, it is food for the hungry, drink for the thirsty, raiment for the naked: It gives to the traveler and the stranger where to lay his head. By it we may supply the place of a husband to the widow, and of a father to the fatherless. We may be a defense for the oppressed, a means of health to the sick, of ease to them that are in pain; it may be as eyes to the blind, as feet to the lame....

All the instructions which are necessary for this may be reduced to three plain rules....

I. Gain All You Can

Gain all you can, by common sense, by using in your business all the understanding which God has given you. It is amazing to observe how few do this; how men run on in the same dull track with their forefathers.... It is a shame for a Christian not to improve upon them, in whatever he takes in hand. You should be continually learning, from the experience of others, or from your own experience, reading, and reflection, to do everything you have to do better today than you did yesterday. And see that you practice whatever you learn, that you may make the best of all that is in your hands.

II. Save All You Can

Having gained all you can, by honest wisdom and unwearied diligence, the second rule of Christian prudence is, "Save all you can." Do not throw the precious talent into the sea.... Do not throw it away in idle expenses, which is just the same as throwing it into the sea. Expend no part of it merely to gratify the desire of the flesh, the desire of the eye, or the pride of life.... Daily experience shows, the more they are indulged, they increase the more....

And why should you throw away money upon your children, any more than upon yourself, in delicate food, in gay or costly apparel, in superfluities of any kind? Why should you purchase for them more pride or lust, more vanity, or foolish and hurtful desires? They do not want any more; they have enough already; nature has made ample provision for them: Why should you be at farther expense to increase their temptations and snares, and to pierce them through with more sorrows?

....How amazing then is the infatuation of those parents who think they can never leave their children enough! What! Cannot you leave them enough of arrows, firebrands, and death? Not enough of foolish and hurtful desires? Not enough of pride, lust, ambition, vanity.... Give each what would keep him above want, and bestow all the rest...for the glory of God....

III. *Give All You Can*
The directions which God has given us, touching the use of our worldly substance, may be comprised in the following particulars. If you desire to be a faithful and a wise steward, out of that portion of your Lord's goods which he has for the present lodged in your hands, but with the right of resuming whenever it pleases him, first provide things needful for yourself—food to eat, raiment to put on, whatever nature moderately requires for preserving the body in health and strength.

Secondly, provide these for your wife, your children, your servants, or any others who pertain to your household. If when this is done there be an overplus left, then "do good to them that are of the household of faith." If there be an overplus still, "as you have opportunity, do good unto all men...."

If, then, a doubt should at any time arise in your mind concerning what you are going to expend, either on yourself or any part of your family, you have an easy way to remove it. Calmly and seriously inquire, "In expending this, am I acting according to my character? Am I acting herein, not as a proprietor, but as a steward of my Lord's goods?"

....Gain all you can, without hurting either yourself or your neighbour, in soul or body, by applying hereto with unintermitted diligence, and with all the understanding which God has given you.

Save all you can, by cutting off every expense which serves only to indulge foolish desire; to gratify either the desire of flesh, the desire of the eye, or the pride of life; waste nothing, living or dying, on sin or folly, whether for yourself or your children.

And then give all you can, or, in other words, give all you have to God. Do not stint yourself.... Render unto God not a tenth, not a third, not half; but all that is God's, be it more or less.

Random Reminiscences of Men and Events
by John Rockefeller

This 1909 book is a short autobiographical sketch by America's original grand philanthropist. Its last two chapters—"The Difficult Art of Giving" and "The Benevolent Trust"—outline Rockefeller's vision for improving society through charitable gifts. In the following excerpt, the great donor discusses principles of the "best philanthropy."

The novelty of being able to purchase anything one wants soon passes, because what people most seek cannot be bought with money. These rich men we read about in the newspapers cannot get personal returns beyond a well-defined limit…. They cannot gratify the pleasures of the palate beyond very moderate bounds, since they cannot purchase a good digestion; they cannot lavish very much money on fine raiment for themselves or their families without suffering from public ridicule; and in their homes they cannot go much beyond the comforts of the less wealthy without involving them in more pain than pleasure. As I study wealthy men, I can see but one way in which they can secure a real equivalent for money spent, and that is to cultivate a taste for giving where the money may produce an effect which will be a lasting gratification….

A man of business may often most properly consider that he does his share in building up a property which gives steady work for few or many people; and his contribution consists in giving to his employees good working conditions, new opportunities, and a strong stimulus to good work. Just so long as he has the welfare of his employees in his mind and follows his convictions, no one can help honoring such a man. It would be the narrowest sort of view to take, and I think the meanest, to consider that good works consist chiefly in the outright giving of money.

The best philanthropy, the help that does the most good and the least harm, the help that nourishes civilization at its very root, that most widely disseminates health, righteousness, and happiness, is not what is usually called charity. It is, in my judgment, the investment of effort or time or money, carefully considered with relation to the power of employing people at a remunerative wage, to expand and develop the resources at hand, and to give opportunity for progress and healthful labor where it did not exist before. No mere money-giving is comparable to this in its lasting and beneficial results.

If, as I am accustomed to think, this statement is a correct one, how vast indeed is the philanthropic field! It may be urged that the daily vocation of life is one thing, and the work of philanthropy quite another. I have no sympathy with this notion. The man who plans to do all his giving on Sunday is a poor prop for the institutions of the country....

I know of men who have followed out this large plan of developing work, not as a temporary matter, but as a permanent principle. These men have taken up doubtful enterprises and carried them through to success often at great risk, and in the face of great skepticism, not as a matter only of personal profit, but in the larger spirit of general uplift....

Probably the most generous people in the world are the very poor, who assume each other's burdens in the crises which come so often to the hard-pressed. The mother in the tenement falls ill and the neighbor in the next room assumes her burdens. The father loses his work, and neighbors supply food to his children from their own scanty store. How often one hears of cases where the orphans are taken over and brought up by the poor friend whose benefaction means great additional hardship! This sort of genuine service makes the most princely gift from superabundance look insignificant indeed. The Jews have had for centuries a precept that one-tenth of a man's possessions must be devoted to good works, but even this measure of giving is but a rough yardstick to go by. To give a tenth of one's income is well nigh an impossibility to some, while to others it means a miserable pittance. If the spirit is there, the matter of proportion is soon lost sight of. It is only the spirit of giving that counts, and the very poor give without any self-consciousness....

If the people can be educated to help themselves, we strike at the root of many of the evils of the world. This is the fundamental thing, and it is worth saying even if it has been said so often that its truth is lost sight of in its constant repetition.

The only thing which is of lasting benefit to a man is that which he does for himself. Money which comes to him without effort on his part is seldom a benefit and often a curse. That is the principal objection to speculation—it is not because more lose than gain, though that is true—but it is because those who gain are apt to receive more injury from their success than they would have received from failure. And so with regard to money or other things which are given by one person to another. It is only in the exceptional case that the receiver is really benefited. But, if we can help people to help themselves, then there is a permanent blessing conferred.

Men who are studying the problem of disease tell us that it is becoming more and more evident that the forces which conquer sickness are within the body itself, and that it is only when these are reduced below the normal that disease can get a foothold. The way to ward off disease, therefore, is to tone up the body generally; and, when disease has secured a foothold, the way to combat it is to help these natural resisting agencies which are in the body already. In the same way the failures which a man makes in his life are due almost always to some defect in his personality, some weakness of body, or mind, or character, will, or temperament. The only way to overcome these failings is to build up his personality from within, so that he, by virtue of what is within him, may overcome the weakness which was the cause of the failure. It is only those efforts the man himself puts forth that can really help him.

We all desire to see the widest possible distribution of the blessings of life. Many crude plans have been suggested, some of which utterly ignore the essential facts of human nature, and if carried out would perhaps drag our whole civilization down into hopeless misery. It is my belief that the principal cause for the economic differences between people is their difference in personality, and that it is only as we can assist in the wider distribution of those qualities which go to make up a strong personality that we can assist in the wider distribution of wealth. Under normal conditions the man who is strong in body, in mind, in character, and in will need never suffer want. But these qualities can never be developed in a man unless by his own efforts, and the most that any other can do for him is, as I have said, to help him to help himself.

We must always remember that there is not enough money for the work of human uplift and that there never can be. How vitally important it is, therefore, that the expenditure should go as far as possible and be used with the greatest intelligence!

I have been frank to say that I believe in the spirit of combination and cooperation when properly and fairly conducted in the world of commercial affairs, on the principle that it helps to reduce waste; and waste is a dissipation of power. I sincerely hope and thoroughly believe that this same principle will eventually prevail in the art of giving as it does in business.

On *The Gospel of Wealth* by Andrew Carnegie
In this oft-cited essay, one of America's great industrialists makes a case for wise charity, and pleas for the wealthy to give their money away while they are still able to guide its use. Below see Wake Forest University professor James Otteson's commentary on Carnegie's insights as published in *Conversation on Philanthropy* (2009). You can read Carnegie's original text in full at carnegie.org/publications/the-gospel-of-wealth/

Andrew Carnegie (1835-1919) was one of the wealthiest men in the world during his lifetime, and indeed one of the wealthiest men in the history of the world, in inflation-adjusted terms. In 1901 Carnegie sold his interest in U.S. Steel to J. P. Morgan for $480,000,000, the equivalent of more than $10 billion today, of which approximately $250 million (some $5 billion today) went directly to Carnegie himself. But Carnegie was not only a single-minded businessman. He also reflected deeply on the obligations people of wealth have toward their needier brethren.

In 1889 Carnegie wrote an essay, "The Gospel of Wealth," in which he argued against what he called "indiscriminate almsgiving." He began with the claim that there is a legitimate and important distinction between deserving and non-deserving poor. Some people, Carnegie argued, are poor through no fault of their own: sometimes circumstances conspire against one, making it difficult to get ahead despite one's best efforts. Such people, Carnegie said, deserve our help. On the other hand, some people are poor because of decisions they made that led to bad consequences. These, Carnegie thought, do not deserve our help. But because indiscriminate almsgiving does not heed this distinction, it rewards not only behavior that should be rewarded—such as effort, industry, and persistence— but also behavior that should not be rewarded—such as imprudence, irresponsibility, and idleness. Carnegie minces no words about this: "It were better for mankind that the millions of the rich were thrown into the sea than so spent as to encourage the slothful, the drunken, the unworthy."

According to Carnegie, the wealthy person who gives to those asking for money without first determining whether the proposed recipient is deserving actually causes not one but two kinds of bad consequences. First, he encourages the undeserving to continue in their wayward behavior, by decreasing the costs of indulgence, and second, he discourages the deserving from continuing their industry and effort, by showing them that it is pointless. If they receive reward regardless of whether they put forth effort, why, all else being equal, would people want to continue putting forth effort? Thus in addition to enabling the idle and irresponsible poor to remain idle and irresponsible, the indiscriminate almsgiver works to increase their numbers by spreading a "moral infection" that slowly but inexorably converts their industrious brethren to consider the less noble but "easier path" of dependence. These facts, Carnegie thought, licensed calling indiscriminate almsgiving a "cancer" on society and indeed characterizing its effects as "evil."

Carnegie was well aware that his position faces the practical problem of how to know whether a person asking for money is deserving. Even more difficult is to know whether a representative of the poor who is asking for money intends to, and in fact will, give the money only to those who deserve it. It is precisely this difficulty of gathering crucial information that Carnegie thought made effective giving such a daunting prospect: "Unless the individual giver knows the person or family in misfortune, their habits, conduct, and cause of distress, and knows that help given will aid them to help themselves, he cannot act properly." However, because he believed that the "man of wealth" should become a "trustee and agent for his poorer brethren" and "he who dies rich dies disgraced," the moral imperative becomes urgent: find those who deserve help, find ways of giving that actually help them, and do it now.

Carnegie's suggested avenues of help included founding museums, concert halls, libraries, and even universities—things that ministered not to people's immediate material or physical needs but instead to the higher aspects of their humanity. Critics derided his suggestions for just this reason: what need has a hungry man for a library? He cannot, after all, eat the books. But Carnegie's aim was to address not what merely kept people alive....

When we offer someone a meal or money without asking how he got to his sorry state or offering to work together on strategies to rise out of it, we may stave off his hunger for a while, but our obligations to him are not yet fulfilled. We intend to refrain from judging him or embarrassing him, but by not engaging him in these serious conversations we treat him as if bodily needs are all there is to him. Asking him to give an account of himself and his actions, by contrast, displays our understanding that he is a reasoning and accountable creature; it manifests our belief that, whatever difficulties he may face, he is capable of taking steps to address them. It shows that we understand that his life is his own; it treats him like an adult; it treats him like a human being.

On "The Best Fields for Philanthropy" by Andrew Carnegie

In this essay, Carnegie opined on where public good could most readily be done by donors. The full essay is available at: jstor.org/stable/25101907. Below are thoughts from philanthropy scholar Leslie Lenkowsky (originally in *Philanthropy* magazine's Winter 2011 issue) about how Carnegie's own main foundation, the Carnegie Corporation, is doing today at honoring his views.

Andrew Carnegie warned of the perils the wealthy faced if they were insufficiently philanthropic during their lifetimes.... In 1911, during his 76th year, Carnegie realized that he was at risk of this fate himself. Despite having already given $150 million away, he had seen his fortune grow more rapidly and remained an extremely wealthy man. As a result, with initial gifts totaling $125 million (close to $3 billion today), he established the Carnegie Corporation.... This marked the beginning of the modern era of foundation philanthropy.... More than size and scope made the Carnegie Corporation stand out. It also embraced a philosophy of giving known as "scientific philanthropy," which sought to apply the knowledge of experts, particularly those in the medical and social sciences, to the problems donors wanted to address....

During his own lifetime, Carnegie tried to practice what he preached. He established a number of scholarly and research institutes which bear his name: the Carnegie Institution for Science, the Carnegie Foundation for the Advancement of Teaching, and the Carnegie Institute of Technology (today known as Carnegie Mellon University). Convinced of the power of music for worship, he helped churches purchase over 7,500 organs. He created organizations designed to encourage the peaceful resolution of international conflicts, including the Carnegie Endowment for International Peace and the Carnegie Council for Ethics in International Affairs....

By using their wealth "to produce the most beneficial results for the community," those who enjoyed the fruits of the economic system could ensure that the rest of society gained, too.... But not merely through any kind of giving.... The "best fields for philanthropy"...included supporting universities, libraries, hospitals, meeting halls, and recreational facilities. Simply giving money to the needy was not on the list.... Throughout the rest of his life, he...would help people cultivate their talents and take advantage of the opportunities he believed the economic system offered.

....The Carnegie Corporation kept its focus in the years after the Second World War chiefly on social problems, particularly education....

As Washington began to address poverty and other social issues, however, the Carnegie Corporation's attention turned increasingly toward trying to affect public policy.... Andrew Carnegie had seen his philanthropy as an alternative to government, preventing the potentially harmful growth of the public sector in response to the perceived injustices produced by the economic system.... Progress in helping those left behind by the economic system—the same economic system that conferred such great benefits on Andrew Carnegie and others—had been slow to achieve. Some at the Corporation started to wonder if it could be accomplished at all....

Since Vartan Gregorian, a former president of Brown University, took the helm in 1997, the Corporation has concentrated on its traditional interests of improving teacher education and school curricula. It has also continued a long tradition of challenging the educational establishment by giving support to charter schools, working to link teacher pay to student performance, and undertaking other reform efforts....

Yet in important ways, the Corporation's work has departed from its founder's vision. Although it remains riveted on curing social and political inequalities, it has come to regard them less as the unfortunate byproduct of an otherwise successful and worthy economic system, and more as symptoms of fundamental flaws that require substantial changes to the system itself.... The idea that philanthropy—or, for that matter, public policy—should make distinctions between those who deserve help and those who do not has all but vanished.

These departures are an outgrowth of the Corporation's aligning its grantmaking with the views of experts. By looking to the social sciences and other scholarly disciplines to guide its programs, it inevitably acquired the perspectives and biases such expertise possessed.... The lesson for today's philanthropists is not that expertise should be ignored, but that it must be handled with care.

....The centennial of the Carnegie Corporation is also a reminder that what Andrew Carnegie is most often remembered for today—his call for the wealthy to give their fortunes away during their lifetimes—is one of the few goals he failed to achieve. That is why he created the Corporation. But what he really ought to be remembered for has frequently been forgotten.... The responsibility of the wealthy is not only to use their fortunes to help others, but to do so in ways that affirm the value, and enable others to take advantage of, the opportunities the United States afforded an immigrant like him. To Carnegie, philanthropy was made possible by the American political and economic system—and philanthropy was best used when it enabled others to likewise benefit from the nation's opportunities.

Money Well Spent by **Paul Brest and Hal Harvey**
Former Hewlett Foundation head Paul Brest is a leading advocate of the modern style of philanthropy variously known as "strategic," "measured," or "transformational." In his book with Hal Harvey, Brest offers suggestions on how to organize one's giving so as to improve the chances of having prominent effects. This review by philanthropy journalists Matthew Bishop and Michael Green (*Philanthropy* Spring 2009) gives a flavor of his argument.

The philanthropic sector has been reluctant to acknowledge anything except success over the years, which makes *Money Well Spent* such a refreshing change. From the first page of this thoughtful and comprehensive how-to guide to effective giving, Paul Brest and Hal Harvey learn from philanthropic failures as well as triumphs....

There are two important things about failure, say the authors. First, if philanthropy is really society's risk capital, then "some promising philanthropic investments do not succeed and should not succeed if philanthropy is taking appropriate risks." If you do not have failures, you are not doing your job.

Second, how you fail matters. The Robert Wood Johnson Foundation's $90 million, 15-year Fighting Back initiative—which ultimately did little to tackle drug and alcohol abuse—is, they say, a smart failure because the foundation evaluated the program, learned, and shared the knowledge. In contrast, the authors offer up the $500 million Annenberg Challenge, which started out with the wrong assumptions and kept plowing ahead regardless....

When it comes to measurement and metrics, Brest and Harvey are fans of Social Return on Investment, giving examples from New York's hedge-fund-driven Robin Hood Foundation and from the Acumen Fund, which invests philanthropic dollars in for-profit firms in the developing world, to illustrate how this approach can be applied in practice.

Within the nonprofit sector, there is still a lot of pushback against this approach, which some critics feel borrows too heavily from the business world.... Brest and Harvey are alive to the critique, even quoting Einstein to the effect that, "not everything that counts can be counted and not everything that can be counted counts." Yet, as they say, too often complaining about the difficulty of measurement is just an easy cop out.

Give Smart **by Thomas Tierney and Joel Fleishman**
A 2012 book that looks at the big questions that should guide donors who want to get results. Philanthropy Roundtable president Adam Meyerson summarizes the work below.

Tierney and Fleishman argue that "philanthropy's natural state is underperformance." A common trap is "fuzzy-headedness" and ambiguity, the failure of donors to clarify what they are trying to achieve. Another frequent error is to "underestimate what it will actually cost to deliver results and underinvest in the capacity required to make those results a reality." The authors are especially critical of the "nonprofit starvation cycle," the unwillingness of many funders to provide the general operating support that enables grantees to improve their internal systems and management.

Generosity alone will not achieve results, the authors contend. What is needed is generosity informed by rigor, discipline, and strategy. Tierney and Fleishman provide wise, jargon-free guidance about six questions they argue that every philanthropist must wrestle with:

What are my values and beliefs?
What is "success" and how can it be achieved?
What am I accountable for?
What will it take to get the job done?
How do I work with grantees?
Am I getting better?

Some of their useful observations: "In philanthropy, excellence is self-imposed. Unless you demand outstanding performance from yourself, no one else will demand it of you."

"Donors intent on achieving results need to be up-front, clear-minded, and realistic about matching the time frames for their grants with what they're trying to accomplish. Many of the problems philanthropists address require multi-year, or even multi-decade, solutions."

"The measures that matter are the ones that inform and improve decisions. If you cannot connect a given measure to a decision that you (or your grantee) needs to make, it's probably unnecessary."

Changing names to protect confidentiality, Tierney and Fleishman tell cautionary stories of foundations that have deeply disappointed their creators. They point to three common problems in foundations that depart from the original donors' wishes: donors who fail to articulate clearly the mission and principles of their giving, the hiring of staff who behave as if they are giving away their own money, and the creation of family foundations when different family members have vastly different values and charitable priorities.

The authors also understand the fundamental importance of philanthropic freedom for effectiveness in giving. "One of the most compelling arguments for maintaining the broad freedom from external accountability that philanthropists enjoy is that it affords them the freedom to experiment and take risks. Risks that business and government entities cannot, or will not, accept. In fact, philanthropy has served as society's 'risk capital' for more than a century."

What Your Money Means by Frank Hanna
In this personal book, a prominent living donor offers guidance on why we have money, what our money calls us to be, how to shield ourselves and our loved ones from the dangers inherent in wealth, and how to give wisely. Following is a glimpse from philosopher George Weigel's review of the book (*Philanthropy* Fall 2008).

A primer on the meaning of wealth, in which Hanna thinks aloud with his readers about material possessions—and what it means to have a lot of them.... At the outset of his book, he defines his position crisply while throwing down the gauntlet to his readers:

> It's simply not right for those of us who have money to take it for granted. Each of us has to confront the reality of our money and seek to discern its meaning, not only in our own lives but in the overall scheme of things. Either we discover its meaning and live in accordance with that meaning, or rid ourselves of it, because, like fire, it will harm us if we don't use it as it's meant to be used.

...*What Your Money Means* then draws a distinction between what Hanna calls "the fundamentals" and what he terms "non-essential wealth." The "fundamentals" include "all the things money can buy to ensure that persons develop as they ought and become as productive as they can be as individuals and citizens." The "fundamentals" will, obviously, differ from case to case, and in every instance, it's a judgment of prudence when enough is enough.... He is interested in constructing a moral calculus, so that we can determine with integrity what is, for each of us, "non-essential wealth"—and then proceed to give that surplus away. *All of it....*

Hanna makes a serious argument for a philanthropy that is not self-perpetuating, but rather deliberately self-exhausting.

"Non-essential wealth," he argues, is both a danger and an opportunity. It can corrupt those we love by denying them the opportunity to grow into economically responsible actors. It can stifle initiative. It can build barriers to humility and gratefulness. It can create a warped sense of personal identity constructed around vanity possessions, just as it can lead to irrational guilt. On the other hand, "non-essential wealth" gives us the opportunity to do a lot of good, and to enhance our own prospects of living a good life in the process....

The trick, of course, is doing this intelligently, so that our philanthropy serves genuinely good ends. Here, Hanna offers some useful advice on thoughtful charitable giving. The originality of his proposal, however, lies not in his "ten rules of thumb for donors," but in his argument that we should, in effect, give it all away: now, and not at some point in the future determined by our heirs or by the charitable foundations we create.... "We should undertake a lifetime distribution program that will enable us to give away most (if not all) of our non-essential wealth by the time we die."

....In Frank Hanna's considered view, that's a responsibility that can't be generationally outsourced.

The Intelligent Donor's Guide to College Giving
by Anne Neal and Michael Poliakoff

For donors who specifically want to support colleges and universities, the second edition of this short book is a clearly written guide that will help you make sure you get what you pay for. Step-by-step strategies for avoiding common mistakes, plus lots of case histories depicting college giving done well.

CASE STUDIES AND
THE HISTORY OF U.S. GIVING

Casebook for The Foundation
by Joel Fleishman, Scott Kohler, and Steven Schindler
Duke University academics explore 100 of the highest-achieving foundation initiatives of all time, stretching from 1901 to 2002, and touching many fields—medicine, education, employment, law enforcement, ecology, overseas aid, and others. They are all archived online at cspcs.sanford.duke.edu/learning-resources/publications/casebook-foundation-great-american-secret

What Makes Charity Work **edited by Myron Magnet**
Twelve journalistic essays that unwrap instructive philanthropic cases—past and present, successes and failures. For instance, "Why the Boy Scouts Work," "Once We Knew How to Rescue Poor Kids," "What Good is Pro Bono?," and "How Businessmen Shouldn't Help the Schools." A sample from "At Last, a Job Program That Works" by Kay Hymowitz:

Strive's funders, the largest of which is the Clark Foundation, range from the left-wing Aaron Diamond Foundation to the conservative Smith Richardson Foundation. But the organization doesn't take government money, believing that the strings attached to it strangle just those qualities that led to Strive's commendation by the Government Accounting Office in 1996 as one of six job training programs in the U.S. that work. For instance, says Rob Carmona, because of how the government pays its job training providers, "If a person drops out, you don't get paid. It's your goal to keep that person at all costs, so you make excuses for him every day, even if you know he's going out and smoking a joint during lunch." One 35-year-old woman confirmed this picture during a lunch break at Strive: "I've been to other job training programs, and they're not strict enough. They just smile nice at you."

This contrast with other programs helps put Strive's sometimes abrasive toughness in a different light. If, unlike many programs, it demands a great deal of emotional endurance from its participants, it is also unlike those programs in giving much support in return....

Strive staff make no apologies for their basic "there-is-no-better-training-for-work-than-work" philosophy. Given the background of their clientele, they encourage a hard-nosed realism about their immediate opportunities. Jusino tells the group in the middle of the first week: "There are lots of programs out there that'll sell you dreams: you can be an astronaut or something. We don't sell you dreams. I guarantee you, if you follow the program, we'll get you a job making more than you are making now. That's all."

Irving Brown, who has hired more than 50 Strive graduates over the past year for his company, Choice Courier, confirms the success of this lesson. "Strive people understand what's expected of them, and you don't have to reinvent them. They understand that this is a job to give them discipline and basic skills, which they can translate into a more meaningful job in the future. They know they're captains of their own fate. Of the people I've hired, I'd say 75 percent are still here after a year, and the others have gone on to better positions."

In his final book, sociologist Christopher Lasch argued for an "ethos of respect" to supplant what he saw as the prevailing "ethos of compassion" toward the poor. Underlying the prodding, teasing, and confrontation, it is just this kind of respect that Strive displays toward its clients. Insisting on realism, plainspokenness, and clear, impersonal standards of conduct, its staff members neither patronize nor condescend, for they truly believe in the capacities of their clients.... Rather than merely pitying the poor as victims and thereby reinforcing their helplessness, Strive instead believes in their competence and appeals to their ability to climb atop their miserable circumstances and see new possibilities. It's a tough climb, but for those willing and able to make it, it works wonders.

Golden Donors by **Waldemar Nielsen**
Nielsen explores the 36 largest foundations in America at the time of the book's publication in 1986. An overview from Adam Meyerson:

One of the few books about philanthropy that everybody in the field should read, the *Golden Donors* by Waldemar Nielsen, though somewhat dated today, remains a goldmine of intelligent insights about the achievements, failures, and promise of organized philanthropy. Not all readers will agree with Nielsen's biases toward progressive "scientific" philanthropy or his sharply opinionated pronouncements about individual foundations, but philanthropic novices and old hands alike will find much to learn....

Perhaps his harshest criticism is reserved for business leaders whose business minds desert them when they turn to philanthropy:

> In moving from the profit-making to the not-for-profit sphere, they with few exceptions forgot their accumulated skills entirely.... They went for advice mostly to their lawyers and accountants. On the substance of what the foundations might do and how it might be best structured to accomplish it, they either consulted no one or turned to their minister, or wife, or child, or relied on friends and associates as ignorant about philanthropic matters as they themselves.... Staffing was most often an afterthought, frequently with the result that the directorship fell to someone—a failed but amiable executive of the donor's company or the retired head of a local college—with credentials that were at best coincidental.

This beautifully written book challenges foundations to pursue excellence, to set standards, and to make commitments to great causes.

> These strange and wonderful inventions have a unique freedom from the dependency of other institutions on markets or constituencies that cripple their capacity to take the long view and to bring a competent and disinterested approach to the search for complex problems.... It is a waste of important potential if foundations do not make use of the special freedoms they have been given: to take the long view; to back a promising but unproven idea, individual, or institution; to take an unpopular or unorthodox stand; to facilitate change rather than automatically endorsing the status quo...to act and not merely react; to initiate, even to gamble and dare.

American Philanthropy by **Robert Bremner**
Though published more than 50 years ago, for many in this field it remains the preferred single-volume history on the rise of charitable giving in the U.S.

BIOGRAPHIES OF SOME GREAT DONORS

Titan: The Life of John D. Rockefeller, Sr. by Ron Chernow
A highly readable, comprehensive, and fair biography of one of America's most successful business moguls and history's most influential philanthropist. Some details adapted from a review by Martin Wooster in *Philanthropy* magazine's September/October 1998 issue:

The wealth John Rockefeller created has endowed scores of charities, many of whom were not created by the Rockefeller family. For example, Stephen Harkness, one of Rockefeller's early partners, dropped out of Standard Oil and became one of the first important philanthropists. Henry Folger was a director of Standard Oil, and his wealth went to the Folger Shakespeare Library.

John Rockefeller's life was extremely interesting. Born in 1839, the long-lived man came of age before the Civil War yet lived to enjoy the lubricious comedies of Jean Harlow before his death in 1937. Ron Chernow ably retells his story in a way that is balanced, fair, and respectful.

Most people have two sets of questions about Rockefeller. Was his wealth obtained honestly? And was his philanthropy useful?

Chernow conclusively shows that Rockefeller was no "robber baron," but that journalists of the era had trapped Rockefeller in a game he could not win. Rockefeller's virtues were repeatedly turned into vices by the press and the state. Unlike most of the wealthy men and women of his era, Rockefeller lived simply, practicing thrift until extreme old age. Because he did not build large mansions with his fortune, Ida Tarbell condemned Rockefeller as a "social cripple." In 1915, when he spent too long in Cleveland comforting his dying wife, the state of Ohio rewarded his fidelity to his spouse by declaring that Rockefeller was a legal resident of Ohio that year, and presenting him with a million-dollar state tax bill.

The automobile ensured that Rockefeller's wealth would mushroom after his retirement in 1897. When he retired, Rockefeller was worth about $100 million. But as the automobile changed from a rich man's toy into a working man's necessity, demand for gasoline relentlessly increased. Consumer demand quickly pushed Rockefeller's wealth to $900 million in 1912 dollars, or about $25 billion today.

Rockefeller would leave his wealth to a giant foundation. And due to the machinations of Rockefeller's philanthropic adviser Frederick Gates and his attorney Starr Murphy, the Rockefeller Foundation would not have to follow the ideas of its founder. Gates and Murphy agreed that neither wanted to have to answer to Rockefeller.

The Foundation did not neglect Rockefeller's ideas entirely. Like Andrew Carnegie, Rockefeller realized that charity often leads to dependency. "It is a great problem," Rockefeller once wrote, "to learn how to give without weakening the moral backbone of the beneficiary." So Rockefeller's wealth was not simply redistributed. It was Gates's decision to use much of the money on medical research, on the grounds that medicine was non-political, useful, and did not attract many donors at the time. The Rockefellers created what is now Rockefeller University, which has funded many useful medical discoveries.

Titan is a well-written and highly entertaining account. John Rockefeller was a great man and a great philanthropist, and his greatness has been clouded by misinformation spread by his foes. Ron Chernow has ably scraped away falsehoods surrounding Rockefeller's life and ideals. The result is that John Rockefeller is seen not as a villain or an angel, but as a flawed man whose innovations helped Americans lead happier and more productive lives.

A Gift of Freedom: How the John M. Olin Foundation Changed America by John Miller

A book-length history of one of America's most effective twentieth-century foundations, respected by friend and foe alike for its influence on the nation's intellectual life. An extract from a January/February 2006 review in *Philanthropy*:

The John M. Olin Foundation stayed very small and conventional for the first two decades of its life. Most of its patron's giving was directed to hospitals, museums, his alma mater Cornell. The unrest of the Vietnam era changed that dramatically. Olin decided to channel his money, as Miller writes, "primarily toward scholars and activists who understood the principles of market capitalism and were capable of influencing opinions and debate." Miller summarizes principles practiced by Olin that any foundation can learn from:

  ○ Long-term commitments to grantees

◦ A strong commitment to donor intent
◦ A united board
◦ Excellent staff
◦ Term-limiting the foundation so it would have its effect quickly and then close

A Gift of Freedom shows us that even a relatively small foundation can, with a term limit and a strong-willed donor, achieve greatness.

You Need a Schoolhouse by **Stephanie Deutsch, and**
Julius Rosenwald: The Man Who Built Sears, Roebuck and Advanced the Cause of Black Education in the American South by **Peter Ascoli**
Biographies, both by family members, of the donor who built 5,357 schoolhouses for African-American children who would otherwise have grown up in ignorance in the first half of the twentieth century. Drawing from Ascoli's book, Martin Wooster chronicles the exchange between Rosenwald and Booker T. Washington that launched this hugely successful philanthropic effort to relieve the effects of Jim Crow abandonment of blacks by local governments in the South (*Philanthropy*, May/June 2006):

In a September 1912 letter, Washington urged Rosenwald to assist in the building of six rural schools in Alabama. He proposed that the schools would cost $600 apiece and that Rosenwald pay half of this.... "It is the best thing for the people themselves to build schoolhouses in their own community," Washington concluded. "Many people who cannot give money would give a day's work, and others would give material in the way of brick, nails, lime, etc." Rosenwald agreed to pay for half the cost of the six schools. By the time of his death he had paid for thousands more.

And here is a snip from Juan Williams's review of Stephanie Deutsch's *You Need a Schoolhouse* in the Spring 2012 issue of *Philanthropy*:

Julius Rosenwald believed that education, combined with hard work and self-reliance, was the foundation for personal success. That worldview would later be called the American Dream, the ethos that all citizens can rise in America if they work hard enough. Rosenwald boiled America's racial disparity down to the educational differential between black and white. That led him to build schools.

"Rosenwald schools were a haven from prejudice. Their black teachers and principals were loving and supportive. Many children knew their parents and neighbors had raised money and in some cases even done the physical work of building the schools," writes Deutsch…. A free education for generations of black people bettered the lives of millions of Americans, and set the nation on the course to the 1954 *Brown v. Board of Education* decision.

George Eastman: A Biography **by Elizabeth Brayer**
This Pulitzer Prize-nominated biography profiles the business success and vast philanthropy of the founder of Eastman Kodak, whose charities included MIT, the Eastman School of Music, the University of Rochester, the Hampton and Tuskegee Institutes, dental clinics across the globe, and other projects, many of them launched anonymously.

Foundation Builders: Brief Biographies of Twelve Great Philanthropists **by Martin Morse Wooster**
Includes chapters on famous donors like Andrew Carnegie, John Rockefeller, George Eastman, Henry Ford, and Andrew Mellon. Available at philanthropyroundtable.org/guidebook/foundation_builders

Tuxedo Park: A Wall Street Tycoon and the Secret Palace of Science That Changed the Course of World War II **by Jennet Conant**
A fascinating biography of the man who financed rural electrification, anticipated the 1929 stock market crash, then used his resulting fortune for science and defense philanthropy.

PHILANTHROPY AND
THE AMERICAN CHARACTER

Who Really Cares? Who Gives, Who Doesn't, and Why it Matters
by Arthur Brooks
We all know we should give to charity, but who actually does, and why?
A prominent policy expert uncovers the surprising associations among
family structure, faith, political views, and giving. One chapter presents
evidence that giving is linked to increased personal happiness, individual
health, and national wealth. Snippets from the *Philanthropy* review of
September/October 2006:

About three out of four American families give charitable gifts each year.
Brooks finds that the most generous donors have four key traits: religious
faith, skepticism about the government in economic life, strong families, and
personal entrepreneurism. Where these converge, dollars flow freely toward
charitable causes.

If you want to predict giving patterns, first look at a person's religious
convictions. People who worship nearly every week give away three and a
half times more money each year than people who only go once or twice
a year. For two otherwise identical families earning $49,000 in 2000, the
religious one gave $2,210 vs. $642. But religious people don't just give to
their churches and synagogues. They are more likely to give to non-religious
causes as well, whether it's the PTA or the symphony, and they are twice as
likely to volunteer.

Political orientation is another powerful factor in charitable giving.
Conservative households donate 30 percent more money to charity than
liberal households, and they are more likely to volunteer as well. Why the
difference? Brooks found that liberals view government redistribution as a
"form of charity," which they believe exonerates them from further giving.

The continent of Europe has had a longer time to play out the consequences
of heavy government spending. Americans give three and a half times as
much as the Dutch to charity, seven times as much as the Germans, and
fourteen times as much as the Italians. Tocqueville's America is still alive
and well today.

Whether or not people give charitably has everything to do with
entitlement mentality. In a fascinating comparison, Brooks looks at the giving
patterns of the poorest Americans. The working poor give away three times

as much of their money as people on welfare, even though they have exactly the same income. Apparently receiving entitlement payments cripples the impulse to aid others.

> **The Greater Good: How Philanthropy Drives the American Economy and Can Save Capitalism by Claire Gaudiani**
> The U.S. is a rich nation in no small part because we are generous. And expanded generosity is crucial to keeping our country healthy and thriving in the future. Here is part of a short reflection on the book (*Philanthropy* January/February 2005):

Instead of mucking about in the swamp of current philanthropic jargon about effectiveness, efficiency, and accountability, Claire Gaudiani drives right at the fundamental questions surrounding charity, wealth, and politics. In the first half of her book she argues that philanthropy has fueled American economic success. Her basic claim: "Most people think that Americans are generous because we are rich. The truth is that we are rich, in significant part, because we are generous."

But in the book's second half, the party's over. Gaudiani fears that as the economy chugs along, the bottom 40 percent of Americans will feel left farther behind and the lives of the rich more "gated." In response, she calls upon wealthy individuals to partner with local communities in order to put capital into the hands of the poor.

For all of the moral language that she uses in praise of philanthropy, though, she does not quite recognize that solutions to today's problems must likewise involve moral character rather than material goods. Redistribution of wealth will not solve problems of the soul. Moreover, today's givers are moved much more by identification or affiliation with those they give to, rather than by fear or guilt.

One of the best things Gaudiani's argument could do, as Alexis de Tocqueville urged in his *Memoir on Pauperism*, would be to renew and strengthen the "moral tie" between giver and receiver, rich and poor. That can only happen through individualized charity that respects the dignity of both the one who gives and the one who receives.

PURSUING PHILANTHROPY LIKE A BUSINESS

Good to Great and the Social Sectors **by Jim Collins**
A short book by the prominent management consultant in which he takes his discoveries on the factors that allow companies to perform at a high level and applies them to philanthropy.

Philanthrocapitalism **by Matthew Bishop & Michael Green**
Examines the "venture investing" movement, which combines for-profit techniques with nonprofit goals. The book includes interviews with a host of investors like Bill Gates, Ted Turner, George Soros, Michael Bloomberg, and others. A piece from a spinoff article by the authors in *Philanthropy* Fall 2009:

The movement we have described as "philanthrocapitalism" is all about harnessing the best techniques in business for doing good. One of the leading examples of this movement is Legacy Venture, a Palo Alto fund that raised $40 million from individuals willing to commit that every penny the firm makes for them by investing in Silicon Valley would go to philanthropy. Within ten years, the firm had more than $700 million under management. Legacy's job is taking the capital that wealthy individuals have set aside for philanthropy and making it work as hard as possible in terms of financial returns. "We are investing for maximum profitability, and then all the dollars go to philanthropy," says partner Alan Marty.

The firm hosts a regular series of seminars that connect investors with leading thinkers in philanthropy and social enterprise, such as Nobel Peace laureate and micro-finance pioneer Muhammad Yunus, and Teach For America founder Wendy Kopp. Maybe even more important is the opportunity to learn from each other. "Our investor community includes both experienced and aspiring philanthropists," says co-founder Russ Hall.

"Madison Avenue Mercies"
by Nicholas Kristof and Sheryl WuDunn
The virtues of advertising, overhead, and other wicked ways of doing good (*Philanthropy*, Spring 2015):

When considering whether to support a nonprofit, one of the basic bits of information many people look for is its Charity Navigator rating and the proportion of its revenues consumed by administration, particularly salaries. They also see overhead and marketing as a drain that should be absolutely minimized.

Administrative expenses can indeed be relevant, but what truly matters is not overhead but impact. There's no point in funding an AIDS vaccine effort that saves on overhead by using unreliable third-rate laboratory equipment. One shortcoming of Charity Navigator ratings has been that charities often respond by systematically underinvesting in anything overhead-related, skimping on computers, personnel training, evaluation, marketing, and talented people.

We asked Charlie MacCormack, who formerly ran Save the Children, about overhead at nonprofits, and he was blunt: "Our uncompetitive salaries make it almost impossible for people to develop real careers; our underinvestment in staff development hampers performance; and our creaky knowledge management and information systems undermine potential results.... Donors resist funding these kinds of activities and consider program-to-overhead ratios to be proxies for organizational quality."

Forced to squeeze their overhead, aid groups cut corners in ways that undermine the mission. Without the funds or expertise to do rigorous evaluations, they're often groping in the dark to determine what works best.

"Business Marries Charity!" by Howard Husock
The hopes and hazards of bringing market mechanisms to philanthropy (*Philanthropy*, Spring 2015):

"Social-impact investing"—venture capitalism, more or less, that aims for a mix of human and economic returns—is becoming all the rage. At first blush, the term "impact investing" may seem redundant. All financial investments are made with the intention of having an impact. The twist here is a desire among some idealistic investors, philanthropists, foundations, and financial institutions to meld moneymaking with societal improvement.

It's a growing niche. Some $8 billion in impact investments were made just in 2012, and interest has grown since then. The movement enjoys buzz from the highest levels of government, philanthropy, and venture capital. A blue-ribbon group of donors recently suggested that "the power of markets can help to scale solutions to some of our most urgent problems."

Factoring in nontraditional returns like social effects leads to a range of expectations about profits. Some impact investors expect standard market returns, while others will accept below-market returns along with the social effect they desire. Sometimes this trade-off is masked with the claim that the investor is seeking his or her return over "a longer time horizon." Or that, in the memorable phrase of one impact investor, this is "philanthropy in which you lose your money slowly."

"Giving Made Easy" by Joanne Florino
Donor-advised funds are bringing new convenience to philanthropy (*Philanthropy*, Spring 2015):

A donor-advised fund offers efficiency and flexibility. It allows money the chance to grow while it is invested in the market. It gives even small donors access to accumulated knowledge on the best nonprofits. It makes it easy for families to transmit values and teach younger members how to engage in creative giving. The most important factor driving philanthropists to donor-advised funds may be simplicity.

Today over one thousand organizations offer donor-advised funds in the U.S., housing over $50 billion in charitable assets. The funds sponsored by companies like Fidelity, Schwab, and Vanguard have grown so rapidly, thanks to their ease of use, that they now rank among America's largest charitable conduits. Donor-advised funds now outnumber private foundations by more than two to one in the U.S.

"Donor-advised funds are attractive to generous people and actually encourage them to set aside more for charity," states Brent Christopher of the Communities Foundation of Texas.

"Stronger Together" by Evan Sparks
Donors are increasingly using expert intermediaries to bundle and target their giving (*Philanthropy*, Spring 2015):

Groups that aggregate together the donations of many givers, then steer them into carefully chosen charities, have become extremely popular of late. The Charter School Growth Fund and the NewSchools Venture Fund, for instance, have invested some $435 million in charter schools in recent years. Collaboration with other donors allows a giver to have big effects relatively quickly.

Aggregators help givers in a variety of other ways. In an increasingly complex charitable landscape, donors are looking for trusted judgment. Banding together is a solution to the problem of not having enough time to deeply research a field. The intermediary organization takes responsibility for finding the best practitioners, and the donor provides the resources.

"If you're a donor and you don't have the time, network, or resources to go find the best entrepreneurial educators in the private market, that's our job. That's what we will be doing," says Rob Birdsell of the Drexel Fund, a new group that will bundle together donations to expand the number and quality of Catholic schools. He encourages donors to think of it like a private equity fund—an opportunity to work with experts to achieve results not possible without both the experts and the capital.

Another driver of aggregation is efficiency. "It's all about minimizing transaction costs," says one adviser. Philanthropic aggregators can "get the grant reporting done, follow up on how recipients are doing, cut the check," she adds. "They're better set up to run smaller grants."

"Alms Alchemy" by Liz Essley Whyte
The National Christian Foundation's ability to turn unusual contributions to gold is creating a new trove of generosity (*Philanthropy*, Spring 2015):

The National Christian Foundation was set up in 1982 and ran for a dozen years with a staff of just two. Then in the mid-'90s, it started accepting gifts beyond simple cash and stocks. Demand for converting more complex assets into charitable gifts boomed. The foundation has now given out $5.3 billion in grants.

President David Wills estimates that of the roughly $2.2 billion the foundation holds right now, $500 million of it is in the form of non-liquid assets. In addition to receiving real estate and various kinds of stock, NCF is also a leader in helping donors give away part or all of entire businesses. NCF employs about 20 experts—tax lawyers and financial gurus—to help make non-cash gifts happen.

"It used to be in the fundraising world that donors would never give the tree, but would just give the fruit," Wills says. Now nonprofits can get trees as well as fruit.

"Catalytic Philanthropy" by Mark Kramer
Rather than leaving to charitable organizations all responsibility for finding solutions to social problems, ambitious donors can set in motion their own fixes, this journal article suggests. Full text at: ssireview.org/articles/entry/catalytic_philanthropy

"Virtuous Capital: What Foundations Can Learn from Venture Capitalists" by Christine Letts, William Ryan, & Allen Grossman
This *Harvard Business Review* article argues that funders should not only write checks to nonprofits but help them develop their organizational capacity—as venture capitalists do for small businesses. Available here: hbr.org/product/virtuous-capital-what-foundations-can-learn-from-v/an/97207-PDF-ENG

THE ROLE OF MORAL ISSUES IN CHARITABLE SUCCESS

The Tragedy of American Compassion by Marvin Olasky

This important book excavates lost history on how poverty can—and cannot—be fought effectively. It concludes that the real problem with much contemporary aid is not that it is too stingy but that it doesn't address, in a personal way, the damaged hearts and souls that are at the root of much economic failure. The author's interview on C-SPAN with Brian Lamb can be viewed at: c-span.org/video/?62813-1/book-discussion-tragedy-american-compassion

"In Praise of Do-It-Yourself Do-Good" and "Broken Windows Philanthropy," both by William Schambra

Two short essays representative of many others produced by a leading critic of the current taste for large-scale, "root causes," measurement-driven, "change the world" philanthropy. He prescribes a humbler, more local, more personal style of helping which accepts the difficulty and sometimes undesirability of transforming people and social institutions. "Broken Windows Philanthropy" can be read at: hudson.org/research/8795-james-q-wilson-and-broken-windows-philanthropy. Following is a section from "In Praise of..." (from the book *Giving Well, Doing Good*) where Schambra warns against turning over national problem-solving to distant experts and elites.

The central premise of twentieth-century philanthropy is that the "ungodly bright" (to use Warren Buffett's term) are somehow better equipped to solve society's problems than are everyday citizens. The notion that citizens themselves could and should play a central role in solving their own problems is, of course, reflected in Alexis de Tocqueville's understanding of American democracy.

Tocquevillian or civic renewal philanthropy would reach out quietly but actively into the communities it wishes to assist, harvesting "street wisdom" about which groups genuinely capture a community's self-understanding of its problems. Such groups will more than likely have duct tape on their industrial carpeting and water stains on their ceilings. They will not be able to draft clever, eye-catching fundraising brochures or grant proposals. They will not have sophisticated accounting systems, or be able to lay out a schedule of measurable outcomes. They will not speak the language of the social sciences, but more often than not, the language of sin and spiritual redemption. They will not be staffed by well-paid credentialed experts, but rather by volunteers whose chief credential is that they themselves have managed to overcome the problem they are now helping others to confront. No matter what the group's formal charter states, it will minister to whatever needs present themselves at the door, even if it means being accused of inefficiency or mission drift. For each person is treated not as an inadequately self-aware bundle of pathologies, but rather as a unique individual, a citizen possessed of a soul, demanding a respectful, humane response to the entire person.

This approach turns completely on its head the still-entrenched orthodoxy of progressive philanthropy. Indeed, it looks suspiciously like charity—the antiquated, discredited approach which nonetheless honored and ministered personally to the individual before it. Charity does indeed deal with "mere symptoms" because they are what people themselves consider important, rather than with root causes visible only to experts who can "see through" the client. Because civic renewal philanthropy tackles social problems individual by individual, neighborhood by neighborhood, and because it relies on and entrusts ordinary, public-spirited citizens, familiar with the communities of which they are a part, to lead the way—to identify and resolve their own problems in their own way—this approach will not appeal to the ungodly bright.

It is hardly surprising that the immensely wealthy today should find appealing the century-old vision of putting massive funding into cutting-edge technology in order to deliver the decisive, "knock-out punch" to some vexing social problem. Perhaps a handful, however, will come to appreciate the lessons of the past century, that there are no knock-outs in the effort to improve society, and the search for them can readily take ugly turns. By funding more concrete, immediate, community-based efforts of the sort described by Tocqueville, however, it would be possible to make modest headway against social ills. It would also contribute to a much loftier purpose, the revival of civic engagement and democratic self-governance in America, perhaps thereby helping to insure the survival of our democratic republic. But to appreciate the importance of that goal, it is necessary to transcend the narrow, scientific knowledge of the ungodly bright. It requires instead a kind of prudence or wisdom that aims at an attainable good, while accepting and working with, rather than trying to see through the bewildering variety of human needs. It thus fully respects and helps to preserve democratic citizenship and human dignity. This would be the philanthropy, not of the ungodly bright, but rather of the godly wise.

The Triumphs of Joseph by Robert Woodson
Readers of this book meet a string of neighborhood heroes who are struggling not only against the problems of urban poverty but also against bureaucratic notions of social service fashionable among philanthropists and government officials. Here is an adaptation from the book in which Woodson explains how grassroots donor-funded social ministries can help the underclass:

Our welfare problem is part of a larger crisis in America. Every year, more American blacks are killed in urban violence by other blacks than the total number of blacks who died in service throughout nine years of the Vietnam war. Today, little children can stand at the scene of a homicide calmly eating ice cream cones.

And the moral dissolution that is devastating our low-income minority neighborhoods has also begun gnawing away at white, upper-income society. Carroll O'Connor, Gloria Vanderbilt, and George McGovern lost children to substance abuse or suicide. Margaux Hemingway was found dead after a long struggle with alcohol and bulimia. If race and poverty cause social breakdown, then why do we have cases like the Menendez brothers, who gunned down their affluent parents in cold blood? Why are there so many wealthy people in drug rehab? Many Americans live in lavish homes that echo with emptiness, and many wealthy children experience the same moral confusion as poor kids.

The good news is that solutions to our welfare problem, and the larger moral crisis to which it is linked, do exist. But the ultimate answers lie beyond traditional responses like job training, education, subsidized housing, food assistance, or racial reconciliation. To locate solutions to our most dangerous social diseases we must look in some new places.

For there are embers of health and restoration even among the ruins of today's inner-city neighborhoods. To make use of the hope they offer, we must open ourselves to new kinds of authority and expertise. Some of today's most promising community healers have come out of our prisons, out of drug addiction, out of dysfunctional families and crime-ridden neighborhoods. Many have themselves fallen into trouble—but then recovered through their faith in God.

Many of these moral healers are helping—with meager resources—persons who conventional service-providers have given up on, with an effectiveness that eclipses conventional remedies. For example, a faith-based substance-abuse program established in San Antonio, Texas, by a recovered drug addict named Freddie Garcia has freed 13,000 drug abusers and alcoholics from their addictions. It operates at a cost of only $80 per person, per day, yet has a 70 percent success rate, in contrast to conventional therapeutic programs for substance abusers that charge up to $600 a day per client yet have far lower success rates.

Why haven't we heard more about these social healers? Why haven't we tapped their approaches to address not only the needs of the underclass but also the problems of apathy, despair, and isolation that are wrenching families of every race, ethnicity, and income bracket?

The main reason, simply put, is elitism. The moral and religious approaches emphasized by healers like Pastor Garcia are looked down upon by many in our cultural establishment, who prefer to view the poor as hapless victims waiting to be rescued by experts and monthly checks. Establishment poverty industries will not easily relinquish their "ownership" of social problems, particularly to any solutions that compete with their clinical, government-transfer-based approach.

But some private groups and individuals are exploring less conventional methods of aiding the underclass. Moral healers have successfully addressed problems that everyone agrees are at the core of our meltdown—the degeneracy that gets expressed in violence, drug addiction, sexual license, and family disloyalty.

I was the founder of a policy institute looking for ways to combat poverty. For two years, I hosted town meetings around the country and invited local leaders to show me strategies of personal and community revitalization that have been effective. I still don't entirely understand how privately funded faith-based organizations reach into the heart of the most severely damaged individuals and transform them. But overwhelming evidence shows they can do just that.

From Native American reservations in New Mexico, to black inner-city neighborhoods, to rural white mining towns, to Hispanic barrios, I've talked to people who were in prison, who had infected their own sons with drugs, who were prostitutes, shattered people who experts said were beyond reach but whom I saw transformed. I met a white man who told me that for seven years while he was a police officer he was addicted to violence—against those he arrested, and against his own family. But he found his way to a grassroots ministry and his life was remade. He has now been violence-free for seven years.

Even within the most devastated social terrain, the embers of spiritual renewal are alive in the work of thousands of grassroots moral leaders. If these embers can be nourished by those who have wealth and influence, the flames of revitalization can sweep across the nation like a brushfire, bringing life and hope where there is now only cynicism, confusion, and despair.

> ### *Poverty and Compassion* by Gertrude Himmelfarb
> This Victorian history compares the guiding lights behind the Christian Salvation Army and the socialist Fabians, traces the development of concepts such as unemployment and the poverty line, and concludes that the material and moral dimensions of poverty were inseparable in the minds of the Victorians. These paragraphs drawn from Peter Berger's review in *Commentary* (December 1991) give some sense of the book:

The Victorian Age has had a bad press among intellectuals: the very adjective has come to be synonymous with all that is repressed, hypocritical, moralistically meddlesome. The same view holds in the area of social reform: the Victorians oppressively imposed their bourgeois values on a reluctant working class, and were particularly addicted to the habit which American liberals now call "blaming the victim."

This disagreeable stereotype has been challenged before, but never in a more exhaustive and sustained fashion than by the eminent historian Gertrude Himmelfarb. She has demonstrated just how short the stereotype falls of complex reality....

An argument that recurs throughout this book concerns the "moral imperialism" of Victorian social thought. It has been a common notion, and not only on the Left, that the Victorian reformers sought to impose middle-class values and styles of life on the poor. Miss Himmelfarb rejects this view. The "respectability" so dear to the Victorians was not just a value of the bourgeoisie. On the contrary, it was at the core of the aspirations and the culture of the working class itself....

While reiterating that the problems of the Victorians were different from our own, Himmelfarb does look at the "lessons" they may hold for us. Most importantly, she proposes that the Victorians were right in insisting that poverty is a multi-layered phenomenon, and right in insisting that it has a centrally important moral component. Both insights have been lost in much of 20th-century social thought and policy. It is not the Victorians but many of our own contemporaries who can be fairly described as "moral imperialists."

In Miss Himmelfarb's own words: "After making the most arduous attempt to objectify the problem of poverty, to divorce poverty from any moral assumptions and conditions, we are learning how inseparable the moral and material dimensions of that problem are. And after trying to devise social policies that are scrupulously neutral and 'value-free,' we are finding these policies fraught with moral implications that have grave material and social consequences."

THE POWER OF GRASSROOTS CIVIL SOCIETY

"Civil and Uncivil Societies" by Niall Ferguson

In a lecture delivered at the Royal Society of Edinburgh, a prominent historian and Harvard professor discussed the value of private initiative in civil society. It may be read in its entirety at bbc.co.uk/programmes/articles/1n02Kr5c1XCGkZbw8wvbv5s/niall-ferguson-civil-and-uncivil-societies. Here is a condensation by The Philanthropy Roundtable:

Nearly ten years ago I bought a house on the coast of South Wales. But there was a catch. The lovely stretch of coastline in front of it was hideously strewn with rubbish. Thousands of plastic bottles littered the sands and rocks. Plastic bags fluttered in the wind, caught on the thorns of the Burnet roses.

Dismayed, I asked the locals: who's responsible for keeping the coastline clean?

"Well, the council is supposed to do it," one of them explained, "but they don't do nothing about it, do they?"

I took to carrying and filling black bin-liners whenever I went for a walk. But it was a task far beyond the capacity of one man. And that was when it happened: I asked for volunteers.

Well, the first beach clear-up was a modest affair. The second was more of a success.... It was when the local branch of the Lions Club became involved, however, that the breakthrough came. I had never heard of the Lions Club. I learned that it's originally an American association, not unlike the Rotary Club. Both were founded by Chicago businessmen about a century ago and both are secular networks whose members dedicate their time to various good causes.

The Lions brought a level of organization and motivation that far exceeded my earlier improvised efforts. As a result of their involvement, the shoreline was transformed. The plastic bottles were bagged and properly disposed of; the roses were freed from their ragged polyethylene wrappings.

Together, spontaneously, without any public sector involvement, without any profit motive, without any legal obligation or power, we had turned a depressing dumping ground back into a beauty spot. Now I ask myself: How many other problems could be solved in this simple and yet satisfying way?

...In his best-selling book *Bowling Alone*, my Harvard colleague Robert Putnam detailed the drastic declines, between around 1960 or 1970 and the late 1990s, in a long list of indicators of social capital:

- Attendance at a public meeting on town or school affairs: down 35 percent.
- Service as an officer of a club or organization: down 42 percent.
- Service on a committee for a local organization: down 39 percent.
- Membership of parent-teacher associations: down 61 percent.
- The average membership rate for 32 national chapter-based associations: down by almost 50 percent.
- Membership rates for men's bowling leagues: down 73 percent.

...It is something Alexis de Tocqueville anticipated, in what is perhaps the most powerful passage in the whole of *Democracy in America*. Here he vividly imagines a future society in which associational life has died:

> An innumerable multitude of men, all equal and alike, incessantly endeavouring to procure the petty and paltry pleasures with which they glut their lives. Each of them, living apart, is as a stranger to the fate of all the rest; his children and his private friends constitute to him the whole of mankind. As for the rest of his fellow citizens, he is close to them, but he does not see them....
>
> Above this race of men stands an immense and tutelary power, which takes upon itself alone to secure their gratifications and to watch over their fate. That power is absolute, minute, regular, provident, and mild. It would be like the authority of a parent if, like that authority, its object was to prepare men for manhood; but it seeks, on the contrary, to keep them in perpetual childhood....

Tocqueville was surely right...the state—with its seductive promise of security from the cradle to the grave—was the real enemy of civil society.... Over the past 50 years governments encroached too far on the realm of civil society....

Like Tocqueville, I believe that spontaneous local activism by citizens is better than central state action not just in terms of its results, but more importantly in terms of its effect on us as citizens. For true citizenship is not just about voting, earning, and staying on the right side of the law.

It is also about participating in the troop—the wider group beyond our families—which is precisely where we learn how to develop and enforce rules of conduct. In short, to govern ourselves; to educate our children; to care for the helpless; to fight crime; to clear the beach of rubbish....

We humans live in a complex matrix of institutions. There is government. There is the market. There is the law. And then there is civil society.... Once this matrix worked astonishingly well, with each set of institutions complementing and reinforcing the rest. That, I believe, was the key to Western success in the eighteenth, nineteenth, and twentieth centuries. But the institutions in our times are out of joint.

It is our challenge in the years that lie ahead to restore them. It is time, ladies and gentlemen, to clear up the beach.

Democracy in America by Alexis de Tocqueville

French observer Alexis de Tocqueville visited pioneer America and wrote deathless descriptions of what makes the nation exceptional. The bulwark of our democracy, he discovered, is citizens who voluntarily pool their money, expertise, and labor to improve society. Here is a relevant bit:

Americans of all ages, stations in life, and all types of dispositions are forever forming associations.... of a thousand different types—religious, moral, serious, futile, very general and very limited, immensely large and very minute. Americans combine to give fetes, found seminaries, build churches, distribute books, and send missionaries to the antipodes. Hospitals, prisons, and schools take shape in that way. Finally, if they want to proclaim a truth or propagate some feelings by the encouragement of a great example, they form an association. In every case, at the head of any new undertaking where in France you would find the government, or in England some great lord, in the United States you are sure to find an association....

If some obstacle blocks the public road halting the circulation of traffic, the neighbors at once form a deliberative body; this improvised assembly produces an executive authority which remedies the trouble.... Associations are formed to combat exclusively moral troubles: intemperance is fought in common. Public security, trade and industry, and morals and religion all provide the aims for associations in the United States....

The first time that I heard in America that one hundred thousand men had publicly promised never to drink alcohol liquor, I thought it more of a joke than a serious matter.... In the end I came to understand that these hundred thousand Americans, frightened by the progress of drunkenness around them, wanted to support sobriety by their patronage. They were acting in just the same way as some great lord who dresses very plainly to encourage a contempt of luxury among simple citizens. One may fancy that if they had lived in France, each of these hundred thousand would have made individual representations to the government asking it to supervise all the public houses throughout the realm....

Many of my contemporaries.... claim that as the citizens become weaker and more helpless, the government must become proportionately more skilled and active, so that society should do what is no longer possible for individuals. They think that answers the whole problem, but I think they are mistaken....

What political power could ever carry on the vast multitude of lesser undertakings which associations daily enable American citizens to control? ....The more government takes the place of associations, the more will individuals lose the idea of forming associations and need the government to come to their help. That is a vicious circle of cause and effect....

The morals and intelligence of a democratic people would be in as much danger as its commerce and industry if ever a government wholly usurped the place of private associations. Feelings and ideas are renewed, the heart enlarged, and the understanding developed only by the reciprocal action of men upon another.... A government, by itself, is equally incapable of refreshing the circulation of feelings and ideas among a great people.

Reclaiming the American Dream by **Richard Cornuelle**
This groundbreaking 1965 work revived the idea, at a time of rising centralism, that individuals and communities can often solve their problems more effectively than government bureaucracies. Below is a substantial extract from the book. You can also read a condensation of a related talk that Cornuelle delivered to The Philanthropy Roundtable in 1999 at: philanthropyroundtable.org/topic/philanthropic_freedom/ want_real_community_stick_to_a_human_scale

For a long time it seemed that the free society and the good society could be realized together in America. This, I think, was the American dream. And for a hundred years and more, it worked.

We wanted, from the beginning, a free society, free in the sense that every man was his own supervisor and the architect of his own ambitions. So our founders took pains to design a government with limited power, and then carefully scattered the forces which could control it.

We wanted as well, with equal fervor, a good society—a humane, responsible society in which helping hands reached out to people in honest distress, in which common needs were met freely and fully. In pursuit of this ambition, Americans used remarkable imagination. We created a much wider variety of new institutions for this purpose than we built to insure political freedom. As a frontier people, accustomed to interdependence, we developed a genius for solving common problems. People joined together in bewildering combinations to found schools, churches, opera houses, co-ops, hospitals, to build bridges and canals, to help the poor. To see a need was, more often than not, to promote a scheme to meet it better than had ever been done before.

The American dream was coming true. Each part of it supported another part. We were free because we limited the power of government. We prospered because we were free. We built a good society because our prosperity yielded surplus energy which we put directly to work to meet human needs. Thus, we didn't need much government, and because we didn't, we stayed uniquely free. A sort of supportive circle, or spiral, was working for us.

The part of the system least understood, then as now, was the network of non-governmental institutions which served public needs. They did not leave an easy trace for historians to follow. [Nonetheless] they took on almost any public job and so became the principal way Americans got things done.... Citizens, acting on their own, took the heavy load. Local and state government took most of what was left. We rarely needed the federal government, a distant thing to the frontiersman. We limited government, not only because people knew its limitations and wanted it limited, but because we left little for it to do....

[But today] the private citizen has come to feel that technical progress creates public problems faster than it solves them—so many that only government seems big enough to work on them.... This attitude was born out of the Depression.... Our habit of sending difficult problems to Washington quickly became almost a reflex. A one-way flow of responsibility to the federal government, begun by Depression remedies, has continued and gained speed....

This rather sudden disappearance of any evident alternative to government action profoundly affected our national life. It broke the spiral I referred to earlier.... Humanity and freedom seem now to be in permanent conflict....

It quickly became fashionable to speak of American life in terms of only two "sectors": the public sector, which is a prejudicial euphemism for government, and the private sector, which is profit-seeking commerce. We leave out the third sector in our national life, the one which is neither governmental nor commercial. We ignore the institutions which once played such a decisive part in the society's vibrant growth. By assuming a major role in meeting public needs, thus leaving less to government, the third sector once made it possible for us to build a humane society and a free society together.

The important third force deserves a name. It is a distinct, identifiable part of American life, not just a misty area between commerce and government. I have come to call it "the independent sector." After some years of work among the people and organizations operating in this sector, no other word seems to express its unique, intrepid character as well....

When you push back the curtain that has strangely hidden the independent sector from the public eye, one surprise follows another. You notice dozens of agencies that serve you daily. The sector's dimensions are fantastic, its raw strength awesome. . . .

Sometimes the independent impulse shows itself in humble, simple ways, as when our new neighbors brought a pot of soup and offered to sit with the baby when we moved into our tract house in San Mateo.

Sometimes it shows itself boldly and professionally, as when the National Foundation for Infantile Paralysis set out to conquer polio with dimes—and did it.

Sometimes the independent sector deals with small pleasures, as when my wife's Garden Guild attends to the floral decorations at our church.

But often it deals with grave problems, as when Stanford Research Institute designs weapons system and strategy on which our defense depends.

Sometimes independent action is impulsive, as when thousands of Americans mailed $600,000 to Dallas Patrolman J. D. Tippit's grief-stricken wife and $78,000 to the assassin's stunned young widow. But often it is highly systematic, as when the Ford Foundation coaches colleges and universities in the complexities of long-range capital planning.

Sometimes the independent sector does menial, dirty work, as when volunteer hospital aides empty the bedpans and bandage the oozing sores of patients in hospitals all across the country. But often it does what is most gracious and aesthetic, as when the Guggenheim family builds a magnificent museum....

Sometimes independent action is highly individual. Leo Seligman of Memphis, who learned about prison life the hard way in a Nazi concentration camp, has met 786 parolees at prison gates in Tennessee with bus fare, lunch, and a helping hand. But it is often highly organized. The Boy Scouts can tell you to the penny how much it takes to set up a troop....

Sometimes the independent sector provides our luxuries. Most of our opera houses are independent institutions, and independent symphonies provide cultural leaven in more than 1,200 American communities. Sometimes it provides desperate necessities, as when Salvation Army centers give a meal to men who would otherwise sleep hungry in the street....

The independent sector is a kaleidoscope of human action. It takes a thousand forms and works in a million ways. And a tremendous raw strength undergirds its rich variety.... Americans have developed a rich variety of organizations through which they arrange their time, energy, and ingenuity for public service....

Hundreds of fraternal and service organizations...not only march in parades but also send needy youngsters to college.... There are nearly 3,500 independent hospitals, and thousands more independent nursing homes. There are 1,357 private colleges and universities enrolling 1.7 million students, and more than 17,000 private schools....

The independent sector has the power to do these formidable things. But, curiously, as its strength has increased we have given it less and less to do, and assigned more and more common tasks to government.... a natural competitor. Both sectors operate in the same industry: public service and welfare. Sometimes, over the years, leaders on each side have sensed their competitive positions and built a fascinating record of both creative competition and deliberate collusion. The quality of life in the U.S. now depends largely on the revival of a lively competition between these two natural contenders for public responsibility. The struggle would enhance the effectiveness of both....

The very idea of competition with government is, by a weird public myth, thought to be illegitimate, disruptive, divisive, unproductive, and perhaps immoral. [This] came along fairly recently. Just 50 years ago, the Rockefeller Foundation and the Carnegie Corporation together spent twice as much for education and social services as did the entire federal government. Voluntary agencies took the lion's share of public responsibility....

[Today] many believe that the independent sector's main function is to assist the government in its effort to take more responsibility, often by providing pilot projects and press agentry.... Thus the independent sector now mainly promotes its government competitor. The test of a good citizen is not that he takes responsibility, but that he successfully sends it to Washington....

Far from being illegitimate, lively competition with government is essential if our democratic institutions are to work sensibly.... Without competition, the bureaucracy can't make government efficient or even sensibly decide what it needs to do.... Innovation painfully disrupts its way of life. Reform comes only through competitive outsiders who force steady, efficient adjustment to changing situations.

Independent sector leaders genially speak of complementing government, not competing with it—as if monopoly were good and competition destructive—thus unwittingly conspiring against the public interest.... The independent sector will grow strong again when its leaders realize that its unique indispensable natural role in America is to compete with government. It must be as eager as government to take on new public problems. It must be imaginative, vigorous, persistent. Independent groups must line up in Washington, not begging for help but looking for bigger jobs to do....

The independent sector will be cut back further, perhaps abolished, if it fails to compete aggressively in public service.... Already in America, government is tightening its grip on the independent sector. It is challenging the tax-exempt status of foundations, making new efforts to "regulate" almost all private groups.... The government is eyeing foundation treasuries hungrily. Every year the pressures mount for closer government control....

The logic of the foundation-busters is formidable. Foundations, they argue, have money because they don't pay taxes. So, it is said, they are really spending tax money. Officials elected by all the people should control tax money, this argument says, not foundation trustees....

But the foundation is more than a mechanical alternative to government action—and far more than an arm of the welfare state suitable only to test out and lobby for new federal programs. The foundation is an instrument forged by citizens who transfer profit from the commercial sector and put it directly to work as risk capital for the general betterment of the society. To say or imply that the foundation exists only on the sufferance of government is to reason from the premise that government is the whole society. Here is a special version of the untenable notion that the citizen and all his institutions are creatures of the state, not the other way around.

The Quest for Community by **Robert Nisbet**

In this excerpt from Nisbet's classic book, he argues that bigger is not better in social reform. He notes the benefits of smaller-scale organizations and their ability to console, soften, and enrich life. Larger, bureaucratic institutions can often be less socially wholesome than more modest human-scale philanthropy, he argues.

Lewis Mumford has written in *The Culture of Cities...*

> We need, in every part of the city, units in which intelligent and
> cooperative behavior can take the place of mass regulations, mass
> decisions, mass actions, imposed by ever remoter leaders and
> administrators. Small groups: small classes: small communities:
> institutions framed to the human scale.... 20 communities with a
> population of 50,000 people would not merely be more adequately
> governed, probably, than one city that contained a million: it would,
> for example, give an opportunity for 20 mayors or city managers,
> against one in the big center. This rule holds true in every other
> part of society. We demand the impossible in the way of direction
> and specialized service from a few people, and we fail to demand the
> possible from those who are better equipped to handle adequately a
> smaller job. With our overgrown institutions, overgrown colleges,
> overgrown corporations, overgrown cities, is it any wonder that we
> easily become the victims of propaganda machines, routineers?

...The necessity of decentralization is by no means confined to the
structure of the political state, great as the need there may be. Decentralization
is just as necessary in the operation of the other great associations of modern
society—the industrial corporation, the labor union, the large church, the
profession, and the great university....

The labor union, the legal or medical association, or the church will
become as centralized and as remote as the national state itself unless these
great organizations are rooted in the smaller relationships which give
meaning to ends of the large associations.... No large association will remain
an object of personal allegiance, no matter how crucial its goals may be,
unless it is constantly sensitive to the existence of the informal but potent
relationships of which it is really composed....

There is the kind of state that seeks always to extend its administrative
powers and functions into all realms of society, always seeking a higher degree
of centralization in the conduct of its operations, always tending toward a wider
measure of politicization of social, economic, and cultural life. It does not do
this in the name of power but of freedom—freedom from want, insecurity, and
minority tyranny. It parades the symbols of progress, people, justice, welfare,
and devotion to the common man.... Increasingly, in this type of state, the basic
needs for education, recreation, welfare, economic production, distribution, and
consumption, health, spiritual and physical, and all other services of society are
made aspects of transfer. This comes to be accepted by almost everyone....

But there is also the kind of state that seeks…to maintain a pluralism of functions and loyalties in the lives of its people.…It is a state that seeks to diversify and decentralize its own administrative operations and to relate these as closely as possible to the forms of spontaneous association.… It seeks cultural diversity, not uniformity. It does not make a fetish of either social order or personal adjustment, but it recognizes…meaningful relationships of kinship, religion, occupation, profession, and locality.…

Either type of state may be labeled democratic and humanitarian. But the.… first type of state is inherently monolithic and absorptive and, however broad its base in the electorate and however nobly inspired its rulers, must always border upon despotism. The second type of state is inherently pluralist and, whatever the intentions of its formal political rulers, its power will be limited.

CHARITY IN LITERATURE

The Perfect Gift and
Giving Well, Doing Good, **both edited by Amy Kass**
Two collections of readings, mostly literary, that explore the enterprise
of philanthropy. Selections range from the classic to the contemporary,
and include considerations of why, how, to whom, and what we should
give. A few nuggets from Joseph Bottum's review of *The Perfect Gift* in
the March/April 2003 issue of *Philanthropy*:

This book's 52 brief readings attack the sentimental assumption that good
intentions suffice to guarantee good philanthropy. "Gifts," Kass insists, "are
equally conducive to benefit and harm, to joy and sorrow."

Half the book's readings are drawn from literature. There are five sections:

- Why should I give?
- How should I give?
- To whom or for what shall I give?
- What should I give?
- Can giving be taught?

Arguably the most difficult issue involved in giving is whether, at
its deepest level, philanthropy is primarily about the recipients or the
donors? Many of Kass's selections—from O. Henry's almost perfect
comedy "The Chair of Philanthromathematics" to Dorothy Parker's
surprisingly powerful "Song of the Shirt, 1941"—raise the issue sharply.

O. Henry's "Two Thanksgiving Day Gentleman" inverts the moral status of
the giver and the receiver (and then, in his typical style, inverts it once again in a
trick ending). Tales from Sylvia Warner, Henri Barbusse, and Pierre Mac Orlan
examine the goal of philanthropy. Stephen Leacock's comic "Mr. Plumter, B.A.,
Revisits the Old Shop" and John O'Hara's more sober masterpiece "Memorial
Fund" unite to tear away the mask from donations made to colleges. Edith
Wharton seems motivated by kindness and Dorothy Parker by cruelty, but both
their stories in *The Perfect Gift* are soul-wrenching exposures of human action.

And here is Scott Walter's brief description of *Giving Well, Doing Good*
(*Philanthropy*, Spring 2008):

Anyone who ever gave an allowance to a 10-year-old knows how hard it is to do good by giving away money. As the money multiplies, so do the problems. The difficulty has been noted many times, but few people have probed it in pursuit of wisdom.

Enter Amy Kass and her book of 82 brief readings, averaging perhaps three pages, with authors ranging from Plato to Henry James to Muhammad Yunus, the godfather of microlending.

The collection is organized into six topical sections:

- *Goals and Intentions*—What should philanthropy aim to do? Readings from Tocqueville, Dostoevsky, W. E. B. DuBois, Pope Benedict XVI
- *Gifts, Donors, Recipients*—What sort of obligations does a grant imply for givers and receivers? Aristotle, Seneca, Maimonides, Thomas Paine
- *Bequests and Legacies*—Shelley, E. M. Forster, Shakespeare, Henry James, Julius Rosenwald, Waldemar Nielsen
- *Effectiveness*—Tolstoy, Andrew Carnegie, Irving Kristol, Chekhov, Hawthorne
- *Accountability*—Plato, Wordsworth, Robert Frost, Emerson, Ralph Ellison, Benjamin Franklin
- *Philanthropic Leadership*—Lao Tzu, Aeschylus, Lincoln, Jane Addams, Paul Ylvisaker

Our Mutual Friend by **Charles Dickens**
The Warden by **Anthony Trollope**
Middlemarch by **George Eliot**
These beloved novels provide examples of themes which many nineteenth-century writers wrestled with, and which are at the heart of philanthropy: questions of compassion, of charity, and of what constitutes a kind versus an unkind intervention in the life of another person.

THE SPECIAL CASE OF
CORPORATE PHILANTHROPY

"Business and Philanthropy" by Irving Kristol
Businesses have no obligation to give away money, writes think-tank
scholar Irving Kristol, and if they choose to they should do so in
ways that serve the interests of their enterprise. This should include
support for people and organizations devoted to the preservation of a
strong private sector (*Wall Street Journal*, March 21, 1977):

When David Packard and William Simon made the perfectly reasonable
suggestion that corporations look before they give, and discriminate among
friend, neutral, and foe in their philanthropy, they were denounced in the
most vehement terms by universities which seemed to think they had some
kind of *right* to that money.

They have no such right. If they want money from any particular
segment of the population, it is their job to earn the good opinion of that
segment. If they are indifferent to that good opinion, they will just have
to learn to be indifferent to the money too. That's the way it is, and that's
the way it's supposed to be, in a free society where philanthropy is just
as free as speech.

Many businessmen—most, I imagine—will find this line of thought
congenial enough, but will still end up uneasy and confused. Where do
we go from here, they will ask? For the sad truth is that the business
community has never thought seriously about its philanthropy, and
doesn't know how.

Some corporate executives seem to think that their corporate philanthropy
is a form of benevolent charity. It is not. An act of charity refines and elevates
the soul of the giver—but corporations have no souls to be saved or damned.
Charity involves dispensing your own money, not your stockholders'.
When you give away your own money, you can be as foolish, as arbitrary,
as whimsical as you like. But when you give away your stockholders' money,
your philanthropy must serve the longer-term interests of the corporation.
Corporate philanthropy should not be, cannot be, disinterested.

One such corporate interest, traditionally recognized, is usually
defined as "public relations," but can more properly be described as
meeting one's communal responsibilities. This involves donations

to local hospitals, welfare funds, and other benevolent organizations active in the community where the corporation resides. In a sense, this philanthropy is mandated by community opinion, and there are few interesting or controversial decisions about it for the executives to make.

In addition to such mandated philanthropic expenditures, however, there are the controllable expenditures. These latter reflect a movement beyond communal responsibility to "social responsibility." Different corporations may well have different conceptions of such "social responsibility," and there is nothing wrong with that. But most corporations would presumably agree that any such conception ought to include as one of its goals the survival of the corporation itself as a relatively autonomous institution in the private sector....

A positive step would be for corporations to give support to those elements...which do believe in the preservation of a strong private sector.... men and women who are not necessarily "pro-business," and who may not be much interested in business at all, but who are interested in individual liberty and limited government who are worried about the collectivist tendencies in the society....

"How can we identify such people, and discriminate intelligently among them?" corporate executives always inquire plaintively. Well, if you decide to go exploring for oil, you find a competent geologist. Similarly, if you wish to make productive investments in the intellectual and educational worlds, you find competent intellectuals and scholars— "dissident" members as it were, of the New Class—to offer guidance. Yet few corporations seek any such advice on their philanthropy. How many large corporations make use of academic advisory committees for this purpose? Almost none, so far as I can determine.

This is a melancholy situation, for in any naked contest with the New Class, business is a certain loser. Businessmen who cannot even persuade their own children that business is a morally legitimate activity are not going to succeed, on their own, in persuading the world of it. You can only beat an idea with another idea, and the war of ideas and ideologies will be won or lost *within* the New Class, not against it. Business certainly has a stake in this war—but for the most part seems blithely unaware of it.

"The Social Responsibility of Business Is to Increase Its Profits" by Milton Friedman
A classic 1970 *New York Times Magazine* essay where Nobel-winner Milton Friedman insists that, when it comes to corporations, the most "pro-social" use of funds is to make the business thrive, not to give money to nonprofits. For the full text go to colorado.edu/studentgroups/libertarians/issues/friedman-soc-resp-business.html

"The Competitive Advantage of Corporate Philanthropy" by Michael Porter and Mark Kramer
Rather than making PR-driven corporate donations, companies should give to improve their competitive standing, urges this *Harvard Business Review* article. ExxonMobil makes large donations to improve roads in developing countries where it operates. The film studio DreamWorks trains students in skills required by the entertainment industry. Tech-dependent businesses may donate to institutions that improve math and science skills. Full text is available at hbr.org/2002/12/the-competitive-advantage-of-corporate-philanthropy/ar/pr

The Market for Virtue: The Potential and Limits of Corporate Social Responsibility by **David Vogel**
A 2005 book-length assessment of the movement for "corporate social responsibility" by a Berkeley professor who concludes that while it has achieved some success in improving labor, human rights, and environmental practices in developing countries, there are limits and substantial costs to "socially responsible" business behavior.

RESPECTING THE INTENTIONS OF DONORS

ProtectingDonorIntent.com
This is a rich collection of articles and information for donors serious about keeping their philanthropy focused on the causes they support, even after they have passed away. Includes a detailed Resource Library, numerous magazine articles, interviews, book reviews, and other useful material.

"When Philanthropy Goes Wrong" by Adam Meyerson
The text below, condensed from a March 9, 2012 essay in the *Wall Street Journal*, sketches the risks when donors fail to carefully define the purposes and future control of their foundations.

Entrepreneur and philanthropist Chuck Feeney made news in 2011 when his foundation donated $350 million to Cornell University. What underlay this huge gift from Atlantic Philanthropies was Mr. Feeney's refusal to fall into a trap that has snared many other philanthropists.

When a foundation is set up to dribble out its funds in perpetuity, there is a high risk it will eventually drift into projects the donor did not believe in. Recognizing this, Mr. Feeney has insisted on giving away money fast to do good now.

"Giving while living" is his way of making certain his funds support causes he believes in. It's not simple. By the end of 2016, when he intends it to cease making grants, the Atlantic Philanthropies will have to donate more than $2 million every working day to exhaust its more than $2 billion of assets. The Feeney method is not the only way to avoid having charitable gifts go to the wrong places, but he is absolutely right to be wary. One of the great scandals in modern philanthropy is that trustees and staff of grantmaking institutions all too often pay little attention to the principles governing their founders' charitable giving.

Consider oil magnate J. Howard Pew (1882-1971). The 1957 charter of the J. Howard Pew Freedom Trust spelled out that Pew intended to "acquaint the American people" with "the evils of bureaucracy," "the values of a free market," and "the paralyzing effects of government controls on the lives and activities of people." Pew also wanted to "inform our people of the struggle, persecution, hardship, sacrifice, and death by which freedom of the individual was won." Many recent initiatives from the successor Pew Charitable Trusts—such as its crusades for campaign finance regulation, universal early childhood education, and recognition of the dangers of global climate change—have little connection to J. Howard's worldview and philanthropic goals.

The Ford Foundation is one of the best examples of donor neglect. Henry Ford (1863-1947) had a fairly well-articulated philosophy of giving, both in his writings and interviews—e.g., "I do not believe in giving folks things. I do believe in giving them a chance to make things for themselves"—and in the record of his generous contributions during his lifetime to organizations such as Detroit's Henry Ford Hospital.

But he left no instructions on the purposes of the Ford Foundation. Henry's grandson, Henry Ford II, was later to write his famous 1977 resignation letter from the board of the Ford Foundation, after years of frustration over its anti-free-enterprise grants. His words have haunted philanthropists ever since: "The foundation is a creature of capitalism, a statement that, I'm sure, would be shocking to many professional staff people in the field of philanthropy. It is hard to discern recognition of this fact in anything the foundation does."

Founding donors themselves are often partly to blame for any departures from their principles, thanks to open-ended statements of their philanthropic intent. Insurance magnate John MacArthur (1897-1978) gave his trustees no instructions at all. "I'll make the money," he told them. "You people, after I'm dead, will have to learn how to spend it."

The initial board of the MacArthur Foundation was described by one of its members as "mostly a bunch of Midwestern businessmen devoted to free enterprise and opposed to more government controls." The founder's son Rod, much more politically liberal than his father, seized control of the board and shaped much of the foundation's future direction.

But changes in a foundation's strategy may not only be ideological. In 2012 the Barnes Foundation moved its extraordinary collection of impressionist and post-impressionist masterpieces to a new Philadelphia museum substantially different in character from the intimate art school envisioned by Dr. Albert Barnes. Serious mistakes in funding and governance by Barnes when he set up his foundation allowed this to happen.

In 2008, Princeton University agreed to pay $100 million to settle a lawsuit charging it with ignoring the mission of the Robertson Foundation, whose 1961 gift of $35 million—which would grow to an endowment of nearly $900 million—dramatically expanded the graduate-level Woodrow Wilson School of Public and International Affairs. Students were supposed to be prepared for government service, especially in international affairs. But in recent decades only 14 percent of its graduates took such jobs.

To avoid such problems, donors—whether large or small—need to take concrete action to safeguard their philanthropic principles:

○ Clearly define your charitable mission. Write it down in your founding documents. Add a long written or oral record about your likes and dislikes in charitable giving.
○ Choose trustees and staff who share your fundamental principles. Family members, friends, and close business associates such as lawyers, bankers, and accountants may not be good choices, unless you share the same worldview.
○ Separate your philanthropic interests from your interests in maintaining control of your company. Donor intent frequently suffers when the two are mixed, as happened at the Ford Foundation.
○ Give generously while you're alive and able to guide and oversee your gifts. If you establish a foundation, strongly consider a sunset provision, perhaps a generation or two after your death.
○ If you do establish a foundation in perpetuity, create strong procedures for electing future trustees who share your principles, and make respect for donor intent part of their fiduciary duty.

"Letter to an Aspiring Philanthropist" by Randy Richardson
Some brief advice from an experienced foundation head on what he calls the "Perpetuity Temptation" (*Philanthropy* Spring 1997):

You are nearing 70. Your body and your doctor have finally convinced you you're mortal. Coming from modest circumstances, you have created a business empire and vast wealth. Your legacy—and gratitude to the nation and the economic system that made your success possible—is much on your mind. Several close friends with similar histories have created foundations, which has started you thinking.

I've had some experience organizing and running a foundation. Perhaps what I learned may help you up the learning curve while you're still in the thinking stage. Let's start with the Perpetuity Temptation.

Many large foundations—Ford, Rockefeller, Carnegie—were created by men and women who could not resist the shade of immortality that is conveyed by creating an institution with perpetual life. Perhaps you feel the tug of the same temptation. A word of caution, however: in the majority of foundations and charitable trusts granted an unlimited existence, their grants now aid a fulsome roster of causes the founder (that would be you) would never have supported.

In a surprisingly short period after its establishment, your foundation is prone to fall under the control of its staff and/or its staff-selected trustees. That perpetuity remains common is due to an inability to realize that there are dramatic differences between business boards and charity boards. You doubtless have bright business associates. Resist the urge to decorate your beginning board with such folk unless they share your objectives and match your enthusiasm for whatever philanthropic endeavor you choose. There are many business executives whose conduct on charity boards betrays an apparent belief that activities outside business do not merit the full use of their brains. These men and women frequently join a foundation board for the sole purpose of having it fund their favorite charities.

When choosing trustees and staff, look for the same kind of wits that you've noticed in the business executive who takes over a failing major company and turns it into a winner. All too often people in your position turn the management of their foundation over to a retired boyhood chum who managed the shipping department in one of their companies. Shoot for more than this.

"Principles of Public Giving" by Julius Rosenwald

In this *Atlantic* article, one of the great early philanthropists strongly encourages donors to resist setting up permanent bureaucracies that dribble out money in their name for centuries, and to instead give more rapidly to address the needs of their present time, preferably while they are alive to guide the spending wisely. Here is a synopsis by Martin Wooster of Rosenwald's thinking and influence on this question (*Philanthropy*, July/August 1998):

Julius Rosenwald consistently warned of the dangers of perpetuity in foundations. As early as 1909, in an address to the Associated Jewish

Charities of Chicago, Rosenwald warned about the dangers of charities that might have "outlived their usefulness." In a 1913 address to the American Academy of Political and Social Science he said, "I am opposed to the permanent or what might be styled the never-ending endowment. Permanent endowment tends to lessen the amount available for immediate needs; and our immediate needs are too plain and too urgent to allow us to do the work of future generations."

Rosenwald also made sure that his own philanthropy had a strict time limit, imposing the condition that the Julius Rosenwald Fund spend itself out of existence 25 years after his death. "By adopting a policy of using the Fund within this generation, we may avoid those tendencies toward bureaucracy and a formal or perfunctory attitude toward the work which almost inevitably develop in organizations which prolong their existence indefinitely. Coming generations can be relied upon to provide for their own needs as they arise."

In 1929 Rosenwald took his case against perpetuity to the press with the publication of "Principles of Public Giving," the first of two essays in *The Atlantic*. The article created a sensation in the philanthropic world— Rosenwald received hundreds of letters from colleagues who headed philanthropies and universities, a surprising number of whom agreed with him.

Rockefeller Foundation president George Vincent, for example, wrote that the case against "specific permanent endowments" has "been proved over and over again." Edward Filene, the department store magnate who founded the Twentieth Century Fund, declared Rosenwald one of America's ten most important business executives because his "business experience has led him to see through the shams of philanthropy and the pretenses of greatness which so often go with the accidental accumulation of great wealth." Robert Brookings, founder of the Brookings Institution, told Rosenwald that the wealth he had given away "was insignificant" compared to "the value of this idea" of term limits for foundations.

Yet Rosenwald's ideas had relatively little actual influence at the time. Rosenwald did persuade John Rockefeller to loosen some restrictions on grants he made to the University of Chicago so it could remove the funds from its endowment and spend them immediately. And the Rockefeller Foundation spent some of its endowment for a few years during the Depression.

But however much Edward Filene, Robert Brookings, or George Vincent professed to agree with Rosenwald, they did nothing to end the lives of the Twentieth Century Fund, the Brookings Institution, or the Rockefeller Foundation, all of which still exist.

The Julius Rosenwald Fund, however, spent itself out of existence in 1948, a decade before it was legally required to do so. "At the close of the work," noted the fund's historians, "the trustees and officers were more convinced than ever that Mr. Rosenwald had been wise in his stipulation that the foundation should complete its work in a generation. They felt that the Fund had been more effective with a short life than it could have been as a perpetual endowment. Its officers and trustees were not preoccupied with saving funds and conserving capital. They did not have time to grow stale nor to build themselves into a routinized bureaucracy."

***Protecting Donor Intent: How to Define and Safeguard Your Philanthropic Principles* by Jeffrey Cain**
A short guidebook from The Philanthropy Roundtable which examines many practical aspects of making sure a foundation stays true to the principles and interests of the donor, even after he or she passes from the scene. Available here: philanthropyroundtable.org/guidebook/ protecting_donor_intent/foundation_management

***Should Foundations Exist in Perpetuity?* Heather Higgins & Michael Joyce**
One way to prevent a philanthropy from drifting into work contrary to what the donor intended is to spend all the funds and close the enterprise within the founder's lifetime or within a reasonable interval after. This short debate considers the merits of that approach, versus a perpetual trust. Higgins argues foundations should sunset. Joyce counters that under the right conditions they can be trusted to carry out the wishes of their founders into the indefinite future.
Available here: philanthropyroundtable.org/guidebook/should_ foundations_exist_in_perpetuity/debates_in_philanthropy

Starting a Private Foundation: Carrying Out the Donor's Intent
by Paul Rhoads and Stephanie Denby
A short guide to the nitty-gritty of establishing a foundation that will respect its donor's intent. Details the benefits and drawbacks of the conventional foundation, tax considerations, choice of location, and many other practical issues. Walks donors through the planning stage, initial funding, and opening meetings, as well as explaining the basics of record-keeping, grant guidelines, and more. Available here: PhilanthropyRoundtable.org/guidebook/starting_a_private_foundation

On Clawing Back Donor Intent After It Has Been Lost at a Foundation
Some cautionary examples from the experience of the Daniels Fund— one of the few foundations that managed to reclaim its donor's intent after straying. By Evan Sparks in *Philanthropy*, Fall 2011.

Not long after the attack on Pearl Harbor, Bill Daniels was commissioned as a carrier-based fighter pilot. He flew a Grumman Hellcat in the invasion of North Africa, and a Chance Vought Corsair in the desperate battles for Guadalcanal, Midway, and the Coral Sea. He earned the Bronze Star for saving the lives of crewmates after a kamikaze attack trapped them below the decks of the *USS Intrepid*. In Korea, he would serve his nation once again behind the controls of a Grumman F9 Panther. Indeed, Daniels often said that it was his military service that most defined him as a person.

Daniels passed away in 2000. Two years later, the Smithsonian National Air and Space Museum sent a grant inquiry to the Daniels Fund, the $1 billion foundation Daniels had endowed upon his death, requesting funding for an educational exhibit featuring World War II aircraft. In declining the request, the program officer explained that it would be inappropriate to fund a project featuring "instruments of war." When it was pointed out that Daniels had flown the same type of aircraft to defend the cause of freedom, the program officer nonetheless insisted that the request be declined, since the exhibit featured planes designed to "kill people."

"It was a wake-up call," recalls John Saeman, who was then a member of the Daniels Fund board and who later served as chairman. Saeman was one of Daniels' best friends. He had watched as Daniels spent the final years of his life carefully defining his intentions for the philanthropy that would bear his name. After Daniels died in 2000, his estate transferred to the fund, making it one of the largest foundations in the nation. And now, two short years after its founding, the Daniels Fund seemed not to understand—at times, even to disregard—the intentions of Bill Daniels.

"We had to get into the inner workings and understand what was happening internally," continues Saeman. "We had to make some corrections. We had to make sure people who were responsible for the grantmaking—as well as the board—knew exactly what Bill stood for and what he would have wanted to accomplish."

That realization by the board triggered something rare, if not unique, in the annals of American philanthropy. It triggered a process of recovery and restoration, of rediscovering Bill Daniels' intent for his foundation and instituting a process by which it would be protected in the future.

"Bill Daniels was bigger than life in this community, and the people adored him and the press loved to write about him," explains Linda Childears, current president of the foundation. "When he died, his billion-dollar bequest to the foundation was front-page news. The community pressure was instant and intense."

To ramp up scholarship programs, the fund sought guidance from a Washington-based organization that focuses on college access for the underprivileged. "In the early scholarship program, we knew that Bill wanted to find a certain kind of Daniels Scholar—a highly motivated young person who just needed that opportunity," says Childears. "He was looking for a diamond in the rough. But the experts' solution was to run a college prep program."

Early on, a decision was made to open satellite offices in the three states other than Colorado where the Daniels Fund operated—Utah, New Mexico, and Wyoming—and to staff them with local grantmaking professionals. It didn't take long before the satellite offices began to present challenges. "The scholarship program was handled completely differently in all four states," says Childears. "There was no consistency, and brand integrity would have been important to Bill."

As each of the state satellite offices undertook different approaches to grantmaking, the brand integrity issues became ever more visible. The board grew increasingly concerned that the approaches were not always aligned with donor intent. "The staff at each office considered different factors when deciding whether to fund an organization," says Childears. "It was clear that some of the factors being considered were not ones that would have been important to Bill, who was primarily concerned about the focus and effectiveness of the organization."

A troubling thought began to haunt the board. "It didn't take all that long," reflects Childears, "but all of a sudden, the Daniels Fund was starting to look like someone else's foundation." In 2002—two short years after the death of Bill Daniels—the board began to implement changes.

First they hired a new president. Hank Brown had known Bill Daniels for decades through Colorado politics and a mutual interest in charitable activities. The two shared similar backgrounds and values. Brown had been decorated for military service as a forward air observer in the Vietnam War, had served as a Republican member of Congress in both the U.S. House and Senate, and had served as president of the University of Northern Colorado.

"The staff was not familiar with Bill's beliefs," says Brown. "They had unilaterally decided to stop supporting certain organizations, disregarding entirely the fact that Bill had admired and funded those exact organizations during his lifetime." Board member Jim Nicholson agrees: "You had a bunch of young professionals who weren't familiar with Bill Daniels—who didn't know him, who didn't know his soul."

Bill Daniels needed to be front and center at the Daniels Fund, the board decided. The first order of business was to explain—to themselves, their successors, and the world—exactly who Bill Daniels was and what he wanted to do with his money. Then they would have to create a set of institutional safeguards to keep him front and center.

The problem was not that Bill Daniels had failed to clarify his wishes. In many ways, he had made his wishes very explicit—down to the percentage of the annual payout that would go to his selected funding areas and states. But, as his board was discovering, Daniels did not leave very much guidance on the principles that should govern the foundation's grantmaking.

Fortunately, Daniels had a long, clear history of generosity. He endowed scholarships—often in the name of a friend—at colleges and universities across the nation. He personally paid college tuition for many young people he met who were in need. He supported homeless programs, he started Young Americans Bank, and he funded the construction of the Daniels Children's Center at the Betty Ford Center (where, in 1986, he had overcome his own addiction to alcohol).

Daniels was also clear about his wishes in his personal giving. "Very seldom did a check ever go out that didn't have a letter with it," says Saeman. The letter would say clearly what he was giving the gift for and why. "Bill was quite a prolific writer," he says. "We felt confident that we had a large body of evidence to refer to, in addition to his written directions to the board."

The board began a painstaking review of Daniels's correspondence, speeches, and writing. It commissioned researchers to track down any and all available material. As new items became available, they were catalogued and cross-indexed. The board was determined to have as comprehensive a set of primary source documents as it could get.

"Here's an example," offers Childears. "In the incorporating documents, Bill said he wanted to fund 'innovative education programs.' Well, there isn't a nonprofit in America that doesn't claim to have one! It actually doesn't give a lot of direction. So what did Bill really mean? Well, look at the second half of the sentence—'such as charter schools and voucher programs.' When you look into his letters and read his correspondence, it becomes very apparent what he was talking about. Basically, it was what we would call school reform."

Another example concerns funding ethics programs at business schools. "Bill indicated he wanted to support ethics programs," explains Saeman. "Well, 'ethics' is a pretty broad word. Every school in the country has an ethics program; everybody believes in some kind of ethics. But we wanted to make sure that we were supporting the kinds of ethics programs that Bill would support, not just anything that called itself an 'ethics program.'"

So what did Bill Daniels mean by "ethics"? "We went through his files, his letters, and, just as importantly, his actions," continues Saeman. "The board concluded that Bill was fundamentally guided by principle-based ethics. He believed that there are certain principles—man's integrity, honesty—that are inviolable. He believed in the reality of absolute ethical principles, and the need of all people to follow them. We concluded that Bill would have wanted to fund programs that conformed to standards of right and wrong."

"It took us a couple of years to get to the point where the whole board could say, 'I think every word in here describes our guy,'" adds Childears. "It required us to get away from experiences we'd had and boil it down to characteristics—his style, his values, his principles."

The result: a thorough set of documents describing who Daniels was and what he wanted to do with his money. "Preserving Donor Intent" outlines Daniels's written instructions (in the fund's bylaws), along with his principles and beliefs, his giving during his lifetime, and interpretive comments by the board. Another document, "Understanding the Man Behind the Daniels Fund" is longer, identifying 11 core characteristics of Daniels (such as integrity and patriotism) and pointing to examples of these characteristics in his life, quotations from his writings, and implications for the Daniels Fund.

Assembling these materials on Daniels and his intent was utterly necessary, the board realized, but it would not be sufficient. The documents needed to become operational, to be integrated into the legal structure and, more importantly, the culture of the Daniels Fund. "It had to start with the board establishing Bill's intent as a matter of governance," says Saeman. "It had to permeate the whole organization."

The first order of business was to require all board members to acknowledge, in writing, that they had read and understood the full set of materials on Bill Daniels, and that they agreed to set aside their personal views or preferences when acting on behalf of the Daniels Fund and ensure that it fulfilled Bill Daniels's intentions and ideals. Staff members are required to sign a similar document. To emphasize the continuing nature of this commitment, at each annual board retreat a director prepares a presentation reflecting on the donor and his purposes.

The fund makes a concerted effort to recruit employees who will honor Daniels's intent. "It's enormously important to get people who haven't worked only in the nonprofit sector," says Brown. "People who are attracted to foundation work are not typically entrepreneurs," adds Childears, whose background before Daniels was in commercial banking.

Finally, the board instituted a new mechanism for its own succession. Board members serve a four-year term and are eligible for a second. "If your term is up and you want to run again, the nominating committee chair conducts a peer review, and then it goes to a board vote," explains Childears. "It's unusual, it's not easy at all, but it does get to what we're trying to do, which is hold each other accountable to donor intent."

As befits a cable television pioneer, there's a lot of video footage of Daniels. His fund's website hosts videos of him talking about his values and principles. The fund has also commissioned a book about Daniels's life and philanthropy, in order to reach wider audiences. Drawing on the video archive and the board's collection of his letters and writings, the fund produced an interactive presentation on Daniels's life, achievements in business and public service, philanthropy, and personal values. It plays at kiosks at Daniels Fund headquarters and at places he loved and helped fund. This allows future generations of his grantees to learn about their benefactor.

The Great Philanthropists and the Problem of Donor Intent by **Martin Morse Wooster**
This compact book provides history's worst examples of disrespect for donor intent as well as happier stories of donor intent preserved.

Donor Intent Resource Library
For philanthropists with a particular interest in protecting donor intent, The Philanthropy Roundtable has assembled this specialized online library of readings that get into many details. Go to philanthropyroundtable.org/topic/donor_intent/donor_intent_resource_library

IN DEFENSE OF PRIVATE GIVING

"America is Built on Giving" by Adam Meyerson
Philanthropic freedom is an indispensable part of political freedom.
Adopted from *Imprimis*, January 2010.

Historically, Americans did not raise funds by appealing to donors' guilt, or by urging them to "give back" to society. Instead, they appealed to their fellow citizens' ideals and aspirations, their religious principles, and their desire to create. The tradition of private generosity in America has always been central to our free society.

For instance, thousands of voluntary donations from the farm families of the Midwest made it possible for Hillsdale College to be independent, which in turn gave it the freedom to challenge prevailing cultural and political wisdom. Following another philanthropic creation, Oberlin, Hillsdale was the second American college to grant four-year liberal-arts degrees to women. Founded at a time when Michigan public schools were officially segregated by race, Hillsdale was also the first American college to prohibit in its charter any discrimination on the basis of race, religion, or sex. Without the independence that comes from private support, Hillsdale would not have been able to provide this leadership.

The creation of Hillsdale College was part of a larger philanthropic movement. Every town in our decentralized republic wanted its own college, both to promote economic opportunity and to encourage citizen leadership. Former Librarian of Congress Daniel Boorstin cites an amazing statistic: in 1880, the state of Ohio, with three million inhabitants, had 37 colleges; by contrast, England, with 23 million people, had four degree-granting institutions. It was philanthropy that enabled colleges across America to grow and flourish. I could offer similar examples about hospitals, refuges for animals, the arts, youth programs, and grassroots problem-solving of all sorts. Private charitable giving sustains all of these institutions and gives them the freedom to make their own decisions.

Private charitable giving is also at the heart and soul of public discourse in our democracy. It makes possible our great think tanks, whether left, right, or center. Name a great issue of public debate today: climate change, the role of government in health care, school choice, stem cell research, same-sex marriage. On all these issues, private philanthropy enriches debate by enabling organizations with diverse viewpoints to articulate and spread their message.

One reason America is so charitable is because we respect the freedom and the ability of individuals, and associations of individuals, to make a difference. Americans don't wait for government or experts or the local nobleman to solve our problems; we find solutions ourselves.

The late Milton Friedman once noted that "economic freedom is an end in itself" and that "economic freedom is also an indispensable means toward the achievement of political freedom." We can similarly say that freedom in philanthropic arrangements is an end in itself, but is also an indispensable means toward the achievement of political freedom.

Necessary, Important, and in Jeopardy
by Daniel Patrick Moynihan
A warning on the subject of government vs. private social aid. What follows is an excerpt from the late Senator's March 5, 1980 address to the charter meeting of the new philanthropic organization Independent Sector.

I am here to tell you that you are necessary. You are important. And you are in some jeopardy....

There grew up in the nineteenth century the stern notion that there ought to be no public or common provision really of any kind, that individuals were on their own.... There also arose as a kind of a parallel heresy the idea of the all-encompassing state. These two opposed, incompatible, and, in terms of human experience, almost unrecognizable sets of ideas still grip much of the world....

But out of a recognition that this is not the way people have lived or should live, there arose the notion of the independent sector, or mediating institutions— the Red Cross in war and the Audubon Society in peace, the Theatre Association, the Community Chest, the foundling hospitals, the Brooklyn Jewish Hospital, Columbia Presbyterian. This kind of mediating institution began to be something characteristically associated with British and with American life....

[Then] the public sector began to grow—first, to keep the private sector from too great a monopoly of power, and then to acquire a condition of its own and a dynamic of its own.

I think many of you will remember reading Joseph Schumpeter's last great book in 1948 in which he said how this wonderfully creative civilization which we have produced in North America and Western Europe is going to come to an end—not in some great apocalyptic Armageddon in which one class takes over another class and destroys all classes. No. It will come to an end through the slow but steady conquest of the private sector by the public sector.

There is nowhere that this is more in evidence and more advanced than with respect to the non-government enterprises of public concern which you represent. Little by little, you are being squeezed out of existence or slowly absorbed....

I had not fully understood the depth of the animosity which the state has commenced to acquire toward your very existence until three years ago. Senator Packwood and I introduced legislation that would provide a measure of tax aid to persons who send their children to non-governmental schools. Fifteen years ago, it would not have been thought such a horrible idea, or at least the language and the techniques used in opposition would not have been thought inappropriate. In 1964, when John Gardner was the Secretary of HEW, the Democratic platform called for this kind of assistance. In response to that acknowledgment, a major government program to aid elementary and secondary schools came into being. It came into being because it was said...that this aid would be distributed all across the spectrum from the private to the government schools.

But the reality turned out to be that only government schools got it and once they got it, they wanted more, and as they wanted more, they wanted others to have less. An institutional dynamic took place, in which people of the most gentle miens and benevolent dispositions set out to destroy these competitors because they did not control them.

"Destroy" is not too strong a term. You should have heard the language used, the insinuations made, above all, the ultimate insinuation of a statist tendency which is to say, "These institutions are un-American. They are non-governmental."

...Private institutions really aren't private anymore. Many are primarily supplied by government funds. Their private leadership is nominal, their fundraising scarcely exists. And on the edges, it is thought to be inappropriate. As a matter of fact, the tipping point comes when it is clear that the government would prefer that you didn't get any money which wasn't governmental, because it's not controlled.

Now, that's happening here. Think of your own institutions and how much money you now get from public sources. I talked the other day with the head of Catholic Charities, the national organization, who reported that last year something momentous happened to Catholic Charities. For the first time, more than 50 percent of its budget came from government. More than half. In time, there cannot be any outcome to that encroachment save governmental control.

We have two possibilities: One is the disappearance of the independent sector, or—just as powerful a possibility—its subversion, so that it only appears to continue. And in fact, this day is upon us. We don't want that and we don't have to have it…. There is a time, that has come, to insist that the federal government not take away your opportunity to exist through contributions. Else it will surely do so. The most seemingly forward-looking attitudes somehow transmute when they get to Washington.

Have you all heard of the idea of tax expenditures? Do you know you're a tax expenditure? And that every dollar that is deducted through a contribution to United Way is a tax expenditure? It seemed like a good idea to discover what [monies] are not paid in taxes by individuals because they're used for other things. [Now] the idea [is] surfacing that the government owns your income and permits you to retain a certain amount. That's the real tax expenditure—what you are allowed to keep….

If you're allowed to keep it, then it wasn't yours in the first place, was it? It belongs to the state. The state will consume it if you don't fight back….

Something of the most profound concern to American society is at issue, and that is our tradition of a plural, democratic society. It would be the final irony if, in the name of good purposes, government ended up destroying liberty in the society. But that can happen, and that is what seems to me is your job to make certain does not happen.

Beware the Concept of "Tax Expenditures"
by Peter Berger and Richard Neuhaus

A cautionary about using the slippery term "tax expenditures" to describe the measures that protect private charities from taxation, from the book *To Empower People*.

The relatively new concept of tax expenditures…has been infiltrated into public policy. It is calculated, for example, that a certain amount of revenue is lost to the government because a private college is tax exempt. The revenue lost is called a tax expenditure. This may seem like an innocuous bit of bookkeeping, but the term expenditure implies that the college is in fact government-subsidized (a tax expenditure is a kind of government expenditure) and therefore ought to be governmentally controlled. This implication, which is made quite explicit by some bureaucrats, is incipiently totalitarian. The logic is that all of society's wealth really belongs to the government and that the government should therefore be able to determine how all wealth—including the wealth exempted from taxation—should be used. The concept of tax expenditure should be used, if at all, as a simple accounting device having no normative implications.

"The Great Charitable Myth" by Heather Higgins
On the danger of treating philanthropic dollars as public money. Originally published in The Huffington Post, March 2, 2012.

In the midst of public debates on fairness, tax rates, and debt reduction, there is a fallacy, deliberately promoted by some, that undermines honest discourse. It is this: private charitable contributions should be classified and treated as "public money." If allowed to perpetuate, this bait and switch could lead to real and negative consequences for every charitable organization and donation made in this country.

The argument goes that because charitable organizations are tax exempt and donations to charitable organizations are tax deductible, the government misses out on some potential revenue. Lost revenue constitutes a subsidy, and subsidies, as we know, are done with government money. This argument relies on the semantic slipperiness of the word "subsidy," eliding its different meanings, and more deeply assumes that all our income first belongs to the government, which only chooses to let us keep some of it.

Two noted legal scholars, John Tyler from the Kauffman Foundation and Evelyn Brody from the Chicago-Kent College of Law, set out to make a definitive, legal case for what are, and are not, private charitable assets in this country. Their findings are published in the book *How Public Is Private Philanthropy? Separating Reality from Myth*, which strengthens the case that private charitable dollars are private.

Why does this matter? One current point of contention comes from political officials who wish to commandeer private resources to support their view of the public good. And we are increasingly seeing state officials go after revenue or pursue political gain under the guise that charitable organizations are "public" because they have state charters. The authors resoundingly prove that although charities have state charters, this does not make them any more "public" bodies than publicly traded companies. It just means the organizations must obey the law and be responsible for what they say they are going to do. Period.

But the real meat and potatoes over this "public money" debate is centered around tax exemptions and charitable deductions. Some claim that because charitable organizations are tax exempt and receive tax-deductible contributions, those benefits qualify activists and the government to have a say in their decision making and operations....

Charity flourished in this country long before there even was an income tax and the concern about deductions, because most charitable giving isn't driven primarily by tax considerations. Donations to charitable institutions receive tax benefits as recognition that these are private monies that could have been spent on self, that instead are pursuing public purposes.

Herein the next challenge: who defines public purpose? Certain self-styled watchdogs would very much like to limit what qualifies in order to give preference to the causes and types of organizations they hold most dear. Soup kitchens over art and music programs? Social justice over inner city education? The environment over medical research? Who would ultimately do the picking? What would be their criteria? Do we really want these decisions politicized and manipulated?

"How Foundations Should and Should Not Be Held Accountable" by Adam Meyerson

The independence of foundations must be protected, says this extract from the Fall 2009 issue of *Philanthropy*.

Foundations are accountable to government authorities for compliance with the tax laws. But otherwise foundations are accountable solely to their trustees. Unlike elected officials, they are not accountable to the voters. Unlike businesses, they do not have to meet a market test. This limited external accountability is the great strength of foundations. It gives them the independence and freedom to do something bold, unpopular, unconventional.

Independence allows foundations to investigate unconventional hypotheses in medical research, to support new energy technologies with uncertain market prospects, and to finance innovative social enterprises such as Teach For America long before they become popular.

Limited external accountability can lead to laziness, complacency, insularity, arrogance, and mediocrity. It therefore becomes all the more important for foundation donors and trustees to set and enforce high standards of excellence. Philanthropy can also benefit greatly from feedback from grantees, self-assessment tools, voluntary codes of conduct, high-level journalism about philanthropy, and thoughtful criticism from academic experts, strategy consultants, and watchdog groups.

But it is one thing to say that foundations should be open to outside perspectives. It is quite another to require that outsiders have the authority to determine what foundations can and cannot do. Independence of foundation action is central to philanthropic creativity. We lose it at our peril.

"The Politics of Giving" by Katherine Mangu-Ward

A *Reason* magazine editor interviews Adam Meyerson for their March 2010 issue about American philanthropy and the importance of the charitable deduction.

Reason: What do you say to people who object to the fact that tax-exempt donations are going to the opera or to Harvard when there are genuinely needy people in the world?

Meyerson: We've had a long tradition where, so long as they make contributions to genuinely charitable causes, Americans can decide where and how to give away their money voluntarily. We're talking about voluntary action here. They could spend it on their yachts, but they want to give their money to other institutions.

Philanthropy and charitable giving are central to American life and have been since the beginning of the republic.

Reason: Charities in America get preferential tax status. Various players argue that this means charitable organizations are, in some sense, funded with public money. Once you accept that premise, strange things begin to happen. Some politicians want "their" money back, to spend on other things. And activist groups argue that private charities should be more heavily regulated.

Meyerson: We have been hearing more and more of that. Some prominent legislators have been saying that tax preferences amount to a gift from the government. And politicians put extra-legislative pressure on foundations and other donors to give to their favorite causes. It's almost a kind of blackmail where political leaders threaten harmful legislation unless their favorite causes are funded.

Reason: You're referring to things like the Foundation Diversity and Transparency Act in California.

Meyerson: There's wonderful diversity within the philanthropic sector. That diversity mostly takes place between or among organizations, not necessarily within organizations. An organization called the Greenlining Institute turned its attention to private philanthropy four years ago with a plan to "democratize philanthropy" by stocking the boards of private charities with minority members. Its targets are large foundations, and its mission is to redirect private foundation assets to advance its own goals through its preferred organizations. These actions are conducted without regard for the mission of the private foundation or its right to direct its assets to causes consistent with donor intent.

Even with something like intellectual diversity, you don't necessarily want widely different theories in one charity of what the mission of the organization is supposed to be. It's a nightmare recipe for paralysis within organizations. It would be inappropriate to require, let's say, a Jewish or a Catholic or a Mormon foundation to have members from another faith on its board. It would be inappropriate to require that family foundations have non-family members on their board. If there's a Latino family foundation, does it have to have Anglos on its board in order to make wise decisions about, let's say, Arizona? That's both false and insulting. Should a liberal foundation be required to put conservatives on its board? It can if it wants, but it defeats the whole purpose of philanthropy to require that kind of decision.

Reason: Talk a little bit about the relationship between big charities and the little guys.

Meyerson: A few years ago there was a disturbing set of proposals to actually abolish the little guys. Eliot Spitzer, who was then attorney general in New York, actually proposed that foundations with less than $20 million in assets should not be allowed to exist. One argument he made was that there were too many foundations, and it was hard for the IRS and state attorneys general to monitor and keep track of all of them. And Spitzer was not alone in this. In 2005 the then-chairman of a large philanthropic association made a similar proposal in an article in the *Chronicle of Philanthropy*, saying that we shouldn't have foundations with less than $1 million in assets.

Just as in business, you often start small in philanthropy and you do a lot of learning by doing. It would be devastating to philanthropic learning to close off the opportunity to begin one's foundation on a small scale, quite apart from the outrageous assault on freedom that's involved.

Several years ago, there was a white paper proposed by the Senate Finance Committee staff proposing that tax-exempt status be contingent upon accreditation. Having seen the dangers of accreditation in higher education—for instance, in the Thomas Aquinas College case, where the regional monopoly sought to deny accreditation to a college because it didn't approve of its Great Books curriculum—we resisted this very strongly and argued that that was a very serious threat to philanthropic freedom.

More recently the IRS is proposing to get involved in assessing the governance of foundations and even their effectiveness, something that it has no statutory authority to do. There's a serious proposal to create a self-regulatory agency under the control of the IRS, and we fear that that would be an open invitation for the kind of cartelization impulses that we sometimes see in industry.

Reason: For-profit charity sounds like an oxymoron, but it's become increasingly common.

Meyerson: We're seeing an entrepreneurial explosion in philanthropic services and in new kinds of giving. Some of these are for-profit. Some of these are nonprofit. Probably the most important new feature we're seeing is that business minds, really exceptional business minds, are coming into philanthropy now. Some of them are coming in directly as philanthropists, as living donors, but others are applying business models to philanthropy.

One of the most exciting features that we're seeing is the growth of intermediary organizations. They receive money from donors and then give it out themselves, across many fields. We're seeing specialized services in the arts, in international giving. There are left-wing intermediaries. There are libertarian intermediaries. We're seeing more information, more giving opportunities, more analytical structures for giving. We think it's very important to protect this kind of entrepreneurial creativity.

Reason: Government and philanthropy often compete to service the same needs. Is government pushing charity from some places where it has traditionally been?

Meyerson: We do frequently see a kind of crowding out in which philanthropists withdraw from a particular field if government is present. But we frequently see a contrary development as well, which is that government is not always very good at what it does and so the problems aren't always solved.

For instance, in the field of K-12 education there's $500 billion of government spending. And yet we're seeing more and more new philanthropists come into that field pushing ideas of choices and competition and high standards and new models of recruiting and compensating teachers and principals. Even in a field that's tremendously dominated by government, you see philanthropists coming in to find solutions for problems, such as the education of low-income children, that were not being solved by government.

We see this in the field of medical research as well, which is overwhelmingly dominated by government. Smart philanthropists are finding that they can have an enormous contribution by pursuing alternative hypotheses or doing things that government is not doing.

Reason: Obama has spoken of putting public money into charities that work. What do you make of that?

Meyerson: We think there's a danger in trying to bring the private charitable sector under the control of government. It can be very self-defeating and even suicidal to become too dependent on government money. I think it's important for philanthropists to develop alternative ways besides government funding of expanding successful private-sector programs.

"The Myth of the 'Third' Sector" by Irving Kristol

Philanthropy is part of the private sector and needs to be defended against centralizing impulses, says distinguished social critic Irving Kristol in this excerpt from a 1980 speech to the Council on Foundations:

It is now generally said and widely thought that the foundation world constitutes a "third sector" in American society. There is, it is said, the private sector, consisting of business enterprise; the public sector, consisting of government; and then we have the third, not-for-profit sector, of which the foundations are the animating core. I would like to suggest to you that there is no third sector. Foundations are part and parcel of the private sector. They are flesh of the flesh, bone of the bone, blood of the blood of the private sector. The notion that foundations in some way constitute a sector of their own, different from, above, and superior to the other two sectors is an act of pride which will only go before a fall. That fall may consist in the fact that foundations will end up depriving themselves of their sustenance, which comes from the various parts of the private sector. Foundations are creations of the private sector.

In fact, there are only two sectors in our society: the private sector and the governmental sector. The voluntary associations in our nation do not make up a third sector; they are part of the private sector. Churches are part of the private sector. Fraternal organizations are part of the private sector. Even political parties are part of the private sector. There is no high ground which foundations can occupy and from which they can look down upon the other sectors and then try to think up policies, methods of improving the world, which are somehow disinterested in a way that those of the other two sectors are not....

Foundations came into existence originally to do all the things that needed to be done that the government did not do in the nineteenth and early twentieth centuries. That was the right thing for foundations to do at that time. However, the situation has changed today. We have had a reversal. There is almost nothing you can suggest which government is not eager to do. And it seems to me that foundations, therefore, have a special responsibility to be wary of government and to be a lot more solicitous of their own sector, which, I repeat, is the private sector....

To the degree that our society becomes more centralized, to the degree that government becomes more intrusive in all the affairs of our lives, to that degree, foundations are going to end up in fact being adjuncts of government or being assimilated into government.

Even now it is said—and I have heard foundation executives say it, and I think most people here would probably say it—that the money you people spend is public money, and therefore you have a public responsibility. Now, in what sense is the money you spend public? Under the tax laws, the contributions made to foundations are deductible from income. If you say that that money is public money, you are saying: "Well, the government has the right to all our money, but it doesn't exercise this right at all times or in all respects. It leaves some of that governmental money for us to spend, and therefore we have a public responsibility attached to that money." I think that is socializing money in rhetoric prior to socializing it in fact.

The money you people spend is private money. It is not public money. Money that the government does not take is ours. You can have whatever public responsibilities you wish to assume with that private money. But it is private money. It is the lifeblood of your organizations, and I think it is time foundations gave a little more thought to the source of that life blood and to what might be done to making that life blood a little more abundant.

"Democracy in Action" by Stephen Carter
Individuals acting as donors measure community needs differently than centralized policy makers, says a Yale law school professor (Bloomberg View, November 23, 2011).

The deduction for charitable contributions is one of the oldest in the tax laws, dating back to the War Revenue Act of 1917.... The theory behind the deduction, as Representative Carl Curtis, a Nebraska Republican, noted during World War II, is that charitable giving is "exempt from taxation" because it represents "an expenditure for the public good."

Curtis had it right. Charitable giving represents spending for precisely the same purpose that the government spends: to promote the general welfare. The difference is that the individual who gives to charity might measure the needs of the community by different calipers than centralized policy makers, and will therefore contribute to a different set of causes.

These millions of individual decisions lead to a diversity in spending that would be impossible if we adopted the theory that the only money spent for the public good is the money spent by the state.

[It's easy to] misunderstand the purpose and function of the deduction. Its principal beneficiaries are not those who give, but those who receive. If I donate money directly to a local soup kitchen rather than requiring it to wade through the layers of paperwork and volumes of regulation required for obtaining even the mere chance of a direct government subsidy, everyone is better off—especially those who eat there....

The charitable deduction also helps resolve an information problem: Government officials, no matter how well-intentioned, cannot know all the places where donations are needed, or the form that will be most useful. The deduction is democracy in action. By encouraging individuals to make their own choices on how to spend money for the public good, the deduction makes society as a whole better off. Let's keep it that way.

"Preserving National Values Through the Charitable Deduction" by Robert Shiller

Yale economics professor Robert Shiller argues in a December 15, 2012 *New York Times* column that "instead of curtailing the charitable deduction, we should be aiming to make it an even bigger part of our culture."

Our nation has been defined as both self-reliant and charitable. We trust one another, and not just the government, to make important decisions and to take action. Self-reliant does not mean selfish: while it is important that we manage our personal finances responsibly, we also have a deep tradition of giving to others. Many of us believe that we have obligations to others that only we can interpret, through our own consciences.

"The Rising Threat to the Charitable Deduction" by Howard Husock

A warning against viewing the charitable deduction as "just one more 'tax expenditure,'" by Howard Husock in *Forbes*, December 14, 2012.

As the fiscal cliff looms, representatives of U.S. nonprofit organizations are circling the wagons to defend the charitable tax deduction from Congressional action to cap or otherwise limit it. Well they should. The $300 billion, highest per capita among OECD nations, in annual philanthropic giving provides the lifeblood for medical research, higher education, the arts, and a range of programs that assist and uplift the poor. Even a relatively modest change long favored by the Obama White House—limiting the tax benefit of a charitable donation to 28 percent of its value, even for those paying higher tax rates—would, it's been estimated, reduce charitable giving by some $3 billion. An overall cap on tax deductions of all kinds could have even more drastic effects.

"What's Behind Recent Attacks on the Charitable Tax Deduction?" by Joanne Florino
Does the government know how to spend money better than private citizens? Do uniform monolithic solutions to social problems trump diversity and experimentation? From an open letter published by the Triad Foundation:

The assertion by some that the charitable tax deduction isn't that important to charity can't be left unchallenged. Whether a private donation comes from a billionaire or a middle-class American, the charitable deduction is an important incentive. And it benefits the charitable recipient far more than it does the giver. A person who gives away $100, even if you subtract the maximum deduction of $35, is still giving away $65 for the good of someone else. And the ultimate beneficiary of that generosity, whether seated at a soup kitchen or at the local ballet, still enjoys what the full amount of the gift can provide.

It is becoming increasingly apparent that attacks on the charitable deduction are based on the beliefs that the government knows how to spend money better than private citizens, that the public sector can pick winners and losers in the charitable sector, and that monolithic solutions trump diversity and experimentation. If we choose to go down this rocky and treacherous path, we send a clear message to our country that a strong civil society isn't really that important when our government has other problems.

Those who are attempting to divide the sector suggest that some charitable gifts are "better" than others. So let's be clear that donations to the Family Reading Partnership or an art museum or science center are not about putting food in the stomachs of hungry families. But they may well be about feeding undernourished souls or educating those who might otherwise be denied that experience.

The charitable deduction continues to be a powerful incentive for those who contribute to all the causes that individual donors believe will make their communities, their country, and their world a better place.

We cannot allow this foundation of strong civic participation to be altered forever. We must make sure our political leadership values private giving and charity as much as those whom they serve do.

RESULTS
of
AN ORIGINAL 2015 NATIONAL POLL

Comparatively little polling has been conducted on big questions at the heart of voluntary giving. So in 2015 The Philanthropy Roundtable commissioned a survey of 1,000 American likely voters over age 18. Results and brief analysis follow.

The graphs show nationwide results. In places where citizens of a certain age or origin or viewpoint gave answers that differ in interesting ways from the overall result, we mention that in the commentary.

The firm Pulse Opinion Research used random selection, oversamples, and a dynamic weighting program to ensure that the respondents represented the overall U.S. population in terms of sex, age, race, political preference, religion, family structure, education, income, and other factors. The margin of sampling error for the full results is plus or minus 3 percentage points at a 95 percent confidence level.

Question 1:

When it comes to voluntarily giving money to a charitable cause, are Americans more generous, less generous, or about as generous as people in other developed nations?

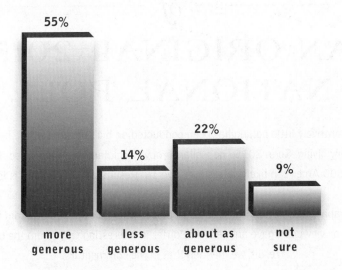

A large minority of Americans—45% in total—don't realize that their country is all by itself at the front of the pack in the practice of making voluntary donations to others. For the actual hard numbers, see the last chart in the section that follows this one, Statistics on U.S. Generosity. You'll see that the level of charitable offerings in the U.S. ranges from roughly twice what takes place in lands like Britain and Canada to almost *20 times* the rate of Italians and Germans.

Interestingly, younger Americans ages 18-39 (who often think of themselves as more globally aware) are actually far less likely than compatriots 40 and over to appreciate how much their country differs from others on this front.

This slight blind spot may help explain why younger citizens, in some of the sub-detail behind Question 5, are more willing to countenance efforts that push fellow Americans to give more.

Would your first choice for solving a social problem in America be to use government or to use philanthropic aid?

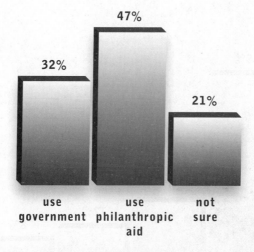

47%

32%

21%

use
government

use
philanthropic
aid

not
sure

Another area where Americans are distinctive is in attitudes toward fixing social problems. Our strong preference is to pull the lever of private aid wherever possible, instead of relying on government.

This is partly just a response to what we see around us: in crucial areas like medical care, disaster relief, college education, family life, addiction treatment, sharing the arts, expanding home ownership, and so forth, the most effective actors are often charitable and voluntary groups, not state agencies.

Predictably, the biggest split on this question is by political viewpoint. Overall, men and women alike prefer private aid as their first choice, as do people of all ages and religions. But while Republicans and Independents prefer philanthropy over government by more than 2:1, Democrats run against the trend by picking government over philanthropy by 51% to 31%.

Question 3:

Which is more cost-effective in promoting social good—private charities or government?

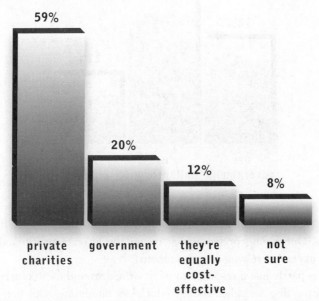

One thing the public is pretty clear on—charities are much better at stretching a dollar and avoiding waste.

Here, political liberals are even starker outliers. Individuals who use that label to describe themselves think 37% to 34% that government will be more cost-effective. They are the sole exception: Both sexes, all races, all religions, all education and income levels—indeed, every other demographic category we measured—agree that private aid will be more efficient.

Is it important that Americans continue to give money and time to charities?

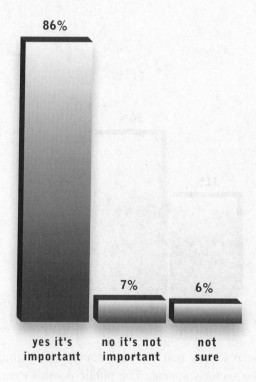

86%

7%

6%

yes it's
important

no it's not
important

not
sure

In opinion polling, results this strong are rare. So underline it: Americans think charitable giving is very important to keeping their country healthy and successful.

Question 5:

As a personal matter, *not* as a matter of law, should people be encouraged to contribute a larger percentage of their income to charity?

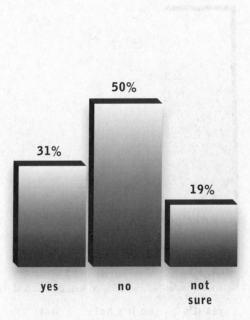

At the same time, it's clear that the voluntary part of voluntarism is a crucial part of the sector's appeal. The public doesn't even want to be *encouraged* to increase donations, so you can be dead certain it doesn't want to be pushed into mandatory do-gooding.

This presents something of a dilemma to charity boosters. Even while the country has gotten much richer over the last century, the fraction of national income donated has held basically constant. While a vastly larger number of actual dollars is handed over, thanks to economic growth, it's still about the same percentage of our adjusted gross income that we give away now compared to a generation ago. (See Graph 1 in our Statistics section.)

Should tax deductions for charitable contributions be eliminated or capped because they cost the government tax revenue, OR should tax deductions for charitable contributions be protected because they encourage people to help others in voluntary and selfless ways?

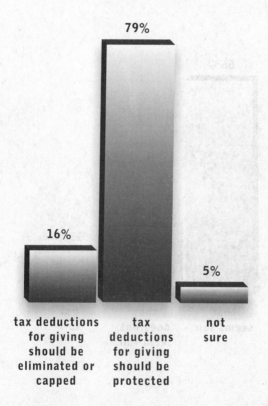

79%

16%

5%

tax deductions
for giving
should be
eliminated or
capped

tax
deductions
for giving
should be
protected

not
sure

Americans consider it entirely reasonable and indeed desirable that when someone gives money to charity rather than consuming it or saving it for himself, he should be allowed to deduct that from his income. This is overwhelmingly supported by every demographic slice in our polling sample.

Our examination of historical polling further shows that this sentiment has been firmly lodged in the national bosom for decades, at about the same level as captured in our survey question above.

Question 7:

Is it fair that the tax deduction for charitable contributions could result in one family paying less tax than another family with the same income, just because the first family gave more to charity?

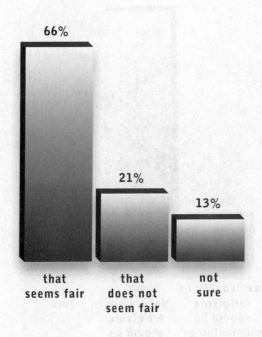

66%

21%

13%

that
seems fair

that
does not
seem fair

not
sure

More evidence that Americans have no objection to tax deductions for charity, even when it results in unequal payments to the government. Support for the charitable deduction has actually strengthened a bit compared to 2003, when a similar question was asked in a national poll.

Would capping or eliminating the tax deduction for donations have a negative effect on charities and the people they serve?

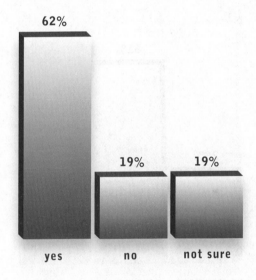

Some political figures suggest the charitable tax deduction could be capped or eliminated without damaging the flow of donations to charitable works. The public disagrees.

Question 9:

Does the government need to place stricter controls on how charities, donors, and foundations operate, OR does the government need to allow charities, donors, and foundations wide opportunities to find new and better ways of solving social problems?

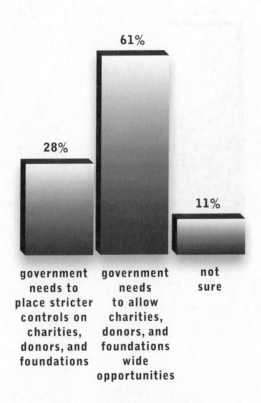

government needs to place stricter controls on charities, donors, and foundations	government needs to allow charities, donors, and foundations wide opportunities	not sure
28%	61%	11%

Voters aren't wanting more regulation of charity. Not even self-described liberals (40% "control 'em" vs. 43% "leave 'em alone") or Democrats (40% to 48%) tip in favor of more policing and direction.

When it comes to addressing the most pressing issues of our day, which social sector do you trust most— entrepreneurial companies, nonprofit charities, or government agencies?

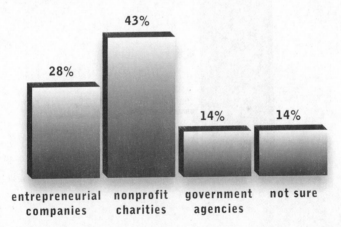

entrepreneurial companies	nonprofit charities	government agencies	not sure
28%	43%	14%	14%

Charities enjoy an extraordinary public trust. People have more confidence in their ability to deliver on tough assignments than competing organizations.

It's intriguing to see that there is almost *no* partisan or ideological split on this question—Republicans and Democrats, conservatives and liberals, give nonprofit charities almost the same vote of endorsement. It's between the other two entities where there is a huge political gulf. The preferences among Republicans: 42% for entrepreneurial companies, 43% for nonprofit charities, 4% for government agencies. Among Democrats: 13% for entrepreneurial companies, 46% for nonprofit charities, 28% for government agencies.

Question 11:

Do you agree or disagree with the following? It is in my power to improve the welfare of others, by personally giving or volunteering.

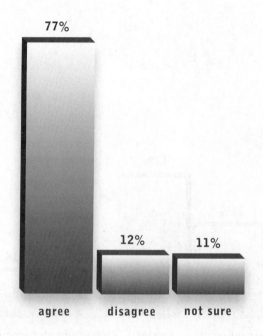

You see here the strong confidence of Americans that individual acts of kindness will make a real difference in the lives of others. The only subset of the population that diverges slightly from this powerful view is high-school dropouts—and even they still say by 51% to 27% that personal good deeds will help the recipient.

Thinking about your own personal giving, which charitable cause do you give most to?

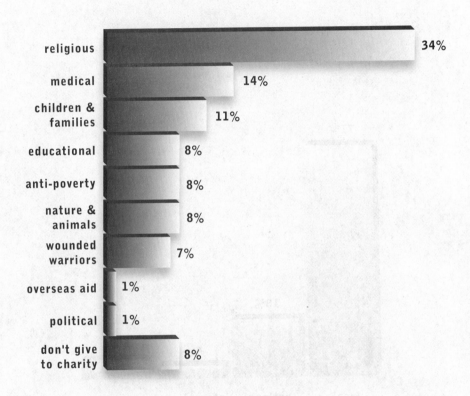

religious	34%
medical	14%
children & families	11%
educational	8%
anti-poverty	8%
nature & animals	8%
wounded warriors	7%
overseas aid	1%
political	1%
don't give to charity	8%

In descending order, you can see here how people prioritize charitable causes when it comes time to share their own dollars. Religious charities are, and always have been, the ones Americans are most willing to contribute to. In addition to serving spiritual needs, of course, religious charities are often leaders in other fields listed above. Many of the best medical and overseas charities, for instance, are religious. The Salvation Army and Habitat for Humanity are top anti-poverty charities, Catholic schools bring donor dollars to more poor children than any other educational charity. Much of today's aid for the homeless is a product of churches. And so forth.

Question 13:

When you make a charitable contribution, are you more likely to give to local causes, national causes, or international causes?

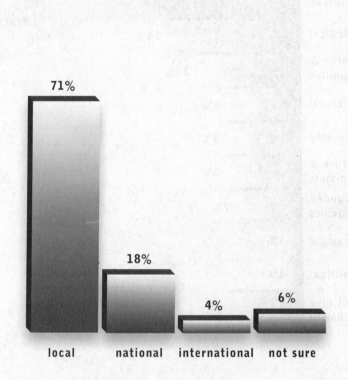

U.S. givers send lots of money overseas, but their first impulses are to think locally and act locally. This is true of *all* of the country's demographic groups—though compared to others, evangelical Christians and younger people are more likely to give internationally, and liberals are significantly more likely to give at the national level.

How much does society as a whole benefit when Americans donate money to charity—a large amount, a moderate amount, only a little, or not at all?

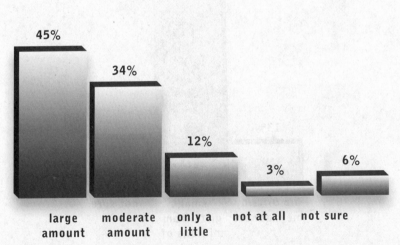

| large amount | moderate amount | only a little | not at all | not sure |
| 45% | 34% | 12% | 3% | 6% |

Here again we see evidence of the overwhelming confidence of people in the efficacy, honesty, and value of our nation's charitable giving. Within this powerful trend there are some variations. There is a clear influence by education: The response "society benefits a large amount" rises on a straight line from 30% among high-school dropouts right up to 55% among those with graduate degrees, while the combined "only a little/not at all" response tumbles from 36% among dropouts to just 8% among the highly educated. Democrats are also less enthusiastic, with 38% describing the benefit of charitable donations as "large" and 40% choosing "moderate"—compared to 52% "large" and 31% "moderate" among Republicans.

Question 15:

Between two general categories of giving—big gifts by megadonors, or small gifts from millions of everyday citizens—which is more important to America?

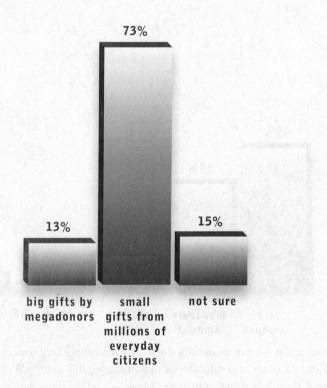

73%

13%   15%

big gifts by   small   not sure
megadonors   gifts from
                 millions of
                 everyday
                 citizens

Our national sample believes that even more than the big checks from moguls it is the flurries of $20 and $100 bills that make U.S. giving distinctive and powerful. Only among the young and high-school dropouts are there noticeably more votes for the big gifts—and even within those two groups it is fewer than one out of every five persons who name megadonors as more important.

STATISTICS

on

U.S. GENEROSITY

In this section you'll find charts and graphs laying out the most important numbers in American philanthropy. They document how much we give, how that has changed over time, what areas we give to, and what mechanisms we use to donate. There are figures here on where charities get their money, how many people (and of what type) offer volunteer labor, the demographic factors that influence generosity (income, marriage, education, race, ideology), and how various states and cities differ. The top foundations and donor-advised funds are ranked by their giving. We present surprising information on overseas aid, and statistics on how the U.S. compares to other countries when it comes to donating to charity.

Graph 1:

Real Rise in U.S. Giving
charitable donations after adjustment for inflation

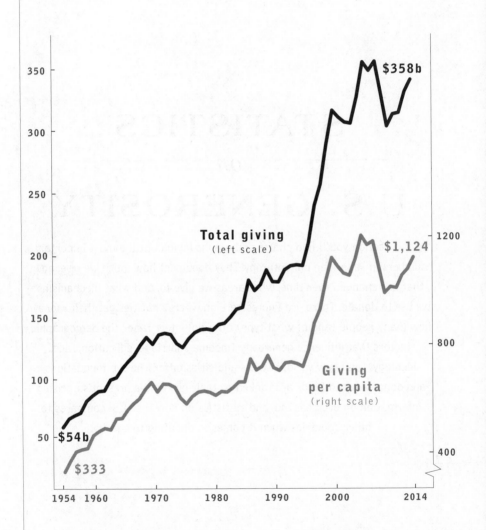

Source: Giving USA; *U.S. Bureau of the Census; CPI inflation adjustments by the editor.*

After adjusting for inflation, charitable giving by Americans is more than 6½ times as big in 2014 as it was 60 years earlier.

Of course, one reason total giving went up is because the U.S. population almost doubled. But if we recalculate inflation-adjusted charitable giving on a *per capita* basis, we see that has also soared: by almost 3½ times. Charitable causes are very lucky to have a remarkably expansive American economy behind them, and a standard of living that refuses to stagnate.

What if we calculate charitable giving as a proportion of all national production (GDP)? The math reveals that over the last 60 years, donations as a proportion of our total annual output increased—but only very slightly. For most of the last lifetime, giving has hovered right around 2 percent of our total national treasure.

Two percent of GDP is a huge sum, particularly in comparison to other countries (see details on that at Graph 27). But it's interesting that even as we have become a much wealthier people in the post-WWII era, the fraction we give away hasn't risen. There seems to be something stubborn about that 2 percent rate.

Graph 2:

Percentage of U.S. Donations Going to Various Causes

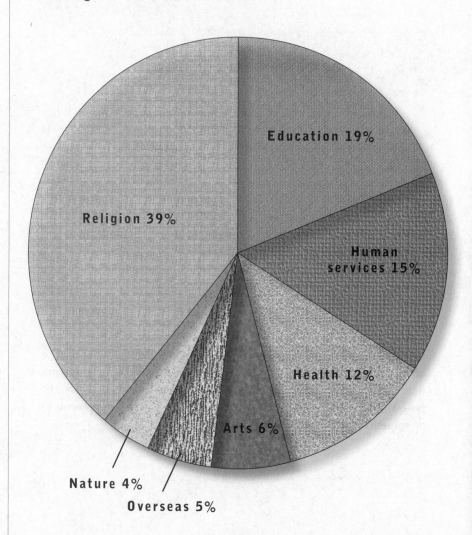

Education 19%

Human services 15%

Religion 39%

Health 12%

Arts 6%

Nature 4%

Overseas 5%

Source: Editor calculations from Giving USA *data for 2014.*
Note: Giving that is not to a cause but rather to a mechanism that will later give it to a cause
(like a family foundation, a donor-advised fund, or the United Way) is not included here.

eligious causes are, and always have been, Americans' favorite charitable targets. Of course, "Religion" is a very broad category. Some of those funds are used to support houses of worship and clergy, to maintain the faith, and to proselytize future generations. Much religious charity, however, ultimately goes into sub-causes like relief for the poor, medical care, education, or aid sent to low-income countries or victims of disaster.

Keep in mind too that religious charities tend to have less access to supplemental funds than other nonprofits. Hospitals and colleges charge users fees to supplement their donated income; other nonprofits sell goods; many museums charge admission; some charities receive government grants. Churches and religious charities, however, operate mostly on their donated funds depicted in this graph.

Graph 3:

Sources of U.S. Charitable Giving

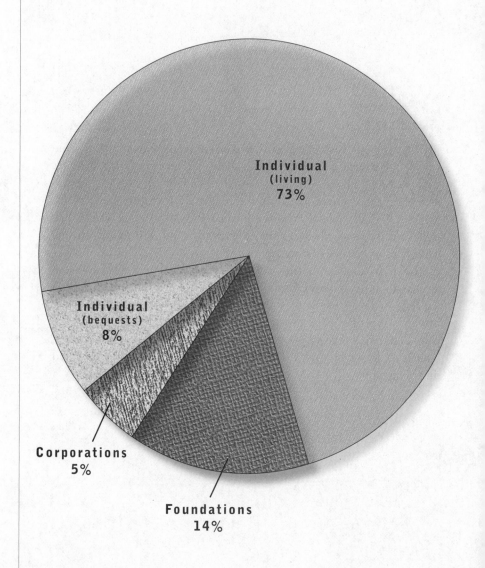

Source: Giving USA *data for 2014.*

It's easy, amid press stories about the projects of large foundations or corporations, to forget that the vast bulk of American philanthropy is carried out by individuals. Between individual donations and bequests in wills, personal gifts come to *over four times as much*, every year, as what behemoths like the Gates, Ford, Walton, etc. foundations plus corporations give away.

Graph 4:

Growth of Public Charities

501(c)(3)s registered with the IRS

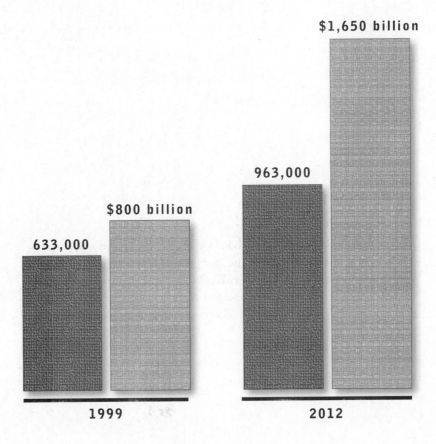

$1,650 billion

963,000

$800 billion

633,000

1999

2012

Number   Revenues

Source: *National Center for Charitable Statistics.*

The number of nonprofits, and their revenues, have both grown quickly in recent years.

Graph 5:

% of U.S. Workforce
Employed in Nonprofit Sector

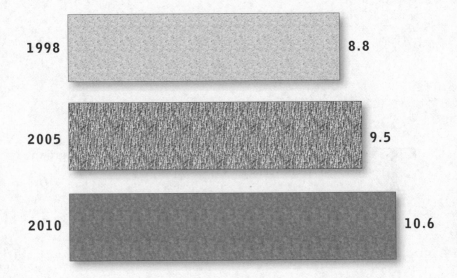

1998   8.8

2005   9.5

2010   10.6

Source: National Center for Charitable Statistics.

onprofits have grown faster than government and faster than the business sector over the last generation, even during boom periods.

The figures charted here actually underestimate the fraction of American manpower that goes into charitable work—because they show only paid employment, while volunteers carry out a large share of the labor poured into these groups. Various calculations of the cash value of donated labor suggest that roughly an additional 50 percent of the work done by charities takes place "off the books" because it is produced voluntarily. You'll find more statistics on American volunteering in Graphs 8 and 9.

Graph 6:

Output of Nonprofit Sector

as % of U.S. GDP

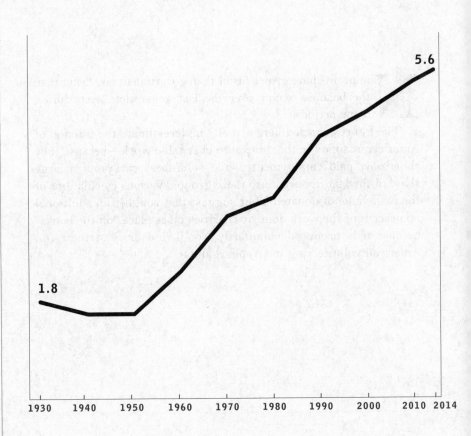

5.6

1.8

1930 1940 1950 1960 1970 1980 1990 2000 2010 2014

Source: U.S. Bureau of Economic Analysis.

haritable activity is becoming a bigger and bigger part of America's total economy. For perspective, consider that annual U.S. defense spending totals 4.5 percent of GDP. The nonprofit sector surpassed the vaunted "military-industrial complex" in economic scope way back in 1993.

Our charitable world is actually even bigger than this graph indicates, because its output is underestimated in several ways. The official annual statistics ignore the fact that about a third of the charitable workforce is unpaid (volunteers), and therefore invisible to the tabulators of economic activity. Also, the unusual definition of the nonprofit sector that is employed by the U.S. Bureau of Economic Analysis results in many charities that are officially registered with the IRS getting their annual output counted as part of the business sector, rather than as charitable activity.

Nonetheless, even the partial measure graphed here makes clear that philanthropic work has become a big part of our national output.

Graph 7:

Sources of Revenue of Public Charities

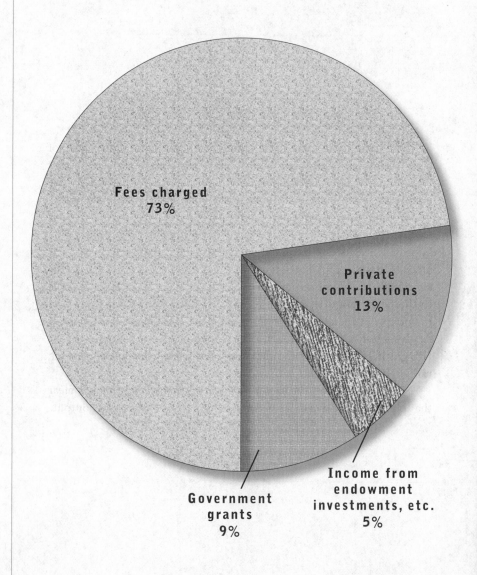

Fees charged
73%

Private
contributions
13%

Government
grants
9%

Income from
endowment
investments, etc.
5%

Source: IRS 2012 data compiled by National Center for Charitable Statistics.

The underappreciated fact illustrated starkly here is that many charities sell things—from used clothes to admission tickets to college educations—and rely heavily on those market revenues to keep their doors open. You can see that government grants are not a large portion of the income of U.S. public charities as a whole—annual donations plus income from invested gifts are twice as big. Of course there are also substantial government fees paid to charities as reimbursements through programs like Medicare and Medicaid. Within the "Fees charged" slice of this pie, a little more than two thirds of the money collected was private, but close to a third came from some level of government that was paying for a charitable service rendered.

Graph 8:

Volunteering in the U.S

annual number of volunteers	**63 million individuals**
% of population volunteering	**26 percent of all adults**
average time given by volunteers	**233 hours per year**
total time volunteered in the U.S.	**8.1 billion hours**

Source: *U.S. Bureau of Labor Statistics, 2013 data.*

This data comes from detailed time logs that statisticians ask householders to keep. In less strict definitions like phone surveys, more like 45 percent of the U.S. population say they volunteered some time to a charitable cause within the last year.

Current estimates of the dollar value of volunteered time range from $163 billion per year to more than twice that, depending on how you count.

Volunteering is closely associated with donating cash as well. One Harris study showed that Americans who volunteered gave 11 times as much money to charity in a year as those who did not volunteer.

Graph 9:

Demographics of Voluntarism

% of various groups volunteering

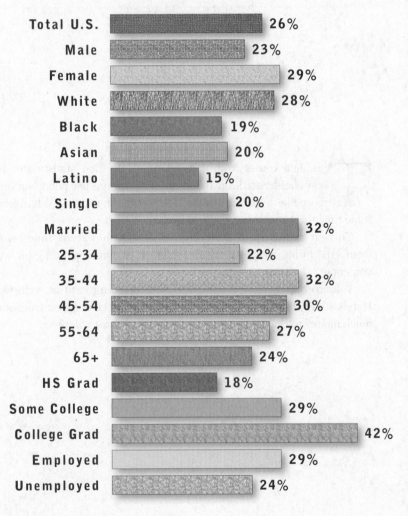

Group	%
Total U.S.	26%
Male	23%
Female	29%
White	28%
Black	19%
Asian	20%
Latino	15%
Single	20%
Married	32%
25-34	22%
35-44	32%
45-54	30%
55-64	27%
65+	24%
HS Grad	18%
Some College	29%
College Grad	42%
Employed	29%
Unemployed	24%

Source: *U.S. Department of Labor, 2010 data.*

All patterns courtesy of GraphicsFuel.com

Volunteering takes place at very different levels among different segments of the population. Women volunteer more than men, whites more than blacks or Latinos, married persons much more than singles. Younger and older people lag well behind 35- to 55-year-olds. The more educated are vastly likelier to give of their time. And unemployed persons don't use their extra hours to volunteer—they actually do less than those who are also holding down jobs.

Graph 10:

Proportion of Households
that Donate to Charity in a Given Year

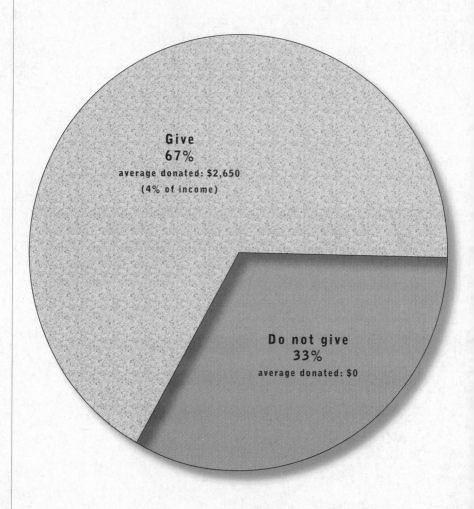

Give
67%
average donated: $2,650
(4% of income)

Do not give
33%
average donated: $0

Source: Panel Study of Income Dynamics data, adjusted to 2014 dollars.

C haritability is not evenly distributed. The two thirds of households who give money actually average a hefty 4 percent of their income in gift-making. It is the other third of the population giving nothing who pull down the national average.

Graph 11:

Percentage of Households Giving to Charity By Annual Income

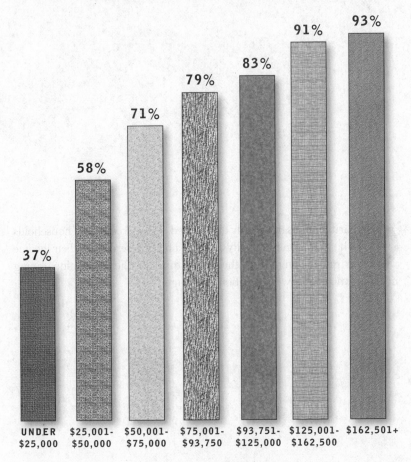

37%	58%	71%	79%	83%	91%	93%
UNDER $25,000	$25,001- $50,000	$50,001- $75,000	$75,001- $93,750	$93,751- $125,000	$125,001- $162,500	$162,501+

Average donation among those who do give

(percentage of income)

$934 (12%)	$1,760 (5%)	$2,064 (3%)	$2,475 (3%)	$2,566 (2%)	$3,469 (3%)	$5,805 (2%)

Source: Panel Study of Income Dynamics data, in "The Market for Charitable Giving" by John List, Journal of Economic Perspectives. *Editor's adjustment to 2014 dollars.*

n interesting pattern emerges if one studies giving by income level. As incomes rise, more and more of the people in that bracket make gifts to charity. The sizes of their gifts tend to rise as well. However: if you look at average donations as a fraction of funds available, they tend to level off at around 2-3 percent of income.

The exception to this pattern comes at the bottom of the income spectrum. Low-income households are the only ones in America where a majority do not give money to charity. Among the minority of poor who *do* give, however, a significant number are sacrificial donors—sharing double-digit portions of their incomes.

These sacrificial givers generally fall into two categories. Lots are religious, who tithe or otherwise give generously even when they have modest means. Others are elderly persons who have modest annual earnings yet are able to give because they have savings or paid-for homes and other assets that incline them to generosity.

Graph 12:

Influence of Marriage and Education on Likelihood of Charitable Giving

all other demographic variables held constant

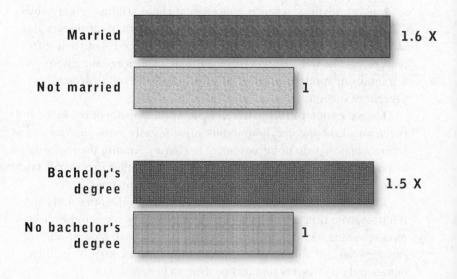

Married	1.6 X
Not married	1
Bachelor's degree	1.5 X
No bachelor's degree	1

Source: 2012 regression analysis done by Giving USA.

Just as with volunteering (Graph 9), certain factors have a strong influence on willingness to make donations. Religion (see next graph), marriage, and education are foremost among the factors that incline people to generosity. For this graph, all other variables like income, age, race, geography, and so forth were held constant. After those adjustments, it could be seen that married people give to charity at *1.6 times* the rate of counterparts who are identical in every other way except that they are unmarried. Likewise, people who have completed college are *1.5 times* as likely to give compared to an otherwise equivalent person without that education.

Graph 13:

Religion and Charitable Giving

all other demographic variables held constant

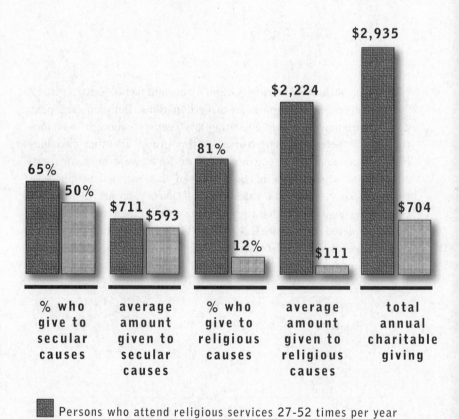

				$2,935

Persons who attend religious services 27-52 times per year

Persons who never attend religious services

Source: Panel Study of Income Dynamics data analyzed by the Center on Wealth and Philanthropy. Adjusted to 2014 dollars by the editor.

eligious faith is a central influence on giving. Religious people are much more likely than the non-religious to donate to charitable causes—including secular causes— and they give much more.

This chart holds all other demographic variables like income, race, education, etc. constant, so that when religious and non-religious counterparts are compared they are true peers in every other way. And the results show that persons who attend religious services twice a month or more give over four times as much as persons who never attend services.

We know the religious are also far more likely to volunteer. Among Americans who have volunteered within the last year, three quarters belong to a religious organization, one quarter do not.

Graph 14:

Heavy vs. Light Charitable Giving by Party Registration

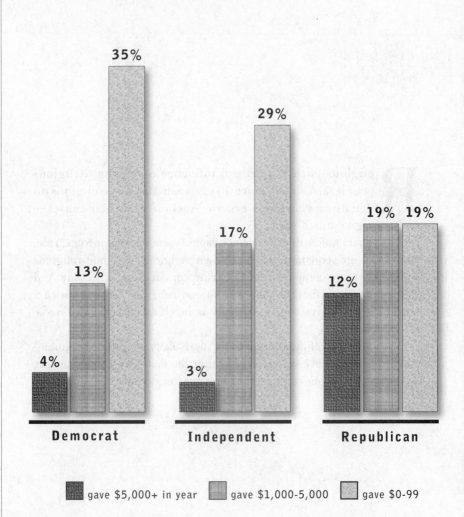

Source: Zogby poll 2005.

Among Democrats, Independents, and Republicans alike, almost exactly half of the group averaged $100-$999 in annual charitable donations at the time of this 2005 poll. There was virtually no difference among the parties in the size of that moderate-giving group, so those results were not included in the graph to the left.

If, however, you zero in on giving that is heavier or lighter than the middle range (the bars pictured here), you find that the parties differ a lot. Democrats and Independents both had many zero-to-very-light givers (less than $100 for the year), and modest numbers of heavier givers. Republicans, in comparison, had comparatively few skinflints, and numerous serious donors—31 percent sharing at least $1,000 with charity, versus 17 percent among Democrats, and 20 percent among Independents.

Graph 15:

Income and Giving by Ideology

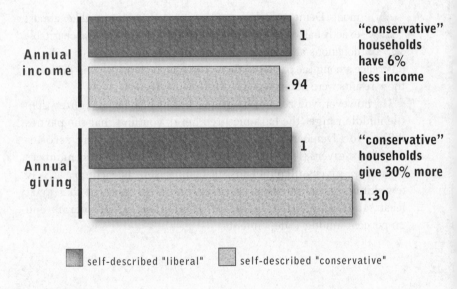

Source: *Social Capital Community Benchmark Survey, Roper Center, 2000 data.*

As individual donors, conservatives are hearty givers—as made clear in this graph, the one previous, and many other data sets.

When it comes to running foundations, though, liberals tend to control the reins. Matched analyses of the major American foundations reported in the book *The New Leviathan* found 82 foundations whose staff took a clear conservative orientation in their giving, and 122 foundations whose staff operated with a clear liberal orientation. The conservative-controlled foundations had assets of $10 billion in 2010, from which they gave away $832 million annually. That same year, the liberal-controlled foundations had assets of $105 billion (more than ten times their conservative counterparts), and gave away $8.8 billion annually (11 times as much as conservative counterparts).

Many foundations end up espousing the priorities and orientations of their staff rather than the principles of the donor behind the foundation. As this has become more widely understood, some new foundations have made efforts to protect "donor intent" and be sure that funds are expended on causes compatible with the founder's views. There has also been a sharp jump of interest in "sunset" foundations—which spend all their money relatively close to the donor's lifetime, rather than existing in perpetuity, where capture by staff becomes almost inevitable. See the text accompanying Graph 18 for more details on sunsetting.

Graph 16:

Generosity of States

giving as % of adjusted gross income

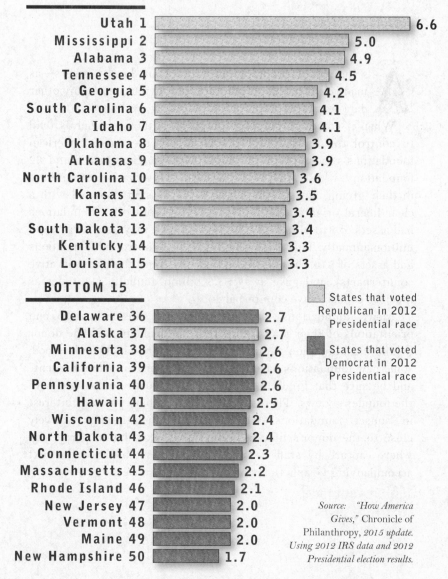

TOP 15

Utah 1	6.6
Mississippi 2	5.0
Alabama 3	4.9
Tennessee 4	4.5
Georgia 5	4.2
South Carolina 6	4.1
Idaho 7	4.1
Oklahoma 8	3.9
Arkansas 9	3.9
North Carolina 10	3.6
Kansas 11	3.5
Texas 12	3.4
South Dakota 13	3.4
Kentucky 14	3.3
Louisana 15	3.3

BOTTOM 15

Delaware 36	2.7
Alaska 37	2.7
Minnesota 38	2.6
California 39	2.6
Pennsylvania 40	2.6
Hawaii 41	2.5
Wisconsin 42	2.4
North Dakota 43	2.4
Connecticut 44	2.3
Massachusetts 45	2.2
Rhode Island 46	2.1
New Jersey 47	2.0
Vermont 48	2.0
Maine 49	2.0
New Hampshire 50	1.7

States that voted Republican in 2012 Presidential race

States that voted Democrat in 2012 Presidential race

Source: "How America Gives," Chronicle of Philanthropy, 2015 update. Using 2012 IRS data and 2012 Presidential election results.

For the analysis graphed here, the *Chronicle of Philanthropy* analyzed official IRS data on income and giving, right down to the county level. The results showed that rural states, and specifically the Bible Belt and Mormon West, give more of themselves for charity. Other ways of measuring, carried out by different groups using alternate statistical sources, have shown essentially the same pattern. Though it comes as a surprise to some observers, it is not Americans in the high-income, urban, liberal states like Massachusetts or California who are our most generous citizens. Rather it is residents of middle-American, conservative, moderate-income, religiously active regions who step up the most.

Several observers have pointed out the political twist to this reality. When it reported its findings, the *Chronicle of Philanthropy* noted that the states that rank highest in charitable giving all voted Republican in the 2012 Presidential election, while all but a couple of the least generous states voted for the Democrat (that's what the color coding to the left reflects). Economist Arthur Brooks, author of the detailed charity analysis *Who Really Cares*, likewise states that "the electoral map and the charity map are remarkably similar." He notes "there is a persistent sterotype about charitable giving in politically progressive regions of America: while people on the political right may be hardworking and family-oriented, they tend not to be very charitable toward the less fortunate," while, "those on the political left care about vulnerable members of society, and are thus the charitable ones…. This stereotype is wrong."

Brooks points out that these differences go beyond just what households donate in money. He cites studies showing that conservatives are more likely to do things like donate blood, and to volunteer. Much of this difference he credits to the comparative religiosity of conservatives. The fact that liberals call for government to help others while conservatives feel called to help directly also seems to factor into differences in behavior.

Graph 17:

Generosity of Cities

giving as % of adjusted gross income

TOP 15

Salt Lake City 1	5.5
Memphis 2	5.1
Birmingham, AL 3	4.8
Atlanta 4	4.0
Nashville 5	3.9
Jacksonville, FL 6	3.8
Oklahoma City 7	3.7
Dallas-Ft. Worth 8	3.6
Charlotte 9	3.4
Virginia Beach 10	3.3
Houston 11	3.2
Indianapolis 12	3.2
Louisville 13	3.2
San Antonio 14	3.1
Orlando 15	3.1

BOTTOM 15

Austin 36	2.6
Minneapolis-St. Paul 37	2.6
New York 38	2.6
Columbus, OH 39	2.6
Seattle 40	2.5
Philadelphia 41	2.5
San Diego 42	2.4
Sacramento 43	2.4
Pittsburgh 44	2.4
San Francisco 45	2.4
Buffalo 46	2.3
Boston 47	2.3
San Jose 48	2.2
Providence, RI 49	1.9
Hartford 50	1.9

Source: "How America Gives," Chronicle of Philanthropy, 2015 update. Based on 2012 IRS data.

A pattern similar to what the previous graph showed for states is also clearly visible in this data on giving levels in America's 50 biggest cities. It is residents of our Mormon and southern Bible Belt metro areas who are our most generous citizens. Meanwhile, many of our very wealthiest urban areas—like San Francisco and Boston—rank low on generosity.

Note here the interesting divergence between Dallas and Austin. Those two cities, just 180 miles apart, share the same economic climate, exact same levels of state taxation, same basic cost of living. Where they differ rather sharply is in culture. The fact that Dallasites give almost 40 percent more to charity than Austinites underlines the powerful influence on charitable behavior exerted by factors like religious practice and political ideology.

Graph 18:

Foundation Numbers and Giving

1975-2013

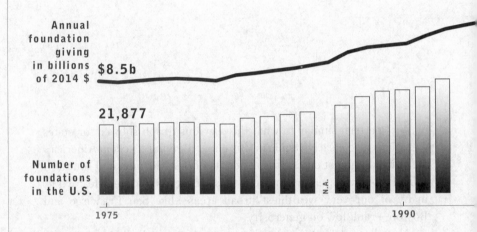

Annual
foundation
giving
in billions
of 2014 $ **$8.5b**

21,877

Number of
foundations
in the U.S.

N.A.

1975   1990

The number of private foundations, and the heft of their endowments and annual giving, have soared over the last generation.

Americans are generally happy with the growing activity of foundations in solving problems—a 2009 poll asked community leaders who have had professional contact with the charitable sector whether they thought foundations have too much, too little, or the right amount of influence on issues in their community; 51 percent answered "too little," 42 percent said "the right amount," and just 7 percent said "too much." Our own survey research in 2015 found the public inclined to give foundations and the rest of the philanthropic sector wide latitude to operate free of government regulation or interference; see Question 9 in our section "Results of an Original 2015 National Poll."

At the same time, Americans don't place foundations at the heart of our philanthropic efforts. They view small gifts from millions of

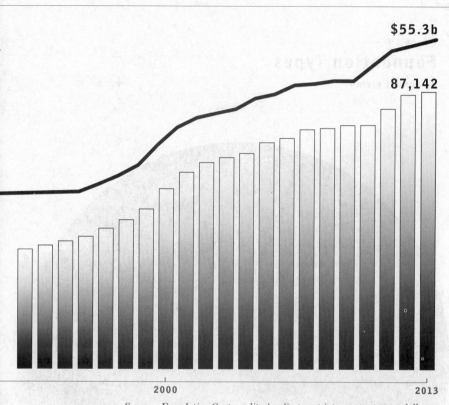

$55.3b

87,142

2000   2013

Source: Foundation Center; editor's adjustment into constant 2014 dollars.

everyday donors as far more important than the big initiatives of foundations (Question 15 in our national poll). And as a factual matter they are entirely right, as Graph 3 in this section shows.

There is, however, a considerable knowledge gap when it comes to the details of how foundations operate. Only about one American out of ten, and half of community leaders, can name an extant foundation when asked by pollsters.

One interesting trend in the growth of foundations is for donors to set them up so that they spend themselves out of existence within a generation, rather than letting them exist in perpetuity. In 2010, a quarter of the assets in America's 50 largest foundations were in trusts that will sunset—compared to only 5 percent 50 years ago. Spending down allows a foundation to have a larger, quicker effect than trickling out funds indefinitely. And it reduces the likelihood of the organization drifting into purposes not approved by the donor (a problem discussed at Graph 15).

Graph 19:

Foundation Types

by annual giving

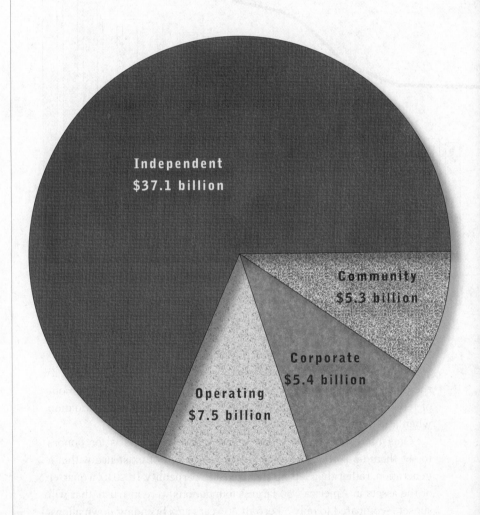

Independent
$37.1 billion

Community
$5.3 billion

Corporate
$5.4 billion

Operating
$7.5 billion

Source: Foundation Center; 2013 data.

raditional independent foundations are by far the largest institutional givers. Community foundations pool donations from many donors within a region; there are more than 780 sprinkled across the country. Corporate foundations are a long-time presence in U.S. philanthropy. Operating foundations are a special subset that spend most of their money running their own programs, rather than disbursing funds to other charitable operators. Leading examples of some of these foundations are presented in the three graphs following.

Graph 20:

Top 50 Independent Foundations

by 2013 giving

Bill & Melinda Gates Foundation	$3,320,725,374
Ford Foundation	$560,335,883
Susan Thompson Buffett Foundation	$450,319,788
Foundation to Promote Open Society	$380,512,799
Robert Wood Johnson Foundation	$337,561,658
Walton Family Foundation	$311,719,212
David and Lucile Packard Foundation	$295,015,267
W. K. Kellogg Foundation	$294,891,874
Gordon and Betty Moore Foundation	$272,332,512
Lilly Endowment	$270,300,000
William and Flora Hewlett Foundation	$240,100,000
Andrew W. Mellon Foundation	$234,372,144
John and Catherine MacArthur Foundation	$218,542,721
Leona and Harry Helmsley Charitable Trust	$210,352,475
Bloomberg Philanthropies	$204,007,709
California Endowment	$182,809,047
Simons Foundation	$179,640,382
Robert W. Woodruff Foundation	$155,816,887
Rockefeller Foundation	$137,817,790
Carnegie Corporation of New York	$130,380,545
Kresge Foundation	$130,183,827
Duke Endowment	$127,729,045
Charles Stewart Mott Foundation	$114,442,289
Eli & Edythe Broad Foundation	$111,692,581

Source: Foundation Center.

John and James Knight Foundation	$107,825,135
John Templeton Foundation	$105,248,596
Howard G. Buffett Foundation	$103,284,879
Sherwood Foundation	$101,964,342
Jerome L. Greene Foundation	$100,947,352
Robertson Foundation	$99,597,042
Richard King Mellon Foundation	$99,152,041
Annie E. Casey Foundation	$98,681,016
Harry and Jeanette Weinberg Foundation	$96,929,767
Conrad N. Hilton Foundation	$92,000,000
McKnight Foundation	$86,598,229
Starr Foundation	$83,168,245
Edward C. Johnson Fund	$82,350,200
Alfred P. Sloan Foundation	$82,091,585
Laura and John Arnold Foundation	$80,519,024
William Penn Foundation	$80,099,460
JPB Foundation	$78,051,333
Doris Duke Charitable Foundation	$75,080,723
Brown Foundation	$74,487,624
Druckenmiller Foundation	$74,469,500
Michael and Susan Dell Foundation	$72,785,040
Annenberg Foundation	$70,030,812
James Irvine Foundation	$69,000,000
Houston Endowment	$64,484,305
Schusterman Family Foundation	$64,025,508
Wallace Foundation	$61,462,148

Graph 21:

Top 50 Community Foundations
by 2013 giving

Silicon Valley Community Foundation	$362,390,000
Greater Kansas City Community Foundation	$234,274,371
Foundation For The Carolinas	$180,272,727
California Community Foundation	$164,428,000
Chicago Community Trust	$150,313,429
New York Community Trust	$144,241,100
Community Foundation for Greater Atlanta	$134,633,871
Tulsa Community Foundation	$110,512,000
Boston Foundation	$105,365,000
Greater Houston Community Foundation	$98,934,435
Columbus Foundation	$95,963,350
Community Foundation for National Capital Region	$95,397,756
San Francisco Foundation	$86,830,000
Communities Foundation of Texas	$82,493,000
Cleveland Foundation	$81,368,990
Omaha Community Foundation	$75,638,463
Greater Cincinnati Foundation	$69,133,479
Oregon Community Foundation	$66,052,201
Seattle Foundation	$65,653,979
Denver Foundation	$64,306,537
Marin Community Foundation	$62,536,631
Community Foundation of Greater Memphis	$58,341,057
Saint Paul Foundation	$54,752,338
Minneapolis Foundation	$52,591,314

Source: Foundation Center.

Community Foundation for Southeast Michigan	$52,560,486
San Diego Foundation	$50,669,000
Orange County Community Foundation	$46,816,000
Community Foundation of Middle Tennessee	$46,607,415
Pittsburgh Foundation	$42,569,107
Community First Foundation	$40,864,094
Arizona Community Foundation	$38,633,992
East Bay Community Foundation	$38,521,288
Central Indiana Community Foundation	$35,371,279
Baton Rouge Area Foundation	$35,351,731
Greater St. Louis Community Foundation	$33,338,981
Dallas Foundation	$33,204,208
Community Foundation Serving Richmond	$32,429,867
New Hampshire Charitable Foundation	$31,818,211
Community Foundation for NE Florida	$30,647,352
Greater Milwaukee Foundation	$30,050,000
Hartford Foundation for Public Giving	$29,828,016
Community Foundation of New Jersey	$28,395,393
Community Foundation of Louisville	$28,285,522
Rhode Island Foundation	$28,267,948
Delaware Community Foundation	$28,100,711
Hawaii Community Foundation	$27,361,979
Oklahoma City Community Foundation	$25,867,694
Community Foundation of Greater Des Moines	$25,228,667
Philadelphia Foundation	$24,679,393
Community Foundation for Greater New Haven	$23,670,346

Graph 22:

Top 50 Corporate Foundations

by 2013 giving

Bristol-Myers Squibb Patient Foundation	$811,433,684
Abbvie Patient Foundation	$783,366,952
Lilly Cares Foundation	$697,004,928
Merck Patient Program	$686,800,564
Genentech Access To Care Foundation	$680,278,040
Johnson & Johnson Patient Foundation	$611,680,261
GlaxoSmithKline Patient Foundation	$599,953,667
Pfizer Patient Foundation	$515,726,553
Novartis Patient Foundation	$452,745,445
Sanofi Foundation for North America	$284,044,399
Wells Fargo Foundation	$186,775,875
Walmart Foundation	$182,859,236
Boehringer Ingelheim Foundation	$179,977,010
Bank of America Charitable Foundation	$175,299,789
GE Foundation	$124,512,065
JPMorgan Chase Foundation	$115,516,001
Genzyme Charitable Foundation	$78,603,357
Citi Foundation	$78,372,150
ExxonMobil Foundation	$72,747,966
Coca-Cola Foundation	$69,658,157
Caterpillar Foundation	$55,998,836
Teva Cares Foundation	$49,164,295
PNC Foundation	$48,269,009
Johnson & Johnson Cos. Foundation	$46,445,669

Source: Foundation Center.
Note: Includes operating foundations run by pharmaceutical companies.

Intel Foundation	$45,318,315
Freddie Mac Foundation	$44,822,806
Verizon Foundation	$43,374,615
UPS Foundation	$42,895,860
MetLife Foundation	$42,488,850
Merck Company Foundation	$41,823,400
Google Foundation	$39,606,000
Goldman Sachs Foundation	$36,658,124
Bayer U.S. Patient Foundation	$34,927,912
PepsiCo Foundation	$31,730,571
Harold Simmons Foundation	$31,398,545
Bristol-Myers Squibb Foundation	$31,251,274
Blue Shield of California Foundation	$31,167,629
Newman's Own Foundation	$30,000,000
Emerson Charitable Trust	$29,059,957
General Motors Foundation	$27,627,768
General Mills Foundation	$26,898,325
Prudential Foundation	$26,859,858
Eli Lilly & Co. Foundation	$26,199,135
Valero Energy Foundation	$26,073,777
Duke Energy Foundation	$26,051,888
Nationwide Insurance Foundation	$25,558,922
Medtronic Foundation	$24,108,117
U.S. Bancorp Foundation	$23,292,965
Reckitt Benckiser Patient Foundation	$22,288,109
Ford Motor Company Fund	$21,970,680

Graph 23:

Donor-Advised Fund Growth

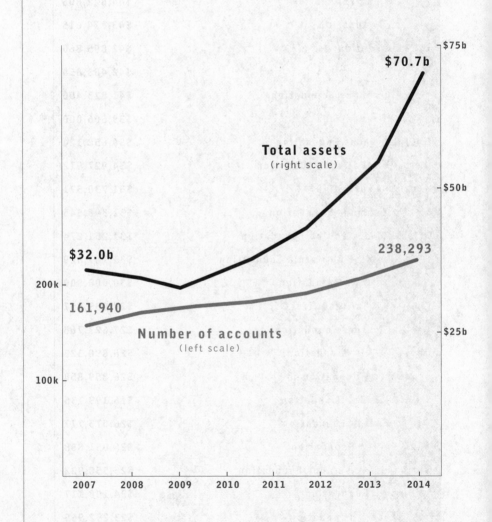

Total assets
(right scale)

$70.7b

$75b

$50b

$32.0b

238,293

200k

161,940

$25b

Number of accounts
(left scale)

100k

2007   2008   2009   2010   2011   2012   2013   2014

Source: National Philanthropic Trust.

oday's very fastest-growing instrument for giving money to charitable causes is the donor-advised fund. DAFs provide givers a much simpler alternative to setting up a private foundation. Donor-advised funds now outnumber private foundations by more than two to one, and in 2014 they funneled close to $13 billion to charities favored by their contributors. DAFs are both efficient and effective: the average fund now pays out in annual charitable grants a full 22 percent of the assets contained in the fund. That's three or four times the rate at which typical foundations pay out.

Graph 24:

Top Ten Donor-Advised Funds

Today's ten largest sponsors	Type of group
Fidelity Charitable Gift Fund	commercial
Schwab Charitable Fund	commercial
Vanguard Charitable Endowment Fund	commercial
Silicon Valley Community Foundation	community
National Christian Foundation	affinity
National Philanthropic Trust	affinity
Jewish Communal Fund	affinity
New York Community Trust	community
Greater Kansas City Community Foundation	community
Renaissance Charitable Foundation	commercial

Source: Chronicle of Philanthropy *2012 data; 2015 Giving Report,* Fidelity Charitable.

There are many sponsors of donor-advised funds. Most community foundations around the country offer them. So do various affinity groups like the National Christian Foundation and the many local Jewish giving federations. Today's fastest-growing sponsors of DAFs are commercial investment companies. They have made it exceptionally convenient for Americans to put away money for charity, keep it growing healthily while specific recipients are being planned, and then dispatch the donations efficiently with a few clicks of a mouse. The hundreds of thousands of individuals who have established accounts at Fidelity Charitable had granted $19 billion to charities as of 2014, with the total rising fast.

Graph 25:

Private Donations for Overseas Aid

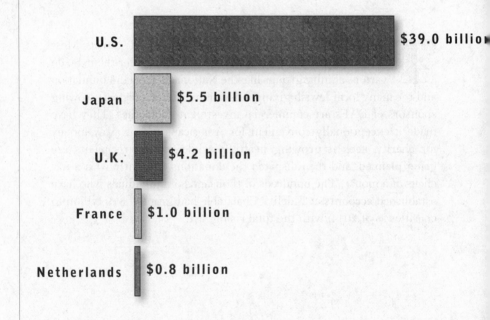

Source: Estimates by Center for Global Prosperity, Hudson Institute, 2011 data.

mericans are much more willing than other peoples to voluntarily donate money to help the poor and stricken in foreign lands. The figures here depict private charitable giving in various forms.

Of course there are other ways that a nation can give to less developed countries in addition to private philanthropy—official government aid, remittances to families back home by immigrants, private business investment, etc. See Graph 26 and its text for more on this subject. When you add up all of these sources of aid, the U.S. comes out far ahead of any other nation, sending $300 billion overseas annually to developing countries.

Graph 26:

U.S. Overseas Assistance

**Private donations
for overseas aid:
$39.0 billion**

Sources of this:
* charities 36%
* religious groups 19%
* corporations 19%
* foundations 12%
* volunteers 9%
* colleges 5%

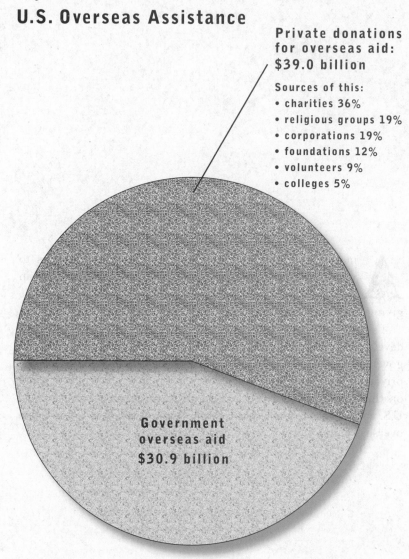

Government
overseas aid
$30.9 billion

Source: Hudson Institute Index of Global Philanthropy and Remittances *2013; 2011 data.*

Few people realize that private giving is now a much bigger part of how Americans aid the poor in foreign lands than official government aid. The $39 billion of annual aid depicted here comes from a variety of sources: private charities, religious groups, corporate giving, foundations, volunteers, etc.

Another very large source of economic assistance to the overseas poor, which we have chosen not to depict here but which has been painstakingly estimated in the Hudson Institute report from which this data is taken, is remittances sent back home by U.S. immigrants from poor lands. These amount to over a hundred billion dollars every year, and are more important to family welfare, health, and education in many underdeveloped countries than either private or governmental charity.

Anyone trying to understand the financial flows that aid the poor overseas must also consider one final element: private investment in developing countries. More than $108 billion of U.S. capital was committed to projects in poor nations in 2011, with for-profit aspirations. This job- and growth-creating money is probably the most important form of all of international sharing.

Graph 27:

Giving Levels, by Country

annual private philanthropy as a % of GDP

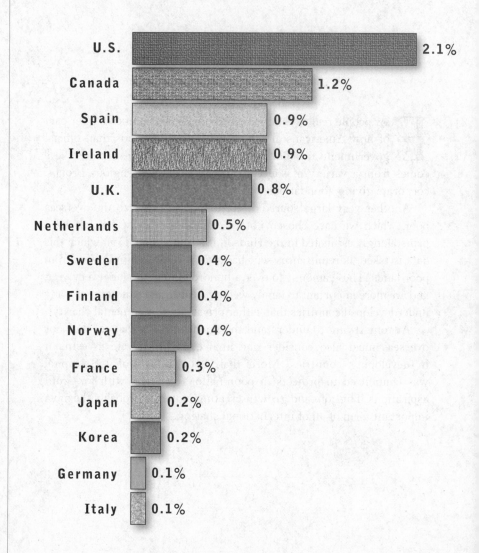

Country	%
U.S.	2.1%
Canada	1.2%
Spain	0.9%
Ireland	0.9%
U.K.	0.8%
Netherlands	0.5%
Sweden	0.4%
Finland	0.4%
Norway	0.4%
France	0.3%
Japan	0.2%
Korea	0.2%
Germany	0.1%
Italy	0.1%

Source: Giving USA, *Johns Hopkins Center for Civil Society Studies;*
data drawn from various recent years.

A number of studies have been undertaken to compare the charitable giving of various countries in fair ways—adjusting for differences in standards of living, population, and so forth. All end up showing about the same relationship that is charted here: Americans are about twice as generous in their private giving as kissing cousins like the British and Canadians, and up to 20 times as charitable as the residents of some other developed nations. Americans also volunteer more than almost any other wealthy people.

WHO GIVES MOST

to

CHARITY?

By Karl Zinsmeister

From Alaskan bush villages to center-city Manhattan, local-scale philanthropy unfolds every day in nearly all American communities. At first glance this modest, unsplashy, omnipresent giving may seem mundane. Yet such microphilanthropy leaves deep imprints in almost every corner of American life, due to its sheer density and the intimate ways in which it is delivered.

The fireworks show that delighted your town this week. The children's hospital where the burned girl from down the street was saved. The Rotary scholarship that allowed you to become dear friends with a visiting Indonesian graduate student. The church-organized handyman service that keeps your elderly mother in her home. The park that adds so much to your family life. These gifts, products of modest offerings from local foundations or groups of community donors, accumulate in powerful ways to make our daily existences safer, sweeter, more interesting.

It is easy to think of philanthropy as something done by the very wealthy, or big foundations, or prosperous companies. Actually, of the $358 billion that Americans gave to charity in 2014, only 14 percent came from foundation grants, and just 5 percent from corporations. The rest—81 percent—came from individuals.

And among individual givers in the U.S., while the wealthy do their part (as you'll see later in this essay), the vast predominance of offerings come from average citizens of moderate income. Between 70 and 90 percent of all U.S. households donate to charity in a given year, and the typical household's annual gifts add up to between two and three thousand dollars.

This is different from the patterns in any other country. Per capita, Americans voluntarily donate about *seven times* as much as continental Europeans. Even our cousins the Canadians give to charity at substantially lower rates, and at *half* the total volume of an American household.

There are many reasons for this American distinction. Foremost is the fact that ours is the most religious nation in the industrial world. Religion motivates giving more than any other factor. A second explanation is our deep-rooted tradition of mutual aid, which has impressed observers like Tocqueville since our founding days. Third is the potent entrepreneurial impulse in the U.S., which generates overflowing wealth that can be shared, while simultaneously encouraging a "bootstrap" ethic that says we should help our neighbors pull themselves up (partly because, in our freewheeling economy, we could be the ones who need help next time).

But what lies beneath our high national average? Do subgroups of the U.S. population vary in their giving, and if so, how much? What exactly do we know about who gives in America, and what motivates them?

Dissecting who is generous and who is not can be controversial. And not all of the research agrees. So we have methodically waded through heaps of studies and drawn out for you the clearest findings. You're about to learn what today's best social science has to say about the geography, demography, and economics of generosity in America. Some of it will surprise you.

HOW U.S. REGIONS VARY

There have been several attempts to compare the charitable giving of different U.S. states and regions. The most straightforward measures match the itemized charitable donations of local taxpayers to their incomes (both pulled from official IRS figures). The Fraser Institute and the Catalogue for Philanthropy have each used variations of this method to reveal what fraction of their annual resources residents are giving away to philanthropic causes, versus consuming or saving for themselves.

These "giving ratios" reveal a consistent pattern. Measured by how much they share out of what they have available, the most generous Americans are not generally those in high-income, urban, liberal states like California or

Top ten states: Fraction of their income that residents give to charity

2010	national rank	2004
Utah	1	Wyoming
Wyoming	2	Utah
Georgia	3	Tennessee
Alabama	4	Arkansas
Maryland	5	Texas
South Carolina	6	Alabama
Idaho	7	Oklahoma
North Carolina	8	Mississippi
Tennessee	9	South Dakota
New York	10	New York

Source: Fraser Institute (2010 IRS data), Catalogue of Philanthropy (2004 IRS data)

	Bottom ten states: Fraction of their income that residents give to charity	
2010	**national rank**	**2004**
Louisiana	41	New Mexico
New Mexico	42	Iowa
Alaska	43	Ohio
Rhode Island	44	Hawaii
Hawaii	45	Montana
Vermont	46	Vermont
New Hampshire	47	Wisconsin
Maine	48	New Hampshire
North Dakota	49	Rhode Island
West Virginia	50	Maine

Source: Fraser Institute (2010 IRS data), Catalogue of Philanthropy (2004 IRS data)

Massachusetts. Rather, people living in states that are more rural, conservative, religious, and moderate in income are our most generous givers. (See the two charts above for listing of the top and bottom givers.)

This same pattern is seen in data very different from the IRS returns. The Panel Study of Income Dynamics is a high-quality microstudy of several thousand U.S. households that are representative of the national population, and whose characteristics have been tracked in detail by researchers over a period of years. When income and charitable giving are compared among this carefully documented group, the willingness to "give until it hurts" can be seen to vary sharply by locale.

In the PSID statistics, the top regions for donations as a percent of income are the Mountain West, the East South Central states (Tennessee, Alabama, Mississippi, Kentucky), the West North Central states (South Dakota, North Dakota, Iowa, Kansas, Minnesota, Missouri, Nebraska), and the West South Central states (Arkansas, Texas, Oklahoma, Louisiana). The least giving region was New England, closely trailed by the Middle Atlantic states (New Jersey, Pennsylvania, New York). The variations are not triv-

Giving by region	
	national rank
Mountain	1
East South Central	2
West North Central	3
West South Central	4
South Atlantic	5
Pacific	6
East North Central	7
Middle Atlantic	8
New England	9

Source: Panel Study of Income Dynamics

ial: the top group of Utah, Idaho, Wyoming, Arizona, Colorado, Montana, Nevada, and New Mexico were more than *twice* as generous as the residents of New England or the Mid-Atlantic region. (See "Giving by region" above.)

MAJOR STUDY RELEASED

A third take on this topic was assembled by the *Chronicle of Philanthropy*. Its study "How America Gives" analyzed IRS income and giving data right down to the level of individual counties in the U.S. The researchers used the latest IRS returns available—2012 in their most recently published update. (More details on the results can be seen in Graphs 16 and 17 of this book's "Statistics on U.S. Generosity" section.)

The results? Not much different from the portraits above. Using four large regional groupings, "How America Gives" reported that Southerners are America's most sacrificial givers, while Northeasterners are substantially less generous.

Giving in four major regions	
	percentage of adjusted gross income donated to charity
South	5.2
West	4.5
Midwest	4.3
Northeast*	4.0

*New England plus New Jersey, New York, and Pennsylvania
Source: How America Gives

Regional results are above. Below are the top and bottom ten states for giving, according to the *Chronicle* calculations. Once again, the biggest givers are found to be concentrated in "Bible Belt" states in the South or where Mormons make up a large portion of the population.

Top ten states for giving	
	giving as % of adjusted gross income
Utah	6.6
Mississippi	5.0
Alabama	4.9
Tennessee	4.5
Georgia	4.2
South Carolina	4.1
Idaho	4.1
Oklahoma	3.9
Arkansas	3.9
North Carolina	3.6

Source: How America Gives, January 2015 update

On the other hand, scant-giving households are heavily concentrated in relatively wealthy and secular New England.

Bottom ten states for giving	
	giving as % of adjusted gross income
Hawaii	2.5
Wisconsin	2.4
North Dakota	2.4
Connecticut	2.3
Massachusetts	2.2
Rhode Island	2.1
New Jersey	2.0
Vermont	2.0
Maine	2.0
New Hampshire	1.7

Source: *How America Gives, January 2015 update*

This effect holds up not only across states but also in major cities. For instance, denizens of Salt Lake City, Birmingham, Memphis, Nashville, and Atlanta donate from 4 to 6 percent of their discretionary income to charity, while counterparts in Boston, Hartford, and Providence average just 2 percent. Silicon Valley is legendary for its wealth, yet lags badly in charity—the *Chronicle* data show San Jose and San Francisco falling near the bottom among our 50 biggest cities, giving away just 2.2 percent and 2.4 percent, respectively, of their income.

There are about the same number of people in urban, high-education San Francisco County as there are in the rural, religious state of South Dakota, economist Arthur Brooks once noted. And families in these two regions give almost exactly the same amount to charity every year. Yet because the average family income is about $45,000 in South Dakota compared to $81,000 in San Francisco, the typical South Dakota household is actually giving away 75 percent more of its income every year than a San Fran counterpart.

STRUGGLING TO EXPLAIN NEW ENGLAND'S LAG

A few years ago, some Bostonians chagrined by these findings created a study which tried to further "rebalance" the national statistics, which they felt did not fully reflect the willingness to give in their region. They used their own methods for adjusting income downward to compensate for high taxes and living costs, and they created estimates of additional giving by persons who don't itemize their contributions on their taxes. Their results are quite different from all other measures.

Boston-model re-estimates of top and bottom states for giving	
	national rank after income is adjusted and giving is extrapolated for non-itemizers
New York	1
Utah	2
Maryland	3
Connecticut	4
California	5
New Jersey	6
Hawaii	7
Wyoming	8
Virginia	9
North Carolina	10
Ohio	41
Wisconsin	42
South Dakota	43
Vermont	44
Iowa	45
New Mexico	46
West Virginia	47
New Hampshire	48
North Dakota	49
Maine	50

Source: The Boston Foundation

In this more synthetic data, evidence of scant giving in New England remains, but the top and bottom groups are otherwise much more jumbled and difficult to see patterns in.

The Boston data have not been widely embraced, for a variety of reasons. About 80 percent of all charitable dollars are captured in the itemized giving data from the IRS (which provide the backbone for the "Generosity Index" and "How America Gives" studies cited earlier). And a large proportion of the donations that are not itemized come from religious conservatives who do not reside heavily in the regions the Boston analysts aim to bolster. These factors leave many observers skeptical of statistical manipulations that reorder the clear trends seen in the IRS data—which are hard measures, not extrapolations or statistical models like the Boston numbers.

One intriguing pattern that emerges from the Boston data is a class stratification in New England when it comes to charitable giving. Among people making $100,000 or more in 2003, New Englanders were actually more generous than the national average. Yet among people in the middle-income band ($25,000 to $99,999), New Englanders fell *below* the national average in giving. And among the low-income (less than $25,000 of annual income in 2003), New Englanders were notoriously skin-flinty, giving at less than *half* the national average for that income group. All of this may reflect the region's lower level of religious belief, a factor which, as we'll see, dramatically lifts giving, even among the comparatively poor.

RED STATE VERSUS BLUE STATE

A strong pattern that makes some commentators uneasy is the fact that, as Brooks put it, "the electoral map and the charity map are remarkably similar." Or to quote the *Chronicle of Philanthropy*'s 2012 summary of its giving research, "the eight states that ranked highest voted for John McCain in the last presidential contest…while the seven lowest-ranking states supported Barack Obama."

In addition to this political tinge, there are many other fascinating demographic and cultural patterns in the national giving statistics. For instance, the PSID survey shows that while New Englanders rank dead last in percentage of income donated to charity, their *participation rate* (fraction of the population who give something) is actually higher than in any other region. New Englanders reflect, and indeed may lead, the extraordinary American propensity to donate to others. They just don't give as much as residents of other regions.

Some other results emerging from statistical regression of the PSID data: All other things being equal, the self-employed give less to charity. So do people who have moved residences more than the norm. Residents of rural areas and small towns, on the other hand, donate at higher levels.

The demographic characteristic most likely to increase giving to charitable causes is marriage. Compared to the unmarried, married households were 62 percent more giving in 2011. This was after all other factors like income, race, region, etc. were statistically adjusted for, using base data from the government's Consumer Expenditure Survey.

Surprisingly, people who volunteer at secular organizations are a bit under-giving, in regressions of the PSID statistics. Meanwhile, persons who volunteer at religious organizations are dramatically bigger donors of money.

Religious practice is the behavioral variable most consistently associated with generous giving. Charitable effort correlates strongly with the frequency with which a person attends religious services. Evangelical Protestants and Mormons in particular are strong givers. Compared to Protestant affiliation, both Catholic affiliation and Jewish affiliation reduce the scope of average giving, when other influences are held constant.

Finer-grain numbers from the PSID show that the faithful don't just give to religious causes; they are also much more likely to give to secular causes than the non-religious. Among Americans who report that they "never" attend religious services, just less than half give any money at all to secular causes. People who attend services 27-52 times per year, though, give money to secular charities in two thirds of all cases. (See page 1138.)

Sociologist Robert Putnam has chronicled the many pro-social and philanthropic overflow effects of religious practice. Not only is half of all American personal philanthropy and half of all volunteering directly religious in character, but nearly half of all associational membership in the U.S. is church-related. Religious practice links us in webs of mutual knowledge, responsibility, and support like no other influence.

Indeed, faith is as important as basic financial success in increasing giving. And religious conviction is often what separates one sub-group from another when it comes to charitable practice. For instance, African Americans, who are generally more religious than whites, are consequently 18 percent bigger givers when households of the same income, region, education, and so forth are compared.

GIVING BY INCOME LEVEL

The curve charting charitable generosity by income takes on an unexpected U-shape largely thanks to the faith factor described above. People with means, as you might expect, are substantial givers. Middle-class Americans donate a little less. But the lower-income population surprises by giving more than the middle—and in some measures even more than the top. (As a *percentage* of available income, that is. In absolute dollars, those in higher income groups give much, much more money.)

The graph below combines results from six different studies of how giving varies as income changes. Each study uses somewhat different definitions of income, different universes of households, measured in different years, so they are not strictly comparable, but I have made some basic standardizations and converted results to present-day dollars so readers can observe the general trend uncovered by each of these analyses: If you measure charitable donations as a fraction of the donor's income, giving is most robust at the top and bottom of the earnings spectrum.

People are generally more philanthropic toward the end of their lives, when they tend to have more savings, time, and motivation to help others. (Giving peaks at ages 61-75, when 77 percent of households donate, compared

Charitable giving's u-curve

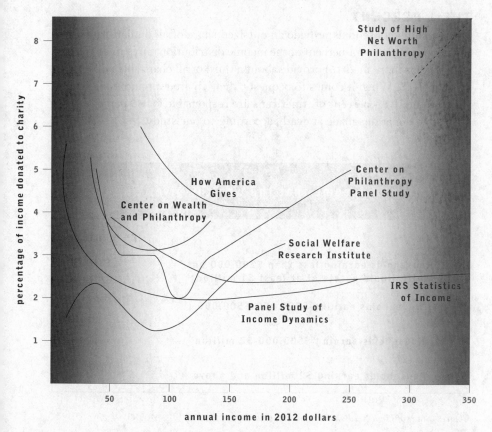

to just over 60 percent among households headed by someone 26-45 years old.) Some of the low-income givers charted on my "u-graph" are undoubtedly retirees who, while their annual incomes are modest, have accumulated wealth that allows them to be generous donors.

The other factor accounting for the high level of donations among low-income Americans is that a significant minority of them are religious tithers who powerfully push up the group average through sacrificial giving. If you look at what fraction of each group gives, various studies show that the *rate* of donation among low-income persons is actually half or less of what it is for the rest of the population. Only about a third of low-income individuals give any money at all in a year. But those who *are* givers tend to be extremely generous, with a third or half of them giving at least 5 percent of their income. These sacrificial givers motivated heavily by religion are found much more among what might be called the working class (households making $25,000-$45,000 in current dollars) than among the truly poor.

THE 1 PERCENT

High-income households provide an outsized share of all philanthropic giving. Those in the top 1 percent of the income distribution (any family making $394,000 or more in 2015) provide about a third of all charitable dollars given in the U.S. When it comes to bequests, the rich are even more important: the wealthiest 1.4 percent of Americans are responsible for 86 percent of the charitable donations made at death, according to one study.

Portion of income that the wealthy give to charity	
	percentage
Households earning less than $200,000 but with liquid assets of at least $1 million	9.7
Households earning $200,000-$500,000	8.6
Households earning $500,000-$2 million	8.3
Households earning $2 million and above	14.0

Source: *Study of High Net Worth Philanthropy (2005, 2007, 2009)*

At the top of the income spectrum, charitable giving bumps upward both in dollars and as a fraction of income. The fullest study of wealthy donors is done every two years by the Lilly Family School of Philanthropy at Indiana University. The chart on the opposite page averages findings from three of its recent reports.

The very wealthy, this shows, give away a much larger chunk of their earnings than others. These robust rates of giving are elevated, however, by the extreme generosity of a subset of the rich. While donations to charity are almost universal among wealthy households (more than 97 percent make some annual gift, according to the Indiana data), data show that many of those gifts are comparatively modest. Others are extraordinarily copious— and these push up the donation average.

If instead of the *average* percentage of income given away by wealthy households, we look at the *median* percentage (meaning that half gave more than this amount, and half gave less), the wealthy appear less magnanimous. From 2007-2011, the median wealthy household (having annual income of $200,000+ or assets of $1 million+) gave away 3.4 percent of its income.

Interestingly, when rich people live in separate enclaves they are not as generous as when they live interspersed in normal communities. The "How America Gives" study showed that when households earning $200,000 a year make up more than 40 percent of the residents of a particular ZIP code, they give just 2.8 percent of their discretionary income to charity. If they live in more mixed neighborhoods and towns, though, they give an average of closer to 5 percent.

Physical separation and economic stratification corrode social cooperation and generosity. In towns, villages, and cities where Americans of differing fortunes live in more traditional combinations, though, generosity flourishes. And for many Americans, the resulting giving seems to be deeply connected to satisfaction in life.

"I came to realize that expanding my philanthropic activities could be both meaningful and fun," successful oil businessman Jim Calaway told *Philanthropy* magazine in 2015. "Making a lot of money and spending it on yourself is not a lot of fun," he noted in an earlier interview with the *Chronicle of Philanthropy*. "What is a lot of fun is to live modestly so that you can give to the common good. That's where happiness really lies."

Why is
CHARITABLE ACTIVITY TAX-PROTECTED?
(Think Freedom, Not Finances)

By Alex Reid

Periodically, some politician seeking increased government revenues will propose to chop down the tax deduction for charitable contributions. Were this to happen, U.S. charities would lose billions of dollars. We as American citizens, however, stand to lose much more than that if the tax protections long afforded to charitable giving were to be withdrawn.

The charitable deduction protects our freedom to create and operate institutions that make up a civil society separate from government. Electing representatives is not our sole means of expressing ourselves and contributing to national success. As citizens of a free country we also have the right to act directly in the public sphere. The many private organizations that act within our borders—educating, assisting individuals, influencing culture, addressing social needs—are the ultimate bedrock underlying our democratic system.

The individual deduction for donations to these civic organizations, and the income-tax exemption for charitable operations, are more than just tax rules. They form a vital legal boundary between the state and civil society. They are not subsidies for civil society, but rather fences that keep government from interfering in a sector that is vital to our national freedom.

Income taxes are the contributions we make to the public good indirectly by force of law. Charitable donations are the contributions we make to the public good directly and voluntarily. Direct giving through donations, and indirect giving through taxes, are dual aspects of our right to self-governance. Altering the charitable deduction would renegotiate the fundamental relationship between citizens and the state, and undermine our ability to shape our own society.

IS THERE MORE TO THE PUBLIC SECTOR THAN GOVERNMENT?

In recent years, our deficit-ridden federal government has been coveting the billions of dollars that citizens send annually to charities. For several years in a row, President Obama proposed cutting the income-tax deduction for charitable giving. Congress entertained some of its own proposals for capping, eliminating, or altering the charitable deduction as part of tax reform.

Policymakers sometimes justify these changes by claiming that the charitable deduction is a government *subsidy* for charity. A more accurate understanding is that the charitable deduction is simply an accounting mechanism to ensure that your income is measured accurately. Money you give away for public benefit is neither part of your income nor the government's money to claim. Any income tax requires a charitable deduction as a matter of principle, because funds given away for the public good are not part of a taxpayer's personal resources.

The state doesn't sponsor and subsidize civil society using tax revenue. It is individuals who create civil society using their own funds. The state simply avoids interfering when it eschews taxing of those transactions.

Some activists say that charitable contributions should be taxed because they are a form of personal consumption. If the donor feels good about himself for giving money away, he has "consumed" the warm glow that comes from being a donor. The rejoinder to this is that the economic value of the charitable contribution actually settles on the recipient of the gift, not the donor. When I buy and eat a pint of ice cream, I literally consume some of my income. When I give money to a disaster-relief fund or cancer hospital, the person whose home or body has been ravaged consumes the funds. I may get a good feeling from both experiences, but the private gulping and the giving to others are wholly different acts.

At its core, the issue of whether charitable contributions should be included in the tax base is a matter of values as much as economics. It is a question of what the relationship should be between citizen and state. If you believe that a citizen's right to elect representatives is all that's needed for self-governance, then interfering with citizens' direct contributions to the public good may not bother you. Under this view, charitable contributions are a luxury that a democratic government may choose to indulge through charitable deductions when it is wealthy, or eliminate when it is poor. Not only does income belong to the state, but so does philanthropy; the donor's choice is irrelevant.

On the other hand, if you believe that citizens should have the freedom to contribute directly to the public good without government interference, that civil society is an end in itself, and that civic engagement is healthy for democracy, then charitable contributions should not be treated as part of the tax base. The donor's right to support independent organizations is part of his fundamental freedom, as valuable as his right to vote.

CITIZEN, PRIVATE CHARITY, STATE

Kamal Jahanbein has a vision. He believes that everyone in the world should have the right to prosper, to speak his or her mind, and to petition the government for redress. Born in Iran, Kamal derives tremendous personal satisfaction from the American system of philanthropy which enables him to enact his vision of the public good without interference from anyone, a precious freedom to those with experience living under an oppressive regime.

Kamal runs a neighborhood pub in Washington, D.C., called the Saloon. The most surprising thing about this popular business is the sign on the door that says, "The Saloon will be closed for the month of August while we go to Africa to do some good." After 20 years of nurturing his now-profitable business, Kamal began building schools in some of the world's poorest towns. He has now completed more than 16 schools around the world, as well as medical facilities and homes, in places like Bafang, Cameroon; Rio Dulce, Guatemala; and Pakua, Laos. By his own estimate, Kamal has given away more than $1.5 million and countless hours to his humanitarian projects. Hundreds of names on the bricks that line his pub belong to individuals who have contributed to his philanthropic projects.

When Kamal builds a school, he seeks to give the gift of self-empowerment, the strength to strive against forces that seem greater than oneself—to have the confidence of David in a world full of Goliaths. Before he begins, Kamal asks representatives from the village where the school will be built to raise 10 percent of the funds from their own pockets, "so they are invested in the project." Then Kamal helps the village negotiate with the local government to provide the teachers, furniture, and equipment necessary to operate the school. When the project is complete, Kamal makes sure the village representatives have copies of the contract with the government so that they can enforce it. "You have never seen such a beautiful sight as a government minister's office filled with determined mothers, waving their contracts and demanding the teachers that they were promised," he said, smiling.

Talking to Kamal, you realize that giving to charity is a radical act. It is defining what is good for society, and putting your money where your mouth is. Marshaling resources for the good of society is also what governments do, which is why there can be a tension between charities and political officials. The ability to create an institution to accomplish a particular vision of the public good creates a locus of power that is separate and apart from the governmental authority. Government is about centralized power; charity is about local problem-solving.

Before there is government, there is charity: ordinary people gathering together to provide for the common good by helping the needy, healing the sick, teaching the ignorant. At its core, charity is about self-reliance. The charitable institutions we create are manifestations of our right to self-governance that is truly by the people, for the people.

A nation can be judged by the amount of charity it permits within its borders. A government that represents its citizens' best interests is not threatened by the additional exercise of self-governance. On the contrary, the exercise of self-reliance by the citizenry strengthens civil society, the stuff of which democracies are made.

Competition between the government and nonprofits to best represent the public interest dates to the founding of America. It is perhaps understandable, given human jealousies, why the government should prefer to control the vast resources of the private nonprofit sector, and to manipulate their contributions to serve government purposes in public policy. But that is not the system of self-rule enshrined in our Constitution. In fact, that is just the sort of government that our founders fought and died to rebel against.

THE RIGHT OF SELF-GOVERNANCE

Americans tend to chafe against restraints on our liberty to speak, act, worship, or band together, even if these acts are heretical or otherwise controversial. Nor do we wait for government to become involved when we perceive a problem. We act on our own, or in concert, to solve it as we see fit. Our ability to define what is wholesome and necessary for the public good, as individuals or self-organized groups, is the essence of American freedom. And making charitable contributions without government interference or taxation is an important part of this original right.

> There is a fashionable argument at present that the charitable deduction is a subsidy from the state. That's entirely wrong.

America's passion for self-governance is manifest in our many associations. We have more than 1.5 million tax-exempt organizations, including 900,000 public charities, 100,000 private foundations, and 600,000 other types of nonprofit organizations, including chambers of commerce, fraternal organizations, and civic leagues, and roughly 320,000 religious congregations. Many associations are effective; many are not. Some last a century; some never get off the ground. But in America, that is our business, not the government's. We are free to create, free to operate, and free to terminate our associations as we please.

Since our nation's founding, the federal government and private associations have been rivals, and the lines of battle have shifted back and forth over the years. Today we take it for granted that private associations serving the public benefit may compete with the federal government. That, however, is a freedom that was hard-fought and won by previous generations.

In 1816, the state of New Hampshire attempted to seize control of Dartmouth College, a private university established by charitable contributions in 1754 for the purpose of educating Native Americans and other people of New Hampshire. The motivation for taking over Dartmouth was political. The Jeffersonians had won the New Hampshire governorship and state legislature in the election of 1812. The trustees of Dartmouth College, however, were members of the opposition Federalist party, and the state sought to replace them with loyal Jeffersonians.

The Jeffersonians argued that the government should have the right to control charitable contributions. As Thomas Jefferson himself explained in a letter he wrote to New Hampshire Governor William Plumer in 1816, a private gift to accomplish a public purpose such as education is, in effect, a gift to the people, and as the people's representative, the democratically elected government of New Hampshire should have the right to oversee the gift. Jefferson believed that state control of Dartmouth was critical to ensure that Dartmouth educated the future leaders of New Hampshire in a manner meeting state approval. Why should a state controlled by Jeffersonians allow a Federalist educational agenda to continue?

Jefferson saw no need to protect Dartmouth from government interference because he believed that democracy itself guaranteed that the government's purposes and those of Dartmouth College would always be synchronous. He wrote, "the idea that institutions, established for the use of the nation cannot be touched or modified, even to make them answer their end, because of rights gratuitously supposed to be in those employed to manage them in trust for the public, may, perhaps, be a salutary provision against the abuses of a monarch, but it is most absurd against the nation itself."

The college challenged the state in the Supreme Court. Daniel Webster, a Dartmouth alumnus, argued the case for Dartmouth's freedom to operate from government interference—even when that government is a democracy. He said, "Shall our state legislature be allowed to take that which is not their own, to turn it from its original use, and apply it to such ends or purposes as they, in their discretion, shall see fit? Sir, you may destroy this little institution; it is weak; it is in your hands! You may put it out; but if you do, you must carry on with your work! You must extinguish one after another, all those great lights of science, which, for more than a century, have thrown their radiance over the land! It is, sir, as I have said, a small college, and yet there are those who love it."

Spoken just 40 years after the signing of the Declaration of Independence, Webster's words resonated deeply with those present.

Writing for the Court, Chief Justice John Marshall was moved to agree with Webster. He found that the state could not replace the trustees of Dartmouth College, because doing so would interfere with the charitable contributions of Dartmouth's donors. Dartmouth was a vehicle through which individual donors pooled their resources to accomplish public benefits they deemed appropriate, and the Constitution gave the state no right to interfere with such a private contract. A gift to accomplish a public benefit is not a gift to the government, and doesn't allow the state to interfere with the institution created by the gift.

It would be difficult to overstate the importance of the *Dartmouth* decision in shaping American civil society over the past two centuries. With one stroke, the Supreme Court severed the public and private spheres, making clear that under our Constitution the government could not direct private associations to implement government policy. After *Dartmouth*, private associations were free to operate autonomously, to accomplish whatever public purposes they choose, constrained only by the legal framework of the tax law, general laws against fraud, discrimination, and so forth, and their ability to obtain resources from charitable donors.

The great flourishing of private associations for the public benefit that followed the *Dartmouth* decision has been the hallmark of American civil society ever since. Writing a couple decades after *Dartmouth*, French philosopher Alexis de Tocqueville observed that public-benefit associations are the foundation on which American democracy rests. Private associations working for the public benefit are not just signs of a healthy democracy, he concluded, they are its *cause*.

THE TAX MAN COMETH

The power struggle between charities and the government continues to this day. The difference is that today, the battle is waged through the tax law. Nearly 100 years after the *Dartmouth* case, Congress gained the power to tax income through ratification of the 16th Amendment to the Constitution. It enacted the corporate and individual income taxes in 1913. Previous attempts to enact an income tax, dating back to the Civil War, all exempted charitable organizations from taxation, as our current code does. The individual deduction for contributions to charities was first introduced in 1917, and has been in place since. This protection of charities and charitable contributions from taxation was a manifestation of the unwritten social contract that private giving should be excluded from the tax base out of deference to the sovereignty of American citizens.

That is very different from the claim made in some quarters today that our present partial tax protections of charitable contributions are a gift from the state—a subsidy. The historic understanding is also completely at odds with today's fashionable argument that, as a contributor, the government has a right to decide how much charity to subsidize, which recipients to support, and how best to manage them.

Those who believe the charitable contribution deduction is a subsidy from the state often argue that the purpose of subsidizing charitable goods and services such as education, poverty relief, scientific research, and health care is because the government would have to provide these things if charities did not. The problem with this view is that if the purpose of the charitable deduction is to serve governmental purposes, then the charities should also be under government control. Under this view, charities should be subject to the rules that apply to government contractors, and the government should have rights to direct and supervise charitable actions.

As yet, the government does not tell charities what goods and services to provide, when and where to provide them, or how much they should cost. The government cannot hire and fire charities at will, reward the ones it favors, or dock the ones that displease officials. The government so far has no right to appoint a charity's board of directors or to select its officers. The government cannot refuse to subsidize charities controlled by individuals the government does not like. When a new government is elected, disfavored charities do not lose their tax benefits, and loyal charities do not get extra credit. (These are not just theoretical worries, but real dangers—as shown by recent actions like IRS discrimination against social-welfare organizations affiliated with the Tea Party, and HHS Secretary Sebelius's phone calls asking companies to give money to new charities operated by former Obama campaign staff to help implement Obamacare.)

> Charitable contributions are protected from taxation in order to keep government from entangling itself with the exercise of individual freedom.

Under current law, anyone can form a charity, regardless of his or her experience, expertise, or political persuasion. To secure tax exemption and be eligible to receive deductible contributions, all that is required is that the organization promise the Internal Revenue Service that it will primarily conduct activities that further its charitable purpose, not intervene in political campaigns or engage in excessive amounts of lobbying, and not distribute profits to shareholders. To maintain its tax exemption, the organization simply must file annual information returns and continue to operate as promised. The government may periodically audit the organization to confirm that it is not breaking its promises, but beyond that the government is supposed to stay out of the picture, and let charities govern themselves and pursue their own purposes. All of that existing practice would be very different if the charitable deduction was accepted as a government subsidy rather than a bulwark against government intrusion.

Moreover, there is another crucial flaw in the idea that protecting charity from taxation represents a government subsidy. Many of the objects of American charity—like religious flourishing—are things our government cannot Constitutionally subsidize. That's why the Supreme Court has expressly rejected subsidy theory as an explanation of the charitable exemption from income tax—because it cannot be reconciled with the clauses of the Constitution protecting free exercise of religion and forbidding establishment of an official church.

The Court has found that tax exemption of churches is not a favor granted to churches, but a democratic necessity to ensure that the state does not infringe on individuals' religious freedom. As Chief Justice Burger wrote in *Walz v. Tax Commission of the City of New York*: "The exemption creates only a minimal and remote involvement between church and state, and far less than taxation of churches. It restricts the fiscal relationship between church and state, and tends to complement and reinforce the desired separation insulating each from the other."

In other words, churches are exempt from tax not because the government is underwriting religion, but because it is vital, Constitutionally, that a free and fair government stay out of their business—which is best accomplished by tax exemption.

SUBSIDY OR IMMUNITY?

This, then, is the crucial point: Charitable contributions must be protected from taxation not because the government wishes to subsidize charitable activity, but because government intrusion in this sector would dangerously entangle the state with the exercise of individual freedom. Through charitable contributions, Americans make real many of our Constitutionally protected rights—creating organizations that engage in freedom of speech, freedom of association, freedom to practice religion. The civil society we build through our nonprofit institutions is not just some sweetener of our quality of life. It is fundamental to our democracy, a replenishing source of nourishment to individual freedom.

The justification for the charitable deduction is akin to the intergovernmental immunity from taxation that the Supreme Court recognized in *McCulloch v. Maryland*, where Justice Marshall famously wrote that "the power to tax involves the power to destroy." Just as the principles of federalism constrain the federal government's power to tax the states and the states' power to tax the federal government, the individual freedoms the Constitution guarantees to American citizens who engage in civil society by creating and funding nonprofit organizations should likewise block intrusive government manipulation of charity via taxation.

Although someone focused only on the federal budget might not care whether the charitable deduction is justified as a subsidy or as an immunity from tax, these diametrically opposed justifications are built on entirely different understandings of the relationship between citizen and state. And legislative action growing out of these two different interpretations could eventually lead to dramatically different results in American society.

Tax subsidies are things the government chooses not to tax in order to encourage behavior that the government supports. The government may manipulate these as it sees fit. *Tax immunity* is a framework that strictly limits the government's ability to control and collect revenue from an activity. The charitable deduction, which protects the vital role of civil society in America, should be understood as a tax immunity, not a subsidy. It is crucial that donors and lovers of liberty in America protect this traditional understanding and not fall into the trap of letting it be redefined as a subsidy, not even a benevolent one.

Charities do not normally provide goods and services to help the government. In fact, they often provide goods and services that the government cannot or will not provide, and even things the government does not like. Philanthropy in America is rich with examples of citizens acting where government has refused to act. It was charitable giving that educated Native Americans at Dartmouth and Hamilton colleges. It was private givers who set up thousands of schools for African Americans when the state was scorning them during the Jim Crow era. It was Rockefeller donations that eliminated hookworm in the U.S. when embarrassed hot-weather state governments refused to acknowledge that such parasites were endemic among their residents. Philanthropists like Bill Gates pursued vaccines for diseases like malaria when that was too costly for government or insufficiently profitable for corporations to pursue.

Charitable giving has even repeatedly spawned movements that fundamentally alter the complexion of democracy. Reforms ranging from abolition to women's suffrage to protections for religious conscience to tort reform have all been inaugurated by philanthropy. In each case, the government has been more adversary than contributor, until the government itself was changed by the movement.

So today's debate over the charitable deduction is about much, much more than taxes and deficits. The charitable deduction is a main artery within our body politic. It nourishes American civil society and gives strength to our democracy. It gives form and substance to our basic freedom of self-governance—a right that is not fully discharged by our ability to elect representatives. It is not a luxury we can do without.

If the charitable deduction were eliminated, Americans would no doubt continue to give generously at some level. But that is not the point. The charitable deduction does not exist to subsidize good works, though the good effects are many. Rather, we shield private donations from the brunt of taxation in order to limit government interference with our personal choices on how best to further the public interest. The charitable deduction is a mechanism for ensuring that the government does not lay claim to that which it should not own: private gifts devoted to the good of the people.

The charitable deduction is a negotiated bargain between citizens and the state, establishing a delicate balance of power. We have accepted limits on how much money we may contribute, on the types of property that can be given, on the arrangements that constitute a gift, on the broad sectors we may give to, and on what the recipients are forbidden to do with our gifts. But, historically and philosophically, there are more reasons to argue that the charitable deduction should be expanded today than that it should be further circumscribed.

Sacrificing the charitable deduction is not a wise, safe, or acceptable means of improving today's warped federal finances. The appropriation of charitable revenue by the federal government would be a profound renegotiation of the relationship between the American government and our civil society. Bluntly, such a drastic move would run counter to the entire history and spirit of American democracy.

> Sacrificing the charitable deduction to improve federal finances would be a profound renegotiation of the relationship between the government and our civil society, a drastic move running counter to the spirit and longstanding practice of American democracy.

Alex Reid is a tax attorney in Washington, D.C., and former counsel to the Joint Committee on Taxation of the U.S. Congress.

INDEX

Council on Foreign Relations 210
Council on Foundations 1088
counseling 279, 408, 415, 439,
    646-647, 660, 662, 673, 711,
    746-747, 757, 762-764, 774,
    907, 973
counter-intelligentsia 223
Cournand, André 327
Cousins, Tom 1000
Covenant House 223, 762
Cowles, Alfred 689
Craft, Joe 83
Crane, Ed 876
Crazy Horse Memorial 1007-1008
"Creating Order from Chaos"
    978-979
Creating Original Music 985
Creative Capital Foundation 481
Creative Commons 390
Crick, Francis 330, 663
crime 43, 72, 309, 342, 424, 600,
    652, 680, 682, 711, 759, 760,
    847, 855, 862, 872, 996, 998,
    1000-1001, 1054
        criminals 24, 61, 163, 711, 760,
        810, 1000
Cristo Rey Jesuit High School
    725, 739
Crocker, Ruth 217, 219
Cromartie, Michael 735
crop production 956
Crossnore 780
Crow Museum 501
crowdfunding 58, 472
Cru 737, 740, 767-768
Crusaders 821, 948
cryogenic surgery 322
cryptology 690-691
Crystal Bridges Museum of
    American Art 474-475

Crystal City 225
CSX Railroad 588
CU-Boulder 823
Cuba 233, 700, 884, 913
Cultural Literacy 418
culture 7, 12, 34-37, 39, 44, 58, 112,
    223, 228-229, 276, 332, 394, 405,
    426, 446-447, 463, 466, 472, 480,
    483, 500-501, 508-509, 517-518,
    523-524, 526, 551, 556-557, 641,
    660, 664, 685, 726, 730, 752, 755,
    787, 850, 865, 913, 923, 948,
    957, 963, 996, 998, 1000, 1007,
    1009, 1050, 1060, 1077, 1091,
    1147, 1184
The Culture of Cities 1060
Cumberland Gap 586
Cummings, Bill 83
Cummings, Joyce 83
Cummins Engine
    Company 510
Cunningham, Ann 554-555
Cuny, Fred 941
Cuomo, Andrew 361
Curti, Merle 451, 903, 967-968
Cutter, Carl 530
Cutting, Fulton 906
CVS Pharmacy 985
Cyprus 800
Cystic Fibrosis Foundation 286
Czech Republic 66, 938, 1007
D. K. G. Institute of Musical Art 539
D.C. 50, 144, 162, 176, 189-190,
    225, 227, 244, 323, 373-374, 385,
    395, 400-401, 404, 424, 468, 476,
    498, 501, 522, 528, 540, 543,
    551-552, 619, 657, 726, 728,
    734-735, 739, 751, 780, 826,
    846-848, 860, 869-870, 875-876,
    881, 908, 923, 988, 1186, 1193

Siam 175, 800

sickle-cell disease 320

Siebel, Stacey 85, 277

Siebel, Tom 85, 277, 307, 574

Siebel Foundation, Thomas and
Stacey 277

Siebel Dinosaur Complex 575

Sierra Club 599, 627, 883, 911

Sierra Leone 894, 913

Sierra Nevada 230, 911

Silicon Graphics 287

Silicon Valley 189, 231, 357, 375,
384, 385, 393, 401, 597, 640,
821, 872, 973-974, 1041, 1154,
1160, 1175

Silicon Valley Community
Foundation 974, 1154, 1160

Silverstein, Craig 85

Simmons, Ellen 477

Simmons Foundation, Harold 1157

Simmons, Matthew 477

Simon, Bill 224, 762

Simon, William E. 82, 89, 182,
222-224, 398, 972, 1064

Simon Center for the Professional
Military Ethic 398

Simon Prize for Philanthropic
Leadership, William E. 82, 972

Simons, James 85, 284, 294, 389,
661, 852

Simons, Marilyn 85

Simons Center for Quantitative
Biology 284

Simons Center for Systems
Biology 284

Simpson, Louis 258

Sinclair, Upton 903

Singer, Paul 85, 840

Singer, Peter 26

Singer Sewing Company 524

Singh, Manmohan 71

Sinquefield, Jeanne 376, 984

Sinquefield, Rex 376, 984

Sinquefield Charitable
Foundation 984

Sioux Valley Hospitals and Health
System 273

Sirico, Robert 747

Sisters of Charity 352, 801

Sisters of Life 745-746

Sisters of Life Guild 746

Sisters of Mercy 102, 785

Sisters of the Blessed Sacrament
101-102, 785-786

Sisters of the Blessed Sacrament for
Negroes and Indians 102

Sitt, Joseph 923

Six Day War 771

Skid Row 656, 673

Skidmore College 386

Skocpol, Theda 907

Skoll, Jeff 36, 85, 644, 842-843,
852, 974

Slager, David 768

Slamon, Dennis 280

Slater Fund, John 73, 439

Slave's Friend 915

slavery 24, 128, 342, 417, 453, 709,
799, 806, 810, 909, 911-916
owners 709, 799
riot 460
slavers 24, 913
slaves 14, 25, 72, 239, 243, 460,
475, 572, 703, 709, 716, 799,
809, 912-915, 926

Sleepy Hollow 519

Sloan, Alfred 328, 663, 904, 1153

Sloan Foundation, Alfred P.
663, 1153

Sloan, Alfred Jr. 904

Society of St. Vincent de Paul
701, 797
sociology 237, 295
Socrates Sculpture Park 975
Socratic-style discussion 391
Soderbergh, Steven 494
soldiers 78, 121, 177, 233, 298, 313,
331, 333, 476-477, 683, 698, 701,
703-704, 713, 717, 794-795, 902,
907, 926-927
Soldiers' Home cottage 225, 227,
476-477
Solidarity movement 949
Solomon, Lon 752
Solzhenitsyn, Aleksandr 236, 761
sonar 905
Sommers, Christina 896
Sons of Liberty 717
Soon-Shiong, Michelle 85
Soon-Shiong, Patrick 85
Soros, George 74-75, 85, 600, 841,
843-844, 846, 848, 933, 937,
941-943, 948-949, 1041
South America 135, 801
South Bronx 668
South Carolina 161, 229, 290, 431,
496, 585, 604, 607, 804, 860, 993,
1011, 1144, 1171, 1174
Charleston 496, 554, 604, 607,
804, 993
Hilton Head 290
South Carolina Policy Council 860
South Dakota 19, 173, 266, 274,
606, 647-648, 1007, 1144,
1171-1172, 1175-1176
South Korea 66, 399, 928
South Sudan 926
South Sudbury, Massachusetts 124
South Vietnam 675
Southbridge, Massachusetts 516

Southeast Asia 501, 731, 964
Southern Baptist Convention 764
southern California 18, 219-221,
300, 483, 511, 541, 623, 656, 671,
842, 883
Southern California Center for
Law in the Public Interest 883
Southern Miss 20, 170, 173
Southern Power Company 105, 431
Southerners 206, 450, 910, 912,
914, 1173
Southside Community Hospital 338
Soviet Union 149, 427-428, 505,
596, 700, 743, 756, 772, 866, 874,
898, 904, 908, 945, 949, 961
Sowell, Thomas 428, 857, 904
space shuttle *Discovery* 989
SpaceIL 922
SpaceShipOne 185
SpaceX 659
Spain 66, 524, 675, 928, 1166
Spanish-American War 233, 333,
698, 701, 964
Spanish-speaking 652
Sparks, Evan 101, 106, 153, 185,
198, 232, 237, 240, 355, 563, 724,
920, 1044, 1073
special education
406, 414, 734
Special Forces 58, 245
Special Research Aid Fund for
Deposed Scholars 682
Speed Art Museum 508
Speed family 508
Spelman Seminary 414, 793
Spencer, Herbert 94
Speyer, James 957
spinal trauma 312, 338
Spink, Charles 974
Spink, Edie 975

324-325, 327, 329-330, 333-334,
339-340, 342, 345, 351, 358, 360,
364, 369-370, 372, 374, 377-378,
384-385, 388, 396, 399, 406, 409,
413-414, 419-420, 422, 424,
428-430, 432, 434, 438-439, 445,
455, 460, 469, 473-474, 479-486,
492-493, 502, 506, 516, 526,
533-535, 539-540, 542-543, 548,
551, 554, 572, 577, 580, 583, 588,
590, 593, 601, 604, 608, 611, 616,
619, 622, 625, 631, 635, 637-638,
641-642, 645, 648-650, 652,
654-656, 659-660, 662-665,
668-670, 672-673, 675, 677, 681,
684-686, 689-690, 695-696, 698,
702, 705-707, 709, 711, 715-717,
719-720, 724, 726-728, 732-733,
737, 739, 742-744, 747-749, 751,
753, 756-759, 762-764, 767,
769-770, 774-776, 779-780,
782-786, 792, 795-796, 801, 806,
816, 818, 824-826, 829, 831-833,
838, 842, 847, 851, 858, 860,
862-863, 870, 872-873, 875, 879-
880, 882, 885-888, 891-896, 902,
911, 921, 923, 925, 928-929, 931,
933, 936-937, 940, 943-944,
948-949, 952-956, 960, 965, 969,
978, 980, 984, 986, 994, 1000,
1002, 1005-1006, 1008-1009,
1012, 1014, 1019, 1021-1023,
1025, 1027, 1029, 1032,
1037-1038, 1041, 1044, 1050,
1055-1059, 1071-1072, 1077,
1088, 1123, 1125, 1188
    work-study programs 725,
      739, 740
    habits 481
worker's compensation 910

WorkFaith Connection 749
Working Seminar on Poverty 996
World Bank 898, 933
World Book Encyclopedia 186
World Congress of Muslim
  Philanthropists 730
World Health Organization 282, 941
World Series 152, 766
World Trade Center 785
World Vision 33, 761, 769-770,
  924, 946
World War I 54, 94, 143, 148, 150,
  165, 209, 215, 609, 691, 694,
  700-701, 776, 778, 795, 904-906,
  960-961
World War II 15, 32, 107, 119, 151,
  166-168, 195-196, 235, 318-319,
  321, 331, 409, 425, 427, 430, 475,
  483, 501, 532, 653, 681, 686, 691,
  700, 707, 726, 771, 778, 784, 815,
  873, 900-901, 958, 961, 1038,
  1073, 1090
Worster, Donald 911
Wortham Foundation 567
Wright, Frank Lloyd 504, 524
Wright, Karen 550
Wrigley, Julie 606
writers 108, 242, 276, 422, 428, 480,
  491, 494, 508, 531, 542, 620, 663,
  833, 870, 872, 876, 1063
writing skills 652
WuDunn, Sheryl 1042
Wyatt-Brown, Bertram 709,
  799, 913
Wycliffe, John 728
Wyeth, Andrew 508
Wyeth, N. C. 464, 508
Wyoming 99, 209, 617, 1074, 1171,
  1173, 1176
    Jackson Hole 612

ABOUT

The

PHILANTHROPY
ROUNDTABLE

THE PHILANTHROPY ROUNDTABLE is America's leading network of charitable donors working to strengthen our free society, uphold donor intent, and protect the freedom to give. Our members include individual philanthropists, families, corporations, and private foundations.

MISSION

The Philanthropy Roundtable's mission is to foster excellence in philanthropy, to protect philanthropic freedom, to assist donors in achieving their philanthropic intent, and to help donors advance liberty, opportunity, and personal responsibility in America and abroad.

PRINCIPLES

- Philanthropic freedom is essential to a free society
- A vibrant private sector generates the wealth that makes philanthropy possible
- Voluntary private action offers solutions to many of society's most pressing challenges
- Excellence in philanthropy is measured by results, not by good intentions
- A respect for donor intent is essential to long-term philanthropic success

SERVICES

World-class conferences

The Philanthropy Roundtable connects you with other savvy donors. Held across the nation throughout the year, our meetings assemble grantmakers and experts to develop strategies for excellent local, state, and national giving. You will hear from innovators in K-12 education, economic opportunity, higher education, national security, and other fields. Our Annual Meeting is the Roundtable's flagship event, gathering the nation's most public-spirited and influential philanthropists for debates, how-to sessions, and discussions on the best ways for private individuals to achieve powerful results through their giving. The Annual Meeting is a stimulating and enjoyable way to meet principled donors seeking the breakthroughs that can solve our nation's greatest challenges.

Breakthrough groups

Our Breakthrough groups—focused program areas—build a critical mass of donors around a topic where dramatic results are within reach. Breakthrough groups become a springboard to help donors achieve lasting effects from their philanthropy. Our specialized staff of experts helps grantmakers invest with care in areas like anti-poverty work, philanthropy for veterans, and family reinforcement. The Roundtable's K-12 education program is our largest and longest-running Breakthrough group. This network helps donors zero in on today's most promising school reforms. We are the industry-leading convener for philanthropists seeking systemic improvements through competition and parental choice, administrative freedom and accountability, student-centered technology, enhanced teaching and school leadership, and high standards and expectations for students of all backgrounds. We foster productive collaboration among donors of varied ideological perspectives who are united by a devotion to educational excellence.

A powerful voice
The Roundtable's public-policy project, the Alliance for Charitable Reform, works to advance the principles and preserve the rights of private giving. ACR educates legislators and policymakers about the central role of charitable giving in American life and the crucial importance of protecting philanthropic freedom—the ability of individuals and private organizations to determine how and where to direct their charitable assets. Active in Washington, D.C., and in the states, ACR protects charitable giving, defends the diversity of charitable causes, and battles intrusive government regulation. We believe the capacity of private initiative to address national problems must not be burdened with costly or crippling constraints.

Protection of donor interests
The Philanthropy Roundtable is the leading force in American philanthropy to protect donor intent. Generous givers want assurance that their money will be used for the specific charitable aims and purposes they believe in, not redirected to some other agenda. Unfortunately, donor intent is usually violated in increments, as foundation staff and trustees neglect or misconstrue the founder's values and drift into other purposes. Through education, practical guidance, legislative action, and individual consultation, The Philanthropy Roundtable is active in guarding donor intent. We are happy to advise you on steps you can take to ensure that your mission and goals are protected.

Must-read publications
The Almanac of American Philanthropy is our authoritative new resource—a compilation of the greatest givers, greatest achievements, and greatest ideas in the field.

Philanthropy, the Roundtable's quarterly magazine, is packed with useful and beautifully written real-life stories. It offers practical examples, inspiration, detailed information, history, and clear guidance on the differences between giving that is great and giving that disappoints.

We also publish a series of guidebooks that provide detailed information on the very best ways to be effective in particular aspects of philanthropy. These guidebooks are compact, brisk, and readable. Most focus on one particular area of giving—for instance, improving teaching, charter-school expansion, support for veterans, programs that get the poor into jobs, investing in public policy, and other topics of interest to grantmakers. Real-life examples, hard numbers, first-hand experiences of other donors, recent history, and policy guidance are presented to inform and inspire savvy donors.

JOIN THE ROUNDTABLE!

When working with The Philanthropy Roundtable, members are better equipped to achieve long-lasting success with their charitable giving. Your membership in the Roundtable will make you part of a potent network that understands philanthropy and strengthens our free society. Philanthropy Roundtable members range from Forbes 400 individual givers and the largest American foundations to small family foundations and donors just beginning their charitable careers. Our members include:

- Individuals and families
- Private foundations
- Community foundations
- Venture philanthropists
- Corporate giving programs
- Large operating foundations and charities that devote more than half of their budget to external grants

Philanthropists who contribute at least $100,000 annually to charitable causes are eligible to become members of the Roundtable and register for most of our programs. Roundtable events provide you with a solicitation-free environment.

For more information on The Philanthropy Roundtable or to learn about our individual program areas, please call (202) 822-8333 or e-mail main@PhilanthropyRoundtable.org.

Also available from
The Philanthropy Roundtable:
Wise Giver's Guides

Catholic School Renaissance:
A Wise Giver's Guide to Strengthening a National Asset
By Andy Smarick and Kelly Robson

Clearing Obstacles to Work:
A Wise Giver's Guide to Fostering Self-Reliance
By David Bass

Agenda Setting: A Wise Giver's Guide to Influencing Public Policy
By John J. Miller and Karl Zinsmeister with Ashley May

Excellent Educators:
A Wise Giver's Guide to Cultivating Great Teachers and Principals
By Laura Vanderkam

From Promising to Proven:
A Wise Giver's Guide to Expanding on the Success of Charter Schools
By Karl Zinsmeister

Closing America's High-achievement Gap: A Wise Giver's Guide to Helping Our
Most Talented Students Reach Their Full Potential
By Andy Smarick

Blended Learning: A Wise Giver's Guide to Supporting Tech-assisted Teaching
By Laura Vanderkam

Serving Those Who Served:
A Wise Giver's Guide to Assisting Veterans and Military Families
By Thomas Meyer

Protecting Donor Intent:
How to Define and Safeguard Your Philanthropic Principles
By Jeffrey Cain

Transparency in Philanthropy
By John Tyler

How Public Is Private Philanthropy?
By Evelyn Brody and John Tyler

KARL ZINSMEISTER, *series editor*
For all current and future titles, visit PhilanthropyRoundtable.org/guidebook

ABOUT
—— *the* ——
AUTHOR

Karl Zinsmeister oversees all magazine, book, and website publishing at The Philanthropy Roundtable in Washington, D.C. He also founded and advises the Roundtable's program on philanthropy for veterans and servicemembers. Karl has authored 11 books, including two different works of embedded reporting on the Iraq war, a book on charter schools, a storytelling cookbook, even a graphic novel published by Marvel Comics. He has also made a PBS feature film and written hundreds of articles for publications ranging from the *Atlantic* to the *Wall Street Journal*. Earlier in his career he was a Senate aide to Daniel Patrick Moynihan, the J. B. Fuqua Fellow at the American Enterprise Institute, and editor in chief for nearly 13 years of *The American Enterprise* magazine. From 2006 to 2009 Karl served in the West Wing as the President's chief domestic policy adviser and director of the White House Domestic Policy Council. He is a graduate of Yale University, and also studied at Trinity College Dublin.